THE KODANSHA

# KANJI LEARNER'S COURSE

## A Step-by-Step Guide to Mastering 2300 Characters

**Andrew Scott Conning**
Foreword by Jack Halpern

Kodansha USA

Published by Kodansha USA, Inc.,
451 Park Avenue South, New York, NY 10016.

Distributed in the United Kingdom and
continental Europe by Kodansha Europe Ltd.

Printed in Canada
18 17 16 15    6 5 4 3 2

COVER DESIGN BY Andrew Lee

### Library of Congress Cataloging-in-Publication Data

Conning, Andrew Scott.
   The Kodansha Kanji learner's course : a step-by-step guide to
   mastering 2300 characters / Andrew Scott Conning ; foreword
   by Jack Halpern.
      pages cm
      ISBN 978-1-56836-526-8 (pbk.)
      1. Japanese language—Textbooks for foreign speakers—Eng-
   lish.  I. Title. II. Title: Kanji learner's course.
   PL539.5.E5C68 2013
   495.61'1—dc23
                                                2013037071

www.kodanshausa.com

THE KODANSHA
# KANJI LEARNER'S COURSE

# CONTENTS

# FOREWORD

Sino-Japanese characters, or kanji, consist of logically interrelated parts that form a systematic network of interlinked symbols representing both meanings and sound. They function as an integrated system, rather than as a set of disconnected symbols that must be memorized by rote.

The traditional approach to making sense of this system has been through the study of *etymology*. A character's etymology and how it relates to its modern meaning is often an interesting story that helps the learner memorize the character. What typifies the etymological approach is that it is based on historical facts to explain how each component contributes to the character's meaning. This is the approach that I use in my book *Kanji no saihakken* (Rediscovering Kanji), which introduces the "Atomic Theory of Chinese Characters." As I illustrate there, knowledge of etymology can be of genuine value to learners when presented in groups of kanji that share the same phonetic component.

In this kanji course, Andrew Scott Conning aims to make learning kanji as straightforward as possible by effectively adapting etymological information to pedagogical purposes. What he has produced is not merely a list of mnemonics, but an integrated, self-guiding, self-reinforcing course that offers a comprehensive system for interpreting the main meaning(s) of each character from its graphical constituents. While it generally preserves the historical meaning of each graphical component, or *grapheme*, it breaks free from rigid adherence to etymology.

This combination of discipline and flexibility allows the author to tap into rich etymological sources while offering learners effective shortcuts for remembering character meanings. The wisdom in fusing a conservative adherence to etymological convention at the grapheme level (*across* characters) with a liberal transcendence of it at the character-formation level (*within* characters) will become apparent in due course.

To illustrate the effectiveness of this approach, consider the character 東 (**EAST**). We can visualize 東 as the "sun" (日) rising behind a "tree" (木) in the **EAST**. Using this interpretive (but historically inaccurate) approach, the learner has little difficulty in memorizing this character's meaning. In reality, 東 originates from 𣍼, a picture of a bag pierced through by a stick used in ancient times for carrying water bags. Since 東 is pronounced *dong* in Chinese, it was "borrowed" and assigned the meaning **EAST**, also pronounced *dong*, without relation to its original meaning.

It is no doubt easier to remember this character with the *interpretive* approach by associating the meaning **EAST** with the concrete image of "the sun rising behind a tree." To most kanji learners—who are primarily interested in efficient memorization—the loss of historical authenticity is of little consequence.

Now let us consider how the etymological and interpretive approaches compare across a group of related characters, using a series based on the element 己.

Etymological sources for 己 provide meanings such as "arrow," "spool," "winding," or "bending." Unfortunately for the learner, how these meanings are related to modern *character* meanings such as SELF (己) and WRITE DOWN (記) is far from straightforward, and is indeed a matter of scholarly debate.

The author's solution is to borrow from etymology the notion of "winding" or "bending" (easily visible in the shape of 己) to produce a concrete image of a kneeling human body with the head bent forward. He then combines this image with the meaning of 己 as an independent character (SELF) by assigning to 己 the graphemic meaning of "kneeling self."

Let's see how this works. The image of a kneeling and bowed figure works well for 己 as an independent character, given the humility expected of a Japanese speaker in referring to one's SELF. To learn the character for WRITE DOWN (記), the learner simply visualizes 己 as the "kneeling self" kneeling before a writing desk, writing down "words" (言). Likewise, the notion of DISCIPLINE (紀) can be visualized as the "kneeling self" using a "rope" (糸) to restrain oneself. Similarly, the abstract idea of REFORM (改) can be seen in the image of striking oneself with a "rod" (攵), while the meaning RISE (起) is represented in the image of the "kneeling self" rising abruptly in order to "run" (走).

It is clear that studying characters organized in groups like the above is more effective than memorizing each one in isolation. The 己-series illustrates the creative, flexible, and etymologically informed way in which this course allows users to associate a single grapheme with a diverse set of meanings. The power of this method lies in invoking *concrete imagery* adapted to the needs of explaining contemporary meanings while maintaining etymological authenticity on the grapheme level.

In my capacity as the editor-in-chief of several kanji dictionaries and author of a book on kanji etymology, several features of this innovative course struck me as particularly remarkable.

First and foremost, the concrete imagery helps the learner memorize the meanings of complex characters from their graphical components. As can be seen from the annotations for 東 and for the 己-series, such imagery serves as a powerful mnemonic because it leaves a lasting impression on the mind.

Second, the *sequence* in which the kanji are introduced represents a breakthrough in kanji pedagogy. The meaning of each grapheme is explained *before* it appears as a component of other characters, ensuring that the learner understands all component parts when learning new kanji.

Third, the mnemonic effect is reinforced by presenting graphically similar characters together, rather than as isolated units, which provides a smooth, streamlined course of study that is both easy to follow and mnemonically self-reinforcing.

Fourth, this course links the mnemonic annotations to semantically accurate, concise mnemonic keywords that encapsulate each character's *core meaning*. Derived from my own *Kodansha Kanji Learner's Dictionary*, the core meanings allow the learner to accurately grasp the character's meanings as a concise conceptual unit. This is another feature that distinguishes this course from every other kanji self-teaching method.

Fifth, special attention is given to learning each kanji in a *differentiated* way; that is, learning the characters in a mutually contrastive manner that connects their graphical distinctions to their underlying semantic differences. The author thus immunizes the learner from what is perhaps the greatest source of difficulty arising at the intermediate and advanced stages of study, which is the confusion produced by multitudes of look-alike characters.

To see an example, the reader can flip to entry 0814, which focuses learners' attention on the distinction between kanji based on 句, 可, and 司. Groups of kanji based on 可 and 司 immediately follow; moreover, a second group based on 可 is appropriately cross-referenced. This approach allows the learner to associate the meaning of each character with the features that distinguish it from graphically similar characters.

Finally, while the meanings of graphemes are rooted in historical etymology, the annotations for individual kanji are defined by their eclectic use of a variety of mnemonic techniques, such as concrete imagery, semantic analysis, historical etymology, and other techniques. The guiding principle is practicality, rather than rigid adherence to a theoretical principle.

This is not the first time that a mnemonic approach has been applied to the learning of kanji. However, the present course surpasses previous works in the thorough approach it takes and in the skillful balance it strikes between etymological authenticity and the practical needs of the learner. The innovative use of concrete imagery, the emphasis on differentiation, the effective sequence of presentation, and the mnemonically effective core meanings round out the course, making it the most effective kanji learning tool available today.

Saitama, Japan

## Jack Halpern
CEO of The CJK Dictionary Institute

# PREFACE

The purpose of this course is to assist the non-native learner in remembering the basic meanings of Sino-Japanese characters (kanji), and in applying kanji-based vocabulary in a communicative context.

In its coverage, arrangement, and pedagogical approach, this course reflects the assumption that the user's overriding goal is not to find the shortest route to some elementary or intermediate stage of kanji proficiency, but to find the most efficient and reliable route to genuine literacy. It contains all 2136 *Joyo* ("regular-use") kanji plus 164 of the most useful non-Joyo characters, specially arranged to maximize efficiency of acquisition. Each kanji is accompanied by an explanation of how to remember its meaning so as to distinguish it from similar ones. Many explanations involve the use of visualization and concrete imagery, but some rely on other mnemonic techniques, as appropriate. The goal throughout is to offer pragmatic, time-saving solutions to remembering the kanji.

I sincerely hope that this course will help learners on their way toward a more direct and profound understanding of Japan and its people, whose generosity, support, and everyday kindness provided this work's foundation as well as its inspiration.

The preparation of this text was made possible by a Japanese Ministry of Education research fellowship and the institutional support of the University of Tokyo, for which I am indebted to Professor Takeo Funabiki. Most of the research and writing took place at the Tokyo Metropolitan Library, the Japan Foundation Library, the Okayama Prefectural Library, and the libraries of Harvard University and the University of Tokyo. My sincere thanks to the librarians of these institutions for their assistance. I am also grateful to Mr. Yasuhiro Takeda of the Ministry of Education's Agency for Cultural Affairs, for his patient help with my numerous requests for information while his agency was preparing the revisions to the Joyo Kanji List.

I wish to express my warm appreciation to Michael Staley and his colleagues at Kodansha, who turned this text from a mere concept into a reality; Jack Halpern of the CJK Dictionary Institute, who generously granted permission to reprint material from the *Kodansha Kanji Learner's Dictionary*; the staff of the CJK Dictionary Institute, who provided invaluable assistance with the preparation of the readings index; Kay Yokota, who edited the manuscript with consummate expertise; Toyoko Kon, who skillfully designed the layout; Roo Heins, Chikako Imoto, and Ayumi Minowa, who proofread every page with care and perseverance. I am especially grateful to Hiroko Takahashi, Tadamasa Iwai, Hideki Shiromoto, Taeko Shiromoto, Fuminori Nagasawa, Katsuo Nagasawa, Kunio Matsushita, James Mark Shields, Rebecca Givens Rolland, Andrew Smith Lewis, Paloma Escalante Gonzalbo, and E. Anthony Fessler for their advice, personal support, and motivating example; and above all to my family, whose constant support allowed this project to reach completion.

# INTRODUCTION

Non-native learners of Japanese have long wished for a simple and reliable way to remember the meanings of Sino-Japanese characters, or kanji. Over the years, a number of exceptionally insightful students of the kanji—people such as Michael Pye, James Heisig, Jack Halpern, and Kenneth Henshall—have pointed the way toward this goal.* These scholars understood from their own experience that it is more efficient for adults to learn kanji through an interpretive mnemonic approach than through the mechanical repetition used by schoolchildren. Their pioneering efforts have helped generations of learners overcome the kanji barrier.

My purpose in creating this course has been to extend previous work by developing a comprehensive and pedagogically sound method for remembering the meanings of all the characters required for genuine literacy in Japanese. I have pursued this objective in a variety of ways, such as by introducing characters in a streamlined and pedagogically effective sequence, by explaining the meanings of graphical components step by step, by summarizing character meanings in concise keywords to facilitate memorization, by applying mnemonic techniques pragmatically and opportunistically, by highlighting the contrastive features of graphically similar characters, and by using concrete imagery to make the meanings of many difficult characters immediately apparent. In these and other ways, I hope that the present volume will help lower the kanji barrier once more.

What follows is a complete kanji course for non-native learners. Its primary goal is to help you remember the basic meanings of each kanji. But it also helps you actively apply each kanji's principal meanings and readings by learning a few sample vocabulary words, carefully chosen to illustrate the kanji's uses and to help you employ it in everyday communication. Finally, by indicating each kanji's stroke order, explaining the component parts of the kanji step by step, and teaching you how to differentiate among graphically similar kanji, this course offers a solid foundation for learning how to write kanji accurately. It thus offers not simply a series of memory aids but an integrated system for studying the kanji.

---

*Pye, M. *The Study of Kanji: A Handbook of Japanese Characters*. Tokyo: Hokuseido, 1971.
Heisig, J. *Remembering the Kanji I: A Complete Course on How Not to Forget the Meaning and Writing of Japanese Characters*. Tokyo: Japan Publications Trading Co., 1977.
Halpern, J. 漢字の再発見 *Kanji no saihakken* [Rediscovering Kanji]. Tokyo: Shodensha, 1987.
Henshall, K. *A Guide to Remembering Japanese Characters*. Rutland, VT: Charles E. Tuttle Co., 1988.

# BACKGROUND AND BASICS

## Kanji and the Japanese Language

The earliest attempts to write the Japanese language used imported Chinese characters, irrespective of their meaning, as phonetic symbols for similar native sounds. As these complex ideographs proved unsuitable for the transcription of a polysyllabic tongue, the Japanese soon invented a much simpler set of phonetic symbols (the kana: first hiragana, and later katakana), but retained the kanji for the many words borrowed from Chinese. They also began using kanji to denote native Japanese words of similar meaning, this time without regard to phonetic similarity, so that many kanji came to have both a Chinese-derived pronunciation (the *on-yomi*, used in reading words borrowed from China) and an unrelated native pronunciation (the *kun-yomi*, used in reading native words). Having thus become associated primarily with meanings rather than sounds, kanji could be used to represent the stem of a polysyllabic Japanese verb or adjective whose inflected portion could be represented by kana. In this way Japanese came to be written in a mixture of kana and kanji.

Today, kanji are used mainly for Chinese-derived nouns, proper nouns, and the stems of verbs and adjectives. Hiragana are used for all types of native words not written in kanji, and for the inflected endings following a kanji stem, known as *okurigana* (for example, the く in 巻く). Katakana are used mainly for loanwords, names of species, sound-mimicking words, and emphasis (like italics).

In this mixed scheme, the main function of kanji is to represent basic meanings, rather than sounds. It is for this reason that in learning Japanese it is useful to systematically study character meanings as an independent task. Thus the primary focus of this course will be to help you associate each kanji's graphical form with its meaning.

There are several ways to do this. The easiest way is simply to see in the kanji a direct representation of either an object (as in the simple pictograms 田 **RICE FIELD** and 火 **FIRE**) or an idea (as in the ideograms 上 **ABOVE** and 下 **BELOW**). However, simple pictograms and ideograms represent only a small percentage of the kanji in use today. Their primary importance lies, rather, in their function as building blocks from which the vast majority of kanji are assembled.

## Kanji Structure and Its Analysis

A few words regarding the structure of kanji are now in order. Most kanji are composed of multiple building blocks, or *graphemes*—meaningful contrastive graphical units. A simple example is the kanji for (**cultivated**) **FIELD** (畑), which combines the kanji (which in this context we would call the "graphemes") for *fire* (火) and *rice field* (田) (as in the main entries, I shall use *italics* to refer to grapheme meanings and CAPITALS to refer to meanings of entire kanji).

To identify the meaning of these "complex" kanji, it is necessary to interpret the clues provided by their component graphemes. However, because of the complicated evolution in the meanings and graphical form of many kanji, these clues are not readily organized into a coherent system. The challenge is made still more difficult by the necessity of remembering every kanji in such a way as to clearly distinguish it from all others. Herein lies the central problem this text is intended to solve: that of devising a comprehensive system of mnemonic clues that allows you to remember distinctly and reliably the meaning(s) of all the kanji needed for fluent reading in Japanese.

In the most common type of kanji, a semantic (meaning-bearing) grapheme is combined with a phonetic (sound-bearing) grapheme, producing a character with one clue as to its meaning and another as to its sound. For example, consider the kanji 舶. This is an example of a "left-right pattern" kanji, in which typically the grapheme at the left is the semantic component, while the one at the right is the phonetic component. Thus 舟 indicates the character has something to do with *boats*, while 白 suggests the Chinese-derived reading ハク (kanji readings are indicated by kana, which needless to say should be learned first). As it turns out, 舶 means OCEANGOING SHIP and is indeed pronounced ハク.

Of course, the clue to the kanji's meaning, 舟, still leaves open a broad range of meanings associated with *boats*. For all we know, 舶 could mean ROWBOAT, CANOE, WARSHIP, RUDDER, GUNWALE, NAVIGATE, or anything else having to do with *boats*. The only thing that distinguishes 舶 from other kanji sharing 舟 is the phonetic clue 白, which we must therefore use as a secondary clue to its meaning (incidentally, 白 means *white*). One way to do this is to associate *white* with the foamy wake churned up by a large OCEANGOING SHIP. This is an example of semantic analysis—more on this in a moment.

Before we turn our attention exclusively to the issue of remembering kanji meanings, let me lower any expectations I may have raised regarding the possibility of determining a kanji's *on-yomi* based on its phonetic clue. While some phonetic hints like 白 are very useful, most are not. To give an extreme example, though all of the characters 税, 鋭, 説, 脱, and 閲 have the *same* phonetic element (兌), each of them has a *different* primary reading: 税 (ゼイ), 鋭 (エイ), 説 (セツ), 脱 (ダツ), and 閲 (エツ). Alas, these irregularities are as much the rule as the exception, because of both historical changes in the pronunciation of Chinese and the fact that the Japanese borrowed characters over a period of hundreds of years and from different linguistic regions within China. Given this situation, you should not concern yourself with learning the *on-yomi* in the same systematic way in which you learn kanji meanings, but instead simply absorb them in the process of learning the Chinese-derived compounds in which the kanji appear. The exception to this guidance is the set of 600 or so kanji listed in Appendix 2 (p. 611).

## The Meanings of Component Graphemes

Each grapheme is introduced the first time it appears, so it is not necessary for you to learn the meanings of the different graphemes before beginning to learn those of whole characters. Once you have learned a new grapheme, you will start to run into it in learning more complex characters, which will naturally reinforce its meaning. For convenient reference, the appendixes contain a Table of Grapheme Meanings (p. 624), but you will hardly need to use it if you proceed through the course in the assigned sequence.

In the way we piece together the hints provided by a kanji's component graphemes, we shall be under no obligation to etymological authenticity. Nevertheless, for the meanings of the graphemes *themselves*, I have chosen to adhere to tradition for the most part. This is not out of any pretense at conventionality, but rather because the traditional meanings are generally the ones most consistently useful as memory aids, as will become apparent in due course. Now and then, especially where it was useful to have a visual mnemonic, I have ignored the traditional meaning. Also, I have occasionally given myself license to treat as a "grapheme" a certain distinguishing set of strokes even though it has not traditionally been considered a distinct unit. Similar exceptions are detailed in the Table of Grapheme Meanings.

As you progress through the course, terms less precise than "grapheme" (such as "element," "construction," "part," etc.) appear more frequently. I do avoid the term "radical," which in its strict sense refers to that portion of a character that is designated by tradition as its semantic root, or to any of 214 forms that are deemed eligible to serve this function. In keeping with this course's expedient approach to remembering kanji, we shall not be particularly concerned with knowing which part of a kanji is designated by tradition as its radical. For purposes of looking up a kanji in a Japanese dictionary organized according to the historical radicals, you may find each kanji's radical and radical number in the reference data section of its main entry (see p. 18, "Explanation of Sample Entry" ❸).

# PEDAGOGICAL APPROACH

This course provides a comprehensive system for remembering the core meanings of all the kanji needed for genuine literacy in Japanese. The solution arrived at is an eclectic mix of mnemonic techniques, relying above all on visualization, and paying special attention to the problem of distinguishing look-alike kanji—a problem that that bedevils so many advanced learners.

## Eclecticism

The pedagogical approach of this course is defined above all by its eclecticism. It does not attempt to rigidly apply a single method method (such as etymology or semantic analysis) to the study of every kanji. Instead, it uses an opportunistic approach, taking advantage of whatever method offers the most efficient and reliable way to remember a kanji's meaning. Different strategies are appropriate to different kanji. Some are easy to remember as pictograms. Others are best approached by linking together the meanings of their component graphemes. Still others are best learned by considering their etymology, or by focusing attention on one of their distinctive features, or by applying some ad hoc method. For this reason, the first guiding principle of this course is that the way a character is learned should be adapted pragmatically to the particular qualities of the character, and to those of similar characters from which it must be distinguished.

## Semantic Analysis

Earlier we associated 舶 with the meaning OCEANGOING SHIP by letting *white* (白) suggest the foamy wake churned up by a large *boat* (舟). This is an example of semantic analysis, in which we use the meanings of individual graphemes to construct an idea representing the meaning of the character as a whole. This technique sometimes provides the most straightforward way to remember a character, and we shall exploit it in those cases.

Unfortunately, there is often so little logical connection between a kanji's combination of graphemes and its meaning that almost any method of remembering the character is easier than trying to analyze the graphemes semantically. Consider the kanji for FALL (落), which contains graphemes for *grass* (艹) and *water* (氵), as well as a phonetic grapheme (各) that by itself means *each* or *every*. Using semantic analysis, we might try to associate the kanji's parts with its meaning through a conceptual statement such as "*every* drop of *water* FALLS on *grass*." Quite apart from its oddness, this statement has two significant disadvantages from a mnemonic standpoint. First, it is *indirect*: rather than allowing us to immediately recognize the meaning of the character in its visual image, it forces us first to pass through an intermediate

stage of cognition. Second, it is *abstract*: it exists only in the mind, rather than in the physical form of the kanji. In short, the analytical method merely substitutes the task of remembering kanji with the perhaps more difficult task of remembering abstract conceptual statements removed from the kanji's concrete form.

## Visualization

For this reason, the approach used in this course is to apply some form of visual interpretation to complex kanji whenever it is practical to do so, while generally (but not always) respecting the individual grapheme meanings. The key to this method is the use of concrete imagery to supplement (and occasionally replace) the semantic face value of a kanji (that is, the meaning one might gather from the meanings of its component graphemes), so that its core meaning may be immediately apprehensible in its graphical form.

This approach allows us to simplify the many complex kanji that do not present a straightforward semantic interpretation. To make this work, we must often treat graphemes as visible images even when their meaning as stand-alone kanji cannot be visualized. For example, though 各 means **EACH** when used as an independent kanji, we shall give it the concrete, visible meaning *cabin* whenever it functions as a component grapheme *inside another kanji*. This allows us to perceive the meaning of 落 directly in its graphical form: simply visualize a *grass* (艹)–covered *cabin* (各) rooftop from which *water* (氵) **FALLS** during a heavy rain.

There are countless kanji like 落 that are hard to master because one of their graphemes represents an abstraction. This problem is solved for you in this course by the substitution of concrete, visible meanings for many of these graphemes. When appearing as a component part inside other kanji, 夕 will thus generally be treated as *evening moon* rather than *evening*, 良 as *good boy* rather than *good*, 己 as *kneeling self* rather than *self*, etc. This substitution of concrete imagery for abstract ideas allows us to make use of grapheme meanings in a consistent and organized way even as we create distinctive images from complex kanji.

For the simple kanji, the use of our visual memory is all but automatic. This course does, however, provide tips for visualizing kanji that have been so drastically stylized, simplified, and reproportioned over the centuries that their pictographic origins are no longer obvious. For example, to see an image of the **MOON** in 月, we can associate the gently curving left-hand stroke with a crescent. This course will offer you many similar opportunities to visualize the distinctive feature(s) of a kanji in a meaningful way.

Here let me emphasize an important point made in the preceding pages—that this course will ask you deliberately to take a simple-minded, *sensory* approach to learning most kanji. For adult learners, it may feel like a waste of mental capacity to prioritize lower-order cognition when more abstract forms of thinking are available for solving a problem. And yet in learning kanji, you will find that seeking a clarifying sense of order at a higher level of abstraction is in fact counterproductive. Simply put, your brain is not wired to memorize 2300 abstractions. It is therefore generally advantageous to slide down the scale of complexity and learn kanji as concrete visual representations. Needless to say, some kanji do require more abstract levels of thinking. But in order to simplify your overall task, I have assigned concrete, easily visualized meanings to most graphemes.

## Etymology

Occasionally, knowing the historical development of a character, or something about its original context or intent, provides the most straightforward way of

remembering its meaning. For example, it is perhaps easiest to remember that 泊 means STAY OVERNIGHT if we consider that it was originally used to refer to an anchorage, *white* (白) *water* (氵) indicating the place where the surf breaks upon land. Whenever we take advantage of such opportunities, our primary concern shall not be whether our understanding of the etymology is historically accurate, but whether it helps us remember the character's meaning in modern Japanese.

## Sensory and Emotional Impressions

The mnemonic approach followed in this course reflects the assumption that the mind is far better at remembering ideas that are accompanied by sensory and emotional impressions than those that are arrived at through logical abstraction. In addition to turning kanji into vivid images that suggest their core meanings, many of the mnemonics in these pages will aim to produce other physical and emotional responses, for example, the annotations for 駆 DRIVE (1388), 挑 PROVOKE (1832), and 拷 TORTURE (1956).

## Differentiation

As your stock of kanji grows, the number of confusing similarities among them will also grow. Because the magnitude of this problem does not become apparent until the later stages, learners often make the costly mistake of starting out with simplistic methods of memorization based on an unrealistically small character set (say, five hundred or a thousand characters). These methods are quite convenient as long as each kanji is easily distinguishable, but turn out not to be sophisticated enough to accommodate the more advanced kanji that come along later and blur the lines of distinction that have initially been drawn. Any learner who aspires toward genuine literacy in Japanese does well to avoid such methods, for they only prove to be an impediment in the long run.

The learning method followed in this course pays specific attention—from the beginning—to the specific qualities that distinguish a kanji from similar ones. Wherever differentiation is an issue, you will learn to recognize the meaning of a kanji precisely in those features that set it apart from others with which it might be confused. This outcome is achieved not only through the use of explicit instructions, but also through meticulous cross-referencing and the arrangement of kanji in graphically related groupings. These features focus your attention on the contrastive attributes of each character as you learn it, and thus save you from having to relearn it in a different way after you encounter confusingly similar kanji at a more advanced stage.

## A Few More Words about Eclecticism

The method outlined above is not a formal or academic approach. The formal study of kanji etymology, while a rewarding pursuit in its own right, is generally not an efficient method for remembering kanji meanings. This course assumes that your goal is not to study the kanji by the most intellectually sophisticated means, but to be able to use them in the shortest possible time. For this purpose, no method of learning a kanji is too unscholarly, provided it helps you recognize the kanji's meaning. On the other hand, should you decide later to look up etymologies, you will encounter no special barriers for having used the method introduced here.

This method is also not a systematic approach—except in its systematic flexibility and pragmatism. Each kanji presents a unique challenge; for this reason, the study of kanji is ill served by the rigid application of one theory of learning

or another. While methodological consistency offers a certain impression of rigor (which perhaps explains why most earlier kanji-learning systems of similar scope have followed more or less strict etymological or analytical approaches), the sacrifice of any pretense at methodological purity is one that I happily make. Surely it is the most sensible response to the lack of predictability in the relationship between component parts of kanji and the meanings kanji have acquired in modern Japanese. There is no consistent set of rules that governs this relationship, no one key that can be turned to unlock the meaning of every character.

## FEATURES OF THIS COURSE

The primary goal of this course is to help you learn and remember the basic meanings of each kanji. It is also designed to familiarize you with the principal pronunciations of each kanji as you learn its core meaning(s), and to actively apply both the meanings and the pronunciations in learning a few sample vocabulary words. As it provides in one place the basic meanings, pronunciations, stroke order, and other information on each kanji, this text can also be used as a basic dictionary.

For an exhaustive listing of meanings, pronunciations, or vocabulary containing the kanji, you should consult a comprehensive kanji dictionary. Likewise, to learn about kanji etymology or for detailed instruction on how to write kanji, you should consult specialized treatments. A brief summary of the principles of stroke direction and stroke order is provided in Appendix 1 (p. 609).

### Coverage

The 2300 entries in this course contain all 2136 kanji in the Ministry of Education, Culture, Sports, Science and Technology's Joyo (regular-use) Kanji List (revised 2010), plus 164 of the most useful kanji not designated in the list. In selecting these 164, I first included all non-Joyo kanji appearing in the Test Content Specifications for Level 1 of the Japanese Language Proficiency Test (JLPT). While the administrators of the JLPT have decided no longer to issue these Test Content Specifications, the latest-issued edition (2006) provided an objective criterion of some practical significance. With a few exceptions, the kanji added from the JLPT list are in fact among the most useful of the non-Joyo kanji.

Beyond that, I selected another roughly one hundred kanji for their general usefulness and/or ease of acquisition. To be included, a kanji had to rate favorably according to a simple cost/benefit assessment: How much time would it take to learn and remember this character? How much benefit would there be to remembering it? To assess a character's "benefit"—which weighed more heavily than "cost"—I consulted a variety of authoritative kanji frequency rankings. Because of the biases inherent in these rankings, I included a limited number of lower-ranking kanji that in my personal judgment were important for you to learn. Conversely, I excluded some kanji that might have merited inclusion based on their frequency ranking alone. Most of these fell into one of the following categories:

(a) *Jinmeiyo (name-use) kanji.* Knowing the meanings of personal and place names is largely irrelevant to language comprehension. I have therefore included Jinmeiyo kanji on the basis of whether they are important for understanding words. For information on other Jinmeiyo kanji, I refer you to Halpern (see "An Ideal Companion Resource," below). The section "How to Study the Kanji" (p. 24) includes some advice on how to handle name kanji in your reading.

(b) *Kanji which appear almost exclusively in a single compound.* You should not study these kanji for their own sake, but instead simply learn the compounds. Kanji in this category appear in this course only if they belong to the Joyo Kanji List.

(c) *Kanji for plant and animal species.* Some of these, such as 桂 (かつら, Japanese Judas tree), would clearly deserve to be included if frequency were the sole criterion. But there is little point in trying to remember a kanji for a species of tree when one doesn't even know what the tree looks like. I thus leave the bulk of these kanji to be pursued by those with a specialized interest (the important ones can be found in Halpern).

The question of "cost" (that is, How much time would it take to learn and remember this character?) was secondary, but it did influence my selection. Among the non-Joyo kanji, those which are visually distinctive, or which otherwise lend themselves to an easy or intuitive mnemonic, are more likely appear in these pages than those which do not.

## Sequence

The order in which you learn the kanji is perhaps as important as the method by which you learn them. I urge you therefore to take a few moments to familiarize yourself with the logic behind the arrangement of kanji in this course.

A basic premise is that you will start with the first kanji and learn the kanji in sequence. Each grapheme is introduced the first time it appears (or, in a few cases, the first time you need to notice it), so that if you go through the entries in order you can build up your kanji vocabulary cumulatively, and will not need to search other parts of the text for the meaning of one of a kanji's component parts. These component parts often consist of whole kanji appearing earlier in the list. Studying the entries out of sequence inevitably leads one into mnemonic explanations that assume knowledge one does not have (for this reason, those with some prior study of the kanji should at least read through the explanations from the beginning). That said, it never hurts to flip ahead and preview later entries, especially to look up unknown kanji in the course of one's reading.

Another reason to follow the sequence is that I have deliberately arranged the kanji to maximize the efficiency with which the adult learner can learn to read authentic Japanese. Most kanji learner's texts, making an unfortunate compromise with the system of graded kanji levels that prevails in Japanese language instruction, separate graphically similar kanji into different groups based on frequency rankings, proficiency test requirements, or the Ministry of Education, Culture, Sports, Science and Technology's kanji grades for Japanese schoolchildren. However, for the adult learner, it makes more sense (a) to learn kanji graphemes step by step, so that one does not learn a complex kanji without first learning the component parts to be used in interpreting its meaning; and (b) to learn kanji in logical groupings based on similarities in graphical form (and sometimes meaning or reading), so that one can give significance to the features that distinguish one kanji from another, *as one learns them.* These graphical groupings also permit the learner to acquire kanji more seamlessly and efficiently than sequences that give no regard to such groups.

Because this course arranges the kanji in accordance with pedagogical principles rather than externally defined grades, it offers the most streamlined and straightforward program of study for learning *all* the kanji needed for genuine literacy, but not necessarily the shortest route to some artificial milestone of kanji

competency (such as mastering the kanji required for the beginning and intermediate levels of the JLPT). I urge you to take the long view. You have a large edifice to build, and it will be better to build it patiently, according to one grand plan, than to rush yourself to complete one or two small rooms only to find that you have seriously delayed or distorted the overall project.

You will notice that the sample compounds ("didactic vocabulary") for each kanji contain only the kanji itself and such others as have already been introduced (this is another reason to study the kanji in the sequence provided). As far as possible, I have included sample vocabulary using each of the kanji's most important meanings and/or readings. Because the didactic compounds can use only such characters as have already appeared, some characters (especially those having multiple meanings and/or readings, and therefore additional didactic requirements) appear later in the sequence than their importance would otherwise dictate. This fact should matter little to the learner whose ultimate goal is real-world literacy.

To the extent allowed by the above considerations, I have *also* attempted to arrange the kanji in general order of frequency, so that you can learn as early as possible the kanji you are most likely to encounter in your reading. Let me emphasize here that the frequency factor carries less weight in the sequence than the other pedagogical considerations explained above. Nonetheless, it has not been ignored. For the benefit of novice learners, all of the hundred most important kanji appear early on. Also, while the imperative of grouping related kanji causes individual kanji to appear earlier or later in the sequence than frequency would otherwise dictate, *the groups themselves* appear in rough order of their aggregate frequency, within the constraints imposed by the step-by-step introduction of graphemes and the availability of sample vocabulary. In this way, the character sequence for this course achieves what perhaps no other sequence has done: it follows a rational pedagogy by introducing character components step by step and related kanji together, yet also introduces the most important characters early on and maintains a general correlation with frequency throughout. I sincerely hope that this volume's unique kanji sequence—quite apart from its mnemonic methods—will in some measure increase the efficiency with which students of Japanese can learn and remember the kanji.

## Explanation of Sample Entry

A sample character entry appears below, with annotations:

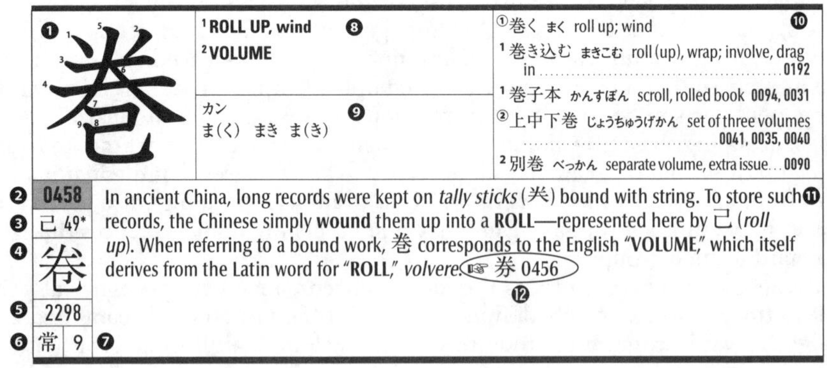

| | | | |
|---|---|---|---|
| ❶ 巻 | ¹ ROLL UP, wind  ❽ <br> ² VOLUME | カン ❾ <br> ま(く) まき ま(き) | ①巻く まく roll up; wind  ❿ <br> ¹ 巻き込む まきこむ roll (up), wrap; involve, drag in .......0192 <br> ¹ 巻子本 かんすぼん scroll, rolled book 0094, 0031 <br> ②上中下巻 じょうちゅうげかん set of three volumes ....................0041, 0035, 0040 <br> ² 別巻 べっかん separate volume, extra issue... 0090 |

❷ **0458**
❸ 己 49*
❹ 巻
❺ 2298
❻ 常 9 ❼

In ancient China, long records were kept on *tally sticks* (关) bound with string. To store such ⓫ records, the Chinese simply **wound** them up into a **ROLL**—represented here by 己 (*roll up*). When referring to a bound work, 巻 corresponds to the English "**VOLUME**," which itself derives from the Latin word for "**ROLL**," *volvere.* ☞ 券 0456
⓬

❶ *Head character.* The font used here simulates brush-stroke form, allowing you to learn to write the character naturally by following the image provided. Numbers indicate the point where each stroke is initiated, and its order.

❷ *Entry number.*

❸ *Radical* (the "root" grapheme by which kanji are arranged in Japanese dictionaries) *and radical number.* An explanation and complete listing of these radicals can be found in the back matter of Halpern. Some radicals will appear in a different form here than they do in the head character; for example, the three-stroke radical 艹 in 茎 appears in its six-stroke parent form 艸. For kanji that lost their radicals in the orthographic reforms that followed the Second World War, a substitute radical from the simplified form is given, followed by an asterisk.

❹ *A nonstandard form* of the character. Most of these are traditional forms (正字, せいじ) now used only in names but still found in prewar writing and certain other contexts. Some are alternative forms (異体字, いたいじ). For characters having both a traditional and an alternative form, I have listed the traditional form. I have not listed traditional forms that are not substantively different from standard forms (e.g., those differing only by the use of 辶 in place of 辶). Where appropriate, notes on nonstandard forms are given in the mnemonic annotations.

❺ *Entry number in* The Kodansha Kanji Learner's Dictionary: Revised and Expanded, edited by Jack Halpern.

❻ *List status,* indicated by one of three characters:
常: Appears in the Joyo (常用) or "regular-use" list
名: Appears in the Jinmeiyo (人名用) or "name-use" list
外: *Hyogai* (表外) or "off-list" (does not appear in either list)

❼ *Stroke count.*

❽ *Meaning(s),* adapted from *The Kodansha Kanji Learner's Dictionary.* Each kanji is shown with up to three basic meanings, consisting of a "mnemonic keyword" in large capitals and additional senses in lowercase type. The mnemonic keyword provides a concise idea for ease of memorization. The additional senses are intended to supplement the keyword by clarifying the kanji's general meaning and usage; do not concern yourself with memorizing these.

The term "mnemonic keyword" refers only to the word or phrase in large capitals while "(basic) meaning" refers to an entire numbered meaning (where no additional senses are provided in lowercase type, the two terms are equivalent). In the mnemonic annotations, "M1," "M2," and "M3" refer to the numbered meanings 1, 2, and 3.

Within one meaning, commas generally separate similar senses and semicolons more divergent ones. In practice, the great difference between Japanese and English often made arbitrary the choice between comma and semicolon.

❾ *Readings,* borrowed from *The Kodansha Kanji Learner's Dictionary.* All of the characters' officially recognized readings are included. Following the usage of Japanese dictionaries, *on* readings are listed first, in katakana, followed by *kun* readings, in hiragana (in this course *kun* readings appear on a separate line). The portion of the *kun* reading that would normally be written in hiragana (*okurigana*) appears in parentheses. The *okurigana* are written to indicate verb and adjective inflections or to clarify pronunciation in ambiguous cases.

Readings marked with an asterisk are not officially recognized in the official Joyo Kanji List. However, asterisks are not used for the readings of characters that themselves are not recognized in the Joyo list.

For a more comprehensive listing of readings, and information on special readings for each character, see Halpern.

❿ *Didactic vocabulary* including kana reading and concise English equivalent, adapted from the *Kodansha Kanji Learner's Dictionary*. Kanji compounds include only characters that have been learned previously, and are followed by cross-references to the main entry, or entries, of such kanji. Due to space limitations, only the principal meanings of each sample vocabulary word are given.

> ①巻く まく roll up; wind
> ¹巻き込む まきこむ roll (up), wrap; involve, drag in ...........0192
> ¹巻子本 かんすぼん scroll, rolled book 0094, 0031
> ②上中下巻 じょうちゅうげかん set of three volumes ...........0041, 0035, 0040
> ²別巻 べっかん separate volume, extra issue...0090

For kanji with multiple meanings, superscript numerals to the left of the word indicate the meaning to which the vocabulary item corresponds. Circled superscript numerals (or circles without numerals in the case of kanji that do not have multiple meanings, or whose meanings overlap in the vocabulary item in question) indicate words that are useful to commit to memory as an illustration of either a reading, a numbered meaning, or both.

Where a compound forms a -な or -の type adjective, the -な or -の suffix is included. Moreover, many substantives are shown in verb form with する, or in adverb form with に. These variations follow Halpern and are intended to highlight important usages and to clarify the kanji's meaning.

The × indicates a kanji in the didactic vocabulary that does not have its own entry in this course, such as the kanji 鹸 in 石けん (石鹸ˣ, せっけん). In such cases, the word is first shown with the unlisted kanji replaced by hiragana (following the official usage for non-Joyo kanji)—except when the kanji is used only for its phonetic value, or other cases in which hiragana would never be used. Note, however, that this practice is not followed in the vocabulary for kanji that *themselves* do not belong to the Joyo list, even though you may find these written in mixed kanji-kana form following official usage (for example, the sample compound for the non-Joyo 繍 1614 is shown only as 刺繍, ししゅう, even though you will sometimes see it written as 刺しゅう).

The following functional labels, appearing at the front of the English equivalent in brackets, are used to clarify usage: archaic, vi (intransitive verb), vt (transitive verb), math (mathematics), familiar, baseball, grammar, literary, elegant, honorific, humble, slang.

⓫ *Mnemonic and other annotations.* Specific formatting conventions are followed in the annotations. **BOLDFACE CAPS** are reserved for appearances of the entry character's mnemonic keyword (additional senses forming part of the character meaning appear in **boldface** without capitalization). REGULAR CAPS are used when

> In ancient China, long records were kept on *tally sticks* (关) bound with string. To store such records, the Chinese simply **wound** them up into a **ROLL**—represented here by 己 (*roll up*). When referring to a bound work, 巻 corresponds to the English "**VOLUME,**" which itself derives from the Latin word for "ROLL," *volvere.* ☞ 券 0456

citing the mnemonic keyword of another character for purposes of comparison or reference, but not in indicating the meaning of another character subsumed as a grapheme in the entry character. *Italics* are used to refer to the meaning of a component grapheme, when that meaning has been established as conventional within this course (i.e., *italics* would not be used for a one-time interpretation of a grapheme). *Italics* are also used for referring to the meaning of another character when it is subsumed as a grapheme in the entry character. They are also occasionally used for foreign loanwords; their intent will be clear from context. Finally, underlining is used for emphasis.

The following abbreviations are used in the mnemonic annotations section:

- "S1," "S2," etc.: stroke 1, stroke 2, etc. (as indicated in the stroke-order diagram)
- "S3-6," "S9-11," etc.: strokes 3 through 6, strokes 9 through 11, etc.
- "V1," "V4," etc.: first didactic vocabulary entry, fourth didactic vocabulary entry, etc.
- "M1," "M2," etc.: meaning 1, meaning 2, etc., in entries with multiple numbered meanings
- "cf.:": compare with

⑫ *Cross-reference to look-alike or other easily confused character(s).*  ☞ 券 0456
In some entries, the symbol ☞ at the end of the annotations section refers you to one or more characters with which the entry character can easily be confused, followed by their entry numbers. Usually this draws your attention to similarities in form (e.g., between 部 and 陪), but occasionally it alerts you to potentially confusing similarities in meaning (e.g., 泣 **CRY** and 涙 **TEAR**) or in two characters' mnemonic imagery or logic. For reference purposes, these cross-references have been provided even when they are redundant with those made in the annotation text.

The aim of these cross-references is to help you become aware of features that distinguish a kanji from its look-alikes, to pay special attention to those features, and when possible to associate some aspect of the kanji's meaning with them. This process, critical to mastering kanji, is done far more efficiently if one notes these similarities and differences from the beginning than if one is left to stumble upon them later.

## Appendixes

Familiarize yourself with the contents of the appendixes before you begin the course, so that you can take advantage of them as you study. They contain the following:

1. *Basic Principles of Stroke Direction and Stroke Order.*

2. *Regular On-Yomi Groups.* The *on* reading of roughly a quarter of the kanji in this course can be learned reliably by mastering a limited number of phonetic components. Take advantage of these low-hanging fruit by consulting this table from time to time as you proceed through the course. Groups are listed in the same order in which their phonetic components appear in the main entries.

3. *Selected Compounds with Irregular Readings.* A list of common compounds with irregular readings, issued by the Ministry of Education, Culture, Sports, Science and Technology. This can be left for the later stages of your kanji study.

4. *Understanding Kanji Compounds.* Use this section to familiarize yourself with the underlying patterns that guide the formation of compound words from individual kanji. Since most kanji appear far more frequently in such compounds than independently, one needs to learn compounds to be able to actively use the kanji. Consult this section relatively early on in the course.

5. *Kanji for Countries and Regions.* Lists thirty of the most frequently encountered kanji used as abbreviations for countries or regions. Consult this appendix when you're ready to try reading a newspaper.

6. *Table of Grapheme Meanings.* As mentioned earlier, each grapheme is explained the first time it appears in a kanji entry. Consult this appendix if you've forgotten the meaning assigned to a grapheme, and to find the place where it is first introduced.

7. *Table of Related and Look-Alike Kanji.* Use this table to practice differentiating among kanji that are graphically similar, or present other potentially confusing similarities. To find a kanji's *kun* homophones, consult its entry in Halpern.

8. *Table of Nonstandard Forms.* You will encounter nonstandard forms in proper nouns, in pre-1946 texts, and in words containing kanji belatedly added to the Joyo Kanji List. Familiarity with these forms will also help you read many non-Joyo kanji. Use this table to familiarize yourself with the nonstandard forms and, at an advanced stage of study, to test your ability to recognize them. You can also use this table to look up the standard forms of any nonstandard forms you come across.

9. *Summary of Changes to the Joyo Kanji List (2010).* Includes a full list of kanji added to (or removed from) the Joyo Kanji List, a list of newly recognized readings, and other information on this important revision to the official list of "regular-use" kanji.

10. *Table of Jinmeiyo (Name-Use) Kanji.* Consult this table as you begin wading into authentic Japanese texts. Of the kanji you will encounter that are not introduced in this course, the majority will be name-use kanji. This table is also useful for finding the entry number of the hundred-odd name-use kanji introduced in this course. Note that I have not included a table of the Joyo kanji, because all of them are included in the course. The official updated Joyo Kanji List is available online.

11. *Table of Hyogai (Off-List) Kanji.* Lists the kanji introduced in this course that do not appear in either the Joyo or Jinmeiyo lists, with their entry numbers.

## Indexes
Three indexes—stroke count, radical, and readings—are provided for your convenience. Information on how to locate a kanji is provided at the beginning of each index, and summarized inside the back cover.

## An Ideal Companion Resource: *The Kodansha Kanji Learner's Dictionary*
When I first approached Kodansha regarding the possibility of putting together a kanji learner's course, I suggested designing it as a complementary resource to *The Kodansha Kanji Learner's Dictionary*, which I personally had found extremely useful in learning the kanji. Thanks to the cooperation of Kodansha—and the Dictionary's editor in chief, Jack Halpern, who gave permission to reprint character meanings,

readings, and a selection of sample vocabulary—learners now have access to an ideally matched pair of kanji study resources: a step-by-step learner's course with the kanji arranged for sequential study, and a conveniently sized learner's dictionary with in-depth character meanings that clarify how each character is used in forming compound words.

While this *course* may certainly be used as a stand-alone resource, I strongly encourage you to use it concurrently with Halpern's *Kanji Learner's Dictionary*. Among the features that make Halpern an ideal companion resource to this volume are the following:

1. *In-depth character meanings.* This *Kanji Learner's Course* provides the core meaning of each kanji, including one or more keywords for memorization and, where necessary, enough additional senses to clarify the character's usage. For the more important characters, however, there are significantly more senses and uses than the scope of this volume allows for. Halpern's *Kanji Learner's Dictionary* allows the user to discover that the greater part of the contribution kanji make to the Japanese language lies in the semantic richness of the several hundred most productive characters. While their entries each occupy but a single frame in this volume, they often fill an entire page in Halpern. The present volume provides a useful method of remembering these characters' core meanings, but it gives only a partial view of their applications and range of meaning. It is therefore best used in conjunction with a dictionary providing complete and precise explanation of how each kanji is used, for which Halpern is the superlative source among portable volumes. For those interested in a reference volume, Halpern's *Kodansha Kanji Dictionary* is recommended.

2. *Cross-referencing of* kun*-reading homophones.* These cross-references identify characters that are related but usually not identical in meaning, such as those having the *kun* reading おさ(める): 収める (take in), 納める (put away, put in place), 治める (govern), and 修める (master). Comparing these related words and characters helps the learner develop a deeper and more precise understanding of their meanings, and overcome one of the trickier challenges of the written language.

3. *Jinmeiyo kanji and name readings.* Halpern includes the full set of Jinmeiyo kanji, as well as special name readings for Joyo kanji.

4. *Full English equivalents for uses of characters as independent* on-*reading words.* These allow the learner to begin making use of a kanji's *on* reading even without knowing any of its compounds. The independent *on*-reading words receive less attention than they deserve in most Japanese-language learning materials, and offer the opportunity to master a character's *on* reading through communicative usage.

5. *Full English equivalents for uses of characters as* kun-*reading words or word elements.* These also allow the learner to make immediate use of a kanji before knowing any of its compounds, and to master a character's readings through communicative usage.

6. *Functional labels.* These clarify, among other things, how a kanji is used differently as a prefix, as a suffix, as a component of compounds, or as an independent word.

7. *Explanatory and supplementary glosses.* These clarify the specific sense, range of usage, and syntactical function of kanji-based words.

# HOW TO STUDY THE KANJI

I have prepared this course with the assumption that you will start with the first kanji and study the characters in the assigned sequence. If you have previously studied kanji, you should at least read through the annotations from the beginning in order to lay the groundwork for learning and remembering the challenging kanji introduced later on. The annotations assume knowledge of what has come before.

## Step-by-Step Method

Each time you begin studying a new character, proceed as follows:

1. Take a moment to study its form carefully, and compare it with similar-looking kanji appearing on the same page or adjacent pages (before or after).

2. Read the annotation. Some annotations will instruct you to review an earlier entry that provides information that is in one way or another foundational to learning the present entry (this information will be found in the earlier entry's annotation section). Often only part of the earlier annotation will be relevant, but it will generally be clear which part. If you've forgotten the meaning of a component grapheme, look it up by stroke count in the Table of Grapheme Meanings, which will refer you to the entry where the grapheme was introduced.

3. After reading the annotation, look over the kanji again. Allow plenty of time for the images or ideas in the annotation to work their way into your memory. Try to see the meaning of the kanji in some aspect of its appearance or its component parts. Staring at it is not a waste of time.

4. Study the kanji's meaning(s) (see "Learning Meanings," below). If more than one meaning is given, consider how the different meanings may be interrelated. Focus on remembering the capitalized mnemonic keywords.

5. Study the kanji's reading(s) (see "Learning Readings," below). If kanji containing the same phonetic component appear immediately before or after the kanji you are studying (as they often will), note whether the other kanji have similar or identical *on-yomi*.

6. If any cross-references are provided at the end of the annotation (indicated by a pointing hand), make note of any similarities or differences with the kanji you are studying. Train your eye to recognize the distinctions, and practice associating these with the respective meanings of each character, as suggested by the annotations.

7. Practice writing the kanji several times in the stroke order provided—even if you are not interested in learning how to write kanji—in order to fix its form in your memory. Mastering orthodox stroke order is important to be able to count strokes accurately (useful for looking up the kanji in dictionaries), and to read cursive writing.

   To practice, start by tracing over the head character with a capped pen. Maintain continuous contact with the paper throughout each stroke. Then write the character, imitating the head character as closely as you can. Note especially how component parts are modified in form or proportion in order to accommodate other parts. To maintain consistent proportion, use the printed manuscript paper (原稿用紙, げんこうようし) the Japanese use. This paper provides squares of regular size, which helps you avoid the bad habit of writing high stroke-count characters larger than low stroke-count characters.

As you write the character, remind yourself of the mnemonic association between the kanji's form and its meaning(s). Also, if the kanji contains a grapheme you are writing for the first time, practice writing it until you can reproduce it from memory.

If the head character is a nonstandardized form (this will be mentioned in the annotation), you should also practice writing it according to the standardized form shown in the variant field below the head character. For example, for 剝 0609, you should practice writing the standardized form 剥.

8. Study the didactic vocabulary provided (see "Learning Didactic Vocabulary," below). If necessary, review other kanji appearing in the vocabulary using the cross-reference numbers provided. For sample words in which the kanji is followed by *okurigana* (a kana-based inflectional ending), note which portion of the inflected word is written in *okurigana*. For example, you should note in entry 0081 that みずから is written 自ら, not 自から or 自ずから.

9. Familiarize yourself with the traditional or alternative form of the kanji, if there is one.

10. If you have a digital device handy, you can practice inputting the didactic vocabulary using a Japanese text input method, find sample sentences on the Internet, etc.

11. Proceed as above until you have reached the end of the page. Then, test yourself on the kanji appearing on the *previous* page (see "Self-Testing," below).

12. Every *n* pages, test yourself on the *previous* set of *n* pages, where *n* equals the average number of pages you are studying per day. For example, if you are studying five pages per day, then on completing page 80, test yourself on pages 71–75 (see "Self-Testing," below).

## Learning Meanings

As mentioned in the sample entry, you should concern yourself only with memorizing the capitalized mnemonic keyword(s), not the additional senses listed in lower case. The mnemonics are designed to suggest the ideas encapsulated in the keywords.

Following Halpern, each basic meaning consolidates a variety of related senses into a concise conceptual unit. This summarizing function, together with the clear division of each kanji's senses into discrete numbered meanings, allows you to avoid the confusion students have long encountered in learning the more semantically rich kanji.

In studying the meanings of these more versatile kanji, try to see how their ramifying senses are related through a core idea. Halpern is particularly helpful for this task (the more important the kanji, the more likely you will find a significant amount of additional information there). The keywords given in Halpern are not always identical to those given here, but the general meanings given in the two texts are consistent.

For characters with multiple meanings, these meanings appear in general order of their importance. Note, however, that the mnemonic annotations will often start with a lower-ranked meaning when this aids learning and retention. This is especially the case when the lower-ranked meaning is in fact the original meaning of the kanji, and is for that reason (a) more directly related to the kanji's graphical

form, and/or (b) more intuitively related to the kanji's various subsenses. For example, the kanji 朗 has two basic meanings: CHEERFUL and CLEAR/bright. While CHEERFUL is the more important meaning in modern Japanese, CLEAR/bright is in fact the original meaning, which not surprisingly is more directly associated with the kanji's semantic hints, "*good* (良) + *moon* (月)." The mnemonic therefore instructs you first to think of a "*good moon*" as being CLEAR and bright, and then to associate this image with the primary meaning CHEERFUL, via the idea of brightness.

As you study, always keep in mind that the mnemonics should not be learned for their own sake. Their only purpose is to serve as a temporary bridge between the kanji's graphical appearance and its meaning(s).

There is no doubt that for many kanji you will end up coming up with a more useful mnemonic than I have done. While this course will give you a reliable way of remembering 2300 kanji, it will certainly not provide the best way of remembering every kanji for every person. In preparing this kanji curriculum, I have had to insert generic mnemonics in place of some personal mnemonics that were specific to my own experience and thus of absolutely no use to you. I encourage you to reverse this process by replacing some generic mnemonics with ones grounded in your own stock of knowledge and experience. Here our one rigid rule, that of being flexible, applies as always.

That said, you should also bear in mind that the reasoning behind a particular mnemonic will not always be apparent at first. In some cases, I have deliberately forgone an obvious mnemonic in favor of one that will help you distinguish the kanji from similar ones introduced later. Also, the above exhortations toward flexibility notwithstanding, it won't do you any good to be gratuitously inconsistent. If you make up a new interpretation of a grapheme nearly every time you run across it, you will soon end up making your job harder rather than easier. Except when there is good reason to ignore an established meaning, it is best to stick to it. Moreover, if you find that a mnemonic hasn't worked, it is usually more efficient to enhance the existing mnemonic than to completely replace it, lest you get the new mnemonic confused with the old one. With these cautions in mind, you are certainly encouraged to adapt this mnemonic system to include your own special insights. In time you will identify the mnemonic strategies that work best for you.

## Learning Readings

One of the more daunting things about learning kanji is that many characters can be read in several different ways. The best approach is not to concern yourself with memorizing the readings for their own sake. Instead, focus on learning didactic vocabulary, and simply learn new kanji readings as you learn new words. Do memorize at least *one* didactic vocabulary word (and thus one reading) the very first time you study a kanji, since this will make it easy for you to produce it on a keyboard, to look it up in an electronic dictionary, or to find it in the readings index of a paper dictionary (or this book). For kanji with both *on-yomi* and *kun-yomi*, I recommend in general that you memorize a didactic vocabulary word for each.

The appendix "Regular *On-Yomi* Groups" lists roughly 550 characters whose readings can be learned reliably by mastering a limited number of phonetic components. I encourage you to take full advantage of this list as you proceed through the course.

## Learning Didactic Vocabulary

The didactic vocabulary for each kanji was chosen with the following purposes in mind, in general order of priority:

(a) to illustrate the basic meanings of the entry character;
(b) to illustrate the principal readings of the entry character;
(c) to create opportunities to put the kanji into practice in an everyday context;
(d) to provide high-frequency or instructive vocabulary words containing the kanji; and
(e) to review previously learned characters, especially recently learned ones.

As suggested by the hierarchy of this list, high-frequency samples were given somewhat less priority than samples that illustrate an important reading or meaning of the entry kanji. This reflects the overall scope and purpose of this volume, which is to serve not as a dictionary but as a tool for gaining a solid understanding of the kanji themselves.

An important feature of this course is that the didactic vocabulary of kanji having more than one basic meaning is arranged in the order of those meanings, and is labeled with a superscript numeral for cross-referencing with the meanings. This feature allows you to reinforce your understanding of the separate meanings and grasp how each one is used, emulating in a limited way one of the most distinctive and didactically useful features of Halpern's dictionary. Note that I have not numbered sample words that in my judgment corresponded equally with more than one numbered meaning, or did not correspond with any numbered meaning.

Do not neglect to briefly study the didactic vocabulary words, as these will help you not only build a more sophisticated sense of the kanji's meaning but also assimilate the meanings and readings of the kanji you have already learned.

I further recommend that you memorize at least one vocabulary word for each kanji, right from the beginning, so that you will not simply attempt to memorize the kanji as a detached entity. For this purpose, I have suggested one or two sample words to memorize for most kanji, by means of inserting a superscript circle to the left of selected vocabulary entries. In some cases, I have suggested three sample words, particularly when a kanji has several important meanings or readings. The words not marked in this way as "suggested" are provided more for the purpose of illustration than for systematic study. Learn these and other kanji-based words through your general study and communicative use of the language, once you've learned the kanji's basic meaning.

Memorizing the suggested words will create opportunities for you to use the kanji in practice, and will help reinforce the individual meanings when more than one exists. For example, it is easier and more natural to remember the kanji 態 (タイ) as the タイ of 状態 (じょうたい, state) and 態度 (たいど, attitude, posture) than to remember it on its own as a kanji with the two basic meanings STATE and POSTURE. The sample words help you ground your learning of the kanji's meaning(s) and reading(s) in concrete examples that can be used in real-life communication.

The vocabulary items also serve as ready identifiers for referring to a kanji verbally. For example, a speaker referring to a kanji pronounced サイ would typically clarify the reference by saying "the サイ of さいばん" (裁判の裁), "the サイ of れんさい" (連載の載), "the サイ of ぼんさい" (盆栽の栽), etc. For kanji with *kun* readings, a *kun* word would serve the same purpose.

I have chosen the suggested vocabulary entries to help you learn and remember the basic meaning(s) and principal readings of each kanji, and to point out particularly useful or instructive words that will allow you to begin communicating through kanji, whether actively or passively. While the suggested words will not be the most useful ones for everyone in every case, I felt it would be advantageous

for you to have some sound basis for selection when an overriding criterion does not present itself. I encourage you to replace them with any words familiar to you from other contexts.

I have not included vocabulary suggestions when I felt there was no particular justification for recommending one word over others. Nor have I included them in the first fifty entries, whose didactic vocabulary is of limited usefulness as a result of the requirement of using only such kanji as have already been introduced.

The didactic vocabulary assumes knowledge of hiragana and katakana, as well as some knowledge of Japanese grammar. Familiarity with word endings and the use of transitive and intransitive verbs is particularly important, as knowledge of the latter will allow you to make sense of examples such as 花を傷める (はなをいためる, spoil a flower) and 傷んだトマト (いたんだトマト, rotten tomato). Always compare the examples given in the didactic vocabulary with the forms listed in the readings field.

Some didactic compounds have irregular readings not listed in the readings field. These can be personal names (e.g., 正男, まさお), place names (北京, ペキン), or words with irregular readings (一人, ひとり). Of this last group, many appear in the appendix "Selected Compounds with Irregular Readings." These compounds combine characters chosen for their semantic value for writing a pre-existing Japanese word, without regard to their phonetic value. For example, 大人 (*big + person*) corresponds to the meaning of the indigenous Japanese word for "adult," おとな, even though 大 is never read as オト and 人 is never read as ナ. A limited number of such compounds, known as *ateji* (suitable characters), appear in this course, including some which also have a regular *on* reading with the same meaning or a related one. An example of the latter case is 今日 (*present/this + day*). Its regular *on* reading (こんにち) means "today" as in "in this day and age," while its irregular *kun* reading (きょう) means "today" as in "this day."

## Learning to Write Kanji

This course is appropriate both for those who aim to learn how to write kanji by hand and for those who are happy just to produce them on a keyboard. The step-by-step introduction of graphemes, and the unwavering emphasis on learning to differentiate among graphically similar kanji, will make it much easier for you to write kanji accurately. At the same time, learning the reading of at least one didactic vocabulary word per kanji will make it easy for you to produce kanji with a keyboard. While this course assumes that your first priority is to learn to *read* the kanji in the shortest time possible, you should still practice writing every kanji as you learn it (if only for the purpose of better recognizing it), and learn to write all the graphemes from memory.

## Learning Nonstandard Forms

It is helpful to be able to recognize traditional forms, not only because of their use in names, but also because kanji not included in the Joyo list (or belatedly added to it) often appear in traditional form.

In many cases, postwar revisions were applied to all of the characters based on a revised form. Thus, the short stroke deleted from the traditional form 者 to make the revised form 者 was also deleted from 諸, 緒 and other traditional forms based on 者. In some cases, different traditional forms (such as the crowns of 榮 and 學) were conflated into a single revised form (栄/学), rendering the origin of some revised characters unclear.

## Self-Testing

The kanji entries in the main section of this course have been laid out in regular columns to allow you to test your recollection of the kanji after you have learned them. By preparing a card of the proper dimensions, you can cover up all of the entry to the right of the kanji, and test your recollection of its mnemonic keyword(s). By cutting a small notch into the side of your self-testing card, you can also test yourself on the didactic vocabulary (the superscript circles to the left of the suggested vocabulary entries allow you to limit your self-testing to these words). The same card can be used with the appendixes, at an advanced stage of study, to test your ability to differentiate among related or look-alike kanji, to recognize nonstandard forms, and to pronounce compounds with irregular readings. Both the Radical Index and the Table of Related and Look-Alike Kanji facilitate self-testing by bringing together groups of related kanji in a different sequence from that used in the main entries. You can simulate the use of flash cards by testing yourself on these kanji in random order and checking off those you have mastered.

## Making the Transition into Reading

This course is designed to reduce the difficulty of initially acquiring the kanji, but it is no replacement for using the kanji by reading real Japanese. You should not attempt to complete the entire course before doing so, or without concurrently studying grammar and other aspects of the language. The 1200-kanji mark is a realistic point at which to plunge into some kind of authentic reading material. This inevitably will expose you to many kanji outside your 1200, which will serve as an impetus to continue adding to that number. It will also tell you what other areas you may need to improve in your knowledge of the language generally.

If you find these first forays into authentic reading too halting, you may be tempted simply to redouble your efforts at studying kanji rather than to apply what you already know. In fact you should pursue the two tasks together, immersing yourself in reading ever deeper as your supply of kanji increases. For one thing, this will help you maintain your knowledge of the kanji you have already studied. In addition, it will force you to explore senses and applications of kanji that go beyond the core meanings provided in this volume.

If you read authentic texts, you will encounter kanji not covered in this course. Make a mental note of these, and perhaps write them in the margin of the Table of Related and Look-Alike Kanji, next to a group of similar kanji. It is helpful just to know that they exist. Do not worry about studying these in the same systematic way you study the kanji in this course. Instead, focus on learning the compounds that contain them. If such a compound contains another kanji that *is* covered in this course, make a note of the compound at that entry.

You may prefer to use a graded reader, or a website that allows you to read Japanese webpages even without having an advanced vocabulary. While this course is not designed specifically to be used with graded readers, it is certainly possible to do so. When you run across kanji you haven't studied yet, you can always flip ahead and preview their entries. But don't let flipping ahead degenerate into skipping around—always go back to the place in the sequence where you left off, and continue forward in order.

Ultimately, you should keep the goal of 2300 kanji firmly in mind, and eventually press on to the end, always reviewing as necessary. Completing the course will create the space in your memory for these 2300 kanji, and hundreds more you will encounter elsewhere, to fit together in an organized way. Naturally, you may prefer

at first to set a goal of 1000 or 1200. But in the long run, while a partial knowledge of the kanji may help you complete a college course or pass an intermediate-level proficiency exam, it will not allow you to read authentic Japanese texts with real fluency. Every aspect of this course reflects the assumption that your ultimate goal in studying kanji is to read authentic texts.

When you begin reading real Japanese, you will notice that a large portion of the kanji unfamiliar to you will be those found in names. Before long you will learn to identify personal names within a text. To pick out name kanji more easily, do cast your eye over the Table of Jinmeiyo Kanji in the appendixes. Compare these kanji with similar kanji you have already learned. Be aware that they exist. If any seem familiar, by all means look them up in Halpern or elsewhere. Practice pronouncing the personal or place names in which they appear. Write them out a few times. When you encounter a name in your reading, try to guess its pronunciation, or part of it. If there are *furigana*, read the name out loud. The important thing is to become familiar with the more common pronunciations of the name kanji—not their meanings.

## A Final Note

In the early stages, you will no doubt find many of the memory aids superfluous. Indeed, to remember the most unique, vivid, or frequently encountered kanji, you hardly need a mnemonic system in the first place. These early stages will impart the useful lesson that a memory aid is only to be used as long as it is needed.

Later on—during the long, critical period in which you know too few kanji to be literate and yet too many to keep track of without help—this text will be a source of order, clarity, handy solutions, and encouragement in the belief that your goal can be achieved. It will also make remembering many of the complicated, the unintuitive, and the look-alike characters as painless, or almost as painless, as remembering the easy ones.

Still, no matter how useful any part of this course may turn out to be, it is not intended to be an end in itself, but merely a temporary expedient by which you may, in a reasonable amount of time, learn to read kanji naturally and without conscious effort. That feat shall be a testimony to the energy and perseverance you bring to this task, far more than to the method provided in the pages that follow.

THE KODANSHA
# KANJI LEARNER'S COURSE

| 日 | **¹ SUN**<br>**² DAY**<br>**³ JAPAN**<br><br>ニチ ジツ<br>ひ -び -か | **²** 日々 ひび daily; days<br>**²** ____ ひにち date; number of days (also written 日にち)<br>**²** 日に日に ひにひに day by day, every day<br>**²** ある日 あるひ one day, a certain day<br>**³** 日ソ にっソ Japan and the Soviet Union, Japanese-Soviet |
|---|---|---|

**0001**

日 72

2606

常 4

We begin with the most common character and the source of all life, the SUN. 日 depicts the SUN with a line drawn along its equator. It also means DAY, as well as JAPAN (as an abbreviation for 日本 [にほん]). In the didactic vocabulary, note the symbol 々, which means "repeat last character"; thus, 日々=日日.

| 一 | **ONE**<br><br>イチ イツ<br>ひと- ひと(つ) | 一日 いちにち one day...........................0001<br>ついたち 1st of the month<br>一々 いちいち one by one; in detail<br>一つ ひとつ one (of something)<br>一つずつ ひとつずつ one at a time |
|---|---|---|

**0002**

一 1

2850

常 1

The next three entries, representing the numbers ONE, TWO, and THREE, are classic examples of Chinese characters as ideographs—written symbols that represent abstract ideas. But one could also argue that they are in fact pictographs, representing ONE, TWO, or THREE fingers. ☞ 壱 2115

| 二 | **TWO**<br><br>ニ<br>ふた ふた(つ) | 二日 ふつか two days; 2nd of the month....0001<br>二メートル にメートル 2 meters<br>二ラウンド にラウンド two rounds, Round 2<br>レモン二つ レモンふたつ two lemons<br>一つ二つ ひとつふたつ one or two..........0002 |
|---|---|---|

**0003**

二 7

1688

常 2

The first didactic vocabulary word (hereafter, "VI") is one of the many words whose pronunciation cannot be derived from the readings listed in these entries. A selection of compounds with irregular readings appears in Appendix 3. ☞ 弐 0110

| 三 | **THREE**<br><br>サン<br>み み(つ) みっ(つ) | 三つだけ みっつだけ just three<br>三日 みっか three days; 3rd (of the month) 0001<br>三日まで みっかまで by the 3rd...............0001<br>二三日 にさんにち two or three days...0003, 0001<br>三グラム さんグラム three grams |
|---|---|---|

**0004**

一 1

1689

常 3

As these first four entries have made clear, the didactic compounds include only such kanji as have been introduced previously.

| 十 | **TEN** | 二十 にじゅう twenty ...........................**0003** |
| | | はたち twenty years old |
| | ジュウ ジッ- | 十日 とおか ten days; 10th of the month ....**0001** |
| | とお と | 二十日 はつか twenty days; 20th of the month |
| | | ......................................................**0003, 0001** |
| | | 一から十まで いちからじゅうまで without |
| | | exception .........................................**0002** |

| **0005** | We now skip forward to the kanji for **TEN**, so that we can start learning two-digit compounds |
| 十 24 | in the didactic vocabulary. Cross your hands in the shape of 十: two hands = **TEN** fingers. |
| | As a component grapheme (a meaningful contrastive unit within a character), 十 can also |
| | denote *abundant/complete*, *cross shape/cross-shaped*, or *needle*. |
| **2855** | |
| 常 2 | |

| 四 | **FOUR** | 四日 よっか four days; 4th of the month.....**0001** |
| | | 十四 じゅうし (=じゅうよん) fourteen ...........**0005** |
| | シ | 四十四 しじゅうし (=よんじゅうよん) forty-four **0005** |
| | よ よ(つ) よっ(つ) よん | 十四日 じゅうよっか fourteen days; 14th of the |
| | | month...............................................**0005, 0001** |
| | | 四ミリ よんミリ 4 millimeters |

| **0006** | The kanji for **FOUR** is based on a square, which has **FOUR** sides. Needless to say, you really |
| 口 31 | have no need of memory aids for such elemental kanji as these numerals. But you may rest |
| | assured that this course will grow in usefulness in proportion to the number of kanji you try |
| | to learn. ☞ 匹 1801 |
| **2620** | |
| 常 5 | |

| 五 | **FIVE** | 五日 いつか five days; 5th of the month.....**0001** |
| | | 四、五日 し、ごにち four or five days....**0006, 0001** |
| | ゴ | 五十五 ごじゅうご fifty-five ..................**0005** |
| | いつ いつ(つ) | 五つほど いつつほど around five |
| | | ダイヤの五 ダイヤのご five of diamonds |

| **0007** | You can approximate this shape using **FIVE** fingers: first, hold out the first three fingers of |
| 二 7 | your right hand, then lay the first two fingers of your left hand across them. ☞ 丑 0590 |
| **2892** | |
| 常 4 | |

| 六 | **SIX** | 六日 むいか six days; 6th of the month......**0001** |
| | | 六日ぶりに むいかぶりに for the first time in |
| | ロク | six days..............................................**0001** |
| | む む(つ) むっ(つ) むい | 十六 じゅうろく sixteen ......................**0005** |
| | | 六つ むっつ six; six years old |
| | | 六トン ろくトン 6 tons |

| **0008** | To repeat, you really do not need memory aids for these most basic kanji, but if you wish |
| 八 12 | to use one for 六, you might see S1 (stroke 1, as marked in the head character) as the letter |
| | "i," and S3–4 as the intersecting lines of the letter "x," spelling the "ix" of **SIX**. Note that the |
| | stroke-order numbers in the head character are placed at the starting point of each stroke. |
| | ☞ 穴 0397 |
| **1710** | |
| 常 4 | |

| SEVEN | | |
|---|---|---|
| シチ<br>なな　なな(つ)　なの | 七日 なのか (=なぬか) seven days; 7th of the month............0001 |
| | 十七日 じゅうしちにち (=じゅうななにち) seventeen days; 17th of the month ............0005, 0001 |
| | 七十五 ななじゅうご (=しちじゅうご) seventy-five ............0005, 0007 |
| | 七五三 しちごさん the lucky numbers; festival for children of three, five, and seven .....0007, 0004 |

**0009**　一 1

Write a numeral **7** European-style, with a line slicing through the middle. Then turn it upside down.

2854<br>常 2

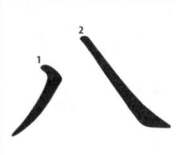

| EIGHT | | |
|---|---|---|
| ハチ<br>や　や(つ)　やっ(つ)　よう | 八日 ようか eight days; 8th of the month ...0001 |
| | 十八日 じゅうはちにち eighteen days; 18th of the month......0005, 0001 |
| | 八ユーロ はちユーロ eight euros |
| | 一か八か いちかばちか all or nothing, hit or miss ............0002 |

**0010**　八 12

Put your **EIGHT** fingers (no thumbs) together in prayer (actually, <u>almost</u> together, imitating 八). Inside other kanji, 八 will sometimes mean *split*, so the *split* between S1 and S2 deserves special attention. Note that in these annotations, *italics* indicate meanings of component graphemes, whereas CAPS indicate mnemonic keywords of whole kanji.

2536<br>常 2

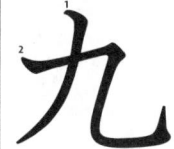

| NINE | | |
|---|---|---|
| キュウ　ク<br>ここの　ここの(つ) | 九日 ここのか nine days; 9th of the month...0001 |
| | 九十九 きゅうじゅうきゅう ninety-nine.........0005 |
| | 九九 くく multiplication table |
| | 九つ ここのつ nine (of something) |
| | 九日から ここのかから starting on the 9th...0001 |

**0011**　乙 5

The trick with this entry is distinguishing it from 力 0084 POWER. To do so, associate the wide, round hook at the end of S2 with the loop in the arabic numeral **9**. ☞ 力 0084, 丸 0012

2858<br>常 2

| ROUND | | |
|---|---|---|
| ガン<br>まる　まる(い)　まる(める) | 一丸となって いちがんとなって as one, all together............0002 |
| | 日の丸 ひのまる Rising Sun flag ............0001 |
| | 丸い まるい round, spherical |
| | 丸める まるめる make round, roll up |

**0012**　丶 3

Similar to 0011, so let the difference between them (S3) suggest the meaning. Because S3 curves slightly, we can see it as part of the circumference of a circle (geometrically speaking, an arc of about 20°), suggesting the meaning **ROUND**. Pencil 丸 into the margin of this page, then draw a dotted line to complete the imaginary circle. ☞ 刃 0087, 九 0011

2883<br>常 3

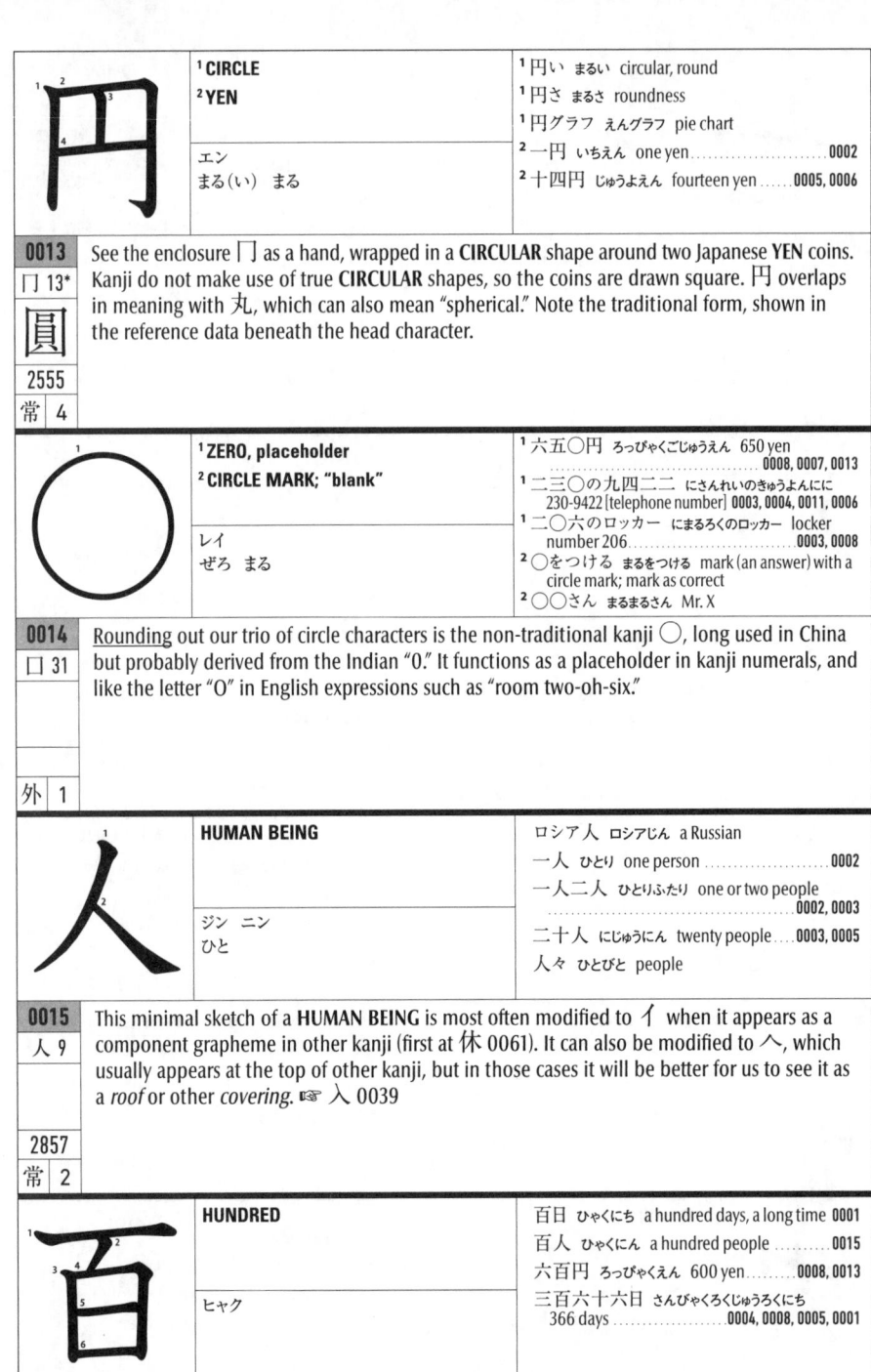

| 円 | **[1] CIRCLE** **[2] YEN** | [1] 円い まるい circular, round |
|---|---|---|
| | | [1] 円さ まるさ roundness |
| | | [1] 円グラフ えんグラフ pie chart |
| | エン | [2] 一円 いちえん one yen.....................0002 |
| | まる(い) まる | [2] 十四円 じゅうよえん fourteen yen ......0005, 0006 |

**0013**
口 13*

圓

2555
常 | 4

See the enclosure 冂 as a hand, wrapped in a **CIRCULAR** shape around two Japanese **YEN** coins. Kanji do not make use of true **CIRCULAR** shapes, so the coins are drawn square. 円 overlaps in meaning with 丸, which can also mean "spherical." Note the traditional form, shown in the reference data beneath the head character.

| ○ | **[1] ZERO, placeholder** **[2] CIRCLE MARK; "blank"** | [1] 六五〇円 ろっぴゃくごじゅうえん 650 yen .....................................0008, 0007, 0013 |
|---|---|---|
| | | [1] 二三〇の九四二二 にさんれいのきゅうよんにに 230-9422 [telephone number] 0003, 0004, 0011, 0006 |
| | レイ | [1] 二〇六のロッカー にまるろくのロッカー locker number 206.....................0003, 0008 |
| | ぜろ まる | [2] 〇をつける まるをつける mark (an answer) with a circle mark; mark as correct |
| | | [2] 〇〇さん まるまるさん Mr. X |

**0014**
口 31

外 | 1

Rounding out our trio of circle characters is the non-traditional kanji ○, long used in China but probably derived from the Indian "0." It functions as a placeholder in kanji numerals, and like the letter "O" in English expressions such as "room two-oh-six."

| 人 | **HUMAN BEING** | ロシア人 ロシアじん a Russian |
|---|---|---|
| | | 一人 ひとり one person ......................0002 |
| | | 一人二人 ひとりふたり one or two people .............................................0002, 0003 |
| | ジン ニン | 二十人 にじゅうにん twenty people....0003, 0005 |
| | ひと | 人々 ひとびと people |

**0015**
人 9

2857
常 | 2

This minimal sketch of a **HUMAN BEING** is most often modified to 亻 when it appears as a component grapheme in other kanji (first at 休 0061). It can also be modified to へ, which usually appears at the top of other kanji, but in those cases it will be better for us to see it as a *roof* or other *covering*. ☞ 入 0039

| 百 | **HUNDRED** | 百日 ひゃくにち a hundred days, a long time 0001 |
|---|---|---|
| | | 百人 ひゃくにん a hundred people ..........0015 |
| | | 六百円 ろっぴゃくえん 600 yen..........0008, 0013 |
| | ヒャク | 三百六十六日 さんびゃくろくじゅうろくにち 366 days .....................0004, 0008, 0005, 0001 |

**0016**
白 106

1746
常 | 6

See the number **100**, turned sideways. A little line attaches the 1 to the place-holding zeroes.

| 千 | **THOUSAND** | 千人 せんにん a thousand people..........0015 |
| | | 一千 いっせん one thousand..............0002 |
| | | 三千 さんぜん three thousand...........0004 |
| | セン | 八千円 はっせんえん 8000 yen ........0010, 0013 |
| | ち | 千々に ちぢに in pieces |

**0017**
十 24

Think of this as a stylized letter T, to represent the distinct sound "th" in **"THOUSAND."** Like the Greek letter for the same sound $\theta$ (theta), it has a line running across the center. Write the word **"THOUSAND"** a few times, replacing "th" with 千, and it should stick. ☞ 千 0408

2881
常 | 3

| 万 | **TEN THOUSAND, myriad, all** | 万人 ばんにん (=ばんじん) all people........0015 |
| | | 万一 まんいち if by any chance.............0002 |
| | | 一万 いちまん ten thousand................0002 |
| | マン バン | 百万 ひゃくまん one million.................0016 |
| | | 三万円 さんまんえん 30,000 yen.......0004, 0013 |

**0018**
一 1*
萬

As a temporary expedient, see 一 (*one*) plus an upside-down numeral 4, suggesting a 1 with four zeroes after it: **TEN THOUSAND.** The mnemonic should shortly become unnecessary for this frequently seen kanji. Often used generically to mean a number that is so large as to be practically countless. ☞ 方 0173

2542
常 | 3

| 口 | **MOUTH** | 人口 じんこう population....................0015 |
| | | 一口 ひとくち a mouthful....................0002 |
| | | 口コミ くちコミ word of mouth |
| | コウ ク | 口パク くちパク lip synch |
| | くち | 口にする くちにする eat; say, speak of |

**0019**
口 30

Depicts a **MOUTH.** As we saw with 円, even a round object like **MOUTH** is drawn as a square in the kanji. Just as the English word **MOUTH** can refer to the end of a river or the entrance to a cave, 口 can refer to any mouth-like opening. Thus as a grapheme, 口 will sometimes mean *opening* or *entrance*.

2865
常 | 3

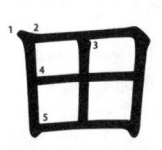

| **RICE FIELD** | 田んぼ (田圃ˣ) たんぼ rice field |
| | ガス田 ガスでん gas field |
| | 三田 みた Mita [surname]...................0004 |
| デン | 田口 たぐち Taguchi [surname]............0019 |
| た | |

**0020**
田 102

Here we look down from the sky on a **RICE FIELD**, divided into four equal plots. As we'll see later at 男 0092, 田 will also be able to take on the meaning *head* when it appears as a grapheme. The ˣ appearing after 圃 in the first sample compound indicates that this kanji is not introduced in this course.

2617
常 | 5

| 目 | [1] **EYE** [2] **ITEM; subdivision; order**<br><br>モク ボク<br>め -め ま- | [1] 一目 ひとめ (=いちもく) a look, a glimpse.....0002<br>[1] 人目 ひとめ attention, public notice.........0015<br>[1] 目つき めつき look, expression<br>[2] 五十人目 ごじゅうにんめ fiftieth person<br>................................0007, 0005, 0015<br>[2] 六日目 むいかめ the sixth day..........0008, 0001 |
|---|---|---|

| **0021**<br>目 109<br><br><br>2619<br>常 5 | This kanji depicts an **EYE** propped up sideways; the middle section represents the iris. It also has a second meaning that is more abstract, but just as easy to see: each of the three rectangles represents one **ITEM** in a list three items long. See *The Kodansha Kanji Learner's Dictionary* by Jack Halpern for additional nuances of this and many other important kanji. Now a word about formatting: in the didactic vocabulary section, the superscript [1] in [1] 一目 indicates that this example illustrates meaning [1] **EYE**. |
|---|---|

| 川 | **RIVER**<br><br>セン<br>かわ | ボルガ川 ボルガがわ Volga River<br>川べり かわべり riverbank<br>川口 かわぐち mouth of a river.............0019<br>　　　　かわぐち Kawaguchi [surname]<br>川田 かわだ (=かわた) Kawada (= Kawata)<br>　　　[surname].................................0020 |
|---|---|---|

| **0022**<br>巛 47<br><br>巛<br><br>0001<br>常 3 | Depicts a **RIVER**, with banks at the left and right, and water flowing through the middle. See 山 0037 and 河 0818 for sample compounds using this character's *on-yomi* (Chinese-derived reading). ☞ 河 0818 |
|---|---|

| 月 | [1] **MOON** [2] **MONTH**<br><br>ゲツ ガツ<br>つき | [2] 一月 いちがつ January ........................0002<br>[2] 　　ひとつき (=いちげつ) one month<br>[2] 三月八日 さんがつようか March 8<br>................................0004, 0010, 0001<br>[2] 月日 がっぴ date.............................0001<br>[2] 　　つきひ time, days |
|---|---|---|

| **0023**<br>月 74<br><br><br>2556<br>常 4 | Focus on the curves of the two upright lines and let them suggest a crescent **MOON**: the line at left outlines the dark portion of the sphere, while the line at right outlines the bright portion. 月 will frequently be incorporated as a component grapheme in other characters, where it can also mean *meat, flesh,* or *body part* (see 肉 0216). |
|---|---|

| 明 | [1] **BRIGHT, cheerful** [2] **CLEAR**<br><br>メイ ミョウ<br>あ(かり) あか(るい) あか(るむ)<br>あか(らむ) あき(らか) あ(ける) -あ(け)<br>あ(く) あ(くる) あ(かす) | [1] 明月 めいげつ bright moon, full moon; harvest<br>　moon...................................................0023<br>[1] 明るい あかるい bright, light; clear; cheerful<br>[2] 明らかな あきらかな clear, distinct, apparent<br>明日 あす (=あした) tomorrow................0001<br>明くる日 あくるひ the following day .........0001 |
|---|---|---|

| **0024**<br>日 72<br><br><br>0756<br>常 8 | This is our first two-grapheme kanji. In it we see the *sun* (日) shining on the *moon*, making it brilliantly **BRIGHT** and **CLEAR**. Notice how the two forms have been compressed; this is because all kanji must occupy a square space of regular size. In the next entry, which combines <u>three</u> graphemes, 日 will become even narrower. |
|---|---|

| 曜 | DAY OF THE WEEK | 日曜(日) にちよう(び) Sunday ................. 0001 |
|---|---|---|
| | | 月曜(日) げつよう(び) Monday ......... 0023, 0001 |
| | | 曜日 ようび day of the week ................. 0001 |
| | ヨウ | 七曜 しちよう seven days of the week ....... 0009 |

| 0025<br>日 72 | 隹 is a *small bird* (S11 shows its head and beak, S12 its breast, S13–18 its tucked-back wings). ヨヨ also looks like a pair of wings—let them suggest the bird's flapping movement. Combined with 日 *day*, the image depicts the little bird taking flight from one day to the next, to the next, as the **DAYS OF THE WEEK** fly by. ☞ 濯 1328, 躍 1327 |
|---|---|
| 1014<br>常 18 | |

| 火 | FIRE | 火曜(日) かよう(び) Tuesday ............ 0025, 0001 |
|---|---|---|
| | | 火口 かこう crater ............................ 0019 |
| | | ひぐち cause of a fire |
| | カ | 口火 くちび fuse; pilot burner; cause (of a war) .......... 0019 |
| | ひ -び ほ- | 火田 かでん slash-and-burn agriculture .... 0020 |

| 0026<br>火 86 | A pyramid-shaped bonfire, from which flames leap to the left and right. As a grapheme, 火 means *fire* or *burn*, and takes either the narrowed form 火 or the completely different form 灬, resembling four fingers of flame. |
|---|---|
| 2911<br>常 4 | |

| 水 | WATER | 火水 ひみず (as opposite as) fire and water 0026 |
|---|---|---|
| | | 水口 みずぐち spout, nozzle ................. 0019 |
| | | 水田 すいでん paddy field, rice field ........ 0020 |
| | スイ | 水曜(日) すいよう(び) Wednesday ...... 0025, 0001 |
| | みず みず- | 月水 げっすい Mondays and Wednesdays ... 0023 |

| 0027<br>水 85 | Looks roughly like 川 0022 RIVER pinched from both sides, making **WATER** splash out. Though it can appear in this form as a grapheme, it almost always changes to the completely different form 氵, easily recognizable as drops of water. ☞ 氷 1690 |
|---|---|
| 0003<br>常 4 | |

| 木 | ¹TREE<br><br>²WOOD | 木曜(日) もくよう(び) Thursday .......... 0025, 0001 |
|---|---|---|
| | | 1月7日(木) いちがつなのか(もく) January 7 (Thursday) ............................ 0023, 0001 |
| | | 火木 かもく Tuesdays and Thursdays ........ 0026 |
| | ボク モク | ² 木目 きめ (=もくめ) (wood) grain ............. 0021 |
| | き こ- | ² 一木 いちぼく one tree ...................... 0002 |

| 0028<br>木 75 | Another simple pictograph. Besides **TREE**, 木 also means **WOOD** or **timber**. In its narrower grapheme form (木) the fourth stroke is foreshortened. To make sense of V4, see the entry for 目 in Halpern (2619). |
|---|---|
| 2901<br>常 4 | |

**¹ METAL**
**² GOLD**
**³ MONEY**

キン　コン
かね　かな-　-がね

¹ 口金　くちがね　metal clasp, snap; metal cap ... 0019
² 金メダル　きんメダル　gold medal
³ お金　おかね　money
金曜(日)　きんよう(び)　Friday .............. 0025, 0001
月水金　げっすいきん　Mondays, Wednesdays, and Fridays ................................. 0023, 0027

| 0029 | |
|---|---|
| 金 167 | In addition to **GOLD**, **METAL**, and **MONEY**, 金 is also the "Fri" in "Friday." Visualize it as a stack of gold bars kept under a *roof* (ヘ) (S6–7 show the gold's glitter). The basic meaning is **GOLD** (hence **MONEY**), but 金 can also convey the more generic meaning **METAL**. The grapheme form (釒) carries the more general meaning. |
| 1771 | |
| 常 8 | |

**SOIL, land**

ド　ト
つち

土曜(日)　どよう(び)　Saturday .............. 0025, 0001
土日　どにち　Saturday and Sunday, weekend ................................................. 0001
土木　どぼく　engineering works .............. 0028
土人　どじん　aborigines ...................... 0015
土いじり　つちいじり　fiddling with dirt, puttering in the garden

| 0030 | |
|---|---|
| 土 32 | See this as a sprout coming forth from the surface of the **SOIL**. Its shades of meaning extend to **earth**, **land**, **ground**, etc. As with 金 and numerous other kanji, the *hen* (left-hand grapheme) form of 土 (圡) is written with its last horizontal stroke sloping upward, to make way for the *tsukuri* (right-hand grapheme) to extend leftward (as in 場 0445).　☞ 士 0350 |
| 2875 | |
| 常 3 | |

**¹ BASIS, origin, root**
**² BOOK**
**³ THIS**

ホン
もと

本土　ほんど　mainland ...................... 0030
日本　にほん (=にっぽん)　Japan ................ 0001
あの人の本　あのひとのほん　that person's book ................................................. 0015
³ 本人　ほんにん　the person himself, the said person ........................................ 0015
本日　ほんじつ　today, this day .............. 0001

| 0031 | |
|---|---|
| 木 75 | To 木 **TREE** a stroke was added to indicate the tree's **roots**. This gradually developed into the meaning **BASIS**. The **root** or **BASIS** of movies, plays, and many other things is in **BOOKS**. The visual focus should be on S5, suggesting an **origin**, a source, a **BASIS**. Indicating the time or place in which the speaker is **BASED**, 本 also means **THIS**. |
| 本 | |
| 2937 | |
| 常 5 | |

**EAST**

トウ
ひがし

東日本　ひがしにほん　eastern Japan ....0001, 0031
東口　ひがしぐち　east exit ...................... 0019
東アジア　ひがしアジア　East Asia
東チモール　ひがしチモール　East Timor

| 0032 | |
|---|---|
| 木 75 | This character can be broken down into two component graphemes. Visualize the *sun* (日) rising from behind a *tree* (木): **EAST**. An *on-yomi* compound appears in the next entry. |
| 2987 | |
| 常 8 | |

| 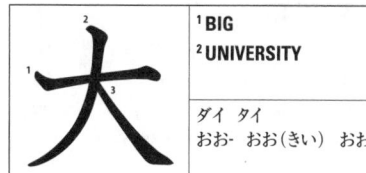 ² 大 ¹ <br> ダイ タイ <br> おお- おお(きい) おお(いに) | ¹ **BIG** <br> ² **UNIVERSITY** | ¹ 大金 たいきん large sum of money .......... 0029 <br> ¹ 大きい おおきい big, grand <br> ¹ 大いに おおいに very, highly <br> ² 大人 おとな adult .............................. 0015 <br> ² 東大 とうだい University of Tokyo (short for 東京大学) .................................................. 0032 |
|---|---|---|

| **0033** <br> 大 37 <br><br> 2882 <br> 常 3 | Stretch out your arms, and spread out your legs: make yourself **BIG**. The second meaning **UNIVERSITY** comes from 大's use as an abbreviation for 大学 (だいがく, university or, literally, "big school"). As a grapheme, 大 can also appear as 六 as in 暮 1342. |
|---|---|

|  ¹ 小 ² ³ <br> ショウ <br> ちい(さい) こ- お- | **SMALL** | 小の月 しょうのつき month with thirty or fewer days .................................................. 0023 <br> 大小 だいしょう large and small; size ........ 0033 <br> 小口 こぐち small lot, small sum [amount]; end, edge ................................................ 0019 <br> 小川 おがわ brook, streamlet .............. 0022 <br> 小さい ちいさい small |
|---|---|---|

| **0034** <br> 小 42 <br><br> 0002 <br> 常 3 | Now bring your legs back together, and pull your arms back down: make yourself **SMALL**. As a grapheme, 小 can also appear as ⺍ or ⺌, though we'll treat those graphemes as visual elements and ignore their etymological derivation from 小. |
|---|---|

| ⁴ 中 ¹ ² ³ <br> チュウ ジュウ <br> なか | ¹ **MIDDLE** <br> ² **IN, throughout** <br> ³ **CHINA** | ¹ 中東 ちゅうとう Middle East .................. 0032 <br> ¹ 中ヒール ちゅうヒール medium-high heel <br> ² 中に なかに in; in the middle of; between, among <br> ² 日中 にっちゅう during the day ............... 0001 <br> ³ にっちゅう Japan and China, Japanese-Chinese |
|---|---|---|

| **0035** <br> 丨 2 <br><br> 2902 <br> 常 4 | Right down the **MIDDLE**. 中 also serves as an abbreviation for **CHINA**, the **MIDDLE** Kingdom. **IN**, the second meaning (hereafter, "M2"), is likewise related to **MIDDLE**. To start, then, you might simply memorize the keyword "**MIDDLE**." |
|---|---|

|  ¹ ³ 生 ² ⁴ ⁵ <br> セイ ショウ <br> い(きる) い(かす) い(ける) う(まれる) う(まれ) うまれ う(む) お(う) は(える) は(やす) き なま なま- | ¹ **LIFE, grow** <br> ² **BE BORN, give birth to** <br> ³ **STUDENT** | ¹ 人生 じんせい human life, life ................ 0015 <br> ¹ 一生 いっしょう a lifetime, all one's life ...... 0002 <br> ¹ 生ビール なまビール draft beer <br> ² 生まれる うまれる be born <br> ³ 東大生 とうだいせい student of the University of Tokyo ............................................ 0032, 0033 |
|---|---|---|

| **0036** <br> 生 100 <br><br> 2933 <br> 常 5 | Behold a young plant springing up from the ground and growing its first leaf. See **BIRTH** and **LIFE** symbolized in this first leaf, which you should make the focal point of this character. This entry has as many readings as any character you'll find, but as explained in the Introduction, you need not trouble yourself to memorize readings for their own sake. Instead, focus on expanding your vocabulary, and let your repertoire of kanji readings grow naturally as you acquire new words. That said, for 生, I suggest you memorize セイ, ショウ, and なま from the start. Numerous examples to illustrate other readings can be found in Halpern. |
|---|---|

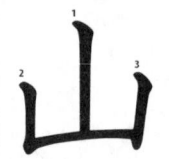

| | MOUNTAIN | 火山 かざん volcano.........................0026 |
| | | 山水 さんすい landscape.....................0027 |
| | | 山川 さんせん mountains and rivers.........0022 |
| | サン | 小山 こやま hill.............................0034 |
| | やま | 山々 やまやま mountains; very much |

| 0037 | Three towering **MOUNTAIN** peaks. Some typefaces obscure the fact that the left and bottom |
| 山 46 | lines are written in a single stroke. This is a good reminder that you should practice writing |
| | the basic forms you are learning until you can reproduce them from memory. Follow the |
| | stroke-order numbers shown in the head character. |
| 2544 | |
| 常 3 | |

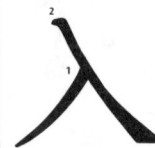

| | ¹ **GO OUT** | ¹ 出る でる go out, depart; go to, be present |
| | ² **PUT OUT** | ¹ 出口 でぐち exit.............................0019 |
| | | ¹ 日の出 ひので sunrise....................0001 |
| | シュツ スイ | ² 出す だす put out, produce; expose |
| | で(る) -て だ(す) -だ(す) | ² 出生 しゅっしょう (=しゅっせい) birth...........0036 |

| 0038 | Visualize the actions **GO OUT** and **PUT OUT** right in the character, by seeing one character |
| 凵 17 | for *mountain* (山) rising out of another. The lower mountain **PUTS OUT** the upper; the upper |
| | mountain **GOES OUT** from the lower. Imitate this action a couple of times with three fingers |
| | from each hand, and the image should stick. |
| 2934 | |
| 常 5 | |

| | ¹ **ENTER** | ¹ 入る いる enter |
| | ² **PUT IN** | ¹ はいる enter; join; contain; have; begin |
| | | ¹ 入口 いりぐち entrance.....................0019 |
| | ニュウ | ² 入れる いれる put in, let in; accommodate; accept |
| | い(る) -い(る) -い(り) い(れる) | ² 入金 にゅうきん payment, deposit...........0029 |
| | -い(れ) はい(る) | |

| 0039 | The projecting line at the top (distinguishing 入 from 人 0015) indicates the onward flow of |
| 入 11 | a river that has just absorbed a tributary. See one river's flow **ENTER** the other's. Note that the |
| | distinction between 入 and 人 is especially noticeable in the handwritten form: in 入, the |
| | right-hand stroke dominates; in 人, the left-hand stroke dominates. ☞ 人 0015 |
| 2859 | |
| 常 2 | |

| | DOWN, lower, below | 下水 げすい sewerage, drainage...........0027 |
| | | 目下 めした subordinate...................0021 |
| | | もっか now, at present |
| | カ ゲ | 川下 かわしも downstream, downriver......0022 |
| | した しも もと さ(げる) さ(がる) | 川田さんの下に かわださんのもとに under Ms. |
| | くだ(る) くだ(り) くだ(す) -くだ(す) | Kawada's supervision.................0022, 0020 |
| | くだ(さる) お(ろす) お(りる) | |

| 0040 | In 下 and 上 (the next entry), the long horizontal stroke indicates a baseline, and the short |
| 一 1 | horizontal stroke (sloping downward, in 下's case) indicates the relative position either |
| | below or above that baseline. 下 means **DOWN** below. 上 means **UP** above. By now you |
| | will have noticed that capitalized words not shown in boldface indicate keywords for other |
| | entries. |
| 2862 | |
| 常 3 | |

| | **UP, rise, raise, above** | 上下 じょうげ high and low; rise and fall; first and second (volumes) ........................ 0040 |
|---|---|---|
| | | 目上 めうえ one's superiors, one's seniors; one's elders ................................................ 0021 |
| | ジョウ ショウ | 川上 かわかみ upstream, upriver ........... 0022 |
| | うえ -うえ うわ- かみ あ(げる) -あ(げる) あ(がる) -あ(がる) あ(がり) -あ(がり) のぼ(る) のぼ(り) のぼ(せる) のぼ(す) | 上がる あがる go up, rise; be finished |
| | | 上る のぼる go up |

| 0041 | Having explained this kanji in the previous entry, I will use this space to explain something about the next one: Note that the asterisks after the readings や(める)* and や(む)* indicate that these readings are not officially recognized in the Ministry of Education's Joyo (regular-use) Kanji List. This does not stop writers from using them. |
|---|---|
| 一 1 | |
| 2876 | |
| 常 3 | |

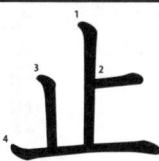

| | **STOP** | 中止する ちゅうしする suspend, stop, discontinue, cancel ........................................... 0035 |
|---|---|---|
| | | 止まる とまる [vi] stop |
| | シ | 止まり木 とまりぎ perch, roost; footrail ...... 0028 |
| | と(まる) -ど(まり) と(める) -と(める) -ど(め) や(める)* や(む)* | 止める とめる [vt] stop |
| | | やめる stop (performing an action) |

| 0042 | Let S1–2 suggest the figure of a man holding out his arms to **STOP** himself. To distinguish from 上, see S3 as another man pushing him from behind. The bottom stroke will be the first man's *feet*, which he is using to **STOP** himself (we'll revert to 止's primitive meaning of *foot* only when it appears inside other kanji, such as in 走 0140 RUN and 歩 0679 WALK). |
|---|---|
| 止 77 | |
| 2545 | |
| 常 4 | |

| | **RIGHT, upright, correct, exact** | 正本 せいほん original document; authenticated facsimile ...................................... 0031 |
|---|---|---|
| | | 大正 たいしょう Taisho (era) (reign of Emperor Taisho, 1912–26) ................................ 0033 |
| | セイ ショウ | 正月 しょうがつ New Year's holiday; January ... 0023 |
| | ただ(しい) ただ(す) まさ まさ(に) | 正しい ただしい right, correct |
| | | 正に まさに just, exactly; surely, certainly |

| 0043 | See S1 as a line that is added at the top of 止 to ensure that all the strokes are set at **RIGHT** angles. It is there to make certain that the vertical lines are perfectly **upright**, and that every angle is **exactly** 90°. The image of straightness also suggests the English word **correct**, which derives from the Latin word for "straight," *rectus*. |
|---|---|
| 止 77 | |
| 2926 | |
| 常 5 | |

| | [1]**FOOT, leg; step** [2]**SUFFICE** | [1] 一足 いっそく one pair (of shoes/socks) ..... 0002 |
|---|---|---|
| | | [1] ひとあし a step |
| | | [1] 足下 あしもと at/under one's feet; gait, pace, step ................................................ 0040 |
| | ソク | [1] 土足 どそく shoes ............................. 0030 |
| | あし た(りる) た(る) た(す) | [2] 千円で足りる せんえんでたりる A thousand yen will suffice ...................... 0017, 0013 |

| 0044 | Represents the Japanese word あし, which conflates the English words "foot" and "leg." Here we add a head (口) to the image of a body with outstretched arms we saw at 止. 止 appears in a modified form here, with "high heels" to emphasize the **FEET** and legs. While the earlier image emphasized the idea of STOPPING, this image emphasizes the **FEET**. |
|---|---|
| 足 157 | |
| 1873 | |
| 常 7 | |

| | |
|---|---|
| **FIX, decide, settle** | 一定する いっていする fix, define, unify .... 0002 |
| | 定木 じょうぎ ruler [cf. 規 0624].............0028 |
| | 定める さだめる fix, decide, settle |
| テイ ジョウ | 定め さだめ law; decision; destiny; certainty |
| さだ(める) さだ(まる) さだ(か) | 定かに さだかに clearly |

| | |
|---|---|
| **0045** | 宀 means *roof* or *house* (S1 suggests a chimney). Here the *roof* has been added to **FIX** the lower portion in place (modified from 正 0043). In 正 we added the top stroke to set the figure RIGHT; that achieved, we now add 宀 to **FIX** it in place. |
| 宀 40 | |
| 1916 | |
| 常 8 | |

| | |
|---|---|
| **¹HAND, arm; labor; skill** | ¹入手する にゅうしゅする obtain, procure ....0039 |
| **²PERFORMER OF AN ACTION, -er** | ¹手中に しゅちゅうに in the hands.............0035 |
| | ¹上手な じょうずな skillful, proficient.........0041 |
| シュ | ¹下手な へたな unskillful, clumsy............0040 |
| て て- -て た- | ¹人手 ひとで hand, manpower................0015 |
| | ²やり手 やりて doer, dealer, highly capable person |

| | |
|---|---|
| **0046** | Depicts a HAND. This is usually abbreviated to 扌 as a grapheme, which we'll interpret as either *hand* or *arm*. See 話 0053, 買 0352, and 投 0517 for examples of compounds using M2. |
| 手 64 | |
| 2907 | |
| 常 4 | |

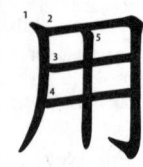

| | |
|---|---|
| **¹EMPLOY, use** | ¹用いる もちいる employ, use |
| **²THINGS TO DO, business** | ¹用人 ようにん steward, manager.............0015 |
| | ¹用水 ようすい tap [irrigation] water.........0026 |
| ヨウ | ¹日用 にちよう everyday use ..................0001 |
| もち(いる) | ²用がある ようがある have things to do |

| | |
|---|---|
| **0047** | Because it will often appear inside more complex kanji, it is wise to give this kanji the concrete, visible meaning *container*, by picturing the crisscrossing lines as the intersecting staves and hoops of a barrel or bucket. For the present entry, simply let the image of a bucket suggest the notion of **EMPLOYING** an instrument or having **THINGS TO DO**. |
| 用 101 | |
| 2569 | |
| 常 5 | |

| | |
|---|---|
| **¹WITHOUT** | ¹無人の むじんの uninhabited; unmanned...0015 |
| **²NOTHING** | ¹無用 むよう useless; unnecessary; forbidden |
| | ................................................0047 |
| | ²無にする むにする bring to naught |
| ム ブ | 金が無い かねがない have no money.......0029 |
| な(い) | 無口 むくち taciturnity, reticence ...........0019 |

| | |
|---|---|
| **0048** | 灬 means *fire* (see 火 0026). Imagine what's above it as a bookcase, utterly consumed in the flames, leaving **NOTHING**. ☞ 焦 1654, 舞 0961 |
| 火 86 | |
| 1832 | |
| 常 12 | |

| 不 | NOT, un- | 不用 ふよう of no use ............................ 0047 |
|---|---|---|
| | | 不正 ふせい injustice, wrong, illegality ..... 0043 |
| | | 不定 ふていの uncertain, indefinite ...... 0045 |
| | フ ブ | 不足 ふそく insufficiency; want; dissatisfaction ............................ 0044 |

**0049**
一 1

Representing negation, 不 can be seen as a bird attempting to fly directly upward but being halted by S1. Up, up into the sky we go ... **NOT**. This character is sometimes interchangeable with 無 when the reading is ブ.

2890
常 4

| 回 | ¹ TURN ROUND | ¹ 回る まわる [vi] turn around |
|---|---|---|
| | ² TIME | ¹ 回す まわす [vt] turn around |
| | | ¹ 上回る うわまわる exceed, go/be over ....... 0041 |
| | カイ エ | ¹ 手回り てまわり at hand; personal [items] ... 0046 |
| | まわ(る) -まわ(る) -まわ(り) まわ(す) | ² 一回 いっかい one time, once .............. 0002 |
| | -まわ(す) まわ(し)- -まわ(し) | |

**0050**
口 31

**TURN ROUND** this wheel-like shape in your imagination. As you do, count each **TIME** it turns round: one **TIME ROUND**, two **TIMES ROUND**, three **TIMES ROUND** ...

回

2630
常 6

| 言 | ¹ SAY | ① 言う いう say, speak, state; call, refer to |
|---|---|---|
| | ² SPEECH, word | ¹ 言い回し いいまわし expression, turn of phrase ............................ 0050 |
| | | ¹ 言明 げんめい declaration, announcement ... 0024 |
| | ゲン ゴン | ② 無言 むごん silence, muteness ............. 0048 |
| | い(う) こと | ² 一言 ひとこと (=いちげん, いちごん) a word ... 0002 |

**0051**
言 149

See the four horizontal lines as sound waves emanating from the small mouth (口) at the bottom, indicating **SPEECH**. As a grapheme, 言 will mean *say*, *speech*, or *word*. Starting in this entry, a superscript circle indicates suggested words to memorize in the didactic vocabulary section. Meaning numbers appear inside circles when both apply. See entry 0222 for an important vocabulary word using ゲン.

1698
常 7

| 舌 | TONGUE | 舌ぼう(舌鋒ˣ) ぜっぽう (sharp) tongue |
|---|---|---|
| | | じょう舌 (饒ˣ舌) じょうぜつ garrulity, loquacity |
| | | ○舌を出す したをだす stick out one's tongue ............................ 0038 |
| | ゼツ | 舌がもつれる したがもつれる one's tongue gets |
| | した | twisted |

**0052**
舌 135

This pictograph, stylized over the centuries, shows a *mouth* at the bottom and a **TONGUE** sticking out towards the top (it reminds one of the expression "forked tongue"). To remember the on-yomi, memorize the compound appearing at 毒 0133. ☞ 古 0254

1871
常 6

45

**SPEAK**

ワ
はな(す) はなし

○話す はなす speak; tell
手話 しゅわ sign language...................0046
話し手 はなして speaker, person speaking...0046
話し中 はなしちゅう while talking, busy
　[telephone line]............................0035
話が無い はなしがない nothing to say......0048

| 0053 | To **SPEAK**, we must produce a flow of sound in our vocal cords, and adjust this sound using the tongue. Both ingredients are present here, in their compacted grapheme forms. Train your eye to see the *tongue* (舌) jutting out to regulate the sound waves (S1–4). The difference between 話 and 言 0051 is roughly that between "talk" and "say" in English. |
| 言 149 | |
| **1388** | |
| 常 13 | |

**1 ACTIVE**
**2 LIVE, lead one's life**

カツ

①活用する かつようする utilize, apply; conjugate, inflect..................................0047
1 活火山 かつかざん (=かっかざん) active volcano
....................................0026, 0037
②生活 せいかつ life, existence; livelihood....0036

| 0054 | We now encounter the grapheme version of *water* (氵), introduced at 水 0027. In this character it indicates a moist *tongue*, suggesting **LIFE** and, by extension, **ACTIVITY**. |
| 水 85 | |
| **0345** | |
| 常 9 | |

**1 GO, proceed**
**2 ACT, perform**
**3 LINE (of print)**

コウ ギョウ アン
い(く) ゆ(く) -ゆ(き) -ゆき -い(き)
-いき おこな(う)

①行く いく (=ゆく) go, proceed; attend
1 行く手 ゆくて one's way, ahead (of one)....0046
②行う おこなう act, do, perform; practice, carry out
2 言行 げんこう speech and conduct..........0051
③二行 にぎょう two lines (of text)............0003

| 0055 | At the top see two intersecting roads. Let this suggest **GO** and, by extension, **ACT**. For M3, let the space between S4 and S5 suggest a **LINE** of text. In the margin, copy 行 big enough that you can write a **LINE** of text in the space between S4 and S5, then write something in. The usual grapheme form, 彳, will suggest *go* or *act*. |
| 行 144 | |
| **0187** | |
| 常 6 | |

**HEART, mind, center, core**

シン
こころ -ごころ

本心 ほんしん one's true mind, one's real intention; one's conscience................0031
○中心 ちゅうしん center, middle ..............0035
心中 しんちゅう heart, mind, true motives...0035
　　　　しんじゅう lovers' suicide, double suicide
心行くまで こころゆくまで to one's heart's content...................................0055

| 0056 | Primitive picture of a **HEART** organ, surrounded by various arterial valves. The meaning extends to **spirit** and **mind**, so when it appears as a grapheme (sometimes in this form, but frequently as 忄, and infrequently as 㣺), we may call it either *heart* or *mind*. |
| 心 61 | |
| **0004** | |
| 常 4 | |

| 耳 | EAR | <sup>○</sup>耳目 じもく eyes and ears; one's attention...0021 |
| | | 中耳 ちゅうじ inner ear......................0035 |
| | | 耳かき みみかき earpick |
| | ジ<br>みみ | 耳たぶ みみたぶ earlobe |

| 0057<br>耳 128<br><br>2948<br>常 6 | Differing from 目 in the way its top, bottom, and right-hand strokes jut out, 耳 represents the three sections of the outer **EAR**. With an earlobe projecting down from the bottom right, 耳 looks like someone's right **EAR**, or your own left **EAR** seen in the mirror. 耳's writing is unusual, so practice it carefully—you'll need it for writing other kanji. |

| 又 | <sup>1</sup> AGAIN; also<br><br><sup>2</sup> OR, in other words<br><br>また また- また(の)- | <sup>①</sup>又明日 またあした See you tomorrow...0024, 0001<br><sup>1</sup> 又の日 またのひ another day................0001<br><sup>②</sup>又は または or; in other words |

| 0058<br>又 29<br><br>2853<br>常 2 | Derives from a picture of one hand crossed over another hand, implying the idea of duplication (**AGAIN**), as well as alternate choices (**OR**). As a grapheme, 又 will usually mean *hand*.<br>☞ 亦 0773 |

| 取 | TAKE<br><br>シュ<br>と(る) と(り) と(り)- とり- -ど(り) | 取水 しゅすい drawing water................0027<br>取り入れる とりいれる take in; harvest;<br>　accept, adopt................................0039<br>取り上げる とりあげる take/pick up; confiscate;<br>　deliver (a baby); accept, listen to; adopt<br>　(a proposal)................................0041<br>取り出す とりだす take out, get out, pick up ...0038<br>日取り ひどり schedule.....................0001 |

| 0059<br>又 29<br><br>1162<br>常 8 | See this as a *hand* (又) reaching out to **TAKE** someone's *ear* (耳; note the slight difference from 耳). You will notice in these mnemonic annotations a strong preference for the active participle, such as "reaching" in the previous sentence. These "-ing" verbs, while not the most elegant choice, help us see actions taking place and avoid abstract statements. |

| 身 | <sup>1</sup> BODY<br><br><sup>2</sup> ONE'S PERSON<br><br><sup>3</sup> SOCIAL POSITION<br><br>シン<br>み | <sup>1</sup> 心身 しんしん mind and body..............0056<br><sup>①</sup>出身 しゅっしん one's place of origin.........0038<br><sup>2</sup> 身の上 みのうえ one's career, one's fortune...0041<br><sup>②</sup>身の回り みのまわり one's person, personal<br>　circle/belongings.........................0050<br><sup>3</sup> 小身 しょうしん humble position.............0034 |

| 0060<br>身 158<br><br>2977<br>常 7 | See as a **BODY** with a long cane (S7) carried on **ONE'S PERSON**. The image of standing with a cane also suggests **SOCIAL STANDING**. Take special care to learn 身's unusual writing. |

| | **REST, suspend** | ○休日 きゅうじつ holiday, day off..............0001 |
| | | 定休(日) ていきゅう(び) regular holiday |
| | | ........................................................0045, 0001 |
| | | 休止 きゅうし pause, standstill, dormancy; rest |
| | | ........................................................0042 |
| | キュウ | ○休み やすみ rest, recess; suspension; vacation, |
| | やす(む) やす(まる) やす(める) | holiday; absence |

| **0061** | Now we'll learn the first of many characters incorporating イ, a compact form of 人 0015 |
| 人 9 | HUMAN BEING. We'll usually refer to イ as *man*, which is less abstract, and which allows us to |
| | contrast it with 女 *woman* (see 0093). Here see a *man* **RESTING** against a *tree* (木). Its sloping |
| **0037** | branches make a comfortable bed to **REST** on. ☞ 体 0062 |
| 常 6 | |

| | **¹BODY** | ¹身体 しんたい (=からだ) body..............0060 |
| | **²FORM** | ①人体 じんたい human body..............0015 |
| | | ¹大体 だいたい outline; generally, roughly, on |
| | | the whole..............0033 |
| | タイ テイ | ¹体の中 からだのなか inside the body........0035 |
| | からだ | ²正体 しょうたい one's true shape; consciousness |
| | | ........................................................0043 |

| **0062** | Here the focus shifts to the tree's roots or physical *basis* (see 本 0031). A *man* (イ)'s physical |
| 人 9* | *basis* is his **BODY**. ☞ 休 0061 |
| 體 | |
| **0055** | |
| 常 7 | |

| | **¹BELIEVE, trust** | ①信用 しんよう trust, credit, confidence......0047 |
| | **²MESSAGE, signal** | ¹信心 しんじん faith, belief, piety..............0056 |
| | | ¹入信 にゅうしん joining the faith..............0039 |
| | | ¹不信 ふしん distrust, discredit..............0049 |
| | シン | ¹信じる(=信ずる) しんじる (=しんずる) believe; |
| | | believe in |

| **0063** | Review 言 0051. Here we observe the mouth *speaking* a **MESSAGE** to a *man* (イ), who **trusts/** |
| 人 9 | **BELIEVES** it. See 受 0065, 書 0079, and 通 0159 for sample compounds using M2 **MESSAGE**. |
| **0084** | |
| 常 9 | |

| | **ATTACH, be attached to, hand over** | 付言 ふげん postscript, additional remarks 0051 |
| | | ○付く つく attach (to), adhere (to); be connected with |
| | | 付ける つける attach, fasten; put (one thing on |
| | | another) |
| | フ | 付け足す つけたす add on, append........0044 |
| | つ(ける) -つ(ける) -づ(ける) つ(け) つ(け)- | 身に付ける みにつける acquire (knowledge), |
| | -つ(け) -づ(け) つけ つ(く) -づ(く) | learn..............0060 |
| | つ(き) -つ(き) -つき -づ(き) -づき | |

| **0064** | In 寸 see a man reaching out his arm (S3), carrying a small object (S5) (this is also an inde- |
| 人 9 | pendent kanji we shall meet at entry 0381). Here, see the *outstretched arm* **ATTACH** (or **hand** |
| | **over**) this small object to the *man* at the left. Take a moment to visualize the arm **ATTACHING** |
| **0019** | the object, sticking it on, **handing** it over, delivering it. ☞ 附 2214 |
| 常 5 | |

| | RECEIVE, accept | ○受信 じゅしん reception (of radio waves); receipt of a message...............................0063 |
|---|---|---|
| | | ○受ける うける receive, accept |
| | | 受け身 うけみ passiveness; passive voice...0060 |
| | ジュ う(ける) -う(け) う(かる) | 受け入れる うけいれる accept, consent to; receive, accommodate...............0039 |
| | | 受付 うけつけ receipt; reception desk.......0064 |

| 0065 | The opposite of "hand over" is "**RECEIVE**." Here we meet two new graphemes. *Claw* (⍦), at |
|---|---|
| 又 29 | the top, derives from 爪 0201 CLAW. ⌒, in the middle, looks like ⌒ *roof* without the chimney, and means *cover*. See a *claw* (⍦) handing over the *cover* and a *hand* (又) RECEIVING it. |
| 2146 | ☞ 愛 0778, 授 1123 |
| 常 8 | |

| | ¹ **TO THE ... OF** ² **BY MEANS OF** | ①以下 いか not more than, under; the following ...............................0040 |
|---|---|---|
| | | ¹ 以上 いじょう not less than; beyond; the above-mentioned; now that; that's all.....0041 |
| | イ もっ(て)* | ¹ 二人以上 ふたりいじょう two or more people ...........................0003, 0015, 0041 |
| | | ² これを以て これをもって with this; because of this |

| 0066 | The primary meaning of this kanji is **TO THE ... OF**. This is a rather abstract idea, but with a little |
|---|---|
| 人 9 | imagination we can actually <u>see</u> it in 以. Copy 以 on a piece of scratch paper such that S4 is the length of your hand. Place your left hand edgewise over S4, palm facing the bottom of the page (you'll have to bend your fingers backward a bit). Your thumb should be hanging down in the position of S5. Now make a sweeping motion in the direction your thumb is |
| 0026 | pointing. Anywhere **TO THE** southeast **OF** S4 is indicated in the phrase "**TO THE ... OF**" (the area |
| 常 5 | occupied by S1–3 is left out). See Halpern for information on M2 **BY MEANS OF**. ☞ 似 1354 |

| | ¹ **STAND** ² **ESTABLISH** | ①中立 ちゅうりつ neutrality....................0035 |
|---|---|---|
| | | ①立つ たつ stand, rise |
| | | ¹ 立ち上がる たちあがる stand up, rise to one's feet ..........................................0041 |
| | リツ リュウ た(つ) -た(つ) た(ち)- た(てる) -た(てる) た(て)- たて- -た(て) -だ(て) -だ(てる) | ¹ 立ち話 たちばなし chatting while standing up ...............................................0053 |
| | | 立てる たてる stand, make stand, establish |

| 0067 | Depicts a **STANDING** person. For a sample compound using M2, see 設 0520 ... Now to prepare |
|---|---|
| 立 117 | for the next entry (部), we need to learn the grapheme β, which derives from a drawing of a hillside. When it appears at the right side of a kanji it will denote *town*; at the left (as in 陸) it |
| 1723 | will denote *hill(s)*. To allow β to suggest both meanings, visualize it as the town's perimeter walls on the straight side, and as the hills outside of town on the curving side. While on the *town* side |
| 常 5 | the hills have been landscaped into a sheer wall, on the outside the *hills* maintain their natural contours. In both cases, β acts as a barrier separating a town from the outlying wilderness ... |

| | SECTION, division, department | ○一部 いちぶ part, portion, section; a copy (of printed matter)...........................0002 |
|---|---|---|
| | | 上部 じょうぶ upper part [section]; top; surface 0041 |
| | | 東部 とうぶ east, eastern part..............0032 |
| | ブ | 部下 ぶか subordinate........................0040 |
| | | ...の部に入る ...のぶにはいる fall under the heading of; be classed among.............0039 |

| 0068 | (Continued) ... Here β appears at the right, so the other graphemes (*person standing* and |
|---|---|
| 邑 163 | *mouth*) appear in the *town* position, <u>inside</u> the barrier. When you see *person standing* above *mouth*, imagine a *very short person standing on a box*. Thus here we observe a short person |
| 1498 | attempting to scale the wall to escape the city. He's not tall enough to surmount the wall from the ground, so he divides the task into two **SECTIONS**, ascending the first **SECTION** with |
| 常 11 | a box and the second **SECTION** under his own power. ☞ 陪 1263 |

| | | ¹ TIMES, -fold<br>² DOUBLE | ¹ 人一倍話す ひといちばいはなす speak twice as much as others .................. 0015, 0002, 0053 |
| | | | ① 二倍 にばい double ........................ 0003 |
| | | バイ | ¹ 二倍以上 にばいいじょう at least twice as much ............................ 0003, 0066, 0041 |
| | | | ² 倍にする ばいにする double |

| **0069**<br>人 9 | We bring in 倍 at this point to show that the *very short person standing on a box* can also appear at the right, in which case the kanji will be pronounced バイ (as in 陪 1263, the inverse of the last entry). Here the *very short person* encounters a *man* of average height, **DOUBLE** his own. Again, the box is his equalizer. ☞ 位 0577 |
| **0090**<br>常 10 | |

| | | ¹ BECOME; form<br>² ACHIEVE | ¹ 成立する せいりつする come into existence; be formed, be organized ...................... 0067 |
| | | | ² 大成する たいせいする achieve greatness ... 0033 |
| | | セイ ジョウ<br>な(る) な(す) -な(す) | ○ 成人 せいじん adult, grown-up .............. 0015 |
| | | | 成る なる become, form, consist of; be accomplished |
| | | | 成す なす form, make; accomplish |

| **0070**<br>戈 62 | The next two characters introduce the graphemes 弋 and 戈, which we shall conflate under the label *spear*. 弋 can be seen as a spear thrower (the dot stroke shows the spearhead). Here, 戈 appears with an extra stroke (戊), which we'll interpret as an optional "guide" that helps the weapon reach its target accurately. To 戊 we need only add the angled stroke at the left (S3) to complete 成. Thus S3's function is to *complete the form*. As a mnemonic, let S3 trigger the idea of **BECOMING** whole or **ACHIEVING** completeness, as in the word 成人 せいじん (coming of age, adult), which we might associate with "attaining one's spear." |
| **2964**<br>常 6 | |

| | | ¹ REPLACE, substitute<br>² GENERATION, age<br>³ CHARGE, fare | ○ 代わる かわる substitute, take the place of |
| | | | 代える かえる substitute, replace (something) with (another) |
| | | ダイ タイ<br>か(わる) か(わり) -が(わり) か(える)<br>よ しろ | 身の代金 みのしろきん ransom ........ 0060, 0029 |
| | | | 大正の代 たいしょうのよ Taisho era ... 0033, 0043 |
| | | | タクシー代 タクシーだい taxi fare |

| **0071**<br>人 9 | From the idea of "axing" a person, we can perceive the concept "**REPLACE**" in this image of "giving a *man* (イ) the *spear* (弋)." **REPLACE** is intuitively related to the other two meanings: just as one **GENERATION** (or age) "replaces" another, a **CHARGE** (i.e., a fee) "replaces" the resources spent in rendering a service. ☞ 伐 1361 |
| **0018**<br>常 5 | |

| | | KING | 王手 おうて check, checkmate .............. 0046 |
| | | | メディア王 メディアおう media magnate |
| | | | 王を立てる おうをたてる enthrone a king ... 0067 |
| | | オウ | 王のように おうのように like a king |

| **0072**<br>玉 96 | A common etymological interpretation provides an easy way to remember 王. From top to bottom, the horizontal lines originally represented heaven, man, and earth. The vertical line represented the symbolic union of all three in the **KING**. |
| **2895**<br>常 4 | |

| | **GEM; round or spherical object** | 水玉 みずたま polka dots .................... 0027 |
|---|---|---|
| | | 百円玉 ひゃくえんだま hundred-yen coin ................................................ 0016, 0013 |
| | | シャボン玉 シャボンだま soap bubble |
| | ギョク<br>たま たま- -だま | 目玉 めだま eyeball; loss leader ............. 0021 |
| | | 玉にきず(玉に疵×) たまにきず flaw in the crystal, fly in the ointment |

**0073**
玉 96

See S5 as the *king* (王)'s **GEM**. When 玉 is used as the *hen* (left-side, usually meaning-bearing grapheme) in other kanji (such as 理 0532), it loses the short "gem" stroke, but nonetheless denotes *gem* or, more generally, a *round/spherical object*. The *on* (Chinese-derived) reading ギョク is unique in this course.

2919
常 5

---

| | **TREASURE** | ○宝玉 ほうぎょく gem ............................ 0073 |
|---|---|---|
| | | 東宝スタジオ とうほうスタジオ Toho [film] Studios ................................ 0032 |
| | ホウ<br>たから | 宝くじ たからくじ lottery |

**0074**
宀 40

See 宀 *roof* as an indication of the unusual value of the *gem* the king holds in 宝. The roof is present to protect this special **TREASURE**. Write 宝 and 玉 in alternation: in 玉, you are depicting an average GEM, in 宝, a rare **TREASURE**, demanding protection.

1910
常 8

---

| | **COUNTRY** | 王国 おうこく kingdom ..................... 0072 |
|---|---|---|
| | | 国王 こくおう king ........................... 0072 |
| | | 国宝 こくほう national treasure ............. 0074 |
| | コク<br>くに | ○国立 こくりつ national (park, etc.) .......... 0067 |
| | | ○国々 くにぐに nations |

**0075**
囗 31

囗 means *border*, though we shall be flexible and see it more generally as an *enclosure* or precinct, or sometimes a box. Here it indicates the *enclosure* around a king and his gems (the crown jewels, if you wish): the borders of his **COUNTRY**.

2659
常 8

---

| | **WHITE** | ○白い しろい white |
|---|---|---|
| | | 白人 はくじん white person, Caucasian ...... 0015 |
| | | 白日 はくじつ broad daylight ................. 0001 |
| | ハク ビャク<br>しろ しら- しろ(い) | 白金 しろがね silver; silver coin ............. 0029<br>はっきん platinum |
| | | ○明白な めいはくな clear, plain, obvious ...... 0024 |

**0076**
白 106

Let S1 suggest a blinding **WHITE** beam radiating from the *sun* (日). Kanji in which 白 appears at the right generally have the *on* reading ハク. This and other such groups are listed in Appendix 2, a resource you will want to take full advantage of as you study the kanji.
☞ 自 0081

2929
常 5

**EMPEROR**

コウ オウ

皇国 こうこく [archaic] Japan ............... 0075

| 0077 | |
|---|---|
| 白 106 | A *white* (白) crown atop the head of a *king* (王) signals a still more exalted status: **EMPEROR**. Don't just link the elements semantically, but rather <u>visualize</u> the crowned head. Useful compounds to learn appear at 居 0255 and 天 0270. ☞ 星 0755 |
| 2223 | |
| 常 9 | |

---

**WHOLE, all**

ゼン
まった(く) すべ(て)

全国 ぜんこく the whole country ........... 0075
○全部 ぜんぶ all, the whole; wholly, entirely ................................................. 0068
万全の ばんぜんの perfect, infallible, absolutely secure ........................................ 0018
○全く まったく entirely, utterly
全ての すべての all, entire, whole

| 0078 | |
|---|---|
| 人 9* | As we learned earlier, 入 is a flattened form of 人, but it will be simpler to see it as a *roof* or other covering (overlapping in meaning with 宀 and 冖). In 王 we have the union of heaven, man and earth in the *king*. Here, see 入 as emphasizing this wholeness. **All** three parts are covered under this one roof—the **WHOLE** thing. |
| 全 | |
| 1743 | |
| 常 6 | |

---

**¹WRITE**

**²BOOK**

ショ
か(く) -が(き) -がき

①書く かく write
¹書き取り かきとり dictation ............... 0059
¹信書 しんしょ correspondence, letter ........ 0063
①白書 はくしょ white paper .................... 0076
²全書 ぜんしょ comprehensive treatise; complete works ........................................ 0078

| 0079 | |
|---|---|
| 日 73 | See a three-fingered hand (⺕) holding a pen and **WRITING** on a pad of paper. Etymology teaches us that S7–10 do not in fact represent 日 *sun* but the obsolete 曰 *say*—we'll ignore both and instead see a stack of writing paper. 書 and 本 0031 both mean **BOOK**: 書 suggests a product of writing, while 本 suggests a product made from the material of a tree. |
| 2314 | |
| 常 10 | |

---

**¹AFFAIR**

**²ABSTRACT THING**

ジ ズ
こと

¹火事 かじ fire .................................. 0026
¹無事に ぶじに without incident ............ 0048
①用事 ようじ things to do, errands, business ... 0047
²行く事にする いくことにする decide to go ... 0055
²書く事が無い かくことがない There is nothing to write about ........................... 0079, 0048

| 0080 | |
|---|---|
| J 6 | This time see the hand turn the pen upward, holding in the air some **THING** it has skewered. Exactly what the hand is holding up should be left vague, for 事 does not in fact refer to a physical object, but to an **ABSTRACT THING** or **AFFAIR**. Remember, the hand goes at the top for WRITING (書), at the bottom for holding a **THING** (事) up in the air. ☞ 物 0172 |
| 2986 | |
| 常 8 | |

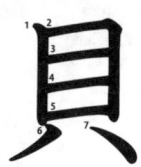

| SELF | 自白 じはく confession........................0076 |
|---|---|
| | ○自体 じたい itself; one's own body..........0062 |
| | 自信 じしん self-confidence..................0063 |
| | 自明の じめいの self-evident, obvious......0024 |
| ジ シ<br>みずか(ら) おの(ずから)* | ○自ら みずから oneself |

**0081**
自 132

The much-stylized result of what began as a drawing of a nose. It will be wise to retain this association, for in Japan one points to the nose to indicate one's **SELF**, and 自 appears later in the kanji for NOSE 1558 and BAD SMELL 1560. Take S1 as that little stubby thing you see in front of your *eyes* (目) when you look at the world: your nose. ☞ 白 0076

2954
常 6

| SHELLFISH | 宝貝 たからがい cowrie shell.................0074 |
|---|---|
| | ホラ貝 ホラがい conch shell |
| | 貝ボタン かいボタン shell button |
| かい | |

**0082**
貝 154

Ignore *eye* (目) and see the whole character as a striated **SHELLFISH**, with two little legs for scampering across the seabed. As a grapheme, 貝 often means *money* or *wealth*, from the use of seashells as a primitive form of currency. ☞ 見 0083, 具 0837

2200
常 7

| SEE | ○一見 いっけん a look, a glance; apparently...0002 |
|---|---|
| | ○見る みる see, view |
| | 見出し みだし headline, heading, caption; title;<br>index...............................0038 |
| ケン<br>み(る) み(える) み(せる) | 見える みえる be visible; look like, appear; be<br>able to see |
| | 見せる みせる show, let see; pretend |

**0083**
見 147

This character is similar to 貝, so focus on what distinguishes them. 儿 is a <u>real</u> pair of *legs*, longer and more flexible than the little stubs the shellfish scurries around on. 目 thus stands taller in 見, the better to SEE. From here on we'll usually assign 儿 the meaning *human legs*, or simply *legs*, but now and then also *roots* (when they depict the "legs" of a plant). ☞ 貝 0082

2201
常 7

| POWER, strength, force | ○体力 たいりょく physical strength............0062 |
|---|---|
| | 活力 かつりょく vital force, vitality, energy...0054 |
| | 百人力 ひゃくにんりき the strength of a hundred<br>men; great strength..................0016, 0015 |
| リョク リキ<br>ちから | 力む りきむ strain (oneself), show one's best effort |
| | ○力を入れて ちからをいれて with effort<br>[emphasis]...............................0039 |

**0084**
力 19

See as a heavy iron plow (handle on the upper left, cutting blade on the lower right), and imagine the **POWER** that **forces** it through the hard-packed soil at the end of the dry season. Though we visualize a plow, the meaning it conveys is **POWER**. Contrast with 九 0011: 力's blade must angle backward, not forward, or it could not plow ahead smoothly. ☞ 九 0011, 刀 0085

2860
常 2

| 刀 | SWORD | 大刀 たいとう long sword.....0033 |
| | | ○小刀 こがたな (=しょうとう) pocketknife......0034 |
| | | 山刀 やまがたな machete.....0037 |
| | トウ | 日本刀 にほんとう Japanese sword ....0001, 0031 |
| | かたな | 刀の付いた かたなのついた (equipped) with a blade.....0064 |

| 0085 | Derives from a drawing of a **SWORD**. Similar to the previous entry, so here let the simplified handle shift our visual focus to the blade. As before, see the cutting edge on the lower right. As a grapheme, 刀 is usually modified to 刂, which we shall associate with *swords, knives, cutting,* and *slicing.* ☞ 力 0084, 九 0011, 刃 0087 |
| 刀 18 | |
| 2534 | |
| 常 2 | |

| 切 | CUT, sharp | 一切の いっさいの all, entire, whole.....0002 |
| | | ○大切な たいせつな important, weighty; valuable.....0033 |
| | | ○切る きる cut, slice, sever |
| | セツ サイ | 切れる きれる be cut (off); run out, expire |
| | き(る) -き(る) き(り) -き(り) -ぎ(り) | ケーキ一切れ ケーキひときれ a piece of cake |
| | き(れる) -き(れる) き(れ) -き(れ) | .....0002 |
| | -ぎ(れ) | |

| 0086 | Recall the slashing line in the European-style handwritten numeral **7** (see 0009). Here see the *sword* (刀) making the sideways **CUT** across the numeral. This entry clearly illustrates an important rule for writing kanji: in writing "left-right" kanji, we must generally make the left side more compact than the right. |
| 刀 18 | |
| 0015 | |
| 常 4 | |

| 刃 | BLADE | 刀刃 とうじん sword blade.....0085 |
| | | ○白刃 はくじん drawn sword.....0076 |
| | | 自刃する じじんする die by one's own sword |
| | ジン | .....0081 |
| | は | 刀の刃 かたなのは edge of a sword.....0085 |
| | | よく切れる刃 よくきれるは a sharp blade ...0086 |

| 0087 | See S3 as a slash made across the *sword* (刀) by the blade of another. Feel and hear the cutting sharpness of the razor-edged **BLADE** as it leaves this mark. This mark should suggest the lacerating edge of the **BLADE**, whereas 刀 means SWORD in general. Practice writing both characters in turn until you've internalized the difference. ☞ 刀 0085, 丸 0012 |
| 刀 18 | |
| 2537 | |
| 常 3 | |

| 分 | ¹DIVIDE | ①分ける わける divide into parts, distribute |
| | ²PART | ②部分 ぶぶん part, section, portion.....0068 |
| | ³MINUTE | ² 身分 みぶん social position; rank, identity...0060 |
| | ブン フン ブ | ² 自分 じぶん self, oneself.....0081 |
| | わ(ける) わ(け) わ(かれる) わ(かる) | ³ 二十分 にじゅっぷん (=にじっぷん) twenty |
| | わ(かつ) | minutes.....0003, 0005 |

| 0088 | Here *sword* cuts up not a 7 (七, as in 切 0086), but an 8 (八). We learned before that as a grapheme 八 0010 can take on the meaning of *split*. See the *sword splitting,* or **DIVIDING,** the top of the character into two **PARTS.** Associate **MINUTE** (the time unit) with the idea of **DIVIDING** time into **PARTS.** ☞ 公 0089 |
| 刀 18 | |
| 1713 | |
| 常 4 | |

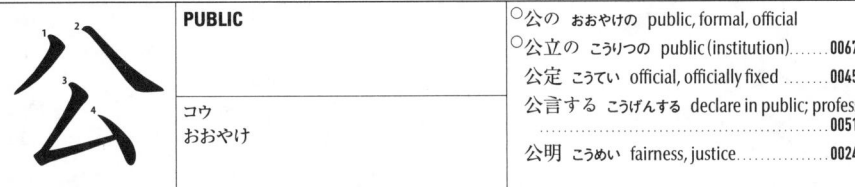

| 公 | **PUBLIC** | ○公の おおやけの public, formal, official |
|---|---|---|
| | | ○公立の こうりつの public (institution).......**0067** |
| | | 公定 こうてい official, officially fixed .........**0045** |
| | コウ | 公言する こうげんする declare in public; profess |
| | おおやけ | ...............................................................**0051** |
| | | 公明 こうめい fairness, justice..............**0024** |

| **0089** | Here we add the grapheme ム, another drawing of the *nose*, more convincing than the one |
|---|---|
| ハ 12 | we saw a while ago at 自 0081. As we did then, we should associate the nose with the *self*, for we shall also take ム to mean *self* or *private*. Thus 公 gives us *split* (ハ) and *private*: see a *private* place *splitting* its doors wide open to welcome the **PUBLIC**. ☞ 分 0088 |
| **1715** | |
| 常 4 | |

| 別 | **¹ SEPARATE**<br>**² ANOTHER** | ①別々に べつべつに separately |
|---|---|---|
| | | **¹** 分別する ぶんべつする classify, distinguish; divide, separate ...........................**0088** |
| | | ①別れる わかれる separate, part from |
| | ベツ | **²** 別人 べつじん another [different] person...**0015** |
| | わか(れる) | **²** 別の本 べつのほん another [different] book ...............................................................**0031** |

| **0090** | Picking up where we left off at 刀, 刂 gives us *cutting* or *slicing*. At the left we find a single |
|---|---|
| 刀 18 | grapheme meaning *bone*, deriving from an old drawing of a skeleton showing head and body. Imagine the *sword* chopping it into two **SEPARATE** parts. Now, a note about 刂 and kanji structure: As we saw in the Introduction, in most left-right kanji, the *hen* is the semantic element, while the *tsukuri* is the phonetic element (though the phonetic hint is often not use- |
| **1032** | ful in Japanese). There are a few exceptions to this positioning, including 刂, which despite |
| 常 7 | being a semantic element appears at the right. ☞ 列 0718, 号 0300 |

| 長 | **¹ LONG**<br>**² CHIEF, senior** | **¹** 身長 しんちょう stature, height ...............**0060** |
|---|---|---|
| | | ①成長 せいちょう growth .........................**0070** |
| | | ①長い ながい long |
| | チョウ | **¹** 長話 ながばなし long talk.....................**0053** |
| | なが(い) | **②** 部長 ぶちょう division chief .................**0068** |

| **0091** | To visualize both **LONG** and **CHIEF**, see 長 as an old man with **LONG** locks of hair streaming |
|---|---|
| 長 168 | to the right. The more **senior** he gets, the **LONGER** his hair grows. S5 shows his outstretched arms, while the lower part of the character shows the pleats of his garments (see 衣 0700 GARMENT). Note that the main vertical line is written in two strokes (S1, S6). ☞ 辰 0510 |
| **2212** | |
| 常 8 | |

| 男 | **MAN** | 男二人 おとこふたり two men/males...**0003, 0015** |
|---|---|---|
| | | 男らしい おとこらしい manly, masculine |
| | | ○長男 ちょうなん eldest son ....................**0091** |
| | ダン ナン | 三男 さんなん third son........................**0004** |
| | おとこ | 正男 まさお Masao [male given name]......**0043** |

| **0092** | It is natural to associate **MAN** with *rice fields* (田) and *plow* (力), but it's more direct just to |
|---|---|
| 田 102 | see the top as a **MAN**'s large head and the bottom as his legs, running. From this point on, the grapheme 田 will be able to take the meaning *head* in addition to *rice field*. |
| **2199** | |
| 常 7 | |

**WOMAN**

ジョ ニョ ニョウ
おんな め

○長女 ちょうじょ eldest daughter ............. 0091
男女 だんじょ men and women, both sexes 0092
皇女 こうじょ imperial princess ............. 0077
女人 にょにん woman ........................ 0015
女の人 おんなのひと woman ............... 0015

| 0093 | The product of many modifications on an ancient drawing of a kneeling **WOMAN**, facing toward our left. In today's version, it will be easier to see her facing forward or toward our right, crossing one leg behind the other in an elegant feminine curtsy. Contrast her gentle curtsy with the POWER(力)-ful forward motion in 男. |
|---|---|
| 女 38 | |
| 2884 | |
| 常 3 | |

¹ **CHILD, son**
² **NOUN SUFFIX, small object**

シ ス
こ -こ -(っ)こ

¹ 子女 しじょ children, sons and daughters ... 0093
①女子／女の子 じょし／おんなのこ girl ...... 0093
①男子／男の子 だんし／おとこのこ boy ...... 0092
¹ 王子 おうじ prince ......................... 0072
² 玉子 たまご egg [cf. 卵 1141] ............. 0073

| 0094 | An infant **CHILD**, recognizable by his oversize head and arms outstretched for hugging. 子 is written in three strokes. ☞ 予 0163 |
|---|---|
| 子 39 | |
| 2872 | |
| 常 3 | |

¹ **LIKE**
² **FAVORABLE**

コウ
この(む) す(く) よ(い)* い(い)*

①好み このみ taste, liking; choice; wish
①大好き だいすき very fond of ............... 0033
¹ 女好き おんなずき fondness for women;
　　amorous man ........................... 0093
² お人好し おひとよし good-natured person 0015
² 好事 こうじ fortune; good deed ............ 0080

| 0095 | The analytical mnemonic "*women* (女) LIKE *children* (子)" is straightforward enough to do the trick here, but I encourage you to *see* the *woman* and *child* LIKING each other. Notice how *woman* changes in the *hen* form. One *on-yomi* compound is provided here; a more useful one to memorize appears at 物 0172. |
|---|---|
| 女 38 | |
| 0184 | |
| 常 6 | |

¹ **PEACEFUL**
² **INEXPENSIVE**

アン
やす(い) やす(まる) やす やす(らか)

①安心 あんしん peace of mind, relief ......... 0056
¹ 安定な あんていな stable, composed ....... 0045
¹ 安らかな やすらかな peaceful, tranquil
②安い やすい inexpensive, cheap
² 十円安 じゅうえんやす down ten yen [foreign
　　exchange market] .................. 0005, 0013

| 0096 | Depicts a *woman* in a **PEACEFUL** state, at home (under the *roof*). Don't try to memorize an abstract statement like "A *woman* feels peaceful under a *roof*"; instead, <u>see</u> the PEACE and calm in the picture of the woman under the roof. When applied to products for sale, 安 means INEXPENSIVE, as in promoting financial PEACE of mind. |
|---|---|
| 宀 40 | |
| 1859 | |
| 常 6 | |

| 案 | PROPOSAL, plan, idea | 案出する あんしゅつする think out, contrive, devise ........................................ 0038 |
| | | 立案する りつあんする make a plan, devise, draft .......................................... 0067 |
| | アン | ○案を立てる あんをたてる draft a proposal ... 0067 |
| | | 案の定 あんのじょう as feared, sure enough ... 0045 |
| | | 案ずる (=案じる) あんずる (=あんじる) ponder; worry over |

**0097**
木 75

*Peacefulness* (安) at the top of a *tree* (木): this is where the woman goes to **think out**, **design**, and **plan** a PROPOSAL (the three verbs all refer to secondary meanings). 案 has a rather businesslike connotation, so don't imagine her loafing around up there.

1960
常 | 10

---

| 字 | CHARACTER | 活字 かつじ movable type, printing type ... 0054 |
| | | 字体 じたい character form, type ............ 0062 |
| | | ○ローマ字 ローマじ Roman letters |
| | ジ | 正字 せいじ traditional form of a kanji ...... 0043 |
| | あざ | 大きな字 おおきなじ large character/print... 0033 |

**0098**
子 39

Here too we find some serious work going on. See the *child* (子) at home under her *roof* (宀), practicing her **CHARACTERS**. With that image, let me remind you to write out the kanji as you learn them, even if you don't plan to learn how to write them by heart. ☞ 字 1542

1860
常 | 6

---

| 学 | ¹ STUDY ² SCHOOL | ¹学力 がくりょく scholarship, scholastic ability ................................................ 0084 |
| | | ①学生 がくせい student ...................... 0036 |
| | | ①学ぶ まなぶ study, learn |
| | ガク | ②大学 だいがく university .................... 0033 |
| | まな (ぶ) | ² 入学する にゅうがくする enter a school, matriculate ................................ 0039 |

**0099**
子 39
學

ツ is a variant of 小 *small*, but is actually used here as shorthand for the cumbersome eleven-stroke crown on the old version 學. We'll interpret ツ flexibly, according to the image we want to give the kanji. Here, see little bits of knowledge cramming themselves into the head of this **STUDYING SCHOOL** *child*. Distinguish ツ from ⺺ *claw*.

2211
常 | 8

---

| 父 | FATHER | ○父子 ふし father and child ................. 0094 |
| | | 代父 だいふ godfather ...................... 0071 |
| | フ | ○父の日 ちちのひ Father's Day .............. 0001 |
| | ちち | お父さん おとうさん father, daddy, papa |

**0100**
父 88

**FATHER**'s slanting eyebrows, long pointy nose, and 八-shaped moustache.

1714
常 | 4

| | ¹ WRITINGS, learning, culture<br>² LETTER, script<br><br>ブン　モン<br>ふみ | ① 文書 ぶんしょ (=もんじょ) document, letter, note .................. 0079<br>¹ 文学 ぶんがく literature, letters ............. 0099<br>¹ 文明 ぶんめい civilization, culture .......... 0024<br>² 文字 もじ character, letter ................ 0098<br>　もんじ character, letter; writings |
|---|---|---|

**0101**
文 67

See a person sitting behind a desk with crossed legs, **WRITING LETTERS**. The desktop is high, so we can't see the writer's body; only her head pops out at the top. 文 means **LETTERS** both in the sense of "written symbols" and in that of "correspondence." Fix the images of 文 and 父 in your memory, so that the next entry will not jar them loose.

1708
常 4

---

| | ¹ INTERCOURSE, association<br>² CROSS, intersect, interchange<br><br>コウ<br>まじ(わる)　まじ(える)　ま(じる)<br>ま(ざる)　ま(ぜる)　-か(う)　か(わす) | ¹ 国交 こっこう diplomatic relations ........... 0075<br>① 交じる (=交ざる) まじる (=まざる) [vi] be mingled, intermingle<br>② 交わす かわす exchange<br>② 交代する こうたいする take turns, alternate, relieve (someone) .......................... 0071<br>² 交付する こうふする hand over, deliver, grant .................. 0064 |
|---|---|---|

**0102**
亠 8

To avoid confusing this entry with the last two, focus on how it has even more **intersecting** lines than the others. 交 picks up all their crissCROSSING lines and combines them into one kanji meaning **CROSS** and **INTERCOURSE**. Now practice writing all three in turn, repeating their meanings out loud as you go. In later entries, 亠 will take the meaning *lid*.

1738
常 6

---

| | ¹ SCHOOL<br>² PROOFREAD<br><br>コウ | ① 学校 がっこう school ......................... 0099<br>¹ 小学校 しょうがっこう primary school ... 0034, 0099<br>¹ 校長 こうちょう principal, schoolmaster ..... 0091<br>¹ 女子校 じょしこう girls' school .......... 0093, 0094<br>② 校正 こうせい proofreading ................ 0043 |
|---|---|---|

**0103**
木 75

An important meaning of 交 is *associate*. 木, the *hen* form of 木 0028 TREE, can imply *wood* or things made of it. Thus 校 suggests a *wooden* building for *associating* or socializing with others: **SCHOOL**. It's also where we go to have our written work **PROOFREAD**.

0840
常 10

---

| | MOTHER<br><br>ボ<br>はは | ○ 母子 ぼし mother and child ................ 0094<br>　父母 ふぼ father and mother, parents ...... 0100<br>　母校 ぼこう alma mater, one's old school... 0103<br>○ 母の日 ははのひ Mother's Day .............. 0001<br>　お母さん おかあさん mother, mommy, mama |
|---|---|---|

**0104**
母 80

MOTHER's breasts.

2917
常 5

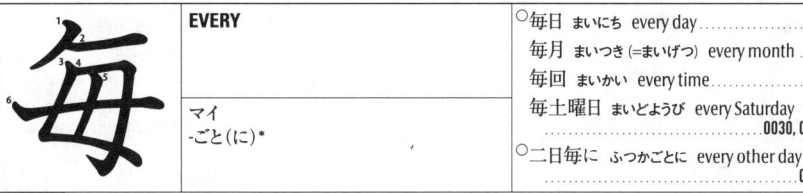

| | EVERY | ○毎日 まいにち every day .................... 0001 |
|---|---|---|
| | | 毎月 まいつき (=まいげつ) every month ...... 0023 |
| | | 毎回 まいかい every time ................... 0050 |
| | | 毎土曜日 まいどようび every Saturday |
| | | ............................ 0030, 0025, 0001 |
| | マイ | ○二日毎に ふつかごとに every other day |
| | -ごと(に)* | ............................ 0003, 0001 |

| 0105 | ⼂ is a version of イ *man*, inverted and turned sideways. We shall follow the etymological |
|---|---|
| 母 80 | meaning here, but in other cases interpret it flexibly. The bottom portion is 母 MOTHER, but |
| 毎 | with her nipples combined into one stroke. This combination implies **EVERY**, for **EVERY** *man* |
| 1751 | has a *mother*. |
| 常 6 | |

| | SEA | 大海 たいかい (=おおうみ) ocean ............. 0033 |
|---|---|---|
| | | 海上 かいじょう oceangoing, maritime, marine |
| | | ............................................ 0041 |
| | | カスピ海 カスピかい Caspian Sea |
| | カイ | ○日本海 にほんかい Sea of Japan ........ 0001, 0031 |
| | うみ | ○海の日 うみのひ Ocean Day [Japanese national |
| | | holiday, third Monday in July] ............. 0001 |

| 0106 | This kanji incorporates the previous one in its entirety. In such cases, it is generally best to use the |
|---|---|
| 水 85 | subsumed character as an integral whole, this being one way in which we simplify complex kanji. |
| 海 | Thus here we treat 毎 as *every* (rather than *man* + *mother*), producing the mnemonic "*Every* drop |
| 0344 | of *water* (氵) flows to the **SEA**." When you find kanji split between left and right, you can normally |
| 常 9 | use the *hen* as a semantic hint and the *tsukuri* as a phonetic hint. But to repeat, the phonetic ele-ment is often not very useful in Japanese; witness the *on-yomi* of 海 and 毎. In any case, we must use the *tsukuri* as a secondary semantic clue if we are to make sense of the character. |

| | PERSON | 信者 しんじゃ believer ...................... 0063 |
|---|---|---|
| | | 話者 わしゃ speaker ......................... 0053 |
| | | ○学者 がくしゃ scholar, learned person ...... 0099 |
| | | 本学の者です ほんがくのものです (I am) from |
| | シャ | [with] this university ................... 0031, 0099 |
| | もの | ○よそ者 よそもの outsider |

| 0107 | Review 土 0030. Diagonal S4 points under the *soil*, so take 耂 to mean (literally) *buried* |
|---|---|
| 老 125 | *underground* or (figuratively) *old*. Let 者 suggest a **PERSON** growing *old* from exposure to |
| 者 | the *sun* (日). Note the tiny extra stroke in the old form, which also appears in the old forms |
| 2765 | of the many kanji that incorporate 者. |
| 常 8 | |

| | ¹ MANUFACTURE; workmanship, work | ¹ 人工 じんこう man-made ................... 0015 |
|---|---|---|
| | ² CONSTRUCTION | ¹ 工学 こうがく engineering ................. 0099 |
| | | ¹ 大工 だいく carpenter ..................... 0033 |
| | | ②工事 こうじ construction .................. 0080 |
| | コウ ク | ² 工事中 こうじちゅう Under Construction [sign] |
| | | ............................ 0080, 0035 |

| 0108 | Imagine that this character depicts an I beam, as viewed from one end. I beams are **MANU-** |
|---|---|
| 工 48 | **FACTURED** at steel plants and used in the **CONSTRUCTION** of buildings. When we find 工 |
| 工 | used as a grapheme, we can give it either of these meanings, or the related meanings *work* |
| 2866 | or *workmanship*. Do not confuse with the katakana エ. |
| 常 3 | |

| | |
|---|---|
| **¹FORM, style, manner** | ①正式に　せいしきに　formally, regularly.......0043 |
| **²CEREMONY, rite** | **¹**...式に　...しきに　after the fashion |
| **³FORMULA** | **²**成人式　せいじんしき　coming-of-age ceremony .......................................0070, 0015 |
| シキ | ②入学式　にゅうがくしき　school entrance ceremony .......................................0039, 0099 |
| | **³**公式　こうしき　formula; formality............0089 |

| 0109 | Here we combine 工 *workmanship* with 弋 *spear*. The meanings **FORM, style, CEREMONY,** and **FORMULA** can all be derived from the underlying concept of an *action done according to a prescribed form*, so let 工 suggest the spear-thrower's professional workmanship in performing his act *according to prescribed form*. ☞ 弐 0110, 武 0111 |
|---|---|
| 弋 56 | |
| 2623 | |
| 常　6 | |

| | |
|---|---|
| **TWO (in legal documents)** | 金弐阡×円　きんにせんえん　the sum of two thousand yen.........................0029, 0013 |
| ニ | |

| 0110 | A special set of kanji exists for writing numbers in bank notes and other legal documents, so as to prevent people from adding a stroke here or there to easily altered characters like 一 and 二. A few of them appear in the Joyo Kanji List and thus in this course. Here, the number **TWO** (二) is hidden in the lower left of the character. ☞ 式 0109, 武 0111, 二 0003 |
|---|---|
| 弋 56* | |
| 貳 | |
| 2752 | |
| 常　6 | |

| | |
|---|---|
| **MILITARY; warrior** | ○武力　ぶりょく　military power.................0084 |
| | ○武者　むしゃ　warrior, soldier..................0107 |
| ブ　ム | 武人　ぶじん　warrior............................0015 |
| | 文武　ぶんぶ　literary and military............0101 |

| 0111 | See a **MILITARY** man stepping forward to *stop* (止) an invader with his *spear*. Following the principle mentioned in the annotation for 取 0059, we deliberately avoid the more concise but abstract statement, "**MILITARY** men *stop* invaders with *spears*." ☞ 式 0109, 弐 0110 |
|---|---|
| 止 77 | |
| 2764 | |
| 常　8 | |

| | |
|---|---|
| **THREAD** | ○金糸　きんし　gold thread.......................0029 |
| | 一糸もまとわずに　いっしもまとわずに　without a stitch of clothing on, stark naked...........0002 |
| シ | 生糸　きいと　raw silk.............................0036 |
| いと | ○糸口　いとぐち　beginning, first step; clue....0019 |
| | 白い糸　しろいいと　white thread..............0076 |

| 0112 | Here we encounter for the first time the grapheme 幺, which you should learn to see as a *child*. In 糸, visualize S4–6 as **THREADS** the *child* is playing with. ☞ 系 1077 |
|---|---|
| 糸 120 | |
| 絲 | |
| 1866 | |
| 常　6 | |

**BEFORE, ahead**

ゼン
まえ -まえ

以前　いぜん　before, ago, since .............0066
事前　じぜん　before the fact .................0080
前者　ぜんしゃ　the former....................0107
○前回　ぜんかい　last time.......................0050
○の前に　のまえに　ahead of, before

| 0113 | Here for the first time we'll let 月 denote *meat* (see 肉 0216 for this derivation). `丷` derives |
|---|---|
| 刀 18 | from 八 (EIGHT), and S3 is 一 (ONE), but instead visualize two strips of *meat* that have been *sliced* ( 刂 ) and placed in front of a line. See 月 and 刂 behind the line, and `丷` **ahead** of or **BEFORE** the line. |
| 1957 | |
| 常 9 | |

**AFTER, later, rear, behind**

ゴ　コウ
のち　うし(ろ)　うしろ　あと　おく(れる)

○以後　いご　after this, from now on, in future;
　　thereafter ....................................0066
事後　じご　after the fact, ex post facto .......0080
○後者　こうしゃ　the latter.......................0107
後回し　あとまわし　deferment, postponement
　　.........................................................0050
後ろから　うしろから　from behind

| 0114 | Now we add the grapheme 夂. When we find it at the bottom of a kanji, we'll take it to mean |
|---|---|
| 彳 60 | *crossed legs*. Here 彳 (from 行 0055) indicates that you're trying to *go* somewhere, but your *child* (幺) is lagging **behind AFTER** you with *crossed legs*. At 条 0119 we'll add a second meaning for 夂. |
| 0321 | |
| 常 9 | |

¹**NOON**

²**(sign of) THE HORSE**

ゴ

午前　ごぜん　morning, a.m.................0113
午前中　ごぜんちゅう　in the morning; all
　　morning..............................0113, 0035
午後　ごご　afternoon, p.m....................0114
正午　しょうご　noon.............................0043

| 0115 | Originally depicting the head of a *horse*, 午 came to mean **NOON** because the sign of **THE** |
|---|---|
| 十 24 | **HORSE** was the central sign of the twelve Chinese horary or zodiac signs, corresponding to the middle of the day. We might ignore such trivia, but 午's similarity to 牛 CATTLE (in the next entry) presses us to see the difference between them in the variation between the head of a horse and that of a bovine. Naturally this is the male's horn, which you should see in the pro- |
| 1720 | truding tip of S4 in 牛 CATTLE. 午 has no such horn, but like 牛 it does have a tag clipped to |
| 常 4 | one ear (S1). Use 馬 0336 for referring to an actual horse. ☞ 牛 0116, 干 0408, 年 0117 |

**CATTLE**

ギュウ
うし

水牛　すいぎゅう　water buffalo .............0027
牛後　ぎゅうご　rump of a cow ...............0114
○子牛　こうし　calf...............................0094

| 0116 | Like 午, 牛 depicts the animal's head. A bull's horns are on the sides of its head, but here |
|---|---|
| 牛 93 | see them symbolized in the middle (top of S4), so as to distinguish 牛 from 午. See 乳 0160 and 肉 0216 for other *on-yomi* compounds. ☞ 午 0115, 丑 0590 |
| 2903 | |
| 常 4 | |

| 年 | **YEAR** | 年中無休 ねんじゅうむきゅう open all year ............0035, 0048, 0061 |
|---|---|---|
| | ネン<br>とし | ○年代 ねんだい age, era, period; date........0071<br>(生)年月日 (せい)ねんがっぴ (birth)date<br>.............0036, 0023, 0001<br>長年 ながねん many years..............0091<br>○年上の としうえの older, senior.............0041 |

| **0117**<br>干 51<br><br><br>1752<br>常 6 | 午 0115, marking the return of the sun to the top of the sky each day, represents the completion of one rotation by the earth. Similarly, 年 marks the return of the sun to the same position in the sky each **YEAR**, representing the completion of the earth's revolution around the sun. It has an extra horizontal stroke, so we can interpret the two lower horizontal strokes as the tropics of Cancer and Capricorn. Let the short vertical stroke represent the sun's path from directly over one tropic, to directly over the other tropic, and back. ☞ 午 0115 |
|---|---|

| 件 | **MATTER, case** | ○用件 ようけん matter (of business), things to be done ..................0047 |
|---|---|---|
| | ケン | 事件 じけん affair, incident, case, event.....0080<br>案件 あんけん matter, case, item.............0097<br>五十件 ごじゅっけん (=ごじっけん) fifty cases,<br>fifty items ...........................0007, 0005<br>その件について そのけんについて Regarding<br>that matter |

| **0118**<br>人 9<br><br><br>0035<br>常 6 | A *man* (亻)'s *cow* (牛) is his own **MATTER**. ☞ 伴 0743 |
|---|---|

| 条 | **ARTICLE, section, clause; strip** | 条目 じょうもく article, stipulation .............0021 |
|---|---|---|
| | ジョウ | ○条件 じょうけん condition(s), term(s); item,<br>proviso ..................................0118<br>信条 しんじょう principle, creed, article of faith<br>..............................................0063<br>条文 じょうぶん text (of a regulation), provision<br>..............................................0101<br>一条 いちじょう a line; a matter; a quotation 0002 |

| **0119**<br>木 75<br><br>條<br><br>1882<br>常 7 | Review 後 0114. Now when we find 夂 at the <u>top</u> of a kanji, we'll see it as an *angled rooftop* viewed from one end. Picture using **strips** of wood from the *tree* (木) below it for constructing the gable formed by S2–3. Associate this image of linear **strips** of wood with the image of lines or **ARTICLES** in a document. ☞ 柔 0688 |
|---|---|

| 化 | **CHANGE INTO, convert** | 化成 かせい chemical synthesis, transformation<br>..............................................0070 |
|---|---|---|
| | カ ケ<br>ば(ける) ば(かす) | ○化学 かがく chemistry........................0099<br>コンピュータ化 コンピュータか computerization<br>○化ける ばける change oneself into, take the<br>form of; disguise oneself<br>化かす ばかす bewitch, deceive |

| **0120**<br>ヒ 21<br><br><br>0012<br>常 4 | ヒ means *spoon* (cf. 匙 1682), but sometimes, as here, we shall see it as a *person who has fallen on his rear*. See the standing person at the left **CHANGE INTO** the seated person at the right. Do not confuse ヒ with 七 SEVEN. |
|---|---|

| 花 | **FLOWER** | ○国花 こっか national flower.................0075 |
| | | 花見 はなみ flower [cherry blossom] viewing |
| | | .................................................0083 |
| | カ | ○花火 はなび fireworks.........................0026 |
| | はな | 生け花 いけばな flower arrangement....0036 |
| | | お花 おはな flower; flower arrangement |

| 0121 | ㅛ, resembling two blades of grass sticking out of the ground, implies that a kanji has something to do with *grass, herbs,* or, more generally, *plants.* Thus ㅛ and 化 (*change*) suggest plants that transform themselves: **FLOWERING** plants. Note that in kanji that are split between top and bottom, the semantic clue generally appears at the top. |
| 艸 140 | |
| **1894** | |
| 常 | 7 | |

| 北 | **NORTH** | ○北部 ほくぶ north, northern part...........0068 |
| | | 北東 ほくとう northeast....................0032 |
| | | 北北東 ほくほくとう north by northeast ......0032 |
| | ホク | 東北 とうほく Tohoku (northeastern Honshu) |
| | きた | .................................................0032 |
| | | ○北口 きたぐち north exit.....................0019 |

| 0122 | The figure at the left resembles the *seated person* at the right, in mirror image. We thus visualize two people sitting back-to-back on the **NORTH** pole. Draw 北 on a piece of scratch paper above a small coin-size circle representing the earth, and take a few moments to fix this image in your memory. The *on* reading ホク is unique in this course. ☞ 比 0123 |
| ヒ 21 | |
| **0176** | |
| 常 | 5 | |

| 比 | ¹**COMPARE, contrast, match** | ①無比 むひ incomparable, peerless, unparalleled |
| | ²**PHONETIC [hi]** | .................................................0048 |
| | | ¹比を見ない ひをみない unparalleled.......0083 |
| | | ①比べる くらべる compare, contrast |
| | ヒ | ¹Aと比べて エーとくらべて compared with A |
| | くら(べる) | ² 日比 にちひ Japan and the Philippines; |
| | | Japanese-Filipino ............................0001 |

| 0123 | Here the figure at the left looks even more like the *seated person* at the right, and they face the same way. Think of them as lining up with one another to **COMPARE** their shape and size. Used in place names not for its meaning but for its phonetic value (thus M2), 比 is the source for *hi* (ひ, ヒ) in the kana syllabaries. ☞ 北 0122, 此 1756 |
| 比 81 | |
| **0014** | |
| 常 | 4 | |

|  | **BACK; stature** | ○背部 はいぶ back.............................0068 |
| | | 背比べ せいくらべ comparison of statures...0123 |
| | | ○背中 せなか back.............................0035 |
| | ハイ | ○背く そむく go against, disobey |
| | せ せい そむ(く) そむ(ける) | 背ける そむける turn (one's face) away |

| 0124 | From 北, we have *people sitting back-to-back on the North Pole.* To that we add *flesh* (月), to refer literally to their **BACKS** (the body part). As the image suggests, 背 is also used to mean *turning one's BACK on someone/something.* ☞ 脊 2153, 皆 1427 |
| 肉 130 | |
| **2230** | |
| 常 | 9 | |

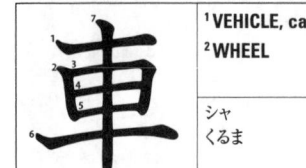

| 車 | ¹ VEHICLE, car<br>² WHEEL<br><br>シャ<br>くるま | ① 車体 しゃたい body (of a car) .............. 0062<br>¹ 人力車 じんりきしゃ rickshaw, human-pulled cart<br>............................ 0015, 0084<br>¹ 下車する げしゃする alight, get off .......... 0040<br>① 車で行く くるまでいく go by car .............. 0055<br>² 水車 すいしゃ waterwheel .................... 0027 |

| 0125<br>車 159<br><br><br>2976<br>常 7 | A bird's-eye view of a chariot gives us the character for **VEHICLE**. As in the original Chinese model, the chariot has only one axle (S7). We can clearly discern a **WHEEL** on either side (S1 and S6), and a chassis in between. |

| 気 | ¹ GAS<br>² SPIRIT<br><br>キ ケ | ① 気体 きたい gas, vapor ...................... 0062<br>¹ 大気 たいき atmosphere .................... 0033<br>² 本気 ほんき seriousness, earnestness ...... 0031<br>² やる気 やるき motivation, willingness,<br>　mind [determination] to do (something)<br>② 気に入る きにいる like, be pleased with .... 0039 |

| 0126<br>気 84<br>氣<br>2751<br>常 6 | S1-2 are イ sideways, but see 气 as lines of vapor (like in the Japanese symbol for hot springs ), escaping from an enclosure (S4) in which an active **GAS** is contained. The "メ" (米 in the old form) shows the **GAS** floating around to every corner of the container, revealing the vital energy and **SPIRIT** of this genie in a bottle. |

| 汽 | STEAM<br><br>キ | ○ 汽車 きしゃ (steam) train ..................... 0125 |

| 0127<br>水 85<br>滊<br>0234<br>常 7 | *Water* (氵) + *gas* (气): **STEAM**. |

| 性 | ¹ NATURE, innate quality<br>² SEX, gender<br>³ -ITY<br><br>セイ ショウ | ¹ 人の性 ひとのせい human nature .......... 0015<br>① 本性 ほんしょう (true) nature, (true) personality<br>............................ 0031<br>² 男性 だんせい male/man .................... 0092<br>② 性別 せいべつ distinction of sex; gender... 0090<br>③ 安定性 あんていせい stability .......... 0096, 0045 |

| 0128<br>心 61<br><br><br>0266<br>常 8 | Review 心 0056. 忄 denotes *heart/mind* and 生 denotes *life/be born*. Together these clues suggest the *heart/mind* we are *born* with, that is, our **NATURE**. |

| | (cultivated) FIELD | 田畑 たはた (=てんばた) fields and rice paddies .... 0020 |
|---|---|---|
| 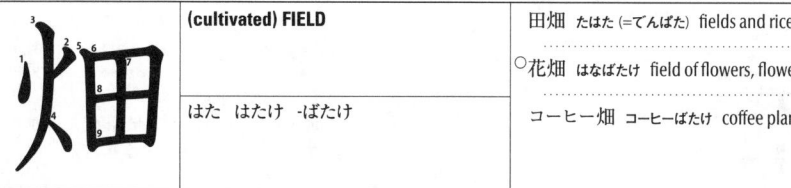 | | ○花畑 はなばたけ field of flowers, flower garden .... 0121 |
| | はた　はたけ　-ばたけ | コーヒー畑 コーヒーばたけ coffee plantation |

| 0129 | Review 火 0026. The present entry means **CULTIVATED FIELD**: see a *rice field* (田) *burned* to |
|---|---|
| 田 102 | clear it for cultivation. Compare 火 with 忄 from the previous entry, noting the difference in |
| | the direction of the second short stroke (S2). |
| 0812 | |
| 常 9 | |

|  | BLUE; green | ○青年 せいねん youth, young man .... 0117 |
|---|---|---|
| | | ○青い あおい blue, green |
| | | 青白い あおじろい pale, pallid .... 0076 |
| | セイ ショウ | 青ざめる あおざめる become pale |
| | あお　あお-　あお(い) | |

| 0130 | The color indicated by 青 is a broad one, ranging from **BLUE** to **green** in their lighter shades. |
|---|---|
| 青 174 | It also suggests "youth." See a young, blue/green *plant* growing on the *moon* (the *growing* |
| 青 | *plant* is simplified here from 生 0036). As a grapheme in other kanji, 青 will sometimes lend |
| 2152 | connotations of *clarity*, *purity*, or *calm*, which we can associate with a *clear, pure, calm,* **BLUE** |
| 常 8 | sky. ☞ 責 0831 |

| | WHEAT | ○小麦 こむぎ wheat .... 0034 |
|---|---|---|
| | | 大麦 おおむぎ barley .... 0033 |
| | | ライ麦 ライむぎ rye |
| | バク | 麦畑 むぎばたけ wheat field .... 0129 |
| | むぎ | 蕎ˣ麦 そば buckwheat noodles, soba; buckwheat |

| 0131 | *Growing plant* + *crossed legs* (夂). Picture **WHEAT** waving back and forth in the wind, firmly |
|---|---|
| 麥 199 | planted in the earth with *crossed legs*. ☞ 表 0705 |
| 麥 | |
| 2133 | |
| 常 7 | |

|  | ¹ ELEMENT | ①水素 すいそ hydrogen .... 0027 |
|---|---|---|
| | ² PLAIN, bare | ²素手 すで bare hands .... 0046 |
| | | ②素足 すあし bare feet .... 0044 |
| | ソ ス | ²素人 しろうと amateur, novice, outsider .... 0015 |

| 0132 | Be flexible about exactly what kind of *growing plant* you imagine, for here it yields not wheat |
|---|---|
| 糸 120 | grain but *thread* (see 糸 0112), as if it were cotton. Imagine yourself pulling the thread down- |
| | ward, leaving the poor plant utterly without a stitch, in its **PLAIN**, naked, most **ELEMENTAL** |
| 2171 | state. ☞ 索 1735 |
| 常 10 | |

| | | POISON | 毒素 どくそ toxin ....................................0132 |
|---|---|---|---|
|  | | | 毒舌 どくぜつ wicked tongue, abusive language<br>..............................................................0052 |
| | | | 毒ガス どくガス poison gas |
| | | ドク | ○中毒 ちゅうどく poisoning; addiction ........0035 |
| | | | 気の毒な きのどくな pitiable, miserable;<br>regrettable, too bad.................................0126 |

| 0133 | Think of yourself as a child, approaching this strange *growing plant* out of innocent curios- |
|---|---|
| 母 80 | ity. Suddenly your *mother* jumps between you and the plant, her arms outstretched (S8) to |
| 毒 | block your approach. The plant is **POISONOUS**. It will help if this image of a mother's urgent |
| | intervention induces a tinge of dread, for 毒 is the Japanese skull and crossbones. |
| 2150 | |
| 常 8 | |

| | | AHEAD (of), previous | ○先月 せんげつ last month ....................0023 |
|---|---|---|---|
| 先 | | | 先行する せんこうする precede, go ahead of...0055 |
| | | | 三キロ先に さんキロさきに 3 kilometers ahead<br>..............................................................0004 |
| | | セン | 刃先 はさき edge of a blade ....................0087 |
| | | さき ま(ず)* | ○行き先 いきさき (=ゆきさき) one's destination 0055 |

| 0134 | Since we saw the sprout appear through the soil back at 土, it has grown a leaf (S1) and roots |
|---|---|
| 儿 10 | (儿, a plant's *legs*). Picture this leaf as the plant's leading edge, physically **AHEAD** of the rest |
| | of the plant. |
| 2123 | |
| 常 6 | |

| | | WASH | 水洗 すいせん flushing, washing ............0027 |
|---|---|---|---|
| 洗 | | | ○洗車 せんしゃ carwash ........................0125 |
| | | | ○洗う あらう wash, cleanse |
| | | セン | 手洗い てあらい lavatory, restroom .........0046 |
| | | あら(う) | |

| 0135 | *Water*(氵) + *ahead of*(先): **WASH**. The logic of this character is obvious—as natural as wash- |
|---|---|
| 水 85 | ing one's hands before a meal. ☞ 洪 0358 |
| 0350 | |
| 常 9 | |

| | | ORIGIN | 元素 げんそ element, chemical element ...0132 |
|---|---|---|---|
| 元 | | | ○元気 げんき vigor, energy; spirits; health...0126 |
| | | | 元金 がんきん principal, capital .............0029 |
| | | ゲン ガン | 火の元 ひのもと origin of a fire..............0026 |
| | | もと | ○元々 もともと originally, from the first; by nature |

| 0136 | See S1 as a thing (any thing) and S2–4 as the **ORIGIN** of or basis for that thing. S2 can be seen |
|---|---|
| 儿 10 | as the ground and S3–4 as roots, suggesting the idea of genesis. |
| 1690 | |
| 常 4 | |

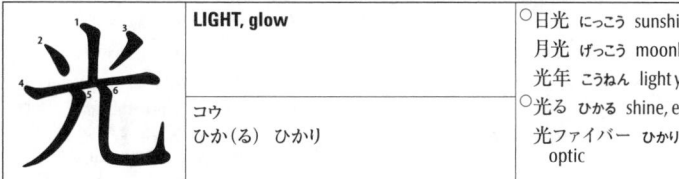

**LIGHT, glow**

コウ
ひか（る）　ひかり

○日光　にっこう　sunshine, sunlight.............0001
　月光　げっこう　moonlight......................0023
　光年　こうねん　light year.......................0117
○光る　ひかる　shine, emit light
　光ファイバー　ひかりファイバー　optical fiber, fiber-optic

---

**0137**

儿 10

2121

常 6

At 金 we let the two dot strokes at the bottom suggest GOLD's glitter. Here we see a candle with three glowing rays of **LIGHT** (ⵗ). ⵗ is a variant of 小 0034, but we'll use it as a visual element distinguished by the way the three lines radiate from (or converge upon) a single point. Distinguish from ⵌ and ⵘ. ☞ 晃 2240

---

**GO AWAY, leave; go by, elapse**

キョ　コ
さ（る）　-さ（る）

○去る　さる　go away, leave; go by, elapse; get rid of
　洗い去る　あらいさる　wash away.............0135
　立ち去る　たちさる　leave, walk out...........0067
　取り去る　とりさる　take away, leave out......0059
○去年　きょねん　last year.......................0117

---

**0138**

厶 28

1850

常 5

Review 公 0089. Here we see the *self* (厶) go "under*ground* (土)," in order to "get away from it all," to just **GO AWAY**.

---

**¹ LAW**

**² METHOD, way**

ホウ　ハッ-　ホッ-

①法案　ほうあん　bill, legislative proposal......0097
¹ 法学　ほうがく　law, jurisprudence.............0099
¹ 法学部　ほうがくぶ　law department/school
　..............................................0099, 0068
² 手法　しゅほう　technique, mechanism, style....0046
² 生活法　せいかつほう　way of life, art of living
　..............................................0036, 0054

---

**0139**

水 85

0295

常 8

According to one theory, the first states and **LAWS** arose along with the need to control the flow of water in dry regions with rivers flowing through them. Here *water* (氵) turns *go away* (去) into "*flow away*," which, in keeping with our theory, we can associate with the need for control, or **LAW**. Connect with M2 **METHOD** via the idea of control or discipline.

---

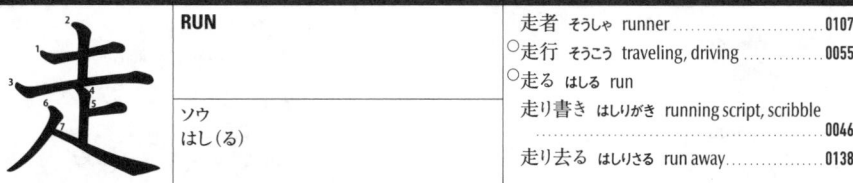

**RUN**

ソウ
はし（る）

　走者　そうしゃ　runner........................0107
○走行　そうこう　traveling, driving.............0055
○走る　はしる　run
　走り書き　はしりがき　running script, scribble
　..............................................0046
　走り去る　はしりさる　run away................0138

---

**0140**

走 156

1877

常 7

走

*Foot* (review 止 0042 and 足 0044) and *ground* (土). Associate this image of a foot hitting the ground with the phrase "hit the ground **RUNNING**."

| | ¹ THE PRESENT, the said, this/that<br>² HIT (the mark); correspond to; allot | ① 当日 とうじつ the appointed day, that day...0001<br>² 本当の ほんとうの true, real, genuine .......0031<br>② 当たる あたる hit (the mark) |
| | トウ<br>あ(たる) あ(たり) あ(てる) あ(て) | ² 日当たり ひあたり exposure to the sun......0001<br>² 一日当たり千円 いちにちあたりせんえん<br>a thousand yen a day ......0002, 0001, 0017, 0013 |

| **0141**<br><br>小 42*<br><br>當<br><br>1865<br>常 6 | At the bottom is a trimmed variant of ⇒ *three-fingered hand* (in other contexts we shall see ⇒/∃ as a *claw*, *pitchfork*, or *shovel*). At 光 we let the three radial lines ⌄ suggest light rays radiating outward; here see them converging inward, like three darts **HITTING THE MARK** of a bull's eye painted on one's *hand*. To assimilate M1 **THE PRESENT**/this, see the darts as pointing to one's present time or location, or the thing one is referring to. |

| | THINK, feel; wish | ○ 思案する しあんする think, consider, reflect<br>....................0097<br>○ 思う おもう think, feel; wish<br>思い付く おもいつく think of, hit upon......0064<br>思い切る おもいきる resign oneself to, give up;<br>resolve, determine............0086<br>思い出 おもいで recollections, memory....0038 |
| | シ<br>おも(う) | |

| **0142**<br><br>心 61<br><br><br>2221<br>常 9 | A *head* pictured above a *heart* (see 男 0092 and 心 0056). Between the *head* and the *heart* we can find a range of ideas from **THINK** to **feel** to **wish**. ☞ 恩 1728 |

| | ¹ EARLY<br>² QUICK | ¹ お早う おはよう Good morning!<br>¹ 早立ち はやだち early morning departure...0067<br>¹ 早めに はやめに a little early, with time to spare<br>² 早口 はやくち fast talking...................0019<br>○ 早々 そうそう (=はやばや) quickly, without delay;<br>early |
| | ソウ サッ-<br>はや(い) はや はや- はや(まる)<br>はや(める) | |

| **0143**<br><br>日 72<br><br><br>2120<br>常 6 | At 土 0030 we learned to see 十 as a cross-shaped plant sticking out of the ground. Here we look out over the eastern horizon and see the *sun* rising over a *plant*: it is **EARLY**. M2 **QUICK** is an easily associated meaning. |

| | GRASS | 毒草 どくそう poisonous plant ..............0133<br>○ 草木 そうもく (=くさき) trees and plants, vegeta-<br>tion..................0028<br>草書 そうしょ cursive writing ...............0079<br>草案 そうあん (rough) draft.................0097<br>草花 くさばな (=そうか) flowering plant ......0121 |
| | ソウ<br>くさ くさ- -ぐさ | |

| **0144**<br><br>艸 140<br><br><br>1953<br>常 9 | To refer to **GRASS** we throw in some *grass* to the vegetation obscuring the *early* morning sun. Practice writing the last two entries in turn, and distinguishing their meanings. |

| 朝 | ¹ MORNING<br>² DYNASTY<br><br>チョウ<br>あさ | ¹ 早朝 そうちょう early morning ............... 0143<br>¹ 朝日 あさひ rising sun, morning sun(light)... 0001<br>① 毎朝 まいあさ every morning ............... 0105<br>¹ 朝早く あさはやく early in the morning ...... 0143<br>② 王朝 おうちょう dynasty, Imperial regime ... 0072 |

| **0145**<br>月 74<br>朝<br>1513<br>常 12 | Here the *sun* rises through two *cross-shaped plants* while the *moon* is still visible, signaling **MORNING**. To remember M2, let the rising sun of **MORNING** suggest the dawn and rise of a **DYNASTY**. ☞ 胡 0258, 期 0486 |

| 潮 | (morning) TIDE<br><br>チョウ<br>しお | 潮水 しおみず seawater ..................... 0027<br>潮入り しおいり coming in of the tide ....... 0039 |

| **0146**<br>水 85<br><br>0675<br>常 15 | *Water* of the *morning*: morning TIDE. See 満 0179, 干 0408 and 汐 0268 for sample *on-yomi* compounds. ☞ 湖 0259 |

|  | SHAPE, material form<br><br>ケイ ギョウ<br>かた -がた かたち | ○体形 たいけい form, figure ................. 0062<br>○人形 にんぎょう doll ..................... 0015<br>形成する けいせいする form, make up, mold<br> ........................... 0070<br>○形だけ かたちだけ merely for appearances [form]<br>花形 はながた floral pattern; leading, popular<br> ........................... 0121 |

| **0147**<br>彡 59<br><br>0749<br>常 7 | Two more graphemes to pick up here. See 开 as a *torii* (a Japanese shrine gate), distinguished by its parallel crossing lintels. We shall interpret 彡 flexibly, depending on the image we wish to make from the character. Here let it suggest three strikes of the stonemason's chisel, giving **SHAPE** to the gate. ☞ 彫 1279 |

|  | ¹ START, generate<br>² EMIT, issue<br>³ OPEN UP, develop<br><br>ハツ ホツ<br>た(つ)* | ¹ 発明 はつめい invention, contrivance ....... 0024<br>¹ 発つ たつ start (on a journey), depart<br>² 発する はっする emit, radiate<br>² 発行する はっこうする publish, issue ........ 0055<br>③ 発見 はっけん discovery, revelation ....... 0083 |

| **0148**<br>癶 105<br>發<br>2222<br>常 9 | 癶 means *outspread legs*. The image of *spreading out* or **OPENING UP** is reinforced by the legs of the *torii* gate, which here **OPEN UP** much more than in the previous entry. To associate the image with M1-2, see the point where the legs are joined as the **STARTING** point, from which something is issued or **EMITTED**, from which the whole character **OPENS UP**. |

| | ¹ ABANDON, abolish<br>² WASTE<br><br>ハイ<br>すた(れる) | ① 廃止する　はいしする　abandon, abolish......0042<br>¹ 廃案　はいあん　rejected bill/project..........0097<br>¹ 全廃　ぜんぱい　total abolition................0078<br>① 廃れる　すたれる　fall into disuse<br>² 廃ガス　はいガス　waste gas |
|---|---|---|

| 0149 | 广 (*slanting roof* or *shelter*) differs from 厂 (*cliff*) only by the dot stroke at the top. While 発 means START/generate; OPEN UP/develop, etc., 廃 means virtually the opposite: ABANDON/abolish; WASTE. Thus see 广 negating the earlier kanji's meaning: what was earlier *started up* and *developed* is now ABANDONED in a storage *shelter*, WASTING AWAY. |
|---|---|
| 广 53 | |
| 2712 | |
| 常 12 | |

|  | SOUND<br><br>オン　イン<br>おと　ね | ○発音　はつおん　pronunciation................0148<br>本音　ほんね　one's real intentions..........0031<br>○母音　ぼいん (=ぼおん)　vowel.................0104<br>子音　しいん (=しおん)　consonant..........0094<br>○足音　あしおと　sound of footsteps..........0044 |
|---|---|---|

| 0150 | *Man standing* on the *sun*. 音 appears in two later kanji meaning DARK, so though it means SOUND by itself, we'll reap benefits later if we can also let it suggest the absence of light. The *man standing* on the *sun* succeeds in blocking the light but produces an ear-splitting scream of pain from the heat. He can make it dark, but his SOUND gives him away. |
|---|---|
| 音 180 | |
| 1783 | |
| 常 9 | |

| | ¹ MIND, thoughts; opinion; will<br>² MEANING, sense<br><br>イ | ① 意見　いけん　opinion, view................0083<br>¹ 好意　こうい　goodwill, favor, kindness.......0095<br>¹ 用意する　よういする　prepare, make arrange-<br>ments................................0047<br>¹ 不意に　ふいに　by surprise; all of a sudden...0049<br>² 文意　ぶんい　meaning (of a passage), purport<br>..........................................0101 |
|---|---|---|

| 0151 | As with 海 and 廃, we can simplify this kanji by using the meaning of another kanji (音) lying inside it. We thus have the "*sound*" inside your *heart*: your MIND or MEANING. A useful compound for M2 appears at 味 0273. |
|---|---|
| 心 61 | |
| 1834 | |
| 常 13 | |

|  | ¹ MAKE, produce, cultivate<br>² WORK, do<br><br>サク　サ<br>つく(る)　つく(り)　-づく(り) | ① 作成する　さくせいする　make, produce, prepare<br>..........................................0070<br>¹ 麦作　むぎさく　wheat cultivation............0131<br>① 作る　つくる　make, create; grow<br>² 作用　さよう　action, operation, function; effect<br>..........................................0047<br>² 作法　さほう　manners, etiquette, decorum...0139 |
|---|---|---|

| 0152 | We'll interpret 乍 as a *saw*. Here see a *man* (亻) with a *saw* WORKING/MAKING something. Let the word "saw" suggest the *on* readings サ and サク, one or both of which apply to all the kanji in this course that contain 乍. |
|---|---|
| 人 9 | |
| 0052 | |
| 常 7 | |

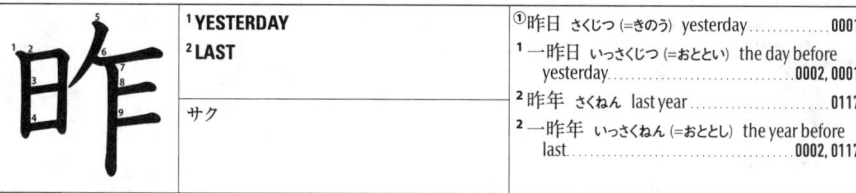

| 昨 | ¹ YESTERDAY<br>² LAST<br><br>サク | ①昨日 さくじつ (=きのう) yesterday ............. 0001<br>¹ 一昨日 いっさくじつ (=おととい) the day before yesterday .......................... 0002, 0001<br>² 昨年 さくねん last year ........................ 0117<br>² 一昨年 いっさくねん (=おととし) the year before last ................................. 0002, 0117 |

**0153**
日 72

**0795**
常 9

*Saw* (乍) off a *day* (日), and it's **YESTERDAY**.

| 雨 | RAIN<br><br>ウ<br>あめ あま- | ○雨水 あまみず (=うすい) rainwater ............ 0027<br>雨上がり あめあがり just after a rainfall ..... 0041<br>雨が止んだ あめがやんだ It stopped raining ................................................ 0042<br>大雨 おおあめ heavy rain ...................... 0033<br>小雨 こさめ drizzle ............................ 0034 |

**0154**
雨 173

**2983**
常 8

Picture this as a **RAIN**cloud. Other sample compounds using the *on-yomi* appear at 林 0240 and 季 0395.

| 電 | ELECTRICITY<br><br>デン | ○電気 でんき electricity; electric light ........ 0126<br>電力 でんりょく electric power, electricity ... 0084<br>発電 はつでん generation of electricity ..... 0148<br>電話 でんわ telephone; phone call .......... 0053<br>電車 でんしゃ train, electric train, trolley .... 0125 |

**0155**
雨 173

**2431**
常 13

At the top we have a *raincloud* (雨). At the bottom, a thundercloud with a lightning bolt shooting out of it: **ELECTRICITY**. ☞ 雷 0900

| 頁 | PAGE<br><br>ケツ<br>ペーじ | 一頁 いちページ page 1, one page ........... 0002<br>九十頁 きゅうじゅっページ (=きゅうじっページ) page 90, ninety pages ............. 0011, 0005<br>頁付け ページづけ pagination ............... 0064<br>五百頁の本 ごひゃくページのほん book of five hundred pages ................. 0007, 0016, 0031 |

**0156**
頁 181

**1795**
名 9

By itself means **PAGE**. Practice by penciling in after page numbers and pronouncing the number in Japanese followed by "*peeji.*" 頁 seldom appears by itself but is found in many other kanji, where we shall give it the meaning *head*: see the wide *head* (S1) attached to the top of a *shellfish* (see 貝 0082), via a stubby neck. ☞ 頁 1158, 首 0157, 夏 0363

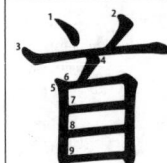

| 首 | ¹ **HEAD** ² **NECK** ³ **LEADER** シュ くび | ① 部首 ぶしゅ radical (of a Chinese character) 0068 ² バイオリンの首 バイオリンのくび neck of a violin ② 手首 てくび wrist ............................0046 ³ 元首 げんしゅ ruler, sovereign ............0136 ³ 首長 しゅちょう leader, chief ............0091 |
| --- | --- | --- |

| 0157 首 185 | Here 頁's two feet have been removed and replaced by two hairs on top of its **HEAD**. 首 also means **HEAD** in the sense of **LEADER**, as well as **NECK**. Practice writing 頁 and 首 until the two images are clear and distinct in your mind. ☞ 頁 0156 |
| --- | --- |
| 1956 常 9 | |

| 道 | **WAY** ドウ トウ みち | 水道 すいどう waterworks [supply]; channel ............................0027 気道 きどう air passage ............0126 ○書道 しょどう calligraphy, penmanship ....0079 人道 じんどう humaneness, humanity ......0015 北海道 ほっかいどう Hokkaido (island and prefecture) ............0122, 0106 |
| --- | --- | --- |

| 0158 辵 162 | Here *head* rides atop 辶, which we shall see as a vehicle with the driver and front wheels visible at the left and a long bed stretching out to the right. To assimilate the characters containing 辶 (or its four-stroke variant, 辶), it's best just to see it as an image of forward motion or conveyance, rather than to focus on its semantic label (though for convenience, we'll refer to it as a *truck*). As Halpern notes, 道 means **WAY** not only as in "road," but also as in "**WAY** of moral conduct" or "the **WAY** of an art." Visualize the *head* guiding the *conveyance* along the proper **WAY**. ☞ 通 0159 |
| --- | --- |
| 2701 常 12 | |

| 通 | ¹ **PASS (through)** ² **COMMUNICATE** ツウ ツ とお(る) とお(り) -とお(り) -どお(り) とお(す) とお(し) -どお(し) かよ(う) | ① 通る とおる pass (by), get through ¹ 通す とおす let pass (by); admit; carry through ① 通学 つうがく attending school; commuting to school ............0099 ² 通信 つうしん correspondence, communication ............0063 ² 交通 こうつう traffic; communication; transportation ............0102 |
| --- | --- | --- |

| 0159 辵 162 | 用 0047 means *container* when used as a grapheme. See マ as a bent arm carrying the *container*, with its elbow pointing forward to indicate progress (unlike ム in 公 0089). Thus regard 甬 as *carrying/moving forward*. In this entry we observe *carrying forward* on a *conveyance*, illustrating the ideas **PASS (through)** and **COMMUNICATE**. ☞ 道 0158 |
| --- | --- |
| 2678 常 10 | |

| 乳 | **MILK, breast** ニュウ ちち ち | ○牛乳 ぎゅうにゅう cow's milk ............0116 母乳 ぼにゅう mother's milk ............0104 ○乳首 ちくび (=ちちくび) teat, nipple ............0157 乳母 うば wet nurse ............0104 乳母車 うばぐるま baby carriage ............0104, 0125 |
| --- | --- | --- |

| 0160 乙 5 | As we saw back at 受 0065, 爫 *claw* derives from 爪 0201. See a *claw* holding a small *child* to a pendulous *breast* (乚), feeding it breast **MILK**. ☞ 浮 0613, 孔 1559 |
| --- | --- |
| 1306 常 8 | |

| | | |
|---|---|---|
|  BEAN, pea<br><br>トウ　ズ<br>まめ　まめ- | ○豆乳　とうにゅう　soybean milk .............0160<br>○豆本　まめほん　miniature book .............0031<br>　青豆　あおまめ　green peas .................0130<br>○大豆　だいず　soybean.........................0033<br>　小豆　あずき　adzuki bean ..................0034 | |

**0161**
豆 151

Picture a **BEAN** (□) popping out of its pod. Because 豆 is often used to refer to small things, we'll sometimes give it the diminutive-sounding label *pea*.

1700
常 7

| | | |
|---|---|---|
|  HEAD, top, beginning<br><br>トウ　ズ<br>あたま　かしら　-がしら | 頭部　とうぶ　head.............................0068<br>出頭する　しゅっとうする　attend, present oneself<br>　..............................................0038<br>○先頭　せんとう　forefront, head, top..........0134<br>頭上　ずじょう　overhead......................0041<br>○頭に入れる　あたまにいれる　keep in mind...0039 | |

**0162**
頁 181

*Bean + head*. The visual focus on *head* is naturally always at the top, S8. Here it is given a mirror reflection in S1 of *bean*, to emphasize the idea of **HEAD**. Like 刂, 頁 is a *tsukuri* that nonetheless functions as a semantic clue. The grapheme at the left therefore serves as the phonetic clue; compare the *on-yomi* of 豆 and 頭.

1450
常 16

| | | |
|---|---|---|
|  IN ADVANCE<br><br>ヨ<br>あらかじ（め）* | 予言　よげん　prediction, forecast ............0051<br>予言者　よげんしゃ　prophet, prognosticator<br>　.......................................0051, 0107<br>予見　よけん　foresight........................0083<br>○予定　よてい　schedule, plan, prearrangement;<br>　expectation; estimate ....................0045<br>予め　あらかじめ　in advance | |

**0163**
亅 6*

豫

The forward-pointing elbow we saw at 通 0159 is replicated here. See both the top and bottom parts of 予 pointing ahead in time, that is, **IN ADVANCE**. ☞ 矛 0164, 子 0094

1719
常 4

| | | |
|---|---|---|
|  HALBERD<br><br>ム<br>ほこ | ○矛先　ほこさき　spearhead; the aim (of an attack);<br>　the brunt (of an argument).................0134 | |

**0164**
矛 110

To distinguish this from the previous entry, see the diagonal stroke S5 as a long, pointy **HAL-BERD**. Practice writing out 矛 several times, reminding yourself each time that the last stroke makes this character **HALBERD**. See the *on-yomi* compound at 盾 1551. ☞ 予 0163

1732
常 5

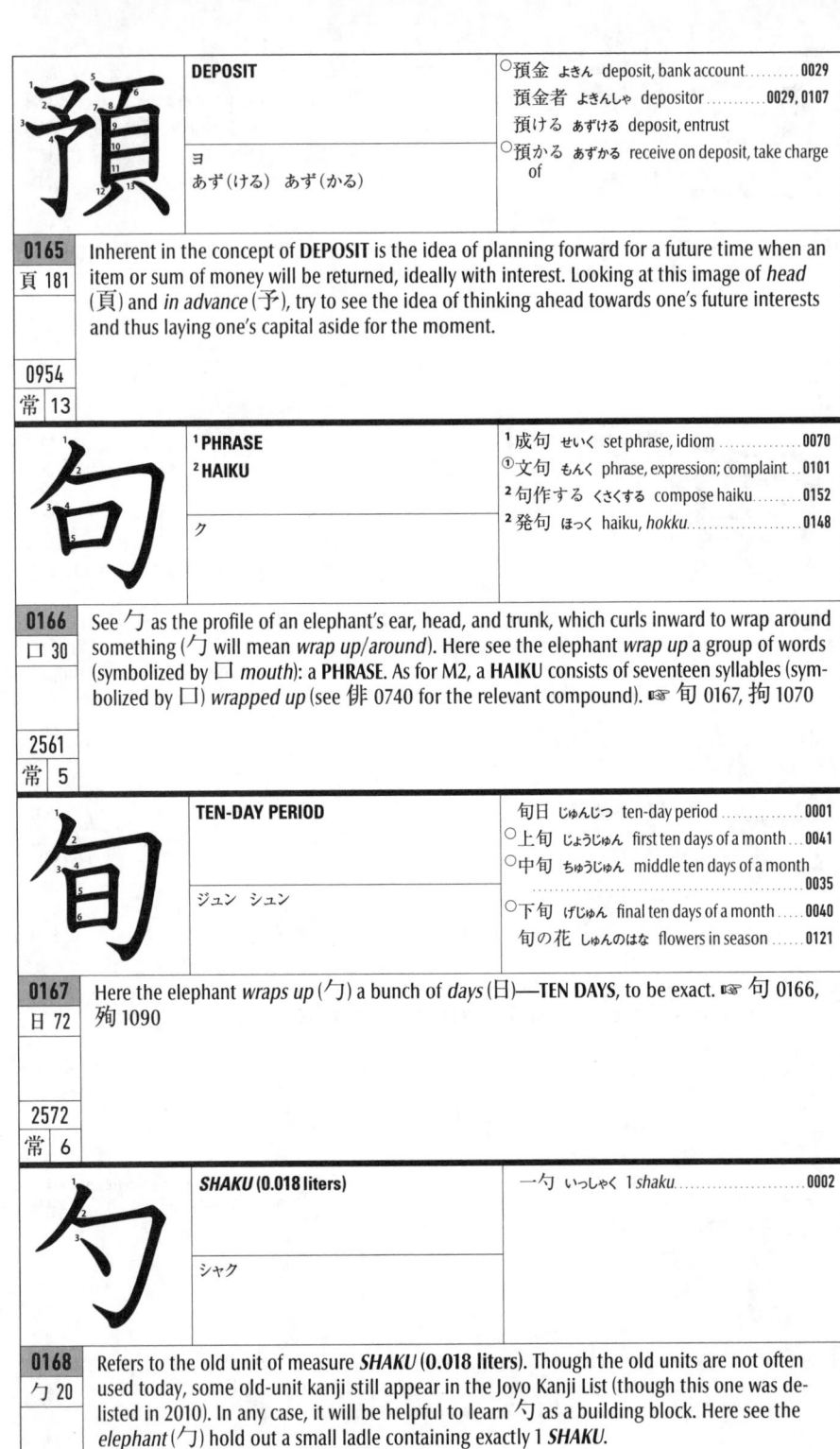

| | | |
|---|---|---|
| 預 | **DEPOSIT** | ○預金 よきん deposit, bank account..........0029 |
| | | 預金者 よきんしゃ depositor............0029, 0107 |
| | | 預ける あずける deposit, entrust |
| | ヨ | ○預かる あずかる receive on deposit, take charge |
| | あず(ける)　あず(かる) | of |

**0165**
頁 181

Inherent in the concept of **DEPOSIT** is the idea of planning forward for a future time when an item or sum of money will be returned, ideally with interest. Looking at this image of *head* (頁) and *in advance* (予), try to see the idea of thinking ahead towards one's future interests and thus laying one's capital aside for the moment.

0954
常 13

| | | |
|---|---|---|
| 句 | **¹PHRASE** | ¹成句 せいく set phrase, idiom...............0070 |
| | **²HAIKU** | ①文句 もんく phrase, expression; complaint...0101 |
| | | ²句作する くさくする compose haiku.........0152 |
| | ク | ²発句 ほっく haiku, *hokku*...................0148 |

**0166**
口 30

See 勹 as the profile of an elephant's ear, head, and trunk, which curls inward to wrap around something (勹 will mean *wrap up/around*). Here see the elephant *wrap up* a group of words (symbolized by 口 *mouth*): a **PHRASE**. As for M2, a **HAIKU** consists of seventeen syllables (symbolized by 口) *wrapped up* (see 俳 0740 for the relevant compound). ☞ 旬 0167, 拘 1070

2561
常 5

| | | |
|---|---|---|
| 旬 | **TEN-DAY PERIOD** | 旬日 じゅんじつ ten-day period...............0001 |
| | | ○上旬 じょうじゅん first ten days of a month...0041 |
| | | ○中旬 ちゅうじゅん middle ten days of a month |
| | ジュン　シュン | .................0035 |
| | | ○下旬 げじゅん final ten days of a month...0040 |
| | | 旬の花 しゅんのはな flowers in season......0121 |

**0167**
日 72

Here the elephant *wraps up* (勹) a bunch of *days* (日)—**TEN DAYS**, to be exact. ☞ 句 0166, 殉 1090

2572
常 6

| | | |
|---|---|---|
| 勺 | ***SHAKU* (0.018 liters)** | 一勺 いっしゃく 1 *shaku*.....................0002 |
| | シャク | |

**0168**
勺 20

Refers to the old unit of measure ***SHAKU*** **(0.018 liters)**. Though the old units are not often used today, some old-unit kanji still appear in the Joyo Kanji List (though this one was de-listed in 2010). In any case, it will be helpful to learn 勺 as a building block. Here see the *elephant* (勹) hold out a small ladle containing exactly 1 *SHAKU*.

2540
外 3

| 的 | ¹ TARGET<br>² ADJECTIVAL SUFFIX<br><br>テキ<br>まと | ① 目的 もくてき object, purpose.............0021<br>① 的に当たる まとにあたる hit the target......0141<br>② 公的 こうてき public, official.............0089<br>² 全体的に ぜんたいてきに in general, on the<br>　　whole.............0078, 0062<br>² 文学的 ぶんがくてき literary.............0101, 0099 |
|---|---|---|

| **0169**<br>白 106<br><br>1040<br>常 \| 8 | Let *white* (白) suggest the *elephant* (勹)'s tusk (S8), the poacher's **TARGET**. This kanji also serves as a **SUFFIX FOR FORMING ADJECTIVES**, which we can associate with the attributive relationship between *white* and *elephant's tusk*. |
|---|---|

| 約 | ¹ PROMISE<br>² SHORTEN, summarize<br>³ APPROXIMATELY<br><br>ヤク | ① 予約 よやく reservation, preengagement...0163<br>¹ 公約 こうやく public pledge.............0089<br>¹ 条約 じょうやく treaty.............0119<br>² 約言 やくげん contraction, abbreviation,<br>　　simplest terms.............0051<br>③ 約三年 やくさんねん about three years<br>　　.............0004, 0117 |
|---|---|---|

| **0170**<br>糸 120<br><br>1177<br>常 \| 9 | We saw 糸 *thread* at the bottom at 素 0132; now we find it at the left, where it usually is. Picture the *elephant* (勹) pulling on the *thread* (i.e., **SHORTENING** it) to tighten a knot (i.e., a **PROMISE**). Associate **APPROXIMATELY** with the idea of **SHORTENING** the figures required for measurement. |
|---|---|

| 勿 | DO NOT, not, never<br><br>モチ　モッ-<br>なか(れ) | 勿体無い もったいない wasteful; be more than<br>　　one deserves.............0062, 0048<br>...勿れ ...なかれ Do not... |
|---|---|---|

| **0171**<br>勹 20<br><br>2547<br>名 \| 4 | Rarely used as an independent kanji in Japanese—just remember the meaning **DO NOT** from the phrase 勿論 (もちろん, of course or, literally, "unarguably," from 勿 **DO NOT** and 論 0942 ARGUE). More importantly, we must add 勿 to our alphabet of graphemes. As it resembles 勹 with hair, see it as a *woolly mammoth*, or just a furry beast in general. |
|---|---|

| 物 | THING<br><br>ブツ　モツ<br>もの　もの- | 物的な ぶってきな material, physical.......0169<br>○ 書物 しょもつ book, volume.............0079<br>○ 好物 こうぶつ favorite dish.............0095<br>○ 物事 ものごと things, matter; everything...0080<br>本物 ほんもの real thing [stuff], genuine article<br>　　.............0031 |
|---|---|---|

| **0172**<br>牛 93<br><br>0777<br>常 \| 8 | This is the first kanji we have seen with 牜, which is the *hen* form of 牛 0116 CATTLE. Unlike 事 0080, which refers to abstract things, 物 generally refers to <u>material</u> **THINGS**, aptly illustrated by a pair of substantial creatures, a *cow* and a *woolly mammoth* (勿). ☞ 事 0080 |
|---|---|

**¹ DIRECTION, side; locality; person**
**² WAY, method**
**³ SQUARE**

ホウ
かた -かた -がた

¹ …の方に …のほうに in the direction of …, toward …
¹ あの方 あのかた that gentleman/lady, he, she
① 方言 ほうげん dialect, regional speech......0051
② 方法 ほうほう method, way; system; means; process................................................0139
³ 正方形 せいほうけい square............0043, 0147

| 0173 | See a **person** (M1) with his arms outstretched, running toward a particular **DIRECTION** or |
|---|---|
| 方 70 | side. Let **DIRECTION** suggest **locality** and **WAY**. M3 **SQUARE** can be remembered by association with **side**. As a grapheme, 方 will usually mean *person*, and may sometimes mean *direction* or *side*. Written in four strokes. ☞ 万 0018 |
| 1709 | |
| 常 4 | |

---

**DEFEND AGAINST**

ボウ
ふせ(ぐ)

防止する ぼうしする prevent, hold in check 0042
○予防 よぼう prevention, protection, precaution ................................................0163
防音 ぼうおん soundproof................0150
国防 こくぼう national defense............0075
○防ぐ ふせぐ prevent, ward off, protect (against)

| 0174 | Review 部 0068. Now ß appears at the left, so 方 is outside the barrier, on the other side |
|---|---|
| 阜 170 | of the *hills* surrounding the town. See a brave *person* (方) running outside the barrier to **DEFEND** the town behind him **AGAINST** attackers. |
| 0242 | |
| 常 7 | |

---

**FACE; facet; surface; mask**

メン
おも おもて つら

○正面 しょうめん façade, front ................0043
方面 ほうめん direction, district; field, sphere ................................................0173
川面 かわづら (=かわも) surface of a river....0022
法的な面 ほうてきなめん the legal aspect ................................................0139, 0169
○面白い おもしろい interesting, amusing ....0076

| 0175 | See the box at the bottom as a **FACE**. The three small white boxes down the center depict the |
|---|---|
| 面 176 | forehead, nose, and chin (S7 shows the eyes and S8 the mouth). The empty spaces on either side are the cheeks. ☞ 画 0176 |
| 1796 | |
| 常 9 | |

---

**¹ PICTURE; draw; kanji stroke**
**² DRAW UP A PLAN**

ガ カク

① 画面 がめん picture; television field; screen 0175
¹ 山水画 さんすいが landscape painting ................................................0037, 0027
¹ 画一的な かくいつてきな uniform, standardized ................................................0002, 0169
¹ 字画 じかく kanji strokes; stroke count......0098
○画する かくする mark off, demarcate; plan, map out

| 0176 | Distinguish from 面 by seeing a **PICTURE** being lowered from above into a frame (the space |
|---|---|
| 田 102 | separating the central shape from the outer enclosure, not present in 面, can be seen as the picture "frame"). With **PICTURE** we associate **draw**, which in turn leads us to **kanji stroke**, and **DRAW UP A PLAN**. See compounds for M2 at 企 0502 and 計 0555. ☞ 面 0175 |
| 畫 | |
| 2586 | |
| 常 8 | |

| | BOTH | | 両面 りょうめん both sides | 0175 |
| | | ○ | 両方 りょうほう both | 0173 |
| | | | 両手 りょうて both hands | 0046 |
| | リョウ | | 両用 りょうよう dual use | 0047 |
| | | | 車両 しゃりょう vehicle, car | 0125 |

| **0177** | This kanji's axial symmetry suggests its meaning. See how **BOTH** sides are joined to a central axis, by which they hang from a single horizontal stroke at the top. Other than the minute serif at the end of S3, **BOTH** sides hang in perfect equilibrium. Ignore *mountain* (S4–6) and just focus on the balance between **BOTH** sides. ☞ 岡 0178 |
| 一 1* | |
| 兩 | |
| 2949 | |
| 常 6 | |

| | HILL | ○ | 岡山 おかやま Okayama [city and prefecture] | 0037 |
| | | | 岡本 おかもと Okamoto [surname] | 0031 |
| | おか | | 岡田 おかだ Okada [surname] | 0020 |
| | | | 上岡 かみおか Kamioka [surname] | 0041 |

| **0178** | Here the two sides don't hang from a top horizontal stroke as in 両, so there is less visual emphasis on the balance between both sides. Instead we have two small strokes (S3–4) suggesting two minuscule climbers standing on top of the *mountain*. The mountain itself is rather undersized—it's more of a **HILL**. ☞ 両 0177 |
| 山 46 | |
| 堽 | |
| 2584 | |
| 常 8 | |

| | FULL, whole | | 満月 まんげつ full moon | 0023 |
| | | | 満潮 まんちょう high tide | 0146 |
| | | ○ | 満足 まんぞく satisfaction, contentment | 0044 |
| | マン | | 円満な えんまんな perfect, harmonious, well-rounded | 0013 |
| | み(ちる) み(つ) み(たす) | ○ | 水を満たす みずをみたす fill (a glass) with water | 0027 |

| **0179** | 氵 implies that now what hangs balanced on *both* sides (両) is a pair of *water* pails we've just **FILLED** at the river. The pails are heavy when they're **FULL**, so we've added *grass* padding (S4–6) around the pole (S7) we use to carry the pails. Note that 氵, covering the full extent of the kanji, overrides 艹 semantically. |
| 水 85 | |
| 滿 | |
| 0553 | |
| 常 12 | |

| | FACE | ○ | 顔面 がんめん face | 0175 |
| | | | 洗顔 せんがん washing one's face | 0135 |
| | | | 顔付き かおつき countenance; expression, look | 0064 |
| | ガン | ○ | 素顔 すがお face without makeup; true face | 0132 |
| | かお | | 丸顔 まるがお round face | 0012 |

| **0180** | 彦 resembles the *very short person* from 部 0068, except that now his face has grown whiskers (彡). Combined with 頁 *head*, this means **FACE**. ☞ 須 1928 |
| 頁 181 | |
| 顏 | |
| 1608 | |
| 常 18 | |

| | ¹GIVE BIRTH<br>²PRODUCE | ①産む うむ give birth (to), bear |
|---|---|---|
| | | ①出産する しゅっさんする give birth (to), bear **0038** |
| | | ②生産 せいさん production, manufacture....**0036** |
| | サン | ²国産 こくさん domestic production .........**0075** |
| | う(む) う(まれる) うぶ- | ²物産 ぶっさん product, produce.............**0172** |

| 0181 | Following the pattern of the previous entry, here we observe a *very short woman* standing on |
|---|---|
| 生 100 | the delivery table, **GIVING BIRTH** to a new *life* (生). |

産

2812
常 11

| | **SAME, similar** | 同一 どういつ sameness, identity............**0002** |
|---|---|---|
| | | 同好 どうこう similar tastes ....................**0095** |
| | | ○同意 どうい consent, approval...............**0151** |
| | ドウ | 同上 どうじょう as above, ditto...............**0041** |
| | おな(じ) | ○同じ おなじ same, similar |

| 0182 | The line (S3) and the box (S4–6) are on the **SAME** side of the enclosure. ☞ 向 0183, 司 0820 |
|---|---|
| 口 30 | |

仝

2578
常 6

| | **TURN TOWARD, direction; other side** | 意向 いこう intention, inclination...........**0151** |
|---|---|---|
| | | ○方向 ほうこう direction, bearing; course ....**0173** |
| | | 向く むく [vi] face; turn toward |
| | コウ | ○向かう むかう [vi] face; head toward |
| | む(く) む(き) -む(き) む(ける) -む(け) | 向こう むこう the other side; the other party |
| | む(かう) む(こう) む(こう)- | |

| 0183 | Now the "line" has **TURNED TOWARD** the **other side**. Practice writing out 同 and 向 in turn, |
|---|---|
| 口 30 | remembering what is signified by the location of the short "line." ☞ 同 0182, 尚 0184 |

2627
常 6

| | ¹STILL (MORE)<br>²VALUE HIGHLY | ¹尚早 しょうそう premature................**0143** |
|---|---|---|
| | | ①尚の事 なおのこと all the more, still more..**0080** |
| | | ¹ この方が尚面白い このほうがなおおもしろい |
| | ショウ | This is more interesting still .....**0173, 0175, 0076** |
| | なお* | 尚又 なおまた moreover, also ................**0058** |

| 0184 | Compared to 向, 尚 has **STILL MORE** strokes on the other side of the enclosure. Taking 向 |
|---|---|
| 小 42 | as a baseline, see the additional strokes suggesting **STILL (MORE)**. Also see them adding extra |
| | **VALUE** to 尚, thus suggesting M2. Borrowing the next entry 高 HIGH, we can make a com- |
| | pound for M2: 高尚 (こうしょう, noble, refined). Also see 古 0254. ☞ 向 0183, 宵 1293, |
| | 肖 1288 |

1919
常 8

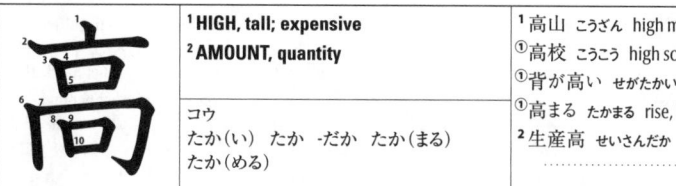

| 高 | ¹ **HIGH, tall**; expensive<br>² **AMOUNT, quantity**<br><br>コウ<br>たか(い)　たか　-だか　たか(まる)<br>たか(める) | ¹ 高山 こうざん high mountain, lofty peak....0037<br>①高校 こうこう high school...................0103<br>①背が高い せがたかい (he/she) is tall........0124<br>①高まる たかまる rise, be raised; increase<br>² 生産高 せいさんだか (amount of) output, yield<br>..................................................0036, 0181 |

**0185**
高 189
髙
1803
常 10

Derives from a picture of a **tall** building: we can see the entrance at the bottom, a window on the second story, and a roof **HIGH** up on top. To connect with M2, see a "high" **AMOUNT** of stuff piled up. As a grapheme 高 will mean *high* or *tall*, and will sometimes be abbreviated to the roof and second story window, as in 京 0245.

| 圧 | **PRESSURE; overwhelm**<br><br>アツ | ○圧力 あつりょく pressure.....................0084<br>水圧 すいあつ water pressure...............0027<br>汽圧 きあつ steam pressure.................0127<br>大気圧 たいきあつ atmospheric pressure<br>..................................................0033, 0126<br>圧する あっする pressure, oppress; overwhelm |

**0186**
土 32
壓
2563
常 5

See the *cliff* exert overwhelming **PRESSURE** on the *soil* beneath it. Do not confuse 圧 with the name-use kanji 庄 FEUDAL VILLAGE (no other kanji differ only by 广 *slanting roof/shelter* vs. 厂 *cliff*). Also, note that the *on* reading アツ is unique in this course.

| 地 | ¹ **GROUND, land**<br>² **PLACE**<br><br>チ ジ | ①土地 とち land ..............................0030<br>¹ 地下の ちかの underground, subterranean<br>..................................................0040<br>² 地方 ちほう district, region, area............0173<br>②地元 じもと local area, local end............0136<br>² 見地 けんち standpoint, viewpoint..........0083 |

**0187**
土 32

0181
常 6

Now we see 土 at the left for the first time (notice how its form changes). See 也 as a scorpion: at the top right hangs its menacing stinger, filled with venom and poised to strike. The *scorpion* is on guard, for its *land* has been invaded. Imagine the scorpion backed up into a corner, holding its **GROUND**.

| 池 | **POND, reservoir**<br><br>チ<br>いけ | ○用水池 ようすいち reservoir............0047, 0027<br>電池 でんち electric cell, battery............0155<br>池田 いけだ Ikeda [surname] ................0020<br>池上 いけがみ Ikegami [surname]..........0041<br>小池 こいけ Koike [surname] ................0034 |

**0188**
水 85

0191
常 6

If the right side of S4 is the scorpion's stinger, the left side is its mouth. See the *scorpion* (也) stick its mouth into a **POND** of drinking *water* (氵). 池 also refers to **reservoirs** or cisterns.

| OTHER | 他方 たほう other side [hand]; on the other hand............0173 |
|---|---|
| | 他面 ためん other side; on the other hand 0175 |
| タ | 他人 たにん another person, other people; stranger.............0015 |
| ほか | 他国 たこく foreign countries.............0075 |
| | ○その他 そのた (=そのほか) the others, the rest |

| 0189 | One can only know oneself by contrasting oneself with "the OTHER." A *man* (イ) placed side-by-side with a *scorpion* (也) makes a graphic image of OTHER-ness. The stroke order for 也 may seem unnatural to you at first, another reminder that it is important to practice writing out each kanji on a pad of paper as you learn it. |
|---|---|
| 人 9 | |

0023
常 5

---

| GATHER, collect | 集金 しゅうきん collecting money............0029 |
|---|---|
| | ○集中する しゅうちゅうする concentrate, focus; converge............0035 |
| シュウ | 中上全集 なかがみぜんしゅう the complete works of Nakagami............0035, 0041, 0078 |
| あつ(まる) あつ(める) つど(う) | ○集まる あつまる [vi] gather, meet; be collected |
| | 集う つどう [vi] gather, meet |

| 0190 | Recall 隹 *small bird* from 曜 0025. Here imagine a whole flock of *small birds* GATHERING in a *tree* (木). ☞ 隻 1658 |
|---|---|
| 隹 172 | |

2413
常 12

---

| ADVANCE | 進行する しんこうする advance, make progress, go forward............0055 |
|---|---|
| | 進学 しんがく advancing to the next level of schooling............0099 |
| シン | ○進化 しんか evolution, progress............0120 |
| すす(む) すす(める) | ○進む すすむ advance, make progress, go forward |
| | 進める すすめる [vt] advance, move forward |

| 0191 | *Small bird* (隹) in *motion* (辶): an intuitive image for ADVANCE. |
|---|---|
| 辵 162 | |

2689
常 11

---

| ¹ MOVE INWARD, into | ①込む こむ put into; go into; be crowded |
|---|---|
| ² EMPHATIC VERBAL SUFFIX | ¹入り込む はいりこむ go into, penetrate......0039 |
| | ¹見込み みこみ outlook, prospects, promise............0083 |
| -こ(む) こ(む) こ(み) -こ(み) こ(める) | ¹込める こめる put into, include |
| | ¹心を込めて こころをこめて with all one's heart............0056 |

| 0192 | *Motion* 辶 + *enter* (入): MOVE INWARD. Examples of M2 can be found at 刈 0524, 冷 0675, 眠 1009, and 煮 1188. |
|---|---|
| 辵 162 | |

2608
常 5

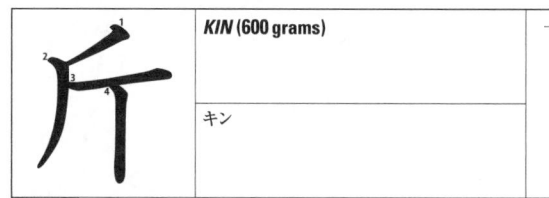

| | **KIN (600 grams)** | 一斤 いっきん one *kin*........................0002 |
|---|---|---|
| | キン | |

**0193**
斤 69

See as picture of a hacksaw standing on end: S1 is the handle and S4 is the blade. We'll mainly use it as a grapheme meaning *hacksaw* or *cut*. The independent kanji, seldom used, represents the former unit of measure *KIN* (**about 600 grams**), easy enough to remember if we consider that a *hacksaw* weighs about one *KIN*. ☞ 丘 0906, 斥 1707

2551
常 4

| | **¹ NEAR**<br>**² RECENT** | ¹ 付近 ふきん neighborhood, environs, vicinity ...........0064 |
|---|---|---|
| | キン<br>ちか(い) | ①近道 ちかみち shortcut........................0158<br>¹ 身近な みぢかな close to one, familiar ......0060<br>² 近年 きんねん recent years, late years .......0117<br>②近代 きんだい modern [recent] times .......0071 |

**0194**
辵 162

*Cut* (斤) + *motion* (辶): **NEAR**. To have something **NEAR**by *cuts* the *motion* required to get there. M2 **RECENT** means "**NEAR** in time." ☞ 辺 0195

2634
常 7

| | **¹ VICINITY, side**<br>**² BORDERLAND, outer regions** | ¹ 近辺 きんぺん vicinity, neighborhood ......0194 |
|---|---|---|
| | ヘン<br>あた(り) -べ | ①どの辺? どのへん? Where/Whereabouts?<br>①一昨年辺り いっさくねんあたり the year before last or thereabouts.............0002, 0153, 0117<br>①川辺 かわべ riverside........................0022<br>² 辺地 へんち remote place........................0187 |

**0195**
辵 162

*Slice* (刀) + *motion* (辶): **VICINITY**. To be in the **VICINITY** of something *slices* the *motion* required to get there. While 近 NEAR refers to a shortness of distance, 辺 **VICINITY** refers to the space next to something, or the "side" of something. Thus it can also refer to **BORDER-LANDS** and **outer regions**, places which are by no means near. ☞ 近 0194

邊
2607
常 5

| | **MOST, -est** | 最高の さいこうの maximum, supreme, highest ........................0185 |
|---|---|---|
| | サイ<br>もっと(も) | 最大の さいだいの biggest, largest, greatest ..0033<br>○最後の さいごの last, final ........................0114<br>最近 さいきん recently........................0194<br>○最も大事な事 もっともだいじなこと the most important thing........................0033, 0080 |

**0196**
日 73

*Take* (取) + *sun* (日). In English we refer to a superlative feat as "shooting the moon" and a superlative gift as "giving someone the moon," but in the kanji, *taking* the *sun* is the superlative act, the **MOST** one can do. As in 書 0079 and some other kanji, 日 technically derives from 曰 *say*, but we shall ignore this etymological distinction in every case.

2181
常 12

| | PLATE | ○皿洗い さらあらい dishwashing; dishwasher .................... 0135 |
|---|---|---|
| 皿 | | スープ皿 スープざら soup plate |
| | さら | 受け皿 うけざら saucer ...................... 0065 |

| 0197 | Here we observe a **PLATE** with food on it, like a slice of layer cake. We'll mostly see it as a grapheme used in other characters, such as the two that follow. |
|---|---|
| 皿 108 | |
| 2916 | |
| 常 5 | |

| | BLOOD | ○出血 しゅっけつ bleeding; hemorrhage ..... 0038 |
|---|---|---|
| 血 | | 無血の むけつの bloodless, without bloodshed .................................................. 0048 |
| | ケツ | 高血圧 こうけつあつ high blood pressure .................................................. 0185, 0186 |
| | ち | ○血だらけ ちだらけ covered in blood |
| | | 血止め ちどめ styptic...................... 0042 |

| 0198 | A single drop of **BLOOD** on a *plate* (皿). |
|---|---|
| 血 143 | |
| 2955 | |
| 常 6 | |

| | WARM | 温血 おんけつ warm-blooded .............. 0198 |
|---|---|---|
| 温 | | 水温 すいおん water temperature .......... 0027 |
| | | ○気温 きおん atmospheric temperature ..... 0126 |
| | オン | 体温 たいおん body temperature.......... 0062 |
| | あたた(か) あたた(かい) あたた(まる) | 日光で温まる にっこうであたたまる be warmed in |
| | あたた(める) | the sun.................................. 0001, 0137 |

| 0199 | *Water* (氵) on a *plate* (皿) under the *sun* (日). ☞ 盟 1305, 湯 0446, 湿 0200 |
|---|---|
| 水 85 | |
| 温 | |
| 0554 | |
| 常 12 | |

| | MOIST | ○湿気 しっけ (=しっき) humidity, moisture .... 0126 |
|---|---|---|
| 湿 | | 湿地 しっち damp ground, swamp .......... 0187 |
| | | ○湿す しめす dampen, moisten |
| | シツ | タオルを湿す タオルをしめす dampen a towel |
| | しめ(る) しめ(す) | 湿っぽい しめっぽい damp, humid; gloomy, depressing |

| 0200 | 业 looks a little like the water on the plate in 温 0199 evaporating under the sun's warmth. See the evaporating **MOISTURE** fill the air, making everything muggy and damp. ☞ 温 0199 |
|---|---|
| 水 85 | |
| 濕 | |
| 0555 | |
| 常 12 | |

| 爪 | **CLAW, nail, plectrum** | 爪先 つまさき tip of a toe, tiptoe ............ 0134 |
| | | ○爪切り つめきり nail clipper ................ 0086 |
| | つめ つま- | 爪立つ つまだつ stand on tiptoe ......... 0067 |

**0201**
爪 87

Here we find three **CLAWS** extending from a paw. We have already encountered the grapheme version ⺤ at 受 0065 and 乳 0160. ☞ 瓜 0202

2605
常 | 4

| 瓜 | **MELON, gourd** | ○瓜二つ うりふたつ as alike as two melons... 0003 |
| | | 水瓜 すいか watermelon .................... 0027 |
| | カ / うり | |

**0202**
瓜 97

Picture S4–5 as a slice of **MELON** speared by the middle claw. The "名" in the reference data section indicates that this kanji appears in the Japanese government's Jinmeiyo (人名用, name-use) Kanji List. Entries marked "常" appear in the Joyo (常用) Kanji List. ☞ 爪 0201

2626
名 | 5

| 巾 | **CLOTH** | ○頭巾 ずきん hood, kerchief |
| | キン | |

**0203**
巾 50

See as a bolt of **CLOTH** rolled around a central tube. ☞ 市 0205

2879
常 | 3

| 布 | ¹ **CLOTH** | ¹ 布巾 ふきん dishcloth, napkin ............... 0203 |
| | ² **SPREAD** | ①画布 がふ canvas .......................... 0176 |
| | | ①布地 ぬのじ cloth ......................... 0187 |
| | フ / ぬの | ² 発布する はっぷする promulgate .......... 0148 |
| | | ² 分布 ぶんぷ distribution.................. 0088 |

**0204**
巾 50

See 𠂇 as a *hand* (S1 are the fingers pointing downward and S2 is the thumb reaching out to the right). Like 巾, 布 means **CLOTH**. It also means **SPREAD**, so visualize the *hand* **SPREAD-ING** out the *cloth*. Now a word about grapheme meanings. As we add graphemes, we shall start to accumulate more of them that mean the same thing (e.g., for *hand* we have already learned the forms 手, 扌, 又, ⺤, and ⇒, and there are others yet to come). While this may seem confusing at first, do not be overly concerned. Once you get used to seeing these forms, you will have no trouble recognizing them.

2566
常 | 5

| | ¹CITY ²MARKET | ①市立 しりつ (=いちりつ) municipal............0067 |
|---|---|---|
| | | ¹市長 しちょう mayor.........................0091 |
| | | ¹市電 してん municipal railway.........0155 |
| | シ いち | ②朝市 あさいち morning market.........0145 |
| | | ² のみの市 のみのいち flea market |

| 0205 | In typical printed fonts, this character appears to have a single central stroke, but is actually composed of 亠 *lid* and 巾 *cloth*. Picture a bolt of *cloth* stored under a *lid* in an old-fashioned **MARKET**. As for M1, a **CITY** is defined by the presence of a **MARKET**. ☞ 巾 0203 |
|---|---|
| 巾 50 | |
| 1724 | |
| 常 5 | |

| | HANG, suspend | ○吊る つる hang, suspend |
|---|---|---|
| | | 吊り上げる つりあげる lift, raise; jack up (prices) .........................................0041 |
| | | ズボン吊り ズボンつり suspenders |
| | チョウ つ(る) つ(り) つ(るす) | 吊り目 つりめ slanted [upturned] eyes ......0021 |
| | | 首吊り くびつり hanging (by the neck) ......0157 |

| 0206 | Visualize *cloth* (巾) **HANGING** from a "loop" (口), like one of those hotel-room hangers with the loop-and-pin hook. The "外" in the reference data section indicates that this is a 表外 *hyogai* (off-list) kanji, meaning that it is not included in either the Joyo list or the Jinmeiyo list. |
|---|---|
| 口 30 | |
| 外 6 | |

| | SPRING | 泉水 せんすい fountain.....................0027 |
|---|---|---|
| | | ○温泉 おんせん hot spring...............0199 |
| | | 温泉地 おんせんち hot spring (area)...0199, 0187 |
| | セン いずみ | アルカリ泉 アルカリせん alkaline spring |

| 0207 | Visualize the meaning of this kanji even as you retain the semantic values of *white* (白) and *water* (水). Rather than relying on an abstraction like "*white water* signals a **SPRING**," it is better to perceive this meaning directly by seeing the *white* froth welling up from the *water* at the **SPRING**'s source. Whenever possible, we should let a kanji represent its meaning pictorially rather than detaching the meaning from the image through the use of a conceptual mnemonic phrase. Here, while 白 does mean *white*, it also represents a visible object, the *white* foam of bubbly water. |
|---|---|
| 水 85 | |
| 洤 | |
| 2224 | |
| 常 9 | |

| | ¹PLAIN, field ²ORIGINAL, primitive | ①高原 こうげん plateau.....................0185 |
|---|---|---|
| | | ¹原田 はらだ Harada [surname].........0020 |
| | | ²原作 げんさく original (work).........0152 |
| | ゲン はら | ²原案 げんあん original bill/plan.........0097 |
| | | ②原子 げんし atom.........................0094 |

| 0208 | Again, let *white* (白) play a dual semantic/pictographic role, this time as a *white* parachute. 小 can also play a dual role, as a *small* skydiver, who drops from the edge of a *cliff* 厂 down to the wide-open **PLAIN** below. Associate with M2 **ORIGINAL/primitive** by thinking of **PLAINS** and **fields** as the **ORIGIN** of our sustenance. |
|---|---|
| 厂 27 | |
| 2593 | |
| 常 10 | |

**SOURCE, origin**

ゲン
みなもと

源泉 げんせん fountainhead, source........0207
水源 すいげん headwaters.................0027
○電源 でんげん power source, electrical outlet
.................................................0155
○川の源 かわのみなもと headwaters..........0022
その源は明らかではない そのみなもとはあきらか
ではない It is of obscure origin............0024

**0209**
水 85

Overlaps with M2 of 原 above. Here the *water* (氵) image emphasizes the idea of **origin** or **SOURCE**, by suggesting the **SOURCE** or fountainhead of a *water*way in a high *plain*.

0600
常 | 13

---

**LINE**

セン

○電線 でんせん electric wire.................0155
無線 むせん wireless, radio.................0048
光線 こうせん ray (of light), beam.........0137
前線 ぜんせん front lines; (weather) front...0113
東海道線 とうかいどうせん Tokaido (railway)
Line.............................0032, 0106, 0158

**0210**
糸 120

Let 糸 *thread* suggest the straight **LINE** along which the water rises up at this *spring* (泉). See it *spring* straight up in a **LINE**, right from the bottom straight up to the top. The presence of the *water* is important to this character, as we shall see in the next entry. ☞ 綿 0211

1273
常 | 15

---

**COTTON**

メン
わた

綿布 めんぷ cotton cloth.................0204
原綿 げんめん raw cotton.................0208
○木綿 もめん cotton, cotton cloth..........0028
○綿を入れる わたをいれる wad with cotton...0039

**0211**
糸 120

帛系

The difference between *water* (水) and *cloth* (巾) changes everything here, so make that your visual focus. 巾 shows us that we're looking not at a spring but at a **COTTON** plant. Again 白 *white* can play a dual semantic/pictorial role, as a *white* **COTTON** boll. See the *white* boll being spun into **COTTON** *thread* and *cloth*. ☞ 線 0210, 錦 0213

1254
常 | 14

---

**SILK**

ケン
きぬ

人絹 じんけん artificial silk; rayon..........0015
絹布 けんぷ silk, silk cloth.................0204
○絹糸 けんし (=きぬいと) silk thread..........0112
正絹 しょうけん (pure) silk.................0043
絹地 きぬじ silk fabrics.................0187

**0212**
糸 120

Here let *flesh* (月) suggest a silkworm, spinning *thread* (糸) out of its *mouth* (口). See the **SILK** *thread* issuing out of the worm's *mouth* and dangling down the left side.

1243
常 | 13

**BROCADE**

キン
にしき

絹の錦 きぬのにしき silk brocade ............0212
錦の金糸 にしきのきんし gold thread of a
brocade ......................................0029, 0112

| 0213 | Gold (金) woven through white (白) cloth (巾) makes **BROCADE**. ☞ 綿 0211 |
| 金 167 | |
| 1549 | |
| 常 16 | |

**¹WISH**
**²ASK A FAVOR**

ガン
ねが(う)

¹ 大願 たいがん ambition.....................0033
¹ 心願 しんがん heartfelt wish ...............0056
② 出願 しゅつがん application ................0038
○ 願う ねがう wish, hope for; pray; request
願い事 ねがいごと one's wish/request......0080

| 0214 | "Original (原) head (頁)": in other words, the thing one wanted to begin with, one's **WISH**. |
| 頁 181 | ☞ 碩 1918 |
| 1637 | |
| 常 19 | |

**INSIDE**

ナイ ダイ
うち

内線 ないせん internal (phone) line, extension
.....................................................0210
内耳 ないじ inner ear........................0057
○ 内部 ないぶ interior, inner parts............0068
以内 いない within, less than................0066
○ 早い内 はやいうち while it is early, soon ....0143

| 0215 | See S3-4 penetrate **INSIDE** the enclosure. ☞ 丙 1523 |
| 冂 13* | |
| 內 | |
| 2914 | |
| 常 4 | |

**FLESH**

ニク

肉体 にくたい body, flesh..................0062
肉的 にくてき physical, of the body..........0169
○ 牛肉 ぎゅうにく beef.........................0116
肉付けする にくづけする flesh out ..........0064
肉入れ にくいれ ink pad .....................0039

| 0216 | A picture of **FLESH**: see a rectangular steak with a pair of wishbone-shaped bones. Abbreviated in grapheme form to 月 meat/flesh, which is identical to moon/month (the meaning we attach to 月 will depend on the character). Note that the on reading ニク is unique in this course. |
| 肉 130 | |
| 2756 | |
| 常 6 | |

**WILD BOAR**

チョ
いのしし い

猪口 ちょこ sake cup, small cup.............0019
猪武者 いのししむしゃ foolhardy warrior; hotspur
.................................................................0111, 0107
猪首 いくび bull neck......................0157

**0217**
犬 94

猪

0489
名 11

犭 (a variant of 犬 0293) is a semantic grapheme that refers to *dogs* or other smallish four-legged creatures. Picture a *person* (者 0107) out walking his four-legged ... **WILD BOAR**.
☞ 豚 0218

---

**PIG**

トン
ぶた

○豚肉 ぶたにく pork.............................0216
子豚 こぶた piglet.............................0094
豚足 とんそく pig's feet....................0044
○豚カツ とんカツ pork cutlet

**0218**
豕 152

0889
常 11

Turn 犭 *dog/four-legged creature* into 豕 *pig* by adding a stroke at the top for the railing of a **PIG** pen, and a few extra strokes at the bottom for **PIG**lets, scrambling toward their mother's teats from every direction. 豕 is no longer used by itself; the kanji used for **PIG** combines it with the general classifier 月 *meat*. ☞ 猪 0217

---

¹**HOUSE, home**
²**FAMILY, House**

カ ケ
いえ や うち゜

①家事 かじ household affairs, housework ...0080
①自分の家 じぶんのいえ one's own house
.................................................................0081, 0088
² 家宝 かほう family treasure, heirloom......0074
②家の人 うちのひと my husband; one's family...0015
作家 さっか writer, novelist, author.........0152

**0219**
宀 40

1963
常 10

The *roof* (宀) over the *pig* (豕) shows us that the *pig* has come inside the **HOUSE**! See 我 just ahead for an example of the reading や.

---

**EGO, I**

ゴ
われ わが- あ-

吾人 ごじん [literary] we......................0015
吾子 あこ my child............................0094

**0220**
口 30

2132
名 7

吾 is used to refer to oneself. See it as a stylized way of writing the word "**EGO**": like the letters "N" and "Y" that blend together on the New York Yankees' baseball cap, see in 吾 an uppercase "E" blended together with a lowercase "g" and "o." Note that kanji incorporating 五 are pronounced ゴ.

**SELF**

ガ
われ わ わ(が)- わが-

○自我 じが self, ego ...........................0081
　無我 むが self-effacement, selflessness......0048
○我々 われわれ we
　我が国 わがくに our country...................0075
○我が家 わがや our home [household] .....0219

| 0221 | See as a *hand* (扌) holding a *spear* (戈), and picture a man carrying his own spear, knowing he must fend for himSELF. |
| 戈 62 | |
| 2971 | |
| 常 7 | |

**¹WORD**
**²LANGUAGE**
**³TELL**

ゴ
かた(る) かた(らう)

①用語 ようご terminology; diction, wording; vocabulary.................................0047
¹語源 ごげん word source, etymology........0209
②言語 げんご language.......................0051
③語る かたる tell, speak
³物語 ものがたり story, tale, legend ..........0172

| 0222 | The *ego* (吾) speaking *words* (言): **WORD; LANGUAGE; TELL.** |
| 言 149 | |
| 1402 | |
| 常 14 | |

**TRANSMIT**

デン
つた(わる) つた(える) つた(う)
-づた(い)

○伝言 でんごん verbal message, word .......0051
　代々伝わる だいだいつたわる be transmitted [handed down] from generation to generation ...................................................0071
○電気を伝える でんきをつたえる conduct electricity ................................0155, 0126
　手伝う てつだう help, assist, lend a hand ...0046

| 0223 | Visualize 云 as a towering cumulonimbus *cloud*. In this character, a *man* (亻) **TRANSMITS** data through "the *cloud*." ☞ 仏 0811, 仁 1094 |
| 人 9 | |
| 傳 | |
| 0029 | |
| 常 6 | |

**TURN, roll over; turn into**

テン
ころ(がる) ころ(げる) ころ(がす)
ころ(ぶ)

○回転する かいてんする revolve, rotate, turn 0050
　自転車 じてんしゃ bicycle...............0081, 0125
　転向 てんこう turn, conversion, about-face...0183
○転がる ころがる roll over
○転ぶ ころぶ fall over

| 0224 | Review 車 0125. Here, the *car* (車)'s wheels **TURN/roll over** quickly, producing a *cloud* of smoke. ☞ 軌 0690 |
| 車 159 | |
| 轉 | |
| 1346 | |
| 常 11 | |

| ART, craft; performance | 工芸 こうげい technical art, technology.....0108 |
| | 手芸 しゅげい handicrafts, manual arts......0046 |
| | 文芸 ぶんげい literature, art and literature 0101 |
| ゲイ | ○芸者 げいしゃ geisha.........................0107 |
| | 芸をする豚 げいをするぶた pig that does tricks |
| | .........................................0218 |

| 0225 | Flowery *grass* (艹) embellishing a *cloud*: **ART**. |
| 艹 140 | |
| 藝 | |
| 1892 | |
| 常 7 | |

| ¹ MEET, gather | ①会話 かいわ conversation...................0053 |
| ² SOCIETY | ¹会見 かいけん interview, audience.........0083 |
| | ①会う あう meet, encounter |
| カイ エ | ²学会 がっかい academic society............0099 |
| あ(う) あ(わせる) | ²会長 かいちょう president, chairman.......0091 |

| 0226 | Visualize *clouds* (云) gathering under a *roof* (亼): **MEET**. As for M2, a **SOCIETY** is a **MEETING** of people on a large scale. Note the traditional form. |
| 人 9* | |
| 會 | |
| 1741 | |
| 常 6 | |

| ¹ COMBINE, join | ¹集合する しゅうごうする gather, assemble; call |
| ² FIT | together..............................0190 |
| | ②合意 ごうい mutual agreement [consent]...0151 |
| ゴウ ガッ- カッ- | ②合う あう fit, come together |
| あ(う) -あ(う) あ(い) あい- -あ(い) | ²話し合う はなしあう speak together, talk over |
| -あい あ(わす) あ(わせる) -あ(わせる) | .........................................0053 |
| | 合わせる あわせる combine, join; match; collate |

| 0227 | Here treat 亼 as a kind of lid. To avoid having to work S3 (一) by itself into the mnemonic of every kanji that has S1-3 in it, just see S1-3 as an image of a lid *fitting* snugly on top of something. Thus in 合 we see *fit* and *opening* (口): picture **joining** or **COMBINING** the snugly fitting lid to the *opening*. The similar widths of S3 and S5 show a good **FIT**. |
| 口 30 | |
| 1740 | |
| 常 6 | |

| ¹ PRESENT, now | ①今まで いままで till now, so far, up to the present |
| ² THIS | ①今日 こんにち today, these days............0001 |
| | ② きょう today |
| コン キン | ²今月 こんげつ this month....................0023 |
| いま | ²今回 こんかい this time; lately..............0050 |

| 0228 | S4 depicts a sundial and its shadow, indicating the time. S1-3 give us *fit*, so 今 suggests the *fitting* (i.e., applicable) *time*: the **PRESENT**. Assimilate M2 **THIS** as an extended idea of **THIS PRESENT** moment. As a grapheme inside other kanji, 今 will mean *now*. ☞ 今 0229 |
| 人 9 | |
| 1712 | |
| 常 4 | |

| | COMMAND | |
|---|---|---|
| | | 法令 ほうれい laws and ordinances, statute 0139 |
| | | ○発令 はつれい pronouncement.............0148 |
| | | 伝令 てんれい messenger....................0223 |
| | レイ | 国王令 こくおうれい royal decree......0075, 0072 |

**0229**
人 9

See as a picture of a bell, used for giving **COMMANDS**. S1–2 form the bell's cup, which is extended down the right side by angled S4. The focal point is S5, the clapper, which sets 令 apart from 今. Picture someone lying in bed and clanging S5 against the lip of the bell to **COMMAND** the presence of a servant. ☞ 今 0228, 命 0232

**1725**
常 5

---

| | THOUGHTS, mind, wish | |
|---|---|---|
| | | 信念 しんねん belief, faith...................0063 |
| | | 念頭 ねんとう mind..........................0162 |
| | | 念願 ねんがん one's heart's desire.........0214 |
| | ネン | ○念入りな ねんいりな careful, elaborate....0039 |
| | | 無念 むねん regret, vexation, chagrin......0048 |

**0230**
心 61

See the sundial's shadow pointing at what is *presently* (今) on one's *mind* (心): one's **THOUGHTS**. Also means **thoughtfulness** or **attention**, meanings which are easy to see in 念 by recalling the phrase "presence of mind."

**1773**
常 8

---

| | SEAL; mark | |
|---|---|---|
| | | 印肉 いんにく stamp pad, ink pad...........0216 |
| | | 代印する だいいんする sign [seal] by proxy..0071 |
| | | ○ゴム印 ゴムいん rubber stamp |
| | イン | ○無印 むじるし unbranded, generic...........0048 |
| | しるし -じるし | 日印 にちいん Japan and India, Indian-Japanese |
| | | ....................................................0001 |

**0231**
卩 26

See a hand 𦥑 holding a **SEAL** (卩). Because the end of S5 points back upward, picture 卩 as one of those self-inking stamps in which the stamp die retracts upward to re-ink, and only flips back downward when you press down. 印 **SEAL** refers not only to the instrument but also to the mark made. Used phonetically for the イン in "India."

**0733**
常 6

---

| | ¹ ORDER, command | ①命令 めいれい command, order; edict, decree |
|---|---|---|
| | ² LIFE | .................................................0229 |
| | ³ FATE | ¹用命 ようめい command, order............0047 |
| | | ②生命 せいめい life.........................0036 |
| | メイ ミョウ | ² 命取りの いのちとりの fatal, deadly.........0059 |
| | いのち | ³ 本命 ほんめい probable winner, most likely |
| | | candidate.......................................0031 |

**0232**
口 30

Here we might try to visualize an **ORDER** from heaven deciding one's **LIFE**. へ suggests "coming down from heaven." 卩 is a *seal*, used here to issue **ORDERS**, or to "*seal* one's **FATE**" (from a visual standpoint, the direct, top-down line made by S8 helps represent an **ORDER** coming down). 口 *mouth* suggests breath, as in "breath of **LIFE**." M3 **FATE** is an **ORDER** coming down from heaven to decide one's **LIFE**. ☞ 令 0229

**1772**
常 8

| 亡 | **DECEASED**<br><br>ボウ モウ<br>な(い) な(き)- | 亡父 ぼうふ late father ......................0100<br>亡者 もうじゃ the deceased...............0107<br>○亡命 ぼうめい exile............................0232<br>亡命者 ぼうめいしゃ exile, exiled person<br>................................................0232, 0107<br>○亡き人 なきひと the deceased .............0015 |
|---|---|---|

| 0233<br>亠 8<br><br>2874<br>常 3 | Visualize as the outline of a coffin, seen from one end: **DECEASED**. As a grapheme, 亡 will take the meanings *die* or *lose*. |
|---|---|

|  米 | **¹RICE**<br>**²AMERICA**<br><br>ベイ マイ<br>こめ | ¹米作 べいさく rice crop ......................0152<br>①米を作る こめをつくる grow rice ...........0152<br>①白米 はくまい white [polished] rice ..........0076<br>②米国 べいこく USA ............................0075<br>² 日米 にちべい Japan and the USA, Japanese-American ................................................0001 |
|---|---|---|

| 0234<br>米 119<br><br>2958<br>常 6 | Depicts a bundled stack of **RICE** stalks. As the picture suggests, 米 refers to rice before it has been cooked; cooked rice has its own kanji (飯 0377). Based on an older pronunciation, 米 was once used phonetically for the メ in "**AMERICA**"; it is now used as an abbreviation for the entire word. |
|---|---|

|  粒 | **GRAIN**<br><br>リュウ<br>つぶ | ○粒子 りゅうし particle, grain ..................0094<br>素粒子 そりゅうし elementary particle 0132, 0094<br>米粒 こめつぶ grain of rice...................0234<br>○雨粒 あまつぶ raindrop.......................0154<br>一粒の麦 ひとつぶのむぎ a grain of wheat<br>[barley]...........................................0002, 0131 |
|---|---|---|

| 0235<br>米 119<br><br>1213<br>常 11 | Here *rice* appears in the more compact form 米. See a *person standing* (立) next to a bundled stack of *rice* stalks and picking off an individual **GRAIN** of rice. |
|---|---|

|  和 | **¹HARMONIOUS**<br>**²PEACE, calm**<br>**³JAPAN**<br>ワ オ<br>やわ(らぐ) やわ(らげる) なご(む)<br>なご(やか) | ¹和気 わき harmonious atmosphere.........0126<br>①和合 わごう harmony, concord; union......0227<br>²和らぎ やわらぎ abatement, alleviation; peacefulness<br>②和やかな なごやかな peaceful, mild, gentle<br>³ 大和 やまと Yamato (old name for Japan)...0033 |
|---|---|---|

| 0236<br>口 30<br><br>1044<br>常 8 | 禾 is a variant on 米, and can be seen as a bundled stack of rice stalks that has been bound neatly across the top with a string (S1), such that S1-2 of 米 disappear. It will mean *rice* or *grain*. Here, see *rice* being put into a person's *mouth* (口) to **calm** him down and preserve the **PEACE** and **HARMONY**. Used in 大和 (やまと), homeland of the Japanese state, and as an abbreviation for **JAPAN**. ☞ 知 0560 |
|---|---|

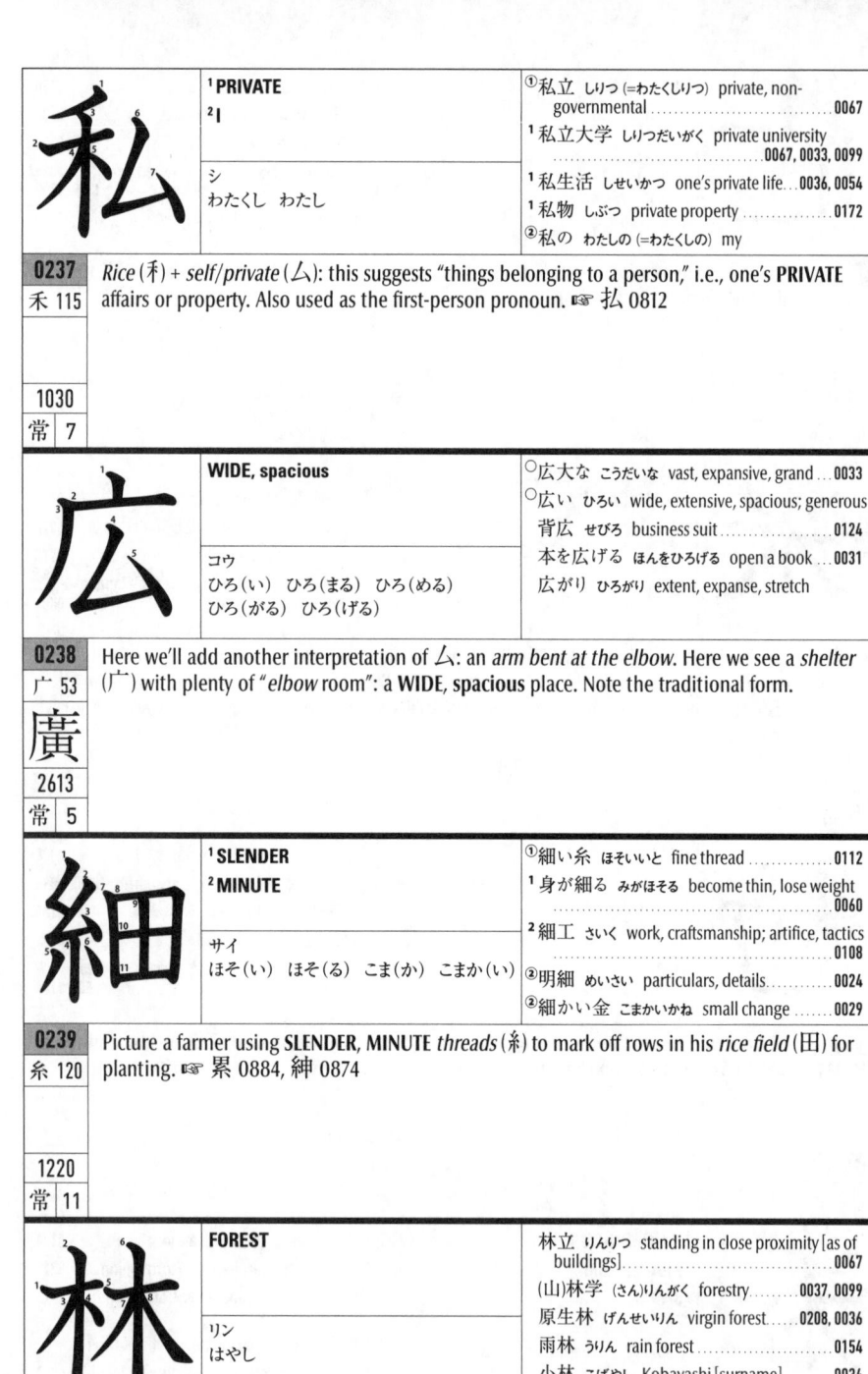

| | ¹ **PRIVATE**<br>²**I** | ①私立 しりつ (=わたくしりつ) private, non-governmental ............................. 0067<br>¹ 私立大学 しりつだいがく private university<br>...................................... 0067, 0033, 0099 |
| | | ¹ 私生活 しせいかつ one's private life...0036, 0054 |
| | シ<br>わたくし わたし | ¹ 私物 しぶつ private property ....................... 0172<br>②私の わたしの (=わたくしの) my |

| 0237<br>禾 115 | Rice (禾) + self/private (厶): this suggests "things belonging to a person," i.e., one's **PRIVATE** affairs or property. Also used as the first-person pronoun. ☞ 払 0812 |
| 1030<br>常 7 | |

| | **WIDE, spacious** | ○広大な こうだいな vast, expansive, grand ... 0033<br>○広い ひろい wide, extensive, spacious; generous |
| | | 背広 せびろ business suit ..................... 0124 |
| | コウ<br>ひろ(い) ひろ(まる) ひろ(める)<br>ひろ(がる) ひろ(げる) | 本を広げる ほんをひろげる open a book ... 0031<br>広がり ひろがり extent, expanse, stretch |

| 0238<br>广 53 | Here we'll add another interpretation of 厶: an *arm bent at the elbow*. Here we see a *shelter* (广) with plenty of "*elbow* room": a **WIDE**, **spacious** place. Note the traditional form. |
| 廣<br>2613<br>常 5 | |

| | ¹ **SLENDER**<br>² **MINUTE** | ①細い糸 ほそいいと fine thread ............... 0112<br>¹ 身が細る みがほそる become thin, lose weight<br>........................................... 0060 |
| | | ² 細工 さいく work, craftsmanship; artifice, tactics<br>........................................... 0108 |
| | サイ<br>ほそ(い) ほそ(る) こま(か) こまか(い) | ②明細 めいさい particulars, details........... 0024<br>②細かい金 こまかいかね small change ....... 0029 |

| 0239<br>糸 120 | Picture a farmer using **SLENDER**, **MINUTE** *threads* (糸) to mark off rows in his *rice field* (田) for planting. ☞ 累 0884, 紳 0874 |
| 1220<br>常 11 | |

| | **FOREST** | 林立 りんりつ standing in close proximity [as of buildings].................................. 0067 |
| | | (山)林学 (さん)りんがく forestry........... 0037, 0099 |
| | リン<br>はやし | 原生林 げんせいりん virgin forest...... 0208, 0036<br>雨林 うりん rain forest ....................... 0154 |
| | | 小林 こばやし Kobayashi [surname]......... 0034 |

| 0240<br>木 75 | Two *trees*: **FOREST**. |
| 0765<br>常 8 | |

| 森 シン もり | **THICK WOODS** | ○森林 しんりん forest, woodland ............ 0240<br>森林学 しんりんがく forestry ............ **0240, 0099**<br>青森 あおもり Aomori [city and prefecture] 0130<br>森田 もりた Morita [surname] ............ 0020 |
|---|---|---|

**0241**
木 75

Three *trees*: **THICK WOODS**. Practice writing and pronouncing the compounds 森林 (しんりん) or 森林学 (しんりんがく) to help yourself assimilate the respective *on-yomi*.

2184
常 12

---

| 松 ショウ まつ | **PINE** | 青松 せいしょう green pine ............ 0130<br>松林 まつばやし pine forest ............ 0240<br>松原 まつばら pine grove ............ 0208<br>松本 まつもと Matsumoto [city in Nagano prefecture] ............ 0031<br>高松 たかまつ Takamatsu [city in Kagawa prefecture] ............ 0185 |
|---|---|---|

**0242**
木 75
枩
0769
常 8

This is the first of numerous tree species we shall learn that combine the classifier 木 *tree* with another element at the right. *Public* (公) suggests a tree that is available to all, a fitting description of the **PINE**, one of the most widely distributed, widely used tree species.

---

| 竹 チク たけ | **BAMBOO** | ○竹林 ちくりん (=たけばやし) bamboo grove ....0240<br>竹の子 たけのこ bamboo shoots ............ 0094<br>竹細工 たけざいく bamboo work, bamboo crafts ............ 0239, 0108<br>竹内 たけうち Takeuchi [surname] ............ 0215<br>竹刀 しない bamboo sword ............ 0085 |
|---|---|---|

**0243**
竹 118

A pair of tall **BAMBOO** shoots with leaves at the top. The grapheme form ⺮ appears in many kanji, often suggesting the idea of *counting, figuring,* or *keeping records,* from the ancient use of bamboo for tally sticks and writing tablets. In other kanji, ⺮ will refer to instruments made of bamboo.

0201
常 6

---

| トツ みやこ | [1] **METROPOLIS, capital**<br>[2] **METROPOLIS OF TOKYO** | ①都会 とかい city, town ............ 0226<br>[1] 大都会 だいとかい large city ............ 0033, 0226<br>[2] 都内 とない in Tokyo metropolis ............ 0215<br>[2] 都立 とりつ metropolitan, under control of the Tokyo Metropolitan Government ............ 0067<br>○都合 つごう convenience, circumstances; in all, altogether ............ 0227 |
|---|---|---|

**0244**
邑 163
都
1505
常 11

Review 部 0068 and 防 0174. Here we find *person* (者 0107) on the *town* side of the *walls around the edge of town* (阝). This entry thus depicts *persons* in a *town*, by which it implies **METROPOLIS** or **capital**. This kanji is also used as an abbreviation for the capital, **TOKYO**.

| [1] CAPITAL [2] TOKYO [3] KYOTO<br><br>キョウ ケイ | [1] 京都 きょうと Kyoto.............................0244<br>[1] 東京 とうきょう Tokyo.............................0032<br>[1] 北京 ぺきん Beijing, Peking.................0122<br>[2] 上京する じょうきょうする go to Tokyo........0041<br>[3] 京大 きょうだい Kyoto University............0033 |
|---|---|

| **0245**<br>亠 8<br>京<br>1766<br>常 8 | From the roof and upper-story window of 高 0185 we derive *tall*. Behold a *tall* building supported by a post (S6) with two diagonal buttresses (S7–8): the legislative assembly building. Used in the names of the old **CAPITAL** 京都 **KYOTO** and the new **CAPITAL** 東京 **TOKYO**, and as an abbreviation for each. |
|---|---|

| **POLITICAL ADMINISTRATION**<br><br>セイ ショウ<br>まつりごと | ○行政 ぎょうせい administration ..............0055<br>行政命令 ぎょうせいめいれい administrative<br>　order .................................0055, 0232, 0229<br>内政 ないせい domestic administration, internal<br>　affairs.................................................0215<br>法政 ほうせい administration of justice.....0139<br>家政 かせい home economy................0219 |
|---|---|

| **0246**<br>攵 66<br><br>1058<br>常 9 | Review 後 0114 and 条 0119. Now we'll learn the four-stroke 攵, which resembles three-stroke 夂 but generally appears at the right, rather than at the top or bottom. Picture 攵 as a hand holding "the rod" (S6 here) for *striking* things. In 政, *strike* implies decisive action, and 正 *correctness*, creating a symbolic ideal for **POLITICAL ADMINISTRATION**. |
|---|---|

| [1] URBAN PREFECTURE (Kyoto or Osaka) [2] GOVERNMENT OFFICE<br><br>フ | ① 京都府 きょうとふ Kyoto prefecture....0245, 0244<br>[1] 府立の ふりつの prefectural.................0067<br>② 政府 せいふ government, administration..0246<br>[2] 国府 こくふ National Government (of China); provincial capital...........................0075 |
|---|---|

| **0247**<br>广 53<br><br>2654<br>常 8 | Review 付 0064. Picture a man *handing over* (付) a document under the *slanting roof* (广) of a **GOVERNMENT OFFICE**. Most often seen in 政府 (せいふ, government, administration). Also refers to the prefectures of **Kyoto** and **Osaka**. Note that kanji incorporating 付 are pronounced フ. ☞ 守 0648 |
|---|---|

| [1] DOOR [2] HOUSEHOLD<br><br>コ<br>と | ① 戸口 とぐち door, doorway...................0019<br>[1] 雨戸 あまど shutter ...........................0154<br>[1] ガラス戸 ガラスど glass door<br>② 一戸 いっこ one house, one household ....0002<br>[2] 戸別に こべつに each house, from house to<br>　house ................................................0090 |
|---|---|

| **0248**<br>戸 63<br>戸<br>1691<br>常 4 | Visualize as a doorframe, suggesting **DOOR**. Note that 戸 also refers to **HOUSEHOLD**, in the same sense implied by the English phrase "going from door to door." Seeing the visible portion as a door <u>frame</u> will help in certain characters where it is used as a grapheme to suggest the top part of a structure. The related grapheme 尸 is associated in some characters with *buttocks*. We shall take advantage of that meaning when the opportunity arises, but on the whole it will be most helpful to let both 戸 and 尸 suggest *doorframe* or *the top part of a structure/roof*. |
|---|---|

| | ¹ **PLACE, point, part** | ① 近所 きんじょ neighborhood.............0194 |
|---|---|---|
| 所 | ² **PARTICLE OF NOMINALIZATION, "-ation"** | ① 長所 ちょうしょ strong point.............0091 |
| | | ① 今の所 いまのところ at present, so far.......0228 |
| | ショ | ¹ 預かり所 あずかりしょ (=あずかりじょ) cloakroom |
| | ところ -ところ どころ | .............0165 |
| | | ² 所信 しょしん one's belief, one's opinion....0063 |

| 0249 | Imagine that in ancient China, every man kept a *hacksaw* (斤) outside his front *door* (戸). 所, a typical image of the entrance to a house, would have been a natural way to represent the idea of a particular **PLACE** or point. V5 illustrates 所's use in producing noun forms: thus 所信 "**point** of believing" = "belief." |
|---|---|
| 戸 63 | |
| 所 | |
| 0752 | |
| 常 8 | |

| | **COME TO; utmost** | ○至る いたる come to, reach; lead to |
|---|---|---|
| 至 | | 至東京 いたるとうきょう to Tokyo [as on the edge of a map].............0032, 0245 |
| | シ | ○至上 しじょう supremacy.............0041 |
| | いた(る) | 至上命令 しじょうめいれい categorical imperative .............0041, 0232, 0229 |
| | | 至大 しだい immense.............0033 |

| 0250 | Review 不 0049. S1-3 derive from an ancient picture of a bird flying not up towards the sky (as in 不) but down towards the ground. This image shows the bird as it arrives at or **COMES TO** the ground (土). Symbolizing the furthest point to which one can go, 至 also means **utmost**. As a grapheme, 至 will mean *arrive* or *come to*. |
|---|---|
| 至 133 | |
| 1869 | |
| 常 6 | |

| | ¹ **BRING ABOUT, lead to** | ① 一致 いっち accord, agreement.............0002 |
|---|---|---|
| 致 | ² **DO HUMBLY** | ¹ 致命的 ちめいてき fatal.............0232, 0169 |
| | | ¹ 合致 がっち agreement, concurrence.......0227 |
| | チ | ② お願い致します おねがいいたします (I) humbly request.............0214 |
| | いた(す) | どう致しまして どういたしまして You are welcome |

| 0251 | As 政 0246 implies, 攵 *strike* can also suggest the more general idea of *taking direct action upon something*. Here we *take direct action* to make something *arrive* or *come to* pass: **BRING ABOUT**. Picture a hand *striking* the bird to **BRING ABOUT** its downfall (in the most literal sense). Also used as a humble form of する (do). ☞ 到 0940 |
|---|---|
| 至 133 | |
| 1202 | |
| 常 10 | |

| | ¹ **HOUSE; roof** | ① 家屋 かおく house, building.............0219 |
|---|---|---|
| 屋 | ² **SMALL SHOP** | ¹ 屋上 おくじょう roof.............0041 |
| | | ¹ 部屋 へや room, chamber.............0068 |
| | オク | ² 米屋 こめや rice shop, rice merchant.......0234 |
| | や | ② 肉屋 にくや butcher shop, butcher.............0216 |

| 0252 | Review 0248 to compare 戸 and 尸. Picture someone *arriving* (至) through the *door* of a **SMALL SHOP**, which in Japan may very well double as a family **HOUSE**. Here seeing 尸 as not only a *doorframe* but also the *top part of a structure* (see 0248) helps us visualize the secondary meaning **roof**. ☞ 室 0253 |
|---|---|
| 尸 44 | |
| 2669 | |
| 常 9 | |

**ROOM, chamber**

シツ
むろ

| | | |
|---|---|---|
| 温室 | おんしつ | greenhouse ....................0199 |
| 室温 | しつおん | room temperature ..........0199 |
| 和室 | わしつ | Japanese-style room..........0236 |
| ○室内 | しつない | indoors .........................0215 |
| 皇室 | こうしつ | imperial family [household]...0077 |

**0253**

宀 40

Here *arrive* (至) under a *roof* (宀) indicates a **ROOM** or chamber. To distinguish from 屋, it may help to associate HOUSE with the "more complete" covering 尸 and **ROOM** with the "more limited" covering 宀. ☞ 屋 0252, 窒 1565

1943
常 | 9

---

**OLD**

コ
ふる(い) ふる- -ふる(す)

| | | |
|---|---|---|
| ○古代 | こだい | ancient times, antiquity........0071 |
| 尚古 | しょうこ | veneration for times of old....0184 |
| 古今 | ここん | ancient and modern times.....0228 |
| ○古い | ふるい | old, outdated |
| 古本屋 | ふるほんや | used book store...0031, 0252 |

**0254**

口 30

Picture a tombstone, covered with a cross. It means **OLD**. There are numerous kanji that subsume this one, starting with the next entry. While their *on-yomi* vary slightly (コ, ゴ, キョ, and ク—not including the 商 テキ group 1118–22), it is useful to remember that the vowel is always short. ☞ 占 0348, 舌 0052

1728
常 | 5

---

**¹ BE PRESENT**

**² RESIDE**

キョ
い(る) -い お(る)*

| | | |
|---|---|---|
| ①居る | いる | be present, be home |
| ¹ 長居 | ながい | long visit [stay].................0091 |
| ² 同居する | どうきょする | live together..........0182 |
| ②別居する | べっきょする | live separately.......0090 |
| ² 皇居 | こうきょ | imperial palace .................0077 |

**0255**

尸 44

This kanji sometimes means simply **BE PRESENT**, but more often it means <u>BE PRESENT over a long period</u>, or **RESIDE**. Think of someone **BEING PRESENT** behind the same *door* "of old" (古), i.e., from long ago. ☞ 届 1528, 屈 1834

2653
常 | 8

---

**¹ BUREAU, office**

**² LIMITED PART, locality**

**³ SITUATION**

キョク

| | | |
|---|---|---|
| ¹ 水道局 | すいどうきょく | waterworks bureau |
| | | ................0027, 0158 |
| ①当局 | とうきょく | the authorities concerned...0141 |
| ②局部 | きょくぶ | limited part, localized area ...0068 |
| ² 局所 | きょくしょ | (limited) part, local..........0249 |
| ③政局 | せいきょく | political situation...........0246 |

**0256**

尸 44

冂 resembles 勹, but there is no ear, so this is <u>not</u> the wrapping elephant. Picture 尸 as an overarching administrative structure. The strokes beneath it indicate a **LIMITED PART** or space within that structure. See the structure narrow down in stages from 尸 to 冂 and finally to 口, which represents a particular **BUREAU** or office at the local level, like a post office or telephone exchange. 口 can also be seen to represent the "current **SITUATION**," enveloped in the context of wider, long-term trends.

2636
常 | 7

| | | |
|---|---|---|
| 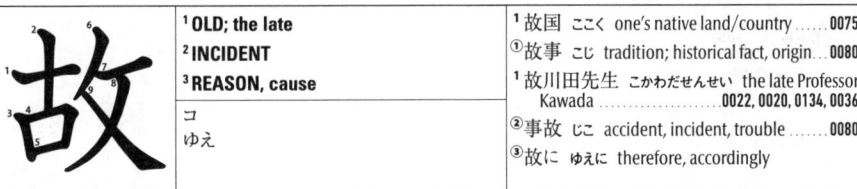 **故** <br> コ <br> ゆえ | **¹ OLD; the late** <br> **² INCIDENT** <br> **³ REASON, cause** | ¹故国 ここく one's native land/country ......0075 <br> ①故事 こじ tradition; historical fact, origin...0080 <br> ¹故川田先生 こかわだせんせい the late Professor Kawada .................0022, 0020, 0134, 0036 <br> ②事故 じこ accident, incident, trouble .......0080 <br> ③故に ゆえに therefore, accordingly |

| 0257 | Means **OLD** or **the late** (i.e., "not around anymore"). Picture *striking* (夊) something into its tombstone (古)-marked grave. The action itself helps us to remember M2 **INCIDENT**. We can also visualize M3 **REASON**/cause, as we can see the **cause** at the right (夊) and the effect at the left (古). Incidentally, be sure not to confuse 夊 with 女 WOMAN. |
|---|---|
| 夊 66 | |
| 1056 | |
| 常 9 | |

| | | |
|---|---|---|
|  **胡** <br> コ ゴ ウ | **NATIVES OF ANCIENT CHINA** | ○胡国 ここく ancient countries in the north or west of China; barbarous country ..........0075 <br> 胡瓜 きゅうり cucumber.....................0202 <br> 胡椒× こしょう pepper <br> 胡錦濤× こきんとう Hu Jintao [Chinese Communist Party general secretary 2002–12]......0213 |

| 0258 | Associate **ANCIENT CHINA** with its *old* (古), *lunar* (月) calendar. 胡 is used in some words referring to things that came to Japan from **ANCIENT CHINA**, such as 胡麻 (ごま, sesame; see 麻 0852) and 胡椒 (こしょう, pepper; 椒 unlisted). It is also a common Chinese surname. ☞ 朝 0145 |
|---|---|
| 月 74 | |
| 1057 | |
| 名 9 | |

| | | |
|---|---|---|
|  **湖** <br> コ <br> みずうみ | **LAKE** | ○湖水 こすい lake ...........................0027 <br> 湖上 こじょう on the lake....................0041 <br> 湖面 こめん lake surface ..................0175 <br> 火口湖 かこうこ crater lake............0026, 0019 <br> 五大湖 ごだいこ The Great Lakes [Lakes Superior, Michigan, Huron, Ontario, and Erie]...0007, 0033 |

| 0259 | Try to visualize the *waters* (氵) of a **LAKE** lapping up on *ancient Chinese* (胡) shores. It helps if you can fill out the scene with details from your own imagination. ☞ 潮 0146 |
|---|---|
| 水 85 | |
| 0551 | |
| 常 12 | |

| | | |
|---|---|---|
| 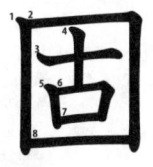 **固** <br> コ <br> かた(める) かた(まる) かた(まり) <br> かた(い) | **¹ SOLID** <br> **² FIRM** | ①固体 こたい solid, solid matter ............0062 <br> ¹固化 こか solidification .....................0120 <br> ²固定 こてい fixed, stationary................0045 <br> 固める かためる [vt] harden, solidify; strengthen <br> ○固い かたい firm, stiff, fast |

| 0260 | See a *tombstone* (古) packed inside a box for delivery. Naturally this must be a very **SOLID**/ **FIRM** box. ☞ 箇 0261 |
|---|---|
| 口 31 | |
| 2658 | |
| 常 8 | |

| 箇 | **COUNTER FOR ITEMS; item** | 二箇所 にかしょ two places ............0003, 0249 |
|---|---|---|
| | | ○一箇月 いっかげつ one month ........0002, 0023 |
| | カ | 箇条 かじょう items, articles ................0119 |
| | | 箇条書き かじょうがき itemization .....0119, 0079 |

| 0261 | Review 竹 0243. Here we use our bamboo tally sticks to **COUNT** the number of tombstone |
|---|---|
| 竹 118 | packages we'll be shipping; the kanji itself means **COUNTER FOR ITEMS**. In V3–4 it simply |
| 个 | means **item**. Now often replaced by ケ or カ. ☞ 固 0260, 筒 1838 |
| 2356 | |
| 常 14 | |

| 個 | ¹ **INDIVIDUAL, single unit** | ①個人 こじん individual ........................0015 |
|---|---|---|
| | ² **GENERAL COUNTER (for things or articles)** | ¹ 個性 こせい individuality .................0128 |
| | | ¹ 個室 こしつ private room ..................0253 |
| | コ カ* | ² りんご一個 りんごいっこ one apple ..........0002 |
| | | ² 二個所 にかしょ two places/points ....0003, 0249 |

| 0262 | Here see an **INDIVIDUAL** man (亻) opening a box with a **single** tombstone (古) he has |
|---|---|
| 人 9 | ordered for his personal use. Picture him **COUNTING** to make sure he has received the right |
| 个 | number. Interchangeable with the previous entry for counting certain kinds of articles, in |
| 0100 | which case 個 is pronounced カ and can be replaced by ケ or カ. |
| 常 10 | |

| 且 | **AS WELL AS, moreover, both ... and ...** | 尚且つ なおかつ and yet; moreover, also ...0184 |
|---|---|---|
| | | 且つ又 かつまた moreover, also .............0058 |
| | か(つ) | 早く且つ私的にできるから はやくかつしてきにて |
| | | きるから because it can be done quickly and |
| | | privately ..........................0143, 0237, 0169 |

| 0263 | 且 is mainly used as a building block inside other characters, in which case it will mean *ladder*. |
|---|---|
| 一 1 | By itself, it means **AS WELL AS/moreover/both ... and ...**, which can be visualized in the way |
| | the rungs of the ladder add upon each other. |
| 2927 | |
| 常 5 | |

| 組 | ¹ **ORGANIZE** | ①組成 そせい composition, formation, construc- |
|---|---|---|
| | ² **ASSEMBLE** | tion ................................0070 |
| | | ①組合 くみあい union, guild, association .....0227 |
| | ソ | ¹ 四人組 よにんぐみ foursome, the Gang of Four |
| | く(む) くみ -ぐみ | ..................................0006, 0015 |
| | | ² 組み立てる くみたてる assemble, erect .....0067 |
| | | ² 手を組む てをくむ join hands ...............0046 |

| 0264 | 糸 means *thread*, but it can also mean *rope* or *cord*. See 組 as a primitive *ladder* **ASSEMBLED** |
|---|---|
| 糸 120 | from wooden poles by *rope*. When what is bound together is <u>people</u>, the applicable keyword |
| | is "**ORGANIZE**": imagine the *rope* wrapping around a group of people to bind them into one |
| | unit. |
| 1224 | |
| 常 11 | |

| 夕 | **EVENING** | ○今夕 こんせき this evening, tonight .........0228 |
|---|---|---|
| | | ○夕方 ゆうがた evening ......................0173 |
| | | 夕べ ゆうべ evening |
| | セキ | 夕日 ゆうひ setting sun......................0001 |
| | ゆう | 七夕 たなばた Festival of the Weaver [the star Vega]; the Star Festival (July 7) .............0009 |

| **0265** | A variant drawing of *moon* (see 月 0023), which we can see as the **EVENING** moon. As in 月, |
|---|---|
| 夕 36 | see two crescent lines, one outlining the dark portion of the sphere, the other outlining the bright portion. Fewer surface details (i.e., crossing strokes) are visible than in 月, for it is not yet fully dark. As a grapheme, 夕 will mean *evening* or *moon*. |
| 2871 | |
| 常 3 | |

| 外 | **OUTSIDE; remove, come off** | ○外(国)人 がい(こく)じん foreigner ......0075, 0015 |
|---|---|---|
| | | 外交 がいこう diplomacy, foreign relations 0102 |
| | | 以外に いがいに except for, excluding......0066 |
| | ガイ ゲ | ○その外 そのほか besides, in addition; the rest, others |
| | そと ほか はず(す) はず(れる) | ○外す はずす take off, remove; miss, dodge |

| **0266** | Let S4–5 represent an image of one thing slipping off of another (the short stroke at the |
|---|---|
| 夕 36 | right points down and away from the central vertical stroke). 夕 *moon* provides the physical context for this occurrence: picture something **coming off** or being **removed** from the *moon*, falling **OUTSIDE** it. |
| 0163 | |
| 常 5 | |

| 多 | **MANY; most** | 多面 ためん many sides, many phases......0175 |
|---|---|---|
| | | ○多分 たぶん probably, perhaps, maybe.....0088 |
| | | 多目的 たもくてき multipurpose .......0021, 0169 |
| | タ | ○多い おおい many, much |
| | おおい | 多くの人 おおくのひと most people.........0015 |

| **0267** | Doubling the number of *moons* (夕) implies **MANY**. |
|---|---|
| 夕 36 | |
| 尋 | |
| 1858 | |
| 常 6 | |

| 汐 | **EVENING TIDE** | ○潮汐 ちょうせき ebb and flow, tide ...........0146 |
|---|---|---|
| | | ○汐が満ちる前に しおがみちるまえに before the tide comes in...........................0179, 0113 |
| | セキ | |
| | しお | |

| **0268** | *Water* (氵) of the *evening* (夕): **EVENING TIDE**. |
|---|---|
| 水 85 | |
| 0197 | |
| 名 6 | |

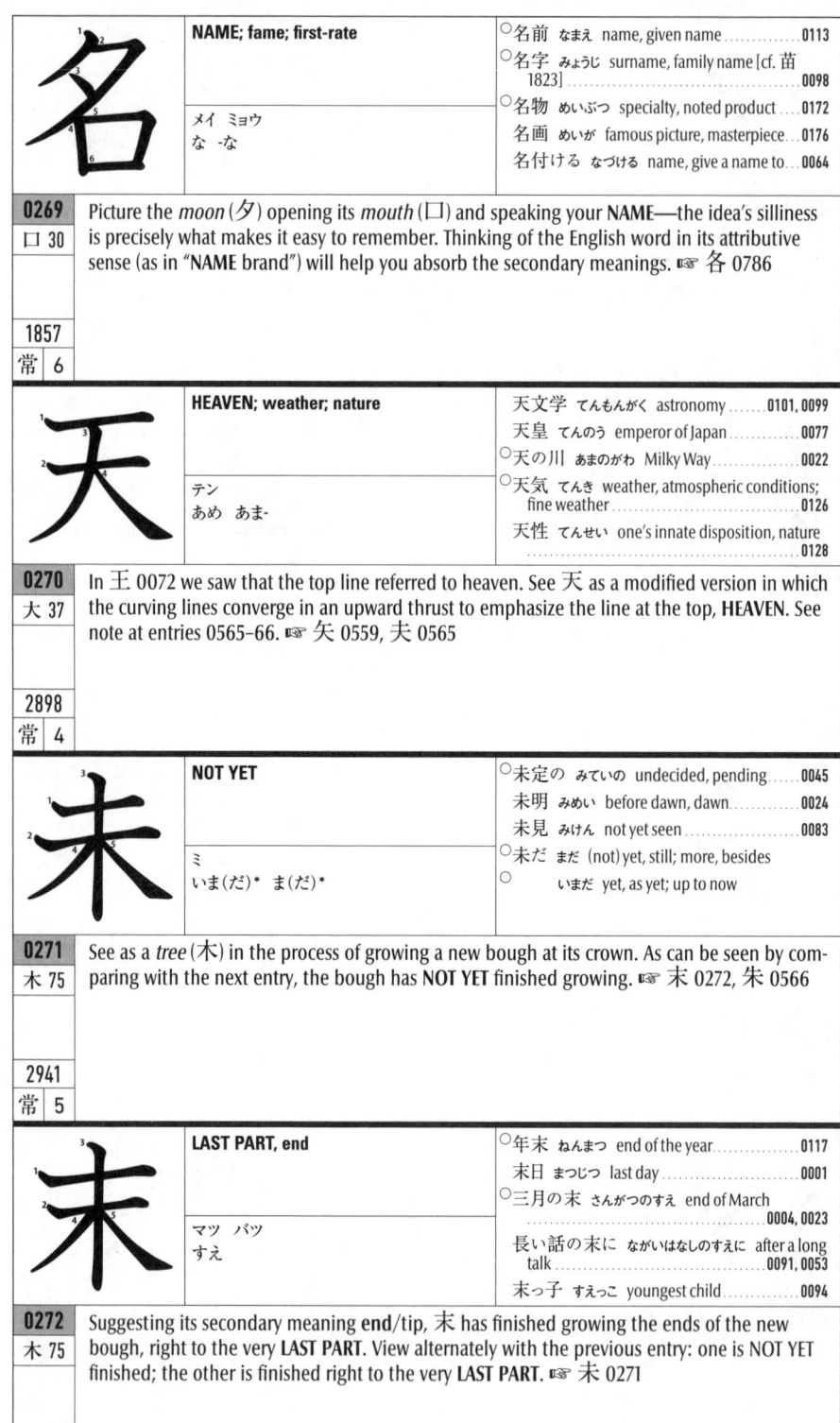

| 名 | **NAME; fame; first-rate** | ○名前 なまえ name, given name..............0113 |
| | | ○名字 みょうじ surname, family name [cf. 苗 1823].........................................0098 |
| | メイ ミョウ | ○名物 めいぶつ specialty, noted product....0172 |
| | な -な | 名画 めいが famous picture, masterpiece...0176 |
| | | 名付ける なづける name, give a name to...0064 |

| **0269** | Picture the *moon* (夕) opening its *mouth* (口) and speaking your **NAME**—the idea's silliness is precisely what makes it easy to remember. Thinking of the English word in its attributive sense (as in "**NAME** brand") will help you absorb the secondary meanings. ☞ 各 0786 |
| 口 30 | |
| **1857** | |
| 常 6 | |

| 天 | **HEAVEN; weather; nature** | 天文学 てんもんがく astronomy.......0101, 0099 |
| | | 天皇 てんのう emperor of Japan............0077 |
| | | ○天の川 あまのがわ Milky Way.................0022 |
| | テン | ○天気 てんき weather, atmospheric conditions; fine weather...............................0126 |
| | あめ あま- | 天性 てんせい one's innate disposition, nature .............................................0128 |

| **0270** | In 王 0072 we saw that the top line referred to heaven. See 天 as a modified version in which the curving lines converge in an upward thrust to emphasize the line at the top, **HEAVEN**. See note at entries 0565–66. ☞ 矢 0559, 夫 0565 |
| 大 37 | |
| **2898** | |
| 常 4 | |

| 未 | **NOT YET** | ○未定の みていの undecided, pending......0045 |
| | | 未明 みめい before dawn, dawn............0024 |
| | | 未見 みけん not yet seen.....................0083 |
| | ミ | ○未だ まだ (not) yet, still; more, besides |
| | いま(だ)* ま(だ)* | ○ いまだ yet, as yet; up to now |

| **0271** | See as a *tree* (木) in the process of growing a new bough at its crown. As can be seen by comparing with the next entry, the bough has **NOT YET** finished growing. ☞ 末 0272, 朱 0566 |
| 木 75 | |
| **2941** | |
| 常 5 | |

| 末 | **LAST PART, end** | ○年末 ねんまつ end of the year...............0117 |
| | | 末日 まつじつ last day ......................0001 |
| | | ○三月の末 さんがつのすえ end of March ....................................................0004, 0023 |
| | マツ バツ | 長い話の末に ながいはなしのすえに after a long talk ........................................0091, 0053 |
| | すえ | 末っ子 すえっこ youngest child..............0094 |

| **0272** | Suggesting its secondary meaning **end**/tip, 末 has finished growing the ends of the new bough, right to the very **LAST PART**. View alternately with the previous entry: one is NOT YET finished; the other is finished right to the very **LAST PART**. ☞ 未 0271 |
| 木 75 | |
| **2940** | |
| 常 5 | |

**TASTE, flavor; contents**

ミ
あじ　あじ(わう)

地味な　じみな　plain, sober, unpretentious . 0187
後味　あとあじ　aftertaste . . . . . . . . . . . . . . . . . . . . . . 0114
切れ味　きれあじ　sharpness, cutting quality 0086
○味わう　あじわう　taste, savor; appreciate, enjoy
○意味　いみ　meaning, intention, significance,
　purport . . . . . . . . . . . . . . . . . . . . . . . . . . . . . . . . . . . 0151

| 0273 | What has *not yet* (未) passed through one's *mouth* (口): this is what one **TASTES**. It is also the mouth's present **contents**. |
|---|---|
| 口 30 | |
| 0247 | |
| 常 8 | |

---

**COME**

ライ
く(る)　きた(る)　きた(す)

○来月　らいげつ　next month, this coming month
　. . . . . . . . . . . . . . . . . . . . . . . . . . . . . . . . . . . . . . . . . . 0023
来日　らいにち　coming to Japan . . . . . . . . . . . . 0001
外来語　がいらいご　loanword, foreign word
　. . . . . . . . . . . . . . . . . . . . . . . . . . . . . . . . . . . 0266, 0222
○来る　くる　come, become
○　　きたる　come, arrive

| 0274 | The word "coming" holds within it the notion "not yet here." So it is with the kanji for **COME**. To *not yet* (未), we add `ヽヽ` (S2-3) to indicate two expected guests that are on their way. See S2-3 **COMING** to the center of the character. In the way they both aim toward the same point, see them **COMING** imminently to the same destination. ☞ 翌 0419 |
|---|---|
| 木 75* | |
| 2975 | |
| 常 7 | |

---

**NEW**

シン
あたら(しい)　あら(た)　あら-　にい-

○新人　しんじん　new talent, rookie; newcomer 0015
新年　しんねん　New Year . . . . . . . . . . . . . . . . . . . . 0117
最新の　さいしんの　newest, latest . . . . . . . . . . . 0196
○新しい　あたらしい　new
○新たに　あらたに　newly, afresh; again

| 0275 | See a person *standing* (立) on top of a *tree* (木), using a *hacksaw* (斤) to saw off some **NEW** branches that are growing there. See only the very **NEW** branches being cut, right at the very tip-top. |
|---|---|
| 斤 69 | |
| 1587 | |
| 常 13 | |

---

¹ **PARENT**
² **RELATIVES**
³ **INTIMATE, friendly**

シン
おや　おや-　した(しい)　した(しむ)

①親子　おやこ (=しんし)　parent and child . . . . . . 0094
①両親　りょうしん　parents . . . . . . . . . . . . . . . . . . . . . 0177
②肉親　にくしん　blood relations . . . . . . . . . . . . . . . 0216
³ 親切な　しんせつな　kind, friendly, obliging . . 0086
③親しい　したしい　intimate, familiar, friendly

| 0276 | Following the pattern of the previous entry, see a **PARENT** (or other older **RELATIVE**) *standing* on top of a *tree, looking* (見) down secretly and with tender **INTIMACY** on its child (or younger **RELATIVE**). |
|---|---|
| 見 147 | |
| 1599 | |
| 常 16 | |

| | **LACK, want** | 欠本 けっぽん missing volume.............0031 |
|---|---|---|
| | | ガス欠 ガスけつ running out of gas |
| | | ○無欠 むけつ flawless.............0048 |
| | ケツ | ○欠ける かける lack, be deficient, be vacant; be broken off |
| | か(ける) か(く) か(かす) | 一人欠けている ひとりかけている one person is missing.............0002, 0015 |

| **0277** | Derives from a picture of a yawning mouth. See the jaws spreading open at the bottom. Like a hatchling's wide-open beak, 欠 easily suggests a **LACK** or want. As a grapheme, 欠 can mean *lack, gap,* or *yawning mouth.* ☞ 欠 0904 |
|---|---|
| 欠 76 | |
| **缺** | |
| 1721 | |
| 常 4 | |

| | **NEXT, second(ary), (numerical) order** | ○次回 じかい next time.............0050 |
|---|---|---|
| | | 次男 じなん second son.............0092 |
| | | 目次 もくじ table of contents.............0021 |
| | ジ シ | ○次ぐ つぐ rank next to, come next/after |
| | つ(ぐ) つぎ | 次のように つぎのように as follows |

| **0278** | 冫 looks like 氵 but has only two strokes. For 次, let the <u>two</u> strokes of 冫 suggest **second(ary)**, so that the whole kanji suggests "a *second* thing to fill the *gap* left by the first," i.e., **NEXT**. When a train conductor uses this word to announce the **NEXT** station, think of it as a *second* station that will fill the *gap* left by the one you've just departed. |
|---|---|
| 欠 76 | |
| 0039 | |
| 常 6 | |

| | **SEAT** | 席を代わる せきをかわる change seats.....0071 |
|---|---|---|
| | | 出席 しゅっせき attendance, presence.....0038 |
| | | ○欠席 けっせき absence, nonattendance.....0277 |
| | セキ | 席次 せきじ order of seats, seating precedence; class standing.............0278 |
| | | 席上で せきじょうて at the meeting; on the occasion.............0041 |

| **0279** | See 廿 as the open mouth of a wood-burning stove. We've fired up the stove to keep warm in our *shelter* (广), and tossed a *cloth* (巾) on the floor for a front-row **SEAT** next to the stove. After studying the next entry, practice writing it in alternation with this one, reminding yourself of their meanings as you do. ☞ 度 0280 |
|---|---|
| 巾 50 | |
| 2683 | |
| 常 10 | |

| | **¹ DEGREE** | ①温度 おんど temperature.............0199 |
|---|---|---|
| | **² TIME** | ¹ 湿度 しつど humidity.............0200 |
| | | ² 毎度 まいど every time, always.............0105 |
| | ド ト タク | ②見る度に みるたびに whenever [each time] one sees (it).............0083 |
| | たび | 二度 にど two degrees/times.............0003 |

| **0280** | See a *hand* (又) shove more fuel into the *stove* (廿) to raise the temperature a few **DEGREES**. 度 also means **TIME** as in "this time" or "the third time." Connect this with M1 by recalling the phrase "by DEGREES," which just means "one **DEGREE** at a **TIME**." Imagine the **DEGREE** measure rising one **TIME** after another as the fire is stoked. ☞ 席 0279 |
|---|---|
| 广 53 | |
| 2670 | |
| 常 9 | |

| | | |
|---|---|---|
|  | **CROSS, ford**<br><br>ト<br>わた(る) -わた(る) わた(す) | ○渡米 とべい going to America .............. 0234<br>○渡来 とらい importation, influx............. 0274<br>○渡る わたる cross, ford<br>渡す わたす carry across (a river); hand over<br>手渡す てわたす hand over (to), give, deliver<br>................................................................. 0046 |

**0281**
水 85

ゝ is a body of *water* that we must **CROSS**. 度 shows the *degrees* of longitude that we must **CROSS** (longitude rather than latitude, for we are moving **CROSS**-wise). Think of **CROSSING** the *degrees* of longitude one at a time on a trans-oceanic voyage.

0560
常 12

| | | |
|---|---|---|
|  | **LIMIT, bounds**<br><br>ゲン<br>かぎ(る) かぎ(り) -かぎ(り) | 限定する げんていする limit, restrict, define... 0045<br>限度 げんど limit, bounds ................. 0280<br>○最大限 さいだいげん maximum ....... 0196, 0033<br>○最小限 さいしょうげん minimum....... 0196, 0034<br>○出来る限り できるかぎり as far as possible<br>................................................................. 0038, 0274 |

**0282**
阜 170

See 艮 as a picture of a little boy. When he's been good, we'll reward him with a "stroke" on top of his head (thus 良 means *good*). But when we "limit" the drawing to 艮, that is, when we "stop" before adding the reward stroke, it means *stop* or *limit*. 限 combines *limit* with *hills around edge of town* (阝) and means **LIMIT** or **bounds**. ☞ 郎 0286

0357
常 9

| | | |
|---|---|---|
|  | **SILVER**<br><br>ギン | ○銀行 ぎんこう bank........................... 0055<br>日銀 にちぎん Bank of Japan (short for 日本銀行)<br>................................................................. 0001<br>水銀 すいぎん mercury, quicksilver ......... 0027<br>銀メダル ぎんメダル silver medal |

**0283**
金 167

*Stop* (艮) just before *gold* (金): **SILVER**.

1534
常 14

| | | |
|---|---|---|
| 根 | **ROOT**<br><br>コン<br>ね -ね | 根本 こんぽん basis, foundation; origin, source<br>................................................................. 0031<br>○根気 こんき perseverance, patience, energy 0126<br>根性 こんじょう nature, temper; willpower; guts<br>................................................................. 0128<br>屋根 やね roof................................... 0252<br>○根回し ねまわし digging around the roots;<br>maneuvering behind the scenes .......... 0050 |

**0284**
木 75

*Stop* (艮) just before the *tree* (木): **ROOTS**.

0841
常 10

103

**GOOD**

リョウ
よ(い) -よ(い) い(い)*

○最良の さいりょうの best, most excellent ....0196
不良 ふりょう badness, inferiority; delinquency
.................................................................0049
良心 りょうしん conscience ...................0056
○良い よい (=いい) good
良い席 よいせき good seats.................0279

| 0285 | See 限 0282: we reward the little boy with a "stroke" on top of his head for **GOOD** behavior. |
| 艮 138 | |
| 2980 | |
| 常 7 | |

**¹YOUNG MAN**
**²MALE NAME SUFFIX**

ロウ

①新郎 しんろう bridegroom.................0275
②一郎 いちろう Ichiro [name of eldest son]....0002
²次郎 じろう Jiro [name of second son].......0278

| 0286 | At the left side we find an abbreviated version of *good*. Unlike 限 0282, where we saw 艮 |
| 邑 163 | outside the town limits, here we see a *good* boy (or in this case, **YOUNG MAN**) staying inside |
| 郎 | the town. ☞ 限 0282 |
| 1184 | |
| 常 9 | |

**CORRIDOR, gallery**

ロウ

○廊下 ろうか corridor, hallway .................0040
画廊 がろう picture gallery .................0176
回廊 かいろう corridor, gallery .................0050

| 0287 | See a good *young man* (郎) walking down a **CORRIDOR** covered by a *slanting roof* (广). |
| 广 53 | |
| 廊 | |
| 2713 | |
| 常 12 | |

**¹EAT**
**²FOOD**

ショク ジキ
く(う) く(らう) た(べる)

①食事 しょくじ meal, dinner.................0080
¹食後に しょくごに after meals .................0114
①食べる たべる eat
¹食う くう eat
²和食 わしょく Japanese-style food............0236

| 0288 | *Good boy* (良) under *roof* (へ): picture a *good* boy who has come home to **EAT**. One is |
| 食 184 | tempted to replace this phrasing with the more concise "*good* boys **EAT** at home," but to |
| | do so would replace a visual description with a conceptual statement. However crisp such a |
| | statement might be, it is better to keep the mnemonic grounded in the kanji's visual image. |
| 1787 | |
| 常 9 | |

| | |
|---|---|
| **DRINK** | ○飲食 いんしょく eating and drinking ........ 0288 |
| | ○飲む のむ drink |
| | 飲み物 のみもの beverage ................. 0172 |
| イン | 飲み水 のみみず drinking [potable] water 0027 |
| の（む） | 飲み屋 のみや bar, tavern ................. 0252 |

**0289**
食 184
飲
1510
常 12

食 is an abbreviated version of 食 EAT. See a *mouth held wide open* (欠) after *eating*, desiring something to **DRINK**. This entry illustrates why the *hen* forms of 艮, 良, and 食 are all abbreviated in this way—so as not to get in the way of *tsukuri* like 欠 which need to extend toward the lower left.

| | |
|---|---|
| ¹ **GOVERNMENT** | ¹ 官用 かんよう government use; government business ................. 0047 |
| ² **GOVERNMENT OFFICIAL** | ¹ 官命 かんめい official order ................. 0232 |
| | ② 長官 ちょうかん director, administrator, chief ................. 0091 |
| カン | ² 外交官 がいこうかん diplomat, foreign service officer ................. 0266, 0102 |

**0290**
宀 40

1912
常 8

Derives from a picture of a **GOVERNMENT OFFICIAL** inside his office, with a drooping, sleeping head (S5–6) and a fat belly (S7–8). A fitting image of **GOVERNMENT** in general. Kanji that contain 官, such as the next entry, are read カン. ☞ 宮 1242

| | |
|---|---|
| **PUBLIC BUILDING** | ○会館 かいかん hall, assembly hall ........... 0226 |
| | 本館 ほんかん main building; this building ... 0031 |
| | 分館 ぶんかん annex, extension ............ 0088 |
| カン | 館長 かんちょう director, superintendent ... 0091 |
| やかた | 館内 かんない in the building ................. 0215 |

**0291**
食 184
舘
1562
常 16

Suggests the *dining* (食) hall of a *government* (官) office, which we can think of as a kind of archetype for a **PUBLIC BUILDING**. Because 館 is unusual in lining up two different *rooftops* across the top, a more focused and direct way to perceive the meaning is to let this juxtaposition be a visual cue for the idea of **BUILDING**.

| | |
|---|---|
| **LODGE** | ○合宿する がっしゅくする lodge together, stay in a camp for training ................. 0227 |
| | 下宿 げしゅく lodging, boarding house ..... 0040 |
| | 宿屋 やどや inn, hotel, lodging house ...... 0252 |
| シュク | ○宿る やどる lodge; dwell in |
| やど やど（る） やど（す） | 子を宿す こをやどす be pregnant with a child ................. 0094 |

**0292**
宀 40

1985
常 11

*One hundred* (百) *persons* (イ) under the same *roof* (宀): a **LODGE**.

| | DOG | ○ 一犬 いっけん one dog .......... 0002 |
|---|---|---|
| | | コリー犬 コリーけん collie |
| | ケン | ○ 小犬 こいぬ puppy, little dog .......... 0034 |
| | いぬ いぬ- | 犬小屋 いぬごや doghouse .......... 0034, 0252 |

**0293**
犬 94
2912
常 4

Picture a **DOG**'s head and neck pointing toward the left, two pairs of legs at the bottom, and a coiled-up tail sticking out to the right. Distinguish from BIG 大 0033 by focusing on S4, the coiling tail. The usual grapheme version is 犭 (introduced back at 猪 0217), which can also mean *smallish four-legged creature*. ☞ 太 0294, 尤 2274

| | ¹ **GREAT, extremely large** | ¹ 太刀 たち long sword .......... 0085 |
|---|---|---|
| | ² **THICK, fat** | ① 太子 たいし crown prince .......... 0094 |
| | | ¹ 太古 たいこ ancient times, remote ages .... 0254 |
| | タイ タ | ② 太い ふとい thick; fat |
| | ふと(い) ふと(る) | ² 太る ふとる grow fat |

**0294**
大 37
1846
常 4

Here let the dot stroke suggest one additional step beyond BIG (大): **GREAT**. That 犬 has the same extra dot stroke underscores the usefulness of seeing it in the upper position as a dog's coiled tail, so as to avoid confusion with 太. Seeing this stroke <u>drop</u> to the lower position suggests heaviness, which we can associate with M2 **THICK**. ☞ 犬 0293

| | ¹ **VESSEL, container** | ① 食器 しょっき tableware .......... 0288 |
|---|---|---|
| | ² **INSTRUMENT** | ① ガラスの器 ガラスのうつわ glass vessel/container |
| | | ② 武器 ぶき weapon .......... 0111 |
| | キ | 器官 きかん organ (of the body) .......... 0290 |
| | うつわ | 器用な きような skillful, ingenious .......... 0047 |

**0295**
口 30
器
2368
常 15

Notice the extra dot stroke in the old form. If we trace 器 back to its origins, we find that it derives from a picture of a *dog* (犬) served up on the center of a table, surrounded by four plates (口), which easily suggest **VESSEL** or **container**. 器 can also be used to refer to any kind of tangible **INSTRUMENT**. ☞ 益 0414

| | ¹ **MISFORTUNE** | ¹ 凶事 きょうじ calamity, misfortune .......... 0080 |
|---|---|---|
| | ² **EVIL** | ② 凶行 きょうこう violence, murder, crime .... 0055 |
| | | ² 凶器 きょうき murder weapon .......... 0295 |
| | キョウ | ² 凶刃 きょうじん assassin's dagger .......... 0087 |
| | | ² 元凶 げんきょう cause of evil, culprit; ringleader .......... 0136 |

**0296**
凵 17
2557
常 4

We saw 凵 before at 画 0176, where it contained a PICTURE. We'll give it the meaning *open container or pit*. Just as the "X" marks over a person's eyes in a drawing indicate he is dead, the "メ" mark here indicates a person who has fallen into an *open pit* and died: an **EVIL MISFORTUNE**. Later we'll associate "メ" with *violent death*. ☞ 区 0297

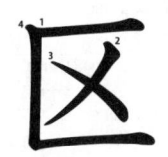

| ¹ DIVIDE INTO SECTIONS<br>² DISTRICT<br>³ WARD, borough<br><br>ク | ¹区分する　くぶんする　divide, subdivide .....0088<br>①区別する　くべつする　distinguish; classify...0090<br>¹区切る　くぎる　punctuate, mark off with a<br>　　comma.................................................0086<br>②地区　ちく　district, area, region, lot .........0187<br>³大田区　おおたく　Ota ward.............0033, 0020 |

**0297**
匸 23
區
2559
常 4

See the crossing lines **DIVIDING** the space inside 匸 **INTO SECTIONS**. If the space were a city, the sections would be called **DISTRICTS** or **WARDS**. The old form reveals the way in which "メ" was used to simplify numerous kanji, including the next entry, after the Second World War. See note at 医 0561. ☞ 凶 0296

| DRAWING, plan<br><br>ズ　ト<br>はか（る） | ○地図　ちず　map...................................0187<br>図書　としょ　books................................0079<br>図書館　としょかん　library..............0079, 0291<br>○意図　いと　intention, aim, plan .............0151<br>合図　あいず　signal, sign......................0227 |

**0298**
囗 31
圖
2645
常 7

Here let 囗 represent the outlines of a **DRAWING** or map. This is a pirate's map, with an "X" to mark the spot of a buried treasure, and a couple of other symbols for nearby landmarks to help the pirates find their way. To absorb 図's more figurative meaning, **plan**, picture yourself **DRAWING** a map of your future, a **plan** for the time to come.

| ¹ NUMERICAL ORDER<br>² WATCH, duty<br><br>バン | ①一番　いちばん　first, first place; most, best...0002<br>¹三番線　さんばんせん　track number 3...0004, 0210<br>²番犬　ばんけん　watchdog.......................0293<br>②交番　こうばん　police box ....................0102<br>²番に当たる　ばんにあたる　be on duty; have<br>　　one's turn..........................................0141 |

**0299**
田 102




2396
常 12

Take 釆 as a *crudely tied rice bundle*—halfway between the basic rice bundle (米) and the neatly tied rice bundle (禾). In this book 釆 will appear only once without 田 below it, at 釈 1506. Here imagine a rotation of sentries who **WATCH** over the *crudely tied rice bundles* left out in a *field*. They take turns in **ORDER**. ☞ 審 1510

| ¹ NUMBER<br>² DESIGNATION, title, name<br>³ SIGN, signal<br><br>ゴウ | ①番号　ばんごう　number, serial number ......0299<br>¹電話番号　でんわばんごう　telephone number<br>　　.....................................0155, 0053, 0299<br>¹315号室　さんいちごごうしつ　room number 315<br>　　.......................................................0253<br>²年号　ねんごう　name of era, reign title.......0117<br>③信号　しんごう　signal; traffic light............0063 |

**0300**
囗 30*
號
1847
常 5

See as a number "05." Means **NUMBER** as in "room number," "train number," etc. With this core idea of "numerical designation," associate the other meanings **DESIGNATION** and **SIGN**. ☞ 別 0090, 呉 1478

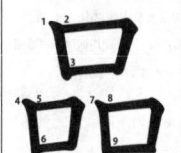

| | ¹ ARTICLE<br>² GRADE OF EXCELLENCE<br>³ CLASSIFICATION<br><br>ヒン<br>しな | ① 作品 さくひん (piece of) work, product......0152<br>① 品物 しなもの article, thing, goods..........0172<br>² 品の良い人 ひんのよいひと person of refined manners ......................0285, 0015<br>② 上品 じょうひん elegance, refinement.......0041<br>³ 品目 ひんもく list of articles/items..........0021 |
|---|---|---|

| **0301**<br>口 30<br><br>品<br><br>1937<br>常 9 | Here we see three **ARTICLES** of merchandise, neatly stacked in their boxes. 品 also means **GRADE OF EXCELLENCE** and **CLASSIFICATION**, meanings which can likewise be visualized in the character: the three boxes represent three **CLASSIFICATIONS**; the highest **GRADE OF EXCELLENCE** is seen in the single (Grade A?) box at the top. |
|---|---|

| | ¹ PLEASURE<br>² COMFORTABLE<br>³ MUSIC<br><br>ガク ラク<br>たの(しい) たの(しむ) | ① 楽しむ たのしむ take pleasure in, enjoy (oneself)<br>② 楽な らくな easy, light; comfortable<br>² 安楽な あんらくな comfortable, carefree, cozy ......................0096<br>③ 音楽 おんがく music......................0150<br>³ 楽器 がっき musical instrument............0295 |
|---|---|---|

| **0302**<br>木 75<br><br>樂<br><br>2460<br>常 13 | Think of a raucous **MUSICAL** celebration centered around a drum set. See the two halves of a hi-hat (白) clanging together as the sound waves (S6-9) shoot out in every direction. 木 can be visualized as the hi-hat's *wooden* stand. The image easily suggests not only **MUSIC** but also fun and enjoyment, **PLEASURE** and **COMFORT**. |
|---|---|

| | DRUG, chemical<br><br>ヤク<br>くすり | 薬品 やくひん medicine, drug; chemicals...0301<br>○薬局 やっきょく drugstore, pharmacy.........0256<br>丸薬 がんやく pill ...........................0012<br>火薬 かやく gunpowder.....................0026<br>○薬屋 くすりや drugstore .....................0252 |
|---|---|---|

| **0303**<br>艸 140<br><br>藥<br><br>2100<br>常 16 | *Grass* (艹) producing *pleasure* (楽): **DRUGS**. |
|---|---|

| | PERIPHERY, around; cycle<br><br>シュウ<br>まわ(り) | ○周辺 しゅうへん environs, outskirts; circumference ......................0195<br>周回 しゅうかい circumference; lap/circling....0050<br>円周 えんしゅう circumference...............0013<br>三周 さんしゅう three rounds [laps] .........0004<br>○周りの人 まわりのひと the people around one ......................0015 |
|---|---|---|

| **0304**<br>口 30<br><br><br>2585<br>常 8 | In the next three characters we'll see 土 above 口, not to be confused with 古 0254. The focus of the present character is 冂, which indicates the **PERIPHERY** around an area of *soil* (土) located behind an *opening* or gate (口). 周 is sometimes used to refer to a lap run **around** a track, so it may help to picture the *soil* as that of a football field. |
|---|---|

| WEEK | ○先週 せんしゅう last week ............... 0134 |
| | 今週 こんしゅう this week ............... 0228 |
| | 来週 らいしゅう next week ............... 0274 |
| シュウ | 週末 しゅうまつ weekend ............... 0272 |
| | 週に三回 しゅうにさんかい three times a week ............... 0004, 0050 |

**0305**
辵 162

Represents the way we go *around* a *cycle* (周) as we *move* forward (辶) through time. When we complete the *cycle* we're back where we started, except that it is one **WEEK** later.

2690
常 11

| ¹ **TONE, note, condition** | ○調子 ちょうし tone, tune, key, note; (health) condition; manner ............... 0094 |
| ² **INVESTIGATE** | 口調 くちょう tone, expression ............... 0019 |
| ³ **PREPARE, make ready** | ○調べる しらべる investigate, look into |
| チョウ | 調合 ちょうごう compounding, mixing, preparation ............... 0227 |
| しら(べる) しら(べ) ととの(う) ととの(える) | ○夕食を調える ゆうしょくをととのえる prepare supper ............... 0265, 0288 |

**0306**
言 149

Think of some very important thing you need to "say," like a marriage vow. Something so important that you keep going *around* and *around* (周) the *words* (言) in search of the precise **TONE**, the perfect **note**. Time and again you **INVESTIGATE**, scrutinizing every *word* as you **PREPARE**. Link the meaning and reading by thinking of ととのえる as "*to*-TONE-*oeru*."

1417
常 15

| ¹ **TIE UP** | ①約束する やくそくする promise, vow ......... 0170 |
| ² **BUNDLE** | ①束ねる たばねる tie up in a bundle |
| | ² 束になって たばになって in a bunch; in a group |
| ソク | ² 花束 はなたば bundle of flowers ............ 0121 |
| たば たば(ねる) つか* | ² 一束十円 ひとたばじゅうえん (=いっそくじゅうえん) ten yen a bundle ............... 0002, 0005, 0013 |

**0307**
木 75

A bunch of *trees* (木) that have been **TIED UP** in a **BUNDLE**.

2978
常 7

| **PUT IN ORDER** | 整地 せいち leveling of ground, soil preparation ............... 0187 |
| | ○調整 ちょうせい regulation, adjustment ..... 0306 |
| | 整形 せいけい orthopedics ............... 0147 |
| セイ | ○整える ととのえる put in order |
| ととの(える) ととの(う) | 整う ととのう be in order |

**0308**
攵 66

The concept **PUT IN ORDER** is readily discernible here. 束 *bundle* represents putting things in bundles as you tidy up. 攵 shows a hand holding a rod (a broomstick?), *taking action*. 正 *correct* suggests putting things in their proper place. ☞ 数 0309

2501
常 16

| | | NUMBER, quantity, count | 数字 すうじ figure, numeral ..................0098 |
|---|---|---|---|
| | | | ○数学 すうがく mathematics ...................0099 |
| | | | 整数 せいすう integer, whole number......0308 |
| | | スウ ス | 数多く かずおおく in large numbers .........0267 |
| | | かず かぞ(える) | ○数える かぞえる count, calculate, enumerate |

| 0309 | Visualize as a *woman* (女) *striking* (攵) bundles of *rice* (米) in order to **count** their **NUMBER**. |
|---|---|
| 攵 66 | ☞ 整 0308, 類 0310, 楼 1957 |
| 數 | |
| 1591 | |
| 常 13 | |

| | | KIND, type | 人類 じんるい mankind, humankind........0015 |
|---|---|---|---|
| | | | ○分類 ぶんるい classification..................0088 |
| | | | 食肉類 しょくにくるい carnivorous animals, |
| | | | Carnivora ....................0288, 0216 |
| | | ルイ | 類語 るいご synonym, related word........0222 |
| | | たぐ(い) | 親類 しんるい relatives, relations............0276 |

| 0310 | We have been given the task of classifying *rice* (米) by **type**. Specifically, we are to separate |
|---|---|
| 頁 181 | the *big* (大) **KINDS** of *rice* from the rest. See the *head* (頁: again, focusing on the top stroke, |
| 類 | here S10) looking over the *rice* and separating the *large* **KIND** from the other **KINDS**. |
| | ☞ 数 0309 |
| 1606 | |
| 常 18 | |

| | | SHOW | 予示する よじする foreshadow...............0163 |
|---|---|---|---|
| | | | 内示 ないじ private [unofficial] announcement |
| | | | ...........................................0215 |
| | | | ○公示 こうじ public [official] announcement 0089 |
| | | ジ シ | ○示す しめす show, display; indicate |
| | | しめ(す) | 示し合わせる しめしあわせる prearrange, |
| | | | conspire......................0227 |

| 0311 | Derives from a picture of an altar to the gods. Laid on top of it is a sacrificial offering (S1). As |
|---|---|
| 示 113 | an independent kanji it now means **SHOW**, a meaning that is easily suggested by this image |
| | of an object lying on top of a table. |
| 1694 | |
| 常 5 | |

| | | PROHIBIT | ○禁止する きんしする prohibit, ban ..........0042 |
|---|---|---|---|
| | | | 禁物 きんもつ taboo.........................0172 |
| | | | 発禁 はっきん prohibition of sale...........0148 |
| | | キン | 禁じる (=禁ずる) きんじる (=きんずる) prohibit |
| | | | 立入禁止 たちいりきんし Keep Out [sign] |
| | | | ...........................0067, 0039, 0042 |

| 0312 | See an *altar to the gods* (示) placed at the edge of a *forest* (林), marking off a sacred, **PRO-** |
|---|---|
| 示 113 | **HIBITED** precinct. |
| 2435 | |
| 常 13 | |

| 礼 | ¹ **ETIQUETTE**<br>² **RITE**<br><br>レイ ライ | ¹ 礼法 れいほう etiquette......................0139<br>¹ お礼 おれい thanks; reward; return present<br>¹ 礼金 れいきん reward, fee, honorarium.....0029<br>① 無礼 ぶれい impolite, rude.................0048<br>² 洗礼 せんれい baptism.......................0135 |
|---|---|---|

**0313**
示 113
禮
0724
常 5

We first saw し back at 乳 0160. From here on, we shall take it to be a *sharp hook*. At the left, ネ is the shorthand form for 示 *altar to the gods*. To remember the meanings **ETIQUETTE** and **RITE**, picture a person presenting a *sharp hook* upon the *altar* to express proper appreciation to the gods. ☞ 札 1694, 祈 0640

| 社 | ¹ **COMPANY**<br>² **SOCIETY**<br>³ **SHINTO SHRINE**<br><br>シャ<br>やしろ | ① 会社 かいしゃ company, corporation, firm...0226<br>¹ 社長 しゃちょう president (of a company)....0091<br>② 社会 しゃかい society, the world.............0226<br>² 社交的な しゃこうてきな sociable, friendly<br>...............................................0102, 0169<br>³ お社 おやしろ village shrine |
|---|---|---|

**0314**
示 113
社
0745
常 7

M3 **SHINTO SHRINE** derives from 社's original denotation of a local (thus 土) guardian deity (ネ). From the idea of the localized group one belongs to, we can obtain the other meanings **COMPANY** and **SOCIETY**.

| 申 | ¹ **REPORT (to a superior)**<br>² **SPEAK HUMBLY**<br><br>シン<br>もうす もうし- | ① 上申する じょうしんする report (to a superior)<br>...............................................0041<br>¹ 内申 ないしん unofficial report.............0215<br>② 申す もうす [humble] say, tell<br>² 申し上げる もうしあげる say, tell, speak humbly;<br>(have the honor to) do.................0041<br>² 申し込む もうしこむ apply; propose.........0192 |
|---|---|---|

**0315**
田 102

2942
常 5

申's meaning (**REPORT** or state something to a superior) is easy to see if S5 is perceived as pointing upward. 日 can be seen as the layers of hierarchy separating oneself (at the bottom) from one's superior. As a grapheme, 申 will mean either *pointing upward*, *piercing through layers*, or both. ☞ 甲 1521, 由 0432

| 神 | **GOD, spirit**<br><br>シン ジン<br>かみ かん- こう- | 神話 しんわ myth, mythology ...............0053<br>○ 神道 しんとう Shinto, the way of the gods...0158<br>神官 しんかん Shinto priest ...............0290<br>神社 じんじゃ Shinto shrine.................0314<br>○ 海の神 うみのかみ god of the sea............0106 |
|---|---|---|

**0316**
示 113
神
0821
常 9

Again see the center line in 申 point upward at something superior to oneself. ネ indicates that in 神, the superior being pointed at is **GOD**. The *on-yomi* follows 申, and adds the voiced-consonant variation ジン.

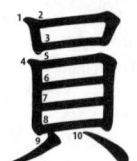

| MEMBER, personnel | 会社員 かいしゃいん company employee, office worker ........................ 0226, 0314 |
|---|---|
| | ○会員 かいいん member .................... 0226 |
| | 全員 ぜんいん all members, entire staff ..... 0078 |
| イン | 定員 ていいん fixed number of regular personnel; capacity ................... 0045 |
| | 満員電車 まんいんでんしゃ train filled to capacity .................. 0179, 0155, 0125 |

**0317**
口 30

Denotes **MEMBERS** or **personnel**, such as those of a company. Typically applied to a person who occupies a basic position and carries out mundane tasks. Indeed, we can perceive one such mundane task here—discussing sums of money. See 貝 *money* being spoken by 口 *mouth*, and associate the image with a clerk, a regular staff **MEMBER**. ☞ 買 0352

1958
常 10

| ¹ QUALITY, nature | ¹ 本質 ほんしつ essence, reality .............. 0031 |
|---|---|
| ² MATTER, substance | ①性質 せいしつ nature, character; property, quality ........................... 0128 |
| ³ PAWN, hostage | ¹ 品質 ひんしつ quality ................... 0301 |
| シツ シチ チ | ②物質 ぶっしつ matter, substance ........... 0172 |
| | ³ 人質 ひとじち hostage, prisoner ............. 0015 |

**0318**
貝 154
质
2445
常 15

Picture two *hacksaws* (斤斤) cutting open a *seashell* (貝) to obtain the **MATTER** or substance inside. More profoundly, they aim to discover the *seashell*'s inner **QUALITY** or nature. To remember M3 **PAWN**, imagine a pawnbroker slicing open a pawned oyster shell to remove the pearl after its depositor defaults on his loan.

| PARTY | ○政党 せいとう political party ................ 0246 |
|---|---|
| | 党首 とうしゅ party chief [leader] ............. 0157 |
| | 党員 とういん party member ................ 0317 |
| トウ | 党大会 とうたいかい party convention 0033, 0226 |
| | 社会党 しゃかいとう Socialist Party ..... 0314, 0226 |

**0319**
儿 10*
黨
2236
常 10

We first saw ⌳ back at 光 0137 and 当 0141. The following six kanji join ⌳ with ⌐, a combination we need to distinguish from that of ⌴ and ⌐ (as in 学 0099). By contrast with ⌴, the three lines in ⌳ are nicely centered, so where we see them above ⌐ we can see the ensemble as a crown or rooftop of formal design—we'll refer to it with the phrase "stately crown" or "stately rooftop." Beneath this decorative crown, the present entry adds 兄 1193, a simple drawing of one's OLDER BROTHER as a head with two legs attached. A *stately crown* has been placed on *older brother*'s head to mark his formal membership in a political **PARTY**.

| HALL, public building | 公会堂 こうかいどう town hall .......... 0089, 0226 |
|---|---|
| | ○食堂 しょくどう dining hall, canteen .......... 0288 |
| | 音楽堂 おんがくどう concert hall ....... 0150, 0302 |
| ドウ | 法堂 ほうどう lecture hall (in a Buddhist temple) .................................. 0139 |
| | 堂々とした どうどうとした dignified, imposing, majestic |

**0320**
土 32

In the context of the similar characters appearing before and after this one, we should make 土 our visual focus. Let it signal the idea of a physical location or place. 口 suggests an *opening* or doorway. Thus we see a *stately rooftop* over a doorway, placed on the *ground* (土), signifying a **HALL** or **public building**. ☞ 常 0321

2246
常 11

| | ¹ NORMAL<br>² REGULAR | ¹ 正常 せいじょう normality, normalcy ........0043<br>¹ 通常の つうじょうの common, ordinary, usual<br>................................................................0159<br>① 常に つねに always, at all times<br>² 常用 じょうよう common use, daily use ......0047<br>② 日常の にちじょうの daily, everyday..........0001 |
| | ジョウ<br>つね とこ- | |

| 0321<br>巾 50 | Here we see clothes *hanging* (see 吊 0206) under the *stately rooftop*. Picture a formal space that has been converted for use as a place for drying laundry. What was once an extraordinary chamber has now become just an ordinary, **NORMAL**, **REGULAR** old place. Remember, 巾 turns this usually special space from <u>formal</u> to <u>normal</u>. ☞ 堂 0320 |
| 2247 | |
| 常 11 | |

| | PRIZE, praise | 賞金 しょうきん prize, award, reward.........0029<br>賞品 しょうひん prize, trophy.................0301<br>受賞者 じゅしょうしゃ prizewinner......0065, 0107<br>○ ノーベル賞 ノーベルしょう Nobel Prize<br>賞を受ける しょうをうける receive a prize....0065 |
| | ショウ | |

| 0322<br>貝 154 | See a *stately crown* placed upon the head of a staff *member*(員): **PRIZE**. ☞ 覚 0325 |
| 2274 | |
| 常 15 | |

| | RECOMPENSE, make up for | 償金 しょうきん reparation, indemnification 0029<br>代償 だいしょう vicarious compensation ....0071<br>○ 無償 むしょう gratuitous, free.................0048<br>○ 償う つぐなう recompense, make up for, atone for |
| | ショウ<br>つぐな(う) | |

| 0323<br>人 9 | See a *prize*(賞) being offered to a *man*(亻) to **RECOMPENSE** him for some harm that he suffered. |
| 0155 | |
| 常 17 | |

| | ¹ PALM OF ONE'S HAND<br>² TAKE CHARGE OF | ① 合掌する がっしょうする join one's hands (as in<br>prayer)...................................................0227<br>¹ 掌中に しょうちゅうに in one's hands .........0035<br>¹ 掌中の玉 しょうちゅうのたま one's treasure<br>................................................................0035, 0073<br>② 車掌 しゃしょう conductor....................0125 |
| | ショウ<br>てのひら• | |

| 0324<br>手 64 | When you see ⺍, ⼍, and 口 above 手 *hand*, ignore the meaning *stately rooftop/crown* and instead see ⺍ as your fingers spread out before you, ⼍ as the balls of your fingers, and 口, right in the middle of the picture, as your **PALM**. Picture gripping something in the **PALM OF YOUR HAND**, like the steering wheel of a car, to **TAKE CHARGE OF** it. |
| 2256 | |
| 常 12 | |

**1 PERCEIVE, sense; realize**
**2 WAKE UP**
**3 COMMIT TO MEMORY**

カク
おぼ(える) さ(ます) さ(める)
さと(る)*

① 自覚する じかくする be conscious of, realize 0081
¹ 味覚 みかく sense of taste .................... 0273
② 覚める さめる [vi] awake, wake up
² 覚ます さます [vt] awake, wake up
③ 覚える おぼえる commit to memory, learn

| 0325 | |
|---|---|
| 見 147 | |
| 覺 | |
| 2258 | |
| 常 12 | |

Like the six preceding kanji, 覚 has 冖, but here ⺌ becomes ⠉, a combination we saw earlier at 学 0099. To remember 覚's meanings **WAKE UP, PERCEIVE,** and **COMMIT TO MEMORY,** see it as a picture of an eyelid, opening. ⠉ are the eyelashes and 冖 is the eyelid, opening wide for the eye to *see* (見) things, be aware of them, learn them, etc. ☞ 賞 0322

---

**AWAKE TO, comprehend**

ゴ
さと(る)

○ 覚悟する かくごする be ready for; be resigned;
　make up one's mind ....................... 0325
悟道 ごどう spiritual enlightenment; philosophy
　................................................. 0158
○ 悟り さとり satori, spiritual awakening

| 0326 | |
|---|---|
| 心 61 | |
| 0379 | |
| 常 10 | |

Like 覚, 悟 refers to **AWAKENING** and can be read さと(る). While 吾 0220 *ego/I* is used to refer to the speaking subject, 悟—adding 忄 *heart*—turns our attention to the subject's consciousness, the seat of one's **AWAKENING** and **comprehension.**

---

**SENSE, feel**

カン

○ 感じる (=感ずる) かんじる (=かんずる) be
　conscious of, feel
感心 かんしん admiration .................... 0056
同感 どうかん same sentiment, sympathy... 0182
感覚 かんかく sense, sensation, feeling ..... 0325
五感 ごかん the five senses ................ 0007

| 0327 | |
|---|---|
| 心 61 | |
| 感 | |
| 2468 | |
| 常 13 | |

Imagine the **SENSATION** as a *guided spear* (戈) rips its way past the *mouth* (口), down the throat and into the *heart* (心) (the image is grisly, but for that very reason hard to forget). See S3 as a miniature representation of the spear, poised in its proper attacking position above the mouth (its position will matter when we learn 惑 1153). ☞ 惑 1153, 憾 1216

---

**CENTER**

オウ

○ 中央 ちゅうおう center .................... 0035
中央口 ちゅうおうぐち central exit ...... 0035, 0019
中央線 ちゅうおうせん Chuo Line [central railway
　line in Tokyo] ....................... 0035, 0210
道央 どうおう central Hokkaido ............. 0158

| 0328 | |
|---|---|
| 大 37 | |
| 2944 | |
| 常 5 | |

This resembles 中 0035 in the way the piercing lines come right up through the **CENTER.** Now notice in the next three entries that 央 loses its left border as the *tsukuri* of 決 and 快, but not of 映. This is easy enough to remember if you bear in mind that 日 has no rightward-pointing stroke competing for this space.

| ¹ REFLECT ² PROJECT | ¹ 湖に山が映る みずうみにやまがうつる the mountain is reflected on the surface of the lake.................0259, 0037 |
| エイ うつ(る) うつ(す) は(える) -ば(え) | ②映画 えいが film, movie.................0176<br>² 上映する じょうえいする screen, show.......0041<br>² 映画をスクリーンに映す えいがをスクリーンにうつす project a movie on a screen.....0176<br>² 夕映え ゆうばえ evening/sunset glow.....0265 |

**0329**
日 72

映

0793
常 9

In a movie theater, the projector is placed in the *center* of the wall opposite the screen, so as to *center* the image. Let 央 here represent a projector piercing through the exact *center* of a wall to **PROJECT** light (suggested by 日) onto a screen. Also means **REFLECT**, which can be thought of as projecting an image back toward its source.

---

| DECIDE, resolve, settle | 決心 けっしん determination, resolution, decision.................0056<br>○決意 けつい resolution, determination.....0151<br>決定 けってい decision, settlement, conclusion.................0045<br>未決 みけつ undecided, to be determined 0271<br>○決める きめる decide, fix, settle |
| ケツ き(める) -ぎ(め) き(まる) | |

**0330**
水 85

決

0233
常 7

Here the surface pierced by 央 is that of *water* ( 氵). Picture a lifeguard diving right into the *center* of the *water* with firm **resolve** and **DECISIVENESS** to rescue a drowning swimmer. The meaning is suggested more by the sharp piercing of the box shape in 央 than by the idea of *center*.

---

| PLEASANT, comfortable, quick | ○快楽 かいらく pleasure, enjoyment.........0302<br>快感 かいかん agreeable sensation, comfort.................0327<br>不快な ふかいな unpleasant, disagreeable 0049<br>快走 かいそう fast running, fast sailing......0140<br>○快く こころよく cheerfully, comfortably; gladly, willingly |
| カイ こころよ(い) | |

**0331**
心 61

0218
常 7

In the *center* of one's *heart* ( 忄) there is a **PLEASANT** feeling. Remember the secondary meaning **quick** by associating **quick**, unobstructed motion with **PLEASURE** and **comfort** (see V4).

---

| ¹ DISTINGUISHED ² ENGLAND | ¹ 英明な えいめいな intelligent, wise.........0024<br>² 英国 えいこく England, Great Britain, the UK.................0075<br>②英語 えいご English.................0222<br>² 英会話 えいかいわ English conversation.................0226, 0053<br>² 和英 わえい Japanese-English [dictionary, translation, etc.].................0236 |
| エイ | |

**0332**
艸 140

1925
常 8

That *grass* ( 艹)-covered isle at the *center* of the world (or at least its time zones): **ENGLAND**. Because 英 is mostly used in reference to the English language, we base the mnemonic on **ENGLAND**, though this character's connection with **ENGLAND** is purely phonetic. Its original meaning is **DISTINGUISHED**.

| | LINE UP, place in a row; average, ordinary | 並立 へいりつ standing abreast............0067 |
|---|---|---|
| | | ○並行 へいこう parallel, going side by side; occurring together............0055 |
| | | ○並の なみの ordinary, average, mediocre |
| | ヘイ<br>なみ な(み) なら(べる) なら(ぶ)<br>なら(びに) | 並木 なみき row of trees, roadside trees....0028 |
| | | ○並べる ならべる [vt] line up, place in order; enumerate |

| **0333**<br>一 1*<br>立<br>1936<br>常 8 | All the strokes in 並 are **LINED UP** in parallel sets. The meaning extends to **average** and **ordinary**, from the idea of being in **LINE** with the standard. Now would be a good time to go back and look over 湿 0200. |
|---|---|

| | **¹ FLAT; impartial; plain**<br>**² CALM** | ①平らな道 たいらなみち level road............0158 |
|---|---|---|
| | | ¹ 公平 こうへい impartiality, fairness............0089 |
| | | ①平社員 ひらしゃいん mere clerk.......0314, 0317 |
| | ヘイ ビョウ<br>たい(ら) -だいら ひら ひら- | ¹ 平年並み へいねんなみ normal [average] year............0117, 0333 |
| | | ②平和 へいわ peace............0236 |

| **0334**<br>干 51<br>平<br>2921<br>常 5 | Marbles can be used like a spirit level to make sure a surface is **FLAT**. See 干 as a bookshelf and ⺍ as two marbles that will stop rolling (i.e., become **CALM**) once the shelf has been made completely **FLAT**. Because 平 can also denote **impartiality** or fairness, we can also let the perfectly balanced shelves suggest the "scales of Justice." ☞ 半 0335 |
|---|---|

| | **HALF** | ○半分 はんぶん half............0088 |
|---|---|---|
| | | 前半 ぜんはん (=ぜんぱん) first half............0113 |
| | | 後半 こうはん second half............0114 |
| | ハン<br>なか(ば) | 二年半 にねんはん two and a half years............0003, 0117 |
| | | ○月半ばに つきなかばに mid-month............0023 |

| **0335**<br>十 24<br>2936<br>常 5 | With ⺍ coming from above the top of the bookshelf this time, it's easier to see them as two karate chops meant to split the shelf in **HALF**. Compare with 平, in which there's no space for karate-chopping. Train your eyes to recognize marble-balancing **FLATNESS** in the previous entry, and shelf-**HALVING** karate chops in this one. ☞ 平 0334 |
|---|---|

| | **HORSE** | ○馬車 ばしゃ horse-drawn carriage, coach, wagon............0125 |
|---|---|---|
| | | 馬力 ばりき horsepower; energy, effort; cart, wagon............0084 |
| | バ<br>うま うま- ま | 馬身 ばしん horse's length............0060 |
| | | 竹馬 ちくば (=たけうま) stilts............0243 |
| | | ○馬小屋 うまごや stable............0034, 0252 |

| **0336**<br>馬 187<br>2809<br>常 10 | A **HORSE** with a long, flowing mane and galloping legs. |
|---|---|

| 尺 | **SHAKU (30.3 centimeters); measure**<br><br>シャク | 一尺 いっしゃく 1 *shaku*............................**0002**<br>°尺八 しゃくはち end-blown bamboo flute (having a traditional standard length of 1.8 *shaku*)<br>..................................................**0010**<br>尺度 しゃくど linear measure; standard .....**0280** |
|---|---|---|

**0337**
尸 44

Inside other kanji we shall usually see 尺 as a *digger* resting his chin on the handle of his shovel (S4). The independent kanji (standing for the old unit of measure **SHAKU**, and by extension **measure** in general) does not appear often, but when it does, we can picture the laborer measuring out a length of **30.3 cm** between his feet and his shovel.

2896
常 4

| 尽 | **EXHAUST, use up**<br><br>ジン<br>つ(くす) -つ(くす) -づ(くし) つ(きる)<br>つ(かす) | °尽力 じんりょく efforts, assistance ...........**0084**<br>不尽 ふじん Yours sincerely..................**0049**<br>°尽くす つくす use up, exhaust<br>言い尽くす いいつくす tell all, exhaust a subject<br>..................................................**0051**<br>尽きる つきる be exhausted; come to an end |
|---|---|---|

**0338**
尸 44*

A *digger*(尺) resting his chin on the handle of his shovel, and dripping sweat (S5–6): **EXHAUSTED**. See note at 参 1238. ☞ 冬 0360

盡
2624
常 6

| 駅 | **STATION**<br><br>エキ | °駅前の えきまえの in front of the station ....**0113**<br>当駅 とうえき this station .....................**0141**<br>駅長 えきちょう stationmaster ...............**0091**<br>駅ビル えきビル station building<br>神戸駅 こうべえき Kobe Station .......**0316, 0248** |
|---|---|---|

**0339**
馬 187

Now the *digger*(尺) is standing behind a *horse*, waiting for his commuter coach to leave the stagecoach **STATION** (駅 now refers to train **STATION**). Note from the old form how 尺 is in fact shorthand for 睪.

驛
1618
常 14

| 鳥 | **BIRD**<br><br>チョウ<br>とり | °鳥類 ちょうるい birds, fowl...................**0310**<br>白鳥 はくちょう swan......................**0076**<br>°鳥肉 とりにく chicken .....................**0216**<br>鳥居 とりい torii, Shinto shrine archway ....**0255**<br>渡り鳥 わたりどり migratory bird............**0281** |
|---|---|---|

**0340**
鳥 196

Observe a **BIRD** with a feather (S1) sticking up from its head (S3–5), and one wing extended backward (S6). It roosts over four hatchlings (S8–11), which point their beaks upward in hopes of nourishment. ☞ 烏 2281

2822
常 11

| | ISLAND | ○半島 はんとう peninsula .................... 0335 |
| --- | --- | --- |
| | | 無人島 むじんとう uninhabited island **0048**, **0015** |
| | トウ | ○島国 しまぐに island nation ............... 0075 |
| | しま | セブ島 セブとう Cebu Island |
| | | 広島 ひろしま Hiroshima (city and prefecture) |
| | | .................... 0238 |

| 0341 | A *mountain* (山) where the *bird* (鳥) alights to rest during its long migration across the sea: an **ISLAND**. |
| --- | --- |
| 山 46 | |
| 嶋 | |
| 2820 | |
| 常 10 | |

| | ¹ ANGLE, corner | ①角度 かくど angle, angular measure, degree |
| --- | --- | --- |
| | ² HORN | .................... 0280 |
| | | ¹ 三角 さんかく triangle ................ 0004 |
| | カク | ¹ 角に切る かくにきる cut into squares ....... 0086 |
| | かど つの | ①四つ角 よつかど street corner, intersection 0006 |
| | | ² ヘラジカの角 ヘラジカのつの horns of a moose [elk] |

| 0342 | See S3–7 as the head of an animal, and S1–2 as its **HORN**. **ANGLE, corner**, edge, antenna, etc. are associated meanings, any of which may apply when we come across 角 as a grapheme inside other kanji. Do not confuse S3–7 in this character with 用 0047. ☞ 色 0528 |
| --- | --- |
| 角 148 | |
| 1761 | |
| 常 7 | |

| | INSECT, worm | 成虫 せいちゅう imago .................... 0070 |
| --- | --- | --- |
| | | ○防虫 ぼうちゅう insect proof, insect repelling |
| | チュウ | .................... 0174 |
| | むし | 毒虫 どくむし poisonous insect ............. 0133 |
| | | ○虫取り むしとり bug catching ............. 0059 |
| | | 水虫 みずむし athlete's foot ............... 0027 |

| 0343 | A rather fantastic depiction of an **INSECT**, but nonetheless morphologically sound: a tail at the bottom, two bulging eyeballs in the middle, and an antenna at the top. As a grapheme in other characters, 虫 will mean either *insect* or *worm*. |
| --- | --- |
| 虫 142 | |
| 蟲 | |
| 2959 | |
| 常 6 | |

| | TOUCH; come in contact with | ○触覚 しょっかく sense of touch ............... 0325 |
| --- | --- | --- |
| | | 触角 しょっかく feeler, antenna ............. 0342 |
| | | 感触 かんしょく (sense of) touch, feeling .... 0327 |
| | ショク | ○触れる ふれる touch, feel; come into contact with |
| | ふ(れる) さわ(る) | ○触る さわる touch, feel |

| 0344 | Etch 触's meaning in your memory by imagining what it would feel like to **TOUCH** this *insect* (虫)'s *antenna* (角) with the tip of your finger. **TOUCH** the tip of your pencil with your fingertip as you observe this *insect's antenna*. ☞ 蟹 2294 |
| --- | --- |
| 角 148 | |
| 觸 | |
| 1376 | |
| 常 13 | |

|  | ¹ TAKE APART<br>² DISSOLVE<br>³ CLARIFY, solve<br><br>カイ ゲ<br>と(く) と(かす) と(ける) | 解体 かいたい dismantling; dissolution;<br>　　dissection................................0062<br>○分解する ぶんかいする take apart; analyze,<br>　　decompose.............................0088<br>解禁 かいきん removal of a ban.............0312<br>解明する かいめいする explain, elucidate....0024<br>○解ける とける [vi] come loose, come undone;<br>　　be solved |
|---|---|---|

| **0345**<br>角 148<br>解<br>1375<br>常 13 | Horn (角) + cut (刀) + cattle (牛). Our job is to **TAKE APART** the cattle, and the first step is to cut off their horn. With this image of dissecting we can associate **DISSOLVING**, as in liquefying a solid, or disbanding a rock group. From there it is not far to the additional meanings **solve** (a problem) and **CLARIFY** (that which is difficult to understand). |
|---|---|

|  | **ALONE, by oneself**<br><br>ドク<br>ひと(り) | ①独立 どくりつ independence, self-reliance...0067<br>¹独身 どくしん single life; celibacy............0060<br>¹独学 どくがく self-study, self-teaching.......0099<br>¹独りぼっちの ひとりぼっちの solitary<br>②日独 にちどく Japan and Germany, Japanese-<br>　　German.................................0001 |
|---|---|---|

| **0346**<br>犬 94<br>獨<br>0354<br>常 9 | Picture an insect (虫)-infested dog (犭) left all **ALONE**. As a remnant of its use in the obsolete kanji transliteration for Germany (独逸, どいつ), 独 is used today in advertising, newspaper headlines, etc., as a space-saving sign for Deutschland. A selected list of kanji abbreviations for countries and regions appears in Appendix 5. |
|---|---|

|  | **SHOP**<br><br>テン<br>みせ | 店長 てんちょう shop manager..............0091<br>○店員 てんいん clerk.......................0317<br>書店 しょてん bookstore...................0079<br>本店 ほんてん main store, head office......0031<br>○お店 おみせ shop, your shop |
|---|---|---|

| **0347**<br>广 53<br><br><br>2657<br>常 8 | See a **SHOP** clerk (S4) standing behind a counter (S6–8), with one arm outstretched (S5) to display an item of merchandise. A slanting roof (广) covers the **SHOP**. |
|---|---|

|  | ¹ OCCUPY, hold<br>² DIVINE<br><br>セン<br>し(める) うらな(う) | ①独占 どくせん exclusive possession, monopoly<br>　　......................................0346<br>¹国家独占 こっかどくせん state monopoly<br>　　.............................0075, 0219, 0346<br>①占める しめる occupy, hold<br>¹独り占め ひとりじめ monopoly, exclusive<br>　　possession.............................0346<br>②占う うらなう divine, tell (someone's) fortune |
|---|---|---|

| **0348**<br>卜 25<br><br><br>1729<br>常 5 | This open-air shop is perfect for a Japanese fortune-teller, who plies his trade over a small table on the sidewalk. See him reach out not to show you merchandise, but to take your hand, in which he'll **DIVINE** your future. Visualize M1 **OCCUPY** by picturing the diviner **holding** down a particularly coveted piece of sidewalk along a busy avenue. ☞ 古 0254 |
|---|---|

| | **POINT, dot** | ○出発点 しゅっぱつてん starting point...0038, 0148 |
|---|---|---|
| | | 点字 てんじ Braille..........................0098 |
| | | 同点 どうてん tie, draw; tie score..........0182 |
| | テン | 点と線 てんとせん points and lines.........0210 |
| | | その点について そのてんについて on that<br>point, in that respect |

| **0349** | Now ignore "fortune-teller" and see the four lines of ⺍ all converging toward a single imagi- |
|---|---|
| 火 86* | nary **POINT** at the center of 口. |

黑占

1793
常 9

---

| | **¹ MILITARY MAN** | ①武士 ぶし samurai, warrior ..................0111 |
|---|---|---|
| | **² MAN OF LEARNING, professional suffix** | ¹ 武士道 ぶしどう the way of the warrior |
| | | ..........................................0111, 0158 |
| | | ² 名士 めいし man of distinction ..............0269 |
| | シ | ² 国士 こくし distinguished citizen............0075 |
| | | ² 力士 りきし sumo wrestler....................0084 |

| **0350** | Compare with 土 0030 SOIL. In the greater length of the crossing stroke here, see a long |
|---|---|
| 士 33 | spear held in the hands of a **MILITARY MAN**, standing on the horizon. Remember: the upper |
| | stroke is longer in **MILITARY MAN** (emphasizing the spear), the lower stroke longer in SOIL |
| | (emphasizing the soil). 士 may also mean **MAN OF LEARNING**. ☞ 土 0030 |

2877
常 3

---

| | **TRADE, commerce** | 商工 しょうこう commerce and industry .....0108 |
|---|---|---|
| | | ○商品 しょうひん goods, products, commodities |
| | | ..........................................0301 |
| | | 商店 しょうてん shop, store ...................0347 |
| | ショウ | ○商う あきなう sell, trade in |
| | あきな(う) | 商い中 あきないちゅう Open [store sign].....0035 |

| **0351** | Here we observe *standing man* (立) holding out 岡, which you can visualize as a wide basket |
|---|---|
| 口 30 | in which he displays his merchandise (to remember how to write 商, it helps to think of |
| | his having *four* [四] little boxes [口] of merchandise). Associate this image with the idea of |
| | conducting **TRADE**. |

1818
常 11

---

| | **BUY** | ○買う かう buy |
|---|---|---|
| | | 買い手 かいて buyer, customer .............0046 |
| | | ○買い物 かいもの shopping; purchases ......0172 |
| | バイ | 買い入れ かいいれ purchase, buying........0039 |
| | か(う) | 買い上げる かいあげる buy, buy up; bid up |
| | | ..........................................0041 |

| **0352** | 罒 looks like 目 0021 laid on its side, but when it appears sideways, it usually means not *eye* |
|---|---|
| 貝 154 | but *net*. Here the *net* represents a shopping bag. 貝 in turn represents shopping *money*, so |
| | together they easily suggest **BUY**. A sample *on-yomi* compound appears in the next entry. |
| | ☞ 員 0317 |

2252
常 12

**売** SELL

バイ
う(る) う(れる)

○商売 しょうばい trade, business, commerce 0351
売買 ばいばい buying and selling, trade.... 0352
売店 ばいてん booth, stand; store.......... 0347
○売る うる sell
売り切れ うりきれ sellout; sold out.......... 0086

**0353**
士 33*

賣

1878
常 7

In the old form 賣, we can see a *man of learning* (士) at the opposite end of the transaction implied in 買 BUY, thus indicating **SELL** (a typical case of "simplification" rendering a kanji less intuitive and thus harder for us to learn). Overcome this by seeing 士 hold out merchandise in 宀 (recalling 商 0351), which then spreads widely (儿) among the public.

---

**続** CONTINUE

ゾク
つづ(く) つづ(ける)

○続行 ぞっこう continuation.................. 0055
続出する ぞくしゅつする appear in succession
.................................................. 0038
○続く つづく [vi] continue, follow, ensue
手続き てつづき procedure, formalities .... 0046
話し続ける はなしつづける keep talking .... 0053

**0354**
糸 120

續

1244
常 13

In the same sense that *thread* (糸) suggests LINE in 線 0210, it can also lend connotations of *continuity*, as it does here. Adding it to the previous entry, we picture a merchant *selling thread* that **CONTINUES** to reel off the spool interminably. Paint an exaggerated mental picture of the threadmonger whose thread just goes on without end. ☞ 継 0848

---

**読** READ

ドク トク トウ
よ(む) -よ(み)

読者 どくしゃ reader, subscriber ............ 0107
読本 とくほん reader, reading book ........ 0031
○読書 どくしょ reading a book, reading....... 0079
○読む よむ read
読み方 よみかた way of reading; reading (of a Chinese character) .......................... 0173

**0355**
言 149

讀

1401
常 14

Picture a *seller* (売) of *words* (言)—your local newsstand clerk or used book seller—purveying materials for us to **READ**.

---

**共** JOINT, together

キョウ
とも とも(に) -ども

公共の こうきょうの public, common ........ 0089
○共通の きょうつうの common, mutual....... 0159
共和国 きょうわこく republic............. 0236, 0075
○母子共に ぼしともに both mother and child
................................................. 0104, 0094
私共 わたくしども [humble] we .............. 0237

**0356**
八 12

2122
常 6

For a good image of a **JOINT** effort, picture 共 as two people competing in a three-legged race: their arms are stretched over each other's shoulders for balance (S1), and they are tied together at the waist (S4). Only the outer two legs are visible. When 共 appears as a grapheme, we shall often use its secondary meaning **together**.

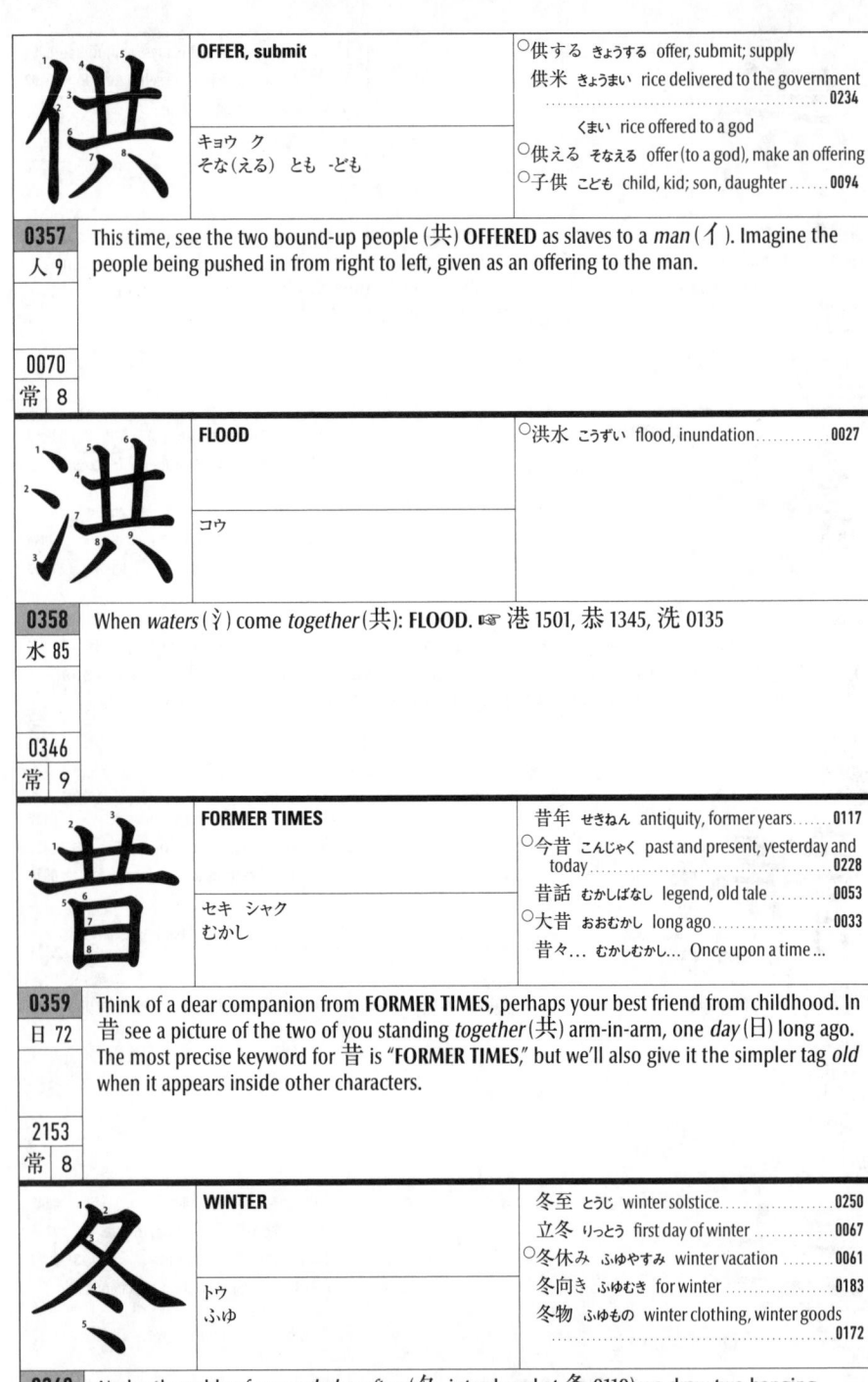

**供** OFFER, submit

キョウ ク
そな(える) とも -ども

○供する きょうする offer, submit; supply
供米 きょうまい rice delivered to the government ....................0234
くまい rice offered to a god
○供える そなえる offer (to a god), make an offering
○子供 こども child, kid; son, daughter .......0094

| 0357 | This time, see the two bound-up people (共) **OFFERED** as slaves to a *man* (イ). Imagine the people being pushed in from right to left, given as an offering to the man. |
| 人 9 | |
| 0070 | |
| 常 8 | |

**洪** FLOOD

コウ

○洪水 こうずい flood, inundation ............0027

| 0358 | When *waters* (氵) come *together* (共): **FLOOD.** ☞ 港 1501, 恭 1345, 洗 0135 |
| 水 85 | |
| 0346 | |
| 常 9 | |

**昔** FORMER TIMES

セキ シャク
むかし

昔年 せきねん antiquity, former years ......0117
○今昔 こんじゃく past and present, yesterday and today ...........................0228
昔話 むかしばなし legend, old tale ..........0053
○大昔 おおむかし long ago ......................0033
昔々... むかしむかし... Once upon a time ...

| 0359 | Think of a dear companion from **FORMER TIMES**, perhaps your best friend from childhood. In 昔 see a picture of the two of you standing *together* (共) arm-in-arm, one *day* (日) long ago. The most precise keyword for 昔 is "**FORMER TIMES**," but we'll also give it the simpler tag *old* when it appears inside other characters. |
| 日 72 | |
| 2153 | |
| 常 8 | |

**冬** WINTER

トウ
ふゆ

冬至 とうじ winter solstice ....................0250
立冬 りっとう first day of winter ............0067
○冬休み ふゆやすみ winter vacation ........0061
冬向き ふゆむき for winter ....................0183
冬物 ふゆもの winter clothing, winter goods ...........................0172

| 0360 | Under the gable of an *angled rooftop* (夂, introduced at 条 0119) we draw two hanging icicles to mean **WINTER**. The easiest way to remember the *on-yomi* for this and the other season kanji is to learn the four-season compound 春夏秋冬 listed at 秋 0364. Also, see the note at 参 1238. ☞ 寒 0361, 修 1676, 尽 0338 |
| 冫 15 | |
| 1851 | |
| 常 5 | |

| | | |
|---|---|---|
|  | **COLD**<br><br>カン<br>さむ(い) | 寒中 かんちゅう midwinter...................0035<br>防寒する ぼうかんする protect from cold....0174<br>○寒気 かんき cold, cold weather.............0126<br>　さむけ chill<br>○寒い さむい cold, chilly |

| 0361 | Icicles in the gable may indicate winter, but icicles <u>inside the house</u> signify true **COLD**. Under 宀 *roof* we see two people bundled *together* (共), with an extra stroke binding their bodies together for extra warmth. And <u>still</u> two icicles hang between their legs. See note at 参 1238. ☞ 冬 0360, 塞 2232 |
|---|---|
| 宀 40 | |
| 2011 | |
| 常 12 | |

| | | |
|---|---|---|
|  | **SPRING**<br><br>シュン<br>はる | 来春 らいしゅん next spring...................0274<br>春分 しゅんぶん vernal equinox.............0088<br>青春 せいしゅん bloom of youth.............0130<br>売春 ばいしゅん prostitution.................0353<br>○春休み はるやすみ spring vacation..........0061 |

| 0362 | Picture the two diagonal strokes as two hands playing the strings of a koto, out in the *sun*shine (日) of **SPRING** after a long winter of practicing indoors. Remember that this koto (表) has <u>three</u> strings, as in 三月 (さんがつ, March), **SPRING**'s first month. |
|---|---|
| 日 72 | |
| 2232 | |
| 常 9 | |

| | | |
|---|---|---|
|  | **SUMMER**<br><br>カ ゲ<br>なつ | 立夏 りっか first day of summer.............0067<br>夏至 げし summer solstice...................0250<br>○夏休み なつやすみ summer vacation........0061<br>夏向き なつむき for summer..................0183<br>常夏 とこなつ everlasting summer...........0321 |

| 0363 | This entry looks like 頁 0156 (grapheme meaning: *head*), only with *crossed legs* (夂). Let this version's more relaxed position remind you of **SUMMER**, the season for rest. Now a reminder about 夂: while at the bottom of a kanji it means *crossed legs*, at the top of a kanji it means *angled rooftop*, as in 冬 above. ☞ 憂 0779, 頁 0156 |
|---|---|
| 夂 35 | |
| 1815 | |
| 常 10 | |

| | | |
|---|---|---|
|  | **AUTUMN**<br><br>シュウ<br>あき | 秋分 しゅうぶん autumnal equinox..........0088<br>今秋 こんしゅう this [next] autumn...........0228<br>○この秋 このあき this [next] autumn<br>春秋 しゅんじゅう spring and autumn; years, age<br>..............................................0362<br>○春夏秋冬 しゅんかしゅうとう four seasons, all year round...........................0362, 0363, 0360 |

| 0364 | At the left, we see a bundled *rice sheaf*, suggesting the completion of the harvest. At the right, a *fire* burns the grain stubble to clear the land for next year's planting. The season is **AUTUMN**. |
|---|---|
| 禾 115 | |
| 穐 | |
| 1054 | |
| 常 9 | |

| | | |
|---|---|---|
| **¹ MAIN**<br>**² LORD, master** | ¹ 主語 しゅご [grammar] subject.............0222 |
| | ① 主に おもに mainly, chiefly; mostly |
| シュ ス | ② 主人 しゅじん master, proprietor; husband...0015 |
| ぬし おも あるじ* | ② 家主 やぬし landlord, landlady.............0219 |
| | ² 買い主 かいぬし buyer, purchaser.............0352 |

**0365**
、 3

主

1696
常 5

This kanji derives from a drawing of an oil lamp or vigil light burned in reverence to a god (S1 is the flame). To remember its modern meaning, simply replace "god" with **LORD**. MAIN is an associated meaning, as in "the **MAIN** man."

---

| | | |
|---|---|---|
| **LIVE, inhabit** | ○ 住所 じゅうしょ one's dwelling, address......0249 |
| | 住居 じゅうきょ house, dwelling, address....0255 |
| | 居住する きょじゅうする live, dwell, reside...0255 |
| ジュウ | ○ どこに住んでいますか どこにすんでいますか |
| す(む) す(まう) -ず(まい) | Where do you live? |
| | 住まい すまい living; dwelling, house |

**0366**
人 9

住

0047
常 7

In the next few characters, see 主 not as "lord" but as the vigil light itself. Here we observe a *man* who has returned to where the *vigil light* burns for him: the place where he **LIVES**. Note carefully the differences between this kanji and the *small bird* grapheme (隹). ☞ 往 0866, 任 0372

---

| | | |
|---|---|---|
| **STATIONED** | 駐日 ちゅうにち stationed in Japan.............0001 |
| | 駐英 ちゅうえい stationed in England........0332 |
| | ○ 駐車する ちゅうしゃする park a car ..........0125 |
| チュウ | 駐車禁止 ちゅうしゃきんし No Parking [sign] |
| | .................0125, 0312, 0042 |

**0367**
馬 187

駐

1622
常 15

Here we see a *horse* (馬) tied out in front next to the *vigil light* (主), indicating that someone will be staying for the night. This character refers to the **STATIONING** of troops or officials. It also refers to the act of parking a car or bicycle, analogous to tying up one's horse.

---

| | | |
|---|---|---|
| **¹ POUR**<br>**² CONCENTRATE, pay attention to** | ¹ 注入する ちゅうにゅうする pour into, inject...0039 |
| | ① 注ぎ込む そそぎこむ pour into, instill .......0192 |
| | ② 注意 ちゅうい attention, care, advice ........0151 |
| チュウ | ² 注目 ちゅうもく attention, notice.............0021 |
| そそ(ぐ) | 注文する ちゅうもんする order, place an order; |
| | request...................................0101 |

**0368**
水 85

注

0287
常 8

Here *water* (氵) is **POURED** on the flame of the vigil light (主). This character also means **CONCENTRATE**, in the sense of **POURING** all one's attention into (something).

| | AMBITION, aim | ○意志 いし will, volition ..................... 0151 |
|---|---|---|
| | | 志向 しこう intention, aim; orientation ..... 0183 |
| | | 同志 どうし like-minded person, comrade .. 0182 |
| | シ | ○志す こころざす aim, have an ambition for |
| | こころざ(す) こころざし | 志を立てる こころざしをたてる set one's mind on (something) ...................... 0067 |

**0369**
心 61

What is **AMBITION**, other than one's *heart* (心), one's spirit, **aiming** upward at something? In 志 we have a vivid picture of this very thing, though to take advantage of it we'll have to ignore the semantic value of 士 this time, and see it as a pointer (or "**aimer**"). Note that the grapheme 士 usually appears at the top, 土 at the bottom or left.

1881
常 | 7

| | MAGAZINE, document | 誌面 しめん page of a magazine ............ 0175 |
|---|---|---|
| | | 誌上て しじょうて in a magazine ........... 0041 |
| | | ニューズウィーク誌 ニューズウィークし *Newsweek* |
| | シ | 日誌 にっし diary ......................... 0001 |
| | | 地誌 ちし topography, geographical description ...................... 0187 |

**0370**
言 149

This character suggests putting down one's *aims* (志) in *words* (言), that is, **documenting** them. It now mostly refers to periodical documents such as **MAGAZINES**. ☞ 記 0427

1406
常 | 14

| | ¹ SERVE | ¹仕官 しかん entering the government service |
|---|---|---|
| | ² DO | ..................... 0290 |
| | | ①仕える つかえる serve (under) |
| | | ②仕事 しごと work, employment, business ... 0080 |
| | シ ジ | ² 仕方 しかた way, method, means .......... 0173 |
| | つか(える) | ² 仕手 して doer; protagonist in a Noh drama |
| | | ..................... 0046 |

**0371**
人 9

See the ordinary *man* (亻) at the left **SERVING** the *man of learning* (士) at the right. Its primary *on-yomi* being シ, 仕 was chosen to stand in for the -ます base of the verb する (**DO**) in kanji compounds such as those in V3–5 (in V3, for example, する 事 becomes 仕事). We may thus think of the ordinary *man* **DOING** something for the *man of learning*. ☞ 任 0372

0021
常 | 5

| | ¹ OFFICE, duty | ①任命 にんめい appointment, nomination ... 0232 |
|---|---|---|
| | ² ENTRUST, leave (up) to | ¹ 主任 しゅにん person in charge, head, chief 0365 |
| | | ¹ 後任 こうにん successor, replacement ....... 0114 |
| | ニン | ②任せる まかせる leave (up) to, entrust with; leave alone |
| | まか(せる) まか(す) | ² 任意の にんいの optional, voluntary; arbitrary |
| | | ..................... 0151 |

**0372**
人 9

壬 resembles 王 *king* but ranks lower: *courtier*. Picture him as a *man of learning* (士) wearing a special headdress (S3 here) to mark his courtly status. This entry shows a *man* (亻) *courtier*, to whom the king **ENTRUSTS** certain **duties/OFFICES**. Compare with the role of the *woman courtier* (see 妊 1845). ☞ 住 0366, 仕 0371

0038
常 | 6

| | |
|---|---|
| **¹BRANCH** | ①支店 してん branch [office/store] .......... 0347 |
| **²SUPPORT, prop up** | ² 支出 ししゅつ expenditure, disbursement....0038 |
| **³BE OBSTRUCTED** | ² 支度する したくする arrange, prepare.......0280 |
| シ | ②支える ささえる support, prop up |
| ささ(える) つか(える) か(う) | ³ つかえる be blocked, be obstructed |

| | |
|---|---|
| **0373** | Start with M1 and M2. These meanings can best be captured by seeing a *hand* propping up (i.e., |
| 支 65 | SUPPORTING) a **BRANCH** (see S1–2, which resemble the plant in 先 minus the leaf and roots, as a |
| | small branch). The key is to see the action of supporting or propping up. Also, because 支 lends |
| | the idea of *skill* to a couple of more complex kanji in which it appears, this image of a hand |
| 1717 | holding up a branch should also suggest the idea of *skillful manipulation*. Note that 支 actually |
| 常 4 | refers to branches of stores, banks, etc.; for those of trees we must use 枝 0965. To perceive M3 **BE** |
| | **OBSTRUCTED**, picture the *hand* choking the *branch*, OBSTRUCTING its escape. ☞ 皮 0595, 枝 0965 |

| | |
|---|---|
| **COUNTER, against, anti-** | ○反発する はんぱつする repulse, repel; oppose |
| | .........0148 |
| | 反日 はんにち anti-Japanese.................0001 |
| | 反する はんする oppose; act contrary to |
| ハン ホン タン | ○反る そる [vi] bend, warp, lean backward |
| そ(る) そ(らす) | 反らす そらす [vt] bend (backward), warp |

| | |
|---|---|
| **0374** | Imagine putting your *hand* (又) against this *cliff* (厂) and pushing with all your might. No |
| 又 29 | matter how hard you push, the *cliff* **COUNTERS** your force. As a grapheme inside other char- |
| | acters, 反 may also mean *oppose*, *opposite*, or *against*. ☞ 皮 0595, 友 0399 |
| 2549 | |
| 常 4 | |

| | |
|---|---|
| **SLOPE** | 坂道 さかみち incline, sloping road..........0158 |
| | ○上り坂 のぼりざか uphill, upward slope.....0041 |
| | 下り坂 くだりざか downhill, downward slope |
| ハン | .................................................0040 |
| さか | |

| | |
|---|---|
| **0375** | Denotes a place where the *earth* (土) *opposes* (反) our forward motion: a **SLOPE**. A sample |
| 土 32 | *on-yomi* compound appears at 登 1054. |
| 0206 | |
| 常 7 | |

| | |
|---|---|
| **SLOPE** | ○大阪 おおさか Osaka (city and prefecture)...0033 |
| | 大阪府 おおさかふ Osaka prefecture...0033, 0247 |
| | ○阪神 はんしん Osaka and Kobe .............0316 |
| ハン | 阪大 はんだい Osaka University ............0033 |
| さか | |

| | |
|---|---|
| **0376** | This time our forward motion is *opposed* (反) by *hills* (阝). This character also means **SLOPE**, |
| 阜 170 | but is used today only in the place name 大阪 (おおさか), or as an abbreviation for it. |
| 0243 | |
| 常 7 | |

| 飯 | ¹ COOKED RICE<br>² MEAL<br><br>ハン<br>めし | ○ご飯 ごはん boiled rice; meal<br>² 朝飯 あさめし (=あさはん) breakfast............0145<br>² 夕飯 ゆうはん (=ゆうめし) evening meal, supper<br>..........................................................0265<br>² 飯店 はんてん (high-class) Chinese restaurant;<br>hotel (in China)..................................0347<br>² 飯を食う めしをくう eat/devour a meal......0288 |

**0377**
食 184
飯
1509
常 12

The construction *"food-against"* can easily bring to mind **COOKED RICE** if we think of rice as a kind of foil or contrast to the other parts of a meal, giving occasional relief to the palate from the spicier flavors. Also, we often physically place other *foods against* rice in order to eat them together. Rice being the staple food, 飯 can also mean **MEAL**.

| 返 | **RETURN, send back**<br><br>ヘン<br>かえ(す) -かえ(す) かえ(る) -かえ(る) | 返金 へんきん repayment.....................0029<br>返信 へんしん reply, answer................0063<br>○返事 へんじ reply, answer..................0080<br>○返す かえす return, send back<br>返る かえる be restored to, return |

**0378**
辵 162

2633
常 7

Suggests *conveying* (辶) something in the *opposite* (反) direction, i.e., **RETURNING**/sending back.

| 雑 | ¹ MISCELLANEOUS<br>² MIXED<br><br>ザツ ゾウ | ① 雑誌 ざっし magazine, journal..............0370<br>¹ 雑木 ぞうき miscellaneous trees...........0028<br>² 雑居地 ざっきょち mixed residential quarter<br>...............................................0255, 0187<br>² 雑音 ざつおん noise; interference, static ...0150<br>雑な ざつな coarse, rough, crude |

**0379**
隹 172
雑
1267
常 14

Picture a **MISCELLANEOUS MIX** of *nine* (九) *small birds* (隹) in a *tree* (木).

|  | **DISORDERED, excessive**<br><br>ラン<br>みだ(れる) みだ(す) | ○乱れる みだれる be disordered, be confused; be<br>chaotic<br>乱雑 らんざつ disorder, confusion...........0379<br>乱用 らんよう abuse, misuse, misappropriation<br>..........................................................0047<br>○反乱 はんらん rebellion, revolt...............0374<br>乱読 らんどく indiscriminate reading........0355 |

**0380**
乙 5
亂
1161
常 7

Recall *sharp hook* (乚) from 礼 0313. To remember the meaning **DISORDERED**, picture a rebellious person whose *tongue* (舌) is pierced with a *sharp hook*. In compounds where it means **excessive**, 乱 is interchangeable with 濫 2030. ☞ 濫 2030

| 寸 ² ¹ ³ | ¹ **A BIT OF**<br>² *SUN* (3.03 cm)<br><br>スン | ①寸前に すんぜんに immediately before......0113<br>¹ 一寸 ちょっと a little bit........................0002<br>² いっすん 1 *sun*<br>②寸法 すんぽう measurements, size; plan....0139<br>² 原寸 げんすん full [actual] size..............0208 |
|---|---|---|

| **0381**<br>寸 41 | At 付 0064 we learned to see 寸 as a man reaching out his arm (S1), carrying a small object (S3). Here our focus is on the small object, for 寸 by itself means "**A BIT OF**" (or, when giving a precise measure, *SUN* [3.03 cm]). When we find 寸 inside other characters, we'll generally focus in one way or another on the *outstretched arm*. |
|---|---|

| **2541**<br>常 3 |
|---|

---

| 寺 | **BUDDHIST TEMPLE**<br><br>ジ<br>てら | 古寺 こじ old temple........................0254<br>国分寺 こくぶんじ state-established provincial<br>　temple................................0075, 0088<br>東大寺 とうだいじ Todaiji [temple]....0032, 0033<br>○お寺 おてら (Buddhist) temple<br>山寺 やまでら mountain temple............0037 |
|---|---|---|

| **0382**<br>寸 41 | See 寸 as a man carrying a small offering to a certain precinct of *land* (土). It must be the **BUDDHIST TEMPLE**. |
|---|---|

| **1853**<br>常 6 |
|---|

---

| 時 | **TIME**<br><br>ジ<br>とき -どき | ○同時に どうじに simultaneously, at the same<br>　time..................................0182<br>一時 いちじ for a time, temporarily; once; one<br>　o'clock................................0002<br>ひととき (=いっとき) time, while, moment<br>時代 じだい age, era, period; antiquity.....0071<br>寸時 すんじ a moment, a minute............0381 |
|---|---|---|

| **0383**<br>日 72 | It is said that in ancient China, **TIME** was kept by sundials located within the precincts of temples. Here then, picture the *sun* (日) showing the **TIME** by shining on a *temple* (寺). |
|---|---|

| **0830**<br>常 10 |
|---|

---

| 持 | **HOLD, have, keep**<br><br>ジ<br>も(つ) -も(ち) も(てる) | ○持つ もつ hold, have; keep, maintain<br>所持する しょじする have about one; possess<br>　........................................0249<br>○支持する しじする support, maintain, back up<br>　........................................0373<br>金持ち かねもち wealthy person.............0029<br>気持ち きもち feeling, sensation, mood....0126 |
|---|---|---|

| **0384**<br>手 64 | 扌 returns us to the image of the man carrying his offering, **HOLDING** it in his *hands*. As any *temple* (寺) might exhort us, let us not go to the *temple* empty-*handed*; we must **have** something with us. |
|---|---|

| **0333**<br>常 9 |
|---|

| 特 | SPECIAL<br><br>トク | ○特別の とくべつの special, particular; extra-ordinary...........0090<br>特定の とくていの specific, particular.......0045<br>特集 とくしゅう special edition, feature (article)...........0373<br>独特な どくとくな peculiar, unique....0346<br>特に とくに particularly, especially |

**0385** 牛 93 — For a memorable image of a truly **SPECIAL** situation, picture a *cow* (牛) walking into the *temple* (寺) and joining in the worship service.

0852 常 10

| 待 | WAIT (for), treat<br><br>タイ<br>ま(つ) -ま(ち) | 待命 たいめい waiting for orders...........0232<br>○待つ まつ wait<br>待ち合わせる まちあわせる wait, meet by appointment...........0227<br>待合室 まちあいしつ waiting room....0227, 0253<br>信号待ち しんごうまち waiting for a traffic light...........0063, 0300 |

**0386** 彳 60 — *Go* (彳) to the *temple* (寺) and **WAIT** for the worship service to begin. ☞ 得 0387, 徒 0870

0323 常 9

| 得 | ¹ ACQUIRE<br>² GAIN, benefit<br><br>トク<br>え(る) う(る) | ①取得する しゅとくする acquire, gain; purchase...........0059<br>² 得意 とくい one's forte; pride; customer....0151<br>² 得になる とくになる bring profit, do (someone) good<br>○得る える (=うる) acquire, gain; can, be able to<br>止むを得ない やむをえない unavoidable...0042 |

**0387** 彳 60 — 旦 1392 shows the sun coming up over the horizon and means **DAWN**. We can thus take the present entry as a kanji version of the expression "the early bird catches the worm": one gets up at *dawn* (旦), goes out (彳), reaches out with one's arm (寸), and **ACQUIRES** something (得). In short, "the dawn goer reaches out and **ACQUIRES**." ☞ 待 0386, 獲 1659

0435 常 11

| 侍 | ¹ ATTEND UPON<br>² SAMURAI<br><br>ジ<br>さむらい | ①近侍 きんじ attendant...........0194<br>¹ 侍女 じじょ lady attendant...........0093<br>² 犬侍 いぬざむらい shameless/depraved samurai...........0293 |

**0388** 人 9 — See a *man* (亻) serving in **ATTENDANCE** at a *temple* (寺). This image of a man serving is one we can easily associate with the second meaning, **SAMURAI**.

0066 常 8

| | POETRY | ○詩人 しじん poet .................................... 0015 |
|---|---|---|
| | | 詩集 ししゅう anthology of poems ........... 0190 |
| | | 詩的な してきな poetic ........................... 0169 |
| シ | | 詩を作る しをつくる compose a poem ...... 0152 |

| 0389 | The beauty and expression of religious sentiment found in scripture surely earn it a place in |
|---|---|
| 言 149 | the most sublime literary genre: *words* (言) of the *temple* (寺) are **POETRY**. ☞ 詠 1693 |
| 1384 | |
| 常 13 | |

| | ¹ IMMEDIATE | ¹ 即売 そくばい spot sale ......................... 0353 |
|---|---|---|
| | ² NAMELY, that is | ¹ 即時 そくじ immediately, promptly ......... 0383 |
| | | ¹ 即金 そっきん immediate cash ............... 0029 |
| | ソク | ①即席 そくせき impromptu; instant ........... 0279 |
| | すなわ(ち)* | ² (A)、即ち (B) (エー)、すなわち(ビー) A, namely [that is], B |

| 0390 | Recall 卩 *seal/stamp*, introduced back at 印 0231. At the left we find the five-stroke *hen* form |
|---|---|
| 卩 26 | of 艮, which here reverts to its visual meaning of *little boy* (see 限 0282). Picture a *little boy* |
| 卽 | who likes to *stamp* things the very instant they are placed before him. As you look at the |
| | character, imagine placing a piece of paper before the boy and his **IMMEDIATELY** (即) stamp- |
| 1036 | ing it. Learn the second meaning **NAMELY** by extension from **IMMEDIATELY**: to say "**NAMELY**" |
| 常 7 | is to say "I will now **IMMEDIATELY** tell you the specific thing I refer to." ☞ 既 1820, 却 0733 |

| | ¹ JOINT, node | ①竹の節 たけのふし node [joint] of a bamboo... 0243 |
|---|---|---|
| | ² SECTION, space; space out, economize | ②節電 せつでん saving electricity ............. 0155 |
| | ³ SEASON, time | ² 前の節て まえのせつて in the former section [stanza] ................................................. 0113 |
| | セツ セチ | ③時節 じせつ season, times; occasion ........ 0383 |
| | ふし -ぶし | ³ 節分 せつぶん eve of the beginning of spring, close of winter ..................................... 0088 |

| 0391 | From *bamboo* (⺮) and *immediately* (即) we obtain the idea of two **SECTIONS** of a *bamboo* |
|---|---|
| 竹 118 | shoot that are *immediately* next to each other. The Chinese in fact made this character to |
| 節 | refer to the **JOINTS** between bamboo sections, as well as to the **SECTIONS** themselves. Being |
| | a good representation of evenly **spaced SECTIONS**, this came also to signify **space out** or |
| 2349 | **economize**, as well as **SEASON**. But it still refers to **JOINTS** or **nodes**, such as the knuckles on |
| 常 13 | the fingers that are holding this book, which resemble **SECTIONS** of bamboo. ☞ 筋 0392 |

| | ¹ MUSCLE; sinew | ①筋肉 きんにく muscle, sinews ................. 0216 |
|---|---|---|
| | ² THREADLIKE STRUCTURE, thread | ¹ 心筋 しんきん myocardium, heart muscle... 0056 |
| | | ² 背筋 せすじ spinal column ..................... 0124 |
| | キン | ②筋道 すじみち reason, thread (of an argument), coherence; systematic method ............. 0158 |
| | すじ | ² 筋書き すじがき plot (of a story), outline; plan .......................................................... 0079 |

| 0392 | This kanji suggests something tough and fibrous like *bamboo* (⺮) that gives *flesh* (月) its |
|---|---|
| 竹 118 | *strength* (力): in short, **MUSCLE** or **sinew**. With the image of **MUSCLE**'s fibrous tissue we can |
| 筋 | associate the more general idea of **THREADLIKE STRUCTURE**, such as coherent logic or plot |
| | (see V4–5). ☞ 節 0391 |
| 2337 | |
| 常 12 | |

| 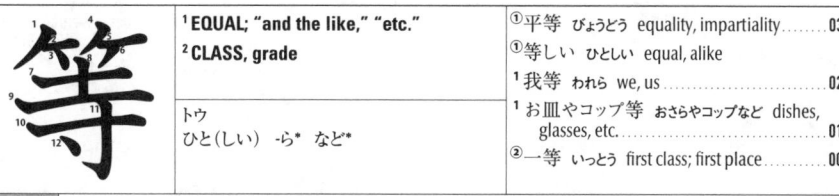 | ¹ **EQUAL**; "and the like," "etc."<br><br>² **CLASS**, grade<br><br>トウ<br>ひと(しい) -ら* など* | ① 平等 びょうどう equality, impartiality........0334<br>① 等しい ひとしい equal, alike<br>¹ 我等 われら we, us .............................0221<br>¹ お皿やコップ等 おさらやコップなど dishes,<br>　　glasses, etc. .............................0197<br>② 一等 いっとう first class; first place..........0002 |

| 0393<br>竹 118<br><br>2339<br>常　12 | Imagine a set of *bamboo* (⺮) tablets inside a *temple* (寺), on which is recorded the **CLASS**/**grade** of each of the monks in training there. One **CLASS**/**grade** consists of all the monks who are presently at the same level, in other words, who are of **EQUAL** rank. To interpret 等 properly, associate **EQUAL** with the idea of "same **grade**." |

|  | **EQUAL, even, uniform**<br><br>キン | 均一な きんいつな uniform, equal, even....0002<br>均等の きんとうの equal, uniform ..........0393<br>均質 きんしつ homogeneity.................0318<br>均整 きんせい symmetry ...................0308<br>○平均 へいきん average, mean; equilibrium,<br>　　balance ..................................0334 |

| 0394<br>土 32<br><br>0207<br>常　7 | This is the only character used in Japanese containing this pair of strokes (S6-7) beneath 勹. Let them suggest a rather crooked equals sign (=), since 均 means **EQUAL**. The two horizontal strokes in 土 reinforce the equals sign. 土 also encourages us to visualize a plot of *land* being leveled out, that is, made "**EQUAL**," even, uniform. |

|  | **SEASON**<br><br>キ | ○季節 きせつ season ........................0391<br>夏季 かき summer, summer season .......0363<br>四季 しき the four seasons.................0006<br>雨季 うき rainy season.....................0154<br>季語 きご season word (in haiku) ..........0222 |

| 0395<br>子 39<br><br>2210<br>常　8 | 禾 is one way to represent *rice*. Here visualize a *baby* (子) *rice* plant maturing into a fully grown one (禾) in **SEASON**. In copying this character, notice how the two graphemes adjust to fit around/inside each other. Do not confuse with the name-use kanji 李 PLUM, a common Chinese and Korean surname. |

|  | **COMMIT**<br><br>イ<br>ゆだ(ねる) | ○委員会 いいんかい committee, commission<br>　........................................0317, 0226<br>公安委員会 こうあんいいんかい public safety<br>　commission ...............0089, 0096, 0317, 0226<br>常任委員会 じょうにんいいんかい standing<br>　committee ..........0321, 0372, 0317, 0226<br>委任する いにんする entrust, delegate, commit 0372<br>委ねる ゆだねる entrust to |

| 0396<br>女 38<br><br>2209<br>常　8 | A man **COMMITS** his *rice* (禾) to a *woman* (女). ☞ 萎 1456 |

| | | HOLE, cave | ○穴居人 けっきょじん cave dweller, caveman ......................................... 0255, 0015 |
|---|---|---|---|
| | 穴 | | ○ボタンの穴 ボタンのあな buttonhole |
| | | ケツ<br>あな | 穴子 あなご conger eel ................................................ 0094 |

| 0397 | Visualize a man walking in the pitch-blackness of a **cave** or other **HOLE**, holding out his arms |
|---|---|
| 穴 116 | lest he bump into something. ☞ 空 0398, 六 0008 |
| 1852 | |
| 常 5 | |

| | | ¹**SKY**<br>²**AIR**<br>³**EMPTY** | ①青空 あおぞら blue sky ........................... 0130 |
|---|---|---|---|
|  | 空 | | ②空気 くうき air; atmosphere ................... 0126 |
| | | | ③部屋を空ける へやをあける clear a room .................................................. 0068, 0252 |
| | | クウ<br>そら あ(く) あ(き) あ(ける) から<br>むな(しい)・ す(く)・ | ³ 空手 からて karate; empty hand ............. 0046 |
| | | | ³ 空車 くうしゃ (empty car) for hire ............ 0125 |

| 0398 | Review 工 0108 and 穴 0397. In 空, we see a worker walking vertiginously along an exposed |
|---|---|
| 穴 116 | I beam, 100 stories up. He holds his arms out to keep his balance, for all around him is nothing but **EMPTY AIR/SKY**. Note that no other kanji in this book has the *on-yomi* クウ. |
| 1913 | ☞ 穴 0397 |
| 常 8 | |

| | | FRIEND | ○友人 ゆうじん friend ............................. 0015 |
|---|---|---|---|
| | 友 | | 親友 しんゆう close friend ....................... 0276 |
| | | | 友好 ゆうこう friendship, amity ............... 0095 |
| | | ユウ<br>とも | ○友だち ともだち friend [cf. 達 1475] |
| | | | メル友 メルとも e-mail friend |

| 0399 | S1–2 (ナ) and S3–4 (又) both depict *hands* (see 又 0058 and 布 0204). 友 thus joins |
|---|---|
| 又 29 | together two *hands* in **FRIENDSHIP**. ☞ 反 0374 |
| 2553 | |
| 常 4 | |

| | | HAVE; exist, there is | ○有名な ゆうめいな famous; notorious ........ 0269 |
|---|---|---|---|
| | 有 | | 有毒 ゆうどく poisonous ........................ 0133 |
| | | | ○有無 うむ existence, presence; yes or no ... 0048 |
| | | ユウ ウ<br>あ(る) | ○有る ある be, exist; have; take place |
| | | | 有り得る ありえる (=ありうる) possible, likely 0387 |

| 0400 | A *hand* (ナ), holding a piece of *meat* (月): hard to beat as an image for the abstract idea |
|---|---|
| 月 74 | **HAVE**. Also means **to exist**. |
| 2576 | |
| 常 6 | |

| 左 | **LEFT**<br><br>サ<br>ひだり | 左方 さほう left side.............................0173<br>左辺 さへん left side.............................0195<br>左足 ひだりあし left leg...........................0044<br>左手 ひだりて left hand..........................0046<br>○左下 ひだりした lower left.......................0040 |
|---|---|---|

| **0401**<br>工 48<br><br>2567<br>常 5 | The kanji for **LEFT** (左) and **RIGHT** (右) both start with the grapheme for *hand* (ナ). For **LEFT**, the most direct solution is to discern a stylized uppercase "L" in the shape at the bottom. |
|---|---|

| 右 | **RIGHT**<br><br>ウ ユウ<br>みぎ | 右方 うほう right side.........................0173<br>右辺 うへん right side ........................0195<br>○左右 さゆう right and left.....................0401<br>右から左へ みぎからひだりへ from right to left;<br>  speedily.................................0401<br>○右上 みぎうえ upper right ....................0041 |
|---|---|---|

| **0402**<br>口 30<br><br>2568<br>常 5 | Right-handers should have no trouble associating the *hand* (ナ) that brings food to the *mouth* (口) with their **RIGHT** hand. Those who eat with their left hand can think of the many cultures in which eating with the **RIGHT** hand is the rule. At this point in the course, I recommend you study Appendix 4. ☞ 石 0403 |
|---|---|

|  | **STONE**<br><br>セキ シャク コク<br>いし | ○宝石 ほうせき gem, jewel.....................0074<br>石けん (石鹸ˣ) せっけん soap<br>一石二鳥 いっせきにちょう kill two birds with one<br>  stone ...........................0002, 0003, 0340<br>○小石 こいし pebble, stone....................0034<br>白石島 しらいしじま Shiraishi Island...0076, 0341 |
|---|---|---|

| **0403**<br>石 112<br><br>2564<br>常 5 | Easily confused with the previous entry. The difference is in the diagonal stroke, which here does not protrude upward. Focus visually on that difference, which separates a drawing of a *hand* from one of a *cliff* (a variation on 厂). In 石, the undivided horizontal line indicates the top of the cliff, the diagonal line its slope. See S3–5 not as a mouth but as a **STONE** rolling down the cliff. Now go back to the previous entry, train your eyes on the protruding point at the top, and fix in your memory that without this projection, this is not a *hand* but a *cliff*. ☞ 右 0402 |
|---|---|

|  | **YOUNG**<br><br>ジャク ニャク<br>わか(い) わか- も(しくは) も(し)ˣ | ○若年 じゃくねん youth, young age............0117<br>○若い わかい young, junior<br>若者 わかもの young person, youth.........0107<br>若し もし if, supposing<br>若しくは もしくは or, either... or |
|---|---|---|

| **0404**<br>艸 140<br><br>1928<br>常 8 | Odd jobs like pulling weeds and grass usually fall to the **YOUNG**. Visualize a **YOUNG** person reaching down with his *right* (右) hand and pulling up some *grass* (艹). ☞ 苦 0405 |
|---|---|

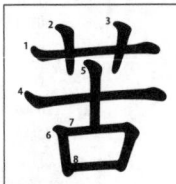

| | ¹SUFFERING, hardship<br>²BITTER<br><br>ク<br>くる(しい) -ぐる(しい) くる(しむ)<br>くる(しめる) にが(い) にが(る) | ¹苦心 くしん pains, efforts, hard work........0056<br>①苦しい くるしい hard, painful; straitened<br>¹親を苦しめる おやをくるしめる cause one's<br>　parents distress.................................0276<br>②苦味 にがみ (=くみ) bitter taste..............0273<br>²苦手 にがて weak point, dislike of .........0046 |
|---|---|---|

| 0405<br>艸 140<br><br>1932<br>常 8 | Enlist your taste buds to create a vivid sensual impression from this character: imagine stuffing your mouth with a fistful of *old* (古), moldy *grass* (艹), and the tongue-shrinkingly **BITTER** taste it would produce. M1 **SUFFERING/hardship** is an intuitive extension from **BITTER.** ☞ 若 0404 |
|---|---|

| | BE, reside<br><br>ザイ<br>あ(る) | 在校生 ざいこうせい (currently) enrolled student<br>　..........................................0103, 0036<br>○不在 ふざい absence .........................0049<br>在日 ざいにち (resident) in Japan..........0001<br>駐在 ちゅうざい residence, stay..............0367<br>テーブルの上に本が在る テーブルのうえにほん<br>　がある There is a book on the table...0041, 0031 |
|---|---|---|

| 0406<br>土 32<br><br>2577<br>常 6 | Now to ナ *hand* we add an extra enclosing stroke (S3) to mean *hold close*. 在 shows the idea of one's *holding close* to a specific piece of *land* (土), to imply **BEING** or **residing** in a particular place. ☞ 存 0407 |
|---|---|

| | EXIST; be aware of, believe<br><br>ソン ゾン | ○存在 そんざい existence, being..............0406<br>生存する せいぞんする exist, live, survive...0036<br>共存 きょうぞん coexistence ...................0356<br>○存じる(=存ずる) ぞんじる(=ぞんずる) believe; be<br>　aware of<br>存分に ぞんぶんに as much as one likes....0088 |
|---|---|---|

| 0407<br>子 39<br><br>2575<br>常 6 | This image of a newborn *child* (子) *held close* (イ) to one's bosom implies **EXISTENCE** (a child **EXISTS** where there was no child before). It also represents the secondary meanings **be aware of** and **believe**, which we can think of as holding an idea in one's bosom, or having an idea **EXIST** in one's mind. ☞ 在 0406 |
|---|---|

| | DRY<br><br>カン<br>ほ(す) ほ(し)- -ぼ(し) ひ(る) | ○干潮 かんちょう ebb tide.....................0146<br>(潮の)干満 (しおの)かんまん ebb and flow, tide<br>　.........................................0146, 0179<br>干天 かんてん drought, dry weather........0270<br>若干 じゃっかん a number of, some, a little...0404<br>○干す ほす [vt] dry |
|---|---|---|

| 0408<br>干 51<br><br>2863<br>常 3 | See 干 as a drying rack with two horizontal poles for hanging the wet laundry up to **DRY.** ☞ 午 0115, 千 0017, 乾 1807 |
|---|---|

| 刊 | **PUBLISH** | ○刊行 かんこう publication..................0055 |
|---|---|---|
| | | 週刊誌 しゅうかんし weekly magazine 0305, 0370 |
| | | 朝刊 ちょうかん morning edition/paper....0145 |
| | カン | 夕刊 ゆうかん evening edition/paper.......0265 |
| | | 未刊の みかんの unpublished..............0271 |

**0409** 刀 18 — Recall リ *cut/slice*, seen earlier at 別 0090 and 前 0113. In 刊, we thus have *dry* (干) and *cut* (リ). *Dry* the ink, then *cut* the pages: **PUBLISH**. ☞ 刑 0722, 判 0744

0167 常 5

| 汗 | **SWEAT** | ○発汗する はっかんする perspire, sweat.....0148 |
|---|---|---|
| | | 汗血 かんけつ sweat and blood............0198 |
| | | ○汗をかく あせをかく sweat, perspire |
| | カン | 汗ばむ あせばむ become slightly sweaty |
| | あせ | 汗だくて あせだくて dripping with sweat |

**0410** 水 85 — *Water* (氵) dripping down to moisten a *dry* (干) face: **SWEAT**. ☞ 汁 0756

0194 常 6

| 竿 | **POLE** | ○竿竹 さおだけ bamboo pole...............0243 |
|---|---|---|
| | | 竹竿 たけざお bamboo pole...............0243 |
| | | 物干し竿 ものほしざお pole for drying laundry |
| | カン | ..................0172, 0408 |
| | さお | |

**0411** 竹 118 — Review 干 0408. *Bamboo* (⺮) **POLES** for *drying* the laundry.

2288 名 9

| 利 | ¹ **ADVANTAGE** ² **PROFIT** | ¹ 有利な ゆうりな advantageous, favorable; profitable..................0400 |
|---|---|---|
| | | ¹ 利用する りようする utilize, make use of....0047 |
| | | ①左利き ひだりきき left-handed; heavy drinker |
| | リ | ..................0401 |
| | き(く) | ² 利子 りし interest..................0094 |
| | | 利く きく work (well), function (properly) |

**0412** 刀 18 — *Rice* (禾) and *cut* (リ) suggest the idea of reaping the **PROFITS** of one's labor. Associate M1 **ADVANTAGE** with M2 **PROFIT**.

1029 常 7

135

| | HARM, hinder | 有害な ゆうがいな harmful, pernicious, noxious .............................................0400 |
|---|---|---|
| | | 公害 こうがい environmental pollution.....0089 |
| | | 害虫 がいちゅう harmful insect ................0343 |
| | ガイ | ○利害 りがい interests, what one stands to gain or lose ...............................0412 |
| | | 害する がいする harm, hinder |

| 0413 | We shall need to distinguish this one from 憲 0417, so it makes sense to focus on 口. Picture the *mouth* consuming a poisonous *plant* (the same one mother was protecting us from in 毒 0133), and think of the **HARM** the plant is causing. ⌂ *roof* provides a scene for the crime; fill out its other details in your imagination. ☞ 割 0416, 善 1213, 憲 0417 |
|---|---|
| ⌂ 40 | |
| 1962 | |
| 常 10 | |

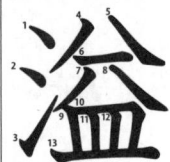

| | BENEFIT, profit | 有益な ゆうえきな beneficial; profitable.....0400 |
|---|---|---|
| | | 公益 こうえき public benefit.................0089 |
| | | 益虫 えきちゅう beneficial insect............0343 |
| | エキ ヤク | ○利益 りえき profit, gains; benefit ...........0412 |
| | ま(す)* | ○益々 ますます increasingly |

| 0414 | Here we are given a vivid image of **BENEFIT**/**profit**: four people reach out their hands (S1, S2, S4, and S5) to help themselves to something served on a *plate* (皿). Note the traditional form, which is incorporated into the next entry (learn to recognize the two forms without distinction). ☞ 器 0295 |
|---|---|
| 皿 108 | |
| 益 | |
| 1978 | |
| 常 10 | |

| | SPILL OVER | 溢水 いっすい inundation ...................0027 |
|---|---|---|
| | | ○溢れる あふれる overflow |
| | | トイレの水が溢れた トイレのみずがあふれた The toilet overflowed ......................0027 |
| | イツ | ○溢れる こぼれる be spilled |
| | あふ(れる) こぼ(れる) こぼ(す) | 溢す こぼす spill |

| 0415 | Now see *liquid* ( 氵 ) **SPILL OVER** the edge of the *plate* (皿) as people hastily help themselves. |
|---|---|
| 水 85 | |
| 溢 | |
| 0601 | |
| 名 13 | |

| | DIVIDE, cut, break | ○分割する ぶんかつする divide up, partition, split..................................0088 |
|---|---|---|
| | | コップを割る コップをわる break a glass |
| | | 三割五分 さんわりごぶ 35%......0004, 0007, 0088 |
| | カツ | ○割れる われる [vi] break; be divided; [math] is divisible |
| | わ(る) わり わ(り) わ(れる) さ(く) | ○割く さく spare (time), set aside |

| 0416 | "Harm-cut" (害 plus 刂) intuitively suggests the idea of **breaking** something, or **DIVIDING** into pieces something which is whole. ☞ 害 0413 |
|---|---|
| 刀 18 | |
| 1611 | |
| 常 12 | |

**CONSTITUTION, code of laws**

ケン

○憲法 けんぽう constitution, constitutional law ...........0139
憲政 けんせい constitutional government...0246
合憲的 ごうけんてき constitutional....0227, 0169
合憲性 ごうけんせい constitutionality 0227, 0128
立憲 りっけん constitutional .................0067

---

**0417**
心 61
憲
2091
常 | 16

Now we shall add a figurative meaning to 罒 (*net*): the *law*. If in English we refer to the law's "long arm," here we might think of its "wide net." Below *roof* (宀) then we have three symbols: *growing plant* (S4–7) for prosperity, *law* for law and order, and *heart* (心) for compassion and human rights. The *roof* that protects all three is the **CONSTITUTION**. ☞ 寧 0438, 害 0413

---

¹ **FEATHER**
² **WING**

ウ
は わ はね

¹ 羽根 はね feather, wing; (fan) blade; shuttle-cock .............0284
②羽化する うかする grow wings, emerge ....0120
②羽音 はおと flapping [whirring] of wings ...0150
○一羽 いちわ one bird/rabbit.............0002
三羽 さんば three birds/rabbits.............0004

---

**0418**
羽 124
羽
0200
常 | 6

We now meet the pictographic character for **WING**. S1 and S4 depict the limbs; S2, S3, S5, and S6 the **FEATHERS**. Compare with the traditional form, as well as the scaled-down version we saw at the top right of 曜 0025. ☞ 弱 0424

---

**THE FOLLOWING**

ヨク

○翌日 よくじつ the following [next] day .......0001
翌年 よくねん (=よくとし) the following [next] year..............0117
翌春 よくしゅん next spring .............0362
翌々日 よくよくじつ two days after............0001
翌朝 よくあさ the following [next] morning 0145

---

**0419**
羽 124
翌
2325
常 | 11

Picture the person at the bottom *standing* up (立), spreading his *wings* (羽) and magically flying to **THE FOLLOWING** time period (for example, 翌年 [よくねん, the next year/the following year]). Note the distinction in usage from 来年 (らいねん), which means "next year" (without "the"). ☞ 習 0420, 笠 0754, 来 0274

---

¹ **LEARN, study**
² **CUSTOM, habit**

シュウ
なら(う) なら(い)

¹ 学習 がくしゅう study, learning .................0099
①習得 しゅうとく learning, acquisition.......0387
①習う ならう learn, study; practice
¹ 習い事 ならいごと (cultural) lessons (music, calligraphy, etc.), practice.................0080
² 常習 じょうしゅう custom, habit .............0321

---

**0420**
羽 124
習
2324
常 | 11

Let *white* (白) *feathers* (羽) bring to mind an image of a young bird (which hasn't yet developed a mature bird's dark plumage), **LEARNING** to fly. Note that the most important compound using M2 **CUSTOM** appears at 慣 1912. ☞ 翌 0419

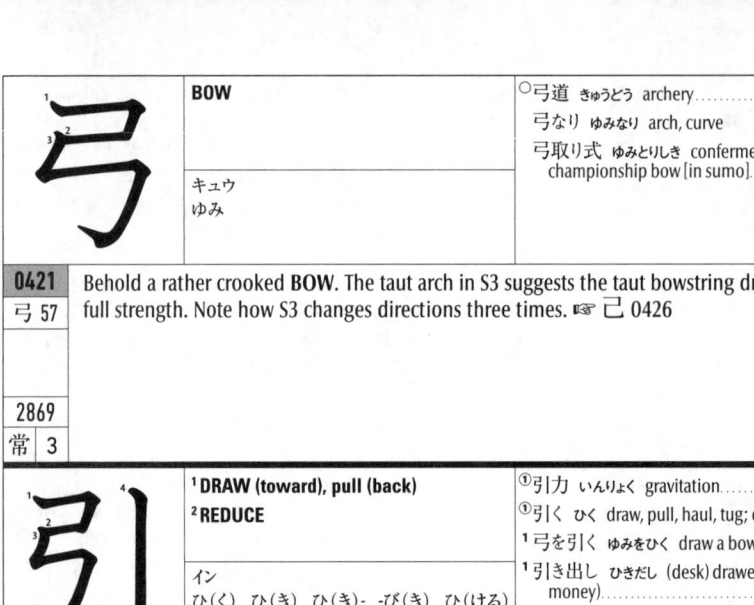

| | **BOW** | ○弓道 きゅうどう archery.........................0158 |
|---|---|---|
| | | 弓なり ゆみなり arch, curve |
| | キュウ<br>ゆみ | 弓取り式 ゆみとりしき conferment of the<br>championship bow [in sumo].........**0059, 0109** |

| **0421**<br>弓 57 | Behold a rather crooked **BOW**. The taut arch in S3 suggests the taut bowstring drawn back at full strength. Note how S3 changes directions three times. ☞ 己 0426 |
|---|---|
| **2869**<br>常 3 | |

| | **¹ DRAW (toward), pull (back)**<br>**² REDUCE** | ①引力 いんりょく gravitation...................0084 |
|---|---|---|
| | | ①引く ひく draw, pull, haul, tug; drag, trail |
| | | ¹ 弓を引く ゆみをひく draw a bow.............0421 |
| | イン<br>ひ（く） ひ（き） ひ（き）- -び（き） ひ（ける） | ¹ 引き出し ひきだし (desk) drawer; withdrawal (of money)................................................0038 |
| | | ² 割り引き わりびき discount..................0416 |

| **0422**<br>弓 57 | See S4 as a kind of *handle* we can use to **DRAW** back the *bow* (弓). When you see 引 on a door, it means **pull** on the handle. M2 **REDUCE** is an extension of the idea "**DRAW back**." |
|---|---|
| **0160**<br>常 4 | |

| | **STRONG** | 強大な きょうだいな mighty, powerful, strong<br>.................................................0033 |
|---|---|---|
| | | ○強調する きょうちょうする emphasize, stress 0306 |
| | | 強引な ごういんな overbearing, coercive ...0422 |
| | キョウ ゴウ<br>つよ（い） つよ（まる） つよ（める）<br>し（いる） | ○根強い ねづよい firmly rooted, deep-rooted<br>.................................................0284 |
| | | ○強いる しいる force, compel, press |

| **0423**<br>弓 57 | The kanji for STRONG (強) and WEAK (弱) are both based on the grapheme for *bow* (弓). Thus we should imagine two *bows*: first, a **STRONG** *bow*, made from the hard exoskeleton of an *insect* (虫) (take S4–5 ム, the katakana for *mu*, to be a kind of *furigana* cue for ムシ), ...(continued in the next entry) |
|---|---|
| **0432**<br>常 11 | |

| | **WEAK** | ○弱点 じゃくてん weak point...................0349 |
|---|---|---|
| | | 弱肉強食 じゃくにくきょうしょく law of the jungle<br>(the strong prey on the weak)...**0216, 0423, 0288** |
| | | 200人弱 にひゃくにんじゃく slightly under two<br>hundred people................................0015 |
| | ジャク<br>よわ（い） よわ（る） よわ（まる） よわ（める） | ○弱気な よわきな timid; weak-spirited; bearish<br>[stock market]...............................0126 |
| | | 火を弱める ひをよわめる turn down the flame<br>.................................................0026 |

| **0424**<br>弓 57 | (Continuing from the previous entry) ... and second, a **WEAK** *bow*, made from a bird's *wings* (羽). ☞ 羽 0418 |
|---|---|
| <br>**1080**<br>常 10 | |

| 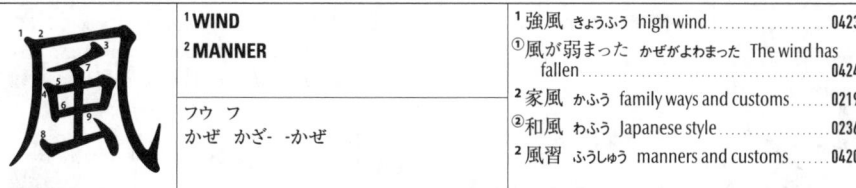 | <sup>1</sup>**WIND**<br><sup>2</sup>**MANNER**<br><br>フウ フ<br>かぜ かざ- -かぜ | <sup>1</sup> 強風 きょうふう high wind.....................0423<br>① 風が弱まった かぜがよわまった The wind has<br>fallen..........................0424<br><sup>2</sup> 家風 かふう family ways and customs........0219<br>② 和風 わふう Japanese style...................0236<br><sup>2</sup> 風習 ふうしゅう manners and customs.......0420 |
|---|---|---|

| **0425**<br>風 182<br><br>2591<br>常 9 | Visualize this as an *insect* (虫) taking shelter from strong **WINDS** under a tent (几). S3 can be thought of as a strap inside the tent to which the insect holds fast, so as to keep from blowing away. By associating the idea of prevailing winds with prevailing styles or customs, we can associate M1 **WIND** with M2 **MANNER**. Now a word about graphemes. To distinguish 几 from 几, let 几's warped shape and bent lower-right corner suggest the force of the wind outside. In other kanji, 几 will signify *wind*. We shall treat the similar but narrower form 几 as a separate grapheme, meaning *tablecloth* or *table* (see, for example, 処 0553 and 飢 1966). |
|---|---|

|  | **ONESELF**<br><br>コ キ<br>おのれ | ○ 自己 じこ oneself, self, ego.................0081<br>自己中心 じこちゅうしん egocentrism<br>.........................0081, 0035, 0056<br>利己 りこ self-interest.....................0412<br>利己的 りこてき self-interested, selfish 0412, 0169<br>○ 己を信じる おのれをしんじる believe in oneself<br>.........................0063 |
|---|---|---|

| **0426**<br>己 49<br><br>2864<br>常 3 | Visualize as your**SELF** in a kneeling position with your head bowed forward—an appropriately humble image for referring to one**SELF**. Your head is at the upper left, shoulders at the upper right, knees at the lower left, and feet at the lower right. When 己 appears as a grapheme in other kanji, we may interpret it as *kneeling self*. ☞ 弓 0421 |
|---|---|

|  | **WRITE DOWN**<br><br>キ<br>しる(す) | 記者 きしゃ journalist, reporter; editor......0107<br>記事 きじ news, article; account............0080<br>○ 記入する きにゅうする enter, fill in (a form)...0039<br>伝記 でんき biography.....................0223<br>○ 記す しるす record, write down |
|---|---|---|

| **0427**<br>言 149<br><br>1321<br>常 10 | Here the *kneeling self* (己) kneels at a writing desk **WRITING DOWN** words (言) in a diary, or 日記 (にっき). ☞ 誌 0370 |
|---|---|

| 紀 | <sup>1</sup>**ERA, age**<br><sup>2</sup>**DISCIPLINE, morals**<br><br>キ | ① 紀元 きげん era; AD, CE .....................0136<br><sup>1</sup> 紀元前 きげんぜん BC, BCE ...........0136, 0113<br><sup>1</sup> カンブリア紀 カンブリアき Cambrian period<br>② 風紀 ふうき public morals..................0425<br><sup>2</sup> 校紀 こうき school discipline ...............0103 |
|---|---|---|

| **0428**<br>糸 120<br><br>1173<br>常 9 | Now visualize the *kneeling self* (己) using *rope* (糸) to restrain himself. Picture the *rope* looping around the back of the knees (middle of S9) to tie 己 down good and tight. Let this image represent the idea of **DISCIPLINE**. Associate M2 **DISCIPLINE** with M1 **ERA** via the idea of sustaining self-restraint over a long period of time. |
|---|---|

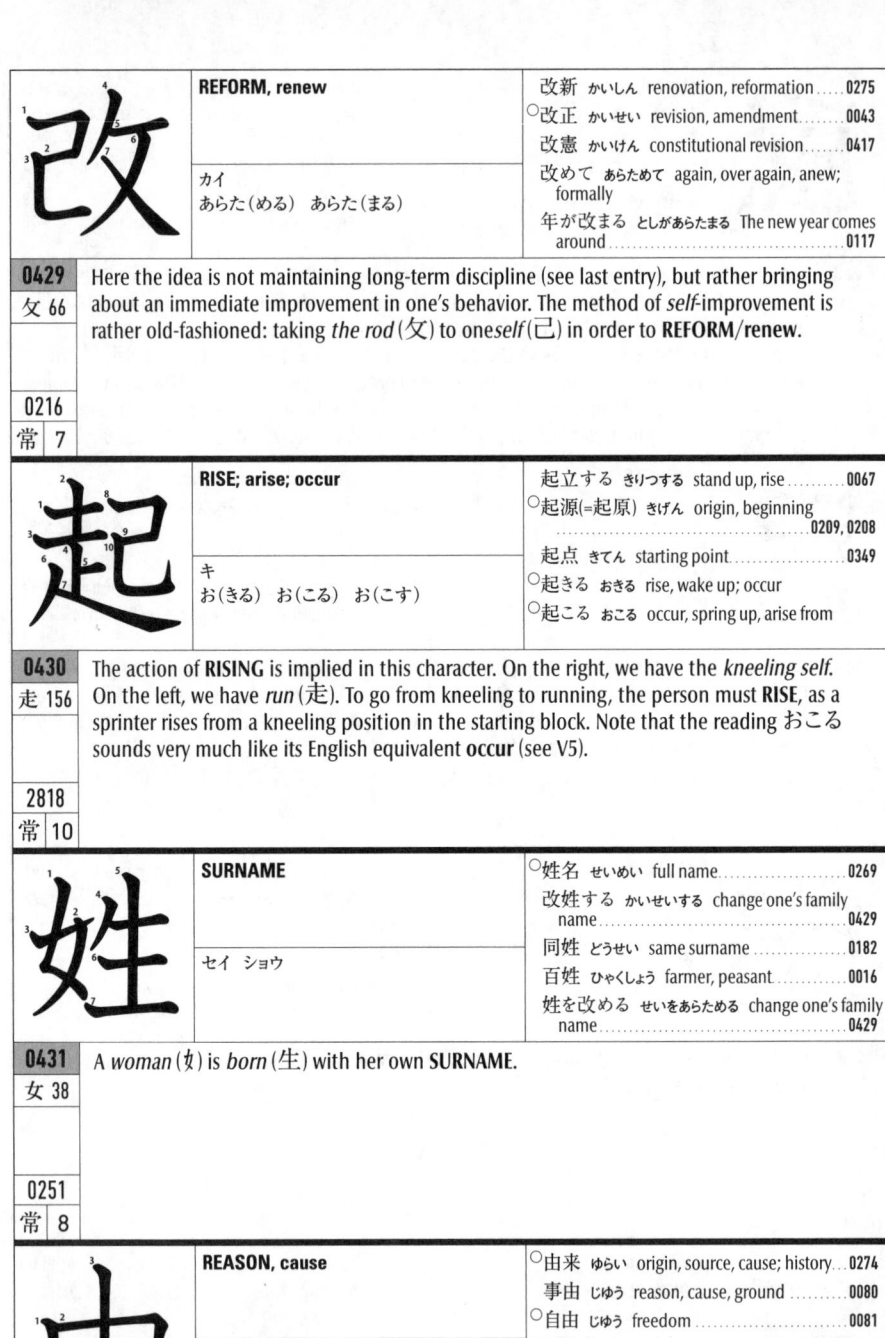

| | REFORM, renew | 改新 かいしん renovation, reformation.....0275 |
| --- | --- | --- |
| 改 | | ○改正 かいせい revision, amendment........0043 |
| | | 改憲 かいけん constitutional revision.......0417 |
| | カイ<br>あらた(める) あらた(まる) | 改めて あらためて again, over again, anew;<br>formally |
| | | 年が改まる としがあらたまる The new year comes<br>around .................0117 |

| **0429**<br>攵 66 | Here the idea is not maintaining long-term discipline (see last entry), but rather bringing about an immediate improvement in one's behavior. The method of *self*-improvement is rather old-fashioned: taking *the rod* (攵) to one*self* (己) in order to **REFORM**/renew. |
| --- | --- |
| 0216<br>常 7 | |

| | RISE; arise; occur | 起立する きりつする stand up, rise.........0067 |
| --- | --- | --- |
| 起 | | ○起源(=起原) きげん origin, beginning<br>.................0209, 0208 |
| | | 起点 きてん starting point.................0349 |
| | キ<br>お(きる) お(こる) お(こす) | ○起きる おきる rise, wake up; occur |
| | | ○起こる おこる occur, spring up, arise from |

| **0430**<br>走 156 | The action of **RISING** is implied in this character. On the right, we have the *kneeling self*. On the left, we have *run* (走). To go from kneeling to running, the person must **RISE**, as a sprinter rises from a kneeling position in the starting block. Note that the reading おこる sounds very much like its English equivalent **occur** (see V5). |
| --- | --- |
| 2818<br>常 10 | |

| | SURNAME | ○姓名 せいめい full name.................0269 |
| --- | --- | --- |
| 姓 | | 改姓する かいせいする change one's family<br>name.................0429 |
| | | 同姓 どうせい same surname .................0182 |
| | セイ ショウ | 百姓 ひゃくしょう farmer, peasant...........0016 |
| | | 姓を改める せいをあらためる change one's family<br>name.................0429 |

| **0431**<br>女 38 | A *woman* (女) is *born* (生) with her own **SURNAME**. |
| --- | --- |
| 0251<br>常 8 | |

| | REASON, cause | ○由来 ゆらい origin, source, cause; history...0274 |
| --- | --- | --- |
| 由 | | 事由 じゆう reason, cause, ground ..........0080 |
| | | ○自由 じゆう freedom .................0081 |
| | ユ ユウ ユイ<br>よし | 不自由 ふじゆう inconvenience; disability;<br>poverty.................0049, 0081 |
| | | 由無き よしなき senseless, meaningless, absurd<br>.................0048 |

| **0432**<br>田 102 | Let this character represent an image of **REASONS**/causes (lying in the square at the bottom) <u>giving rise</u> to a consequence/effect (the stroke that rises out of this square). ☞ 甲 1521, 申 0315 |
| --- | --- |
| 2935<br>常 5 | |

## 油 OIL

ユ
あぶら

○石油 せきゆ petroleum, oil.................0403
原油 げんゆ crude oil............................0208
オリーブ油 オリーブゆ olive oil
油田 ゆでん oilfield.............................0020
大豆油 だいずあぶら soybean oil.....0033, 0161

**0433** 水 85 / 0303 常 8

See S6 as **OIL** spurting up from an oil field. 氵 suggests the category *liquid*.

## 井 WELL

セイ ショウ
い

○油井 ゆせい oil well........................0433
○天井 てんじょう ceiling...................0270
○井戸 いど (water) well...................0248
井上 いのうえ Inoue [surname]........0041
石井 いしい Ishii [surname]............0403

**0434** 二 7 / 2905 常 4

A bird's-eye view of a **WELL**, showing the wooden frame built around it. ☞ 丼 0436

## 囲 ENCLOSE

イ
かこ(む) かこ(う) かこ(い)

○周囲 しゅうい circumference, periphery; surroundings.....................0304
○囲む かこむ enclose, surround
囲まれる かこまれる be surrounded
取り囲む とりかこむ enclose, encircle.......0059
囲いに入れる かこいにいれる place in an enclosure.....................0039

**0435** 口 31 / 圍 / 2643 常 7

Now we add an enclosure around the well, to signify **ENCLOSE**.

## 丼 BOWL (of food)

ドン
どんぶり

天丼 てんどん tempura on rice.............0270
親子丼 おやこどん (=おやこどんぶり) chicken and egg on rice.................0276, 0094
牛丼 ぎゅうどん bowl of rice topped with beef.................0116
丼もの どんぶりもの rice-bowl dishes

**0436** 二 7 / 2945 常 5

Here 井 represents the outlines of a square rice bowl, and the central stroke a piece of meat or fish laid on top of the rice: **BOWL (of food)**. ☞ 井 0434

| | ¹ TOWN SUBSECTION<br>² MISCELLANEOUS COUNTER | ¹ 四丁目 よんちょうめ 4-chome, fourth town/<br>　neighborhood subsection ............0006, 0021<br>² ラーメン三丁 ラーメンさんちょう three bowls of<br>　ramen...............................................0004 |
|---|---|---|
| | チョウ テイ | 丁度 ちょうど just, exactly; as if.............0280 |

**0437**

一 1

Visualize as a T-shaped intersection of two streets. Indeed, this character is used in the word for such an intersection: 丁字路 (ていじろ; we'll learn 路 at entry 0788). Imagine you are looking at an aerial photograph of such an intersection, observing the three **TOWN SUB-SECTIONS** that adjoin there.

2851

常 2

---

| | COURTEOUS; peaceful | ○丁寧な ていねいな polite, courteous.........0437<br>丁寧語 ていねいご polite language [speech]<br>　...............................................0437, 0222 |
|---|---|---|
| | ネイ | 寧日 ねいじつ peaceful day...................0001<br>安寧 あんねい public peace, tranquility.....0096 |

**0438**

宀 40

In 寧 try to perceive the safe, sheltered feeling of a **COURTEOUS** and **peaceful** social environment: over one's *heart* (心), there is a sheltering *roof* (宀); under it, there is the supportive safety *net* (罒) of one's *town subsection* (丁). The *on* reading ネイ is unique in this course.
☞ 憲 0417

2061

常 14

---

| | TOWN, town section | ○町人 ちょうにん townsman, tradesman (in Edo period)<br>　...............................................0015<br>○下町 したまち (downtown) business quarters, old part<br>　of Tokyo...........................................0040 |
|---|---|---|
| | チョウ<br>まち | 前原町三丁目 まえはらちょうさんちょうめ Town/District<br>　of Maehara, Section 3 [part of residential address]<br>　................0113, 0208, 0004, 0437<br>室町時代 むろまちじだい Muromachi period (Japa-<br>　nese historical era, approx. 1336–1573) 0253, 0383, 0071 |

**0439**

田 102

Review 丁 0437. Here, see 田 as a map of a **TOWN**, divided into *town subsections*.

甲

1028

常 7

---

| | LAMP | 灯火 とうか light, lamplight...................0026<br>灯油 とうゆ kerosene, lamp oil ..............0433<br>○電灯 でんとう lamp, electric light............0155 |
|---|---|---|
| | トウ<br>ひ | 灯光 とうこう lamplight.......................0137<br>灯を付ける ひをつける turn on the light....0064 |

**0440**

火 86

*Fire* (火) illuminating an *intersection* (丁): street **LAMP**.

燈

0730

常 6

| | GOVERNMENT AGENCY | ○官庁 かんちょう government office [agency] ...0290<br>都庁 とちょう Tokyo Metropolitan Government Office................................................0244<br>府庁 ふちょう prefectural office (for Osaka-fu and Kyoto-fu)........................................0247<br>文化庁 ぶんかちょう Agency for Cultural Affairs ................................................0101, 0120<br>法王庁 ほうおうちょう the Vatican......0139, 0072 |
|---|---|---|
| | チョウ | |

| 0441 | The character for **GOVERNMENT AGENCY** is written as a *shelter* (广) built over a *town sub-section* (丁). It symbolizes how the **GOVERNMENT AGENCY** "covers" or safeguards this portion of the city. |
|---|---|
| 广 53 | |
| 廳 | |
| 2612 | |
| 常 5 | |

| | STORE UP, save | ○貯金 ちょきん savings, deposit .................0029<br>貯水池 ちょすいち reservoir............0027, 0188 |
|---|---|---|
| | チョ | |

| 0442 | This is the first time we've encountered the narrow *hen* form of 貝 *money*. See *money* being **STORED UP** in the *town subsection* (丁) depository, with a protecting *roof* (宀) visible over it. |
|---|---|
| 貝 154 | |
| 1368 | |
| 常 12 | |

| | ¹ EASY<br>² EXCHANGE<br>³ FORTUNE-TELLING | ①安易な あんいな easy, easygoing............0096<br>¹ 易しい やさしい easy, simple<br>①分かり易い わかりやすい easy to understand ................................................0088<br>² 交易 こうえき trade, commerce .............0102<br>③易者 えきしゃ fortune-teller.................0107 |
|---|---|---|
| | エキ イ<br>やさ(しい) やす(い)* | |

| 0443 | To distinguish from the grapheme 昜 (*difficult*), focus on the lack of a central stroke, which makes it **EASY** for the rays of the *sun* (日) to reach the *woolly mammoth* (勿). By contrast, in 昜 it is *difficult* for the sun's rays to reach it, for they must first break through a barrier. As for M2 and M3, rather than force these into an overburdened mnemonic, learn these meanings through their most fundamental compounds. Thus, for M3 **FORTUNE-TELLING**, V5 易者 (えきしゃ, fortune-teller) should be memorized. Postpone learning M2 **EXCHANGE** until you come to its highest-frequency compound at 貿 1169. |
|---|---|
| 日 72 | |
| 2135 | |
| 常 8 | |

| | DEIGN TO GIVE, bestow | ○賜金 しきん gratuity, grant .................0029<br>下賜する かしする grant, deign to give .....0040<br>○賜る たまわる deign to give, bestow; be awarded, have the honor to receive<br>賜り物 たまわりもの gift, boon.................0172 |
|---|---|---|
| | シ<br>たまわ(る) | |

| 0444 | "*Easy* (易) *money* (貝)" intuitively summarizes the idea of some high authority, such as the emperor, **DEIGNING TO GIVE** or **bestowing** a grant. ☞ 贈 1227, 腸 1985 |
|---|---|
| 貝 154 | |
| 1433 | |
| 常 15 | |

| 場 | PLACE | ○工場 こうじょう (=こうば) factory, plant, workshop .................................................... 0108 |
|---|---|---|
| | | ○場所 ばしょ place, spot, site; space, room ... 0249 |
| | | 出場 する しゅつじょうする take part, participate .................................................... 0038 |
| | ジョウ ば | 場合 ばあい occasion, situation, circumstances, case .................................................... 0227 |
| | | 駐車場 ちゅうしゃじょう parking lot ..... 0367, 0125 |

| **0445** 土 32 場 0512 常 12 | *Land* (土) + *difficult* (易): one's hard-earned **PLACE**. This is not the first time that 土 has lent the sense of a <u>particular</u> area of land (i.e., place), nor will it be the last. |
|---|---|

| 湯 | HOT WATER | ○温湯 おんとう comfortably hot bathwater ... 0199 |
|---|---|---|
| | | 入湯 にゅうとう taking a hot bath ............. 0039 |
| | | ○お湯 おゆ hot water |
| | トウ ゆ | 湯気 ゆげ steam, vapor ..................... 0126 |
| | | 湯元 ゆもと source of a hot spring ........... 0136 |

| **0446** 水 85 0561 常 12 | *Water* (氵) + *difficult* (易): **HOT WATER**. Later we shall learn five more kanji with 易: 揚 1308, 暢 1309, 陽 1310, 瘍 1945, and 腸 1985. ☞ 温 0199, 渇 2267 |
|---|---|

| 門 | GATE | ○正門 せいもん main gate, main entrance ... 0043 |
|---|---|---|
| | | 部門 ぶもん group, division, section; genus 0068 |
| | | 門下生 もんかせい disciple, pupil ..... 0040, 0036 |
| | モン かど | 名門 めいもん prestigious establishment/family .................................................... 0269 |
| | | ○門口 かどぐち entrance, gateway ........... 0019 |

| **0447** 門 169 门 0789 常 8 | The twin leaves of a **GATE**. |
|---|---|

| 間 | SPACE IN BETWEEN, interval | 空間 くうかん space, room ................. 0398 |
|---|---|---|
| | | ○時間 じかん time, period; hour ............. 0383 |
| | | 長い間 ながいあいだ a long time ........... 0091 |
| | カン ケン あいだ ま | ○...の間に ...のあいだに in between ... |
| | | ○間に合う まにあう be in time; answer the purpose; be able to do without ........... 0227 |

| **0448** 門 169 2836 常 12 | See the *sun* (日) shining through the **SPACE IN BETWEEN** the two leaves of the *gate* (門). |
|---|---|

| 閉 | **CLOSE** | ○閉会 へいかい closing a meeting............0226 |
|---|---|---|
| | | 閉口する へいこうする be dumbfounded [stumped], be silenced............0019 |
| | ヘイ と(じる) と(ざす) し(める) し(まる) | 閉店時間 へいてんじかん store closing time ............0347, 0383, 0448 |
| | | ○閉じる とじる [vi & vt] close |
| | | ○閉まる しまる [vi] close, be closed |

**0449** 門 169 閇 2832 常 11

Focusing on the long diagonal stroke (S11) that distinguishes this character from the others in this set, see オ as a kind of crossbar apparatus used to **CLOSE** the *gate* (門). Take some time to associate that distinctive diagonal stroke with the idea of **CLOSING** the gate. ☞ 閇 1365

| 開 | **OPEN** | ○開会 かいかい opening a meeting............0226 |
|---|---|---|
| | | 開閉する かいへいする open and close.....0449 |
| | | 開発する かいはつする develop, open up...0148 |
| | カイ ひら(く) ひら(き) -び(らき) ひら(ける) あ(く) あ(ける) | ○開く ひらく [vi & vt] open |
| | | ○開く あく [vi] open |

**0450** 門 169 開 2835 常 12

Now under *gate* (門) we find a smaller *torii* gate (开), signifying that it is OK to pass through—the gate is **OPEN**. ☞ 関 0451

| 関 | [1] **CONNECT WITH, concern** [2] **BARRIER** | ①関する かんする concern, be connected with |
|---|---|---|
| | | [1] 関わる かかわる be concerned in, affect |
| | | [1] 関節 かんせつ joint............0391 |
| | カン せき -ぜき かか(わる) | ②関東 かんとう Kanto district ("east of the barrier")............0032 |
| | | [2] 大関 おおぜき sumo wrestler of second highest rank............0033 |

**0451** 門 169 關 2842 常 14

Here let us try to perceive **CONNECT WITH** and **BARRIER** in the same image. First, see 关 (not to be confused with 天) as a barricade with two long crossbeams, blocking a *gate* (門). Now, try also to see the crossbeams as **CONNECTING** the two sides of the *gate* (so that no passable space remains between them). ☞ 開 0450

| 問 | **QUESTION, ask** | ○質問 しつもん question............0318 |
|---|---|---|
| | | 学問 がくもん scholarship, learning............0099 |
| | | ○問う とう ask, question |
| | モン と(う) と(い) とん | 問い合わせる といあわせる inquire, check; refer to............0227 |
| | | ○問いかける といかける ask a question |

**0452** 口 30 問 2833 常 11

For the next two kanji, imagine a visitor approaching the *gate* (門). First, he opens his *mouth* (口) to ask a **QUESTION**.

**HEAR; ask**

ブン　モン
き(く)　き(こえる)

見聞 けんぶん experience, observation.....0083
○新聞 しんぶん newspaper.................0275
○聞く きく hear; ask
聞き手 ききて listener, audience...........0046
道を聞く みちをきく ask the way...........0158

| 0453 | (Continuing from the previous entry) After asking the question, the visitor puts forth his *ear* (耳) to **HEAR** the answer. 聞 can also mean **ask** (overlapping with the previous entry). |
| 耳 128 | |
| 2840 | |
| 常 14 | |

**VISIT**

ホウ
おとず(れる)　たず(ねる)

○訪問 ほうもん visit...........................0452
訪日 ほうにち visiting Japan, visit to Japan...0001
来訪する らいほうする visit, call...........0274
○訪れる おとずれる visit, call on
○訪ねる たずねる visit, call on

| 0454 | Review 方 0173 and 防 0174. 訪 here is used to describe **VISITS** such as those of a head of state to another country, so we should try to perceive 訪 as a *person*(方) carrying with him *words*(言) of greeting and warm regard. Remember that the ホウ of ほうもん (see V1) is the only kanji having the phonetic component 方 that is not read ボウ. |
| 言 149 | |
| 1335 | |
| 常 11 | |

**SEND, transmit**

ソウ
おく(る)

返送する へんそうする send back...........0378
○送信 そうしん transmission (of a message)...0063
送別会 そうべつかい farewell party....0090, 0226
○送る おくる send, transmit
見送る みおくる see off.......................0083

| 0455 | Picking up from 関 0451, we now see the *barricades*(关) loaded up on the bed of a *truck* (辶)—someone is **SENDING** them back to the storehouse. 关's horizontal lines, pointing in one direction toward its origin and in the other direction toward its destination, reinforce the idea of **transmit**. ☞ 迸 1211 |
| 辵 162 | |
| 2664 | |
| 常 9 | |

¹ **TICKET**
² **CERTIFICATE**

ケン

¹ 食券 しょっけん food ticket .................0288
①入場券 にゅうじょうけん admission ticket
........................................0039, 0445
¹ 回数券 かいすうけん coupon ticket, carnet
........................................0050, 0309
² 日銀券 にちぎんけん Bank of Japan bond
........................................0001, 0283

| 0456 | 关 depicts an ancient Chinese *tally stick*: a split piece of bamboo used for recordkeeping. See S3–4 as the stick, and let its other strokes illustrate the act of chiseling notches into it. In 券, one *cuts*(刀) a *tally stick*(关) into individual **TICKETS/CERTIFICATES**. Note the traditional forms for this and the next four entries. ☞ 巻 0458 |
| 刀 18 | |
| 券 | |
| 2286 | |
| 常 8 | |

146

# 包

<sup>1</sup>**WRAP**
<sup>2</sup>**ENCOMPASS**

ホウ
つつ(む)

①包む つつむ wrap, pack
<sup>1</sup> 小包 こづつみ parcel, package .............. 0034
<sup>2</sup> 内包 ないほう connotation, intension, comprehension ................................. 0215
②包囲する ほういする surround, envelop .... 0435
　包丁 ほうちょう kitchen knife, carving knife 0437

---

**0457**
勹 20
包
2560
常 5

Recall 勹 *wrap around*, first learned at 句 0166. Here 勹 and 己 both wrap around each other, vividly representing the ideas **WRAP** and **ENCOMPASS**. We thus add the grapheme meaning *wrap/roll up* for 己, which will be useful in the next two entries, and again later on.

---

# 巻

<sup>1</sup>**ROLL UP, wind**
<sup>2</sup>**VOLUME**

カン
ま(く) まき ま(き)

①巻く まく roll up; wind
<sup>1</sup> 巻き込む まきこむ roll (up), wrap; involve, drag in ................................. 0192
<sup>1</sup> 巻子本 かんすぼん scroll, rolled book 0094, 0031
②上中下巻 じょうちゅうげかん set of three volumes ........................... 0041, 0035, 0040
<sup>2</sup> 別巻 べっかん separate volume, extra issue... 0090

---

**0458**
己 49*
巻
2298
常 9

In ancient China, long records were kept on *tally sticks* (关) bound with string. To store such records, the Chinese simply **wound** them up into a **ROLL**—represented here by 己 (*roll up*). When referring to a bound work, 巻 corresponds to the English "**VOLUME**," which itself derives from the Latin word for "**ROLL**," *volvere*. ☞ 券 0456

---

# 圏

**SPHERE, circle, range**

ケン

生物圏 せいぶつけん biosphere ........ 0036, 0172
○(通信)圏外 (つうしん)けんがい out of range (of communication) ............... 0159, 0063, 0266
共産圏 きょうさんけん the Communist bloc ..................................... 0356, 0181
首都圏 しゅとけん national capital region ..................................... 0157, 0244

---

**0459**
囗 31
圏
2714
常 12

*Rolled up* (巻) inside an *enclosure* (囗): **SPHERE, circle, range**. For example, think of a **SPHERE** of influence *rolling up* everything inside it into its **range**, or the signal **range** of a mobile phone company *rolling up* a certain area.

---

# 勝

<sup>1</sup>**WIN**
<sup>2</sup>**EXCEL**

ショウ
か(つ) -が(ち) まさ(る)

①勝利 しょうり victory, triumph, win .......... 0412
<sup>1</sup> 勝者 しょうしゃ winner ...................... 0107
①勝つ かつ win, defeat; gain advantage
<sup>1</sup> 早い者勝ち はやいものかち first come, first served ................................ 0143, 0107
<sup>2</sup> 勝る まさる be better than, excel

---

**0460**
力 19
勝
0918
常 12

We'll treat the right side as 券 0456 CERTIFICATE, though here it contains 力, not 刀. See 勝 as a prize of *meat* and a victory *certificate*, awarded together to the person who **WINS** a competition (i.e., the person who **EXCELS** all others). ☞ 騰 2236, 藤 2235, 謄 2237

**WAR, battle, contest**

セン
いくさ　たたか(う)

戦線　せんせん　(war) front, battle line........0210
○作戦　さくせん　tactics, strategy; (military)
　　maneuvers....................................0152
舌戦　ぜっせん　war of words................0052
決勝戦　けっしょうせん　final round match, finals
　　..................................................0330, 0460
○戦う　たたかう　fight; contest

| 0461 | At the left, see a man with outstretched arms and three sharp projectiles (⺍) on his *head* |
|---|---|

0461
戈 62

戰

1590
常 13

At the left, see a man with outstretched arms and three sharp projectiles (⺍) on his *head* (田). He carries the projectiles for attaching to the *spear* (戈) he holds in front of him, for he is marching off to **WAR**. Note the old form, which shows the pattern for those of kanji based on 単.

---

**SINGLE, simple, unit**

タン

単身　たんしん　alone, by oneself, unaccompanied
　　..................................................0060
単独の　たんどくの　single, independent, sole,
　　lone ...........................................0346
単数　たんすう　[grammar] singular...........0309
○単に　たんに　merely, simply
単なる　たんなる　mere, simple, sheer

0462
小 42*

單

1946
常 9

In the previous entry, 単 carried a spear, and in a later entry (弾 1075) he will carry a bow, but here he's reduced to **simple**, hand-to-hand combat. With no tool for launching his sharpened projectiles, his own body is his **SINGLE** weapon. Take a moment to associate his isolation with this character's core concept, **SINGLE**. ☞ 巣 0601, 卑 2087

---

**SIMPLE**

カン

○簡単な　かんたんな　simple, easy, light.......0462
簡素な　かんそな　plain, simple...............0132
簡易な　かんいな　simple, simplified; easy...0443
簡明な　かんめいな　terse, concise...........0024

0463
竹 118

2374
常 18

Review 間 0448. See a **SIMPLE** *bamboo* (⺮) decoration above a gate with the sun shining through the space between its leaves.

---

過

¹**PASS BY**
²**EXCEED, over-**

カ
す(ぎる)　-す(ぎる)　-す(ぎ)　す(ごす)
あやま(つ)　あやま(ち)

①過去　かこ　the past, bygone days ............0138
²過半数　かはんすう　majority, more than half
　　..................................................0335, 0309
②過つ　あやまつ　err, make a mistake
過ぎる　すぎる　[vi] pass by; elapse; exceed, over-
○過ごす　すごす　[vt] pass (time); let pass; overdo

0464
辵 162

2704
常 12

See 咼 as a tall stack of boxes. Too many boxes have stacked up on the back of this *truck* (辶), **EXCEEDING** the legal limit (i.e., going **over** or **PAST** the limit). As a component part of other kanji, 咼 will mean *exceed/over-*.

| 骨 | **BONE** | ○人骨 じんこつ human bone ................0015 |
|---|---|---|
| | | 白骨 はっこつ bleached bone, skeleton.....0076 |
| | | 骨化 こっか ossification ....................0120 |
| | コツ | 背骨 せぼね backbone, spine ..............0124 |
| | ほね | ○骨組み ほねぐみ skeleton; framework......0264 |

| 0465 | Let S1-4, showing one box shape inside of another, suggest the idea of "inner core." Beneath that, we have ⌒ *cover* and 月 *flesh*, thus giving us "*inner core covered* by *flesh*," implying **BONE**. The reading ほね, which becomes ぼね after vowels, can be associated with the English "bone." ☞ 滑 1493 |
|---|---|
| 骨 188 | |
| 2310 | |
| 常 10 | |

| 昼 | **DAYTIME, midday** | ○昼間 ひるま (=ちゅうかん) daytime, day.......0448 |
|---|---|---|
| | | 白昼 はくちゅう broad daylight ............0076 |
| | | 昼食 ちゅうしょく lunch ....................0288 |
| | チュウ | ○昼ご飯 ひるごはん lunch ...................0377 |
| | ひる | 昼休み ひるやすみ noon recess, lunch break ....................0061 |

| 0466 | Review 尺 0337 and 尽 0338. Here, we see a *digger* (尺) leaning on the handle of his shovel, taking a break under the hot **midday** sun: **DAYTIME**. |
|---|---|
| 日 72 | |
| 晝 | |
| 2668 | |
| 常 9 | |

| 夜 | **NIGHT** | ○夜間 やかん night, nighttime...............0448 |
|---|---|---|
| | | 夜学 やがく night school....................0099 |
| | | 今夜 こんや tonight, this evening ..........0228 |
| | ヤ | 夜昼 よるひる night and day ...............0466 |
| | よ よる | ○夜中 よなか midnight, dead of night........0035 |

| 0467 | Here we perceive the idea of **NIGHT**, first from the fact of the *man* (亻)'s being at home under his *roof* (亠, normally "lid"), and next from 夕 *moon*. S8 represents the *moon*'s long, slow course across the sky at **NIGHT**. Reinforce this by writing S8 very slowly when you practice writing this character. |
|---|---|
| 夕 36 | |
| 1770 | |
| 常 8 | |

| 液 | **LIQUID** | ○液体 えきたい liquid, fluid.................0062 |
|---|---|---|
| | | 廃液 はいえき waste fluid...................0149 |
| | | 血液 けつえき blood ........................0198 |
| | エキ | 乳液 にゅうえき milky lotion; latex ..........0160 |

| 0468 | To associate 液 with **LIQUID**, let 氵 *water* and 夜 *night* suggest dew. |
|---|---|
| 水 85 | |
| 0468 | |
| 常 11 | |

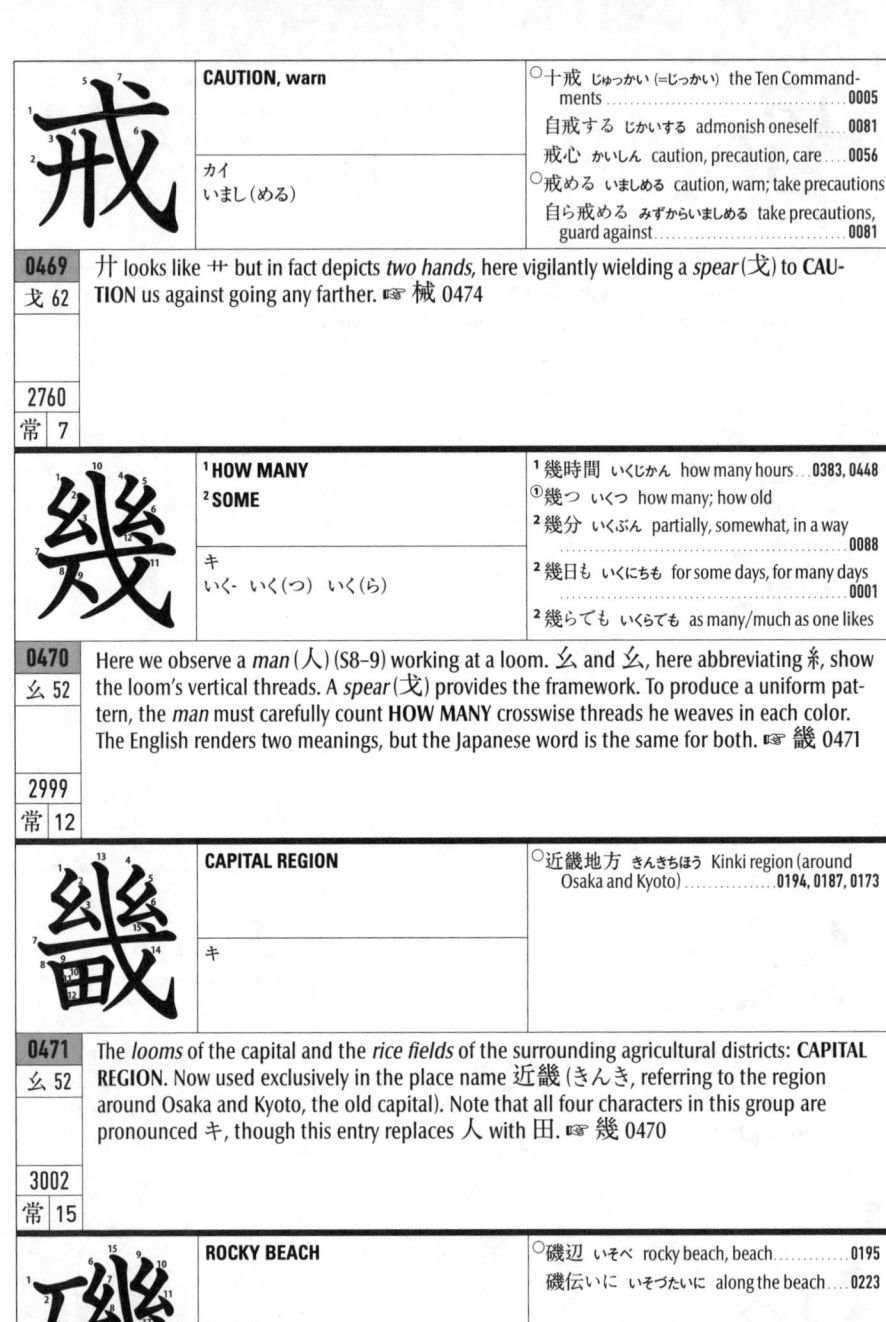

| | CAUTION, warn | ○十戒 じゅっかい (=じっかい) the Ten Commandments .................................................. **0005** |
|---|---|---|
| | | 自戒する じかいする admonish oneself ..... **0081** |
| | | 戒心 かいしん caution, precaution, care ....**0056** |
| | カイ<br>いまし(める) | ○戒める いましめる caution, warn; take precautions |
| | | 自ら戒める みずからいましめる take precautions, guard against............................... **0081** |

| **0469** | 廾 looks like ⧾ but in fact depicts *two hands*, here vigilantly wielding a *spear* (戈) to **CAUTION** us against going any farther. ☞ 械 0474 |
|---|---|
| 戈 62 | |
| **2760** | |
| 常 7 | |

| | ¹ **HOW MANY**<br>² **SOME** | ¹ 幾時間 いくじかん how many hours ...**0383, 0448** |
|---|---|---|
| | | ①幾つ いくつ how many; how old |
| | | ² 幾分 いくぶん partially, somewhat, in a way .................................................. **0088** |
| | キ<br>いく- いく(つ) いく(ら) | ² 幾日も いくにちも for some days, for many days .................................................. **0001** |
| | | ² 幾らでも いくらでも as many/much as one likes |

| **0470** | Here we observe a *man* (人) (S8-9) working at a loom. 幺 and 幺, here abbreviating 糸, show the loom's vertical threads. A *spear* (戈) provides the framework. To produce a uniform pattern, the *man* must carefully count **HOW MANY** crosswise threads he weaves in each color. The English renders two meanings, but the Japanese word is the same for both. ☞ 畿 0471 |
|---|---|
| 幺 52 | |
| **2999** | |
| 常 12 | |

| | **CAPITAL REGION** | ○近畿地方 きんきちほう Kinki region (around Osaka and Kyoto) ..............**0194, 0187, 0173** |
|---|---|---|
| | キ | |

| **0471** | The *looms* of the capital and the *rice fields* of the surrounding agricultural districts: **CAPITAL REGION**. Now used exclusively in the place name 近畿 (きんき, referring to the region around Osaka and Kyoto, the old capital). Note that all four characters in this group are pronounced キ, though this entry replaces 人 with 田. ☞ 幾 0470 |
|---|---|
| 幺 52 | |
| **3002** | |
| 常 15 | |

| | **ROCKY BEACH** | ○磯辺 いそべ rocky beach, beach............**0195** |
|---|---|---|
| | | 磯伝いに いそづたいに along the beach....**0223** |
| | キ<br>いそ | |

| **0472** | 石 *rock* and the cragginess of 幾 together represent **ROCKY BEACH**. |
|---|---|
| 石 112 | |
| **1147** | |
| 名 17 | |

| | | |
|---|---|---|
| | **¹ MACHINE**<br>**² AIRCRAFT**<br>**³ OPPORTUNITY**<br><br>キ<br>はた | ① 機関 きかん engine, machine; agency, facilities, institution .................................... 0451<br>¹ 機器 きき machinery and tools, apparatus ... 0295<br>² 機体 きたい fuselage, body (of an airplane); machine ........................................... 0062<br>③ 機会 きかい opportunity, occasion ......... 0226<br>³ 好機 こうき favorable opportunity, good chance ................................................. 0095 |

| 0473<br>木 75<br><br>0989<br>常 16 | The next two kanji use trees in mechanical devices, hardly to be wondered at given how old kanji are. In this entry we see a *wooden* (木) *loom* (幾), representing literally **MACHINE**, and figuratively **OPPORTUNITY**. Proving the kanji are not incapable of adapting to new purposes, the **MACHINE** that 機 most often refers to today is the **AIRCRAFT**. |
|---|---|

| | | |
|---|---|---|
| | **MECHANICAL CONTRIVANCE**<br><br>カイ | ○ 機械 きかい machine, mechanism ........... 0473<br>機械化 きかいか mechanization ...... 0473, 0120<br>器械 きかい instrument, apparatus, appliance ................................................. 0295 |

| 0474<br>木 75<br><br>0870<br>常 11 | **MECHANICAL CONTRIVANCES** (i.e., tools and machines) can be dangerous, so they usually come with warning labels. With this in mind, it should be easy for you to remember that a *wooden* (木) object with "*caution*" (戒) written on it is a **MECHANICAL CONTRIVANCE**.<br>☞ 戒 0469 |
|---|---|

| | | |
|---|---|---|
| | **FLY; leap**<br><br>ヒ<br>と(ぶ) と(ばす) -と(ばす) | ○ 飛行 ひこう flight, aviation ................. 0055<br>飛行機 ひこうき airplane ............. 0055, 0473<br>○ 飛ぶ とぶ fly; leap<br>飛び上がる とびあがる fly up, jump up ..... 0041<br>飛ばす とばす [vt] fly; make fly, shoot |

| 0475<br>飛 183<br><br>2990<br>常 9 | Behold a bird fluttering its wings in **FLIGHT** (compare with 隹 *small bird* and 羽 WING/FEATHER). |
|---|---|

| | | |
|---|---|---|
| | **¹ FAMILY, clan; surname**<br>**² COURTESY TITLE**<br><br>シ<br>うじ -うじ | ¹ 源氏 げんじ Genji, the Minamoto family/clan ................................................. 0209<br>① 氏神 うじがみ tutelary deity, patron saint ... 0316<br>① 氏名 しめい (full) name ..................... 0269<br>② 故川田氏 こかわだし the late Mr. Kawada ................................................. 0257, 0022, 0020<br>² 同氏 どうし the said person, he/she ......... 0182 |

| 0476<br>氏 83<br><br>2552<br>常 4 | Take S3–4 as an abbreviation for 弋 *spear* (see 成 0070), and S1–2 as a kind of shelter (cf. 广), representing a *home*. Together, *spear* and *home* suggest the idea of protecting one's **FAMILY**. 氏 can also be used as a **COURTESY TITLE** after family names. ☞ 民 0477 |
|---|---|

**PEOPLE, nation, race**

ミン
たみ

市民 しみん citizens, townspeople ..........0205
○国民 こくみん people, nation; the people...0075
民芸 みんげい folkcraft ......................0225
民間 みんかん private citizens; private, unofficial
..............................................0448
○自由の民 じゆうのたみ a free people...0081, 0432

| 0477 | Focus on the difference between the top part of this kanji and the top part of the kanji in the previous entry. Just as 民 is greater than 氏, so too **PEOPLE/nation** is greater than FAMILY/ clan. ☞ 氏 0476 |
| 氏 83 | |
| 2614 | |
| 常 5 | |

**PAPER**

シ
かみ

和紙 わし Japanese paper...................0236
○用紙 ようし blank form, stationery ..........0047
日刊紙 にっかんし daily newspaper ...0001, 0409
○手紙 てがみ letter............................0046
包み紙 つつみがみ wrapping paper.........0457

| 0478 | **PAPER**, deriving from fibrous plants, belongs to the *thread*(糸) *family*(氏). Like 氏, 紙 is pronounced シ. But all the kanji that add an extra horizontal line beneath 氏, which follow presently, are pronounced テイ. 民 differs from both groups in having a box shape at the top and in being pronounced ミン. |
| 糸 120 | |
| 1197 | |
| 常 10 | |

**LOW**

テイ
ひく(い) ひく(める) ひく(まる)

低下する ていかする fall, sink, lower, go down
..............................................0040
低温 ていおん low temperature ............0199
○最低の さいていの lowest ..................0196
○低い ひくい low, short [stature]; humble
低める ひくめる lower, bring down

| 0479 | 氐 adds an extra horizontal line at the base of 氏 and will mean *base* or *foundation*. It is not in use as a stand-alone character. Here it joins with イ to signify **LOW**, through the idea of "low man," or *man* at the *base*. |
| 人 9 | |
| 0057 | |
| 常 7 | |

**RESIST, stand up to**

テイ

抵当 ていとう mortgage, security ............0141
○大抵 たいてい generally, mostly, for the most part.................................................0033

| 0480 | Here picture two stubbornly opposing forces: 扌 pushing hard from left to right, and 氐 digging in and **RESISTING** from its very *foundation*. Try to see the mutual **RESISTANCE** as the *hand* pushes up against something that's rooted firmly to its *base*. The most important compound using this character appears at 抗 1639. |
| 手 64 | |
| 0284 | |
| 常 8 | |

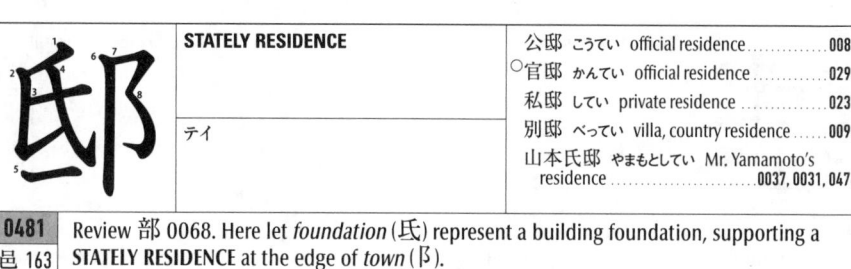

| 邸 | **STATELY RESIDENCE** | 公邸 こうてい official residence.............0089 |
|---|---|---|
| | | ○官邸 かんてい official residence............0290 |
| | | 私邸 してい private residence ...........0237 |
| | テイ | 別邸 べってい villa, country residence......0090 |
| | | 山本氏邸 やまもとしてい Mr. Yamamoto's residence .....................0037, 0031, 0476 |

| **0481** 邑 163 | Review 部 0068. Here let *foundation* (氏) represent a building foundation, supporting a **STATELY RESIDENCE** at the edge of *town* (阝). |
|---|---|
| 1045 常 8 | |

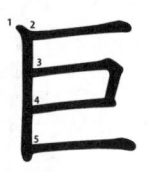

| | **BOTTOM, base** | 海底 かいてい sea bottom...................0106 |
|---|---|---|
| | | ○根底 こんてい root, basis, foundation......0284 |
| | | 心の底から こころのそこから from the bottom of one's heart.....................0056 |
| | テイ そこ | ○川底 かわぞこ riverbed ....................0022 |
| | | どん底 どんぞこ rock bottom |

| **0482** 广 53 | *Foundation* (氏) beneath a *shelter* (广): **BOTTOM**. |
|---|---|
| 2656 常 8 | |

| 巨 | **GIANT** | 巨人 きょじん giant; great person.............0015 |
|---|---|---|
| | | ○巨大 きょだいな huge, gigantic, enormous...0033 |
| | | 巨大分子 きょだいぶんし macromolecule .....................................0033, 0088, 0094 |
| | キョ | 巨体 きょたい gigantic figure.................0062 |
| | | 巨石 きょせき megalith ......................0403 |

| **0483** 二 7 | A letter "E" with a whopping middle stroke, to signify **GIANT**. This and the next entry being new graphemes, now is a good time to reiterate that you should practice writing every new grapheme until you can reproduce it from memory (always follow the established stroke order). |
|---|---|
| 2616 常 5 | |

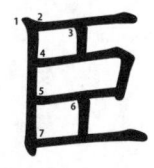

| | **RETAINER, subject** | 臣下 しんか retainer, subject, vassal.........0040 |
|---|---|---|
| | | 家臣 かしん retainer, vassal ..................0219 |
| | | ○臣民 しんみん subjects......................0477 |
| | シン | ○大臣 だいじん minister (of state)............0033 |
| | | 国土交通大臣 こくどこうつうだいじん Minister of Land, Infrastructure, and Tourism .......................0075, 0030, 0102, 0159 |

| **0484** 臣 131 | Resembling a section of brick wall, 臣 can symbolize a faithful, unquestioning "brick in the wall" and thus, by extension, a "loyal servant to one's master": a **RETAINER** or **subject**. |
|---|---|
| 2642 常 7 | |

| 基 | **BASE, foundation** | 基底 きてい base, basis, foundation; [math] base ....................0482 |
| | | 基地 きち base ....................0187 |
| | | ○基本 きほん basis, foundation ..............0031 |
| | キ | データを基にする データをもとにする based on data |
| | もと もとい | ○基づく もとづく be based on |

| **0485** | Recall 共 0356: two people bound TOGETHER for a three-legged race. Here we add two straps around their torsos, to imply the idea of *binding* (we shall postpone learning 其's meaning as a stand-alone kanji until entry 1757). In the present entry, we need to see the idea of *binding* something to the *earth* (土), for it means **BASE** or **foundation**. ☞ 碁 1797, 墓 1340 |
| 土 32 | |
| 2330 | |
| 常 11 | |

| 期 | **¹ TERM, period** | ①期間 きかん term, period....................0448 |
| | **² EXPECT, anticipate** | ¹学期 がっき school term....................0099 |
| | | ¹時期 じき time, season ....................0383 |
| | キ ゴ | ¹期限 きげん time limit, term ..............0282 |
| | | ②期待する きたいする expect, anticipate, hope ....................0386 |

| **0486** | *Bound* (其) to the *moon* (月) implies "tied to the lunar cycle," representing the idea of a fixed **period** or **TERM**. As for M2, it is precisely the lunar cycle's periodicity that allows us to **anticipate/EXPECT** when it will return. Consider this underpinning relationship as you study V5. ☞ 朝 0145 |
| 月 74 | |
| 1520 | |
| 常 12 | |

| 毛 | **HAIR** | ○毛布 もうふ blanket....................0204 |
| | | 羽毛 うもう feathers, plumage, down ........0418 |
| | | 原毛 げんもう raw wool....................0208 |
| | モウ | 不毛の ふもうの barren; infertile............0049 |
| | け | ○毛糸 けいと woolen yarn, wool ..............0112 |

| **0487** | Carefully note each difference between this kanji and 手 0046. In 毛 see a **HAIR** so long it drags across the floor. 手 does no such dragging; it is like a clean, vertical karate chop. Practice writing these two kanji correctly. |
| 毛 82 | |
| 2904 | |
| 常 4 | |

| 尾 | **TAIL** | 尾灯 びとう taillight....................0440 |
| | | 尾行 びこう following, shadowing ..........0055 |
| | | 末尾 まつび end, close ....................0272 |
| | ビ | ○語尾 ごび word ending ....................0222 |
| | お | ○尾を引く おをひく leave a trail ..............0422 |

| **0488** | We shall generally treat 尸 as *door* (see 戸 0248). Sometimes, though, it will be wise to make a concession to the etymological meaning *buttocks*, which is easy enough to see if we visualize 尸 as a leg bent at the knee while seated, with the *buttocks* at the top. Here see a long *hairy* thing hanging down from the *buttocks*: a **TAIL**. |
| 尸 44 | |
| 2635 | |
| 常 7 | |

| RAISE | ○体育 たいいく physical training [education] 0062 |
| | 発育する はついくする grow, develop......0148 |
| | 育つ そだつ be brought up; grow |
| イク | ○育てる そだてる bring up, raise; cultivate |
| そだ(つ) そだ(ち) そだ(てる) | 育む はぐくむ bring up, raise |
| はぐく(む) | |

| 0489 | Take 月 as *flesh*, representing the young flesh of a small child. Above the child is its parent (云), reaching down to grab the child and literally **RAISE** it to adulthood. We see the parent's head (S1), broad shoulders (S2), and arm extending downward, bent at the elbow (S3-4). See the child being physically lifted upward, or **RAISED**. |
| 肉 130 | |
| 毓 | |
| 1764 | |
| 常 8 | |

| SHEEP, goat | 羊肉 ようにく mutton .....................0216 |
| | ○羊毛 ようもう wool .........................0487 |
| | ○子羊 こひつじ lamb ......................0094 |
| ヨウ | 羊の数を数える ひつじのかずをかぞえる count |
| ひつじ | sheep.................................0309 |

| 0490 | Frontal view of a **SHEEP**'s head: at the top are two horns, at the bottom a long muzzle (or the beard of its cousin the **goat**, known in Japanese as 山羊 [やぎ]). |
| 羊 123 | |
| 1870 | |
| 常 6 | |

| ¹OCEAN | ①大洋 たいよう ocean .........................0033 |
| ²WESTERN, foreign | ² 洋画 ようが foreign film; Western painting 0176 |
| | ②洋風 ようふう Western [foreign] style........0425 |
| ヨウ | ² 和洋 わよう Japan and the West ............0236 |
| | ² 洋式 ようしき Western style.................0109 |

| 0491 | One normally does not associate *sheep* with the **OCEAN**. But if we imagine that for the ancient Chinese the *sheep* was not a native animal but one that had been brought from overseas, the link between *water* (氵), *sheep* (羊), and **OCEAN** is not so hard to remember. |
| 水 85 | |
| 0353 | |
| 常 9 | |

| FISH | ○魚類 ぎょるい fishes......................0310 |
| | 金魚 きんぎょ goldfish......................0029 |
| | 人魚 にんぎょ mermaid, merman ..........0015 |
| ギョ | ○魚市場 うおいちば fish market........0205, 0445 |
| うお さかな -ざかな | ○魚屋 さかなや fish shop; fishmonger........0252 |

| 0492 | Visualize as a **FISH** getting caught: S1-2 show a line and hook, S3-7 the fish's body, S8-11 its tail. Note that S1-2 will take a different meaning in other characters we'll learn later, such as 色 0528 and 危 0726. |
| 魚 195 | |
| 1825 | |
| 常 11 | |

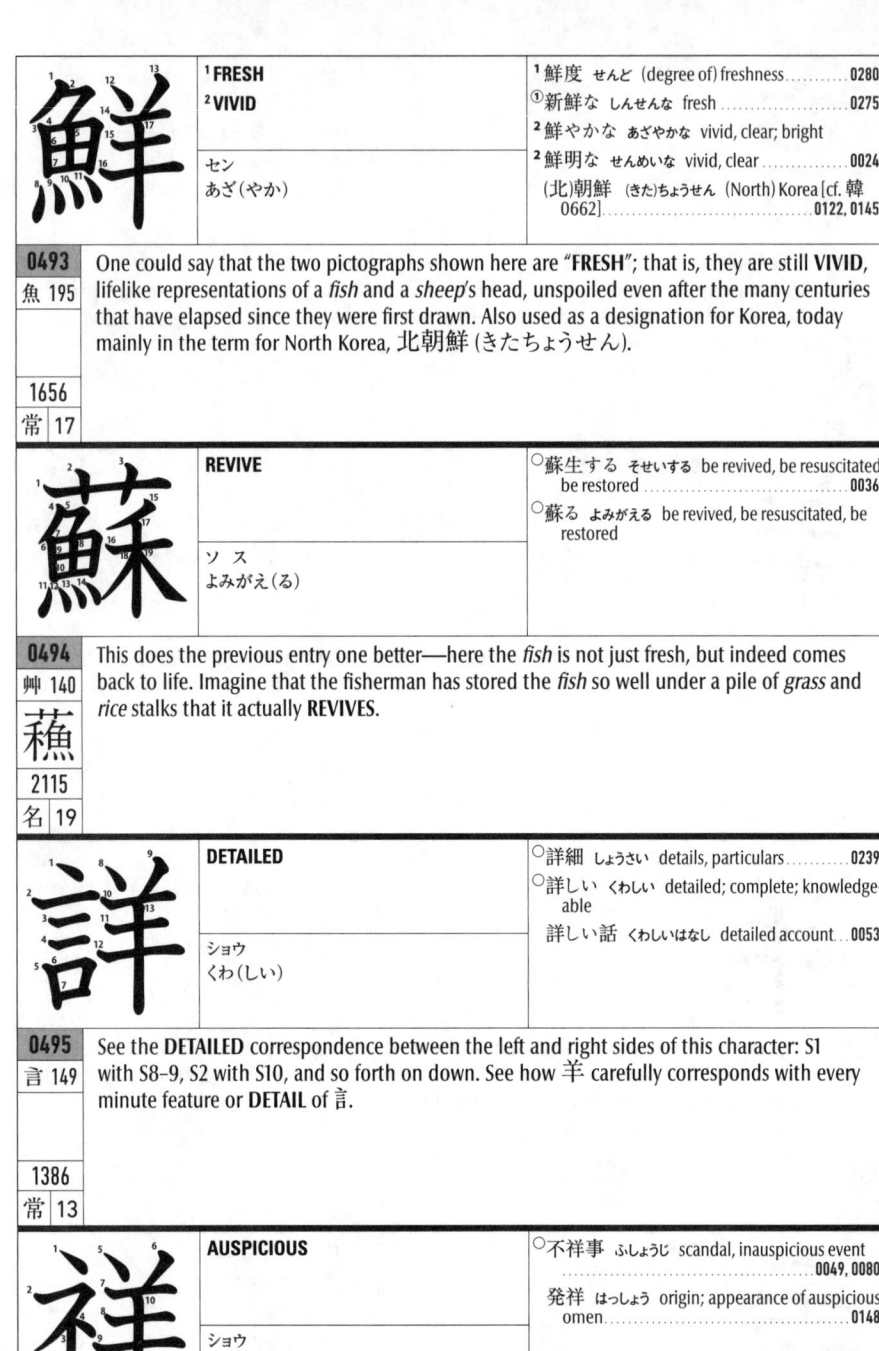

| | ¹ **FRESH** | ¹ 鮮度 せんど (degree of) freshness ............ 0280 |
| --- | --- | --- |
| | ² **VIVID** | ① 新鮮な しんせんな fresh ..................... 0275 |
| | | ² 鮮やかな あざやかな vivid, clear; bright |
| | セン | ² 鮮明な せんめいな vivid, clear ............. 0024 |
| | あざ(やか) | (北)朝鮮 (きた)ちょうせん (North) Korea [cf. 韓 0662] ................................. 0122, 0145 |

| **0493** | |
| --- | --- |
| 魚 195 | One could say that the two pictographs shown here are "**FRESH**"; that is, they are still **VIVID**, lifelike representations of a *fish* and a *sheep*'s head, unspoiled even after the many centuries that have elapsed since they were first drawn. Also used as a designation for Korea, today mainly in the term for North Korea, 北朝鮮 (きたちょうせん). |
| **1656** | |
| 常 17 | |

| | **REVIVE** | ○ 蘇生する そせいする be revived, be resuscitated, be restored ................................. 0036 |
| --- | --- | --- |
| | | ○ 蘇る よみがえる be revived, be resuscitated, be restored |
| | ソ ス | |
| | よみがえ(る) | |

| **0494** | |
| --- | --- |
| 艸 140 | This does the previous entry one better—here the *fish* is not just fresh, but indeed comes back to life. Imagine that the fisherman has stored the *fish* so well under a pile of *grass* and *rice* stalks that it actually **REVIVES**. |
| **2115** | |
| 名 19 | |

| | **DETAILED** | ○ 詳細 しょうさい details, particulars ............ 0239 |
| --- | --- | --- |
| | | ○ 詳しい くわしい detailed; complete; knowledge-able |
| | ショウ | 詳しい話 くわしいはなし detailed account ... 0053 |
| | くわ(しい) | |

| **0495** | |
| --- | --- |
| 言 149 | See the **DETAILED** correspondence between the left and right sides of this character: S1 with S8–9, S2 with S10, and so forth on down. See how 羊 carefully corresponds with every minute feature or **DETAIL** of 言. |
| **1386** | |
| 常 13 | |

| | **AUSPICIOUS** | ○ 不祥事 ふしょうじ scandal, inauspicious event ................................. 0049, 0080 |
| --- | --- | --- |
| | | 発祥 はっしょう origin; appearance of auspicious omen ................................. 0148 |
| | ショウ | |

| **0496** | |
| --- | --- |
| 示 113 | Here we see a *sheep* (羊) being sacrificed at the *altar* (礻) to propitiate the gods. Because it was believed to ensure the gods' favor, the ritual itself came to represent the idea **AUSPICIOUS**. |
| **0855** | |
| 常 10 | |

| | BEAUTIFUL | ○美人 びじん beautiful woman .............. 0015<br>美化 びか beautification.................. 0120<br>美点 びてん good point.................. 0349 |
|---|---|---|
| | ビ<br>うつく(しい) | ○美しい うつくしい beautiful<br>美味しい おいしい delicious, good ....... 0273 |

**0497**
羊 123

1955
常 9

羊 shortens to 羊 to accommodate other graphemes below it, as we observe in this entry and the next one. Remember the meanings of these two kanji based on how they differ. First, 業 (the next entry) is built on 木 *tree*, rather than 大. It also has what can be visualized as a board with four bricks piled on top of it (⠁ in the next entry). Containing lumber and a load of bricks, the next entry suggests WORK. By contrast, the present entry contains a *sheep* (羊) spreading its legs out in two graceful curves (S8–9): BEAUTY. ☞ 業 0498, 実 0499

| | ¹ **WORK**<br>² **BUSINESS**<br>³ **INDUSTRY**<br><br>ギョウ ゴウ<br>わざ | ① 人間業 にんげんわざ work of man..... 0015, 0448<br>¹ 作業 さぎょう work, operation.............. 0152<br>² 事業 じぎょう undertaking, business........ 0080<br>³ 工業 こうぎょう industry, manufacturing .... 0108<br>① 産業 さんぎょう industry ................. 0181 |
|---|---|---|

**0498**
木 75

2265
常 13

The previous entry explains how to associate this character with WORK. The trick is to see the *act* of carrying out a task, in the way the tree-based structure supports the load of bricks. Once you have assimilated this image of WORK, you can associate it with the extended meanings BUSINESS and INDUSTRY. ☞ 美 0497, 実 0499

| | ¹ **REAL, actual, true**<br>² **FRUIT, bear fruit**<br><br>ジツ<br>み みの(る) | ¹ 実用 じつよう practical use, utility .......... 0047<br>① 事実 じじつ fact, reality.................... 0080<br>¹ 実に美しい じつにうつくしい truly beautiful 0497<br>② 実る みのる bear fruit, ripen<br>² 木の実 このみ nut, berry.................. 0028 |
|---|---|---|

**0499**
宀 40

1911
常 8

Picture 宀 as the roof of a granary, and 夫 as a pile of FRUIT, accumulating layer by layer (S4–6) during the harvest, literally the FRUIT of one's labor. Thinking of FRUIT as the <u>realization</u> of one's labor allows us to associate FRUIT with REAL/actual. Note the traditional form. ☞ 美 0497, 業 0498, 果 0599

| | FOSTER, cultivate, raise to maturity<br><br>ヨウ<br>やしな(う) | ○養育する よういくする foster, bring up, educate<br>.................. 0489<br>養子 ようし foster/adopted child.......... 0094<br>養成する ようせいする train, educate, bring up<br>.................. 0070<br>休養 きゅうよう rest, recuperation, relaxation 0061<br>○養う やしなう foster, raise; raise animals |
|---|---|---|

**0500**
食 184

2089
常 15

Recalling that 羊 is an abbreviated version of 羊 *sheep* and that 良 0285 shows us an image of a *good boy*, visualize in this entry a *sheep's* **raising** its *good kid*. See the sheep spread its legs (S7–8) protectively over its young, to FOSTER its safe and healthy development.

|  | ¹MODE, manner, way (of doing), style<br><br>²FORMAL TITLE<br><br>ヨウ<br>さま | ¹ 様式 ようしき mode, manner; style ..........0109<br>① 同様に どうように similarly, in the same way 0182<br>¹ 様子 ようす situation, aspect; appearance;<br>  indication................................0094<br>¹ 有様 ありさま condition, state of affairs; sight 0400<br>² 田中様 たなかさま Ms./Mr. Tanaka ....0020, 0035 |
| --- | --- | --- |

| **0501**<br>木 75<br>様<br>0969<br>常 14 | The right half of this character shows us a **way** of writing 羊 *sheep* and 水 *water* together with a single vertical stroke (also note that in this version of *water*, we write its left-hand portion in two separate strokes). It is easy to imagine that the *sheep* is standing beside a *tree* (木), lowering its head to drink from a pond. Think of this as a funny **MODE**, **style**, or **way** of writing *sheep* and *water* (this is the only character in the course that has this combined form). V5 illustrates the usage of the second meaning, **FORMAL TITLE**. |
| --- | --- |

|  | SCHEME, project, plan<br><br>キ<br>くわだ(てる)　たくら(み)* | 企図 きと plan, scheme, intention ..........0298<br>企画 きかく plan, project ....................0176<br>○企業 きぎょう undertaking, enterprise; company<br>  ................................................0498<br>○企てる くわだてる scheme; undertake, attempt<br>凶行を企てる きょうこうをくわだてる plan/at-<br>  tempt a terrible crime.................0296, 0055 |
| --- | --- | --- |

| **0502**<br>人 9<br><br>1742<br>常 6 | See 人 as a mountain peak, and let 止 suggest a couple of mountain climbers *stopping* on their way to the summit to carefully **plan** a **SCHEME** for reaching the top. Associate 止 *stop* in this character with the deliberate, careful **planning** of a **SCHEME** or **project**. |
| --- | --- |

| 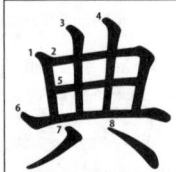 | ¹MUSICAL COMPOSITION<br><br>²CURVE<br><br>キョク<br>ま(がる)　ま(げる) | ¹ 曲調 きょくちょう melody, tone................0306<br>¹ 名曲 めいきょく excellent piece of music, famous<br>  tune ......................................0269<br>① 作曲 さっきょく composition................0152<br>② 曲線 きょくせん curve, curved line ..........0210<br>② 曲がる まがる [vi] curve; warp; turn |
| --- | --- | --- |

| **0503**<br>日 73<br><br>2956<br>常 6 | Visualize 曲 as a pair of notes (S3–4) written on a three-line musical staff, representing a **MUSICAL COMPOSITION**. Now imagine a tune composed of many notes along this staff, a melodious series of **CURVES** bending now higher, now lower, among the staff's straight lines. |
| --- | --- |

| 典 | ¹STANDARD WORK<br><br>²CANON, authority<br><br>テン | ¹ 事典 じてん encyclopedia....................0080<br>¹ 字典 じてん Chinese character dictionary...0098<br>① 古典 こてん classics; old book..............0254<br>² 法典 ほうてん code of laws, statute..........0139<br>² 出典 しゅってん authority, source ............0038 |
| --- | --- | --- |

| **0504**<br>八 12<br><br>2283<br>常 8 | Visualize a two-legged bookshelf, containing the **STANDARD WORKS** or **CANON** of one's discipline. Practice writing this entry and the previous one in alternation, remembering that the character with the two legs is a bookshelf containing the **CANON**. Note also that in the present entry S6 extends out both the left and right sides. |
| --- | --- |

**¹ RISE TO PROSPERITY, rouse up**
**² AMUSEMENT, interest**

コウ キョウ
おこ(る) おこ(す)

¹ 興起する こうきする rise, be in the ascendant; rouse, stir..................0430
① 興業 こうぎょう promotion of industry.......0498
① 国が興る くにがおこる the country prospers 0075
② 興味 きょうみ interest.....................0273
² 興が有る きょうがある be interesting, be fun ..................0400

**0505**
臼 134

2525
常 16

See as three entertainers (S1–13) performing on a stage (S14). S15–16 can be visualized as a pair of viewers in the audience, or a pair of ramps leading up to the stage. Picture a **rousing** performance, one that excites much **interest** and **AMUSEMENT**, and that symbolizes through its vigorous movement the idea of **RISING TO PROSPERITY**. ☞ 輿 0506

---

**PALANQUIN**

ヨ
こし

○神輿 みこし palanquin shrine carried in festivals [cf. 御 0862]...............0316
輿入れ こしいれ bridal procession; bride's marriage into the groom's home...........0039

**0506**
臼 134

2529
名 17

Easily visualized as a covered litter or **PALANQUIN**, with 車 to suggest the idea of a carriage. Most often used in the words 神輿 (V1) and 御輿 (see 御 0862), both read みこし and referring to the "portable shrine" used in Japanese festivals for carrying around a symbolic representation of the local tutelary deity. ☞ 興 0505

---

**DRAGON**

リュウ
たつ

竜神 りゅうじん dragon god, dragon king....0316
○竜骨 りゅうこつ keel.........................0465
竜安寺 りょうあんじ Ryoanji [Zen temple in Kyoto]...............................0096, 0382
竜巻 たつまき tornado.....................0458

**0507**
龍 212
龍
1805
常 10

A mythical monster surfs on a bolt of lighting (cf. 電 0155): behold the **DRAGON**. Pay special attention to the traditional form, which is used in 籠 BASKET (two entries below) and 襲 RAID/INHERIT (1849). Learn to recognize the new and old forms interchangeably.

---

**WATERFALL**

たき

滝川 たきがわ rapids.....................0022
ナイアガラの滝 ナイアガラのたき Niagara Falls

**0508**
水 85
瀧
0607
常 13

Now picture the *dragon* (竜) bathing in the *water* (氵) of a **WATERFALL**.

**籠**

竹 118
**籠**
2383
常 22

0509

**BASKET, confine (oneself) in**

ロウ
かご こ(める) こも(る)

○籠居 ろうきょ living in seclusion, retirement ............................................ 0255

灯籠 とうろう garden lantern; hanging lantern ............................................ 0440

○鳥籠 とりかご bird cage ...................... 0340
○籠る こもる be confined in, seclude oneself

引き籠り ひきこもり a shut-in ............... 0422

This kanji uses the traditional form for *dragon* (龍, which was not standardized with the previous two entries when it was added to the Joyo list). Close your eyes and imagine catching a *dragon* in a great *bamboo* (⺮) **BASKET**, and then **confining** it in that basket for the rest of its days.

---

**辰**

辰 161
2582
名 7

0510

**(sign of) THE DRAGON**

シン
たつ

○辰年 たつどし Year of the Dragon ............ 0117

The character for **(sign of) THE DRAGON** resembles 長 0091 LONG/CHIEF but adds a beard (lower part of S2). We can visualize, then, the long mane and beard often included in Eastern depictions of dragons. 竜 0507 is used to refer to the creature; the present entry refers only to the Chinese horary or zodiac sign associated with it. ☞ 長 0091

---

**農**

辰 161
2353
常 13

0511

**FARMING**

ノウ

○農業 のうぎょう agriculture .................. 0498

農家 のうか farmhouse, farmer ............. 0219

農作 のうさく land cultivation ............... 0152

士農工商 しのうこうしょう warriors, farmers, artisans, and tradesmen [the four classes of Edo-era Japan] ................................. 0350

To perceive the idea of **FARMING** in this character, imagine that 辰 *dragon* has been forced into service as a draft animal, seen here plowing crisscrossing furrows in a farm field, which we'll represent just this once with 曲.

---

**濃**

水 85
0697
常 16

0512

**THICK, concentrated**

ノウ
こ(い)

○濃度 のうど density ........................... 0280

濃化する のうかする concentrate, condense

濃さ こさ depth (of color); thickness, strength [as of coffee]

○濃いスープ こいスープ thick soup

油っ濃い あぶらっこい greasy, oily .......... 0433

The sight of ⺡ *water* flowing beside the *farming* (農) dragon should call to mind an image of **THICK** agricultural runoff, full of muddy sediment and various nutrients, fertilizers, and other additives the farmer mixes into it. Picture a **THICK**, gloppy, **concentrated** syrup.

**ABUNDANT**

ホウ
ゆたか

豊水 ほうすい abundance of water .........0027
豊満な ほうまんな plump, corpulent .......0179
○豊作 ほうさく abundant harvest.............0152
豊年 ほうねん fruitful year.................0117
○豊かな国 ゆたかなくに rich country .......0075

**0513**
豆 151

豐

2352
常 | 13

Here we observe a *pea* (豆)–sized man carrying an **ABUNDANT** harvest on his back.

---

**LUCKY**

キチ キツ

吉日 きちじつ (=きつじつ) lucky day ..........0001
○吉事 きちじ auspicious event ..............0080
吉祥 きちじょう (=きっしょう) auspicious omen..0496
吉凶 きっきょう good or ill luck, fortune .....0296
吉田 よしだ Yoshida [surname].............0020

**0514**
口 30

1855
常 | 6

When we see 士 *military man* standing on a pedestal as in 吉, it will be helpful to see him as a particular kind of military man, the 力士 りきし or sumo wrestler. Here we see the champion of the tournament, standing on a pedestal (口) to be honored—this is his **LUCKY** day. Do not confuse with the *"earth* behind *door"* combination we saw earlier at 周 0304.

---

¹ **STUFF**
² **REPRIMAND**

キツ
つ(める) つ(め) -づ(め) つ(まる)
つ(む)

¹詰める つめる stuff, fill, cram
¹見詰める みつめる gaze at, watch intently...0083
①詰まる つまる be stuffed; be clogged
¹気詰まり きづまり constrained feeling, awkwardness.................................0126
②詰問する きつもんする cross-examine, question closely...................................0452

**0515**
言 149

1380
常 | 13

See the well-upholstered sumo fighter (士) use every gram of his massive weight to **STUFF** these *words* (言) into the box beneath him. This image of cramming something with words also suggests 詰's original meaning of **REPRIMANDING** someone, in the sense of pressing them hard with words of criticism or interrogation.

---

¹ **TIE**
² **CONCLUDE**

ケツ
むす(ぶ) ゆ(う) ゆ(わえる)

¹結束 けっそく unity, union...................0307
①結ぶ むすぶ tie (up), bind
¹結う ゆう dress/do one's hair
²結語 けつご conclusion, concluding remarks.................................0222
②結局 けっきょく after all, finally, in conclusion 0256

**0516**
糸 120

1235
常 | 12

Now we are in the sumo wrestler's dressing room, observing his topknot being **TIED** with *thread* (糸) as he prepares for his match. M2 **CONCLUDE** is a natural extension from **TIE**.

| | **¹ THROW** | **¹ 投石** とうせき  throwing stones ............... 0403 |
|---|---|---|
| | **² SEND IN (to), submit** | **¹ 投手** とうしゅ  pitcher .......................... 0046 |
| | | **①投げる** なげる  throw, cast, pitch; abandon |
| | トウ | **②投書** とうしょ  contribution, letter (from a reader) |
| | な(げる) -な(げ) | .................................................. 0079 |
| | | 投じる(=投ずる) とうじる (=とうずる)  throw, cast, pitch; send in/to; join; invest |

**0517**

手 64

Now we meet the grapheme 殳 *lance*, made up of 又 *hand* and 几, whose three sides can with some effort be seen as representing the outlines of a lance's shaft, viewed from one end (几 by itself means *tablecloth*, but we'll ignore that when it appears inside 殳). Thus here we see 扌 *hand* THROWING a *lance*. SEND IN (to)/submit is a derivative meaning.

0228

常 7

| | **SERVICE, duty, office(r)** | 役所 やくしょ  public [government] office ... 0249 |
|---|---|---|
| | | 役員 やくいん  officer, leader, director ....... 0317 |
| | | 役者 やくしゃ  actor, actress .................. 0107 |
| | ヤク エキ | 役割 やくわり  assigning parts; part, role, duty |
| | | .................................................. 0416 |
| | | ○役に立つ やくにたつ  be useful, be helpful .. 0067 |

**0518**

彳 60

The construction "*lance* (殳) + *action* (彳)" illustrates the idea of carrying out one's military SERVICE.

0217

常 7

| | **SINK, fall in** | 水没する すいぼつする  sink, submerge ..... 0027 |
|---|---|---|
| | | 日没 にちぼつ  sunset ......................... 0001 |
| | | 没頭する ぼっとうする  be absorbed in ...... 0162 |
| | ボツ | ○没入する ぼつにゅうする  be immersed/ absorbed in (one's work) ................... 0039 |
| | | 戦没する せんぼつする  be killed in battle/ action ........................................ 0461 |

**0519**

水 85

Visualize the *lance* (殳) SINKING into the *water* (氵). As 没 is one of only two kanji in this course with the *on* reading ボツ (and the other, 勃 2036, is much less frequently used), one might think of this as the sound of a heavy iron *lance* forcefully splashing as it **falls into water**.

0230

常 7

| | **SET UP, establish** | ○設立する せつりつする  establish, found, set up |
|---|---|---|
| | | .................................................. 0067 |
| | | 設定 せってい  establishment, creation, setting up; setting .............................. 0045 |
| | セツ | 私設の しせつの  private ...................... 0237 |
| | もう(ける) | 設問する せつもんする  pose a question .... 0452 |
| | | ○設ける もうける  set up, establish |

**0520**

言 149

Think of a cavalry battalion, SETTING UP/establishing a formation for battle: 殳 *lance* represents their weaponry and 言 *word* represents their tactical discussions. The reading セツ is easily remembered from the English SET UP.

1338

常 11

| 段 | **STEP, stage** | 石段 いしだん stone steps ......................... 0403 |
| --- | --- | --- |
| | | 五段 ごだん fifth grade (as in karate) ........ 0007 |
| | | 段々畑 だんだんばたけ terraced fields ....... 0129 |
| | ダン | 段取り だんどり program, plan, step, course of action ................................................. 0059 |
| | | ○手段 しゅだん means, way, step .............. 0046 |

**0521**
殳 79
**1059**
常 9

Ｆ can be seen as a long pole with pegs inserted into it. Here we insert *lances* (殳) into the peg holes, to make a series of **STEPS** for climbing.

| 殺 | **KILL** | ○殺人 さつじん murder, homicide ............. 0015 |
| --- | --- | --- |
| | | 自殺 じさつ suicide .............................. 0081 |
| | | 殺害 さつがい (=せつがい) murder, killing, assassination ..................................... 0413 |
| | サツ サイ セツ | ○殺す ころす kill, murder |
| | ころ(す) -ごろ(し) | 人殺し ひとごろし murder; murderer ........ 0015 |

**0522**
殳 79
殺
**1208**
常 10

Back at 凶 0296 EVIL MISFORTUNE we learned to associate the "メ" mark with violent death. Continuing along these lines, here we can see メ as a pair of *slash marks* violently cut into a *tree* (木) with a *lance* (殳), **KILLING** it. ☞ 刹 0523

| 刹 | **TEMPLE** | ○名刹 めいさつ famous temple ............... 0269 |
| --- | --- | --- |
| | | 古刹 こさつ historic temple ................... 0254 |
| | サツ セツ | |

**0523**
刀 18
**1167**
常 8

Again メ suggests *slash marks*, now made by a *sword* (刂). Let this symbolize a *tree* (木)-cutting ritual consecrating the construction of a new **TEMPLE**. An *on-yomi* compound with セツ appears at 那 1410. ☞ 殺 0522, 刈 0524

| 刈 | **CLIP, crop** | 刈り込む かりこむ prune ........................ 0192 |
| --- | --- | --- |
| | | 刈り取る かりとる mow, cut down, reap, harvest ................................................ 0059 |
| | | 羊毛を刈る ようもうをかる shear sheep .............................................. 0490, 0487 |
| | か(る) | 草刈り くさかり mowing, mower ............. 0144 |
| | | 刈り入れ かりいれ harvest ...................... 0039 |

**0524**
刀 18
苅
**0017**
常 4

*Sword* (刂) and *slash marks* (メ): let this image suggest a machete or pair of shears, **cropping** or **CLIPPING** vegetation. ☞ 刹 0523

**PICTURE, painting**

カイ　エ

○絵画　かいが　pictures, paintings, drawings... **0176**
絵本　えほん　picture book ..................... **0031**
絵巻物　えまきもの　picture scroll ....... **0458, 0172**
○大和絵　やまとえ　classical Japanese decorative
　　painting..................... **0033, 0236**
油絵　あぶらえ　oil painting ................... **0433**

| **0525** | Review 会 0226 and 合 0227. Here let 糸 *thread* suggest a canvas, and let 会 *meet* suggest combinations of lines and colors painted on it: **PICTURE.** ☞ 給 0526 |
| 糸 120 | |
| 繪 | |
| 1233 | |
| 常 12 | |

---

**¹ SUPPLY**
**² PAY**

キュウ

¹ 給油　きゅうゆ　supply of oil ..................... **0433**
¹ 自給　じきゅう　self-supply, self-support ....... **0081**
¹ 支給　しきゅう　provision, supply; grant ....... **0373**
² 月給　げっきゅう　monthly pay [salary] ......... **0023**
② 時給　じきゅう　hourly wage ..................... **0383**

| **0526** | Let this character suggest the idea of "*fitting* (合) with *threads* (糸)," i.e., "outfitting," and by extension **SUPPLYING**. When the thing **SUPPLIED** is wages, the English rendering is **PAY** (M2). ☞ 絵 0525, 紹 1106 |
| 糸 120 | |
| 1237 | |
| 常 12 | |

---

**CIRCULAR COMMA PATTERN**

ハ
ともえ

○三つ巴　みつどもえ　circular pattern of three
　　commas; three-sided fight................ **0004**

| **0527** | Depicts a **CIRCULAR COMMA PATTERN** used as a decoration in みこし (see 輿 0506) and other Shinto architecture. Two of them together look like this: ☯. ☞ 巳 2296 |
| 己 49 | |
| 2894 | |
| 名 4 | |

---

色

**¹ COLOR, character**
**² EROS**

ショク　シキ
いろ

① 青色　あおいろ (=せいしょく)　blue ............. **0130**
¹ 顔色　かおいろ (=がんしょく)　complexion,
　　countenance ................................. **0180**
① 特色　とくしょく　characteristic ......... **0385**
¹ 色々な　いろいろな　various kinds of
② 色っぽい　いろっぽい　erotic, amorous

| **0528** | Here 巴 depicts a bent-over body with exposed buttocks. S1–2 suggest engaging in an **EROTIC** act with this object. If we also think of it as an "*iro*-tic" (i.e., colorful) act, we can associate the ideas **EROS** and **COLOR** the same way Japanese speakers do. ☞ 免 1272, 角 0342, 危 0726 |
| 色 139 | |
| 1748 | |
| 常 6 | |

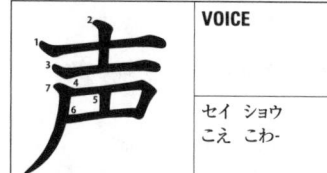

| 声 | **VOICE** | 声調 せいちょう tone of voice, style; tone [in Chinese phonetics] .................... 0306 |
|---|---|---|
| | セイ ショウ こえ こわ- | ○音声 おんせい voice, sound ................ 0151 |
| | | 発声 はっせい vocalization, utterance ...... 0148 |
| | | 声明 せいめい declaration ................. 0024 |
| | | ○読者の声 どくしゃのこえ voice of the reader .......................... 0355, 0107 |

| 0529 | Think of 戸 *door* as a classroom door, this time with a two-paned window at the top. Though the classroom *door* is shut, the booming **VOICE** of a lecturing *man of learning* (士) carries over the *door* (and through the two-paned window), reaching our ears. |
|---|---|
| 士 33* 聲 | |
| 1880 常 7 | |

| 眉 | **EYEBROW** | 眉間 みけん brow, glabella ............... 0448 |
|---|---|---|
| | ビ ミ まゆ | ○眉毛 まゆげ eyebrows .................. 0487 |
| | | 眉をひそめる まゆをひそめる knit one's brows, frown |

| 0530 | An *eye* (目) with an **EYEBROW** over it. |
|---|---|
| 目 109 | |
| 2770 常 9 | |

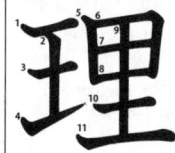

| 里 | ¹ **VILLAGE, countryside** ² **LEAGUE, *RI* (about 3.9 kilometers)** | ¹ 里人 りじん villagers, country folk .......... 0015 |
|---|---|---|
| | リ さと | ①古里 ふるさと hometown, birthplace ....... 0254 |
| | | ¹ 里心 さとごころ homesickness ............. 0056 |
| | | ² 一里 いちり 1 *ri* ...................... 0002 |
| | | ② 千里 せんり 1000 *ri*, a great distance ....... 0017 |

| 0531 | Though 田 and 土 are unified in a single central vertical stroke, visualize them separately as *rice fields* and the *land* adjacent to it, where the **VILLAGE** is located. Also means **LEAGUE/ RI** (about 3.9 kilometers), which may be thought of as the typical distance, in former times, between one **VILLAGE** and the next. |
|---|---|
| 里 166 | |
| 2968 常 7 | |

| 理 | ¹ **REASON, logic** ² **BASIC PRINCIPLE, law** ³ **MANAGE, put in order** | ①合理的な ごうりてきな rational, logical, reasonable ........................... 0227, 0169 |
|---|---|---|
| | リ | ¹ 理由 りゆう reason, cause, ground ......... 0432 |
| | | ² 原理 げんり principle, theory ............. 0208 |
| | | ³ 代理人 だいりにん representative, agent, proxy ................................... 0071, 0015 |
| | | ³ 整理する せいりする put in order, arrange; liquidate; retrench .................... 0308 |

| 0532 | The *hen* form 王 is an abbreviation of 玉 and signifies *gem* or *round/spherical object*. Here 里, made up of 田 and 土, refers to land with orderly parallel lines running through it. Combined with 王, this is meant to suggest the grain of a gemstone, symbolizing **REASON**, **logic**, and **PRINCIPLE**, and by extension **put in order/MANAGE**. ☞ 埋 0533 |
|---|---|
| 玉 96 | |
| 0881 常 11 | |

| | BURY, be buried | 埋設する まいせつする put [lay] underground .......0520 |
|---|---|---|
| | | ○埋没する まいぼつする be buried; fall into oblivion .......0519 |
| | マイ | 土に埋める つちにうめる bury in the ground 0030 |
| | う(める) う(まる) う(もれる) | 生き埋め いきうめ being buried alive .......0036 |
| | | ○埋め立てる うめたてる reclaim, fill in .......0067 |

| 0533 | The only place where villagers desire to **BE BURIED** is in the *earth* (土) of their *village* (里). |
|---|---|
| 土 32 | ☞ 理 0532 |
| 0364 | |
| 常 10 | |

| | ¹ **FIELD** ² **WILD, rustic** | ¹平野 へいや plain(s), open field .......0334 |
|---|---|---|
| | | ①分野 ぶんや field, sphere, area .......0088 |
| | | ②野生 やせい wild .......0036 |
| | ヤ | ²野鳥 やちょう wild fowl, wild bird .......0340 |
| | の の- | 野党 やとう opposition party .......0319 |

| 0534 | Review 予 0163. Here see 予 as a sign posted at the edge of the *village* (里), pointing in the |
|---|---|
| 里 166 | direction of virgin **FIELDS**. **WILD** and **rustic** are cognate meanings. |
| 埜 | |
| 1350 | |
| 常 11 | |

| | **BLACK** | ○黒人 こくじん black person .......0015 |
|---|---|---|
| | | 黒海 こっかい Black Sea .......0106 |
| | | ○黒い くろい black |
| | コク | 黒字 くろじ the black, surplus .......0098 |
| | くろ くろ(い) | 白黒 しろくろ black and white .......0076 |

| 0535 | See ⺌ *fire* burning the *village* until it is **BLACK**. |
|---|---|
| 黒 203 | |
| 黑 | |
| 2388 | |
| 常 11 | |

| | **INDIA INK** | ○水墨画 すいぼくが India-ink painting .0027, 0176 |
|---|---|---|
| | | 墨色 すみいろ India-ink color .......0528 |
| | | ○墨絵 すみえ India-ink painting .......0525 |
| | ボク | お墨付き おすみつき certificate, authorization; |
| | すみ | paper bearing the signature of the shogun or |
| | | feudal lord .......0064 |

| 0536 | So-called "**INDIA INK**" actually comes from the Far East, but may have originally reached |
|---|---|
| 土 32 | Europe via India. Its kanji contains *earth* (土) because it was traditionally manufactured in |
| 墨 | solid blocks, to be dissolved in water at one's desk. Thus *black earth* was written to suggest |
| 2400 | a solidified black pigment: **INDIA INK**. |
| 常 14 | |

| CHILD | 童心 どうしん child's mind [heart] ............ 0056 |
| | 童顔 どうがん baby face ..................... 0180 |
| | ○童話 どうわ nursery tale, fairy tale .......... 0053 |
| ドウ | 学童 がくどう schoolchild ..................... 0099 |
| わらべ | ○童の わらべの children's |

| 0537 | In this and the next entry, see 里 as a person (田 taking on its secondary meaning *head*). |
| 立 117 | Here, picture a **CHILD** *standing* (立) on a grown-up's shoulders. ☞ 章 1459 |
| | |
| 1828 | |
| 常 12 | |

| QUANTITY, weigh(t), measure | ○大量 たいりょう large quantity, great volume ... 0033 |
| | 量産 りょうさん mass production ............ 0181 |
| | 数量 すうりょう quantity, volume ............ 0309 |
| リョウ | 量より質 りょうよりしつ quality before quantity |
| はか(る) | ................................. 0318 |
| | ○量る はかる measure, weigh |

| 0538 | The concept of **QUANTITY** is vividly depicted in 量, in which a person (里) is noticeably |
| 里 166 | squashed under a heavy load (thus also suggesting the character's secondary meaning |
| | **weigh(t)**). ☞ 重 0539 |
| 2180 | |
| 常 12 | |

| ¹**HEAVY** | ①重量 じゅうりょう weight ..................... 0538 |
| ²**PILE ON TOP OF; layer, -ply; duplicate** | ¹ 起重機 きじゅうき crane ............... 0430, 0473 |
| | ①重い おもい heavy, serious |
| ジュウ チョウ | ②重ねる かさねる [vt] pile up; stack in layers |
| え おも(い) おも(り) かさ(ねる) | ² 二重の ふたえの (=にじゅうの) twofold, two-ply |
| かさ(なる) | ................................. 0003 |

| 0539 | 重 vividly conveys both its meanings: **PILE ON TOP OF** (from the seven horizontal lines piled |
| 里 166 | **layer** upon **layer**), and **HEAVY** (from the weight of so many lines all piled up). For examples of |
| | compounds using the チョウ reading, see 尊 0802, 貴 1177, and 慎 1718. ☞ 量 0538, 垂 |
| 2991 | 1004 |
| 常 9 | |

| MOVE | ○動く うごく [vi] move; operate; act |
| | 重い物を動かす おもいものをうごかす move |
| | something heavy ....................... 0539, 0172 |
| ドウ | ○動物 どうぶつ animal ..................... 0172 |
| うご(く) うご(かす) | 不動産 ふどうさん immovable property, real |
| | estate .............................. 0049, 0181 |
| | 感動する かんどうする be moved, be impressed |
| | ................................. 0327 |

| 0540 | To perceive the meaning **MOVE** in this character, try to see *power* (力) dragging a *heavy* (重) |
| 力 19 | weight from left to right. ☞ 働 0541, 勤 1732, 勲 1778 |
| | |
| 1583 | |
| 常 11 | |

| WORK | 実働時間 じつどうじかん actual working hours ...................................0499, 0383, 0448 |
|------|--------|
| ドウ<br>はたら(く) | ○働く はたらく work, labor; operate, function<br>働き手 はたらきて worker, breadwinner.....0046<br>共働き ともばたらき working together; dual income...................................................0356 |

| 0541<br>人 9<br>仂<br>0130<br>常 13 | To the last entry we now add イ, to convey the idea of human labor. See イ busily **WORKING**, helping *move* (動) the heavy weight from left to right. 働 is among the kanji known as 国字 (こくじ, national characters), which the Japanese created themselves based on the Chinese pattern; this is the only one to which they gave a pseudo *on-yomi*. ☞ 動 0540 |
|---|---|

| LABOR | ○労働 ろうどう (manual) labor, toil..............0541<br>労働組合 ろうどうくみあい labor union ...................................0541, 0264, 0227<br>労役 ろうえき labor, work, toil..................0518<br>苦労 くろう difficulties, hardships, labor....0405<br>心労 しんろう cares, worries, anxiety .........0056 |
|------|--------|
| ロウ | |

| 0542<br>力 19<br>勞<br>2205<br>常 7 | To see the meaning **LABOR**, see ⺍ as drops of sweat *covering* (冖) a *plow* (力). The dripping sweat suggests more arduous effort than what we could see in 働 0541, in keeping with the secondary meanings found in Halpern, such as "toil," "pains," and "fatigue." Distinguish the top of this kanji from the top of 受 0065. |
|---|---|

| COOPERATE | ○協力する きょうりょくする cooperate, collaborate ...................................................0084<br>協会 きょうかい association, society .........0226<br>協調 きょうちょう cooperation, harmony....0306<br>農協 のうきょう agricultural cooperative.....0511<br>協定 きょうてい agreement, pact.............0045 |
|------|--------|
| キョウ | |

| 0543<br>十 24<br><br>0074<br>常 8 | Three *plows* together (劦) suggest a **COOPERATIVE** labor project. In fact, all thirty *plows* in the village are cooperating—three *plows* times *ten* (十). ☞ 脇 1993 |
|---|---|

| ¹ VARIETY, type<br>² SEED | ①種類 しゅるい kind, sort, species.............0310<br>¹ 一種の いっしゅの a kind of, a sort of........0002<br>¹ この種の このしゅの this kind of<br>² 種子 しゅし seed, pit.........................0094<br>②話の種 はなしのたね source of conversation ...................................................0053 |
|------|--------|
| シュ<br>たね | |

| 0544<br>禾 115<br><br>1128<br>常 14 | A **SEED** is the *heaviest* (重) part of a sheaf of *grain* (禾). As a **SEED** can be thought of as the extract or essence of an individual species, this character has also come to express the idea of **VARIETY** or type. |
|---|---|

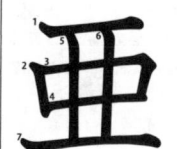

| | ¹ SUB-<br>² PHONETIC [a]<br><br>ア | ① 亜種 あしゅ subspecies ........................0544<br>² 亜細亜 アジア Asia................................0239<br>② 東亜 とうあ East Asia ........................0032 |

**0545**
二 7

亜

2966
常 7

Neatly divided among top, middle, and bottom, with two vertical lines passing between them. In this vertical relation we can perceive the relationship between master (S1) and SUBordinate (S7), mediated by S2–4. Note the traditional forms for this entry and the next one. ☞ 串 1938

| | BAD<br><br>アク オ<br>わる(い) わる- あ(し)* | 悪化する あっかする worsen, deteriorate....0120<br>悪条件 あくじょうけん bad terms .......0119, 0118<br>○最悪 さいあく the worst........................0196<br>○悪い行い わるいおこない bad/evil deed....0055<br>悪口 わるくち (=あっこう) slander, abuse, foul<br>language...................................................0019 |

**0546**
心 61

惡

2393
常 11

The previous entry suggests a thing of *subordinate* rank. Here this refers to the lower regions of one's *heart/mind* (心): the BAD part of one's nature. ☞ 患 1939

| | ¹ IMPORTANT, essential<br>² SUMMARIZE<br>³ REQUIRE, required<br><br>ヨウ<br>い(る) かなめ | 要素 ようそ (essential) element, constituent,<br>factor...................................................0132<br>○重要な じゅうような important, essential,<br>principal.............................................0539<br>要石 かなめいし keystone, cornerstone .....0403<br>○要するに ようするに in a word, in short<br>○金が要る かねがいる I need/want money; It<br>takes money.........................................0029 |

**0547**
襾 146

要

2290
常 9

襾 is officially a variant of 西 0795 WEST, but we'll usually see it as a *box (or basket) with a handle*. Distinguish it now from 亜 above. In this entry, imagine that the *box* is filled with IMPORTANT, REQUIRED items, which weigh down this *woman* (女). As for M2, to SUMMARIZE is to provide the IMPORTANT points. ☞ 妄 1455

| | ¹ PRICE<br>² VALUE<br><br>カ<br>あたい | ① 物価 ぶっか prices (of commodities)........0172<br>¹ 高価な こうかな expensive, high-priced....0185<br>¹ 米価 べいか price of rice .....................0234<br>² 声価 せいか reputation, fame...............0529<br>価千金の あたいせんきんの priceless, invaluable<br>........................................................0017, 0029 |

**0548**
人 9

價

0067
常 8

Just this once, we'll see 襾 as a kind of currency symbol (resembling a dollar sign with two vertical strokes), which a *man* (亻) uses to mark an object's PRICE or VALUE.

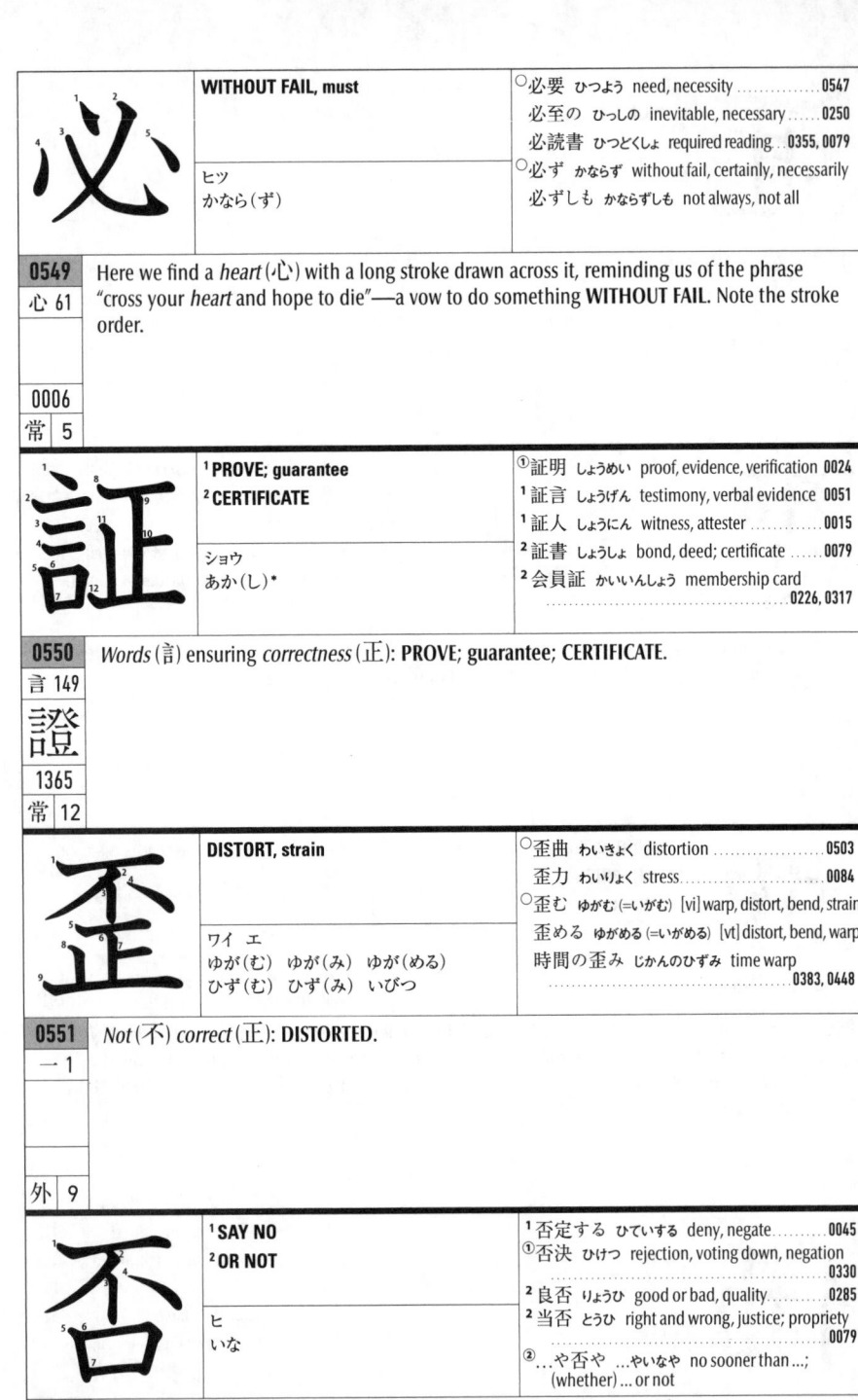

| | WITHOUT FAIL, must | ○必要 ひつよう need, necessity ............. 0547 |
|---|---|---|
| | | 必至の ひっしの inevitable, necessary ...... 0250 |
| | | 必読書 ひつどくしょ required reading ... 0355, 0079 |
| | ヒツ | ○必ず かならず without fail, certainly, necessarily |
| | かなら(ず) | 必ずしも かならずしも not always, not all |

| **0549** | Here we find a *heart* (心) with a long stroke drawn across it, reminding us of the phrase |
|---|---|
| 心 61 | "cross your *heart* and hope to die"—a vow to do something **WITHOUT FAIL**. Note the stroke |
| | order. |
| **0006** | |
| 常 5 | |

| | **¹ PROVE; guarantee** | ①証明 しょうめい proof, evidence, verification 0024 |
|---|---|---|
| | **² CERTIFICATE** | ¹ 証言 しょうげん testimony, verbal evidence 0051 |
| | | ¹ 証人 しょうにん witness, attester ............. 0015 |
| | ショウ | ² 証書 しょうしょ bond, deed; certificate ...... 0079 |
| | あか(し)* | ² 会員証 かいいんしょう membership card |
| | | ...................................... 0226, 0317 |

| **0550** | *Words* (言) ensuring *correctness* (正): **PROVE; guarantee; CERTIFICATE**. |
|---|---|
| 言 149 | |
| 證 | |
| **1365** | |
| 常 12 | |

| | DISTORT, strain | ○歪曲 わいきょく distortion ................. 0503 |
|---|---|---|
| | | 歪力 わいりょく stress ...................... 0084 |
| | | ○歪む ゆがむ (=いがむ) [vi] warp, distort, bend, strain |
| | ワイ エ | 歪める ゆがめる (=いがめる) [vt] distort, bend, warp |
| | ゆが(む) ゆが(み) ゆが(める) | 時間の歪み じかんのひずみ time warp |
| | ひず(む) ひず(み) いびつ | ...................................... 0383, 0448 |

| **0551** | *Not* (不) *correct* (正): **DISTORTED**. |
|---|---|
| 一 1 | |
| 外 9 | |

| | **¹ SAY NO** | ¹ 否定する ひていする deny, negate .......... 0045 |
|---|---|---|
| | **² OR NOT** | ○否決 ひけつ rejection, voting down, negation |
| | | ..................................... 0330 |
| | | ² 良否 りょうひ good or bad, quality .......... 0285 |
| | ヒ | ² 当否 とうひ right and wrong, justice; propriety |
| | いな | ..................................... 0079 |
| | | ② ...や否や ...やいなや no sooner than ...; |
| | | (whether) ... or not |

| **0552** | See the word *"not"* (不) emanating from a *mouth* (口): **SAY NO**. ☞ 呑 2174 |
|---|---|
| 口 30 | |
| **2130** | |
| 常 7 | |

| 処 | **DEAL WITH, dispose of** | ○処理する しょりする manage, deal with, dispose of; process, treat ............................ 0532 |
|---|---|---|
| | | 処分 しょぶん disposal, measure; punishment ...... 0088 |
| | ショ | 処する しょする deal with, dispose of |
| | | 処女 しょじょ virgin, maiden ................. 0093 |

**0553** 几 16* 處 2609 常 5

Review 風 0425, where 几 and 几 are introduced. Visualize 几 as a *tablecloth* draped over a *table* (we shall identify it with both these objects). Here, we drape a *tablecloth* over an *angled rooftop* (夂) to **DEAL WITH** a leak. Only in this entry and the next one will *angled rooftop* not appear at the top of the character. Note the old form.

| 拠 | **GROUNDS, basis** | 拠点 きょてん strongpoint, base ............. 0349 |
|---|---|---|
| | | ○根拠 こんきょ grounds, basis, authority ..... 0284 |
| | | 本拠 ほんきょ base, stronghold, headquarters ...... 0031 |
| | キョ コ | ○証拠 しょうこ proof, evidence ............. 0550 |
| | | 典拠 てんきょ authority ................. 0504 |

**0554** 手 64 據 0276 常 8

In English one might use the word "footing" to refer to one's **basis**. In this kanji, we must think of **basis** not as "footing" but as "handing": picture a sure and solid *hand* (扌) backing up the action of *dealing with* (処) something. Write this and the last entry in turn, recalling that when you add 扌, you refer to the **basis** or **GROUNDS** for dealing with something.

| 計 | ¹**PLAN** ²**COMPUTE, calculate** | ①計画 けいかく plan, project .................. 0176 |
|---|---|---|
| | | ¹設計 せっけい design, plan .................. 0520 |
| | | ²会計 かいけい account, finance, bill ........ 0226 |
| | ケイ | ②合計 ごうけい sum total, total .............. 0227 |
| | はか(る) はか(らう) | ²時計 とけい clock, watch ................ 0383 |

**0555** 言 149 1309 常 9

Of the number kanji, 十 *ten* is among those most often appearing inside other kanji. Here see it as an instrument for **COMPUTING** or **calculating** (by *tens*) the number of *words* (言) in a document. This character also means **PLAN**, from the idea of **calculating** one's actions.
☞ 訂 1024, 診 2165, 討 1023

| 針 | **NEEDLE** | 長針 ちょうしん long [minute] hand .......... 0091 |
|---|---|---|
| | | ○方針 ほうしん course, policy, plan ........... 0173 |
| | | ○針金 はりがね wire ...................... 0029 |
| | シン はり | 針の穴 はりのあな eye of a needle ........... 0397 |

**0556** 金 167 1488 常 10

Here see 十 as a long and pointy *metal* (金) **NEEDLE**. From now on, *needle* will be an alternative grapheme meaning for 十.

**¹WHOLE, total**
**²GENERAL**

ソウ

¹総計する そうけいする total, sum up ........0555
①総合する そうごうする synthesize, integrate
.................................................0227
¹総量 そうりょう gross weight/volume ........0538
²総会 そうかい general meeting .............0226
②総理大臣 そうりだいじん prime minister
.................................0532, 0033, 0484

| 0557 | Let 公 *public* and 心 *heart/mind* represent two opposite realms: public stance and private feeling. See the *thread* stretching from top to bottom to tie together both realms, thus unifying the **WHOLE**, or **GENERAL** totality. |
| 糸 120 | |
| 總 | |
| 1261 | |
| 常 14 | |

**WINDOW**

ソウ
まど

窓外 そうがい outside the window ..........0266
○車窓 しゃそう car window....................0125
窓ガラス まどガラス windowpane
二重窓 にじゅうまど double window...0003, 0539
○窓口 まどぐち teller window, counter; teller,
contact ....................................0019

| 0558 | To get some fresh air to supply your *heart* (心), stick your *nose* (ム) out through a large *hole* (穴): a **WINDOW**. |
| 穴 116 | |
| 窗 | |
| 1986 | |
| 常 11 | |

**ARROW**

シ
や

弓矢 ゆみや (=きゅうし) bow and arrow.......0421
○矢印 やじるし arrow [mark]..................0231
矢先 やさき arrowhead ......................0134
毒矢 どくや poisoned arrow/dart ...........0133
矢野 やの Yano [surname]..................0534

| 0559 | As in 天 0270 we see the curving strokes pointing up toward heaven, but here an **ARROW** blade (S1) has been added to make sure we fly straight there. 矢 will sometimes mean *straight* when it appears as a component inside other kanji. See note at entries 0565–66. ☞ 天 0270, 失 0563, 朱 0566 |
| 矢 111 | |
| 1733 | |
| 常 5 | |

**KNOW**

チ
し(る) し(らせる) し(れる)

○知る しる know, be aware of; perceive
知的 ちてき intellectual, mental ............0169
周知の しゅうちの known to all............0304
○通知する つうちする notify, inform..........0159
知り合い しりあい acquaintance............0227

| 0560 | *Mouth* (口) + *arrow* (矢): the *mouth* of a person who **KNOWS** shoots *arrows*. Once you've associated the *arrow* with "**KNOW**ledge," try to see the *mouth* blowing out *arrows* of true **KNOW**ledge. ☞ 智 1093, 和 0236 |
| 矢 111 | |
| 1041 | |
| 常 8 | |

| | ¹MEDICINE | ¹医学 いがく medical science, medicine......0099 |
|---|---|---|
| | ²DOCTOR | ¹医大 いだい medical college.................0033 |
| | | ¹医薬 いやく medicine, drug.................0303 |
| | イ | ¹医薬品 いやくひん pharmaceuticals, medicines .........................................0303, 0301 |
| | | ②医者 いしゃ doctor.........................0107 |

**0561**
匚 23*
醫
2583
常 7

Imagine the enclosure is a human thorax. The **DOCTOR**'s job is to reach in and pull out the *arrow* (矢). Note that the enclosure has been modified to 匚 from the virtually identical form 匸, seen in the radical field to the left. The same is true for all the kanji in this course having this radical. ☞ 匠 1802

| | SHORT | 短刀 たんとう dagger .........................0085 |
|---|---|---|
| | | ○短期 たんき short term ......................0486 |
| | | 短気 たんき short temper ....................0126 |
| | タン | 短所 たんしょ shortcoming, defect ..........0249 |
| | みじか(い) | ○短い みじかい short |

**0562**
矢 111

1093
常 12

Picture an *arrow* (矢) the length of a *pea* (豆): that's one **SHORT** arrow!

| | ¹LOSE | ¹失業する しつぎょうする lose one's job......0498 |
|---|---|---|
| | ²SLIP | ①失う うしなう lose, miss |
| | | ¹見失う みうしなう lose sight of..............0083 |
| | シツ | ²失言 しつげん slip of the tongue...........0051 |
| | うしな(う) | ②失礼 しつれい rudeness; bad manners; Excuse me.........................................0313 |

**0563**
大 37

2947
常 5

Looks like 矢 0559 ARROW, but here we've **SLIPPED** (up) and gone too far—right past the pearly gates of heaven (天 0270). Like games of guessing in which one is disqualified for going over the mark, in writing 失 we automatically **LOSE**, for our arrow has passed beyond the target. See note at entries 0565-66. ☞ 矢 0559, 夫 0565, 朱 0566

| | IRON | 鉄工 てっこう ironworker; blacksmith.......0108 |
|---|---|---|
| | | 鉄骨 てっこつ steel/iron frame .............0465 |
| | | ○鉄道 てつどう railway.......................0158 |
| | テツ | 地下鉄 ちかてつ subway............0187, 0040 |
| | | 鉄のカーテン てつのカーテン iron curtain |

**0564**
金 167
鐵
1527
常 13

**IRON** is a *metal* (金) that readily rusts or oxidizes, which is to *lose* (失) matter in a chemical reaction with oxygen. ☞ 鋼 2069

**1 HUSBAND**

**2 MALE LABORER**

フ フウ ブ*
おっと

① 夫に代わって　おっとにかわって　on behalf of my husband .......................................................0071
¹ 前夫　ぜんぷ　ex-husband.................................0113
¹ 夫人　ふじん　wife, married lady, Mrs. ........0015
② 農夫　のうふ　peasant, plowman.................0511
² 水夫　すいふ　sailor....................................0027

---

**0565**
大 37

2909
常 4

Memorize the reading *otto* and its meaning, **HUSBAND**. Write *otto* in cursive roman letters the normal way, with a single stroke crossing both t's, then a special way, writing a single t crossed twice, as in 夫. Associate this special "double t" with *otto*. **HUSBAND** easily suggests M2 **MALE LABORER** ... Now a note on differentiating 天 0270, 矢 0559, 失 0563, 夫 0565, and 朱 0566. The last one is unique in having *tree*. The other variations are a) the presence/absence of the pointing arrow blade; and b) whether the upward-sloping strokes end at the top stroke or pierce through it. In 天 the sloping strokes end precisely at the top stroke ... (continued) ☞ 天 0270, 失 0563

---

**VERMILION**

シュ

○朱色　しゅいろ　vermilion, Chinese red .......0528
朱肉　しゅにく　red ink pad ...................0216
朱顔　しゅがん　flushed face....................0180
朱書する　しゅしょする　write in red ..........0079

---

**0566**
木 75

2960
常 6

(Continued)... which we associate with HEAVEN. 矢 adds a pointing ARROW blade to aid our course to this desired destination. 失 overshoots the target and thus LOSES. 夫 has no arrow blade so it can be seen as a cursive "t" crossed twice for doubling, as in *otto*. 夫 cannot mean HEAVEN because the sloping strokes don't end precisely at the top stroke. And as noted above, the present entry can be distinguished from 矢 0559 and 失 0563 by its *tree* grapheme, which suggests that its short S1 is not a pointing arrow blade but a leaf. Though Japan's fall colors are much anticipated, this *leaf* has *not yet* (未) turned **VERMILION**. ☞ 未 0271, 矢 0559, 失 0563

---

**STOCK, stub**

かぶ

株券　かぶけん　share [stock] certificate .......0456
株主　かぶぬし　stockholder.....................0365
株価　かぶか　stock price ......................0548
○株式会社　かぶしきがいしゃ　joint stock corporation...........................0109, 0226, 0314
切り株　きりかぶ　stump........................0086

---

**0567**
木 75

0846
常 10

The word "**STOCK**" derives from the Old English *stoc(c)*, meaning "tree trunk." This kanji likewise refers both to corporate shares and to the stump of a tree. Because the exposed inside of a tree often has a reddish hue, *vermilion* (朱) *tree* (木) can suggest a tree trunk cut down to a stump or **stub**.

---

**FAMILY, tribe**

ゾク

○家族　かぞく　family, household................0219
親族　しんぞく　relative(s) .......................0276
民族　みんぞく　race, people, nation...........0477
アイヌ族　アイヌぞく　the Ainu (people)
ローラー族　ローラーぞく　roller-skating devotees

---

**0568**
方 70

0863
常 11

Here see a *person* (方) holding out a rod (⼀) with *arrows* (矢) hanging from it. Once you have seen the image clearly, associate it with an *arrow*-wielding **tribe** or **FAMILY**. ☞ 旅 0569

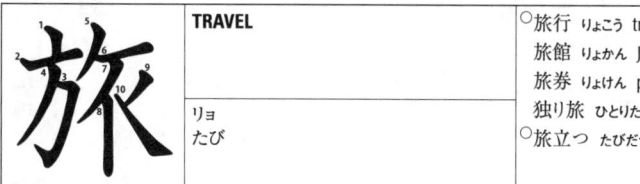

| | | |
|---|---|---|
| TRAVEL | | ○旅行 りょこう travel, trip ...................... 0055 |
| | | 旅館 りょかん Japanese inn ................. 0291 |
| | | 旅券 りょけん passport ........................ 0456 |
| | リョ | 独り旅 ひとりたび solitary travel ............ 0346 |
| | たび | ○旅立つ たびだつ set off on a journey ........ 0067 |

| 0569 | See 𧘇 as the folds and pleats of a garment, similar to 衣 0700 GARMENT. Thus here we see |
|---|---|
| 方 70 | a *person* (方) carrying his *garments* on a journey, neatly illustrating the idea of **TRAVEL**. ☞ 族 0568, 旋 0572 |
| 0829 | |
| 常 10 | |

| | | |
|---|---|---|
| ¹ PLAY | | ①遊楽 ゆうらく amusement ................... 0302 |
| ² TOUR | | ①遊ぶ あそぶ play |
| | | ¹ 遊び場 あそびば playground ............... 0445 |
| | ユウ ユ | ² 遊学 ゆうがく traveling to study, study abroad |
| | あそ(ぶ) あそ(ばす) | ......................................................... 0099 |
| | | ②外遊 がいゆう foreign tour ................... 0266 |

| 0570 | Here picture 方 as the child (子)'s parent. The two are taking a **TOUR** on one of those minia- |
|---|---|
| 辵 162 | ture trains that make leisurely loops around amusement parks. The child wears a hat (宀) for |
| | the outing. Learn to associate the image with fun and **PLAY**. |
| 2709 | |
| 常 12 | |

| | | |
|---|---|---|
| ¹ EXECUTE | | ¹ 施政 しせい administration, government... 0246 |
| ² BESTOW | | ¹ 実施する じっしする carry out, enforce, execute |
| | | ......................................................... 0499 |
| | シ セ | ①施設 しせつ equipment, facilities .......... 0520 |
| | ほどこ(す) | ○施す ほどこす conduct, perform, execute; bestow, apply |
| | | ² 施し ほどこし alms, almsgiving |

| 0571 | Now 方 is a shaman, holding out a *scorpion* (也) at the end of his rod (宀). Using this talis- |
|---|---|
| 方 70 | manic creature, he **EXECUTES** rituals, and **BESTOWS** blessings. |
| 0792 | |
| 常 9 | |

| | | |
|---|---|---|
| GYRATE | | ○旋回 せんかい revolution, rotation, circling |
| | | ......................................................... 0050 |
| | | 旋転 せんてん gyration, revolution, rotation |
| | | ......................................................... 0224 |
| | セン | 旋風 せんぷう whirlwind ....................... 0425 |
| | | 周旋 しゅうせん good offices, mediation .... 0304 |

| 0572 | 疋 is identical to the *right/correct* grapheme in 定 except that it looks like it has broken its |
|---|---|
| 方 70 | "nose." We'll give this the meaning of *broken* or *deformed*. Here see 方 as a showman hold- |
| | ing out a grotesquely *deformed* creature at a one-ring circus, **GYRATING** around the ring in |
| | rapid circles so that all the spectators can see it. ☞ 旅 0569 |
| 0862 | |
| 常 11 | |

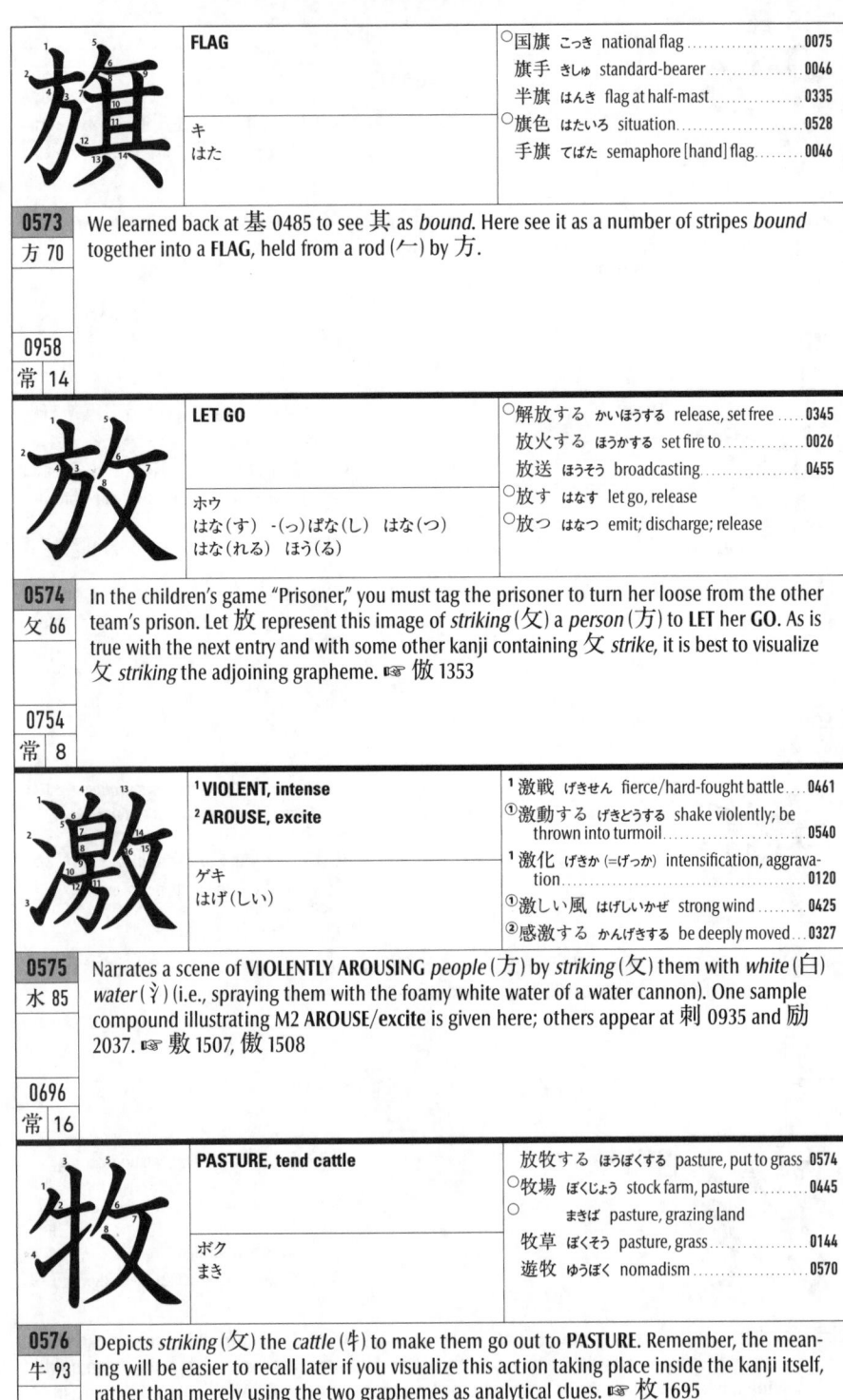

## 旗 — FLAG

キ
はた

○国旗 こっき national flag .................... 0075
旗手 きしゅ standard-bearer ................ 0046
半旗 はんき flag at half-mast ............... 0335
○旗色 はたいろ situation ...................... 0528
手旗 てばた semaphore [hand] flag ........ 0046

**0573**
方 70

We learned back at 基 0485 to see 其 as *bound*. Here see it as a number of stripes *bound* together into a **FLAG**, held from a rod (⺧) by 方.

0958
常 | 14

## 放 — LET GO

ホウ
はな(す) -(っ)ぱな(し) はな(つ)
はな(れる) ほう(る)

○解放する かいほうする release, set free ..... 0345
放火する ほうかする set fire to ............... 0026
放送 ほうそう broadcasting .................. 0455
○放す はなす let go, release
○放つ はなつ emit; discharge; release

**0574**
攵 66

In the children's game "Prisoner," you must tag the prisoner to turn her loose from the other team's prison. Let 放 represent this image of *striking* (攵) a *person* (方) to **LET** her **GO**. As is true with the next entry and with some other kanji containing 攵 *strike*, it is best to visualize 攵 *striking* the adjoining grapheme. ☞ 倣 1353

0754
常 | 8

## 激 — ¹VIOLENT, intense / ²AROUSE, excite

ゲキ
はげ(しい)

¹激戦 げきせん fierce/hard-fought battle .... 0461
①激動する げきどうする shake violently; be thrown into turmoil ...................... 0540
¹激化 げきか (=げっか) intensification, aggravation ........................... 0120
①激しい風 はげしいかぜ strong wind ......... 0425
②感激する かんげきする be deeply moved ... 0327

**0575**
水 85

Narrates a scene of **VIOLENTLY AROUSING** *people* (方) by *striking* (攵) them with *white* (白) *water* (氵) (i.e., spraying them with the foamy white water of a water cannon). One sample compound illustrating M2 **AROUSE/excite** is given here; others appear at 刺 0935 and 励 2037. ☞ 敷 1507, 傲 1508

0696
常 | 16

## 牧 — PASTURE, tend cattle

ボク
まき

放牧する ほうぼくする pasture, put to grass 0574
○牧場 ぼくじょう stock farm, pasture .......... 0445
○ まきば pasture, grazing land
牧草 ぼくそう pasture, grass ................. 0144
遊牧 ゆうぼく nomadism .................... 0570

**0576**
牛 93

Depicts *striking* (攵) the *cattle* (牛) to make them go out to **PASTURE**. Remember, the meaning will be easier to recall later if you visualize this action taking place inside the kanji itself, rather than merely using the two graphemes as analytical clues. ☞ 枚 1695

0776
常 | 8

| | ¹ **RANK**<br>² **POSITION**<br><br>イ<br>くらい ぐらい | ¹ 地位 ちい status, social standing, position 0187<br>①首位 しゅい first place, leading position ....0157<br>¹ 学位 がくい academic degree................0099<br>² 転位 てんい transposition, displacement...0224<br>² 位の低い人 くらいのひくいひと person of low<br>　rank ........................................0479 |

| **0577**<br>人 9 | イ *man* and 立 *stand* suggest "a *man's standing*"; that is, his **RANK**, or the **POSITION** where he *stands*. ☞ 倍 0069 |
| **0045**<br>常 \| 7 | |

| | **CRY**<br><br>キュウ<br>な（く） | 号泣する ごうきゅうする wail, lament ........0300<br>感泣する かんきゅうする weep with emotion, be<br>　moved to tears ...........................0327<br>泣く なく cry, weep, sob<br>泣き顔 なきがお tear-stained face ..........0180<br>泣き声 なきごえ tearful voice, crying ......0529 |

| **0578**<br>水 85 | See *water* (氵) streaming down from the face of a *standing man* (立). He is **CRYING**. ☞ 涙 1020 |
| **0300**<br>常 \| 8 | |

| | **LAUGH, smile**<br><br>ショウ<br>わら（う） え（む） | ○苦笑 くしょう forced/strained smile..........0405<br>○笑う わらう laugh, smile<br>笑い話 わらいばなし funny story .............0053<br>笑む えむ smile; bloom<br>○笑顔 えがお smiling face, smile.............0180 |

| **0579**<br>竹 118 | With a little effort, this can be seen as the squinting eyes and split cheeks of a person who is **LAUGHING** or broadly **smiling**. Note how the first stroke of 夭 differs in angle and direction from that of 天 0270. Except in the special combinations noted in Appendix 1, slanting strokes are always written downward. ☞ 筈 1442 |
| **2300**<br>常 \| 10 | |

| | **EXCLUSIVELY, entirely**<br><br>セン<br>もっぱ（ら） | ○専用 せんよう exclusive/private use..........0047<br>専門 せんもん specialty, profession .........0447<br>専門家 せんもんか specialist..........0447, 0219<br>専売 せんばい monopoly ....................0353<br>専ら本を書いている もっぱらほんをかいている<br>　devoting oneself exclusively to writing a book<br>　........................................0031, 0079 |

| **0580**<br>寸 41 | Recall 寸 *outstretched arm*. See what sits above it (甫) as a large cauldron with a mixer inserted into it (十); we'll refer to this hereafter as a *(mixing) cauldron*. The idea to perceive in this kanji is that this single *outstretched arm* is lifting the **entire** huge *cauldron* by itself (i.e., **EXCLUSIVELY**). ☞ 恵 0581, 博 0983 |
| **2297**<br>常 \| 9 | |

**FAVOR, kindness**

ケイ エ
めぐ(む)

○特恵 とっけい special favor, partiality.........0385
○知恵 ちえ wisdom, intelligence ...........0560
○恵む めぐむ bestow a favor, show kindness to
恵み めぐみ favor; blessing
金を恵む かねをめぐむ give alms ...........0029

| 0581 | A big *cauldron* (甫) full of *heart* (心) (i.e., love) implies **kindness** or **FAVOR**. Note the tradi-tional forms of this entry and the previous one, which set the pattern for characters based on 甫. ☞ 専 0580 |
| 心 61 | |
| 恵 | |
| 2315 | |
| 常 10 | |

**¹ LINK, connect**
**² IN SUCCESSION, in a row**

レン
つら(なる) つら(ねる) つ(れる) -づ(れ)

¹連合 れんごう combination, union, alliance; association ...................................0227
①連れる つれる take along, bring along
②連続する れんぞくする continue, occur in succession .............................0354
²四連勝 よんれんしょう four wins in a row
.............................................0006, 0460
○連ねる つらねる put in a row, join

| 0582 | Visualize as a flatbed *truck* (辶) transporting *cars* (車), and imagine the *cars* lined up **IN SUCCESSION** from front to back on the *truck* bed, **LINKED** together from bumper to bumper. ☞ 運 0584 |
| 辵 162 | |
| 2672 | |
| 常 10 | |

**ARMY, military**

グン

○軍人 ぐんじん soldier, military person.......0015
軍事力 ぐんじりょく military force......0080, 0084
軍部 ぐんぶ military authorities, the military
...........................................0068
空軍 くうぐん air force.........................0398
女性軍 じょせいぐん women's team .....0093, 0128

| 0583 | Suggests an armor-*covered* (冖) *vehicle* (車), and thus **ARMY**. ☞ 運 0584 |
| 車 159 | |
| 1789 | |
| 常 9 | |

**¹ CARRY, transport**
**² MOVE**
**³ FORTUNE, fate**

ウン
はこ(ぶ)

¹運送 うんそう shipping, transportation .....0455
①運ぶ はこぶ carry, transport
②運動 うんどう motion, movement; exercise 0540
³運命 うんめい fortune, fate, destiny .........0232
③運が悪い うんがわるい out of luck..........0546

| 0584 | The *army* (軍) is on the **MOVE**: a flatbed *truck* (辶) is **CARRYING** an armored vehicle towards its assigned position. M1 CARRY is associated with M3 FORTUNE/fate via the notion that **FORTUNE** and fate CARRY us along toward our destiny. ☞ 軍 0583, 連 0582 |
| 辵 162 | |
| 2707 | |
| 常 12 | |

| 蓮 | **LOTUS** | 木蓮 もくれん lily magnolia; cucumber tree; *Magnolia liliflora*....................0028 |
|---|---|---|
| | | ○日蓮 にちれん [thirteenth-century founder of the Nichiren sect of Buddhism].........0001 |
| | | 蓮池 はすいけ lotus pond ..................0188 |
| | レン | ○蓮の花 はすのはな lotus flower.............0121 |
| | はす はちす | 蓮の根 はすのね lotus root ................0284 |

**0585** 艸 140 / 2047 名 13

The **LOTUS** grows very densely across the surface of water, sometimes obscuring the surface of a pond completely. For this reason, we can easily think of a **LOTUS** pond when we see this image of *plants* (艹) *linked* together in tight *succession* (連).

| 隊 | **PARTY, corps** | 軍隊 ぐんたい army, troops .................0583 |
|---|---|---|
| | | 連隊 れんたい regiment .....................0582 |
| | | 楽隊 がくたい musical band................0302 |
| | タイ | ○部隊 ぶたい unit, corps, party, squad......0068 |
| | | 隊を組む たいをくむ form a party, line up...0264 |

**0586** 阜 170 / 0570 常 12

Recall the *pig* grapheme 豕 from 豚 0218. When you see the pig with two strokes added at the top (㒼), see them as the two straps of a backpack passing over its shoulders, and picture it as a specially equipped *pig commando*. 阝 *hills* completes the picture of a hillside encampment of pig commandos: **PARTY/corps.** ☞ 墜 2211

| 呈 | **PRESENT** | 呈上 ていじょう presentation.................0041 |
|---|---|---|
| | | 進呈する しんていする proffer, present .....0191 |
| | | ○呈示する ていじする exhibit, present .......0311 |
| | テイ | 呈する ていする give, present; show, present |

**0587** 口 30 / 1874 常 7

At 皇 0077 we visualized *king* with a *white* crown as EMPEROR. Here imagine a simple gift box 口, **PRESENTED** to the *king* (王) by ceremoniously placing it on top of his head! This kanji must be compared carefully with 提 1679 PRESENT, which it resembles in both meaning and appearance. ☞ 是 1678, 程 0588, 提 1679

| 程 | ¹ **EXTENT** ² **ESTABLISHED FORM** | ①程度 ていど degree, extent, standard.......0280 |
|---|---|---|
| | | ¹ 旅程 りょてい itinerary; distance to be covered ...............0569 |
| | | ①程々 ほどほど moderately |
| | テイ | ² 工程 こうてい process of manufacture, work schedule, amount of work ................0108 |
| | ほど -ほど | ②過程 かてい process, course .................0464 |

**0588** 禾 115 / 1100 常 12

In former times, *rice* (禾) was *presented* (呈) to the king as tribute. For each vassal's tribute there was a fixed measure or **EXTENT**, as well as an **ESTABLISHED FORM** and procedure for presenting it to the king. Thus let "*presenting rice*" suggest the carefully measured **EXTENT** of one's rice tribute and the precisely patterned **FORM** for presenting it. ☞ 呈 0587, 聖 0589

| | |
|---|---|
| **¹ HOLY** | ①聖書 せいしょ Bible......................................0079 |
| **² SAINT** | ¹ 神聖な しんせいな holy, sacred, divine.......0316 |
| | ¹ オリンピックの聖火 オリンピックのせいか |
| セイ | Olympic flame/torch .......................0026 |
| | ² 聖ペテロ せいペテロ St. Peter |

| 0589 | A wise *king* (王) turns his *ear* (耳) toward the *mouth* (口) of a **HOLY** man/**SAINT**. ☞ 程 0588 |
|---|---|
| 耳 128 | |
| 2464 | |
| 常 13 | |

| | |
|---|---|
| **(sign of) THE OX** | ○丑年 うしどし Year of the Ox ....................0117 |
| チュウ | |
| うし | |

| 0590 | Like 牛 0116 CATTLE, the sign of **THE OX** is pronounced うし. In 丑 we view a long-horned OX head-on, such that the vertical lines represent both the sides of its body and its legs. Its head is lowered, so all we see is its back (upper box), its long horns (S3), and its tail sticking out at the upper left. S4 is the ground. ☞ 牛 0116, 五 0007 |
|---|---|
| 一 1 | |
| 2889 | |
| 名 4 | |

| | |
|---|---|
| **STRING, cord** | 紐付き ひもつき strings attached, conditional |
| | ......................................................0064 |
| | 口紐 くちひも drawstring [as for closing a bag] |
| チュウ ジュウ | ......................................................0019 |
| ひも | 組紐 くみひも braid..............................0264 |
| | 紐を結ぶ ひもをむすぶ tie a string ..........0516 |

| 0591 | 糸 represents a **STRING** for tying up the *ox* (丑). |
|---|---|
| 糸 120 | |
| 1190 | |
| 外 10 | |

| | |
|---|---|
| **¹ LEATHER** | ①革紐 かわひも leather strap .................0591 |
| **² REFORM, change** | ¹ 牛革 ぎゅうかわ cowhide, oxhide ...........0116 |
| | ² 革新 かくしん innovation, reform, renovation |
| カク かわ | ......................................................0275 |
| | ②革命 かくめい revolution.....................0232 |
| | ² 改革 かいかく reform, reformation..........0429 |

| 0592 | Visualize an animal skin converted to **LEATHER** and stretched out for drying. S1–4 show an intact head with horns, the box beneath it shows the portion of the skin covering the thorax, and the bottom portion of the character shows the skin of the hind limbs and tail. Associate M2 **REFORM**/change with the idea of converting an animal skin into **LEATHER**. ☞ 華 1012 |
|---|---|
| 革 177 | |
| 2163 | |
| 常 9 | |

**SHOES**

カ
くつ

| | | |
|---|---|---|
| 軍靴 | ぐんか military shoes, combat boots | ...0583 |
| ○靴下 | くつした socks, stockings | ...0040 |
| 運動靴 | うんどうぐつ sneakers | ...0584, 0540 |
| 靴墨 | くつずみ shoe polish | ...0536 |
| 靴紐 | くつひも shoelaces | ...0591 |

| 0593 | *Leather*(革) *changes*(化) into **SHOES**. |
|---|---|
| 革 177 | |
| 1586 | |
| 常 13 | |

**SUITCASE, bag**

ホウ
かばん

| | | |
|---|---|---|
| 鞄持ち | かばんもち private secretary, lackey | 0384 |
| 青い鞄 | あおいかばん blue bag | ...0130 |
| 旅行鞄 | りょこうかばん traveling case | ...0569, 0055 |

| 0594 | *Leather*(革) *wrapping*(包): **SUITCASE/bag**. This kanji incorporates the traditional form of 包 |
|---|---|
| 革 177 | 0457. |
| 鞄 | |
| 1594 | |
| 名 14 | |

**SKIN; leather**

ヒ
かわ

| | | |
|---|---|---|
| 皮革 | ひかく leather, hides | ...0592 |
| ○皮肉 | ひにく cynicism, sarcasm; irony | ...0216 |
| 毛皮 | けがわ fur | ...0487 |
| 牛皮 | ぎゅうひ cowhide, oxhide | ...0116 |
| ○バナナの皮 | バナナのかわ banana peel | |

| 0595 | Recall 厂 *cliff*. Notice there's an extra serif at the right edge of the *cliff* here (一), which suggests that the cliff is especially craggy. S3 traces the line of a *hands*(又)–first slide down the *craggy cliff*, a line now marked by a trail of scraped-off **SKIN**. ☞ 支 0373, 反 0374 |
|---|---|
| 皮 107 | |
| 2615 | |
| 常 5 | |

**BREAK**

ハ
やぶ(る) やぶ(れる)

| | | |
|---|---|---|
| 破約 | はやく breach of contract | ...0170 |
| ○破局 | はきょく collapse, catastrophe | ...0256 |
| 読破する | どくはする read through (to the end) ...0355 | |
| 囲みを破る | かこみをやぶる break through a siege | ...0435 |
| ○破れる | やぶれる be torn; be ruined | |

| 0596 | *Rock*(石) **BREAKING** through *skin*(皮). |
|---|---|
| 石 112 | |
| 1064 | |
| 常 10 | |

| | THIRD PERSON PRONOUN, boyfriend/<br>girlfriend | 彼我 ひが he/she and I, they and we, both<br>sides...................................................0221 |
|---|---|---|
| | | 彼等 かれら they ......................................0393 |
| | | ○彼氏 かれし he; boyfriend......................0476 |
| | ヒ<br>かれ かの | ○彼女 かのじょ she; girlfriend ................0093 |

| **0597**<br>イ 60 | Because 彼 is used to refer to one's **boyfriend** or **girlfriend**, you'll remember it best by linking its elements (*go/act* and *skin*) with a memorable personal story involving your own beau or belle. |
|---|---|
| **0259**<br>常 8 | |

| | WAVE, undulation | 波止場 はとば wharf, quay .............0042, 0445 |
|---|---|---|
| | | 波長 はちょう wavelength.........................0091 |
| | | ○電波 でんぱ electromagnetic waves, radio<br>waves...................................................0155 |
| | ハ<br>なみ | 短波 たんぱ shortwave ............................0562 |
| | | ○波形 なみがた wavy shape......................0147<br>はけい waveform |

| **0598**<br>水 85 | Let "*water*(氵)'s *skin*(皮)" suggest the texture of the water's surface, formed by **WAVES**. |
|---|---|
| **0292**<br>常 8 | |

| | ¹ **FRUIT, result**<br>² **ACCOMPLISH; come to an end** | ¹ 果実 かじつ fruit, berry........................0499 |
|---|---|---|
| | | ¹ 成果 せいか result, fruit, outcome...........0070 |
| | | ①結果 けっか result, outcome, consequence 0516 |
| | カ<br>はた(す) -はた(す) は(てる)<br>-は(てる) は(て) | ² 果たす はたす carry out, accomplish |
| | | ②果てる はてる come to an end |

| **0599**<br>木 75 | Visualize this character as a square-shaped cluster of **FRUIT** (田) growing on a *tree* (木). Now take a few moments to associate this concrete image of **FRUIT** with the figurative ideas "come to **FRUITION**," result, **ACCOMPLISH**, and **come to an end**. ☞ 某 2121, 呆 0647, 実 0499 |
|---|---|
| **2982**<br>常 8 | |

| | ¹ **ASSIGNMENT, task, lesson**<br>² **ASSIGN, impose, levy** | ¹ 人事課 じんじか personnel section....0015, 0080 |
|---|---|---|
| | | ①課長 かちょう section chief .....................0091 |
| | | ①課目 かもく school subject, course...........0021 |
| | カ | ¹ 課程 かてい course, curriculum ..............0588 |
| | | ² 課する かする impose (a tax or other obligation) |

| **0600**<br>言 149 | The time has come to pick the *fruit* (果), and a corvée has been **levied** upon us. See 言 as the *words* of a plantation foreman **imposing** on us our **task**, and **ASSIGNING** each of us to a specific work crew. When 課 is used in reference to a course of study, the English rendering would not be **task** but **lesson**. ☞ 謀 2122 |
|---|---|
| **1423**<br>常 15 | |

| | NEST | 巣立つ　すだつ　leave one's nest; become independent ....................................0067 |
|---|---|---|
| 巣 | ソウ<br>す | 古巣　ふるす　old nest, one's former haunt...0254 |
| | | ○空き巣　あきす　empty nest; sneak thief......0398 |
| | | クモの巣　クモのす　spiderweb |
| | | 巣籠もる　すごもる　nest.........................0509 |

| 0601 | ⺍ suggests a few twigs arranged at the top of a *fruit* (果) tree: a **NEST**. There are not many words using 巣's *on-yomi*, but you can find one at 卵 1141 and another at 窟 1843. |
|---|---|
| 小 42* | ☞ 単 0462, 菓 0602 |
|  | |
| 1987 | |
| 常 11 | |

| | CONFECTIONERY | お菓子　おかし　confectionery, cake, sweets 0094 |
|---|---|---|
| 菓 | カ | 菓子屋　かしや　confectionery shop....0094, 0252 |
| | | ○和菓子　わがし　Japanese-style confection<br>.........................................0236, 0094 |
| | | ○洋菓子　ようがし　Western-style confection<br>.........................................0491, 0094 |

| 0602 | With a little processing (namely, adding an *herbal* garnish ⺿), *fruit* (果) becomes **CONFECTIONERY**. ☞ 巣 0601 |
|---|---|
| 艹 140 | |
| 1997 | |
| 常 11 | |

| | TEA | 茶菓　さか (=ちゃか)　tea and cakes, refreshments<br>.........................................0602 |
|---|---|---|
| 茶 | チャ　サ | ○茶道　さどう (=ちゃどう)　tea ceremony.........0158 |
| | | 茶の間　ちゃのま　living room..................0448 |
| | | 茶の湯　ちゃのゆ　tea ceremony................0446 |
| | | 茶色　ちゃいろ　light brown....................0528 |

| 0603 | Visualize as a small **TEA** arbor with a mossy (i.e., *grass* [⺿]-covered) *roof* (ハ). Inside the arbor, a *tree*, its branches separated, suggests a **TEA** bush with its leaves picked off. The *on* reading チャ is unique in this course. |
|---|---|
| 艹 140 | |
| 1948 | |
| 常 9 | |

| | ¹ WORLD, public<br>² AGE, generation | ①世の中　よのなか　the world, society, life ....0035 |
|---|---|---|
| 世 | セイ　セ<br>よ | ①世間　せけん　world society; the public, people<br>.........................................0448 |
| | | ¹ 出世　しゅっせ　success in life; promotion ....0038 |
| | | ②世紀　せいき　century .........................0428 |
| | | ² 世代　せだい　generation......................0071 |

| 0604 | See S1 and S5 as a great celestial Creator, reaching out Its hand (S1) to hold the whole **WORLD** (S2–4). In this same sense of creator and created, now see S1 and S5 as a parent holding its child (S2–4), a vivid image of one **generation** or **AGE** begetting the next. In time, the small "L" shape at the center (S2 and S4) will replace the large "L" shape below it (S5). |
|---|---|
| 一 1 | |
| 世 | |
| 2932 | |
| 常 5 | |

**LEAF**

ヨウ
は

万葉集 まんようしゅう *Collection of Myriad Leaves* [ancient poetry anthology]....**0018, 0190**
葉っぱ はっぱ leaf, foliage
葉巻 はまき cigar....................................**0458**
○葉書 はがき postcard...........................**0079**
言葉 ことば word, term; wording; language
......................................................**0051**

| 0605 | |
|---|---|
| 艸 140 | |
| 2024 | |
| 常 | 12 |

Intuitively suggests the foliage (艹) that sprouts forth from a *tree* (木) in successive *generations* (世): **LEAF**. Until you are able to immediately perceive the character's meaning in its image, use *generation* as a semantic clue suggesting the part of the tree that periodically renews itself. ☞ 棄 0606

**ABANDON, throw away**

キ
す(てる)*

○廃棄 はいき discarding, abolition, annulment
......................................................**0149**
破棄する はきする break (a treaty), annul...**0596**
放棄する ほうきする abandon, resign.......**0574**
投棄する とうきする abandon, give up, throw away.................................................**0517**
○棄てる すてる abandon, give up, throw away

| 0606 | |
|---|---|
| 木 75 | |
| 1835 | |
| 常 | 13 |

Recall 厶 *reach down with bent arm*, introduced back at 育 0489. Here see someone *reaching down with a bent arm* to place a piece of trash into a wastebasket (世) built on top of a short *tree* (木). This illustrates the act of **throwing away** or **ABANDONING** something. ☞ 葉 0605, 帯 1232

**GREEN**

リョク ロク
みどり

○緑色 みどりいろ (=りょくしょく) green ..........**0528**
緑茶 りょくちゃ green tea, Japanese tea.......**0603**
緑青 ろくしょう verdigris, copper [green] rust
......................................................**0130**
葉緑素 ようりょくそ chlorophyll.........**0605, 0132**
濃緑色 のうりょくしょく dark green......**0512, 0528**

| 0607 | |
|---|---|
| 糸 120 | |
| 1259 | |
| 常 | 14 |

彐 is another version of *three-fingered hand*, seen before at 書 0079 and at 当 0141. Now picture using three fingers to dip a *thread* (糸) into an algae-filled pool of *water* (this is the five-stroke version of *water* we first saw in 様 0501), so as to dye it **GREEN**. ☞ 緣 0610

**RECORD, register**

ロク

○記録する きろくする record, register; set a record
......................................................**0427**
録音 ろくおん sound recording................**0150**
録画 ろくが video recording...................**0176**
目録 もくろく catalog............................**0021**
付録 ふろく appendix, supplement..........**0064**

| 0608 | |
|---|---|
| 金 167 | |
| 1554 | |
| 常 | 16 |

Here picture 金 as a photosensitive *metal* plate that has been exposed to light. Now picture using *three fingers* (彐) to dip the plate into a special *water*-based chemical solution that will permanently fix the **RECORDED** image. While 緣 and 錄 were decades ago modified to 緑 and 録, the next entry is still officially listed in its old form.

| | | |
|---|---|---|
| **STRIP OFF, peel off, come off** | ○剥く むく peel, take off | |
| | 剥ぎ取る はぎとる strip off, tear off ........0059 | |
| | 剥き身 むきみ shellfish removed from the shell ................................0060 | |
| ハク<br>は(げる) は(がれる) は(ぐ) は(がす)<br>む(ける)* む(く)* | 引き剥ぐ ひきはぐ peel off, strip off ........0422 | |

| | |
|---|---|
| **0609**<br>刀 18<br>**剥**<br>1494<br>常 10 | Learn to recognize this kanji interchangeably with 剝, an accepted variant. In 緑 and 録 we dipped objects into water in order to fix a color or a recorded image upon them. Now we reverse the process, dipping an object in water to loosen its coating, then using a *knife* (刂) to **STRIP** it clean. A sample *on-yomi* compound appears at 奪 1657. |

| | | |
|---|---|---|
| ¹ **RELATION**<br>² **EDGE** | ¹ 無縁の むえんの unrelated; having no relatives ................................0048 | |
| | ¹ 血縁 けつえん blood relation ................0198 | |
| | ①縁を切る えんをきる sever relations ........0086 | |
| エン -ネン<br>ふち | ②皿の縁 さらのふち edge of a dish ..........0197 | |
| | ²縁辺 えんぺん border, edge; relations ....0195 | |

| | |
|---|---|
| **0610**<br>糸 120<br>**縁**<br>1269<br>常 15 | Here a *hand* (彐) uses a *rope* (糸) to leash a *pig* to the **EDGE** of its pigsty, visible at S9. See S9 not only as the **EDGE** of the sty but also as the point of **RELATION** between the *pig* and its master. Take a moment to let the two English words fuse into one image in the kanji, depicting something that is at once an **EDGE** and a point of **RELATION**. ☞ 緑 0607 |

| | | |
|---|---|---|
| **MEDIATE, lie between; shellfish** | 介する かいする help, support, aid | |
| | ○介入 かいにゅう intervention ................0039 | |
| | 介在する かいざいする lie between ........0406 | |
| カイ | 介意する かいいする worry about; concern oneself about............................0151 | |
| | お節介 おせっかい meddling; busybody ...0391 | |

| | |
|---|---|
| **0611**<br>人 9<br>**介**<br>1711<br>常 4 | Though 介 resembles the umbrella-like shape of a jellyfish, see へ as a hard shell, for 介 sometimes denotes **shellfish**, as in 魚介 (ぎょかい, fish and shellfish, seafood). Its principal meaning, **MEDIATE/lie between**, is visible in the way the long tentacles (S3–4) **lie between** the two halves of the shell. Visualize the tentacles interposing themselves between the two opposed halves and **MEDIATING** between them. |

| | | |
|---|---|---|
| ¹ **WORLD, area**<br>² **BOUNDS, boundary** | ①世界 せかい world, universe ................0604 | |
| | ¹ 政界 せいかい political world/circles ........0246 | |
| | ¹ 業界 ぎょうかい industry, business world ...0498 | |
| カイ | ¹ 学界 がっかい academic world/circles ....0099 | |
| | ②限界 げんかい boundary, limit, bounds ....0282 | |

| | |
|---|---|
| **0612**<br>田 102<br>**界**<br>2220<br>常 9 | As in the last entry, 介's tentacles *lie between* two halves, here interposing themselves between two *rice fields* (田). This illustrates the idea of a **boundary** between two **areas** or **WORLDS**. Bear in mind that 界 refers more often to the **WORLD** delimited by a **boundary** than to the **boundary** itself. ☞ 畏 2096 |

| | **FLOATING, transient** | ○浮力 ふりょく buoyancy, lift ..................... 0084 |
|---|---|---|
| | | 浮き上がる うきあがる float, rise to the surface ........................................................ 0041 |
| | | 浮世絵 うきよえ ukiyo-e, Japanese woodblock prints ("pictures of the floating world") **0604, 0525** |
| | フ | ○心に浮かぶ こころにうかぶ come across one's mind ............................................... 0056 |
| | う(く) う(かれる) う(かぶ) う(かべる) | ボートを浮かべる ボートをうかべる launch a boat |

| **0613** | A *claw* (⼎) tries to push a *baby* under *water* (comparing the heights of 氵 and 子, the *baby* appears momentarily to be submerged), but the *baby*'s body fat keeps making it **FLOAT** to the surface. This would be a good time to review 乳 0160. ☞ 乳 0160, 将 0614 |
|---|---|
| 水 85 | |
| **0393** | |
| 常 10 | |

| | **GENERAL OFFICER** | ○将軍 しょうぐん commander, general, shogun ........................................................ 0583 |
|---|---|---|
| | | 将校 しょうこう officer, commissioned officer ........................................................ 0103 |
| | ショウ | 大将 たいしょう admiral, general; old chap ... 0033 |
| | | 主将 しゅしょう captain ........................... 0365 |
| | | ○将来 しょうらい future; in the future .......... 0274 |

| **0614** | 扌 is short for 爿, visible in the traditional kanji forms of this entry and the two that follow. 爿 is an unlisted kanji meaning "half of a split tree trunk" (we'll see the other half at 片 0922). On this basis, take 扌 to mean a *wooden block* or *tablet* for carrying important messages, here grasped by a *claw* (⼎) at the end of an *outstretched arm* (寸). Visualize a **GENERAL OFFICER** holding out a *tablet* with important instructions and commands for his subordinates. 将 also has the meaning "will" or "about to occur," restricted to V5 and compounds built from it. ☞ 奨 0615, 浮 0613 |
|---|---|
| 寸 41 | |
| 将 | |
| **0415** | |
| 常 10 | |

| | **ENCOURAGE, promote** | 奨学 しょうがく promotion of scholarship ... 0099 |
|---|---|---|
| | | ○奨学金 しょうがくきん scholarship/grant ........................................................ 0099, 0029 |
| | ショウ | |

| **0615** | Let 大 *big* suggest a "grand" (magnanimous) gesture from the *general officer* (将) down toward his subordinates: kind words of **ENCOURAGEMENT**. To visualize this kanji's meaning clearly, it's useful to *see* the *grand* gesture moving from top to bottom, as from a position of higher status toward one of lower status. ☞ 装 1591, 将 0614, 醤 2128 |
|---|---|
| 大 37 | |
| 奬 | |
| **2474** | |
| 常 13 | |

| | ¹**FORM, shape** | ①形状 けいじょう shape, form, configuration ... 0147 |
|---|---|---|
| | ²**CONDITION, state** | ¹液状の えきじょうの liquefied .............. 0468 |
| | ³**LETTER, note** | ²商状 しょうじょう market condition .......... 0351 |
| | ジョウ | ③礼状 れいじょう thank-you letter ............. 0313 |
| | | 白状 はくじょう confession ................... 0076 |

| **0616** | If one's *dog* (犬) could etch out a message on a *wooden tablet* (爿), what would it write? Imagine the dog of someone you know writing a **LETTER** of complaint about its living **CONDITIONS**. Associate M1 **FORM**/shape with M2 **CONDITION**/state. ☞ 壮 1589 |
|---|---|
| 犬 94 | |
| 狀 | |
| **0244** | |
| 常 7 | |

| 病 | ILLNESS | ○病気 びょうき illness, disease .................0126 |
|---|---|---|
| | | 病室 びょうしつ patient/sick room...........0253 |
| | ビョウ ヘイ | 病状 びょうじょう condition of a disease/patient |
| | や(む) -や(み) やまい | ...................................................0616 |
| | | ○病む やむ fall ill, suffer from |
| | | 病は気から やまいはきから The mind is the root |
| | | of sickness and health ................0126 |

**0617**

疒 104

2791

常 10

疒 looks like 广 with a pair of infectious pustules growing on it, and means *illness*. 丙 will be introduced at 1523, but for the purposes of this entry we can treat it as a variation on 内 *inside*. The image here is thus of an *illness* penetrating *inside* one's body, which merely reinforces the sense **ILLNESS**.

| 症 | PATHOLOGICAL CONDITION, -osis | 病症 びょうしょう nature of a disease .........0617 |
|---|---|---|
| | | 重症 じゅうしょう serious illness...............0539 |
| | | ○症状 しょうじょう symptom ...................0616 |
| | ショウ | ダウン症 ダウンしょう Down syndrome |

**0618**

疒 104

2794

常 10

The "*correct*" (正) (i.e., formal) term for *illness*: PATHOLOGICAL CONDITION/-osis.

| 痛 | ¹ PAIN | ¹ 痛覚 つうかく sense of pain.................0325 |
|---|---|---|
| | ² ACUTE | ①頭痛 ずつう headache.......................0162 |
| | | ①痛い いたい painful, sore |
| | ツウ | ②痛切に つうせつに acutely, keenly..........0086 |
| | いた(い) いた(む) いた(ましい) | ² 痛快 つうかい thrill, keen pleasure.........0331 |
| | いた(める) | |

**0619**

疒 104

2799

常 12

Review 通 0159. In the present entry, we see *illness* (疒) swiftly *moving forward* (甬) into the body: ACUTE PAIN.

| 憶 | REMEMBER, think | ○記憶 きおく memory, recollection...........0427 |
|---|---|---|
| | | |
| | オク | |

**0620**

心 61

0691

常 16

As a grapheme in the next three entries, 意 (see 0151) will take the sense *thought*. Here, a *mind* (忄) REMEMBERS or **thinks** *thoughts* (意). An additional sample compound appears below at 測 0627. Note that all three kanji in which 意 appears in the phonetic position are pronounced オク. ☞ 臆 0621, 憶 0622

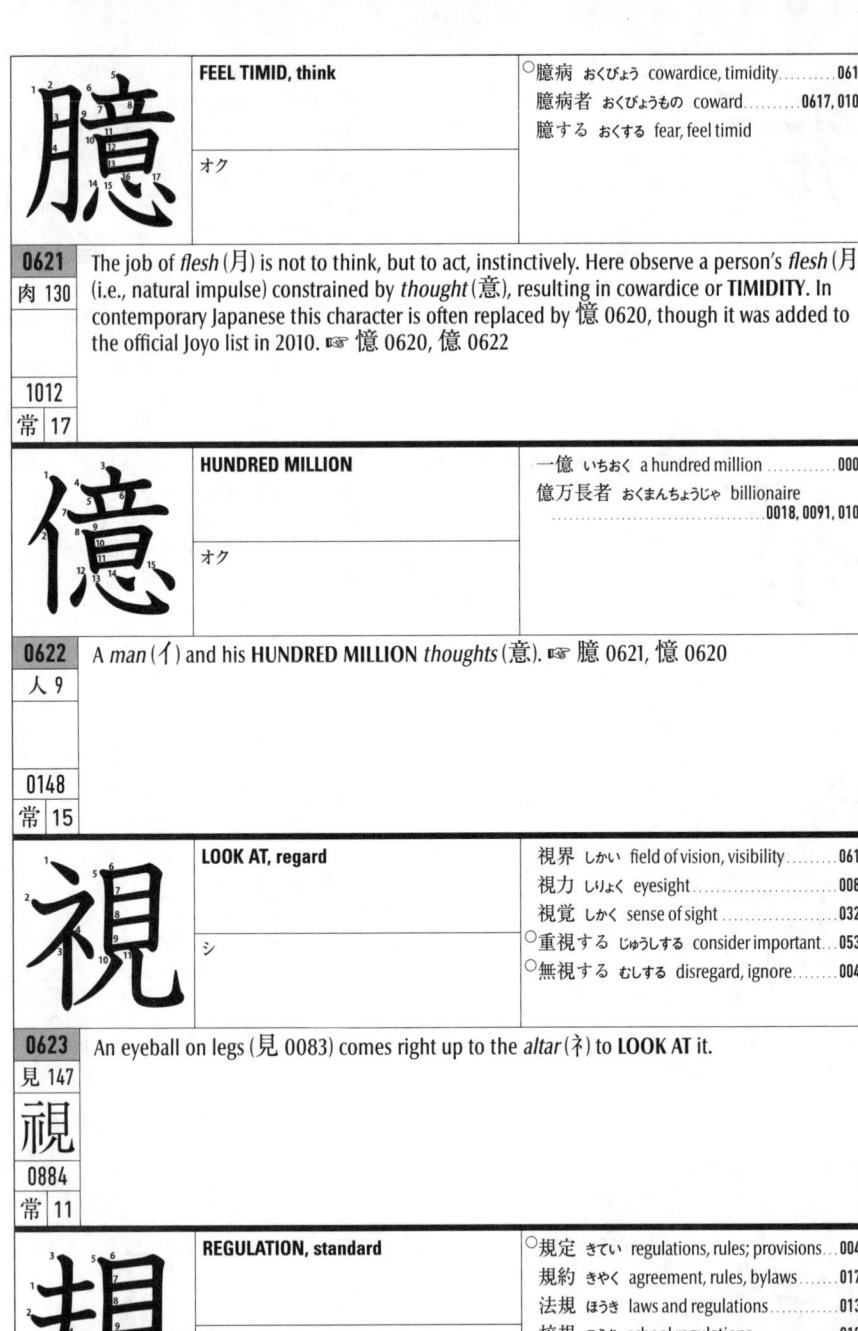

| | | | |
|---|---|---|---|
| **臆** | **FEEL TIMID, think** | ○臆病 おくびょう cowardice, timidity..........0617 | |
| | | 臆病者 おくびょうもの coward..........0617, 0107 | |
| | オク | 臆する おくする fear, feel timid | |

**0621**
肉 130

The job of *flesh* (月) is not to think, but to act, instinctively. Here observe a person's *flesh* (月) (i.e., natural impulse) constrained by *thought* (意), resulting in cowardice or **TIMIDITY**. In contemporary Japanese this character is often replaced by 憶 0620, though it was added to the official Joyo list in 2010. ☞ 憶 0620, 億 0622

1012
常 | 17

| | | | |
|---|---|---|---|
| **億** | **HUNDRED MILLION** | 一億 いちおく a hundred million ............0002 | |
| | | 億万長者 おくまんちょうじゃ billionaire | |
| | オク | ..........0018, 0091, 0107 | |

**0622**
人 9

A *man* (亻) and his **HUNDRED MILLION** *thoughts* (意). ☞ 臆 0621, 憶 0620

0148
常 | 15

| | | | |
|---|---|---|---|
| **視** | **LOOK AT, regard** | 視界 しかい field of vision, visibility..........0612 | |
| | | 視力 しりょく eyesight..........................0084 | |
| | | 視覚 しかく sense of sight ....................0325 | |
| | シ | ○重視する じゅうしする consider important...0539 | |
| | | ○無視する むしする disregard, ignore........0048 | |

**0623**
見 147

An eyeball on legs (見 0083) comes right up to the *altar* (ネ) to **LOOK AT** it.

0884
常 | 11

| | | | |
|---|---|---|---|
| **規** | **REGULATION, standard** | ○規定 きてい regulations, rules; provisions...0045 | |
| | | 規約 きやく agreement, rules, bylaws........0170 | |
| | | 法規 ほうき laws and regulations............0139 | |
| | キ | 校規 こうき school regulations.............0103 | |
| | | 定規 じょうぎ ruler, rule, square [cf. 定 0045] | |
| | | ..........................................0045 | |

**0624**
見 147

Imagine a martinetish *husband*/father (夫), keeping a watchful eye (見) on his wife and children to make sure they follow the rules and **REGULATIONS** of the household.

0890
常 | 11

**RULE, law**

ソク

| | | |
|---|---|---|
| ○規則 | きそく rule, regulation | 0624 |
| 法則 | ほうそく law, rule | 0139 |
| 原則 | げんそく principle | 0208 |
| 反則 | はんそく violation of rules, infringement | 0374 |
| 自民党則 | じみんとうそく rules of the Liberal Democratic Party | 0081, 0477, 0319 |

**0625**

刀 18

The possession of property or *money* (貝) requires the rule of law. Here リ signifies the enforcement of **RULES** and laws, standing beside 貝 to protect it. Take a moment to allow the character's image to find a snug niche in your memory, letting リ be a visible symbol of **RULES** and **laws**.

1311

常 9

---

**SIDE**

ソク
がわ

| | | |
|---|---|---|
| 右側 | みぎがわ (=うそく) right side | 0402 |
| 側聞する | そくぶんする learn by hearsay | 0453 |
| ○側面 | そくめん side, flank; side, aspect | 0175 |
| 内側 | うちがわ inside, interior | 0215 |
| ○向かい側 | むかいがわ opposite side, across (the street) | 0183 |

**0626**

人 9

To the above image we now add a *man* (イ), who attempts to approach the *money* (貝) on the opposite **SIDE** from リ. Think of him as being literally on the "wrong **SIDE** of the *law*." ☞ 測 0627

0120

常 11

---

¹ **MEASURE, gauge**
² **CONJECTURE, estimate**

ソク
はか(る)

| | | |
|---|---|---|
| ①測定する | そくていする measure, gauge | 0045 |
| ¹ 測量 | そくりょう measurement, surveying | 0538 |
| ¹ 気温を測る | きおんをはかる measure the (atmospheric) temperature | 0126, 0199 |
| ² 予測 | よそく estimate, forecast, prediction | 0163 |
| ² 憶測 | おくそく conjecture, speculation, guess | 0620 |

**0627**

水 85

*"Rules/laws* for *water"* implies a system of weights and **MEASURES** to govern the trade of measurable substances (e.g., liquids 氵). **MEASURE** can easily be associated with **gauge**, **estimate**, and **CONJECTURE**. Note that both characters incorporating 則 follow its *on* reading, ソク. ☞ 側 0626

0558

常 12

---

**THINK; deliberate; study**

コウ
かんが(える) かんが(え)

| | | |
|---|---|---|
| 考案 | こうあん idea, plan; project | 0097 |
| ○思考 | しこう thinking, thought, consideration | 0142 |
| 考古学 | こうこがく archaeology | 0254, 0099 |
| ○考える | かんがえる think; deliberate; study | |
| 考え方 | かんがえかた way of thinking, view | 0173 |

**0628**

老 125

Recall 耂 *old/buried underground.* 与 easily suggests the numeral *5*. Now consider how sometimes one must get away from mundane distractions for a period of sustained, concentrated thought. Along these lines, 考 can suggest to us the idea of escaping *underground* for *5* minutes to carefully **THINK** about something. ☞ 老 0629

2753

常 6

**OLD**

ロウ
お(いる) ふ(ける)

| | | |
|---|---|---|
| ○老人 ろうじん old person, old folks | ......... | **0015** |
| 老若 ろうにゃく the old and the young | ...... | **0404** |
| 老化 ろうか aging | ............ | **0120** |
| ○老いる おいる grow old | | |
| ○老ける ふける grow old | | |

**0629**
老 125

2754
常 | 6

屮 *old/buried underground* and ヒ *fallen person* (see 化 0120) depict an **OLD** person fallen into his grave. From this kanji, 屮 itself takes the meaning *old*. ☞ 考 0628

---

**FILIAL PIETY**

コウ

| | | |
|---|---|---|
| 孝行 こうこう filial piety | ............... | **0055** |
| ○親孝行 おやこうこう filial piety | ...... | **0276, 0055** |
| 孝心 こうしん filial devotion/affection | ...... | **0056** |
| 孝子 こうし filial child | .................. | **0094** |
| 不孝 ふこう (=ふきょう) lack of filial piety, undutifulness | ........... | **0049** |

**0630**
子 39

2761
常 | 7

This image of a *child* (子) assuming a submissive position beneath his *elders* (屮) vividly depicts the notion of **FILIAL PIETY**.

---

¹ **THICK**
² **KIND**

コウ
あつ(い)

| | | |
|---|---|---|
| ¹ 濃厚な のうこうな thick, dense, heavy, rich | ... | **0512** |
| ① 厚い あつい thick, bulky | | |
| ② 厚意 こうい kindness, favor | ................. | **0151** |
| ² 厚志 こうし kindness, kind thought/intention | ................ | **0369** |
| ² 温厚な おんこうな gentle, courteous | ........ | **0199** |

**0631**
厂 27

2588
常 | 9

We can visualize both this character's meanings. Start with the idea that a **KIND** child is one who buries his selfish desires in order to put others above himself. Now see a *child* (子) suppressing himself beneath a *cliff* (厂) and two **THICK** layers of earth (日). Thus the multiple strata above 子 represent both **THICKNESS** and **KINDNESS**.

---

¹ **TEACH; inform**
² **RELIGION**

キョウ
おし(える) おそ(わる)

| | | |
|---|---|---|
| ① 教育 きょういく education, teaching | ........ | **0489** |
| ¹ 教室 きょうしつ classroom, class | ............. | **0253** |
| ① 教える おしえる teach; tell, inform | | |
| ² 教会 きょうかい church | ................. | **0226** |
| ² 布教する ふきょうする spread (a religion) | ... | **0204** |

**0632**
攵 66
敎

1356
常 | 11

From 孝 0630 we have an image of an *older* person above a *child*. Here the *older* person wields 攵 *the rod*, the better to **TEACH** the *child* a lesson (you may prefer to think of it as the teacher's pointer). M2 **RELIGION** comes from the idea of **TEACHING**. Do not confuse with the name-use kanji 敦 KINDLY; HARD WORKING.

| 完 | COMPLETE | 完全な かんぜんな perfect, complete, whole 0078 |
|---|---|---|
| | | ○完成する かんせいする complete; be completed .......... 0070 |
| | カン | 完結 かんけつ completion, conclusion, finish .......... 0516 |
| | | 完投する かんとうする [baseball] pitch a complete game .......... 0517 |
| | | 未完の みかんの incomplete, unfinished .... 0271 |

| 0633 | 元 0136 suggests the *origin* or foundation of a building. Just add a *roof* (宀) to COMPLETE the structure. ☞ 宗 0636 |
|---|---|
| 宀 40 | |
| 1883 | |
| 常 7 | |

| 院 | INSTITUTION | ○病院 びょういん hospital .......... 0617 |
|---|---|---|
| | | 入院する にゅういんする be hospitalized .... 0039 |
| | | 大学院 だいがくいん graduate school 0033, 0099 |
| | イン | 両院 りょういん both Houses (of the legislature) .......... 0177 |
| | | 寺院 じいん temple .......... 0382 |

| 0634 | Picture some kind of INSTITUTION being *completed* (完) in the *hills outside of town* (阝). They're just lowering the roof onto it now. It wouldn't hurt to visualize a specific INSTITUTION you know of, located in the *hills* surrounding some town (see the sample vocabulary for ideas). The reading イン can be associated with INSTITUTION. |
|---|---|
| 阜 170 | |
| 0410 | |
| 常 10 | |

| 奈 | PHONETIC [na] | 奈良 なら Nara (city and prefecture) .......... 0285 |
|---|---|---|
| | | 奈良時代 ならじだい Nara period (Japanese historical era, approx. 710–94 CE) .......... 0285, 0383, 0071 |
| | ナ | 神奈川 かながわ Kanagawa (prefecture) .......... 0316, 0022 |

| 0635 | Best remembered as the ナ in 奈良 (なら), ancient capital of Japan. See it as an *altar* (示) rising up to a *great* (大) height, depicting Nara's great temple 東大寺 (とうだいじ), the largest in the nation. Note that this character is the source for *na* (な, ナ) in the kana syllabaries. |
|---|---|
| 大 37 | |
| 1905 | |
| 常 8 | |

| 宗 | RELIGIOUS SECT | ○宗教 しゅうきょう religion, faith, creed .......... 0632 |
|---|---|---|
| | | 改宗 かいしゅう conversion; proselytism .... 0429 |
| | | 日蓮宗 にちれんしゅう Nichiren sect (of Buddhism) .......... 0001, 0585 |
| | シュウ ソウ | 宗門 しゅうもん sect, doctrine .......... 0447 |
| | | 宗家 そうけ (=そうか) family head; originator .......... 0219 |

| 0636 | The *roof* (宀) above the *altar* (示) suggests an individual house of worship, that is, a particular RELIGIOUS SECT. ☞ 崇 1645, 完 0633, 察 0639 |
|---|---|
| 宀 40 | |
| 1915 | |
| 常 8 | |

**FESTIVAL, worship**

サイ
まつ(る) まつ(り) まつり

| | |
|---|---|
| 祭礼 さいれい (religious) festival | 0313 |
| ○祭日 さいじつ holiday, festival day | 0001 |
| 文化祭 ぶんかさい culture festival | 0101, 0120 |
| 祭る まつる worship, enshrine | |
| ○祭り まつり festival | |

**0637**

示 113

2329
常 | 11

The top of this character is a new grapheme for us, not to be confused with 癶 (see 発 0148). It derives from a picture of a *hand* (S5–6) placing an offering of *meat* (S1–4) above an *altar* (示), representing the ideas of **worship** and (by extension) **FESTIVAL**.

---

**¹VERGE, edge**
**²OCCASION**

サイ
きわ ‐ぎわ

| | |
|---|---|
| ①際立つ きわだつ be conspicuous, be prominent | 0067 |
| ¹窓際の席 まどぎわのせき window seat | 0558, 0279 |
| ¹交際 こうさい association, friendship | 0102 |
| ①国際 こくさい international | 0075 |
| ②食事の際に しょくじのさいに when eating | 0288, 0080 |

**0638**

阜 170

0646
常 | 14

Recall that items placed to the right of 阝 are located in the *hills just outside town*. Based on ancient geomantic and religious ideas, the Japanese located most temples (and therefore most *festivals*) in such marginal areas, so 際 graphically illustrates the **edge** or **VERGE** of town. We may also think of this trip to a little-visited place as a special **OCCASION**, a special time for getting away from the usual town-bound routines and living on the **edge**.

---

**¹INSPECT, observe**
**²GUESS, judge**

サツ

| | |
|---|---|
| ①視察 しさつ inspection, observation | 0623 |
| ¹詳察 しょうさつ detailed observation | 0495 |
| ²察知する さっちする infer, gather | 0560 |
| ²考察する こうさつする consider, contemplate, study | 0628 |
| ②察する さっする guess, conjecture, judge; sympathize with | |

**0639**

宀 40

2062
常 | 14

See 宀 as a god presiding over the sacrificial *festival* rite (祭), **INSPECTING**, observing, **judging**, and trying to **GUESS** what on earth the people are doing. ☞ 審 1510, 宗 0636

---

**PRAY**

キ
いの(る)

| | |
|---|---|
| 祈願する きがんする pray, implore | 0214 |
| ○祈念 きねん prayer | 0230 |
| 祈り いのり prayer | |

**0640**

示 113

祈

0779
常 | 8

Recall from 所 0249 that in former times a *hacksaw* (斤) was an essential item that all households would have. Also, scripture taught that God rewards those who demonstrate their faith by offering up to Him their most basic possessions. Thus offering one's *hacksaw* at the *altar* (ネ) made an intuitive image for **PRAYER**. ☞ 礼 0313

| 祖 | ANCESTOR | ○祖先 そせん ancestor, forefather ............ 0134 |
|---|---|---|
| | ソ | 祖国 そこく one's native country............ 0075 |
| | | 元祖 がんそ originator, pioneer ............ 0136 |
| | | 祖父 そふ grandfather ..................... 0100 |
| | | 祖母 そぼ grandmother..................... 0104 |

**0641** 示 113 祖 0823 常 9

Traditionally people in China believed that their **ANCESTORS** became gods. And sure enough, here we see a *ladder*(且) leading up to the top of the *altar*(ネ), symbolically representing the **ANCESTORS'** joining the gods in heaven. Note that kanji in which 且 appears at the right (i.e., in the phonetic position) are read ソ.

| 助 | HELP, save | 助手 じょしゅ assistant, helper............... 0046 |
|---|---|---|
| | ジョ | ○助言 じょげん advice..................... 0051 |
| | たす(ける) たす(かる) すけ | 助教員 じょきょういん assistant teacher ....... 0632, 0317 |
| | | ○助ける たすける help; save |
| | | 助け出す たすけだす rescue (someone) from ....... 0038 |

**0642** 力 19 1037 常 7

Building on 動 0540, we can visualize here a *strong* person (力) dragging along a *ladder*(且) from left to right, rushing to **HELP** or **save** someone in distress.

| 仲 | ¹ INTERMEDIARY ² PERSONAL RELATIONS | ①仲介者 ちゅうかいしゃ intermediary, mediator, agent.................... 0611, 0107 |
|---|---|---|
| | チュウ | ¹仲人 なこうど go-between, matchmaker....0015 |
| | なか | ¹仲買 なかがい brokerage; middleman......0352 |
| | | ②仲間 なかま fellow, comrade, associate.....0448 |
| | | ²仲が良い なかがよい be on good terms ....0285 |

**0643** 人 9 0028 常 6

Reading left to right, we get "*man*(イ) in the *middle*(中)": **INTERMEDIARY**. Reading right to left, we get "in the *middle* of *men*": **PERSONAL RELATIONS**. Note that this entry and the next two all follow 中 in their *on-yomi*.

| 忠 | LOYALTY, faithfulness | ○忠実 ちゅうじつ faithfulness, devotion, honesty ....0499 |
|---|---|---|
| | チュウ | 忠孝 ちゅうこう loyalty and filial piety........0630 |
| | | 尽忠 じんちゅう loyalty ..................... 0338 |
| | | 忠臣 ちゅうしん loyal subject................. 0484 |

**0644** 心 61 2154 常 8

Depicts **LOYALTY** or faithfulness, that is, the idea of keeping one's assigned purpose in the very *middle* (中) of one's *heart* (心), before all other things.

| | OPEN SEA | ○沖合 おきあい open sea, offshore, offing....0227<br>二キロ沖 にキロおき 2 kilometers offshore<br>..............................................................0003 |
|---|---|---|
| | チュウ<br>おき | |

**0645**
水 85

沖

0232
常 7

Way out there in the *middle* (中) of the *water* (氵): the **OPEN SEA**.

---

| | PRESERVE, maintain, guarantee | 保持する ほじする maintain, preserve, retain...0384<br>保存する ほぞんする preserve, store, keep, save<br>...............................................................0407<br>保育 ほいく nurture, upbringing; nursing ......0489<br>○保証する ほしょうする guarantee .................0550<br>○平和を保つ へいわをたもつ preserve peace<br>..........................................................0334, 0236 |
|---|---|---|
| | ホ<br>たも(つ) | |

**0646**
人 9

Derives from a picture of a mother carrying a baby on her back. The baby's wrapping eventually became conflated with the grapheme for tree, but see 木 as crisscrossing straps the mother has carefully tied around her baby to hold it safe and close to her body, **PRESERVING** it and sustaining it wherever she goes.

0077
常 9

---

| | DUMB, dumbfounded | ○呆れる あきれる be amazed, be astounded<br>呆れ顔 あきれがお dumbfounded expression<br>...............................................................0180<br>呆れ果てる あきれはてる be astounded, be<br>stupefied..................................................0599<br>呆気 あっけ amazement, stupefaction ......0126 |
|---|---|---|
| | ホウ ボウ<br>あき(れる) | |

**0647**
口 30

Continuing from the previous entry, we now see the swaddled baby left alone. Think of how the baby can neither think nor speak for itself, and you should have little trouble remembering that this character means **DUMB**. See 然 0760 and 阿 0819 for sample *on-yomi* compounds. ☞ 果 0599

外 7

---

| | PROTECT, watch over, keep | ○保守的 ほしゅてき conservative........0646, 0169<br>○守る まもる protect, watch over, keep<br>規則を守る きそくをまもる keep to/observe the<br>regulations .............................0624, 0625<br>身を守る みをまもる defend oneself.........0060<br>子守り こもり babysitting; babysitter .......0094 |
|---|---|---|
| | シュ ス<br>まも(る) まも(り) もり -もり | |

**0648**
宀 40

Review 寸 0381. Beneath a *roof* (宀) we see an *outstretched arm* holding a small object (寸). Visualize the roof **PROTECTING** or **watching over** the vulnerable little object. Remembering this idea, practice writing 守 and 寸 in turn. ☞ 府 0247

1861
常 6

| 団 | COLLECTIVE, group, organization | 団体 だんたい group, collective; organization ............ 0062 |
|---|---|---|
| ダン トン | | 団地 だんち (public) housing development ............ 0187 |
| | | 集団 しゅうだん group, collective ............ 0190 |
| | | 軍団 ぐんだん (army) corps ............ 0583 |
| | | 布団 ふとん futon, bed quilt ............ 0204 |

| 0649 | The *small object* (寸)'s *enclosure* inside 囗 graphically reminds us of an individual's inclusion (or confinement) within a larger **COLLECTIVE**. |
|---|---|
| 囗 31 | |
| 團 | |
| 2628 | |
| 常 6 | |

| 対 | ¹ **OPPOSITE, counter to; in relation to**<br>² **OPPOSE** | ¹ 対面する たいめんする meet, face ............ 0175 |
|---|---|---|
| タイ<br>つい | | ¹ 人に対して親切 ひとにたいしてしんせつ kind toward others ............ 0015, 0276, 0086 |
| | | ① 対になる ついになる form a pair |
| | | ² 対決 たいけつ confrontation, showdown ... 0330 |
| | | ② 反対する はんたいする oppose, object (to) 0374 |

| 0650 | 夂 varies slightly from 文, but we'll see them the same way, as a person working behind a desk (see 0101). 対 depicts the notion of "**OPPOSITE** sides" or "**OPPOSING** roles": 寸 holds out an object to deliver it (as in 付 0064), while 夂 sits behind a desk and receives it. Bear in mind that 対 does not mean "deliver" or "receive"; it means **OPPOSE**. |
|---|---|
| 寸 41 | |
| 對 | |
| 0735 | |
| 常 7 | |

| 村 | **VILLAGE** | 農村 のうそん farm village ............ 0511 |
|---|---|---|
| ソン<br>むら | | 村会 そんかい village assembly ............ 0226 |
| | | 市町村 しちょうそん cities, towns, and villages; municipalities ............ 0205, 0439 |
| | | 村人 むらびと villager ............ 0015 |
| | | 八木村 やぎむら Yagi village ............ 0010, 0028 |

| 0651 | Visualize as an *outstretched arm* (寸) pulling up a *tree* (木) to clear land and build a **VILLAGE**. ☞ 材 0654 |
|---|---|
| 木 75 | |
| 邨 | |
| 0738 | |
| 常 7 | |

| 才 | ¹ **TALENT**<br>² **-YEARS OLD** | ¹ 才気 さいき talent ............ 0126 |
|---|---|---|
| サイ | | ¹ 英才 えいさい talent, genius; gifted person 0332 |
| | | ① 天才 てんさい (person of) genius ............ 0270 |
| | | ² 十二才 じゅうにさい twelve years old ... 0005, 0003 |
| | | ² 十八才未満 じゅうはっさいみまん under eighteen years old ............ 0005, 0010, 0271, 0179 |

| 0652 | Refers to the natural gift of genius or **TALENT**, or the possessor of such a gift. See a person reaching out with one arm (S3), a person of such **TALENT** that she can reach out and attain anything she sets her sights on. Also used as the suffix "**-YEARS OLD**," shorthand for the homophonous 歳 2041. ☞ 丈 0657 |
|---|---|
| 手 64 | |
| 2880 | |
| 常 3 | |

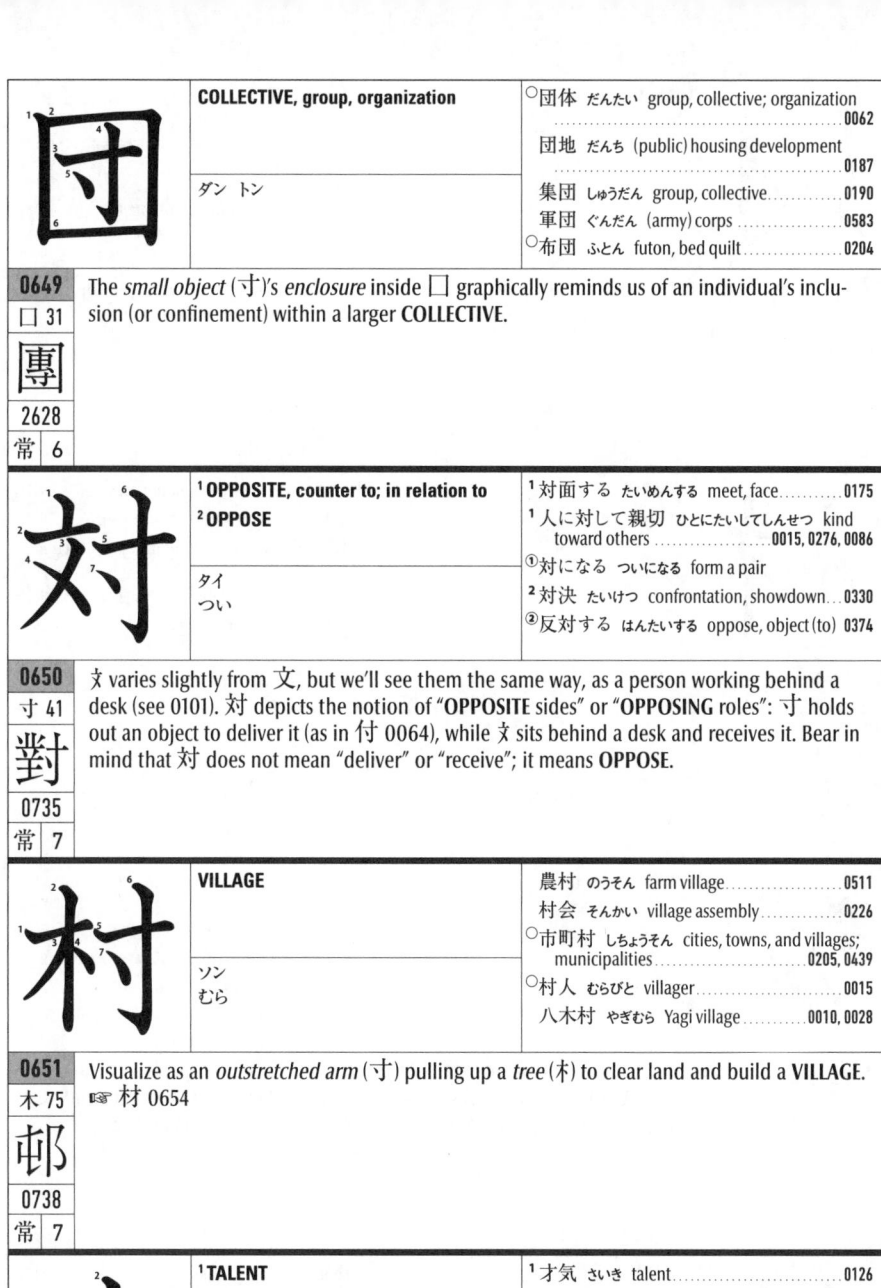

| 財  **WEALTH; property**<br><br>ザイ　サイ | 財政 ざいせい public finance, financial affairs ...... 0246<br>財界 ざいかい business world, economic circles ...... 0612<br>財布 さいふ purse, wallet ...... 0204<br>○財産 ざいさん property, fortune, wealth .... 0181<br>財団 ざいだん endowed institution, foundation ...... 0649 |
|---|---|

| **0653**<br>貝 154<br><br>賎<br><br>1326<br>常 10 | See the idea of **WEALTH** in the *talented person* (才)'s reaching out and grabbing *money* (貝). Note that 才 is written a little differently as a *tsukuri*—basically a narrower version of the katakana 才. |
|---|---|

| 材 **¹TIMBER**<br>**²MATERIAL**<br><br>ザイ | ①材木 ざいもく timber, lumber, logs ...... 0028<br>¹ 木材 もくざい wood, timber, lumber ...... 0028<br>②取材 しゅざい news gathering, data collection ...... 0059<br>² 人材 じんざい capable/talented person .... 0015<br>² 教材 きょうざい teaching materials ...... 0632 |
|---|---|

| **0654**<br>木 75<br><br>杁<br><br>0740<br>常 7 | See the idea of **TIMBER** (or more generically, **MATERIAL**), in the *talented person* (才)'s reaching out and grabbing a *tree* (木). ☞ 村 0651, 枕 0656, 杖 0658 |
|---|---|

| 沈 **SINK, submerge**<br><br>チン<br>しず(む)　しず(める) | ○沈没する ちんぼつする sink, go to the bottom ...... 0519<br>沈下 ちんか subsidence, sinking ...... 0040<br>浮沈 ふちん rise and fall; ups and downs ... 0613<br>○日が沈む ひがしずむ The sun sets ...... 0001<br>沈める しずめる sink, send to the bottom, submerge |
|---|---|

| **0655**<br>水 85<br><br><br>0231<br>常 7 | To remember this character, it is sufficient to focus on S6, which seems to represent the arcing trajectory of an object that **submerges** under *water* (氵). Notice how the object **SINKS** to the very bottom of 氵. S7, for its part, seems to represent the act of reaching bottom. |
|---|---|

| 枕 **PILLOW**<br><br>まくら | 枕元 まくらもと bedside ...... 0136<br>○枕カバー まくらカバー pillowcase<br>枕木 まくらぎ railroad tie ...... 0028<br>本を枕にして ほんをまくらにして using a book as a pillow ...... 0031<br>枕草子 まくらのそうし *The Pillow Book* [eleventh-century collection of musings] ...... 0144, 0094 |
|---|---|

| **0656**<br>木 75<br><br><br>0759<br>常 8 | Here the long, curving stroke (S7) suggests a soft, rounded **PILLOW** positioned next to a *tree* (木) to give it a soft landing after it is cut. Now as you practice writing the character, imagine the *tree* laying its head down into that gently sloping stroke for a good night's sleep.<br>☞ 材 0654, 杖 0658, 枕 1695 |
|---|---|

|  | ¹ **STATURE; measure**<br>² **STOUT**<br><br>ジョウ<br>たけ | ①背丈 せたけ stature, height ...............0124<br>¹ 丈比べ たけくらべ comparison of statures...0123<br>² 丈夫な じょうぶな healthy, robust; stout, solid<br>...............0565<br>②大丈夫 だいじょうぶ safe, sure, all right<br>...............0033, 0565<br>² 気丈な きじょうな stouthearted, courageous 0126 |

| **0657**<br>一 1<br><br>2885<br>常 3 | Originally representing a unit of **measure** (roughly 3 meters), 丈 can be seen as three yard-sticks laid across one another. If a man measured 3 meters tall we would say he is a man of great **STATURE**. If he measured 3 meters around we would call him **STOUT**. ☞ 才 0652 |

|  | **CANE, staff**<br><br>ジョウ<br>つえ | 杖がないと立っていられない つえがないとたっていられない (He) can't stand without a cane<br>...............0067<br>竹の杖 たけのつえ bamboo rod.............0243<br>松葉杖 まつばづえ crutches.............0242, 0605 |

| **0658**<br>木 75<br><br>0736<br>名 7 | Building on the last entry, here see three *wooden* **CANES**, each about a meter long. ☞ 材 0654, 枕 0656, 枚 1695 |

|  | **GREAT, eminent**<br><br>イ<br>えら(い) | ○偉大な いだいな great, mighty, grand ......0033<br>偉丈夫 いじょうふ towering/great man; hero<br>...............0657, 0565<br>偉業 いぎょう great work/achievement .....0498<br>○偉い人 えらいひと great man, extraordinary<br>character...............0015<br>偉がる えらがる be self-important, be conceited |

| **0659**<br>人 9<br><br>0128<br>常 12 | This kanji introduces a new grapheme, 韋 *leather*. Like the earlier grapheme we learned for *leather*, 革 0592, 韋 has parts corresponding to the main thorax area of the flayed skin (口), a head with horns (at the top), as well as hind limbs and a tail (at the bottom). Practice writing 革 and 韋 until you can reproduce them from memory. For the present entry, try to visualize a **GREAT** and **eminent** *man* (イ) wearing an impressive *leather* cape. The more vividly you imagine this picture, the better you will remember the kanji. |

|  | **LATITUDE; woof/weft**<br><br>イ | ○緯度 いど latitude...............0280<br>緯線 いせん line(s) of latitude ..............0210<br>北緯 ほくい north latitude ...............0122 |

| **0660**<br>糸 120<br><br>1285<br>常 16 | Let us imagine that the Chinese chose to combine 糸 with 韋 to represent **woof/weft** (the crosswise threads in weaving) because of the latter's many horizontal lines (S8, S9, S11, S12, S13, S15). Now let the same lines represent the lines of **LATITUDE** running around the globe. Write this kanji, sketch a globe next to it, and connect the lines. ☞ 経 1257 |

| | **GUARD** | 衛生 えいせい hygiene, sanitation, preservation of health ............................0036 |
|---|---|---|
| | | 衛生的 えいせいてき sanitary, hygienic ............................................0036, 0169 |
| | エイ | ○防衛 ぼうえい defense, protection .......0174 |
| | | 守衛 しゅえい guard, doorkeeper...........0648 |
| | | 前衛 ぜんえい vanguard; forward player....0113 |

| **0661** | Review 行 0055. Here the left and right sides of 行 are split apart by a third element. When |
|---|---|
| 行 144 | this happens, see them as *either side of a road* (行). In the present entry, visualize 韋 as a |
| 衞 | protective layer of *leather* laid over the road, to **GUARD** it from damage. |
| **0686** | |
| 常 16 | |

| | **(SOUTH) KOREA** | ○韓国 かんこく South Korea ...................0075 |
|---|---|---|
| | | 大韓民国 だいかんみんこく Republic of Korea ............................................0033, 0477, 0075 |
| | カン | 日韓 にっかん Japan and South Korea, Japanese-South Korean .............................0001 |
| | | 訪韓 ほうかん visit to South Korea...........0454 |

| **0662** | 卓 (from 朝 0145) suggests *morning*. Imagine a ship that arrives at Japan's western shore every |
|---|---|
| 韋 178 | *morning* with a shipment of *leather* (韋) from **KOREA**. At length "*morning leather*" comes to |
| | signify **KOREA**. Don't confuse with 朝, used in the old term for "Korea" 朝鮮 (ちょうせん) |
| | and in the modern term for "North Korea," 北朝鮮 (きたちょうせん). |
| **1575** | |
| 常 18 | |

| | ¹ **DIFFER; be wrong** | ①違う ちがう differ; disagree; be wrong |
|---|---|---|
| | ² **VIOLATE** | ¹ 食い違い くいちがい difference (in opinion), cross-purposes .............................0288 |
| | | ¹ 違和感 いわかん uncomfortable feeling ............................................0236, 0327 |
| | イ | ②違反 いはん violation (of the law); breach...0374 |
| | ちが(う) ちが(い) ちが(える) | ² 違法 いほう illegality, unlawfulness.........0139 |
| | -ちが(える) | |

| **0663** | Think of the wildest person you know. Someone who **VIOLATES** every rule—except that of |
|---|---|
| 辵 162 | always being **DIFFERENT** from others. Now picture that person driving down the street in a |
| | *vehicle* (辶) with an all-*leather* (韋) exterior. Paint in your mind a picture of **DIFFERING** and |
| | **VIOLATING** around the image of a *leather*-covered car. |
| **2716** | |
| 常 13 | |

| | **HOLD (in one's arms)** | ○介抱する かいほうする nurse, care for.......0611 |
|---|---|---|
| | | ○抱く だく hug, embrace, hold in one's arms |
| | | いだく harbor (suspicion), entertain (hope), cherish; hold in one's arms, hug |
| | ホウ | ○抱える かかえる hold in one's arms |
| | だ(く) いだ(く) かか(える) | 抱き抱える だきかかえる hold, carry, embrace |

| **0664** | Review 包 0457 **WRAP**, and note that all kanji incorporating that character are pronounced |
|---|---|
| 手 64 | ホウ. The present entry indicates *wrapping* in one's *arms* (扌): **HOLD.** ☞ 抱 1070 |
| **0271** | |
| 常 8 | |

|  | **HEAVY GUN** | 砲火 ほうか gunfire ...........................0026 |
|---|---|---|
| | | 発砲する はっぽうする fire, discharge (a gun) ..................................................0148 |
| | ホウ | 大砲 たいほう gun, cannon, artillery .......0033 |
| | | 対戦車砲 たいせんしゃほう antitank gun ........................................0650, 0461, 0125 |
| | | ○鉄砲 てっぽう gun, firearm ...............0564 |

| 0665 | Associate this image with the act of loading a **HEAVY GUN** with a projectile. Let *stone* (石) represent the projectile, and let *wrap* (包) suggest the act of "packing" it, if you will, into the **HEAVY GUN**. |
|---|---|
| 石 112 | |
| **1065** | |
| 常 10 | |

| 泡 | **BUBBLE, foam** | 発泡 はっぽう foaming, effervescence.......0148 |
|---|---|---|
| | | 気泡 きほう air bubble, bubble ................0126 |
| | | ○水泡 すいほう bubble, foam ................0027 |
| | ホウ あわ | ○泡立つ あわだつ bubble, foam ...............0067 |

| 0666 | *Liquid* (氵) that *wraps around* (包) a spherical volume of air: **BUBBLE**. |
|---|---|
| 水 85 | |
| **0296** | |
| 常 8 | |

| 丹 | **CINNABAR RED; wholeheartedly** | ○丹念な たんねんな painstaking, assiduous, diligent.......................................0230 |
|---|---|---|
| | タン | 丹心 たんしん sincerity .......................0056 |

| 0667 | Let S4 indicate a waistline and S3 the organ located at the center of the upper body—the heart—here representing the color **CINNABAR RED**. Associate **wholeheartedly** with the idea of one's heart burning bright **RED** with sincerity. ☞ 舟 0668, 凡 1629 |
|---|---|
| 丶 3 | |
| 丹 | |
| **2897** | |
| 常 4 | |

|  | **SMALL BOAT** | ○舟行 しゅうこう navigation, going by ship ...0055 |
|---|---|---|
| | | 舟運 しゅううん transportation by water .....0584 |
| | | ○小舟 こぶね small craft .......................0034 |
| | シュウ ふね ふな- -ぶね | 舟大工 ふなだいく boatbuilder........0033, 0108 |
| | | 渡し舟 わたしぶね ferryboat.................0281 |

| 0668 | A bird's-eye view of a kayak (representing **SMALL BOAT**) gliding straight down toward the bottom of this page. S6 shows the kayaker's double-bladed paddle. The short stroke at the top can be thought of as a rudder, to help distinguish this from 丹. As a grapheme, 舟 will simply mean *boat*. ☞ 丹 0667 |
|---|---|
| 舟 137 | |
| **2965** | |
| 常 6 | |

**SHIP**

セン
ふね　ふな-　-ぶね

○船長 せんちょう (ship) captain ................ 0091
風船 ふうせん balloon ........................ 0425
商船 しょうせん merchant ship, trading vessel
........................................ 0351
助け船 たすけぶね lifeboat; help ............ 0642
船旅 ふなたび (sea) voyage ................ 0569

| | |
|---|---|
| **0669**<br>舟 137<br>船<br>1229<br>常 11 | Picture the right half of this character as a pair of hands (or sticks) rolling a hoop. Here then we have a *boat* (舟) large enough for a child to *roll a hoop* around its deck: a **SHIP**. As you practice writing this character, imagine *rolling a hoop* round and round the deck of a big **SHIP**. The right half of this character will come up again at 沿 1348 and 鉛 2067. ☞ 般 0671 |

**OCEANGOING SHIP**

ハク

船舶 せんぱく ship, vessel; craft ............ 0669
舶用機関 はくようきかん marine engine
........................... 0047, 0473, 0451
○舶来品 はくらいひん imported goods, foreign-
made articles ................ 0274, 0301

| | |
|---|---|
| **0670**<br>舟 137<br><br>1228<br>常 11 | Here we observe an even larger *boat* (舟), big enough to leave a long, frothy wake of *white* (白) seawater: an **OCEANGOING SHIP**. |

**SORT, kind**

ハン

○一般の いっぱんの general, universal, common
........................................ 0002
一般向け いっぱんむけ for the general public
................................... 0002, 0183
全般の ぜんぱんの whole, general, overall 0078
万般 ばんぱん all things, all sorts of matters 0018
先般 せんぱん the other day, some time ago 0134

| | |
|---|---|
| **0671**<br>舟 137<br><br>1203<br>常 10 | We have just seen three different boats, but now we see a unique sort of boat, one for transporting *lances* (殳). Indeed, this *boat* for *lances* is so <u>one of a kind</u> that the meaning of this character is **kind** or **SORT**. ☞ 航 1640, 船 0669, 搬 0672 |

**CARRY**

ハン

○搬送 はんそう conveyance .................... 0455
搬出する はんしゅつする carry out ........... 0038
搬入する はんにゅうする carry in ............ 0039
運搬する うんぱんする carry, transport, convey,
deliver .................................. 0584

| | |
|---|---|
| **0672**<br>手 64<br><br>0592<br>常 13 | Here we see the *boat* (舟) for *lances* (殳) arriving to the waiting *hands* (扌) of the longshore-man, who must unload the lances and **CARRY** them by *hand*. Be deliberate about associating 扌 with **CARRY**, lest you confuse this entry with the previous one. ☞ 盤 0673, 般 0671 |

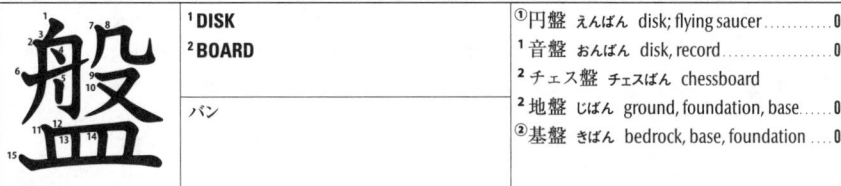

| 盤 | ¹ **DISK** ² **BOARD** バン | ① 円盤 えんばん disk; flying saucer ............ 0013 <br> ¹ 音盤 おんばん disk, record ................ 0150 <br> ² チェス盤 チェスばん chessboard <br> ² 地盤 じばん ground, foundation, base ...... 0187 <br> ② 基盤 きばん bedrock, base, foundation .... 0485 |

| **0673** <br> 皿 108 <br><br> 2481 <br> 常 15 | Visualize 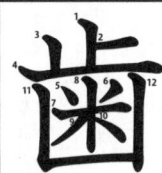 as a **DISK** or **BOARD** on which the "*boat* for *lances*" (般) is loaded. ☞ 搬 0672, 盆 1302 |

| 歯 | **TOOTH** シ は | 歯石 しせき tartar, dental calculus ............ 0403 <br> ○歯医者 はいしゃ dentist ................ 0561, 0107 <br> 入れ歯 いれば dentures ................ 0039 <br> 虫歯 むしば decayed tooth ................ 0343 <br> 歯車 はぐるま cog, toothed wheel .......... 0125 |

| **0674** <br> 齒 211 <br> 齒 <br> 2185 <br> 常 12 | First study the traditional form, which easily suggests two rows of **TEETH** inside a mouth. Now try to visualize 歯 the same way. 止 can be used to remember the reading シ, but to complement the **TEETH** image, let S2 represent a nose. One *on-yomi* compound is provided here, but a more useful one to memorize appears at 科 0759. |

| 冷 | **COLD** レイ <br> つめ(たい) ひ(える) ひ(や) <br> ひ(ややか) ひ(やす) ひ(やかす) <br> さ(める) さ(ます) | ○冷水 れいすい cold water ................ 0027 <br> 冷害 れいがい damage from cold weather . 0413 <br> 冷戦 れいせん Cold War ................ 0461 <br> ○冷え込む ひえこむ get colder, get chilled ... 0192 <br> ○スープが冷めた スープがさめた The soup has cooled |

| **0675** <br> 冫 15 <br><br> 0061 <br> 常 7 | We first encountered 冫 at 次 0278. Now we shall learn a new meaning for it: showing 冫 congealed into two strokes, it can also represent *ice*. In the present entry, we observe *ice commanding* (令) (i.e., forcing) everything around it to be **COLD**. |

| 齢 | **AGE** レイ | ○年齢 ねんれい age, years ................ 0117 <br> 高齢者 こうれいしゃ elderly person .... 0185, 0107 <br> 老齢 ろうれい old age ................ 0629 <br> 学齢 がくれい school age ................ 0099 <br> 月齢 げつれい moon's age ................ 0023 |

| **0676** <br> 齒 211 <br>  <br> 1675 <br> 常 17 | The unmistakable signs of **AGE**: long *teeth* (歯) and giving *commands* (令). |

**LITTLE, few**

ショウ
すく(ない) すこ(し)

○少々 しょうしょう a little, a few, slightly
多少 たしょう a little, somewhat............0267
少年 しょうねん boy ........................0117
○少なくとも すくなくとも at least
○少しも すこしも (not) at all

| 0677 | Focus on S4, which indicates something <u>under</u> *small* (小): **LITTLE**. |
| 小 42 | |
| 2915 | |
| 常 4 | |

**SAND**

サ シャ
すな

砂金 さきん gold dust.....................0029
砂場 すなば sandbox.....................0445
砂時計 すなどけい hourglass.........**0383, 0555**
砂粒 すなつぶ grain of sand...........0235
砂利 じゃり gravel, ballast...............0412

| 0678 | *Little* (少) *stones* (石): **SAND**. Though two *on-yomi* compounds are provided here, a more |
| 石 112 | useful one to memorize appears at 漠 1338. ☞ 沙 1747 |
| 1047 | |
| 常 9 | |

**WALK, step**

ホ ブ フ
ある(く) あゆ(む)

○歩行者 ほこうしゃ pedestrian..........0055, 0107
歩道 ほどう sidewalk, footpath.............0158
進歩 しんぽ progress, advancement, improvement ..................................0191
○歩く あるく walk, go on foot
歩む あゆむ [elegant] walk

| 0679 | At 走 0140 we saw that the image of a foot hitting the ground means RUN. Here, the construction *"little foot"* suggests **WALKING** rather than running. Note that the traditional forms of this and the next entry actually have one <u>fewer</u> stroke than the modern versions. |
| 止 77 | |
| 歩 | |
| 2141 | |
| 常 8 | |

**HAVE RELATIONS WITH**

ショウ

○交渉 こうしょう negotiation, bargaining, discussion ...................................0102
干渉 かんしょう interference, intervention...0408
渉外 しょうがい public relations.............0266

| 0680 | We must *walk* (歩) across the *water* (氵) to **HAVE RELATIONS WITH** the people on the other side. |
| 水 85 | |
| 渉 | |
| 0482 | |
| 常 11 | |

| | ¹ **MINISTRY**<br>² **SAVE, cut down on, leave out**<br>³ **INTROSPECT, reflect**<br><br>セイ　ショウ<br>かえり(みる)　はぶ(く) | ¹ 厚生労働省　こうせいろうどうしょう　Ministry of Health, Labor, and Welfare 0631, 0036, 0542, 0541<br>² 省エネルギー　しょうエネルギー　energy conservation<br>②省く　はぶく　leave out; save, cut down<br>③省みる　かえりみる　reflect upon oneself<br>③反省　はんせい　reflection, introspection.....0374 |

**0681**
目 109

This kanji has three very different meanings. Start by associating the meaning **SAVE**/**cut down on** with the idea of using *few* (少) *items* (目). Now think of a government **MINISTRY** forced by budget cuts to **reflect** (**INTROSPECT**) on how to **cut down on** its expenses.

2164
常 | 9

---

| | ¹ **ASPECT; physiognomy**<br>² **MUTUAL**<br>³ **MINISTER (of state)**<br><br>ソウ　ショウ<br>あい- | ①様相　ようそう　aspect, phase, condition......0501<br>² 相違　そうい　difference, disparity.............0663<br>² 相当する　そうとうする　correspond to, be suitable for.................................................0141<br>②相手　あいて　partner, opponent.............0046<br>③外相　がいしょう　foreign minister.............0266 |

**0682**
目 109

*Eye* and *tree*: picture a government **MINISTER**, observing the goings-on at his ministry from behind a *tree*, judging the overall **ASPECT** (i.e., outer appearance) of the situation from behind the scenes. The other meaning, **MUTUAL**, is visible in the mutuality between the three vertical sections of 木 and 目: the top section of 目 corresponds to the crown of the *tree* (S1 and above), the middle section to the branches (S3–4), and the bottom section to the trunk (lowest part of S2). This can be reinforced by writing 木 and 目 on scratch paper and drawing a dotted line to connect the upper, middle, and lower sections of each. ☞ 租 1515

0808
常 | 9

---

| | **CONCEIVE, think**<br><br>ソウ　ソ | 発想　はっそう　conception.....................0148<br>○思想　しそう　thought, conception, idea......0142<br>理想　りそう　ideal .............................0532<br>予想　よそう　expectation, conjecture, prospect .................................................0163<br>回想　かいそう　recollection, reminiscence....0050 |

**0683**
心 61

Here 心 is added to show us the thoughts and contemplations in the *minister* (相)'s *heart* as he observes the situation. 想 connotes more deliberate thought than does 思 0142 THINK, so we summarize its meaning with the word "CONCEIVE."

2462
常 | 13

---

| | **APPELLATION**<br><br>ショウ | ○名称　めいしょう　appellation, name, title......0269<br>称号　しょうごう　title, degree ..................0300<br>自称する　じしょうする　call/style oneself .....0081<br>称する　しょうする　name, designate; claim, pretend<br>対称　たいしょう　symmetry......................0650 |

**0684**
禾 115

稱

The next two kanji have both been simplified using 尔, but are otherwise unrelated (note how their old forms differ). Because 尔 lacks any meaning or consistent origin, a sensible way to approach these two kanji is simply to master the meaning and reading of one compound. For this entry, the logical choice is V1, which reinforces the keyword "APPELLATION." ☞ 弥 0685

1075
常 | 10

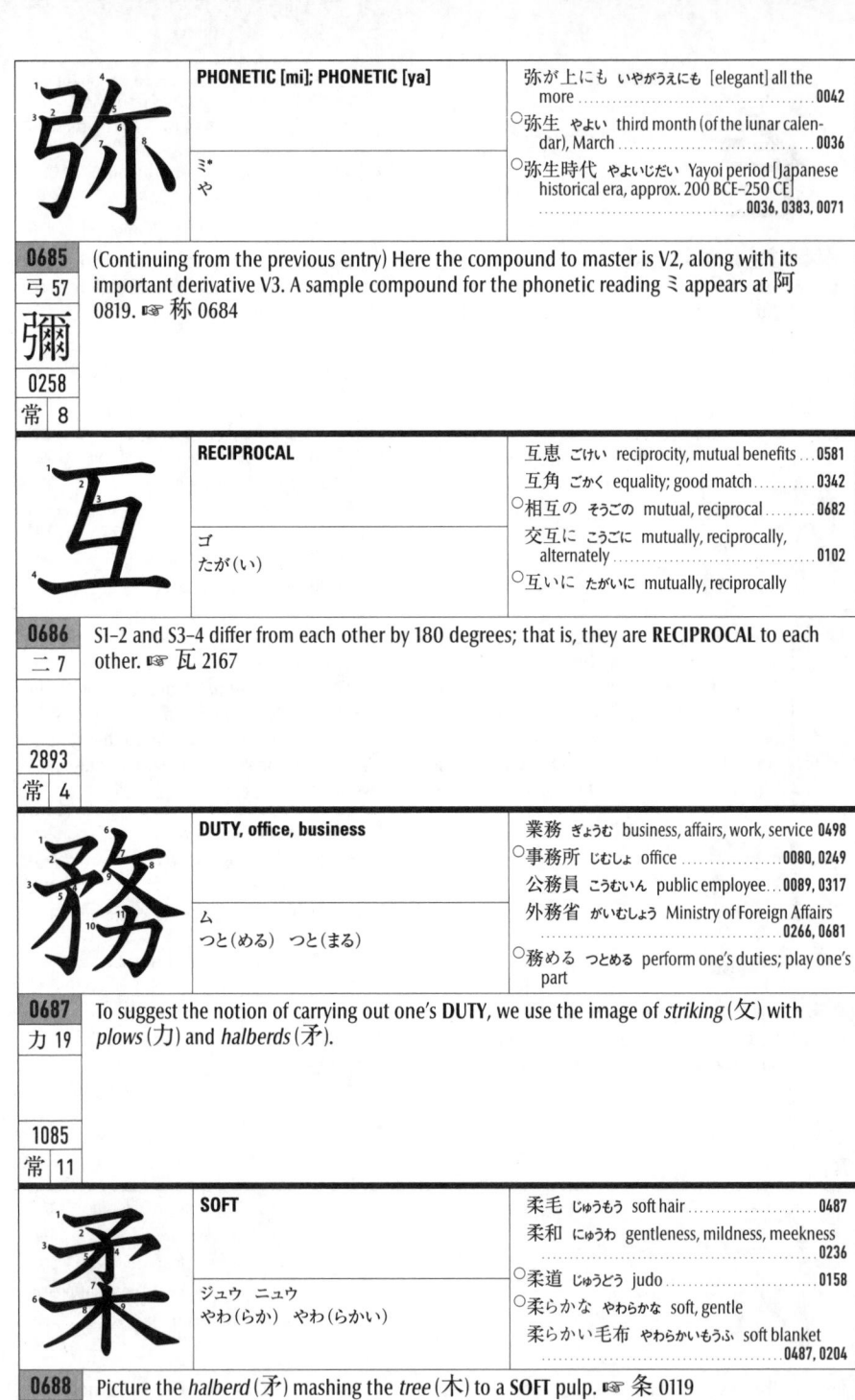

| 弥 | **PHONETIC [mi]; PHONETIC [ya]**<br><br>ミ\*<br>や | 弥が上にも いやがうえにも [elegant] all the more ............................................ 0042<br>○弥生 やよい third month (of the lunar calendar), March ...................................... 0036<br>○弥生時代 やよいじだい Yayoi period [Japanese historical era, approx. 200 BCE–250 CE] ................................. 0036, 0383, 0071 |
|---|---|---|

**0685**
弓 57

彌

0258
常 | 8

(Continuing from the previous entry) Here the compound to master is V2, along with its important derivative V3. A sample compound for the phonetic reading ミ appears at 阿 0819. ☞ 称 0684

| 互 | **RECIPROCAL**<br><br>ゴ<br>たが(い) | 互恵 ごけい reciprocity, mutual benefits ... 0581<br>互角 ごかく equality; good match ........... 0342<br>○相互の そうごの mutual, reciprocal ......... 0682<br>交互に こうごに mutually, reciprocally, alternately ............................................ 0102<br>○互いに たがいに mutually, reciprocally |
|---|---|---|

**0686**
二 7

S1–2 and S3–4 differ from each other by 180 degrees; that is, they are **RECIPROCAL** to each other. ☞ 瓦 2167

2893
常 | 4

| 務 | **DUTY, office, business**<br><br>ム<br>つと(める) つと(まる) | 業務 ぎょうむ business, affairs, work, service 0498<br>○事務所 じむしょ office ................. 0080, 0249<br>公務員 こうむいん public employee...0089, 0317<br>外務省 がいむしょう Ministry of Foreign Affairs ............................................ 0266, 0681<br>○務める つとめる perform one's duties; play one's part |
|---|---|---|

**0687**
力 19

To suggest the notion of carrying out one's **DUTY**, we use the image of *striking* (攵) with *plows* (力) and *halberds* (矛).

1085
常 | 11

| 柔 | **SOFT**<br><br>ジュウ ニュウ<br>やわ(らか) やわ(らかい) | 柔毛 じゅうもう soft hair ...................... 0487<br>柔和 にゅうわ gentleness, mildness, meekness ............................................ 0236<br>○柔道 じゅうどう judo .......................... 0158<br>○柔らかな やわらかな soft, gentle<br>柔らかい毛布 やわらかいもうふ soft blanket ............................................ 0487, 0204 |
|---|---|---|

**0688**
木 75

Picture the *halberd* (矛) mashing the *tree* (木) to a **SOFT** pulp. ☞ 条 0119

1797
常 | 9

| | **SOFT** | ○軟化 なんか softening; weakening..........0120 |
|---|---|---|
| | | 軟骨 なんこつ cartilage.....................0465 |
| | | 柔軟な じゅうなんな soft, pliable, flexible....0688 |
| | ナン | ○軟らかな やわらかな soft, tender |
| | やわ（らか） やわ（らかい） | 軟らかい若葉 やわらかいわかば soft young leaf |
| | | ................................................0404, 0605 |

| **0689** 車 159 | Picture a plush luxury *car*（車）opening a *yawning*（欠）side door, inviting you to sit down on its **SOFT** leather seats. |
|---|---|
| **1345** 常 11 | |

| | **TRACK, path** | 軌道 きどう track, railway; planetary orbit....0158 |
|---|---|---|
| | | 軌条 きじょう rails.............................0119 |
| | キ | 常軌 じょうき usual course, beaten track ....0321 |

| **0690** 車 159 | *Car*（車）+ *nine*（九）: picture a busy railway corridor with nine **TRACKS**. ☞ 転 0224 |
|---|---|
| **1312** 常 9 | |

| | **¹ EAVES** | **¹** 軒下 のきした under the eaves.............0040 |
|---|---|---|
| | **² COUNTER FOR HOUSES** | ①軒並み のきなみ row of houses; all round, across the board.....................................0333 |
| | | ②四軒 よんけん four houses ..................0006 |
| | ケン | **²** 一軒家 いっけんや solitary house; private home |
| | のき | ................................................0002, 0219 |
| | | **²** 数軒 すうけん several houses ..............0309 |

| **0691** 車 159 | A *car*（車）stays *dry*（干）beneath the **EAVES** of a house. ☞ 幹 1808 |
|---|---|
| **1328** 常 10 | |

| | **¹ AXLE** | **¹** 車軸 しゃじく wheel axle, axle ..............0125 |
|---|---|---|
| | **² AXIS** | **²** 軸線 じくせん axis, shaft line ..............0210 |
| | | **²** 地軸 ちじく axis of the earth...............0187 |
| | ジク | ②回転軸 かいてんじく axis of revolution |
| | | ................................................0050, 0224 |
| | | **²** 左右軸 さゆうじく lateral axis..........0401, 0402 |

| **0692** 車 159 | Review 車 0125 VEHICLE. Now see 由 as a close-up diagram of one side of the vehicle, at the point where the **AXLE** juts out of the chassis. The wheel is left off, to expose the **AXLE**. The reading ジク is unique in this course. |
|---|---|
| **1371** 常 12 | |

| | **COMPARE** | ○比較する ひかくする compare with, draw a comparison . . . . . . . . . . . . . : . . . . . . . . . . . .0123 |
|---|---|---|
| | カク | 比較的 ひかくてき comparative . . . . . . .0123, 0169 |
| | | 比較文学 ひかくぶんがく comparative literature . . . . . . . . . . . . . . . . . . . . . . . . . . . . . 0123, 0101, 0099 |
| | | 比較言語学 ひかくげんごがく comparative linguistics . . . . . . . . . . . . . . .0123, 0051, 0222, 0099 |

| **0693** | Picture a couple of hot-rodders "*crossing*(交) *wheels*(車)" down at the street corner to |
|---|---|
| 車 159 | **COMPARE** their custom jobs. Used almost exclusively in the word 比較 (ひかく, comparison). |
| | Make an effort to remember that 較 (カク) is the only character based on 交 that is not |
| | pronounced コウ. |
| **1397** | |
| 常 13 | |

| | **STORAGE CHAMBER** | 金庫 きんこ strong box, cashbox . . . . . . . . . . .0029 |
|---|---|---|
| | コ ク | ○車庫 しゃこ car shed, garage . . . . . . . . . . . . . . .0125 |
| | | 宝庫 ほうこ treasure house, treasury . . . . . . . .0074 |
| | | 文庫 ぶんこ library; collection of literary works; box for stationery . . . . . . . . . . . . . . . . . . . . . . . . . .0101 |
| | | 在庫 ざいこ stock, inventory . . . . . . . . . . . . . . . . .0406 |

| **0694** | In this character, and a few others you will learn later on, 广 *shelter* will be a *garage*. A *car* |
|---|---|
| 广 53 | (車) stored in a *garage* is a natural image for **STORAGE CHAMBER**. |
| **2682** | |
| 常 10 | |

| | **STORE, storehouse** | 貯蔵 ちょぞう storage, preservation . . . . . . . . .0442 |
|---|---|---|
| | ゾウ | ○冷蔵庫 れいぞうこ refrigerator . . . . . . . . . .0675, 0694 |
| | くら | 蔵書 ぞうしょ one's library, book collection 0079 |
| | | 大蔵省 おおくらしょう Ministry of Finance . . . . . . . . . . . . . . . . . . . . . . . . . . . . . . . . . . . .0033, 0681 |
| | | 蔵相 ぞうしょう Minister of Finance . . . . . . . . . .0682 |

| **0695** | Observe a *retainer*(臣) holding a *guided spear*(戈), standing guard over **STORES** of food |
|---|---|
| 艸 140 | (from *plants* ⊥). ☞ 臓 1974 |
| 藏 | |
| **2088** | |
| 常 15 | |

| | **STOREHOUSE** | ○倉庫 そうこ warehouse, storehouse . . . . . . . . .0694 |
|---|---|---|
| | ソウ | 船倉 せんそう ship's hold . . . . . . . . . . . . . . . . . .0669 |
| | くら | 米倉 こめぐら rice granary . . . . . . . . . . . . . . . . . .0234 |
| | | 武器倉 ぶきぐら armory . . . . . . . . . . . . . . .0111, 0295 |
| | | ○倉渡し くらわたし ex-warehouse . . . . . . . . . . . . .0281 |

| **0696** | Take S3-7 as a variant of 戸 *door*. 口 *opening* completes the image of a *door*. A place for |
|---|---|
| 人 9 | storing things safely under a *roof*(亼) and behind a *door*: a **STOREHOUSE**. |
| **1807** | |
| 常 10 | |

**CREATE**

ソウ
つく(る)

創作する そうさくする create, produce; write 0152
創世記 そうせいき Genesis .............0604, 0427
独創的 どくそうてき original, creative .0346, 0169
○創立する そうりつする establish, organize, start
................................................................0067
創設 そうせつ establishment, founding.....0520

| 0697 | To remember that this character means **CREATE**, picture **CREATING** a *storehouse* (倉) by carving it with one's *sword* ( 刂 ) out of a giant block of wood. Be sure to paint a vivid picture in your mind's eye, remembering that 刂 is not used destructively here, but **CREAT**ively. |
|---|---|
| 刀 18 | |
| 1610 | |
| 常 12 | |

**¹ NOTIFY**
**² ACCUSE**

コク
つ(げる)

¹ 申告 しんこく report, statement, notification
................................................................0315
¹ 戒告 かいこく caution, warning, reprimand 0469
①広告 こうこく public notice; advertisement 0238
①告げる つげる notify, tell
² 告発 こくはつ accusation, prosecution,
indictment................................................0148

| 0698 | First recall the image of a one-leaved plant from 先 0134. Now imagine what things people do when only plants are watching them, what things plants would **ACCUSE** them of if only they had *mouths* (口) to **ACCUSE** with. Of what unspeakable deeds would they **NOTIFY** us? |
|---|---|
| 口 30 | |
| 2134 | |
| 常 7 | |

**MAKE, build**

ゾウ
つく(る) つく(り) ・づくり

○創造 そうぞう creation .......................0697
造船 ぞうせん shipbuilding .................0669
木造の もくぞうの wooden..................0028
○造る つくる make, build
防火造り ぼうかづくり fireproof construction
................................................................0174, 0026

| 0699 | If plants did have mouths, one thing they would surely *accuse* (告) us of is removing them from their land whenever we decide to **build** something. See the *accusing* plant issuing its accusations toward us as we *cart* (辶_) it off to the compost factory so we can **MAKE** a **building** where it once stood. |
|---|---|
| 辵 162 | |
| 2679 | |
| 常 10 | |

**GARMENT, clothing**

イ エ*
ころも

○衣類 いるい clothes, garments ..............0310
衣食住 いしょくじゅう food, clothing, and shelter;
the necessities of life.................0288, 0366
外衣 がいい outer garment ..................0266
法衣 ほうい (=ほうえ) sacerdotal robe........0139
羽衣 はごろも robe of feathers..............0418

| 0700 | See 亠 as a person's head and shoulders, and the rest as the folds and pleats of his **GARMENTS**. 長 0091 and 旅 0569 show a couple of variations on the pleated **GARMENT** image. Soon we shall encounter still other variations, including 衤 (used at the left) and 衣 (used at top and bottom simultaneously). |
|---|---|
| 衣 145 | |
| 1736 | |
| 常 6 | |

| | **DEPEND ON** | ○依存する いぞんする (=いそんする) depend on, rely on .......................... 0407 |
| | | 依拠 いきょ basis, grounds; dependence ... 0554 |
| | イ　エ | 依願 いがん at one's own request .......... 0214 |

| **0701** | In the Japanese expression for "food, clothing, and shelter," clothing comes first (see V2 of the previous entry). Truly, a *man* (イ) **DEPENDS ON** his *clothing* (衣). See 帰 1018 for an *on-yomi* compound using the reading エ. |
| 人 9 | |
| 0065 | |
| 常 8 | |

| | **BAG** | 風袋 ふうたい packing, tare ................. 0425 |
| | | ○紙袋 かみぶくろ paper bag .................. 0478 |
| | | 手袋 てぶくろ gloves ........................ 0046 |
| | タイ | 浮き袋 うきぶくろ air bladder; life buoy, float ................................................. 0613 |
| | ふくろ | 足袋 たび Japanese (digitated) socks, *tabi* 0044 |

| **0702** | A **BAG** is a kind of clothing for the items we put inside it. This character puts *clothing* (衣) at the bottom, to represent a **BAG**, and *replace* (代) above it, to represent the things we place and replace into the **BAG**. Take a moment to visualize the *replace*able contents going into and out of their "*clothing*," that is, their **BAG**. ☞ 装 1591 |
| 衣 145 | |
| 2245 | |
| 常 11 | |

| | **COMMEND, praise** | 褒賞 ほうしょう prize, reward ................. 0322 |
| | | ○褒美 ほうび reward, prize .................... 0497 |
| | | 過褒 かほう excessive praise ................. 0464 |
| | ホウ | ○褒める ほめる praise, commend |
| | ほ(める) | 褒め言葉 ほめことば words of praise 0051, 0605 |

| **0703** | 衣 is a variant of 衣 *clothing*. 保 here falsely suggests the clothes are meant to *preserve*; in fact, they are meant as gifts conveying **praise** and **COMMENDATION** upon the young mother and baby (see 保 0646), like clothes presented with compliments at a baby shower. Note the long vowel in the *on-yomi*, contra 保. ☞ 裏 0704 |
| 衣 145 | |
| 褒 | |
| 1841 | |
| 常 15 | |

| | **REAR, reverse, inside** | ○裏面 りめん (=うらめん) back, reverse, other side, inside; background ......................... 0175 |
| | | 裏側 うらがわ back/reverse/other side, wrong side ........................................... 0626 |
| | リ　うら | ○裏切る うらぎる betray, double-cross ........ 0086 |
| | | 裏付け うらづけ endorsement; backing; proof ................................................. 0064 |
| | | 裏通り うらどおり back street ................. 0159 |

| **0704** | First imagine that to hide our *village* (里) from a marauding band of outlaws, we've covered it up with *clothing* (衣). Now see how the *village* lies hidden **inside**/at the **REAR** of the *clothing*. ☞ 褒 0703 |
| 衣 145 | |
| 裡 | |
| 1836 | |
| 常 13 | |

| | ¹ EXPRESS, manifest | ① 表示する　ひょうじする　indicate, show, express ................0311 |
| | ² SURFACE, outside, front | ① 表す　あらわす　express, manifest |
| | ³ TABLE, chart | ² 表裏　ひょうり (=おもてうら)　front and rear, |
| | | ヒョウ | both sides; duplicity ..................0704 |
| | おもて -おもて あらわ(す) あらわ(れる) | ② 表の戸　おもてのと　street/front door .......0248 |
| | | ³ 図表　ずひょう　chart, diagram ................0298 |

| 0705 |  Start by comparing this kanji with the previous one, its opposite. Here the cover of clothing |
| 衣 145 | has been lifted off the top, turning inside to **outside**. A *growing plant* (S1–4) rises out of the |
| | covering *clothing* to **EXPRESS** itself on the **SURFACE**. As for M3, **TABLE/chart** derives from the |
| | idea of **EXPRESSING** something so that it is easily visible. ☞ 麦 0131 |
| 2151 | |
| 常 8 | |

| | ¹ ACTUAL, present | ¹ 現状　げんじょう　present condition(s) .........0616 |
| | ² APPEAR | ① 現在　げんざい　present time, now; present tense |
| | | | ...........0406 |
| | | ¹ 現金　げんきん　cash ......................0029 |
| | ゲン | ② 表現する　ひょうげんする　express, represent...0705 |
| | あらわ(れる)　あらわ(す) | ② 現れる　あらわれる　appear, emerge |

| 0706 | Like the entries before and after, 現 is used for writing あらわ(れる)/あらわ(す) (as usual, |
| 玉 96 | each *kun-yomi* homophone has its own particular range of usage). 現's special sense is |
| | **APPEAR**: here a *gem* (王) **APPEARS** to our *sight* (見). Being right before our eyes, it also sug- |
| | gests M1 **ACTUAL**/present. Recall that the *hen* form 王 is shorthand for 玉 0073. |
| 0879 | |
| 常 11 | |

| | ¹ AUTHOR | ¹ 著作する　ちょさくする　write, author .........0152 |
| | ² CONSPICUOUS | ① 著者　ちょしゃ　author, writer ...............0107 |
| | | ① 著す　あらわす　author, write |
| | チョ | ² 著名　ちょめい　prominence, eminence, |
| | あらわ(す)　いちじる(しい) | distinction ....................0269 |
| | | ② 著しい　いちじるしい　remarkable, conspicuous |

| 0707 | Here we observe a *person* (者) using blades of *grass* (艹) to write: an **AUTHOR**. Her action |
| 艸 140 | of expressing things clearly and visibly in writing makes them **CONSPICUOUS**. ☞ 箸 1443, |
| 著 | 暑 1444, 署 1445 |
| 1993 | |
| 常 11 | |

| | ¹ SYSTEM | ① 制度　せいど　system, organization, institution |
| | ² CONTROL | | ...............0280 |
| | | ¹ 体制　たいせい　system, structure, organization |
| | | | ...............0062 |
| | セイ | ² 規制する　きせいする　regulate, control ......0624 |
| | | ² 制限　せいげん　restriction, limit ...........0282 |
| | | ² 産制　さんせい　birth control ...............0181 |

| 0708 | Taking your cue from 生 *growing plant,* see in 制 a leaf, branches, and roots (ignore the |
| 刀 18 | similarity with 市). Then see 刂 trimming away (i.e., **CONTROLLING** or regulating) any excess |
| | growth among these. Finally, learn M1 **SYSTEM** as something that **CONTROLS** the functioning |
| | of an institution or process. ☞ 刺 0935, 製 0709 |
| 1170 | |
| 常 8 | |

**MANUFACTURE**

セイ

製作 せいさく manufacture, production ....0152
製造業 せいぞうぎょう manufacturing industry
.................................................0699, 0498
○製品 せいひん manufactured goods, product
.................................................0301
製薬 せいやく drug manufacture .............0303
日本製の にほんせいの made in Japan 0001, 0031

---

**0709**

衣 145

2441

常 14

*Clothing* was among the first products made by systematic, industrial processes. It is no surprise, then, that *system* (制) and *clothes* (衣) in combination refer to the systematic making of things, or **MANUFACTURING**. Picture the *clothing* at the bottom of the character being *systematically* produced. ☞ 裂 0720, 制 0708

---

**FIRST**

ショ
はじ(め) はじ(めて) はつ はつ- うい-
-そ(める) -ぞ(め)

初期 しょき early stage, beginning; initial...0486
○最初 さいしょ first, outset, beginning........0196
初めての はじめての first, first-time
○初飛行 はつひこう maiden flight ......0475, 0055
○夜が明け初める よがあけそめる day begins to
dawn ..............................0467, 0024

---

**0710**

刀 18

1031

常 7

In ネ one can vaguely discern 衣 0700, of which it is a variant (do not confuse ネ with ネ). In the same way the Japanese expression 皮切り (かわきり, "cutting the leather") conveys the idea of "beginning," this image of taking a *sword* (刀) to *cloth* represents the **FIRST** step in making a garment. While no two kanji will differ by ネ and ネ alone, you should remember that ネ comes from 衣 while ネ comes from 示 0311.

---

**NAKED**

ラ
はだか

裸体 らたい nude body, nudity .............0062
○全裸 ぜんら stark naked, nude .............0078
○裸の はだかの naked, bare, undressed
裸馬 はだかうま barebacked horse.........0336
裸足 はだし barefoot, bare feet.............0044

---

**0711**

衣 145

1120

常 13

*Clothing* (ネ) hanging on *fruit* (果) tree: **NAKED**.

---

**¹ DIFFICULT**
**² DISASTER**
**³ FAULT, criticize**

ナン
かた(い) -がた(い) むずか(しい)

①難病 なんびょう incurable disease .............0617
①難しい むずかしい difficult
①解き難い ときがたい hard to solve............0345
² 難民 なんみん refugee, displaced person...0477
³ 難詰する なんきつする blame, censure ......0515

---

**0712**

隹 172

難

1632

常 18

Picture 莫 as a *Han-dynasty Chinese scholar-official*. His high status is marked by the laurel 艹 he wears on his head. S7–8 show his arms joined at his abdomen, one hand inserted into the open portion of the opposite sleeve in his gown. Notice his spread legs. The other kanji using 莫 (and a version with legs joined, 堇), appear at 1730–34; preview these now. The present entry depicts a *small bird* (隹) making life **DIFFICULT** for a poor *Han scholar-official*. See how the bird painfully torments him by pecking at his ears. This image also serves us well for the act of **FAULTING** or **criticizing**. Learn M2 **DISASTER** as an extension of M1 **DIFFICULTY**.

| 准 | **JUNIOR** | ○准教員 じゅんきょういん junior/assistant teacher .................................... 0632, 0317 |
|---|---|---|
| | ジュン | |

| 0713 | Our challenge here is to keep this kanji distinct from the next one, which has the same reading, similar writing, and one similar meaning. Focus on 冫 (the next entry has 氵), once more letting it suggest *second(ary)* (see 次 0278). You thus obtain a *second*-ranking (i.e., **JUNIOR**) *bird* (隹). The reading ジュン is easy to associate with *JUNIOR*. ☞ 準 0714 |
|---|---|
| 冫 15 | |
| 0108 | |
| 常 10 | |

| 準 | **¹ STANDARD, level** **² QUASI-** | ¹ 準則 じゅんそく regulations, standard ....... 0625 |
|---|---|---|
| | | ¹ 水準 すいじゅん level, standard; water level 0027 |
| | | ① 基準 きじゅん standard, criterion, basis ..... 0485 |
| | ジュン | ② 準決勝 じゅんけっしょう semifinal ....... 0330, 0460 |
| | | ² 準会員 じゅんかいいん associate member .................................... 0226, 0317 |

| 0714 | In Japanese the ideas **level** and **STANDARD** are expressed in the word "water level" (水準, すいじゅん). To perceive the above meanings in this kanji, see a *bird* (隹) sipping *water* (氵) from a river, whose **level** is marked by S12. S13 indicates the river's maximum range of fluctuation, revealing that it is almost at high water; this suggests M2 **QUASI-**. ☞ 准 0713 |
|---|---|
| 水 85 | |
| 準 | |
| 2486 | |
| 常 13 | |

| 備 | **PROVIDE (for), furnish** | 軍備 ぐんび military preparations, armaments .................................... 0583 |
|---|---|---|
| | | ○準備する じゅんびする provide for, prepare for .................................... 0714 |
| | ビ | 予備 よび reserve, spare; preparation, preliminaries .................................... 0163 |
| | そな(える) そな(わる) | 設備する せつびする equip/provide (with) ... 0520 |
| | | ○備える そなえる provide for, stock, furnish |

| 0715 | To perceive here the idea of **PROVIDING for** a rainy day, visualize this *man* (亻) gathering food provisions (from *plants* 艹) inside a *container* (用), and hanging it from the edge of a *cliff* (厂). This may seem like an odd place to store his provisions, but in fact he will only need them when he has been pushed to "the edge." |
|---|---|
| 人 9 | |
| 0126 | |
| 常 12 | |

| 死 | **DIE** | ○死亡 しぼう death .................................... 0233 |
|---|---|---|
| | | 死去 しきょ death, passing away ............. 0138 |
| | | 過労死 かろうし death from overwork 0464, 0542 |
| | シ | 死を覚悟する しをかくごする be prepared to die .................................... 0325, 0326 |
| | し(ぬ) し(に)- | ○死ぬ しぬ die, pass away |

| 0716 | 歹 means *bone* or *death*. Let the first stroke represent ground level, so that 夕 is buried underground. Here it takes 匕 *fallen person* underground with it, representing the act of **DYING**. ☞ 苑 0729 |
|---|---|
| 歹 78 | |
| 2952 | |
| 常 6 | |

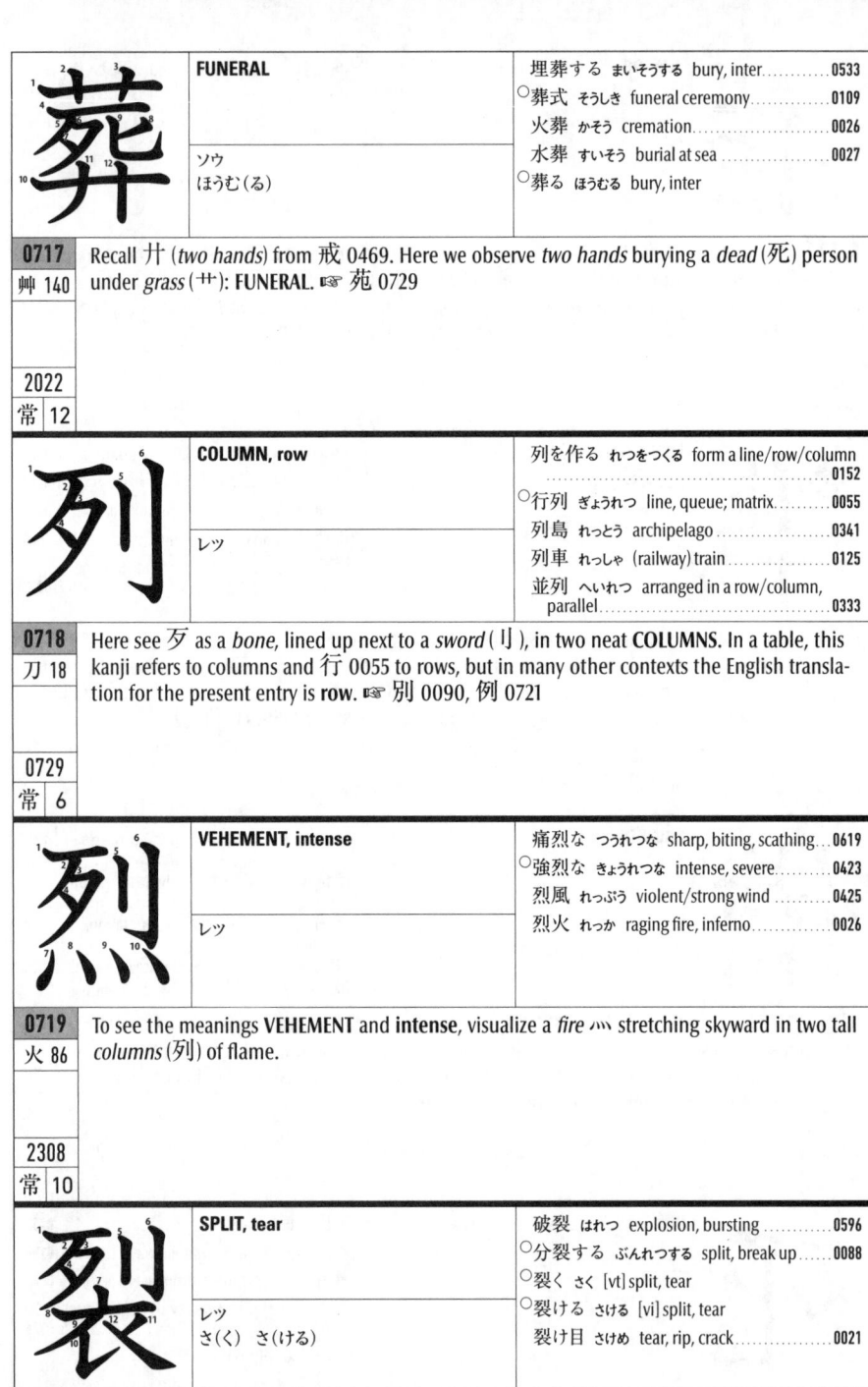

| | FUNERAL | 埋葬する まいそうする bury, inter............0533 |
|---|---|---|
| 葬 | | ○葬式 そうしき funeral ceremony............0109 |
| | | 火葬 かそう cremation....................0026 |
| | ソウ | 水葬 すいそう burial at sea.................0027 |
| | ほうむ（る） | ○葬る ほうむる bury, inter |

| 0717 | Recall 廾 (*two hands*) from 戒 0469. Here we observe *two hands* burying a *dead* (死) person under *grass* (艹): **FUNERAL**. ☞ 苑 0729 |
|---|---|
| 艸 140 | |
| 2022 | |
| 常 12 | |

| | COLUMN, row | 列を作る れつをつくる form a line/row/column ............0152 |
|---|---|---|
| 列 | | ○行列 ぎょうれつ line, queue; matrix.........0055 |
| | レツ | 列島 れっとう archipelago..................0341 |
| | | 列車 れっしゃ (railway) train.................0125 |
| | | 並列 へいれつ arranged in a row/column, parallel................0333 |

| 0718 | Here see 歹 as a *bone*, lined up next to a *sword* (刂), in two neat **COLUMNS**. In a table, this kanji refers to columns and 行 0055 to rows, but in many other contexts the English translation for the present entry is **row**. ☞ 別 0090, 例 0721 |
|---|---|
| 刀 18 | |
| 0729 | |
| 常 6 | |

| | VEHEMENT, intense | 痛烈な つうれつな sharp, biting, scathing...0619 |
|---|---|---|
| 烈 | | ○強烈な きょうれつな intense, severe.........0423 |
| | レツ | 烈風 れっぷう violent/strong wind .........0425 |
| | | 烈火 れっか raging fire, inferno............0026 |

| 0719 | To see the meanings **VEHEMENT** and **intense**, visualize a *fire* 灬 stretching skyward in two tall *columns* (列) of flame. |
|---|---|
| 火 86 | |
| 2308 | |
| 常 10 | |

| | SPLIT, tear | 破裂 はれつ explosion, bursting ...........0596 |
|---|---|---|
| 裂 | | ○分裂する ぶんれつする split, break up......0088 |
| | レツ | ○裂く さく [vt] split, tear |
| | さ（く） さ（ける） | ○裂ける さける [vi] split, tear |
| | | 裂け目 さけめ tear, rip, crack.................0021 |

| 0720 | When you see this character, imagine **SPLITTING** or **tearing** the *garment* (衣) into the two "*columns*" 列 (i.e., strips) above it. ☞ 製 0709 |
|---|---|
| 衣 145 | |
| 2347 | |
| 常 12 | |

| | EXAMPLE, precedent | ○前例 ぜんれい precedent; above example...0113 |
|---|---|---|
| | | 常例 じょうれい usual practice, established custom...................................................0321 |
| | | 例外 れいがい exception.............................0266 |
| | レイ | 例の れいの usual; that, (the one) in question |
| | たと(える) | ○例えば たとえば for example |

| 0721 | Following the **EXAMPLE/precedent** set by 歹 and 刂, 人 *person* becomes 亻 here and assumes an upright position in line with the others. Make an effort to remember that 例 (レイ) is the only character based on 列 that is not pronounced レツ. ☞ 列 0718, 倒 0941 |
|---|---|
| 人 9 | |
| 0071 | |
| 常 8 | |

| | PENALTY | ○刑務所 けいむしょ prison.............0687, 0249 |
|---|---|---|
| | | 刑期 けいき prison term.......................0486 |
| | | 死刑 しけい capital punishment, death penalty ...................................................0716 |
| | ケイ | 処刑 しょけい execution, punishment.......0553 |
| | | 刑事 けいじ (police) detective.............0080 |

| 0722 | Imagine that a traditional **PENALTY** in Japan was to be tied to a *torii* (开) and hacked with a *sword* (刂). ☞ 判 0744, 刊 0409, 研 0724 |
|---|---|
| 刀 18 | |
| 0734 | |
| 常 6 | |

| | TYPE, model | ○典型 てんけい type, pattern, model, exemplar ...................................................0504 |
|---|---|---|
| | | 典型的な てんけいてきな typical.......0504, 0169 |
| | | 体型 たいけい form, figure.....................0062 |
| | ケイ | 大型 おおがた large size; large model.......0033 |
| | かた -がた | 血液型 けつえきがた blood type.......0198, 0468 |

| 0723 | One way to associate this construction with the meanings **TYPE** and **model** is to let "*penalty* (刑) + *earth* (土)" suggest the idea of pounding or "punishing" a malleable material like clay to shape it into a predefined mold. |
|---|---|
| 土 32 | |
| 2292 | |
| 常 9 | |

| | [1] **GRIND** [2] **RESEARCH** | ①研ぐ とぐ grind, polish |
|---|---|---|
| | | [1] 研ぎ石 とぎいし whetstone, knife sharpener ...................................................0403 |
| | | [1] 研米機 けんまいき rice polisher.......0234, 0473 |
| | ケン | ②研学 けんがく study...........................0099 |
| | と(ぐ) | |

| 0724 | Picture using the *stone* (石) to **GRIND** the *torii* (开) to a smooth polish. To associate M1 **GRIND** with M2 **RESEARCH**, think of the latter as the polishing of one's understanding. A sample compound is provided here for M2, but more important ones appear at 修 1676 and 究 1710. ☞ 刑 0722 |
|---|---|
| 石 112 | |
| 研 | |
| 1046 | |
| 常 9 | |

**MISFORTUNE, trouble**

ヤク

| | |
|---|---|
| 厄日 やくび unlucky day, critical day | 0001 |
| 厄年 やくどし climacteric/critical year, unlucky year | 0117 |
| ○厄介 やっかい trouble, annoyance | 0611 |
| 大厄 たいやく great misfortune; grand climacteric | 0033 |

**0725**
厂 27

2550
常 4

This character shows us a *cliff* (厂) with a body lying below it, hunched over, its back and neck broken (巳). It signifies **MISFORTUNE**. Do not confuse 巳 *broken body* with 卩 *seal*, introduced back at 印 0231. ☞ 危 0726

---

**DANGEROUS**

キ
あぶ(ない) あや(うい) あや(ぶむ)

| | |
|---|---|
| ○危機 きき crisis, emergency | 0473 |
| 危害 きがい injury, harm; danger, risk | 0413 |
| ○危ない(=危うい) あぶない (=あやうい) dangerous, insecure | |
| 命が危ない いのちがあぶない (one's) life is in danger | 0232 |
| 危ぶむ あやぶむ fear, apprehend | |

**0726**
卩 26

2755
常 6

Picture S1–2 as a man who peers down over the edge of a *cliff* (厂). Realizing what happened to the poor man in the last entry, he suddenly senses **DANGER**. ☞ 厄 0725, 色 0528

---

**MODEL**

ハン

| | |
|---|---|
| ○規範 きはん standard, norm, criterion | 0624 |
| 範例 はんれい example | 0721 |
| 典範 てんぱん model, standard; law, code | 0504 |
| 範囲 はんい range, scope | 0435 |
| 広範囲 こうはんい wide range | 0238, 0435 |

**0727**
竹 118

2364
常 15

Recall that kanji with 𥫗 sometimes have to do with *keeping records*. Here a notorious case of a *chariot* (車) running over someone (leaving a *broken body* 巳) has been recorded on a *bamboo* scroll as an admonitory **MODEL** or example of what occurs when one ignores the rules of safe driving.

---

**HOLD A GRUDGE, resent**

エン オン
うら(む)• うら(み)• うら(めしい)•

| | |
|---|---|
| ○怨念 おんねん deeply held grudge | 0230 |
| ○怨む うらむ hold a grudge, resent [cf. 恨 1217] | |

**0728**
心 61

2227
常 9

夗 combines 夕 (which resembles 歹 *death/bone*) and 巳 *broken body*. We can treat 夗 as a variation on 死 *death*. It combines here with *heart/mind* (心) to represent the idea of wishing someone were *dead*: **HOLD A GRUDGE/resent**. A compound using the reading エン appears at 恨 1217. うらむ (V2 here) is usually written with the latter kanji.

**IMPERIAL GARDEN**

エン　オン
その

内苑　ないえん　inner garden (of the imperial palace) ......0215
外苑　がいえん　outer garden (of the imperial palace) ......0266

**0729**
艸 140

Here we find *grass* growing from the soil in which *dead bodies* (死) are buried. Imagine that they are the remains of deceased emperors, for this character refers to **IMPERIAL GARDENS**. ☞ 宛 0730, 死 0716, 葬 0717

1926
名 8

**ADDRESS**

あ(てる)　-あ(て)　-あて

○宛先　あてさき　address, addressee ......0134
宛名　あてな　addressee, address ......0269
外来語に字を宛てる　がいらいごにじをあてる　assign Chinese characters to a foreign word ......0266, 0274, 0222, 0098
宛て字　あてじ　phonetic substitute, false substitute character ......0098
オレンジを一人宛三個　オレンジをひとりあてさんこ　three oranges per person ......0002, 0015, 0004, 0262

**0730**
宀 40

Means **ADDRESS**, in the sense of directing to or assigning to. Here we can see the *dead bodies* (死) being assigned to a location under a certain *roof* (宀), that is, a specific numbered location (an **ADDRESS**) where they will be kept until identified. ☞ 苑 0729

1908
常 8

**BOWL, cup**

ワン

○茶碗　ちゃわん　teacup; rice bowl ......0603
お碗　おわん　bowl

**0731**
石 112

In a full dinner service, each dish is assigned to a specific course of a meal. Thus in this entry a *stone* 石 (standing for ceramics and glass) that is *addressed* (宛) to a part of a meal represents **BOWLS** or cups. ☞ 腕 0732

1110
名 13

**ARM**

¹ ARM
² ABILITY

ワン
うで

¹腕力　わんりょく　muscular strength ......0084
①上腕　じょうわん　upper arm ......0041
¹腕時計　うでどけい　wrist watch ......0383, 0555
②腕前　うでまえ　skill, ability, capacity ......0113
²腕利き　うできき　person of ability ......0412

**0732**
肉 130

By evolving to walk upright, humans freed up two limbs for *addressing* to other tasks. Here "*body part* (月) + *address* (宛)" suggests that *body part* which, not otherwise occupied, can be assigned to whatever task we may wish to carry out: the **ARM**. As for M2, just as 手 0046 HAND can signify "skill," so too 腕 ARM can signify **ABILITY**. ☞ 碗 0731

0919
常 12

| | ELIMINATE, reject | 売却する ばいきゃくする sell off, dispose of by sale...........................0353 |
| --- | --- | --- |
| | | 却下する きゃっかする reject, dismiss, turn down ...........................0040 |
| | キャク | 棄却する ききゃくする reject, renounce .....0606 |
| | | ○返却する へんきゃくする return .............0378 |

| 0733 | For this and the next entry, we go from 巳 *broken body* back to 卩 *seal*. Here let *seal* and *go away* (去 0138) suggest an expulsion or deportation order stamped by a high authority; that is, an order to **ELIMINATE** or **reject**. ☞ 脚 0734, 即 0390 |
| --- | --- |
| 卩 26 | |
| 卻 | |
| 1034 | |
| 常 7 | |

| | LEG | 脚部 きゃくぶ leg(s) [as of a table]............0068 |
| --- | --- | --- |
| | | ○三脚 さんきゃく tripod...........................0004 |
| | | 脚注 きゃくちゅう footnote.......................0368 |
| | キャク キャ | 脚本 きゃくほん script, playbook, scenario...0031 |
| | あし | 三本脚の犬 さんぼんあしのいぬ three-legged dog...........................0004, 0031, 0293 |

| 0734 | Think of the **LEG** as the *body part* (月) for *eliminating* (却) things, as in "kicking them out" or "punting them away." ☞ 却 0733 |
| --- | --- |
| 肉 130 | |
| 0887 | |
| 常 11 | |

| | OFFENSE, violation | 犯行 はんこう criminal act, crime, offense...0055 |
| --- | --- | --- |
| | | ○犯人 はんにん criminal, offender............0015 |
| | | 防犯 ぼうはん crime prevention ..............0174 |
| | ハン | ○法を犯す ほうをおかす violate the law .......0139 |
| | おか(す) | 女を犯す おんなをおかす rape a woman....0093 |

| 0735 | This character shows the scene of a criminal **OFFENSE**: a *dog* (犭) has just killed a man, leaving only his *broken body* (巳). |
| --- | --- |
| 犬 94 | |
| 0175 | |
| 常 5 | |

| | CRAZY, mad (about) | 狂気の きょうきの insane, mad, crazy........0126 |
| --- | --- | --- |
| | | ○狂犬病 きょうけんびょう rabies............0293, 0617 |
| | | 殺人狂 さつじんきょう homicidal maniac ...........................0522, 0015 |
| | キョウ | 女に狂う おんなにくるう run mad after a girl 0093 |
| | くる(う) くる(おしい) くる(わす) くる(わせる) | 狂おしい思い くるおしいおもい maddening thought...........................0142 |

| 0736 | To remember that this character means **CRAZY**, let *"dog king"* suggest a crowned werewolf. Take a few moments to picture 王 at the right going **mad** and turning into 犭 at the left. |
| --- | --- |
| 犬 94 | |
| 0241 | |
| 常 7 | |

**PRISON**

ゴク

| | |
|---|---|
| 獄衣 ごくい prison uniform | 0700 |
| 獄死 ごくし death in prison | 0716 |
| 出獄 しゅつごく release from prison | 0038 |
| 獄中記 ごくちゅうき diary written in prison | 0035, 0427 |
| ○地獄 じごく hell; inferno | 0187 |

| 0737 |
|---|
| 犬 94 |
| 0644 |
| 常 14 |

犭 *dog* and 犬 *dog* are used here as a disdainful way to represent two locked-up convicts. Imagine the *words* (言) they speak to each other, inside the **PRISON**. Might they be trash-talking one another, or rather collaborating on a plan for escaping their impoundment?

**IS NOT, non-, un-, wrong**

ヒ

| | |
|---|---|
| ○非常 ひじょう emergency, calamity | 0321 |
| 非常口 ひじょうぐち emergency exit | 0321, 0019 |
| 非礼 ひれい impoliteness | 0313 |
| 非難 ひなん criticism, blame | 0712 |
| 非とする ひとする condemn, denounce | |

| 0738 |
|---|
| 非 175 |
| 0790 |
| 常 8 |

This image of two virtually identical objects facing opposite directions intuitively represents the ideas **NOT**, **non-**, **un-**, and **wrong**.

¹**EXCLUDE, reject**
²**DISCHARGE, excrete**

ハイ

| | |
|---|---|
| ①排他的な はいたてきな exclusive, cliquish, clannish | 0189, 0169 |
| ¹排日 はいにち anti-Japanese | 0001 |
| ²排出 はいしゅつ discharge, exhaust, evacuation | 0038 |
| ²排水 はいすい drainage; displacement (of ships) | 0027 |
| ②排気ガス はいきガス exhaust gas | 0126 |

| 0739 |
|---|
| 手 64 |
| 0446 |
| 常 11 |

See a *hand* (扌) **EXCLUDING** or **rejecting** something by making the *"not"* signal (非). Learn M2 **DISCHARGE** as an extension of M1. ☞ 批 0746, 俳 0740

**HAIKU, actor**

ハイ

| | |
|---|---|
| ○俳句 はいく haiku (seventeen-syllable poem) | 0166 |
| 俳人 はいじん haiku poet | 0015 |

| 0740 |
|---|
| 人 9 |
| 0094 |
| 常 10 |

Here we see a *man* (亻) composing or acting out fiction (i.e., that which *"is not"* 非): he is an **actor** or **HAIKU** poet. A sample compound for the **actor** sense appears at 優 0780. ☞ 排 0739

| | CRIME, sin | 犯罪 はんざい offense, crime ............... 0735 |
|---|---|---|
| | | ○無罪の むざいの not guilty, innocent ....... 0048 |
| | | ○有罪の ゆうざいの guilty ..................... 0400 |
| | ザイ | 罪業 ざいごう sin, iniquity .................. 0498 |
| | つみ | 罪人 つみびと sinner ........................ 0015 |
| | | ざいにん criminal, offender |

| 0741 | To remember that this kanji means **CRIME**, visualize 罒 as the tiny, barred window of a prison cell and 非 as the bars of the sliding cell door, just now about to slam shut. To remember this kanji's reading, I suggest you memorize the antonym pair V2 and V3, though V1 is more common than these. |
|---|---|
| 网 122 | |
| 2264 | |
| 常 13 | |

| | PUNISHMENT, heaven's vengeance | ○罰金 ばっきん fine ........................ 0029 |
|---|---|---|
| | | 刑罰 けいばつ penalty, punishment ........ 0722 |
| | | 処罰 しょばつ punishment, penalty ........ 0553 |
| | バツ バチ | 罰する ばっする punish |
| | | 罰当たりな ばちあたりな sacrilegious ....... 0141 |

| 0742 | Again we have the barred prison cell window (罒), now shown with *words* of sentencing (言), and the *sword* of the executioner (刂), symbolizing **PUNISHMENT**. |
|---|---|
| 网 122 | |
| 2266 | |
| 常 14 | |

| | ACCOMPANY | ○同伴する どうはんする accompany, go with |
|---|---|---|
| | | ........................ 0182 |
| | | ○伴う ともなう accompany, go with, attend |
| | ハン バン | 友人を伴って ゆうじんをともなって accompanied |
| | ともな(う) | by a friend ............................ 0399 |

| 0743 | See a *man* (亻) **ACCOMPANIED** by his "better *half*" (半). Note that all kanji in this course containing 半 have the *on* reading ハン, though a few of these may also be read バン. ☞ 件 0118 |
|---|---|
| 人 9 | |
| 0044 | |
| 常 7 | |

| | ¹JUDGE, decide | ①判決 はんけつ judicial decision, judgment, |
|---|---|---|
| | ²PERSONAL SEAL | sentence .............................. 0330 |
| | | ¹判事 はんじ judge ......................... 0080 |
| | | ¹判定する はんていする judge, decide ....... 0045 |
| | ハン バン | ¹判じる はんじる judge, decide, interpret |
| | | ②判子 はんこ personal seal; seal impression 0094 |

| 0744 | The English word **decide** derives from the Latin *caedere* or "cut," for when people **decide**, they "cut off" one option in favor of another. Similarly, the kanji for **JUDGE/decide** suggests "*cut* (刂) in *half* (半)." To remember M2, associate the act of affixing one's **PERSONAL SEAL** with the idea of **deciding** in favor of something. ☞ 刑 0722, 刊 0409 |
|---|---|
| 刀 18 | |
| 1038 | |
| 常 7 | |

| 評 | COMMENT, evaluate | 評判 ひょうばん fame, reputation............0744 |
|---|---|---|
| | | 好評 こうひょう favorable criticism, public favor ....................0095 |
| | ヒョウ | 映画評 えいがひょう film review .......0329, 0176 |
| | | ○評価 ひょうか evaluation, appraisal .........0548 |
| | | 大方の評では おおかたのひょうでは according to public opinion ........0033, 0173 |

**0745**
言 149
Recall that 平 0334 resembles "the scales of Justice." Here, we observe *words* (言) that weigh or assess something on a *scale* of value, that is, words of **evaluation** or **COMMENTARY**.

1361
常 12

| 批 | CRITICIZE, comment | ○批評 ひひょう criticism, comment............0745 |
|---|---|---|
| | | 批評家 ひひょうか critic, reviewer.....0745, 0219 |
| | ヒ | 批難 ひなん criticism, blame.................0712 |
| | | 批判 ひはん criticism, comment ............0744 |
| | | 批准する ひじゅんする ratify .................0713 |

**0746**
手 64
Imagine using the fingers of your *hand* (扌) to point out the relative merits and faults of two things you are *comparing* (比): **CRITICIZE/comment.** ☞ 排 0739

0223
常 7

| 帥 | COMMANDER IN CHIEF | ○元帥 げんすい marshal, general ............0136 |
|---|---|---|
| | | 総帥 そうすい commander in chief..........0557 |
| | スイ | |

**0747**
巾 50
Review 官 0290 GOVERNMENT OFFICIAL. We'll treat 𠂤 as a variation on *official* (officials), one not working in an office (no 宀), but sporting a feather in his cap (S1) to indicate high status. *Cloth* (巾) can in this instance represent an army's flag, marking 𠂤 as the army's *"flag officer"* or highest authority, its **COMMANDER IN CHIEF**. ☞ 師 0748

1185
常 9

| 師 | MASTER, teacher | ○教師 きょうし teacher, instructor .............0632 |
|---|---|---|
| | | 師範 しはん teacher, master, coach..........0727 |
| | シ | 医師 いし doctor, physician, surgeon.....0561 |
| | | 牧師 ぼくし pastor, minister, priest..........0576 |
| | | 絵師 えし painter, artist......................0525 |

**0748**
巾 50
Of still higher status than the COMMANDER IN CHIEF (帥) is his **MASTER** or **teacher** (師), who gets to carry not only a flag but also a teacher's pointer (S7), for pointing to the blackboard during strategy lessons. Practice writing the two kanji in alternation, learning to identify their meanings by the presence or absence of the teacher's pointer. ☞ 帥 0747

1211
常 10

| | ¹ SEAT<br>² SIT | ① 座席 ざせき seat..............................0279<br>¹ 座布団 ざぶとん (floor) cushion........0204, 0649<br>² 正座する せいざする sit upright/straight...0043<br>② 座る すわる sit down<br>口座 こうざ (bank) account..................0019 |
| ザ<br>すわ(る) | |

| **0749**<br>广 53 | See two people (人人) occupying **SEATS** on either side of a bench under a shelter (广). |
| 2686<br>常 10 | |

| | SIT | 対坐する たいざする sit face to face..........0650<br>独坐 どくざ sitting alone ....................0346 |
| ザ<br>すわ(る) | |

| **0750**<br>土 32 | In Chinese, 坐 means "sit" while 座 means "seat," but in Japanese the latter has come to fulfill both functions. The former still persists in a few kanji compounds in which it refers to the action, **SIT**. ☞ 卒 0751 |
| 2970<br>名 7 | |

| | ¹ GRADUATE, come to an end<br>² PRIVATE, soldier | ① 卒業 そつぎょう graduation..................0498<br>¹ 東大卒 とうだいそつ graduate from the<br>　University of Tokyo....................0032, 0033<br>¹ 高卒 こうそつ high school graduate.........0185<br>¹ 卒する そっする die, pass on<br>② 一等卒 いっとうそつ private first class 0002, 0393 |
| ソツ | |

| **0751**<br>十 24<br>卆 | Informed by 座 0749, try to visualize two **PRIVATES** wearing flat-topped service caps, sitting on a bench and listening to a **GRADUATION** speech. Their **soldier**'s training has **come to an end**. ☞ 坐 0750, 率 0752 |
| 1769<br>常 8 | |

| | ¹ RATE, proportion<br>² LEAD, command | ① 比率 ひりつ ratio, percentage ..............0123<br>¹ 利率 りりつ interest (rate) ...................0412<br>¹ 率を定める りつをさだめる fix the rate.......0045<br>² 引率する いんそつする lead, command ....0422<br>② 率いる ひきいる lead, command |
| ソツ リツ<br>ひき(いる) | |

| **0752**<br>玄 95 | 亠 is a *lid*, S6–9 are sound waves (see 楽 0302), 幺 is a *child*, and 十 is *ten*. Together they mean **LEAD/command**, from the idea of keeping a *lid* on *ten noisy children*. For M1, think of how a numerator determines (i.e., "**commands**") a proportion/**RATE**. ☞ 卒 0751, 牽 1736 |
| 1820<br>常 11 | |

**UMBRELLA**

サン
かさ

○傘下 さんか under the umbrella (of), affiliated, subsidiary............0040
鉄傘 てっさん iron dome...........0564
雨傘 あまがさ umbrella............0154
日傘 ひがさ parasol............0001

| 0753 | Behold an **UMBRELLA**. |
| 人 9 | |
| 1829 | |
| 常 12 | |

**BAMBOO HAT**

リュウ
かさ

雨笠 あまがさ rain hat.............0154
○竹笠 たけがさ bamboo hat.............0243
笠原 かさはら Kasahara [surname].............0208
小笠原 おがさわら Ogasawara [surname]
.............0034, 0208
笠森 かさもり Kasamori [surname].............0241

| 0754 | Here we see 竹 *bamboo* used as an old-fashioned conical **BAMBOO HAT** by a *standing person* (立). Because a **BAMBOO HAT** serves to shield its wearer from rain or the sun's rays, 笠 was given the same Japanese reading as the kanji for UMBRELLA, shown in the previous entry. ☞ 翌 0419 |
| 竹 118 | |
| 2320 | |
| 名 11 | |

**STAR, celestial body**

セイ ショウ
ほし -ぼし

星座 せいざ constellation.............0749
星条旗 せいじょうき the Stars and Stripes
.............0119, 0573
火星 かせい Mars.............0026
○衛星 えいせい satellite, moon.............0661
○星占い ほしうらない astrology.............0348

| 0755 | **STARS** are the source of life. Visualize a **STAR**'s life-giving energy here in the way the *sun* (日) shines down on a *growing plant* (生). ☞ 皇 0077 |
| 日 72 | |
| 2156 | |
| 常 9 | |

¹ **JUICE**
² **SOUP**

ジュウ
しる -しる

①果汁 かじゅう fruit juice.............0599
①レモンの汁 レモンのしる lemon juice
²出し汁 だしじる broth, stock.............0038
肉汁 にくじゅう meat juice, gravy.............0216

| 0756 | *Ten* (十) cups of *water* (氵) to make **JUICE** or **SOUP**. ☞ 斗 0757, 汗 0410 |
| 水 85 | |
| 0173 | |
| 常 5 | |

| 斗 | <sup>1</sup> DIPPER <br> <sup>2</sup> TO (18 liters) <br><br> ト | <sup>1</sup> 北斗七星 ほくとしちせい the Big Dipper ..............................0122, 0009, 0755 <br> <sup>2</sup> 二斗 にと 2 *to* ..............................0003 |
|---|---|---|

| **0757** <br> 斗 68 <br><br> 2554 <br> 常 4 | Depicts a **DIPPER**, with two drops of water (S1–2) to represent its contents. We might think of it as containing the volume of one **TO** (**18 liters**, equivalent to 10 升 *SHO* 1051). As a component grapheme in other kanji, 斗 may also mean *measure*. ☞ 汁 0756 |
|---|---|

| 料 | <sup>1</sup> FEE <br> <sup>2</sup> MATERIALS <br><br> リョウ | ① 料金 りょうきん charge, rate, fee, fare ........0029 <br> <sup>1</sup> 有料／無料 ゆうりょう／むりょう for a fee/for free ..............................0400, 0048 <br> <sup>2</sup> 原料 げんりょう raw material ..............0208 <br> <sup>2</sup> 食料 しょくりょう food, foodstuffs ............0288 <br> ② 料理 りょうり cooking, cuisine; handling....0532 |
|---|---|---|

| **0758** <br> 斗 68 <br><br> 1187 <br> 常 10 | Depicts the act of scooping up a measure of *rice* (米) with a *dipper* (斗). Think of it as a vendor collecting a **FEE** by scooping up a measure of his client's rice (as in V1), or a cook scooping up **MATERIALS** for a meal (as in V5). ☞ 科 0759 |
|---|---|

| 科 | **SUBJECT OF STUDY** <br><br> カ | ○ 科学 かがく science..............................0099 <br> 歯科 しか dentistry ..............................0674 <br> 理科 りか science; science department.....0532 <br> 教科 きょうか school subject; course of study, curriculum..............................0632 <br> 科する かする inflict, levy (a fine, etc.) |
|---|---|---|

| **0759** <br> 禾 115 <br><br> 1053 <br> 常 9 | Learn to recognize the meaning of this kanji just by the way it differs from the last one. In 料 we collected <u>roughly bundled</u> *rice* (米), which suggests raw MATERIALS. Here, we collect <u>neatly bundled</u> *rice* (禾, see 和 0236), which suggests a more technologically advanced stage, one requiring the disciplined training of a **SUBJECT OF STUDY**. ☞ 料 0758 |
|---|---|

| 然 | <sup>1</sup> "-LIKE," "-ly" (modifier-forming suffix) <br> <sup>2</sup> SO, in that way <br><br> ゼン ネン | ① 平然と へいぜんと calmly, quietly...........0334 <br> <sup>1</sup> 全然 ぜんぜん wholly, totally, completely; (not) at all ..............................0078 <br> <sup>2</sup> 天然の てんねんの natural..................0270 <br> ② 自然 しぜん nature..............................0081 <br> <sup>2</sup> 当然 とうぜん naturally, as a matter of course ..............................0141 |
|---|---|---|

| **0760** <br> 火 86 <br><br> 2423 <br> 常 12 | It is probably easiest for English speakers to learn the meaning of 然 by thinking of it as adding the sense of **-LIKE** or **-ly** to the character preceding it. Now we normally don't think of *dogs* (犬) as *meat* (月, written here as in 祭 0637), but if one were cooked up and served to us, our outlook might change. Here, picture a *fire* (灬) making a *dog* "*meat*-**LIKE**." ☞ 黙 0762 |
|---|---|

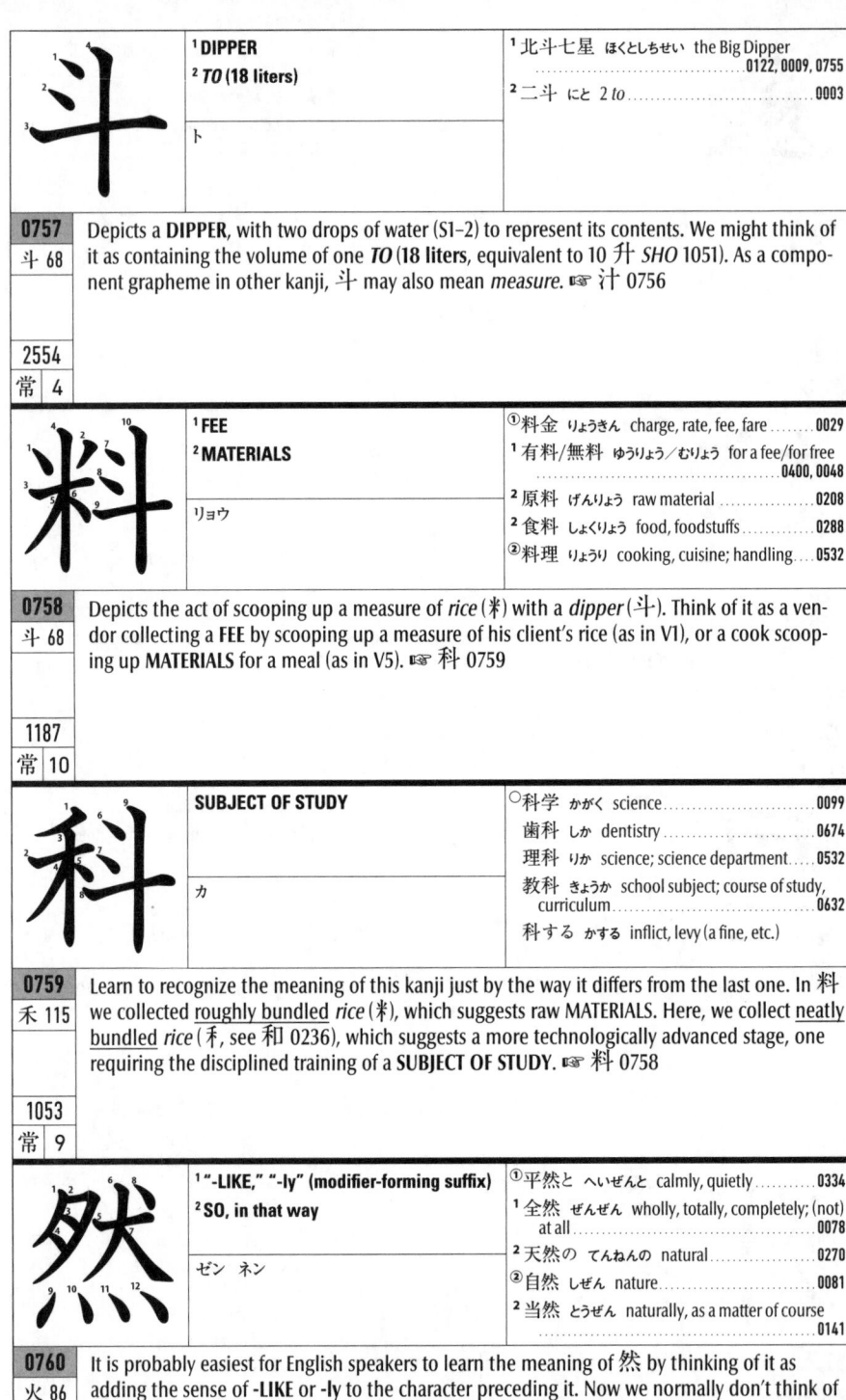

**BURN**

ネン
も(える) も(やす) も(す)

○燃料 ねんりょう fuel ............................ 0758
内燃機関 ないねんきかん internal combustion engine ..................... 0215, 0473, 0451
○燃える もえる [vi] burn
燃え尽きる もえつきる [vi] burn out, be burned up ........................ 0338
燃やす もやす [vt] burn

| 0761 | A little etymology is in order here. Since the previous entry pictured a *fire* (灬) but then came also to mean something unrelated to *fire*, 火 was added here to make a kanji that would unambiguously refer to **BURNING**. Practice writing the two kanji in turn, learning to identify their meanings by the presence or absence of 火. |
|---|---|
| 火 86 | |
| 0995 | |
| 常 16 | |

**SILENT, tacit**

モク
だま(る)

○沈黙 ちんもく silence, reticence ............. 0655
黙読する もくどくする read silently .......... 0355
黙とう (黙禱ˣ) もくとう silent prayer
○黙る だまる become silent, shut one's mouth

| 0762 | At 0535 we learned that *fire* (灬) turned a *village* (里) BLACK (黒). Here it turns the village's dogs (犬) **SILENT**. ☞ 獣 0763, 然 0760 |
|---|---|
| 黒 203 | |
| 黙 | |
| 2494 | |
| 常 15 | |

**BEAST**

ジュウ
けもの

○獣医 じゅうい veterinarian ....................... 0561
野獣 やじゅう wild animal, wild game ........ 0534
獣道 けものみち animal trail ................... 0158

| 0763 | Picture 𤢈 as a wild, hairy **BEAST**, standing his ground muzzle-to-muzzle with a *dog* (犬). Be sure to visualize 𤢈 as a large and dangerous creature, lest you confuse this kanji with the next one. ☞ 黙 0762 |
|---|---|
| 犬 94 | |
| 獸 | |
| 1673 | |
| 常 16 | |

**HUNTING**

リョウ

○猟師 りょうし hunter ............................. 0748
猟季 りょうき hunting season ................ 0395
猟犬 りょうけん hound, hunting dog ........ 0293
禁猟 きんりょう hunting/shooting ban ...... 0312
猟をする りょうをする hunt, shoot

| 0764 | 巤 is a simplified variant of 鼠 2263 RAT, here being **HUNTED** by a *dog*-like creature (犭). ☞ 狩 0766 |
|---|---|
| 犬 94 | |
| 獵 | |
| 0491 | |
| 常 11 | |

漁

**FISHING**

ギョ リョウ

○漁師 りょうし fisherman ........ 0748
○漁業 ぎょぎょう fishing industry ........ 0498
漁船 ぎょせん fishing boat ........ 0669
漁場 ぎょじょう fishing ground, fishery ........ 0445

**0765**
水 85

0631
常 14

Visualize here the act of hauling a *fish* (魚) out of *water* (氵), that is, **FISHING.**

---

狩

**HUNT**

シュ
か(る) か(り) -が(り)

○狩猟 しゅりょう hunting, hunt ........ 0764
狩猟期 しゅりょうき hunting season ........ 0764, 0486
狩人 かりゅうど (=かりうど) hunter ........ 0015
○狩りに行く かりにいく go hunting ........ 0055
潮干狩り しおひがり shell gathering (at low tide) ........ 0146, 0408

**0766**
犬 94

0356
常 9

A **HUNTING** *dog* (犭) *watches over* (守) his master's quarry until the hunter arrives to claim it.
☞ 猟 0764

---

猛

**FEROCIOUS, intensive**

モウ

猛犬 もうけん ferocious dog ........ 0293
猛獣 もうじゅう savage beast ........ 0763
○猛烈な もうれつな violent, vehement, fierce ........ 0719
猛然と もうぜんと fiercely ........ 0760
猛毒 もうどく deadly poison ........ 0133

**0767**
犬 94

0490
常 11

I suggest that visualizing 皿 as the *dog* (犭)'s lower teeth sinking into a *child* (子) may better evoke the idea **FEROCIOUS** than picturing the dog serving himself a child on a *plate*.

---

煙

**SMOKE**

エン
けむ(る) けむり けむ(い)

○禁煙 きんえん No Smoking [sign]; giving up smoking ........ 0312
節煙 せつえん moderation in smoking ........ 0391
煙になる けむりになる vanish in thin air
○煙い けむい smoky
煙草 たばこ tobacco; cigarette ........ 0144

**0768**
火 86
烟
0936
常 13

We've learned to see 覀 as a box (see 要 0547), but here we're better off seeing it as a cloud of **SMOKE**, billowing up over the *earth* (土) where a *fire* (火) burns.

|  | **BURN, roast**<br><br>ショウ<br>や(く) や(き) や(き)- -や(き) や(ける) | 燃焼 ねんしょう combustion, burning ....... 0761<br>○全焼する ぜんしょうする be burnt down..... 0078<br>焼身自殺 しょうしんじさつ burning oneself to<br>　　death .......................... 0060, 0081, 0522<br>○焼き鳥 やきとり grilled chicken ............ 0340<br>夕焼け ゆうやけ sunset glow................. 0265 |

| **0769**<br>火 86<br>焼<br>0909<br>常 12 | Visualize 堯 as a fire with three leaping flames. S10–12, representing the base of the fire, resembles 元 0136 (ORIGIN or base). Together with 火, this easily suggests **BURN** or **roast**.　☞ 暁 0770 |

| 暁 | **DAWN**<br><br>ギョウ<br>あかつき | 暁天 ぎょうてん dawn, sky at dawn........... 0270<br>暁星 ぎょうせい morning star, Venus......... 0755<br>今暁 こんぎょう at daybreak today .......... 0228<br>○暁の空 あかつきのそら dawning sky.......... 0398 |

| **0770**<br>日 72<br>暁<br>0892<br>常 12 | Three "flames" (i.e., rays) of *sun*shine (日) rising up over the horizon at **DAWN**. ☞ 焼 0769 |

| 旧 | **FORMER, old**<br><br>キュウ | 旧制 きゅうせい old system, old style ........ 0708<br>旧姓 きゅうせい one's former name, née .... 0431<br>○旧式 きゅうしき old style, old type ........... 0109<br>新旧の しんきゅうの old and new............. 0275<br>旧ソ連 きゅうソれん former Soviet Union ....0582 |

| **0771**<br>日 72*<br>舊<br>0005<br>常 5 | 日 marks the present *day*. S1 marks a time before that (i.e., to the left on the calendar): **FORMER** times. When 旧 appears as a grapheme inside other characters, we'll generally refer to it by the term *old*. |

|  | **CHILD**<br><br>ジ ニ | ○児童 じどう child, juvenile.................. 0537<br>二才児 にさいじ two-year-old child ...0003, 0652<br>○小児科 しょうにか (department of) pediatrics<br>　　.......................................0034, 0759<br>乳児 にゅうじ infant, baby, suckling ......... 0160<br>育児 いくじ infant rearing, nursing of children<br>　　.................................................. 0489 |

| **0772**<br>儿 10<br>兒<br>2203<br>常 7 | Once a generation comes of age, it sets about reproducing itself. This character depicts a new generation arising to take the place of an *old* (旧) one. See a newborn **CHILD** trying to balance himself on two little *legs* (儿). At the top is his head, looking just like his *old* man. |

**ALSO**

エキ
また

彼も亦良い人だ かれもまたいいひとだ He is a nice man, too.....................0597, 0285, 0015

私も亦 わたしもまた I also, me too ...........0237

**0773**
亠 8

1734
名 6

Used infrequently as an independent kanji meaning **ALSO**, an idea that we may associate with the "repetition" of the base strokes: first two on the inside (S3–4), then **ALSO** two on the outside (S5–6). More important to us is its use as a grapheme, for which we shall visualize it as *flames* (S3–6, resembling 灬) *heating a griddle* (S2). ☞ 赤 0774, 又 0058

---

**RED**

セキ シャク
あか あか- あか(い) あか(らむ)
あか(らめる)

○赤十字 せきじゅうじ Red Cross...........0005, 0098
赤軍 せきぐん Red Army......................0583
赤外線 せきがいせん infrared rays.....0266, 0210
○赤らむ あからむ become red
赤字 あかじ deficit, red figures...............0098

**0774**
赤 155

1876
常 7

Associate this character with the color **RED** by letting the cross (十) at the top suggest a **RED** cross (the medical relief symbol), kept **RED** hot on a *flame-heated griddle* (亦). ☞ 亦 0773

---

変

¹ **CHANGE, variation**
² **ABNORMAL**

ヘン
か(わる) か(わり) か(える)

①変化 へんか change, variety; declension ...0120
¹ 変動 へんどう change, fluctuation...........0540
①変わる かわる change, be different
¹ 変える かえる change, revise
² 変人 へんじん eccentric person, crank ......0015

**0775**
夂 34*

變

1782
常 9

Here let 夂 *crossed legs* suggest passiveness or stasis. Then imagine applying a *hot griddle* (亦) to a changeless *cross-legged* person to force them into **CHANGE**. M2 **ABNORMAL** can be thought of as "**CHANGED** from the normal." Note in the old forms for this and the next two entries how 亦 simplifies the 糸-言-糸 construction.

---

**BARBARIAN**

バン

蛮人 ばんじん savage, barbarian; aboriginal
....................................................0015
蛮族 ばんぞく savage tribe .................0568
○野蛮な やばんな savage, barbarous.........0534

**0776**
虫 142

蠻

1827
常 12

Think of cooking a meal of *insects* (虫) on a *hot griddle* (亦) as a most **BARBARIAN** act.

| | (romantic) LOVE | 失恋 しつれん unrequited love .............. 0563 |
|---|---|---|
| | | 恋う こう love |
| | | 恋する こいする love, fall in love with |
| | レン | ○恋人 こいびと lover, sweetheart ............ 0015 |
| | こ(う) こい こい(しい) | 初恋 はつこい first love ................. 0710 |

| **0777** | A *heart* (心) burning like the fire under a *hot griddle* (亦): **(romantic) LOVE**. The *on-yomi* |
|---|---|
| 心 61 | compound to memorize appears in the next entry. ☞ 愛 0778 |
| 戀 | |
| 1804 | |
| 常 10 | |

| | LOVE | ○恋愛 れんあい romantic love ................ 0777 |
|---|---|---|
| | | 愛称 あいしょう nickname, pet name ....... 0684 |
| | | 愛国心 あいこくしん patriotism, nationalism |
| | | ...................................... 0075, 0056 |
| | アイ | 愛する あいする love, be fond of |
| | いと(しい)* | ○愛しい いとしい darling, beloved |

| **0778** | Review 受 0065. Here what is handed over is one's *heart* (心)—even if the *cross-legged* (夂) |
|---|---|
| 心 61 | recipient appears unmoved—for this is true **LOVE**. ☞ 受 0065, 恋 0777 |
| 2191 | |
| 常 13 | |

| | ¹ **BE ANXIOUS, worry** | ①憂国 ゆうこく patriotism, concern for one's |
|---|---|---|
| | ² **GRIEF** | country.............................. 0075 |
| | | ①将来を憂える しょうらいをうれえる worry about |
| | | the future...................... 0614, 0274 |
| | ユウ | ¹ 憂い うれい anxiety, trouble, worry |
| | うれ(える) うれ(い) う(い) う(き) | ² うい melancholy, sad |
| | | ² 物憂い ものうい languid, melancholy ...... 0172 |

| **0779** | Here we observe a *heart* **AGGRIEVED**, caught between the burden of a thousand-pound weight |
|---|---|
| 心 61 | (S1-6, resembling 百 0016 HUNDRED, but with an extra zero) and the passive emotionless- |
| | ness of its *cross-legged* beloved (夂). Observing its predicament, we can easily perceive its |
| | **ANXIETY** and **GRIEF**. ☞ 夏 0363 |
| 1842 | |
| 常 15 | |

| | ¹ **SUPERIOR** | ①優先 ゆうせん preference, priority .......... 0134 |
|---|---|---|
| | ² **ACTOR** | ¹ 優勝する ゆうしょうする win, be victorious.... 0460 |
| | ³ **KIND** | ①優れた学者 すぐれたがくしゃ eminent scholar |
| | | ..................................... 0099, 0107 |
| | ユウ | ² 俳優 はいゆう actor, actress ................ 0740 |
| | やさ(しい) すぐ(れる) | ③優しい やさしい gentle, kind |

| **0780** | Think of 亻 here as a **SUPERIOR** and **KIND** *man* who comes to aid an *anxious/grieving* heart |
|---|---|
| 人 9 | (憂). For M2 **ACTOR**, it suffices to learn the three compounds 俳優 (はいゆう, actor, actress), |
| | 女優 (じょゆう, actress), and 男優 (だんゆう, actor). Learn these three words as a set. |
| 0156 | |
| 常 17 | |

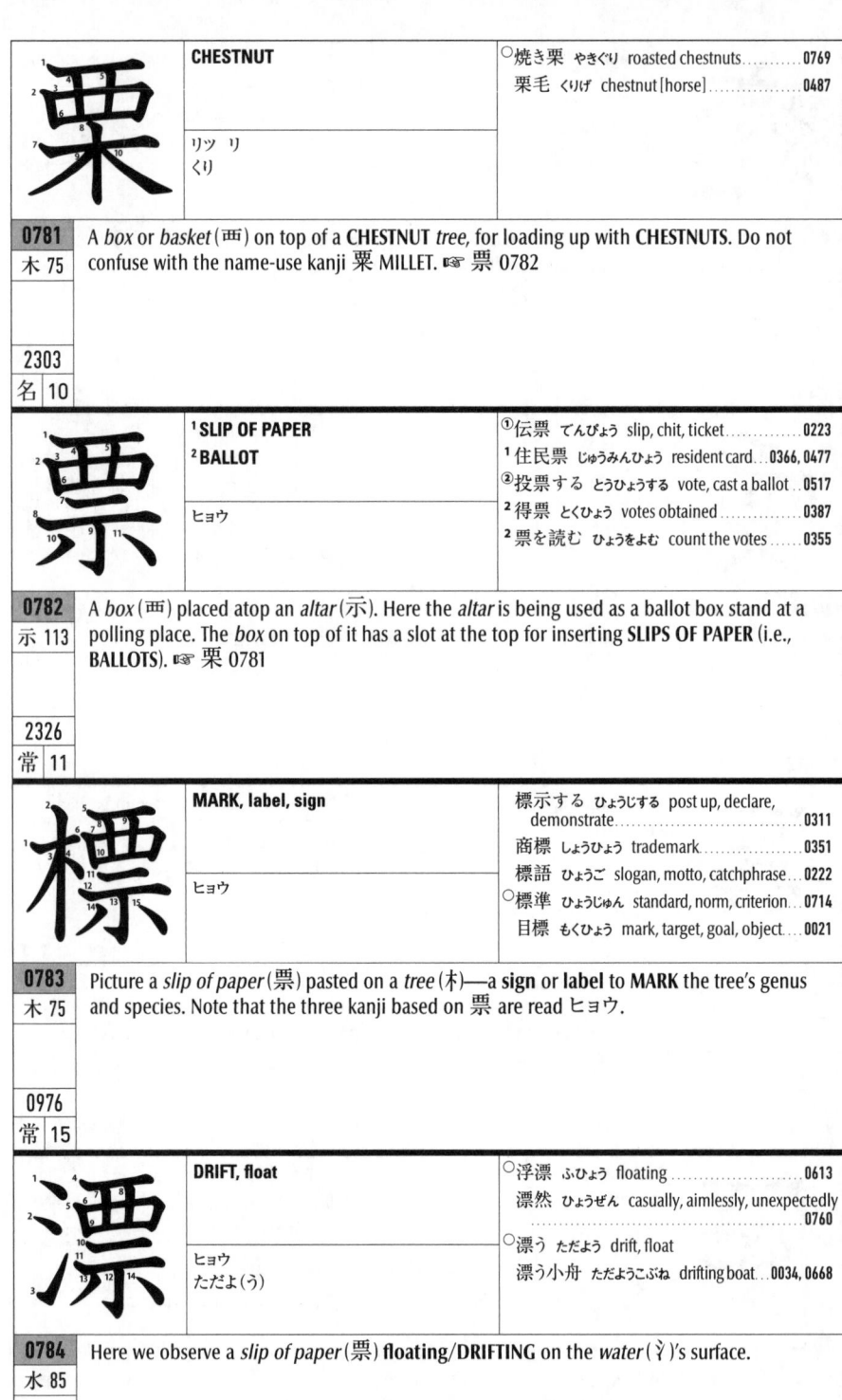

| | CHESTNUT | ○焼き栗 やきぐり roasted chestnuts............0769 |
| | | 栗毛 くりげ chestnut [horse].................0487 |
| | リツ リ | |
| | くり | |

**0781**
木 75

A *box* or *basket* (覀) on top of a **CHESTNUT** *tree,* for loading up with **CHESTNUTS.** Do not confuse with the name-use kanji 粟 MILLET. ☞ 票 0782

**2303**
名 10

---

| | ¹ **SLIP OF PAPER** | ①伝票 でんぴょう slip, chit, ticket.............0223 |
| | ² **BALLOT** | ¹ 住民票 じゅうみんひょう resident card...0366, 0477 |
| | | ②投票する とうひょうする vote, cast a ballot ..0517 |
| | ヒョウ | ² 得票 とくひょう votes obtained .............0387 |
| | | ² 票を読む ひょうをよむ count the votes ......0355 |

**0782**
示 113

A *box* (覀) placed atop an *altar* (示). Here the *altar* is being used as a ballot box stand at a polling place. The *box* on top of it has a slot at the top for inserting **SLIPS OF PAPER** (i.e., **BALLOTS**). ☞ 栗 0781

**2326**
常 11

---

| | MARK, label, sign | 標示する ひょうじする post up, declare, demonstrate.................0311 |
| | | 商標 しょうひょう trademark.................0351 |
| | | 標語 ひょうご slogan, motto, catchphrase...0222 |
| | ヒョウ | ○標準 ひょうじゅん standard, norm, criterion...0714 |
| | | 目標 もくひょう mark, target, goal, object....0021 |

**0783**
木 75

Picture a *slip of paper* (票) pasted on a *tree* (木)—a **sign** or **label** to **MARK** the tree's genus and species. Note that the three kanji based on 票 are read ヒョウ.

**0976**
常 15

---

| | DRIFT, float | ○浮漂 ふひょう floating .......................0613 |
| | | 漂然 ひょうぜん casually, aimlessly, unexpectedly ................0760 |
| | ヒョウ | ○漂う ただよう drift, float |
| | ただよ(う) | 漂う小舟 ただようこぶね drifting boat...0034, 0668 |

**0784**
水 85

Here we observe a *slip of paper* (票) floating/**DRIFTING** on the *water* (氵)'s surface.

**0632**
常 14

**TRANSFER**

セン

○遷都 せんと transfer of the capital............0244
左遷 させん relegation, demotion .........0401
○変遷 へんせん changes, vicissitudes .......0775

**0785**
乏 162

2735
常 15

Visualize the three lines of 大 (S7-9) as ropes wrapping around the objects above and below (which just so happen to be *wrap* 己 and *box* 西). 大 ties these objects onto the bed of a *truck* (辶), which is used to **TRANSFER** them to a new location. The three ropes join in a knot at the center of 大. ☞ 遭 1880, 選 1502

**EACH, every, all; various**

カク
おのおの

○各自 かくじ each/every individual ..........0081
各国 かっこく each country; various countries ..........0075
各地 かくち every place; various places .....0187
各一部 かくいちぶ one copy each .....0002, 0068
○各の考えて おのおののかんがえて at individual discretion ..........0628

**0786**
口 30

1856
常 6

Review 条 0119. Here, the *angled rooftop* (夂) shelters a square building. We'll use this concrete image for 各, under the label *cabin*, when it appears inside other kanji. By itself it means **EACH/every**; to perceive this idea it may help to focus visually on how **EACH** rafter attaches to a wall, or vice versa. ☞ 客 0787, 名 0269

¹**VISITOR**
²**CUSTOMER**

キャク カク

¹訪問客 ほうもんきゃく visitor, caller ....0454, 0452
¹客室 きゃくしつ guest room, stateroom......0253
¹来客 らいきゃく visitor, guest.................0274
²常客 じょうきゃく regular customer ..........0321
○お客さん おきゃくさん visitor, guest; customer, client; spectator; passenger; outsider

**0787**
宀 40

1939
常 9

The extra *roof* (宀) indicates a host's special solicitude for the esteemed **VISITOR** occupying his guest *cabin* (各). ☞ 各 0786

**ROAD, way**

ロ -じ

○道路 どうろ road, street, way................0158
路地 ろじ alley, lane......................0187
線路 せんろ (railway) line, track ............0210
通路 つうろ passage, pathway, aisle ......0159
旅路 たびじ journey ........................0569

**0788**
足 157

1394
常 13

Visualize 𧾷 as a person *stepping* down a **ROAD** that leads to a *cabin* (各). The reading ロ can be associated with **ROAD** (but remember that the vowel is short).

| | <sup>1</sup> **NORM, standard**<br><sup>2</sup> **STATUS, rank**<br><sup>3</sup> **CHARACTER**<br><br>カク コウ | ①合格する ごうかくする pass (an examination), qualify...............0227<br><sup>2</sup> 格が上がる かくがあがる be promoted to a higher rank ..............0041<br>②価格 かかく price, cost.................0548<br>③性格 せいかく character, personality ........0128<br>格子 こうし latticework, lattice, grid.......0094 |
|---|---|---|

**0789**

木 75

Only *trees* (木) of standard height, straightness, and hardness may be used in building *cabins* (各). Thus let *"cabin tree"* represent the idea of a **standard** or **NORM**. Trees that meet this **standard** earn a corresponding **STATUS** or **rank**. Associate M3 **CHARACTER** with M2 **STATUS**, via the idea of one's personal standing.

**0835**

常 | 10

---

| | <sup>1</sup> **INTERLINK**<br><sup>2</sup> **ENTWINE**<br><br>ラク<br>から(む)　から(める)　から(まる) | ①連絡 れんらく connection, contact; communication......0582<br><sup>1</sup> 短絡 たんらく short circuit...........0562<br><sup>2</sup> 籠絡する ろうらくする inveigle, ensnare, entice ......0509<br>②絡み合う からみあう intertwine, interlock...0227<br><sup>2</sup> 絡まり からまり entanglement |
|---|---|---|

**0790**

糸 120

Here we use *string* (糸) to **ENTWINE** or **INTERLINK** the *cabin* (各)'s rafters with its supporting walls. The reading からまり (V5, entanglement) can be associated with the tangled legs of fried calamari.

**1238**

常 | 12

---

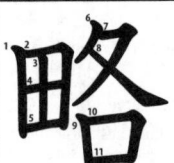

| | <sup>1</sup> **LEAVE OUT, abridge**<br><sup>2</sup> **STRATEGY; seize**<br><br>リャク | <sup>1</sup> 略語 りゃくご abbreviation ...........0222<br>①省略する しょうりゃくする omit, abbreviate...0681<br><sup>1</sup> 略す りゃくす abbreviate; leave out<br>②戦略 せんりゃく strategy, stratagem.......0461<br><sup>2</sup> 政略 せいりゃく political maneuvering ......0246 |
|---|---|---|

**0791**

田 102

Imagine a group of *field* officers inside a *cabin* (各), devising a battle*field* (田) **STRATEGY**. Naturally, their **STRATEGIZING** revolves around which of the *field*'s four quadrants to **seize**, and which to **LEAVE OUT**. Incidentally, this is the only kanji in this course with the reading リャク.

**1081**

常 | 11

---

| | <sup>1</sup> **STATELY BUILDING**<br><sup>2</sup> **CABINET (of a government)**<br><br>カク | <sup>1</sup> 閣下 かっか Your/His Excellency.........0040<br><sup>1</sup> 天守閣 てんしゅかく castle-tower; dungeon, keep.........0270, 0648<br><sup>1</sup> 銀閣寺 ぎんかくじ Ginkakuji [temple] ......0283, 0382<br>②内閣 ないかく government cabinet........0215 |
|---|---|---|

**0792**

門 169

A *cabin* (各) framed inside a *gate* (門) depicts a **STATELY BUILDING**. As you look at this kanji, picture an imposing edifice, set well back from the *gate* on extensive grounds, that offers the space and privacy to which those of high rank are accustomed. A group of government ministers meets privately in this stately *cabin*: the **CABINET**.

**2841**

常 | 14

| | FALL, fail | ○落下 らっか fall, drop, descent ............... 0040 |
|---|---|---|
| | | 低落する ていらくする fall, depreciate, go down |
| | | ................................................... 0479 |
| | | ○落ちる おちる fall, drop; fail |
| | ラク | 落ち葉 おちば fallen leaves ................ 0605 |
| | お(ちる) お(ち) お(とす) | 落とす おとす let fall, drop; remove |

| 0793 | Visualize *water* (氵) **FALLING** off the *grass* (艹) roof of this *cabin* (各). Now we have learned |
|---|---|
| 艸 140 | eight characters containing 各, which leaves only 賂 1229 and 酪 2126. |
| **2019** | |
| 常 12 | |

| | SOUTH | ○南北 なんぼく north and south, north-south 0122 |
|---|---|---|
| | | 南部 なんぶ south(ern) part; south ......... 0068 |
| | | 東南 とうなん southeast ...................... 0032 |
| | | 南蛮 なんばん southern barbarians, Europeans |
| | ナン ナ | arriving to Japan from the south (in the |
| | みなみ | sixteenth to eighteenth centuries) .......... 0776 |
| | | ○南口 みなみぐち south exit ................. 0019 |

| 0794 | Visualize this as a kind of chart of the earth, marking **SOUTH** with the symbol for *sheep* |
|---|---|
| 十 24 | (abbreviating 羊), in reference to the sheep pastures of Patagonia. |
| **1791** | |
| 常 9 | |

| | WEST | 西部 せいぶ western part; the West......... 0068 |
|---|---|---|
| | | 大西洋 たいせいよう Atlantic Ocean ... 0033, 0491 |
| | | ○西洋 せいよう the West ..................... 0491 |
| | セイ サイ | 北西 ほくせい northwest ...................... 0122 |
| | にし | ○西側 にしがわ west side; Western European |
| | | countries and America ...................... 0626 |

| 0795 | Picture S1 as the horizon and 口 as the sun, now set below it in the **WEST**. S4–5 point down- |
|---|---|
| 襾 146 | ward, suggesting the sun's downward course over the western horizon. ☞ 酉 0796 |
| **2951** | |
| 常 6 | |

| | (sign of) THE ROOSTER | ○酉年 とりどし Year of the Rooster ............ 0117 |
|---|---|---|
| | | 酉の方角 とりのほうがく west .......... 0173, 0342 |
| | | 酉の市 とりのいち "Rooster Day"; year-end fair |
| | ユウ | ................................................... 0205 |
| | とり | |

| 0796 | This character appears frequently as a component grapheme, where it signifies *liquor* or |
|---|---|
| 酉 164 | *ferment*. We can visualize it as a mostly empty bottle with a large stopper (S1, S4–5). As an |
| **2969** | independent kanji, it is the horary sign of **THE ROOSTER**. ☞ 西 0795 |
| 名 7 | |

**ALCOHOLIC DRINK**

シュ
さけ さか-

酒造 しゅぞう sake brewing; distilling .......0699
飲酒 いんしゅ drinking (alcoholic drinks)...0289
お酒 おさけ sake; alcoholic drink, wine, liquor, beer
酒屋 さかや sake dealer, liquor store........0252
酒場 さかば bar, barroom, pub, tavern .....0445

| 0797 | *Liquid* ( 氵) poured from a *liquor bottle* (酉): **ALCOHOLIC DRINK.** ☞ 酒 0798 |
| 水 85 | |
| 0403 | |
| 常 10 | |

**SPRINKLE, wash**

シャ サイ

○お洒落な おしゃれな stylishly dressed.......0793
洒落る しゃれる dress up stylishly; play on words, be witty ...............................0793
洒落たヘアスタイル しゃれたヘアスタイル fashionable hairstyle..........................0793
洒落者 しゃれもの dandy, fop.........0793, 0107

| 0798 | Resembles 酒, but now the bottle is empty. The few drops that remain ( 氵) are not enough to drink, only to **SPRINKLE** on the floor. ☞ 酒 0797 |
| 水 85 | |
| 外 9 | |

¹ **DISTRIBUTE**
² **PUT IN ORDER, manage**

ハイ
くば(る)

①配る くばる distribute, allot
¹ 配給 はいきゅう distribution, supply; rationing ................................................0526
¹ 配電盤 はいでんばん distributing board, switchboard ............................0155, 0673
² 手配 てはい arrangement, preparation.....0046
②支配する しはいする control, manage, govern ................................................0373

| 0799 | Visualize *kneeling* down (己) to **DISTRIBUTE** *liquor* (酉) to a group of seated guests. With this image of carefully allocating the liquor we can associate M2 **PUT IN ORDER/manage.** |
| 酉 164 | |
| 1330 | |
| 常 10 | |

¹ **ACID**
² **OXYGEN**

サン
す(い)

①酸性 さんせい acidity .......................0128
¹ 酸い すい sour, acid
¹ 酸っぱい すっぱい sour, acid
②酸素 さんそ oxygen.......................0132
² 酸化 さんか oxidation .......................0120

| 0800 | Take 夋 to mean *sharp stimulus*: ム is a *nose* and 儿—just in 変—are acrid vapors entering the nostrils (from stinky feet at the end of the *crossed legs* 夂). We thus obtain "*ferment* (酉) + *sharp stimulus* (夋)," signifying **ACID.** Also refers to the element **OXYGEN**, once associated with the formation of **ACIDS.** ☞ 俊 1440, 唆 1441 |
| 酉 164 | |
| 1415 | |
| 常 14 | |

| | DELAY | ○猶予する ゆうよする postpone, delay, extend; hesitate ........................0163 |
|---|---|---|
| | ユウ | |

| 0801 | 酉 depicts a *ceremonial liquor bottle*, distinguished by the ornaments on its stopper (S4–5 in this entry), which you may wish to visualize as a pair of precious jewels. To associate this character with the meaning **DELAY**, imagine a *dog* (犭) who has been slowed down by a few sips from the *ceremonial liquor bottle*. |
|---|---|
| 犬 94 | |
| 0566 | |
| 常 12 | |

| | HONOR, esteem | ○尊重する そんちょうする respect, esteem, value ........................0539 |
|---|---|---|
| | | 自尊心 じそんしん self-respect, pride..0081, 0056 |
| | ソン | ○尊い たっとい (=とうとい) exalted, august |
| | たっと(い) とうと(い) たっと(ぶ) | 神を尊ぶ かみをたっとぶ revere God ........0316 |
| | とうと(ぶ) | 尊父 そんぷ your father ....................0100 |

| 0802 | This character conveys the ideas **HONOR** and **esteem** by showing an *outstretched arm* (寸) holding aloft the *ceremonial liquor bottle* (酉) for an **HONORED**/esteemed authority figure. ☞ 遵 0803, 導 0804 |
|---|---|
| 寸 41 | |
| 2029 | |
| 常 12 | |

| | OBEY | ○遵守する じゅんしゅする observe, obey, follow, conform to...........................0648 |
|---|---|---|
| | ジュン | 遵法 じゅんぽう law observance.............0139 |

| 0803 | Here let 辶 suggest following in the path of an *honored* or *esteemed* authority figure (尊), i.e., **OBEYING** one's superior. Take a moment to absorb from this image the idea of **OBEYING** an authority. ☞ 尊 0802, 導 0804 |
|---|---|
| 辵 162 | |
| 2732 | |
| 常 15 | |

| | GUIDE, conduct | ○導入する どうにゅうする lead into, bring into ........................0039 |
|---|---|---|
| | | 主導 しゅどう initiative, leadership ..........0365 |
| | | 教導する きょうどうする instruct, teach, train ........................0632 |
| | ドウ | 半導体 はんどうたい semiconductor...0335, 0062 |
| | みちび(く) | ○導く みちびく guide, conduct |

| 0804 | Here we observe an *outstretched arm* (寸) **GUIDING** something along its *way* (道). Like 道 0158, this entry is read ドウ. ☞ 遵 0803, 尊 0802 |
|---|---|
| 寸 41 | |
| 2509 | |
| 常 15 | |

**RESPECT, revere**

ケイ
うやま(う)

敬老 けいろう respect for the aged ........... 0629
○尊敬 する そんけいする respect, esteem, honor ....... 0802
敬称 けいしょう honorific title, term of respect ....... 0684
敬語 けいご honorific language, polite speech ....... 0222
○敬う うやまう respect, revere, honor

| 0805 |
| 攵 66 |

At the left we see a circus elephant, with a phrase in its mouth (see 句 0166 PHRASE) and a *grass* (艹) laurel on its head. At the right we see a *rod*-bearing hand (攵), that of the beast's master. Imagine this laurelled, phrase-uttering circus elephant bowing before its master to show its **RESPECT**. Stick with this image in the next two entries.

| 1517 |
| 常 12 |

---

**¹ GUARD AGAINST**
**² WARN**

ケイ

①警察 けいさつ police ..................... 0639
¹警官 けいかん police officer ............. 0290
¹警視庁 けいしちょう Metropolitan Police Department ............... 0623, 0441
²警告 けいこく warning, admonition ......... 0698
警戒 けいかい caution, warning; guard, vigilance ............... 0469

| 0806 |
| 言 149 |

(Continuing from the previous entry) Now the master issues a stern *word* (言) of **WARNING** to the circus elephant, to **GUARD AGAINST** any disrespectful behavior. ☞ 驚 0807

| 2512 |
| 常 19 |

---

**SURPRISE**

キョウ
おどろ(く) おどろ(かす)

一驚 いっきょう astonishment, surprise ...... 0002
○驚がく (驚愕×) きょうがく astonishment, surprise, shock
○驚く おどろく be surprised; be frightened
驚くべき おどろくべき astonishing, wonderful
驚かす おどろかす surprise; frighten

| 0807 |
| 馬 187 |

As part of the circus act, a *horse* 馬 suddenly bolts out of its stable to **SURPRISE** the poor elephant. V2 驚がく (きょうがく, sometimes written with the unlisted kanji 愕, ガク) is suggested for memorization, but compounds with listed kanji appear later at 異 0882 and 嘆 1731. ☞ 警 0806

| 2513 |
| 常 22 |

---

**SCATTER, disperse; unrestrained**

サン
ち(る) ち(らす) -ち(らす) ち(らかす)
ち(らかる) ち(らばる)

○解散 かいさん breakup, dispersion; dissolution ....... 0345
○散らす ちらす [vt] scatter, disperse, break up
食い散らす くいちらす eat untidily, eat a bit of everything ............... 0288
部屋を散らかす へやをちらかす litter a room ............... 0068, 0252
散歩 さんぽ leisurely stroll, walk ......... 0679

| 0808 |
| 攵 66 |

昔 depicts *flesh* (月) attached *together* (S1-4, from 共), which we can interpret to mean *Siamese twins*. Now imagine that you *strike* (攵) the *Siamese twins* to "**SCATTER**" (i.e., separate) them. ☞ 撒 2186

| 1518 |
| 常 12 |

**BOLDLY**

カン
あ (えて)• あ (えず)•

○敢然と かんぜんと boldly, bravely ...........0760
敢行 かんこう decisive [daring] action.......0055
果敢な かかんな bold, daring; resolute.....0599
敢えてする あえてする dare to do; do anyway
取り敢えず とりあえず as a temporary measure,
for now.............................................0059

| 0809 | See the act of **BOLDLY** *striking* (攵) someone in the *ear* (耳), which swells presently into a *cauliflower ear* 耳. |
| 攵 66 | |
| 1522 | |
| 常 12 | |

¹ **SEVERE**
² **SOLEMN**

ゲン ゴン
おごそ (か) きび (しい)

¹ 厳格な げんかくな severe, strict, rigorous ...0789
①厳禁 げんきん strictly prohibited ...........0312
①厳しい きびしい severe, strict, rigorous
②厳かな おごそかな solemn, dignified
² 尊厳 そんげん dignity, sanctity ..............0802

| 0810 | First let ⍩ on top of 厂 suggest wildflowers growing at the edge of a *cliff*, and imagine an unwary child running over to pick them. Now think of his parent's **SEVERE** reprimand, starting with a *cauliflower ear* (耳)-inducing blow (攵) to the head. |
| 小 42* | |
| 嚴 | |
| 2804 | |
| 常 17 | |

**BUDDHA**

ブツ フツ*
ほとけ

神仏 しんぶつ gods and Buddha; Shinto and
Buddhism...........................................0316
○仏教 ぶっきょう Buddhism.......................0632
念仏 ねんぶつ Buddhist invocation, prayer to
Amitabha ...........................................0230
○仏様 ほとけさま Buddha; deceased person...0501
日仏 にちふつ Japan and France, Japanese-
French................................................0001

| 0811 | Earlier we linked *nose* 厶 with "self"; here, it just means *nose*. Imagine a giant **BUDDHA** statue, such as the famous ones at Nara or Kamakura. Then see a *man* (亻) climbing up the statue and discovering he's only the size of **BUDDHA's** *nose*. 仏 also refers to France, from its use in the old transliteration 仏蘭西 (ふらんす). ☞ 払 0812, 伝 0223 |
| 人 9 | |
| 佛 | |
| 0010 | |
| 常 4 | |

¹ **CLEAR AWAY**
² **PAY**

フツ
はら (う) -はら (い) -ばら (い)

①払底 ふってい shortage.........................0482
¹ 払い落とす はらいおとす brush off, shake off
.........................................................0793
¹ 厄払い やくばらい exorcism....................0725
² 払い込む はらいこむ pay in, pay up.........0192
②支払い しはらい payment, payout, defrayment
.........................................................0373

| 0812 | See a *hand* (扌) reaching up to **CLEAR AWAY** the mucus from a runny *nose* (厶). **PAY** is an associated meaning, from the idea of **CLEARING AWAY** one's debts. Note the traditional forms for this entry and the one before. ☞ 仏 0811, 拡 0813, 私 0237 |
| 手 64 | |
| 拂 | |
| 0171 | |
| 常 5 | |

**ENLARGE, widen**

カク

○拡大する かくだいする magnify, enlarge, expand .......... 0033

拡散 かくさん scattering, diffusion .......... 0808

拡声器 かくせいき (loud)speaker, megaphone .......... 0529, 0295

軍拡 ぐんかく expansion of armaments .......... 0583

| 0813 | A *hand* (扌) opening *wide* (広): widen/**ENLARGE**. ☞ 払 0812 |
| 手 64 | |
| 擴 | |
| 0273 | |
| 常 8 | |

¹**POSSIBLE, -able; worthy of**
²**APPROVE**

カ

①可燃ゴミ かねんゴミ burnable trash .......... 0761

¹不可欠 ふかけつ indispensable .......... 0049, 0277

¹可愛い かわいい lovable, darling, sweet ... 0778

②可決 かけつ approval/adoption of a bill ... 0330

²可否 かひ right or wrong, propriety .......... 0552

| 0814 | Make the "okay" gesture with your right hand, forming a circle (口) with your thumb and |
| 口 30 | forefinger and wrapping your three other fingers above and around that circle, roughly |
| | matching this character. By learning to see the idea of "okay" in 可, we can easily remember |
| | that it means **POSSIBLE** and **APPROVE**. Now a few notes about differentiating |
| 2562 | graphemes. Ignore the similarity between this entry's outer frame and 勹 *wrap up* (the |
| 常 5 | elephant's "ear" is an indispensable part of the latter; to review see 句 0166). Also, carefully |
| | note the difference between this entry and 司 0820, ... (continued below) ☞ 司 0820 |

¹**WHAT**
²**HOW MANY, several**

カ
なに なん なに- なん-

①幾何学 きかがく geometry .......... 0470, 0099

¹何時ですか なんじですか What time is it? ... 0383

¹何事 なにごと whatever, what .......... 0080

②何才ですか なんさいですか How old are you? .......... 0652

²何時間 なんじかん several hours .......... 0383, 0448

| 0815 | (Continuing from the previous entry) ... which contains an extra horizontal stroke above 口, |
| 人 9 | and whose enclosure is written in a single stroke. Except for 阿 (0819) and the 奇 group |
| | (which starts at 1329), the *on-yomi* of characters based on 可 is カ, while that of characters |
| | based on 司 0820 is シ... Now let us address the present entry. Nonverbal communication |
| 0048 | (like the "okay" gesture 可) is by nature rather vague. Here a *man* (亻), not understanding |
| 常 7 | exactly what someone means by the gesture, comes up and asks, "**WHAT?**" ☞ 伺 0821 |

**TORMENT; severe**

カ
いじ (め)* いじ (める)* いら*
さいな (む)*

○苛烈な かれつな severe, intense .......... 0719

苛性の かせいの caustic .......... 0128

○苛める いじめる bully, torment

苛む さいなむ torment

苛立つ いらだつ become irritated .......... 0067

| 0816 | Here let 可 *okay* suggest the overly acquiescent attitude of a bullying victim. The bully **TOR-** |
| 艸 140 | **MENTS** him by piling *grass* (艹) on his shoulders, to which he meekly replies, "okay." |
| | ☞ 荷 0817 |
| 1929 | |
| 常 8 | |

| | LOAD, cargo | |
|---|---|---|
| | カ | 入荷 にゅうか arrival of goods (at a shop) ...0039 |
| | に | ○在荷 ざいか stock, goods on hand ..........0406 |
| | | ○荷物 にもつ baggage, luggage, load........0172 |
| | | 荷造り にづくり packing.....................0699 |
| | | 荷を下ろす にをおろす take a load off ......0040 |

| 0817 艸 140 | Combines the two previous entries, vexingly. Our best option may be to see イ and 可 working together to carry a heavy **LOAD** of *grass*. Remind yourself that when イ and 可 carry the load of *grass* together it means **LOAD**, while making 可 carry it alone is just *torment*.<br>☞ 苛 0816 |
|---|---|
| 1972 | |
| 常 10 | |

| | RIVER | |
|---|---|---|
| | カ | 河川 かせん rivers..............................0022 |
| | かわ | ○運河 うんが canal...........................0584 |
| | | 銀河 ぎんが Milky Way; galaxy .............0283 |
| | | 河底 かわぞこ riverbed .......................0482 |
| | | 河原 かわら dry riverbed, river beach .......0208 |

| 0818 水 85 | Unlike seawater, **RIVER** water is okay for drinking. Thus "*okay* (可) *water* (氵)" means **RIVER**.<br>☞ 川 0022 |
|---|---|
| 0298 | |
| 常 8 | |

| | PHONETIC [a] | |
|---|---|---|
| | ア | 阿部 あべ Abe [surname]....................0068 |
| | | 阿倍 あべ Abe [surname]....................0069 |
| | | 阿呆 あほう (=あほ) fool, idiot..............0647 |
| | | 阿弥陀ˣ あみだ Amitabha; lottery; wearing<br>a hat on the back of the head .............0685 |
| | | 南阿 なんあ South Africa....................0794 |

| 0819 阜 170 | This character is used phonetically for ア, and is the only character based on 可 (other than the 奇 group starting at 1329) not pronounced カ. Making special note that this entry is the single exception will make it easier to remember that the others are all read カ. Memorize its reading from the surnames listed in VI–2. |
|---|---|
| 0305 | |
| 名 8 | |

| | OFFICIATE, administer | |
|---|---|---|
| | シ | 司書 ししょ librarian ........................0079 |
| | | 司祭 しさい Catholic priest, rabbi ..........0637 |
| | | 司会する しかいする preside; emcee .......0226 |
| | | ○司法 しほう administration of justice........0139 |
| | | 上司 じょうし superior officer, superior ......0041 |

| 0820 口 30 | A view from above of an official's tidy desktop: S1 outlines the shape of her desk, while S2 represents her pen and 口 her writing pad, all arranged at neat 90-degree angles. Let this image symbolize the act of **administering** or **OFFICIATING**. As noted earlier, all kanji based on 司 are read シ. 司 is even used phonetically for シ, as in 寿司 すし. ☞ 同 0182, 可 0814 |
|---|---|
| 2538 | |
| 常 5 | |

**INQUIRE, pay a visit**

シ
うかが(う)

○伺う うかがう inquire (about), be told; pay a visit
伺い うかがい question, inquiry; consulting the oracle; call, visit
いつお伺いしましょうか いつおうかがいしましょうか When shall I call on you?
…と伺った …とうかがった I heard that…

| 0821 | |
|---|---|
| 人 9 | |
| 0053 | |
| 常 7 | |

When you come across 司 as a component grapheme in kanji such as the present entry, you can visualize it as the *desk of an official or administrator*. Here we observe a *man* (イ) standing before the *official's desk*. He is **paying a visit** to the official to **INQUIRE** about some matter. Sample *on-yomi* compounds for this entry appear later at 候 1675 and 奉 2103. ☞ 何 0815

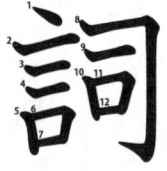

**WORDS**

シ

作詞 さくし writing lyrics.....................0152
品詞 ひんし part of speech..................0301
○動詞 どうし verb...............................0540
○名詞 めいし noun..............................0269

| 0822 | |
|---|---|
| 言 149 | |
| 1363 | |
| 常 12 | |

See the **WORDS** (言) spoken at an *official's desk* (司).

**RAISE ANIMALS**

シ
か(う)

○飼育する しいくする raise (animals), breed, rear
.......................................................0489
飼料 しりょう fodder..........................0758
○(犬を)飼う (いぬを)かう keep (a dog)........0293
羊飼い ひつじかい shepherd.................0490
放し飼い はなしがい grazing; letting (a dog) run free......................................................0574

| 0823 | |
|---|---|
| 食 184 | |
| 飼 | |
| 1529 | |
| 常 13 | |

"*Administer* (司) + *food* (食)": **RAISE ANIMALS.**

**COUNTER FOR BOOKS**

サツ サク

冊数 さっすう number of books..............0309
○一冊 いっさつ one volume ..................0002
小冊子 しょうさっし booklet, pamphlet
.....................................................0034, 0094
分冊 ぶんさつ separate volume...............0088
別冊 べっさつ separate volume, extra issue 0090

| 0824 | |
|---|---|
| 冂 13 | |
| 册 | |
| 2925 | |
| 常 5 | |

**BOOKS** in a bookcase. Do not confuse with 而 *roots*, introduced at 耐 2109. ☞ 札 1694

| 嗣 | **HEIR** | ○嗣子 しし heir, successor .................... 0094 |
| | | 皇嗣 こうし imperial heir, crown prince ...... 0077 |
| | シ | |

**0825**
口 30

Picture the greedy **HEIR** of an official approaching the *official's desk* (司) with a hungry *mouth* (口) and a stack of *books* (冊) containing a long testament listing all of the possessions he hopes to inherit, if he can only get the official to sign it.

1532
常 13

---

| 覗 | **PEEK, come into view** | ○覗く のぞく peek, look into; stick out, peek through |
| | | 窓から外を覗く まどからそとをのぞく look out the window ............................. 0558, 0266 |
| | シ | 覗き穴 のぞきあな peephole ................. 0397 |
| | のぞ(く) | おへそが覗いている おへそがのぞいている (Your) belly button is showing |

**0826**
見 147

Until now all of the graphemes adjoining 司 *official's desk* have approached it from the visitor's side, the left. Here a *seeing* eye (見) sneaks around the back of the desk to **PEEK** into the *official's* drawers.

外 12

---

| 歌 | ¹**SONG** ²**JAPANESE POEM** | ¹ 歌詞 かし words/lyrics of a song ............ 0822 |
| | | ①歌手 かしゅ singer .......................... 0046 |
| | | ①歌う うたう sing, recite |
| | カ | ² 短歌 たんか tanka, Japanese verse ......... 0562 |
| | うた うた(う) | ² 和歌 わか Japanese poem, tanka .......... 0236 |

**0827**
欠 76

Now we return to the カ (可) group—remember, when there's no desk pen, and the enclosure is written in two strokes, it's カ, not シ, and it's *okay*, not *official's desk*. To learn the present entry, make the *okay* gesture (可) with both hands, put them in front of your *gaping mouth* (欠) like two megaphones, and **SING** a **SONG** through them.

詞
1621
常 14

---

| 唄 | **DITTY** | 小唄 こうた ditty, ballad .................... 0034 |
| | | 子守唄 こもりうた lullaby .............. 0094, 0648 |
| | うた うた(う) | ○唄う うたう recite, sing |

**0828**
口 30

Here 口 sings a little **DITTY**, with conch *shell* (貝) accompaniment.

0358
常 10

| | ¹**BEAR**<br>²**LOSE**<br><br>フ<br>ま(ける) ま(かす) お(う) | ①負う おう bear on the back; take upon oneself<br>¹負荷 ふか load, burden ................... 0817<br>¹抱負 ほうふ aspiration, ambition ............ 0664<br>②負ける まける lose, be defeated<br>②勝負 しょうぶ victory or defeat; match, game<br>............................................. 0460 |
|---|---|---|

| **0829**<br>貝 154<br><br><br>1799<br>常\|9 | Simply see ク as something bearing down upon and overwhelming 貝 *shellfish*. To correctly perceive in this kanji the meanings **BEAR** and **LOSE**, we must take the perspective of the *shellfish*, who **LOSES** to ク and who must **BEAR** the burden of ク on top of him. Now is a good time to go back and review 買 0352. ☞ 貞 1867, 敗 0830 |
|---|---|

| | **BE DEFEATED**<br><br>ハイ<br>やぶ(れる) | ○敗北 はいぼく defeat, setback ................... 0122<br>敗戦 はいせん lost battle, defeat ............ 0461<br>失敗 しっぱい failure, mistake ................... 0563<br>二勝三敗 にしょうさんぱい two wins, three losses<br>............................................. 0003, 0460, 0004<br>○敗れる やぶれる be defeated, lose |
|---|---|---|

| **0830**<br>攵 66<br><br><br>1342<br>常\|11 | There must be something about *shellfish* and losing, because this character also means **BE DEFEATED**. While the previous entry suggests *bearing* the burden of defeat, this one points rather to the <u>act</u> of **BEING DEFEATED**, with its image of a *striking rod* (攵) beating a *shellfish* (貝). ☞ 負 0829 |
|---|---|

| | ¹**RESPONSIBILITY**<br>²**BLAME, censure**<br><br>セキ<br>せ(める) | ①責任 せきにん responsibility, liability ....... 0372<br>¹責務 せきむ responsibility and obligation... 0687<br>¹重責 じゅうせき heavy responsibility ......... 0539<br>²自責 じせき self-accusation ................... 0081<br>②責める せめる blame, censure |
|---|---|---|

| **0831**<br>貝 154<br><br><br>2176<br>常\|11 | See 龶 as onerous layers of **RESPONSIBILITY** or **BLAME**, mounting up on the poor *shellfish* (貝). When we find 責 inside other kanji, we can simply interpret it as a graphic representation of *mounting layers*. ☞ 貴 1177, 青 0130 |
|---|---|

| | **ACCUMULATE**<br><br>セキ<br>つ(む) -づみ つ(もる) つ(もり) | 重積 じゅうせき piling up ...................... 0539<br>○積む つむ pile up; stow aboard<br>積み上げる つみあげる pile up, accumulate<br>............................................. 0041<br>○面積 めんせき area, square measure ........ 0175<br>積もり つもり intention, purpose |
|---|---|---|

| **0832**<br>禾 115<br><br><br>1142<br>常\|16 | Informed by the previous entry, see *mounting layers* of *rice* (禾) **ACCUMULATING** on top of the *shellfish*. A good *on-yomi* compound to memorize for this character appears at 累 0884. |
|---|---|

| 債 | ¹ DEBT<br>² BOND | ①負債 ふさい debt, liabilities ................ 0829<br>¹ 債務 さいむ debt, obligation, liabilities..... 0687<br>②債券 さいけん bond, debenture ............ 0456<br>国債 こくさい national bonds; national debt/<br>loan ....................................... 0075<br>公債 こうさい public bond; public loan ..... 0089 |
| | サイ | |

| 0833<br>人 9 | Picture a *man* (イ) burdened by *mounting layers* (責) of **DEBT**. ☞ 借 1220 |
| 0135<br>常 13 | |

| 漬 | **PICKLE, immerse** | ○漬ける つける pickle, preserve; immerse, dip<br>漬け物 つけもの pickles, pickled vegetables<br>.......................................... 0172<br>大根漬け だいこんづけ pickled daikon (radish)<br>................................... 0033, 0284<br>手を水に漬ける てをみずにつける immerse/<br>dip one's hand in water............. 0046, 0027 |
| | つ(ける) つ(かる) -づ(け) -づけ | |

| 0834<br>水 85 | Here think of 氵 as brine, and try to picture 龶 weighing down 貝 so as to keep it **immersed** for **PICKLING**. Notice how 貝 is literally pushed down to the bottom of 氵.<br>☞ 潰 1178, 清 0974 |
| 0636<br>常 14 | |

| 紡 | **SPIN, make yarn** | ○紡糸 ぼうし spinning; spun cotton/wool ... 0112<br>紡毛 ぼうもう carded wool ................. 0487<br>綿紡 めんぼう cotton spinning............. 0211<br>○綿を糸に紡ぐ めんをいとにつむぐ spin cotton<br>into yarn .............................. 0211, 0112 |
| | ボウ<br>つむ(ぐ) | |

| 0835<br>糸 120 | Earlier we learned to see 方 as a *person* running toward one side. Here he drags behind him a *thread* (糸), which by running around he **SPINS** into **yarn**. |
| 1189<br>常 10 | |

| 績 | **ACHIEVEMENTS; spin thread** | ○成績 せいせき results, record, achievement 0070<br>実績 じっせき (actual) result, positive achieve-<br>ments ..................................... 0499<br>業績 ぎょうせき achievements, business results<br>.......................................... 0498<br>不成績 ふせいせき poor result, underachieve-<br>ment .............................. 0049, 0070<br>紡績 ぼうせき spinning ..................... 0835 |
| | セキ | |

| 0836<br>糸 120 | This kanji's original meaning was **spin thread**. First visualize 責 as a spool, each of its seven horizontal lines representing one loop of *thread* around the spool, drawn from 糸. Now imagine the loops of thread accumulating one by one from the bottom up as the spool winds around, symbolizing a person's cumulative **ACHIEVEMENTS**. |
| 1288<br>常 17 | |

241

**IMPLEMENT, tool**

グ

| 道具 どうぐ tool, implement; furniture .....0158 |
| 用具 ようぐ tool, instrument, appliance ....0047 |
| ○家具 かぐ furniture.........................0219 |
| 具体的な ぐたいてきな concrete, specific |
| .....................................0062, 0169 |
| 絵の具 えのぐ colors, oils, paint ..........0525 |

| 0837 | Restaurants serving whole lobster or crab usually provide special utensils for removing the flesh from the shell. Visualize S6 as a special **IMPLEMENT** splitting apart a *shellfish* (貝). |
| 八 12 | |
| 具 | ☞ 貝 0082 |
| 2208 | |
| 常 8 | |

**TRUE, genuine**

シン
まま-

| 真意 しんい true meaning; real intention...0151 |
| 真相 しんそう truth, facts, real situation .....0682 |
| ○真実 しんじつ truth, reality .................0499 |
| ○真ん中 まんなか center, middle ............0035 |
| 真正面 ましょうめん right in front ......0043, 0175 |

| 0838 | Here, building on the last entry, we use both the *implement* at the bottom (S8) and a dagger at the top (S1-2) to pry open the *shellfish* and discover the **TRUTH** hiding inside. This is similar to the way we learned 質 0318, so you may wish to review that entry. |
| 目 109 | |
| 眞 | |
| 1813 | |
| 常 10 | |

¹**STRAIGHT, direct, upright**
²**PUT STRAIGHT, correct**

チョク ジキ ジカ•
ただ(ちに) なお(す) -なお(す)
なお(る) す(ぐ)•

| ①直線 ちょくせん straight line.................0210 |
| ¹ 正直に しょうじきに honestly, frankly ........0043 |
| ①直ちに ただちに straight away, at once |
| ②直す なおす set right, fix |
| ² やり直す やりなおす do over again |

| 0839 | The English words **direct** and **correct** derive from the Latin word for "straight," *rectus*. As we did with 正 0043, we should <u>see</u> **STRAIGHTNESS**, **correctness**, and **uprightness** in this kanji. See S8 as a carpenter's square, and 目 as a graduated scale, both of which this character's architect must have included so as to keep it perfectly **STRAIGHT**. |
| 目 109 | |
| 2539 | |
| 常 8 | |

**PLANT**

ショク
う(える) う(わる)

| ○植物 しょくぶつ plant, vegetation ...........0172 |
| 植民 しょくみん colonization..................0477 |
| 植民地 しょくみんち colony, settlement |
| .............................................0477, 0187 |
| ○植える うえる plant, grow |
| 植え木 うえき garden plant, potted plant...0028 |

| 0840 | Depicts the act of setting a *tree* (木) perfectly *upright* (直) when **PLANTING** it. Interchangeable with the next entry for V2 植民 しょくみん (colonization). |
| 木 75 | |
| 0903 | |
| 常 12 | |

| 殖 | **MULTIPLY** | ○生殖 せいしょく reproduction, procreation ... 0036 |
| | | 殖産 しょくさん increase of production; |
| | | enhancement of one's fortune ............. 0181 |
| | | 殖民 しょくみん colonization ................ 0477 |
| | ショク | ○財産が殖える ざいさんがふえる become rich |
| | ふ(える) ふ(やす) | .................................................. 0653, 0181 |
| | | 貯金を殖やす ちょきんをふやす increase one's |
| | | savings ................................ 0442, 0029 |

| **0841** | Imagine a depopulated rural town desperate to raise its census count in order to augment a |
| 歹 78 | government subsidy. This kanji suggests the novel solution of **MULTIPLYING** the population |
| | by standing all the *dead* (歹) *upright* (直), so that the census-taker will mistakenly count |
| | them as living inhabitants. ☞ 増 1223 |
| **0907** | |
| 常 12 | |

| 値 | **VALUE, worth** | ○価値 かち value, merit, worth ............. 0548 |
| | | 数値 すうち numerical value ............... 0309 |
| | | ○値上げ ねあげ price hike ................ 0041 |
| | チ | 値切る ねぎる beat down the price, bargain |
| | ね あたい | .................................................. 0086 |
| | | ○価する あたいする be worth, deserve, merit |

| **0842** | "*Upright* (直) *man* (イ)" suggests a man of **VALUES**. Note that the sense is not "having prin- |
| 人 9 | ciples," but rather finding **VALUE** or **worth** in something. |
| **0091** | |
| 常 10 | |

| 置 | **PLACE, put in place; leave in place** | ○位置 いち position, place ................. 0577 |
| | | 設置する せっちする establish, found, set up |
| | | .................................................. 0520 |
| | チ | 放置する ほうちする leave alone; neglect ... 0574 |
| | お(く) -お(き) | ○置く おく put in place; leave behind |
| | | 物置き ものおき closet, storeroom, shed ... 0172 |

| **0843** | Many train cars have luggage shelves made of *nets* of cord or steel. In this character, try to |
| 罓 122 | visualize the act of **PLACING** your luggage *straight/upright* (直) on a *net* (罒) shelf. |
| **2262** | |
| 常 13 | |

| 県 | **PREFECTURE** | ○県立 けんりつ prefectural ................. 0067 |
| | | 県民 けんみん citizens of a prefecture ....... 0477 |
| | | 県知事 けんちじ prefectural governor |
| | ケン | .................................................. 0560, 0080 |
| | | 都道府県 とどうふけん urban and rural |
| | | prefectures ........................ 0244, 0158, 0247 |
| | | 愛知県 あいちけん Aichi prefecture ... 0778, 0560 |

| **0844** | Here we take S1–2 of 直 0839, split it into three pieces (vertical piece plus horizontal piece |
| 目 109* | which splits between left and right), and use them to erect a **PREFECTURAL** office, following |
| 縣 | the same post-and-buttress design we used for CAPITAL 京 0245, but without the *tall*ness |
| | (亠). This makes for a structure that is upright (cf. 直) without being "uppity." |
| **2294** | |
| 常 9 | |

| | ¹ **STATE, province** ² **SANDBAR** | ¹ 州政府 しゅうせいふ state government 0246, 0247 |
|---|---|---|
| | | ¹ 州立大学 しゅうりつだいがく state-run college ............................................0067, 0033, 0099 |
| | シュウ す | ¹ 州都 しゅうと state capital ..............0244 |
| | | ① テキサス州 テキサスしゅう state of Texas |
| | | ② 砂州 さす sandbar, sandbank ..............0678 |

**0845**
巛 47

The odd-numbered strokes are **SANDBARS** that appear in the middle of the river when the water is low. For rivers that mark the boundary between **STATES**, this raises the tricky question of which **STATE** each **SANDBAR** belongs to. ☞ 洲 0846

**0040**
常 | 6

---

| | **SANDBAR** | ○ 砂洲 さす sandbar, sandbank ..............0678 |
|---|---|---|
| | | 座洲する ざすする strand, run aground ....0749 |
| | シュウ す | |

**0846**
水 85

Interchangeable with the previous entry for the sense **SANDBAR**. ☞ 州 0845

**0352**
名 | 9

---

| | **CONTACT, join, meet** | 接触 せっしょく contact, touch................0344 |
|---|---|---|
| | | 接続 せつぞく connection, joining ..........0354 |
| | | ○ 直接に ちょくせつに directly.................0839 |
| | セツ つ(ぐ) | 接する せっする come in contact; adjoin |
| | | ○ 接ぐ つぐ piece together, splice |

**0847**
手 64

妾 is an unlisted kanji that means *concubine* (think of it as a man *standing* [立] on a *woman* [女], holding her down in her lowly status). In the present entry, he reaches out with his *hand* (扌) to have physical **CONTACT** with his low-ranking mistress.

**0460**
常 | 11

---

| | **SUCCEED, follow** | ○ 継続する けいぞくする continue, last, maintain ........................................................0354 |
|---|---|---|
| | | 後継 こうけい succession; successor, heir...0114 |
| | | 中継 ちゅうけい relay, rebroadcasting .......0035 |
| | ケイ つ(ぐ) | ○ 家を継ぐ いえをつぐ succeed to a house....0219 |
| | | 受け継ぐ うけつぐ inherit, succeed to ......0065 |

**0848**
糸 120

Review 続 0354. In this entry, we have a sheaf of *rice* (米), baled into a box with baling *cord* (糸) for bequeathing to one's **SUCCESSOR**. ☞ 断 0849, 繍 1614, 続 0354

**1242**
常 | 13

| | **¹ CUT OFF, refuse** <br> **² DECIDE, resolve** | ① 断つ たつ cut off, sever; abstain from |
|---|---|---|
| | | **¹** 切断する せつだんする cut off, sever........**0086** |
| | | ② 判断 はんだん judgment, decision .........**0744** |
| | ダン <br> た（つ） ことわ（る） | **²** 決断 けつだん decision, determination, resolution.................**0330** |
| | | ○ 断る ことわる refuse, reject; give advance notice, inform |

| **0849** | While 糸 in the previous entry suggests continuation, 斤 *hacksaw* here signals ending. Picture 斤 sawing right through the box (along S3). With this image, associate both M1 **CUT OFF** and M2 **DECIDE**, which in fact derives from the Latin words for **CUT** (*caedere*) and **OFF** (*de*). Remember, 糸 signals continuation, while 斤 signals discontinuation. ☞ 継 0848 |
|---|---|
| 斤 69 | |
| 斷 | |
| 1355 | |
| 常 | 11 |

| | **RESPOND, correspond** | ○ 対応する たいおうする correspond to, answer to; be equivalent; deal/cope with.............**0650** |
|---|---|---|
| | | 反応する はんのうする react, respond ......**0374** |
| | | 応接 おうせつ reception [as of guests] ......**0847** |
| | オウ <br> こた（える） | 応用 おうよう practical application ..........**0047** |
| | | 応える こたえる strike home, have an effect on; repay, reward |

| **0850** | Let *shelter* (广) + *heart/mind* (心) suggest one's mental or emotional **RESPONSE** on entering a secluded, sheltered place. As 応 refers to **RESPONDING** to, acting in accordance with, or being suitable for a given demand or situation, we can also associate it with the English word **correspond**. |
|---|---|
| 心 61 | |
| 應 | |
| 2640 | |
| 常 | 7 |

| | **¹ BED** <br> **² FLOOR** | **¹** 起床する きしょうする get up, rise...........**0430** |
|---|---|---|
| | | ① 温床 おんしょう hotbed ..................**0199** |
| | | **¹** 床に入る とこにはいる get into bed........**0039** |
| | ショウ <br> とこ ゆか | ② 床の間 とこのま alcove...................**0448** |
| | | ② 床の上に ゆかのうえに on the floor .........**0041** |

| **0851** | Let 木 represent the *wooden* **FLOOR** or **BED** inside a *shelter* (广). ☞ 麻 0852 |
|---|---|
| 广 53 | |
| 牀 | |
| 2641 | |
| 常 | 7 |

| | **¹ HEMP** <br> **² BECOME NUMB** | **¹** 亜麻 あま flax ........................**0545** |
|---|---|---|
| | | **¹** 大麻 たいま hemp; paper amulet used in Shinto rites...................**0033** |
| | | **¹** 胡麻 ごま sesame..........................**0258** |
| | マ <br> あさ | ① 麻布 あさぬの (=あさふ, まふ) hemp cloth, linen ................**0204** |
| | | ② 麻薬 まやく narcotic, drug .................**0303** |

| **0852** | HEMP *"trees"* growing in a *shelter,* i.e., a greenhouse. ☞ 床 0851 |
|---|---|
| 麻 200 | |
| 2694 | |
| 常 | 11 |

| | **PERSONAL HISTORY** | ○学歴 がくれき academic background........0099 |
| | | 病歴 びょうれき case history, patient's record...0617 |
| | | 戦歴 せんれき war record.................0461 |
| | レキ | 略歴 りゃくれき summarized personal background, bio..................0791 |
| | | 社歴 しゃれき company history............0314 |

| **0853** | Here we'll ignore the 广/厂 distinction in order to take advantage of 厤 *hemp*. In Japan one fills out a standard **PERSONAL HISTORY** form (履歴書 [りれきしょ, see 履 1871]) when applying for a job. If 歴 were any indication of the form's content, we would expect it to ask the applicant, "When did you *stop* (止) smoking *hemp* (厤)?" ☞ 暦 0854 |
| 止 77 | |
| 歴 | |
| 2600 | |
| 常 14 | |

| | **CALENDAR** | ○西暦 せいれき Christian Era, AD.............0795 |
| | | 旧暦 きゅうれき old (lunar) calendar .........0771 |
| | | ○暦の上では こよみのうえでは according to the calendar .................0041 |
| | レキ こよみ | 花暦 はなごよみ floral calendar.............0121 |

| **0854** | Again we'll use 麻 *hemp* without distinguishing between 广 and 厂. Here, a *hemp*-paper chart of the *days* (日): a **CALENDAR**. Later, we'll learn three more kanji based on 麻: 魔 2095, 摩 2099, and 磨 2100. Those three all use 广 and are, like 麻, read マ, while the present two use 厂 and are read レキ. ☞ 歴 0853 |
| 日 72 | |
| 暦 | |
| 2599 | |
| 常 14 | |

| | ¹ **ATTEND (to)** | ¹ 臨席 りんせき presence, attendance........0279 |
| | ² **CONFRONT** | ¹ 臨床 りんしょう clinical .................0851 |
| | | ①会合に臨む かいごうにのぞむ be present at/ attend a meeting.........0226, 0227 |
| | リン のぞ(む) | ② 臨時の りんじの temporary, provisional, special ...............0383 |
| | | ² 臨機応変 りんきおうへん adaptation to circumstances.........0473, 0850, 0775 |

| **0855** | Recall 臣 0484 RETAINER. In this entry, we observe the *retainer* dutifully **CONFRONTING**/ **ATTENDING TO** a problem that has arisen in connection with some *articles* of merchandise (品) produced by his master's factory. 个 indicates 臣's purposeful forward gaze as he CON- FRONTS the situation. ☞ 監 2027 |
| 臣 131 | |
| | |
| 1470 | |
| 常 18 | |

| | **GARDEN** | ○公園 こうえん park, public garden...........0089 |
| | | 楽園 らくえん paradise...................0302 |
| | | 動物園 どうぶつえん zoological park..0540, 0172 |
| | エン その | 植物園 しょくぶつえん botanical garden.... 0840, 0172 |
| | | ○花園 はなぞの flower garden..............0121 |

| **0856** | Here we observe an enclosed **GARDEN**, inside which we find, of course, *soil* (土), but also a square fountain (口), as well as a *garment* (S9-12, yet another variation on 衣 0700), which might represent a picnic blanket. The enclosed portion of this character should not be confused with 哀 1860. |
| 口 31 | |
| 園 | |
| 2722 | |
| 常 13 | |

| | DISTANT | 遠方 えんぽう great distance; distant place....**0173** |
| | | ○遠足 えんそく excursion, hike, long walk....**0044** |
| | | 遠心力 えんしんりょく centrifugal force |
| | | ...................................................**0056, 0084** |
| | エン オン | 遠近法 えんきんほう perspective [in art] |
| | とお(い) | ...................................................**0194, 0139** |
| | | ○遠い とおい distant, remote |

| **0857** | Building on the previous entry, we now see the garden lifted out of its enclosure, loaded on a |
| 辶 162 | *truck* (辶), and transported to a **DISTANT** place. ☞ 還 1550 |
| 2715 | |
| 常 13 | |

| | ¹ **GIVE, grant** | ①与える あたえる give, grant; inflict |
| | ² **TAKE PART IN** | ①供与する きょうよする offer, present, submit |
| | | ...................................................**0357** |
| | | ¹ 給与する きゅうよする grant; pay (a salary)....**0526** |
| | ヨ | ②関与する かんよする take part in, participate in, |
| | あた(える) | be concerned in................................**0451** |
| | | ² 与党 よとう party in power...................**0319** |

| **0858** | Earlier we saw the bottom part of 考 0628 as a numeral 5. The 5-like figure here is virtually |
| 一 1* | the same, except that its first stroke is written left to right, and at no angle. Here let it stand |
| 與 | for a 5-dollar **GIFT**, held out by the arm (S3) of its donor. Associate M2 **TAKE PART IN** with the |
| 2887 | idea of making a 5-dollar entry "donation." ☞ 写 0859 |
| 常 3 | |

| | **COPY** | 写生 しゃせい sketching from nature; portrayal |
| | | ...................................................**0036** |
| | | 写実 しゃじつ objective description; realism **0499** |
| | シャ | ○写真 しゃしん photograph...................**0838** |
| | うつ(す) うつ(る) | ○写真を写す しゃしんをうつす take a photo...**0838** |
| | | ○写真に写る しゃしんにうつる be photographed, |
| | | appear in a photograph ...................**0838** |

| **0859** | Now the arm (S5) holds the 5-dollar bill to the screen of a **COPY** machine, closes the *cover* |
| 宀 14* | (宀), and **COPIES** it. ☞ 与 0858 |
| 寫 | |
| 1726 | |
| 常 5 | |

| | **MOVE, shift** | ○移動する いどうする move, shift, transfer...**0540** |
| | | 移植 いしょく transplanting...................**0840** |
| | | 移民 いみん migration; migrant............**0477** |
| | イ | ○東京に移る とうきょうにうつる move to Tokyo |
| | うつ(る) うつ(す) | ...................................................**0032, 0245** |
| | | 病気を移す びょうきをうつす transmit an illness |
| | | ...................................................**0617, 0126** |

| **0860** | You must take *lots* (多) of *rice* (禾) with you when you **MOVE**. |
| 禾 115 | |
| 1087 | |
| 常 11 | |

**WHOLESALE**

おろ(す) おろし おろ(し)

○卸す おろす sell wholesale
卸て買う おろしてかう buy wholesale ........0352
卸商 おろししょう wholesaler.................0351
卸売り おろしうり wholesale ...............0353
卸値 おろしね wholesale price .............0842

| 0861 | Here a *seal* (刂) stamps bills of sale while *cattle* (牛) *stop* (止) to unload their cargo at a WHOLESALE market. ☞ 御 0862 |
| 刂 26 | |
| 1315 | |
| 常 9 | |

**GENERAL HONORIFIC TERM**

ギョ ゴ
おん- お-\* み-\*

御苑 ぎょえん imperial garden.............0729
御用 ごよう your order, your business ......0047
御中 おんちゅう Messrs.......................0035
御手洗い おてあらい lavatory, restroom
...........................................0046, 0135
お御輿 おみこし palanquin shrine (carried in festivals) [cf. 輿 0506] .....................0506

| 0862 | You'll see 御 dozens of times for every one time you'll see 卸 0861, so ignore the latter here. In fact, you only need to associate the image of 御 with its pronunciation, which you'll hear constantly used as an HONORIFIC prefix. Simply let 彳 *go* remind you of the reading ゴ, and the meaning will take care of itself. ☞ 卸 0861 |
| 彳 60 | |
| 0529 | |
| 常 12 | |

**COMPOUND, double, duplicate**

フク

複数 ふくすう plural.........................0309
複合 ふくごう compound, composite, complex
...........................................0227
○複雑な ふくざつな complicated, complex, involved.....................................0379
複製 ふくせい duplication, reproduction...0709
複写 ふくしゃ copy, duplication.............0859

| 0863 | 复 means *overlap, duplicate, double, fold,* etc., and can be visualized as a person with a cap (ㅗ), a *sunny* expression on his face (日), and—most importantly—underlined crossed (i.e., overlapping) *legs* (夂). This whole kanji represents *folded* (复) *clothing* (衤) and means COMPOUND, double, or duplicate. |
| 衣 145 | |
| 1132 | |
| 常 14 | |

**BELLY**

フク
はら なか\*

腹部 ふくぶ abdomen, belly.................0068
腹痛 ふくつう abdominal pain..............0619
○切腹 せっぷく hara-kiri, suicide by disembowelment........................................0086
○腹を立てる はらをたてる get angry, take offense
...........................................0067
○お腹空いた おなかすいた (I'm) hungry .....0398

| 0864 | We can interpret this character as "*doubled* (复) *flesh* (月)" or "*folds* of flesh." It means BELLY. |
| 肉 130 | |
| 0949 | |
| 常 13 | |

| 復 | RETURN TO, repeat | 復活 ふっかつ revival, rebirth, resurrection **0054** |
|---|---|---|
| | | 回復 かいふく recovery, restoration; rehabilita-tion.........................**0050** |
| | フク | ○復習 ふくしゅう review.........................**0420** |
| | | 反復 はんぷく repetition; reiteration.......**0374** |
| | | 旧に復する きゅうにふくする be restored to the former condition......................**0771** |

| **0865** | "*Go*(彳) + *duplicate*(复)" means "go back to"—in other words, **RETURN TO** or repeat. |
|---|---|
| 彳 60 | |
| 復 | |
| 0527 | |
| 常 12 | |

| 往 | GO ON, proceed; pass away | ○往復 おうふく going and returning; round trip........................**0865** |
|---|---|---|
| | | 往来 おうらい come-and-go, traffic; road, street........................**0274** |
| | オウ | 右往左往する うおうさおうする go this way and that, move about in confusion........**0402, 0401** |
| | | 往時 おうじ bygone days.....................**0383** |
| | | 往古より おうこより from time immemorial...**0254** |

| **0866** | Recall 主 *main/lord*. Let "*lord* + *go*(彳)" suggest that the *lord* **GOES ON** to the next world, that is, **passes away**. ☞ 住 0366, 征 0868, 従 0869 |
|---|---|
| 彳 60 | |
| 徃 | |
| 0261 | |
| 常 8 | |

| 柱 | PILLAR, mainstay | ○電柱 でんちゅう power pole.................**0155** |
|---|---|---|
| | | 円柱 えんちゅう cylinder, column, shaft......**0013** |
| | | 門柱 もんちゅう gatepost.....................**0447** |
| | チュウ | 柱時計 はしらどけい grandfather clock........................**0383, 0555** |
| | はしら | ○大黒柱 だいこくばしら central pillar (of a house); mainstay..........................**0033, 0535** |

| **0867** | "*Main*(主) *tree*(木)": **PILLAR/mainstay**. |
|---|---|
| 木 75 | |
| 0797 | |
| 常 9 | |

| 征 | CONQUER, invade | 征戦 せいせん military expedition..........**0461** |
|---|---|---|
| | | ○出征する しゅっせいする go to war...........**0038** |
| | | 遠征 えんせい (punitive) expedition, invasion; tour.........................**0857** |
| | セイ | 征夷×大将軍 せいいたいしょうぐん Commander in Chief of the Expeditionary Force Against the Barbarians.................**0033, 0614, 0583** |

| **0868** | 彳 here refers to *going* into action and 正 refers to *right*eousness, together implying a campaign, such as a crusade, with allegedly righteous motivations. It means **CONQUER** or invade. ☞ 往 0866, 従 0869 |
|---|---|
| 彳 60 | |
| 0262 | |
| 常 8 | |

249

**FOLLOW, obey**

ジュウ ショウ ジュ
したが(う) したが(える)

従者 じゅうしゃ follower, attendant............0107
従的 じゅうてき subordinate, secondary.....0169
○従来の じゅうらいの former, existing........0274
○従う したがう follow, attend on; obey
…に従って …にしたがって in accordance with …;
in proportion to …

| 0869 | Here S4–5 change the meaning from CONQUER (征) to <u>being conquered</u>—that is, having to **FOLLOW** or **obey** someone. Therefore, we should see S4–5 as beating down the conqueror's "righteous" cause. Practice writing the two kanji in alternation, learning to identify their meanings by the presence or absence of these two strokes. ☞ 往 0866, 征 0868, 徒 0870 |
|---|---|
| 彳 60 | |
| 従 | |
| 0376 | |
| 常 10 | |

¹**FOLLOWER, pupil**
²**FELLOW(S)**
³**GOING ON FOOT**

ト

¹仏教徒 ぶっきょうと Buddhist (faithful) 0811, 0632
¹学徒 がくと student, follower................0099
①生徒 せいと pupil, student...................0036
²徒党 ととう clique, faction, conspirators....0319
③徒歩五分 とほごふん five minutes on foot
.................................0679, 0007, 0088

| 0870 | 彳 represents a person walking behind (i.e., **FOLLOWING ON FOOT**) another person who is *running* (走). Generally speaking, this kanji means **GOING ON FOOT** or "useless" when it is at the front (i.e., attributive position) of a compound, and **FOLLOWER** or **pupil** when it is at the rear of a compound. ☞ 待 0386, 従 0869 |
|---|---|
| 彳 60 | |
| 0377 | |
| 常 10 | |

**VERTICAL**

ジュウ
たて

○縦の たての vertical, longitudinal
縦書き たてがき vertical writing ............0079
縦軸 たてじく vertical axis, y-axis............0692
○縦断 じゅうだん cutting vertically............0849
縦線 じゅうせん vertical line, bar [in music]... 0210
たてせん vertical line

| 0871 | Think of 糸 *thread* as a plumb line. What does a plumb line *obey* (従)? **VERTICALITY**. |
|---|---|
| 糸 120 | |
| 縦 | |
| 1286 | |
| 常 16 | |

¹**EXTEND**
²**POSTPONE**

エン
の(びる) の(べる) の(べ) の(ばす)

①延長 えんちょう extension, prolongation,
continuation ........................0091
²延期 えんき postponement, deferment.....0486
○延びる のびる be extended, be prolonged
延べる のべる [vt] extend; postpone
延ばす のばす [vt] extend, prolong; postpone

| 0872 | Here we encounter two new graphemes: a new variant of 正 (which we'll conflate with the usual version), and ㄠ (which depicts a long stride and means *stretch one's legs* or *stretch*, and is not to be confused with 辶). In this entry, we have "*stretch straight*," which suggests **EXTENDING** something fully. ☞ 延 0877 |
|---|---|
| ㄠ 54 | |
| 2646 | |
| 常 8 | |

| 伸 | **STRETCH, grow**<br><br>シン<br>の(びる) の(ばす) の(べる) | ○二伸 にしん postscript, P.S..................**0003**<br>続伸する ぞくしんする continue to rise......**0354**<br>○伸びる のびる [vi] stretch, extend, spread, grow, develop<br>伸ばす のばす [vt] stretch, elongate, extend, spread<br>引き伸ばす ひきのばす stretch out, elongate; enlarge (photographs)....................**0422** |
|---|---|---|

| **0873**<br>人 9<br><br>0054<br>常 7 | Imagine the *man* (イ) **STRETCHING** his body to *pierce through layers* (申) (concretely, imagine him **STRETCHING** as high as he can to try to force his head through the ceiling). Note that all kanji incorporating 申 have the *on-yomi* シン. |
|---|---|

| 紳 | **GENTLEMAN**<br><br>シン | ○紳士 しんし gentleman......................**0350**<br>紳士用 しんしよう men's (clothing, etc.)<br>................................**0350, 0047**<br>紳士靴 しんしぐつ men's shoes........**0350, 0593**<br>紳商 しんしょう merchant prince, rich merchant<br>................................**0351** |
|---|---|---|

| **0874**<br>糸 120<br><br>1221<br>常 11 | Imagine that the distinction of a **GENTLEMAN** is to have his initials sewn into his shirts. Here the long vertical line (S11) shows us the *thread* (糸) *piercing* (申) down through the shirt fabric to mark the owner's **GENTLEMANLY** status. ☞ 細 0239 |
|---|---|

| 縮 | **SHRINK, curl up**<br><br>シュク<br>ちぢ(む) ちぢ(まる) ちぢ(める)<br>ちぢ(れる) ちぢ(らす) | 伸縮 しんしゅく expansion and contraction...**0873**<br>○縮小 しゅくしょう reduction, curtailment, cut **0034**<br>短縮 たんしゅく shortening, contraction......**0562**<br>○縮む ちぢむ [vi] shrink, contract<br>縮れる ちぢれる [vi] be wavy, curl; be wrinkled |
|---|---|---|

| **0875**<br>糸 120<br><br>1290<br>常 17 | Review 宿 0292. The present entry tells us that the *threads* (糸) in *lodge* (宿) linens are all **SHRUNK**/curled up from being washed every day. |
|---|---|

| 誕 | **BE BORN**<br><br>タン | ○誕生 たんじょう birth, nativity.................**0036**<br>誕生日 たんじょうび birthday...........**0036, 0001**<br>生誕 せいたん birth, nativity.................**0036** |
|---|---|---|

| **0876**<br>言 149<br><br>1430<br>常 15 | Let 延 suggest the fully *extended* (i.e., spread) legs of a mother giving **BIRTH**, and 言 the crying of a baby **BEING BORN**. Note that S8 in this entry (and S1 in the next entry) must be written from right to left (except for the special combinations noted in Appendix 1, always write slanting strokes downward). ☞ 艇 0879 |
|---|---|

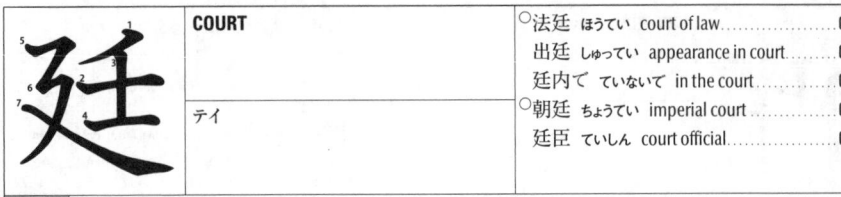

| COURT | ○法廷 ほうてい court of law .................... 0139 |
| テイ | 出廷 しゅってい appearance in court ........ 0038 |
| | 廷内で ていないで in the court ............... 0215 |
| | ○朝廷 ちょうてい imperial court ............... 0145 |
| | 廷臣 ていしん court official .................... 0484 |

| 0877 | Recall 壬 *courtier*, introduced at 任 0372. Here we observe the *courtier* striding around the **COURT** to *stretch his legs* (廴). ☞ 延 0872, 庭 0878 |
| 廴 54 | |
| 2631 | |
| 常 7 | |

| ¹ COURTYARD | ¹校庭 こうてい schoolyard, campus ........... 0103 |
| ² GARDEN | ²庭園 ていえん garden, park ................. 0856 |
| テイ | ² 石庭 せきてい rock garden ................. 0403 |
| にわ | ²庭師 にわし gardener ....................... 0748 |
| | 家庭 かてい home, family, household ... 0219 |

| 0878 | To the previous entry we now add 广 to indicate a protective enclosure encompassing the *court*: a **COURTYARD**. ☞ 廷 0877 |
| 广 53 | |
| 2684 | |
| 常 10 | |

| BOAT | ○舟艇 しゅうてい boat, craft .................... 0668 |
| テイ | 艇身 ていしん boat length .................... 0060 |
| | 艇庫 ていこ boat house ...................... 0694 |
| | 艇長 ていちょう coxswain, captain (of a submarine) ................................ 0091 |
| | 警備艇 けいびてい guardship ......... 0806, 0715 |

| 0879 | Picture an aristocratic garden of the Heian era, with an open pavilion that stretches out over a pond. From the shade of the pavilion, the members of the imperial *court* (廷) view a passing **BOAT** (舟). Note that both characters incorporating 廷 follow its *on* reading, テイ. ☞ 誕 0876 |
| 舟 137 | |
| 1246 | |
| 常 13 | |

| ¹ UNFOLD, develop | ¹展開 てんかい unfolding, development; deployment .............................. 0450 |
| ² DISPLAY | ¹ 発展 はってん expansion, development; prosperity ............................... 0148 |
| テン | ¹ 伸展する しんてんする expand, extend ..... 0873 |
| | ²展示する てんじする put on display, exhibit 0311 |
| | ² ダリ展 ダリてん Dali exhibition |

| 0880 | The root meaning of **DISPLAY** is **UNFOLD**, so M1 and M2 in fact refer to the same action. Perceive that action in this kanji by visualizing a *door* (尸) with a *noren* partition **UNFOLDED/ DISPLAYED** beneath it. The *noren* is made of *cloth* (S8–10, a three-stroke variant of 衣), split at the bottom but stitched *together* (S4–7, from 共) across the top. |
| 尸 44 | |
| 2681 | |
| 常 10 | |

| | ¹ PALACE | ¹ 殿堂 てんどう hall, palace, shrine; sanctuary... **0320** |
| | ² FORMAL HONORIFIC TITLE | ¹ 御殿 ごてん palace ............................ **0862** |
| | | ② 殿下 でんか His Imperial Highness ........ **0040** |
| | デン テン | ² 殿様 とのさま feudal lord.................... **0501** |
| | との -どの | ² 山田太郎殿 やまだたろうどの Taro Yamada, Esq. |
| | | ......................... **0037, 0020, 0294, 0286** |

**0881**
殳 79

First note how 屍 differs from the previous entry. See it as a closed door (a *door* that is joined "*together*" (共) with its door frame), specifically, the closed gate of a PALACE, now under attack by a unit of *lancers* (殳). Also used as an exalted HONORIFIC TITLE.

1593
常 13

| | DIFFERENT | ○ 異常な いじょうな abnormal, unusual, extraordinary ................................... **0321** |
| | | 驚異 きょうい wonder, marvel, miracle ...... **0807** |
| | イ | 異例 いれい singular case, exception ....... **0721** |
| | こと こと(なる) | 異にする ことにする differ, be different |
| | | ○ 異なる ことなる different, be different from |

**0882**
田 102

Two DIFFERENT ways of arranging six sticks: 田 and 共 (let's think of sticks—rather than brushstrokes—because 田 is written in five strokes, not six).

2241
常 11

| | WING | 翼状 よくじょう wing-shaped.................. **0616** |
| | | ○ 左翼 さよく left wing...................... **0401** |
| | | ○ 右翼 うよく right wing .................... **0402** |
| | ヨク | 主翼 しゅよく wing (of an aircraft)........... **0365** |
| | つばさ | ○ 翼を広げる つばさをひろげる spread the wings |
| | | ....................................... **0238** |

**0883**
羽 124

Two very *different* (異) *wings* (羽): the left WING, and the right WING. ☞ 糞 1892

2373
常 17

| | ¹ CUMULATE | ① 累積 るいせき accumulation ................. **0832** |
| | ² ENCUMBER | ¹ 累計 るいけい total........................... **0555** |
| | | ¹ 累犯者 るいはんしゃ repeat offender...**0735, 0107** |
| | ルイ | ¹ 累進 るいしん successive promotions; progressive (tax, etc.) ............................... **0191** |
| | | ² 連累 れんるい involvement, implication....**0582** |

**0884**
糸 120

Visualize an entire *rice field* (田) CUMULATING on top of a single *thread* (糸), ENCUMBERING it. See 係 1078 for another compound using M2. ☞ 細 0239

2242
常 11

| | ¹ BASE<br>² SMALL FORT<br><br>ルイ | ¹ 三塁 さんるい  third base.................0004<br>①満塁ホームラン まんるいホームラン  grand-slam<br>　　　　home run..........................0179<br>②土塁 どるい  earthwork, parapet...........0030 |
|---|---|---|

| 0885<br>土 32<br>畾<br>2250<br>常 12 | Here we can see the four **BASES** of a baseball diamond (S6-9), with 土 *earth* in the foreground (the infield) and 田 *field* in the background (the outfield). Comparing with the traditional form, note that S6-9 are written in lieu of writing the upper grapheme two more times; this simplification also occurs in 渋 1234 and 摂 1235. |
|---|---|

| | **OFFICIAL**<br><br>リ | 官吏 かんり  government official.............0290<br>公吏 こうり  public official ...................0089<br>○吏員 りいん  official...........................0317 |
|---|---|---|

| 0886<br>口 30<br>2963<br>常 6 | Hind view of an **OFFICIAL**'s horse (S1 is its head, S2-4 are its body, and the bottom two lines are its legs). Though we see a horse, it is (as a stand-alone kanji) only a symbol of **OFFICIAL-DOM**. The next five kanji all resemble this one, so compare them as you go, linking each one's distinctive features with its meaning. ☞ 使 0887, 史 0888, 更 0889 |
|---|---|

| | ¹ USE<br>² ENVOY, dispatch<br><br>シ<br>つか(う) つか(い) -つか(い) -づか(い) | ①使用する しようする  use, employ, apply ....0047<br>¹ 使用中 しようちゅう  in use, occupied...0047, 0035<br>①使い方 つかいかた  how to use, usage.......0173<br>² 大使 たいし  ambassador.....................0033<br>² 天使 てんし  angel............................0270 |
|---|---|---|

| 0887<br>人 9<br>0072<br>常 8 | Seeing here a *man* (イ) about to mount the *official's horse*, we should perceive it as being **USED**/dispatched on a mission. We can easily remember M2 **ENVOY** as a <u>person who is dispatched</u>. Again, be sure to review similarities and distinctions as you proceed through this tricky set of kanji (ending at 硬 0891). ☞ 史 0888, 吏 0886, 便 0890 |
|---|---|

| | **HISTORY**<br><br>シ | 史上に しじょうに  in history, in the annals...0041<br>史料 しりょう  historical materials/records...0758<br>史書 ししょ  history book......................0079<br>史学者 しがくしゃ  historian.............0099, 0107<br>○世界史 せかいし  world history........0604, 0612 |
|---|---|---|

| 0888<br>口 30<br>2946<br>常 5 | See this as the dead body of an *official's horse*, now in an advanced state of decomposition. It has been dead so long, in fact, that the remains of its head (see 吏 above) have now disappeared. Visualize this kanji as something that has long since passed away, and you should be able to remember that it means **HISTORY**. ☞ 吏 0886, 使 0887 |
|---|---|

| 更 | **1 RENEW, replace**<br>**2 FURTHERMORE**<br>**3 GROW LATE**<br><br>コウ<br>さら　さら(に)　ふ(ける)　ふ(かす) | ① 更新する こうしんする renew, renovate .....0275<br>1 変更する へんこうする alter, change, modify<br> ................................................0775<br>2 尚更 なおさら still more, all the more .......0184<br>② 更に さらに furthermore; still more<br>3 更ける ふける grow late, wear on |
|---|---|---|

| **0889**<br>日 73<br><br>2967<br>常　7 | After an *official's horse* (吏) ages, it retires and begins a new career in postal delivery. As this entry shows, it is renovated (i.e., **RENEWED**) for its new career by having its head raised (note how it now sits at the very top of the central vertical stroke), and by having a mailbag tied onto its back—visible here as a second layer on its body, which should be our visual focus. Train your brain to let this "new" or "additional" layer on the horse's body remind you of the ideas **RENEWAL** and **FURTHERMORE**. M3 **GROW LATE** can also be associated with the idea of adding on. ☞ 吏 0886, 便 0890 |
|---|---|

| 便 | **1 CONVENIENT**<br>**2 POSTAL DELIVERY, transportation service, flight**<br>**3 EXCRETA**<br><br>ベン　ビン<br>たよ(り) | ① 便利な べんりな convenient, handy, useful 0412<br>1 不便な ふべんな inconvenient .............0049<br>② 次の便 つぎのびん next post; next flight ...0278<br>② 便り たより news, tidings; correspondence, letter<br>③ 便器 べんき toilet bowl, urinal.............0295 |
|---|---|---|

| **0890**<br>人 9<br><br>0075<br>常　9 | This kanji's meanings are diverse. Lay a foundation for all of them by perceiving in 便 an image, building on 更 0889, of a <u>postal delivery horse departing on its route</u>. We know that it is on its way, because the postman (亻) has now arrived to lead it away (contra 更). This image serves us well for M2 **POSTAL DELIVERY**, and for the modern **transportation services** to which this kanji now refers, such as trains and **flights**. Also, the idea of **DELIVERY** is easy to associate with the way the body "sends out" **EXCRETA** (M3). **CONVENIENCE** (M1) can be associated with our original image of a postal delivery horse departing on its route, via the idea of timely **transportation service** departures. ☞ 使 0887, 更 0889 |
|---|---|

|  | **HARD**<br><br>コウ<br>かた(い) | 硬度 こうど hardness .........................0280<br>硬化する こうかする harden, stiffen.........0120<br>硬骨 こうこつ hard bone; firmness ..........0465<br>○ 強硬 きょうこう firm (attitude), unbending; drastic (measure)..............................0423<br>○ 硬い石 かたいいし hard stone...............0403 |
|---|---|---|

| **0891**<br>石 112<br><br>1095<br>常　12 | Before studying this entry, take a moment to take stock of the following: (1) 吏 is an OFFICIAL's horse, while 更 has been "RENEWED" for postal delivery; and (2) 使 shows a horse being USED/dispatched, while 便 shows a POSTAL DELIVERY horse departing on its route … Now to address the present entry, 硬: let 石 suggest the **HARD** *stones* the *postal delivery horse* must tread upon. Once you've practiced writing this kanji, cover up the definitions for entries 0886–91 and test yourself. Go randomly through the six entries, pick out their distinguishing features, and see if you can relate these to the kanji's meaning(s). |
|---|---|

|  | **1 ABILITY; function**<br>**2 NOH DRAMA**<br><br>ノウ | 1 才能 さいのう talent, ability .................0652<br>① 能力 のうりょく ability, capacity, faculty......0084<br>1 機能 きのう function, faculty.................0473<br>1 可能な かのうな possible, feasible ..........0814<br>② 能楽 のうがく Noh drama.................0302 |
|---|---|---|

| **0892**<br>肉 130<br><br>1207<br>常　10 | 月 here gives us the semantic category *body part*, encouraging us to see 厶 as an *arm bent at the elbow* (recall 広 0238). Complete the image by also seeing the two ヒs as limbs. We thus visualize a body with bendable limbs that point in various directions, symbolizing diverse **ABILITIES**/functions. M2 **NOH DRAMA** is an exhibition of dramatic **ABILITY**. |
|---|---|

**¹ STATE, condition**
**² POSTURE, attitude**

タイ

①状態 じょうたい state, condition, appearance, situation, aspect.............0616
¹ 事態 じたい situation, state of affairs.........0080
¹ 実態 じったい actual conditions, state.......0499
¹ 形態 けいたい shape, form, structure, morphology.............0147
②態度 たいど attitude, posture..............0280

| 0893 | |
|---|---|
| 心 61 | While 能 in the previous entry represents an *able* body, adding 心 here redirects our attention to the <u>state of *mind*</u> supporting the able body, like that of the martial artist, whose mental state underlies his physical ability. Associate both M1 **STATE**/**condition** and M2 **POSTURE**/**attitude** with this image of a person's enabling <u>state of mind</u>. ☞ 態 0894 |
| **2478** | |
| 常 14 | |

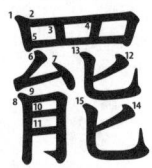

**BEAR**

くま

白熊 しろくま polar bear.....................0076
黒熊 くろくま black bear.....................0535
熊本 くまもと Kumamoto (city and prefecture).............0031

| 0894 | |
|---|---|
| 火 86 | See 灬 as **BEAR** claws protracting from the end of 能's various limbs (see 0892). ☞ 態 0893 |
| **2479** | |
| 常 14 | |

**DISCONTINUE**

ヒ
や(める)*

○罷業 ひぎょう work stoppage, strike.........0498
○罷める やめる discontinue

| 0895 | |
|---|---|
| 网 122 | To perceive the idea **DISCONTINUE** here, visualize 罒 as a curtain just now beginning to fall on a *Noh drama* (能). ☞ 羅 0896 |
| **2272** | |
| 常 15 | |

**¹ LINE UP, arrange**
**² PHONETIC [ra]**

ラ

¹ 羅列する られつする arrange, itemize......0718
①羅針盤 らしんばん compass............0556, 0673
² 曼×陀×羅 まんだら mandala
² 天麩×羅 てんぷら tempura.................0270

| 0896 | |
|---|---|
| 网 122 | Here we observe a *bird* (隹) holding *thread* (糸) in its beak and **LINING** it **UP** in three straight columns to make a *net* (罒). Focus visually on the three neatly **arranged** columns at the top. ☞ 罷 0895 |
| **2278** | |
| 常 19 | |

**CLOUD**

ウン
くも　-ぐも

雲海　うんかい　sea of clouds .................0106
雲間　くもま　rift between clouds ............0448
○雨雲　あまぐも　rain clouds ....................0154
入道雲　にゅうどうぐも　cumulonimbus 0039, 0158
キノコ雲　キノコぐも　mushroom cloud

| 0897 | Review 伝 0223. Here we combine *rain* (⻗) and *cloud* (云) into the kanji for **CLOUD**. 雷雲 (らいうん, see 雷, just ahead) is probably a more useful *on-yomi* compound to memorize than VI. ☞ 曇 0898 |
|---|---|
| 雨 173 | |
| 2415 | |
| 常 12 | |

**CLOUDY**

ドン
くも（る）

○曇天　どんてん　cloudy weather ..............0270
○曇る　くもる　become cloudy
曇り空　くもりぞら　cloudy sky ................0398
曇りがち　くもりがち　cloudy
花曇り　はなぐもり　cloudy weather in springtime
.................................................0121

| 0898 | *Clouds* (雲) blocking out the *sun* (日): **CLOUDY**. ☞ 雲 0897 |
|---|---|
| 日 72 | |
| 2195 | |
| 常 16 | |

**SNOW**

セツ
ゆき

雪上車　せつじょうしゃ　snowmobile ....0041, 0125
○新雪　しんせつ　fresh snow ....................0275
雪合戦　ゆきがっせん　snowball fight ...0227, 0461
雪祭り　ゆきまつり　Snow Festival ............0637
○初雪　はつゆき　first snow of the season ......0710

| 0899 | See ⺕ as a shovel, scooping up **SNOW** that falls from a snow *cloud* (⻗). |
|---|---|
| 雨 173 | |
| 2406 | |
| 常 11 | |

**THUNDER**

ライ
かみなり

○雷雨　らいう　thunderstorm ....................0154
雷電　らいでん　thunder and lightning, thunder-
bolt .........................................0155
雷雲　らいうん　thundercloud ................0897
地雷　じらい　land mine .......................0187
○雷親父　かみなりおやじ　irascible old man
.................................................0276, 0100

| 0900 | Recall that 电 in 電 0155 represents lightning. In this entry, there is no lightning bolt (乚) extending down toward the earth, so we only hear **THUNDER**. ☞ 電 0155 |
|---|---|
| 雨 173 | |
| 2432 | |
| 常 13 | |

**ZERO**

レイ

| | |
|---|---|
| 零度 れいど | zero degrees, freezing point...0280 |
| 零下 れいか | below zero, sub-zero...........0040 |
| ○零時 れいじ | twelve o'clock .................0383 |
| 零点 れいてん | (score of) zero ...............0349 |
| 零勝二敗 れいしょうにはい | 0 wins, 2 losses |
| | .................0460, 0003, 0830 |

| 0901 | Focus on 人, visualizing it as a solid, sweeping *roof* that permits exactly **ZERO** drops of *rain* (雨) to penetrate into the house—a **ZERO**-tolerance roof, if you will. The *on-yomi* follows 令, 冷, and 齢. |
|---|---|
| 雨 173 | |
| 2433 | |
| 常 13 | |

---

**QUAKE, tremble**

シン
ふる(う) ふる(える)

| | |
|---|---|
| ○地震 じしん | earthquake .....................0187 |
| 震動 しんどう | shock, tremor, vibration......0540 |
| 震源地 しんげんち | epicenter..........0209, 0187 |
| 震度 しんど | seismic intensity ..............0280 |
| ○震える ふるえる | tremble, shudder |

| 0902 | Review 辰 0510. Here, a powerful, *dragon*-like *rain*storm (雨) causes everything to **tremble** and **QUAKE**. |
|---|---|
| 雨 173 | |
| 2443 | |
| 常 15 | |

---

**SWING, wave, wield, pretend**

シン
ふ(る) ぶ(る) ふ(り) -ぶ(り)
ふ(るう) ふ(れる)

| | |
|---|---|
| ○振動 しんどう | vibration ......................0540 |
| 不振 ふしん | dullness, depression, stagnation, slump ..........................0049 |
| ○手を振る てをふる | wave one's hand.........0046 |
| 腕を振るう うでをふるう | show one's ability...0732 |
| 死んだ振りをする しんだふりをする | play dead ...0716 |

| 0903 | Vividly imagine the *hand* (扌) taking the *dragon* (辰) by its beard (lower part of S5) and **SWINGING** it violently in circles, its long mane **waving** in the air behind it. |
|---|---|
| 手 64 | |
| 0388 | |
| 常 10 | |

---

**OF LONG DURATION**

キュウ ク
ひさ(しい)

| | |
|---|---|
| ○持久 じきゅう | endurance......................0384 |
| 久遠 くおん | eternity .......................0857 |
| ○久しい ひさしい | long, longstanding |
| 久しい昔 ひさしいむかし | a long time ago....0359 |
| 久し振りに ひさしぶりに | after a long time, for the first time in a long while...........0903 |

| 0904 | Visualize as a person taking a **LONG** stride. ☞ 欠 0277 |
|---|---|
| ノ 4 | |
| 2867 | |
| 常 3 | |

**FLOURISH; be bustling**

シン
にぎ（わう）　にぎ（やか）

賑わう　にぎわう　flourish, prosper, be bustling
○賑やか　にぎやか　bustling

| 0905 | Picture a **bustling, FLOURISHING** downtown market where merchants busily exchange *dragons* (辰) for *seashells/money* (貝). |
| 貝 154 | |
| 1409 | |
| 名 14 | |

**HILL**

キュウ
おか

○砂丘　さきゅう　sand dune, sand hill ............ 0678
火口丘　かこうきゅう　volcanic cone ...... 0026, 0019
丘辺　おかべ　vicinity of a hill ................. 0195
○丘の上に　おかのうえに　on top of a hill ...... 0041

| 0906 | See this as a *hacksaw* 斤 thrust into the top of a **HILL** to stake a claim to it. ☞ 斤 0193, 兵 0907 |
| 一 1 | |
| 邱 | |
| 2931 | |
| 常 5 | |

**SOLDIER**

ヘイ　ヒョウ

兵士　へいし　soldier ........................ 0350
○兵隊　へいたい　soldier; troops ............... 0586
兵卒　へいそつ　private, common soldier .... 0751
兵役　へいえき　military service ............... 0518
兵器　へいき　arms, weapon, ordnance ..... 0295

| 0907 | Picture S6–7 as two **SOLDIERS** crawling up a *hill* (丘) battle-style, preparing to take it over from the party who claimed it with his hacksaw in the previous entry. Practice writing this entry and the last one in alternation, learning to identify their meanings by the presence or absence of S6–7. ☞ 丘 0906 |
| 八 12 | |
| 2207 | |
| 常 7 | |

**HIGH MOUNTAIN, peak**

ガク
たけ

岳友会　がくゆうかい　mountaineering club
.................................. 0399, 0226
○山岳　さんがく　mountains ................... 0037
北岳　きただけ　Mt. Kita ..................... 0122
朝日岳　あさひだけ　Mt. Asahi ........... 0145, 0001

| 0908 | When you put a *hill* 丘 on top of a *mountain* 山, you get an especially **HIGH MOUNTAIN**, a **peak** that stands out above the rest of the range. ☞ 峰 1378 |
| 山 46 | |
| 嶽 | |
| 2213 | |
| 常 8 | |

**BEACH**

ヒン
はま

| | | |
|---|---|---|
| ○海浜 | かいひん seashore, seaside, beach | 0106 |
| ○浜辺 | はまべ beach, seashore | 0195 |
| 砂浜 | すなはま sandy beach, sands | 0678 |
| 浜風 | はまかぜ beach wind | 0425 |
| 浜伝いに | はまづたいに along the beach | 0223 |

**0909**
水 85

濱
0394
常 10

Review 兵 0907. Here we observe *soldiers* (兵) emerging from the *water* (氵) to crawl up a sand dune on the **BEACH**, trying desperately to establish a beachhead. Note the traditional form, which is based on 賓 1962.

---

**HUT, building**

シャ

| | | |
|---|---|---|
| 兵舎 | へいしゃ barracks | 0907 |
| ○宿舎 | しゅくしゃ lodgings, quarters | 0292 |
| 校舎 | こうしゃ school building | 0103 |
| 駅舎 | えきしゃ station building | 0339 |
| 田舎 | いなか country, rural district | 0020 |

**0910**
人 9*

舎
1774
常 8

This character contains the "*earth* behind *door*" combination we saw back at 周 0304 (do not confuse with 吉 0514 LUCKY). Here we see a simple *roof* over an *earthen* floor with a *door* in the front: a **HUT**.

---

**ANOTHER TIME**

サイ サ
ふたた(び)

| | | |
|---|---|---|
| 再度 | さいど another time, a second time | 0280 |
| 再開 | さいかい reopening, resumption | 0450 |
| ○再生 | さいせい reclamation; regeneration; resuscitation; playback | 0036 |
| 再来週 | さらいしゅう the week after next | 0274, 0305 |
| ○再び読む | ふたたびよむ reread | 0355 |

**0911**
冂 13

2950
常 6

*Work* (工) another *month* (月): **ANOTHER TIME**. Learn to write this kanji by heart, as it will appear inside others you'll learn soon. The reading ふたたび combines ふたつ (see 二 0003 TWO) and たび (see 度 0280 TIME).

---

**TIGER**

コ
とら

| | | |
|---|---|---|
| ○虎穴 | こけつ tiger's den; dangerous place | 0397 |
| 虎口 | ここう tiger's den; dangerous place | 0019 |
| ○虎の巻 | とらのまき key, crib, pony; secret (of a trade) | 0458 |

**0912**
虍 141

虍
2766
常 8

Picture 虍 as the entrance to a **TIGER**'s lair, located beneath a *craggy cliff* (review 皮 0595). At the top of the entrance appear the lowercase letters "r" and "t," for *regnum tigrium* (realm of the **TIGER**). The full character includes 儿 *human legs*, suggesting a half-eaten person.

**(sign of) THE TIGER**

イン
とら

○寅年 とらとし Year of the Tiger.................0117

| 0913 | While the previous entry is used to refer to TIGER the animal, this one refers to the horary |
|---|---|
| ⼧ 40 | sign of **THE TIGER**. Picture a tiger-skin trophy, hung on a wall under someone's *roof*. S4 represents its head, S10–11 the skin of its hind legs. Its stripes make a crossing design on its back (田). ☞ 冥 1592 |
| 1981 | |
| 名 11 | |

**PERFORM**

エン

主演する しゅえんする play the leading part 0365
上演する じょうえんする put on stage........0041
○出演する しゅつえんする appear on stage,
　perform.................................................0038
独演 どくえん solo performance.............0346
ロミオを演じる ロミオをえんじる play the part of
　Romeo

| 0914 | Like all cats, tigers do not like to get wet. Create a scene in your imagination of a circus |
|---|---|
| 水 85 | **PERFORMANCE** involving a trainer with a *water* hose and a *tiger*. If you prefer to see a tiger <u>skin</u>, as in the last entry, the story works just as well with a human actor dressed in a tiger's skin and **PERFORMING** its role. The reading エン can be associated with the English word "EN-tertain." |
| 0630 | |
| 常 14 | |

**YELLOW**

コウ オウ
き こ-

黄河 こうが Yellow River......................0818
○黄色 きいろ (=こうしょく, おうしょく) yellow.....0528
黄金 こがね (=おうごん) gold; money........0029
黄身 きみ egg yolk.............................0060

| 0915 | A reasonable way to remember that this kanji means **YELLOW** is to picture a girl wearing |
|---|---|
| 黄 201 | blonde pigtails (either end of S1) and a yellow *tiger*-skin dress. Note the variant forms for this and the next entry. |
| 黄 | |
| 2177 | |
| 常 11 | |

横

¹ **SIDEWAYS, across**

² **ARBITRARY, despotic**

オウ
よこ

①横断する おうだんする cross, traverse.......0849
¹ 縦横に じゅうおうに (=たてよこに) vertically and
　horizontally; freely.............................0871
¹ 横軸 よこじく X-axis, horizontal axis........0692
² 横行する おうこうする be rampant, overrun,
　swagger, strut...................................0055
②専横 せんおう arbitrariness, despotism.....0580

| 0916 | Picture a *wooden* (木) barricade painted *yellow* (黄) for easy visibility, laid out **SIDEWAYS** |
|---|---|
| 木 75 | across the road. Once you've given your mind enough time to fix the association between *yellow wood* and **SIDEWAYS/across**, associate **SIDEWAYS** with **ARBITRARY/despotic** through the notion of running contrary to the normal, reasonable course. ☞ 構 0917 |
| 横 | |
| 0979 | |
| 常 15 | |

| | ¹ **CONSTRUCT, frame**<br>² **MIND, care about** | ¹ 構成 こうせい composition, construction, formation, organization .......................... 0070<br>① 構造 こうぞう structure, construction, framework ........................................................ 0699 |
|---|---|---|
| | コウ<br>かま(える) かま(う) | ¹ 構想する こうそうする conceive, contrive; plan... 0683<br>① 構える かまえる set up (a house); assume a posture, make ready<br>² 構わない かまわない do not care/mind |

| **0917**<br>木 75 | First note how 黄 YELLOW differs from this entry's 冓. The latter is composed of 丯, which we'll see as a scaffold, and 再 *"again,"* which suggests "repeating" the scaffold, i.e., assembling a multilevel structure. Now associate 木 *lumber* and 冓 *scaffolding structure* with CONSTRUCT. MIND/care about relates to CONSTRUCT via the idea of "taking a stand." ☞ 横 0916 |
|---|---|
| **0962**<br>常 14 | |

| | **LECTURE** | ○講演 こうえん lecture........................... 0914<br>講堂 こうどう lecture hall, auditorium........ 0320<br>講座 こうざ lectureship, (professor's) chair; course of study ............................. 0749 |
|---|---|---|
| | コウ | 講師 こうし speaker, lecturer.................. 0748<br>講話 こうわ lecture, discourse .............. 0053 |

| **0918**<br>言 149 | Think of a LECTURE as a multilevel *structure* (冓) of *words* (言). Note that this set of four kanji with the phonetic component 冓 are all pronounced コウ. ☞ 譲 1662 |
|---|---|
| **1463**<br>常 17 | |

| | **PURCHASE** | 購買 こうばい purchase, buying ............. 0352<br>購読 こうどく subscription.................... 0355<br>○購入 こうにゅう purchase, buying ............ 0039<br>購書 こうしょ purchasing books.............. 0079 |
|---|---|---|
| | コウ | |

| **0919**<br>貝 154 | Here let 冓 *scaffolding structure* suggest a neatly arranged stack of *shells* (貝, representing *money*) on a store counter, used to PURCHASE something. |
|---|---|
| **1467**<br>常 17 | |

| | **CHANNEL, ditch** | 側溝 そっこう channel, ditch, gutter ......... 0626<br>排水溝 はいすいこう drainage, canal... 0739, 0027<br>○海溝 かいこう sea trench...................... 0106<br>溝レール みぞレール grooved rail |
|---|---|---|
| | コウ<br>みぞ | |

| **0920**<br>水 85 | Picture 氵 as a CHANNEL of *water,* and 冓 as *scaffolding structure* built alongside the CHANNEL to restrain the earth so that the water can pass smoothly. |
|---|---|
| **0604**<br>常 13 | |

| | ¹ TEMPORARY, provisional<br>² FAKE | ① 仮に かりに provisionally; for example;<br>supposing that<br>¹ 仮設の かせつの temporary; hypothetic ... 0520 |
|---|---|---|
| | カ ケ<br>かり かり- | ① 仮定 かてい assumption, supposition ...... 0045<br>² 仮面 かめん mask, disguise ................. 0175<br>仮名 かな kana, Japanese syllabary ........ 0269<br>かめい pseudonym, alias |

| 0921<br>人 9<br>假<br>0034<br>常 6 | Sometimes you just need something to "lean on" **TEMPORARILY** or **provisionally** for the purpose of accomplishing a specific task at hand, even though you will replace it later. Here a *man* (イ) leans *against* (反) something **TEMPORARY**. We can also think of it as **FAKE**, since it is just a provisional substitute, not the real thing. |
|---|---|

|  | ¹ FRAGMENT<br>² ONE OF TWO | ① 断片 だんぺん fragment, piece ............. 0849<br>¹ 破片 はへん fragment, broken piece, scrap 0596<br>² 片面 かためん one side, one face ........... 0175 |
|---|---|---|
| | ヘン<br>かた- かた | ② 片道 かたみち one-way ..................... 0158<br>片仮名 かたかな katakana script ...... 0921, 0269 |

| 0922<br>片 91<br><br>2910<br>常 4 | Review 将 0614. The present entry gives the second half of the split tree trunk (the first half 丬, seen earlier in the notes for 将, is generally simplified to 丬). The two halves appear together in kanji like 淵 1492. By comparing with 淵, we can see 片 by itself as a mere **FRAGMENT** of the original, **ONE** part **OF TWO**. |
|---|---|

| | ¹ PRINTING PLATE<br>² PUBLISHING, printing | ¹ 版画 はんが woodcut print ................. 0176<br>¹ 木版 もくはん woodblock printing, wood<br>engraving ............................ 0028 |
|---|---|---|
| | ハン | ② 出版 しゅっぱん publishing; publication .... 0038<br>² 初版 しょはん first edition ................. 0710<br>² 英語版 えいごばん English edition .... 0332, 0222 |

| 0923<br>片 91<br><br>0775<br>常 8 | Continuing from the previous entry, note that both halves of the split tree trunk, 片 and 丬, can signify *wooden block* or *tablet* inside other kanji. In this entry, we observe the act of **PRINTING** by placing a sheet of paper (not shown) *against* (反) a *wooden block* (片). M2 **PUBLISHING** is a derivative meaning. |
|---|---|

|  | ¹ BOARD<br>² PLATE | ① 黒板 こくばん blackboard .................. 0535<br>¹ 土の上に板を置く つちのうえにいたをおく<br>place boards on the dirt ........ 0030, 0041, 0843 |
|---|---|---|
| | ハン バン<br>いた | ① 床板 ゆかいた floorboard ................. 0851<br>¹ どぶ板 どぶいた boards covering a drainage ditch<br>² 鉄板 てっぱん iron plate ................. 0564 |

| 0924<br>木 75<br><br>0762<br>常 8 | Think of a **BOARD** or **PLATE** as a piece of *wood* (木) you set things *against* (反). In English we would not say "against" but "on" (as in "on board"), but to learn this kanji, try to think of setting things *against* a board or a plate, such as writing "*against*" a blackboard (V1) or frying "*against*" an iron plate (V5). |
|---|---|

**ENGAGE IN SALES**

ハン

○販売する はんばいする sell, market.........0353
自動販売機 じどうはんばいき vending machine
..............0081, 0540, 0353, 0473
再販 さいはん resale.......................0911
販路 はんろ market, outlet...............0788
市販 しはん marketing....................0205

| 0925 | Here 貝 represents an offer of *money* from a buyer, while 反 represents the *opposite* activity, |
| 貝 154 | that of **ENGAGING IN SALES**. |
| 1343 | |
| 常 11 | |

---

**¹ RIGHTEOUSNESS**
**² MEANING, sense**
**³ SUBSTITUTE, artificial**

ギ

① 義理 ぎり sense of duty/honor, obligation,
debt of gratitude; justice; courtesy.........0532
② 定義 ていぎ definition.....................0045
² 講義 こうぎ lecture.........................0918
³ 義歯 ぎし artificial tooth, denture.......0674
③ 義父 ぎふ father-in-law; foster father, stepfather
..............0100

| 0926 | Review 我 0221 SELF. Here the *self* demonstrates its **RIGHTEOUSNESS** by sacrificing a *sheep* |
| 羊 123 | (羊) to God. This surrendering of a material possession in favor of a spiritual principle sym- |
| | bolizes the idea of **MEANING**. M3 **SUBSTITUTE/artificial** comes from the idea of having the |
| 2052 | same **MEANING** or significance while not actually being the thing itself. |
| 常 13 | |

---

**¹ DISCUSS**
**² LEGISLATIVE BODY**

ギ

① 議決 ぎけつ decision, resolution...........0330
¹ 会議 かいぎ conference, meeting, council..0226
² 議会 ぎかい assembly, national assembly...0226
② 議院 ぎいん House, Diet Chamber.........0634
² 議員 ぎいん member of an assembly, Diet
member..............0317

| 0927 | Represents people's *speaking* (言) of *righteousness* (義), that is, **DISCUSSING** the right thing |
| 言 149 | to do. Note that all the kanji that incorporate 義 are pronounced ギ. |
| 1480 | |
| 常 20 | |

---

**CEREMONY, rite**

ギ

○ 儀式 ぎしき ceremony, rite, ritual...........0109
葬儀 そうぎ funeral service/rites.............0717
礼儀 れいぎ etiquette, courtesy, propriety,
manners..............0313
礼儀正しい れいぎただしい polite.....0313, 0043
行儀 ぎょうぎ manners, behavior...........0055

| 0928 | "*Man* (亻) + *righteousness* (義)" represents a man conducting a *rite* or **CEREMONY**, i.e., a |
| 人 9 | customary act felt to honor a *righteous* principle. Needless to say, the homophony of **rite** and |
| | *righteousness* can be helpful here. |
| 0147 | |
| 常 15 | |

## 犠 — SACRIFICE

ギ

犠飛 ぎひ [baseball] sacrifice fly ............0475

**0929**
牛 93

犠義

1010
常 | 17

Like the sheep in 義 RIGHTEOUS, the *cattle* (牛) are **SACRIFICED** to honor a *righteous* principle. The sample compound to memorize appears in the next entry.

---

## 牲 — SACRIFICE

セイ

○犠牲 ぎせい sacrifice .....................0929
犠牲者 ぎせいしゃ victim.............0929, 0107

**0930**
牛 93

0813
常 | 9

A *cow* (牛)'s *life* (生) is meant to be **SACRIFICED**. This kanji only appears as part of VI, so focus on learning that compound, rather than the kanji per se.

---

## 旨 — PURPORT, gist, aim

シ
むね うま(い)*

○要旨 ようし gist, summary, abstract; purport 0547
本旨 ほんし main object, true aim...........0031
主旨 しゅし gist, main point, substance .....0365
その旨を書き送る そのむねをかきおくる write
　(someone) to that effect..............0079, 0455
旨い うまい skillful, good at, wise; delicious

**0931**
日 72

1744
常 | 6

Refers to the essence or substance of something. Recalling from 化 0120 that ヒ means *spoon*, picture scooping out a *spoonful* of glistening golden *sun* (日) to examine its substance, its **gist**. The substance or **gist** of a person's remarks is their **PURPORT**.

---

## 指 — ¹FINGER / ²POINT (out)

シ
ゆび さ(す) -さ(し)

¹ 指の節 ゆびのふし finger joints.............0391
②指す さす point (with one's finger)
②指定する していする designate, appoint ...0045
² 指示する しじする instruct; indicate, point to
　...................................................0311
² 目指す めざす aim for, have an eye on......0021

**0932**
手 64

0337
常 | 9

Now imagine that a *hand* (扌) extends a **FINGER** and **POINTS** at something noticed in the *spoonful* of sun (previous entry). The meaning is not obvious here, so to remember it you must form a vivid mental image. Kanji in this course are not usually grouped by *kun-yomi*, but note that さ(す) homophones appear below at 刺 0935 and 差 0937. ☞ 脂 1994

**BRANDISH, wave**

キ

指揮する しきする conduct; command ..... 0932
○指揮者 しきしゃ conductor; commander
.................................................. 0932, 0107
発揮する はっきする display, demonstrate; put
to use .................................. 0148

| 0933 | See a *hand* (扌) **waving** orders at an *army* (軍). Imagine that it **BRANDISHES** something, such as a baton of command. |
| 手 64 | |

0538
常 | 12

**SHINE BRILLIANTLY**

キ
かがや(く)

輝度 きど brightness .......................... 0280
輝々 きき brilliance
光輝有る こうきある shining, brilliant, splendid
.................................................. 0137, 0400
○輝く かがやく shine brilliantly, glitter, light up
輝かしい かがやかしい bright, brilliant
.................................................. 0060

| 0934 | Like its boots, the *army's* armored vehicles (軍) **SHINE BRILLIANTLY** in the *light* (光) of the sun. |
| 車 159 | |

1280
常 | 15

**PIERCE, stab**

シ
さ(す) さ(さる) さ(し) さし

刺殺する しさつする stab to death .......... 0522
刺激 しげき stimulus; stimulation, excitation
.................................................. 0575
○名刺 めいし calling card ...................... 0269
○虫に刺される むしにさされる be stung by an
insect ................................... 0343
刺身 さしみ sashimi, sliced raw flesh (esp. of fish)
.................................................. 0060

| 0935 | 朿 looks like 木 with two thorns sticking out of it, and means *stab*. Together, 朿 and 刂 (*cut*) unambiguously denote **PIERCE/stab**. Do not confuse 朿 *stab* with 束 0307 BUNDLE. ☞ 制 0708 |
| 刀 18 | |

1171
常 | 8

**¹ SCHEME, plan**
**² MEASURE**

サク

¹ 政策 せいさく policy, political measures .... 0246
¹ 方策 ほうさく plan, policy, scheme .......... 0173
¹ 策略 さくりゃく artifice, stratagem, scheme ... 0791
②対策 たいさく countermeasure, counterplan 0650
² 施策 しさく measure, execution of a policy ... 0571

| 0936 | During World War II, the Japanese Imperial Army devised a **SCHEME** by which civilians would defend the homeland from foreign invaders by *stabbing* (朿) them with *bamboo* (⺮) spears. You can interpret this kanji to represent that **SCHEME/MEASURE**, or any other one people might use to take a "*stab*" at a problem. |
| 竹 118 | |

2338
常 | 12

| | DIVERGENCE, difference | 格差 かくさ differential, disparity............0789<br>○交差点 こうさてん crossing, intersection ("point of convergence and divergence").....0102, 0349<br>時差 じさ time difference....................0383<br>二分の差 にふんのさ a difference of two minutes...............................0003, 0088<br>○差す さす extend (one's hand); offer; hold (an umbrella); wear (in one's belt or hair) |
|---|---|---|
| | サ<br>さ(す) さ(し) | |

| **0937**<br>工 48 | Starts off like 羊, but then the line that points downward **DIVERGES** to the left (S7). Informed by 左 0401, let 工 suggest a stylized uppercase "L," for divergence to the "Left." See S7 as an arm held out at an angle to (i.e., **DIVERGING** from) the rest of the body, as if to extend a hand to someone, or to hold an umbrella (see V5). ☞ 着 0938, 羞 1671 |
|---|---|
| 2821 | |
| 常 10 | |

| | ¹ PUT ON (clothes)<br>² ARRIVE<br>³ STICK, adhere | 着る きる [vi] put on clothes, dress, wear<br>○着物 きもの clothes, kimono.................0172<br>○駅に着く えきにつく arrive at the station....0339<br>着信 ちゃくしん arrival (of mail, phone call, etc.) 0063<br>○接着 せっちゃく adhesion, gluing.........0847 |
|---|---|---|
| | チャク ジャク<br>き(る) -ぎ き(せる) -き(せ) つ(く)<br>つ(ける) | |

| **0938**<br>羊 123 | Visualize this as the act of **PUTTING ON** a wool cap: 羊 *sheep* provides the wool and S7 shows the visor, shielding the *eyes* (目). Speaking from the cap's perspective, we would not say that you **PUT** it **ON**, but that it **ARRIVES** on your head (M2). Then it **STICKS** there (M3). ☞ 差 0937, 看 0939, 羞 1671 |
|---|---|
| 2826 | |
| 常 12 | |

| | OBSERVE, keep an eye on | ○看板 かんばん signboard, sign...............0924<br>看破する かんぱする see through, penetrate ...............................................0596<br>看取する かんしゅする perceive, detect; see through..................................0059<br>○看病する かんびょうする nurse, care for....0617<br>看守 かんしゅ jailer, prison guard.........0648 |
|---|---|---|
| | カン | |

| **0939**<br>目 109 | Here what shields the *eye* (目) is not a wool cap but a *hand* (S1-4, modified from 手). We shield our eyes when we are intent on watching something in spite of a glaring light. Along these lines, we should see in this kanji the act of closely watching something, such as **OBSERVING** a hospital patient or **keeping an eye on** children. ☞ 着 0938, 羞 1671 |
|---|---|
| 2771 | |
| 常 9 | |

| | ARRIVE | ○到着 とうちゃく arrival........................0938<br>到来 とうらい arrival, advent..............0274<br>殺到する さっとうする rush in, pour in; descend on....................................0522<br>到底 とうてい after all, in the long run.......0482 |
|---|---|---|
| | トウ | |

| **0940**<br>刀 18 | Review 至 0250 through 屋 0252. Here we see a *sword* (刂) slicing through something until it *comes to* (至) the ground, which symbolizes the act of **ARRIVING**. V1 will test whether you've learned to distinguish the previous two entries. ☞ 倒 0941, 致 0251 |
|---|---|
| 1163 | |
| 常 8 | |

| | **TOPPLE** | 卒倒する そっとうする faint, fall unconscious 0751 |
|---|---|---|
| | | ○倒産 とうさん insolvency, bankruptcy; breech birth...........................................0181 |
| | | 圧倒する あっとうする overwhelm, overpower, crush..............................................0186 |
| | トウ<br>たお(れる) -だお(れ) たお(す) | 後に倒れる うしろにたおれる fall backward...0114 |
| | | 共倒れ ともだおれ falling together, mutual ruin ..................................................0356 |

| **0941** | Informed by the previous entry, let this one suggest a *man* (イ) *"arriving"* to the ground (到), |
|---|---|
| 人 9 | i.e., TOPPLING over. ☞ 到 0940, 例 0721 |
| **0106** | |
| 常 10 | |

| | ¹ **ARGUE, discuss**<br>² **THEORY, view** | ¹ 議論 ぎろん argument, discussion ..........0927 |
|---|---|---|
| | | ¹ 結論 けつろん conclusion ...................0516 |
| | | ①論じる(=論ずる) ろんじる (=ろんずる) argue, discuss |
| | ロン | ² 進化論 しんかろん theory of evolution...0191, 0120 |
| | | ² 世論 せろん (=よろん) public opinion........0604 |

| **0942** | Review 冊 0824. 侖 shows a stack of *books* under a *roof* (the single line beneath the roof |
|---|---|
| 言 149 | just shows the roof *fitting* on top; see 合 0227). We'll let this represent *library*, and, by exten- |
| | sion, *careful study*. For this entry, learn to associate *words* (言) and *careful study* (侖) with |
| | **ARGUMENT** and **THEORY**. ☞ 諭 0946 |
| **1424** | |
| 常 15 | |

| | **MORALS** | ○倫理 りんり ethics, morals, code of conduct ..................................................0532 |
|---|---|---|
| | | 倫理学 りんりがく ethics, moral philosophy ...........................................0532, 0099 |
| | リン | 不倫な ふりんな immoral, illicit .............0049 |
| | | 人倫 じんりん humanity, morality; human relations ...........................................0015 |

| **0943** | Here we observe a *man* (イ) of *careful study*, that is, a man of deep **MORAL** sensitivity and |
|---|---|
| 人 9 | reflection, one who thinks carefully about his actions and the difference between right and |
| | wrong. |
| **0103** | |
| 常 10 | |

| | ¹ **WHEEL**<br>² **RING** | ①車輪 しゃりん wheel.............................0125 |
|---|---|---|
| | | ¹ 駐輪場 ちゅうりんじょう bicycle parking lot ...........................................0367, 0445 |
| | | ² 輪状の りんじょうの ring-shaped, annular...0616 |
| | リン<br>わ | ² 輪投げ わなげ quoits, ringtoss.............0517 |
| | | ②指輪 ゆびわ (finger) ring ...................0932 |

| **0944** | These days many communities have "tool libraries" that lend out tools to the public. This |
|---|---|
| 車 159 | kanji suggests a *wheel library*. Imagine that stacked on its bookshelf (冊) are not books but |
| | **WHEELS** (車)! The reading リン sounds like M2 **RING**. ☞ 輪 0945 |
| **1436** | |
| 常 15 | |

| | TRANSPORT | | | 輸送する ゆそうする transport, convey......0455 |
|---|---|---|---|
| | | | 運輸 うんゆ transport(ation), conveyance...0584 |
| | ユ | | ○輸出 ゆしゅつ export, exportation..........0038 |
| | | | ○輸入 ゆにゅう import, importation.........0039 |
| | | | 禁輸 きんゆ embargo.......................0312 |

**0945**
車 159
輸
1454
常 16

Recalling 前 0113, we take 俞 to be *sliced* (刂) *meat* (月). The "roof *fitting* on top" (from 合 0227) indicates that the meat is covered (i.e., packaged). The whole kanji thus shows us a *vehicle* (車) TRANSPORTING *packages of sliced meat* (俞). All kanji incorporating 俞 are pronounced ユ. ☞ 輸 0944

---

| | ADMONISH, instruct | | 諭旨 ゆし official suggestion or instruction..0931 |
|---|---|---|
| | | ○教諭 きょうゆ teacher, instructor.............0632 |
| | ユ | ○諭す さとす admonish, instruct |
| | さと(す) | 諭し さとし guidance, admonition |
| | | 教え諭す おしえさとす give guidance.......0632 |

**0946**
言 149
諭
1446
常 16

Visualize as *words* (言) of warning, printed on the label of a *package of sliced meat* (俞), ADMONISHING us and **instructing** us. ☞ 論 0942

---

| | PLEASED | | ○愉快な ゆかいな pleasant, delightful.......0331 |
|---|---|---|
| | | 愉色 ゆしょく pleased look, cheerful expression |
| | | ....................................................0528 |
| | ユ | 愉楽 ゆらく pleasure, joy.....................0302 |
| | | 不愉快な ふゆかいな unpleasant, disagreeable, |
| | | cheerless..................................0049, 0331 |

**0947**
心 61
愉
0534
常 12

Think of this *heart* (忄) as being PLEASED at the prospect of consuming this *package of sliced meat* (俞). ☞ 癒 0948

---

| | HEAL, soothe | | ○平癒 へいゆ recovery, restoration to health...0334 |
|---|---|---|
| | | 癒着 ゆちゃく adhesion, conglutination; |
| | | connection, collusion.......................0938 |
| | ユ | 癒える いえる be healed, be soothed |
| | い(やす) い(える) | ○癒す いやす heal, soothe |
| | | 心の癒し こころのいやし healing/soothing of |
| | | the mind.....................................0056 |

**0948**
疒 104
癒
2806
常 18

Think of an *illness* (疒) resulting from a deficiency in meat protein, then see the *sliced meat* (俞) going to the *heart* (心, i.e., insides) of an *ill* person to HEAL and **soothe** him. ☞ 療 0952, 愉 0947

| | ¹ STAND, pedestal, platform<br>² COUNTER FOR MACHINES AND VEHICLES<br>³ TAIWAN<br><br>ダイ タイ | ¹ 荷台 にだい carrier, bed (of a truck).........0817<br>① 台所 だいどころ kitchen .....................0249<br>¹ 台地 だいち plateau, tableland.............0187<br>② 自動車十台 じどうしゃじゅうだい ten cars<br>.................0081, 0540, 0125, 0005<br>³ 日台 にったい Japan and Taiwan, Japanese-<br>Taiwanese.........................0001 |
|---|---|---|

**0949**
口 30*

臺

1731
常 | 5

Here 口 represents a flat-topped structure and ム an *elbow*, resting on it. This kanji thus aptly depicts a **STAND**, **pedestal**, or **platform** on which we can place things. It is also used as a **COUNTER FOR MACHINES AND VEHICLES** because these tend to be solid, boxy objects, just like the square **STAND** shown here.

| | ¹ GOVERN, bring under control<br>² CURE<br><br>ジ チ<br>おさ(める) おさ(まる) なお(る)<br>なお(す) | ① 政治 せいじ government, administration,<br>politics.............................0246<br>¹ 治安 ちあん public peace and order .......0096<br>① 国を治める くにをおさめる govern a country,<br>manage a state ...................0075<br>² 治癒 ちゆ healing, cure, recovery...........0948<br>② 病気が治った びょうきがなおった The illness has<br>been cured.........................0617, 0126 |
|---|---|---|

**0950**
水 85

0297
常 | 8

To remember the kanji for **GOVERN/bring under control**, think of a unit of riot control officers standing on a *platform* (台) and blasting protesters with a *water* (氵) cannon. M2 **CURE** comes from the idea of **bringing** a disease **under control**. ☞ 沿 1348, 冶 0951

| | **WORK METALS**<br><br>ヤ | ○ 冶金 やきん metallurgy.......................0029 |
|---|---|---|

**0951**
冫 15

0062
常 | 7

Recall from 冷 0675 that 冫 sometimes means *ice*. Since this kanji signifies **METALWORKING**, we'll let *ice* suggest the cooling of smelted metal, which once solidified is placed upon a *platform* (台, i.e., an anvil) for hammering. Additional sample compounds appear at 陶 1372 and 鍛 2064. ☞ 治 0950

| | **TREAT, medicate**<br><br>リョウ | ○ 治療する ちりょうする treat, cure.............0950<br>療法 りょうほう method of treatment, remedy<br>.................................0139<br>療養中 りょうようちゅう under medical care, in<br>recuperation.....................0500, 0035<br>医療 いりょう medical treatment/care.......0561<br>施療 せりょう free medical treatment........0571 |
|---|---|---|

**0952**
疒 104

2803
常 | 17

Informed by 楽 0302 PLEASURE and 大 0033 BIG, take 尞 to mean *big fun*. Here it refers to the *big fun* provided by powerful pain relievers used to **TREAT** the *ill* (疒). Note that all four kanji incorporating 尞 are pronounced リョウ. ☞ 癒 0948

| 僚 | COLLEAGUE, official | 僚友 りょうゆう comrade, colleague, fellow worker .....0399 |
|---|---|---|
| | リョウ | ○同僚 どうりょう colleague, associate, fellow official .....0182 |
| | | 閣僚 かくりょう cabinet members .....0792 |
| | | ○官僚 かんりょう government official(s); bureaucracy, officialdom .....0290 |
| | | 官僚的 かんりょうてき bureaucratic ....0290, 0169 |

**0953** 人 9 / 0143 / 常 14

Let "*man*(イ) + *big fun*(尞)" remind you of a certain playful coworker/**COLLEAGUE**.

| 瞭 | CLEAR | ○明瞭な めいりょうな clear, plain, lucid .......0024 |
|---|---|---|
| | リョウ | 一目瞭然の いちもくりょうぜんの immediately clear, obvious .....0002, 0021, 0760 |

**0954** 目 109 / 1145 / 常 17

**CLEAR** viewing—*big fun*(尞) for the *eyes*(目).

| 寮 | DORMITORY | ○学生寮 がくせいりょう student dormitory .....0099, 0036 |
|---|---|---|
| | リョウ | 寮生 りょうせい boarder .....0036 |
| | | 寮長 りょうちょう dormitory leader .....0091 |
| | | 独身寮 どくしんりょう company dormitory for unmarried employees .....0346, 0060 |
| | | 寮に住む りょうにすむ live in a dormitory ...0366 |

**0955** 宀 40 / 2079 / 常 15

*Big fun*(尞) occurring under a *roof*(宀): **DORMITORY**.

| 始 | BEGIN | ○開始する かいしする begin, commence, open .....0450 |
|---|---|---|
| | シ はじ(める) -はじ(める) はじ(まる) | 原始的な げんしてきな primitive, primeval .....0208, 0169 |
| | | ○始める はじめる begin, start, originate; embark on |
| | | 歩き始めた あるきはじめた began walking...0679 |
| | | 始まり はじまり beginning |

**0956** 女 38 / 0252 / 常 8

Visualize a *woman*(女) setting about (i.e., **BEGINNING**) the task of preparing a meal at the kitchen *platform*(台), i.e., the kitchen counter.

| | END | ○最終 さいしゅう last, the end; final............0196 |
| | | 終点 しゅうてん last stop, terminus..........0349 |
| | | 始終 しじゅう from beginning to end, at all times |
| | | ............................................................0956 |
| | シュウ | 終戦 しゅうせん end of the war..............0461 |
| | お(わる) -お(わる) お(える) | ○終わる おわる [vi] end, finish |

| **0957** | Recall 冬 0360 WINTER. Now think of a spool of *thread* as having four seasons, starting from |
| 糸 120 | spring, when you reel off the first few inches, all the way to *winter*, when the spool stops |
| | unwinding and you've come to the very **END**. |
| 1223 | |
| 常 11 | |

| | ¹ **FINISH** | ①終了する しゅうりょうする end, complete; expire |
| | ² **COMPREHEND** | .......................................................0957 |
| | | ¹ 満了する まんりょうする expire, become due 0179 |
| | | ¹ 未了 みりょう unfinished, incomplete........0271 |
| | リョウ | ②了解 りょうかい understanding; consent....0345 |
| | | ² 了知する りょうちする know, understand, |
| | | appreciate..............................................0560 |

| **0958** | Recall that 子 depicts an infant *child* with its arms outstretched for hugging. Now imagine |
| J 6 | that an important part of an infant's training is to learn how to lie with its arms tucked in (了), |
| | rather than flailing around at the sides (子). In this kanji we see a child who has finished this |
| | learning process: **FINISH; COMPREHEND**. |
| 2852 | |
| 常 2 | |

| | ¹ **AGREE TO, be told** | ①了承 りょうしょう acknowledgement, understand- |
| | ² **RECEIVE** | ing..........................................................0958 |
| | | ¹ 承知する しょうちする consent to; forgive; know, |
| | | understand..............................................0560 |
| | ショウ | ² 承継 しょうけい succession....................0848 |
| | うけたまわ(る) | ² 伝承 でんしょう tradition, legend............0223 |
| | | ②承る うけたまわる [humble] hear, listen to, be told |

| **0959** | The three lines running across the center of this kanji are a unique feature, so an easy short- |
| 手 64 | cut is to perceive these lines as transmitting something from left to right, and imagine that |
| | the right side **RECEIVES** it, accepts it, **AGREES TO** it, etc. It may help at first to sketch this kanji |
| | in the margin, replacing S3–5 with arrows. ☞ 蒸 0960 |
| 0007 | |
| 常 8 | |

| | **STEAM, be steamed** | 蒸気 じょうき steam, vapor...................0126 |
| | | ○蒸発 じょうはつ evaporation, volatilization; |
| | | mysterious disappearance.................0148 |
| | | ○蒸す むす steam; be stuffy |
| | ジョウ | 蒸し菓子 むしがし steamed cake......0602, 0094 |
| | む(す) む(れる) む(らす) | 飯を蒸らす めしをむらす steam boiled rice..0377 |

| **0960** | Visualize this character as the act of **STEAMING** vegetables: see 艹 as the vegetables, S4–8 as |
| 艸 140 | a variation on *water* (水), and S9 as a metal plate, heated by a *fire* (灬). |
| | ☞ 承 0959, 煮 1188, 燕 1741 |
| 2043 | |
| 常 13 | |

**DANCE**

ブ
ま(う) -ま(う) まい

○舞台 ぶたい stage..............................0949
舞曲 ぶきょく dance music, music and dancing
..............................0503
○舞を舞う まいをまう perform a dance
振る舞う ふるまう conduct oneself; entertain, treat..............................0903
見舞う みまう ask for, visit (a sick person)....0083

| 0961 | 舛 136 | 1844 | 常 15 |

舛 means *dance*. See it as two legs, one of which takes a *dance* step to our left. The portion above it in this entry recalls 無 0048 NOTHING, but here we can just see it as a skirt hanging over the *dancing* legs, to complete the image of **DANCING**. ☞ 無 0048

**NEIGHBOR**

リン
とな(る) となり

○隣人 りんじん neighbor..............................0015
隣国 りんごく neighboring country..........0075
隣接した りんせつした neighboring, adjoining, adjacent..............................0847
○隣り合う となりあう adjoin, be next door to each other..............................0227

| 0962 | 阜 170 | 0700 | 常 16 |

To remember the kanji for **NEIGHBOR**, picture a noisy party taking place on the other side of a wall. Here see β, which we normally see as the boundary between a town and the outlying hills, as a thin wall separating your house from your **NEIGHBOR**'s. On the other side, there is food (米) and *dancing* (舛).

**BLINK; instant**

シュン
またた(く)

○瞬間 しゅんかん instant, moment, second...0448
瞬時 しゅんじ instant, moment..............0383
一瞬 いっしゅん instant, moment ..........0002
○瞬く またたく wink, blink; twinkle, flicker
瞬く間に またたくまに in the blink of an eye 0448

| 0963 | 目 109 | 1151 | 常 18 |

Recall that at 覚 0325 we saw ⺌ as eyelashes and 冖 as an open eyelid. Here the eyelashes (⺍) have an extra stroke (of mascara?), and the eyelid *dances* (舛) up and down (i.e., **BLINKS**) flirtatiously. It is only logical that 目 should replace 見 here, as this kanji does not have to do with *sight* but with the *eye* itself.

**DREAM**

ム
ゆめ

夢想 むそう dream, vision; daydream.......0683
夢中で むちゅうで as if in a dream; madly, like crazy; intently ..............................0031
○悪夢 あくむ nightmare, bad dream..........0546
○夢を見る ゆめをみる dream, have a dream...0083
夢枕に ゆめまくらに in a dream..............0656

| 0964 | 夕 36 | 2046 | 常 13 |

Informed by the previous entry, visualize S1-10 as a heavy eyelid, now closing in the *evening* (夕), to sleep, perchance to **DREAM**. Note that the bottom of the character contains 冖 *lid* and 夕 *evening*, not 歹 *death/bone*.

| | | BRANCH | 枝葉 しよう (=えだは) branches and leaves; minor details.....0605 |
| --- | --- | --- | --- |
| 枝 シ えだ | | | 枝切り えだぎり pruning.....0086 |
| | | | 枝豆 えだまめ green soybeans, edamame...0161 |

| 0965 | Review 支 0373 BRANCH. When 支 is combined with 木, it refers to a *tree* BRANCH. |
| --- | --- |
| 木 75 | ☞ 支 0373, 肢 1991 |

| 0767 | |
| --- | --- |
| 常 8 | |

| | | SKILL, craft | 技能 ぎのう skill, ability, capacity.....0892 |
| --- | --- | --- | --- |
| 技 ギ わざ | | | ○技師 ぎし engineer, technician.....0748 |
| | | | 演技 えんぎ acting, performance.....0914 |
| | | | 特技 とくぎ one's special talent/skill.....0385 |
| | | | ○得意技 とくいわざ one's special talent/skill .....0387, 0151 |

| 0966 | Recall that *skill* is a secondary meaning of both 手 0046 (abbreviated here to 扌) and 支 0373. |
| --- | --- |
| 手 64 | The present entry thus refers to manual SKILLS and crafts. ☞ 伎 0967 |

| 0221 | |
| --- | --- |
| 常 7 | |

| | | PERFORMANCE | 伎楽 ぎがく ancient mask show.....0302 |
| --- | --- | --- | --- |
| 伎 キ ギ* | | | ○歌舞伎 かぶき Kabuki.....0827, 0961 |

| 0967 | A *man* (亻) PERFORMING a *skill* (支). ☞ 技 0966 |
| --- | --- |
| 人 9 | |

| 0036 | |
| --- | --- |
| 常 6 | |

| | | DIVERGE, fork | 分岐 ぶんき divergence, ramification, forking .....0088 |
| --- | --- | --- | --- |
| 岐 キ | | | ○分岐点 ぶんきてん junction.....0088, 0349 |
| | | | 多岐 たき many branches, many divergences .....0267 |
| | | | 岐路 きろ forked road, crossroad.....0788 |

| 0968 | A *mountain* (山) road *branching* (支) in two: DIVERGE/fork. |
| --- | --- |
| 山 46 | |

| 0214 | |
| --- | --- |
| 常 7 | |

| | MOUNTAIN PASS | 峠道 とうげみち road over a mountain pass 0158 |
|---|---|---|
| 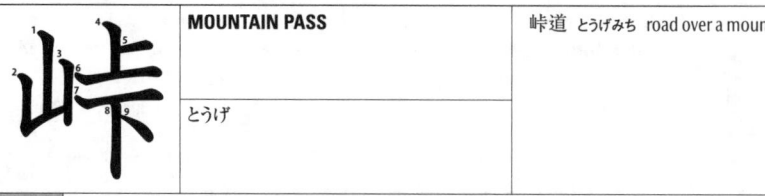 | とうげ | |

| 0969 | Shows a lofty *mountain* (山) peak and a low **PASS** off to its right, at S6–7. Picture a group of hikers coming up *over* (上) the **PASS** then *down* (下) the other side. |
|---|---|
| 山 46 | |
| 0319 | |
| 常 9 | |

| | MOUND | 岐阜 ぎふ Gifu (city and prefecture) ........ 0968 |
|---|---|---|
| 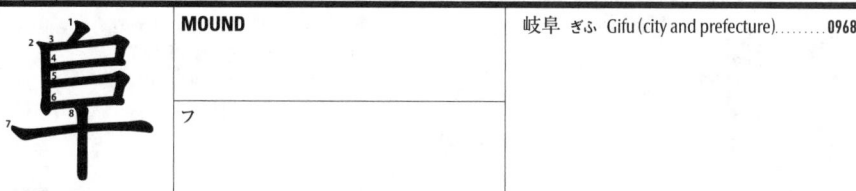 | フ | |

| 0970 | Picture this as a *high-ranking official* (𠂤, see 帥 0747) sitting atop a **MOUND** of earth. The **MOUND** must be located in 岐阜 (ぎふ, a prefecture in central Japan), for we are likely to only see 阜 in this one place-name, at least within Japan. |
|---|---|
| 阜 170 | |
| 2284 | |
| 常 8 | |

| | ¹ URGENT<br>² HURRY<br>³ SUDDEN | ¹ 至急に しきゅうに urgently, with all haste, at once ........................................ 0250 |
|---|---|---|
| | | ² 急行 きゅうこう express (train/bus); going in a hurry ........................................ 0055 |
| | キュウ<br>いそ (ぐ) いそ (ぎ) | ②急ぐ いそぐ [vi] hurry, hasten |
| | | ³ 急病 きゅうびょう sudden illness ............. 0617 |
| | | ○急な きゅうな urgent; hasty; sudden; steep |

| 0971 | See 刍 as a pair of hands **URGENTLY** pressing down on a *heart* (心). The reason they are in such a **HURRY** is that the heart is not beating. |
|---|---|
| 心 61 | |
| 1800 | |
| 常 9 | |

| | CONTEND, struggle for | ○戦争 せんそう war, battle ............. 0461 |
|---|---|---|
| | | 争議 そうぎ dispute, strike ............. 0927 |
| | | 論争 ろんそう dispute, argument ........... 0942 |
| | ソウ<br>あらそ (う) | ○争い あらそい dispute, struggle |
| | | 竜虎の争い りゅうこのあらそい well-matched contest ........................... 0507, 0912 |

| 0972 | Now see the pair of hands (刍) **CONTEND**/**struggle** with each other over control of a rod (亅). |
|---|---|
| 亅 6* | |
|  | |
| 1749 | |
| 常 6 | |

**¹ EMOTION, feeling**
**² ACTUAL CONDITIONS**

ジョウ セイ
なさ(け)

¹ 感情 かんじょう feelings, emotion............0327
① 表情 ひょうじょう expression, look............0705
¹ 同情 どうじょう sympathy, compassion......0182
① 情け無い なさけない unfeeling, cruel; pitiful,
  wretched; shameful.........................0048
² 事情 じじょう circumstances, conditions,
  situation.........................................0080

| 0973 | Review 青 0130 BLUE. Here *"blue heart"* suggests "the blues," i.e., EMOTION/feeling. Associate this with M2 **ACTUAL CONDITIONS** via the idea of one's current state of mind or mood. Note that while most of the kanji containing 青 have two *on* readings, they all share the reading セイ. |
|---|---|
| 心 61 | |
| 0439 | |
| 常 11 | |

**CLEAR, pure**

セイ ショウ
きよ(い) きよ(まる) きよ(める)

清水 せいすい pure/clear water.............0027
　　しみず spring water
清酒 せいしゅ (refined) sake.................0797
○ 清書 せいしょ fair/clean copy.............0079
○ 清まる きよまる be cleansed

| 0974 | As we saw at 0130, 青 sometimes lends connotations of *clarity* or *purity* to a kanji in which it appears. This entry suggests **pure, CLEAR** *water* (氵). ☞ 漬 0834 |
|---|---|
| 水 85 | |
| 0479 | |
| 常 11 | |

**CLEAR SKY**

セイ
は(れる) は(れ) は(れ)- -ば(れ)
は(らす)

快晴 かいせい fine weather.................0331
○ 晴天 せいてん fine weather, cloudless sky..0270
○ 晴れる はれる [vi] clear up
晴れの日 はれのひ fine day; formal occasion
　..................................................0001
晴らす はらす dispel (doubts or gloom), clear
  away

| 0975 | *Sun* (日) and *blue* (青) sky: **CLEAR** weather. |
|---|---|
| 日 72 | |
| 晴 | |
| 0893 | |
| 常 12 | |

**¹ REFINED; precise, meticulous**
**² ESSENCE**
**³ SPIRIT**

セイ ショウ

¹ 精油 せいゆ refined oil; essence............0433
¹ 精製 せいせい refining; careful manufacture
  ..................................................0709
¹ 丹精 たんせい efforts, pains.................0667
² 精液 せいえき semen, sperm.................0468
③ 精神 せいしん spirit; mind, soul; motive....0316

| 0976 | Imagine that the finest, innermost essence of a grain of rice is light blue, a color you would discover if you meticulously refined the rice grain. Using this image, we can associate *blue* (青) *rice* (米) with **precise, meticulous REFINING**, and with the innermost **ESSENCE** or **SPIRIT** of something. |
|---|---|
| 米 119 | |
| 精 | |
| 1248 | |
| 常 14 | |

| 請 | REQUEST | |
|---|---|---|
| | セイ シン<br>こ(う) う(ける) | ○申請 しんせい application, petition, request ............0315<br>要請する ようせいする request, demand ...0547<br>請願 せいがん petition ..................0214<br>○請う こう ask, request<br>○請ける うける undertake |

**0977**
言 149
請
1426
常 15

"*Blue* (青) *word* (言)" means a *pure* word, i.e., a sincere **REQUEST**.

| 静 | QUIET, still | |
|---|---|---|
| | セイ ジョウ<br>しず- しず(か) しず(まる) しず(める) | 静止する せいしする stand still .............0042<br>○冷静な れいせいな cool, calm, dispassionate ...............0675<br>静物画 せいぶつが still-life picture ...0172, 0176<br>○静かな しずかな quiet, still; tranquil<br>気を静める きをしずめる compose oneself...0126 |

**0978**
青 174
靜
1539
常 14

As we have seen, 青 *blue* can also imply *calm*, as in *blue* sky. Here a *struggle* (争) is *calmed*, resulting in **QUIET** stillness.

| 浄 | CLEAN, pure | |
|---|---|---|
| | ジョウ | 清浄な せいじょうな pure, clean .............0974<br>○浄化 じょうか purification, cleansing ........0120<br>浄書 じょうしょ clean copy...................0079<br>浄水場 じょうすいじょう water purification plant ...................0027, 0445<br>浄土宗 じょうどしゅう Pure Land Sect (of Buddhism)..................0030, 0636 |

**0979**
水 85
淨
0342
常 9

Water that sits in stagnant pools is likely to be contaminated, but water that flows underground or over rocks is likely to be clean and pure. This character points to the same phenomenon by suggesting that "*water* (氵) through *struggle* (争) becomes **CLEAN**."

| 算 | CALCULATE | |
|---|---|---|
| | サン | ○計算 けいさん computation, calculation....0555<br>精算 せいさん exact calculation; settlement of accounts ..................0976<br>算数 さんすう arithmetic; calculation .......0309<br>予算 よさん budget; estimate...............0163<br>算盤 そろばん abacus....................0673 |

**0980**
竹 118

Recall that 𥫗 sometimes implies *counting* or *figuring*. Here picture 目 as an abacus (see V5), manipulated by *two hands* (廾) to **CALCULATE** something. ☞ 鼻 1558

2359
常 14

**ANSWER**

トウ
こた（える）　こた（え）

| | | |
|---|---|---|
| 応答 | おうとう answer, response, reply | 0850 |
| 問答 | もんどう questions and answers; catechism | 0452 |
| ○回答 | かいとう answer, reply | 0050 |
| 解答 | かいとう answer, solution | 0345 |
| ○質問に答える しつもんにこたえる answer a question | | 0318, 0452 |

| 0981 | Here 合 suggests that the information written on a certain *bamboo* (⺮) tablet "*fits*"—in other words, that it **ANSWERS** correctly. |
|---|---|
| 竹 118 | |
| 2340 | |
| 常 12 | |

**SYMBOL, mark; tally stick**

フ

| | | |
|---|---|---|
| ○符号 | ふごう sign, mark, symbol | 0300 |
| 終止符 | しゅうしふ period (.) | 0957, 0042 |
| 音符 | おんぷ note; phonetic grapheme of a kanji | 0150 |
| 割符 | わりふ tally, check | 0416 |
| 切符 | きっぷ ticket | 0086 |

| 0982 | Refers to the act of *attaching* (付) a **SYMBOL** or **mark** to a *bamboo* (⺮) **tally stick**. Once this kanji makes sense to you, take a moment to review 券 0456. |
|---|---|
| 竹 118 | |
| 2319 | |
| 常 11 | |

博

¹ **EXTENSIVE (knowledge)**
² **DOCTOR, PhD**

ハク　バク

| | | |
|---|---|---|
| ①博士 | はくし (=はかせ) doctor, PhD | 0350 |
| ①博物館 | はくぶつかん museum | 0172, 0291 |
| ¹博愛主義 | はくあいしゅぎ philanthropy, altruism | 0778, 0365, 0926 |
| ¹博学 | はくがく extensive learning, erudition | 0099 |
| ²医博 | いはく doctor of medicine, MD | 0561 |

| 0983 | Review 専 0580, noting the extra dot stroke here. 十 *ten* can lend connotations of *abundance* or *completeness* (just think of the word 十分 [じゅうぶん, full, enough; plentiful]). In this kanji, 十 (*complete*) and 専 (*entire*) together denote **EXTENSIVE**, such as the **EXTENSIVE KNOWLEDGE** of a **DOCTOR/PhD**. ☞ 専 0580, 縛 0984 |
|---|---|
| 十 24 | |
| 0129 | |
| 常 12 | |

**BIND, restrain**

バク
しば（る）

| | | |
|---|---|---|
| ○束縛する | そくばくする restrain, restrict, bind, fetter | 0307 |
| きつく縛る | きつくしばる fasten tightly | |
| 縛り上げる | しばりあげる tie up | 0041 |
| ○縛る | しばる bind, tie; restrain | |

| 0984 | From here on, we'll revert to simply visualizing 専 as a *cauldron* borne by an *outstretched arm* (see 専 0580). In this entry, picture it being **BOUND** with *cord* (糸). Do not confuse this entry's 縛る (しばる, bind, tie; restrain) with 絞る (しぼる, wring) in 1414, or 搾る (しぼる, squeeze) in 1415. ☞ 博 0983 |
|---|---|
| 糸 120 | |
| 1282 | |
| 常 16 | |

## RECORD BOOK

ボ

簿記 ぼき bookkeeping .......................0427
○名簿 めいぼ register/list of names ..........0269
計算簿 けいさんぼ account book......0555, 0980
家計簿 かけいぼ housekeeping account book
.........................................0219, 0555
通信簿 つうしんぼ report card .........0159, 0063

| 0985 |
| 竹 118 |
| 芲 |
| 2377 |
| 常 19 |

Now シ fills the *cauldron* (専), for soup. On a *bamboo* (⺮) **RECORD BOOK** we register how many cauldrons of soup we make. Now note from this series how we add an extra dot stroke above 専 whenever we include it as a component inside more complex kanji. Also note how this does not occur with 穂 1314, which is based on 恵 0581. ☞ 薄 0986, 籍 1910

## THIN, scanty

ハク
うす(い) うす- -うす うす(める)
うす(まる) うす(らぐ) うす(ら)-
うす(れる)

厚薄 こうはく (relative) thickness ............0427
○薄弱な はくじゃくな weak, feeble, frail .......0424
薄情な はくじょうな unfeeling, heartless, cruel
.........................................0973
○薄い うすい thin, weak, scant
水で薄める みずでうすめる water down ....0027

| 0986 |
| 艸 140 |
| 2093 |
| 常 16 |

Imagine putting just a few weak *herbs* (艹) into a large *cauldron* (専) of *water* (シ, i.e., broth) and you should be able to remember that this character means **THIN/scanty**. Practice writing this entry in alternation with the last one, and learn to derive their meanings from the uppermost grapheme. ☞ 薄 0985

## GATHER

サイ

采配 さいはい baton symbolizing authority or
command.................................0799
采配を振る さいはいをふる direct, command
.................................0799, 0903

| 0987 |
| 木 75 |
| 2147 |
| 常 8 |

Depicts a *claw* (⺥) collecting *trees* (木), and means **GATHER.**

## VEGETABLE

サイ
な

○野菜 やさい vegetables, greens.............0534
菜食 さいしょく vegetable diet...............0288
菜園 さいえん vegetable garden ............0856
前菜 ぜんさい hors d'oeuvre................0113
○青菜 あおな greens .......................0130

| 0988 |
| 艸 140 |
| 2004 |
| 常 11 |

*Plants* (艹) for *gathering* (采): **VEGETABLES.** Note that all three characters incorporating 采 follow its *on* reading, サイ.

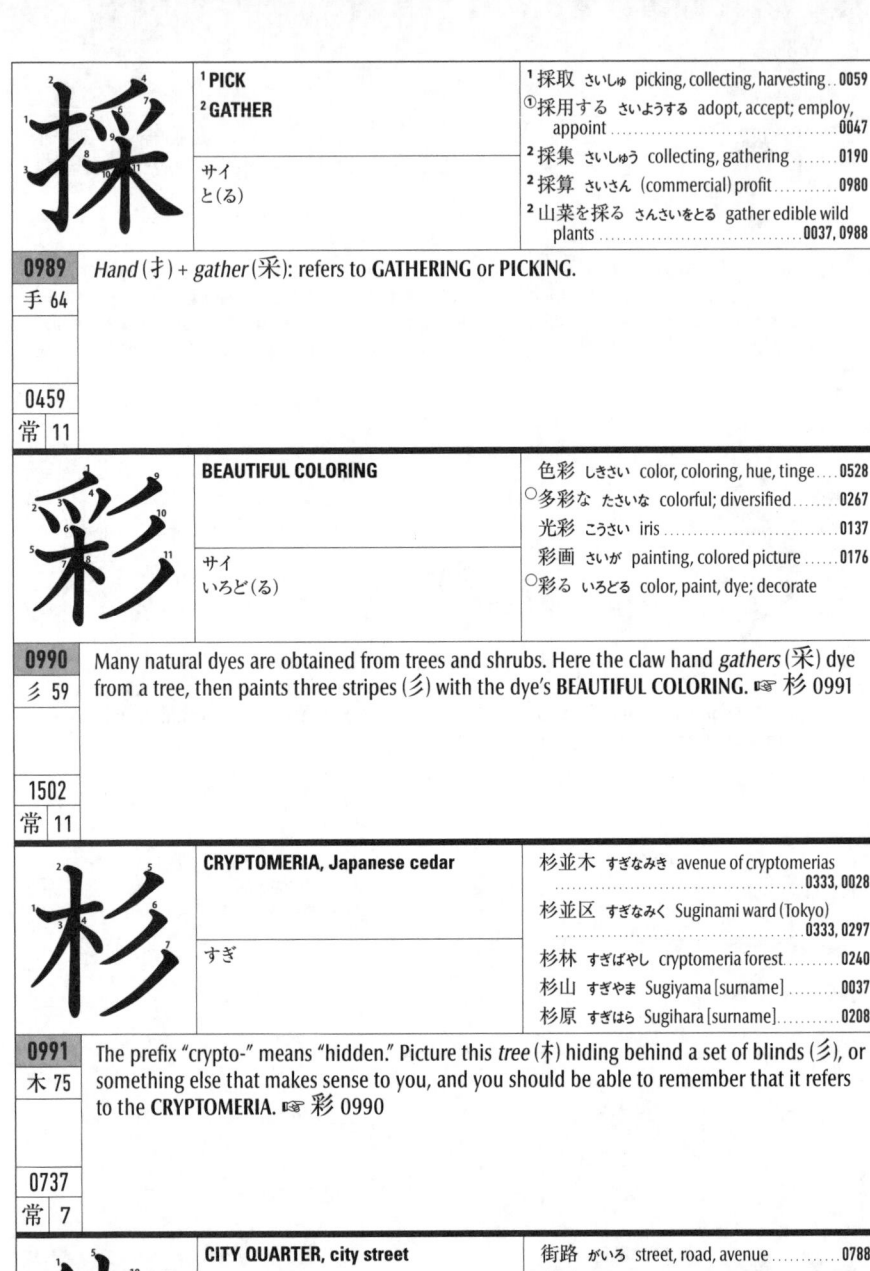

| | | |
|---|---|---|
| 採 | ¹ **PICK**<br>² **GATHER**<br><br>サイ<br>と(る) | ¹ 採取 さいしゅ picking, collecting, harvesting..0059<br>①採用する さいようする adopt, accept; employ, appoint ................................................0047<br>² 採集 さいしゅう collecting, gathering ........0190<br>² 採算 さいさん (commercial) profit............0980<br>² 山菜を採る さんさいをとる gather edible wild plants .................................................0037, 0988 |

**0989** 手 64 / 0459 常 11

*Hand*(扌) + *gather*(采): refers to **GATHERING** or **PICKING**.

| | | |
|---|---|---|
| 彩 | **BEAUTIFUL COLORING**<br><br>サイ<br>いろど(る) | 色彩 しきさい color, coloring, hue, tinge....0528<br>○多彩な たさいな colorful; diversified........0267<br>光彩 こうさい iris ...................................0137<br>彩画 さいが painting, colored picture ......0176<br>○彩る いろどる color, paint, dye; decorate |

**0990** 彡 59 / 1502 常 11

Many natural dyes are obtained from trees and shrubs. Here the claw hand *gathers* (采) dye from a tree, then paints three stripes (彡) with the dye's **BEAUTIFUL COLORING**. ☞ 杉 0991

| | | |
|---|---|---|
| 杉 | **CRYPTOMERIA, Japanese cedar**<br><br>すぎ | 杉並木 すぎなみき avenue of cryptomerias ................................................0333, 0028<br>杉並区 すぎなみく Suginami ward (Tokyo) ................................................0333, 0297<br>杉林 すぎばやし cryptomeria forest..........0240<br>杉山 すぎやま Sugiyama [surname] ........0037<br>杉原 すぎはら Sugihara [surname]..........0208 |

**0991** 木 75 / 0737 常 7

The prefix "crypto-" means "hidden." Picture this *tree* (木) hiding behind a set of blinds (彡), or something else that makes sense to you, and you should be able to remember that it refers to the **CRYPTOMERIA**. ☞ 彩 0990

| | | |
|---|---|---|
| 街 | **CITY QUARTER, city street**<br><br>ガイ カイ<br>まち | 街路 がいろ street, road, avenue ............0788<br>街道 かいどう thoroughfare, highway....0158<br>○商店街 しょうてんがい shopping center, shopping street ...........................0351, 0347<br>街灯 がいとう street lamp ......................0440<br>○街角 まちかど street corner..................0342 |

**0992** 行 144 / 0528 常 12

Back at 衛 0661 we learned to see (彳亍) as *either side of a road*. Here, *soil* (土) is piled up in the middle to widen the road into an important avenue. Thus amplified, this kanji is suitable for referring to relatively busy **CITY QUARTERS** and streets. ☞ 掛 1117

| | PRACTICAL ART, technique | ○技術 ぎじゅつ technique, art, skill; technology ............0966 |
|---|---|---|
| | | 芸術 げいじゅつ art, the arts ..............0225 |
| | ジュツ | 美術 びじゅつ art, fine arts ..............0497 |
| | | 手術 しゅじゅつ surgical operation ..........0046 |
| | | 柔術 じゅうじゅつ jujitsu, jujutsu ..............0688 |

| 0993 | In the variant of 木 appearing here, the lower branches are detached, and a small leaf grows |
|---|---|
| 行 144 | at the top. This is a *noteworthy tree*, worthy of special attention (such as building a *road* around it!). The idea to perceive is the technical skill (i.e., **PRACTICAL ART**) involved in building *either side of a road* (彳亍) <u>around</u> the *noteworthy tree*. ☞ 述 0994, 桁 2229 |
| 0433 | |
| 常 11 | |

| | STATE, mention | 口述する こうじゅつする dictate ..............0019 |
|---|---|---|
| | | 供述 きょうじゅつ testimony, statement; confession ..............0357 |
| | | ○前述の通り ぜんじゅつのとおり as stated above ..............0113, 0159 |
| | ジュツ の(べる) | ○述べる のべる state, mention |
| | | 詳しく述べる くわしくのべる expound ......0495 |

| 0994 | Now the *noteworthy tree* is carried off on a *truck* (辶) for exhibition, the purpose being to |
|---|---|
| 辵 162 | **STATE/mention** its special qualities to the public. The idea you need to see here is that of <u>bringing forward something worthy of note</u>. ☞ 術 0993, 途 1000 |
| 2648 | |
| 常 8 | |

| | ¹REMAINING, left over<br>²EXCESS | ¹余地 よち room, space, margin ..............0187 |
|---|---|---|
| | | ¹余波 よは secondary effect, aftereffect ......0598 |
| | | ²余分 よぶん excess, extra, surplus ..........0088 |
| | | ②余計な よけいな excess, surplus; needless ...0555 |
| | ヨ あま(る) あま(り) あま(す) | ○余る あまる be in excess, remain over |

| 0995 | Visualize as a woodsman (S5) carrying a pile of wood (S3–4) back into his cabin (suggested by |
|---|---|
| 人 9 | *roof* へ). S6–7 show two pieces, in **EXCESS** of what he could carry, that have fallen out of his grasp. **REMAIN** is an associated meaning, from the idea of being **left over**. Focus on associating S6–7 with **EXCESS/left over**. |
| 餘 | |
| 1757 | |
| 常 7 | |

| | RID OF | 除去する じょきょする rid of, remove, eliminate ..............0138 |
|---|---|---|
| | | ○除雪する じょせつする remove snow ........0899 |
| | | 排除 はいじょ exclusion, removal, elimination ..............0739 |
| | ジョ ジ のぞ(く) | ○除く のぞく rid of; exclude, omit |
| | | 月曜日を除いて げつようびをのぞいて excepting Mondays ..............0023, 0025, 0001 |

| 0996 | Now, having learned from the previous entry, the woodsman decides to get **RID OF** the *excess* |
|---|---|
| 阜 170 | (余) pieces in the *hills* (阝), rather than schlep them down toward the cabin in a futile effort. Picture him dumping out S9–10 on the hillside. As you learn this set of characters based on 余, note that their *on-yomi* all have short vowels. ☞ 隙 1876 |
| 0412 | |
| 常 10 | |

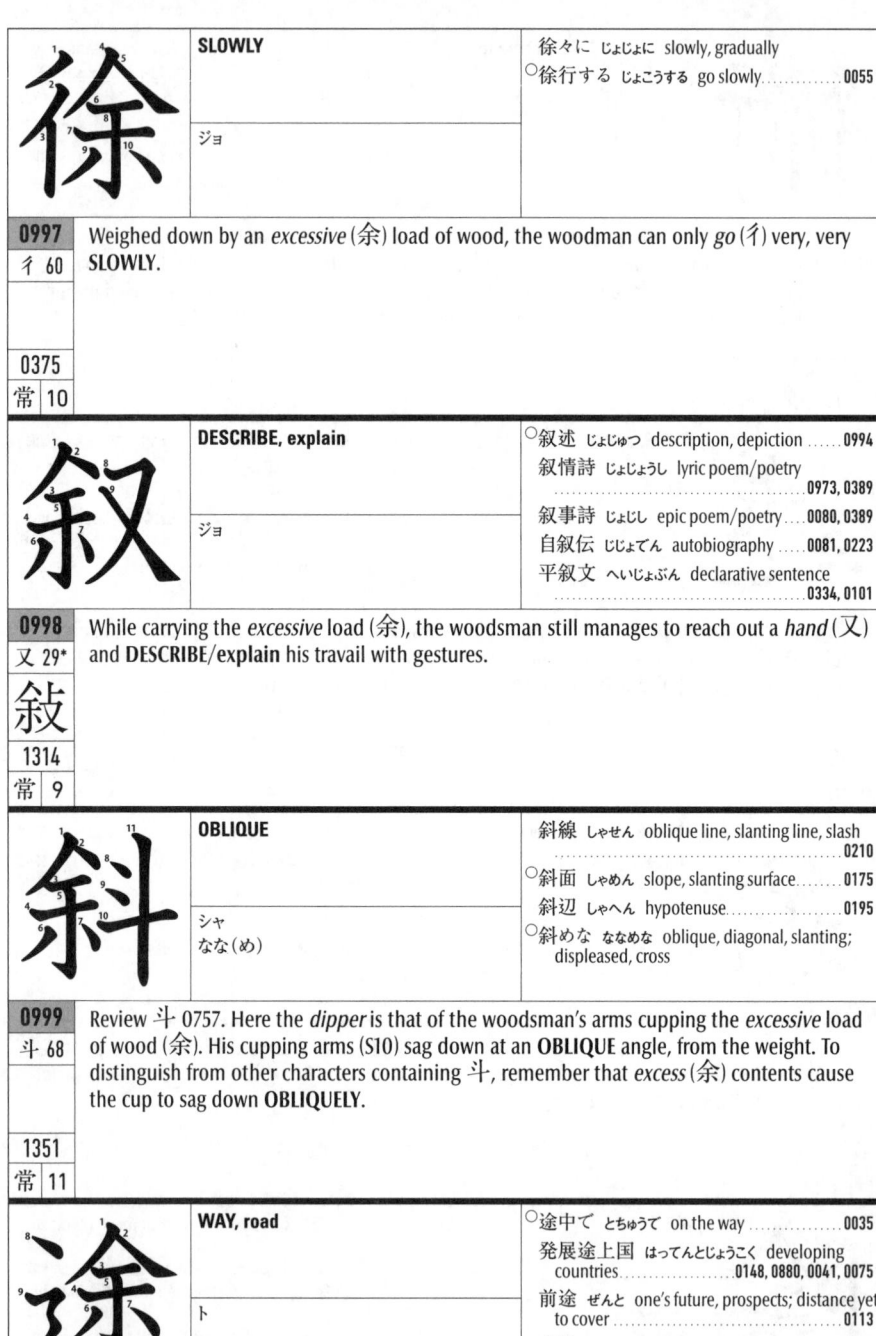

| | SLOWLY | 徐々に　じょじょに　slowly, gradually |
|---|---|---|
| 徐 | ジョ | ○徐行する　じょこうする　go slowly............0055 |

**0997**
イ 60

Weighed down by an *excessive* (余) load of wood, the woodman can only *go* (イ) very, very **SLOWLY**.

0375
常 | 10

---

| | DESCRIBE, explain | ○叙述　じょじゅつ　description, depiction......0994 |
|---|---|---|
| 叙 | ジョ | 叙情詩　じょじょうし　lyric poem/poetry...........0973, 0389 |
| | | 叙事詩　じょじし　epic poem/poetry......0080, 0389 |
| | | 自叙伝　じじょでん　autobiography......0081, 0223 |
| | | 平叙文　へいじょぶん　declarative sentence......0334, 0101 |

**0998**
又 29*

敍

While carrying the *excessive* load (余), the woodsman still manages to reach out a *hand* (又) and **DESCRIBE**/explain his travail with gestures.

1314
常 | 9

---

| | OBLIQUE | 斜線　しゃせん　oblique line, slanting line, slash......0210 |
|---|---|---|
| 斜 | シャ | ○斜面　しゃめん　slope, slanting surface........0175 |
| | なな(め) | 斜辺　しゃへん　hypotenuse......0195 |
| | | ○斜めな　ななめな　oblique, diagonal, slanting; displeased, cross |

**0999**
斗 68

Review 斗 0757. Here the *dipper* is that of the woodsman's arms cupping the *excessive* load of wood (余). His cupping arms (S10) sag down at an **OBLIQUE** angle, from the weight. To distinguish from other characters containing 斗, remember that *excess* (余) contents cause the cup to sag down **OBLIQUELY**.

1351
常 | 11

---

| | WAY, road | ○途中で　とちゅうで　on the way......0035 |
|---|---|---|
| 途 | ト | 発展途上国　はってんとじょうこく　developing countries......0148, 0880, 0041, 0075 |
| | | 前途　ぜんと　one's future, prospects; distance yet to cover......0113 |
| | | 方途　ほうと　means, way, measure......0173 |
| | | 用途　ようと　use, service, application........0047 |

**1000**
辵 162

Here, instead of trudging back through the forest, the woodsman has decided just to put the *excessive* load (余) on the back of his *truck* (辶) and head back via the **road/WAY**.
☞ 述 0994, 逾 1555

2676
常 | 10

**APPLY ON A SURFACE, paint**

ト
ぬ(る) ぬ(り)

○塗料 とりょう paint ...............................0758
塗布する とふする apply (an ointment) ....0204
○塗る ぬる lay on, paint
塗り絵 ぬりえ picture for coloring ..........0525
塗り物 ぬりもの lacquerware................0172

| 1001 | Visualize *excessively* (余)—i.e., sloppily—spreading a *liquid* ( 氵) over the *ground* (土): APPLY ON A SURFACE/paint. ☞ 漆 1002 |
|---|---|
| 土 32 | |
| 2473 | |
| 常 13 | |

**LACQUER**

シツ
うるし

○漆器 しっき lacquerware...................0295
○漆塗り うるしぬり lacquering, japanning; lacquer ware.......................................1001

| 1002 | See the sap of a LACQUER *tree* (木) dripping down in splashing drops, like *water* (氺, 氵). 氺 is the five-stroke version of *water* we first saw at 様 0501. ☞ 塗 1001, 泰 2105, 添 1344 |
|---|---|
| 水 85 | |
| 0637 | |
| 常 14 | |

**HERMIT, immortal mountain fairy**

セン

○仙人 せんにん immortal mountain fairy; hermit, recluse ............................0015
仙術 せんじゅつ fairy magic................0993
神仙 しんせん supernatural being..........0316
酒仙 しゅせん heavy drinker................0797
仙台 せんだい Sendai (city in Miyagi prefecture) ..................................0949

| 1003 | *Man* (亻) living in the *mountains* (山): HERMIT. |
|---|---|
| 人 9 | |
| 0020 | |
| 常 5 | |

**HANG DOWN, dangle**

スイ
た(れる) た(らす) た(れ) -た(れ)

○垂直の すいちょくの vertical, perpendicular 0839
垂線 すいせん perpendicular line ..........0210
○垂れる たれる hang down, dangle
雨垂れ あまだれ raindrops................0154
垂らす たらす hang down, suspend

| 1004 | Picture wet clothes (S4-5) HANGING DOWN/dangling from a drying rack. ☞ 重 0539, 乗 1005 |
|---|---|
| 土 32 | |
| 2985 | |
| 常 8 | |

| | RIDE; get on | ○乗車する じょうしゃする get aboard.........0125 |
|---|---|---|
| | | 乗客 じょうきゃく passenger..................0787 |
| | | ○船に乗る ふねにのる board a ship.........0669 |
| | | タクシー乗り場 タクシーのりば taxi stand...0445 |
| | ジョウ | 波乗り なみのり surfing.................0598 |
| | の(る) -の(り) の(せる) | |

| 1005 | Use the diagonal strokes 8 and 9 to visualize this entry differently from the previous one. In |
|---|---|
| ノ 4 | the rectangle at the center, picture a subway car (recalling 車 0125), stopped at a crowded |
| 乗 | station platform (S6). No sooner does its door open than three phalanxes of busy commuters |
| | (S7-9) push forward to **get on** for a **RIDE**. ☞ 垂 1004 |
| 2992 | |
| 常 9 | |

| | ¹ COMBINE | ①兼任 けんにん holding two or more posts...0372 |
|---|---|---|
| | ² CANNOT, find it difficult to | ¹ 兼業 けんぎょう side business.............0498 |
| | | ¹用事と遊びを兼ねる ようじとあそびをかねる |
| | | combine business with pleasure |
| | ケン | ....................0047, 0080, 0570 |
| | か(ねる) -か(ねる) | ².-兼ねる -かねる [verbal suffix] cannot, find it difficult to |
| | | ②待ち兼ねる まちかねる can't wait.........0386 |

| 1006 | Recalling 書 0079, see the act of trying to write with two pens at once (i.e., to **COMBINE** them), |
|---|---|
| 八 12 | an act so difficult as to represent the idea **CANNOT**. As Halpern notes, the independent verb |
| 兼 | 兼ねる (かねる) means "serve two functions" (M1), while the suffix -兼ねる (-かねる) |
| | means "find it difficult to ..." (M2). The reading -かねる sounds like **CANNOT**. |
| 1979 | |
| 常 10 | |

| | SURPLUS | 余剰 よじょう surplus, remainder, residue...0995 |
|---|---|---|
| | | 剰余 じょうよ surplus, remainder, balance...0995 |
| | | 剰員 じょういん superfluous member.........0317 |
| | ジョウ | ○過剰 かじょう surplus, excess.................0464 |

| 1007 | At rush hour, some trains are so crowded that not everyone can *get on* (乗). For this reason, |
|---|---|
| 刀 18 | platform agents stand ready to *"cut"* (刂) away **SURPLUS** passengers so that the doors may |
| 剰 | close. See the three converging lines at the lower left as **SURPLUS** to be cut away by 刂. |
| 1584 | |
| 常 11 | |

| | SLEEP | 仮睡 かすい nap, doze......................0921 |
|---|---|---|
| | | 午睡 ごすい nap, afternoon sleep.........0115 |
| | | 一睡もしなかった いっすいもしなかった had a |
| | | sleepless night ..........................0002 |
| | スイ | 睡蓮 すいれん water lily....................0585 |

| 1008 | Over an *eye* (目) an eyelid *hangs down* (垂), signifying **SLEEP**. The *on-yomi* compound to |
|---|---|
| 目 109 | memorize appears in the next entry. |
| | |
| 1108 | |
| 常 13 | |

| **SLEEP** | ○睡眠 すいみん sleep, slumber...............1008 |
| | 不眠 ふみん sleeplessness, insomnia.......0049 |
| | 冬眠 とうみん hibernation...................0360 |
| ミン | 安眠 あんみん peaceful sleep ................0096 |
| ねむ(る)　ねむ(い) | 眠り込む ねむりこむ fall asleep .............0192 |

| 1009 | The *people* (民, see 0477) are ignorant; they do not awaken to the ways in which they are |
| 目 109 | deceived. Truly, the *eyes* (目) of the *people* **SLEEP**. The *on-yomi* follows 民. ☞ 眼 1092 |
| 1061 | |
| 常 10 | |

| **MAIL** | ○郵便 ゆうびん mail service, mail, postal matter |
| | ...............................................0890 |
| | 郵便局 ゆうびんきょく post office.......0890, 0256 |
| | 郵貯 ゆうちょ postal savings (short for 郵便貯 |
| ユウ | 金)........................................0442 |
| | 郵政 ゆうせい postal system.................0246 |
| | 郵袋 ゆうたい mailbag.......................0702 |

| 1010 | Picture a **MAIL** bag *dangling* (垂) from the *wall around the edge of town* (阝), right where |
| 邑 163 | the stagecoach passes. |
| 1506 | |
| 常 11 | |

| **SPINDLE** | ○紡錘 ぼうすい spindle .......................0835 |
| | 錘形の つむがたの spindle-shaped, fusiform |
| | ...............................................0147 |
| スイ | |
| つむ | |

| 1011 | A tapered piece of *metal* (金) *hangs down* (垂) for spinning thread: a **SPINDLE**. This character |
| 金 167 | was removed from the Joyo list in 2010. |
| 1559 | |
| 外 16 | |

| ¹ **FLOWER** | ¹ 華道 かどう flower arrangement...........0158 |
| ² **MAGNIFICENT** | ②華やかな はなやかな flowery, gay, brilliant |
| ³ **CHINA** | ² 華々しい はなばなしい brilliant, magnificent |
| カ　ケ | ③中華料理 ちゅうかりょうり Chinese cuisine |
| はな | ...................................0035, 0758, 0532 |

| 1012 | Just as wet clothes *hang down* over a drying rack at 垂 1004, so hangs here an elaborate |
| 艸 140 | arrangement of *plants* (⺿) and **FLOWERS** upon a trellis (S4–10), signifying both flowery |
| | **MAGNIFICENCE** and the splendor of **CHINA**. We'll encounter this character again inside 嘩 |
| | 1400. ☞ 革 0592 |
| 1973 | |
| 常 10 | |

| | INVADE, violate | ○侵入 しんにゅう invasion, raid, trespass, intrusion ............................0039 |
|---|---|---|
| | | 侵犯 しんぱん invasion; violation ...........0735 |
| | | 侵害 しんがい infringement, violation ......0413 |
| | シン<br>おか(す) | 表現の自由を侵す ひょうげんのじゆうをおかす<br>violate the freedom of expression<br>...................0705, 0706, 0081, 0432 |

| 1013 | 㞢 suggests one *hand* (彐) *covering* (宀) another *hand* (又). Here a *man* (亻) covers another person's hand with his own, symbolizing **INVASION** or violation. Note that all three kanji incorporating 㞢 are pronounced シン. |
|---|---|
| 人 9 | |
| 0085 | |
| 常 9 | |

| | SOAK, immerse | ○浸水 しんすい inundation, submergence...0027 |
|---|---|---|
| | | 浸出 しんしゅつ percolation, exudation, effusion<br>.......................0038 |
| | | ○浸す ひたす [vt] soak, steep, immerse; moisten |
| | シン<br>ひた(す) ひた(る) | 牛乳に浸したパン ぎゅうにゅうにひたしたパン<br>bread dunked in milk.................0116, 0160 |
| | | 空想に浸る くうそうにひたる indulge in fantasies<br>.......................0398, 0683 |

| 1014 | Here one *hand* (彐) *covers* (宀) another *hand* (又) which it pushes under *water* (氵), immersing/**SOAKING** it. ☞ 漫 1135 |
|---|---|
| 水 85 | |
| 0401 | |
| 常 10 | |

| | GO TO SLEEP | 寝台 しんだい bed, sleeping berth ..........0949 |
|---|---|---|
| | | ○寝室 しんしつ bedroom .....................0253 |
| | | 寝具 しんぐ bedclothes, bedding ...........0837 |
| | シン<br>ね(る) ね(かす) ね(かせる) | ○寝る時間 ねるじかん bedtime .........0383, 0448 |
| | | 寝かす ねかす put to sleep; lay down |

| 1015 | The whole story of **GOING TO SLEEP** is here: one enters a *house* (宀), lies down on a long wooden tablet (爿), lays one hand over the other (㞢) on his belly, and **GOES TO SLEEP**. |
|---|---|
| 宀 40 | |
| 寝 | |
| 2034 | |
| 常 13 | |

| | SWEEP (away) | ○掃除 そうじ cleaning.........................0996 |
|---|---|---|
| | | 掃除機 そうじき vacuum cleaner.......0996, 0473 |
| | | 清掃 せいそう cleaning .......................0974 |
| | ソウ<br>は(く) | ○掃く はく sweep |
| | | 掃き出す はきだす sweep out...............0038 |

| 1016 | The structure 帚 shows a *hand* (彐) *covering* (宀) a *cloth* (巾). We'll take it to mean *washcloth* (帚). In the present entry, *hand* (扌) and *washcloth* signify **SWEEP (away)**. |
|---|---|
| 手 64 | |
| 0464 | |
| 常 11 | |

| | ADULT WOMAN, wife | 主婦 しゅふ housewife........................0365 |
|---|---|---|
| | | 婦人 ふじん woman, lady, female...........0015 |
| | | 夫婦 ふうふ husband and wife, married couple |
| | | ........................................0565 |
| | フ | 掃除婦 そうじふ charwoman, cleaning woman |
| | | ..............................1010, 0996 |
| | | 産婦人科医 さんふじんかい obstetrician and |
| | | gynecologist........0181, 0015, 0759, 0561 |

| 1017 | Though I disclaim once and for all any tolerance for the anachronistic gender associations |
|---|---|
| 女 38 | built into this ancient script, I shall not attempt to ignore them. Here the image of a *woman* |
| | (女) holding a *washcloth* (帚) denotes **ADULT WOMAN** or **wife**. |
| 0426 | |
| 常 11 | |

| | RETURN (home) | 帰国する きこくする return to one's country....0075 |
|---|---|---|
| | | 復帰する ふっきする return, be restored, revert |
| | | ........................................0865 |
| | | 帰る かえる return (to one's original position), |
| | キ | come back, come home |
| | かえ(る)  かえ(す) | 帰り道 かえりみち the way back, return trip 0158 |
| | | 帰す かえす let (someone) return, send |
| | | (someone) home, dismiss |

| 1018 | S1–2 resemble 刂 *sword*, but the old form (歸) reveals that these strokes are in fact an |
|---|---|
| 刀 18* | abbreviation. In the way S2 turns, perceive the idea of "turning back." With *washcloth* (帚) to |
| 歸 | represent domesticity, this character suggests the idea of "turning back toward one's domicile," |
| | or **RETURNING (home)**. |
| 0113 | |
| 常 10 | |

| | RETURN, give back | 返戻する へんれいする return, give back....0378 |
|---|---|---|
| | | 戻す もどす return, give back |
| | | 払い戻し はらいもどし refund, repayment....0812 |
| | レイ | 取り戻す とりもどす take back, regain, restore |
| | もど(す)  もど(る) | ........................................0059 |
| | | 戻る もどる return, come/go back |

| 1019 | Suggests a hero's triumphant **RETURN**—this time through the *big* (大) *door* (戸). |
|---|---|
| 戸 63 | |
| 戻 | |
| 1699 | |
| 常 7 | |

| | TEAR | 感涙 かんるい tears of intense emotion.....0327 |
|---|---|---|
| | | 落涙する らくるいする shed tears............0793 |
| | | 涙目 なみだめ teary eyes.....................0021 |
| | ルイ なみだ | 空涙 そらなみだ crocodile tears.............0398 |
| | | 涙ぐむ なみだぐむ be moved to tears |

| 1020 | Here drops of *water* ( 氵) suggest a **TEAR**ful *return* (戻). ☞ 泣 0578 |
|---|---|
| 水 85 | |
| 泪 | |
| 0399 | |
| 常 10 | |

| | SHOOT, radiate | 射的 しゃてき target practice, shooting......0169 |
| --- | --- | --- |
| | | 発射する はっしゃする discharge, shoot, launch .........................................................0148 |
| | シャ<br>い(る) さ(す)* | 反射 はんしゃ reflection .......................0374 |
| | | ○注射 ちゅうしゃ injection, shot............0368 |
| | | ○目を射る光 めをいるひかり light shining into/<br>piercing one's eyes.................0021, 0137 |

| **1021**<br>寸 41 | We already recognize 寸 as an *outstretched arm* delivering a small object. Here observe the outstretched arm of a police officer, delivering (i.e., **SHOOTING**) a bullet at the *body* (身) of an escaping criminal. ☞ 謝 1022 |
| --- | --- |
| **1327**<br>常 10 | |

| | ¹ THANK<br>² APOLOGIZE | ①感謝 かんしゃ gratitude, thanks.............0327 |
| --- | --- | --- |
| | | ¹ 謝礼 しゃれい remuneration, reward; thanks .........................................................0313 |
| | シャ<br>あやま(る) | ¹ 月謝 げっしゃ monthly fee ....................0023 |
| | | ②謝罪 しゃざい apology.......................0741 |
| | | ②謝る あやまる apologize |

| **1022**<br>言 149 | Continuing from the previous entry: Before the bullet arrives, the criminal offers a belated *word* (言) of **APOLOGY**. M1 **THANK** is a cognate meaning. ☞ 射 1021 |
| --- | --- |
| **1465**<br>常 17 | |

| | ¹ STUDY, examine<br>² SUPPRESS BY ARMED FORCE | ¹ 討議 とうぎ discussion, debate, deliberation 0927 |
| --- | --- | --- |
| | | ①討論 とうろん debate, discussion, argument 0942 |
| | | ² 征討 せいとう subjugation, conquest .......0868 |
| | トウ<br>う(つ) | ² 掃討する そうとうする wipe out (the enemy) 1016 |
| | | ②討つ うつ suppress by armed force, attack |

| **1023**<br>言 149 | Here visualize an *arm reaching out* (寸) to grasp *words* (言), signifying an aggressive effort to **STUDY/examine** something that has been written or said (M1). It may also signify an aggressive attempt to **SUPPRESS** words of protest (M2). A good *on-yomi* compound to memorize appears at 検 1029, just ahead. ☞ 計 0555, 訂 1024 |
| --- | --- |
| **1324**<br>常 10 | |

| | REVISE, correct | ○訂正する ていせいする correct, amend, revise .........................................................0043 |
| --- | --- | --- |
| | | 改訂する かいていする revise, edit ..........0429 |
| | テイ | 校訂する こうていする revise................0103 |

| **1024**<br>言 149 | Earlier we learned to see 丁 as a *T-shaped intersection* or *town subsection*. Now we add the meaning *nail*, anticipating 釘 2078 NAIL (this will only apply to the narrow-headed version, such as appears here). This entry suggests *nailing* down one's *words* (言), that is, making them precise by **REVISING/correcting** them. ☞ 計 0555, 診 2165, 討 1023 |
| --- | --- |
| **1310**<br>常 9 | |

| | STRIKE, (emphatic verbal prefix) | 打楽器 だがっき percussion instrument...0302, 0295 |
|---|---|---|
| | | 本塁打 ほんるいだ [baseball] home run...0031, 0885 |
| | | ○打倒する だとうする overthrow, knock down, defeat .....................0941 |
| | ダ | ○打ち込む うちこむ strike/drive into, ram down; devote oneself to, be absorbed in .............0192 |
| | う(つ) う(ち)- | 打ち切る うちきる put an end to, break off, finish .....................0086 |

| 1025 | *Hand* (扌) hammering *nail* (丁): **STRIKE**. See it happening in your mind's eye. |
|---|---|
| 手 64 | |
| 0170 | |
| 常 5 | |

|  | STRIKE, attack; shoot | 打撃 だげき blow, strike....................1025 |
|---|---|---|
| | | 射撃する しゃげきする shoot, fire at....1021 |
| | | ○反撃 はんげき counterattack................0374 |
| | ゲキ | ○撃つ うつ strike, attack; shoot |
| | う(つ) | 撃ち破る うちやぶる defeat, crush..........0596 |

| 1026 | Visualize an aggressive fist (手)-first **attack** into an opposing force made up of armored *cars* (車) and *lancers* (殳). The increasing width of S12–14 gives the character something of a 3-D quality, visually suggesting a **STRIKING** fist. ☞ 繋 1576 |
|---|---|
| 手 64 | |
| 擊 | |
| 2492 | |
| 常 15 | |

|  | WIPE | ○拭く ふく wipe, dry |
|---|---|---|
| | | ○拭う ぬぐう wipe |
| | | 手拭い てぬぐい handkerchief, towel.......0046 |
| | ショク | 口拭き くちふき napkin.......................0019 |
| | ふ(く) ぬぐ(う) | 払拭する ふっしょくする (=ふっしきする) sweep, wipe away..................................0812 |

| 1027 | Review 式 0109. As when waxing a floor or washing a window, the *hands* (扌) must *follow prescribed form* (式) when **WIPING**. |
|---|---|
| 手 64 | |
| 0338 | |
| 常 9 | |

|  | TRY, test | 試食 ししょく sampling (of food) .............0288 |
|---|---|---|
| | | ○試運転 しうんてん test run .............0584, 0224 |
| | | 試合 しあい match, game ....................0227 |
| | シ | ○試み こころみ trial, attempt, test |
| | こころ(みる) ため(す) | ○試してみる ためしてみる give (something) a try |

| 1028 | It is best to associate this character's meaning of **TRY**/test with a **test** in school, in which one must speak or write *words* (言) *according to a prescribed form* (式). ☞ 誠 1299 |
|---|---|
| 言 149 | |
| 1385 | |
| 常 13 | |

**EXAMINE, investigate**

ケン

| | |
|---|---|
| 点検 てんけん inspection, examination | 0349 |
| 車検 しゃけん automobile inspection | 0125 |
| ○検討する けんとうする examine, study, investigate | 1023 |
| 検察 けんさつ criminal investigation | 0639 |
| 検事 けんじ public prosecutor | 0080 |

| 1029 | |
|---|---|
| 木 75 | |
| 検 | |
| 0898 | |
| 常 12 | |

Earlier we learned to see 吏 as an *official's horse* (0886). The right half of the present entry shows a similar form, with a *roof* over it to suggest *horse stable*. In this sequence of five characters based on *stable*, the one with 木 *wood* refers to the construction process, in which we must carefully **EXAMINE** the building materials.

**TEST, examine**

ケン ゲン

| | |
|---|---|
| 験算 けんざん verification of accounts, checking figures | 0980 |
| ○試験 しけん test, examination | 1028 |
| 受験する じゅけんする take an examination | 0065 |
| 体験する たいけんする experience, go through, (actually) feel | 0062 |
| 実験 じっけん experiment | 0499 |

| 1030 | |
|---|---|
| 馬 187 | |
| 驗 | |
| 1628 | |
| 常 18 | |

Next to be **examined** are the *horses* themselves (馬). Here we take one out for a **TEST** ride. Note the traditional form, whose pattern is followed by the other kanji in this group. Also note that all the kanji in this group have the *on-yomi* ケン, though the present entry is read ゲン in a few compounds.

¹**DANGEROUS**
²**STEEP**

ケン
けわ(しい)

| | |
|---|---|
| ①危険な きけんな dangerous | 0726 |
| ¹ 険悪な けんあくな dangerous, threatening, hostile, serious | 0546 |
| ¹ 保険 ほけん insurance | 0646 |
| ² 険路 けんろ steep pass | 0788 |
| ②険しい けわしい steep; craggy; severe, grim | |

| 1031 | |
|---|---|
| 阜 170 | |
| 險 | |
| 0495 | |
| 常 11 | |

Horses are a precious commodity, so it is of some concern that this particular *stable* should be perched so **DANGEROUSLY** on a **STEEP** *hill* (阝).

**FRUGAL**

ケン

| | |
|---|---|
| 倹約 けんやく economy, frugality, thrift | 0170 |
| ○節倹 せっけん economy, frugality, thrift | 0391 |

| 1032 | |
|---|---|
| 人 9 | |
| 儉 | |
| 0098 | |
| 常 10 | |

The *man* (亻) who works at the stable (the stable hand), notorious for his poverty, also symbolizes the virtues of **FRUGAL** living.

**SWORD**

ケン
つるぎ

刀剣 とうけん sword......................0085
○真剣 しんけん real sword; seriousness ......0838
剣道 けんどう fencing, swordsmanship, kendo
.......................0158
剣客 けんきゃく (=けんかく) swordsman, fencer
.......................0787
○剣を研ぐ つるぎをとぐ sharpen a sword.....0724

| 1033 | Now picture a **SWORD** (刂) slicing the *stable* right in two. |
| 刀 18 | |

劔

1493
常 | 10

**VALLEY**

コク
たに

空谷 くうこく lonely valley ..................0398
谷川 たにがわ valley stream, mountain stream
.......................0022
谷水 たにみず valley water, rill.............0027
谷底 たにそこ bottom of a ravine, valley bottom
.......................0482
○谷間 たにま valley, gorge.................0448

| 1034 | Picture a **VALLEY** in the mountains. S1–2 are the slopes of distant peaks, S3–4 the outlines of |
| 谷 150 | a widening **VALLEY**, and 口 a pond or field in the middle of it. Compare with 合 0227, which |
| | has an extra stroke under its "lid" to complete the image of FIT. The key contrast, of course, is |
| | the presence or absence of mountain peaks in the background. |

1758
常 | 7

**DESIRE**

ヨク
ほっ（する）　ほ（しい）

○食欲 しょくよく appetite (for food) ..........0288
物欲 ぶつよく worldly desires...............0172
意欲 いよく volition, will, desire............0151
平和を欲する へいわをほっする wish for peace
.......................0334, 0236
○欲しがる ほしがる desire, wish for

| 1035 | In the mountain *valley* (谷) dwells a community of simple peasant folk. Though they lead |
| 欠 76 | a happy life there, they know there are luxuries in the city that they lack. Here we see their |
| | *wide-open mouths* (欠), symbolizing people's insatiable **DESIRE** for more. |

慾

1341
常 | 11

**BATHE**

ヨク
あ（びる）　あ（びせる）

○浴室 よくしつ bathroom...................0253
入浴する にゅうよくする bathe, take a bath 0039
○浴びる あびる [vi] bathe; be bathed in
浴びせる あびせる [vt] pour (water) on; shower (abuse) upon
浴衣 ゆかた (=よくい) informal summer kimono
.......................0700

| 1036 | Here picture **BATHING** in the *water* (氵) of a pond or stream in a *valley* (谷) among mountains. |
| 水 85 | ☞ 溶 1038 |

0404
常 | 10

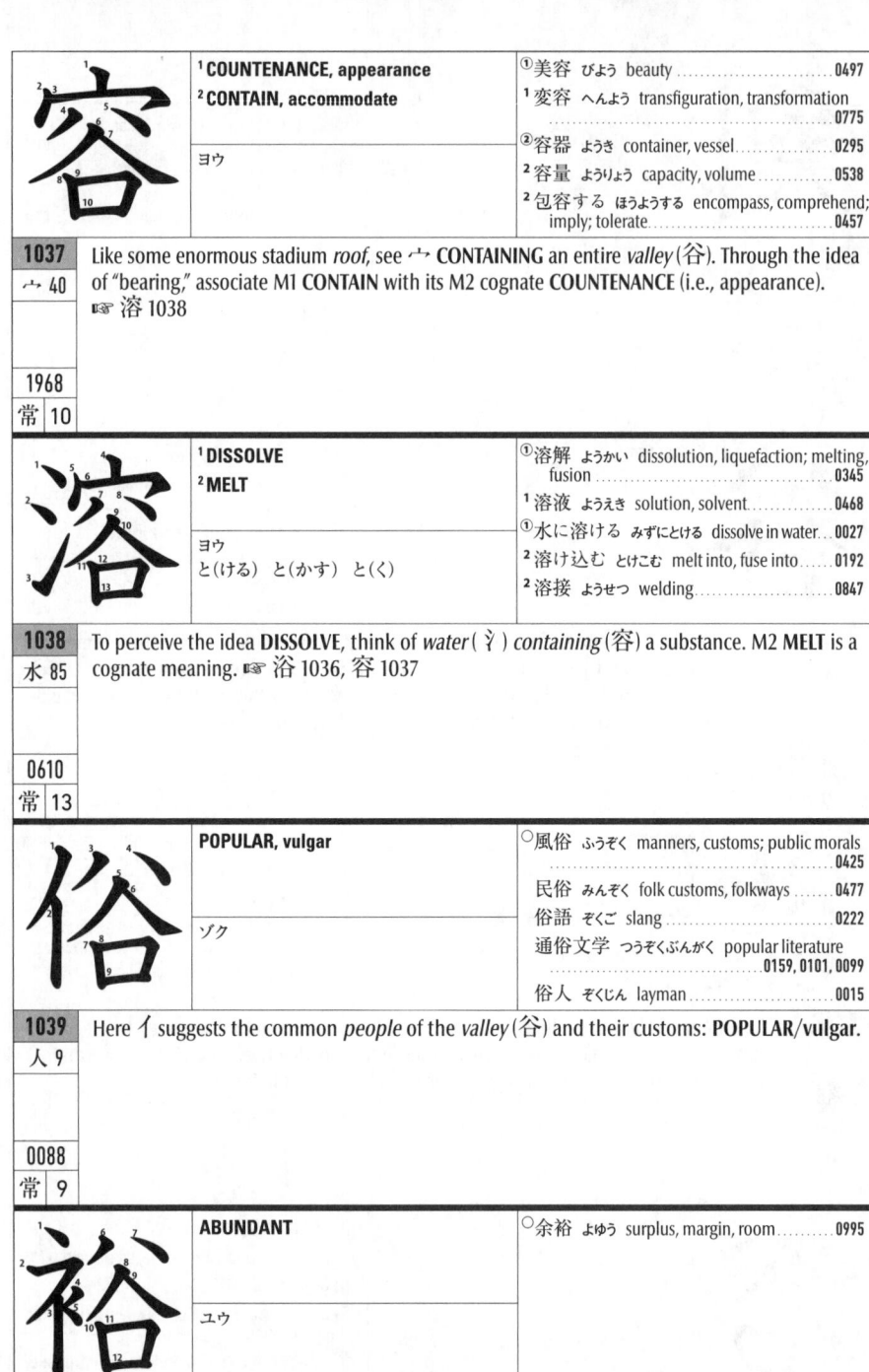

## 容

¹ **COUNTENANCE, appearance**
² **CONTAIN, accommodate**

ヨウ

① 美容 びよう beauty ................................................ 0497
¹ 変容 へんよう transfiguration, transformation ........................................ 0775
② 容器 ようき container, vessel .................. 0295
² 容量 ようりよう capacity, volume .............. 0538
² 包容する ほうようする encompass, comprehend; imply; tolerate .............................. 0457

| 1037 | Like some enormous stadium *roof*, see ⼧ CONTAINING an entire *valley* (谷). Through the idea of "bearing," associate M1 CONTAIN with its M2 cognate COUNTENANCE (i.e., appearance). ☞ 溶 1038 |
| ⼧ 40 | |
| 1968 | |
| 常 10 | |

## 溶

¹ **DISSOLVE**
² **MELT**

ヨウ
と(ける) と(かす) と(く)

① 溶解 ようかい dissolution, liquefaction; melting, fusion ................................................ 0345
¹ 溶液 ようえき solution, solvent ................ 0468
① 水に溶ける みずにとける dissolve in water ... 0027
² 溶け込む とけこむ melt into, fuse into ...... 0192
² 溶接 ようせつ welding ............................ 0847

| 1038 | To perceive the idea **DISSOLVE**, think of *water* (氵) *containing* (容) a substance. M2 **MELT** is a cognate meaning. ☞ 浴 1036, 容 1037 |
| 水 85 | |
| 0610 | |
| 常 13 | |

## 俗

**POPULAR, vulgar**

ゾク

○ 風俗 ふうぞく manners, customs; public morals ................................................ 0425
民俗 みんぞく folk customs, folkways ....... 0477
俗語 ぞくご slang ................................ 0222
通俗文学 つうぞくぶんがく popular literature
............................................ 0159, 0101, 0099
俗人 ぞくじん layman ............................ 0015

| 1039 | Here 亻 suggests the common *people* of the *valley* (谷) and their customs: **POPULAR/vulgar**. |
| 人 9 | |
| 0088 | |
| 常 9 | |

## 裕

**ABUNDANT**

ユウ

○ 余裕 よゆう surplus, margin, room .......... 0995

| 1040 | The people in the *valley* (谷) make their own *clothing* (衤) from local materials, freely available all around them. Thus *clothing* in the *valley* is **ABUNDANT**. See 富 1481 and 福 1484 for additional sample compounds. |
| 衣 145 | |
| 1104 | |
| 常 12 | |

| 寛 | **LENIENT** | 寛大な かんだいな generous, magnanimous, lenient ........................................0033 |
| | | ○寛容な かんような tolerant, liberal, generous ........................................................1037 |
| | カン | 寛厳 かんげん lenience and severity ........0810 |

**1041**
宀 40
寛
2031
常 13

This is the only kanji in this course in which "grass-crown" (艹) is <u>itself</u> crowned. Let us use this fact thus: see the *grass* as a kind of padding to soften the pressure of the heavy *roof* (宀) placed atop this fragile *seeing* eyeball (見). In this way the character symbolizes **LENIENCE**.

| 甘 | **SWEET** | ○甘味料 かんみりょう sweetener.........0273, 0758 |
| | | 甘酸 かんさん sweetness and bitterness; pain and pleasure...................................0800 |
| | カン | ○甘い あまい sweet; indulgent; overly optimistic |
| | あま(い) あま(える) あま(やかす) | 甘口の あまくちの sweet (wine), mild (tobacco) ........................................................0019 |
| | | 甘やかす あまやかす pamper, spoil |

**1042**
甘 99
2930
常 5

Derives from a picture of an open mouth with a **SWEET** (S4) laid on the tongue. Think of a sugary candy melting on your tongue as you let this image find a place in your memory.

| 紺 | **DARK BLUE** | ○紺色 こんいろ dark blue, navy blue..........0528 |
| | | 紺屋 こうや (=こんや) dyer; dyer's shop......0252 |
| | | 濃紺 のうこん dark blue, navy blue..........0512 |
| | コン | 紺の背広 こんのせびろ blue business suit ........................................................0124, 0238 |

**1043**
糸 120
1219
常 11

To connect *sweet* (甘) and **DARK BLUE**, imagine a bowl of *sweet* blueberries spilling on a dyer's *thread* (糸) and turning it all sweet blueberry blue. Thrilled by this discovery, the dyer decides to make all **DARK BLUE** thread in this way.

| 紅 | **CRIMSON** | 紅白 こうはく red and white .................0076 |
| | | 紅葉 こうよう fall colors.......................0605 |
| | | もみじ fall colors; Japanese maple |
| | コウ ク | ○紅茶 こうちゃ black tea.......................0603 |
| | べに くれない | ○口紅 くちべに lipstick, rouge.................0019 |
| | | 薄紅 うすくれない light crimson, pink........0986 |

**1044**
糸 120
1174
常 9

The next four entries require us to visualize a series of actions being taken with an *I beam* (工). Here, informed by his serendipitous discovery of a dye for DARK BLUE (紺), the dyer learns to dye *threads* **CRIMSON** by rubbing them against a rusting iron *I beam*.

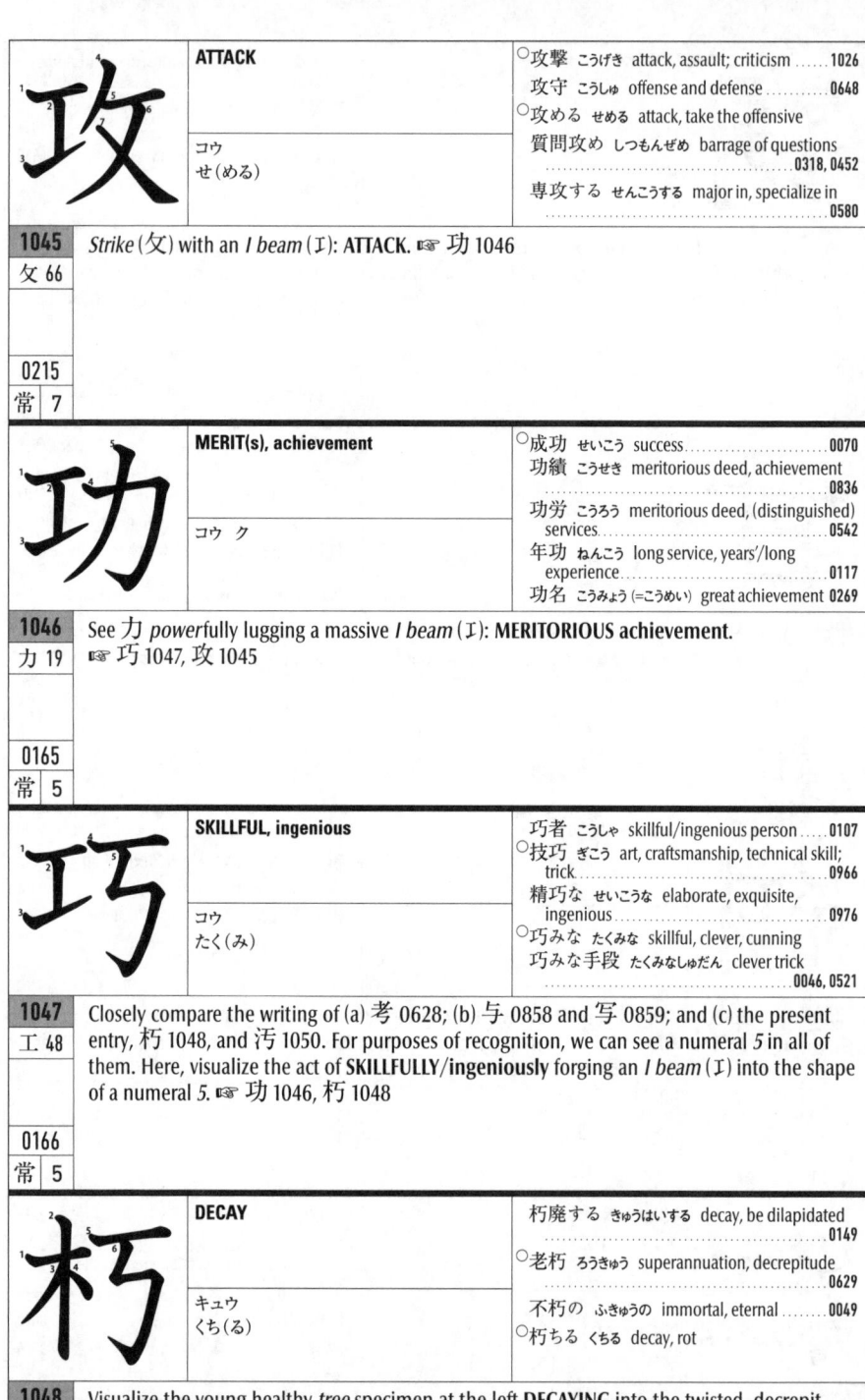

| 攻 | **ATTACK** | ○攻撃 こうげき attack, assault; criticism ...... 1026 |
| | | 攻守 こうしゅ offense and defense .......... 0648 |
| | | ○攻める せめる attack, take the offensive |
| | コウ | 質問攻め しつもんぜめ barrage of questions |
| | せ(める) | .................................................... 0318, 0452 |
| | | 専攻する せんこうする major in, specialize in |
| | | .................................................................. 0580 |

| **1045** | *Strike* (攵) with an *I beam* (工): **ATTACK.** ☞ 功 1046 |
| 攵 66 | |
| 0215 | |
| 常 7 | |

| 功 | **MERIT(s), achievement** | ○成功 せいこう success ........................ 0070 |
| | | 功績 こうせき meritorious deed, achievement |
| | | .................................................................. 0836 |
| | | 功労 こうろう meritorious deed, (distinguished) |
| | コウ ク | services .................................................. 0542 |
| | | 年功 ねんこう long service, years'/long |
| | | experience ............................................. 0117 |
| | | 功名 こうみょう (=こうめい) great achievement 0269 |

| **1046** | See 力 *powerfully* lugging a massive *I beam* (工): **MERITORIOUS achievement.** |
| 力 19 | ☞ 巧 1047, 攻 1045 |
| 0165 | |
| 常 5 | |

| 巧 | **SKILLFUL, ingenious** | 巧者 こうしゃ skillful/ingenious person ..... 0107 |
| | | ○技巧 ぎこう art, craftsmanship, technical skill; |
| | | trick .................................................... 0966 |
| | | 精巧な せいこうな elaborate, exquisite, |
| | コウ | ingenious .............................................. 0976 |
| | たく(み) | ○巧みな たくみな skillful, clever, cunning |
| | | 巧みな手段 たくみなしゅだん clever trick |
| | | .......................................................... 0046, 0521 |

| **1047** | Closely compare the writing of (a) 考 0628; (b) 与 0858 and 写 0859; and (c) the present |
| 工 48 | entry, 朽 1048, and 汚 1050. For purposes of recognition, we can see a numeral *5* in all of |
| | them. Here, visualize the act of **SKILLFULLY**/ingeniously forging an *I beam* (工) into the shape |
| | of a numeral *5*. ☞ 功 1046, 朽 1048 |
| 0166 | |
| 常 5 | |

| 朽 | **DECAY** | 朽廃する きゅうはいする decay, be dilapidated |
| | | .................................................................. 0149 |
| | | ○老朽 ろうきゅう superannuation, decrepitude |
| | | .................................................................. 0629 |
| | キュウ | 不朽の ふきゅうの immortal, eternal ........ 0049 |
| | くち(る) | ○朽ちる くちる decay, rot |

| **1048** | Visualize the young healthy *tree* specimen at the left **DECAYING** into the twisted, decrepit |
| 木 75 | numeral *5*-shaped specimen at the right, looking like some old, warped bristlecone pine. Do |
| | not confuse 朽ちる (くちる) with 腐る (くさる) 2183 (both mean "decay"). ☞ 巧 1047 |
| 0727 | |
| 常 6 | |

| | **WITHER** | ○枯死 こし withering, dying ................. 0716 |
|---|---|---|
| | | 枯れ葉 かれは dead/withered leaf ......... 0605 |
| | | ○枯れ木 かれき dead/withered tree ........ 0028 |
| | コ | 夏枯れ なつがれ summer inactivity, summer slump ................................. 0363 |
| | か(れる) か(らす) | 木枯らし こがらし cold wintry wind ......... 0028 |

| **1049** | An *old* (古) *tree* (木), **WITHERING**. |
|---|---|
| 木 75 | |
| **0801** | |
| 常 9 | |

| | **DIRTY, defile** | 汚物 おぶつ dirt, filth, impurities ........... 0172 |
|---|---|---|
| | | ○汚名 おめい bad name, ill fame, disgrace ... 0269 |
| | | 汚す けがす defile, disgrace, desecrate |
| | オ | 汚す よごす make dirty, soil, defile |
| | けが(す) けが(れる) けが(らわしい) よご(す) よご(れる) きたな(い) | ○汚い きたない dirty, soiled; foul, base, obscene |

| **1050** | While this entry shares the crossing stroke with 与 0858 and 写 0859, the writing of its |
|---|---|
| 水 85 | 5 shape follows that of 巧 1047 and 朽 1048. When you see the crossed numeral *5* with *water* (氵), think of the crossing stroke as **defiling** the *5* (i.e., making it **DIRTY**), so that we feel compelled to take the *water* and wash out the offending stroke. |
| **0196** | |
| 常 6 | |

| | ***SHO* (1.8 liters)** | 一升 いっしょう 1 *sho* ....................... 0002 |
|---|---|---|
| | ショウ ます | |

| **1051** | Earlier we learned to see 廾 as *two hands* (see 戒 0469, 葬 0717, and 算 0980). Now we |
|---|---|
| 十 24 | add the meaning *twenty* (double *ten* 十). Here imagine a 2-liter container with gradations marked at every deciliter (0.1 liters). At full capacity, it would be filled to the *twentieth* mark. Start with *20* deciliters (廾) then pour a little out (S1): **1.8 liters.** ☞ 弁 1052 |
| **2906** | |
| 常 4 | |

| | ¹ **SPEAK, argue** | ¹ 答弁する とうべんする reply, answer; defend oneself ................................. 0981 |
|---|---|---|
| | ² **MANAGE** | ¹ 関西弁 かんさいべん Kansai dialect ......... 0451, 0795 |
| | ³ **VALVE** | ① 代弁する だいべんする speak/act for another ... 0071 |
| | ベン | ² 弁償する べんしょうする compensate, indemnify ..................................... 0323 |
| | | ³ 安全弁 あんぜんべん safety valve ......... 0096, 0078 |

| **1052** | This is the modern simplified form of three distinct kanji: 辯 (**SPEAK**), 辨 (**MANAGE**), and 瓣 |
|---|---|
| 廾 55 | (**VALVE**). We can perceive the first two meanings together by seeing ム as a courtroom attorney's *elbow* leaning on the jury box balustrade (廾) as he **MANAGES** his client's case/**SPEAKS** his closing **argument** (see V3 here and V5 at 護 1661). ☞ 升 1051 |
| 辯 | |
| **1730** | |
| 常 5 | |

**ASCEND, rise in rank**

ショウ
のぼ(る)

上昇する じょうしょうする ascend, rise........0041
○昇進する しょうしんする be promoted, rise in rank ................................0191
昇格する しょうかくする be promoted to a higher status.....................0789
昇給 しょうきゅう salary raise .................0526
○位が昇る くらいがのぼる rise in rank........0577

| 1053 | See the *sun* **ASCEND**/*rise* up over 升, just the way it rose over 十 in 早 0143 EARLY and 朝 0145 MORNING. Also compare with 旦 1392 DAWN. |
| 日 72 | |
| 2139 | |
| 常 8 | |

---

**¹ ASCEND, climb**
**² ATTEND, appear**
**³ REGISTER**

トウ ト
のぼ(る)

①山を登る やまをのぼる climb a mountain...0037
¹ 登坂 とうはん climbing a hill ................0375
②登場する とうじょうする come on stage; appear ..............................0445
③登録 とうろく registration ...................0608
³ 登記簿 とうきぼ register...............0427, 0985

| 1054 | We saw at 発 0148 that 癶 means *outspread legs*. Here we see a *bean* (豆) spread out its legs like a rock climber, stretching to reach a pair of good footholds from which to **ASCEND** a rock face. M2 **ATTEND**/**appear** can be thought of as "**climbing**" into the place where one is awaited, and M3 **REGISTER** as "**climbing**" into the books. |
| 癶 105 | |
| 2251 | |
| 常 12 | |

---

**LIMPID**

チョウ
す(む) す(ます) -す(ます)

清澄な せいちょうな clear, lucid; serene .....0974
○明澄な めいちょうな unclouded, clear, limpid ..................................0024
○澄む すむ become clear
澄んだ水 すんだみず limpid water..........0027
見澄ます みすます observe carefully, watch intently.................................0083

| 1055 | As impurities settle to the bottom, **LIMPID** *water* (氵) *climbs* (登) to the top. |
| 水 85 | |
| 澂 | |
| 0674 | |
| 常 15 | |

---

**¹ FILL**
**² ALLOT**

ジュウ
あ(てる)

¹ 充満する じゅうまんする be full..............0179
①充分(=十分)な じゅうぶんな full, enough; plentiful.......................0088, 0005
¹ 拡充 かくじゅう expansion, amplification....0813
¹ 充員 じゅういん reserves......................0317
②充てる あてる allot, assign

| 1056 | Review 育 0489. Here the parent 云 must cope with the "hollow legs" of adolescence (儿). See the parent reach down with a *bent arm* (厶) to **FILL** the hungry child's *legs* with his full **ALLOTMENT** of nourishment. |
| 儿 10 | |
| 1737 | |
| 常 6 | |

| | GUN, rifle | 銃撃 じゅうげき shooting (down) ............. 1026 |
|---|---|---|
| | | ○銃砲 じゅうほう firearm ........................ 0665 |
| | | 猟銃 りょうじゅう hunting gun ................. 0764 |
| | ジュウ | 短銃 たんじゅう pistol ......................... 0562 |
| | | 機関銃 きかんじゅう machine gun ...... 0473, 0451 |

| **1057** | This combination suggests *filling* (充) something made of *metal* (金), and refers to the act of |
|---|---|
| 金 167 | loading a **GUN**. |
| **1535** | |
| 常 14 | |

| | ¹ UNITE, subjugate | ¹統一 とういつ unity, coordination, standardiza- |
|---|---|---|
| | ² INTERCONNECTED SYSTEM | tion .............................................. 0002 |
| | | ①統制 とうせい control, regulation ............ 0708 |
| | | ①統べる すべる unite, unify |
| | トウ | ² 血統 けっとう lineage, bloodline ............. 0198 |
| | す（べる） | ②伝統 でんとう tradition, convention ......... 0223 |

| **1058** | "*String* (糸) + *fill* (充)" suggests tying together fully/completely: **UNITE**. M2 **INTERCONNECTED** |
|---|---|
| 糸 120 | **SYSTEM** should be learned by extension from M1. |
| **1239** | |
| 常 12 | |

| | ¹ FLOW | ①流れる ながれる flow; [of time] pass; float |
|---|---|---|
| | ² CURRENT | ①流通 りゅうつう circulation; flow ............. 0159 |
| | ³ STYLE | ¹ 上流 じょうりゅう upper stream (of a river); upper |
| | リュウ ル | class ............................................. 0041 |
| | なが（れる） なが（れ） なが（す） | ² 電流 でんりゅう electric current ............. 0155 |
| | -なが（す） | ³ 三島流の みしまりゅうの in the style of Mishima |
| | | ............................................ 0004, 0341 |

| **1059** | Picking up from 充 1056, we now find the parent's *bent arm* (厶) reaching down to flush a |
|---|---|
| 水 85 | toilet, releasing a **FLOW** or **CURRENT** of *water* (氵) resembling a river (川) (note, however, that |
| | S10 curls to the right and then up). Associate M3 **STYLE** with M2 **CURRENT**. |
| **0400** | |
| 常 10 | |

| | SULFUR | ○硫酸 りゅうさん sulfuric acid ................... 0800 |
|---|---|---|
| | | 硫黄 いおう sulfur ............................. 0915 |
| | | 硫黄島 いおうじま Iwo Jima (island) ... 0915, 0341 |
| | リュウ | |

| **1060** | **SULFUR** is associated with volcanism, suggested here by *flowing rock* (石) (the meaning *flow-* |
|---|---|
| 石 112 | *ing* is borrowed from 流). ☞ 硝 1290 |
| **1096** | |
| 常 12 | |

**BLIND**

モウ

| | | |
|---|---|---|
| 盲人 もうじん blind person | | 0015 |
| ○盲目 もうもく blindness | | 0021 |
| 盲信 もうしん blind belief | | 0063 |
| 盲学校 もうがっこう school for the blind | | 0099, 0103 |
| 色盲 しきもう color blindness | | 0528 |

| 1061 | *Dead* (亡) *eyes* (目): **BLIND**. Review 亡 0233 if necessary. |
|---|---|
| 目 109 | |
| 1767 | |
| 常 8 | |

**FORGET**

ボウ
わす (れる)

| | |
|---|---|
| ○忘失する ぼうしつする forget, lose | 0563 |
| 忘年会 ぼうねんかい year-end party | 0117, 0226 |
| 忘却する ぼうきゃくする forget | 0733 |
| ○忘れる わすれる forget | |
| 忘れ物 わすれもの lost item, something left behind | 0172 |

| 1062 | The only difference between this character and the next one is whether *heart/mind* drops below 亡 or squeezes beside it. To keep them distinct, associate 忘 **FORGET** with the *mind's* dropping or falling, and 忙 BUSY with its being tightly squeezed by time demands. In the first *dies* knowledge; in the second *dies* time to think. ☞ 忙 1063 |
|---|---|
| 心 61 | |
| 1753 | |
| 常 7 | |

**BUSY**

ボウ
いそが (しい)

| | |
|---|---|
| ○多忙な たぼうな busy | 0267 |
| 忙殺される ぼうさつされる be very busily occupied, be worked to death | 0522 |
| 忙しさ いそがしさ busyness | |
| ○仕事で忙しい しごとでいそがしい be busy with one's work | 0371, 0080 |

| 1063 | (See previous entry) ☞ 忘 1062 |
|---|---|
| 心 61 | |
| 0188 | |
| 常 6 | |

**WILD, barren; devastated, ruined**

コウ
あら (い) あら- あ (れる) あ (らす)
-あ (らし)

| | |
|---|---|
| ○荒天 こうてん stormy weather | 0270 |
| 荒廃 こうはい desolation, waste, ruin | 0149 |
| ○荒れる あれる become rough; run wild; be devastated | |
| 荒い波 あらいなみ raging waves, stormy seas | 0598 |
| 荒っぽい あらっぽい rough, wild, rude | |

| 1064 | *Grass* (艹) + *die* (亡) + *river* (川): picture a **WILD** river **devastating** the vegetation in its path. Note again how the third stroke of what we are here calling *river* differs from that of 川 0022 RIVER. |
|---|---|
| 艸 140 | |
| 1950 | |
| 常 9 | |

**FLURRIED, hurried**

コウ
あわ(てる) あわ(ただしい)

○慌てる あわてる be flurried, be confused, be in a hurry
慌てて あわてて in confusion, in hot haste
大慌て おおあわて total fluster, hot haste...**0033**
慌てるな あわてるな Calm down!; Hold your horses!
慌ただしい あわただしい flurried, confused; busy, hurried

| 1065 | |
|---|---|
| 心 61 | *Wild* (荒)–*minded* (忄): **FLURRIED/hurried**. A sample *on-yomi* compound appears at 恐 1633. |
| 0532 | |
| 常 12 | |

¹ **HOPE**
² **LOOK AFAR**

ボウ モウ
のぞ(む)

①欲望 よくぼう desire, craving.............**1035**
¹ 要望 ようぼう demand, request.............**0547**
¹ 失望する しつぼうする be disappointed, despair.............**0563**
①望む のぞむ hope for, desire
² 展望する てんぼうする have a view of.......**0880**

| 1066 | |
|---|---|
| 月 74 | A *king* (王) believes the members of his line ascend to the *moon* (月) after they *die* (亡). Picture the king **LOOKING** up at the moon **AFAR**, **HOPING** to find his ancestors and a place where he might go in death. |
| 2390 | |
| 常 11 | |

¹ **RARE**
² **ASPIRE**

キ
まれ*

¹ 希元素 きげんそ rare element.........**0136, 0132**
①希少な きしょうな scarce, rare .............**0677**
①希な まれな rare, uncommon, scarce
¹ 希薄な きはくな dilute, thin, rare, sparse.....**0986**
②希望 きぼう hope, wish, aspiration.........**1066**

| 1067 | |
|---|---|
| 巾 50 | At 殺 0522 we learned to see メ as a pair of *slash marks*. Here see it as an "*x*" marking this **RARE** *cloth* (布) as forbidden, for its scarcity. Naturally, such an object is one people **ASPIRE** to possess. |
| 1763 | |
| 常 7 | |

**RARE**

キ ケ
まれ

稀代の きたいの (=きだいの) uncommon, rare
.........**0071**
稀有な けうな (=きゆうな) rare, unusual, uncommon.........**0400**
○稀少な きしょうな scarce, rare .............**0677**
稀薄な きはくな dilute, thin, rare, sparse....**0986**
○稀な まれな rare, uncommon, scarce

| 1068 | |
|---|---|
| 禾 115 | One ought not to take one's *rice* (禾) for granted; often enough it has been a **RARE** commodity. Interchangeable with the previous entry when that one means rare. |
| 1099 | |
| 名 12 | |

| | LUMP TOGETHER | 一括する いっかつする lump together, sum up .................................0002 |
|---|---|---|
| **括** | | ○総括的 そうかつてき all-inclusive, all-embracing .........................0557, 0169 |
| カツ | | 包括する ほうかつする include, comprehend, comprise.................0457 |
| | | 統括する とうかつする generalize ...........1058 |

| 1069 | Imagine the *hand* (扌) rolling the *tongue* (舌) **TOGETHER** in a **LUMP**. |
|---|---|
| 手 64 | |
| 0334 | |
| 常 9 | |

| | ARREST | 拘禁する こうきんする detain, confine, imprison .................................0312 |
|---|---|---|
| **拘** | | ○拘置 こうち detention, confinement, arrest 0843 |
| コウ | | 拘束 こうそく restriction, restraint, binding...0307 |
| かか(わる)* | | ○拘わる かかわる adhere to, stick to |
| | | ...にも拘わらず ...にもかかわらず in spite of ..., regardless of ... |

| 1070 | Recall the **PHRASE**-speaking elephant from 句 0166. Such an elephant is bound to cause public commotion, leading ultimately to his **ARREST**. This act is symbolized here by *hand* (扌), presumably that of the animal warden. ☞ 抱 0664, 句 0166 |
|---|---|
| 手 64 | |
| 0274 | |
| 常 8 | |

| | PICK UP | ○拾得する しゅうとくする pick up, find ........0387 |
|---|---|---|
| **拾** | | 拾い上げる ひろいあげる pick up; pick out 0041 |
| シュウ ジュウ | | 拾い集める ひろいあつめる gather, collect 0190 |
| ひろ(う) | | ○石を拾う いしをひろう pick up a stone .......0403 |

| 1071 | To learn this kanji, think of your *hand* (扌) as "*fitting*" (合) itself to an object whenever it **PICKS** one **UP**. Close and **PICK UP** this book, and notice how your *hand fits* itself to the precise shape of the book in order to do so. ☞ 捨 1072 |
|---|---|
| 手 64 | |
| 0339 | |
| 常 9 | |

| | DISCARD | 取捨 しゅしゃ adoption or rejection, choice 0059 |
|---|---|---|
| **捨** | | 四捨五入 ししゃごにゅう rounding (to the nearest integer) ..........................0006, 0007, 0039 |
| シャ | | ○捨てる すてる discard, throw away, abandon |
| す(てる) | | 捨て子 すてご abandoned child ...........0094 |
| | | 見捨てる みすてる forsake, desert ..........0083 |

| 1072 | Review 舎 0910. Here, a *hand* (扌) tosses a piece of garbage into the earth-floored *hut* (舎): **DISCARD**. ☞ 措 1219, 拾 1071 |
|---|---|
| 手 64 | |
| 0461 | |
| 常 11 | |

| 孤 | **SOLITARY** | ○孤独の こどくの solitary, lonely, alone......0346 |
| | | 孤立 こりつ isolation ........................0067 |
| | | 孤客 こかく lone traveler.................0787 |
| | コ | 孤島 ことう solitary island................0341 |
| | | 孤児 こじ orphan ...........................0772 |

| **1073** | Review 瓜 0202. This *child* (子) is anxious to find a **SOLITARY** place where he will be left |
| 子 39 | alone to eat his *melon*. ☞ 弧 1074 |
| **0317** | |
| 常 9 | |

| 弧 | **ARC** | 弧状の こじょうの arc-shaped................0616 |
| | | ○括弧 かっこ parentheses, brackets .........1069 |
| | | 弧線 こせん arc (of a circle)................0210 |
| | コ | 弧形 こけい arc............................0147 |
| | | 円弧 えんこ circular arc; arc of a circle ......0013 |

| **1074** | Think of drawing a bowstring until the *bow* (弓) is bent into a *melon* (瓜)-shaped **ARC**. Prac- |
| 弓 57 | tice writing this entry in alternation with the last one, and learn to determine their meanings |
| **0320** | from the variable component. ☞ 孤 1073 |
| 常 9 | |

| 弾 | ¹ **PROJECTILE, bullet** | ①弾丸 だんがん shot, bullet, shell............0012 |
| | ² **SPRING BACK; play on (stringed** | ¹ 砲弾 ほうだん cannonball, shell ............0665 |
| | **instruments)** | ②弾む はずむ spring back, rebound; be animated |
| | ダン | ....................................0084, 0128 |
| | ひ(く) -ひ(き) はず(む) たま | ² 弾力性 だんりょくせい elasticity; flexibility |
| | | ②弾く ひく play on (stringed instruments) |

| **1075** | Review 戦 0461 and 単 0462. Here see the man's outstretched arms drawing back the *bow* |
| 弓 57 | (弓) at full force and firing a **PROJECTILE** from among those stored on top of his head. Hear |
| 弾 | the bowstring **SPRING BACK** into place as he does this—a pleasant sound like that made by |
| **0524** | **playing on a stringed instrument.** |
| 常 12 | |

| 禅 | **ZEN** | ○禅宗 ぜんしゅう Zen sect .....................0636 |
| | | 座禅 ざぜん Zen meditation................0749 |
| | ゼン | 禅寺 ぜんでら Zen temple..................0382 |

| **1076** | Review 学 0099. Here think of ⺍ as **ZEN** *enlightenment* from *God* (ネ). Picture the man with |
| 示 113 | his arms spread out in **ZEN** meditation and the pieces of enlightenment coming down into |
| 禅 | his head. |
| **0947** | |
| 常 13 | |

| | ¹ SYSTEM, interrelated group<br>² LINEAGE, descent | ①体系 たいけい system, organization.........0062<br>¹ 系列 けいれつ order, succession; series.....0718<br>②系図 けいず genealogy, pedigree...........0298<br>² 直系 ちょっけい direct descent line ..........0839<br>² 日系ブラジル人 にっけいブラジルじん Brazilians of Japanese descent................0001, 0015 |
| | ケイ | |

| 1077 | Let S1 represent the point where a yarn spinner attaches a fiber to a post. That becomes the origin of the *thread* that he spins from the fiber. Now picture a long unbroken *thread descending* down from this point, symbolizing an unbroken ancestral **LINEAGE** (recall from 続 0354 that 系 will sometimes suggest *continuity*). This image of a shared organizing line can also symbolize any **interrelated group** or **SYSTEM**. ☞ 系 0112 |
|---|---|
| 糸 120 | |
| 1701 | |
| 常 7 | |

| | ¹ CONNECT, relate to<br>² PERSON IN CHARGE | ①関係 かんけい relation, relationship, connection ...........................0451<br>¹ 連係 れんけい connection, linking, contact 0582<br>¹ 係わる かかわる be concerned in, affect<br>¹ 係累 けいるい dependent(s), encumbrance(s) ...........................0884<br>②会計係 かいけいがかり accountant, treasurer ...........................0226, 0555 |
| | ケイ<br>かか(る) かかり -がかり かか(わる)* | |

| 1078 | Building on the previous entry, we now see a *man* (亻) who is **CONNECTED**/related to the *system*/*lineage* (系). To build from M1 to M2, think of the **PERSON IN CHARGE** of an activity as the person whose work is **related to** that activity (see V5). |
|---|---|
| 人 9 | |
| 0078 | |
| 常 9 | |

| | GRANDCHILD | 皇孫 こうそん imperial grandchild...........0077<br>王孫 おうそん royal grandson................0072<br>○子孫 しそん descendant, offspring .........0094<br>天孫 てんそん descendant of a god .........0270<br>○お孫さん おまごさん your grandchild |
| | ソン<br>まご | |

| 1079 | The *child* (子) at the end of the *lineage* (系): **GRANDCHILD**. |
|---|---|
| 子 39 | |
| 0370 | |
| 常 10 | |

| | SUSPEND | 懸垂 けんすい suspension; chin-ups........1004<br>懸案 けんあん pending question/problem...0097<br>懸念 けねん anxiety, concern, fear ..........0230<br>○一生懸命 いっしょうけんめい with all one's might ...................0002, 0036, 0232<br>賞金を懸ける しょうきんをかける offer a prize ...................0322, 0029 |
| | ケン ケ<br>か(ける) か(かる) | |

| 1080 | See 心 as **SUSPENDED** perilously from the bottom of 縣, a fragile thread extending from each of its five points of attachment to a corresponding point of attachment above it (it might help to sketch this in the margin, with more space separating 心). Focus visually on this set of corresponding points and use it as a visual shortcut to the idea **SUSPEND**. |
|---|---|
| 心 61 | |
| 2532 | |
| 常 20 | |

| | ONE-SIDED, partial | 偏食 へんしょく unbalanced diet............0288 |
|---|---|---|
| | | ○偏見 へんけん prejudice, biased view, narrow view.................................0083 |
| | | 偏愛 へんあい partiality, favoritism.........0778 |
| | ヘン<br>かたよ(る) | ○偏る かたよる be one-sided, be prejudiced, be unfair |
| | | 偏った考え かたよったかんがえ partial view..0628 |

| **1081** | From 冊 0824 BOOK we know to see 冊 as a bookcase. When we find it set inside 戸 we shall call it *framed bookcase*, not to be confused with 侖 *library*. Here we see a *man* (亻) leaning up against the *framed bookcase* (i.e., leaning to ONE SIDE). The reading かたよる (be ONE-SIDED) can be thought of as かた (direction/side, one of two) + よる (lean). |
|---|---|
| 人 9 | |
| 0116 | |
| 常 11 | |

| | **1** ALL OVER, everywhere<br>**2** COUNTER FOR TIMES | **1** 遍在 へんざい omnipresence, ubiquity.....0406 |
|---|---|---|
| | | ①遍歴 へんれき travels, pilgrimage...........0853 |
| | | **1** 満遍なく まんべんなく evenly, equally; without exception; all over..........................0179 |
| | ヘン | ①一遍 いっぺん once.............................0002 |
| | | **2** 何遍も なんべんも several/many times, very often............................................0815 |

| **1082** | A *framed bookcase* (扁) on a *truck* (辶). Depicts a mobile library, whose purpose is to transport books ALL OVER/everywhere. To learn M2 COUNTER FOR TIMES, I suggest you simply practice counting out loud the times you do something, using いっぺん, にへん, さんべん ... |
|---|---|
| 辵 162 | |
| 2703 | |
| 常 12 | |

| | **1** COMPILE, edit<br>**2** KNIT | ①編集 へんしゅう editing, compilation........0190 |
|---|---|---|
| | | **1** 編成する へんせいする form, compose, compile ...........................................0070 |
| | | **1** 改編する かいへんする reorganize, remodel .............................................0429 |
| | ヘン<br>あ(む) -あ(み) | ②編む あむ knit |
| | | **2** 編み物 あみもの knitting, knitted goods..0172 |

| **1083** | Suggests knitting books together with *thread* (糸): in a figurative sense, COMPILE/**edit**; in a literal sense, KNIT. Note that the *on-yomi* for all kanji based on 扁 is ヘン. |
|---|---|
| 糸 120 | |
| 1270 | |
| 常 15 | |

| | VOLUME; chapter, part | 前篇 ぜんぺん first volume/part............0113 |
|---|---|---|
| | | 後篇 こうへん last volume/part, sequel.....0114 |
| | | 続篇 ぞくへん sequel.........................0354 |
| | ヘン | ○短篇 たんぺん short (as in "short story")....0562 |
| | | 一篇の作品 いっぺんのさくひん one work/piece (of literature)....................0002, 0152, 0301 |

| **1084** | 竹 suggests *keeping records* or *counting*. In this instance we are enumerating segments of literature stored in a *framed bookcase* (扁): VOLUMES, **chapters**, or **parts**. This kanji has not been officially standardized with the previous three, so appears here with the traditional form 扁, whose first stroke is written from right to left. |
|---|---|
| 竹 118 | |
| 篇 | |
| 2365 | |
| 名 15 | |

| | WIDESPREAD, common | 普遍 ふへん universality, generality .........1082 |
|---|---|---|
| | | 普遍的な ふへんてきな universal, omnipresent, ubiquitous....................................1082, 0169 |
| | フ | 普請 ふしん building, construction .........0977 |
| | | ○普通の ふつうの normal, regular, ordinary...0159 |
| | | 普段の ふだんの usual, ordinary...........0521 |

| 1085 | Recall 並 0333 LINE UP, whose secondary meaning is "average, ordinary." Joining this with 日 sun, we can perceive the idea of "*lining up* with everything else under the *sun*," in other words, **common** or **WIDESPREAD**. ☞ 善 1213 |
|---|---|
| 日 72 | |
| 2028 | |
| 常 12 | |

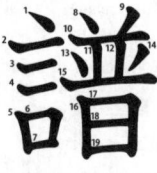

| | SYSTEMATIC RECORD; musical score | ○年譜 ねんぷ chronological record...........0117 |
|---|---|---|
| | | 譜代 ふだい successive generations; hereditary Tokugawa daimyo............................0071 |
| | フ | 系譜 けいふ genealogy, family tree .........1077 |
| | | 家譜 かふ genealogy, pedigree ............0219 |
| | | ○楽譜 がくふ (sheet of) music, musical score 0302 |

| 1086 | *Widespread* (普) *words* (言): suggests words spread over a wide period, as in covering a subject systematically over a period of time. Such **SYSTEMATIC RECORDS** include those of all the events that have occurred in an era (a chronology, V1), all the persons that have lived in a family (a genealogy, V3-4), and all the notes in a musical composition (a **score**, V5). |
|---|---|
| 言 149 | |
| 1476 | |
| 常 19 | |

| | EMPLOYMENT, post | ○職業 しょくぎょう occupation, vocation, profession ...................................0498 |
|---|---|---|
| | | 職務 しょくむ duty, duties, function .........0687 |
| | ショク | 職場 しょくば place of work...................0445 |
| | | 無職の むしょくの unemployed..............0048 |
| | | 現職 げんしょく present post; incumbent ...0706 |

| 1087 | Take 戠 (戈 *spear* + 立 *stand* + 日 *sun*) as a *spear-bearing guard standing in the sun.* His **EMPLOYMENT** is to protect the community using his *ears* (耳). Following the practice of community policing, he listens not only for sounds of disorder, but also for insights from the people who live or work in the area. ☞ 織 1088, 識 1089 |
|---|---|
| 耳 128 | |
| 1297 | |
| 常 18 | |

| | WEAVE | 織機 しょっき (=おりき) loom .................0473 |
|---|---|---|
| | | ○組織 そしき organization, system; constitution, construction; tissue.........................0264 |
| | ショク シキ | ○織る おる weave |
| | お(る) お(り) おり -おり -お(り) | 織物 おりもの cloth, textile, fabric...........0172 |
| | | 目の細かな織り めのこまかなおり fine texture .............................................0021, 0239 |

| 1088 | (Continuing from the previous entry) With little to do but listen, the guard is more or less idle. To keep himself occupied, he has taken to **WEAVING** with his *spear* and *thread* (糸). ☞ 職 1087, 識 1089 |
|---|---|
| 糸 120 | |
| 1295 | |
| 常 18 | |

| | ¹ DISCRIMINATE, discern<br>² KNOWLEDGE, learning<br><br>シキ | ①意識する いしきする be conscious of, be aware of ........ 0151<br>¹ 識別する しきべつする discriminate, discern **0090**<br>②知識 ちしき knowledge ........ **0560**<br>² 博識 はくしき extensive knowledge ......... **0983**<br>² 常識 じょうしき common sense, common knowledge ........ **0321** |
|---|---|---|

| **1089**<br>言 149<br><br>1477<br>常 \| 19 | (Continuing from 1087–88) 言 indicates the *words* the guard hears in his community policing work, representing **KNOWLEDGE**. Associate M1 **DISCRIMINATE** with M2 **KNOWLEDGE** via the idea of **discernment**. Now review this set of kanji based on 戠. Learn to associate the variable component with the meaning of each. ☞ 職 1087, 織 1088 |
|---|---|

| | **DIE A MARTYR**<br><br>ジュン | 殉職 じゅんしょく dying at one's post ........ **1087**<br>◯殉教 じゅんきょう martyrdom ........ **0632**<br>殉教者 じゅんきょうしゃ martyr ........ **0632, 0107**<br>殉国 じゅんこく dying for one's country ...... **0075** |
|---|---|---|

| **1090**<br>歹 78<br><br>0849<br>常 \| 10 | Recall 歹 *death* and 旬 0167 TEN DAYS. The present entry originally referred to the practice of following one's master into death. We can thus imagine that, upon the master's death, a servant was within *ten days* to **DIE A MARTYR**. ☞ 旬 0167 |
|---|---|

| | **RETREAT**<br><br>タイ<br>しりぞ(く) しりぞ(ける) | 退職 たいしょく retirement, resignation ..... **1087**<br>◯退院 たいいん discharge from a hospital ... **0634**<br>退廃 たいはい degeneration, decadence ... **0149**<br>◯退く しりぞく retreat; retire<br>退ける しりぞける repel, beat back |
|---|---|---|

| **1091**<br>辵 162<br><br>2665<br>常 \| 9 | 艮 means *stop* (see 限 0282), while 辶 suggests forward movement. We thus obtain "stop forward movement": **RETREAT**. |
|---|---|

| | **EYE**<br><br>ガン ゲン<br>まなこ め* | 近眼 きんがん nearsightedness ........ **0194**<br>眼科 がんか ophthalmology ........ **0759**<br>◯眼識 がんしき insight, discrimination ....... **1089**<br>千里眼 せんりがん clairvoyance ........ **0017, 0531**<br>団栗眼 どんぐりまなこ goggle eyes, round eyes ........ **0649, 0781** |
|---|---|---|

| **1092**<br>目 109<br><br>1084<br>常 \| 11 | 目 provides the meaning for the entire character—**EYE**—so it may be useful to visualize 艮 simply as an eyelid, goggle, or other protection to "*stop*" objects that might strike the *eye*. ☞ 眠 1009 |
|---|---|

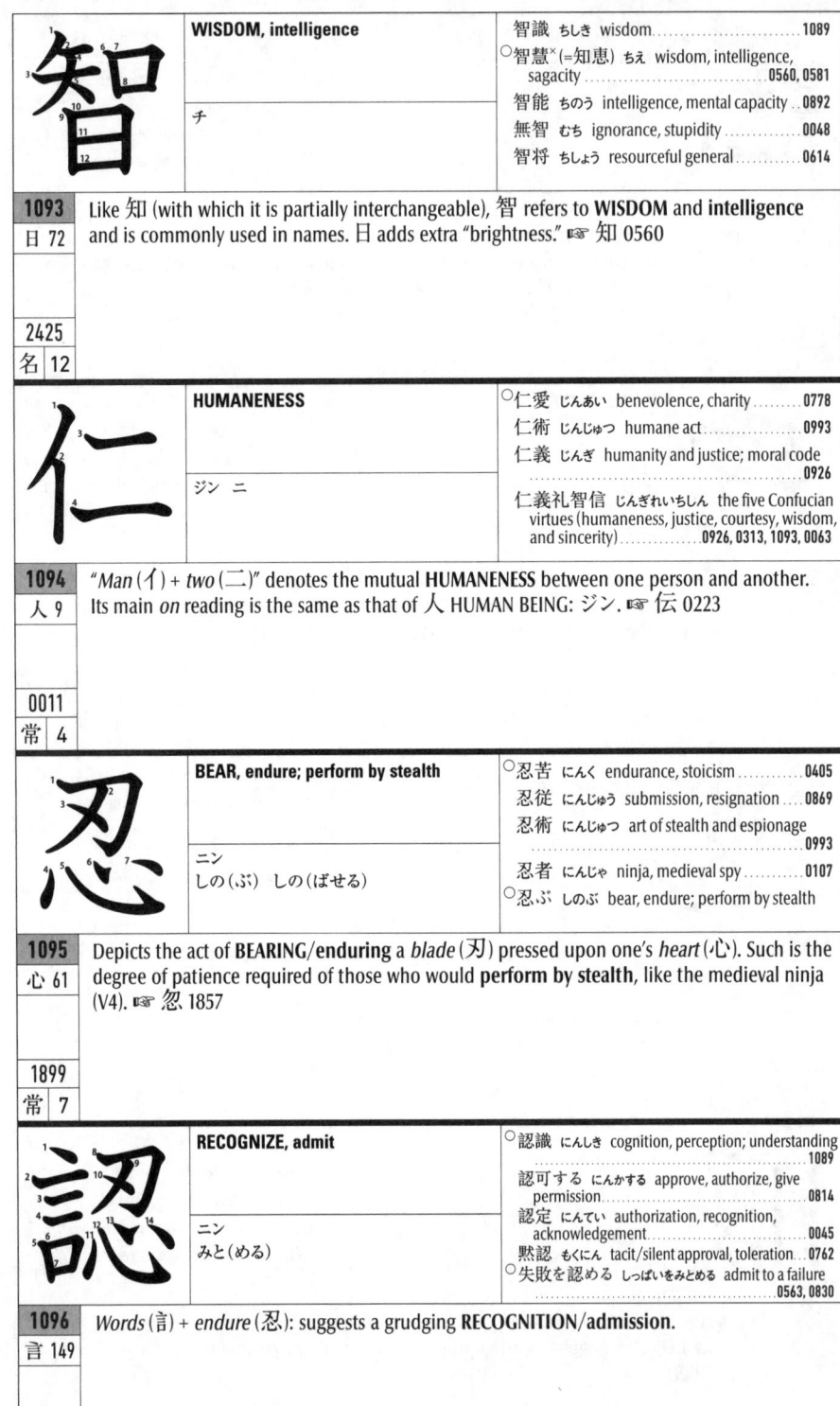

| | | WISDOM, intelligence | 智識 ちしき wisdom............................1089 |
|---|---|---|---|
| 智 | | | ○智慧× (=知恵) ちえ wisdom, intelligence, sagacity....................0560, 0581 |
| | | チ | 智能 ちのう intelligence, mental capacity ..0892 |
| | | | 無智 むち ignorance, stupidity ..............0048 |
| | | | 智将 ちしょう resourceful general............0614 |

| **1093** | Like 知 (with which it is partially interchangeable), 智 refers to **WISDOM** and **intelligence** |
|---|---|
| 日 72 | and is commonly used in names. 日 adds extra "brightness." ☞ 知 0560 |
| 2425 | |
| 名 12 | |

| | | HUMANENESS | ○仁愛 じんあい benevolence, charity..........0778 |
|---|---|---|---|
| 仁 | | | 仁術 じんじゅつ humane act..................0993 |
| | | ジン ニ | 仁義 じんぎ humanity and justice; moral code ..........................................0926 |
| | | | 仁義礼智信 じんぎれいちしん the five Confucian virtues (humaneness, justice, courtesy, wisdom, and sincerity)..............0926, 0313, 1093, 0063 |

| **1094** | "Man (亻) + two (二)" denotes the mutual **HUMANENESS** between one person and another. |
|---|---|
| 人 9 | Its main *on* reading is the same as that of 人 HUMAN BEING: ジン. ☞ 伝 0223 |
| 0011 | |
| 常 4 | |

| | | BEAR, endure; perform by stealth | ○忍苦 にんく endurance, stoicism ............0405 |
|---|---|---|---|
| 忍 | | | 忍従 にんじゅう submission, resignation ....0869 |
| | | ニン | 忍術 にんじゅつ art of stealth and espionage ..........................................0993 |
| | | しの(ぶ) しの(ばせる) | 忍者 にんじゃ ninja, medieval spy ..........0107 |
| | | | ○忍ぶ しのぶ bear, endure; perform by stealth |

| **1095** | Depicts the act of **BEARING**/**enduring** a *blade* (刃) pressed upon one's *heart* (心). Such is the |
|---|---|
| 心 61 | degree of patience required of those who would **perform by stealth**, like the medieval ninja |
| | (V4). ☞ 忍 1857 |
| 1899 | |
| 常 7 | |

| | | RECOGNIZE, admit | ○認識 にんしき cognition, perception; understanding ..........................................1089 |
|---|---|---|---|
| 認 | | | 認可する にんかする approve, authorize, give permission..............................0814 |
| | | ニン | 認定 にんてい authorization, recognition, acknowledgement........................0045 |
| | | みと(める) | 黙認 もくにん tacit/silent approval, toleration...0762 |
| | | | ○失敗を認める しっぱいをみとめる admit to a failure ..........................................0563, 0830 |

| **1096** | *Words* (言) + *endure* (忍): suggests a grudging **RECOGNITION**/**admission**. |
|---|---|
| 言 149 | |
| 1404 | |
| 常 14 | |

| 求 | SEEK | 求職 きゅうしょく seeking employment........1087 |
|---|---|---|
| | | 求人 きゅうじん job posting....................0015 |
| | | ○請求 せいきゅう demand, request, claim ....0977 |
| | キュウ | 要求する ようきゅうする require, demand, |
| | もと(める) | request.....................................0547 |
| | | ○求める もとめる seek, pursue |

| 1097 水 85 | Visualize a drowning person **SEEKING** help, splashing desperately as he struggles to keep his head above the *water*(氺)'s surface (S1). |
|---|---|
| 2974 常 7 | |

| 救 | SAVE, rescue | 救命 きゅうめい lifesaving....................0232 |
|---|---|---|
| | | 救世主 きゅうせいしゅ the Savior, the Messiah |
| | | ....................................0604, 0365 |
| | | 救助 きゅうじょ rescue, relief................0642 |
| | キュウ | ○救急車 きゅうきゅうしゃ ambulance.....0971, 0125 |
| | すく(う) | ○救う すくう save, rescue |

| 1098 攵 66 | Now visualize **SAVING/rescuing** the drowning person, by reaching out to him with *the rod* (攵). Note that both characters incorporating 求 follow its *on* reading, キュウ. |
|---|---|
| 1358 常 11 | |

| 球 | BALL, globe | ○地球 ちきゅう the Earth....................0187 |
|---|---|---|
| | | 眼球 がんきゅう eyeball ....................1092 |
| | | 野球 やきゅう baseball ....................0534 |
| | キュウ | 球場 きゅうじょう ballpark ................0445 |
| | たま | ○球拾い たまひろい picking up balls; poor player |
| | | ....................................1071 |

| 1099 玉 96 | We have already learned that 𤣩 is the *hen* form of 玉 and signifies *gem* or, more generally, *round/spherical object*. The latter applies here: visualize a water polo player splashing around in the water with a **BALL**. ☞ 玩 2219 |
|---|---|
| 0880 常 11 | |

| 屯 | STATION TROOPS | ○駐屯する ちゅうとんする be stationed, occupy |
|---|---|---|
| | | ....................................0367 |
| | トン | |

| 1100 屮 45 | This character can be interpreted as a combination of 七 *seven* and 山 *mountain*. Picture *seven* **TROOPS STATIONED** on a *mountain*. |
|---|---|
| 2908 常 4 | |

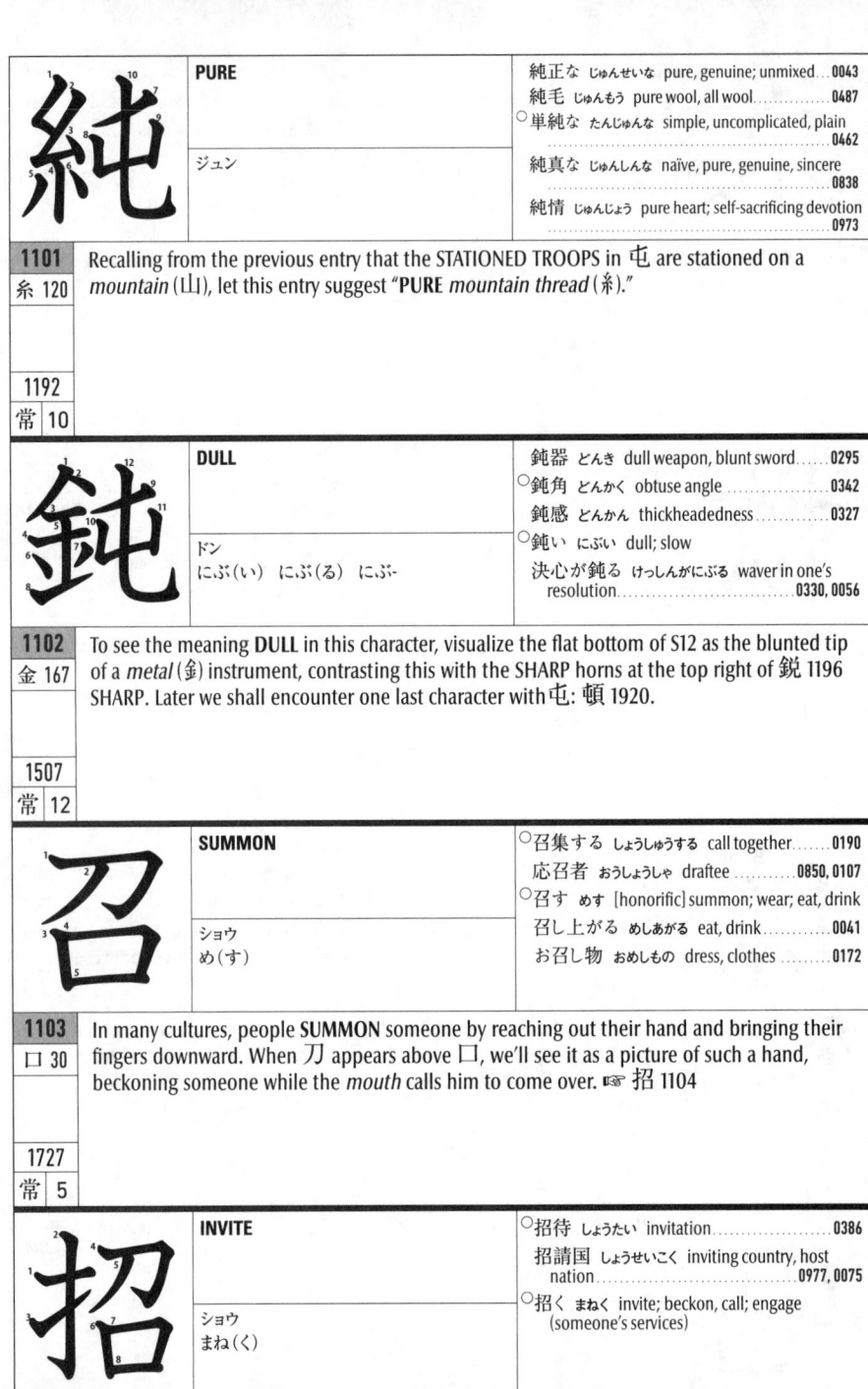

| | PURE | 純正な じゅんせいな pure, genuine; unmixed...0043 |
|---|---|---|
| 純 | | 純毛 じゅんもう pure wool, all wool............0487 |
| | | ○単純な たんじゅんな simple, uncomplicated, plain........0462 |
| | ジュン | 純真な じゅんしんな naïve, pure, genuine, sincere........0838 |
| | | 純情 じゅんじょう pure heart; self-sacrificing devotion........0973 |

| **1101** | Recalling from the previous entry that the STATIONED TROOPS in 屯 are stationed on a *mountain* (山), let this entry suggest "**PURE** *mountain thread* (糸)." |
|---|---|
| 糸 120 | |
| **1192** | |
| 常 10 | |

| | DULL | 鈍器 どんき dull weapon, blunt sword......0295 |
|---|---|---|
| 鈍 | | ○鈍角 どんかく obtuse angle ...........0342 |
| | | 鈍感 どんかん thickheadedness.........0327 |
| | ドン | ○鈍い にぶい dull; slow |
| | にぶ(い) にぶ(る) にぶ- | 決心が鈍る けっしんがにぶる waver in one's resolution............0330, 0056 |

| **1102** | To see the meaning **DULL** in this character, visualize the flat bottom of S12 as the blunted tip of a *metal* (金) instrument, contrasting this with the SHARP horns at the top right of 鋭 1196 SHARP. Later we shall encounter one last character with 屯: 頓 1920. |
|---|---|
| 金 167 | |
| **1507** | |
| 常 12 | |

| | SUMMON | ○召集する しょうしゅうする call together.......0190 |
|---|---|---|
| 召 | | 応召者 おうしょうしゃ draftee .........0850, 0107 |
| | | ○召す めす [honorific] summon; wear; eat, drink |
| | ショウ | 召し上がる めしあがる eat, drink............0041 |
| | め(す) | お召し物 おめしもの dress, clothes .........0172 |

| **1103** | In many cultures, people **SUMMON** someone by reaching out their hand and bringing their fingers downward. When 刀 appears above 口, we'll see it as a picture of such a hand, beckoning someone while the *mouth* calls him to come over. ☞ 招 1104 |
|---|---|
| 口 30 | |
| **1727** | |
| 常 5 | |

| | INVITE | ○招待 しょうたい invitation...........0386 |
|---|---|---|
| 招 | | 招請国 しょうせいこく inviting country, host nation............0977, 0075 |
| | ショウ | ○招く まねく invite; beckon, call; engage (someone's services) |
| | まね(く) | |

| **1104** | Building on the previous entry, picture the *hand* (扌) making a beckoning motion to **INVITE** someone to come over. To refer to the act of literally beckoning with the hand, we would use this character (see V3); the previous entry carries the formal sense SUMMON. ☞ 召 1103, 拐 1784 |
|---|---|
| 手 64 | |
| **0281** | |
| 常 8 | |

## 沼 MUDDY POND

ショウ
ぬま

湖沼 こしょう lakes and marshes ............0259
○沼地 ぬまち swampland, bogland, marshland
................................................0187

**1105**
水 85
0302
常 8

Think of as *water* (氵) being *summoned* (召) into a **MUDDY POND** to keep the tadpoles nice and moist. Note that all kanji in this course incorporating 召 follow its *on* reading, ショウ, except 超 below, where it is surrounded by an enclosure. ☞ 沢 1504

## 紹 INTRODUCE

ショウ

○紹介する しょうかいする introduce, present
................................................0611
紹介状 しょうかいじょう letter of introduction
................................................0611, 0616
自己紹介 じこしょうかい self-introduction
................................................0081, 0426, 0611

**1106**
糸 120
1222
常 11

For this entry see 糹 as a bearded man (S1 shows his brow, S2 starts at his nose and ends at his jaw, and S4–6 show his flowing beard). Here one *summons* (召) a friend, in order to **INTRODUCE** her to this distinguished bearded gentleman. ☞ 給 0526

## 詔 IMPERIAL EDICT

ショウ
みことのり

詔令 しょうれい imperial edict............0229
○詔書 しょうしょ imperial edict............0079
大詔 たいしょう imperial rescript/mandate...0033
大事な詔 だいじなみことのり important imperial
edict................................0033, 0080

**1107**
言 149
1366
常 12

*Summoning* (召) all subjects to come listen to some important *words* (言): gather round for the **IMPERIAL EDICT**.

## 勅 IMPERIAL DECREE

チョク

勅語 ちょくご imperial rescript............0222
詔勅 しょうちょく imperial edict............1107

**1108**
力 19
勅
1319
常 9

Like the Roman *fasces*, 束 *bundle* can represent a ruler's coercive power. Here we see 力 *power* issuing from this source of authority: **IMPERIAL DECREE**.

| | |
|---|---|
| **LUMINOUS, enlightened** | 昭々たる しょうしょうたる [rare] bright, clear; obvious, plain |
| | ○昭和 しょうわ Showa era (reign of Emperor Showa, 1926–89) . . . . . . . . . . . . . . . . . . . . . . . . . . . **0236** |
| ショウ | 昭和天皇 しょうわてんのう Emperor Showa (Hirohito) . . . . . . . . . . . . . . . **0236, 0270, 0077** |

| 1109 | See the *sun* (日) being *summoned* (召) to shine on one spot and make it **LUMINOUS**. The |
|---|---|
| 日 72 | original meaning of "**emitting light**" is now rare; today, this character is generally used only in reference to the Showa emperor and era (V2–3), in which it denotes "**enlightened (rule)**" (see Halpern). ☞ 照 1110 |
| 0796 | |
| 常 9 | |

| | |
|---|---|
| **¹ ILLUMINATE** | ①照明 しょうめい illumination, lighting . . . . . . . **0024** |
| **² EXAMINE BY COMPARISON** | ¹ 照射 しょうしゃ irradiation . . . . . . . . . . . . . . . . . . . . **1021** |
| | ①照らす てらす illuminate, shine on |
| ショウ | ² 照合する しょうごうする verify, compare, collate |
| て(る) て(らす) て(れる) | . . . . . . . . . . . . . . . . . . . . . . . . . . . . . . . . . . . . . . . . . . . **0227** |
| | ②対照 たいしょう contrast, comparison; control (of an experiment) . . . . . . . . . . . . . . . . . . . . . . . . . . **0650** |

| 1110 | Here both *sun* (日) and *fire* (灬) are *summoned* (召) to **ILLUMINATE** a scene. The flickering |
|---|---|
| 火 86 | flames in this entry denote that 照 physically shines, whereas 昭 1109 emits only figurative light. Associate M1 **ILLUMINATE** with M2 **EXAMINE BY COMPARISON**, via the idea of "shedding light" on two things by comparing them with one another. ☞ 昭 1109 |
| 2461 | |
| 常 13 | |

| | |
|---|---|
| **SURPASS, super-, ultra-** | ○超自然的な ちょうしぜんてきな supernatural . . . . . . . . . . . . . . . . . . . . . . . . . . . . **0081, 0760, 0169** |
| | 超国家的な ちょうこっかてきな supranationalistic . . . . . . . . . . . . . . . . . . . . . . **0075, 0219, 0169** |
| チョウ | 超大型 ちょうおおがた extra-large . . . . . . **0033, 0723** |
| こ(える) こ(す) | ○超える こえる surpass, exceed, excel |
| | 超す こす surpass, exceed, be more than |

| 1111 | This kanji starts by *running* (走), then *summons* (召) an even higher level of effort: **super-/** |
|---|---|
| 走 156 | **ultra-/SURPASS**. Note that this is the only kanji in which 召 is bounded by an enclosure, and thus the only one not read ショウ. Now practice all the kanji from 召 1103 to here (except 勅 1108), using the variable elements to guide you to their meanings. |
| 2824 | |
| 常 12 | |

| | |
|---|---|
| **GO BEYOND** | 超越する ちょうえつする transcend, surpass 1111 |
| | ○優越 ゆうえつ superiority, supremacy . . . . . . . **0780** |
| | ○越える こえる cross over; surmount; surpass |
| エツ | ○越す こす cross over; overcome |
| こ(す) -こ(す) -ご(し) こ(える) -ご(え) | 引っ越す ひっこす move (to a new house) . . . **0422** |

| 1112 | Recall 戈 *guided spear*, first encountered back at 成 0070. Here its left-hand stroke (S8) |
|---|---|
| 走 156 | doubles back, so as not to trail across the enclosure (走). In this kanji, picture a javelin thrower committing a foul by *running* **BEYOND** the end line after his throw. Also used as an abbreviation for Vietnam (to the Chinese, a land "**BEYOND** the South" 越南). |
| 2825 | |
| 常 12 | |

# 趣

| | |
|---|---|
| **¹ PURPORT, gist, meaning**<br>**² FLAVOR, distinctive charm**<br><br>シュ<br>おもむき | ①趣旨 しゅし purpose, aim; purport, meaning..0931<br>¹趣意 しゅい purpose, aim; purport, meaning, point .........0151<br>²情趣 じょうしゅ mood, sentiment, artistic effect .........0973<br>²野趣 やしゅ charms of the countryside......0534<br>②趣の有る おもむきのある tasteful, elegant...0400 |

**1113**
走 156

2827
常 | 15

PURPORT refers to the **meaning** or **gist** a communication intends to "carry forth," from the Latin *pro* (forth) and *portare* (carry). We can perceive "carry forth" here if we visualize S7 as a ramp (built for *running* down) and 取 as *taking* something down it. 趣 also refers to the intrinsic quality of what is carried forth—its **distinctive charm** or **FLAVOR**.

---

| | |
|---|---|
| **PROCEED TO**<br><br>フ<br>おもむ(く) | ○赴任 ふにん proceeding to a new post......0372<br>○赴く おもむく proceed to<br>死地に赴く しちにおもむく ride into the jaws of death.........0716, 0187 |

**1114**
走 156

2816
常 | 9

The next four entries include the grapheme 卜, which we'll interpret as *pointing downward*. Here, 卜 points downward (and forward) from S7, which as in the previous entry we visualize as a ramp built for *running* down. Thus the picture we obtain is that of **PROCEEDING** down the ramp. Note the similarity with 趣 1113, both graphically and in the *kun-yomi*.

---

# 訃

| | |
|---|---|
| **DEATH REPORT**<br><br>フ | 訃音 ふいん report of a death .........0150<br>訃告 ふこく obituary.........0698 |

**1115**
言 149

1308
常 | 9

Again simply see 卜 as *pointing downward*. Here a *word* (言) comes down from heaven: **DEATH REPORT**. A useful compound appears at 報 1472.

---

| | |
|---|---|
| **SIMPLE**<br><br>ボク | 純朴な じゅんぼくな simple and honest .....1101<br>○朴直な ぼくちょくな simple and honest, artless, naïve .........0839<br>素朴な そぼくな simple, naïve, artless ......0132<br>質朴な しつぼくな simple, plain, unsophisticated .........0318 |

**1116**
木 75

0725
常 | 6

Here we can ignore the grapheme meaning and just note how 卜 is **SIMPLER** than 木.

| | ¹ SET (on) ² HANG, fasten | ¹ はかりに掛ける はかりにかける weigh on a scale |
|---|---|---|
| | | ¹ そこに布が掛かっている そこにぬのがかかっている The cloth is spread over there ............. 0204 |
| | | ¹ 水を掛ける みずをかける sprinkle water on (something) ............................................. 0027 |
| | か(ける) -か(ける) か(け) -か(け) -が(け) か(かる) -か(かる) -が(かる) か(かり) -が(かり) かかり -がかり | ② 掛け軸を掛ける かけじくをかける hang up a hanging scroll ............................................. 0692 |
| | | ² 掛け時計 かけどけい wall clock ............. 0383, 0555 |

| 1117 手 64 | In traditional Japanese buildings, framed pictures and documents are hung on the highest part of a wall and face downward. Here see the *hand* (扌) **SET/HANG** an object on a high *earthen* (土) wall, pointing *downward* (卜) so that it can be observed from below. ☞ 街 0992 |
|---|---|
| 0449 常 11 | |

| | **PICK, pluck** | 摘発する てきはつする expose, lay bare, disclose ............................................. 0148 |
|---|---|---|
| | | 摘出する てきしゅつする extract, remove; point out ............................................. 0038 |
| | テキ つ(む) | 摘要 てきよう summary ............................. 0547 |
| | | ○指摘する してきする point out ............. 0932 |
| | | ○摘む つむ pick, pluck, gather |

| 1118 手 64 | Review 商 0351 TRADE. The following five entries use the similar form 商, which contains 古 (*old*) in the merchant's basket, and is associated with the reading テキ. We shall interpret 商 as a *fruit merchant carrying an old basket*. Here, the merchant reaches up with his *hand* (扌) to **PICK** a fruit and put it in his basket. |
|---|---|
| 0629 常 14 | |

|  | **DROP** | 滴下する てきかする drip, trickle ............. 0040 |
|---|---|---|
| | | 点滴 てんてき falling drops of water; intravenous drip ............................................. 0349 |
| | テキ しずく したた(る) | ○雨滴 うてき raindrop ............................. 0154 |
| | | 一滴の水 いってきのみず a drop of water ............................................. 0002, 0027 |
| | | ○滴る したたる drip, drop, trickle |

| 1119 水 85 | 氵 suggests **DROPS** of juice **DRIPPING** from the bottom of the *fruit merchant's old fruit basket* (商). A few of the fruits have split open. |
|---|---|
| 0640 常 14 | |

| | **LEGITIMATE WIFE/CHILD** | ○嫡子 ちゃくし legitimate child ............. 0094 |
|---|---|---|
| | | 廃嫡 はいちゃく disinheritance ............. 0149 |
| | | 嫡男 ちゃくなん heir, eldest son; legitimate son ............................................. 0092 |
| | チャク | 嫡孫 ちゃくそん descendants of one's eldest son ............................................. 1079 |
| | | 嫡嗣 ちゃくし legitimate heir ............. 0825 |

| 1120 女 38 | Here the *fruit merchant* (商) appears with his **LEGITIMATE WIFE** (女). |
|---|---|
| 0620 常 14 | |

| | FIT, suit | ○適当な てきとうな suitable, fitting; irresponsible ............ 0141 |
|---|---|---|
| | | 適切な てきせつな fitting, appropriate, adequate ............ 0086 |
| | テキ | 適量 てきりょう proper/moderate quantity ... 0538 |
| | | 適性 てきせい aptitude ...................... 0128 |
| | | 適する てきする suit, fit |

| **1121** | Now the *fruit merchant* (商) loads his *old basket* on a *truck* (辶) to carry it to market. The |
|---|---|
| 辵 162 | way to visualize the meaning of this character is to perceive how the merchant and his basket |
| | **FIT** precisely inside the space afforded by the bed of the truck. |
| **2726** | |
| 常 14 | |

| | ENEMY | ○敵意 てきい hostility, enmity ................ 0151 |
|---|---|---|
| | | 強敵 きょうてき powerful enemy [rival] ...... 0423 |
| | | 敵対する てきたいする oppose, fight against ............ 0650 |
| | テキ | |
| | かたき | 敵に掛かる てきにかかる attack the enemy 1117 |
| | | ○敵討ち かたきうち vendetta, revenge ....... 1023 |

| **1122** | There's always an **ENEMY** at the market, ready to sell the same fruit at a lower price. This pic- |
|---|---|
| 攵 66 | ture of *striking* (攵) one's rival <u>fruit merchant</u> (商) (perhaps overturning his tray and spilling |
| | all his merchandise on the floor?) is an evocative image of rivalry and confrontation. |
| **1648** | |
| 常 15 | |

| | ¹ CONFER<br>² INSTRUCT | ①授与する じゅよする grant, give, confer ..... 0858 |
|---|---|---|
| | | ¹ 授受 じゅじゅ giving and receiving .......... 0065 |
| | | ①学位を授ける がくいをさずける award a degree ............ 0099, 0577 |
| | ジュ | ² 授業 じゅぎょう teaching, instruction; lesson ............ 0498 |
| | さず(ける) さず(かる) | ² 教授 きょうじゅ teaching; professor ......... 0632 |

| **1123** | To 受 0065 RECEIVE we add *hand* (扌) to refer to the party that **CONFERS**. Practice writing |
|---|---|
| 手 64 | these two kanji in alternation, learning to identify their meanings by the presence or absence |
| | of 扌 (also note the correspondence between the readings うける and さずける). M2 **INSTRUCT** |
| | comes from the idea of **CONFERRING** knowledge. ☞ 受 0065, 援 1124 |
| **0448** | |
| 常 11 | |

| | AID, give a hand | ○援助 えんじょ aid, assistance, help .......... 0642 |
|---|---|---|
| | | 援軍 えんぐん relieving force, reinforcements ............ 0583 |
| | | 支援 しえん support, backing, aid .......... 0373 |
| | エン | 応援 おうえん aid, reinforcement; support; cheering ............ 0850 |
| | | 後援する こうえんする give support/backing ............ 0114 |

| **1124** | Take the right-hand portion of this character to mean *give*: in it, a *claw* (爫) gives a baton (S8) |
|---|---|
| 手 64 | to one's *friend* (友). Adding *hand* (扌) here, we obtain "*give a hand*," or **AID**. ☞ 授 1123 |
| **0536** | |
| 常 12 | |

**DAMSEL, young lady of noble birth**

エン
ひめ

才媛 さいえん talented girl, accomplished woman, girl with scholastic ability .........**0652**
たちばな媛(橘⁼媛) たちばなひめ Tachibana-hime (name of a woman in a Japanese myth)
愛媛県 えひめけん Ehime prefecture...**0778, 0844**

| 1125 | "*Giving* (爰) a *woman* (女)": here a **DAMSEL/young lady of noble birth** is given away as a concubine to a king or powerful warlord, in order to advance her family's interests. |
|---|---|
| 女 38 | ☞ 姫 2196 |
| 0519 | |
| 常 12 | |

**SLACK, loose**

カン
ゆる(い) ゆる(やか) ゆる(む)
ゆる(める)

○緩和 かんわ easing, relief, alleviation.......**0236**
緩行 かんこう going slowly...................**0055**
○緩い ゆるい slack, loose
緩やかな坂 ゆるやかなさか gentle slope....**0375**
歩調を緩める ほちょうをゆるめる slacken one's pace...................................**0679, 0306**

| 1126 | A *thread* (糸) that "*gives* (爰)": **SLACK/loose.** The reading ゆるむ (slacken) can be associated with "giving you room." |
|---|---|
| 糸 120 | |
| 1272 | |
| 常 15 | |

**WARM**

ダン
あたた(か) あたた(かい) あたた(まる)
あたた(める)

暖冬 だんとう mild winter ....................**0360**
○温暖な おんだんな warm, mild........**0199**
地球温暖化 ちきゅうおんだんか global warming
....................**0187, 1099, 0199, 0120**
暖かな毛布 あたたかなもうふ warm blanket
....................................**0487, 0204**
○部屋を暖める へやをあたためる heat the room
....................................**0068, 0252**

| 1127 | The *sun* (日) *gives* (爰) **WARMTH.** |
|---|---|
| 日 72 | |
| 0922 | |
| 常 13 | |

**VIEW**

カン

○観光 かんこう sightseeing ...................**0137**
外観 がいかん external appearance.........**0266**
楽観的 らっかんてき optimistic .......**0302, 0169**
○価値観 かちかん (sense of) values...**0548, 0842**
世界観 せかいかん world view, outlook on the world...............................**0604, 0612**

| 1128 | Since he can't speak to us, this *small bird* (隹) carries an *arrow* (stylized from 矢) for pointing at things. Here he points at something to guide our *sight* (見) toward it. He is asking us to **VIEW** it. Note the traditional form, whose pattern is followed by the traditional forms of the next three entries. |
|---|---|
| 見 147 | |
| 觀 | |
| 1659 | |
| 常 18 | |

| | URGE, promote | 勧告 かんこく advice, counsel, recommendation ............. 0698 |
|---|---|---|
| | | 勧業 かんぎょう encouragement of industry .. 0498 |
| | カン | ○勧める すすめる urge, promote; offer |
| | すす(める) | 行く様に勧める いくようにすすめる encourage (someone) to go............................ 0055, 0501 |
| | | 酒を勧める さけをすすめる offer liquor ...... 0797 |

| 1129 | "*Pointing bird*(隹) + *strong*(力)": imagine the bird is giving us his "strong recommendation"; |
|---|---|
| 力 19 | that is, he is **URGING**/**promoting** something. |
| 勧 | |
| 1645 | |
| 常 13 | |

| | ¹**RIGHT** | ①権利 けんり right; authority; privilege ....... 0412 |
|---|---|---|
| | ²**POWER, authority** | ¹ 人権 じんけん human rights ................. 0015 |
| | | ² 政権 せいけん political power, administrative power ...................................... 0246 |
| | ケン ゴン | ² 権力 けんりょく power, authority, influence. 0084 |
| | | ² 越権する えっけんする overstep one's authority ...................................... 1112 |

| 1130 | Think of the *pointing bird*(隹) pointing at the *tree*(木) to claim his natural **RIGHT** or privilege |
|---|---|
| 木 75 | to inhabit it. M2 **POWER/authority** is a cognate meaning. Note that this is the only character |
| 権 | in which the *pointing bird* appears at the right, which you should associate with the fact that |
| 0977 | it is the only one not pronounced カン. |
| 常 15 | |

| | **JOYOUS** | ○歓楽 かんらく pleasure, merriment .......... 0302 |
|---|---|---|
| | | 歓楽街 かんらくがい pleasure quarter 0302, 0992 |
| | | 歓声 かんせい cheers, shouts of joy ......... 0529 |
| | カン | 歓待 かんたい warm welcome ................. 0386 |
| | | 歓送 かんそう warm sendoff.................. 0455 |

| 1131 | *Pointing bird*(隹) with *wide open beak*(欠): **JOYOUS** singing. |
|---|---|
| 欠 76 | |
| 歡 | |
| 1650 | |
| 常 15 | |

| | **CRANE** | 鶴首する かくしゅする look forward to ...... 0157 |
|---|---|---|
| | | ○千羽鶴 せんばづる string of a thousand folded paper cranes.......................... 0017, 0418 |
| | カク* | 鶴の一声 つるのひとこえ the last word (leader's final decision) ...................... 0002, 0529 |
| | つる | |

| 1132 | Notice how the variation on 隹 in the next two characters differs from that of the previous |
|---|---|
| 鳥 196 | four. Think of it as having a neck so long that its head juts out of the *cover*(SI-2) placed over |
| 鶴 | it. 鳥 *bird* indicates that the present entry refers to a bird species. Thus we obtain *bird species* |
| 1641 | + *long-necked bird*: **CRANE**. |
| 常 21 | |

| | | |
|---|---|---|
| **CERTAIN, definite** | | ○確認 かくにん confirmation ..................1096 |
| | | 確実な かくじつな certain, reliable; sound, solid ...............................0499 |
| | | 正確な せいかくな accurate, precise, exact..0043 |
| カク たし(か) たし(かめる) | | ○確かに たしかに certainly, surely |
| | | 確かめる たしかめる ascertain, confirm |

| **1133** | 石 *rock* offers a solid, reliable place for the *long-necked bird* (隹) to alight, thus suggesting the meaning **CERTAIN**/**definite**. Now note that both characters based on *long-necked bird* are read カク, while the modal reading for characters based on *pointing bird* (隹) is カン. ☞ 礁 1655 |
|---|---|
| 石 112 | |
| **1135** | |
| 常 15 | |

| | | |
|---|---|---|
| **¹ARROGANT** | | ¹慢心 まんしん self-conceit; pride ...........0056 |
| **²SLUGGISH** | | ①自慢 じまん pride, self-praise, vanity ........0081 |
| | | ¹我慢 がまん patience, endurance; self-restraint ...............................0221 |
| マン | | ②慢性の まんせいの chronic..................0128 |
| | | ²緩慢な かんまんな slack, slow-moving, inactive ...............................1126 |

| **1134** | Visualize 曼 as an *arrogant, lazy person*: 日 depicts his dour face; 罒 his crossed arms, and 又 his crossed legs (resembling 夂)—a position from which he proudly refuses to budge. 忄 tells us that the present entry refers to his mentality: **ARROGANT** and **SLUGGISH**. |
|---|---|
| 心 61 | |
| **0625** | |
| 常 14 | |

| | | |
|---|---|---|
| **¹RAMBLING** | | ¹漫遊する まんゆうする make a leisurely tour 0570 |
| **²COMIC** | | ¹散漫な さんまんな desultory, vagrant, vague 0808 |
| | | ①放漫 ほうまん laxity, looseness, indiscretion 0574 |
| マン | | ②漫画 まんが cartoon, comic strip ...........0176 |
| | | ²漫才 まんざい comic dialogue, *manzai*......0652 |

| **1135** | This character's core meaning is **RAMBLING**—think of *arrogant, lazy* (曼) *water* (氵), meandering along neglectfully. Associate this with M2 **COMIC** via the idea of pursuing idle fun rather than a focused objective. ☞ 浸 1014 |
|---|---|
| 水 85 | |
| **0633** | |
| 常 14 | |

| | | |
|---|---|---|
| **(sign of) THE HARE** | | 卯月 うづき fourth month (of the lunar calendar), April........................................0023 |
| | | ○卯年 うさぎどし (=うどし) Year of the Hare ....0117 |
| ボウ う | | |

| **1136** | Depicts two long *rabbit ears*, a natural symbol for the horary **sign of THE HARE** in the Sino-Japanese Zodiac. ☞ 卯 1141 |
|---|---|
| 卩 26 | |

| | |
|---|---|
| **0177** | |
| 名 5 | |

| 抑 | SUPPRESS | ○抑制する よくせいする control, suppress, inhibit 0708 |
|---|---|---|
| | | ○抑圧する よくあつする oppress, repress, suppress ................................................ 0186 |
| | | ○抑える おさえる suppress, hold down |
| | ヨク | 抑え難い おさえがたい irrepressible, uncontrollable ................................................ 0712 |
| | おさ(える) | 反乱を抑える はんらんをおさえる stifle a rebellion ........................................ 0374, 0380 |

| 1137 | This entry contains the four-stroke version of *rabbit ears* (as distinct from the five-stroke version |
|---|---|
| 手 64 | in the previous entry). Now if a man had *rabbit ears*, he'd feel rather embarrassed about it. |
| | He'd reach up with his *hand* (扌) and try to hold them down (i.e., **SUPPRESS** them). |
| 0229 | |
| 常 7 | |

| 仰 | LOOK UP (to) | ○仰視する ぎょうしする look up ............... 0623 |
|---|---|---|
| | | 信仰する しんこうする believe in, have faith ................................................ 0063 |
| | | 仰ぐ あおぐ look up (to), respect; turn to |
| | ギョウ コウ | ○仰向け あおむけ facing upward, belly up ... 0183 |
| | あお(ぐ) おお(せ) | 仰せ おおせ wishes or command of a superior |

| 1138 | Normal human ears are attached on either side of the head, but *rabbit ears* are attached right |
|---|---|
| 人 9 | up on top. Visualize the *man* (イ) **LOOKING UP** at his towering *rabbit ears*. |
| 0032 | |
| 常 6 | |

| 迎 | WELCOME; go out to meet | ○歓迎 かんげい warm welcome ............... 1131 |
|---|---|---|
| | | 送迎する そうげいする welcome and send off ................................................ 0455 |
| | | ○迎える むかえる welcome; go out to meet |
| | ゲイ | 出迎える でむかえる go out to meet ......... 0038 |
| | むか(える) | 迎え撃つ むかえうつ fight the attack of an enemy ............................................... 1026 |

| 1139 | Here we see the *rabbit* being sent out on a *truck* (辶) to **WELCOME** an arriving guest. |
|---|---|
| 辵 162 | |
| 2632 | |
| 常 7 | |

| 柳 | WILLOW | 花柳 かりゅう geisha, courtesans; red-light district .......................................... 0121 |
|---|---|---|
| | | 花柳界 かりゅうかい red-light district ... 0121, 0612 |
| | | 枝垂れ柳 しだれやなぎ weeping willow ................................................ 0965, 1004 |
| | リュウ | 柳本 やなぎもと Yanagimoto [surname] ..... 0031 |
| | やなぎ | |

| 1140 | We now go back to the original five-stroke *rabbit ears*. It would be far-fetched to try to associ- |
|---|---|
| 木 75 | ate *rabbit* with **WILLOW**, so instead see two *drooping branches* (卯) hanging from a weeping |
| | **WILLOW**. |
| 0803 | |
| 常 9 | |

| | EGG | 抱卵 ほうらん incubation..................0664 |
|---|---|---|
| | | ○卵黄 らんおう yolk.......................0915 |
| | | 産卵 さんらん egg-laying, spawning.........0181 |
| ラン | | 卵巣 らんそう ovary.......................0601 |
| たまご | | 卵焼き たまごやき fried egg, omelette.......0769 |

| 1141 | A stylized depiction of two ova. ☞ 卯 1136 |
|---|---|
| 卩 26 | |
| 0751 | |
| 常 7 | |

| | ¹ SCATTERED | ①疎開 そかい dispersal, evacuation...........0450 |
|---|---|---|
| | ² ESTRANGED | ¹ 過疎 かそ depopulation....................0464 |
| | | ² 疎遠 そえん estrangement, alienation, neglect |
| | ソ | ..........................................0857 |
| | うと(い) うと(む) | ②疎い うとい estranged, distant |
| | | ² 疎む うとむ neglect, estrange |

| 1142 | Back at 旋 0572 we saw the grapheme 疋, but 疋 here is not quite like that, or 止, or 正, so we'll give it a unique interpretation. See it as a woman reaching out her arms (S2) to hand back a *bundle*(束) of flowers to a man who seeks her affection. The image depicts **ESTRANGE-MENT**. Link this with M2 **SCATTERED** via the idea of pushing away. |
|---|---|
| 疋 103 | |
| 疎 | |
| 1091 | |
| 常 12 | |

| | QUICK | 急速に きゅうそくに swiftly, rapidly, promptly 0971 |
|---|---|---|
| | | 快速 かいそく high speed; rapid (local) train 0331 |
| | | ○高速道路 こうそくどうろ expressway, freeway |
| | ソク | ..............................0185, 0158, 0788 |
| | はや(い) はや- はや(める) はや(まる) | ○足を速める あしをはやめる quicken one's pace |
| | すみ(やか) | ........................................0044 |
| | | ○速やかに すみやかに quickly, immediately |

| 1143 | Visualize this as a *truck*(辶) transporting *bundles*(束, i.e., bouquets) of flowers, and think about how **QUICKLY** it must travel for the bouquets to arrive fresh. ☞ 迅 1146 |
|---|---|
| 辵 162 | |
| 2674 | |
| 常 10 | |

| | ¹ SLOW | ①足が遅い あしがおそい be slow-footed .....0044 |
|---|---|---|
| | ² LATE | ②遅着 ちちゃく late arrival...................0938 |
| | | ² 遅生まれ おそうまれ born after April 1 (school |
| | チ | age group cutoff date)....................0036 |
| | おく(れる) おく(らす) おそ(い) | ②乗り遅れる のりおくれる miss (a train).......1005 |
| | | 返事を遅らす へんじをおくらす defer one's reply |
| | | ........................................0378, 0080 |

| 1144 | By contrast with the previous entry, the *sheep*(羊) *truck*(辶) moves **SLOWLY**, since the sheep are transported "on the hoof" (尸 is an enclosure the trucker uses to keep them from jumping off the truck bed). Imagine looking over at this **SLOW**-moving truck as you pass it on the highway. ☞ 達 1475 |
|---|---|
| 辵 162 | |
| 遅 | |
| 2700 | |
| 常 12 | |

## 辻

**CROSSROAD**

つじ

辻店 つじみせ street stall .................... 0347
辻堂 つじどう roadside shrine .............. 0320
辻野 つじの Tsujino [surname] ............. 0534
辻本 つじもと Tsujimoto [surname] ......... 0031

---

**1145**
辵 162

辻

2750
名 | 6

Suggests a *truck* (辶) arriving at a **CROSSROAD** (十). The head character shows the form 辶, which appears in kanji that have not been officially simplified to 辶 (mainly kanji that are not on the Joyo list, but also a few belatedly added to it, such as 遜 2060). It is always acceptable to replace 辶 with 辶.

---

## 迅

**SWIFT**

ジン

○迅速な じんそくな swift, rapid ............... 1143

---

**1146**
辵 162

2621
常 | 6

Recall 几 *wind* (from 風 0425), here abbreviated to a single stroke. This character suggests flying like the *wind* through a *crossroad* (辻), and means **SWIFT**. ☞ 訊 1637, 速 1143

---

## 加

**ADD (to), join**

カ
くわ(える) くわ(わる)

○加法 かほう [math] addition ................. 0139
○加える くわえる add
加工 かこう processing, manufacturing ..... 0108
加害者 かがいしゃ assailant, assaulter 0413, 0107
集まりに加わる あつまりにくわわる take part in a gathering ................................. 0190

---

**1147**
力 19

0024
常 | 5

Think of starting with 口 *mouth* (suggesting a person's voice or influence?) and then **ADD-ING** 力 as a rein*force*ment (**joining** its *strength* to that of 口).

---

## 減

**DECREASE, subtract**

ゲン
へ(る) へ(らす)

○減法 げんぽう [math] subtraction ........... 0139
○減る へる [vi] decrease, lessen
○減少する げんしょうする decrease, reduce, lessen
.............................................. 0677
加減 かげん addition and subtraction; degree, extent; adjustment ....................... 1147
食事を減らす しょくじをへらす cut down on (one's) meals ..................... 0288, 0080

---

**1148**
水 85

0548
常 | 12

Review 感 0327. The present entry suggests how the *mouth-piercing guided spear* (咸) **DECREASES** the amount of *water* (氵) in the mouth. Note that 咸 is obsolete by itself. ☞ 滅 1149

## EXTINGUISH, destroy

メツ
ほろ（びる）　ほろ（ぶ）　ほろ（ぼす）

撃滅する　げきめつする　destroy, exterminate...1026
○全滅　ぜんめつ　annihilation, total destruction
.................................................................0078
点滅する　てんめつする　[of light] go on and off,
blink......................................................0349
滅びて行く民族　ほろびていくみんぞく　dying race
.................................................0055, 0477, 0568
○敵を滅ぼす　てきをほろぼす　destroy the enemy
.................................................................1122

| 1149 | Suggests a *flaming* (火) *guided spear* (戈) being **EXTINGUISHED** as it falls into *water* (氵). A visual shortcut is to focus on 灭, which suggests putting something on a flame to **EXTINGUISH** it. No other kanji in this course has the reading メツ. ☞ 滅 1148 |
| --- | --- |
| 水 85 | |
| 0606 | |
| 常 13 | |

## ¹ MIGHT, power; majesty
## ² THREATEN BY FORCE

イ

¹ 威力　いりょく　power, might, authority.......0084
①権威　けんい　authority, power..................1130
¹ 威厳　いげん　solemn dignity.................0810
¹ 威儀　いぎ　dignity, dignified manner.......0928
² 威圧　いあつ　coercion..........................0186

| 1150 | As we did back at 感 0327, see the short horizontal stroke (S3 here) as a miniature representation of the *guided spear*. Here it is held above a *woman* (女)'s head as a **THREATENING** display of **MIGHT**. The most important compound using M2 appears in the next entry. |
| --- | --- |
| 女 38 | |
| 2993 | |
| 常 9 | |

## INTIMIDATE

カク

○威嚇する　いかくする　intimidate, threaten...1150

| 1151 | Visualize *red* (赤)–hot words of **INTIMIDATION** emanating from the *mouth* (口). |
| --- | --- |
| 口 30 | |
| 0702 | |
| 常 17 | |

## A CERTAIN

ワク
あ（る）　ある（いは）

○或る人　あるひと　a certain person, someone　0015
或る程度　あるていど　to a certain extent
.................................................0588, 0280
○或いは　あるいは　perhaps; or
或いはそうかもしれない　あるいはそうかもしれない
It may be so
今日或いは明日　きょうあるいはあす　today or
tomorrow................................0228, 0001, 0024

| 1152 | Now we return to the ordinary *spear* (戈), without the optional "guide" of 戊. Again see the short cross stroke (S5 here) as a depiction of the spear. Unguided, it "misses" its proper position above the *mouth* (see 感 0327). This kanji's meaning is too abstract to be visualized, so you might simply remember the phrase "**A CERTAIN** misguided spear." ☞ 惑 1153 |
| --- | --- |
| 戈 62 | |
| 2763 | |
| 名 8 | |

**BEWILDERED, led astray**

ワク
まど(う)

惑乱 わくらん bewilderment, confusion .... 0380
○惑星 わくせい planet .......................... 0755
当惑 とうわく perplexity, confusion .......... 0141
○惑う まどう be bewildered
戸惑い とまどい loss of orientation, bewilderment .................................. 0248

| 1153 | |
|---|---|
| 心 61 | Combining *"a certain misguided spear"* (或) from the previous entry with 心 to indicate a person's *mental* state, we obtain **BEWILDERED/led astray**. ☞ 感 0327, 或 1152 |
| 2427 | |
| 常 12 | |

**BOUNDED AREA, district**

イキ

域内の いきないの within the area .......... 0215
○地域 ちいき region, area ..................... 0187
区域 くいき zone, area; limits ............... 0297
全域 ぜんいき the whole area, entire region 0078
聖域 せいいき holy/sacred precincts, sanctuary ........................................... 0589

| 1154 | |
|---|---|
| 土 32 | Recall that 土 can refer to a physical location or place. Here it refers to an entire *area*: like a misdirected golf ball that lands in the next fairway, *"a certain misguided spear"* (或) flies into the next **district/BOUNDED AREA**. The *on* reading イキ is unique in this course. ☞ 城 1298 |
| 0421 | |
| 常 11 | |

**TAKE IN, gain, seize**

シュウ
おさ(める) おさ(まる)

収容する しゅうようする accommodate, receive (guests) .................................. 1037
収得する しゅうとくする take possession of ... 0387
○収入 しゅうにゅう income, earnings, receipts 0039
収支 しゅうし earnings and expenditures .... 0373
○勝利を収める しょうりをおさめる win, gain a victory .................................. 0460, 0412

| 1155 | |
|---|---|
| 又 29* | Visualize as a *hand* (又) holding out an offering receptacle (S1–2) to **TAKE IN** contributions to a collection. |
| 0016 | |
| 常 4 | |

¹ **PAY**
² **ACCEPT**
³ **PUT IN PLACE**

ノウ ナッ- ナ ナントウ
おさ(める) -おさ(める) おさ(まる)

①納入 のうにゅう payment; delivery .......... 0039
¹ 分納 ぶんのう payment/delivery in installments .................................. 0088
² 納受する のうじゅする accept, receive ....... 0065
³ 収納 しゅうのう storing; harvesting; receipt 1155
③倉庫に納める そうこにおさめる store in a warehouse .............................. 0696, 0694

| 1156 | |
|---|---|
| 糸 120 | The core idea to perceive here is **PUT IN PLACE**: visualize the top of S9 as a *thread* (糸) protruding from a box (S7–8), then picture pulling or pushing it inside the box so that it is **PUT IN PLACE**. Pulling it inside from the bottom (toward oneself) represents M2 **ACCEPT**; pushing it inside from the top (away from oneself) represents M1 **PAY**. |
| 1195 | |
| 常 10 | |

**OFFER, donate**

ケン　コン

献身 けんしん self-sacrifice, devotion ........ **0060**
献呈 けんてい presentation ................ **0587**
献金する けんきんする donate money ...... **0029**
○献血 けんけつ blood donation ............ **0198**
献立 こんだて menu, preparations .......... **0067**

| 1157 | Here the *South* (南) **OFFERS** a *dog* (犬) (to the North) as a token of peace and cordial relations. |
|---|---|
| 犬 94 | |
| 獻 | |
| 1588 | |
| 常 13 | |

---

**TRIBUTE**

コウ　ク
みつ（ぐ）

○貢献する こうけんする contribute to, serve ... **1157**
年貢 ねんぐ land tax ...................... **0117**
○貢ぐ みつぐ support, contribute (financially or materially)
貢ぎ みつぎ tribute
貢ぎ物 みつぎもの tribute .................... **0172**

| 1158 | **TRIBUTE** delivered to support the lord's *construction* (工) projects. Visualize *money* (貝) bearing a heavy *I beam* (工), representing the idea of supporting the *construction* projects financially. ☞ 頁 0156 |
|---|---|
| 貝 154 | |
| 1970 | |
| 常 10 | |

---

**COVET**

ドン
むさぼ（る）

○貪欲な どんよくな greedy ..................... **1035**
○貪る むさぼる covet, crave
貪り食う むさぼりくう devour ................. **0288**

| 1159 | "*Money* (貝), *now* (今)!": **COVETOUS**. |
|---|---|
| 貝 154 | |
| 1821 | |
| 常 11 | |

---

**GET**

セイ
もら（う）

○貰う もらう receive; get (someone) to do (something)
教えて貰う おしえてもらう get (someone) to teach you (something) ................. **0632**
貰い手 もらいて receiver, recipient .......... **0046**
貰い物 もらいもの (received) gift ............ **0172**

| 1160 | *Money* (貝) + *generation* (世): think of one generation **GETTING** (inheriting) wealth from the previous generation. |
|---|---|
| 貝 154 | |
| 2259 | |
| 名 12 | |

| | POOR | 貧相 ひんそう unhealthy-looking, scrawny **0682** |
|---|---|---|
| 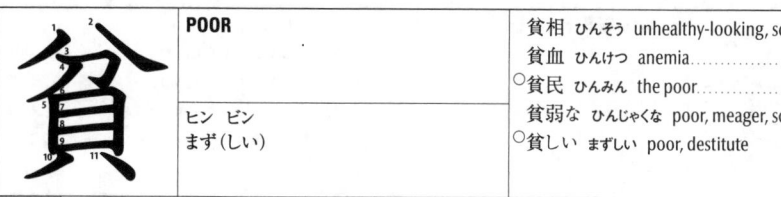 | | 貧血 ひんけつ anemia ....................... **0198** |
| | | ○貧民 ひんみん the poor ...................... **0477** |
| | ヒン ビン | 貧弱な ひんじゃくな poor, meager, scanty... **0424** |
| | まず(しい) | ○貧しい まずしい poor, destitute |

| **1161** 貝 154 | *Money*(貝) *divided*(分) among many household members: **POOR**. The most useful *on-yomi* compounds appear at 困 1723 and 乏 1758. |
|---|---|
| **1822** 常 11 | |

| | ¹**WAGES** | ¹労賃 ろうちん wages, pay ...................... **0542** |
|---|---|---|
| 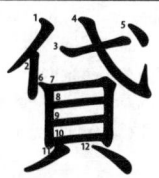 | ²**CHARGES** | ¹賃金 ちんぎん wages, pay ...................... **0029** |
| | | ¹賃上げ ちんあげ wage increase ............. **0041** |
| | チン | ②家賃 やちん (house) rent ................... **0219** |
| | | ² 運賃 うんちん passenger fare, freight charges .................................................. **0584** |

| **1162** 貝 154 | Review 任 0372. The present entry refers to the *money*(貝) received as payment for carrying out one's *duties*(任): **WAGES/CHARGES**. ☞ 貸 1163 |
|---|---|
| **2350** 常 13 | |

| | LEND, loan; rent out | ○賃貸 ちんたい lease, hiring out, charter .....**1162** |
|---|---|---|
|  | | 貸与 たいよ loan, lending ................... **0858** |
| | | ○貸す かす lend, loan; rent out |
| | タイ | 貸し出し中 かしだしちゅう for rent; out on loan .................................................. **0038, 0035** |
| | か(す) か(し)- かし- | 貸し室 かししつ room for rent ............... **0253** |

| **1163** 貝 154 | Review 代 0071. In **renting**, an owner *charges*(代) *money*(貝) in exchange for **LENDING** property. ☞ 賃 1162, 貨 1164 |
|---|---|
| **2254** 常 12 | |

| | ¹**MONEY, currency** | ¹硬貨 こうか coin, metallic currency..........**0891** |
|---|---|---|
| | ²**GOODS; freight** | ①通貨 つうか currency ...................... **0159** |
| | | ²百貨店 ひゃっかてん department store .................................................. **0016, 0347** |
| | カ | ②貨物 かもつ freight, cargo, goods ...........**0172** |
| | | ²貨車 かしゃ freight car ....................... **0125** |

| **1164** 貝 154 | The idea expressed here is *money*(貝)'s function as a medium of exchange—it can be exchanged for (i.e., "*changed into*" 化) anything. In this way 貨 can signify both **MONEY** and **GOODS**. Note that all kanji incorporating 化 have the *on* reading カ. ☞ 貸 1163 |
|---|---|
| **2175** 常 11 | |

| | RESOURCES, capital | ○資源 しげん resources ............................ 0209 |
|---|---|---|
| | | 資金 しきん funds, capital ................... 0029 |
| | | 資本 しほん funds, capital ................... 0031 |
| | シ | 投資 とうし investment .......................... 0517 |
| | | 資料 しりょう materials, data ................. 0758 |

| **1165** | Review 次 0278 NEXT. Here we see *money* (貝) applied toward the *next* thing, expressing the |
|---|---|
| 貝 154 | idea of **RESOURCES/capital** producing future wealth. |
| **2351** | |
| 常 13 | |

| | ¹ APPROVE OF | ①賛成 さんせい approval, agreement, support |
|---|---|---|
| | ² PRAISE | ........................................ 0070 |
| | | ¹ 賛否 さんぴ approval or disapproval, yes or no |
| | | ........................................ 0552 |
| | サン | ¹ 賛助 さんじょ backing, support, approval... 0642 |
| | | ² 賛美 さんび praise, admiration .............. 0497 |
| | | ² 賞賛する しょうさんする laud, praise, commend |
| | | ........................................ 0322 |

| **1166** | Here 夫 signifies *man laborer* (see 0565). Observe *money* (貝) being given to a pair of *man* |
|---|---|
| 貝 154 | *laborers* to **PRAISE** them for their hard work. ☞ 替 1167 |
| 賛 | |
| **2446** | |
| 常 15 | |

| | REPLACE, substitute for | 代替 だいたい substitution ................... 0071 |
|---|---|---|
| | | ○交替 こうたい alternation, shift, change ...... 0102 |
| | | ○替える かえる replace, change to something new |
| | タイ か(える) | 両替 りょうがえ exchange of money .......... 0177 |
| | か(え)- か(わる) | 替わる かわる be replaced, change places with |

| **1167** | Distinguishing from the previous entry, 日 here suggests *"day laborers"*—laborers who are |
|---|---|
| 日 73 | **REPLACED** from one day to the next. The two laborers are identical, so one could easily |
| | **REPLACE** the other. ☞ 賛 1166 |
| **2424** | |
| 常 12 | |

| | ¹ SUBMERGE | ①潜水 せんすい diving ........................... 0027 |
|---|---|---|
| | ² LURK | ①潜る もぐる submerge; get in |
| | | ² 潜入 せんにゅう infiltration ................... 0039 |
| | セン | ² 潜在の せんざいの latent, potential ......... 0406 |
| | ひそ(む) もぐ(る) | ②潜む ひそむ lurk, lie concealed; be latent |

| **1168** | *"Replace"* (替, i.e., displace) *water* (氵): **SUBMERGE**. |
|---|---|
| 水 85 | |
| 潜 | |
| **0680** | |
| 常 15 | |

| | TRADE | ○貿易 ぼうえき trade, commerce............0443 |
|---|---|---|
| | | 貿易会社 ぼうえきがいしゃ trading firm |
| | | ....................0443, 0226, 0314 |
| | ボウ | 貿易風 ぼうえきふう trade wind........0443, 0425 |
| | | 世界貿易センター せかいぼうえきセンター World |
| | | Trade Center....................0604, 0612, 0443 |

**1169**
貝 154

At the top of this character we find a hook (S1–3) and sword (S4–5), here being **TRADED** in for cold cash (貝). Back at 易 0443 I asked you to wait until this entry to learn that character's second meaning EXCHANGE; now try to learn that meaning as you study the sample compounds.

2255
常 | 12

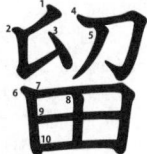

| | ¹ **KEEP IN PLACE** | ¹ 拘留 こうりゅう penal detention............1070 |
|---|---|---|
| | ² **STAY; reside** | ¹ 抑留 よくりゅう detainment, detention, arrest |
| | | ....................1137 |
| | | ① 留める とめる keep in place, fasten |
| | リュウ ル | ② 留学する りゅうがくする study abroad.......0099 |
| | と(める) -と(める) -ど(め) と(まる) | ² 家に留まる いえにとどまる stay home.......0219 |
| | とど(まる)* | |

**1170**
田 102

Here visualize the hook (S1–3) and sword (S4–5) slotting themselves into sections of this *rice field* (田) with the objective of **KEEPING** themselves **IN PLACE**. Picture them digging themselves in for a long **STAY**.

2235
常 | 10

| | **ACCUMULATE** | ○蒸溜 じょうりゅう distillation..................0960 |
|---|---|---|
| | | ○溜まる たまる [vi] accumulate, heap up |
| | | 切手を溜める きってをためる collect stamps |
| | リュウ | ....................0086, 0046 |
| | た(まる) た(める) | 家賃を溜める やちんをためる let the rent fall |
| | | into arrears....................0219, 1162 |
| | | 溜め池 ためいけ reservoir, pond............0188 |

**1171**
水 85

*Water* (氵) *staying in place* (留): **ACCUMULATE.**

0608
名 | 13

| | **CONGRATULATE** | ○賀状 がじょう greeting card..................0616 |
|---|---|---|
| | | 年賀状 ねんがじょう New Year's greeting card |
| | | ....................0117, 0616 |
| | ガ | 賀正 がしょう New Year's congratulations...0043 |

**1172**
貝 154

*Adding* (加) *money* (貝): think of a financial gift made to **CONGRATULATE** a person or couple on an auspicious occasion.

2253
常 | 12

| | **LAY ACROSS** | ○架設する かせつする construct, erect, install **0520** |
|---|---|---|
| | | 架空の かくうの overhead, aerial; fictitious **0398** |
| | | 画架 がか easel.............................**0176** |
| | カ | 十字架 じゅうじか cross, crucifix........**0005, 0098** |
| | か(ける) か(かる) | ○電線を架ける てんせんをかける lay a wire |
| | | ............................**0155, 0210** |

| **1173** | Refers to **LAYING** a bridge or wire **ACROSS** the space between two sides of something, such |
|---|---|
| 木 75 | as a river (see Halpern). It can also refer to other flat, spanning forms such as a shelf or a |
| | stretcher. To perceive these meanings, visualize S6 as **LAID ACROSS** the top of the *tree* (like a |
| **2226** | bridge or wire), holding up 力 and 口 (like a shelf). |
| 常 9 | |

| | **DYE, stain; infect** | ○染みる しみる soak into, permeate |
|---|---|---|
| | | 黒く染まる くろくそまる be dyed black.......**0535** |
| | | 汚染 おせん pollution, contamination .....**1050** |
| | セン | ○感染 かんせん infection ....................**0327** |
| | そ(める) -ぞ(め) -ぞめ そ(まる) | 伝染病 でんせんびょう infectious disease |
| | し(みる) -じ(みる) し(み) | ............................**0223, 0617** |

| **1174** | Let this suggest a *liquid* (氵) **DYE** derived from a certain *tree* (木). *Nine* (九) suggests soaking |
|---|---|
| 木 75 | repeatedly so as to fix the **DYE**. |
| **2229** | |
| 常 9 | |

| | **PEAR** | 梨花 りか pear blossoms.................**0121** |
|---|---|---|
| | | 梨果 りか pome.........................**0599** |
| | | ○梨の実 なしのみ pear.....................**0499** |
| | リ* | 山梨 やまなし Yamanashi (prefecture).......**0037** |
| | なし | |

| **1175** | This *tree* (木) offers up *profit* (利) in the form of delicious **PEARS**. You'll most often see this in |
|---|---|
| 木 75 | the place name 山梨 (やまなし), a prefecture to the north of Mt. Fuji. The *on-yomi* follows |
| | 利 (リ). |
| **2392** | |
| 常 11 | |

| | **PERSON OF EXCELLENCE** | 傑物 けつぶつ great man, outstanding figure |
|---|---|---|
| | | ............................**0172** |
| | | 女傑 じょけつ heroine, lady of character ....**0093** |
| | ケツ | ○傑作 けっさく masterpiece, magnum opus; |
| | | blunder ............................**0152** |
| | | 傑出する けっしゅつする excel, stand out....**0038** |
| | | 傑人 けつじん outstanding person ..........**0015** |

| **1176** | 舛 normally means *dance* (see 舞 0961), but here we'll see it as data occupying adjacent cells |
|---|---|
| 人 9 | in an **EXCEL** spreadsheet, framed by S10 and S11. Picture the *man* (亻) **EXCELLING** at **EXCEL**, |
|  | neatly lining up the data into an organized spreadsheet (桀). ☞ 俊 **1440** |
| **0133** | |
| 常 13 | |

| | ¹ **NOBLE; precious** <br> ² **YOUR HONORABLE** <br><br> キ <br> たっと(い) とうと(い) たっと(ぶ) <br> とうと(ぶ) | ①貴ぶ とうとぶ (=たっとぶ) value highly <br> ¹ 貴い命 とうといのち (=たっといのち) precious life ................................0232 <br> ¹ 貴族 きぞく nobility, noble ................0568 <br> ①貴重な きちょうな precious, valuable ........0539 <br> ² 貴社 きしゃ your company ...............0314 |

| **1177** <br> 貝 154 <br><br> 2260 <br> 常 12 | Review 質 0318 and 真 0838. In the *middle* (中) of the *shell* (貝) lies something **precious** and **NOBLE** (a pearl). Visualize S5 as a formal tray on which we place the **precious** object obtained from the *middle* of the *shell*. M2 reflects this character's use in certain honorific phrases. ☞ 貴 0831 |

| | **CRUSH, break** <br><br> カイ <br> つぶ(す) つぶ(れる) | 潰滅する かいめつする be destroyed, be annihilated ................................1149 <br> 倒潰 とうかい collapse, destruction, crumbling ................................0941 <br> ○潰す つぶす crush, smash; butcher, kill; ruin, wreck <br> 時間を潰す じかんをつぶす kill time...0383, 0448 <br> 潰れる つぶれる be crushed, break; be worn down; be ruined |

| **1178** <br> 水 85 <br><br> 0677 <br> 常 15 | Depicts the instant we **CRUSH** the shell to obtain its *precious* (貴) contents, when *water* (氵) comes spattering out. ☞ 潰 0834 |

| | **LEAVE BEHIND, bequeath** <br><br> イ ユイ | ○遺産 いさん inheritance, bequest, heritage 0181 <br> 遺族 いぞく bereaved family ...............0568 <br> 遺体 いたい remains, body, corpse ........0062 <br> ○遺言 ゆいごん will, testament...............0051 <br> 後遺症 こういしょう sequela, aftereffect (of a disease) ................................0114, 0618 |

| **1179** <br> 辵 162 <br><br> 2731 <br> 常 15 | *Conveying* (辶) *precious* (貴) things forward to future generations: **LEAVE BEHIND/bequeath**. ☞ 遣 1180 |

| | ¹ **DISPATCH, envoy** <br> ² **USE** <br><br> ケン <br> つか(う) -つか(い) -づ(かい) <br> つか(わす) | ①分遣 ぶんけん detachment, detail ..........0088 <br> ¹ 先遣する せんけんする send ahead .........0134 <br> ¹ 遣わす つかわす dispatch, send <br> ②遣う つかう use, spend <br> ² 心遣い こころづかい consideration, anxiety ................................0056 |

| **1180** <br> 辵 162 <br><br> 2717 <br> 常 13 | S1–5 suggests the *precious* item recovered from 貴, similarly placed on a formal tray (S5). Here we **DISPATCH** a *government official* (𠭏) or **envoy** to "*convey* (辶)" this item to an important allied power. Associate M1 **DISPATCH** with M2 **USE** via the idea of putting something to use. ☞ 遺 1179, 追 1181 |

| 追 | **CHASE, follow** | ○追求する ついきゅうする pursue .............1097 |
| | | 追放する ついほうする banish, purge, exile **0574** |
| | | 追加 ついか addition, appendix, supplement |
| | | .............................................................**1147** |
| | ツイ | ○追う おう chase, pursue, follow |
| | お(う) | 追い越す おいこす outrun, pass, overtake...**1112** |

| **1181** | 𠂤 indicates a *high-ranking official* (see 帥 0747), here using the official *truck* (辶) to **CHASE** |
| 辵 162 | a crime suspect. ☞ 遣 1180, 迫 1182 |
| 2667 | |
| 常 9 | |

| 迫 | **PRESS, urge; draw near** | ○切迫する せっぱくする draw near, press; become |
| | | acute, grow tense ..............................**0086** |
| | | 強迫 きょうはく coercion, compulsion .......**0423** |
| | | 圧迫する あっぱくする press, oppress, pressure |
| | ハク | .............................................................**0186** |
| | せま(る) | 迫害 はくがい persecution, oppression .....**0413** |
| | | ○迫る せまる press, urge; draw near |

| **1182** | *Advancing* (辶) + *white* (白): let this suggest **PRESSING** on someone so intensely that he turns |
| 辵 162 | *white* (i.e., the blood gets **PRESSED** out of him). ☞ 追 1181 |
| 2647 | |
| 常 8 | |

| 泊 | **STAY OVERNIGHT** | 宿泊 しゅくはく lodging.........................**0292** |
| | | 外泊 がいはく staying out overnight.........**0266** |
| | | ○一泊 いっぱく overnight/one-night stay ....**0002** |
| | ハク | ○泊まる とまる stay overnight, lodge, stay at |
| | と(まる) と(める) | 友人を泊める ゆうじんをとめる put a friend up |
| | | for the night ...........................**0399, 0015** |

| **1183** | This character was originally used to refer to an anchorage, "*white* (白) *water* (氵)" indicating |
| 水 85 | the place where the surf breaks upon land. This is the place one can moor one's ship and |
| | **STAY OVERNIGHT.** |
| 0293 | |
| 常 8 | |

| 伯 | **¹ OLDER SIBLING OF PARENT** | ①伯父 おじ (=はくふ) uncle (older than one's |
| | **² COUNT, earl** | parent) [cf. 叔 2043] .........................**0100** |
| | | ¹ 伯母 おば (=はくぼ) aunt (older than one's |
| | | parent) [cf. 叔 2043].........................**0104** |
| | ハク | ² 前島伯 まえじまはく Count Maejima...**0113, 0341** |

| **1184** | Here we see a *man* (亻) with a completely *white* (白) head of hair, conveying the general |
| 人 9 | sense of "senior figure." Used in compounds referring to an **OLDER SIBLING OF ONE'S PARENT,** |
| | or to a **COUNT** or **earl.** ☞ 叔 2043 |
| 0043 | |
| 常 7 | |

| | BEAT, rhythm | ○拍手 はくしゅ applause, clapping ............0046 |
|---|---|---|
| | | 拍車 はくしゃ spur, rowel spur..............0125 |
| | | 拍動 はくどう pulsation, pulsebeat .........0540 |
| | ハク ヒョウ | ○拍子 ひょうし time, beat, rhythm; chance, the moment....................0094 |
| | | 三拍子 さんびょうし simple triple time..0004, 0094 |

**1185** 手 64 / 拍 / 0269 / 常 8
Ignore 白 *white*; instead, visualize 日 as a drum, and S4 as the motion of the *hand* (扌) striking it: **BEAT.**

| | CONDOLE; mourn | 弔意 ちょうい condolence, mourning .......0151 |
|---|---|---|
| | | ○弔問 ちょうもん condolence call.............0452 |
| | | ○弔う とむらう condole; mourn |
| | チョウ / とむら(う) | |

**1186** 弓 57 / 2888 / 常 4
A *bow* (弓) crying a cataract of tears (S4): **CONDOLE/mourn.**

| | BOIL (over) | ○沸点 ふってん boiling point................0349 |
|---|---|---|
| | | ○沸く わく [vi] boil (over), seethe, be excited |
| | | 沸かす わかす [vt] boil, make hot, stimulate |
| | フツ / わ(く) わ(かす) | 湯沸かし ゆわかし kettle, water heater.....0446 |

**1187** 水 85 / 0291 / 常 8
A *bow* (弓) crying two cataracts of tears (S7–8), from the agony of being **BOILED** in *water* (氵).

| | BOIL, cook | ○煮沸 しゃふつ boiling.....................1187 |
|---|---|---|
| | | ○煮る にる [vt] boil, cook |
| | | 煮込む にこむ boil well; stew, cook together ....................0192 |
| | シャ / に(る) -に に(える) に(やす) | 煮える にえる [vi] boil, be cooked |
| | | 煮やす にやす [vt] boil down |

**1188** 火 86 / 煮 / 2426 / 常 12
*Person* (者) being **BOILED**/cooked on a *fire* (灬). ☞ 蒸 0960, 薫 1779

**SPEND**

ヒ
つい(やす) つい(える)

○生活費 せいかつひ living expenses, cost of living ........................ 0036, 0054
燃費 ねんぴ (gas) mileage ................. 0761
費用 ひよう expenses, outlay .............. 0047
○費やす ついやす expend, consume; waste
費える ついえる be wasted

| | |
|---|---|
| **1189** | (Picking up from 沸 1187) Crying over how much *money* (貝) one has **SPENT**. |
| 貝 154 | |
| **2261** | |
| 常 12 | |

**YOUNGER BROTHER**

テイ ダイ デ
おとうと

義弟 ぎてい younger brother-in-law ........ 0926
弟子 でし disciple, pupil, apprentice ...... 0094
門弟 もんてい pupil, disciple ............... 0447
師弟 してい master and pupil .............. 0748
○弟さん おとうとさん your younger brother

| | |
|---|---|
| **1190** | Two brothers sometimes like to spike their hair. Here we see the **YOUNGER BROTHER**, the crybaby (from 弔 1186) who carries around a toy halberd (S7, from 矛 0164). S1–2 show his spiked hair. Eventually, you should learn to recognize this character simply by the presence of the spiked hair, which distinguishes it from the next entry. ☞ 第 1191 |
| 弓 57 | |
| **1759** | |
| 常 7 | |

**ORDINAL NUMBER PREFIX; order**

ダイ

○第一 だいいち the first, No. 1; the best; to begin with, above everything else ............... 0002
第三者 だいさんしゃ third party ....... 0004, 0107
第六感 だいろっかん the sixth sense, intuition ........................ 0008, 0327
次第 しだい order; circumstances, reasons; as soon as ....................... 0278
落第する らくだいする fail an examination... 0793

| | |
|---|---|
| **1191** | Your main challenge in recognizing this kanji and the previous one will be to have a reliable way of associating the variable element with the meaning. Here, then, simply learn to associate 𥫗 (*bamboo for counting*) with this kanji's function as the **ORDINAL NUMBER PREFIX**. Take a few moments to practice distinguishing these two. ☞ 弟 1190 |
| 竹 118 | |
| **2318** | |
| 常 11 | |

**SHAVE**

テイ
そ(る) す(る)

○剃る そる (=する) shave
剃り立て そりたて (=すりたて) freshly shaven ........................ 0067
剃り落す そりおとす (=すりおとす) shave off... 0793
剃刀 かみそり razor .......................... 0085

| | |
|---|---|
| **1192** | *Little brother* (弟) using a *knife* ( 刂 ) to **SHAVE** off the spikes in his hair. |
| 刀 18 | |
| | |
| 外 9 | |

| 兄 | **OLDER BROTHER** | ○兄弟 きょうだい (=けいてい) brothers (and sisters) .................... 1190 |
|---|---|---|
| | | 父兄 ふけい one's father and older brothers; guardians .................... 0100 |
| | | 義兄 ぎけい older brother-in-law .......... 0926 |
| | ケイ キョウ | ○兄さん にいさん older brother |
| | あに | 兄貴 あにき older brother; one's senior ..... 1177 |

| 1193 | Now we meet the **OLDER BROTHER**, who has gotten rid of his spikes for this portrait (see 弟 1190). To distinguish this from the next entry, remember that **OLDER BROTHER** has *human legs* (儿). ☞ 只 1194 |
|---|---|
| 儿 10 | |
| 1848 | |
| 常 5 | |

| 只 | ¹ **FREE OF CHARGE** <br> ² **JUST, only; ordinary** | ¹ 只乗り ただのり free ride ..................... 1005 |
|---|---|---|
| | | ¹ 只働き ただばたらき working for nothing .... 0541 |
| | | ②只今 ただいま just now; at present, presently; I'm home! .................... 0228 |
| | シ | ² 只の人 ただのひと common person, man in the street .................... 0015 |
| | ただ ただ- | ² 只事ではない ただごとではない It is no common case .................... 0080 |

| 1194 | Picture a "zero" (0) walking around on a pair of stubby legs (ハ). The meanings this character expresses range from "costs nothing" (**FREE OF CHARGE**) to "nothing more than/no different than" (**JUST/only**) to "nothing special" (**ordinary**). ☞ 兄 1193 |
|---|---|
| 口 30 | |
| 1849 | |
| 名 5 | |

| 税 | **TAX** | ○税金 ぜいきん tax, duty; rates ................ 0029 |
|---|---|---|
| | | 税込み ぜいこみ tax included ............... 0192 |
| | | 所得税 しょとくぜい income tax ........ 0249, 0387 |
| | | 付加価値税 ふかかちぜい value-added tax .................... 0064, 1147, 0548, 0842 |
| | ゼイ | 税を納める ぜいをおさめる pay a tax ........ 1156 |

| 1195 | Here again we have *older brother*, this time with spiked hair (兄). This character suggests paying one's *rice* (禾) to *Big Brother*: **TAX**. |
|---|---|
| 禾 115 | |
| 税 | |
| 1101 | |
| 常 12 | |

| 鋭 | **SHARP** | ○鋭角 えいかく acute angle .................... 0342 |
|---|---|---|
| | | 先鋭な せんえいな radical; acute, sharp ..... 0134 |
| | | 鋭利な えいりな sharp, keen; acute, sharp, clever .................... 0412 |
| | エイ | 精鋭 せいえい best/pick, choice .............. 0976 |
| | するど(い) | ○鋭いナイフ するどいナイフ sharp knife |

| 1196 | Clearly depicts **SHARP**: starts with 金 to suggest something *metal*, then gives us an older brother with two **SHARP** pointy spikes on his head. It is useful to practice this character together with 鈍 1102 DULL, using the compounds 鋭角 (えいかく, acute angle) and 鈍角 (どんかく, obtuse angle) to learn their *on-yomi*. ☞ 尖 1563 |
|---|---|
| 金 167 | |
| 鋭 | |
| 1544 | |
| 常 15 | |

| | |
|---|---|
| **¹EXPLAIN; preach**<br>**²THEORY, view** | ①説明 せつめい explanation, description....0024<br>¹説教 せっきょう preaching; scolding.........0632<br>①説く とく explain; preach; persuade |
| セツ　ゼイ<br>と(く) | ²仮説 かせつ hypothesis.....................0921<br>²説を立てる せつをたてる put forward a theory<br>............................................0067 |

| 1197 | Older brother (兄, here with *spiked hair*) always seems to have a **THEORY**, a way to **EXPLAIN** |
|---|---|
| 言 149 | just about anything. In 言 see the various **THEORIES** and **EXPLANATIONS** emanating from his |
| 説 | mouth. |
| 1405 | |
| 常 14 | |

| | |
|---|---|
| **¹REMOVE**<br>**²ESCAPE FROM** | ¹剝脱する はくだつする strip (off), deprive...0609<br>①靴を脱ぐ くつをぬぐ take off one's shoes...0593<br>¹脱毛 だつもう hair removal; falling out of hair<br>............................................0487 |
| ダツ<br>ぬ(ぐ)　ぬ(げる) | ②脱退 だったい withdrawal, secession........1091<br>²脱税 だつぜい tax evasion...................1195 |

| 1198 | This character seems to refer to the way older brothers always walk around with their shirts |
|---|---|
| 肉 130 | off, flaunting their muscles: *older brothers with spiked hair* (兄) **REMOVE** their clothing to |
| 脱 | expose their *flesh* (月). M2 is a cognate meaning. |
| 0886 | |
| 常 11 | |

| | |
|---|---|
| **REVIEW, inspect** | ○検閲 けんえつ censorship; inspection, review<br>............................................1029<br>校閲 こうえつ revision, reviewing, editing...0103 |
| エツ | 閲兵 えっぺい inspection of troops..........0907<br>観閲 かんえつ inspection of troops..........1128 |

| 1199 | Older brother with spiked hair (兄) at the gate (門) to the clubhouse, **REVIEWING** all little |
|---|---|
| 門 169 | brothers in a rigorous **inspection** before they will be allowed to enter. |
| 閲 | |
| 2845 | |
| 常 15 | |

| | |
|---|---|
| **CELEBRATE, congratulate** | 祝賀 しゅくが celebration; congratulation...1172<br>○祝日 しゅくじつ holiday, festival day.........0001<br>祝儀 しゅうぎ celebration; congratulatory gift; tip<br>............................................0928 |
| シュク　シュウ<br>いわ(う) | 祝卒業 しゅくそつぎょう Congratulations,<br>　graduates!.......................0751, 0498<br>○祝い いわい celebration; congratulation |

| 1200 | Older brother (兄) standing at an altar (ネ), representing his family in marking a happy occa- |
|---|---|
| 示 113 | sion and thanking God for it: **CELEBRATE**. |
| 祝 | |
| 0822 | |
| 常 9 | |

| 況 | **CONDITIONS, state of affairs** | ○状況 じょうきょう state of affairs, conditions, circumstances ............................. 0616 |
|---|---|---|
| | | 戦況 せんきょう war situation, progress of a battle ............................. 0461 |
| | キョウ | 市況 しきょう market conditions ............................. 0205 |
| | | 好況 こうきょう brisk market, prosperity .... 0095 |
| | | 不況 ふきょう depression, slump, recession 0049 |

| **1201** | People often refer to their present personal or financial **CONDITIONS** using phrases like "under water" or "keeping my head above water." Here let the level of *water* (氵) around *older brother* (兄) suggest his current **CONDITIONS** or **state of affairs**. |
|---|---|
| 水 85 | |
| 0299 | |
| 常 8 | |

| 悦 | **DELIGHTED** | ○悦楽 えつらく pleasure, joy ................... 0302 |
|---|---|---|
| | | 満悦 まんえつ great joy, rapture ............. 0179 |
| | | 愉悦 ゆえつ joy ............................. 0947 |
| | エツ | 法悦 ほうえつ religious exultation; ecstasy 0139 |

| **1202** | With so many advantages over his siblings, what can be in the *heart* (忄) of *older brother with spiked hair* (兄) but **DELIGHT**? |
|---|---|
| 心 61 | |
| 悦 | |
| 0378 | |
| 常 10 | |

| 克 | **OVERCOME** | 下克上 げこくじょう the junior dominating/supplanting the senior ................ 0040, 0041 |
|---|---|---|
| | | 相克する そうこくする struggle with each other, conflict ............................. 0682 |
| | コク | ○克己 こっき self-denial, self-control ......... 0426 |
| | | 克明 こくめい scrupulousness, diligence .... 0024 |

| **1203** | Imagine that you have **OVERCOME** your dominant *older brother* (兄) by stabbing a dagger (S1–2) into the top of his head. The most useful compound containing this character appears at 服 1471. |
|---|---|
| 儿 10 | |
| 1760 | |
| 常 7 | |

| 競 | **COMPETE** | ○競走する きょうそうする compete, contend, vie ............................. 0140 |
|---|---|---|
| | | 競輪 けいりん bicycle race ................... 0944 |
| | キョウ ケイ | 競技 きょうぎ match, contest, game; sporting event ............................. 0966 |
| | きそ(う) せ(る) | ○競う きそう compete with, vie |
| | | 競る せる make a bid for |

| **1204** | Two small boys *stand* (𱔼) on the shoulders of their *older brothers* (兄) and **COMPETE** in a jousting match. |
|---|---|
| 立 117 | |
| 1639 | |
| 常 20 | |

**OLDER SISTER**

シ
あね

| | |
|---|---|
| 実姉 じっし one's true (older) sister | 0499 |
| 義姉 ぎし older sister-in-law | 0926 |
| 令姉 れいし your older sister | 0229 |
| 姉上 あねうえ older sister | 0041 |
| ○姉さん ねえさん older sister; waitress, girl; miss | |

**1205**
女 38

**OLDER SISTER:** *girl* (女) who is old enough to go to the *market* (市) and take care of the shopping.

0253
常 | 8

---

**YOUNGER SISTER**

マイ
いもうと

| | |
|---|---|
| ○姉妹 しまい (=きょうだい) sisters | 1205 |
| 義妹 ぎまい younger sister-in-law | 0926 |
| 弟妹 ていまい younger brothers and sisters | 1190 |
| 妹さん いもうとさん your younger sister | |

**1206**
女 38

Review 未 0271. Here, *girl* (女) who has *not yet* (未) reached maturity: **YOUNGER SISTER.**

0250
常 | 8

---

**PEARL**

シュ

| | |
|---|---|
| 珠玉 しゅぎょく jewel, gem | 0073 |
| ○真珠 しんじゅ pearl | 0838 |
| 珠算 しゅざん calculation on the abacus | 0980 |
| 数珠 じゅず Buddhist rosary | 0309 |

**1207**
玉 96

Review 朱 0566. Here see a *gem* (王) resting upon the *vermilion* (朱) tissue of a mollusk's mantle—a **PEARL.**

0854
常 | 10

---

**SPECIAL**

シュ
こと

| | |
|---|---|
| ○特殊な とくしゅな special, unique | 0385 |
| 殊勝な しゅしょうな laudable, praiseworthy | 0460 |
| ○殊に ことに especially, above all | |
| 殊更に ことさらに especially; intentionally, deliberately | 0889 |

**1208**
歹 78

For funerary rites, people favor **SPECIAL** articles and ornamentation. Here let "*death* (歹) + *vermilion* (朱)" suggest a **SPECIAL** vermilion shroud in which to bury a deceased person. Note that both of these kanji incorporating 朱 in the phonetic position follow its *on* reading, シュ.

0850
常 | 10

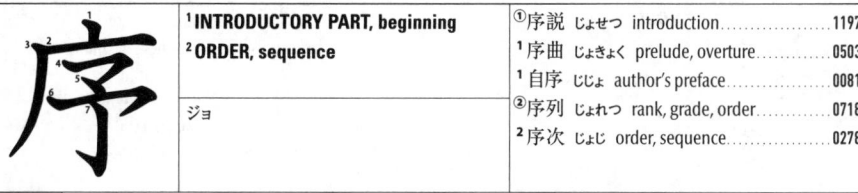

| 序 | **1 INTRODUCTORY PART, beginning**<br>**2 ORDER, sequence**<br><br>ジョ | ① 序説 じょせつ introduction.................1197<br>**1** 序曲 じょきょく prelude, overture...........0503<br>**1** 自序 じじょ author's preface................0081<br>② 序列 じょれつ rank, grade, order..........0718<br>**2** 序次 じょじ order, sequence.................0278 |

| **1209**<br>广 53<br><br>2639<br>常 7 | Review 予 0163. Let *slanting roof* (广) + *in advance* (予) suggest the front of a building, the part one enters first: **INTRODUCTORY PART/beginning**. This easily suggests M2, because an **ORDER/sequence** always starts from the **beginning**. |

| 秩 | **ORDER**<br><br>チツ | ○秩序 ちつじょ order, discipline; method, system<br>...................................1209 |

| **1210**<br>禾 115<br><br>1073<br>常 10 | Represents the **ORDER** obtained through the social contract: citizens *lose* (失) some *rice bundles* (禾) (i.e., taxes) in exchange for law and **ORDER**. |

| 迭 | **ALTERNATE**<br><br>テツ | ○更迭する こうてつする reshuffle, change [as of government officials], exchange places....0889 |

| **1211**<br>辵 162<br><br>2650<br>常 8 | Combines one grapheme for *advancing* (辶) and another for *losing* (失) ground. One step forward, one step back, one step forward, one step back ...: **ALTERNATE**. ☞ 送 0455 |

| 喜 | **HAPPY**<br><br>キ<br>よろこ (ぶ) よろこ (ばす) | ○喜悦 きえつ delight, rapture, joy ...........1202<br>歓喜する かんきする rejoice, be greatly delighted ...........................1131<br>○喜ぶ よろこぶ be happy, be delighted<br>大喜び おおよろこび great joy, delight......0033<br>親を喜ばす おやをよろこばす make one's parents happy.............................0276 |

| **1212**<br>口 30<br><br>2008<br>常 12 | 壴, not to be confused with 豆 0161, means *drum*. Picture it as a large drum standing on its side: S4–6 show the drum skin, while 士 *military man* represents a drummer standing atop the drum (in certain Japanese festivals, there truly are drums so big that people stand on them). Combining *drum* with *mouth* (S10–12), 喜 suggests music and singing, and means **HAPPY**. |

| 善 GOOD | 善良な ぜんりょうな good, virtuous ..........0285 |
|---|---|
| | 善意 ぜんい good intention; favorable sense ..........0151 |
| | ○改善 かいぜん improvement, amelioration 0429 |
| ゼン よ(い) | 善と悪 ぜんとあく good and evil ............0546 |
| | ○善い行い よいおこない good deed ..........0055 |

| 1213 口 30 譱 2030 常 12 | Look at this character's traditional form, provided in the reference data section of this entry. See the present-day simplified form as an "improved" form that consolidates the two 言 graphemes. In this consolidation and improvement, this character symbolizes **GOOD**. ☞ 害 0413, 普 1085 |
|---|---|

| 繕 MEND | ○繕う つくろう mend, repair |
|---|---|
| | 繕い つくろい mending, darning |
| ゼン つくろ(う) | |

| 1214 糸 120 1296 常 18 | *Thread* (糸) making something *good* (善) again: **MEND**. An *on-yomi* compound appears at 修 1676. Note that both characters incorporating 善 follow its *on-yomi*, ゼン. |
|---|---|

| 膳 SMALL FOOD TABLE, tray | ○お膳 おぜん low four-legged tray for serving food |
|---|---|
| | お膳立てをする おぜんだてをする set the table, prepare for..........0067 |
| ゼン | 配膳する はいぜんする set (a place at) the table ..........0799 |
| | 二の膳 にのぜん second course; side dish ..........0003 |

| 1215 肉 130 1000 常 16 | Picture *good* (善) *meat* (月) served on an old-fashioned Japanese dining tray: **SMALL FOOD TABLE/tray**. |
|---|---|

| 憾 STRONGLY REGRET | ○遺憾な いかんな regrettable ..........1179 |
|---|---|
| カン | |

| 1216 心 61 0690 常 16 | Adds another *heart* (忄) to *sense/feel* (感). Let this suggest an even more strongly felt emotion: **STRONGLY REGRET**. This would be a good time to review not only 感 0327 but also 惑 1153. ☞ 感 0327 |
|---|---|

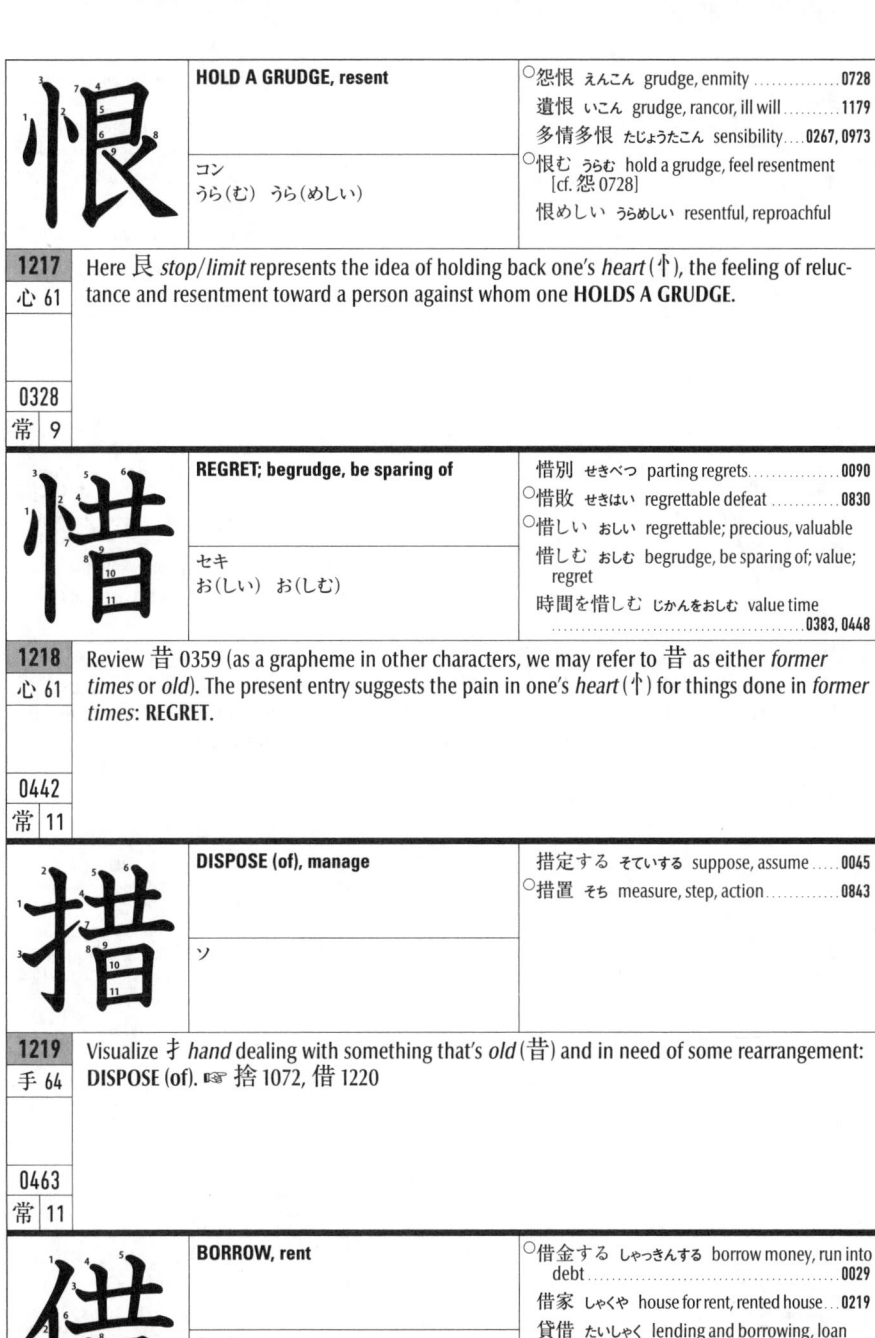

## 恨

**HOLD A GRUDGE, resent**

コン
うら(む) うら(めしい)

怨恨 えんこん grudge, enmity .............. 0728
遺恨 いこん grudge, rancor, ill will .......... 1179
多情多恨 たじょうたこん sensibility .... 0267, 0973
恨む うらむ hold a grudge, feel resentment
　　[cf. 怨 0728]
恨めしい うらめしい resentful, reproachful

| 1217 | Here 艮 *stop/limit* represents the idea of holding back one's *heart* (忄), the feeling of reluctance and resentment toward a person against whom one **HOLDS A GRUDGE**. |
| 心 61 | |
| 0328 | |
| 常 9 | |

## 惜

**REGRET; begrudge, be sparing of**

セキ
お(しい) お(しむ)

惜別 せきべつ parting regrets ................ 0090
惜敗 せきはい regrettable defeat ............ 0830
惜しい おしい regrettable; precious, valuable
惜しむ おしむ begrudge, be sparing of; value; regret
時間を惜しむ じかんをおしむ value time
　　.................................................. 0383, 0448

| 1218 | Review 昔 0359 (as a grapheme in other characters, we may refer to 昔 as either *former times* or *old*). The present entry suggests the pain in one's *heart* (忄) for things done in *former times*: **REGRET**. |
| 心 61 | |
| 0442 | |
| 常 11 | |

## 措

**DISPOSE (of), manage**

ソ

措定する そていする suppose, assume ..... 0045
措置 そち measure, step, action ............. 0843

| 1219 | Visualize 扌 *hand* dealing with something that's *old* (昔) and in need of some rearrangement: **DISPOSE (of)**. ☞ 捨 1072, 借 1220 |
| 手 64 | |
| 0463 | |
| 常 11 | |

## 借

**BORROW, rent**

シャク
か(りる)

借金する しゃっきんする borrow money, run into debt ............................................ 0029
借家 しゃくや house for rent, rented house ... 0219
貸借 たいしゃく lending and borrowing, loan
　　.................................................. 1163
賃借する ちんしゃくする hire, lease .......... 1162
借りる かりる borrow, get a loan; hire, rent

| 1220 | Have you ever known a man who never <u>bought</u> his own new things, but always <u>borrowed</u> other people's old things? Picture that *man* (亻) here, standing beside all of his *old* (昔) **BORROWED** stuff. Do not confuse with 債 0833, which is both graphically and semantically similar. ☞ 債 0833, 措 1219 |
| 人 9 | |
| 0104 | |
| 常 10 | |

| | MIXED UP | 交錯した こうさくした entangled, complicated ..........0102 |
|---|---|---|
| | | ○錯覚 さっかく false perception, (optical) illusion ..........0325 |
| | サク | 錯角 さっかく alternate interior angles ......0342 |
| | | 錯乱 さくらん derangement, confusion......0380 |
| | | 倒錯 とうさく perversion, inversion..........0941 |

| 1221 | Iron rusts when it combines with oxygen. Think of *metals* (金) reacting chemically as they get *old* (昔), thereby getting **MIXED UP** with other substances. |
|---|---|
| 金 167 | |
| 1555 | |
| 常 16 | |

| | BEFORE, formerly | 曽祖父 そうそふ (=ひいじじ) great-grandfather ..........0641, 0100 |
|---|---|---|
| | | 曽祖母 そうそぼ (=ひいばば) great-grandmother ..........0641, 0104 |
| | ソウ ソ ゾ | 曽孫 そうそん (=ひまご) great-grandchild ....1079 |
| | | 未曽有 みぞう unprecedented ........0271, 0400 |

| 1222 | When used inside other kanji, 曽 will mean *build up*: see how its layers *build up* from 日 through 田, with ㇚ pointing still further up. On the infrequent occasions when it is used as a stand-alone kanji, its core meaning is **BEFORE**, which we can associate with the layers of accumulated experience that came **BEFORE**. Learn to recognize the old form 曾. |
|---|---|
| 八 12 | |
| 曾 | |
| 1823 | |
| 常 11 | |

| | INCREASE | 増加する ぞうかする increase, multiply, rise 1147 |
|---|---|---|
| | | 増減 ぞうげん increase and decrease, rise and fall 1148 |
| | | ○急増 きゅうぞう sudden/rapid increase......0971 |
| | ゾウ | ○量が増える りょうがふえる increase in quantity ..........0538 |
| | ま(す) ま(し) ふ(える) ふ(やす) | 人手を増やす ひとでをふやす add staff ..........0015, 0046 |

| 1223 | A pile of *earth* (土) *building up* (曽): **INCREASE**. ☞ 殖 0841 |
|---|---|
| 土 32 | |
| 増 | |
| 0619 | |
| 常 14 | |

| | STRATUM | 成層圏 せいそうけん stratosphere .....0070, 0459 |
|---|---|---|
| | | ○社会層 しゃかいそう stratum of society 0314, 0226 |
| | | 知識層 ちしきそう the intellectual class ..........0560, 1089 |
| | ソウ | ○高層ビル こうそうビル high-rise (building)...0185 |
| | | 一層 いっそう all the more, still more........0002 |

| 1224 | An easy shortcut to recognizing this character is to visualize the rectangular layer at the top as the highest **STRATUM**, toward which the horizontal layers in 曽 *build up*. From a certain ideological viewpoint, the shape of 尸 is suggestive of society's upper crust in the way it encloses and appears to keep a lid on the lower strata. |
|---|---|
| 尸 44 | |
| 層 | |
| 2728 | |
| 常 14 | |

**HATE**

ゾウ
にく(む) にく(い) にく(らしい)
にく(しみ)

○憎悪 ぞうお abhorrence, hatred ............. 0546
憎まれ口 にくまれぐち offensive [abusive]
　language ................................... 0019
憎まれっ子 にくまれっこ bad [naughty] child 0094
生憎 あいにく unfortunately; I am sorry, but...
　.............................................. 0036
○憎しみ にくしみ hatred, enmity

| 1225 | 忄 here suggests feelings. Feelings of antipathy *building up* (曾) in one's *heart*: **HATRED**. |
| 心 61 | |

憎
0626
常 14

**BONZE, priest**

ソウ

僧職 そうしょく priesthood .................... 1087
○僧院 そういん monastery, temple ........... 0634
小僧 こぞう priestling; servant boy; kid, brat 0034
破戒僧 はかいそう sinful priest, depraved monk
　......................................... 0596, 0469
禅僧 ぜんそう Zen priest/monk ............. 1076

| 1226 | A *man* (亻) *building up* (曾) his moral self-discipline and good karma: **BONZE**. |
| 人 9 | |

僧
0138
常 13

**PRESENT A GIFT**

ゾウ ソウ
おく(る)

贈呈 ぞうてい presentation .................. 0587
贈答品 ぞうとうひん present, gift ...... 0981, 0301
○贈与 ぞうよ donation, presentation ........ 0858
○贈り物 おくりもの present, gift ............. 0172
花を贈る はなをおくる give flowers .......... 0121

| 1227 | *Money* (貝) *building up* (曾) on a table at which gifts are offered at a ceremony: **PRESENT A GIFT.** ☞ 賜 0444 |
| 貝 154 | |

贈
1472
常 18

**BRIBE**

ワイ
まかな(う)

○収賄 しゅうわい acceptance of a bribe, corruption
　.............................................. 1155
贈賄する ぞうわいする bribe, corrupt ....... 1227
贈収賄 ぞうしゅうわい corruption, bribery
　......................................... 1227, 1155
○賄う まかなう provide meals/board, cater; meet,
　cover, pay

| 1228 | "*There is* (有) *money* (貝)"—memorize this as a phrase used by the unscrupulous as an indirect way of offering a **BRIBE**. |
| 貝 154 | |

1390
常 13

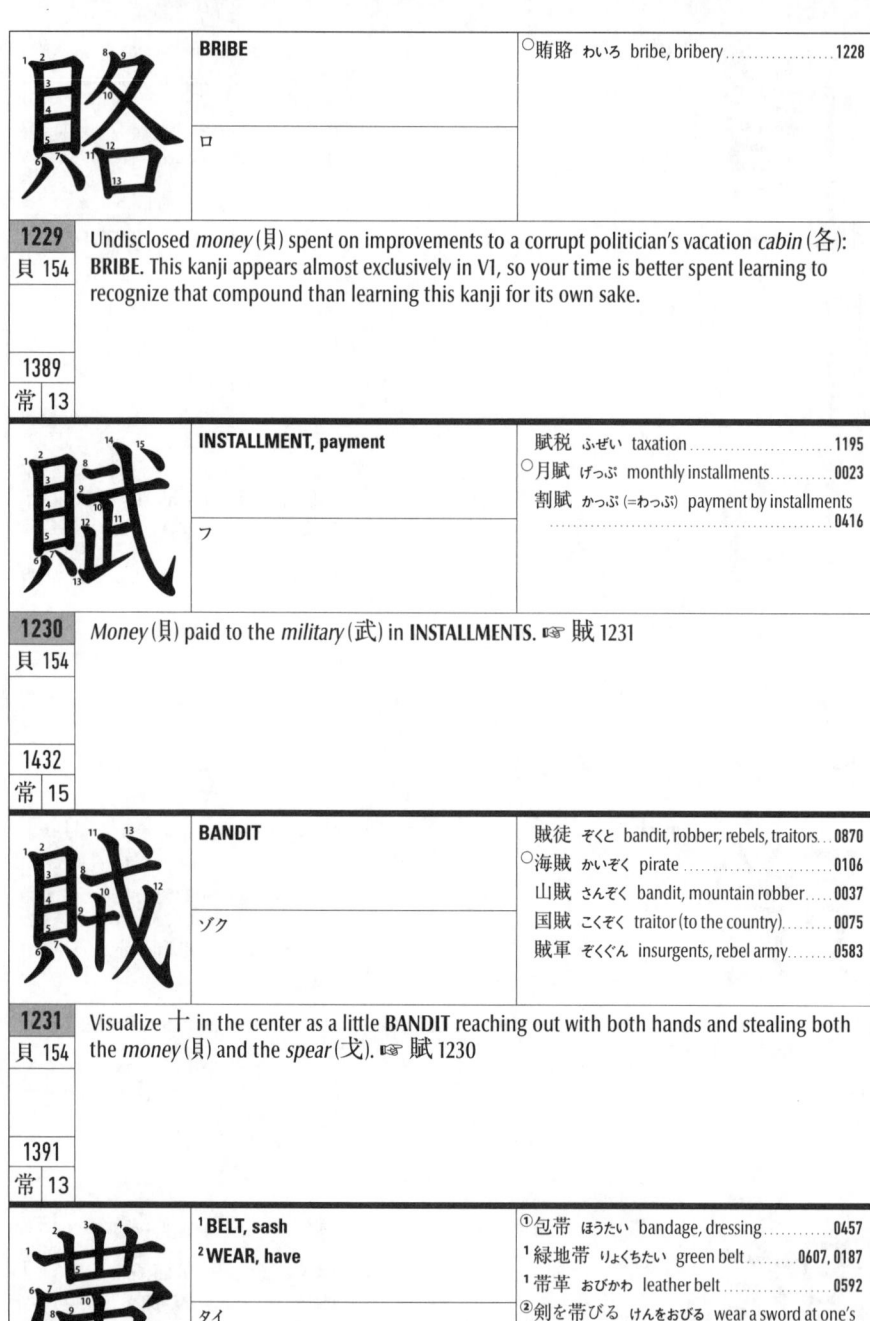

**BRIBE**

ロ

○賄賂 わいろ bribe, bribery.................1228

| 1229 | Undisclosed *money*(貝) spent on improvements to a corrupt politician's vacation *cabin*(各): **BRIBE**. This kanji appears almost exclusively in VI, so your time is better spent learning to recognize that compound than learning this kanji for its own sake. |
| 貝 154 | |
| 1389 | |
| 常 13 | |

**INSTALLMENT, payment**

フ

賦税 ふぜい taxation.........................1195
○月賦 げっぷ monthly installments...........0023
割賦 かっぷ (=わっぷ) payment by installments
.................................................0416

| 1230 | *Money*(貝) paid to the *military*(武) in **INSTALLMENTS**. ☞ 賊 1231 |
| 貝 154 | |
| 1432 | |
| 常 15 | |

**BANDIT**

ゾク

賊徒 ぞくと bandit, robber; rebels, traitors...0870
○海賊 かいぞく pirate.........................0106
山賊 さんぞく bandit, mountain robber......0037
国賊 こくぞく traitor (to the country).........0075
賊軍 ぞくぐん insurgents, rebel army........0583

| 1231 | Visualize 十 in the center as a little **BANDIT** reaching out with both hands and stealing both the *money*(貝) and the *spear*(戈). ☞ 賦 1230 |
| 貝 154 | |
| 1391 | |
| 常 13 | |

**¹ BELT, sash**
**² WEAR, have**

タイ
お(びる) おび

①包帯 ほうたい bandage, dressing............0457
¹緑地帯 りょくちたい green belt.........0607, 0187
¹帯革 おびかわ leather belt...................0592
②剣を帯びる けんをおびる wear a sword at one's side...............................................1033
² 付帯的な ふたいてきな incidental, accessory
.................................................0064, 0169

| 1232 | Review 共 0356. Here we see <u>three</u> people **WEARING** a single waist**BELT** (S6–7) and *cloth* skirt (巾). ☞ 棄 0606, 帝 1418 |
| 巾 50 | |
| 2237 | |
| 常 10 | |

**¹ STAGNATE, be left undone**
**² STAY**

タイ とどこおる

① 沈滞 ちんたい stagnation, dullness.........0655
¹ 滞納 たいのう nonpayment, delinquency....1156
① 滞る とどこおる stagnate, be left undone
② 滞在 たいざい stay, sojourn.............0406
² 滞留 たいりゅう sojourn, stay.............1170

| 1233 | *Belt* (帯) constricting the flow of *water* (氵): **STAGNATE; STAY.** |
| 水 85 | |
| 滞 | |
| 0609 | |
| 常 13 | |

**¹ NOT GO SMOOTHLY**
**² ASTRINGENT juice (of unripe persimmons)**

ジュウ
しぶ しぶ(い) しぶ(る)

① 渋滞 じゅうたい delay, retardation, stagnation
.........1233
¹ 交通渋滞 こうつうじゅうたい traffic jam
.........0102, 0159, 1233
² 渋茶 しぶちゃ strong tea.............0603
② 渋い しぶい astringent; glum; sober (color); refined
答えを渋る こたえをしぶる be reluctant to answer
.........0981

| 1234 | Refers to the **ASTRINGENT**, puckery taste of unripe persimmons. S8–11, converging on one point, suggest the contracting action of the tongue caused by a puckery flavor, and offer a visual shortcut to M2. This relates to M1 **NOT GO SMOOTHLY** via the idea of pulling tightly together—and *stopping* up (止)—as in a traffic jam (V2). See note at 塁 0885. |
| 水 85 | |
| 澁 | |
| 0471 | |
| 常 11 | |

**¹ TAKE IN**
**² ACT AS REGENT**

セツ
と(る)*

① 摂取する せっしゅする take (in), ingest, absorb
.........0059
¹ カロリーの摂取量 カロリーのせっしゅりょう
caloric intake.............0059, 0538
² 摂政 せっしょう regency; regent.............0246
² 摂関家 せっかんけ line of regents.....0451, 0219
摂氏 (=セ氏) せっし (=セし) Celsius, centigrade
.........0476

| 1235 | Related graphically and semantically to 取 0059, and (unofficially) sharing with it the reading とる. Refers to **TAKING IN** nutrition, so picture the *hand* (扌) **TAKING IN** the *ear* (耳) as food and S10–13 as the ear now dissolved in the stomach. Associate M2 **ACT AS REGENT** with **TAKING IN** someone else's responsibility. See note at 塁 0885. |
| 手 64 | |
| 攝 | |
| 0595 | |
| 常 13 | |

**¹ DO; act**
**² SAKE, benefit**

イ
ため* な(す)*

¹ 為政者 いせいしゃ statesman.........0246, 0107
① 行為 こうい act, deed, conduct.............0055
¹ 不正を為す ふせいをなす commit an injustice
.........0049, 0043
¹ 為替 かわせ money order, exchange.........1167
② ...の為に ...のために for the sake of...

| 1236 | Visualize as a galloping team of horses. In the horses' purposeful galloping, see an image of determined action done to attain an objective. The horses **DO** (M1), but they don't "just do it"; they **DO** with a specific interest in mind, a "**SAKE.**" |
| 火 86* | |
| 爲 | |
| 2994 | |
| 常 9 | |

**FALSIFY, deceive**

ギ
いつわ（る）にせ

○偽造 ぎぞう forgery, fabrication ............. 0699
偽証 ぎしょう perjury ......................... 0550
○偽る いつわる falsify, deceive
○偽物 にせもの sham, imitation, fake, forgery
................................................................ 0172

| | |
|---|---|
| **1237**<br>人 9<br>偽<br>0114<br>常 11 | Think of a *man* (亻) **deceiving** his *team of horses* (為) (e.g., "We're almost there, boys!").<br>☞ 擬 1352 |

¹ **PARTICIPATE**
² **VISIT A HOLY PLACE; go somewhere; refer to**

サン
まい（る）

①参加する さんかする participate, join ....... 1147
¹ 参戦 さんせん participation in a war ........ 0461
②参る まいる [humble] go/come; visit a holy place
² 遅参 ちさん lateness, tardiness ............. 1144
² 参考 さんこう reference, consultation ....... 0628

| | |
|---|---|
| **1238**<br>ム 28<br>参<br>1778<br>常 8 | In this kanji try to visualize the act of **VISITING A HOLY PLACE** (specifically, a Shinto shrine). Take 大 as a *large* shrine hall, and ム as the 千木 (ちぎ) crossbeams on the ridge of its roof. S6–8, evoking a sense of perspective in the way they get smaller as they go up, suggest the act of approaching the shrine from a distance. This image also serves us well for the secondary sense **go somewhere** (and likewise **refer to**, which is to "**go somewhere** for additional information"). It also suggests M1 **PARTICIPATE**, from the idea of participating in a shrine ceremony. |

¹ **MISERABLE, wretched**
² **CRUEL**

サン ザン
みじ（め）

①惨事 さんじ disaster, tragic incident, catastrophe
................................................................ 0080
¹ 惨状 さんじょう pitiful situation ............ 0616
¹ 惨敗 ざんぱい miserable defeat ............. 0830
①惨めな思いをする みじめなおもいをする feel
miserable ................................................ 0142
² 惨殺する ざんさつする murder cruelly,
slaughter ................................................ 0522

| | |
|---|---|
| **1239**<br>心 61<br>惨<br>0441<br>常 11 | Let S9–11 suggest repeated waves of pain penetrating ever deeper into one's *heart* (忄): **MISERABLE; CRUEL**. Now a note on differentiating some look-alike kanji: Note how the direction and number of sloping strokes differs between 冬 0360/終 0957/寒 0361/尽 0338 (two strokes, written downward from left to right), and 参 1238/惨 1239/修 1676 (three strokes, written downward from right to left). Two strokes are written downward from left to right, whereas three strokes are written downward from right to left. Practice writing these kanji, noting especially the differences between 冬 (based on three-stroke 夂) and 修 (based on four-stroke 攵). |

**PHONETIC [ro]**

ロ

○風呂 ふろ bath ................................. 0425
語呂 ごろ sound harmony ................. 0222

| | |
|---|---|
| **1240**<br>口 30<br><br>1872<br>常 7 | This character is used phonetically to represent the sound ロ (*ro*). See it as one katakana sign ロ (*ro*) stacked upon another, and remember it as the ロ of ふろ (bath, V1). Also used in V2 語呂 (ごろ), which juxtaposes two rhyming syllables as a way to signify the meaning of "sound harmony" or euphony. |

| | COMPANION | ○伴侶 はんりょ partner, companion...........0743 |
| | | 僧侶 そうりょ Buddhist monk.................1226 |
| | リョ | |

**1241**
人 9

The word "**COMPANION**" originally referred to the person with whom one would break bread (Latin: *panis*). This makes it a good keyword for a kanji that can refer not only to a partner (V1) but also to a Buddhist monk (V2). 呂 gives us a clear image of two similar forms standing side-by-side; with イ, this easily suggests a pair of **COMPANIONS**.

0083
常 9

| | ¹ROYAL PALACE | ¹王宮 おうきゅう king's palace, royal palace....0072 |
| | ²SHINTO SHRINE | ¹宮内庁 くないちょう Imperial Household Agency |
| | | .................................................0215, 0441 |
| | キュウ グウ ク | ²神宮 じんぐう Shinto shrine; Grand Shrine at Ise |
| | みや | .................................................0316 |
| | | ²宮参り みやまいり shrine visit .................1238 |
| | | 子宮 しきゅう uterus, womb .................0094 |

**1242**
宀 40

In the next two entries visualize 呂 as a large two-story structure. With a *roof* over it (宀), it represents a **ROYAL PALACE** or large **SHINTO SHRINE**. ☞ 官 0290

1964
常 10

| | ¹OPERATE, manage | ①営業する えいぎょうする do business, trade in |
| | ²BARRACKS, camp | .................................................0498 |
| | | ¹運営する うんえいする operate, manage....0584 |
| | エイ | ¹名古屋市営 なごやしえい operated by the city |
| | いとな(む) | of Nagoya.................0269, 0254, 0252, 0205 |
| | | ①営む いとなむ manage, operate |
| | | ²兵営 へいえい barracks .................0907 |

**1243**
小 42*

營

The next three entries follow 学 0099 and 覚 0325 as far as S5, but derive from traditional forms crowned by two fires 火 (contrast 營 with 學). For this "fire-crown" group, we'll visualize ⺍ as *glowing fire*, *shining lights*, or *brilliant flowers*. Here they are *shining lights*, indicating that this two-story establishment (呂) is open for business, i.e., now **OPERATING**. Connect this with M2 by thinking of a **BARRACKS** or camp as a place for conducting military **OPERATIONS**.

2257
常 12

| | FIREFLY | 蛍火 けいか (=ほたるび) light of a firefly .....0026 |
| | | 蛍雪 けいせつ diligent study.................0899 |
| | | 蛍光 けいこう fluorescent.................0137 |
| | ケイ | ○蛍光灯 けいこうとう fluorescent lamp/light |
| | ほたる | .................................................0137, 0440 |
| | | ○蛍の光 ほたるのひかり firefly glow; "Auld Lang |
| | | Syne".................0137 |

**1244**
虫 142

*Glowing fire* (⺍) + *insect* (虫): **FIREFLY**.

螢

2248
常 11

| | **¹ FLOURISH, thrive** **² GLORY** エイ さか(える) は(え) -ば(え) は(える) | ① 栄える さかえる flourish, thrive ① 栄養 えいよう nutrition, nourishment........0500 ² 栄光 えいこう glory...........................0137 ² 栄転 えいてん promotion....................0224 ² 見栄え みばえ appearance, show, display...0083 |
|---|---|---|

| **1245** 木 75 榮 2231 常 \| 9 | *Tree* (木) covered in *brilliant flowers* (ハ): **FLOURISH/thrive; GLORY.** |
|---|---|

| | **HONOR, glory** ヨ ほま(れ) | 栄誉 えいよ honor, glory, distinction........1245 ○ 名誉 めいよ honor, glory; dignity............0269 名誉教授 めいよきょうじゅ honorary professor, professor emeritus.............0269, 0632, 1123 ○ 国の誉れ くにのほまれ national glory........0075 |
|---|---|---|

| **1246** 言 149 譽 2193 常 \| 13 | The next two entries also use ハ to abbreviate their old crowns, but note how these differ from "fire-crown" above. In any case, stick with the image of *brilliant flowers*. Here *big* (大, from S4-6) *brilliant flowery words* confer **HONOR/glory.** Do not confuse 誉れ (ほまれ, glory) with 褒める (ほめる, praise, 0703). |
|---|---|

| | **¹ NOMINATE, cite** **² NOTEWORTHY ACT** **³ RAISE (one's hand)** キョ あ(げる) あ(がる) | ① 挙用する きょようする appoint..............0047 ① 例を挙げる れいをあげる cite an example...0721 ² 快挙 かいきょ brilliant achievement, heroic deed/feat...............................0331 ³ 挙手 きょしゅ raising/holding up one's hand; salute................................0046 ³ 手を挙げろ てをあげろ Stick 'em up!........0046 |
|---|---|---|

| **1247** 手 64 擧 2169 常 \| 10 | First visualize the *hand* (手) **RAISING** a *big* (S4-6) bundle of *brilliant flowers* for people to see. Then associate this image of **RAISING** an object up for public appreciation with M1 **NOMINATE.** This in turn relates to M3 **NOTEWORTHY ACT,** which may be cause for one's being **NOMINATED** for something. ☞ 拳 1248 |
|---|---|

| | **FIST** ケン ゲン° こぶし | 拳骨 げんこつ fist.............................0465 鉄拳 てっけん clenched fist..................0564 拳銃 けんじゅう pistol, handgun..............1057 ○ じゃん拳 じゃんけん rock-paper-scissors ○ 拳を固める こぶしをかためる close one's fist 0260 |
|---|---|---|

| **1248** 手 64 2316 常 \| 10 | Note carefully the differences between this and the previous entry. One difference is that this entry has an extra horizontal stroke. That gives us five tightly packed horizontal strokes, one for each knuckle in a tightly closed **FIST.** Use the greater density of horizontal strokes (as compared to 挙 above) as a visual cue. ☞ 拳 1247 |
|---|---|

# 桜

**CHERRY**

オウ
さくら

○桜花 おうか cherry blossoms ..................0121
○桜の木 さくらのき cherry tree ..................0028
　山桜 やまざくら wild cherry tree ..............0037
　桜井 さくらい Sakurai [surname] ..............0434

**1249**
木 75

櫻

0842
常 | 10

A shower of **CHERRY** blossoms (ソソ) falls over a *woman* (女)'s body from a **CHERRY** *tree* (木).

---

# 妥

**COME TO TERMS**

ダ

○妥協 だきょう compromise, agreement,
　understanding .....................................0543
　妥結 だけつ compromise, agreement,
　understanding .....................................0516
　妥当な だとうな proper, appropriate ........0141

**1250**
女 38

2128
常 | 7

Visualize a *claw* (⼨) stroking a *woman* (女)'s head, in a gesture of concession or compromise: **COME TO TERMS**. Note the difference between ⼨ here and ソソ in the previous entry.

---

# 咲

**BLOOM**

さ(く) -ざ(き)

○桜が咲いている さくらがさいている the cherries
　are in bloom .......................................1249
　咲き溢れる さきこぼれる blossom profusely 0415
　早咲き はやざき early blooming, early flowering
　..........................................................0143
　狂い咲く くるいざく bloom out of season ...0736

**1251**
口 30

0310
常 | 9

Earlier we saw 关 as a barricade (see 関 0451 and 送 0455). In the next two entries, however, visualize it as *blossoms* (S4–5) from *heaven* (天). Here let *mouth* (口) suggest blowing, and perceive blossoms being blown from heaven (i.e., falling from the sky) at **BLOOMING** time.

---

# 朕

**IMPERIAL WE**

チン

朕の ちんの Our

**1252**
月 74

0856
常 | 10

This character corresponds to the imperial first-person pronoun チン. Think of it as combining *blossoms from heaven* (关) with the idea of incarnation (from 月 *flesh*): "**WE** who incarnate heavenly blossoms ..."

| | **STEM, stalk** | ○球茎 きゅうけい bulb, corm .................... 1099 |
|---|---|---|
| | | 地下茎 ちかけい subterranean shoot, rootstock .......................................... 0187, 0040 |
| | ケイ | 長い茎の有るバラ ながいくきのあるバラ long-stemmed rose ........................ 0091, 0400 |
| | くき | 水茎 みずくき writing brush .................... 0027 |

| 1253 | Recall that 土 represents a cross-shaped *plant*. 又 depicts a *hand*, which here winds the plant into a straight fiber. Thus 圣, which replaces the old form 坙, signifies *straight*. With ⁺⁺ here, it refers to the *straight* part of a *plant*: the **STEM** or **stalk**. For this character and the ones that follow, use the straight vertical stroke of 土 as a visual shortcut to the meaning *straight*. |
|---|---|
| 艸 140 | |
| 莖 | |
| 1931 | |
| 常 8 | |

| | **¹ PATH** | ①径路 けいろ path; process .................... 0788 |
|---|---|---|
| | **² DIAMETER** | ¹ 小径 しょうけい (=こみち) path, lane .......... 0034 |
| | | ②直径 ちょっけい diameter .................... 0839 |
| | ケイ | ² 半径 はんけい radius .................... 0335 |
| | | ² 口径 こうけい caliber, bore; diameter ....... 0019 |

| 1254 | *Go* (彳) + *straight* (圣): **PATH; DIAMETER.** |
|---|---|
| 彳 60 | |
| 徑 | |
| 0260 | |
| 常 8 | |

| | **MYSTERIOUS** | 怪聞 かいぶん strange rumor, scandal ...... 0453 |
|---|---|---|
| | | ○怪物 かいぶつ monster; ghost, goblin; mysterious figure .................... 0172 |
| | カイ ケ* | 怪獣 かいじゅう monster; beast .................... 0763 |
| | あや(しい) あや(しむ) | ○怪しい あやしい doubtful; suspicious; strange; mysterious; uncanny |
| | | 怪我 けが injury, wound; accident .......... 0221 |

| 1255 | This character is **MYSTERIOUS** in that, unlike the other characters in this group based on 圣, its *on-yomi* is not ケイ and its meaning does not suggest any intuitive relationship with *straight*. The **MYSTERY** is solved if we consider that it is the only character in this group that did not derive from a simplification of 坙, the origin of said reading and meaning. This character is easily recognized in that only 忄 *heart/mind* among the radicals in this set is germane to the meaning **MYSTERIOUS**. Needless to say its **MYSTERIOUS**ness is a useful mnemonic for its abnormal reading. |
|---|---|
| 心 61 | |
| 恠 | |
| 0264 | |
| 常 8 | |

| | **LIGHT** | 軽量 けいりょう light weight .................... 0538 |
|---|---|---|
| | | ○軽食 けいしょく light meal, snack .................... 0288 |
| | | 軽視する けいしする make light of, despise; neglect .................... 0623 |
| | ケイ | ○軽い かるい light, slight |
| | かる(い) かろ(やか) | 軽やか かろやか light, airy |

| 1256 | A *car* (車) feels "heavy" when one must steer it back and forth. By contrast, a *car* moving *straight* (圣) feels **LIGHT**. |
|---|---|
| 車 159 | |
| 輕 | |
| 1372 | |
| 常 12 | |

| | | |
|---|---|---|
| **¹ PASS THROUGH, longitude**<br>**² MANAGE**<br>**³ SUTRA, scripture**<br><br>ケイ キョウ<br>へ(る) た(つ)* | ① 経験 けいけん experience .................. 1030<br>¹ 経緯 けいい longitude and latitude; particulars,<br>  course of events ................................ 0660<br>¹ 時間が経つ じかんがたつ Time goes by<br>  .......................................... 0383, 0448<br>¹ 十年を経て じゅうねんをへて after ten years<br>  .......................................... 0005, 0117<br>② 経営 けいえい management .............. 1243 | |

| 1257 |
|---|
| 糸 120 |
| 經 |
| 1218 |
| 常 11 |

Associate *straight* (圣) *thread* (糸) with a continuous line or "thread" **PASSING** down **THROUGH** space or time, such as a line of **longitude**, the long columns in which Buddhist **SUTRAS** were recorded, the long-term **MANAGEMENT** of an organization's affairs, or the act of **PASSING THROUGH** a location or one's own life experience. The most important compound for M2 appears in 1260 below. A simple example for M3 is お経 (おきょう, sutra). See Halpern for many more didactic examples. ☞ 緯 0660

| | | |
|---|---|---|
| **EQUAL, uniform**<br><br>セイ | 均斉 きんせい symmetry .................. 0394<br>○ 一斉に いっせいに all together, all at once,<br>  simultaneously................................ 0002 | |

| 1258 |
|---|
| 斉 210 |
| 齊 |
| 1768 |
| 常 8 |

Earlier we learned to see 文 as a person sitting behind a desk with crossed legs, which we can associate here with studying. S6–7 resemble an equals sign. This can be taken to suggest a **uniform** curriculum of study, but I suggest you simply use it as a visual cue for **EQUAL** (cf. 均 0394). Note the old forms for the next four entries. ☞ 斎 1259

| | | |
|---|---|---|
| **¹ OBSERVE RELIGIOUS ABSTINENCE**<br>**² STUDY (room)**<br><br>サイ | ① 斎戒 さいかい purification .................. 0469<br>¹ 斎日 さいじつ day of religious abstinence ... 0001<br>¹ 斎場 さいじょう funeral parlor .............. 0445<br>² 書斎 しょさい study, library.................. 0079 | |

| 1259 |
|---|
| 斉 210 |
| 齋 |
| 1817 |
| 常 11 |

Replaces the equals sign in the previous entry with an *altar* (示), thus suggesting the idea of "studying religiously": **OBSERVE RELIGIOUS ABSTINENCE; STUDY (room).** ☞ 斉 1258

| | | |
|---|---|---|
| **¹ SETTLE, pay back, come to an end**<br>**² RELIEVE, save**<br><br>サイ<br>す(む) -ず(み) -ずみ す(まない)<br>す(ます) -す(ます) す(ませる) | ① 返済する へんさいする repay; reimburse ... 0378<br>¹ 完済 かんさい full payment, liquidation .... 0633<br>① 済む すむ be settled, be concluded<br>² 救済する きゅうさいする relieve, save, deliver<br>  .......................................... 1098<br>○ 経済 けいざい economy, economics ........ 1257 | |

| 1260 |
|---|
| 水 85 |
| 濟 |
| 0478 |
| 常 11 |

"*Water* (氵) + *equal* (斉)" suggests the level surface of still, **SETTLED** water. Associate the actions of **paying** someone **back** or **SETTLING** an account with the idea of "leveling the waters." Next, associate M1 **SETTLE** with M2 **RELIEVE/save**, via the idea of resolving an unsettled situation.

| | PREPARATION, medicine | ○薬剤 やくざい medicine, drugs ..............0303 |
| --- | --- | --- |
| | | 調剤する ちょうざいする prepare medicines 0306 |
| | | 調合剤 ちょうごうざい preparation, mixture |
| | | ..............................................0306, 0227 |
| | ザイ | ○洗剤 せんざい detergent, cleanser ..........0135 |
| | | 殺虫剤 さっちゅうざい insecticide ......0522, 0343 |

| 1261 | Equal (斉) doses *sliced* (刂) by the pharmacist's razor: **PREPARATION/medicine**. ☞ 剤 1262 |
| --- | --- |
| 刀 18 | |
| 劑 | |
| 1491 | |
| 常 10 | |

| | DISSECT | ○解剖する かいぼうする dissect, anatomize, |
| --- | --- | --- |
| | | conduct an autopsy; analyze................0345 |
| | | 解剖学 かいぼうがく anatomy..........0345, 0099 |
| | ボウ | 生体解剖 せいたいかいぼう vivisection |
| | | ..............................................0036, 0062, 0345 |

| 1262 | Recall *very short person* from 部 0068 and 倍 0069, standing on top of a box to make him-self taller. Here picture *slicing* (刂) him apart from the box: **DISSECT**. ☞ 剤 1261 |
| --- | --- |
| 刀 18 | |
| 1492 | |
| 常 10 | |

| | ATTEND UPON A SUPERIOR | ○陪食 ばいしょく dining with a superior ......0288 |
| --- | --- | --- |
| | | 陪席 ばいせき sitting with one's superior...0279 |
| | | 陪侍 ばいじ attending on the nobility; retainer |
| | バイ | ..............................................0388 |

| 1263 | Appears much less often than 部 0068, so our goal is to be able to recognize when *very short person* appears in the unaccustomed position in relation to 阝. Let this special situation suggest that the *very short person* is showing special deference to 阝 in letting it go first, as if he were **ATTENDING UPON A SUPERIOR**. The most important compound using this character appears at 審 1510. ☞ 部 0068 |
| --- | --- |
| 阜 170 | |
| 0492 | |
| 常 11 | |

| | CULTIVATE | ○培養する ばいようする cultivate, culture, |
| --- | --- | --- |
| | | incubate ....................................0500 |
| | | ○培う つちかう raise; cultivate |
| | バイ | 愛国心を培う あいこくしんをつちかう foster a |
| | つちか(う) | patriotic spirit ....................0778, 0075, 0056 |

| 1264 | The *very short person*, being close to the *ground* (土), specializes in **CULTIVATION**. The reading つちかう (cultivate) in V2 is easily remembered by thinking of it as "raising the soil": つち (soil) + かう (raise animals, see 飼 0823). Note that kanji in which 咅 appears at the right (i.e., in the phonetic position) are pronounced バイ. |
| --- | --- |
| 土 32 | |
| 0420 | |
| 常 11 | |

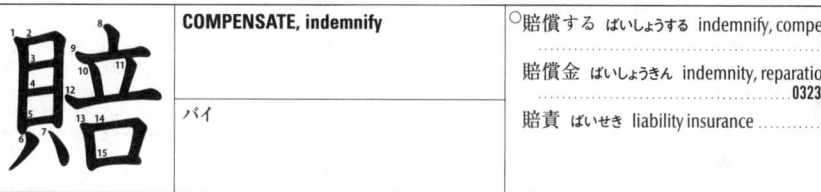

| 賠 | COMPENSATE, indemnify | ○賠償する　ばいしょうする　indemnify, compensate ......................................................0323 |
| | | 賠償金　ばいしょうきん　indemnity, reparation .............................................0323, 0029 |
| | バイ | 賠責　ばいせき　liability insurance ...........0831 |

| **1265** | Here we offer *money*(貝) to the *very short person* to **COMPENSATE/indemnify** him for his always having to stand on top of a box. |
| 貝 154 | |
| 1431 | |
| 常 15 | |

| 貼 | STICK ON, paste | 貼付する　ちょうふする (=てんぷする)　stick(on), paste, append .........................................0064 |
| | | ○貼る　はる　stick(on), paste |
| | チョウ　テン* | 貼り合わせる　はりあわせる　paste together 0227 |
| | は(る)　-ば(り) | 貼り付ける　はりつける　stick(on), paste, append .........................................................0064 |
| | | 貼り紙　はりがみ　sticker, label, poster........0478 |

| **1266** | Review 占 0348. Convinced that like attracts like, the *fortune-teller* attempts to draw more *money*(貝) his way by **pasting** a seashell to the wall of the building behind his booth. |
| 貝 154 | |
| 1369 | |
| 常 12 | |

| 粘 | STICKY | 粘土　ねんど　clay ..................................0280 |
| | | 粘液　ねんえき　mucus ...........................0470 |
| | | 粘着剤　ねんちゃくざい　glue, adhesive 0940, 1261 |
| | ネン | ○粘る　ねばる　be sticky; persevere |
| | ねば(る) | 粘り強い　ねばりづよい　tenacious, stick-to-itive; persistent .................................................0423 |

| **1267** | To keep a firm grip on your hand, the *fortune-teller*(占) applies **STICKY** *rice*(米) to it. Stare at 粘 a moment and imagine the **STICKINESS**. To avoid confusing with the previous entry, remember that while here the *rice* itself is **STICKY**, in 貼 the seashell is just STUCK ON. |
| 米 119 | |
| 黏 | |
| 1212 | |
| 常 11 | |

| 衡 | BALANCE, weigh | ○均衡　きんこう　balance, equilibrium...........0394 |
| | | 平衡　へいこう　equilibrium, balance .........0334 |
| | | 度量衡　どりょうこう　weights and measures ..........................................................0280, 0538 |
| | コウ | |

| **1268** | Interpret the center of this character as a *big-tailed fish*(魚 *fish* + 大 *big*). Here he is being **weighed** on an old-fashioned scale. The **weight** is determined when the left and right sides (行) are in **BALANCE**. ☞ 衝 1567 |
| 行 144 | |
| 0687 | |
| 常 16 | |

**EXCHANGE; replace**

カン
か(える) -か(える) か(わる)

換気 かんき ventilation.........................0126
変換 へんかん change, conversion, transformation
..................................................0775
○交換する こうかんする exchange, interchange,
barter, substitute...........................0102
ドルを円に換える ドルをえんにかえる convert dollars
into yen.....................................0013
○乗り換える のりかえる change (trains), transfer...1005

| 1269 | Take 奐 as a variant of *big-tailed fish*, introduced in the previous entry. Here picture the *hand* |
|---|---|
| 手 64 | EXCHANGING one *big-tailed fish* for another. |
| 0537 | |
| 常 12 | |

**CALL (out)**

カン

召喚する しょうかんする summon, cite,
subpoena.....................................1103
喚問 かんもん summons.....................0452
○喚声 かんせい shout, yell, scream, clamor...0529

| 1270 | Anyone who has seen the carp that swim in Japanese gardens has been impressed by the size |
|---|---|
| 口 30 | of their mouths, and the manner in which they use them to demand food. Here imagine a |
| | *big-tailed carp* (奐) opening its *mouth* (口) to CALL (out) for food. |
| 0503 | |
| 常 12 | |

¹ **BREAK OFF, cut off**
² **COME TO AN END**
³ **WITHOUT MATCH**

ゼツ
た(える) た(やす) た(つ)

¹ 絶縁 ぜつえん breaking off relations; insulation,
isolation......................................0610
① 連絡を絶つ れんらくをたつ sever the connection
..........................................0582, 0790
② 通信は絶えた つうしんはたえた correspondence has
ceased..................................0159, 0063
² 絶滅 ぜつめつ extermination; extinction...1149
③ 絶対 ぜったい absoluteness; absolute; absolutely
..................................................0650

| 1271 | Recall 色 0528 COLOR/EROS. Let us assume that coloring *thread* (糸) weakens it, making it |
|---|---|
| 糸 120 | more likely to BREAK OFF. M1 BREAK OFF clearly relates to M2 COME TO AN END, which in |
| | turn relates to M3 WITHOUT MATCH, via the idea of something reaching its acme. |
| 1240 | |
| 常 12 | |

**EXEMPTION, license, escape**

メン
まぬか(れる) まぬが(れる)

免税 めんぜい tax exemption................1195
○御免 ごめん (your) pardon; decline; refusal;
permission...................................0862
免状 めんじょう license, diploma.............0616
免職 めんしょく dismissal, release............1087
○免れる まぬかれる (=まぬがれる) be exempted
from; escape

| 1272 | 免 may have derived the meaning **escape** from the swiftness of the RABBIT 免/兔 (unlisted), |
|---|---|
| ル 10 | in which we can discern the rabbit's long ears, large eyes, and long legs, with a separate |
| 兔 | stroke added for a carrot. The present entry lacks the carrot, but will still mean *escaping* |
| | *rabbit* as a grapheme. The mnemonic keyword for 免 as a stand-alone kanji is "**EXEMPTION.**" |
| 1779 | ☞ 色 0528 |
| 常 8 | |

**LET SLIP, deviate from the norm**

イツ

逸球 いっきゅう muffed ball, missed ball .... 1099
逸機する いっきする miss a chance, lose an
  opportunity...................................0473
○逸脱 いつだつ deviation, departure from the
  norm ...........................................1198
放逸 ほういつ self-indulgence, looseness....0574
逸品 いっぴん superb article..................0301

| 1273 | |
|---|---|
| 辵 162 | Here we observe *escaping rabbit* (免) slipping off the back of a *truck* (辶), signifying **LET SLIP**. See the next entry for further explanation. ☞ 勉 1274 |
| 逸 | |
| 2688 | |
| 常 11 | |

**ENDEAVOR**

ベン

○勉強 べんきょう study, hard work; selling cheap
  ...................................................0423
勉強家 べんきょうか hard worker.......0423, 0219
勉強不足 べんきょうぶそく insufficient study/
  diligence.........................0423, 0049, 0044
勉学 べんがく study...........................0099

| 1274 | |
|---|---|
| 力 19 | Learn to recognize this kanji by how it differs from the last one. In the previous entry, there is nothing to pin down the *escaping rabbit* (免), so he slips off the back of the truck. Here a strong *force* (力) pins him down, preventing his escape and "forcing" him to **ENDEAVOR**. Train your eye to notice whether *escaping rabbit* is pinned down or not. ☞ 逸 1273 |
| 勉 | |
| 2829 | |
| 常 10 | |

**EVENING**

バン

毎晩 まいばん every evening/night .........0105
○晩ご飯 ばんごはん supper ..................0377
一晩中 ひとばんじゅう all night long ...0002, 0035
晩年 ばんねん late in life .....................0117
晩に ばんに in the evening

| 1275 | |
|---|---|
| 日 72 | The *sun* (日) *escapes* (免): **EVENING**. |
| 晩 | |
| 0891 | |
| 常 12 | |

**PERMIT, authorize**

キョ
ゆる(す)

○許可 きょか permission, approval, authorization
  ...................................................0814
許容する きょようする tolerate, allow, permit 1037
免許 めんきょ license, permit .................1272
特許 とっきょ patent; concession ...........0385
○許す ゆるす permit, authorize; forgive, pardon

| 1276 | |
|---|---|
| 言 149 | Review 午 0115. Employers **PERMIT**/**authorize** their workers to *speak* (言) at the *Hour of the Horse* (午)—the *noontime* break. ☞ 詐 1794 |
| | |
| 1337 | |
| 常 11 | |

**¹PHENOMENON, outward manifestation; image**

**²ELEPHANT**

ショウ ゾウ

¹気象 きしょう atmospheric phenomena, weather conditions ........................................0126

①現象 げんしょう phenomenon .................0706

¹対象 たいしょう object (of study), subject, target ........................................0650

¹印象 いんしょう impression ....................0231

②アフリカ象 アフリカぞう African elephant

| 1277 | Resembles an **ELEPHANT**, complete with a trunk (S1–2), two large ears (S3–6), and a fly-consuming bird (S11) perched on its back. Being such a plainly visible image, this is also an apt representation of M1 **PHENOMENON/outward manifestation; image.** ☞ 像 1278 |
| 豕 152 | |
| 1831 | |
| 常 12 | |

**IMAGE, likeness**

ゾウ

映像 えいぞう (TV) picture, image; reflection ........................................0329

画像 がぞう portrait, likeness ..............0176

○想像する そうぞうする imagine ............0683

○仏像 ぶつぞう image of Buddha; Buddhist statue ........................................0811

自画像 じがぞう self-portrait ..........0081, 0176

| 1278 | Here see the *man* (亻) sculpting an **IMAGE** in the likeness of the *elephant* (象). Imagine the elephant posing in the last entry and the human sculptor here copying its **IMAGE** in a statue (see V1 in the next entry). The previous entry represents the PHENOMENON itself; this entry is a **likeness** made in its **IMAGE.** ☞ 象 1277 |
| 人 9 | |
| 0144 | |
| 常 14 | |

**CARVE, engrave**

チョウ
ほ(る) -ぼ(り)

○彫像 ちょうぞう carved statue .................1278

彫金 ちょうきん metal carving, chasing ......0029

○彫る ほる carve, engrave

木彫り きぼり woodcarving ..................0028

浮き彫り うきぼり (high) relief ..............0613

| 1279 | At 形 0147 we learned to visualize 彡 as a chiseling action. Now review 周 0304, which brings to this entry the sense of *periphery/around*. We thus obtain an image of going around the periphery of an object chiseling (彡) it: **CARVE/engrave.** ☞ 形 0147 |
| 彡 59 | |
| 1503 | |
| 常 11 | |

**SCENE, outlook**

ケイ

○背景 はいけい background; backing; (stage) scenery, setting, scene ...........0124

風景 ふうけい scenery, landscape, view ......0425

夜景 やけい night view/scene ..............0467

○景気 けいき things, times; business conditions ........................................0126

景色 けしき scenery, landscape ..........0528

| 1280 | Picture this as a panoramic vista of the *capital* (京) with the *sun* (日) in the background shining down on it: **SCENE/outlook.** |
| 日 72 | |
| 2179 | |
| 常 12 | |

**SHADOW, image, silhouette**

エイ
かげ

- ○影像 えいぞう image; shadow, phantom....**1278**
- 人影 じんえい (＝ひとかげ) human figure; shadow of a person................................**0015**
- 投影 とうえい cast shadow; projection......**0517**
- 影を映す かげをうつす mirror the image (of) ................................**0329**
- ○面影 おもかげ face; vestige, traces..........**0175**

| 1281 | Here 彡 can be visualized as rays of light projecting a *scene*(景) onto a movie screen: SHADOW/silhouette/image. |
| 彡 59 | |
| 1671 | |
| 常 15 | |

**PHOTOGRAPH**

サツ
と(る) -ど(り)

- ○撮影 さつえい photographing, shooting (of a film) ................................**1281**
- 特撮 とくさつ special effects.................**0385**
- ○写真を撮る しゃしんをとる take a picture ................................**0859, 0838**

| 1282 | Ignore 最 0196 MOST and instead derive the meaning from the constituent graphemes, 取 representing *take* and 日 (*sun*) representing light. The entire character thus represents the act of using one's *hand*(扌) to "take" some light: **PHOTOGRAPH**. |
| 手 64 | |
| 0671 | |
| 常 15 | |

**SET ABOUT, enter upon**

シュウ ジュ
つ(く) つ(ける)

- ○就職 しゅうしょく finding employment.......**1087**
- 就任 しゅうにん assumption of office........**0372**
- 就学する しゅうがくする enter school........**0099**
- ○職に就く しょくにつく take up employment..**1087**
- 役に就ける やくにつける place (someone) in a position................................**0518**

| 1283 | 尤 recalls 沈 0655 SINK. Here let the sinking trajectory of S10 suggest *settle*. We can thus visualize a person's arriving in the *capital*(京) to *settle* into a new job: **SET ABOUT/enter upon**. |
| 尤 43 | |
| 1512 | |
| 常 12 | |

**COOL**

リョウ
すず(しい) すず(む)

- 涼気 りょうき cool air............................**0126**
- 涼風 りょうふう (＝すずかぜ) cool breeze......**0425**
- ○清涼な せいりょうな cool, refreshing.........**0974**
- ○涼しい すずしい cool, refreshing
- 涼む すずむ cool oneself

| 1284 | See drops of *water*(氵) being sprinkled on the *capital*(京) to keep it **COOL**. |
| 水 85 | |
| 涼 | |
| 0477 | |
| 常 11 | |

| | WHALE | ○鯨肉 げいにく whale meat...............0216 |
| | | 鯨油 げいゆ whale oil ....................0433 |
| | | 鯨飲する げいいんする drink heavily......0289 |
| | ゲイ | 鯨類 げいるい cetaceans ...................0310 |
| | くじら | 鯨座 くじらざ the Whale, Cetus...........0749 |

| **1285** | A *capital* (京) *fish* (魚): **WHALE**. |
| 魚 195 | |
| | |
| **1661** | |
| 常 19 | |

| | SEPARATE | 隔絶する かくぜつする be separated, be isolated |
| | | ...............................................1271 |
| | | ○遠隔の えんかくの distant, remote, far......0857 |
| | | 隔週に かくしゅうに every other week.........0305 |
| | カク | ○隔てる へだてる separate; partition |
| | へだ(てる)　へだ(たる) | 隔たる へだたる be apart, be distant |

| **1286** | Iodine is most commonly found in solution. See S4–7 as "Io," representing an iodine crystal. |
| 阜 170 | Here it is dropped into a tripod cauldron (S8–13), in which the iodine atoms are **SEPARATED** |
| | (in the polar directions indicated by S10 and S11). See next entry for further explanation. The |
| | reading へだたる suggests "to **SEPARATE** as far apart as <u>head</u> and <u>tail</u>." ☞ 融 1287 |
| **0615** | |
| 常 13 | |

| | ¹ FUSE | ¹ 溶融 ようゆう melting, fusion.................1038 |
| | ² FINANCE | ①融合 ゆうごう fusion............................0227 |
| | | ②金融 きんゆう finance, circulation of money...0029 |
| | ユウ | ² 融資 ゆうし financing, advance of funds, loan |
| | | ...............................................1165 |
| | | ² 融通 ゆうずう financing, accommodation; |
| | | flexibility........................................0159 |

| **1287** | (Continuing from the previous entry) These two kanji are more or less opposite in meaning. |
| 虫 142 | In 隔, 阝 points down: the iodine crystal drops into the cauldron and its atoms are SEPA- |
| | RATED. In 融, 虫 points up: the iodine atoms rise out of the solution and **FUSE** back |
| | together. M1 **FUSE** relates to M2 **FINANCE** via the idea of "making ends meet." ☞ 隔 1286 |
| **1626** | |
| 常 16 | |

| | LIKENESS | ○肖像 しょうぞう portrait, likeness ...........1278 |
| | | 肖像画 しょうぞうが portrait...........1278, 0176 |
| | | 不肖 ふしょう not like one's father; unworthy; |
| | ショウ | [humble] I, myself............................0049 |

| **1288** | Here try to visualize the act of chiseling a hard material into a **LIKENESS**. S1–3 can be seen as |
| 肉 130 | strokes of the chisel coming down on the sculpture, or, alternatively, fragments or sparks fly- |
| | ing up from it (compare this with 当 0141, 形 0147, and 彫 1279). As a component grapheme, |
| | 肖 will most often represent *sparks* or *fragments*. ☞ 尚 0184 |
| **1887** | |
| 常 7 | |

|  | **¹ EXTINGUISH, disappear**<br>**² SPEND, consume**<br><br>ショウ<br>き(える) け(す) | ①消防 しょうぼう firefighting ................. 0174<br>¹ 消滅 しょうめつ extinction, disappearance ... 1149<br>①消える きえる be extinguished, vanish<br>¹ 消す けす extinguish; turn off<br>² 消費する しょうひする consume, spend ..... 1189 |
|---|---|---|

| **1289**<br>水 85<br><br>0402<br>常 10 | (Continuing from the previous entry) Here we see *water* (氵) being poured on the hot *sparks* (肖) to **EXTINGUISH** them. M2 **SPEND** is an extended meaning. Note that all characters in which 肖 appears at the right or center are pronounced ショウ. |
|---|---|

|  | **NITER**<br><br>ショウ | 硝石 しょうせき saltpeter ................. 0403<br>硝酸 しょうさん nitric acid ................. 0800<br>○硝薬 しょうやく gunpowder ................. 0303<br>硝煙 しょうえん gunpowder smoke ......... 0768<br>硝子 がらす glass ................. 0094 |
|---|---|---|

| **1290**<br>石 112<br><br>1097<br>常 12 | An important component of gunpowder is **NITER** (potassium nitrate), here represented as a *stone* (石) that produces *sparks* (肖). ☞ 硫 1060 |
|---|---|

|  | **TIP OF A TWIG**<br><br>ショウ<br>こずえ | 松の梢 まつのこずえ top of a pine tree ...... 0242<br>梢を払う こずえをはらう top a tree ........... 0812<br>末梢 まっしょう tip, end; tip of a twig ........ 0272 |
|---|---|---|

| **1291**<br>木 75<br><br>0874<br>名 11 | Now see the three strokes at the top of 肖 as the very **TIPS OF THE TWIGS** at the end of the branches of a *tree* (木), flaring out in every direction like flying *sparks* (肖). |
|---|---|

| 削 | **CUT BY CHIPPING**<br><br>サク<br>けず(る) | ○削除 さくじょ deletion, elimination, cancellation<br>................. 0996<br>研削 けんさく grinding ................. 0724<br>開削 かいさく excavation, cutting, digging ... 0450<br>削減 さくげん curtailment, reduction ....... 1148<br>○削る けずる whittle, shave, cut by chipping |
|---|---|---|

| **1292**<br>刀 18<br><br>1316<br>常 9 | Here a *knife* (刂) **CHIPS** away at hard material, sending *fragments* (肖) flying. Of this set of six characters based on 肖 (including the next entry), this is the only one in which 肖 appears at the left side, rather than at the right or center. That's our hint that this is the one pronounced サク, rather than ショウ. |
|---|---|

| | EARLY EVENING | 春宵 しゅんしょう spring evening ............0362 |
|---|---|---|
| | | ○宵の口 よいのくち early evening............0019 |
| | | 宵の明星 よいのみょうじょう evening star, Venus |
| | ショウ | ..........................................0024, 0755 |
| | よい | 今宵 こよい this evening, tonight ..........0228 |

| 1293<br>宀 40 | Visualize an old-fashioned television set with a rabbit-ears antenna (肖), under the *roof* of a house (宀). The image represents the time of day when people have returned home and are sitting down to watch TV: prime time (**EVENING**). ☞ 屑 1891, 尚 0184 |
|---|---|
| 1967<br>常 10 | |

| | BANQUET | ○宴会 えんかい dinner party, banquet, feast 0226 |
|---|---|---|
| | | 賀宴 がえん banquet......................1172 |
| | | 宴席 えんせき banquet hall, dinner party...0279 |
| | エン | 招宴 しょうえん invitation to a party; party...1104 |
| | うたげ* | 歓迎宴 かんげいえん welcome party ..1131, 1139 |

| 1294<br>宀 40 | The point has already been made that recognizing the anachronistic gender associations inherent in kanji such as this one is not tantamount to endorsing them. This kanji shows a *woman* (女) under a *roof* (宀) all *day* (日) preparing a **BANQUET**. Do not confuse with the name-use kanji 晏 PEACEFUL SUNSET. |
|---|---|
| 1961<br>常 10 | |

| | HOMETOWN | 郷里 きょうり one's old home, native place...0531 |
|---|---|---|
| | | 郷土 きょうど one's birthplace ............0030 |
| | | ○故郷 こきょう (=ふるさと) hometown, birthplace |
| | キョウ ゴウ | ..........................................0257 |
| | さと* | 愛郷心 あいきょうしん love for one's hometown |
| | | ..........................................0778, 0056 |
| | | 望郷の念 ぼうきょうのねん homesickness |
| | | ..........................................1066, 0230 |

| 1295<br>邑 163 | S1–3 is a version of 幺 *child* (see 糸 0112). S4–8 is the abbreviated version of 艮 that we use when something appears to the right of it. Given the presence of 幺 *child*, 艮 here suggests *little boy* (see 限 0282). Observe the two little ones exploring all the way to the *wall* (阝) that surrounds their **HOMETOWN**. |
|---|---|
| 郷<br>0501<br>常 11 | |

| | BANQUET | ○饗宴 きょうえん banquet.....................1294 |
|---|---|---|
| | | 饗応 きょうおう treat, feast, banquet .........0850 |
| | キョウ | 饗する きょうする treat, provide dinner for |

| 1296<br>食 184 | The meals one takes in one's hometown tend to be holiday feasts. Thus "*eat* (食) + *hometown* (郷)" clearly suggests **BANQUET**. The top of this kanji has not been officially standardized in its form with 郷, but you will also see it in standardized form (as in the reference box at left), and can certainly write it that way. ☞ 響 1297 |
|---|---|
| 饗<br>2522<br>名 22 | |

| | **REVERBERATE** | 音響 おんきょう sound, acoustics ............0150 |
|---|---|---|
| | | 反響 はんきょう echo, reverberation; response, repercussions....................0374 |
| | | ○影響 えいきょう influence, effect............1281 |
| 響 | キョウ | 交響曲 こうきょうきょく symphony......0102, 0503 |
| | ひび(く) | ○響く ひびく reverberate |

| **1297** | The fact that the *hometown* (郷) is surrounded by *town walls* (阝) means that *sounds* (音) |
|---|---|
| 音 180 | within the town tend to **REVERBERATE**. Note that both kanji incorporating 郷 follow its |
| 響 | principal *on* reading, キョウ. ☞ 饗 1296 |
| 2504 | |
| 常 20 | |

| | **CASTLE, fort** | ○城下町 じょうかまち castle town........0040, 0439 |
|---|---|---|
| | | 落城 らくじょう fall of a castle ...............0793 |
| 城 | | 大阪城 おおさかじょう Osaka Castle....0033, 0376 |
| | ジョウ | 万里の長城 ばんりのちょうじょう The Great Wall (of China).....................0018, 0531, 0091 |
| | しろ | 城本 しろもと Shiromoto [surname].........0031 |

| **1298** | Review 成 0070 BECOME/ACHIEVE (wholeness). For the present entry, first note that Japa- |
|---|---|
| 土 32 | nese castles consist mainly of long, defensive earthworks. Then imagine the process of build- |
| | ing these great earthen ramparts and think of *earth* (土) *becoming* (成) a **CASTLE**. ☞ 域 1154 |
| 0312 | |
| 常 9 | |

| | **SINCERITY, truth** | 誠実 せいじつ sincerity, honesty, faith......0499 |
|---|---|---|
| | | ○誠意 せいい sincerity, good faith............0151 |
| 誠 | | 忠誠 ちゅうせい faithfulness, fidelity.........0644 |
| | セイ | ○誠に まことに truly, really; very, extremely |
| | まこと | |

| **1299** | When one speaks with **SINCERITY**, *words* (言) *become* (成) reality. ☞ 試 1028 |
|---|---|
| 言 149 | |
| 1382 | |
| 常 13 | |

| | **PROSPER; heap up** | ○盛大な せいだいな prosperous; grand, magnificent..........................0033 |
|---|---|---|
| | | 全盛 ぜんせい prime, zenith.................0078 |
| 盛 | | ○盛る もる heap up; fill (a bowl/tray) |
| | セイ ジョウ | ○　　さかる prosper, thrive |
| | も(る) さか(る) さか(ん) | 盛んな商売 さかんなしょうばい thriving business ...................................0351, 0353 |

| **1300** | A *plate* (皿) *achieves wholeness* (成) or **PROSPERITY** when food is **heaped up** on it. See 成 |
|---|---|
| 皿 108 | as literally **heaped up** on the plate, symbolizing **PROSPERITY**. |
| 2332 | |
| 常 11 | |

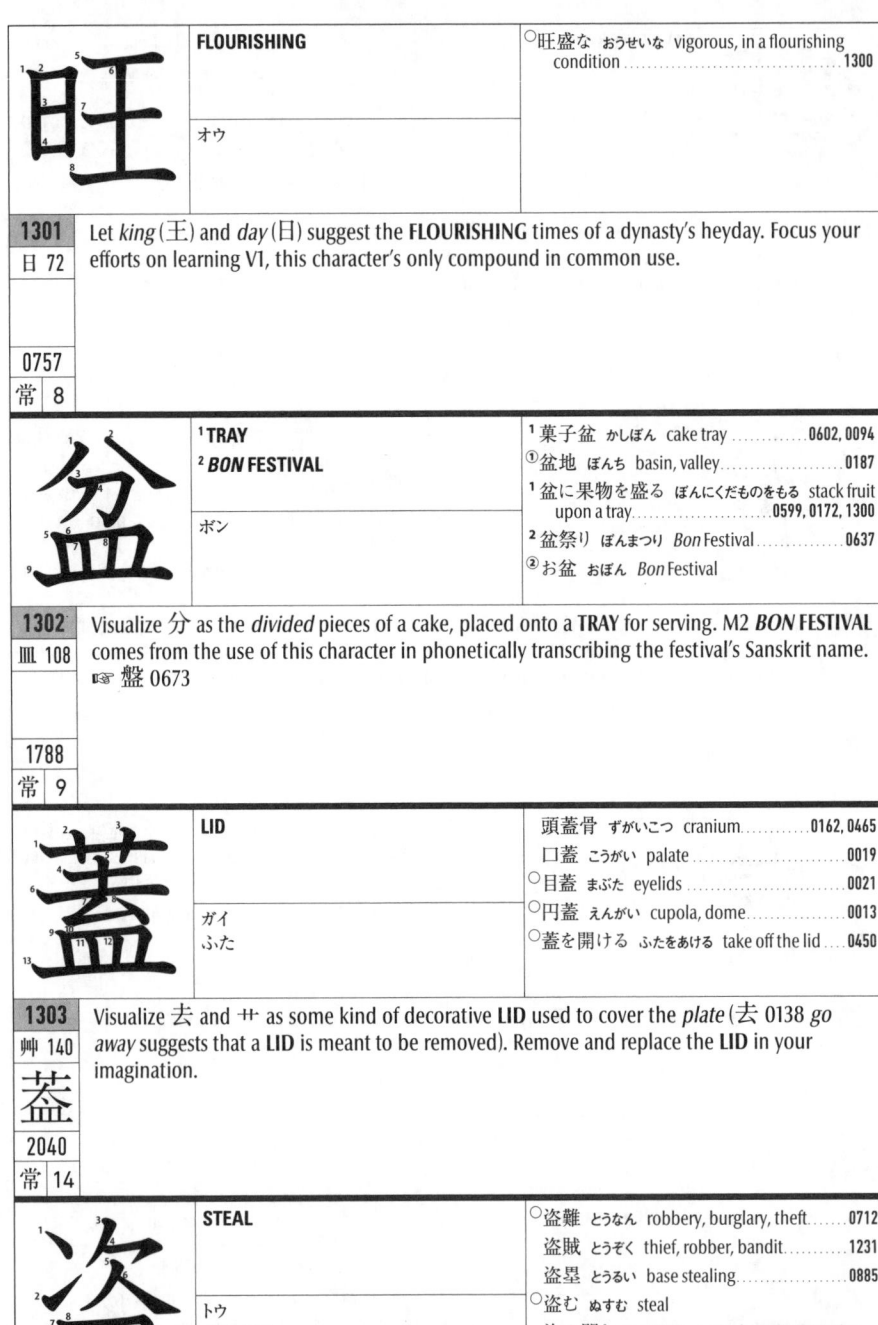

## 旺 FLOURISHING

オウ

○旺盛な　おうせいな　vigorous, in a flourishing condition .................................................. 1300

**1301**
日 72

0757
常 8

Let *king* (王) and *day* (日) suggest the **FLOURISHING** times of a dynasty's heyday. Focus your efforts on learning V1, this character's only compound in common use.

---

## 盆 ¹ TRAY ² *BON* FESTIVAL

ボン

¹ 菓子盆　かしぼん　cake tray ............. 0602, 0094
① 盆地　ぼんち　basin, valley..................... 0187
¹ 盆に果物を盛る　ぼんにくだものをもる　stack fruit upon a tray...................... 0599, 0172, 1300
² 盆祭り　ぼんまつり　*Bon* Festival ............... 0637
② お盆　おぼん　*Bon* Festival

**1302**
皿 108

1788
常 9

Visualize 分 as the *divided* pieces of a cake, placed onto a **TRAY** for serving. M2 *BON* **FESTIVAL** comes from the use of this character in phonetically transcribing the festival's Sanskrit name. ☞ 盤 0673

---

## 蓋 LID

ガイ
ふた

頭蓋骨　ずがいこつ　cranium............. 0162, 0465
口蓋　こうがい　palate ......................... 0019
○目蓋　まぶた　eyelids .......................... 0021
○円蓋　えんがい　cupola, dome................. 0013
○蓋を開ける　ふたをあける　take off the lid .... 0450

**1303**
艸 140

蓋

2040
常 14

Visualize 去 and ⺾ as some kind of decorative **LID** used to cover the *plate* (去 0138 *go away* suggests that a **LID** is meant to be removed). Remove and replace the **LID** in your imagination.

---

## 盗 STEAL

トウ
ぬす(む)

○盗難　とうなん　robbery, burglary, theft........ 0712
盗賊　とうぞく　thief, robber, bandit............ 1231
盗塁　とうるい　base stealing................... 0885
○盗む　ぬすむ　steal
盗み聞き　ぬすみぎき　eavesdropping, tapping .................................................. 0453

**1304**
皿 108

盗

2327
常 11

The Ten Commandments forbid you to **STEAL**, or to "covet anything that is your neighbor's." With these words in mind, let "*next* (次) + *plate* (皿)" suggest the (next door) neighbor's precious china, and associate this with the idea of **STEALING**. ☞ 羨 2040

**ALLIANCE, pact**

メイ

盟約 めいやく pledge, pact, alliance, league .......... 0170

盟友 めいゆう sworn friend .................. 0399

○同盟 どうめい alliance, league, union ....... 0182

連盟 れんめい union, federation, league ... 0582

加盟 かめい participation, affiliation ...... 1147

| 1305 | |
|---|---|
| Ⅲ 108 | Imagine the *sun* (日) and *moon* (月) signing an **ALLIANCE** in rays of light, etched upon a ceremonial *plate* (Ⅲ) as a permanent record of their mutual *pact*. ☞ 温 0199 |
| 2434 | |
| 常 13 | |

---

**SALT**

エン
しお

○塩分 えんぶん salt, salinity ................. 0088

食塩 しょくえん table salt ................. 0288

塩酸 えんさん hydrochloric acid ........... 0800

塩素 えんそ chlorine ................. 0132

塩味 しおあじ salty taste, seasoning ........ 0273

| 1306 | |
|---|---|
| 土 32* | Here visualize ⺈ as a sharp tool used to scrape **SALT** from a block of *earth* (土) and onto a *plate* (Ⅲ). Then imagine putting your *mouth* (口) to the plate, and the **SALTY** flavor you would taste. |
| 鹽 | |
| 0578 | |
| 常 13 | |

---

**WOUND, scar**

ショウ
きず いた(む) いた(める)

○負傷する ふしょうする be injured/wounded, get hurt ................. 0829

傷害 しょうがい injury, bodily harm .......... 0413

中傷 ちゅうしょう slander, libel ............... 0035

花を傷める はなをいためる spoil a flower ... 0121

○傷んだトマト いたんだトマト rotten tomato

| 1307 | |
|---|---|
| 人 9 | Now let us add wound to our salt, if you will. We start with イ, an uninjured *man* standing upright. But then he is shown laid out flat (⺈), experiencing some *difficulty* (昜) (review 昜 0443 if necessary). He has been **WOUNDED**. |
| 0137 | |
| 常 13 | |

---

揚

¹ **RAISE HIGH, exalt**
² **FRY**

ヨウ
あ(げる) -あ(げ) あ(がる)

¹ 揚力 ようりょく lift, lifting power ............. 0084

¹ 意気揚々と いきようようと exultantly, in exalted spirits, proudly ...................... 0151, 0126

①抑揚 よくよう rising and falling (of tones), intonation ......................... 1137

○揚げる あげる raise, hoist; fry in deep fat

² 揚げ物 あげもの fried food ................. 0172

| 1308 | |
|---|---|
| 手 64 | *Hand* (扌) + *difficult* (昜): think of the difficulty of **RAISING** something up **HIGH** with your hand, against the force of gravity. This character for **RAISING HIGH** also applies to the act of **FRYING** food in deep fat, since food generally first sinks in the fat then rises when it's cooked. ☞ 揭 2272 |
| 0542 | |
| 常 12 | |

| | FLUENT | ○流暢な りゅうちょうな fluent, flowing, smooth ..............................1059 |
| | チョウ | |

**1309**
日 72

Use long, piercing S5 as a visual cue for the idea of piercing straight through all *difficulties* (易): **FLUENT**.

**1134**
名 14

---

| | ¹ SUN<br>² POSITIVE | ①太陽 たいよう sun ..............................0294 |
| | | ¹ 陽光 ようこう sunshine, sunlight, sun .......0137 |
| | | ¹ 落陽 らくよう setting sun ....................0793 |
| | ヨウ<br>ひ | ² 陽気な ようきな cheerful, bright, sunny.....0126 |
| | | ②陽性 ようせい positivity......................0128 |

**1310**
阜 170

The next two kanji should be considered together. They both begin with β *hills*, but one means **SUN** while the other means **SHADOW**. A good shortcut to recognizing the one for **SUN** is to notice the *sun* grapheme on the upper right (inside 易 *difficult*, whose meaning we can ignore here). Associate M1 **SUN** with M2 **POSITIVE**.

**0572**
常 12

---

| | ¹ SHADOW<br>² NEGATIVE | ①陰影 いんえい shadow.........................1281 |
| | | ¹ 日陰 ひかげ the shade.....................0001 |
| | | ² 陰惨 いんさん sadness and gloom..........1239 |
| | イン<br>かげ かげ(る) | ² 陰陽 いんよう negative and positive, yin-yang ..............................1310 |
| | | ②陰性 いんせい negativity, dormancy........0128 |

**1311**
阜 170

Continuing from the previous entry, a good shortcut to recognizing that this is the character for **SHADOW/NEGATIVE** is to notice 云 *cloud* at the lower right (the yin-yang opposite of 日 *sun* in the previous entry).

**0494**
常 11

---

| 隠 | HIDE | ○隠居 いんきょ retirement....................0255 |
| | | ○隠す かくす [vt] hide |
| | | 隠し芸 かくしげい hidden talent; parlor trick ..............................0225 |
| | イン<br>かく(す) かく(し)- かく(れる) | 隠れ道 かくれみち hidden path.............0158 |
| | | 戸の陰に隠れる とのかげにかくれる hide behind a door................................0248, 1311 |

**1312**
阜 170

隠

**0645**
常 14

Take the right-hand portion of this character as a version of 急 0971 URGENT/HURRY/SUDDEN. With β, we obtain the idea of *hurrying* into the *hills* to **HIDE**.

| | | |
|---|---|---|
| <sup>1</sup>**CALM**<br><sup>2</sup>**MILD**<br><br>オン<br>おだ(やか) | <sup>1</sup>平穏な へいおんな calm, quiet, tranquil....**0334**<br><sup>1</sup>穏やかな海 おだやかなうみ calm sea........**0106**<br>②穏和な おんわな gentle, mild, genial .......**0236**<br><sup>2</sup>穏当な おんとうな proper, reasonable, moderate<br>........................................................**0141**<br>②穏やかな人 おだやかなひと gentle person **0015** | |

**1313**
禾 115
穏
1141
常 16

Give *rice* (禾, i.e., food) to the *hurried* to **CALM** them.

| | | |
|---|---|---|
| **SPIKE, head of grain**<br><br>スイ<br>ほ | 穂波 ほなみ waving heads of grain...........**0598**<br>○穂先 ほさき spike/ear of grain; spike of a spear;<br> tip of a writing brush...........................**0134**<br>花穂 かすい spike (of flower heads)........**0121**<br>○穂状の すいじょうの shaped like an ear of grain<br>...............................................................**0616**<br>出穂期 しゅっすいき sprouting season (of grain)<br>.....................................................**0038, 0486** | |

**1314**
禾 115
穂
1139
常 15

A **SPIKE** or **head of grain** is represented here by the combination "*rice* (禾) *blessing* (恵)." Review 恵 0581 if necessary. Also see note at 簿 0985.

| | | |
|---|---|---|
| **RICE PLANT**<br><br>トウ<br>いね いな- | ○水稲 すいとう paddy-rice plant ..............**0027**<br>晩稲 ばんとう late-growing rice ..............**1275**<br>稲刈り いねかり rice reaping.................**0524**<br>○稲作 いなさく rice crop; raising rice plants...**0152**<br>稲穂 いなほ ear of rice.......................**1314** | |

**1315**
禾 115
稲
1129
常 14

*Rice* (禾) + *claw* (⺥) + *old* (旧): think of an *old* **RICE PLANT** being *handed* (or in this case "clawed") down from generation to generation, so as to preserve the original seed.

| | | |
|---|---|---|
| **MELANCHOLY**<br><br>シュウ<br>うれ(える) うれ(い) | ○憂愁 ゆうしゅう melancholy, gloom, grief....**0779**<br>郷愁 きょうしゅう homesickness, nostalgia...**1295**<br>ご愁傷様 ごしゅうしょうさま My condolences<br>.......................................................**1307, 0501**<br>愁える うれえる grieve<br>○愁い うれい melancholy | |

**1316**
心 61

*Autumn* (秋) + *mind* (心): autumn mood (**MELANCHOLY**). Note similarity in reading and meaning with 憂 0779. ☞ 悠 1677

2463
常 13

| | | |
|---|---|---|
| **¹ CUT OUT**<br>**² JUDGE, decide, rule**<br><br>サイ<br>た(つ)　さば(く) | ①裁つ　たつ　cut out (a garment), cut (paper)<br>¹ 洋裁　ようさい　Western-style dressmaking...0491<br>②裁く　さばく　judge, decide<br>②裁判　さいばん　trial; judgment, decision ...0744<br>² 独裁　どくさい　dictatorship, autocracy .......0346 | |

| 1317<br>衣 145 | See 𢦏 as a short man (十) holding a *spear* (戈) several times his size. Here he uses the sharp point of the spear to CUT OUT a section of *cloth* (衣). As we have done before (at 判 0744 and 断 0849), we can associate CUTTING with deciding or JUDGING, just as the English word **decide** derives from the Latin word for "cut." |
| 2813<br>常 12 | |

| | | |
|---|---|---|
| **¹ LOAD**<br>**² PUT IN PRINT**<br><br>サイ<br>の(せる)　の(る) | ¹ 積載する　せきさいする　load (with cargo); carry<br>　................................................0832<br>² 記載する　きさいする　record, state, mention 0427<br>②連載　れんさい　serial publication.............0582<br>○載る　のる　be placed upon; appear in print<br>　載せる　のせる　load (with cargo); put in print | |

| 1318<br>車 159 | (Continuing from the previous entry) Here the man LOADS the *spear* onto the roof of a *car* (車). M2 PUT IN PRINT is a cognate meaning. ☞ 戴 1914 |
| 2814<br>常 13 | |

| | | |
|---|---|---|
| **PLANTING**<br><br>サイ | 栽培　さいばい　cultivation, raising, growing 1264<br>植栽　しょくさい　raising trees and plants......0840<br>輪栽　りんさい　rotation of crops .............0944<br>○盆栽　ぼんさい　bonsai (potted dwarf tree)...1302 | |

| 1319<br>木 75 | (Continuing from 1317–18) Here the man PLANTS the *spear* in the ground, so that it will one day grow to become a *tree* (木). Now practice writing and distinguishing the meanings of this set of three kanji based on 𢦏. |
| 2810<br>常 10 | |

| | | |
|---|---|---|
| **AMNESTY**<br><br>シャ | ○赦免　しゃめん　pardon, amnesty, clemency...1272<br>容赦　ようしゃ　pardon, forgiveness, mercy...1037<br>特赦　とくしゃ　amnesty, special pardon ......0385<br>大赦　たいしゃ　amnesty, general amnesty ...0033 | |

| 1320<br>赤 155 | Review 亦 0773 ALSO and 赤 0774 RED. Here, "*striking* (攵) out the *red* (ink) (赤)" suggests forgiving a loan: AMNESTY. |
| 1344<br>常 11 | |

| | TRACE, footprint | 足跡 そくせき (=あしあと) footprint; one's life course.....................................0044 |
|---|---|---|
| | | 遺跡 いせき ruins, remains...................1179 |
| | セキ | 史跡 しせき historic spot/remains...........0888 |
| | あと | 傷跡 きずあと scar, cicatrix ...................1307 |
| | | 城跡 しろあと (=じょうせき) ruins of a castle...1298 |

| **1321** | Seeing ⻊ *leg/foot*, let us visualize S10–11 as a pair of legs and S12–13 as a pair of **footprints** they have left. In this way, ⻊ suggests the general category and S12–13 function as a visual cue for the specific meaning **footprint/TRACE.** ☞ 踪 1322 |
|---|---|
| 足 157 | |
| 1395 | |
| 常 13 | |

| | TRACE, footprint | ○失踪する しっそうする disappear, go missing .................................................0563 |
|---|---|---|
| | | 踪跡 そうせき traces, tracks; whereabouts...1321 |
| | ソウ | |

| **1322** | Using S14–15, we can borrow the same mnemonic we used with S12–13 in the previous entry, which for all intents and purposes has the same meaning. ☞ 跡 1321 |
|---|---|
| 足 157 | |
| 1434 | |
| 常 15 | |

| | SCAR; footprint | ○痕跡 こんせき traces, vestiges.................1321 |
|---|---|---|
| | | 痕跡器官 こんせききかん vestigial organs ..........................................1321, 0295, 0290 |
| | コン | 血痕 けっこん bloodstain........................0198 |
| | あと | 爪痕 つめあと scratch mark ....................0201 |
| | | 傷痕 きずあと (=しょうこん) scar...............1307 |

| **1323** | A body mends itself by producing **SCAR** tissue, so we can think of a **SCAR** as something that "*stops*(艮) *disease*(疒)." **SCAR** relates to the secondary meaning **footprint** through the idea of a mark left behind. |
|---|---|
| 疒 104 | |
| 2795 | |
| 常 11 | |

| | KICK | 一蹴する いっしゅうする flatly reject; easily defeat ..................................................0002 |
|---|---|---|
| | | ○蹴る ける kick |
| | シュウ | 蹴出す けだす kick out.........................0038 |
| | け(る) | 蹴破る けやぶる kick in, break through by kicking ....................................0596 |

| **1324** | 就 1283 refers to the idea of SETTING ABOUT a task or new job. Here visualize ⻊ *foot* **KICK-ING** someone so that they'll "get to work" or "get a job." |
|---|---|
| 足 157 | |
| 1479 | |
| 常 19 | |

**DANCE**

ヨウ
おど（る）　おど（り）

| ○舞踊 ぶよう dancing, dance | 0961 |
| 民踊 みんよう folk dance | 0477 |
| ○踊る おどる dance (energetically) | |
| 踊り手 おどりて dancer | 0046 |
| 盆踊り ぼんおどり *Bon* Festival dance | 1302 |

| 1325 | Recall 甬 *moving forward*, which we first learned at 通 0159 and saw again at 痛 0619. Here, we have *leg* (𝈪) *moving forward*: **DANCE**. |
| 足 157 | |
| 踊 | |
| 1410 | |
| 常 14 | |

---

**TREAD, stand on**

トウ
ふ（む）　ふ（まえる）

| 踏破する とうはする crush underfoot; travel on foot | 0596 |
| ○舞踏 ぶとう dancing | 0961 |
| ○踏む ふむ tread on | |
| 踏切 ふみきり railroad crossing | 0086 |
| 踏まえる ふまえる stand on; be based on | |

| 1326 | Visualize *stepping* (𝈪) on something to squeeze the *water* (水) out of it: **TREAD/stand on**. |
| 足 157 | |
| 踏 | |
| 1435 | |
| 常 15 | |

---

**LEAP, be active**

ヤク
おど（る）

| 飛躍 ひやく leap, jump | 0475 |
| 躍進する やくしんする make rapid progress, advance by leaps and bounds | 0191 |
| 躍動する やくどうする move energetically, throb | 0540 |
| ○活躍 かつやく (great) activity, action | 0054 |
| ○躍る おどる leap, jump | |

| 1327 | Review 曜 0025. Here 𝈪 *leg* indicates a person **LEAPING** in the air to grab the *small bird* before it can fly away. ☞ 曜 0025, 跳 1831, 濯 1328 |
| 足 157 | |
| 1484 | |
| 常 21 | |

---

**RINSE**

タク

| ○洗濯する せんたくする launder, wash | 0135 |
| 洗濯機 せんたくき washing machine | 0135, 0473 |

| 1328 | Picking up again from what was said at 曜 0025, here visualize the *small bird* splashing its wings in *water* (氵), to **RINSE** itself. This would be a good time to go back and review 羽 0418 and 飛 0475. ☞ 曜 0025, 躍 1327 |
| 水 85 | |
| 0711 | |
| 常 17 | |

| 奇 | **UNUSUAL, odd** | 奇異な きいな unusual, strange ............. 0882 |
| | | ○好奇心 こうきしん curiosity ............ 0095, 0056 |
| | | 奇数 きすう odd number ...................... 0309 |
| | キ | 奇跡 きせき miracle, wonder ............... 1321 |
| | | 怪奇 かいき mystery, wonder ............... 1255 |

| **1329** | Review 可 0814. The present entry, and the kanji based on it (which follow below), are |
| 大 37 | not pronounced カ but キ (except 椅 1332 イ). Picture 大 as a *big* man standing with his |
| 竒 | arms and legs stretched out, trying to keep his balance. The key is to perceive something |
| | UNUSUAL/**odd** in the way such a *big* man is balanced atop 可. ☞ 寄 1330 |
| 1902 | |
| 常 8 | |

| 寄 | **¹CONTRIBUTE** | ①寄付 きふ contribution, donation .......... 0064 |
| | **²DRAW NEAR, call on** | ¹寄贈する きぞうする (=きそうする) donate .... 1227 |
| | | ②寄る よる draw near, call on |
| | キ よ(る) | ²近寄る ちかよる go near, approach .......... 0194 |
| | -よ(り) よ(せる) | ²寄せる よせる draw near, allow to approach; |
| | | gather |

| **1330** | Think of this as a charitable home for psychiatric patients — a *roof* (宀) sheltering the *odd* |
| 宀 40 | (奇). The sheltering *roof* signifies the charitable **CONTRIBUTION** of the home's donors and |
| | volunteers; hearing of their good works, many *odd* people **DRAW NEAR**. ☞ 奇 1329 |
| 1983 | |
| 常 11 | |

| 騎 | **RIDE ON HORSEBACK** | 騎馬 きば horse riding ...................... 0336 |
| | | ○騎手 きしゅ rider, horseman, jockey ........ 0046 |
| | | 騎乗の きじょうの mounted, on horseback 1005 |
| | キ | 騎兵 きへい cavalry soldier, cavalry ......... 0907 |
| | | 騎士 きし knight .............................. 0350 |

| **1331** | 奇 shows a big man (大) trying to keep an *odd* balance on top of 可. Here we find him |
| 馬 187 | *oddly* balancing himself on top of a *horse*, i.e., **RIDING ON HORSEBACK**. ☞ 駒 2276 |
| 1629 | |
| 常 18 | |

| 椅 | **CHAIR** | ○椅子 いす chair .............................. 0094 |
| | | 車椅子 くるまいす wheelchair ......... 0125, 0094 |
| | イ | |

| **1332** | Here the big man *oddly* balances himself atop a *wooden* (木) **CHAIR**. Make an effort to |
| 木 75 | remember that 椅 (イ) is the only character based on 奇 that is not pronounced キ. |
| 0896 | |
| 常 12 | |

| | PROMONTORY, cape | 御前崎 おまえざき Cape Omaezaki....**0862, 0113** |
| --- | --- | --- |
| | | 長崎 ながさき Nagasaki (city and prefecture) |
| | | .........................................................**0091** |
| | | 川崎 かわさき Kawasaki [city in Kanagawa |
| | さき | prefecture]..................................**0022** |
| | | 宮崎 みやざき Miyazaki [surname] ..........**1242** |

| **1333** | Here *odd* (奇) *mountain* (山) suggests a mountain that sticks out where no other mountains |
| --- | --- |
| 山 46 | are: **PROMONTORY.** ☞ 岬 1335 |

嵜

0428
常 | 11

| | PROMONTORY, cape | 埼玉 さいたま Saitama (city and prefecture) |
| --- | --- | --- |
| | | .........................................................**0073** |
| | キ゚ | |
| | さい | |

| **1334** | Same meaning, and mnemonic, as the previous entry. *Odd land* sticks out where there is no |
| --- | --- |
| 土 32 | other land: **PROMONTORY.** |

0422
常 | 11

| | CAPE, promontory | 岬の先に みさきのさきに at the tip of a cape **0134** |
| --- | --- | --- |
| | | 岬を回る みさきをまわる round a cape .......**0050** |
| | | 潮岬 しおのみさき Cape Shio.................**0146** |
| | みさき | |

| **1335** | Here it is easiest just to visualize 甲 as a **promontory** or **CAPE** jutting out into a body of water. |
| --- | --- |
| 山 46 | ☞ 崎 1333 |

0255
常 | 8

| | PATTERN, pattern after | 模範 もはん model, pattern, example.......**0727** |
| --- | --- | --- |
| | | 模型 もけい model, pattern, mold ..........**0723** |
| | | 模造 もぞう imitation, counterfeit..........**0699** |
| | | ○模様 もよう pattern, design; appearance, |
| | モ ボ | circumstances ................................**0501** |
| | | 規模 きぼ scale, scope .....................**0624** |

| **1336** | 莫 (not to be confused with 草 (0144) originally depicted the sun (日) setting behind tall |
| --- | --- |
| 木 75 | *grasses* (艹) (to visualize this, let the crossing stroke in 大 suggest the horizon, and the two |
| | curving strokes a sinking motion). We'll take it to mean *no more.* Here, we thus obtain "*tree* |
| | (木) + *no more.*" With no more tree, we can only copy after its **PATTERN.** |

0963
常 | 14

|  | **MEMBRANE**<br><br>マク | 膜状の まくじょうの membranous, filmy.....0616<br>○粘膜 ねんまく mucous membrane..........1267<br>角膜 かくまく cornea.....0342<br>腹膜 ふくまく peritoneum.....0864<br>横隔膜 おうかくまく diaphragm.......0916, 1286 |
|---|---|---|
| **1337**<br>肉 130<br><br>0974<br>常 14 | | *Body part*(月) + *no more*(莫): Suggests the boundary of an organ: **MEMBRANE**. |

|  | **¹ DESERT**<br>**² OBSCURE**<br><br>バク | ①砂漠 さばく desert.....0678<br>² 漠然 ばくぜん obscurity, vagueness, haziness<br>.....0760 |
|---|---|---|
| **1338**<br>水 85<br><br>0598<br>常 13 | | *Water*(氵) + *no more*(莫): **DESERT**. Associate this with M2 **OBSCURE** through the idea of a hazy mirage. ☞ 漢 1730 |

|  | **¹ CURTAIN, tent**<br>**² SHOGUNATE**<br><br>マク バク | ¹ 煙幕 えんまく smoke screen.....0768<br>①開幕 かいまく raising of the curtain; opening scene.....0450<br>¹ 幕を引く まくをひく draw a curtain.....0422<br>②幕府 ばくふ shogunate.....0247<br>² 幕末 ばくまつ closing days of the Tokugawa shogunate.....0272 |
|---|---|---|
| **1339**<br>巾 50<br><br>2044<br>常 13 | | *Cloth*(巾) + *no more*(莫): pulling down the **CURTAIN** at the end of a show. Also means **tent**, which explains M2 **SHOGUNATE**, the English word for the military "tent governments" (幕府 [ばくふ]) of Japan's feudal era. |

|  | **GRAVE**<br><br>ボ<br>はか | 墓地 ぼち graveyard, cemetery, burial grounds<br>.....0187<br>○墓標 ぼひょう grave marker, gravestone ....0783<br>墓石 ぼせき (=はかいし) tombstone..........0403<br>○墓参り はかまいり visit to a grave.....1238 |
|---|---|---|
| **1340**<br>土 32<br><br>2037<br>常 13 | | *Soil*(土) + *no more*(莫): **GRAVE**. ☞ 基 0485 |

**RAISE, collect**

ボ
つの（る）

○募集する　ぼしゅうする　recruit; raise, collect 0190
募金　ぼきん　fund-raising................0029
応募する　おうぼする　apply for, subscribe to,
　　enlist for...............................0850
○募る　つのる　recruit; raise (funds, etc.)

| 1341 | *Strength/force* (力) + *no more* (莫): This means the time has come to **RAISE** new forces/**col-** |
|---|---|
| 力 19 | **lect** new strength. |
| 2013 | |
| 常 12 | |

暮

¹ **DUSK**
² **LIVE**

ボ
く（れる）　く（らす）

¹ 暮色　ぼしょく　dusk, twilight scene...........0528
①薄暮　はくぼ　nightfall, dusk, twilight........0986
¹ 暮れる　くれる　grow dark; come to an end
②暮らす　くらす　live, lead one's life; make a living
² 一人暮らし　ひとりぐらし　living alone...0002, 0015

| 1342 | *Sun* (日) + *no more* (莫): **DUSK**. Associate with M2 **LIVE** by thinking of **DUSK** as an element of |
|---|---|
| 日 72 | daily **LIFE**. |
| 2070 | |
| 常 14 | |

慕

**ADORE**

ボ
した（う）

愛慕　あいぼ　love, attachment...............0778
○慕情　ぼじょう　love, longing................0973
○慕う　したう　adore; long for
慕わしい　したわしい　dear, beloved
故郷を慕う　こきょうをしたう　long for home
　　.......................................0257, 1295

| 1343 | 小 is a variant of 心. It only appears in three kanji in this course; the other two follow. 小 |
|---|---|
| 心 61 | is used to fill a conical space without leaving an unsightly blank space above it (the stroke |
| | order follows 小). In the present entry, we thus have *heart* + *no more*, representing heart- |
| 2069 | breaking **ADORATION**. ☞ 暴 1346 |
| 常 14 | |

**ADD TO, accompany**

テン
そ（える）　そ（う）

○添付する　てんぷする　attach, append, annex
　　.......................................0064
添削　てんさく　correction...................1292
添乗員　てんじょういん　(escort) courier, tour
　　conductor..........................1005, 0317
○添う　そう　accompany
添える　そえる　add to, attach to

| 1344 | In Japan, families offer daily food and drink to the recently deceased to provide their spirits |
|---|---|
| 水 85 | the sustenance they need to reach heaven. Here 小 represents a deceased person's spirit, try- |
| | ing to climb up towards *heaven* (here taking the variant form 夭). We must **ADD** 氵 (symbol- |
| 0485 | izing sustenance) to the spirit to help it reach its goal. ☞ 恭 1345, 漆 1002 |
| 常 11 | |

**RESPECTFUL**

キョウ
うやうや(しい)

○恭敬 きょうけい respect, reverence...........0805
恭賀 きょうが respectful congratulations....1172
恭賀新年 きょうがしんねん Happy New Year
.................................1172, 0275, 0117
○恭しい うやうやしい respectful, reverent

| 1345 | Perceive the meaning **RESPECTFUL** by visualizing a young lady's formal curtsy. As she reaches out with both arms (S1) to spread out her skirt (S5–6), the skirt's wide pleats stretch out before her (小). ☞ 洪 0358, 添 1344 |
| 心 61 | |
| 2172 | |
| 常 10 | |

¹**VIOLENT**
²**DISCLOSE, lay bare**

ボウ バク
あば(く) あば(れる)

①暴力 ぼうりょく violence, force..............0084
¹乱暴 らんぼう violence, roughness; assault 0380
¹暴動 ぼうどう riot, disturbance, uprising....0540
①暴れる あばれる act violently
②暴く あばく disclose (a secret), lay bare

| 1346 | Here think of the *sun* (日) and *water* (氺) coming *together* (共) in **VIOLENT** battle. Also means **DISCLOSE**, from the idea of laying bare the brutal truth. ☞ 爆 1347, 慕 1343 |
| 日 72 | |
| 2194 | |
| 常 15 | |

**EXPLODE**

バク

○爆発 ばくはつ explosion, blast; eruption ...0148
爆弾 ばくだん bomb ...........................1075
爆薬 ばくやく explosives......................0303
爆撃 ばくげき bombing, bombardment ...1026
原爆 げんばく atomic bomb .................0208

| 1347 | Here we observe the *violence* in the previous entry **EXPLODING** into *fire* (火). Practice writing and distinguishing the meanings of this kanji and the one before. ☞ 暴 1346 |
| 火 86 | |
| 1020 | |
| 常 19 | |

**ALONG(SIDE)**

エン
そ(う) -ぞ(い)

○沿線の えんせんの along a railway line .....0210
沿海 えんかい coast, shore ...................0106
○沿う そう lie along (a river), follow along
路線に沿って ろせんにそって along the route/
line .............................................0788, 0210
川沿いに かわぞいに along the riverside ...0022

| 1348 | Review 船 0669. Here, let 氵 represent a body of *water*, and picture *rolling a hoop* **ALONG(SIDE)** it. ☞ 治 0950, 没 0519 |
| 水 85 | |
| 0290 | |
| 常 8 | |

**FOUNDATION STONE**

ソ
いしずえ

礎石 そせき foundation stone, cornerstone 0403
定礎 ていそ laying of a foundation stone...0045
○基礎 きそ basis, foundation ..................0485
礎材 そざい foundation materials..........0654
国家の礎 こっかのいしずえ pillar of state
..........................................0075, 0219

| 1349 | Recall 疋 *broken/deformed*, introduced at 旋 0572. Here it represents the **FOUNDATION** of a building, bent (*deformed*) under the tremendous weight of the lumber assembled on top of it (represented by 林 *forest*). Combining this with 石 *stone*, our keyword for this kanji becomes "**FOUNDATION STONE.**" |
|---|---|
| 石 112 | |
| 1152 | |
| 常 18 | |

**DOUBT, distrust**

ギ
うたが(う)

○疑問 ぎもん question, problem, doubt.....0452
疑惑 ぎわく doubt, suspicion................1153
容疑 ようぎ suspicion........................1037
○疑う うたがう doubt, be suspicious
疑わしい うたがわしい doubtful, suspicious

| 1350 | The katakana spelling of the word ヒマ (free time, idleness; see 暇 1903) across the top is a feature unique to this kanji (and the two that subsume it, which follow). We can therefore take a visual shortcut to its meaning by remembering the maxim "**distrust idleness**" (the keyword for this kanji is "**DOUBT**"). |
|---|---|
| 疋 103 | |
| 1416 | |
| 常 14 | |

**CONGEAL, grow stiff, become absorbed in**

ギョウ
こ(る) こ(らす)

○凝結する ぎょうけつする congeal, coagulate, solidify
..........................................0516
○凝る こる [vi] grow stiff; be absorbed in; be elaborate
凝り性 こりしょう fastidiousness, perfectionism...0128
凝り固まる こりかたまる be fanatical; coagulate, clot
..........................................0260
凝らす こらす [vt] concentrate, strain, elaborate

| 1351 | Recall 冫 *ice* (see 冷 0675 if necessary). One *distrusts* (疑) *ice* because it can make one **grow stiff/CONGEAL.** ☞ 擬 1352 |
|---|---|
| 冫 15 | |
| 0154 | |
| 常 16 | |

**IMITATE**

ギ

擬声語 ぎせいご onomatopoeic word
..........................................0529, 0222
擬人 ぎじん personification, impersonation
..........................................0015
○模擬 もぎ sham, mock, simulated .........1336

| 1352 | The next three kanji are all imitators: they all add a single element to a kanji we already know, and signify "imitate," "copy after," or "resemble." In this entry, see a *hand* (扌), like that of an artist in training, drawing an **IMITATION** of 疑 1350. Do not confuse with 偽 1237, which overlaps in meaning and has the same *on-yomi*. ☞ 偽 1237, 凝 1351 |
|---|---|
| 手 64 | |
| 0706 | |
| 常 17 | |

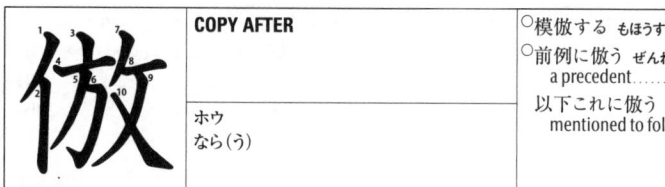

| | COPY AFTER | ○模倣する もほうする imitate, copy ...........1336 |
|---|---|---|
| | ホウ<br>なら(う) | ○前例に倣う ぜんれいにならう follow/copy after a precedent.............................0113, 0721<br>以下これに倣う いかこれにならう The under-mentioned to follow this example ...0066, 0040 |

**1353**　人 9
(Continuing from the first sentence of the previous entry) This entry **COPIES AFTER** 放 0574 by adding イ to it. While 習う (ならう, see 0420) means "to **LEARN** or study," 倣う ならう means "to **COPY AFTER** or follow an example." ☞ 放 0574, 倣 1508

0095　常 10

| | RESEMBLE | 擬似 ぎじ false, pseudo .....................1352 |
|---|---|---|
| | ジ<br>に(る) | ○類似する るいじする resemble, be alike, be similar........................................0310<br>○似る にる resemble, be alike, be similar<br>似合う にあう befit, suit; match well........0227<br>真似する まねする imitate, mimic..........0838 |

**1354**　人 9
(Continuing from the first sentence of 擬 1352) **RESEMBLES** 以 0066. ☞ 以 0066

0046　常 7

| | STRAW SACK | ○土俵 どひょう sumo (wrestling) ring; sandbag ....................................................0030 |
|---|---|---|
| | ヒョウ<br>たわら | ○米俵 こめだわら (straw) rice bag.............0234 |

**1355**　人 9
Review 素 0132. Here, visualize a *man* (イ) whose upper body is naked (S3–6) and who wears nothing but a **STRAW SACK** over his lower body (S7–10, representing his *clothing*). The right side of the character is of course 表 0705, which confirms the idea of the man's *manifesting* himself by wearing nothing but a **STRAW SACK**.

0097　常 10

| | I, myself | ○俺ら おれら we |
|---|---|---|
| | おれ | 俺の おれの my<br>俺に付いてくるな おれについてくるな Stop following me around .....................0040 |

**1356**　人 9
Used by men as an intimate first-person pronoun, though it can carry vulgar connotations. The combination "*man* (イ) + *big* (大) + *lightning* (电)" indeed suggests a rough and boastful way of referring to oneself, along the lines of the tall-talking frontiersman Davy Crockett, who "Greased a great-big streak o' lightnin' with a bottle o' rattlesnake taller (tallow)."

0092　常 10

**HERMITAGE**

アン
いおり

○庵 あん (=いおり) hermitage, secluded cottage
庵室 あんしつ hermitage, secluded cottage 0253
庵主 あんしゅ proprietor of a hermitage ....0365
草庵 そうあん thatched cottage ............0144

| 1357 | |
|---|---|
| 广 53 | While *big* (大) *lightning* (电) strikes outside, we take *shelter* (广) inside a **HERMITAGE**. |
| 2692 | |
| 名 11 | |

¹ **I, myself**
² **MANSERVANT**

ボク

① 僕ら ぼくら we
¹ 僕の ぼくの my
² 忠僕 ちゅうぼく faithful servant............0644
② 従僕 じゅうぼく servant, attendant..........0869
² 家僕 かぼく manservant, house boy .......0219

| 1358 | |
|---|---|
| 人 9 | 美 is kind of a cross between 業 0498 and 美 0497. It combines the "load of bricks" (业) from the former and *big* (大) from the latter, and will mean *big servant*. In the present entry, *man* (亻) and *big servant* combine to mean **MANSERVANT**. More commonly, this kanji is used by men as an informal first-person pronoun. ☞ 撲 1359 |
| 0142 | |
| 常 14 | |

**DEAL A BLOW**

ボク

○打撲傷 だぼくしょう bruise............1025, 1307
撲殺 ぼくさつ clubbing to death............0522
撲滅 ぼくめつ eradication, destruction .....1149
○相撲 すもう sumo wrestling..............0682
大相撲 おおずもう professional sumo wrestling
............0033, 0682

| 1359 | |
|---|---|
| 手 64 | The life of a sumo wrestler in many ways resembles that of a servant. He is forced to live in a "stable" under the control of his seniors and 親方 (おやかた, stable master), who preempts any cash prizes the wrestler may win. Here visualize a sumo bout: the *hand* (扌) **DEALS A BLOW** to a *big servant* (美, sumo wrestler). ☞ 僕 1358 |
| 0666 | |
| 常 15 | |

**STRIKE, slap**

コウ
たた(く)

叩頭 こうとう kowtow (kneel and bow until one's forehead touches the floor)................0162
○キーを叩く キーをたたく strike the keys (of a keyboard)
叩き込む たたきこむ drive in, inculcate .....0192
叩き潰す たたきつぶす smash, pulverize....1178
目叩く めたたく blink, wink; flicker [cf. 瞬 0963]
............0021

| 1360 | |
|---|---|
| 口 30 | Images of a *mouth* before (口) and after (叩) being **STRUCK** (the one on the right has a split lower lip). |
| | |
| 外 5 | |

| | CUT DOWN | ○伐採する ばっさいする lumber, fell, deforest **0989** |
| | | 伐木 ばつぼく felling, cutting, logging......**0028** |
| | | 盗伐 とうばつ secret felling of trees.........**1304** |
| | バツ | 征伐 せいばつ subjugation, conquest ......**0868** |
| | | 討伐 とうばつ suppression (of a rebellion)...**1023** |

| **1361** | Here *man* (亻) and *spear* (戈) combine to mean **CUT DOWN**. Learn to recognize this character by how it differs from the much more common 代 0071. See the additional stroke here as a violent slashing action, **CUTTING** the *man* **DOWN** like a tree. ☞ 代 0071 |
|---|---|
| 人 9 | |
| 0027 | |
| 常 6 | |

| | CLIQUE, clan | 閥族 ばつぞく clan, clique..................**0568** |
| | | ○財閥 ざいばつ financial clique/combine, |
| | | *zaibatsu*......................................**0653** |
| | | 学閥 がくばつ academic clique............**0099** |
| | バツ | 軍閥 ぐんばつ military clique..............**0583** |

| **1362** | The defining quality of **CLIQUES** and **clans** is their exclusivity, vividly represented here in a man's getting *cut down* (伐) trying to pass through a *gate* (門). |
|---|---|
| 門 169 | |
| 2839 | |
| 常 14 | |

| | FIGHT | 戦闘 せんとう battle, fight, combat..........**0461** |
| | | 拳闘 けんとう boxing.........................**1248** |
| | | ○闘争 とうそう fight, conflict..................**0972** |
| | トウ | 春闘 しゅんとう spring labor offensive........**0362** |
| | たたか(う) | ○闘う たたかう fight |

| **1363** | Here we observe a **FIGHT** breaking out under a *gate* (門) between the *pea*-sized guy (豆, see 0161) and the *3-centimeter* guy (寸, see 0381). |
|---|---|
| 門 169* | |
| 鬪 | |
| 2847 | |
| 常 18 | |

| | DARK | 闇夜 やみよ (=あんや) dark night............**0467** |
| | | 真の闇 しんのやみ pitch-darkness..........**0838** |
| | | ○闇市 やみいち black market................**0205** |
| | アン* | 闇相場 やみそうば black-market price......**0682** |
| | やみ | |

| **1364** | Review 音 0150, which we took to mean not only SOUND but also the absence of light. Here the *standing* man blocks the *sun* from passing through the *gate* (門), so that it becomes **DARK**. Use the enclosing quality of 門 as a visual reminder of **DARKNESS**. |
|---|---|
| 門 169 | |
| 2846 | |
| 常 17 | |

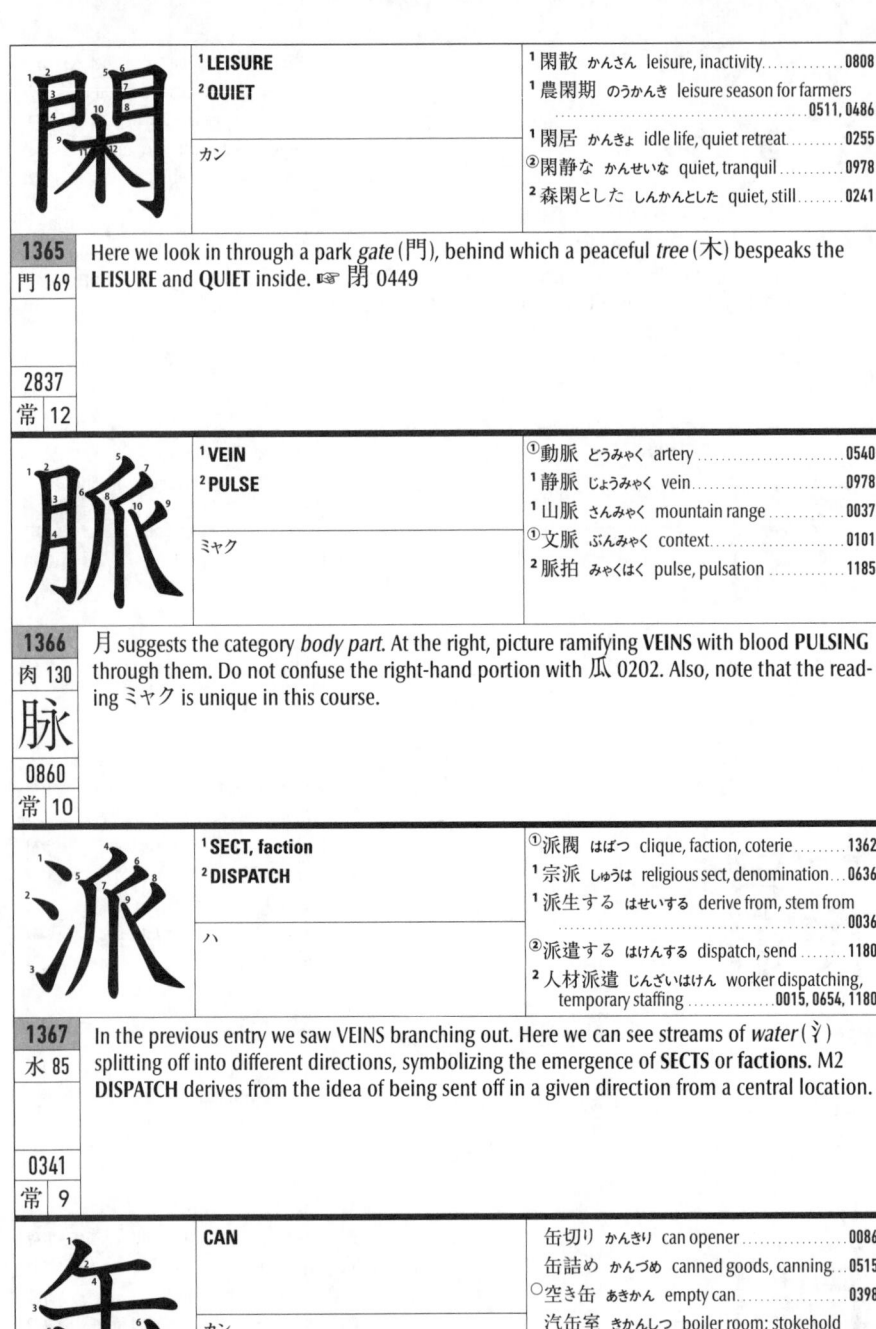

| | | |
|---|---|---|
| 閑 | ¹LEISURE<br>²QUIET<br><br>カン | ¹閑散 かんさん leisure, inactivity............0808<br>¹農閑期 のうかんき leisure season for farmers<br>............................................0511, 0486<br>¹閑居 かんきょ idle life, quiet retreat........0255<br>②閑静な かんせいな quiet, tranquil...........0978<br>²森閑とした しんかんとした quiet, still........0241 |

| 1365 | Here we look in through a park *gate* (門), behind which a peaceful *tree* (木) bespeaks the LEISURE and QUIET inside. ☞ 閉 0449 |
|---|---|
| 門 169 | |
| 2837 | |
| 常 12 | |

| | | |
|---|---|---|
| 脈 | ¹VEIN<br>²PULSE<br><br>ミャク | ①動脈 どうみゃく artery.......................0540<br>¹静脈 じょうみゃく vein......................0978<br>¹山脈 さんみゃく mountain range............0037<br>①文脈 ぶんみゃく context....................0101<br>²脈拍 みゃくはく pulse, pulsation............1185 |

| 1366 | 月 suggests the category *body part*. At the right, picture ramifying VEINS with blood PULSING through them. Do not confuse the right-hand portion with 瓜 0202. Also, note that the reading ミャク is unique in this course. |
|---|---|
| 肉 130 | |
| 脉 | |
| 0860 | |
| 常 10 | |

| | | |
|---|---|---|
| 派 | ¹SECT, faction<br>²DISPATCH<br><br>ハ | ①派閥 はばつ clique, faction, coterie........1362<br>¹宗派 しゅうは religious sect, denomination...0636<br>¹派生する はせいする derive from, stem from<br>............................................0036<br>②派遣する はけんする dispatch, send........1180<br>² 人材派遣 じんざいはけん worker dispatching,<br>temporary staffing..............0015, 0654, 1180 |

| 1367 | In the previous entry we saw VEINS branching out. Here we can see streams of *water* (氵) splitting off into different directions, symbolizing the emergence of SECTS or factions. M2 DISPATCH derives from the idea of being sent off in a given direction from a central location. |
|---|---|
| 水 85 | |
| 0341 | |
| 常 9 | |

| | | |
|---|---|---|
| 缶 | CAN<br><br>カン | 缶切り かんきり can opener.................0086<br>缶詰め かんづめ canned goods, canning...0515<br>○空き缶 あきかん empty can..................0398<br>汽缶室 きかんしつ boiler room; stokehold<br>............................................0127, 0253<br>薬缶 やかん kettle...........................0303 |

| 1368 | Behold a CAN. S1 looks like an opened pull-tab top on a beverage CAN. |
|---|---|
| 缶 121 | |
| 罐 | |
| 1750 | |
| 常 6 | |

## SHAKE

ヨウ
ゆ(れる) ゆ(る) ゆ(らぐ) ゆ(るぐ)
ゆ(する) ゆ(さぶる) ゆ(すぶる)

○動揺 どうよう shaking, trembling; restlessness, disquiet....................0540
○揺れる ゆれる shake, vibrate, swing
揺り起こす ゆりおこす shake up, wake by shaking....................0430

| 1369 | 扌 hand + 爫 claw + can (S8–12): visualize as a bartender's two *hands* firmly holding a mixing *can* and **SHAKING** it. Note that when *can* appears with *claw* it loses its pull-tab top. |
|---|---|
| 手 64 | |
| 搖 | |
| 0543 | |
| 常 12 | |

## POPULAR SONG, chant

ヨウ
うたい うた(う)

○民謡 みんよう folk song/ballad...............0477
童謡 どうよう children's song, nursery rhyme ....................0537
謡曲 ようきょく Noh chant....................0503
歌謡曲 かようきょく popular song......0827, 0503
○謡う うたう recite, chant

| 1370 | Here a *claw* (爫) keeps a beat on a *can*, while a mouth (part of 言) **chants** the *words* (言) of a **POPULAR SONG.** |
|---|---|
| 言 149 | |
| 謠 | |
| 1445 | |
| 常 16 | |

## FAR

ヨウ
はる(か)

遥かな はるかな far, faraway, remote
遥か昔 はるかむかし long ago...............0359
○遥かに はるかに far, far off; a long time ago; by far
遥かに多く はるかにおおく far more.......0267
遥々 はるばる from afar, all the way

| 1371 | Here a *claw* loads *cans* onto a *truck*, to be transported somewhere **FAR** away. |
|---|---|
| 辵 162 | |
| 遙 | |
| 2708 | |
| 名 12 | |

## POTTERY

トウ

○陶器 とうき pottery, porcelain, chinaware...0295
陶芸 とうげい ceramic art....................0225
陶工 とうこう potter, ceramist...............0108
陶の人形 とうのにんぎょう ceramic figurine
....................0015, 0147
陶冶する とうやする train, cultivate.........0951

| 1372 | Think of taking clay from the *hills* (阝), then *wrapping* (勹) your hands around it to shape it into a *can* (缶, i.e., a pot): **POTTERY.** |
|---|---|
| 阜 170 | |
| 0499 | |
| 常 11 | |

| | **SET FORTH, lay out** | ○陳述する ちんじゅつする state, set forth, declare, expound .............................................. 0994 |
| --- | --- | --- |
| | | 開陳する かいちんする state, express (one's opinion) ........................................... 0450 |
| | チン | 陳情 ちんじょう petition, appeal ............. 0973 |
| | | 陳列する ちんれつする exhibit, display .... 0718 |
| | | 陳謝 ちんしゃ apology ........................ 1022 |

| **1373** | In the remainder of this course you will learn a number of characters that incorporate 東 0032 EAST. The meaning EAST is not germane to these characters, so it is better to focus on the way 木 thoroughly penetrates 日, and thereby associate the grapheme 東 with the meaning *all the way through* or *all the way across*. In this entry, *all the way through/across* indicates a thorough description: SET FORTH/lay out. When you see this character, think of hiking to the top of the *hills around the edge of town* (阝) to get the "lay of the land," a vantage point that SETS FORTH or lays out a panoramic view of (i.e., a view extending *all the way across*) the surrounding area. ☞ 陣 1374 |
| --- | --- |
| 阜 170 | |
| 0493 | |
| 常 11 | |

| | **¹ BATTLE FORMATION** **² CAMP** | ¹ 陣形 じんけい battle formation .............. 0147 |
| --- | --- | --- |
| | | ¹ 陣立て じんだて battle array ................. 0067 |
| | | ² 陣営 じんえい camp, quarters ............... 1243 |
| | ジン | ②陣地 じんち encampment, position ......... 0187 |
| | | ² 退陣する たいじんする decamp, withdraw ... 1091 |

| **1374** | Here we observe a *vehicle* (車) driving into the *hills around the edge of town* (阝) to set up a strategic BATTLE FORMATION or CAMP. ☞ 陳 1373 |
| --- | --- |
| 阜 170 | |
| 0411 | |
| 常 10 | |

| | **FALL IN/INTO** | 陥没する かんぼつする sink, fall, cave in .... 0519 |
| --- | --- | --- |
| | | ○陥落する かんらくする fall in, cave in; surrender, fall ............................................. 0793 |
| | カン | 欠陥 けっかん defect, fault, deficiency ...... 0277 |
| | おちい(る) おとし(れる) | ○穴に陥る あなにおちいる fall in a pit ......... 0397 |
| | | 人を陥れる ひとをおとしいれる entrap a person ............................................... 0015 |

| **1375** | Here we can visualize the act of FALLING INTO. From high atop the *hills around the edge of town* (阝), an invading force peers down (S4–5) into the *old* town (see 旧 0771) to plan its attack. It is about to FALL INTO a trap (visualize it FALLING INTO the empty space in the middle of 旧). Think of the reading おちいる (陥る, fall into) as a combination of 落ちる (おちる, fall) and -入る (-いる, verbal suffix like "into" of "FALL INTO"). Think of 陥れる (おとしいれる) as a combination of 落とす (おとす, let fall, drop) and 入れる (いれる, put in). |
| --- | --- |
| 阜 170 | |
| 陥 | |
| 0413 | |
| 常 10 | |

| | **PROSPER, rise** | ○隆々たる りゅうりゅうたる prosperous, thriving; brawny |
| --- | --- | --- |
| | | 隆盛 りゅうせい prosperity ................... 1300 |
| | リュウ | 隆運 りゅううん prosperity, good fortune .... 0584 |
| | | 興隆 こうりゅう prosperity, rise ............... 0505 |
| | | 隆起 りゅうき protuberance, elevation ....... 0430 |

| **1376** | Just as 夂 has represented a *rooftop*, here it represents the top of a *hill* (阝). The top of the hill, in turn, represents not only geographic elevation, but also physical flourishing and material PROSPERITY. 生 *life/be born* suggests the youthful RISE to physical flourishing and PROSPERITY. ☞ 降 1377 |
| --- | --- |
| 阜 170 | |
| 隆 | |
| 0498 | |
| 常 11 | |

| DESCEND, unload | 降下する こうかする descend, fall, drop ....0040 |
| | ○以降 いこう on and after, hereafter..........0066 |
| | ○降りる おりる descend, alight, land |
| コウ | 降ろす おろす discharge, unload |
| お(りる) お(ろす) ふ(る) ふ(り) | ○雨が降っている あめがふっている It is raining ....0154 |

| 1377 | Learn to recognize the meaning of this kanji by how it differs from the previous entry (and |
| 阜 170 | vice versa). Here the lower-right portion is a proxy for 年 *year*, indicating the decline of old age and contrasting with 生 above. After rising to the heights of vigor and PROSPERITY (隆), one in his later *years* may only DESCEND. ☞ 隆 1376 |
| 0414 | |
| 常 10 | |

| PEAK, high mountain | 主峰 しゅほう main peak......................0365 |
| | ○連峰 れんぽう mountain range, series of mountain peaks..........................0582 |
| | 最高峰 さいこうほう highest peak; highest |
| ホウ | authority...........................0196, 0185 |
| みね | 峰伝いに みねづたいに along the ridges....0223 |
| | 峰続き みねつづき succession of peaks .....0354 |

| 1378 | Use the distinctive element 丰 as a cue for the meaning of the next four characters. Here |
| 山 46 | visualize it as a path leading to the top of a high *mountain* (山) PEAK (the crossing strokes depict a series of steps). As in the previous two entries, 夂 represents the summit. ☞ 岳 0908 |
| 0372 | |
| 常 10 | |

| MEET | ○逢着する ほうちゃくする encounter..........0938 |
| | ○逢う あう meet with, see, encounter |
| | 逢い引き あいびき rendezvous, assignation |
| ホウ | ............................................0422 |
| あ(う) | 忍び逢い しのびあい secret rendezvous....1095 |

| 1379 | Borrowing the idea of "path" from the previous entry, see 夆 as a path or line *moving* |
| 辵 162 | *forward* (辶) to MEET someone or something. Note that all four kanji incorporating 夆 are pronounced ホウ. This is another kanji that has not been officially simplified to 辶 (see 辻 1145). Remember, writing 辶 is always acceptable. |
| 2774 | |
| 名 11 | |

| SEW | ○裁縫 さいほう sewing, tailoring ..............1317 |
| | 縫合する ほうごうする suture, stitch (a wound) |
| | ............................................0227 |
| ホウ | ○縫う ぬう sew, stitch |
| ぬ(う) | 傷口を縫う きずぐちをぬう suture a wound ............................................1307, 0019 |
| | 縫い針 ぬいばり sewing needle ..............0556 |

| 1380 | This character subsumes the previous entry 逢 MEET. However, seeing 糸 *thread*, we should |
| 糸 120 | simply take 丰 as a needle and stitches, for SEWING. 辶 might be interpreted as the needle's *forward motion*, but in any case, learn to recognize SEWING from the combination of 糸 and 丰. |
| 1284 | |
| 常 16 | |

| | BEE, wasp | 養蜂 ようほう beekeeping, apiculture........0500 |
|---|---|---|
| | | 蜂起 ほうき revolt.........................0430 |
| | | 働き蜂 はたらきばち worker bee..........0541 |
| | ホウ | 蜂の巣 はちのす beehive.................0601 |
| | はち | 蜂に刺される はちにさされる be stung by a bee |
| | | ...............................0935 |

| 1381 | 虫 *insect* transforms 縫's needle and stitches into a **wasp**'s stinger and stripes. |
|---|---|
| 虫 142 | |
| 1247 | |
| 常 13 | |

| | HONEY; nectar | ○蜂蜜 はちみつ honey .........................1381 |
|---|---|---|
| | | 蜜蜂 みつばち honeybee.....................1381 |
| | | 花蜜 かみつ nectar............................0121 |
| | ミツ | |

| 1382 | Recall 必 *without fail* (review 0549 if necessary). Let 必 suggest *crowded,* from the idea that everyone must crowd together under one *roof*(宀), *without fail*. In this entry we thus have *insects*(虫) *crowded* inside a confining structure, to represent bees in a **HONEY**comb. ☞ 蟹 2294, 密 1383 |
|---|---|
| 宀 40 | |
| 2060 | |
| 常 14 | |

| | ¹ CLOSE, dense, tight<br>² SECRET | ①密度 みつど density ......................0280 |
|---|---|---|
| | | ¹ 密接な みっせつな close, intimate..........0847 |
| | | ¹ 精密 せいみつ precision, accuracy, minuteness |
| | | ...............................0976 |
| | ミツ | ②密輸 みつゆ smuggling, contraband trade 0945 |
| | | ² 密入国 みつにゅうこく illegal entry (into a |
| | | country)...............................0039, 0075 |

| 1383 | (Continuing from the previous entry) *Crowding*(必) inside a confined *mountain* (山) shelter: **CLOSE/dense/tight**. M2 **SECRET** derives from the idea of holding a piece of information **CLOSE** to one's chest. ☞ 蜜 1382 |
|---|---|
| 宀 40 | |
| 1984 | |
| 常 11 | |

| | SECRET | ○秘密 ひみつ secret, mystery; privacy........1383 |
|---|---|---|
| | | 秘書 ひしょ secretary; treasured book ......0079 |
| | | 黙秘する もくひする keep silent, keep secret |
| | | ...............................0762 |
| | ヒ | 神秘 しんぴ mystery............................0316 |
| | ひ(める) | ○心に秘める こころにひめる keep (something) to |
| | | oneself...............................0056 |

| 1384 | One's *rice*(禾) must be kept **SECRET**, *without fail* (必). ☞ 泌 1894 |
|---|---|
| 禾 115 | |
| 祕 | |
| 1074 | |
| 常 10 | |

**EUROPE**

オウ

| | | |
|---|---|---|
| 欧州 | おうしゅう Europe | 0845 |
| ○欧米 | おうべい Europe and America | 0234 |
| 欧亜 | おうあ Europe and Asia | 0545 |
| 西欧 | せいおう Western Europe; the Occident | 0795 |
| 北欧 | ほくおう Northern Europe, Scandinavia | 0122 |

---

**1385**

欠 76

欧

0787

常 8

Recall 区 0297 DIVIDE INTO SECTIONS/DISTRICTS. Here 欠 indicates the *lack* of such division. This we can easily associate with **EUROPE**, ever less divided since the advent of the European Union.

---

**枢** **PIVOT**

スウ

| | | |
|---|---|---|
| 枢要な | すうような pivotal, cardinal | 0547 |
| ○枢軸 | すうじく pivot, axis | 0692 |
| 枢軸国 | すうじくこく the Axis powers | 0692, 0075 |
| 枢密 | すうみつ secret government affairs | 1383 |
| 中枢 | ちゅうすう pivot, center | 0035 |

---

**1386**

木 75

樞

0770

常 8

Here visualize 区 as a board attached to the *tree* (木) by a hinge. Now imagine turning 区 left and right, like a hinged signboard, while 木 stays in place at one central point or **PIVOT**.

---

**殴** **BEAT, thrash**

オウ
なぐ(る)

| | | |
|---|---|---|
| ○殴打 | おうだ blow, beating | 1025 |
| 殴殺する | おうさつする beat to death | 0522 |
| ○殴る | なぐる beat, thrash | |
| 殴り倒す | なぐりたおす knock down | 0941 |
| 横殴り | よこなぐり side sweep, side blow | 0916 |

---

**1387**

殳 79

毆

0788

常 8

Here let 乂 *slash marks* (see 殺 0522) suggest an image of violently **BEATING/thrashing** with a *lance* (殳).

---

**DRIVE**

ク
か(ける) か(る)

| | | |
|---|---|---|
| 駆使する | くしする use liberally, order around | 0887 |
| ○先駆者 | せんくしゃ forerunner, pioneer | 0134, 0107 |
| ○駆ける | かける gallop, dash | |
| 駆け回る | かけまわる bustle about, run about | 0050 |
| 駆け込み乗車 | かけこみじょうしゃ dashing onto a departing train | 0192, 1005, 0125 |

---

**1388**

馬 187

驅

1619

常 14

Here we find *slash marks* (乂) on a *horse*'s hind. Picture a coachman **DRIVING** the horse forward with a violent crack of his whip. ☞ 馳 1389

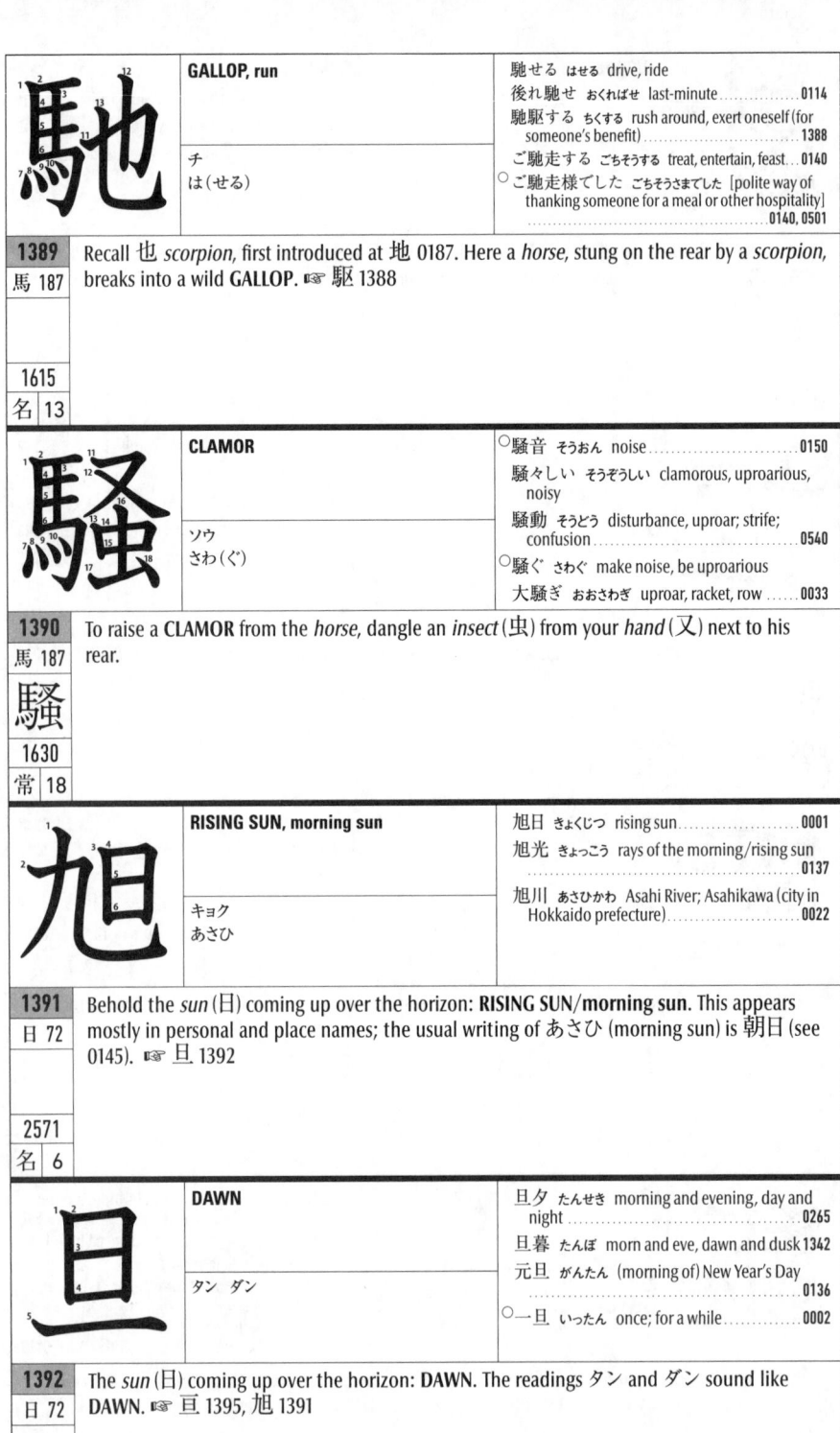

| | **GALLOP, run** | 馳せる はせる drive, ride |
|---|---|---|
| | | 後れ馳せ おくればせ last-minute ............ 0114 |
| | | 馳駆する ちくする rush around, exert oneself (for |
| | | someone's benefit) ...................... 1388 |
| | チ | ご馳走する ごちそうする treat, entertain, feast ... 0140 |
| | は(せる) | ○ ご馳走様でした ごちそうさまでした [polite way of |
| | | thanking someone for a meal or other hospitality] |
| | | ........................................ 0140, 0501 |

| **1389** | Recall 也 *scorpion,* first introduced at 地 0187. Here a *horse,* stung on the rear by a *scorpion,* |
|---|---|
| 馬 187 | breaks into a wild **GALLOP.** ☞ 駆 1388 |
| 1615 | |
| 名 13 | |

| | **CLAMOR** | ○ 騒音 そうおん noise .......................... 0150 |
|---|---|---|
| | | 騒々しい そうぞうしい clamorous, uproarious, |
| | | noisy |
| | | 騒動 そうどう disturbance, uproar; strife; |
| | ソウ | confusion ............................... 0540 |
| | さわ(ぐ) | ○ 騒ぐ さわぐ make noise, be uproarious |
| | | 大騒ぎ おおさわぎ uproar, racket, row ...... 0033 |

| **1390** | To raise a **CLAMOR** from the *horse,* dangle an *insect* (虫) from your *hand* (又) next to his |
|---|---|
| 馬 187 | rear. |
| 騒 | |
| 1630 | |
| 常 18 | |

| | **RISING SUN, morning sun** | 旭日 きょくじつ rising sun .................... 0001 |
|---|---|---|
| | | 旭光 きょっこう rays of the morning/rising sun |
| | | ........................................ 0137 |
| | キョク | 旭川 あさひかわ Asahi River; Asahikawa (city in |
| | あさひ | Hokkaido prefecture) .................... 0022 |

| **1391** | Behold the *sun* (日) coming up over the horizon: **RISING SUN/morning sun**. This appears |
|---|---|
| 日 72 | mostly in personal and place names; the usual writing of あさひ (morning sun) is 朝日 (see |
| | 0145). ☞ 旦 1392 |
| 2571 | |
| 名 6 | |

| | **DAWN** | 旦夕 たんせき morning and evening, day and |
|---|---|---|
| | | night ................................... 0265 |
| | | 旦暮 たんぼ morn and eve, dawn and dusk 1342 |
| | タン ダン | 元旦 がんたん (morning of) New Year's Day |
| | | ........................................ 0136 |
| | | ○ 一旦 いったん once; for a while ............ 0002 |

| **1392** | The *sun* (日) coming up over the horizon: **DAWN**. The readings タン and ダン sound like |
|---|---|
| 日 72 | **DAWN**. ☞ 亘 1395, 旭 1391 |
| 2119 | |
| 常 5 | |

| 但 | **PROVIDED THAT; however**<br><br>ただ(し) | ○但し ただし provided that, on condition that, however, but, only<br>但し書き ただしがき proviso..................0079<br>但し付き ただしつき conditional...............0064<br>ボブは約束はする、但し実行はしない<br>ボブはやくそくはする、ただしじっこうはしない Bob makes promises, but he does not keep them....................0170, 0307, 0499, 0055 |
|---|---|---|

| **1393**<br>人 9<br><br>0056<br>常 7 | Used in writing the conditional conjunction 但し ただし (**PROVIDED THAT**). We might think of a *man* (イ) who was given the freedom to do whatever he pleased in the evening, **PROVIDED** he reported for duty promptly at *dawn* (旦). |
|---|---|

| 担 | **¹ BEAR ON SHOULDER**<br>**² UNDERTAKE, shoulder**<br><br>タン<br>かつ(ぐ) にな(う) | ¹担架 たんか stretcher......................1173<br>¹御輿を担ぐ みこしをかつぐ carry a palanquin/portable shrine..................0862, 0506<br>②担当する たんとうする undertake, be in charge of....................0141<br>² 負担 ふたん burden, charge, responsibility 0829<br>②責任を担う せきにんをになう shoulder responsibility....................0831, 0372 |
|---|---|---|

| **1394**<br>手 64<br>擔<br>0283<br>常 8 | The physical act of carrying something heavy on the shoulder, as a construction worker carries lumber, is not hard to see in this character for **SHOULDERING**. Take S8 as the thumb of a laborer's *hand*, laid over his **SHOULDER** to grasp the stack of two-by-fours (旦) he is **SHOULDERING**. |
|---|---|

| 亘 | **SPAN**<br><br>コウ<br>わた(る) | 幾年にも亘る いくねんにもわたる spanning over so many years...................0470, 0117<br>○数キロに亘る すうキロにわたる spanning over several kilometers...................0309 |
|---|---|---|

| **1395**<br>二 7<br>亙<br>1697<br>名 6 | In 旦 1392 the bottom line represented the eastern horizon, where the sun appears at the beginning of the day. Here we add a second horizontal line, to indicate an arbitrary end point for a time period during which the *sun* (日) **SPANS** the distance between one horizontal line and the next. Try to think of it as a <u>long</u> distance/period. ☞ 旦 1392, 宣 1398 |
|---|---|

| 恒 | **CONSTANT, permanent**<br><br>コウ | ○恒常 こうじょう constancy....................0321<br>恒産 こうさん fixed property....................0181<br>恒星 こうせい fixed star, sidereal............0755<br>恒例 こうれい established custom............0721<br>恒久 こうきゅう perpetuity, permanency.....0904 |
|---|---|---|

| **1396**<br>心 61<br>恆<br>0327<br>常 9 | *Mind* (忄) + *span* (亘): let this suggest **CONSTANCY** of mood or temperament. Note, however, that this character does not refer to a mental state but merely the fact of being **CONSTANT**/permanent. |
|---|---|

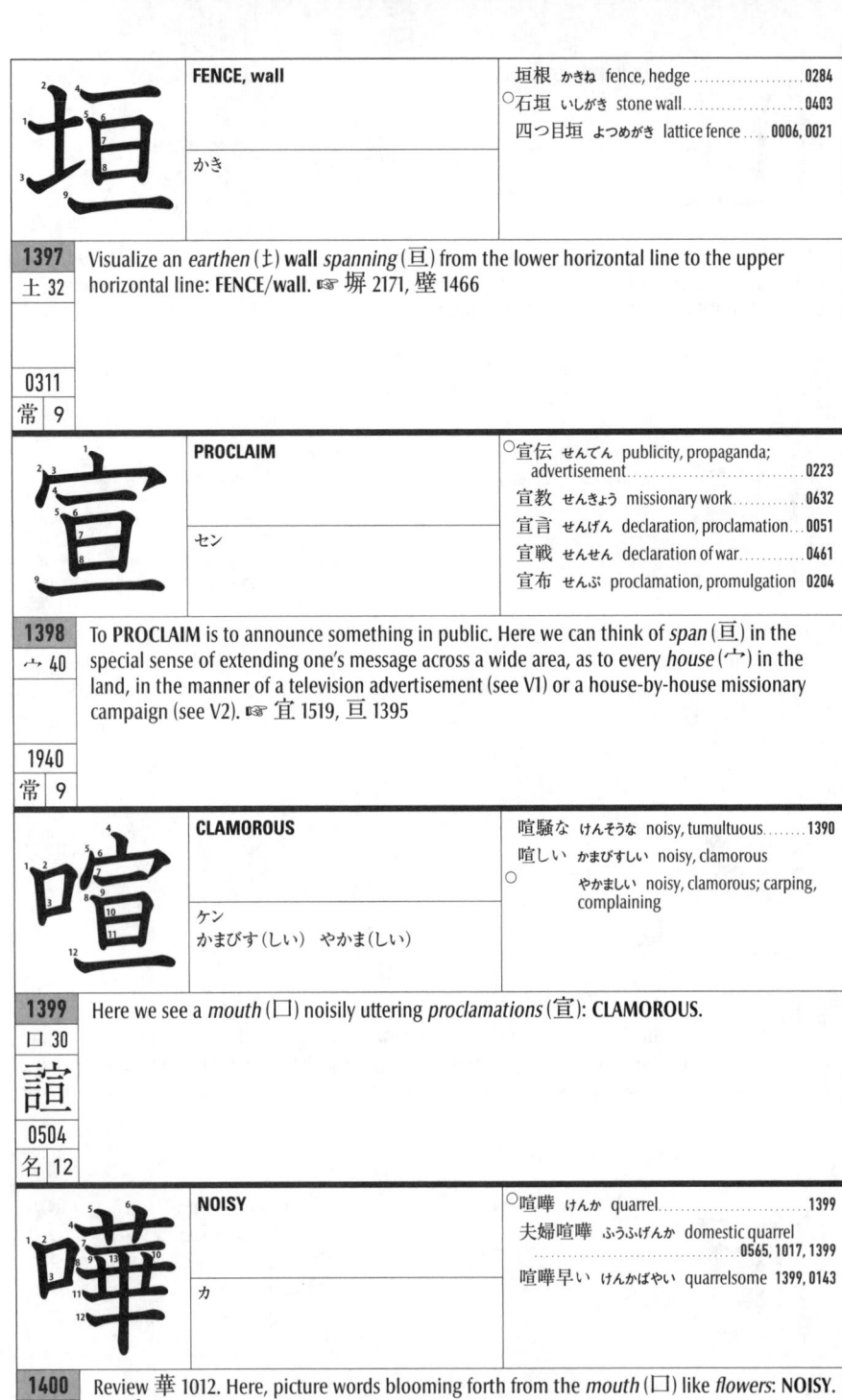

**FENCE, wall**

かき

垣根 かきね fence, hedge ..................0284
○石垣 いしがき stone wall ....................0403
四つ目垣 よつめがき lattice fence .....0006, 0021

| 1397 | |
| --- | --- |
| 土 32 | Visualize an *earthen* (土) **wall** *spanning* (亘) from the lower horizontal line to the upper horizontal line: **FENCE/wall**. ☞ 塀 2171, 壁 1466 |
| 0311 | |
| 常 9 | |

**PROCLAIM**

セン

○宣伝 せんでん publicity, propaganda; advertisement ..................................0223
宣教 せんきょう missionary work .............0632
宣言 せんげん declaration, proclamation ...0051
宣戦 せんせん declaration of war ............0461
宣布 せんぷ proclamation, promulgation 0204

| 1398 | |
| --- | --- |
| 宀 40 | To **PROCLAIM** is to announce something in public. Here we can think of *span* (亘) in the special sense of extending one's message across a wide area, as to every *house* (宀) in the land, in the manner of a television advertisement (see V1) or a house-by-house missionary campaign (see V2). ☞ 宜 1519, 亘 1395 |
| 1940 | |
| 常 9 | |

**CLAMOROUS**

ケン
かまびす(しい) やかま(しい)

喧騒な けんそうな noisy, tumultuous ........1390
喧しい かまびすしい noisy, clamorous
○ やかましい noisy, clamorous; carping, complaining

| 1399 | |
| --- | --- |
| 口 30 | Here we see a *mouth* (口) noisily uttering *proclamations* (宣): **CLAMOROUS**. |
| 諠 | |
| 0504 | |
| 名 12 | |

**NOISY**

カ

○喧嘩 けんか quarrel ..................................1399
夫婦喧嘩 ふうふげんか domestic quarrel
..................................................0565, 1017, 1399
喧嘩早い けんかばやい quarrelsome 1399, 0143

| 1400 | |
| --- | --- |
| 口 30 | Review 華 1012. Here, picture words blooming forth from the *mouth* (口) like *flowers*: **NOISY**. ☞ 唾 1401 |
| 譁 | |
| 0575 | |
| 名 13 | |

| | | |
|---|---|---|
| 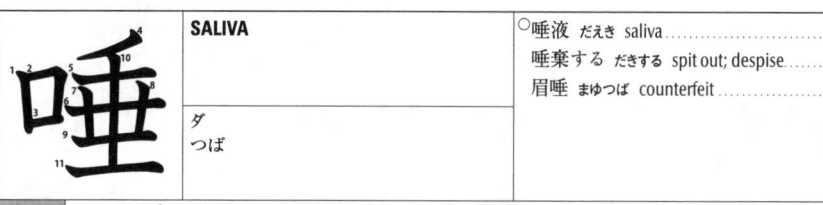 **唾** | **SALIVA**  ダ  つば | ○唾液 だえき saliva .................................... 0468  唾棄する だきする spit out; despise ......... 0606  眉唾 まゆつば counterfeit ...................... 0530 |

| **1401**  口 30  0416  常 11 | Review 垂 1004. Here, imagine **SALIVA** *dangling* (垂) down from the *mouth* (口). To remember the *kun-yomi*, think of all the つば in a tuba-player's mouthpiece. ☞ 嗶 1400 |
|---|---|

| | | |
|---|---|---|
|  **壺** | **JAR, pot**  コ  つぼ | ○油壺 あぶらつぼ oil can ....................... 0433  滝壺 たきつぼ pool beneath a waterfall ..... 0508  骨壺 こつつぼ funerary urn .................. 0465  たこ壺 たこつぼ octopus pot; foxhole  たん壺 たんつぼ spittoon, cuspidor |

| **1402**  土 33  壷  外 11 | Now we add a つぼ for our つば: a **JAR** (spittoon?) for our spit. Picture the *military man* (士) aiming across the room to spit into this wide-bellied **JAR/pot** (resembling 亜 0545). Note in the sample compounds that a spitting-pot is but one of many kinds of **JARS** or **pots** this character can refer to. |
|---|---|

| | | |
|---|---|---|
|  **坪** | **TSUBO (about 3.3 square meters)**  つぼ | 十坪 じっつぼ (=とつぼ) 10 *tsubo* ............ 0005  地坪 じつぼ land area ...................... 0187 |

| **1403**  土 32  0248  常 8 | A different kind of つぼ is the unit for **3.3 square meters**, intuitively referred to here by the combination "*flat* (平) *land* (土)" (regardless of gradient, land for sale must be measured on a flat plane). If you don't remember how to distinguish 平 0334 and 半 0335, now would be a good time to review. |
|---|---|

| | | |
|---|---|---|
|  **畔** | **WATERSIDE**  ハン | ○湖畔 こはん lakeside ....................... 0259  河畔 かはん riverside ...................... 0818  池畔 ちはん edge of a pond ............... 0188  旭川畔 あさひがわはん the banks of the Asahi River .......................... 1391, 0022 |

| **1404**  田 102  1060  常 10 | Here we observe a *rice field* (田) alongside a body of water. *Half* (半) of the *rice field* is on the **WATERSIDE** (the right-hand half, as pictured here). |
|---|---|

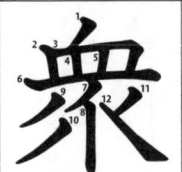

**MULTITUDE**

シュウ　シュ

民衆 みんしゅう populace, the people............ 0477
○ 大衆小説 たいしゅうしょうせつ popular novel, pulp
fiction ........................... 0033, 0034, 1197
公衆電話 こうしゅうでんわ public telephone
.............................. 0089, 0155, 0053
衆議院 しゅうぎいん House of Representatives
.................................... 0927, 0634
アメリカ合衆国 アメリカがっしゅうこく United States
of America ........................... 0227, 0075

| 1405 | |
|---|---|
| 血 143 | The lower portion of this character resembles the right-hand portion of 脈 1366. Here, imagine *blood* (血) "multiplying" along many branching bloodlines, as a single ancestor proliferates into a vast **MULTITUDE**. |
| 2342 | |
| 常 12 | |

**PHONETIC [i]**

イ

伊呂波 いろは *iroha*, the Japanese syllabary
.................................................... 1240
○ 日独伊 にちどくい Japan, Germany, and Italy;
Japanese-German-Italian.............. 0001, 0346
駐伊 ちゅうい stationed in Italy.............. 0367

| 1406 | |
|---|---|
| 人 9 | Visualize ⺕ as a *three-fingered hand* grasping a staff (S6). Here picture it using the staff to trace the katakana letter イ, which was in fact derived from this kanji. 伊 is used to represent the sound イ in kanji-based phonetic spellings, and as an abbreviation for Italy. ☞ 君 1407 |
| 0033 | |
| 名 6 | |

**¹ RULER**
**² FAMILIAR TITLE**
**³ YOU**

クン
きみ　-ぎみ

① 君主 くんしゅ monarch, sovereign ........... 0598
¹ 君臣 くんしん ruler and subject .............. 0484
¹ 君が代 きみがよ imperial reign; "Kimigayo"
(title of Japanese national anthem) ....... 0071
² 平野君 ひらのくん [familiar] Mr. Hirano
.................................... 0334, 0534
③ 君の きみの [familiar] your

| 1407 | |
|---|---|
| 口 30 | (Continuing from the previous entry) The hand wields the *staff* of authority (S4); the *mouth* (口) issues official orders: **RULER.** ☞ 伊 1406 |
| 2762 | |
| 常 7 | |

**GROUP, crowd, flock**

グン
む(れる)　む(れ)　むら　むら(がる)

群衆 ぐんしゅう crowd of people, multitude 1405
群集 ぐんしゅう crowd, mob ................. 0190
○ 魚群 ぎょぐん school of fish ................. 0492
蜂が群がっている はちがむらがっている bees are
swarming................................. 1381
○ 羊の群れ ひつじのむれ flock of sheep ...... 0490

| 1408 | |
|---|---|
| 羊 123 | Here we observe a flock of *sheep* (羊) following their *ruler* (君, the shepherd, who holds a shepherd's staff): **flock/crowd/GROUP.** |
| 1400 | |
| 常 13 | |

**COUNTY**

グン

○郡部 ぐんぶ counties; rural districts.........0068
郡制 ぐんせい county system ...............0708
郡県 ぐんけん counties and prefectures ....0844
名西郡 みょうざいぐん Myozai district...0269, 0795

| 1409 | *Ruler*(君) + *town*(阝). This suggests the ruler of an area centered on a major town: a count. A count rules over a **COUNTY**. ☞ 那 1410, 邦 1411 |
| 邑 163 | |
| 1333 | |
| 常 10 | |

**PHONETIC [na]**

ナ

○旦那 だんな master, husband, patron, protector; sir; donor.........1392
利那 せつな a[the] moment................0523
利那的 せつなてき momentary, fleeting
.........0523, 0169

| 1410 | It suffices to distinguish this character from the ones before and after it, and to note its use in VI, which you should practice writing out and pronouncing. ☞ 郡 1409, 邦 1411 |
| 邑 163 | |
| 0748 | |
| 常 7 | |

**¹ STATE**
**² JAPAN**

ホウ

①連邦 れんぽう federation, confederation, union
.........0582
¹ 盟邦 めいほう ally, allied powers ...........1305
¹ 東邦 とうほう eastern country, Oriental nation; the Orient.........0032
②邦人 ほうじん Japanese, fellow countryman 0015
² 邦楽 ほうがく Japanese music................0302

| 1411 | Think of S1–4 as a fence or palisade. Together with 阝 *walls around the edge of town*, this suggests the boundaries around the territory of an independent political entity, or **STATE**. M2 is an extended meaning. ☞ 那 1410, 郡 1409 |
| 邑 163 | |
| 0750 | |
| 常 7 | |

**SUBURB**

コウ

○郊外 こうがい suburbs, outskirts.........0266
近郊 きんこう suburbs, outskirts ...........0194
断郊競走 だんこうきょうそう cross-country race
.........0849, 1204, 0140

| 1412 | *Crossing*(交) the *walls around the edge of town*(阝) takes you into the **SUBURBS**. Note that, except for 較 0693, all kanji incorporating 交 follow its *on* reading, コウ. |
| 邑 163 | |
| 1181 | |
| 常 9 | |

| | EFFECT | ○効果 こうか effect, efficacy; result............0599 |
| | | 効率 こうりつ efficiency.....................0752 |
| | | 有効な ゆうこうな effective, valid ...........0400 |
| | コウ | 発効する はっこうする take effect, come into force....................0148 |
| | き(く) | ○良く効く よくきく It works/is effective .......0285 |

| **1413** | Crossing/interchanging (交) + strengths (力). Informed by the economic theory of compara- |
| 力 19 | tive advantage, we can derive the idea of **EFFECTIVENESS** from the way this character implies |
| 効 | "exchanging strength with strength," each individual doing what he or she does with the |
| | greatest **EFFECT**. |
| 1164 | |
| 常 8 | |

| | ¹ STRANGLE | ①絞殺する こうさつする strangle, hang .......0522 |
| | ² WRING | ¹絞首刑 こうしゅけい execution by hanging ...........0157, 0722 |
| | | ①首を絞める くびをしめる strangle, wring the neck.....................0157 |
| | コウ | ②お絞り おしぼり wet towel, steamed towel |
| | しぼ(る) し(める) し(まる) | ² 雑巾を絞る ぞうきんをしぼる wring a floorcloth .....................0379, 0203 |

| **1414** | Imagine either end of a rope (糸) looping around someone's neck and then crossing (交): |
| 糸 120 | **STRANGLE; WRING**. As a shortcut, visualize S11–12 as the two ends of the rope closing around |
| 絞 | the neck. Do not confuse 絞る (しぼる, wring) with 縛る (しばる, bind; see 0984), or 搾る |
| | (しぼる, squeeze, extract; see next entry). ☞ 紋 1416 |
| 1236 | |
| 常 12 | |

| | SQUEEZE, extract | 搾油 さくゆ oil expression/extraction.......0433 |
| | | 搾乳 さくにゅう milking.....................0160 |
| | | 圧搾する あっさくする press, compress.....0186 |
| | サク | ○搾取する さくしゅする exploit .................0059 |
| | しぼ(る) | 搾り立てのオレンジジュース しぼりたての オレンジジュース freshly squeezed orange juice ........................0067 |

| **1415** | Imagine you are trying to **extract** a painful splinter from your hand: first you saw (乍) a hole |
| 手 64 | (穴) in your hand (扌), then you **SQUEEZE** out the splinter. Now practice writing and distin- |
| 搾 | guishing the meanings of the three verbs listed at the end of the previous entry. |
| 0594 | |
| 常 13 | |

| | CREST | 家紋 かもん family crest/badge.............0219 |
| | | 紋様 もんよう crest pattern.................0501 |
| | | 紋織り もんおり figured textiles.............1088 |
| | モン | 波紋 はもん ripple; stir, sensation...........0598 |
| | | ○指紋 しもん fingerprint.....................0932 |

| **1416** | Thread (糸) + writing (文): indicates the distinctive insignia "written" in thread on a flag, |
| 糸 120 | uniform, etc.—a CREST. ☞ 絞 1414 |
| 1194 | |
| 常 10 | |

| 菊 | **CHRYSANTHEMUM** | 菊花　きっか　chrysanthemum ..............0121 |
|---|---|---|
| | | 菊人形　きくにんぎょう　chrysanthemum figure [doll] ................................0015, 0147 |
| | キク | 野菊　のぎく　wild chrysanthemum; aster ...0534 |
| | | 白菊　しらぎく　white chrysanthemum .......0076 |
| | | ○菊の御紋　きくのごもん　imperial crest of the chrysanthemum.................0862, 1416 |

**1417**
艹 140

The variety of **CHRYSANTHEMUM** most often seen in Japan is a large, tufty flower. In this kanji, 米 represents the flower's long, tightly gathered petals, while ケ suggests its *elephant*ine size, and 艹 implies *plant*. Note that the chrysanthemum is used in the Japanese Imperial Seal, and that the *on* reading キク is unique in this course.

1999
常 11

---

| 帝 | **EMPEROR** | 帝王　ていおう　monarch, emperor ..........0072 |
|---|---|---|
| | | 皇帝　こうてい　emperor ......................0077 |
| | | ○帝国　ていこく　empire, imperial .............0075 |
| | テイ | 帝国主義　ていこくしゅぎ　imperialism ........0075, 0365, 0926 |
| | みかど* | 帝政　ていせい　imperial government ........0246 |

**1418**
巾 50

Visualize the **EMPEROR**, wearing a special ceremonial belt (S5–6) and *cloth* gown (巾). ☞ 帯 1232

1786
常 9

---

| | ¹ **CONCLUDE, contract** | ①締結する　ていけつする　conclude, contract...0516 |
|---|---|---|
| | ² **TIGHTEN** | ¹ 締約　ていやく　conclusion of a treaty.........0170 |
| | | ①締め切り　しめきり　closing day, deadline; Closed, No Entrance [sign] .................0086 |
| | テイ | ² ベルトを締める　ベルトをしめる　fasten one's belt |
| | し（まる）　し（まり）　し（める）　-し（め） | ² 取り締まる　とりしまる　manage, control; |
| | -じ（め） | superintend ...............................0059 |

**1419**
糸 120

Here let 糸 *cord* represent the cords of the *emperor* (帝)'s belt (S11–12). Now visualize the cords of his belt **TIGHTENING**, symbolic of the uncompromising restrictions on his public and private behavior. M2 **contract/CONCLUDE** is an extended meaning.

1274
常 15

---

| | **GIVE UP** | ○諦める　あきらめる　give up; resign oneself to |
|---|---|---|
| | | 諦め　あきらめ　resignation, acceptance |
| | | 諦観　ていかん　realistic vision, resignation ...1128 |
| | テイ | |
| | あきら（める） | |

**1420**
言 149

Building on the previous entry, now visualize the *emperor*, weary of living under such tight constraints, announcing (言) his abdication: "I **GIVE UP**." Now practice writing and distinguishing the meanings of the last three entries.

1444
常 16

| | ENJOY, receive | |
|---|---|---|
| | | 享受する きょうじゅする enjoy, receive, be given ...... 0065 |
| | | 享有する きょうゆうする enjoy, possess ...... 0400 |
| | | 享楽 きょうらく enjoyment ...... 0302 |
| | キョウ | ○享年 きょうねん age at death ...... 0117 |

| 1421 | Means **ENJOY** in the sense of **receiving** something beneficial. Here we see the *child* (子) **receive** the benefit of some additional *height* (from 高 0185). Now think of the hardships you suffered when you were small, and all the benefits you **ENJOYED** once you grew *tall*. As a grapheme, 享 will mean *growing child*. ☞ 享 1423 |
|---|---|
| 亠 8 | |
| 1765 | |
| 常 8 | |

| | OUTER ENCLOSURE | |
|---|---|---|
| | | ○外郭 がいかく outer enclosure; outline, contour ...... 0266 |
| | | 輪郭 りんかく contour, outline, profile ...... 0944 |
| | カク | 城郭 じょうかく castle, fortress; castle walls, enclosure ...... 1298 |

| 1422 | Here we observe the *growing child* (享) trying unsuccessfully to scale the *walls around the edge of town* (阝): **OUTER ENCLOSURE**. |
|---|---|
| 邑 163 | |
| 1499 | |
| 常 11 | |

| | ¹ INN, restaurant ² PSEUDONYM SUFFIX | |
|---|---|---|
| | | ¹ 亭主 ていしゅ husband; master, host ...... 0365 |
| | | ¹ 亭主関白 ていしゅかんぱく overbearing husband ...... 0365, 0451, 0076 |
| | | ① 旅亭 りょてい inn, hotel ...... 0569 |
| | テイ | ① 料亭 りょうてい high-class restaurant, Japanese restaurant ...... 0758 |
| | | ² 二葉亭 ふたばてい Futabatei [writer's name] ...... 0003, 0605 |

| 1423 | Recall that 丁 0437 depicts a T-shaped intersection, and that 高 0185 depicts a tall building. Now visualize in this character a *tall* **INN**/**restaurant** situated at a *T-shaped intersection*. ☞ 享 1421 |
|---|---|
| 亠 8 | |
| 1785 | |
| 常 9 | |

| | STOP | |
|---|---|---|
| | | ○停止 ていし stop, halt; suspension ...... 0042 |
| | | 停車 ていしゃ stoppage (of a vehicle) ...... 0125 |
| | | 停学 ていがく suspension from school ...... 0099 |
| | テイ | 停職 ていしょく suspension from office ...... 1087 |
| | | バスの停留所 バスのていりゅうじょ bus stop (abbr. バス停) ...... 1170, 0249 |

| 1424 | Picture a *man* (亻) **STOPPING** at the T-shaped intersection where the tall *inn* (亭) is located. |
|---|---|
| 人 9 | |
| 0121 | |
| 常 11 | |

**INSECT**

コン

°昆虫 こんちゅう insect ......................... 0343
昆虫学 こんちゅうがく entomology .....0343, 0099
昆布 こんぶ (=こぶ) sea tangle, kelp ......... 0204

---

**1425**
日 72

We now come to the beginning of a rather formidable snarl of fifteen or so intertwining look-alike characters. To untangle them all, we shall have to take care to review distinctions and similarities as we go. Here, visualize 比 as a pair of **INSECTS** buzzing about on a *sunny*(日) day. ☞ 皆 1427

**2138**
常 8

---

**MIX, mixed up**

コン
ま(じる) -ま(じり) ま(ざる) ま(ぜる)
こ(む)

混血 こんけつ mixed-blood, racial mixture 0198
混合 こんごう mixing, mixture ............... 0227
°混雑 こんざつ confusion, disorder, congestion
.................................................. 0379
混乱 こんらん disorder, confusion, chaos... 0380
°混ぜる まぜる mix, blend, scramble

---

**1426**
水 85

Now picture the *insects*(昆) **MIXING** (reproducing) in *water*(氵).

**0475**
常 11

---

**ALL, everything, everyone**

カイ
みな みんな*

皆目 かいもく altogether, wholly; (not) at all 0021
°皆無 かいむ nothing ........................... 0048
国民皆兵 こくみんかいへい universal conscrip-
tion .................................. 0075, 0477, 0907
皆様 みなさま everybody, ladies and gentlemen
.................................................. 0501
°皆て みなて all/everyone together

---

**1427**
白 106

Take 白 as a variant of 自 (indicating one's *self*), and the pair of seated people (比) as a pair of one's fellows. **ALL** three are gathered together. ☞ 背 0124, 昆 1425

**2160**
常 9

---

**BLOCK CHARACTER STYLE**

カイ

°楷書 かいしょ block [square] style used in writing or printing Chinese characters ............. 0079

---

**1428**
木 75

Refers to the **BLOCK CHARACTER STYLE** used in printing and non-cursive writing, in which *all*(皆) characters are written with the regular straightness of a *tree*(木). Note that all three characters incorporating 皆 follow its *on* reading, カイ.

**0929**
常 13

| | | HARMONY | ○諧調 かいちょう harmony, melody ............0306 |
|---|---|---|---|
| | | | 俳諧 はいかい humorous *waka* poem.......0740 |
| | | カイ | |
| **1429** 言 149 | All (皆) words (言) in agreement: **HARMONY**. | | |
| **1442** 常 16 | | | |

| | | ¹ **FLOOR, story** | ¹三階 さんがい third floor ......................0004 |
|---|---|---|---|
| | | ² **RANK, class** | ○階段 かいだん steps, flight of stairs .........0521 |
| | | | ²段階 だんかい grade, rank, step, stage ....0521 |
| | | | ②階層 かいそう social stratum, class; tier .....1224 |
| | | カイ | ²位階 いかい court, rank ......................0577 |
| **1430** 阜 170 | See 阝 as calling attention to the two levels in 皆 1427: its upper bulge points to the upper **FLOOR/story** occupied by one's two friends (比); its lower bulge points to the lower **FLOOR/story** occupied by one's self (白). M2 **RANK/class** is an extended meaning. ☞ 陛 1431 | | |
| **0569** 常 12 | | | |

| | | **IMPERIAL PALACE STEPS** | ○陛下 へいか His/Her/Your Majesty .........0040 |
|---|---|---|---|
| | | | 天皇陛下 てんのうへいか His Majesty the Emperor, His Imperial Majesty...0270, 0077, 0040 |
| | | ヘイ | |
| **1431** 阜 170 | As in the previous entry, let 阝 suggest different levels. At the top we find a pair of seated people (比), here representing the emperor and empress. Now picture their Highnesses descending the **IMPERIAL PALACE STEPS** toward the *ground* (土). Learn to recognize this kanji and the ones before and after it by how they differ. ☞ 階 1430, 陸 1432 | | |
| **0409** 常 10 | | | |

| | | **LAND** | ○大陸 たいりく continent ......................0033 |
|---|---|---|---|
| | | | 陸兵 りくへい land troops ......................0907 |
| | | | 陸軍 りくぐん army ..............................0583 |
| | | リク | 着陸 ちゃくりく landing, alighting ............0938 |
| | | | 陸上 りくじょう land, ground; shore; track and field ....................................................0041 |
| **1432** 阜 170 | Review 先 0134. In the next few entries, the grapheme 坴 draws our attention to the sub-strate of *earth* (土) situated beneath 先's roots. We'll call it *earth's crust* (not to be confused with 圭). To signify **LAND** (in the sense of "not the sea"), we take *earth's crust* and add *hills* (阝). The reading リク is unique in this course. ☞ 陵 1438, 陛 1431, 睦 1433 | | |
| **0496** 常 11 | | | |

| | FRIENDLY, intimate | 親睦 しんぼく friendliness, amity, intimacy 0276 |
| | | 和睦 わぼく reconciliation, peace ........... 0236 |
| | ボク | 睦む むつむ get along well |
| | むつ(まじい)* むつ(む)* | 睦まじい むつまじい friendly, intimate |
| | | 広尾の睦会 ひろおのむつみかい Hiroo [neighborhood] club/association .......... 0238, 0488 |

| 1433 | This character represents the idea of **intimate** familiarity: an *eye* (目) sees all the way down below the roots and into the *earth's crust* (坴): **intimate/FRIENDLY.** ☞ 陸 1432 |
| 目 109 | |
| 1107 | |
| 常 13 | |

| | ¹ POWER, force<br>² CONDITION, trend | ①勢い良く いきおいよく forcibly, with vigor... 0285 |
| | | ¹ 勢力 せいりょく power, force, influence...... 0084 |
| | | ①大勢 おおぜい crowd, great number of ..... 0033 |
| | セイ | ② 大勢 たいせい general trend |
| | いきお(い) | ² 情勢 じょうせい state of things, situation .... 0973 |

| 1434 | 坴 *earth's crust* and 丸 *round* together make 埶 *the round earth*. This kanji illustrates the idea of **POWER** by showing 力 *power* carrying the whole *round earth* on its back. Associate M1 **POWER** with M2 **CONDITION/trend** via the idea of the current state of one's strength. Now go back and peek at the old form of 芸 0225. ☞ 熱 1435 |
| 力 19 | |
| 2487 | |
| 常 13 | |

| | HEAT, hot | 高熱 こうねつ intense heat; high fever ...... 0185 |
| | | 熱望 ねつぼう fervent hope, earnest desire 1066 |
| | | 熱烈な ねつれつな ardent, fervent ......... 0719 |
| | ネツ | ○情熱 じょうねつ passion, enthusiasm ....... 0973 |
| | あつ(い) | ○熱いコーヒー あついコーヒー hot coffee |

| 1435 | Below *the round earth* (埶) a *fire* (灬) burns: the earth's **HOT** core. The reading ネツ is unique in this course. ☞ 勢 1434, 熟 1436, 塾 1437 |
| 火 86 | |
| 2495 | |
| 常 15 | |

| | MATURE, ripe | ○未熟な みじゅくな unripe, immature; unskilled ........... 0271 |
| | | 円熟した えんじゅくした mature, fully developed ........... 0013 |
| | | 習熟する しゅうじゅくする become practiced (in) ........... 0420 |
| | ジュク | 熟語 じゅくご compound word; phrase, idiom ........... 0222 |
| | う(れる) | ○熟れる うれる ripen, mature |

| 1436 | 享 (*growing child*) and 丸 (*round*) together make 孰 (*well-rounded child*). To this add a low *flame* (灬), for tempering: **MATURE.** ☞ 熱 1435, 塾 1437 |
| 火 86 | |
| 2498 | |
| 常 15 | |

**PRIVATE SCHOOL**

ジュク

塾長 じゅくちょう principal of a private school 0091
塾生 じゅくせい student of a private school…0036
入塾 にゅうじゅく entering a private school…0039
○英語塾 えいごじゅく private school for the study
of English ………………………………0332, 0222
塾を開く じゅくをひらく open a private school 0450

| 1437 | |
|---|---|
| 土 32 | Here 土 shifts our attention to the *place* where the *well-rounded child* (孰) develops: **PRIVATE SCHOOL.** ☞ 熟 1435, 熟 1436 |
| 2490 | |
| 常 14 | |

陵

リョウ
みささぎ

**IMPERIAL MAUSOLEUM, hill**

○丘陵 きゅうりょう hill, hillock ……………0906
陵墓 りょうぼ imperial tomb ……………1340
御陵 ごりょう imperial mausoleum ………0862

| 1438 | |
|---|---|
| 阜 170 | Only 夂 distinguishes this kanji from 陸 1432, so focus on that. Imagine that emperors are buried with *crossed legs* (夂), just as the Egyptian pharaohs were buried with crossed arms. Thus a *hill* (阝, i.e., a tumulus) where one finds *crossed legs buried beneath the roots* (夌) could only be an **IMPERIAL MAUSOLEUM.** ☞ 陸 1432 |
| 0497 | |
| 常 11 | |

**RHOMBUS**

リョウ
ひし

菱形 ひしがた diamond shape, rhombus…0147
○三菱 みつびし Mitsubishi [company name]
………………………………………………0004

| 1439 | |
|---|---|
| 艸 140 | We know not to confuse this character with 陵 1438 IMPERIAL MAUSOLEUM because it has no *hill* (阝) under which to inter an emperor. We thus turn our attention to its shape—wide at the center and narrow at top and bottom—which suggests a **RHOMBUS** ◇. |
| 2003 | |
| 名 11 | |

俊

シュン

**BRILLIANT PERSON**

俊才 しゅんさい genius…………………………0652
○俊傑 しゅんけつ genius, hero……………1176
俊英 しゅんえい talent, genius; gifted person 0332
俊童 しゅんどう brilliant boy, infant prodigy 0537

| 1440 | |
|---|---|
| 人 9 | Review 酸 0800. Here, we have a *"sharply stimulating"* (夋) *person* (亻): **BRILLIANT PERSON.** ☞ 酸 0800, 唆 1441, 傑 1176 |
| 0086 | |
| 常 9 | |

**INSTIGATE**

サ
そそのか(す)

教唆 きょうさ instigation, incitement ........0632
○示唆する しさする suggest, hint ............0311
○唆す そそのかす instigate, egg on, incite
人に悪事を唆す ひとにあくじをそそのかす incite
a person to do something wrong
................................0015, 0546, 0080

**1441**

口 30

A *mouth* (口) giving a *sharp stimulus* (夋), that is, **INSTIGATING** someone to do something. ☞ 俊 1440, 酸 0800

0361
常 10

---

**TO BE EXPECTED**

カツ
はず

¹ ここから見える筈だ ここからみえるはずだ It should be visible from here ..............0083
① その筈だ そのはずだ That is to be expected, You would think so

**1442**

竹 118

Originally this meant "notch of an arrow," but it is mainly used today to express the idea "**TO BE EXPECTED**." Recalling the ancient use of bamboo for keeping records and figures, picture the *tongue* (舌) pronouncing a figure tallied on *bamboo* (⺮), indicating it as one's estimate, as the **EXPECTED** figure. ☞ 箸 1443, 笑 0579

2336
名 12

---

**CHOPSTICKS**

チョ*
はし

○お箸 おはし chopsticks
取り箸 とりばし chopsticks for serving ......0059
火箸 ひばし tongs .............................0026

**1443**

竹 118

箸

Here a *person* (者) uses *bamboo* (⺮) as an instrument for eating or serving: a pair of **CHOP-STICKS**. The final dot stroke, just above 日, appears in 者-based kanji that have not officially been simplified (including 賭 and 儲, just below). As the variant forms indicate, you will also see these kanji written without this final stroke. ☞ 筈 1442, 著 0707

2363
常 15

---

**HOT, summer heat**

ショ
あつ(い)

猛暑 もうしょ fierce heat .......................0767
○暑中 しょちゅう midsummer ..................0035
暑熱 しょねつ heat of summer ...............1435
○蒸し暑い むしあつい sultry, sweltering ......0960
真夏の暑さ まなつのあつさ heat of high summer.................................0838, 0363

**1444**

日 72

暑

The **HOT summer** *sun* (日) scorches this hapless *person* (者). Alternatively, see an *elder* (耂) being scorched between two **HOT summer** *suns*. Though the *on-yomi* of 者 0107 is シャ, most kanji incorporating it on the bottom or right side (as here and in the following entries) are read チョ or ショ, and all have the short vowel. ☞ 著 0707, 署 1445

2182
常 12

| | ¹ GOVERNMENT OFFICE<br>² SIGN ONE'S NAME | ¹ 警察署 けいさつしょ police station.....0806, 0639<br>① 消防署 しょうぼうしょ fire station.......1289, 0174<br>¹ 税務署 ぜいむしょ tax office............1195, 0687<br>② 署名 しょめい signature, autograph.........0269<br>² 代署する だいしょする sign for another.....0071 |
| ショ | |

| 1445<br>网 122<br>署<br>2263<br>常 13 | Review 憲 0417, where we added the meaning *law* for 罒. Here see a *person* (者) inside a **GOVERNMENT OFFICE**, such as a city office or police station. The "wide net of the *law*" covers him; that is, he is under legal authority. For M2, note that **SIGNING ONE'S NAME** puts a person under legal obligation. ☞ 箸 1443, 著 0707, 暑 1444 |

| | **DAWN** | 曙光 しょこう first streak of daylight, dawn...0137<br>○時代の曙 じだいのあけぼの dawn of a new era<br>.............................................0383, 0071<br>曙色 あけぼのいろ yellowish pink............0528 |
| ショ<br>あけぼの | |

| 1446<br>日 72<br>曙<br>1002<br>名 17 | Think of a *government office* (署) near where you live, such as a police station or fire station. Someone is on duty there around the clock—even when the *sun* (日)'s first rays shine upon it at **DAWN**, as depicted here. |

| | **WAGER** | 賭する とする stake, risk; bet, wager<br>賭博 とばく gambling.........................0983<br>○金を賭ける かねをかける bet money........0029<br>賭け かけ bet, wager<br>賭け金 かけきん stakes, bet.................0029 |
| ト<br>か(ける) | |

| 1447<br>貝 154<br>賭<br>1451<br>常 16 | Here we observe a *person* (者) presenting *money* (貝) as a **WAGER**. |

| | **VARIOUS, all kinds of** | 諸島 しょとう archipelago....................0341<br>諸君 しょくん Ladies and Gentlemen, my friends,<br>you .........................................1407<br>○諸国 しょこく various/all countries..........0075<br>諸説 しょせつ various views/theories.......1197<br>諸般の しょはんの various, several, all, every 0671 |
| ショ | |

| 1448<br>言 149<br>諸<br>1427<br>常 15 | *Words* (言) + *people* (者): let this combination suggest the **VARIOUS** languages people speak.<br>☞ 儲 1449 |

**PROFIT**

チョ
もう(ける)　もう(かる)　もう(け)

○儲ける　もうける　profit, make (money)
儲かる　もうかる　yield a profit, be profitable
儲け　もうけ　profit
儲け役　もうけやく　lucrative post..............0518
大儲け　おおもうけ　large profit..............0033

| 1449 | Visualize two *persons* (亻 and 者) exchanging *words* (言) in negotiating a sweet deal: **PROFIT**. |
| 人 9 | ☞ 諸 1448 |

儲

0157
名 18

---

**¹ OUTSET, beginning**
**² LINE, thread (of events)**

ショ　チョ
お

¹ 緒言　しょげん（＝ちょげん）　preface, foreword　0051
¹ 緒戦　しょせん（＝ちょせん）　beginning of hostilities
.............................................................0461
² 由緒　ゆいしょ　history, lineage..............0432
②一緒に　いっしょに　together; at the same time; in
a lump.............................................0002
² へその緒　へそのお　umbilical cord

| 1450 | Visualize the *person* (者) reaching down and taking the near end of the *thread* (that is, its |
| 糸 120 | **beginning** or **OUTSET**), and then following the thread right down the **LINE**, like a detective |
| | following a **thread of events**. It helps to visualize S10 as the **LINE** or **thread of events** being |
| | followed. |

緒

1260
常 14

---

**OLD MAN**

オウ
おきな*

○老翁　ろうおう　old man.......................0629
城本翁　しろもとおう　the revered old Mr.
Shiromoto.........................1298, 0031
翁面　おきなめん　Noh mask for old man char-
acter...........................................0175

| 1451 | Recall 羽 *wings*. Ignore 公's meaning and instead visualize it as a weary **OLD MAN** spreading |
| 羽 124 | his angel wings (S1–2) as he prepares to fly up toward heaven. |

1809
常 10

---

**OLD WOMAN**

バ
ばあ*

○老婆　ろうば　old woman.....................0629
老婆心　ろうばしん　grandmotherly solicitude
.........................................0629, 0056
産婆　さんば　midwife.........................0181
○お婆さん　おばあさん　old woman, old wife,
grandma

| 1452 | A *woman* (女) pounded many times by the *waves* (波) of aging: **OLD WOMAN**. As you begin |
| 女 38 | this set of kanji that incorporate 女 at the bottom, it would be a good idea to review the |
| | ones you have already seen: 委 0396 and 要 0547. ☞ 姿 1453 |

2407
常 11

**FIGURE, appearance; posture**

シ
すがた

容姿 ようし　face and figure, appearance....1037
○姿勢 しせい　posture, position, poise, attitude
.........................................1434
姿態 したい　figure, person; pose...........0893
○姿を消す すがたをけす　disappear...........1289
パジャマ姿て パジャマすがたて　in pajamas

| 1453 | *Woman* (女) + *next/secondary* (次): visualize 次 as the "secondary" **appearance** of the woman, that is, her shadow cast across the floor. In this way let 次 visually represent the outline of the woman's form: her **FIGURE** or **posture**. ☞ 婆 1452 |
|---|---|
| 女 38 | |
| 2291 | |
| 常 9 | |

**ARBITRARY**

シ

恣意 しい　arbitrariness.......................0151
○恣意的 しいてき　arbitrary, as one pleases
.................................0151, 0169

| 1454 | *Mind* (心) + *next/secondary* (次): let this suggest a person who immediately follows through on whatever idea occurs to him: **ARBITRARY**. Note the slight difference between the top portions of this entry and the last one. We shall treat both forms as 次. |
|---|---|
| 心 61 | |
| 2304 | |
| 常 10 | |

**RASH, outrageous**

モウ ボウ

○妄想 もうそう　wild idea, paranoiac delusion
.........................................0683
妄想症 もうそうしょう　paranoia.........0683, 0618
妄信 もうしん　blind belief, credulity.........0009
妄言 ぼうげん (=もうげん)　rash remark, thought-
less words.................................0051

| 1455 | Here 亡 does not suggest a *deceased woman*, but rather a <u>demented</u> one: **RASH/outrageous**. ☞ 要 0547 |
|---|---|
| 女 38 | |
| 1739 | |
| 常 6 | |

**WILT, wither**

イ
なえ(る)　しぼ(む)*　しお(れる)*
しな(びる)*

○萎縮する いしゅくする　wither, waste away...0875
萎縮症 いしゅくしょう　atrophy..........0875, 0618
○萎える なえる　wilt, wither, weaken
萎れる しおれる　wilt, wither; lose heart
萎びる しなびる　wilt, shrivel

| 1456 | Distinguished from 委 0396 by the extra *grass* (艹) piled on top of *rice* (禾), causing 女 to **WILT** visibly under the additional load. ☞ 委 0396 |
|---|---|
| 艸 140 | |
| 1996 | |
| 常 11 | |

| | WIFE | 妻子 さいし one's wife and children, one's family ....0094 |
|---|---|---|
| | サイ<br>つま | ○夫妻 ふさい husband and wife, Mr. and Mrs. 0565<br>森様御夫妻 もりさまごふさい Mr. and Mrs. Mori ....0241, 0501, 0862, 0565<br>良妻 りょうさい good wife....0285<br>○妻にする つまにする marry (a woman) |

| 1457 | Review 婦 1017. Here, visualize a *woman* holding a broom: **WIFE**. |
|---|---|
| 女 38 | |
| 2214 | |
| 常 8 | |

| | TREMENDOUS, terrible | ○凄惨な せいさんな ghastly, gruesome....1239 |
|---|---|---|
| | セイ<br>すご(い)* すさ(まじい)* すご(む)* | 凄絶な せいぜつな horrifying, bone-chilling 1271<br>○物凄い ものすごい tremendous, terrific; terrible, awful....0172<br>凄まじい すさまじい tremendous, terrific; terrible, awful<br>凄くない? すごくない? Pretty awesome, huh? |

| 1458 | Imagine a **TREMENDOUS, terrible** *wife* (妻) who is as cold as *ice* (冫). |
|---|---|
| 冫 15 | |
| 凄 | |
| 0110 | |
| 常 10 | |

| | ¹ CHAPTER; writing<br>² BADGE | ¹ 章句 しょうく passage, chapter and verse....0166 |
|---|---|---|
| | ショウ | ①第一章 だいいっしょう Chapter 1....1191, 0002<br>¹ 文章 ぶんしょう writing, composition, essay; prose....0101<br>②腕章 わんしょう armband, arm badge....0732<br>² 紋章 もんしょう crest, family insignia, coat of arms....1416 |

| 1459 | Imagine the *sound* (音) of a *needle* (十) (see 針 0556) bobbing in and out of a slave's forehead, marking him with a tattoo. This kanji ultimately derives from that barbaric act of inscribing a person with a distinguishing mark or **BADGE**, which later became associated with the idea of **writing** and, by extension, **CHAPTER**. ☞ 童 0537 |
|---|---|
| 立 117 | |
| 1819 | |
| 常 11 | |

| | PROCLAIM MERITS | ○表彰する ひょうしょうする commend (officially), give public recognition....0705 |
|---|---|---|
| | ショウ | |

| 1460 | Here visualize 彡 as a three-striped *badge*, like that worn by military officers of a certain rank. The purpose of the *three-striped badge*, like any military decoration, is to **PROCLAIM** the officer's **MERITS**. See 顕 1921 for an additional sample compound. Note that both kanji incorporating 章 follow its *on* reading, ショウ. |
|---|---|
| 彡 59 | |
| 1647 | |
| 常 14 | |

| | HINDRANCE | ○障害 しょうがい obstacle; (physical) disability **0413** |
|---|---|---|
| | | 故障 こしょう malfunction, breakdown; hindrance, obstacle, accident ........................**0257** |
| | | 障子 しょうじ paper sliding door, *shoji*.......**0094** |
| | ショウ<br>さわ(る) | 保障する ほしょうする (ensure that an undesirable condition does not occur) guarantee, secure, ensure ........................**0646** |
| | | ○障る さわる hinder, interfere with |

| **1461** | |
|---|---|
| 阜 170 | A man in Colombia once operated a mobile library called the Biblioburro using two donkeys— Alfa and Beto. In this character, imagine Alfa and Beto trying to deliver the next *chapter* (章) of a serial novel to an isolated village located on the other side of the *hills* (阝). The *hills* present a **HINDRANCE** to the *chapter*'s progress. ☞ 阻 1517 |
| **0647** | |
| 常 14 | |

| | ¹ **PUNGENT, spicy**<br>² **HARD, painful** | ①辛い からい pungent, hot; salty; dry (wine) |
|---|---|---|
| | | ② つらい painful, bitter |
| | | ¹ 塩辛い しおからい salty ........................**1306** |
| | シン<br>から(い) つら(い)* | ² 辛苦 しんく hardships, trials; labor, trouble **0405** |
| | | ②辛抱 しんぼう patience, endurance ..........**0664** |

| **1462** | |
|---|---|
| 辛 160 | The poor *standing* man (立) undergoes the **HARD** and **painful** ordeal of standing <u>directly</u> on a *needle* (十) (note how this differs from 章 above). The **pain** he feels in his feet is comparable to the sharp pain we feel in our mouths when we eat **PUNGENT** or **spicy** foods. As a grapheme, 辛 will generally go by the label *pain*. ☞ 幸 1470 |
| **1755** | |
| 常 7 | |

| | PRESIDE, manage | ○主宰する しゅさいする preside (over), superintend ........................**0365** |
|---|---|---|
| | | 主宰者 しゅさいしゃ president, chairman, leader ........................**0365, 0107** |
| | サイ | 宰相 さいしょう prime minister ..............**0682** |

| **1463** | |
|---|---|
| 宀 40 | The idea of **PRESIDING** (over) or **managing** is represented here in the act of keeping a *roof* (宀) over (i.e., **managing**) a situation that is inherently *hard* (辛) on those involved. See expressions of protest coming from 辛 but the *roof* keeping the situation under control. |
| **1965** | |
| 常 10 | |

| | SHARP, bitter | 辛辣な しんらつな sharp, biting ............**1462** |
|---|---|---|
| | | ○辣腕な らつわんな sharp, shrewd ..........**0732** |
| | | 辣腕家 らつわんか highly capable person ........................**0732, 0219** |
| | ラツ | 辣油 ラーユ red pepper oil ................**0433** |

| **1464** | |
|---|---|
| 辛 160 | A *bundle* (束) of *spicy* (辛) hot peppers: **SHARP**. The reading ラツ is unique in this course. |
| **1412** | |
| 常 14 | |

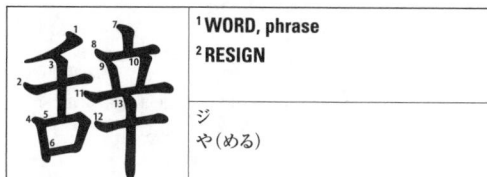

| ¹ WORD, phrase<br>² RESIGN<br><br>ジ<br>や(める) | ① 辞典 じてん dictionary ............................ 0504<br>¹ 辞書 じしょ dictionary ............................ 0079<br>¹ 式辞 しきじ address, speech ................. 0109<br>² 辞職 じしょく resignation ...................... 1087<br>② 会社を辞める かいしゃをやめる quit the<br>　 company ..................................... 0226, 0314 |
| --- | --- |

**1465**
辛 160
辭
1245
常 13

Here let 辛 *hard/painful* suggest "difficult." Now, no movement humans make is so *difficult* as the movements of the *tongue* (舌) in producing **WORDS**. After many years of such *painstaking* **WORD**-uttering, one naturally wants to **RESIGN** and rest one's tongue in a quiet retirement.

| **WALL**<br><br>ヘキ<br>かべ | ○障壁 しょうへき fence, wall; barrier .......... 1461<br>隔壁 かくへき partition, bulkhead; septum 1286<br>城壁 じょうへき castle wall, rampart ......... 1298<br>壁紙 かべがみ wallpaper ........................ 0478<br>○言葉の壁 ことばのかべ language barrier<br>　 .......................................... 0051, 0605 |
| --- | --- |

**1466**
土 32
2515
常 16

Take 辟 to mean *criminal*, represented by the idea of *pain* (辛) attempting to enter one's home through a *door* (尸) or other *opening* (口) (be careful to distinguish this from 辞 above). In the present entry, we observe a *criminal* jumping over an *earthen* (土) **WALL**. ☞ 塀 2171, 垣 1397, 壁 1467

| **MAGNIFICENT JEWEL**<br><br>ヘキ | ○完璧な かんぺきな perfect, flawless .......... 0633 |
| --- | --- |

**1467**
玉 96
2519
常 18

(Continuing from the previous entry) Having scaled the wall, the *criminal* (辟) immediately looks for the house *gems* (玉). Here he sets his sights on a **MAGNIFICENT JEWEL**. ☞ 壁 1466

| **HABIT, quirk**<br><br>ヘキ<br>くせ | 性癖 せいへき predisposition ................. 0128<br>習癖 しゅうへき (bad) habit, habitual practice 0420<br>○悪癖 あくへき (=わるぐせ) bad habit, vice .... 0546<br>飲酒癖 いんしゅへき drinking habit ... 0289, 0797<br>○口癖 くちぐせ way/habit of saying, one's favorite<br>　 phrase ........................................ 0019 |
| --- | --- |

**1468**
疒 104
2805
常 18

*Disease* (疒) and *criminal* (辟) combine to suggest bad **HABITS**.

## 避

**AVOID**

ヒ
さ(ける)

○避難 ひなん refuge, shelter, evacuation .... 0712
避難場所 ひなんばしょ evacuation site ........ 0712, 0445, 0249
回避する かいひする evade, dodge, avoid ... 0050
不可避な ふかひな inevitable ......... 0049, 0814
○避ける さける avoid, evade

**1469**
辵 162
2742
常 16

Here we send a *criminal* (辟) away on a *truck* (⻌) so that we won't run into him anymore: **AVOID.**

## 幸

[1] **GOOD FORTUNE**
[2] **HAPPINESS**

コウ
さいわ(い) さち しあわ(せ)

①幸運 こううん good fortune, good luck ...... 0584
多幸 たこう great happiness; great fortune ... 0267
不幸 ふこう unhappiness; misfortune; bereavement ........ 0049
○幸いな さいわいな happy, blessed
○幸せな夫婦 しあわせなふうふ happy/fortunate couple ........ 0565, 1017

**1470**
干 51
1901
常 8

S4–8 are an abbreviated version of 羊 *sheep* (therefore, the final two strokes do not represent a *needle*, as in the preceding entries). We thus have the "*land* (土) of the *sheep*," a place of rolling green hills of **GOOD FORTUNE** and **HAPPINESS.** ☞ 辛 1462

## 服

[1] **CLOTHES**
[2] **SUBMIT**

フク

[1] 衣服 いふく clothes, dress, clothing ......... 0700
①洋服 ようふく (Western) clothes .............. 0491
②克服する こくふくする conquer, overcome, subjugate ........ 1203
[2] 征服 せいふく conquest, subjugation ....... 0868
[2] 服従 ふくじゅう obedience, submission ..... 0869

**1471**
月 74
0782
常 8

Here visualize 月 as two high shelves for storing one's folded clothes (this *shelf* image for 月 will prove useful again later). Take S5–6 as a coat rack, and S7–8 as the coats that hang from it. Now imagine a **SUBMISSIVE** partner putting away one's **CLOTHES** on these apparatuses. ☞ 報 1472

## 報

[1] **REPORT**
[2] **REQUITE**

ホウ
むく(いる) むく(う)

①情報 じょうほう information .................. 0973
[1] 報告する ほうこくする report, inform ........ 0698
[1] 訃報 ふほう news of a death ................ 1115
[2] 報償 ほうしょう recompense, compensation 0323
②報いる むくいる requite; reward

**1472**
土 32
1515
常 12

*Happiness* (幸) + *coat rack* (𠬝). Imagine a *happy* working woman or man returning home and handing their coat to their partner, who then hangs it on the *coat rack* (the idea to take from this image is that of reciprocal action). The two partners **REPORT** the day's news to each other, and **REQUITE** each other's love. ☞ 服 1471

| | ¹ EXECUTE, perform | ①執る とる perform (duties), carry out |
|---|---|---|
| | ² SEIZE, hold fast to | ①執行する しっこうする execute, carry out....0055 |
| | | ² 固執する こしつする (=こしゅうする) adhere to, persist in ........................................0260 |
| | シツ シュウ | ②執着する しゅうちゃくする (=しゅうじゃくする) be (emotionally) attached to; hold fast to ....0938 |
| | と(る) | ² 執念 しゅうねん tenacity of purpose, vindictiveness ...........................................0230 |

| 1473 | *Happiness* (幸) + *round* (丸): here we might imagine a scene in which an eager child *happily* SEIZES a *round* ball. Connect this with M1 by thinking of **performing** or EXECUTING the seizing action. |
|---|---|
| 土 32 | |
| 1501 | |
| 常 11 | |

| | SINCERE | ○真摯な しんしな sincere, earnest...........0838 |
|---|---|---|
| | シ | |

| 1474 | To *seize* (執) a person's *hand* (手) in a handshake is a sign of **SINCERITY**. |
|---|---|
| 手 64 | |
| 2496 | |
| 常 15 | |

| | ¹ ATTAIN, reach; deliver | ①達成する たっせいする attain, achieve, accomplish ................................0070 |
|---|---|---|
| | ² PLURAL SUFFIX | ¹ 配達 はいたつ delivery .....................0799 |
| | | ¹ 達する たっする attain, reach; deliver (orders) |
| | タツ | ②私達 わたくしたち we ......................0237 |
| | -たち* | ² 友達 ともだち friend(s).....................0399 |

| 1475 | We continue with *happy* (幸), but now give the sheep (羊) its full allotment of three horizontal strokes. Here, think of how *happy* a *truck* (辶) driver feels when he finally **reaches**/ATTAINS his destination. The secondary meaning **deliver** can be thought of as "making (something) **reach**" its destination. ☞ 遅 1144 |
|---|---|
| 辵 162 | |
| 達 | |
| 2706 | |
| 常 12 | |

| | ¹ CHEERFUL | ¹ 朗報 ろうほう good news ...................1472 |
|---|---|---|
| | ² CLEAR, bright | ¹ 明朗な めいろうな cheerful, bright; clean (politics) ....................................0024 |
| | ロウ | ②朗読 ろうどく reading aloud..............0355 |
| | ほが(らか) | ○朗らかに笑う ほがらかにわらう laugh merrily, smile brightly.............................0579 |

| 1476 | A *good* (良) *moon* (月) is **CLEAR** and **bright**. Associate the image with M1 **CHEERFUL** via the idea of **brightness**. |
|---|---|
| 月 74 | |
| 朗 | |
| 1210 | |
| 常 10 | |

**¹ BILLOW, large wave**
**² ROAM, wander**

ロウ

¹ 波浪 はろう waves, billows ..................0598
¹ 風浪 ふうろう wind and waves, heavy seas.. 0425
② 浪人 ろうにん lordless samurai, *ronin*.......0015
² 浮浪者 ふろうしゃ vagabond ...........0613, 0107
² 流浪する るろうする roam about from place to place ................................................1059

| 1477 | Stagnant water tends to be unclean. Thus *"good"* (良) *water* (氵) is water that does not stay in one place, but **ROAMS/drifts about**. The connection with M1 is that a **BILLOW** (a **large wave**) **ROAMS** across the water. The reading ロウ sounds like **ROAM**. |
| --- | --- |
| 水 85 | |
| 0398 | |
| 常 10 | |

**¹ KINGDOM OF WU**
**² GIVE; do for (someone)**

ゴ
く(れる)

① 呉国 ごこく Kingdom of Wu..................0075
¹ 呉音 ごおん Wu reading of Chinese characters ................................................0150
¹ 呉服 ごふく dry goods; drapery .............1471
② 呉れる くれる give; do for (someone)
² 手伝って呉れる? てつだってくれる? Can you help me?.............................0046, 0223

| 1478 | Refers to historical Chinese states in the region around modern Shanghai. For the purpose of reading Japanese, our main goal is to give this a grapheme meaning for use in the next two entries: visualize a person *typing at a keyboard*. Note that while 虞 2001 has no *on-yomi*, the others based on 呉 are pronounced ゴ. ☞ 号 0300 |
| --- | --- |
| 口 30 | |
| 呉 | |
| 2206 | |
| 常 7 | |

**ENJOYMENT**

ゴ

○ 娯楽 ごらく amusement, pastime ...........0302
娯楽街 ごらくがい amusement quarter
................................................0302, 0992
娯楽室 ごらくしつ recreation room....0302, 0253

| 1479 | Visualize a *woman* (女) **ENJOYING** herself as she *types at a keyboard* (呉). |
| --- | --- |
| 女 38 | |
| 娯 | |
| 0366 | |
| 常 10 | |

**MISTAKE**

ゴ
あやま(る) -あやま(る)

○ 誤解 ごかい misunderstanding..............0345
誤報 ごほう misinformation, incorrect report
................................................1472
錯誤 さくご mistake, error...................1221
○ 誤る あやまる make a mistake, err
言い誤る いいあやまる misspeak ...........0051

| 1480 | *Mistyping* (呉) a *word* (言): **MISTAKE**. |
| --- | --- |
| 言 149 | |
| 誤 | |
| 1403 | |
| 常 14 | |

402

| 富 | **RICH** | 富裕 ふゆう wealth, richness..............1040 |
|---|---|---|
| | | 富農 ふのう rich farmer ................0511 |
| | | ○豊富な ほうふな abundant, plentiful, rich...0513 |
| | フ フウ | ○富む とむ be rich; abound in |
| | と(む) とみ | 富の分配 とみのぶんぱい distribution of wealth |
| | | ..........................................0088, 0799 |

**1481** ⼧ 40 — Visualize 畐 as a covered *grain silo* located next to a rice field. The present entry expresses the idea of wealth by putting an entire grain silo under one *roof*(⼧): **RICH**.

2009 常 12

| 副 | **SECONDARY, subordinate** | ○副作用 ふくさよう side effect, reaction 0152, 0047 |
|---|---|---|
| | | 副次的な ふくじてきな secondary......0278, 0169 |
| | | 副詞 ふくし adverb.....................0822 |
| | フク | 副業 ふくぎょう subsidiary business.........0498 |
| | | 副産物 ふくさんぶつ by-product, sideline |
| | | .....................................0181, 0172 |

**1482** 刀 18 — Here we *slice* ( 刂 ) the *grain silo* (畐)'s original supply of grain into subordinate or **SECONDARY** portions. Note that the three kanji in which 畐 appears at one side (rather than in the center, as in 富) have the *on* reading フク.

1581 常 11

| 幅 | **WIDTH, range** | ○振幅 しんぷく amplitude (of vibration)......0903 |
|---|---|---|
| | | 幅広い はばひろい wide, broad............0238 |
| | | 大幅に おおはばに sharply, by a wide margin |
| | フク | .............................................0033 |
| | はば | ○横幅 よこはば breadth.....................0916 |
| | | 幅が利く はばがきく be influential .........0412 |

**1483** 巾 50 — Think of how **WIDE** a *cloth* (巾) you would need to cover the entire *grain silo* (畐).

0523 常 12

| 福 | **FORTUNE** | 福利 ふくり public welfare, prosperity ......0412 |
|---|---|---|
| | | 福音 ふくいん gospel, good news ..........0150 |
| | | 祝福 しゅくふく blessing.....................1200 |
| | フク | ○幸福な こうふくな happy; blessed, fortunate 1470 |
| | | 裕福な ゆうふくな rich, wealthy.............1040 |

**1484** 示 113 — *God* (ネ) filling the *grain silo* (畐): good **FORTUNE**.

0944 常 13

| | **BLESSEDNESS** | ○福祉 ふくし welfare .........................1484 |
|---|---|---|
| | シ | |

**1485**
示 113
祉
0780
常 8

When *God* "remembered" Noah, He *stopped* the rains and promised never again to flood the earth. In this way "*God*(ネ) + *stop*(止)" signifies **BLESSEDNESS**.

---

| | **CALAMITY** | ○禍福 かふく fortune and misfortune ........1484 |
|---|---|---|
| | カ | 禍根 かこん root of evil...................0284 |
| | | 水禍 すいか flood disaster; drowning ......0027 |
| | | 黄禍 こうか Yellow Peril ...................0915 |
| | | 惨禍 さんか terrible disaster; crushing calamity |
| | | ..............................1239 |

**1486**
示 113
禍
0945
常 13

Review 過 0464. Unlike the previous entry, here *God*(ネ) does not *stop*(止) but continues "piling it on" to the point of *excess*(咼), causing a **CALAMITY**. Note that all characters incorporating 咼 are pronounced カ.

---

| | **WHIRLPOOL** | 渦中 かちゅう maelstrom, vortex, whirlpool 0035 |
|---|---|---|
| | カ | ○渦巻き うずまき eddy, whirlpool; coil .......0458 |
| | うず | 渦線 かせん spiral line....................0210 |
| | | 渦紋 かもん whirlpool design ..............1416 |

**1487**
水 85
0550
常 12

*Water*(氵) + *excessive*(咼) (in this case, excessive energy): **WHIRLPOOL**. A shortcut is to see 咼 as a pair of eddies.

---

| | **POT, pan** | ○鍋蓋 なべぶた pot lid....................1303 |
|---|---|---|
| | カ* | 鍋焼き なべやき scalloped; scalloped noodles |
| | なべ | ..............................0769 |
| | | 土鍋 どなべ earthen pot ...................0030 |
| | | シチュー鍋 シチューなべ stew pot/pan, skillet |
| | | 鍋物 なべもの food served in a pot..........0172 |

**1488**
金 167
1564
常 17

Recalling the *excessively* tall stack of boxes in 過 0464, here visualize an *excessively* tall pile of *metal*(金) **POTS** and **pans** in one's sink.

| | | |
|---|---|---|
|  蘭 | **¹ ORCHID**<br>**² HOLLAND**<br><br>ラン | ¹ 蘭栽培法 らんさいばいほう orchidology ............................................1319, 1264, 0139<br>² 蘭国 らんこく Holland..........................0075<br>② 蘭学 らんがく Dutch studies (Edo-era studies of Western texts brought by Dutch traders)...0099 |

| 1489<br>艸 140<br>蘭<br>2114<br>名 19 | Memorize the reading ラン for the next two entries, which differ only by ⧾ and 朮. With so few kanji pronounced ラン, it's easy to associate ラン with **HOLLAND** (オランダ, once written 阿蘭陀 or 和蘭), and by extension with **ORCHID**. Remember that of these two kanji, the one with ⧾ (suggesting *plant species*) refers to **ORCHID**, and thus also to **HOLLAND**. |
|---|---|

| | | |
|---|---|---|
| 欄 | **COLUMN**<br><br>ラン | 広告欄 こうこくらん advertisement column ............................................0238, 0698<br>スポーツ欄 スポーツらん sports section<br>欄外 らんがい margin.........................0266<br>○空欄 くうらん blank column, blank .........0398<br>欄に記入する らんにきにゅうする fill in the blank/column...........................0427, 0039 |

| 1490<br>木 75<br>欄<br>1023<br>常 20 | (Continuing from the previous entry) Here, 朮 resembles a long newspaper **COLUMN** running along the side of a crowded page. |
|---|---|

| | | |
|---|---|---|
| 潤 | **MOIST**<br><br>ジュン<br>うるお(う) うるお(す) うる(む) | ○湿潤な しつじゅんな moist, damp, wet.......0200<br>○潤う うるおう be moistened, be wet; profit<br>利潤 りじゅん profit.............................0412<br>潤い うるおい moisture; profit; tastefulness<br>潤んだ目 うるんだめ eyes moist with tears...0021 |

| 1491<br>水 85<br><br>0676<br>常 15 | Here we look in through the *gates* (門) of the *king* (王)'s palace toward his garden. To keep his garden **MOIST**, the *king* fills luxuriant fountains and pools with *water* (氵). |
|---|---|

| | | |
|---|---|---|
| 淵 | **¹ EDGE**<br>**² DEEP POOL**<br><br>エン<br>ふち | ¹ 淵源 えんげん origin, inception .............0209<br>² 皇居は淵に囲まれている こうきょはふちにかこまれている Deep pools of water surround the imperial palace....................0077, 0255, 0435<br>² 絶望の淵 ぜつぼうのふち the depths of despair ............................................1271, 1066 |

| 1492<br>水 85<br><br>0547<br>名 12 | Review 片 0922. Here, picture trees lining either **EDGE** of a **DEEP POOL**. An image search for 千鳥ヶ淵 (ちどりがふち, an imperial palace moat lined with cherry trees) will no doubt turn up photos to help vivify the image. |
|---|---|

| | ¹ SLIDE ² SMOOTH | ¹ 滑走路 かっそうろ runway............0140, 0788 |
|---|---|---|
| | | ① 滑る すべる slide, glide, slip |
| | | ² 潤滑油 じゅんかつゆ lubricant, lubricating oil ........1491, 0433 |
| | カツ コツ すべ(る) なめ(らか) | ② 円滑な えんかつな smooth, harmonious ...0013 |
| | | ² 滑らかに なめらかに smoothly |

| 1493 | Review 骨 0465 if necessary. Here *water* (氵) slips and **SLIDES SMOOTHLY** along *bone*. |
|---|---|
| 水 85 | ☞ 骨 0465 |
| 0603 | |
| 常 13 | |

| | **PRACTICE, train** | ○ 稽古 けいこ practice, training, drill .........0254 |
|---|---|---|
| | | 稽古着 けいこぎ training suit.........0254, 0938 |
| | | 舞台稽古 ぶたいげいこ dress rehearsal ........0961, 0949, 0254 |
| | ケイ | ○ 滑稽な こっけいな funny, jocular, humorous; laughable, ridiculous ........1493 |

| 1494 | For this character, you need only concern yourself with learning the compounds 稽古 (けいこ) and 滑稽な (こっけいな). |
|---|---|
| 禾 115 | |
| 稽 | |
| 1137 | |
| 常 15 | |

| | **SHOULDER** | ○ 肩章 けんしょう epaulet, shoulder strap .....1459 |
|---|---|---|
| | | 肩に担ぐ かたにかつぐ shoulder, bear.......1394 |
| | | ○ 肩凝り かたこり stiff shoulders.............1351 |
| | ケン かた | 肩書き かたがき title, degree.................0079 |

| 1495 | 戸 frames the top of this character the way the collarbone frames the top of the torso. Visualize S2–3 as the collarbone, S4 as the upper arm extending down from it, and 月 as the *flesh* protected underneath the **SHOULDER**. You might visualize S1 as an epaulet. |
|---|---|
| 肉 130 | |
| 1703 | |
| 常 8 | |

| | **THREATEN** | ○ 脅迫する きょうはくする threaten, intimidate 1182 |
|---|---|---|
| | | 脅迫状 きょうはくじょう intimidating letter ........1182, 0616 |
| | | 脅威 きょうい threat, menace................1150 |
| | キョウ おびや(かす) おど(す) おど(かす) | ○ 脅かす おびやかす threaten, menace |
| | | 脅かす おどかす threaten, intimidate; startle |

| 1496 | Three *powerful* predators (劦) **THREATEN** their prey. They regard it only as *flesh* (月). |
|---|---|
| 肉 130 | ☞ 脇 1993 |
| 1811 | |
| 常 10 | |

| | ASSENT | ○肯定 こうてい affirmation, affirmative.......0045 |
|---|---|---|
| | | 肯定的 こうていてき affirmative.......0045, 0169 |
| | コウ | 首肯する しゅこうする assent, nod.......0157 |

| 1497 | Imagine the *moon* (月) giving its **ASSENT** for some visitors to *stop* (止) on it for awhile. |
|---|---|
| 肉 130 | |
| 2142 | |
| 常 8 | |

| | SET OF TWO, pair | 双肩 そうけん both shoulders.......1495 |
|---|---|---|
| | | 双生児 そうせいじ twins.......0036, 0772 |
| | | ○双方 そうほう both sides/parties.......0173 |
| | ソウ | 一双 いっそう a pair.......0002 |
| | ふた | ○双子 ふたご twins.......0094 |

| 1498 | A pair of *hands*: **SET OF TWO**/pair. |
|---|---|
| 又 29* | |
| 雙 | |
| 0013 | |
| 常 4 | |

| | INLET | 江上 こうじょう bank of a large river.......0041 |
|---|---|---|
| | | ○江湖 こうこ general public, the world.......0259 |
| | | ○入り江 いりえ inlet, cove, creek.......0039 |
| | コウ | 江戸 えど Edo [former name of Tokyo].......0248 |
| | え | 江戸時代 えどじだい Edo period (Japanese |
| | | historical era, approx. 1600–1867) |
| | | .......0248, 0383, 0071 |

| 1499 | Visualize the *water* (氵) flowing into the open space at the left side of 工, which graphically |
|---|---|
| 水 85 | represents an indented seashore, or **INLET**. |
| 0195 | |
| 常 6 | |

| | BAY; curve | 湾口 わんこう bay entrance.......0019 |
|---|---|---|
| | | 湾内 わんない inside the bay.......0215 |
| | | ○東京湾 とうきょうわん Tokyo Bay.......0032, 0245 |
| | ワン | 真珠湾 しんじゅわん Pearl Harbor.......0838, 1207 |
| | | 台湾 たいわん Taiwan.......0949 |

| 1500 | The next two kanji are similar in appearance and meaning. Use 弓 and 己 to distinguish |
|---|---|
| 水 85 | **BAY** (here) from **PORT** (below). To visualize **BAY**, let 弓 suggest a *bow*-shaped **curve** in the |
| 灣 | coastline embracing the *waters* of the sea (the secondary meaning **curve** appears in the word |
| | 湾曲 [わんきょく, curve]). Note how 亦 shortens the old form. ☞ 港 1501 |
| 0562 | |
| 常 12 | |

| | PORT | 港湾局 こうわんきょく Port and Harbor Authority .........................................1500, 0256 |
|---|---|---|
| | | 港口 こうこう harbor entrance...............0019 |
| | コウ | ○空港 くうこう airport.........................0398 |
| | みなと | 入港する にゅうこうする enter a port.........0039 |
| | | ○港町 みなとまち port town ..................0439 |

**1501**
水 85

(Continuing from the previous entry) Recall how 己 can mean *wrap/roll up* (see 包 0457 if necessary). Here, it refers to the way in which ships are "*wrapped up*" *together* (共) inside the break*waters* (氵) of a **PORT**. Remember, *bow* (弓) represents the curved outline of a BAY (湾), whereas *wrap up* (己) signals the full enclosure of a **PORT**. ☞ 洪 0358, 湾 1500

0552
常 12

| | SELECT | 選手 せんしゅ player, representative athlete...0046 |
|---|---|---|
| | | ○選挙 せんきょ election ......................1247 |
| | | 当選 とうせん election to office; winning (a lottery)..............................0141 |
| | セン | ○選ぶ えらぶ select, choose |
| | えら(ぶ) | 選び出す えらびだす select, pick out........0038 |

**1502**
辵 162

Here let 辶 represent a shopping cart. To perceive the idea of **SELECTING**, visualize a pair of *wrapped* (己) items (packages) **SELECTED** from the shelves and placed *together* (共) in the shopping cart. ☞ 遷 0785

2734
常 15

| | SELECT | ○選択する せんたくする select, choose........1502 |
|---|---|---|
| | | 採択する さいたくする adopt, select..........0989 |
| | | 二者択一 にしゃたくいつ either-or choice ....................................0003, 0107, 0002 |
| | タク | |

**1503**
手 64

Review 尺 0337 and 駅 0339 (as with the latter, 尺 *digger* abbreviates 睪 in the old forms of the next several entries). Here the *digger* must **SELECT** which *hand* (扌) to shovel with.

0227
常 7

| | ¹ SWAMP, marsh ² ABUNDANT | ¹ 沼沢 しょうたく marsh, swamp...............1105 |
|---|---|---|
| | | ①沢地 さわち marshy land ...................0187 |
| | | ¹ 長沢 ながさわ Nagasawa [surname].........0091 |
| | タク | ②沢山 たくさん large quantity, plenty.........0037 |
| | さわ | ² 潤沢 じゅんたく abundance, plenty ..........1491 |

**1504**
水 85

氵 signals that *water* gushes forth after the *digger* (尺) sinks his shovel into the earth: **SWAMP**. Associate this with M2 **ABUNDANT** by thinking of the water "overflowing." The meaning **SWAMP** sounds a bit like "さわ-mpu." ☞ 沼 1105

0238
常 7

| | ¹ TRANSLATE<br>² SENSE, meaning<br><br>ヤク<br>わけ | ¹ 訳者 やくしゃ translator.....................0107<br>① 通訳 つうやく interpreting; interpreter......0159<br>¹ 直訳 ちょくやく literal translation ............0839<br>² 訳の分からない言葉 わけのわからないこと<br>　　ば words that make no sense...0088, 0051, 0605<br>　　言い訳 いいわけ apology, excuse, explanation<br>　　.................................................0051 |

| **1505**<br>言 149<br><br>譯<br><br>1340<br>常 11 | Here we observe a *words*(言)–*digger*(尺), or **TRANSLATOR**. His job is to bring the **SENSE** or **meaning** of foreign words to light. |

| | ¹ ELUCIDATE<br>² RELEASE<br><br>シャク | ① 解釈 かいしゃく interpretation, explanation 0345<br>¹ 注釈 ちゅうしゃく annotation, note, comment 0368<br>② 釈放 しゃくほう release, discharge, acquittal 0574<br>² 保釈する ほしゃくする let (a prisoner) out on bail<br>　　.................................................0646 |

| **1506**<br>釆 165<br><br>釋<br><br>1349<br>常 11 | Review 番 0299. Here, imagine the *digger*(尺) unearthing and **RELEASING** a buried cache of *crudely tied rice bundles*. Link this with M2 **ELUCIDATE** via the idea of **RELEASING** clarifying details. |

| | **LAY**<br><br>フ<br>し(く) -し(き) | ○ 敷設 ふせつ construction, laying............0520<br>○ 敷く しく lay, spread; construct<br>　　布団を敷く ふとんをしく make a bed...0204, 0649<br>　　屋敷 やしき mansion, residence; residential lot<br>　　.................................................0252<br>　　敷金 しききん deposit money .................0029 |

| **1507**<br>攵 66<br><br><br>1653<br>常 15 | Review 専 0580. Also, see the note at 簿 0985 about the extra dot stroke at the top. Here, we can visualize the rod-holding hand (攵) **LAYING** a large *mixing cauldron* upon the shoulders of this small *person* (方). ☞ 激 0575, 贄 1509 |

| | **PROUD**<br><br>ゴウ | ○ 傲慢 ごうまん proud, arrogant.................1134 |

| **1508**<br>人 9<br><br><br>0131<br>常 13 | Take 敖 as an abbreviated version of the previous entry, then visualize the small *person* (方) **PROUDLY** carrying the load *laid* upon him. Let イ therefore suggest *man*ly **PRIDE**. This kanji mostly appears in VI, so focus your efforts on learning that compound. ☞ 傲 1353, 激 0575 |

**LUXURY**

ゼイ

○贅沢 ぜいたく luxury, extravagance .......... 1504
贅沢品 ぜいたくひん luxury item ...... 1504, 0301
贅肉 ぜいにく excess fat, flab................ 0216
贅言 ぜいげん redundancy, wordiness ..... 0051

| 1509 | Informed by the previous two entries, visualize *laying* heaps of *money* (貝) upon the small *person* (方): LUXURY. ☞ 敷 1507 |
| 貝 154 | |
| 外 18 | |

¹ **EXAMINE CAREFULLY**
² **TRY**

シン

①審議 しんぎ deliberation, careful consideration ................................................. 0927
¹ 審判 しんぱん (=しんばん) refereeing, judgment; referee, umpire.................... 0744
² 審理する しんりする try, examine, inquire into ................................................. 0532
² 審問 しんもん trial, hearing, interrogation ... 0452
² 陪審 ばいしん jury ......................... 1263

| 1510 | Review 番 0299 WATCH. Here let "*roof* (宀) + *watch*" suggest a sentry or other official carefully questioning a suspect in the privacy of an interrogation room: EXAMINE CAREFULLY. ☞ 察 0639, 番 0299 |
| 宀 40 | |
| 2080 | |
| 常 15 | |

**FEUDAL DOMAIN**

ハン

○藩主 はんしゅ domain lord, daimyo .......... 0365
幕藩体制 ばくはんたいせい (Japanese) feudal system................................. 1339, 0062, 0708
加賀藩 かがはん (Edo-era feudal domain) ............................................. 1147, 1172
藩閥 はんばつ clanship, clan favoritism .... 1362
廃藩 はいはん abolition of the Edo-era feudal system................................ 0149

| 1511 | In feudal Japan, each lord was allotted a DOMAIN endowed with an adequate supply of arable land (here represented by 艹), *water* (氵), and armed men to *watch* over it (番). |
| 艸 140 | |
| 2106 | |
| 常 18 | |

¹ **TURN OVER**
² **RENDER IN ANOTHER FORM, translate**

ホン
ひるがえ(る) ひるがえ(す)

¹ 翻意する ほんいする change one's mind ... 0151
¹ 翻然と ほんぜんと suddenly................ 0760
①翻る ひるがえる turn over; wave, flutter
②翻訳する ほんやくする translate, render .... 1505
² 翻案 ほんあん adaptation.................. 0097

| 1512 | Recall from 番 0299 the idea of *taking turns* or rotating. With 羽 here, we thus get an image of the "alternating" up and down motion of a bird's *wings*: TURN OVER. With this image of TURNING OVER we can easily associate the idea of RENDERING IN ANOTHER FORM, such as translating a document from one language into another. |
| 羽 124 | |
| 1676 | |
| 常 18 | |

## 翔 SOAR

ショウ
かけ(る) と(ぶ)

○飛翔 ひしょう flight, soaring ............... 0475
滑翔機 かっしょうき sailplane, glider ... 1493, 0473
○翔る かける soar, fly
飛び翔る とびかける soar, fly ............... 0475

**1513**
羽 124

1241
名 12

A *winged*（羽）*goat*（羊）taking off: **SOAR**.

---

## 査 LOOK INTO, inspect

サ

査察 ささつ inspection, investigation ....... 0639
査問 さもん inquiry, hearing ............... 0452
調査 ちょうさ investigation, inquiry, survey . 0306
○検査 けんさ inspection, examination, test ... 1029
審査する しんさする examine, investigate, judge
................................................. 1510

**1514**
木 75

2159
常 9

Picture climbing up the *ladder*（且）into the *tree*（木）to **LOOK INTO** something.

---

## 租 LAND TAX

ソ

○租税 そぜい taxes, taxation ............... 1195
地租 ちそ land tax ............... 0187
免租 めんそ tax exemption ............... 1272
貢租 こうそ tribute, annual tax ............... 1158

**1515**
禾 115

1076
常 10

In ancient China **LAND TAXES** were paid in kind, such as in *neatly bundled rice stalks*（禾）. The *ladder*（且）suggests a progressive scale of taxation. Recall that kanji in which 且 appears at the right are pronounced ソ. ☞ 粗 1516, 相 0682

---

## 粗 COARSE

ソ
あら(い) あら-

○粗末な そまつな coarse, crude, humble .... 0272
粗悪な そあくな coarse, crude, bad .......... 0546
粗大な そだいな coarse, rough, unpolished 0033
○粗い細工 あらいさいく rough workmanship
................................................. 0239, 0108
粗造り あらづくり rough work ............... 0699

**1516**
米 119

1214
常 11

Learn to recognize this kanji by how it differs from the previous entry. Compared to the *neat rice bundle*（禾）used for LAND TAX, the "ordinary" *rice bundle*（米）in this kanji seems **COARSE**.
☞ 租 1515

| | | HAMPER, obstruct | ○阻害する そがいする obstruct, check, impede, hamper ............................. 0413 |
|---|---|---|---|
| 阻 | | | 阻止 そし obstruction, check, hindrance .. 0042 |
| | | | 険阻な けんそな steep (mountain pass), precipitous .................................. 1031 |
| | | ソ<br>はば(む) | ○道を阻む みちをはばむ obstruct one's way .. 0158 |
| | | | 成長を阻む せいちょうをはばむ hinder/check the growth of (plants) ........... 0070, 0091 |

**1517**
阜 170 — Visualize climbing the *ladder* (且) to see over the top of the *hills* (阝), which **HAMPER** (i.e., **obstruct**) the view. ☞ 障 1461

0308
常 8

| | | AIM AT | ○狙撃 そげき sniping ........................... 1026 |
|---|---|---|---|
| 狙 | | | ○狙う ねらう aim at |
| | | ソ<br>ねら(う) | 狙い ねらい aim |
| | | | 狙い撃ち ねらいうち sniping ................ 1026 |

**1518**
犬 94 — An ambitious *dog* (犭) who **AIMS** to climb the social *ladder* (且).

0304
常 8

| | | RIGHT, suitable, good, all right | ○便宜 べんぎ convenience, facility ........... 0890 |
|---|---|---|---|
| 宜 | | | 時宜 じぎ right time/occasion .............. 0383 |
| | | | ○宜しい よろしい all right, OK |
| | | ギ<br>よろ(しい)* よろ(しく)* | もし宜しければ... もしよろしければ... If you like ...; If you don't mind ... |
| | | | 宜しくお伝え下さい よろしくおつたえください Please give my best regards ........... 0223, 0040 |

**1519**
宀 40 — Climbing a *ladder* (且) is the **RIGHT**/most **suitable** method for getting on top of a *roof* (宀). ☞ 宜 1398

1909
常 8

| | | ¹ TATAMI, straw mat<br>² FOLD UP | ¹ 畳敷きの部屋 たたみじきのへや straw-matted room ....................... 1507, 0068, 0252 |
|---|---|---|---|
| 畳 | | | ¹ 畳替え たたみがえ refacing tatami mats ..... 1167 |
| | | | ①四畳半の部屋 よじょうはんのへや 4.5-mat room ........................ 0006, 0335, 0068, 0252 |
| | | ジョウ<br>たた(む) たた(み)- たたみ | ②畳む たたむ fold up; shut |
| | | | ² 畳み椅子 たたみいす folding chair .... 1332, 0094 |

**1520**
田 102 — Visualize 田 as four adjoining **TATAMI MATS**. To save space when storing, we **FOLD** them **UP** in a *ladder* (且)–like stack.

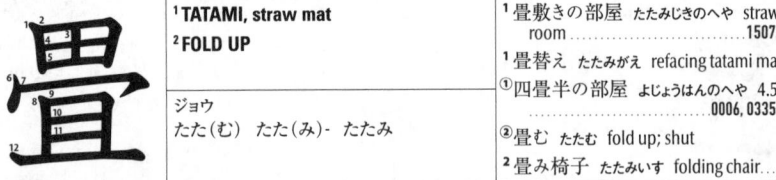

2249
常 12

|  | **¹ SHELL**<br>**² FIRST IN A SERIES**<br><br>コウ カン カ\* | ¹ 甲羅 こうら shell, carapace .................... 0896<br>¹ 甲板 かんぱん (=こうはん) deck ............. 0924<br>①手の甲 てのこう back of the hand .......... 0046<br>¹ 甲骨文 こうこつぶん ancient inscriptions of<br>　　Chinese characters on oracle bones and<br>　　carapaces .................................. 0465, 0101<br>² 甲種 こうしゅ first class, grade A ............. 0544 |
|---|---|---|
| **1521**<br>田 102<br><br>2923<br>常 5 | By | Visualize 日 as a protective **SHELL** (S5 provides a vertical dimension so that we can see the **SHELL** as being "on top," where it can cover underlying soft tissue). Now if you memorize V3, you will know this kanji like the back of your hand. For M2 **FIRST IN A SERIES**, see the note at 丙 1523. ☞ 甲 0315, 由 0432 |

|  | **SECOND IN A SERIES**<br><br>オツ | 乙種 おつしゅ second class, grade B ......... 0544<br>甲と乙 こうとおつ A and B, the former and the<br>　　latter ......................................... 1521<br>乙女 おとめ virgin, maiden ................... 0093<br>乙女座 おとめざ Virgo [constellation]<br>　　.......................................... 0093, 0749 |
|---|---|---|
| **1522**<br>乙 5<br><br>2849<br>常 1 | | By visualizing this as an oddly written numeral 2, it is easy to remember the meaning **SECOND IN A SERIES**. Just as this character roughly approximates the numeral 2, its pronunciation vaguely resembles the word "two": オツ. No other kanji in this course has the reading オツ. ☞ 乞 1805 |

|  | **THIRD IN A SERIES**<br><br>ヘイ | 丙種 へいしゅ third class, grade C ............ 0544<br>○甲乙丙 こうおつへい first, second, and third;<br>　　A, B, and C ............................ 1521, 1522 |
|---|---|---|
| **1523**<br>一 1<br><br>2920<br>常 5 | | We have seen this form before, inside 病 0617. By itself it is the kanji for **THIRD IN A SERIES**. In the context of a series, we can remember that 丙 represents the **THIRD** element by discerning a downward-facing numeral 3 in the lower portion. Similarly, we can discern a numeral 2 in 乙 and a numeral 1 inside 甲. Practice writing and saying V2. ☞ 内 0215 |

| 柄 | **¹ CHARACTER**<br>**² STATUS**<br>**³ HANDLE, grip; shaft**<br><br>ヘイ<br>がら え | ①人柄 ひとがら character, personality ........ 0015<br>¹ 間柄 あいだがら relation, terms ............... 0448<br>¹ 柄の悪い がらのわるい ill-bred ............. 0546<br>②家柄 いえがら social standing of a family; lineage<br>　　............................................... 0219<br>傘の柄 かさのえ umbrella handle ............ 0753 |
|---|---|---|
| **1524**<br>木 75<br><br>0799<br>常 9 | | 丙 here works like a device to measure the *tree* (木)'s **CHARACTER** and **STATUS**. The top of 丙 (S5 here) is used to measure the tree's height (that is, its stature or **STATUS**). The rest of 丙 (内, *inside*) measures what the tree has *inside* (that is, its **CHARACTER**). M3 **HANDLE** is easily recognized in S5. |

| | PUSH, press (down) | 押印する おういんする seal, affix a seal......0231 |
|---|---|---|
| | | ○押す おす push, press (down) |
| | | ○押収 おうしゅう seizure, confiscation.........1155 |
| | オウ | 後押し あとおし pushing; support, backing 0114 |
| | お(す) お(し)- お(っ)- お(さえる) | 押さえる おさえる press down, hold down |

| **1525** | Learn the next two entries by how they differ. Here, 日 has risen too high, so the *hand* (扌) needs to press it **down: PUSH.** ☞ 抽 1526 |
|---|---|
| 手 64 | |
| **0278** | |
| 常 8 | |

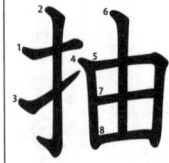

| | DRAW OUT, pull | 抽出する ちゅうしゅつする extract, abstract, educe |
|---|---|---|
| | | ..............0038 |
| | | ○抽選 ちゅうせん drawing of lots, lottery......1502 |
| | チュウ | 抽象的 ちゅうしょうてき abstract .............1277 |

| **1526** | (Continuing from the previous entry) Here, 日 has dropped too low, so the *hand* needs to pull it up: **DRAW OUT.** ☞ 押 1525 |
|---|---|
| 手 64 | |
| **0267** | |
| 常 8 | |

| | LOOK FOR | ○捜査 そうさ criminal investigation, search...1514 |
|---|---|---|
| | | 捜査本部 そうさほんぶ investigation headquar- |
| | | ters ................................1514, 0031, 0068 |
| | | 博捜 はくそう searching far and wide........0983 |
| | ソウ | ○捜す さがす look for |
| | さが(す) | 宝捜し たからさがし treasure hunt...........0074 |

| **1527** | Here you can visualize **LOOKING FOR** an object in the dark with the dim light of a torch. With your left *hand* (扌) you feel for the object; with your right *hand* (又) you carry a torch (申). |
|---|---|
| 手 64 | ☞ 挿 1597 |
| 捜 | |
| **0389** | |
| 常 10 | |

| | ¹ **DELIVER** | ①届ける とどける deliver, give notice |
|---|---|---|
| | ² **REACH** | ¹届け先 とどけさき destination, address......0134 |
| | | ¹欠席届け けっせきとどけ notification of absence |
| | | ........................................0277, 0279 |
| | とど(ける) -とど(け) とど(く) | ②届く とどく reach, arrive |
| | | ² 手の届く所 てのとどくところ within one's reach |
| | | ........................................0046, 0249 |

| **1528** | Visualize 由 as a **DELIVERY** person reaching up with one hand to knock on someone's *door*. M1 **DELIVER** and M2 **REACH** should not be thought of as separate meanings, but rather as |
|---|---|
| 尸 44 | transitive and intransitive senses of the same action. ☞ 届 1834, 居 0255 |
| 届 | |
| **2651** | |
| 常 8 | |

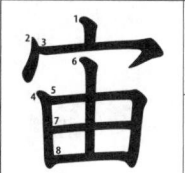

| | | |
|---|---|---|
| **¹ SPACE**<br>**² MIDAIR**<br><br>チュウ | **²** 宙乗り ちゅうのり aerial stunts ............... 1005<br>**²** 宙吊り ちゅうづり hanging in midair ........ 0206<br>②宙返り ちゅうがえり somersault ............... 0378 | |

| 1529<br>宀 40<br><br>1907<br>常 8 | Try to see this as the lid of a box flying into **MIDAIR**. Visualize 由 as a box with a rod that rises up from the inside and pushes the "*roof*" (宀, i.e., lid) of the box into **MIDAIR**, in the same way that a rocket sends a spacecraft into **SPACE**. See 宇 1542 for compounds using M1. |
|---|---|

| | | |
|---|---|---|
| **FLUTE; whistle**<br><br>テキ<br>ふえ | 牧笛 ぼくてき shepherd's pipe ............... 0576<br>汽笛 きてき steam whistle ................... 0127<br>○警笛 けいてき alarm-whistle, horn .......... 0806<br>横笛 よこぶえ flute, fife ...................... 0916<br>○口笛 くちぶえ whistle ...................... 0019 | |

| 1530<br>竹 118<br><br>2323<br>常 11 | In the previous entry I asked you to visualize the central vertical stroke as a rod rising up out of a box. Here see it as air rising up through holes in a *bamboo* (⺮) instrument—a **FLUTE** or whistle. |
|---|---|

| | | |
|---|---|---|
| **SLEEVE**<br><br>シュウ<br>そで | 袖手 しゅうしゅ having one's arms folded in the<br>  sleeves of one's gown ....................... 0046<br>○長袖 ながそで long sleeves ................... 0091<br>○半袖 はんそで short sleeves ................. 0335<br>袖丈 そでたけ sleeve length ................. 0657 | |

| 1531<br>衣 145<br><br>1078<br>常 10 | 衤 indicates *clothing*. Here visualize 由 as a **SLEEVE** with a wrist poking out of it. ☞ 裾 1534 |
|---|---|

| | | |
|---|---|---|
| **COLLAR**<br><br>キン<br>えり | ○開襟シャツ かいきんシャツ wing-collared/<br>  open-neck shirt ....................... 0450<br>半襟 はんえり neckpiece [on a kimono] ..... 0335<br>襟巻き えりまき scarf, muffler ............... 0458<br>○襟を正す えりをただす straighten oneself ... 0043 | |

| 1532<br>衣 145<br><br>1156<br>常 18 | *Clothing* (衤) + *prohibition* (禁): a priest's **COLLAR**. The *on-yomi* follows 禁 0312 キン. Interchangeable with the next entry. |
|---|---|

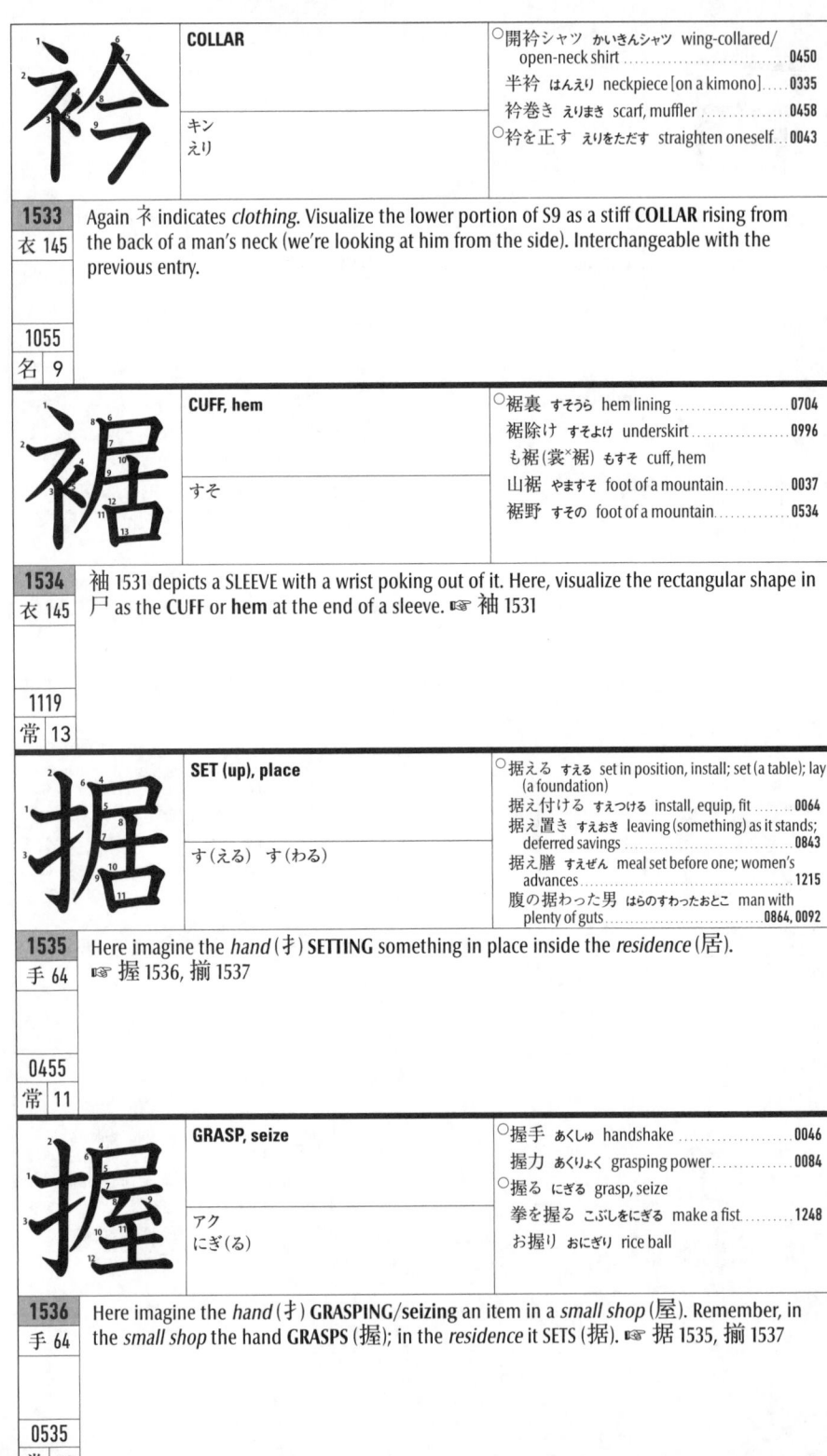

| | COLLAR | | ○開衿シャツ かいきんシャツ wing-collared/ open-neck shirt .......................... 0450 |
|---|---|---|---|
| | | | 半衿 はんえり neckpiece [on a kimono] ..... 0335 |
| | | | 衿巻き えりまき scarf, muffler .................. 0458 |
| | キン | | ○衿を正す えりをただす straighten oneself... 0043 |
| | えり | | |

| 1533 | Again ⻂ indicates *clothing*. Visualize the lower portion of S9 as a stiff **COLLAR** rising from |
|---|---|
| 衣 145 | the back of a man's neck (we're looking at him from the side). Interchangeable with the previous entry. |
| 1055 | |
| 名 9 | |

| | CUFF, hem | | ○裾裏 すそうら hem lining ..................... 0704 |
|---|---|---|---|
| | | | 裾除け すそよけ underskirt ................... 0996 |
| | | | も裾 (裳×裾) もすそ cuff, hem |
| | すそ | | 山裾 やますそ foot of a mountain ........... 0037 |
| | | | 裾野 すその foot of a mountain ............. 0534 |

| 1534 | 袖 1531 depicts a SLEEVE with a wrist poking out of it. Here, visualize the rectangular shape in |
|---|---|
| 衣 145 | 尸 as the **CUFF** or **hem** at the end of a sleeve. ☞ 袖 1531 |
| 1119 | |
| 常 13 | |

| | SET (up), place | | ○据える すえる set in position, install; set (a table); lay (a foundation) |
|---|---|---|---|
| | | | 据え付ける すえつける install, equip, fit ........ 0064 |
| | | | 据え置き すえおき leaving (something) as it stands; deferred savings ............................. 0843 |
| | す(える) す(わる) | | 据え膳 すえぜん meal set before one; women's advances............................................ 1215 |
| | | | 腹の据わった男 はらのすわったおとこ man with plenty of guts ........................... 0864, 0092 |

| 1535 | Here imagine the *hand* (扌) **SETTING** something in place inside the *residence* (居). |
|---|---|
| 手 64 | ☞ 握 1536, 揃 1537 |
| 0455 | |
| 常 11 | |

| | GRASP, seize | | ○握手 あくしゅ handshake ................... 0046 |
|---|---|---|---|
| | | | 握力 あくりょく grasping power .............. 0084 |
| | | | ○握る にぎる grasp, seize |
| | アク | | 拳を握る こぶしをにぎる make a fist ......... 1248 |
| | にぎ(る) | | お握り おにぎり rice ball |

| 1536 | Here imagine the *hand* (扌) **GRASPING**/seizing an item in a *small shop* (屋). Remember, in |
|---|---|
| 手 64 | the *small shop* the hand **GRASPS** (握); in the *residence* it SETS (据). ☞ 据 1535, 揃 1537 |
| 0535 | |
| 常 12 | |

| | **MAKE UNIFORM** | ○揃える　そろえる　make uniform, arrange properly |
|---|---|---|
| | | 揃う　そろう　be uniform/even, match; be complete, make a pair; assemble, be all present |
| | | 家具を揃える　かぐをそろえる　have a suite of furniture..............................................0219, 0837 |
| | セン | 揃い踏み　そろいぶみ　[sumo] stamping on the ring in unison..............................................1326 |
| | そろ（える）　そろ（う）　そろ（い）　-ぞろ（い） | 傑作揃い　けっさくぞろい　full array of masterpieces..............................................1176, 0152 |

| 1537 | Visualize the *hand* (扌) putting in order the items *before* (前) it: **MAKE UNIFORM**. The head character is shown with the old form of 月, reflecting the fact that this name-use list kanji has not officially been standardized (as of this writing). Either way of writing the character is acceptable. ☞ 据 1535, 握 1536 |
|---|---|
| 手 64 | |
| 揃 | |
| 0539 | |
| 名 12 | |

| | **STROKE, soothe** | 愛撫する　あいぶする　caress, love dearly....0778 |
|---|---|---|
| | | ○撫でる　なでる　stroke, pet |
| | ブ | 撫で付ける　なでつける　smooth down......0064 |
| | な（でる） | 撫で肩　なでがた　sloping shoulders.........1495 |

| 1538 | Here the *hand* (扌) turns aches and pains to *nothing* (無): **STROKE/soothe**. |
|---|---|
| 手 64 | |
| 0667 | |
| 名 15 | |

| | **ENTRUST** | ○委託する　いたくする　entrust with, consign...0396 |
|---|---|---|
| | | 信託　しんたく　trust................................0063 |
| | | 結託する　けったくする　conspire with........0516 |
| | タク | 託児所　たくじしょ　day nursery.........0772, 0249 |
| | | 託す　たくす　entrust (a person with a thing) |

| 1539 | Visualize 乇 as a person sitting on the floor with his arms outstretched, relaxing. The picture in this entry is of a person giving *words* (言) of instruction to a subordinate so that he can unburden himself of (i.e., **ENTRUST**) a responsibility, and then be at leisure. ☞ 詫 1541 |
|---|---|
| 言 149 | |
| 1323 | |
| 常 10 | |

| | **DWELLING HOUSE** | 宅地　たくち　land for housing, residential land..............................................0187 |
|---|---|---|
| | | お宅　おたく　your home, your house; you |
| | | 自宅　じたく　one's house, one's home........0081 |
| | タク | ○住宅　じゅうたく　housing, residence .........0366 |
| | | 家宅捜査　かたくそうさ　search of the premises..............................................0219, 1527, 1514 |

| 1540 | A person *relaxing* (乇) in the comfort of his *home* (宀): **DWELLING HOUSE**. ☞ 宇 1542 |
|---|---|
| 宀 40 | |
| 1862 | |
| 常 6 | |

**APOLOGIZE**

タ
わ(びる)　わ(び)

○お詫び　おわび　apology
　お詫びする　おわびする　apologize
　詫びる　わびる　apologize
　詫び状　わびじょう　letter of apology..........0616
　詫び言　わびごと　apology ...................0051

| 1541 | *Words* (言) of **APOLOGY** delivered personally at the *home* (宅) of the offended. ☞ 託 1539 |
| 言 149 | |
| 1387 | |
| 名 13 | |

**UNIVERSE**

ウ

○宇宙　うちゅう　universe, cosmos; (outer) space
　...................1529
　大宇宙　だいうちゅう　macrocosm; the universe
　...................0033, 1529
　宇宙飛行士　うちゅうひこうし　astronaut,
　　cosmonaut...............1529, 0475, 0055, 0350

| 1542 | Note how 于 here differs from 毛 above. We can still picture it as a person spreading his arms widely, only now he is not seated but standing. Here we observe him gazing up at the *roof* (宀) over the world (i.e., the firmament): **UNIVERSE**. ☞ 宅 1540, 字 0098 |
| 宀 40 | |
| 1863 | |
| 常 6 | |

**POTATO**

いも

　ジャガ芋　ジャガいも　potato, white potato
　里芋　さといも　taro............................0531
○焼き芋　やきいも　baked sweet potato........0769

| 1543 | With a slight variation in strokes we move from the cosmic to the most literally terrestrial. Here picture a rhizome spreading its roots widely inside the earth, under a *grass* (艹) covering: **POTATO**. Practice identifying the meanings of these last two kanji from the variable component. |
| 艸 140 | |
| 1868 | |
| 常 6 | |

¹**LONGEVITY**
²**CONGRATULATIONS**

ジュ　ス*
ことぶき

¹長寿　ちょうじゅ　long life, longevity ...........0091
①寿命　じゅみょう　life span......................0232
¹天寿　てんじゅ　one's natural life span ........0270
②新年の寿　しんねんのことぶき　New Year's
　　greetings.............................0275, 0117
　寿司を握る　すしをにぎる　make sushi...0820, 1536

| 1544 | Here 寸 *outstretched arm* holds a long rod (S4), like an elderly man steadying himself on a staff. We add a crossing stroke to the staff for each stage of life completed (childhood, youth, and middle age), so that the staff represents the attainment of **LONGEVITY**. His attainment is cause for **CONGRATULATIONS**. |
| 寸 41* | |
| 壽 | |
| 2979 | |
| 常 7 | |

| | CAST, mint | 鋳鉄 ちゅうてつ iron casting ............... 0564 |
|---|---|---|
| | | ○鋳造 ちゅうぞう casting, minting, coining ... 0699 |
| | | ○鋳る いる cast, mint |
| | チュウ | 鋳物 いもの cast metal, casting ........... 0172 |
| | い(る) | 鋳型 いがた mold, cast, matrix, die ........ 0723 |

| **1545** | Giving a *long-lived* (寿) shape to *metal* (金): **CAST/mint.** ☞ 銭 1585 |
|---|---|
| 金 167 | |
| 鋳 | |
| 1543 | |
| 常 15 | |

| | INSCRIPTION | ○銘文 めいぶん inscription ................... 0101 |
|---|---|---|
| | | 銘記する めいきする bear in mind; inscribe, engrave ................. 0427 |
| | メイ | 感銘 かんめい deep impression ........... 0327 |
| | | 銘柄 めいがら brand name, brand ........... 1524 |
| | | 銘打つ めいうつ engrave an inscription; call (itself) ................... 1025 |

| **1546** | Etching one's *name* (名) in *metal* (金): **INSCRIBE.** |
|---|---|
| 金 167 | |
| 1536 | |
| 常 14 | |

| | ¹ **MIRROR** ² **OPTICAL INSTRUMENT** | ¹ 鏡台 きょうだい dressing table .............. 0949 |
|---|---|---|
| | | ① 鏡に映る かがみにうつる be reflected in a mirror ............... 0329 |
| | キョウ | ② 眼鏡 めがね (=がんきょう) glasses, spectacles 1092 |
| | かがみ | ² 望遠鏡 ぼうえんきょう telescope ........ 1066, 0857 |
| | | ² 双眼鏡 そうがんきょう binoculars ....... 1498, 1092 |

| **1547** | Ancient mirrors were made not of glass but of *metal* (金). If we take S14-19 as a variant of 見 *see*, we obtain an image of someone *standing* (立) before a *metal* object and *seeing* his image: **MIRROR.** M2 is an extended meaning. Distinguish the right half of this character from the two halves of 競 1204. |
|---|---|
| 金 167 | |
| 1576 | |
| 常 19 | |

| | ¹ **BOUNDARY** ² **SITUATION** | ¹ 境界 きょうかい boundary, border ........... 0612 |
|---|---|---|
| | | ① 国境 こっきょう (national) border ........... 0075 |
| | キョウ ケイ | ① 境目 さかいめ border, boundary line; crisis ... 0021 |
| | さかい | ² 境地 きょうち state, stage; field, ground ...... 0187 |
| | | ² 心境 しんきょう frame of mind, mental attitude ................... 0056 |

| **1548** | Suggests *standing* (立) in a high position from which a wide *area* (土) can be *seen* (S9-14). No doubt this originally referred to a border lookout (like one of the towers along the Great Wall), since this kanji means **BOUNDARY.** The kanji for **BOUNDARIES** can also signify **SITUATION**, in the sense of the circumstances that surround us. |
|---|---|
| 土 32 | |
| 0618 | |
| 常 14 | |

| | ¹ RING<br>² SURROUND<br><br>カン | ① 環状の かんじょうの ring-shaped, circular... 0616<br>¹ 環状線 かんじょうせん belt line......... 0616, 0210<br>¹ 一環 いっかん link; part ..................... 0002<br>② 環境 かんきょう environment, surroundings,<br>circumstances ............................. 1548<br>² 環海 かんかい surrounding seas........... 0106 |
|---|---|---|

| **1549**<br>玉 96<br><br>1011<br>常 17 | 王 suggests *gem* or *round object*. Here we might imagine S10 as a **RING**, seen edgewise, resting on a velvet *cloth* stand (see 園 0856) and covered by a protective *net*ting (罒). M2 is a logical extension of M1. |
|---|---|

| | **RETURN**<br><br>カン | 帰還する きかんする return, come home... 1018<br>生還する せいかんする return alive; [baseball]<br>reach home plate .......................... 0036<br>○返還 へんかん return, restoration, repayment<br>............................................. 0378<br>償還 しょうかん repayment, reimbursement.. 0323<br>還暦 かんれき completion of the traditional<br>sexagenary cycle, sixtieth birthday ......... 0854 |
|---|---|---|

| **1550**<br>辵 162<br><br>2743<br>常 16 | **RETURNING** a *ring* (from the previous entry) to its sender. ☞ 遠 0857 |
|---|---|

| | **SHIELD**<br><br>ジュン<br>たて | ○矛盾 むじゅん contradiction ................. 0164<br>矛盾する むじゅんする be contradictory...... 0164<br>盾に取る たてにとる hide behind ........... 0059<br>○後ろ盾 うしろだて backer..................... 0114 |
|---|---|---|

| **1551**<br>目 109<br><br>2590<br>常 9 | Picture this as a soldier sheltering himself underneath a **SHIELD**. |
|---|---|

| | **CIRCULATE**<br><br>ジュン | ○循環 じゅんかん circulation, rotation; cycle.. 1549<br>血液循環 けつえきじゅんかん blood circulation<br>............................... 0198, 0468, 1549<br>悪循環 あくじゅんかん vicious circle.... 0546, 1549<br>景気循環 けいきじゅんかん business cycle<br>............................... 1280, 0126, 1549<br>循環器科 じゅんかんきか cardiology (department)<br>............................... 1549, 0295, 0759 |
|---|---|---|

| **1552**<br>彳 60<br><br>0530<br>常 12 | Since the *shield* (盾) cannot be penetrated, the only choice is to *go* (彳) around it (S1–2 indicate a path around the top). Let this image of "*going*" around" suggest the idea of **CIRCULATING**. |
|---|---|

| | **MAKE THE ROUNDS, go around** | 巡査 じゅんさ police, patrolman ............1514 |
|---|---|---|
| 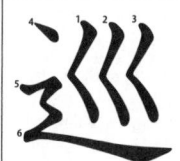 | | 巡察する じゅんさつする patrol, make a round of inspections .................................0639 |
| | | ○巡礼 じゅんれい pilgrimage; pilgrim .......0313 |
| | ジュン | ○巡る めぐる go around; tour |
| | めぐ(る) めぐ(り) | 血の巡り ちのめぐり circulation of blood ...0198 |

| **1553** | Resembles one of those mobile signs used by highway maintenance crews in which a series of arrows (巛) flashes in sequence, directing traffic to **go around**. |
|---|---|
| 巛 47 | |
| 2622 | |
| 常 6 | |

| | **CRAWL** | ○這う はう crawl on all fours, stay flat |
|---|---|---|
|  | | 四つん這い よつんばい on all fours .......0006 |
| | | 横這い よこばい crawling sideways .......0916 |
| | シャ | ツタの葉が壁を這う ツタのはがかべをはう ivy crawls across the wall ................0605, 1466 |
| | は(う) | 淵から這い上がる ふちからはいあがる climb out of the depths ................1492, 0041 |

| **1554** | Focus on how the strokes of 言 lie flat, keeping a low profile as they *move forward* (辶) along the ground: **CRAWL**. As ever, 辶 may be replaced by 辶. |
|---|---|
| 辵 162 | |
| 這 | |
| 2775 | |
| 名 11 | |

| | **RELAY** | ○逓信 ていしん communications ............0063 |
|---|---|---|
| | | 逓送 ていそう forwarding.................0455 |
| | | 逓次 ていじ in order, successively .........0278 |
| | テイ | |

| **1555** | At 巡 1553 I suggested you visualize 巛 as a set of flashing arrows. Here I suggest you visualize the parallel horizontal lines (S3–4) on this *truck* (辶)'s cargo as a sign directing us to keep the cargo moving forward on its way; i.e., to **RELAY** it forward on the next stage of its journey. ☞ 途 1000 |
|---|---|
| 辵 162 | |
| 逓 | |
| 2675 | |
| 常 10 | |

| | **BREATH** | ○一息 ひといき breath; pause, rest; a little bit of effort ........................0002 |
|---|---|---|
| | | 溜め息 ためいき sigh .................1171 |
| | | ○休息 きゅうそく rest, repose .................0061 |
| | ソク | 消息 しょうそく (personal) news, movements; letter.........................1289 |
| | いき | 息子 むすこ son ..........................0094 |

| **1556** | Through the *nose* (自) and down to the *heart* (心) passes the **BREATH** of life. Review 自 0081 if the connection with *nose* is not clear. ☞ 憩 1557, 鼻 1558, 臭 1560 |
|---|---|
| 心 61 | |
| 2301 | |
| 常 10 | |

| | **TAKE A REST** | ○休憩する きゅうけいする take a rest .......... 0061 |
|---|---|---|
| | | 小憩 しょうけい short rest, brief recess ....... 0034 |
| | | 木陰に憩う こかげにいこう take a rest under a tree .................................................. 0028, 1311 |
| | ケイ<br>いこ(い) いこ(う) | ○憩いの場 いこいのば place for relaxation and refreshment ............................... 0445 |

| **1557** | Catching one's *breath* (息) and taking refreshment for one's *tongue* (舌): **TAKE A REST.** ☞ 息 1556 |
|---|---|
| 心 61 | |
| 憩 | |
| 2510 | |
| 常 16 | |

| | **NOSE** | ○鼻音 びおん nasal sound ..................... 0150 |
|---|---|---|
| | | 耳鼻 じび nose and ears ..................... 0057 |
| | | 鼻血 はなぢ nosebleed ....................... 0198 |
| | | 鼻息 はないき snorting; temper; vigor ...... 1556 |
| | ビ<br>はな | ○象の鼻 ぞうのはな elephant's trunk .......... 1277 |

| **1558** | The character for **NOSE** starts with the grapheme *nose* (自), to which is attached a *head* (田), |
|---|---|
| 鼻 209 | into which are inhaled two streams of air (廾), one through each nostril (ignore earlier meanings established for 廾). ☞ 算 0980, 息 1556 |
| 2362 | |
| 常 14 | |

| | **OPEN HOLE** | ○気孔 きこう pore, stoma ..................... 0126 |
|---|---|---|
| | | 鼻孔 びこう nostrils ......................... 1558 |
| | | 排水孔 はいすいこう scupper (hole); osculum .................................................. 0739, 0027 |
| | コウ | 孔子 こうし Confucius ....................... 0094 |

| **1559** | Associate *child* (子) + *sharp hook* (乚) with the predictable result of such a combination: **OPEN** |
|---|---|
| 子 39 | **HOLE.** ☞ 乳 0160 |
| 0158 | |
| 常 4 | |

| | **BAD SMELL** | 体臭 たいしゅう body odor ................... 0062 |
|---|---|---|
| | | 悪臭 あくしゅう offensive odor, stench ....... 0546 |
| | | 臭気 しゅうき offensive odor, stench ....... 0126 |
| | | 酒臭い さけくさい reeking of liquor .......... 0797 |
| | シュウ<br>くさ(い) -くさ(い) にお(う) にお(い) | 素人臭い しろうとくさい amateurish ... 0132, 0015 |

| **1560** | In the next five entries we should interpret 大 visually, although its semantic value *big* can |
|---|---|
| 自 132 | reinforce each image. In all five, see 大's slanting strokes coming together into a vertex that |
| 臭 | points into the element above it. Here, we observe a (*big*) odor converging on one's *nose* (自): |
| 2289 | **BAD SMELL.** ☞ 息 1556, 匂 2245 |
| 常 9 | |

| | SMELL, sniff | ○嗅覚 きゅうかく sense of smell .................. 0325 |
|---|---|---|
| | | 嗅神経 きゅうしんけい olfactory nerve...0316, 1257 |
| | キュウ | ○嗅ぐ かぐ smell, sniff |
| | か（ぐ） | 嗅ぎ出す かぎだす sniff out.................. 0038 |
| | | 嗅ぎ分ける かぎわける sniff out; tell apart by smell ............................................ 0088 |

| **1561** | To the previous entry we add 口 to suggest the sensory perception of a *bad smell* (臭), that is, the act of **SMELLING** or sniffing. This character incorporates the old form of the previous entry, which is based on 犬 rather than 大. 嗅 was not officially standardized to match 臭 when it was added to the Joyo list. |
|---|---|
| 口 30 | |
| 嗅 | |
| 0576 | |
| 常 13 | |

---

| | INNER PART, depths | 奥義 おうぎ (=おくぎ) secret principles, secrets, hidden mysteries.............................. 0926 |
|---|---|---|
| | | ○奥行き おくゆき depth, length .............. 0055 |
| | オウ | 奥歯 おくば molars, back teeth .............. 0674 |
| | おく | 奥日光 おくにっこう the secluded recesses of Nikko..................................0001, 0137 |
| | | ○奥様 おくさま married lady, Mrs.; your wife..0501 |

| **1562** | Here visualize two blitzing columns converging on the **INNER PART** of a property, where the *rice* (米) is stored. |
|---|---|
| 大 37 | |
| 奥 | |
| 2458 | |
| 常 12 | |

---

| | POINTY | ○尖鋭な せんえいな radical; acute, sharp ....1196 |
|---|---|---|
| | | 尖兵 せんぺい advance-guard point; advance detachment.................................0907 |
| | セン | ○尖る とがる (=とんがる) be pointed, be sharp; become irritated |
| | とが（る） とん（がる） | 尖り声 とがりごえ sharp/irate voice..........0529 |
| | | 尖った鼻 とがったはな pointy nose..........1558 |

| **1563** | Here the slanting strokes of 大 taper to a (*small* 小) **POINTY** tip. *Big* at the base, but very *small* at the tip. This kanji is now often replaced in *on-yomi* compounds by 先 0134. ☞ 鋭 1196 |
|---|---|
| 小 42 | |
| 1864 | |
| 名 6 | |

---

| | THRUST; dash forward | 突入する とつにゅうする dash into, thrust into ...................................................0039 |
|---|---|---|
| | | ○突破する とっぱする break through; surmount; exceed ...................................0596 |
| | トツ | 突然 とつぜん abruptly, suddenly, unexpectedly ...................................................0760 |
| | つ（く） | 煙突 えんとつ chimney, smokestack ........0768 |
| | | ○突く つく thrust; push; poke; pierce |

| **1564** | Recall 穴 *hole*. Now see 大 **THRUSTING** upward into the *hole*. ☞ 究 1710 |
|---|---|
| 穴 116 | |
| 突 | |
| 1918 | |
| 常 8 | |

| | ¹CHOKE, plug up<br>²NITROGEN | ①窒息 ちっそく suffocation, asphyxia..........1556<br>②窒素 ちっそ nitrogen........................0132<br>² 窒化物 ちっかぶつ nitride.............0120, 0172 |
| | チツ | |

| **1565**<br>穴 116 | (Continuing from the previous entry) Now see 至 *arriving* at and **plugging up**/**CHOKING OFF** the *hole* in 穴. **CHOKE** relates in a meaningful way to M2 **NITROGEN**, whose gaseous form has been called the "lifeless air," for in it flames expire and men suffocate. ☞ 室 0253 |
| **1980**<br>常 11 | |

| | STEAL | ○窃盗 せっとう theft, larceny..................1304<br>窃盗罪 せっとうざい (charge of) theft, larceny<br>..........................1304, 0741<br>窃盗犯 せっとうはん thief.............1304, 0735<br>窃取 せっしゅ theft, larceny..................0059 |
| | セツ | |

| **1566**<br>穴 116<br>竊<br>1942<br>常 9 | Imagine a thief *cutting* (切) a *hole* (穴) in your bag to **STEAL** your valuables. |

| | COLLIDE | 衝突する しょうとつする collide (with), crash<br>(into); conflict/clash (with)..................1564<br>○衝撃 しょうげき impact, shock, impulse .....1026<br>衝動 しょうどう impulse, urge.................0540<br>緩衝 かんしょう buffer.......................1126 |
| | ショウ | |

| **1567**<br>行 144<br><br>0658<br>常 15 | Review 行 0055. Here, imagine cars speeding down the two intersecting roads and **COLLIDING** "heavily" (重) into each other. ☞ 衡 1268 |

| | PLEDGE | ○契約 けいやく contract, agreement..........0170<br>契約書 けいやくしょ contract document<br>..........................0170, 0079<br>契機 けいき opportunity, chance...........0473<br>○契る ちぎる pledge, promise |
| | ケイ<br>ちぎ(る) | |

| **1568**<br>大 37<br><br>2293<br>常 9 | Here try to visualize the idea of a man's fulfilling his **PLEDGE** to provide for his family. The (*big*) man carries a machete (刀, *sword*) over one shoulder and a *growing plant* (representing grain) over the other. ☞ 喫 1569, 誓 1701 |

| | INGEST | 喫茶店 きっさてん coffee shop, tea house .................... 0603, 0347 |
|---|---|---|
| | キツ | ○喫煙 きつえん smoking ........................ 0768 |
| | | 喫煙席 きつえんせき smoking section 0768, 0279 |
| | | 満喫する まんきつする have enough, enjoy fully ............................................... 0179 |

**1569**
口 30

(Continuing from the previous entry) After the man fulfills his *pledge* (契) by providing grain, a *mouth* (口) INGESTS it. ☞ 契 1568, 潔 1570

0505
常 12

| | IMMACULATE | 清潔な せいけつな clean, neat, pure ........ 0974 |
|---|---|---|
| | | 不潔な ふけつな unclean, dirty, impure .... 0049 |
| | ケツ | ○潔癖 けっぺき love of cleanliness, fastidiousness ............................................... 1468 |
| | いさぎよ(い) | 純潔な じゅんけつな purehearted, immaculate, innocent ............................... 1101 |
| | | ○潔い いさぎよい upright, sportsmanlike; manly, brave |

**1570**
氵 85

From the *growing plants* the man gathered in 1568, we now produce IMMACULATE *thread*: take the raw *growing plant* at the top (S4–7), then scrape off the dirt with a *knife* (刀) and rinse with *water* (氵) to produce IMMACULATE *thread* (糸), issuing from the bottom. ☞ 繁 1575, 繋 1576, 喫 1569

0678
常 15

| | INSULT, disdain | ○侮言 ぶげん words of insult ................ 0051 |
|---|---|---|
| | | 侮る あなどる despise, disdain, hold in contempt, make light of |
| | ブ | ○侮り難い敵 あなどりがたいてき formidable enemy |
| | あなど(る) | ............................................... 0712, 1122 |

**1571**
人 9

侮

Calling (or considering) someone merely an *everyman* (毎 *every* + イ *man*): INSULT/disdain.

0063
常 8

| | JAPANESE APRICOT, *ume* | 梅林 ばいりん (=うめばやし) *ume* grove ....... 0240 |
|---|---|---|
| | | ○梅雨 ばいう (=つゆ) rainy season (of early summer) ............................ 0154 |
| | バイ | 梅雨明け つゆあけ end of the rainy season ............................................... 0154, 0024 |
| | うめ | ○梅干し うめぼし pickled *ume* ................ 0408 |
| | | 梅酒 うめしゅ *ume* brandy ................ 0797 |

**1572**
木 75

梅

A *tree* (木) for *every* (毎) purpose, the *ume* is planted for its celebrated late-winter flowers but also for its fruit, which are used not only as fruit but also for pickles, sauce, liquor, and medicine. For its early summer ripening it gives its name to the East Asian rainy season (see V2).

0833
常 10

| **REPENT, regret** | 悔恨 かいこん regret, repentance............1217 |
| | ○後悔する こうかいする be sorry, regret, repent ............0114 |
| | 悔い改める くいあらためる repent, be penitent ............0429 |
| カイ | 悔し泣き くやしなき crying from vexation, tears |
| く(いる) く(やむ) くや(しい) | of regret............0578 |
| | ○悔しい くやしい vexing, regrettable |

**1573**

心 61

悔

0324

常 | 9

Here think of 毎 *every* in the sense of "all possible." In this way let "*heart* (忄) + *all possible*" suggest wholehearted **REPENTANCE/regret**.

---

| **NIMBLE; alert** | 敏速 びんそく quickness, agility, alacrity....1143 |
| | ○敏感な びんかんな sensitive ................0327 |
| | 鋭敏な えいびんな sharp, keen, sensitive....1196 |
| ビン | 俊敏な しゅんびんな quick-witted............1440 |
| | 敏腕 びんわん ability, capability............0732 |

**1574**

攵 66

敏

1206

常 | 10

As in the previous entry, think of 毎 *every* in the sense of "all possible." With 攵, we can imagine a *striking* action performed with the greatest possible agility: **NIMBLE**.

---

| **THRIVE, be busy; numerous, manifold** | 繁殖する はんしょくする breed, multiply....0841 |
| | ○繁栄する はんえいする thrive, flourish......1245 |
| | 繁盛する はんじょうする thrive, flourish.....1300 |
| ハン | 繁忙 はんぼう pressure of business, busyness |
| | ............1063 |
| | 農繁期 のうはんき busy farming season |
| | ............0511, 0486 |

**1575**

糸 120

繁

2484

常 | 16

As with 潔 several entries back, we can visualize *thread* issuing forth as it is produced. Here a *nimble* (敏) spinner quickly produces large quantities of *thread* (糸), an intuitive image for the concepts **THRIVE, be busy, numerous,** and **manifold**. ☞ 緊 2035, 繋 1576, 潔 1570

---

| **CONNECT, tie together** | ○連繋 れんけい connection, linking, contact 0582 |
| | 繋争 けいそう dispute, contention (of a legal |
| | case)............0972 |
| | 繋留 けいりゅう mooring, anchorage........1170 |
| ケイ | 繋がる つながる be connected |
| つな(ぐ) つな(がる) かか(る) | ○手を繋ぐ てをつなぐ join hands ............0046 |

**1576**

糸 120

繋

外 | 17

Imagine tying the *lances* (殳) to the *car* (車) with *rope* (糸): **CONNECT/tie together**. This character is often replaced by 係 in *on-yomi* compounds. ☞ 繁 1575, 撃 1026, 潔 1570

**GROW THICK**

モ
しげ(る)

○繁茂する　はんもする　grow thick, luxuriate...1575
○茂る　しげる　grow thick, be luxuriant
茂み　しげみ　thicket, brush
生い茂る　おいしげる　grow luxuriantly/thickly
..............................................0036
吉田茂　よしだしげる　Yoshida Shigeru (prime minister, 1946–47 and 1948–54)...0514, 0020

| 1577 | Imagine using the blade at the end of this *guided spear* (戊) to slice your way through a |
|---|---|
| 艸 140 | thicket of tall *grass* (艹): **GROW THICK**. |

栺
1934
常 8

---

**BRIDGE**

キョウ
はし

鉄橋　てっきょう　iron bridge..................0564
○架橋　かきょう　bridge building.............1173
橋脚　きょうきゃく　bridge pier.................0734
○吊り橋(=釣り橋)　つりばし　suspension bridge
..............................................0206, 2132
高橋　たかはし　Takahashi [surname].........0185

| 1578 | 喬, like 高 0185, means *tall*. In ancient China, as today, bridges were among the tallest struc- |
|---|---|
| 木 75 | tures. The character they created for **BRIDGE**, then, implied a *tall* structure made of *wood* (木). Note that this character contains 夭, not 天; S5 must be written from right to left. |

0991
常 16

---

**RECTIFY**

キョウ
た(める)

○矯正　きょうせい　correction, rectification......0043
矯め直す　ためなおす　rectify, reset..........0839
矯風　きょうふう　moral reform................0425
○枝を矯める　えだをためる　straighten a branch
..............................................0965

| 1579 | *Tall* (喬) + *arrow* (矢). Here the *arrow* has been stretched *tall* to make it as straight and narrow |
|---|---|
| 矢 111 | as possible: **RECTIFY**. |

1146
常 17

---

稿

**MANUSCRIPT**

コウ

○原稿　げんこう　manuscript, draft, copy.......0208
稿料　こうりょう　payment for a manuscript...0758
草稿　そうこう　outline, draft..................0144
投稿する　とうこうする　contribute (an article) 0517
寄稿　きこう　contribution (to a newspaper)...1330

| 1580 | Now we return to the more familiar form 高. Picture a *tall* sheet of *rice* (禾) paper (a long |
|---|---|
| 禾 115 | scroll?), on which a **MANUSCRIPT** is written. Note that this entry and the next one, following 高, have the *on* reading コウ, while the two characters above with 喬 are pronounced キョウ. |

槀
1138
常 15

**STRIPE**

コウ
しま

| | | |
|---|---|---|
| 縞柄 | しまがら striped pattern | 1524 |
| 縞馬 | しまうま zebra | 0336 |
| ○縞模様 | しまもよう striped pattern | 1336, 0501 |
| 横縞 | よこじま lateral stripes | 0916 |
| 縦縞 | たてじま vertical stripes | 0871 |

**1581**
糸 120

Again let *tall* (高) suggest long—in this case, a *thread* (糸) running the length of a garment: pin**STRIPE**.

1287
名 16

---

**WRITING PAPER, label**

セン

| | | |
|---|---|---|
| ○便箋 | びんせん stationery, letter paper | 0890 |
| 用箋 | ようせん stationery, blank pad | 0047 |
| 付箋 | ふせん label, tag, adhesive note | 0064 |
| 処方箋 | しょほうせん prescription | 0553, 0173 |

**1582**
竹 118
箋

Imagine *bamboo* (⺮) tags used for labeling one's *spears* (戔): **WRITING PAPER/label.** The traditional form 箋 was retained when this kanji was added in 2010 to the official Joyo list; however, the *spears* portion had decades earlier been simplified to 戋 in the entries that follow. Learn to recognize both versions interchangeably.

2360
常 14

---

¹ **LEAVE BEHIND, remain**
² **RUTHLESS**

ザン
のこ(る) のこ(す)

| | | |
|---|---|---|
| ¹残高 | ざんだか balance, remainder | 0185 |
| ①残業 | ざんぎょう overtime (work) | 0498 |
| ①残る | のこる remain, linger, stay; be left over; survive | |
| ¹残す | のこす leave (behind); reserve, save; leave undone | |
| ²残忍 | ざんにん cruelty, atrocity, brutality | 1095 |

**1583**
歹 78
殘

To organize this set of five characters based on the simplified form 戋, let it represent some kind of vehicle transporting a stack of cargo. See it as facing to the right, and picture the diagonal stroke (S9 here) as a ramp used for unloading various objects. Here it **LEAVES BEHIND** a *dead* body (歹), **RUTHLESSLY** abandoning it to the elements.

0851
常 10

---

**SCAFFOLD**

サン

| | | |
|---|---|---|
| ○桟橋 | さんばし (landing) pier, jetty, wharf | 1578 |
| 桟敷 | さじき reviewing stand, box, gallery | 1507 |

**1584**
木 75
棧

Here 戋 unloads a *tree* (木, i.e., a log), depositing it upright in order to support a **SCAFFOLD.** Note the traditional forms of this whole series of characters based on 戋.

0843
常 10

**MONEY; coin, 0.01 yen monetary unit**

セン
ぜに

金銭 きんせん money, cash .................. 0029
無銭の むせんの penniless, moneyless ..... 0048
○銭湯 せんとう public bath .................. 0446
二円五十銭 にえんごじっせん two yen fifty sen
.................................... 0003, 0013, 0007, 0005
○銭入れ ぜにいれ purse, till .................. 0039

| 1585 | Here 戋 unloads *money*(金), in the form of a long trail of coins: **MONEY/coin.** ☞ 鋳 1545 |
|---|---|

金 167
銭
1537
常 14

---

**PUT INTO ACTION**

セン

○実践する じっせんする put into practice,
    implement ................................. 0499
実践的 じっせんてき practical .......... 0499, 0169

| 1586 | Here 戋 unloads a brave *foot*(𧾷) soldier, who aims his rifle forward as he steps into battle: **PUT INTO ACTION.** |
|---|---|

足 157
践
1396
常 13

---

**SHALLOW**

セン
あさ(い)

○浅海 せんかい shallow sea .................. 0106
浅薄 せんぱく shallowness, superficiality,
    flimsiness ................................. 0986
浅学 せんがく superficial knowledge ........ 0099
○浅い あさい shallow

| 1587 | Here a hose extends down the ramp, covering the street with a **SHALLOW** layer of *water*(氵). ☞ 洩 1588 |
|---|---|

水 85
浅
0349
常 9

---

**LEAK**

エイ セツ
も(る) も(れる) も(らす)

○洩れる もれる [vi] leak(out)
洩らす もらす [vt] leak, divulge
水洩り みずもり leak .................. 0027
秘密を洩らす ひみつをもらす divulge a secret
.................................... 1384, 1383

| 1588 | Visualize 曳 as a person dragging a hose, and *water*(氵) **LEAKING** from it. ☞ 浅 1587, 湧 2006 |
|---|---|

水 85

外 9

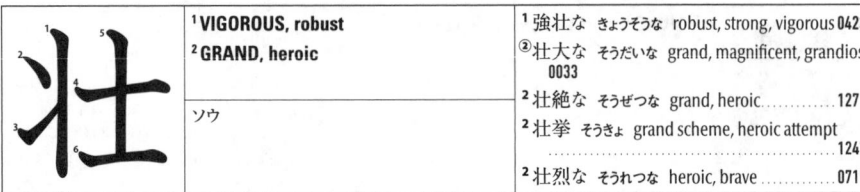

| | ¹ **VIGOROUS, robust**<br>² **GRAND, heroic** | ¹ 強壮な きょうそうな robust, strong, vigorous **0423**<br>② 壮大な そうだいな grand, magnificent, grandiose **0033**<br>² 壮絶な そうぜつな grand, heroic............**1271**<br>² 壮挙 そうきょ grand scheme, heroic attempt<br>..................................................**1247**<br>² 壮烈な そうれつな heroic, brave............**0719** |
|---|---|---|
| | ソウ | |

| **1589**<br>士 33<br><br>壮<br><br>0198<br>常 6 | Review 将 0614 GENERAL OFFICER. In the present entry, we have *wooden tablet* (爿) and *military man* (士). Imagine a **VIGOROUS** *military man* **GRANDLY** and **heroically** carrying the *wooden tablet* entrusted to him by the general officer. Note the variant form of this and the next two entries. ☞ 状 0616 |
|---|---|

| | ¹ **VILLA**<br>² **DIGNIFIED, solemn** | ① 別荘 べっそう villa, country cottage..........**0090**<br>¹ 山荘 さんそう mountain villa.................**0037**<br>¹ 静観荘 せいかんそう Seikan Inn.......**0978, 1128**<br>② 荘厳な そうごんな solemn, sublime.........**0810**<br>² 荘重な そうちょうな solemn, grave, impressive<br>..................................................**0539** |
|---|---|---|
| | ソウ | |

| **1590**<br>艹 140<br><br>荘<br><br>1954<br>常 9 | *Grass* (艹) + *grand* (壮): a stately country **VILLA**. Associate M2 **DIGNIFIED** with the same image. |
|---|---|

| | ¹ **DRESS, disguise**<br>² **FIT OUT, equip** | ① 装う よそおう dress oneself, wear; make up<br>① 服装 ふくそう dress, garments, attire........**1471**<br>¹ 仮装する かそうする disguise oneself.......**0921**<br>② 武装 ぶそう armament......................**0111**<br>² 装置 そうち equipment, device, installation<br>..................................................**0843** |
|---|---|---|
| | ソウ ショウ<br>よそお(う) | |

| **1591**<br>衣 145<br><br>裝<br><br>2344<br>常 12 | Let "*grand* (壮) *clothing* (衣)" suggest the idea of adorning oneself in a special way, such as to create a particular appearance (**DRESSING** up/**disguising** oneself), or to prepare oneself for a certain purpose, such as battle (**FITTING** oneself **OUT**/**equipping** oneself). ☞ 奨 0615, 袋 0702 |
|---|---|

| | **DARK** | 冥途 めいど the other world, realm of the dead<br>..................................................**1000**<br>冥想 めいそう meditation.....................**0683**<br>○冥福 めいふく bliss in the next world, soul's repose..................................................**1484**<br>冥加 みょうが divine protection.............**1147**<br>○冥利 みょうり providence, good luck.......**0412** |
|---|---|---|
| | メイ ミョウ | |

| **1592**<br>冖 14<br><br><br><br>1810<br>常 10 | *Sun* (日) *covered* (冖) under *six* (六) layers: **DARK**. This character refers to darkness only in a metaphorical sense, and is used much less frequently than the next entry. ☞ 寅 0913 |
|---|---|

| 暗 | **DARK** | 暗黒 あんこく darkness .............................0535 |
| | | 〇暗号 あんごう code, password ..............0300 |
| | | 暗証番号 あんしょうばんごう PIN, code number |
| | | .............................................0550, 0299, 0300 |
| | アン | 暗記する あんきする learn by heart, memorize |
| | くら(い) | .............................................................0427 |
| | | 〇暗闇 くらやみ darkness ..........................1364 |

| **1593** | Review 音 0150 and 闇 1364. It is relatively easy to remember that 闇 means DARK, given |
| 日 72 | the enclosing quality of 門. Similarly, 日 here signals that the character refers not to *sound* |
| | but to the absence of light: **DARK**. |
| **0921** | |
| 常 13 | |

| 韻 | **RHYME, melodious tone** | 音韻 おんいん phoneme .........................0150 |
| | | 音韻学 おんいんがく phonology, phonetics |
| | | .............................................................0150, 0099 |
| | | 韻文 いんぶん poetry, verse......................0101 |
| | イン | 〇頭韻 とういん alliteration, head rhyme......0162 |
| | | 〇脚韻 きゃくいん rhyme, end rhyme ..........0734 |

| **1594** | This character's meaning is suggested by the **RHYMING** *on-yomi* of its component parts: 音 |
| 音 180 | 0150 オン/イン and 員 0317 イン. It is helpful to memorize the antonym pair V4 and V5. |
| 韵 | |
| **1609** | |
| 常 19 | |

| 損 | **LOSS; disadvantage** | 〇損失 そんしつ loss...............................0563 |
| | | 損害 そんがい damage, harm.................0413 |
| | | 損な条件 そんなじょうけん unfavorable |
| | | conditions ....................................0119, 0118 |
| | ソン | 〇損なう そこなう lose, damage |
| | そこ(なう) -そこ(なう) そこ(ねる) | 〇見損なう みそこなう fail to see; misjudge ...0083 |
| | -そこ(ねる) | |

| **1595** | Here a mistake committed by the *hand* (扌) of an *employee* (員) results in a **LOSS**. |
| 手 64 | |
| **0596** | |
| 常 13 | |

| 捕 | **CATCH, seize** | 〇捕鯨 ほげい whaling.............................1285 |
| | | 捕手 ほしゅ [baseball] catcher ...............0046 |
| | | 袖を捕らえる そでをとらえる catch a person by |
| | | the sleeve ..........................................1531 |
| | ホ | 〇魚を捕る さかなをとる catch fish ............0492 |
| | と(らえる) と(らわれる) と(る) | 犯人を捕まえる はんにんをつかまえる arrest the |
| | つか(まえる) つか(まる) | culprit .......................................0735, 0015 |

| **1596** | See 甫 as a *fishing net*: S4 here depicts the surface of a body of water, S9 a pole to hold the |
| 手 64 | net underwater, 月 the netting, and S10 a fish leaping out of the water to avoid the net (dis- |
| | tinguish 甫 from the *(mixing) cauldron* seen in 専 0580, 敷 1507, etc.). In the present entry, |
| | we see a *hand* (扌) using a *fishing net* to **CATCH** fish. ☞ 挿 1597, 掴 1602 |
| **0387** | |
| 常 10 | |

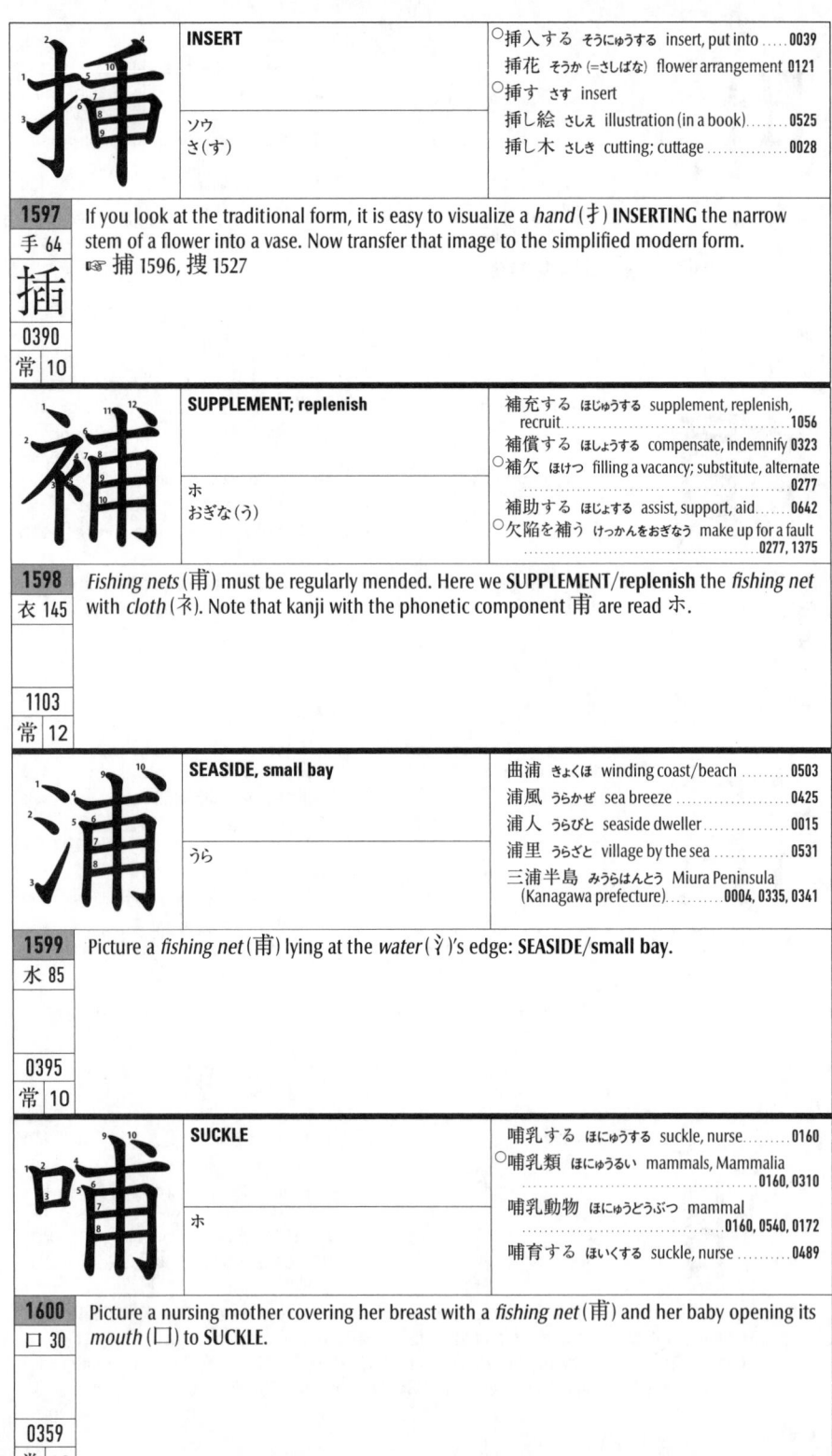

| | INSERT | ○挿入する そうにゅうする insert, put into .....0039 |
|---|---|---|
| 挿 | | 挿花 そうか (=さしばな) flower arrangement 0121 |
| | | ○挿す さす insert |
| | ソウ | 挿し絵 さしえ illustration (in a book)........0525 |
| | さ(す) | 挿し木 さしき cutting; cuttage .............0028 |

**1597** 手 64 挿 0390 常 10

If you look at the traditional form, it is easy to visualize a *hand* (扌) **INSERTING** the narrow stem of a flower into a vase. Now transfer that image to the simplified modern form.
☞ 捕 1596, 捜 1527

| | SUPPLEMENT; replenish | 補充する ほじゅうする supplement, replenish, recruit...............................................1056 |
|---|---|---|
| 補 | | 補償する ほしょうする compensate, indemnify 0323 |
| | | ○補欠 ほけつ filling a vacancy; substitute, alternate ...............................................0277 |
| | ホ | 補助する ほじょする assist, support, aid.......0642 |
| | おぎな(う) | ○欠陥を補う けっかんをおぎなう make up for a fault ...........................................0277, 1375 |

**1598** 衣 145 1103 常 12

*Fishing nets* (甫) must be regularly mended. Here we **SUPPLEMENT**/replenish the *fishing net* with *cloth* (衤). Note that kanji with the phonetic component 甫 are read ホ.

| | SEASIDE, small bay | 曲浦 きょくほ winding coast/beach .........0503 |
|---|---|---|
| 浦 | | 浦風 うらかぜ sea breeze ....................0425 |
| | | 浦人 うらびと seaside dweller...............0015 |
| | うら | 浦里 うらざと village by the sea .............0531 |
| | | 三浦半島 みうらはんとう Miura Peninsula (Kanagawa prefecture)..........0004, 0335, 0341 |

**1599** 水 85 0395 常 10

Picture a *fishing net* (甫) lying at the *water* (氵)'s edge: **SEASIDE**/small bay.

| | SUCKLE | 哺乳する ほにゅうする suckle, nurse........0160 |
|---|---|---|
| 哺 | | ○哺乳類 ほにゅうるい mammals, Mammalia ...........................................0160, 0310 |
| | | 哺乳動物 ほにゅうどうぶつ mammal ...........................................0160, 0540, 0172 |
| | ホ | 哺育する ほいくする suckle, nurse .........0489 |

**1600** 口 30 0359 常 10

Picture a nursing mother covering her breast with a *fishing net* (甫) and her baby opening its *mouth* (口) to **SUCKLE**.

| 舗 | ¹ PAVE<br>² SHOP | ①舗装 ほそう paving............1591<br>¹ 舗道 ほどう pavement, paved street ....0158<br>②店舗 てんぽ shop, store............0347<br>² 老舗 しにせ (=ろうほ) old shop ....0629<br>² 本舗 ほんぽ head office, main shop ....0031 |
| | ホ | |

**1601**
人 9*
舗
1547
常 15

Here we observe a *hut* (舎) where *fishing nets* (甫) are sold. Lots of them. Only fishing nets and more fishing nets, covering everything, all over the **SHOP**. They even cover the *hut's* dirt floor, as a kind of reticulated **PAVEMENT**, and indeed **PAVE** the dirt side street that leads to the **SHOP**.

---

| 掴 | GRASP, clutch | ○掴む つかむ clutch, grasp, hold fast to<br>掴み取る つかみとる grab, seize; acquire, attain<br>............0059<br>掴み つかみ grip<br>一掴み ひとつかみ a handful............0002<br>吊り革に掴まる つりかわにつかまる cling to a<br>strap............0206, 0592 |
| | カク<br>つか(む) つか(まえる) つか(まる) | |

**1602**
手 64
摑
外 11

Picture the *hand* (扌) **GRASPING** the *kingdom* (国). ☞ 捕 1596

---

| 捉 | CATCH, grasp | ○捕捉 ほそく seizure, capture; apprehension;<br>understanding............1596<br>○捉える とらえる seize, capture; grasp, understand<br>意味を捉える いみをとらえる grasp the meaning<br>............0151, 0273<br>捉え所の無い とらえどころのない elusive, subtle<br>............0249, 0048 |
| | ソク<br>とら(える) | |

**1603**
手 64
0391
常 10

Recall the image of 足 as a person with "high heels" to emphasize his FEET/legs (see 0044). Here, visualize a *hand* (扌) trying to **CATCH** 足 by the heel. The mnemonic image notwithstanding, 捉 refers to apprehending ideas, not people; for the latter meaning, use 捕 1596.

---

| | HASTEN, urge | ○促進する そくしんする promote, spur on, facilitate<br>............0191<br>促成 そくせい growth promotion............0070<br>○発達を促す はったつをうながす accelerate<br>development............0148, 1475<br>注意を促す ちゅういをうながす call a person's<br>attention (to)............0368, 0151 |
| | ソク<br>うなが(す) | |

**1604**
人 9
0087
常 9

Here visualize 亻 pushing 足 forward into action: **HASTEN/urge**. Note that both characters that incorporate 足 in the phonetic position follow its *on* reading, ソク.

| | ¹ **BRUSH** | ¹ 毛筆 もうひつ (writing or painting) brush...**0487** |
| | ² **WRITING** | ¹ 画筆 がひつ paintbrush......................**0176** |
| | | ① 筆先 ふてさき brush tip....................**0134** |
| | ヒツ | ¹ 万年筆 まんねんひつ fountain pen....**0018, 0117** |
| | ふて | ② 筆者 ひっしゃ writer........................**0107** |

| **1605** | In 書 0079 WRITE, the tip of the *writing brush* (聿) was trimmed to accommodate the |
| 竹 118 | additional grapheme beneath it. Here (and in the entries that follow), it stretches right down |
| | to the tip. ⺮ suggests a *bamboo* **BRUSH** for **WRITING**. |
| **2335** | |
| 常 12 | |

| | **HARBOR, ferry** | ○津波 つなみ tsunami, tidal wave............**0598** |
| | | 津々浦々に つつうらうらに throughout the land, |
| | シン | in every harbor and every bay...............**1599** |
| | つ | |

| **1606** | Here picture 聿 as a **ferry**'s rudder, writing a foamy wake across the *water* (氵) of the **HARBOR**, |
| 水 85 | as if it were a *writing brush*. |
| **0351** | |
| 常 9 | |

| | ¹ **LAW; commandment** | ① 法律 ほうりつ law............................**0139** |
| | | ¹ 規律 きりつ order, discipline; regulation, law |
| | ² **RHYTHM, tone** | ............**0624** |
| | | ¹ 律儀 りちぎ honesty, faithfulness, loyalty.....**0928** |
| | リツ リチ | ² 律動 りつどう rhythm, rhythmic movement **0540** |
| | | ² 韻律 いんりつ rhythm, meter, measure......**1594** |

| **1607** | 彳 suggests *action*, while 聿 suggests the written rules that regulate it: **LAW**. M2 **RHYTHM** is |
| 彳 60 | a kind of **LAW** governing the arrangement of sounds. |
| **0322** | |
| 常 9 | |

| | **CATCH A CRIMINAL** | ○逮捕 たいほ arrest, capture.................**1596** |
| | | 逮捕状 たいほじょう arrest warrant.....**1596, 0616** |
| | タイ | |

| **1608** | 隶 combines *three-fingered hand* (⺕) with the five-stroke version of *water* (氺). Visualize it |
| 辵 162 | as a *hand spraying water from a hose*. In this entry, imagine a squad of riot officers riding in |
| | on a *truck* (辶) and subduing a gang of looters with *water hoses*: **CATCH A CRIMINAL**. |
| | ☞ 康 1611 |
| **2691** | |
| 常 11 | |

**BUILD**

ケン コン
た(てる) た(て) -だ(て) た(つ)

○建設する けんせつする construct, build .... **0520**
建造 けんぞう construction, building ....... **0699**
○建立 こんりゅう erection, building [as a temple]
........................................................................ **0067**
○建物 たてもの building, structure .......... **0172**
二階建ての家 にかいだてのいえ two-story
house ..............................**0003, 1430, 0219**

| 1609 | Let *"writing brush* (聿) + *stretch* (廴)" suggest an architect's drawing up plans for an expansion: **BUILD.** ☞ 健 1610 |
|---|---|
| 廴 54 | |
| 2661 | |
| 常 9 | |

**ROBUST, healthy**

ケン
すこ(やか)

健在だ けんざいだ be well, be in good health
........................................................................ **0406**
○健全 けんぜん health, soundness .......... **0078**
強健な きょうけんな robust, healthy, strong. **0423**
保健 ほけん (preservation of) health, sanitation
........................................................................ **0646**
○健やかな体 すこやかなからだ healthy body **0062**

| 1610 | *Man* (亻) *building* (建) his body: **ROBUST**/healthy. ☞ 建 1609 |
|---|---|
| 人 9 | |
| 0117 | |
| 常 11 | |

**HEALTHY**

コウ

○健康 けんこう health............................**1610**
健康な けんこうな healthy, well.............**1610**
健康保険 けんこうほけん health insurance
............................................**1610, 0646, 1031**
小康 しょうこう lull, respite, breathing spell (of
peace)..........................................**0034**

| 1611 | Here a *hand sprays water from a hose* (隶) on the plants in a *shelter* (广, i.e., a greenhouse). Associate the image with **HEALTHY** growth. On that note, let me remind you that to keep healthy and strong the kanji expertise you already have, you should by this stage be spending a good part of your study time reading. ☞ 逮 1608, 庸 1612 |
|---|---|
| 广 53 | |
| 2693 | |
| 常 11 | |

**MEDIOCRE**

ヨウ

○庸才 ようさい mediocre talent ............... **0652**
中庸 ちゅうよう the (golden) mean, the middle
path ............................................ **0035**

| 1612 | *Shelter* (广) + *writing brush* (聿) + *moon/month* (月): picture a student who practices calligraphy in his room only once a *month,* and therefore never makes much progress: **MEDIOCRE.** ☞ 康 1611, 粛 1613, 唐 1615 |
|---|---|
| 广 53 | |
| 2697 | |
| 常 11 | |

**¹PURGE**
**²HUSHED; solemnly**

シュク

① 粛清する　しゅくせいする　purge, clean up....0974
¹ 粛正する　しゅくせいする　regulate, enforce
　(discipline).................................................0043
² 静粛　せいしゅく　silence, stillness.............0978
² 厳粛な　げんしゅくな　grave, solemn, austere 0810
② 粛々と　しゅくしゅくと　in solemn silence

| 1613 | Visualize a writer **PURGING** the ink from his *writing brush* (聿) by inserting it into a container of *rice* (米). The rice grains envelop the brush without making the slightest sound, and easily damp any vibrations it might make: **HUSHED**. One can hear the "**HUSH**" in the reading シュク. ☞ 庸 1612 |
|---|---|
| 聿 129 | |
| 肅 | |
| 2996 | |
| 常 11 | |

**EMBROIDERY; brocade**

シュウ

○ 刺繡　ししゅう　embroidery........................0935

| 1614 | Here imagine that the *three-fingered hand* (⺕) holds a needle rather than a brush, and picture it using the *thread* (糸) to stitch an eight-pointed *rice* design (米): **EMBROIDERY**. ☞ 継 0848 |
|---|---|
| 糸 120 | |
| 繡 | |
| 外 17 | |

**TANG DYNASTY**

トウ
から

○ 唐朝　とうちょう　Tang dynasty.................0145
唐詩　とうし　Tang poetry.........................0389
遣唐使　けんとうし　Japanese envoys to Tang
　China...............................................1180, 0887
唐辛子　とうがらし　red pepper.........1462, 0094
○ 唐様　からよう　Chinese style (design)........0501

| 1615 | In this entry the *writing brush* (聿) is trimmed to accommodate 口 *mouth*. The latter symbolizes formal oratory, an art that developed in conjunction with that of writing. The two arts, shown under a *shelter*ing (广) roof, symbolize the great cultural flowering of the **TANG DYNASTY** (China, 618–907 CE). ☞ 庸 1612 |
|---|---|
| 口 30 | |
| 2685 | |
| 常 10 | |

**SUGAR**

トウ

○ 砂糖　さとう　sugar.................................0678
精糖　せいとう　refined sugar, sugar refining 0976
糖分　とうぶん　sugar content....................0088
果糖　かとう　fruit sugar, fructose.............0599
無糖　むとう　sugar-free...........................0048

| 1616 | The technology of sugar refinement arrived to East Asia during the Tang dynasty. The character for **SUGAR** thus combines those for *rice* (米, here suggesting a white granular substance) and *Tang dynasty* (唐). |
|---|---|
| 米 119 | |
| 1281 | |
| 常 16 | |

| 粧 | **APPLY MAKEUP** | ○化粧 けしょうする make up, put on makeup... **0120** |
|---|---|---|
| | | 化粧品 けしょうひん cosmetics.........**0120, 0301** |
| | | 化粧室 けしょうしつ powder room, lavatory |
| | ショウ | ..............**0120, 0253** |
| | | 薄化粧 うすげしょう light makeup...**0986, 0120** |

| **1617** | Note the difference between 圧 0186 and 庄 here. The latter is not a Joyo kanji, so we'll |
|---|---|
| 米 119 | interpret it based on its parts, *earth* (土) and *shelter* (广), and picture an *earthen*ware jar |
| | inside a potter's workshop. Imagine applying a layer of *rice* (米) powder to beautify the jar: |
| | **APPLY MAKEUP.** |
| 1232 | |
| 常 12 | |

| 糧 | **FOOD PROVISIONS** | ○食糧 しょくりょう provisions, food, foodstuffs |
|---|---|---|
| | | ...........**0288** |
| | | 糧道 りょうどう supply of provisions .......**0158** |
| | リョウ ロウ | 衣糧 いりょう clothing and food ..........**0700** |
| | かて | 兵糧 ひょうろう army provisions...........**0907** |
| | | ○心の糧 こころのかて nourishment for the mind/ |
| | | soul ...........**0056** |

| **1618** | Review 量 0538. Here, picture a cargo of *rice* (米) **PROVISIONS** being loaded onto the per- |
|---|---|
| 米 119 | son's head. Compare the sample compounds with V3–5 of 料 0758. |
| 粮 | |
| 1294 | |
| 常 18 | |

| 粉 | **POWDER** | ○粉末 ふんまつ powder.............**0272** |
|---|---|---|
| | | 精粉 せいふん fine powder ..............**0976** |
| | | 製粉 せいふん flour milling..............**0709** |
| | フン | ○小麦粉 こむぎこ (wheat) flour ........**0034, 0131** |
| | こ こな | ○粉薬 こなぐすり powdered medicine ....**0303** |

| **1619** | Picture 分 *dividing* (i.e., pulverizing) the *rice* at the left into rice flour: **POWDER.** |
|---|---|
| 米 119 | |
| 1186 | |
| 常 10 | |

| 紛 | **CONFUSED** | 紛争 ふんそう conflict, strife.............**0972** |
|---|---|---|
| | | ○紛失 ふんしつ loss, misplacement.........**0563** |
| | | 紛れる まぎれる be confused with, be mistaken |
| | フン | for; be diverted from |
| | まぎ(れる) -まぎ(れ) まぎ(らす) | 紛らす (=紛らわす) まぎらす (=まぎらわす) divert, |
| | まぎ(らわす) まぎ(らわしい) | distract; beguile, evade |
| | | ○紛らわしい まぎらわしい confusing, misleading, |
| | | ambiguous |

| **1620** | Here *thread* (糸) suggests logical continuity or coherence. Picture 分 *dividing* the unified |
|---|---|
| 糸 120 | thread into various branches, creating **CONFUSION.** |
| 1191 | |
| 常 10 | |

| | INQUIRE INTO | 紛糾 ふんきゅう complication, disorder, entanglement ............................ 1620 |
|---|---|---|
| | | 糾明 きゅうめい searching examination ..... 0024 |
| | キュウ | ○糾問 きゅうもん cross-examination, arraignment ........................... 0452 |
| | | 糾弾 きゅうだん impeachment, censure ...... 1075 |

**1621**
糸 120

糺

1176
常 9

S7–9 is a form we first saw back at 収 1155, where we visualized it as a receptacle. Here, visualize it as an apparatus for twisting *threads* (糸) into rope. As we twist, we unify the threads into a coherent story line, like detectives reconstructing a "thread" of events. The image thus represents the act of **INQUIRING INTO**. In V1, it denotes twisting.

| | REFINED | ○純粋な じゅんすいな pure, genuine; unalloyed ........................... 1101 |
|---|---|---|
| | | 精粋 せいすい essence, purity ............... 0976 |
| | スイ | 生粋の きっすいの trueborn, pure, genuine .... 0036 |
| | いき | 無粋な ぶすいな lacking in polish; unromantic ........................... 0048 |
| | | 粋な いきな stylish, smart, chic |

**1622**
米 119

粋

1188
常 10

卆 suggests "*nine* (九) times *ten* (十)," or *ninety*. After writing 卆 a few times for practice, review 精 0976. Now whereas the term "quintessence" (or "fifth essence") refers to a substance distilled through five stages of refinement, the present entry suggests a still higher degree of refinement: a grain of *rice* (米) **REFINED** to the *ninetieth* essence!

| | CRUSH UP | ○粉砕する ふんさいする pulverize, shatter, crush ........................... 1619 |
|---|---|---|
| | | 破砕する はさいする crush, smash .......... 0596 |
| | サイ | 玉砕 ぎょくさい death for honor ............. 0073 |
| | くだ(く) くだ(ける) | ○砕く くだく crush, shatter |
| | | 砕ける くだける be crushed; break down, buckle |

**1623**
石 112

砕

1048
常 9

**CRUSH UP** a *stone* (石) into *ninety* (卆) pieces.

| | FRAME | 枠を付ける わくをつける frame, set a frame 0064 |
|---|---|---|
| | | ○枠組み わくぐみ framework, frame .......... 0264 |
| | | 窓枠 まどわく window frame, sash .......... 0558 |
| | わく | 糸枠 いとわく spool ......................... 0112 |
| | | 枠内 わくない within the limits/framework ... 0215 |

**1624**
木 75

枠

0771
常 8

The logs of *ninety* (卆) *trees* (木), all put together: **FRAME**.

**BECOME INTOXICATED**

スイ
よ(う) よ(い)

○麻酔 ますい anesthesia......................0852
酔態 すいたい drunkenness, intoxication...0893
○酔う よう become intoxicated; feel sick
酔っ払う よっぱらう get drunk.............0812
二日酔い ふつかよい hangover, morning after
..............................................0003, 0001

| 1625 | *Ninety* (卆) bottles of *liquor* (酉): **BECOME INTOXICATED.** |
| 酉 164 | |
| 酔 | |
| 1348 | |
| 常 11 | |

**WAKE UP, sober up**

セイ
さ(める)* さ(ます)*

○覚醒剤 かくせいざい stimulant (drug) 0325, 1261
警醒する けいせいする warn, awaken.......0806
醒める さめる [vi] wake up
醒ます さます [vt] wake up
酔い醒める よいざめる sober up.............1625

| 1626 | Review 星 0755 if necessary. A *star* (星, i.e., the sun) shining on you, after *liquor* (酉): **WAKE** |
| 酉 164 | **UP/sober up.** |
| | |
| 1457 | |
| 常 16 | |

**RECIPROCATE, recompense**

シュウ

○報酬 ほうしゅう remuneration, reward; pay...1472
応酬 おうしゅう response, reply; exchange...0850

| 1627 | Picture 酉 here as a bottle of *liquor* placed at one side of a *sandbar*-dotted river (州), an |
| 酉 164 | appealing reward for whoever can cross it: **RECIPROCATE/recompense.** |
| | |
| 1399 | |
| 常 13 | |

**SEVERE, cruel**

コク
ひど(い)*

酷刑 こっけい severe punishment...........0722
酷評 こくひょう severe criticism.............0745
○残酷な ざんこくな cruel, ruthless.............1583
酷暑 こくしょ severe heat.....................1444
○酷い ひどい awful, terrible, severe

| 1628 | *Liquor* (酉) + *accuse* (告): let this suggest **cruel** and **SEVERE** accusations spoken by a drunk |
| 酉 164 | person. |
| | |
| 1414 | |
| 常 14 | |

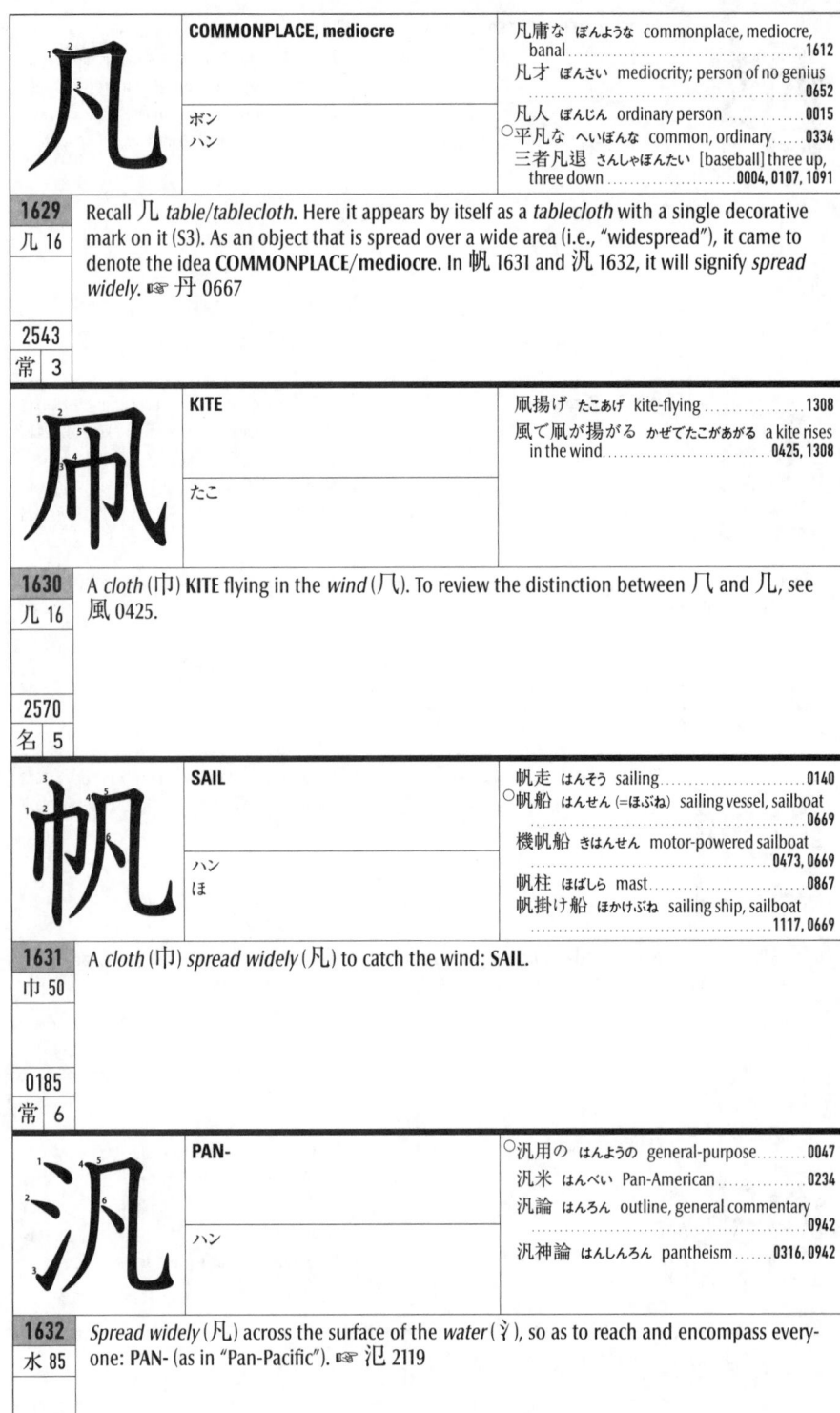

| 凡 | **COMMONPLACE, mediocre** | 凡庸な ぼんような commonplace, mediocre, banal ............................................1612 |
|---|---|---|
| | | 凡才 ぼんさい mediocrity; person of no genius ......................................................0652 |
| | ボン | 凡人 ぼんじん ordinary person ................0015 |
| | ハン | ○平凡な へいぼんな common, ordinary......0334 |
| | | 三者凡退 さんしゃぼんたい [baseball] three up, three down ....................0004, 0107, 1091 |

| **1629** | Recall 几 *table/tablecloth*. Here it appears by itself as a *tablecloth* with a single decorative |
|---|---|
| 几 16 | mark on it (S3). As an object that is spread over a wide area (i.e., "widespread"), it came to |
| | denote the idea **COMMONPLACE/mediocre**. In 帆 1631 and 汎 1632, it will signify *spread* |
| | *widely*. ☞ 丹 0667 |
| **2543** | |
| 常 3 | |

| 凧 | **KITE** | 凧揚げ たこあげ kite-flying ..................1308 |
|---|---|---|
| | | 風で凧が揚がる かぜでたこがあがる a kite rises in the wind............................0425, 1308 |
| | たこ | |

| **1630** | A *cloth* (巾) **KITE** flying in the *wind* (几). To review the distinction between 几 and 几, see |
|---|---|
| 几 16 | 風 0425. |
| **2570** | |
| 名 5 | |

| 帆 | **SAIL** | 帆走 はんそう sailing..........................0140 |
|---|---|---|
| | | ○帆船 はんせん (=ほぶね) sailing vessel, sailboat ..........................................................0669 |
| | ハン | 機帆船 きはんせん motor-powered sailboat ................................................0473, 0669 |
| | ほ | 帆柱 ほばしら mast...........................0867 |
| | | 帆掛け船 ほかけぶね sailing ship, sailboat ................................................1117, 0669 |

| **1631** | A *cloth* (巾) *spread widely* (凡) to catch the wind: **SAIL**. |
|---|---|
| 巾 50 | |
| **0185** | |
| 常 6 | |

| 汎 | **PAN-** | ○汎用の はんような general-purpose..........0047 |
|---|---|---|
| | | 汎米 はんべい Pan-American .................0234 |
| | ハン | 汎論 はんろん outline, general commentary ..........................................................0942 |
| | | 汎神論 はんしんろん pantheism.......0316, 0942 |

| **1632** | *Spread widely* (凡) across the surface of the *water* (氵), so as to reach and encompass every- |
|---|---|
| 水 85 | one: **PAN-** (as in "Pan-Pacific"). ☞ 氾 2119 |
| **0192** | |
| 常 6 | |

**FEAR**

キョウ
おそ(れる) おそ(る) おそ(ろしい)

恐竜 きょうりゅう dinosaur....................0507
○恐慌 きょうこう panic, scare, alarm...........1065
恐縮する きょうしゅくする feel much obliged;
　regret; feel embarrassed ...............0875
○恐れる おそれる fear; stand in awe
恐ろしい おそろしい fearful; marvelous

| 1633 | When it appears next to 工 (the I beam, representing *construction*), let 凡 suggest a carpenter's *table*. The thought of I beams, table saws, and other dangerous objects arouses **FEAR** in one's *heart* (心). |
| 心 61 | |
| 2306 | |
| 常 10 | |

**FEARFUL**

フ
こわ(い) こわ(がる)

○恐怖 きょうふ fear ...........................1633
○怖い こわい fearful, scary; be afraid
怖い顔 こわいかお angry look, grim face ...0180
犬が怖い いぬがこわい be afraid of dogs ...0293
怖がる こわがる be afraid of, be frightened

| 1634 | Imagine unfolding this *cloth* (布) and discovering a beating, bloody *heart* (忄) organ wrapped inside: **FEARFUL!** |
| 心 61 | |
| 0263 | |
| 常 8 | |

**CONSTRUCT**

チク
きず(く)

○建築 けんちく construction, architecture....1609
建築家 けんちくか architect............1609, 0219
構築 こうちく construction, building........0917
新築 しんちく new building.................0275
○築く きずく construct, build

| 1635 | *Bamboo* (⺮) scaffolding + *I beam* (工) + carpenter's *table* (凡, see 1633) + *lumber* (木): finding all these together, we know we must be looking at a **CONSTRUCTION** site. |
| 竹 118 | |
| 2369 | |
| 常 16 | |

**INQUIRE, look for**

ジン
たず(ねる)

○尋問 じんもんする question, examine, interro-
　gate..................................0452
○尋ねる たずねる inquire, look for
理由を尋ねる りゆうをたずねる ask the reason
　...............................0532, 0432
尋ね人 たずねびと missing person .........0015
尋ね求める たずねもとめる seek...........1097

| 1636 | Let *hand* (⺕) and *outstretched arm* (寸) together signify a detective's **looking for** something with both hands. 口 *mouth* suggests the detective's oral questioning, and 工 his professional *workmanship*. Taken as a whole, the ensemble suggests a formal **INQUIRY**. |
| 寸 41 | |
| 2027 | |
| 常 12 | |

| 訊 | INTERROGATE, ask | ○訊問する じんもんする question, examine, interrogate...........................0452<br>反対訊問 はんたいじんもん cross-examination.............................0374, 0650, 0452 |
| --- | --- | --- |
| | ジン<br>たず(ねる) き(く) | ○訊ねる たずねる ask, inquire; look into, investigate<br>道を訊く みちをきく ask the way.............0158 |

| **1637**<br>言 149 | On the right, picture a person standing in a doorway asking questions. See how he steps forward to try to catch his respondent's every *word* (言): **INTERROGATE/ask**. Now usually replaced by the previous entry. ☞ 迅 1146 |
| --- | --- |
| **1320**<br>名 10 | |

| 諮 | CONSULT, ask for advice | ○諮問する しもんする consult, inquire.........0452<br>○諮る はかる consult, ask for advice |
| --- | --- | --- |
| | シ<br>はか(る) | 委員会に諮る いいんかいにはかる submit (a plan) to a committee for deliberation<br>.........................0396, 0317, 0226 |

| **1638**<br>言 149 | A distinctive feature of this kanji is the pair of strokes (冫) sandwiched in the middle. Use that as a visual shortcut to the idea of **CONSULTING/asking for advice**: see 欠 as a person **asking for advice**, and 冫 as information passing from the *words* of advice (言) into the advice-seeker's ear (S10). |
| --- | --- |
| **1443**<br>常 16 | |

| 抗 | RESIST | 抗争 こうそう dispute, resistance.............0972<br>抗議 こうぎ protest, remonstrance, objection.............................0927<br>○抵抗する ていこうする resist, oppose, defy 0480<br>対抗する たいこうする oppose, antagonize, rival; counteract.............................0650<br>不可抗力 ふかこうりょく act of God, irresistible force.....................0049, 0814, 0084 |
| --- | --- | --- |
| | コウ | |

| **1639**<br>手 64 | 亢 shows a flat *table*top with 亠 over it to emphasize the idea of *straightness*. With 扌, it suggests an arm held *straight* out in **RESISTANCE**. Visualize S5 as a resisting stiff arm. Note that all three kanji incorporating 亢 are pronounced コウ. |
| --- | --- |
| **0224**<br>常 7 | |

| 航 | NAVIGATE | 航行 こうこう navigation, cruise.............0055<br>航海 こうかい voyage, ocean navigation....0106<br>航路 こうろ sea route, course.............0788<br>航空 こうくう aviation.........................0398<br>○航空券 こうくうけん plane ticket.......0398, 0456 |
| --- | --- | --- |
| | コウ | |

| **1640**<br>舟 137 | Making sure a *boat* (舟) travels in a *straight* (亢) line: **NAVIGATION**. ☞ 般 0671 |
| --- | --- |
| **1204**<br>常 10 | |

| 坑 | **PIT (of a mine)** | 坑口 こうこう pithead, minehead............0019 |
|---|---|---|
| | | 坑夫 こうふ miner............0565 |
| | | 坑内 こうない (interior of a) mine pit, shaft 0215 |
| | コウ | 金坑 きんこう gold mine............0029 |

| **1641**<br>土 32<br><br>0208<br>常 7 | A *straight* (亢) shaft dug into the *earth* (土): **PIT (of a mine)**. |
|---|---|

| 拝 | **¹ WORSHIP**<br>**² HUMBLY** | ① 参拝する さんぱいする worship, visit a shrine/ temple............1238 |
|---|---|---|
| | | ¹ 礼拝 れいはい (=らいはい) worship; church service............0313 |
| | | ① 拝む おがむ bow in veneration, worship; pay one's respects with joined hands, entreat |
| | ハイ<br>おが(む) | ² 拝見する はいけんする have the honor of seeing, look at............0083 |
| | | ² 拝借する はいしゃくする borrow............1220 |

| **1642**<br>手 64<br><br>0268<br>常 8 | The image at the right suggests the interlocking fingers of *hands* joined in prayer: **WORSHIP**. M2 **HUMBLY** is an extended meaning. |
|---|---|

| 耕 | **TILL** | 耕作する こうさくする cultivate, plow, till ...0152 |
|---|---|---|
| | | 耕具 こうぐ farm implements............0837 |
| | | 耕運機 こううんき cultivator, tiller.....0584, 0473 |
| | コウ<br>たがや(す) | 農耕 のうこう farming............0511 |
| | | 耕す たがやす till, plow |

| **1643**<br>耒 127<br><br>1198<br>常 10 | In this entry, 井 will not represent *well* (see 0434), but instead furrows in a farm field. 耒 is a new grapheme meaning *plow*, which we can visualize here as a three-bladed rotary tiller rolling across those furrows, **TILLING** the soil in a crisscross pattern. The diagonal lines at the lower left (S5–6) show the **TILLED** soil being tossed to one side. |
|---|---|

| 耗 | **WEAR AWAY** | 消耗する しょうもうする consume, exhaust, use up............1289 |
|---|---|---|
| | | 損耗 そんもう wear and tear, deterioration 1595 |
| | モウ コウ | |

| **1644**<br>耒 127<br><br>1199<br>常 10 | (Continuing from the previous entry) Now the rotary tiller (耒) is used to grind up *wool* (毛). Picture how quickly the wool **WEARS AWAY** under the harrowing contact of the rotary tiller. This image is captured well in the sample compound 摩耗する (まもうする, wear away, wear out; see 摩 2099). |
|---|---|

**REVERENCE**

スウ

○崇拝 すうはい worship, adoration............1642
祖先崇拝 そせんすうはい ancestor worship
........................................0641, 0134, 1642
崇敬 すうけい reverence, admiration........0805
崇高な すうこうな lofty, sublime, noble.....0185
尊崇 そんすう reverence, veneration........0802

| 1645 | In Japan, temples have often been built at the base of hills or mountains, the place where man may approach the infinite. Reflecting this practice, this character places a *house of worship* (宗) at the foot of a *mountain* (山) to represent the idea of human **REVERENCE** toward the elevated and the sacred. ☞ 宗 0636 |
|---|---|
| 山 46 | |
| 1990 | |
| 常 11 | |

**ASH**

カイ
はい

重灰 じゅうかい dense ash ...................0539
灰白色 かいはくしょく ash color, light gray
........................................0076, 0528
灰色 はいいろ ash color, gray ...............0528
○灰皿 はいざら ashtray......................0197
火山灰 かざんばい volcano ashes .....0026, 0037

| 1646 | Picture a *fire* (火) producing a great mound of **ASH**, as tall as a *cliff* (厂). ☞ 炭 1647 |
|---|---|
| 火 86 | |
| 2573 | |
| 常 6 | |

¹**COAL**
²**CHARCOAL**
³**CARBON**

タン
すみ

¹炭坑 たんこう coal mine, coal pit ............1641
¹石炭 せきたん coal ............................0403
²木炭 もくたん charcoal......................0028
²炭を焼く すみをやく make charcoal .........0769
③炭素 たんそ carbon..........................0132

| 1647 | Here a *mountain* (山) buries *ash* (灰), compressing it so heavily it turns to **COAL**. Associate the compression of the *ash* here (compared to the previous entry) with the greater density of **COAL** vis-à-vis *ash*. ☞ 灰 1646, 岸 1648 |
|---|---|
| 火 86 | |
| 1947 | |
| 常 9 | |

**SHORE, bank**

ガン
きし

沿岸 えんがん coast, shore..................1348
○海岸 かいがん seashore, beach..............0106
対岸 たいがん opposite bank/shore.........0650
岸壁 がんぺき quay (wall), wharf ............1466
○向こう岸 むこうぎし opposite bank, further shore
........................................0183

| 1648 | Here we observe a high *mountain* (山) *cliff* (厂), with the grapheme 干 to signify *dry*. Seeing the latter, we recognize that this kanji refers to the **SHORE**, in the same sense in which sea-weary sailors might use the expression "dry land" in English. ☞ 炭 1647 |
|---|---|
| 山 46 | |
| 1920 | |
| 常 8 | |

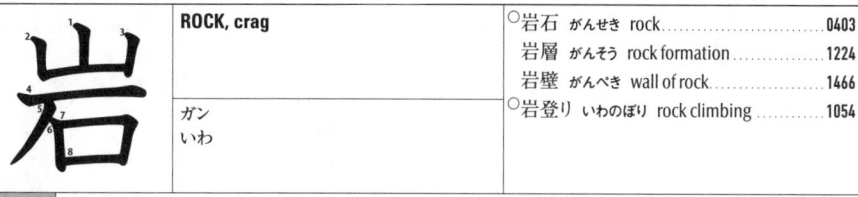

| 岩 | ROCK, crag | ○岩石 がんせき rock.............................0403 |
| | | 岩層 がんそう rock formation.................1224 |
| | | 岩壁 がんぺき wall of rock.......................1466 |
| | ガン | ○岩登り いわのぼり rock climbing.............1054 |
| | いわ | |

| 1649 | Recall that 石 *stone* uses a variation on 厂. Visualize the present entry as a *stone* protruding |
| 山 46 | from the side of a *mountain* (山): **ROCK/crag**. |
| 1921 | |
| 常 8 | |

| 崩 | CRUMBLE | 崩落する ほうらくする collapse; decline.....0793 |
| | | ○崩れる くずれる [vi] crumble, collapse, cave in |
| | | 雪崩 なだれ avalanche, snowslide...........0899 |
| | ホウ | 土砂崩れ どしゃくずれ landslide....0030, 0678 |
| | くず(れる) -くず(れ) くず(す) | 切り崩す きりくずす level (a hill)............0086 |

| 1650 | See 朋 not as two *moons* but as two massive piles of earth pouring down from a *mountain* |
| 山 46 | (山) in a landslide. Two valleys separate the mountain's three peaks; see one pile of earth |
| | **CRUMBLING** down from each valley. A useful *on-yomi* compound to memorize appears at 壊 |
| | 1666. |
| 1989 | |
| 常 11 | |

| 嵐 | STORM | 嵐の前の静けさ あらしのまえのしずけさ the calm |
| | | before a storm...........................0113, 0978 |
| | | 砂嵐 すなあらし sandstorm...................0678 |
| | あらし | |

| 1651 | Behold the *winds* (風) of a **STORM** blowing down from a *mountain* (山). |
| 山 46 | |
| 2012 | |
| 常 12 | |

| 崖 | CLIFF | ○断崖 だんがい palisade, cliff.................0849 |
| | | 断崖絶壁 だんがいぜっぺき sheer cliff |
| | | .................................0849, 1271, 1466 |
| | | 懸崖 けんがい overhanging cliff.............1080 |
| | ガイ | 崖っ縁 がけっぷち cliff's edge; critical moment |
| | がけ | .........................................0610 |
| | | ○崖崩れ がけくずれ landslide.................1650 |

| 1652 | To compose the kanji for **CLIFF**, we visually reinforce *cliff* (厂) with *mountain* (山) and piled |
| 山 46 | layers of *earth* (圭). ☞ 涯 1902 |
| 崖 | |
| 1988 | |
| 常 11 | |

| | ¹ **SPONSOR, make happen** <br> ² **PRESS FOR** <br><br> サイ <br> もよお(す) | ¹ 開催する かいさいする hold/open an event…**0450** <br> ① 主催 しゅさい sponsorship, promotion……**0365** <br> ¹ 催す もよおす hold (an event), give (a dinner), put on (a show) <br> ¹ 催眠 さいみん hypnotism ……………**1009** <br> ② 催促する さいそくする press for, urge, demand ……………………**1604** |
|---|---|---|

| **1653** <br> 人 9 <br><br> 0136 <br> 常 13 | The *man* (亻) at the left has **SPONSORED** a *bird* (隹) reserve in the *mountains* (山). To capture the broad sense of this character, think of the efforts he has made to **PRESS FOR** the reserve's creation and finally **make it happen**. |
|---|---|

| | ¹ **SCORCH** <br> ² **BE IMPATIENT** <br><br> ショウ <br> こ(げる) こ(がす) こ(がれる) あせ(る) | ① 焦げる こげる [vi] scorch, burn <br> ¹ 焦熱 しょうねつ scorching heat……………**1435** <br> ① 焦点 しょうてん focus, focal point; (photographic) focus ………………**0349** <br> ② 焦る あせる be impatient, be in a hurry <br> ² 焦心 しょうしん impatience ……………**0056** |
|---|---|---|

| **1654** <br> 火 86 <br><br> 2412 <br> 常 12 | Imagine how desperately **IMPATIENT** the *bird* (隹) must be as it sits on a *fire* (灬), being **SCORCHED.** ☞ 無 0048, 礁 1655 |
|---|---|

| | **REEF** <br><br> ショウ | 環礁 かんしょう atoll…………………**1549** <br> 暗礁 あんしょう sunken rock; deadlock…**1593** <br> ○ 座礁(=坐礁)する ざしょうする run aground, be stranded ……………………**0749, 0750** <br> 岩礁 がんしょう reef …………………**1649** |
|---|---|---|

| **1655** <br> 石 112 <br><br> 1148 <br> 常 17 | Observe the *bird* (隹) alighting on the *scorching*-hot *rocks* (石) of an exposed **REEF.** ☞ 礁 1133, 焦 1654 |
|---|---|

| | **ROUSE UP** <br><br> フン <br> ふる(う) | 奮起する ふんきする rouse oneself………**0430** <br> 奮然と ふんぜんと resolutely, courageously **0760** <br> 奮闘 ふんとう hard fighting ……………**1363** <br> ○ 興奮 こうふん excitement, agitation, stimulation ………………………**0505** <br> ○ 奮う ふるう rouse up, do energetically |
|---|---|---|

| **1656** <br> 大 37 <br><br> 2090 <br> 常 16 | Visualize the *bird* (隹)'s first sitting passively in a *rice field* (田), then suddenly being **ROUSED UP**, spreading its wings "big" (大), and briskly flying away. Use 大 more as a visual clue than a semantic one: see S2–3 as the bird's wings flapping vigorously as it attempts to **ROUSE** itself **UP.** ☞ 奪 1657 |
|---|---|

**SEIZE, rob**

ダツ
うば(う)

奪還 だっかん recapture, recovery...........1550
○略奪 りゃくだつ pillage, plunder, looting....0791
争奪 そうだつ scramble, contest, struggle...0972
剥奪する はくだつする deprive, divest......0609
○奪う うばう rob, take by force

| 1657 | (Building on the previous entry) Now we see what the *bird* (隹) is getting all roused up about: a predator is reaching up with an *outstretched arm* (寸) to **SEIZE** it before it can fly away. ☞ 奮 1656 |
|---|---|
| 大 37 | |
| 2058 | |
| 常 14 | |

**¹ ONE OF A PAIR**
**² COUNTER FOR SHIPS**

セキ

①隻眼 せきがん one eye......................1092
②一隻 いっせき one ship ....................0002
² 数隻 すうせき several ships.................0309

| 1658 | The traditional form of 双 1498 SET OF TWO was 雙, showing a hand holding a pair of birds. The present entry is used in contrast to that, showing a *hand* holding only <u>one</u> of the *birds*, to signify the idea **ONE OF A PAIR**. It has not been simplified to 又 because such a character already exists (0058). ☞ 集 0190 |
|---|---|
| 隹 172 | |
| 2403 | |
| 常 10 | |

**CATCH GAME**

カク
え(る)

○獲得する かくとくする get, acquire, obtain...0387
捕獲する ほかくする catch (fish); capture, seize
.................................................1596
乱獲 らんかく excessive fishing/hunting....0380
○獲物 えもの spoils, catch, prize.............0172
獲る える hunt, fish

| 1659 | The next three characters include 蒦. Picture it as an adult bird (隹) grasping some grass (艹) within its talons (suggested by 又 *hand*). In the present entry, then, we have *grasp* + *smallish four-legged creature* (犭): **CATCH GAME**. ☞ 得 0387, 穫 1660 |
|---|---|
| 犬 94 | |
| 0699 | |
| 常 16 | |

**HARVEST**

カク

○収穫する しゅうかくする harvest, gather in, reap
.................................................1155
収穫期 しゅうかくき harvest season ....1155, 0486

| 1660 | (Continuing from the previous entry) *Grasp* (蒦) + *rice* (禾): **HARVEST**. ☞ 獲 1659 |
|---|---|
| 禾 115 | |
| 1155 | |
| 常 18 | |

| PROTECT | ○護る まもる guard, protect |
| | 護衛 ごえい guard, escort ....................0661 |
| | 看護婦 かんごふ nurse ...............0939, 1017 |
| ゴ | 保護者 ほごしゃ guardian ............0646, 0107 |
| まも(る)* | ○弁護士 べんごし lawyer, attorney .....1052, 0350 |

| **1661** | (Continuing from 1659–60) This time we observe the bird *grasping* (蒦) the grass and speaking fierce *words* (言) to **PROTECT** its possession. ☞ 讓 1662 |
| 言 149 | |
| 1481 | |
| 常 20 | |

| CEDE, yield | 讓渡 じょうと transfer (of ownership), conveyance |
| | ....................................................0281 |
| | 讓与 じょうよ transfer (of ownership) ........0858 |
| | ○讓歩 じょうほ concession, compromise .....0679 |
| ジョウ | ○讓る ゆずる cede, transfer |
| ゆず(る) | 親讓りの おやゆずりの hereditary ..........0276 |

| **1662** | 襄 at the right is based on the split version of *garment* (衣). Picture it as a garment whose interior has been *padded with fluffy lining* (S10–16). With 言 it refers to the *words* of a compromise-negotiating mediator who inserts soft "padding" between two disputing parties. From this idea the character has come to mean **CEDE/yield**. ☞ 護 1661, 講 0918 |
| 言 149 | |
| 譲 | |
| 1482 | |
| 常 20 | |

| YOUNG LADY | 令嬢 れいじょう your daughter; young lady...0229 |
| | 老嬢 ろうじょう spinster ......................0629 |
| | 交換嬢 こうかんじょう telephone operator |
| | ....................................................0102, 1269 |
| ジョウ | 案内嬢 あんないじょう usherette........0097, 0215 |
| | ○お嬢さん おじょうさん your daughter; young lady |

| **1663** | 女 *woman* + 襄 *pad with fluffy lining* = a padded, fluffy way of addressing a **YOUNG LADY**. Note that 襄 in this series of characters is a simplification of 襄, which shows the "padding" even more clearly. Take some time to practice writing the simplified version, remembering to start and finish with 衣. |
| 女 38 | |
| 嬢 | |
| 0685 | |
| 常 16 | |

| BREW | ○醸造 じょうぞう brewing; distilling ...........0699 |
| | 醸造所 じょうぞうしょ brewery ..........0699, 0249 |
| | 醸成する じょうせいする brew; bring about 0070 |
| ジョウ | ○酒を醸す さけをかもす brew sake...........0797 |
| かも(す) | |

| **1664** | 酉 *liquor* jar + 襄 *pad with fluffy lining* refers to the addition of fermenting agents into a cask: **BREW**. Note that all these kanji incorporating 襄 are pronounced ジョウ. |
| 酉 164 | |
| 醸 | |
| 1483 | |
| 常 20 | |

| | **ARABLE SOIL** | ○土壌 どじょう soil, earth.....................0030 |
| | | 平壌 ピョンヤン (=へいじょう) Pyongyang.....0334 |
| | ジョウ | |

| **1665** | "土 *earth* + 襄 *padded and fluffy*": ARABLE SOIL. ☞ 壌 1666 |
| 土 32 | |
| 壌 | |
| 0683 | |
| 常 16 | |

| | **BREAK DOWN** | 破壊する はかいする break (down), destroy, wreck.....................0596 |
| | | ○崩壊する ほうかいする collapse, crumble, cave in.....................1650 |
| | カイ | 倒壊する とうかいする collapse, be destroyed, crumble.....................0941 |
| | こわ(す) こわ(れる) | 壊す こわす [vt] break (down), destroy |
| | | ○壊れる こわれる [vi] break (down), be broken |

| **1666** | Take S4–10 in the upper right as a variant of 直 *straight/upright*. Combined with 衣 *garment*, it suggests a straight-cut gown. In this entry, imagine that a person's *straight-cut gown* gets caught on the *ground* (土) and tears apart: BREAK DOWN. Note that the right side is a simplification of 裏. ☞ 壌 1665, 懐 1667 |
| 土 32 | |
| 壊 | |
| 0684 | |
| 常 16 | |

| | **¹ BOSOM, embosom**<br>**² LONG FOR** | ¹ 懐中電灯 かいちゅうでんとう flashlight.....................0035, 0155, 0440 |
| | | ¹ 自然の懐 しぜんのふところ bosom of Nature.....................0081, 0760 |
| | カイ | ②懐郷 かいきょう nostalgia, homesickness....1295 |
| | ふところ なつ(かしい) なつ(かしむ) | ②懐かしむ なつかしむ long for, miss |
| | なつ(く) なつ(ける) | ² 人懐かしい ひとなつかしい miss people; long for others' presence.....................0015 |

| **1667** | This character refers to the *heart* (忄) hidden beneath one's *(straight-cut) gown*: BOSOM. Behind the gown, we hide our tears (visible in the traditional form), and shroud our private loves and LONGINGS. ☞ 壊 1666 |
| 心 61 | |
| 懐 | |
| 0689 | |
| 常 16 | |

| | **VIRTUE** | 徳義 とくぎ morality, sincerity.....................0926 |
| | | ○道徳 どうとく morality, morals.....................0158 |
| | | 悪徳 あくとく vice, corruption, immorality...0546 |
| | トク | 美徳 びとく virtue, good deed.....................0497 |
| | | 徳川幕府 とくがわばくふ Tokugawa shogunate.....................0022, 1339, 0247 |

| **1668** | Again, take the upper right as a variant of 直 *straight/upright*. Together with 心, it suggests *upright heart*, which here combines with 彳 *action* to signify virtuous action, or simply VIRTUE. ☞ 聴 1669 |
| 彳 60 | |
| 悳 | |
| 0623 | |
| 常 14 | |

| | **LISTEN** | 拝聴する はいちょうする have the honor of hearing/listening to ......................1642 |
|---|---|---|
| | | ○聴衆 ちょうしゅう audience ...................1405 |
| | | 聴覚 ちょうかく sense of hearing ...........0325 |
| | チョウ | 視聴者 しちょうしゃ viewer, audience...0623, 0107 |
| | き(く) | 民の声を聴く たみのこえをきく listen to the voice of the people ......................0477, 0529 |

| **1669** | *Ear*(耳) + *upright heart*: together these suggest attentive **LISTENING**. ☞ 徳 1668 |
|---|---|
| 耳 128 | |
| 聴 | |
| 1292 | |
| 常 17 | |

| | **SHAME** | ○無恥 むち shameless ........................0048 |
|---|---|---|
| | | 恥骨 ちこつ pubic bone......................0465 |
| | | ○恥じる はじる feel ashamed |
| | チ | 恥知らず はじしらず shameless person .....0560 |
| | は(じる) はじ は(じらう) は(ずかしい) | ○恥ずかしい はずかしい shy; ashamed; shameful |

| **1670** | *Ear*(耳) + *heart*(心): suggests a feeling brought on by the consciousness of others' opinions of us: **SHAME**. Picture a word of reproach passing through the *ear* and causing great distress to the *heart*. |
|---|---|
| 心 61 | |
| 恥 | |
| 1200 | |
| 常 10 | |

| | **SHAME** | 羞恥 しゅうち shame, shyness ...............1670 |
|---|---|---|
| | | 羞恥心 しゅうちしん (sense of) shame..1670, 0056 |
| | シュウ | |

| **1671** | The *ox*(丑 0590) feels **ASHAMED** for associating with the *goat*(羊). See how he hides underneath the goat out of **SHAME**. ☞ 差 0937, 着 0938 |
|---|---|
| 羊 123 | |
| 2823 | |
| 常 11 | |

| | **RANK OF NOBILITY** | ○爵位 しゃくい rank of nobility ............0577 |
|---|---|---|
| | | 公爵 こうしゃく duke, prince..................0089 |
| | | 伯爵 はくしゃく count, earl ...................1184 |
| | シャク | 男爵 だんしゃく baron.........................0092 |

| **1672** | Visualize ⊞ as kind of crown, which ⺥ (*claw*) places on the heads of the two small graphemes appearing at the bottom. Imagine that these two are minor gentry, and that the *claw* bestows upon them the **RANK OF NOBILITY**. |
|---|---|
| 爪 87 | |
| 2197 | |
| 常 17 | |

**FEUDAL LORD**

コウ

| | | |
|---|---|---|
| 侯爵 こうしゃく marquis, marquess | | 1672 |
| 諸侯 しょこう feudal lords | | 1448 |
| 王侯 おうこう princes, royalty, crowned heads | | 0072 |
| 仙台侯 せんだいこう lord of Sendai | | 1003, 0949 |

| 1673 | Picture the right half of this character as the granting of an arrow (矢), i.e., the Crown's bestowal of a feudal title in exchange for military service. With 亻 for *man*, it signifies **FEUDAL LORD.** ☞ 候 1675 |
|---|---|
| 人 9 | |
| 0079 | |
| 常 9 | |

**THROAT**

コウ
のど

| | | |
|---|---|---|
| ○喉頭 こうとう larynx | | 0162 |
| 喉頭蓋 こうとうがい epiglottis | | 0162, 1303 |
| 喉元 のどもと throat | | 0136 |
| 喉が痛い のどがいたい one's throat is sore | | 0619 |
| ○喉を潤す のどをうるおす slake one's thirst | | 1491 |

| 1674 | (Continuing from the previous entry) This time imagine the king shoving the arrow through the *feudal lord* (侯)'s *mouth* (口) and down his **THROAT.** |
|---|---|
| 口 30 | |
| 0506 | |
| 常 12 | |

**¹ SEASON**
**² SEASONAL WEATHER, sign**

コウ
そうろう

| | | |
|---|---|---|
| ¹時候 じこう season, time of the year | | 0383 |
| ²天候 てんこう weather | | 0270 |
| ②症候 しょうこう symptom | | 0618 |
| 候補者 こうほしゃ candidate, applicant | | 1598, 0107 |
| 候 そうろう classical verbal suffix equiv. to *-masu* | | |

| 1675 | Picture a *feudal lord* (侯) using a rod (S3) to divine the weather for this season: **SEASONAL WEATHER; SEASON.** Note that both characters incorporating 侯 follow its *on* reading, コウ. ☞ 侯 1673 |
|---|---|
| 人 9 | |
| 0101 | |
| 常 10 | |

**¹ CULTIVATE (oneself), study**
**² REPAIR**

シュウ　シュ
おさ(める)　おさ(まる)

| | | |
|---|---|---|
| ①研修 けんしゅう study and training | | 0724 |
| ¹修士 しゅうし master, master's degree | | 0350 |
| ①修める おさめる cultivate, practice, study; master | | |
| ²修繕する しゅうぜんする mend, repair | | 1214 |
| ②修理する しゅうりする mend, repair | | 0532 |

| 1676 | Review the note at 参 1238. Here a *man* (亻) *strikes* (攵) himself with a rod (S3) to discipline himself in his efforts at self-improvement. As you write out 彡, imagine that these three lines represent progressive stages of his training, self-improving, or repairing, thus signifying M1 **CULTIVATE (oneself)/study** and M2 **REPAIR.** ☞ 冬 0360 |
|---|---|
| 人 9 | |
| 0105 | |
| 常 10 | |

| | LEISURELY, serene | ○悠々と ゆうゆうと calmly, leisurely; easily, without difficulty; boundlessly |
|---|---|---|
| | | 悠長な ゆうちょうな leisurely, easygoing; tedious ....................................................0091 |
| | ユウ | 悠然として ゆうぜんとして with an air of perfect composure ...............................0760 |

| **1677** | Meaning **LEISURELY/serene**, this character can be seen as a kind of reversal of the previous one. Let *heart* (心) signify compassion toward the disciplined self-improver, mercifully replacing the staged training process (represented by 彡 in the previous entry) with a moment of **LEISURE**. ☞ 愁 1316 |
|---|---|
| 心 61 | |
| 2389 | |
| 常 11 | |

| | RIGHT, correct | ○是非 ぜひ right and/or wrong; by all means, at any cost .........................................0738 |
|---|---|---|
| | | 是非とも ぜひとも at any cost, by some means or other ..........................................0738 |
| | ゼ | 是認 ぜにん approval .........................1096 |
| | | 是正 ぜせい correction.....................0043 |

| **1678** | Suggests the *sun* (日)'s *straight* (正) path through the sky: **RIGHT/correct**. Both **RIGHT** and **correct** derive from the Latin word *rectus*, meaning "straight," which is what we shall call 是 when it appears inside other kanji. These follow presently. ☞ 呈 0587 |
|---|---|
| 日 72 | |
| 2157 | |
| 常 9 | |

| | ¹ **PRESENT, offer** ² **CARRY IN HAND** | ①提案 ていあん proposition, proposal, suggestion ................................................0097 |
|---|---|---|
| | | ¹提出する ていしゅつする present, submit, turn in ..........................................0038 |
| | テイ さ(げる) | ¹提供する ていきょうする offer, tender; sponsor (a show)...................................0357 |
| | | ¹前提 ぜんてい premise, presupposition ....0113 |
| | | ②提げる さげる carry in hand, take with |

| **1679** | One should hold one's *hand* (扌) *straight* (是) out when **PRESENTING** a gift, business card, etc. ☞ 呈 0587 |
|---|---|
| 手 64 | |
| 0540 | |
| 常 12 | |

| | EMBANKMENT | ○堤防 ていぼう bank, embankment, dike....0174 |
|---|---|---|
| | | 突堤 とってい pier, breakwater...............1564 |
| | | 防潮堤 ぼうちょうてい tide embankment, seawall ........................................0174, 0146 |
| | テイ つつみ | 防波堤 ぼうはてい breakwater.........0174, 0598 |

| **1680** | *Straightened* (是) *earth* (土): **EMBANKMENT**. The next entry, by the way, will be one of the last high-frequency kanji you will learn. Once you've learned it, it would be prudent to reduce the time you spend acquiring new kanji, in favor of more reading. You now have more to lose by forgetting kanji you've already learned than to gain by learning new ones. |
|---|---|
| 土 32 | |
| 0515 | |
| 常 12 | |

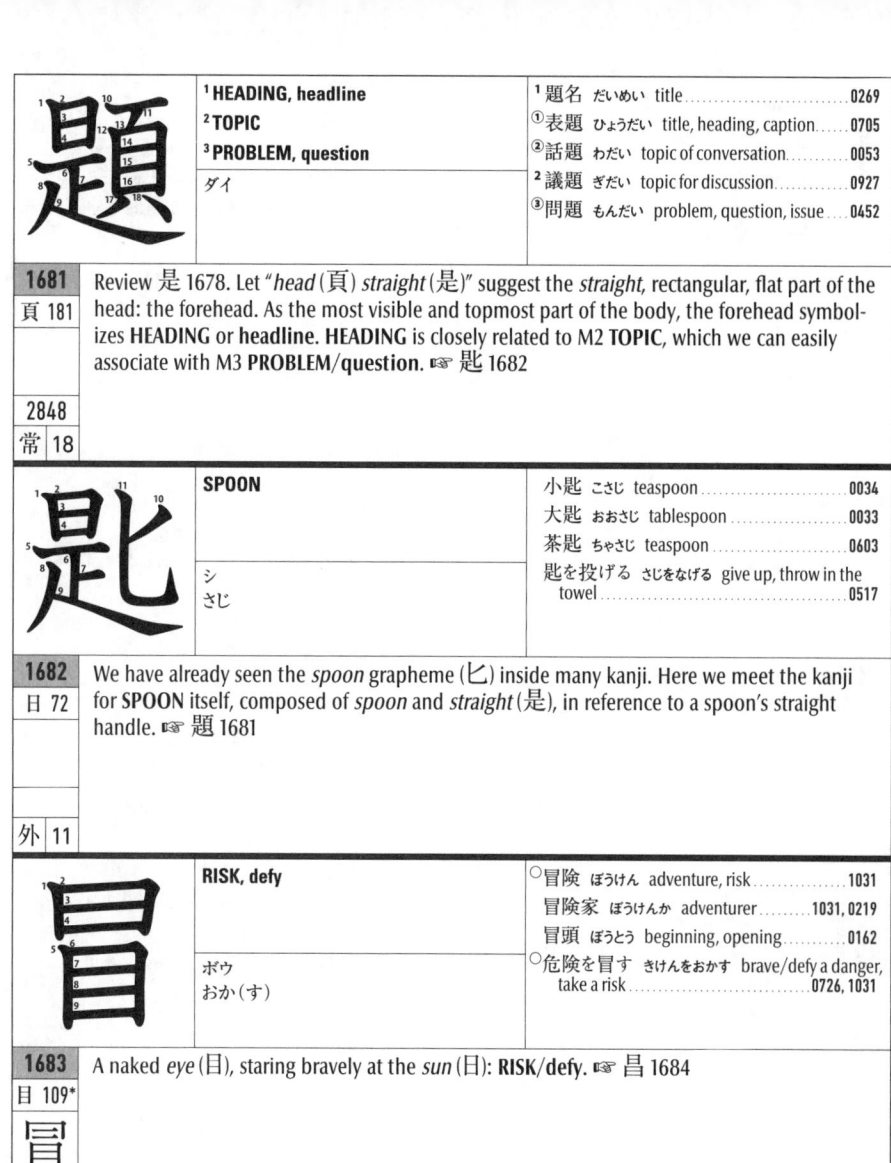

**題**

¹ **HEADING, headline**
² **TOPIC**
³ **PROBLEM, question**

ダイ

| | |
|---|---|
| ¹ 題名 だいめい title | 0269 |
| ① 表題 ひょうだい title, heading, caption | 0705 |
| ② 話題 わだい topic of conversation | 0053 |
| ² 議題 ぎだい topic for discussion | 0927 |
| ③ 問題 もんだい problem, question, issue | 0452 |

**1681**
頁 181

2848
常 18

Review 是 1678. Let "*head* (頁) *straight* (是)" suggest the *straight*, rectangular, flat part of the head: the forehead. As the most visible and topmost part of the body, the forehead symbolizes **HEADING** or **headline**. **HEADING** is closely related to M2 **TOPIC**, which we can easily associate with M3 **PROBLEM/question**. ☞ 匙 1682

---

**匙**

**SPOON**

シ
さじ

| | |
|---|---|
| 小匙 こさじ teaspoon | 0034 |
| 大匙 おおさじ tablespoon | 0033 |
| 茶匙 ちゃさじ teaspoon | 0603 |
| 匙を投げる さじをなげる give up, throw in the towel | 0517 |

**1682**
日 72

外 11

We have already seen the *spoon* grapheme (匕) inside many kanji. Here we meet the kanji for **SPOON** itself, composed of *spoon* and *straight* (是), in reference to a spoon's straight handle. ☞ 題 1681

---

**冒**

**RISK, defy**

ボウ
おか(す)

| | |
|---|---|
| ○冒険 ぼうけん adventure, risk | 1031 |
| 冒険家 ぼうけんか adventurer | 1031, 0219 |
| 冒頭 ぼうとう beginning, opening | 0162 |
| ○危険を冒す きけんをおかす brave/defy a danger, take a risk | 0726, 1031 |

**1683**
目 109*

冒

2155
常 9

A naked *eye* (目), staring bravely at the *sun* (日): **RISK/defy**. ☞ 昌 1684

---

**昌**

**CLEAR, bright**

ショウ

| | |
|---|---|
| ○繁昌 はんじょう prosperity | 1575 |

**1684**
日 72

2140
名 8

Think of how **CLEAR** and **bright** the world would be if we had <u>two</u> *suns* (日). V1 is related to the idea of a **bright** outlook. ☞ 冒 1683

| | **SING, intone** | ○合唱 がっしょう chorus ..........................0227 |
| | | 独唱する どくしょうする sing solo ...........0346 |
| 唱 | | 斉唱する せいしょうする sing in unison......1258 |
| | | 提唱する ていしょうする advocate, propose 1679 |
| | ショウ | ○唱える となえる chant, recite; cheer; advocate |
| | とな(える) | |

| **1685** | Mouth (口) singing *clearly* (昌): **SING/intone**. V5 唱える (となえる) sounds like **intone**. |
| 口 30 | ☞ 晶 1686 |
| | |
| 0418 | |
| 常 11 | |

| | **CRYSTAL** | ○結晶 けっしょう crystallization, crystal; grain; |
| | | fruit(s)...................................................0516 |
| 晶 | | 液晶 えきしょう liquid crystal...................0468 |
| | | 液晶画面 えきしょうがめん liquid crystal display |
| | ショウ | ......................................0468, 0176, 0175 |

| **1686** | Three *suns*: **CRYSTAL** clear. ☞ 唱 1685 |
| 日 72 | |
| | |
| 2183 | |
| 常 12 | |

| | **HEADGEAR** | ○帽子 ぼうし cap, hat...........................0094 |
| | | 帽章 ぼうしょう badge on a cap...............1459 |
| 帽 | | 学帽 がくぼう school cap .......................0099 |
| | | 脱帽 だつぼう taking off one's cap/hat; |
| | ボウ | submission ...................................1198 |

| **1687** | Unlike in 冒 1683, here a piece of *cloth* (巾) is used to protect the *eye* (目) from the *sun* (日)'s |
| 巾 50 | rays: **HEADGEAR**. The *on-yomi* follows 冒. |
| | |
| 0522 | |
| 常 12 | |

| | **BUILDING, ridgepole** | 西棟 にしとう west wing......................0795 |
| | | ○病棟 びょうとう hospital ward................0617 |
| 棟 | | 第三棟 だいさんとう building/block number 3 |
| | | ...........................................1191, 0004 |
| | トウ | 上棟式 じょうとうしき ridgepole-raising cere- |
| | むね むな- | mony...................................0041, 0109 |
| | | ○棟木 むなぎ ridgepole.........................0028 |

| **1688** | Review 陳 1373. In this entry 木 *tree* + 東 *all the way through/across* refers to a **ridgepole**, |
| 木 75 | the beam that runs across the top of a sloping roof, anchoring the rafters on either side. As |
| | the **ridgepole** passes through the whole length of the building, 棟 is most often used in |
| | reference to entire **BUILDINGS**. |
| 0904 | |
| 常 12 | |

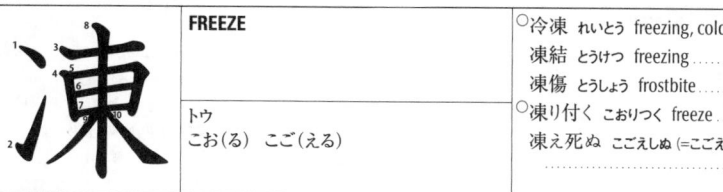

| | FREEZE | ○冷凍 れいとう freezing, cold storage.........0675 |
|---|---|---|
| | | 凍結 とうけつ freezing.........................0516 |
| | | 凍傷 とうしょう frostbite.....................1307 |
| | トウ | ○凍り付く こおりつく freeze ...............0064 |
| | こお(る) こご(える) | 凍え死ぬ こごえしぬ (=こごえじぬ) freeze to death .........0716 |

| **1689** | "Ice (冫) + all the way through (東)": thoroughly **FROZEN**. |
|---|---|
| 冫 15 | |
| 0111 | |
| 常 10 | |

| | ICE | ○氷河 ひょうが glacier.......................0818 |
|---|---|---|
| | | 氷山 ひょうざん iceberg.....................0037 |
| | | 氷枕 こおりまくら ice pillow ...............0656 |
| | ヒョウ | ○氷水 こおりみず ice water; shaved ice .....0027 |
| | こおり ひ | 氷雨 ひさめ [elegant] hail; chilly rain .......0154 |

| **1690** | The only difference between the characters for **ICE** (in this entry) and WATER (水 0027) is S2, |
|---|---|
| 水 85 | which we should therefore visualize as an icicle. ☞ 水 0027, 永 1691 |
| 冰 | |
| 0025 | |
| 常 5 | |

| | ETERNAL, long | 永久 えいきゅう permanence, eternity .......0904 |
|---|---|---|
| | | ○永遠 えいえん eternity......................0857 |
| | | 永住 えいじゅう permanent residence ......0366 |
| | エイ | 永眠 えいみん eternal sleep, death..........1009 |
| | なが(い) | ○永い ながい eternal, long |

| **1691** | To distinguish this character from 氷 1690 ICE and 水 0027 WATER, focus on S1–2. These |
|---|---|
| 水 85 | form a dotted letter "i," as in "infinity": **ETERNAL/long**. ☞ 氷 1690 |
| 1695 | |
| 常 5 | |

| | SWIM | ○水泳 すいえい swimming....................0027 |
|---|---|---|
| | | 泳法 えいほう swimming style ...............0139 |
| | | 背泳 はいえい backstroke ....................0124 |
| | エイ | ○泳ぐ およぐ swim |
| | およ(ぐ) | 平泳ぎ ひらおよぎ breaststroke.............0334 |

| **1692** | Let "long (永) water (氵)" suggest a long and narrow pool for **SWIMMING**. Note that the two |
|---|---|
| 水 85 | characters incorporating 永 follow its *on* reading, エイ. |
| 0289 | |
| 常 8 | |

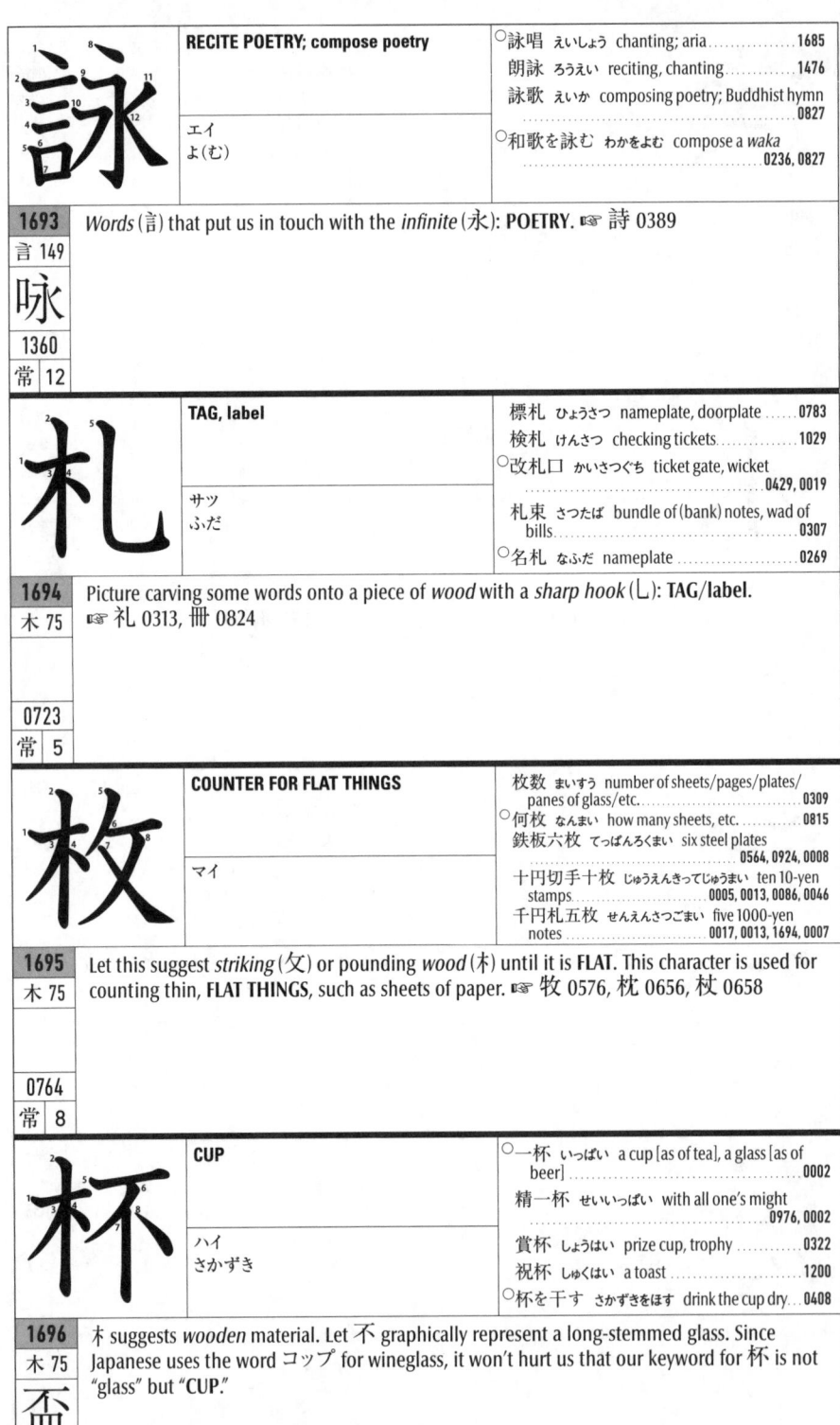

| | RECITE POETRY; compose poetry | ○詠唱 えいしょう chanting; aria.............1685 |
|---|---|---|
| | | 朗詠 ろうえい reciting, chanting.............1476 |
| | | 詠歌 えいか composing poetry; Buddhist hymn |
| | | .............0827 |
| | エイ | ○和歌を詠む わかをよむ compose a *waka* |
| | よ(む) | .............0236, 0827 |

| 1693 | *Words* (言) that put us in touch with the *infinite* (永): **POETRY.** ☞ 詩 0389 |
|---|---|
| 言 149 | |
| 咏 | |
| 1360 | |
| 常 12 | |

| | TAG, label | 標札 ひょうさつ nameplate, doorplate .......0783 |
|---|---|---|
| | | 検札 けんさつ checking tickets.............1029 |
| | | ○改札口 かいさつぐち ticket gate, wicket |
| | | .............0429, 0019 |
| | サツ | 札束 さつたば bundle of (bank) notes, wad of |
| | ふだ | bills. .............0307 |
| | | ○名札 なふだ nameplate .............0269 |

| 1694 | Picture carving some words onto a piece of *wood* with a *sharp hook* (乚): **TAG/label.** |
|---|---|
| 木 75 | ☞ 礼 0313, 冊 0824 |
| | |
| 0723 | |
| 常 5 | |

| | COUNTER FOR FLAT THINGS | 枚数 まいすう number of sheets/pages/plates/ |
|---|---|---|
| | | panes of glass/etc. .............0309 |
| | | ○何枚 なんまい how many sheets, etc. .............0815 |
| | | 鉄板六枚 てっぱんろくまい six steel plates |
| | | .............0564, 0924, 0008 |
| | マイ | 十円切手十枚 じゅうえんきってじゅうまい ten 10-yen |
| | | stamps. .............0005, 0013, 0086, 0046 |
| | | 千円札五枚 せんえんさつごまい five 1000-yen |
| | | notes .............0017, 0013, 1694, 0007 |

| 1695 | Let this suggest *striking* (攵) or pounding *wood* (木) until it is **FLAT.** This character is used for |
|---|---|
| 木 75 | counting thin, **FLAT THINGS**, such as sheets of paper. ☞ 牧 0576, 枕 0656, 杖 0658 |
| | |
| 0764 | |
| 常 8 | |

| | CUP | ○一杯 いっぱい a cup [as of tea], a glass [as of |
|---|---|---|
| | | beer] .............0002 |
| | | 精一杯 せいいっぱい with all one's might |
| | | .............0976, 0002 |
| | ハイ | 賞杯 しょうはい prize cup, trophy .............0322 |
| | さかずき | 祝杯 しゅくはい a toast .............1200 |
| | | ○杯を干す さかずきをほす drink the cup dry...0408 |

| 1696 | 木 suggests *wooden* material. Let 不 graphically represent a long-stemmed glass. Since |
|---|---|
| 木 75 | Japanese uses the word コップ for wineglass, it won't hurt us that our keyword for 杯 is not |
| 盃 | "glass" but "**CUP.**" |
| 0761 | |
| 常 8 | |

## 析

**ANALYZE**

セキ

○分析 ぶんせき analysis ..................... 0088
解析 かいせき analysis, analytical research 0345

| 1697 | Picture using the *hacksaw* (斤) to take the *tree* (木) apart, breaking it down into its constituent elements: **ANALYZE**. ☞ 折 1698 |
| 木 75 | |

0766
常 | 8

---

## 折

¹ **BREAK (OFF)**
² **FOLD, bend**

セツ
お(る) おり お(り) -お(り) お(れる)

①骨折 こっせつ bone fracture ................... 0465
¹ 歯を一本折る はをいっぽんおる break a tooth
.................... 0674, 0002, 0031
² 曲折 きょくせつ bending, winding; zigzags 0503
②折り紙 おりがみ folded paper; the art of paper folding ................... 0478
² 折り返し おりかえし turn, turning point; return (trip); lapel .................... 0378

| 1698 | Notice how the frame of the *hacksaw* (斤) is **bent** (at S5). This, we can imagine, was achieved by the *hand* (扌) at the left, pulling with all its might. Now imagine that it continues **bending** the frame until it either **FOLDS** or **BREAKS OFF**. ☞ 析 1697 |
| 手 64 | |

0225
常 | 7

---

**BREAK, sprain**

ザ
くじ(く)* くじ(ける)*

○挫折 ざせつ frustration, setback ............ 1698
挫傷 ざしょう bruise, sprain, fracture ........ 1307
挫く くじく sprain, break, crush
挫ける くじける be sprained, be broken, be crushed

| 1699 | Visualize the *hand* (扌) getting **BROKEN** or sprained on this pointy object (坐). The *on-yomi* follows 坐 and 座. |
| 手 64 | |

0392
常 | 10

---

**TWIST**

ネン
ひね(る)* ねじ(る)*

○捻挫 ねんざ sprain ..................... 1699
捻出する ねんしゅつする contrive/manage to (do) ................... 0038
○捻る ひねる [vt] twist, turn; contrive a solution (to); easily defeat
捻り潰す ひねりつぶす crush in one's fingers ... 1178
捻る ねじる twist, wrench, screw

| 1700 | Let "*hand* (扌) + *thought* (念)" suggest turning something around and around in one's mind, as if with one's *hand*. It refers to the physical act of **TWISTING**, or the mental act of contriving a solution at some effort. |
| 手 64 | |

0457
常 | 11

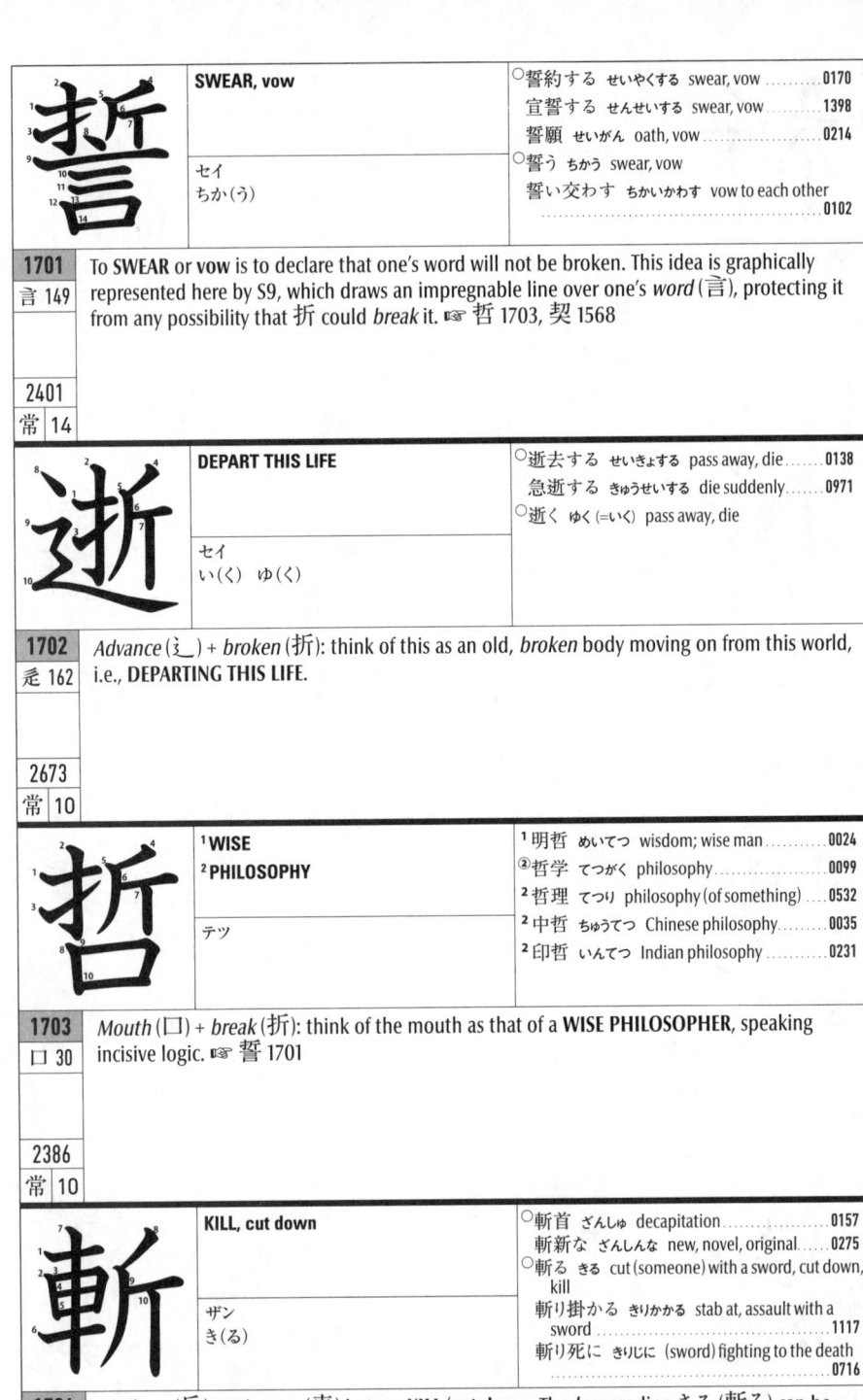

## 誓 — SWEAR, vow

○誓約する せいやくする swear, vow .......... 0170
宣誓する せんせいする swear, vow .......... 1398
誓願 せいがん oath, vow .......... 0214
○誓う ちかう swear, vow
誓い交わす ちかいかわす vow to each other .......... 0102

セイ
ちか(う)

**1701**
言 149

To **SWEAR** or **vow** is to declare that one's word will not be broken. This idea is graphically represented here by S9, which draws an impregnable line over one's *word* (言), protecting it from any possibility that 折 could *break* it. ☞ 哲 1703, 契 1568

**2401**
常 14

## 逝 — DEPART THIS LIFE

○逝去する せいきょする pass away, die .......... 0138
急逝する きゅうせいする die suddenly .......... 0971
○逝く ゆく (=いく) pass away, die

セイ
い(く)　ゆ(く)

**1702**
辶 162

*Advance* (辶) + *broken* (折): think of this as an old, *broken* body moving on from this world, i.e., **DEPARTING THIS LIFE.**

**2673**
常 10

## 哲 — ¹WISE　²PHILOSOPHY

¹明哲 めいてつ wisdom; wise man .......... 0024
②哲学 てつがく philosophy .......... 0099
²哲理 てつり philosophy (of something) .... 0532
²中哲 ちゅうてつ Chinese philosophy .......... 0035
²印哲 いんてつ Indian philosophy .......... 0231

テツ

**1703**
口 30

*Mouth* (口) + *break* (折): think of the mouth as that of a **WISE PHILOSOPHER**, speaking incisive logic. ☞ 誓 1701

**2386**
常 10

## 斬 — KILL, cut down

○斬首 ざんしゅ decapitation .......... 0157
斬新な ざんしんな new, novel, original .......... 0275
○斬る きる cut (someone) with a sword, cut down, kill
斬り掛かる きりかかる stab at, assault with a sword .......... 1117
斬り死に きりじに (sword) fighting to the death .......... 0716

ザン
き(る)

**1704**
斤 69

*Hacksaw* (斤) cutting *car* (車) in two: **KILL/cut down.** The *kun* reading きる (斬る) can be associated, via the idea of **cutting down**, with 切る (きる, cut). Alternatively, it can be associated with the English "**KILL.**"

**1347**
常 11

**GRADUALLY**

ゼン

| | | |
|---|---|---|
| 漸次 ぜんじ gradually | | 0278 |
| ○漸進 ぜんしん gradual advance | | 0191 |
| 漸減 ぜんげん gradual decrease | | 1148 |

**1705**
水 85

After the car is *cut* (斬), drops of motor oil (氵) **GRADUALLY** drain out.

0641
常 14

---

**SHORT WHILE**

ザン
しばら(く)*

| 暫時 ざんじ short while, a moment | 0383 |
|---|---|
| ○暫定の ざんていの provisional, tentative | 0045 |
| 暫定案 ざんていあん provisional plan | 0045, 0097 |
| ○暫く しばらく a while; a good while; for the time being | |
| 暫くですね しばらくですね It's been a while | |

**1706**
日 72

*Cutting* (斬) out a little slice of the *day*—just a **SHORT WHILE**.

2493
常 15

---

**REJECT**

セキ

| ○排斥する はいせきする reject, expel, exclude | 0739 |
|---|---|
| 斥力 せきりょく repulsion, repulsive force | 0084 |

**1707**
斥 69

With S5, this *hacksaw* (斤)'s manufacturer has marked it as defective, and consigned it to scrap. It has been **REJECTED.** ☞ 斤 0193

2565
常 5

---

**[1] APPEAL TO**
**[2] SUE, complain**

ソ
うった(える)

| [1] 上訴する じょうそする appeal to a higher court | 0041 |
|---|---|
| [2] 起訴 きそ prosecution, indictment, litigation | 0430 |
| [2] 公訴 こうそ arraignment, prosecution | 0089 |
| [2] 敗訴 はいそ losing a suit/case | 0830 |
| [2] 訴える うったえる sue; complain | |

**1708**
言 149

*Words* (言) spoken in *rejection* (斥): **SUE/complain**. Also means **APPEAL TO**, from the idea of seeking attention for some adverse condition.

1367
常 12

| | LITIGATE | ○訴訟 そしょう lawsuit, litigation ............1708 |
| | | 刑事訴訟 けいじそしょう criminal lawsuit ............0722, 0080, 1708 |
| | ショウ | 民事訴訟 みんじそしょう civil lawsuit ............0477, 0080, 1708 |
| | | 訟務部 しょうむぶ Litigation Department (of the Ministry of Justice) ............0687, 0068 |

| 1709 言 149 | "Words (言) + public (公)" suggests taking one's claim to a public tribunal: **LITIGATE.** |
| 1339 常 11 | |

| | STUDY EXHAUSTIVELY | ○研究 けんきゅう research, study ............0724 |
| | | 研究室 けんきゅうしつ laboratory ......0724, 0253 |
| | | 究明する きゅうめいする investigate, study 0024 |
| | キュウ きわ(める) | 学究 がっきゅう scholar, student ............0099 |
| | | ○究める きわめる study exhaustively, master |

| 1710 穴 116 | *Nine* (九), the last digit in the decimal system, here suggests "reaching the end," as in exploring a *cave* (穴) to its furthest depths. The full character thus implies getting to the bottom of an unfamiliar subject: **STUDY EXHAUSTIVELY.** ☞ 突 1564 |
| 1885 常 7 | |

| | PUSHED TO THE LIMIT | ○窮地 きゅうち predicament, difficult situation, dilemma ............0187 |
| | | 貧窮 ひんきゅう poverty ............1161 |
| | キュウ | ○窮める きわめる carry to extremity, reach an extreme |
| | きわ(める) きわ(まる) きわ(まり) きわ(み) | 道が窮まる みちがきわまる reach a dead end 0158 |
| | | 窮み無き きわみなき endless, without limit 0048 |

| 1711 穴 116 | Here we observe a *body* (身) contorted into the shape of a *bow* (弓) so as to squeeze itself inside a small *hole* (穴): **PUSHED TO THE LIMIT.** |
| 2078 常 15 | |

| | ¹ EXTREME ² POLE | ¹ 極秘 ごくひ top secret ............1384 |
| | | ①極めて きわめて extremely, very |
| | キョク ゴク | ¹ 栄華の極み えいがのきわみ the apex of prosperity ............1245, 1012 |
| | きわ(める) きわ(まる) きわ(まり) きわ(み) | ②南極圏 なんきょくけん the Antarctic (Circle) ............0794, 0459 |
| | | ² 陽極 ようきょく positive pole, anode ............1310 |

| 1712 木 75 | As a shortcut, see the two horizontal strokes S5 and S12 as **POLAR EXTREMES.** It takes the full length of the *tree* (木) to reach from one end to the other, emphasizing the great distance between them. |
| 0900 常 12 | |

**BOX**

カン
はこ

○函館 はこだて Hakodate [city in Hokkaido]... **0291**
青函トンネル せいかんトンネル Seikan Tunnel [between Aomori and Hakodate]............ **0130**
○投函する とうかんする drop into a mailbox, post ........................................................ **0517**
私書函 ししょばこ post office box...... **0237, 0079**
函に入れる はこにいれる put in a box...... **0039**

| 1713 | Looks like a **BOX**, filled with foam packing peanuts (S3-6), that has just been opened. ☞ 箱 1909 |
| 凵 17 | |
| 凾 | |
| 2587 | |
| 名 8 | |

¹ **PROBE, explore**
² **LOOK FOR**

タン
さぐ（る） さが（す）

①探求 たんきゅう quest, search, pursuit ....... **1097**
¹探究 たんきゅう investigation, search, inquiry ........................................................ **1710**
¹探検 たんけん exploration, expedition ..... **1029**
¹探る さぐる probe, search into, explore
②探す さがす search for (something desired), look for

| 1714 | Treat 厸 as a variant on 穴 *hole*. Now when you see this character, imagine **PROBING** around a *hole* in a *tree* (木) with your *hand* (扌). |
| 手 64 | |
| 0466 | |
| 常 11 | |

**DEEP**

シン
ふか（い） -ぶか（い） ふか（まる）
ふか（める）

○深度 しんど depth ................................. **0280**
深夜 しんや dead of night, midnight ....... **0467**
測深 そくしん sounding...................... **0627**
興味深い きょうみぶかい of great interest ........................................................ **0505, 0273**
○深める ふかめる deepen, intensify

| 1715 | (Continuing from the previous entry) Now imagine that, **DEEP** at the bottom of the *hole* (厸) in the *tree* (木), you feel rain *water* (氵). |
| 水 85 | |
| 0480 | |
| 常 11 | |

**TREMBLE, shudder**

リツ

○慄然として りつぜんとして with horror...... **0760**
戦慄する せんりつする shudder, shiver...... **0461**

| 1716 | Think of the bones in your spine as a string of *chestnuts* (栗, see 0781). With 忄, *chestnuts* thus suggest an emotion you feel in your spine: **shuddering/TREMBLING**. |
| 心 61 | |
| 0589 | |
| 常 13 | |

| 懼 | **FEAR** | ○危懼 きぐ apprehension, misgiving.........0726 |
| | | 絶滅危懼種 ぜつめつきぐしゅ endangered |
| | グ | species....................1271, 1149, 0726, 0544 |

**1717**
心 61

The right-hand portion of this entry is the old form of 具 0837 IMPLEMENT/tool. While the independent kanji 具 was modified as part of the orthographic reforms that followed World War II, the present entry was not so modified when it was added to the Joyo list in 2010. In the same way as 恐 1633, it suggests a **FEAR** of dangerous *tools*. ☞ 慎 1718

0437
常 | 11

| 慎 | **PRUDENT, discreet** | ○慎重 しんちょう prudence, discretion, circum- |
| | | spection................................0539 |
| | | ○慎む つつしむ be prudent, be discreet |
| | シン | 慎み深い つつしみぶかい discreet, prudent, |
| | つつし（む） | modest....................................1715 |

**1718**
心 61

Keeping the *truth* (真) in one's *heart* (忄): **PRUDENT/discreet.** ☞ 懼 1717

愼
0590
常 | 13

| 鎮 | **QUELL, appease** | 鎮圧する ちんあつする quell, suppress.....0186 |
| | | 鎮静剤 ちんせいざい sedative, tranquilizer |
| | | ..................................0978, 1261 |
| | チン | ○鎮痛剤 ちんつうざい anodyne, painkiller |
| | しず（める）　しず（まる） | ..................................0619, 1261 |
| | | ○鎮める しずめる quell, pacify |
| | | 暴動が鎮まった ぼうどうがしずまった |
| | | The riot was put down ...............1346, 0540 |

**1719**
金 167

Pacifying someone with *true* (真) *gold* (釒): **QUELL/appease.**

鎭
1570
常 | 18

| 塡 | **FILL (in)** | 装塡する そうてんする load (a firearm)......1591 |
| | | 補塡する ほてんする compensate for.......1598 |
| | | ○充塡する じゅうてんする fill (up)..............1056 |
| | テン | |

**1720**
土 32

眞 is the old form of 真 0838 TRUE. This portion was not officially standardized with 真 when the present entry was added to the Joyo list in 2010, but the standardized form (填) is also used. Learn to recognize both forms interchangeably. The meaning comes from the idea of **FILLING IN** soil to make the *ground* (土) "true," i.e., level.

填
0581
常 | 13

## 婚 — MARRY

コン

- ○結婚 けっこん marriage ........................0516
- 未婚 みこん unmarried, single ...............0271
- 婚約 こんやく engagement, betrothal ......0170
- 恋愛結婚 れんあいけっこん love marriage ........................0777, 0778, 0516
- 新婚旅行 しんこんりょこう honeymoon ........................0275, 0569, 0055

**1721**
女 38
0427
常 11

*Woman* (女) + *family* (氏, review 0476 if needed) + (wedding) *day* (日): **MARRY**.

## 囚 — PRISONER

シュウ

- ○囚人 しゅうじん prisoner, convict ............0015
- 獄囚 ごくしゅう prisoner, convict ............0737
- 囚衣 しゅうい prison uniform ................0700
- 女囚 じょしゅう female convict ................0093
- 死刑囚 しけいしゅう criminal condemned to death ................................0716, 0722

**1722**
囗 31
2618
常 5

*Man* (人) held inside *enclosure* (囗): **PRISONER**. ☞ 困 1723, 因 1725

## 困 — BE IN TROUBLE

コン
こま(る)

- 困窮 こんきゅう destitution, poverty .........1711
- ○困難 こんなん difficulty, distress, hardship 0712
- 貧困 ひんこん poverty, indigence; lack, need ........................1161
- ○困る こまる be in trouble; be destitute
- 生活に困る せいかつにこまる live in want ........................0036, 0054

**1723**
囗 31
2644
常 7

*Tree* (木) trapped inside *enclosure* (囗), its growth stunted: **IN TROUBLE**. ☞ 因 1725, 囚 1722

## 梱 — PACKAGE, bale

コン

- ○同梱する どうこんする include in a package 0182
- 梱包 こんぽう packaging, crating ............0457
- 梱包材 こんぽうざい packing material ......0457
- 開梱する かいこんする open a package .....0450

**1724**
木 75
外 11

**PACKAGE/bale**: depicts a *tree* (木) before and after being **PACKAGED** inside a box.

**CAUSE**

イン
よ(る)

| | | |
|---|---|---|
| 因果 いんが | cause and effect; karma | 0599 |
| 死因 しいん | cause of death | 0716 |
| ○原因 げんいん | cause, origin | 0654 |
| 要因 よういん | main cause | 0547 |
| ○に因る によ る | caused by, due to | |

| 1725 | To connect this image with the idea of **CAUSATION**, let the *enclosure* (口) suggest **CAUSAL** |
|---|---|
| 口 31 | circumstances, and let 大 suggest the *"big"* (i.e., main) **CAUSE**. ☞ 困 1723, 囚 1722 |

| 2629 | |
|---|---|
| 常 6 | |

---

**MARRIAGE**

イン

| | | |
|---|---|---|
| ○婚姻 こんいん | marriage, matrimony | 1721 |
| 姻族 いんぞく | in-laws, relatives by marriage | |
| | | 0568 |

| 1726 | Suggests that **MARRIAGE** is something a *woman* (女) might *cause* (因). However, if you |
|---|---|
| 女 38 | don't mind conflating 因 with 囚, the image easily suggests a *woman* holding a (*big*) man *prisoner*. V1 is the more common of the two sample compounds, but the easy association between 姻族 (いんぞく) and *"in*-laws" makes V2 mnemonically useful. |

| 0315 | |
|---|---|
| 常 9 | |

---

**THROAT**

イン

| | | |
|---|---|---|
| ○咽喉 いんこう | throat | 1674 |
| 耳鼻咽喉 じびいんこう | ear, nose, and throat | |
| | | 0057, 1558, 1674 |
| 咽頭 いんとう | pharynx | 0162 |
| 咽頭鏡 いんとうきょう | pharyngoscope | 0162, 1547 |

| 1727 | Except where 因 appears at the top (in the next entry), all kanji in this course containing 因 |
|---|---|
| 口 30 | are pronounced イン. Knowing that, you should be able to recognize *mouth* (口) + 因 as the イン of 咽喉 (いんこう, throat). Concern yourself only with learning that compound, and the associative pathway to it from the semantic and phonetic clues of 咽. |

| 0309 | |
|---|---|
| 常 9 | |

---

¹ **GRACE, favor**
² **DEBT OF GRATITUDE**

オン

| | | |
|---|---|---|
| ¹ 恩人 おんじん | benefactor, patron | 0015 |
| ①恩恵 おんけい | benefit, grace, favor, blessing | 0581 |
| ² 恩返し おんがえし | repaying another's kindness | |
| | | 0378 |
| ² 恩給 おんきゅう | pension | 0526 |
| ² 恩知らず おんしらず | ingratitude, ingrate | 0560 |

| 1728 | The English words **GRACE** and **GRATITUDE** refer to either side of the *cause*-effect relationship |
|---|---|
| 心 61 | that exists when a **favor** is given: **GRACE** is the *cause* (因), and **GRATITUDE** is the result. See both sides of this relationship in 恩: 因 represents the (*cause* of) **GRACE**; 心 represents the (resulting) **DEBT OF GRATITUDE**. ☞ 思 0142 |

| 2311 | |
|---|---|
| 常 10 | |

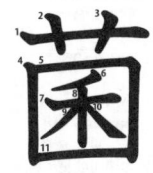

**BACTERIA, germ, fungus**

キン

○細菌 さいきん bacteria, germ, microbe......0239
殺菌する さっきんする sterilize, pasteurize...0522
病菌 びょうきん disease germ, virus.........0617
保菌者 ほきんしゃ germ carrier........0646, 0107
菌を培養する きんをばいようする culture
[cultivate] bacteria....................1264, 0500

| 1729 | Let 艹 suggest a **fungus** or other microorganism growing on a *box* (囗) of *rice* (禾): **BACTERIA/** |
| 艸 140 | **germ/fungus.** |
| 2000 | |
| 常 11 | |

漢

¹**(ancient) CHINESE; Han dynasty**
²**FELLOW, man**

カン

¹漢方薬 かんぽうやく Chinese (herbal) medicine
.....................................0173, 0303
¹漢民族 かんみんぞく Chinese people, Han
ethnicity....................0477, 0568
¹漢語 かんご Chinese-derived word, Chinese
expression...........................0222
①漢字 かんじ Chinese characters, kanji......0098
²好漢 こうかん nice fellow....................0095

| 1730 | Review 難 0712. Here we see the *Han scholar-official* next to *water* (氵). The Han dynasty's |
| 水 85 | power largely rested on its effective control of water, so it is fitting that this character is used |
| 漢 | in reference to the dynasty itself (it also refers more generally to the ancient **CHINESE**). Asso- |
| 0602 | ciate M2 **FELLOW** with the image of the official. ☞ 僅 1734, 漢 1338 |
| 常 13 | |

嘆

**SIGH, lament**

タン
なげ(く) なげ(かわしい)

○嘆息 たんそく sigh............................1556
驚嘆する きょうたんする admire, wonder ...0807
嘆声 たんせい sigh, lamentation; sigh of
admiration...............................0529
○嘆く なげく sigh (in grief or despair), lament
嘆かわしい事態 なげかわしいじたい deplor-
able/lamentable situation ...........0080, 0893

| 1731 | Here imagine the *mouth* (囗) of the *Han scholar-official* letting out a **SIGH** of **lament,** |
| 囗 30 | perhaps over the sovereign's failure to live up to the Confucian ideal of moral leadership and |
| 嘆 | just rule. Like the other kanji using the *scholar-official* with his legs spread apart (難 0712 |
| 0577 | and 漢 1730), the *on-yomi* ends in -AN. |
| 常 13 | |

**SERVICE, work, employment**

キン　ゴン
つと(める)　-づと(め)　つと(まる)

○通勤する つうきんする commute, go to one's
office.........................................0159
転勤する てんきんする be transferred (to
another office)..........................0224
勤務する きんむする serve, be on duty, work ..0687
○勤める つとめる serve, hold a job
勤め先 つとめさき (one's place of) employment
.............................................0134

| 1732 | The following three kanji show the *Han scholar-official* with his legs joined together. Kanji |
| 力 19 | using this version are pronounced キン. Here we observe the *scholar-official* busy at work |
| 勤 | behind a *plow* (力), illustrating the ideas **SERVICE**, **work**, and **employment.** ☞ 動 0540 |
| 1613 | |
| 常 12 | |

**RESPECTFULLY, carefully**

キン
つつし(む)

謹呈する きんていする present respectfully [with compliments] .................................................0587
謹告する きんこくする announce respectfully .................................................................................0698
○謹慎 きんしん penitence; house arrest ......1718
謹賀新年 きんがしんねん Happy New Year .................................................1172, 0275, 0117
○謹む つつしむ be respectful, be humble

| 1733 | Picture the *Han scholar-official* addressing the sovereign with **RESPECTFUL, carefully** chosen *words*(言). Note the traditional form for this entry and the one before: this old form of the *scholar-official* is retained in the next entry. |
| 言 149 | |
| 謹 | |
| 1462 | |
| 常 17 | |

**A FEW, little**

キン
わず(か)

僅々 きんきん merely, no more than
僅少 きんしょう few, little, trifling ............0677
○僅か わずか only, merely, a little

| 1734 | Only **A FEW** *men* (イ) were selected as *Han scholar-officials*. Note how the *scholar-official* differs slightly here from the previous two entries. 僅 was not officially standardized to match them when it was added to the Joyo list, but its standardized form (shown in the variant field) is also accepted. ☞ 漢 1730 |
| 人 9 | |
| 僅 | |
| 0134 | |
| 常 13 | |

**SEARCH FOR**

サク

索引 さくいん index ...............................0422
捜索する そうさくする search for, investigate 1527
探索する たんさくする search for; inquire into, investigate.......................................1714
○検索する けんさくする look up (a word in a dictionary), search for, refer to ............1029
索条 さくじょう cable, rope....................0119

| 1735 | Visualize S1–4 as a person standing at the top of a long shaft, and 糸 as a rope that he's using to **SEARCH FOR** something in the shaft. Now imagine his raising the rope to look at what he's retrieved, in the same way one goes through the results obtained by an internet **SEARCH** (see V4). ☞ 牽 1736, 素 0132 |
| 糸 120 | |
| 2168 | |
| 常 10 | |

**PULL**

ケン
ひ(く)

○牽く ひく pull, tug, haul
○牽引する けんいんする drag, tow, pull ......0422
○牽引力 けんいんりょく traction..............0422
牽引車 けんいんしゃ tractor, tow truck 0422, 0125
牽引療法 けんいんりょうほう traction therapy .............................................0422, 0952, 0139

| 1736 | A distinctive and easily recognizable feature of this character is that ⌐ passes through the middle of it. It is therefore a good idea to focus on this feature and associate it with the character's meaning, **PULL**. Picture ⌐ as a handle by which a *child* (幺) **PULLS** along a *cow* (牛). ☞ 索 1735, 率 0752 |
| 一 8 | |
| 1816 | |
| 名 11 | |

**牢**

¹ PRISON
² HARDNESS

ロウ

①牢獄 ろうごく prison, jail................0737
¹牢屋 ろうや prison, jail.................0252
¹牢破り ろうやぶり jailbreak.............0084
²牢固な ろうこな solid, firm.............0260

| 1737 | Picture a *cow* (牛) under the **HARD** stone *roof* (宀) of the **PRISON** (the "hoosecow," if you will). |
| --- | --- |
| 宀 40 | |
| 外 7 | |

**啓**

¹ ENLIGHTEN
² ADDRESS RESPECTFULLY

ケイ

①啓発する けいはつする enlighten, develop, edify
.........................................0148
²啓上する けいじょうする speak respectfully 0041
①拝啓 はいけい Dear Sir/Madam.............1642
²謹啓 きんけい Dear Sirs, Gentlemen.........1733

| 1738 | Visualize as a face with its *mouth* (口) and right eye (戸) opening wide in response to a *striking* (攵) insight: **ENLIGHTENMENT**. As a form of **RESPECTFUL ADDRESS**, it expresses admiration for the enlightening wisdom of the person one is addressing. |
| --- | --- |
| 口 30 | |
| 2408 | |
| 常 11 | |

**庶**

**MANIFOLD**

ショ

○庶務 しょむ general affairs.............0687
庶務課 しょむか General/Administrative Affairs
    Section.........................0687, 0600
庶事 しょじ various matters.............0080
庶政 しょせい all phases of government.....0246
庶民 しょみん common people, the masses 0477

| 1739 | From 席 0279 and 度 0280, recall the image of 廿 as the open mouth of a woodburning stove. Here, focus on the **MANIFOLD** *flames* (S8–11) beneath the stove. ☞ 燕 1741 |
| --- | --- |
| 广 53 | |
| 2696 | |
| 常 11 | |

**遮**

**INTERRUPT, cut off**

シャ
さえぎ(る)

○遮断する しゃだんする interrupt, intercept,
    block; isolate.....................0849
遮断器 しゃだんき crossing gate, breaker
.........................................0849, 0295
○遮る さえぎる interrupt, obstruct, cut off
道を遮る みちをさえぎる block the way......0158
話を遮る はなしをさえぎる interrupt (someone)
.........................................0053

| 1740 | Picture *manifold* (庶) objects piled on the *truck* (辶), which drives in front of you from the right side, blocking your advance: **INTERRUPT**/cut off. The reading さえぎる (遮る, interrupt, obstruct, cut off) sounds a bit like "side-きる," or "cut (off)" from the side. |
| --- | --- |
| 辵 162 | |
| 2724 | |
| 常 14 | |

**SWALLOW, martin**

エン
つばめ

燕麦 えんばく oats ............................ 0131
燕尾服 えんびふく tailcoat ............ 0488, 1471
○燕の巣 つばめのす swallow's nest .......... 0601

| 1741 | A top-down view into a **SWALLOW**'s nest. In the center rests a tiny **SWALLOW**'s egg (口). ☞ 庶 1739, 蒸 0960 |
| 艸 140 | |
| 2196 | |
| 名 16 | |

**¹ SPARROW**
**² MAHJONG**

ジャク ジャン
すずめ

①燕雀 えんじゃく swallows and sparrows; small birds ................................................ 1741
①雀の巣 すずめのす sparrow's nest .......... 0601
¹ 雀蜂 すずめばち hornet, wasp ............. 1381
②麻雀 マージャン mahjong .................. 0852
² 雀荘 ジャンそう mahjong club .............. 1590

| 1742 | *Little* (少) + *small bird* (隹): **SPARROW**. |
| 隹 172 | |
| 2178 | |
| 名 11 | |

**INFERIOR**

レツ
おと(る)

○劣等感 れっとうかん inferiority complex ........................................... 0393, 0327
劣悪な れつあくな inferior, coarse ........... 0546
優劣 ゆうれつ superiority or inferiority, quality ............................................. 0780
○劣る おとる be inferior to
勝るとも劣らぬ まさるともおとらぬ not at all inferior to .................................. 0460

| 1743 | *Little* (少) + *strength* (力): **INFERIOR**. |
| 力 19 | |
| 2124 | |
| 常 6 | |

**EXCERPT, select**

ショウ

抄出する しょうしゅつする take excerpts ..... 0038
○抄録 しょうろく quotation, summary .......... 0608
抄訳 しょうやく abridged translation ......... 1505
抄本 しょうほん extract, abstract .............. 0031

| 1744 | *Hand* (扌) picking out just a *little* (少): **EXCERPT**/select. |
| 手 64 | |
| 0226 | |
| 常 7 | |

| 秒 | **SECOND** | 秒速10メートル びょうそくじゅうメートル 10 meters per second...............................1143 |
|---|---|---|
| | ビョウ | 秒針 びょうしん second hand..............0556 |
| | | ○秒読み びょうよみ countdown ...........0355 |
| | | 二分二十五秒 にふんにじゅうごびょう 2′25″ ...............................0003, 0088, 0005, 0007 |

| **1745** | Imagine an hourglass with tiny grains of rice, in lieu of sand. Each *little* (少) grain of *rice* (禾) marks one **SECOND** of time. |
|---|---|
| 禾 115 | |
| 1052 | |
| 常 9 | |

| 妙 | **MARVELOUS, wonderful, strange** | 絶妙な ぜつみょうな miraculous, exquisite, superb .......................................1271 |
|---|---|---|
| | ミョウ | 妙案 みょうあん bright idea, excellent plan..0097 |
| | | 妙技 みょうぎ wonderful skill; stunt ........0966 |
| | | 巧妙な こうみょうな skillful, ingenious, clever 1047 |
| | | ○妙に思う みょうにおもう think strange .......0142 |

| **1746** | *Little* (少) *woman* (女): suggests the **MARVELOUS**, **strangely** enchanting beauty of a dainty female figure. |
|---|---|
| 女 38 | |
| 0210 | |
| 常 7 | |

| 沙 | **SAND** | 沙丘 さきゅう sand dune .....................0906 |
|---|---|---|
| | サ | 沙漠 さばく desert...............................1338 |
| | すな | |

| **1747** | *Little* (少) stones next to *water* (氵): **SAND**. The usual character for SAND is 砂 0678; 沙 is generally limited to V1-2 of the next entry. ☞ 砂 0678 |
|---|---|
| 水 85 | |
| 0236 | |
| 常 7 | |

| 汰 | **SIFT OUT** | 沙汰 さた instructions; notice, tidings, rumor; affair ......................................1747 |
|---|---|---|
| | タ | ○ご無沙汰しております ごぶさたしております I haven't seen you for a long time.........0048, 1747 |
| | | とう汰 (淘×汰) する とうたする select, weed out, sift; dismiss, cashier |
| | | 自然とう汰 (淘×汰) しぜんとうた natural selection ...............................................0081, 0760 |

| **1748** | Suggests using *water* (氵) to **SIFT OUT** a relatively "thick" (太) item. For example, imagine washing gravel in a pan to **SIFT OUT** gold or silver. A similar mnemonic works well for the unlisted 淘 (トウ, SELECT) in V3-4, showing an *elephant* (匋) prospector "selecting" out gold or silver by washing gravel in a *can* (缶). |
|---|---|
| 水 85 | |
| 0237 | |
| 常 7 | |

| | BOIL, roast | 湯煎する ゆせんする warm in hot water....0446 |
|---|---|---|
| | | ○煎茶 せんちゃ green tea .................0603 |
| | | 煎じる せんじる boil, decoct |
| | | ○煎る いる parch, fire, roast; boil down |
| | セン | 煎り卵 いりたまご scrambled eggs..........1141 |
| | い(る) | |

| 1749 | BOILING/roasting on a *fire* (灬) *before* (前) eating. This character was not officially standard- |
|---|---|
| 火 86 | ized with 前 when it was added to the Joyo list, but you'll also see it in standardized form. |

煎

2054

常 13

---

| | ROAST, parch | 炒飯 チャーハン fried rice.................0377 |
|---|---|---|
| | | 野菜炒め やさいいため fried vegetables |
| | | .................................0534, 0988 |
| | | ○炒る いる roast, parch, fry, broil |
| | ショウ ソウ | 肉を炒める にくをいためる (stir-)fry meat ...0216 |
| | い(る) いた(める) | |

| 1750 | *Little* (少) *fire* (火): lightly ROAST/parch. |
|---|---|
| 火 86 | |

名 8

---

| | COOK | ○炊事 すいじ cooking........................0080 |
|---|---|---|
| | | 炊婦 すいふ cook, kitchen maid...........1017 |
| | | 自炊 じすい cooking food for oneself .......0081 |
| | | ○炊く たく cook, boil |
| | スイ | 一合炊きの いちごうだきの having a cooking |
| | た(く) -だ(き) | capacity of one *go* (0.18 liters) .......0002, 0227 |

| 1751 | *Gaping mouth* (欠) blowing *fire* (火) on food: COOK. |
|---|---|
| 火 86 | |

0773

常 8

---

| | KINDLE, build a fire | 焚書 ふんしょ book burning.................0079 |
|---|---|---|
| | | 焚く たく kindle, build a fire, burn |
| | | ○焚き火 たきび bonfire....................0026 |
| | | 焚き付け たきつけ kindling, fire lighter.....0064 |
| | フン | 焚き付ける たきつける kindle, build a fire; |
| | た(く) | instigate, stir up .................0064 |

| 1752 | *Forest* (林) over *fire* (火): KINDLE/build a fire. |
|---|---|
| 火 86 | |

2418

名 12

|  | **FIREWOOD**<br><br>シン<br>たきぎ まき* | ○薪炭 しんたん firewood and charcoal .......1647<br>薪水 しんすい cooking.....................0027<br>○薪拾い たきぎひろい firewood gathering ...1071<br>薪を焚く たきぎをたく burn firewood .......1752<br>薪能 たきぎのう fire-lit Noh drama performance<br>.................................................0892 |
|---|---|---|

| **1753**<br>艸 140<br><br>2098<br>常 16 | Review 新 0275. Here the standing person cuts *new* (新) branches for **FIREWOOD**. ⧺ *grass* suggests slender sprigs, just right for kindling. |
|---|---|

|  | **POSSESSIVE PARTICLE**<br><br>ナイ ダイ<br>の すなわ(ち) | ○日乃丸 ひのまる Rising Sun flag .......0001, 0012<br>戦えば乃ち勝つ たたかえばすなわちかつ win<br>every battle fought...................0461, 0460<br>○...乃至... ...ないし... from ... to ...; between ...<br>and ...; ... or ...............................0250 |
|---|---|---|

| **1754**<br>ノ 4<br><br>2535<br>名 2 | This kanji appears as the **POSSESSIVE PARTICLE** の in archaic or archaic-style texts in which kana are not used (note its similarities with the hiragana の and katakana ノ, both of which were derived from this kanji). Other possible uses appear in V2 and V3. Note how S2 changes directions four times. ☞ 之 1755 |
|---|---|

|  | **POSSESSIVE PARTICLE**<br><br>シ<br>の これ | 鳥之巣 とりのす bird's nest ............0340, 0601<br>之は何ですか これはなんですか What is this?<br>.................................................0815 |
|---|---|---|

| **1755**<br>、 3<br><br>2886<br>名 3 | Like the previous entry, this character appears in archaic texts as the **POSSESSIVE PARTICLE** の. V2 provides another possible usage. Do not confuse with the hiragana え. ☞ 乃 1754, 乏 1758, 芝 1759 |
|---|---|

|  | **THIS**<br><br>シ<br>こ(れ) こ(の) | 此れ これ this (thing)<br>此処 ここ here, this place....................0553<br>此の世界 このせかい this world.......0604, 0612 |
|---|---|---|

| **1756**<br>止 77<br><br>0728<br>名 6 | Visualize 此 as two men standing behind a third man (匕), who points toward something. To refer to the object to which he has drawn their attention, he says "**THIS** ..." Inside other kanji, 此 can provide an image of *three men looking at something that has drawn their attention*. ☞ 比 0123 |
|---|---|

| | **THAT** | 其れ それ it, that (thing) |
| | | 其処 そこ there, that place ................. 0553 |
| | | 其の筈だ そのはずだ That is to be expected, |
| | キ | You would think so .................... 1442 |
| | そ(れ) そ(の) | 其の後 そのご after that, thereafter ......... 0114 |

| **1757** | We learned this form back at 基 0485, where we gave it the meaning *bind/bound*. As an |
| 八 12 | independent kanji, it means **THAT**, as in 其の人 (そのひと, that person). Like the preceding |
| | three entries, you won't frequently come across 其 as an independent kanji. |
| **2285** | |
| 名 8 | |

| | **SCANTY, poor** | 欠乏 けつぼう lack, shortage, scarcity ....... 0277 |
| | | 窮乏 きゅうぼう destitution, poverty ......... 1711 |
| | | ○貧乏な びんぼうな poor, destitute ........... 1161 |
| | ボウ | ○乏しい とぼしい scanty, meager |
| | とぼ(しい) | 金が乏しい かねがとぼしい be short of money |
| | | ................................................. 0029 |

| **1758** | S1–2 resemble the mortarboard and tassel of the student's formal gown, which you might |
| ノ 4 | associate with a student's impoverished lifestyle: **SCANTY/poor**. ☞ 之 1755, 芝 1759 |
| **1693** | |
| 常 4 | |

| | **LAWN GRASS** | 芝草 しばくさ lawn ............................ 0144 |
| | | ○芝生 しばふ lawn, turf ...................... 0036 |
| | | 芝居 しばい play, drama ................... 0255 |
| | しば | 芝居小屋 しばいごや playhouse |
| | | ......................... 0255, 0034, 0252 |
| | | 東芝 とうしば Toshiba [company name] ..... 0032 |

| **1759** | When you see 之 with ⺿ *grass*, you might visualize it as a hand-pushed lawn mower: **LAWN** |
| 艸 140 | **GRASS**. ☞ 乏 1758, 之 1755 |
| **1867** | |
| 常 6 | |

| | **REACH TO, extend to; be equal to; as** | ○及ぶ およぶ reach to, amount to |
| | **well as, and** | 言及する げんきゅうする mention, refer to ... 0051 |
| | | ○普及 ふきゅう diffusion, spread ............. 1085 |
| | | 及第する きゅうだいする pass an examination |
| | キュウ | ............................................. 1191 |
| | およ(ぶ) およ(び) および およ(ぼす) | ○A及びB エイおよびビー A and B |

| **1760** | Note the ways in which this form differs from 乃 above. To perceive the idea **REACH TO**, |
| ノ 4* | focus visually on how S2 **REACHES** over **TO** the left, and S3 **REACHES** over **TO** the right. The |
| | way they both **extend to** the other side recalls 廴 *stretch* (introduced back at 延 0872). In |
| | the three entries that follow, 及 will signify *reach*. |
| **2868** | |
| 常 3 | |

| | | |
|---|---|---|
|  | **HANDLE, treat**<br><br>あつか(う) あつか(い) | 上手に扱う じょうずにあつかう handle skillfully .........0041, 0046<br>○扱い方 あつかいかた way to handle .........0173<br>客扱い きゃくあつかい hospitality, entertainment; service .........0787<br>取り扱い とりあつかい handling, dealing, treatment; trading, selling; handling, manipulation, operation; service .........0059 |

| | |
|---|---|
| **1761**<br>手 64<br><br>0189<br>常 6 | Following the previous entry, see how S5 and S6 *reach*. Now visualize the whole kanji as a *hand* (扌) *reaching* out to **HANDLE/treat** something. |

| | | |
|---|---|---|
| 級 | **GRADE, rank**<br><br>キュウ | 等級 とうきゅう class, grade, rank, magnitude 0393<br>○階級 かいきゅう class, estate; rank, grade.....1430<br>上級 じょうきゅう higher grade, advanced class, high class .........0041<br>初級 しょきゅう beginner's class .........0710<br>同級生 どうきゅうせい classmate .......0182, 0036 |

| | |
|---|---|
| **1762**<br>糸 120<br>級<br>1175<br>常 9 | Suggests military insignia, that is, *thread* (糸) that shows one has *reached* (及) a certain **GRADE** or rank. While the previous entry does not have an *on* reading, this one and the one after follow the *on* reading of 及, キュウ. |

| | | |
|---|---|---|
| 吸 | **¹ SUCK**<br>**² BREATHE IN**<br><br>キュウ<br>す(う) | ①吸引する きゅういんする suck (in), absorb; attract .........0422<br>¹ 吸収 きゅうしゅう absorption, assimilation; merger.........1155<br>² 吸入する きゅうにゅうする inhale, breathe in; suck (in); imbibe.........0039<br>② タバコを吸う タバコをすう smoke a cigarette<br>吸い物 すいもの Japanese-style soup.......0172 |

| | |
|---|---|
| **1763**<br>口 30<br><br>0179<br>常 6 | Picture the *mouth* (口) *reaching* (及) out to **SUCK** in/**BREATHE IN** air. Note how two of the three strokes in 及 seem to get **SUCKED** toward 口. The reading す う resembles the sound your mouth makes when you **SUCK** in air, as when you're sipping hot "soooooup" (see V5).<br>☞ 吹 1764 |

| | | |
|---|---|---|
|  | **BLOW, breathe out**<br><br>スイ<br>ふ(く) | 風が吹いている かぜがふいている the wind is blowing.........0425<br>○吹き込む ふきこむ blow into, breathe into...0192<br>笛吹き ふえふき flute player .................1530<br>吹雪 ふぶき snowstorm.......................0899 |

| | |
|---|---|
| **1764**<br>口 30<br><br>0204<br>常 7 | *Mouth* (口) + *gaping mouth* (欠): **breathe out/BLOW**. To distinguish from the previous entry, note how S5 seems to point away from the *mouth*, whereas in the previous entry, two of the three strokes in 及 get sucked toward it. *On-yomi* compounds appear at 鼓 2016 and 奏 2104. ☞ 吸 1763 |

| 呼 | **CALL, send for** | 点呼 てんこ roll call....................0349 |
| | | ○呼吸 こきゅう breathing, respiration.........1763 |
| | | 呼び掛ける よびかける call to; appeal to..1117 |
| | | 呼び出す よびだす call, summon; page....0038 |
| | コ | ○医者を呼ぶ いしゃをよぶ call the doctor |
| | よ(ぶ) | ...................................0561, 0107 |

| **1765** | Visualize the *mouth* (口) **CALLING** to 乎 and getting its attention. Note how, in contrast to 平 |
| 口 30 | 0334, 乎 has two strokes that either lean (S4, in the head character) or hook (S8) toward the |
| | *mouth*, graphically representing how the mouth has attracted its attention. |
| 0246 | |
| 常 8 | |

| 吐 | **SPEW, vomit** | ○吐息 といき sigh, long breath................1556 |
| | | 吐血 とけつ vomiting blood.................0198 |
| | | ○吐く はく spew, vomit; exhale; emit, send forth |
| | ト | 吐き出す はきだす spew, vomit, disgorge....0038 |
| | は(く) | 吐き気 はきけ nausea........................0126 |

| **1766** | *Mouth* (口) ingests *soil* (土), then **SPEWS/vomits.** ☞ 叶 1767 |
| 口 30 | |
| 0180 | |
| 常 6 | |

| 叶 | **BE FULFILLED, fulfill, grant** | 叶う かなう be fulfilled, be realized, be granted |
| | | 叶わない かなわない be unable, be beyond |
| | | one's power |
| | キョウ ギョウ | ○望みが叶う のぞみがかなう have one's wish |
| | かな(う) かな(える) | realized....................................1066 |
| | | 叶える かなえる grant (a request), fulfill |
| | | (expectations), answer (a person's prayer) |

| **1767** | If you visualize 十 as pointing down from the *mouth* (口), it suggests a word coming down |
| 口 30 | from the mouth of a higher-up, **FULFILLING/granting** a subordinate's request. ☞ 吐 1766 |
| 0161 | |
| 名 5 | |

| 叱 | **SCOLD** | 叱責する しっせきする reproach, scold, reprove |
| | | .........................................0831 |
| | | 叱正 しっせい correction of errors..........0043 |
| | シツ | ○叱る しかる scold, rebuke, reprove |
| | しか(る) | 叱られる しかられる be scolded |
| | | 叱り付ける しかりつける rebuke strongly, bawl |
| | | out........................................0064 |

| **1768** | Visualize 口 as the *mouth* of an adult, **SCOLDING** a *seated* child (匕). |
| 口 30 | |
| | |

| 常 5 | |

## 叫 SHOUT

キョウ
さけ(ぶ)

○叫喚 きょうかん shout, cry, scream ........... 1270
絶叫する ぜっきょうする exclaim, scream, shout
................................................ 1271
○叫ぶ さけぶ shout, scream, cry; advocate
叫び声 さけびごえ shout, outcry ........... 0529
改革を叫ぶ かいかくをさけぶ cry loudly for
reform ................................... 0429, 0592

**1769**
口 30

0178
常 6

Visualize 斗 as a hand held up to one's *mouth* (口) to amplify the volume of one's voice while **SHOUTING**. S5 represents the thumb, held out to fit under the chin. S4 and the top of S6 represent the fingers, while the bottom of S6 represents the wrist.

## 吟 RECITE

ギン

吟唱する ぎんしょうする recite, chant ........ 1685
朗吟する ろうぎんする recite, sing ........... 1476
詩吟 しぎん reciting Chinese poems ........ 0389
○吟詠 ぎんえい reciting/chanting a poem; poem
................................................ 1693

**1770**
口 30

0203
常 7

When it appears next to *now* (今), let *mouth* (口) suggest singing or **RECITING** in precise time. ☞ 含 1771

## 含 CONTAIN, include

ガン
ふく(む) ふく(める)

含有する がんゆうする contain, have, hold . 0400
○包含する ほうがんする include, encompass;
imply ................................... 0457
○含む ふくむ contain, include
含める ふくめる include
...を含めて ...をふくめて including...

**1771**
口 30

1756
常 7

A good way to distinguish this from the previous entry is to see the larger 口 here as a box rather than a mouth. This entry thus refers to what is *presently* (今) inside a box, to signify the idea **CONTAIN/include**. Remember, the smaller 口 in the previous entry represents a *mouth*, while the larger 口 in this entry represents a box. ☞ 吟 1770

## 琴 KOTO (Japanese zither)

キン
こと

琴曲 きんきょく koto music ..................... 0503
○琴線 きんせん heartstrings, one's innermost
feelings ................................... 0210
琴を弾く ことをひく play the koto ........... 1075
琴爪 ことづめ artificial fingernail [plectrum] of
ivory used in playing the koto ............ 0201

**1772**
玉 96

2422
常 12

Following 吟 above, 今 suggests playing in precise (musical) time. The top of the character depicts the strings of the **KOTO**.

| | **PERPLEXED, lost** | 迷惑 めいわく trouble, annoyance............1153 |
| | | 迷信 めいしん superstition..................0063 |
| | | 低迷する ていめいする be in a slump........0479 |
| | メイ | ○迷宮 めいきゅう labyrinth, maze............1242 |
| | まよ(う) | ○迷う まよう be perplexed, be lost |

| **1773** | See the eight lines of the *rice* (米) grapheme all pointing in different directions. 辶 indicates that we're trying to go somewhere, but 米 indicates that we don't know which way to go. We're lost/PERPLEXED. |
| 辵 162 | |
| **2663** | |
| 常 9 | |

| | **RIDDLE, enigma** | 謎を解く なぞをとく solve a riddle [mystery] 0345 |
| | | ○謎の なぞの mysterious |
| | | 謎の殺人事件 なぞのさつじんじけん mysterious |
| | なぞ | murder....................0522, 0015, 0080, 0118 |

| **1774** | *Words* (言) that *perplex* (迷): RIDDLE/enigma. Like other new Joyo kanji that contain 辶, this entry was not officially simplified to 辶 when it was added to the Joyo Kanji List. Remember, it is always acceptable to write 辶 in place of 辶. |
| 言 149 | |
| 謎 | |
| **1464** | |
| 常 17 | |

| | **REVERSE, contrary** | ○逆転 ぎゃくてん reversal, turnabout, inversion |
| | | ..........................0224 |
| | | 逆戻り ぎゃくもどり retrogression, going |
| | | backward............................1019 |
| | | 逆説 ぎゃくせつ paradox....................1197 |
| | ギャク | ○逆様 さかさま upside-down, reverse........0501 |
| | さか さか(さ) さか(らう) | 親に逆らう おやにさからう disobey one's parents |
| | | ..........................0276 |

| **1775** | Imagine that S6 started out vertical. Then the *truck* (辶) suddenly sped forward, sending the object loaded on it tumbling backward. 逆 depicts that instant, when the two objects move in REVERSE directions. |
| 辵 162 | |
| **2662** | |
| 常 9 | |

| | **GO BACK IN TIME, go upstream** | ○遡及する そきゅうする retroact................1760 |
| | | 遡及的 そきゅうてき retroactive........1760, 0169 |
| | | 遡上する そじょうする retroact; go upstream |
| | | ..........................0041 |
| | ソ | 遡行する そこうする go upstream..........0055 |
| | さかのぼ(る) | ○遡る さかのぼる go back (in time); go upstream |

| **1776** | To 逆 *reverse* we now add 月 *month*, to suggest the idea of going in reverse <u>through time</u>: GOING BACK IN TIME. |
| 辵 162 | |
| 遡 | |
| **2785** | |
| 常 14 | |

| | MODEL, mold | 塑像 そぞう plastic image; clay figure........1278 |
|---|---|---|
| | | ○塑造 そぞう modeling, molding............0699 |
| | ソ | 彫塑 ちょうそ carving and modeling, plastic arts; clay model...................1279 |

| **1777** | Use the curving shape of S6 and S7 as a visual cue for the idea of giving shape to an object. |
|---|---|
| 土 32 | See both parts of 朔 working together as a **MODEL** to mold a malleable chunk of *earth* (土). |
| 2475 | |
| 常 13 | |

| | MERITORIOUS SERVICE | ○勲功 くんこう distinguished service, merit..1046 |
|---|---|---|
| | | 勲章 くんしょう decoration, order, medal....1459 |
| | クン | 武勲 ぶくん deeds of arms, distinguished military service...................0111 |
| | | 殊勲 しゅくん meritorious deeds, distinguished service...................1208 |

| **1778** | *Moving* (動) directly over searing *flames* (灬): **MERITORIOUS SERVICE**. ☞ 薫 1779, 動 0540 |
|---|---|
| 力 19 | |
| 勳 | |
| 2500 | |
| 常 15 | |

| | BALMY, fragrant | ○薫風 くんぷう balmy breeze.................0425 |
|---|---|---|
| | | 薫煙 くんえん fragrant smoke.................0768 |
| | クン | ○薫り かおり fragrance, aroma |
| | かお(る) | 若葉が薫る わかばがかおる The fresh verdure smells sweet.......................0404, 0605 |

| **1779** | *Herbs* (艹) *piled* (重) atop a *fire* (灬), burning fragrantly: **BALMY/fragrant**. ☞ 煮 1188, 勲 |
|---|---|
| 艸 140 | 1778 |
| 薫 | |
| 2094 | |
| 常 16 | |

| | FRAGRANT | ○芳気 ほうき fragrant scent.................0126 |
|---|---|---|
| | | 芳草 ほうそう fragrant herb.................0144 |
| | ホウ | 芳潤な ほうじゅんな aromatic, rich..........1491 |
| | かんば(しい) | 芳名録 ほうめいろく guest book.......0269, 0608 |
| | | ○芳しい かんばしい fragrant; favorable |

| **1780** | Picture a *person* (方) running through a **FRAGRANT** meadow filled with *herbs* (艹). |
|---|---|
| 艸 140 | |
| 1893 | |
| 常 7 | |

**SWEET SMELL**

コウ キョウ
か かお(り) かお(る)

薫香 くんこう fragrance .......................1779
芳香 ほうこう perfume, fragrance, aroma ....1780
○香水 こうすい perfume .......................0027
香る かおる smell sweet, be fragrant
○花の香り はなのかおり fragrance of flowers 0121

| 1781 | *Bundled rice* (禾), mellowing in the *sun*shine (日): **SWEET SMELL**. |
| 香 186 | |
| 2225 | |
| 常 9 | |

**EXCELLENT**

シュウ
ひい(てる)

○優秀な ゆうしゅうな excellent, superior, best 0780
秀逸 しゅういつ supreme excellence.........1273
俊秀 しゅんしゅう genius, prodigy............1440
秀才 しゅうさい (person of) genius ..........0652
○日本語に秀てる にほんごにひいてる excel in
　　Japanese .........................0001, 0031, 0222

| 1782 | When 乃 (1754) appears inside other kanji, see it as a hand or rod (丿) *pulling* an object (乃) *away* toward the left. Here, we thus have a *rice bundle* (禾) being *pulled away* from "the chaff," to signify **EXCELLENCE**. Now review the differences between 乃 and 及 1760. The reading ひいてる (excel, stand out) sounds like 引いて (ひいて, pulling) + 出る (てる, go out). |
| 禾 115 | |
| 2202 | |
| 常 7 | |

**INDUCE, invite**

ユウ
さそ(う)

○誘惑 ゆうわく temptation, seduction.........1153
勧誘する かんゆうする induce, invite, persuade
　　.............................................1129
誘導する ゆうどうする induce, incite; guide, lead
　　.............................................0804
誘発する ゆうはつする cause, induce, lead to
　　.............................................0148
○誘う さそう invite, ask

| 1783 | This character includes the previous entry in full, but we should still focus visually on 乃 and how its left-hand stroke seems to *pull away*. *Words* (言) attempting to *pull* (someone) *away*: **INDUCE**/invite. |
| 言 149 | |
| 1407 | |
| 常 14 | |

**KIDNAP**

カイ

○誘拐 ゆうかい kidnapping, abduction ......1783
拐帯 かいたい absconding with money.....1232

| 1784 | Do you notice anything odd about this character? By now, you are probably used to seeing *knife* (刀) over *mouth* (口) in kanji based on 召 1103, but here, the *knife* and *mouth* are reversed. In this way, think of this entry as the conceptual opposite of politely **INVITING** (招 1104): **KIDNAPPING**. ☞ 招 1104 |
| 手 64 | |
| 拐 | |
| 0272 | |
| 常 8 | |

| | ¹ **PASS THROUGH**<br>² **SEE-THROUGH, transparent**<br><br>トウ<br>す(く) す(かす) す(ける) | ① 浸透 しんとう permeation, penetration ......1014<br>② 透明な とうめいな transparent ..............0024<br>² 見え透く みえすく be seen right through, be obvious ..........0083<br>² 闇を透かす やみをすかす peer into the darkness ..........1364<br>② 透けるブラウス すけるブラウス sheer blouse |

| **1785**<br>辵 162<br><br>2677<br>常 10 | Here again focus visually on 乃 and how its left-hand stroke seems to pull toward the left. With ⻌ *advance*, we should think of *pulling* or *advancing* through a barrier: **PASS THROUGH**. Also means **SEE-THROUGH/transparent**, from the idea of light **PASSING THROUGH** a barrier. |

| | **CARRY IN HAND, join hands**<br><br>ケイ<br>たずさ(える) たずさ(わる) | ○携帯(電話) けいたい(でんわ) mobile (telephone) ..........1232, 0155, 0053<br>携行する けいこうする carry along, bring ....0055<br>杖を携える つえをたずさえる carry a stick in one's hand..........0658<br>連携 れんけい cooperation, league, concert..0582<br>○提携する ていけいする act in concert with, tie up with..........1679 |

| **1786**<br>手 64<br><br>攜<br>0593<br>常 13 | *Hand* (扌) + *bird* (隹) + *pull away* (乃): here visualize the *hand* carrying the *bird* away (like a portable phone): **CARRY IN HAND**. ☞ 擕 2182 |

| | ¹ **MALE**<br>² **HEROIC**<br><br>ユウ<br>お- おす | ① 雄牛 おうし bull, steer ..........0116<br>① 雄犬 おすいぬ male dog..........0293<br>² 雄弁な ゆうべんな eloquent, fluent ........1052<br>② 英雄 えいゆう hero..........0332 |

| **1787**<br>隹 172<br><br>0920<br>常 12 | Think of 厷 as a *hand* (ナ) placed on a *nose* (ム). Then visualize this character as a **MALE** bravely and **HEROICALLY** placing his hand upon a *bird* (隹)'s *nose* (i.e., beak). ☞ 雌 1788 |

| | **FEMALE**<br><br>シ<br>め- めす | 雌雄 しゆう male and female; victory or defeat ..........1787<br>雌牛 めうし cow..........0116<br>雌花 めばな female flower..........0121<br>○雌犬 めすいぬ female dog, bitch ..........0293 |

| **1788**<br>隹 172<br><br>0971<br>常 14 | Recall from 此 1756 the image of *three men looking at something that has drawn their attention*. Here they are three male birds, gawking at a lovely **FEMALE** *bird* (隹). ☞ 雄 1787 |

**A LITTLE BIT**

サ
いささ（か）

○些事 さじ trifling matter.....................0080
○些細な ささいな slight, trifling, insignificant...0239
些々な ささな trifling, trivial
些か驚きました いささかおどろきました （I) was a
　little surprised.............................0807

| 1789 | Because the top stroke of 二 is narrower than the lower stroke, we can visualize it here as a pyramid shape, narrowing at the top. Notice how there's only **A LITTLE BIT** of space at the top of S7 for the *three men* (此) to fit. |
| 二 7 | |
| 2282 | |
| 名 8 | |

**BRUSHWOOD, firewood**

サイ
しば

○柴刈り しばかり firewood gathering.........0524
柴垣 しばがき brushwood fence.............1397
柴犬 しばいぬ Shiba Inu [kind of dog].......0293
柴田 しばた Shibata [surname].............0020

| 1790 | Here visualize 此 as slender branches at the top of a *tree* (木): **BRUSHWOOD/firewood**. ☞ 紫 1791 |
| 木 75 | |
| 2309 | |
| 名 10 | |

**PURPLE**

シ
むらさき

○紫外線 しがいせん ultraviolet rays.....0266, 0210
紫紺 しこん purplish blue...................1043
紫煙 しえん tobacco smoke.................0768
○紫色 むらさきいろ purple color, purple......0528
赤紫 あかむらさき reddish purple............0774

| 1791 | Here the *three men* (此)'s attention has been drawn by a flamboyant **PURPLE** *thread* (糸). ☞ 柴 1790 |
| 糸 120 | |
| 2348 | |
| 常 12 | |

**HAIR**

ハツ
かみ

○散髪 さんぱつ haircut.........................0808
毛髪 もうはつ hair..............................0487
白髪 しらが (=はくはつ) white/gray hair......0076
髪結い かみゆい hairdresser; hairdressing 0516
○髪の毛 かみのけ hair.........................0487

| 1792 | 髟 means *hair*. Picture 彡 as a *comb*, and S2-4 as long locks of *hair*. With 友 *friend*, this entry depicts a person having her **HAIR** combed by a friend. ☞ 髭 1793 |
| 髟 190 | |
| 2477 | |
| 常 14 | |

| | | |
|---|---|---|
| **BEARD, mustache** | ○髭を剃る　ひげをそる　shave (one's beard) …1192 | |
| | 鼻髭　はなひげ　mustache ………………………1558 | |
| | 髭面　ひげづら　bearded/unshaven face …..0175 | |
| シ | 無精髭　ぶしょうひげ　stubble, unshaven face | |
| ひげ | …………………………………………………0048, 0976 | |

**1793**
髟 190

Distinguish from the previous entry by using ヒ (similar to katakana ヒ) as a quick clue for ひげ (**BEARD**/mustache). ☞ 髪 1792

外 16

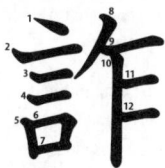

| | |
|---|---|
| **SWINDLE** | 詐取　さしゅ　fraud, swindle ………………0059 |
| | 詐称　さしょう　misrepresentation, false statement |
| サ | …………………………………………………0684 |

**1794**
言 149

Review 0153–54. Here, we fabricate *words* (言) as with a *saw* (乍): **SWINDLE**. A useful compound to memorize appears in the next entry. Remember to associate the English word "saw" with the *on* readings サ and サク, one or both of which apply to all kanji in this course containing 乍. ☞ 許 1276

1362
常 12

| | |
|---|---|
| **DECEIVE** | ○詐欺　さぎ　swindle, fraud ………………1794 |
| | 詐欺師　さぎし　swindler, con artist…..1794, 0748 |
| | ○欺く　あざむく　deceive |
| ギ | 欺き惑わす　あざむきまどわす　deceive and lead |
| あざむ(く) | astray………………………………………1153 |

**1795**
欠 76

Imagine a scenario in which a person has been duped into letting in a robber, who ties him up and then makes off with his valuables. In this kanji we see the person *bound* up (其), his mouth *gaping* (欠) in shock at how he's been **DECEIVED**.

1519
常 12

| | |
|---|---|
| **SHOGI (Japanese chess)** | ○将棋　しょうぎ　shogi, Japanese chess ………0614 |
| | 棋士　きし　professional go/shogi player…..0350 |
| | 棋界　きかい　go circles; shogi circles………0612 |
| キ | 棋譜　きふ　record of a game of shogi/go ….1086 |

**1796**
木 75

In the next two entries, let 其 represent a rectangular grid, on which one plays a game of chess or checkers. The game with the *wooden* (木) pieces is **SHOGI (Japanese chess)**. (Continued in next entry) ☞ 碁 1797

基

0899
常 12

| | **GO (Japanese checkers)** | 碁石 ごいし go stone ............................ 0403 |
|---|---|---|
| | | ○碁盤 ごばん go board, checkerboard ....... 0673 |
| | | 碁会所 ごかいしょ go parlor ............ 0226, 0249 |
| | ゴ | 囲碁 いご (the game of) go ................ 0435 |
| | | 碁を打つ ごをうつ play (a game of) go ..... 1025 |

**1797**
石 112

(Continuing from the previous entry) The game with the *stone* (石) pieces is **GO (Japanese checkers)**. ☞ 基 0485, 棋 1796

**2354**
常 13

| | **EXTREMELY** | ○甚大な じんだいな extremely big; serious; heavy ................................. 0033 |
|---|---|---|
| | | 幸甚である こうじんである be very glad ..... 1470 |
| | | 深甚な しんじんな profound; careful, mature 1715 |
| | ジン | ○甚だ はなはだ extremely, very |
| | はなは(だ) はなは(だしい) | 甚だしい誤解 はなはだしいごかい serious misunderstanding ................... 1480, 0345 |

**1798**
甘 99

Returning to the meaning *bind/bound* for 其, we can visualize in this entry a person *bound* to "the stocks," an **EXTREME** form of punishment. S6 represents the boards locked around the detainee's *legs*, which can be seen dangling below (儿). Associate the image not with punishment, but with the idea of **EXTREMENESS**.

**2296**
常 9

| | ¹ **CHECK, consider** | ¹ 勘定 かんじょう calculation; account, settlement of accounts............................... 0045 |
|---|---|---|
| | ² **INTUITIVE PERCEPTION** | ①勘弁する かんべんする pardon, forgive; tolerate ............................... 1052 |
| | | ² 勘付く かんづく sense (a danger) ............. 1715 |
| | カン | ² 勘の良い人 かんのいいひと person of quick perception ................... 0285, 0015 |
| | | ②勘違い かんちがい wrong guess/impression ... 0663 |

**1799**
力 19

Here we observe the *detainee* (甚) **CHECKING** out the *plow* (力) left next to him, **considering** it for potential use in an escape plot. To the extent that he naturally understands how to make use of the *plow*, the character can also represent the idea of **INTUITIVE PERCEPTION**.

**1582**
常 11

| | **ENDURE, tolerate** | 堪忍する かんにんする have patience, bear with; forgive, pardon ................... 1095 |
|---|---|---|
| | | ○堪える たえる endure, bear |
| | | ○堪え難い たえがたい unbearable ........... 0712 |
| | カン | ○不幸に堪える ふこうにたえる bear up under misfortune................... 0049, 1470 |
| | た(える) たま(る)* | 堪らない たまらない cannot bear; cannot help (doing) |

**1800**
土 32

Finally, picture the *detainee* (甚) suffering the additional humiliation of being pelted by clods of *dirt* (土), hurled at him by scornful passers-by: **ENDURE**.

**0514**
常 12

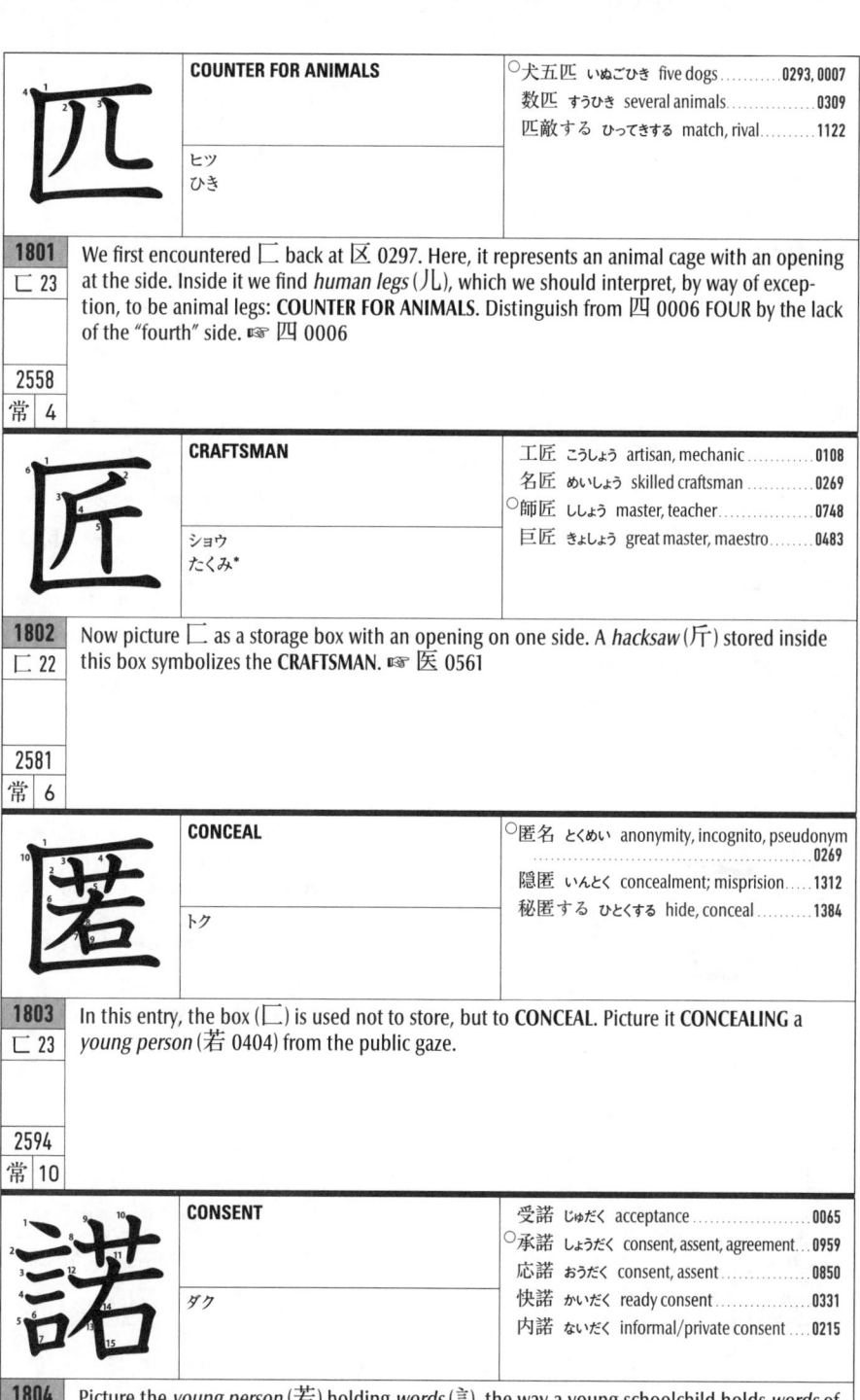

| 匹 | COUNTER FOR ANIMALS | ○犬五匹 いぬごひき five dogs............0293, 0007 |
|---|---|---|
| | | 数匹 すうひき several animals............0309 |
| | ヒツ ひき | 匹敵する ひってきする match, rival............1122 |

| 1801 | We first encountered ⼐ back at 区 0297. Here, it represents an animal cage with an opening at the side. Inside it we find *human legs* (儿), which we should interpret, by way of exception, to be animal legs: **COUNTER FOR ANIMALS**. Distinguish from 四 0006 FOUR by the lack of the "fourth" side. ☞ 四 0006 |
|---|---|
| ⼐ 23 | |
| 2558 | |
| 常 4 | |

| 匠 | CRAFTSMAN | 工匠 こうしょう artisan, mechanic............0108 |
|---|---|---|
| | | 名匠 めいしょう skilled craftsman............0269 |
| | ショウ たくみ* | ○師匠 ししょう master, teacher............0748 |
| | | 巨匠 きょしょう great master, maestro............0483 |

| 1802 | Now picture ⼖ as a storage box with an opening on one side. A *hacksaw* (斤) stored inside this box symbolizes the **CRAFTSMAN**. ☞ 医 0561 |
|---|---|
| ⼖ 22 | |
| 2581 | |
| 常 6 | |

| 匿 | CONCEAL | ○匿名 とくめい anonymity, incognito, pseudonym |
|---|---|---|
| | | ............0269 |
| | | 隠匿 いんとく concealment; misprision.....1312 |
| | トク | 秘匿する ひとくする hide, conceal............1384 |

| 1803 | In this entry, the box (⼖) is used not to store, but to CONCEAL. Picture it **CONCEALING** a *young person* (若 0404) from the public gaze. |
|---|---|
| ⼖ 23 | |
| 2594 | |
| 常 10 | |

| 諾 | CONSENT | 受諾 じゅだく acceptance............0065 |
|---|---|---|
| | | ○承諾 しょうだく consent, assent, agreement...0959 |
| | | 応諾 おうだく consent, assent............0850 |
| | ダク | 快諾 かいだく ready consent............0331 |
| | | 内諾 ないだく informal/private consent....0215 |

| 1804 | Picture the *young person* (若) holding *words* (言), the way a young schoolchild holds *words* of parental **CONSENT** on a permission slip as he reports to school on the day of a field trip. |
|---|---|
| 言 149 | |
| 1418 | |
| 常 15 | |

| | BEG | ○乞う こう beg, pray for |
|---|---|---|
| | | 乞食 こじき beggar..........................0288 |
| | | 物乞い ものごい beggar; begging...........0172 |
| | コツ* コ* | 雨乞い あまごい ritual prayer for rain........0154 |
| | こ(う) | |

| **1805** | Visualize 乙 as a **BEGGAR** kneeling and holding out his hands, and ⼃ as a charitable person |
|---|---|
| 乙 5 | standing above him, holding out an arm (S2) to give him a handout. ☞ 迄 1806, 乙 1522 |
| **1707** | |
| 常 3 | |

| | UP TO, until | 此れ迄 これまで up to/until now..............1756 |
|---|---|---|
| | | 其れ迄 それまで up to/until then..............1757 |
| | | 盗み迄する ぬすみまてする go to the extent of |
| | キツ | stealing..............................1304 |
| | まで | 年末迄に ねんまつまでに by the year's end. 0117, 0272 |
| | | 当然の事をした迄だ とうぜんのことをしたまでだ |
| | | I simply have done what I ought to do |
| | | .........................0141, 0760, 0080 |

| **1806** | *Beggar* (乞) hitching a ride on a *truck* (辶), as far as it will take him: **UP TO/until**. Note that |
|---|---|
| 辵 162 | まで is usually written in hiragana. ☞ 乞 1805 |
| 迄 | |
| **2757** | |
| 名 7 | |

| | DRY | 乾季 かんき dry season.....................0395 |
|---|---|---|
| | | 乾物 かんぶつ dry provisions, groceries....0172 |
| | | ○乾杯する かんぱいする drink a toast, toast...1696 |
| | カン | ○乾く かわく [vi] dry (up) |
| | かわ(く) かわ(かす) | 着物を乾かす きものをかわかす dry clothes |
| | | .........................0938, 0172 |

| **1807** | Alcoholic *beggar* (乞) "**DRYING**" out in the *morning* (from 朝 0145). ☞ 幹 1808, 干 0408 |
|---|---|
| 乙 5 | |
| **1500** | |
| 常 11 | |

| | TRUNK | 根幹 こんかん basis, root; keynote; root and |
|---|---|---|
| | | trunk.............................0284 |
| | | 新幹線 しんかんせん Shinkansen, bullet train |
| | | ............................0275, 0210 |
| | カン | ○幹部 かんぶ executive, (managing) staff....0068 |
| | みき | 主幹 しゅかん editor in chief................0365 |
| | | ○木の幹 きのみき trunk of a tree.............0028 |

| **1808** | Here interpret 干 visually, as a tree **TRUNK** with two sets of branches (see 人 as the tree's |
|---|---|
| 干 51 | canopy). From 朝 0145, recall that the left side of this character depicts the *sun* (日) rising |
| | through two *cross-shaped plants*. Let that image suggest "rising straight up," just as a tree |
| **1531** | **TRUNK** does. ☞ 乾 1807, 軒 0691 |
| 常 13 | |

| | ¹ MANIPULATE ² FIDELITY | ① 操作 そうさ operation, manipulation, handling 0152 |
|---|---|---|
| | | ¹ 操縦する そうじゅうする manage, control; steer; pilot ....................................................... 0871 |
| | | ¹ 体操 たいそう gymnastics, calisthenics .......... 0062 |
| | ソウ みさお あやつ(る) | ① 世論を操る せろんをあやつる manipulate public opinion ............................................ 0604, 0942 |
| | | ② 操を守る みさおをまもる preserve one's chastity; adhere to one's principles ...................... 0648 |

**1809**
手 64

Think of 喿 as a *tree* (木) with fruit (品), which the *hand* (扌) carefully and dexterously picks: **MANIPULATE**. Associate M2 **FIDELITY** with the idea of dependable handling.

0693
常 16

| | DRY OUT | ○乾燥する かんそうする dry out/up, desiccate ....................................................... 1807 |
|---|---|---|
| | | 乾燥機 かんそうき dryer ................. 1807, 0473 |
| | ソウ | 高燥地 こうそうち high and dry ground ........................................................ 0185, 0187 |
| | | 無味乾燥な むみかんそうな dry as dust, insipid opinion ...................................... 0048, 0273, 1807 |

**1810**
火 86

Now we use *fire* (火) to **DRY OUT** the *fruit* (品, following previous entry).

1009
常 17

| | ¹ REEL, spin ² SHIFT ONWARD | ¹ 繰り綿 くりわた ginned cotton .............. 0211 |
|---|---|---|
| | | ² 繰り上げる くりあげる advance, move up ... 0041 |
| | | ² 繰り延べる くりのべる postpone, put off ... 0872 |
| | く(る) | ² やり繰り やりくり tiding over, makeshift |
| | | ② 繰り返す くりかえす repeat, do over again ... 0378 |

**1811**
糸 120

Here, picture 品 as cotton bolls, whose *thread* (糸) is being **spun** onto **REELS**. M2 **SHIFT ONWARD** comes from the idea of shifting thread from a cotton boll or silk cocoon onto a **REEL**. Note that while this entry has no *on-yomi*, the others incorporating 喿 are all pronounced ソウ.

1300
常 19

| | SEAWEED, algae | 藻類 そうるい seaweed, algae ............. 0310 |
|---|---|---|
| | | ○海藻 かいそう seaweed, kelp, marine algae 0106 |
| | ソウ も | 緑藻 りょくそう green algae ................. 0607 |
| | | 藻草 もぐさ water plants ................. 0144 |

**1812**
艸 140

This time, the focus shifts to ⺾ and ⺡, which suggest that 喿 is in this case a *grass*-like plant growing in *water*: **SEAWEED**.

2116
常 19

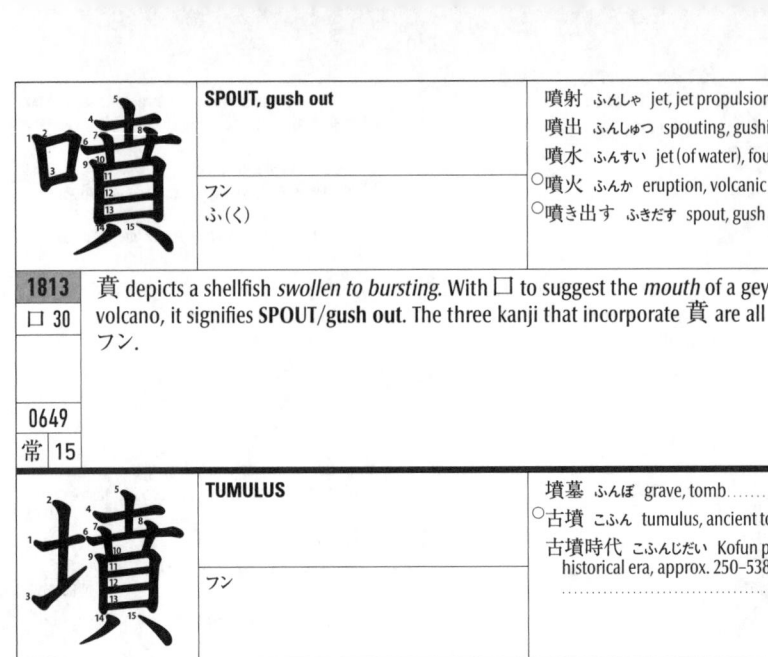

| | SPOUT, gush out | 噴射 ふんしゃ jet, jet propulsion............1021 |
|---|---|---|
| | | 噴出 ふんしゅつ spouting, gushing..........0038 |
| | | 噴水 ふんすい jet (of water), fountain......0027 |
| | | °噴火 ふんか eruption, volcanic activity....0026 |
| | フン ふ(く) | °噴き出す ふきだす spout, gush out.........0038 |

| 1813 | 賁 depicts a shellfish *swollen to bursting*. With 口 to suggest the *mouth* of a geyser or |
|---|---|
| 口 30 | volcano, it signifies **SPOUT/gush out**. The three kanji that incorporate 賁 are all pronounced フン. |
| 0649 | |
| 常 15 | |

| | TUMULUS | 墳墓 ふんぼ grave, tomb...................1340 |
|---|---|---|
| | | °古墳 こふん tumulus, ancient tomb.........0254 |
| | | 古墳時代 こふんじだい Kofun period [Japanese |
| | フン | historical era, approx. 250–538 CE] |
| | | ...................0254, 0383, 0071 |

| 1814 | *Earth* (土) + *swollen to bursting* (賁): **TUMULUS**. |
|---|---|
| 土 32 | |
| 0653 | |
| 常 15 | |

| | INDIGNATION | 義憤 ぎふん righteous indignation..........0926 |
|---|---|---|
| | | 憤激する ふんげきする be enraged..........0575 |
| | | °憤然と ふんぜんと indignantly, in a rage....0760 |
| | | 公憤 こうふん public indignation/resentment |
| | フン いきどおる | ...................0089 |
| | | °憤る いきどおる be indignant |

| 1815 | *Heart* (忄) + *swollen to bursting* (賁): **INDIGNATION**. |
|---|---|
| 心 61 | |
| 0662 | |
| 常 15 | |

| | FANG, tusk | 象牙 ぞうげ ivory.........................1277 |
|---|---|---|
| | | 毒牙 どくが poison fang....................0133 |
| | | 虎が牙を剝いた とらがきばをむいた the tiger |
| | ガ ゲ きば | bared its fangs......................0912, 0609 |

| 1816 | Depicts a **FANG** or **tusk**. Note the slight difference between the independent kanji and the |
|---|---|
| 牙 92 | grapheme version, seen in the next entry. ☞ 芽 1817 |
| 2891 | |
| 常 4 | |

## 芽 BUD

ガ
め

○発芽する はつがする bud, sprout, germinate ...........................................................0148
麦芽 ばくが wheat germ, malt ............0131
新芽 しんめ sprout, bud, shoot.............0275
若芽 わかめ young bud .....................0404
○芽生える めばえる bud, sprout; begin......0036

| 1817 | Slender *fang*(牙) of *grass*(艹): BUD. ☞ 牙 1816 |
| 艹 140 | |
| 芽 | |
| 1927 | |
| 常 8 | |

## 雅 ELEGANT

ガ

○優雅な ゆうがな elegant, graceful, refined...0780
風雅 ふうが elegance, refinement, daintiness ...........................................................0425
雅楽 ががく old Japanese court music ......0302
雅俗 がぞく elegance and vulgarity ............1039

| 1818 | *Bird*(隹) with an ELEGANT, slender, *fang*(牙)-like beak, like a hummingbird's. |
| 隹 172 | |
| | |
| 1106 | |
| 常 13 | |

## 邪 EVIL

ジャ

○邪悪 じゃあく wickedness, vice ..............0546
邪道 じゃどう evil course; heresy.............0158
無邪気 むじゃき innocence, simplicity..0048, 0126
正邪の区別 せいじゃのくべつ discrimination between right and wrong .......0043, 0297, 0090
風邪 かぜ (common) cold ..................0425

| 1819 | Here we observe a *fanged*(牙) beast that has surmounted the town walls and is now inside the *town*(阝). Let this image symbolize EVIL. |
| 邑 163 | |
| | |
| 1039 | |
| 常 8 | |

## 既 ALREADY, previous

キ
すで(に)

既婚の きこんの (already) married ..........1721
既往症 きおうしょう previous illness, medical history....................................0866, 0618
○既成の きせいの established, existing, done..0070
既成事実 きせいじじつ established fact, fait accompli....................0070, 0080, 0499
既に申した様に すでにもうしたように as I have previously stated ......................0315, 0501

| 1820 | At the right, notice how 旡 differs from 牙 of the previous few entries. We shall still see it as a *fang*. Focus on how the *fang* has ALREADY wrapped all the way around the *little boy*(旦)— he's ALREADY done for. Note the variant forms for this and the next two entries. ☞ 即 0390 |
| 旡 71 | |
| 既 | |
| 1079 | |
| 常 10 | |

| | GENERAL, rough | 概略 がいりゃく outline, summary; roughly....**0791** |
|---|---|---|
| | | 概論 がいろん outline, general remarks ....**0942** |
| | | 概括する がいかつする generalize, summarize ............................................**1069** |
| | ガイ | ○概念 がいねん general idea, concept........**0230** |
| | | 一概に いちがいに unconditionally; wholly, indiscriminately............................**0002** |

| **1821** | The *little boy*(旦) is larger than the usual prey, so the *fanged*(旡) beast will have to measure |
|---|---|
| 木 75 | him first to be sure it can actually swallow him. Here we observe the fanged beast using a |
| 概 | piece of *wood*(木) to make a **GENERAL/rough** measure of the size of his quarry. ☞ 慨 1822 |
| 0959 | |
| 常 14 | |

| | DEPLORE | 慨嘆する がいたんする deplore, lament, regret ............................................**1731** |
|---|---|---|
| | | ○憤慨 ふんがい resentment, indignation ....**1815** |
| | ガイ | 慨然と がいぜんと deploringly; indignantly **0760** |

| **1822** | Here a *heart*(忄) **DEPLORES** what is happening to the *little boy*(旦) in 既 1820. Remembering |
|---|---|
| 心 61 | this idea, practice writing this character in alternation with 既 and 概, focusing on distin- |
| 慨 | guishing their meanings. ☞ 概 1821 |
| 0588 | |
| 常 13 | |

| | SEEDLING | 種苗 しゅびょう seedlings, seeds and saplings ............................................**0544** |
|---|---|---|
| | | ○苗木 なえぎ sapling, young tree............**0028** |
| | ビョウ ミョウ* | 苗床 なえどこ seedbed ........................**0851** |
| | なえ なわ- | 苗代 なわしろ bed for rice seedlings, rice nursery ............................................**0071** |
| | | ○苗字 みょうじ surname [cf. 名 0269].........**0098** |

| **1823** | Young *plant*(艹) sprouting in a recently seeded *rice field*(田): **SEEDLING**. |
|---|---|
| 艸 140 | |
| | |
| 1924 | |
| 常 8 | |

| | DEPICT | 描画する びょうがする draw a picture, paint **0176** |
|---|---|---|
| | | 素描 そびょう (rough) sketch .................**0132** |
| | | ○描写 びょうしゃ depiction; portrayal; drawing ............................................**0859** |
| | ビョウ | ○描く えがく depict, draw, paint |
| | えが(く) か(く) | 油絵を描く あぶらえをかく paint in oil....**0433, 0525** |

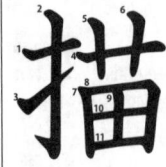

| **1824** | *Hand*(扌) using a *seedling*(苗) as a brush, to **DEPICT** things. |
|---|---|
| 手 64 | |
| | |
| 0445 | |
| 常 11 | |

## 猫 CAT

ビョウ
ねこ

○愛猫家 あいびょうか cat lover ..........0778, 0219
子猫 こねこ kitten..................0094
猫背 ねこぜ stoop, bent back...............0124
猫撫て声で ねこなでごえて in a soft coaxing voice ...................1538, 0529
招き猫 まねきねこ beckoning cat (figurine) 1104

**1825**
犬 94

0488
常 11

A *smallish four-legged creature* (犭), gentle and lithe enough to walk among the *seedlings* (苗): **CAT**. As a visual shortcut, you might associate 艹 with a **CAT**'s whiskers.

---

## 萌 GERMINATE, sprout

ホウ ボウ
も(える) きざ(す)

○萌芽 ほうが germination, beginning; sprout 1817
○萌える もえる sprout, bud
萌黄色 もえぎいろ yellowish green....0915, 0528
○萌す きざす germinate, sprout; show signs of
萌し きざし germination, sprouting; signs

**1826**
艸 140

萠

1995
名 11

Rather than use *bright* from 明, I suggest you visualize *grass* (艹) sprouting atop the *sun* (日) and *moon* (月): **GERMINATE**.

---

## 兆 ¹SIGN, omen; show signs of ²TRILLION

チョウ
きざ(す) きざ(し)

①兆候 ちょうこう symptom, sign; omen .......1675
¹前兆 ぜんちょう omen, sign..................0113
①兆す きざす sprout, show signs of
¹凶事の兆し きょうじのきざし omen of disaster ...................0296, 0080
²二兆円 にちょうえん two trillion yen ...0003, 0013

**1827**
儿 10

0199
常 6

萌す (きざす, previous entry, V4) and 兆す (きざす, V3 here) overlap in signifying "sprout" and "**show signs of**," so see 兆 as a pair of stalks with buds **showing signs of** blossoming. M2 **TRILLION** should be practiced together with 万 0018 TEN THOUSAND and 億 0622 HUNDRED MILLION.

---

## 眺 GAZE

チョウ
なが(める)

○眺望 ちょうぼう view, prospect, outlook .....1066
海を眺める うみをながめる look out over the sea ...................0106
月を眺める つきをながめる gaze at the moon ...................0023

**1828**
目 109

1083
常 11

What is an *eye* (目) to do when placed next to a pair of stalks with flowers that are about to break out of their knobby *buds* (兆), other than **GAZE** at them, as long as it takes, until they finally blossom? The reading ながめる (眺める, gaze) sounds like 長い (ながい, long) + 見る (みる, see, view).

## 逃

**ESCAPE**

トウ
に(げる)　に(がす)　のが(す)
のが(れる)

○逃走　とうそう　flight, escape .................. 0140
逃亡する　とうぼうする　escape, abscond, desert .................. 0233
逃避　とうひ　escape, evasion, flight .......... 1469
○逃げる　にげる　escape, run away
逃がす　にがす　let go, let escape

1829
辵 162
迯
2666
常 9

Picture a dishonest plant lover pulling the *budding stalks* (兆) up from their roots and spiriting them away on the back of a *truck* (辶) to his private flower garden: **ESCAPE**.

## 桃

**PEACH**

トウ
もも

黄桃　おうとう　yellow peach .................. 0915
桃園　ももぞの　peach orchard ................ 0856
○桃色　ももいろ　pink, rose [color] ............ 0528

1830
木 75
0848
常 10

木 suggests *tree* species. What we must memorize, then, is that the tree's *budding* flowers (兆) are those of the **PEACH**. Picture the buds first flowering to attract pollinators, then ripening into big, velvety, juicy, thirst-slaking **PEACHES**.

## 跳

**JUMP, leap**

チョウ
は(ねる)　と(ぶ)　-と(び)

跳躍する　ちょうやくする　jump, leap, spring ... 1327
○跳ねる　はねる　jump, leap, bound
○跳ぶ　とぶ　jump, leap, spring
飛び跳ねる　とびはねる　jump up and down, hop .................. 0475
高跳び　たかとび　high jump .................. 0185

1831
足 157
1392
常 13

See ⻊ as a person getting ready to spring his *legs* and **JUMP** right over the two *budding stalks* (兆). This would be a good time to review 飛 0475 and 踊 1325. ☞ 躍 1327

## 挑

**PROVOKE, challenge**

チョウ
いど(む)

○挑戦　ちょうせん　challenge, defiance .......... 0461
挑発する　ちょうはつする　provoke, incite, excite, stimulate .................. 0148
○戦いを挑む　たたかいをいどむ　challenge (someone) to a fight .................. 0461

1832
手 64
0331
常 9

See the two short crossing strokes of 扌 *hand* (its fingers) **PROVOKING** the *budding stalks* (兆): they are picking at the top-left bud, and in an instant they will have plucked it off. Focus for a moment on the place where the fingers are about to pinch off the helpless bud, and sense the prospect of imminent violence. Now test yourself on this 兆 set.

| 拙 | **CLUMSY** | ○拙劣な せつれつな clumsy, awkward, unskillful ............................................ **1743** |
|---|---|---|
| | | 拙速な せっそくな rough and ready, fast and sloppy................................. **1143** |
| | セツ | 巧拙 こうせつ skill, dexterity, workmanship **1047** |
| | つたな(い) | ○拙い つたない clumsy, unskillful |

| **1833** 手 64 | Here we observe a *hand* (扌) slipping *out* (出) of place, which signifies the idea of **CLUMSI-NESS**. ☞ 掘 1835 |
|---|---|
| **0280** 常 8 | |

| 屈 | **BEND, submit to** | ○屈折 くっせつ bending, turn; refraction.....**1698** |
|---|---|---|
| | | 不屈の ふくつの indomitable, unyielding **0049** |
| | | 窮屈な きゅうくつな cramped; overly formal **1711** |
| | クツ | 屈する くっする bend, yield |
| | かが(む)* かが(める)* | 屈む かがむ bend over, stoop |

| **1834** 尸 44 | Now we shall make use of 尸's additional sense *buttocks*, which we learned back at 尾 0488. The present entry refers to "*putting out* (出) one's *buttocks*," i.e., the act of **BENDING** over. ☞ 届 1528, 居 0255 |
|---|---|
| **2652** 常 8 | |

| 掘 | **DIG** | 掘削する くっさくする dig out, excavate .....**1292** |
|---|---|---|
| | | 採掘 さいくつ mining........................... **0989** |
| | | ○発掘する はっくつする dig, excavate ........**0148** |
| | クツ | ○掘る ほる dig, excavate |
| | ほ(る) | 掘り返す ほりかえす turn up (the soil), tear up (a road) ................................................... **0378** |

| **1835** 手 64 | *Bend* over (屈) and **DIG** with your *hands* (扌). Note that while the next entry has no *on-yomi*, the other three with 屈, including the present entry, are all pronounced クツ. ☞ 拙 1833, 堀 1836 |
|---|---|
| **0454** 常 11 | |

| 堀 | **DITCH** | ○堀川 ほりかわ canal.............................**0022** |
|---|---|---|
| | | 堀割 ほりわり canal, ditch ................... **0416** |
| | | 用水堀 ようすいぼり irrigation ditch...**0047, 0027** |
| | ほり | 外堀 そとぼり outer moat.................... **0266** |

| **1836** 土 32 | Once used interchangeably with the previous entry, but now used only for the noun ほり (**DITCH**), while the previous entry is used for the verb ほる (**DIG**). You can remember this easily by associating 扌 with the action and 土 with the object. Because 堀 is used only for the word ほり, it has no *on-yomi*. ☞ 塀 2171, 掘 1835 |
|---|---|
| **0423** 常 11 | |

| | ¹ SEAL, enclose<br>² ENFEOFF | ①同封する どうふうする enclose (in a letter)...0182<br>¹ 密封する みっぷうする seal hermetically....1383<br>¹ 封を切る ふうをきる break the seal.........0086<br>②封建的な ほうけんてきな feudal, feudalistic<br>.........................1609, 0169<br>² 封建制度 ほうけんせいど feudalism<br>.........................1609, 0708, 0280 |
| --- | --- | --- |
| | フウ ホウ | |

| **1837** | Here we observe an *outstretched arm* (寸) applying two lumps of sticky *earth* (土) to SEAL an |
| --- | --- |
| 寸 41 | envelope (see V2 of the next entry). Associate M2 **ENFEOFF** with M1 **SEAL** through association with the historical process of Enclosure, which "sealed" off common lands so as to turn them into private property. |
| **1182** | |
| 常 9 | |

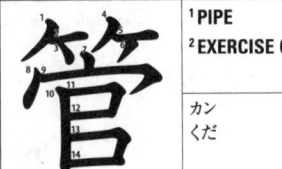

| | TUBE | 円筒 えんとう cylinder.....................0013<br>○封筒 ふうとう envelope.....................1837<br>○筒形 つつがた cylindrical, tube-shaped ...0147<br>筒袖 つつそで tight-sleeved kimono........1531<br>茶筒 ちゃづつ tea caddy.....................0603 |
| --- | --- | --- |
| | トウ<br>つつ | |

| **1838** | When 同 appears under ⺮, visualize it as a cross-sectional view of an insulated TUBE (made |
| --- | --- |
| 竹 118 | of *bamboo*, of course). Also, make an effort to remember that 筒 (トウ) is the only character based on 同 that is not pronounced ドウ. ☞ 箇 0261 |
| **2341** | |
| 常 12 | |

| | ¹ PIPE<br>² EXERCISE CONTROL | ¹ 管状の かんじょうの tubular.................0616<br>○気管 きかん windpipe, trachea.............0126<br>○鉄の管 てつのくだ iron pipe................0564<br>②管理する かんりする administer, manage...0532<br>² 保管する ほかんする take custody of, keep 0646 |
| --- | --- | --- |
| | カン<br>くだ | |

| **1839** | *Bamboo* (⺮) *government official* (官): associate this combination with municipally oper- |
| --- | --- |
| 竹 118 | ated utilities involving bamboo pipes, such as sewerage and water. This should allow you to remember M1 **PIPE**, as well as M2 **EXERCISE CONTROL**, from the idea of governmental control over what passes through the pipes. |
| **2357** | |
| 常 14 | |

| | COFFIN | ○石棺 せっかん sarcophagus.................0403<br>納棺する のうかんする place a body in a coffin<br>.........................1156<br>出棺する しゅっかんする carry the coffin out of<br>the house.........................0038 |
| --- | --- | --- |
| | カン<br>ひつぎ | |

| **1840** | Every *government official* (官) is allotted one *tree* (木) for his **COFFIN**. |
| --- | --- |
| 木 75 | |
| **0897** | |
| 常 12 | |

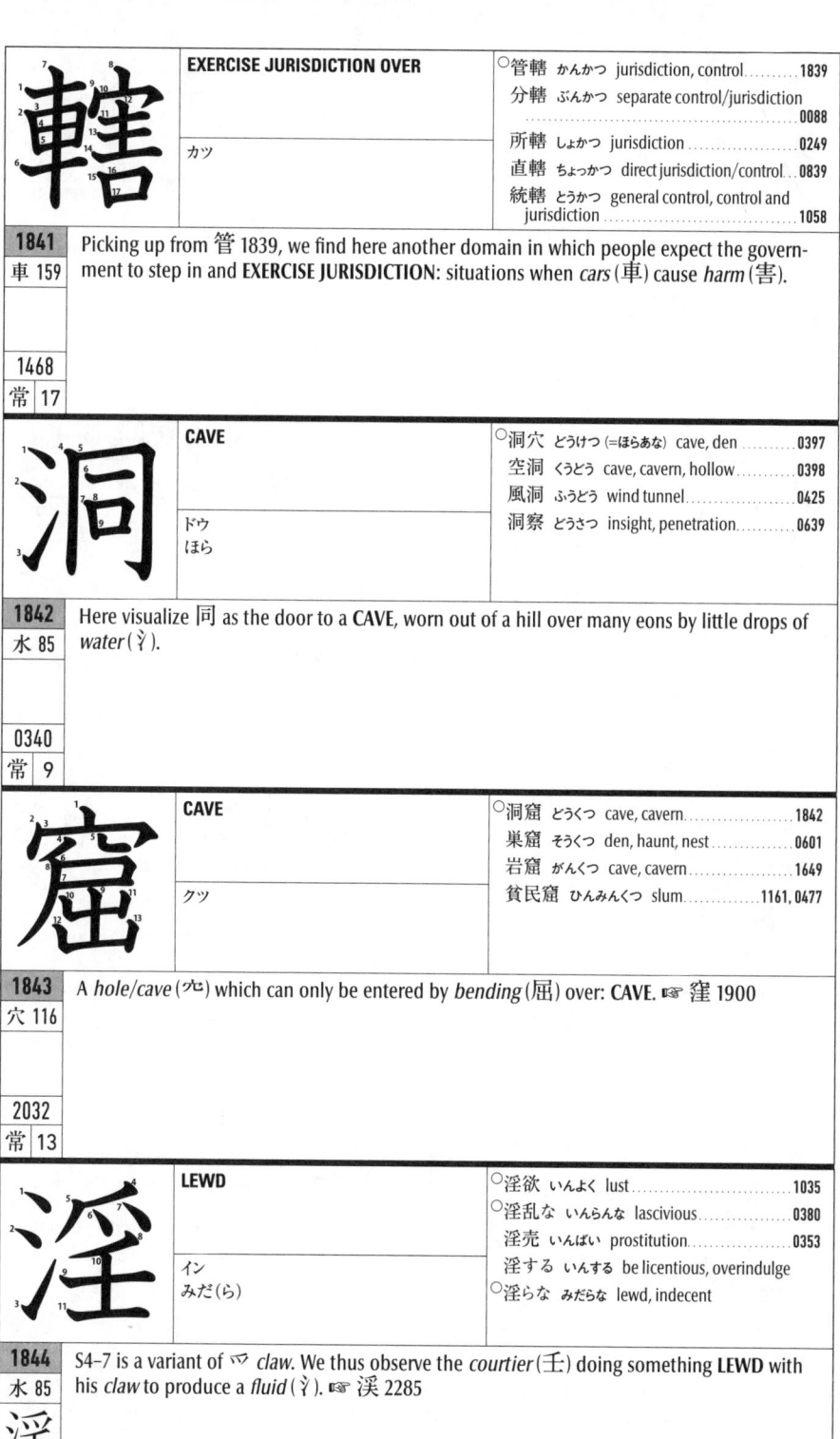

## 1840 轄

**EXERCISE JURISDICTION OVER**

カツ

○管轄　かんかつ　jurisdiction, control..........1839
分轄　ぶんかつ　separate control/jurisdiction
.................................................0088
所轄　しょかつ　jurisdiction..................0249
直轄　ちょっかつ　direct jurisdiction/control...0839
統轄　とうかつ　general control, control and
jurisdiction..........1058

---

**1841**
車 159

1468
常 17

Picking up from 管 1839, we find here another domain in which people expect the government to step in and **EXERCISE JURISDICTION**: situations when *cars* (車) cause *harm* (害).

---

## 洞

**CAVE**

ドウ
ほら

○洞穴　どうけつ (＝ほらあな)　cave, den..........0397
空洞　くうどう　cave, cavern, hollow..........0398
風洞　ふうどう　wind tunnel..................0425
洞察　どうさつ　insight, penetration..........0639

---

**1842**
水 85

0340
常 9

Here visualize 同 as the door to a **CAVE**, worn out of a hill over many eons by little drops of *water* (氵).

---

## 窟

**CAVE**

クツ

○洞窟　どうくつ　cave, cavern..................1842
巣窟　そうくつ　den, haunt, nest..............0601
岩窟　がんくつ　cave, cavern..................1649
貧民窟　ひんみんくつ　slum..........1161, 0477

---

**1843**
穴 116

2032
常 13

A *hole/cave* (穴) which can only be entered by *bending* (屈) over: **CAVE.** ☞ 窪 1900

---

## 淫

**LEWD**

イン
みだ (ら)

○淫欲　いんよく　lust..........................1035
○淫乱な　いんらんな　lascivious..................0380
淫売　いんばい　prostitution..................0353
淫する　いんする　be licentious, overindulge
○淫らな　みだらな　lewd, indecent

---

**1844**
水 85

淫

0470
常 11

S4–7 is a variant of ⺤ *claw*. We thus observe the *courtier* (壬) doing something **LEWD** with his *claw* to produce a *fluid* (氵). ☞ 溪 2285

**BECOME PREGNANT**

ニン

○避妊 ひにん contraception ................. 1469
懐妊 かいにん pregnancy, conception...... 1667
不妊 ふにん sterility .......................... 0049
妊婦 にんぷ pregnant woman.............. 1017
妊産婦 にんさんぷ pregnant women and
nursing mothers ....................... 0181, 1017

| | |
|---|---|
| **1845** | At 任 0372, we saw that the role of the *man courtier* was to be ENTRUSTED with certain |
| 女 38 | duties or OFFICES. By contrast, the role of the *woman courtier* (妊, i.e., the courtesan) is to |
| 妊 | BECOME PREGNANT. ☞ 妖 2176 |
| 0211 | |
| 常 7 | |

---

**CONCEIVE**

シン

○妊娠する にんしんする become pregnant,
conceive ......................................... 1845
妊娠中絶 にんしんちゅうぜつ abortion
....................................... 1845, 0035, 1271

| | |
|---|---|
| **1846** | *Woman* (女) receives *dragon* (辰): CONCEIVE. |
| 女 38 | |
| 0369 | |
| 常 10 | |

---

**LIP**

シン
くちびる

口唇 こうしん lips, labia....................... 0019
○上唇 うわくちびる (=じょうしん) upper lip ...... 0041
下唇 したくちびる (=かしん) lower lip.......... 0040

| | |
|---|---|
| **1847** | A *dragon* (辰) above a *mouth* (口): picture this as a long mustache snaking across a man's |
| 口 30 | upper **LIP**. |
| 唇 | |
| 2385 | |
| 常 10 | |

---

**HUMILIATE**

ジョク
はずかし(める)

侮辱する ぶじょくする insult, treat with contempt
.................................................... 1571
○屈辱 くつじょく humiliation, disgrace, insult 1834
恥辱 ちじょく disgrace, dishonor, shame .... 1670
○辱める はずかしめる humiliate; disgrace

| | |
|---|---|
| **1848** | Visualize **HUMILIATING** the *dragon* (辰) by picking it up and holding it in the air with a |
| 辰 161 | single *outstretched arm* (寸). 辱 is the only kanji in this course with the reading ジョク, |
| | which can therefore be linked with the meaning **HUMILIATE** through the mnemonic phrase |
| | "making a <u>joke</u> out of someone." |
| 2384 | |
| 常 10 | |

| | ¹ RAID<br>² INHERIT | ¹ 襲撃 しゅうげき raid, attack ................... 1026<br>①空襲 くうしゅう air raid ...................... 0398<br>¹ 奇襲 きしゅう surprise attack ............. 1329 |
|---|---|---|
| 襲 | シュウ<br>おそ(う) | ①襲う おそう raid, attack<br>②世襲 せしゅう heredity ...................... 0604 |

| 1849<br>衣 145<br><br>2533<br>常 22 | 龍 is the old form of 竜 0507 DRAGON, but here focus instead on its many layers. See 衣 as a man holding out his arms, trying to withstand layer upon layer of bombs dropped from above in an air **RAID**. With better fortune but no less burden, he can also be seen bearing layer upon layer of material goods, bequeathed from above by a wealthy parent: **INHERIT**. |
|---|---|

| | **PROSTRATE, turn over** | ○伏す ふす prostrate, lie down<br>伏せる ふせる turn downward, lay upside down, turn over<br>屈伏 くっぷく submission, surrender ........ 1834<br>○降伏 こうふく surrender, submission ........ 1377<br>潜伏 せんぷく concealment, hiding; latency 1168 |
|---|---|---|
| 伏 | フク<br>ふ(せる) ふ(す) | |

| 1850<br>人 9<br><br>0030<br>常 6 | Here imagine a *man* (亻) commanding his *dog* (犬) to lie down: **PROSTRATE**. |
|---|---|

| | **HOWL, bark** | ○吠える ほえる howl, bark, bellow, bay<br>吠え声 ほえごえ howl, bark ................. 0529<br>遠吠え とおぼえ howling .................. 0857 |
|---|---|---|
| 吠 | ベイ ハイ<br>ほ(える) | |

| 1851<br>口 30<br><br>外 7 | *Dog* (犬) *mouth* (口): **HOWL/bark**. The reading ほえる (吠える, howl) sounds like "howl." |
|---|---|

| | **BITE, chew** | ○噛む かむ bite, chew<br>噛み切る かみきる bite off ................. 0086<br>噛み傷 かみきず bite wound ............... 1307<br>噛み合う かみあう mesh, engage [as of gears]; bite one another .......................... 0227 |
|---|---|---|
| 噛 | ゴウ コウ<br>か(む) | |

| 1852<br>口 30<br><br>噛<br><br>外 15 | Now that we have learned the kanji for "bark," let us learn the one for **BITE**, which we write as a *mouth* (口) that exposes its *teeth* (歯) so as to cut into something. |
|---|---|

| 班 | **SQUAD** | ○班長 はんちょう squad/group leader .........0091 |
| | | 取材班 しゅざいはん data-collecting party |
| 1 6 7 | | ...........................................................0059, 0654 |
| 2 3 8 9 | ハン | 救護班 きゅうごはん relief party.........1098, 1661 |
| 4 5 10 | | 三つの班に分ける みっつのはんにわける divide |
| | | into three groups.......................0004, 0088 |

| **1853** | Here interpret S5–6 as a variant of 刂 *cut*. We thus obtain *cutting* or dividing *gems* (王). To |
| 玉 96 | associate this image with **SQUAD**, think of a small band of gem robbers who divide their |
| | loot. |
| **0853** | |
| 常 10 | |

| 斑 | **SPOT, speck** | ○斑点 はんてん spot, speck.....................0349 |
| | | 紫斑病 しはんびょう purpura............1791, 0617 |
| | | 母斑 ぼはん mole, birthmark...............0104 |
| | ハン | 雀斑 そばかす freckles.......................1742 |

| **1854** | Think of 文 as a distinctive **SPOT** *"written"* on a *gem* (王). |
| 文 67 | |
| **0911** | |
| 常 12 | |

| 輩 | **FELLOW** | 吾輩 わがはい I................................0220 |
| | | ○先輩 せんぱい one's senior, elder ...........0134 |
| | | ○後輩 こうはい one's junior....................0114 |
| | ハイ | ○同輩 どうはい fellow, comrade, colleague...0182 |
| | | 輩出する はいしゅつする appear in succession, |
| | | one after another ...........................0038 |

| **1855** | See 非 as a pair of chummy **FELLOWS** boarding a taxi (車) after a night at the pub. |
| 車 159 | |
| **2444** | |
| 常 15 | |

| 悲 | **SAD** | 悲壮な ひそうな pathetic, tragic.............1589 |
| | | 悲惨な ひさんな miserable, pitiable, tragic..1239 |
| | | 悲嘆 ひたん grief, sorrow, lamentation.....1731 |
| | ヒ | ○悲観的な ひかんてきな pessimistic....1128, 0169 |
| | かな(しい) かな(しむ) | ○悲しい かなしい sad |

| **1856** | Un- (非) + *heart* (心): disheartened, **SAD**. |
| 心 61 | |
| **2416** | |
| 常 12 | |

| | |
|---|---|
| **1 SUDDENLY, at once** **2 CARELESS** | 1 忽然と こつぜんと suddenly, unexpectedly 0760 |
| | ①忽ち たちまち at once, suddenly |
| | 1 切符は忽ち売り切れた きっぷはたちまちうりきれた the tickets sold out right away |
| コツ たちま(ち) | .....0086, 0982, 0353 |
| | ②粗忽に そこつに carelessly.................1516 |
| | 2 粗忽者 そこつもの careless person...1516, 0107 |

| 1857 | |
|---|---|
| 心 61 | *Woolly mammoth* (勿) + *heart/mind* (心). Associate this with animal instinct, and thus with immediate, unthinking action: **SUDDENLY; CARELESS.** ☞ 忍 1095 |
| 2149 | |
| 名 8 | |

| | |
|---|---|
| **FALL IN LOVE WITH; grow senile** | ○惚れる ほれる fall in love with |
| | 一目惚れ ひとめぼれ love at first sight 0002, 0021 |
| | 聞き惚れる ききほれる listen spellbound ...0453 |
| | 自惚れる うぬぼれる be haughty/conceited |
| コツ ほ(れる) ぼ(ける) | .....0081 |
| | ○惚ける ぼける grow senile [mentally slow] |

| 1858 | |
|---|---|
| 心 61 | *Heart* (忄) + *sudden unthinking action* (忽): **FALL IN LOVE.** |
| 0440 | |
| 名 11 | |

| | |
|---|---|
| **MONKEY, ape** | 類人猿 るいじんえん anthropoid, troglodyte |
| | .....0310, 0015 |
| | ○犬猿の仲 けんえんのなか enmity, loggerheads |
| | .....0293, 0643 |
| | 猿真似 さるまね blind imitation........0838, 1354 |
| エン さる | 猿芝居 さるしばい monkey show; shallow- minded trick.....1759, 0255 |
| | 吠猿 ほえざる howler monkey ...............1851 |

| 1859 | |
|---|---|
| 犬 94 | 袁 is familiar to us from 園 0856 and 遠 0857, where the *garment* had one fewer pleat (note that the reading エン is shared with those two kanji). In this entry, we can ignore *soil* (土) and simply let the garbed *four-legged creature* (犭) suggest a very <u>smart</u> four-legged creature— indeed, a four-<u>handed</u> one: **MONKEY.** |
| 0612 | |
| 常 13 | |

| | |
|---|---|
| **1 SORROW** **2 PITY** | 1 悲哀 ひあい sorrow, sadness.................1856 |
| | ①哀愁 あいしゅう sadness, sorrow, pensiveness |
| | .....1316 |
| | 2 可哀相な かわいそうな poor, pitiable, pathetic |
| アイ あわ(れ) あわ(れむ) | .....0814, 0682 |
| | ②哀れな あわれな pitiable; miserable |
| | 2 哀れむ あわれむ pity, sympathize |

| 1860 | |
|---|---|
| 口 30 | This entry should not be confused with 袁 in the previous entry, or with the enclosed portion of 園 0856 and 遠 0857: here, the top portion is not 土 *land* but the upper part of 衣 *garment*. Picture a person in mourning *dress* (衣) with an open-*mouthed* (口) expression of **SORROW.** ☞ 衰 1861, 衷 1862 |
| 1781 | |
| 常 9 | |

**DECLINE, degenerate**

スイ
おとろ(える)

衰退 すいたい decline, decay, degeneration 1091
○老衰 ろうすい senility ........................... 0629
減衰する げんすいする be attenuated ...... 1148
栄枯盛衰 えいこせいすい prosperity and
decline, rise and fall ............. 1245, 1049, 1300
○衰える おとろえる weaken, lose vigor, become
emaciated

| 1861 | Only S5 distinguishes this entry from the previous one. Think of it as a "wrinkle" added to 哀, |
|---|---|
| 衣 145 | signifying the process of **DECLINING** with age. ☞ 哀 1860, 衷 1862 |
| 1806 | |
| 常 10 | |

**INNER HEART**

チュウ

衷心 ちゅうしん inner heart, inmost feelings 0056
苦衷 くちゅう mental suffering, dilemma.... 0405
○折衷 せっちゅう compromise, eclecticism ... 1698
和洋折衷 わようせっちゅう mixing of Japanese
and Western elements .......... 0236, 0491, 1698

| 1862 | It is easy to perceive the meaning **INNER HEART** if you focus visually on how S5, S6, and S9 |
|---|---|
| 衣 145 | come together at the **INNER HEART** of this character. Now practice writing the last three |
| | entries in alternation, recognizing the meaning of each in its distinctive feature. |
| | ☞ 哀 1860, 衰 1861, 喪 1863 |
| 1802 | |
| 常 9 | |

**¹ MOURNING**
**² LOSS**

ソウ
も

①喪服 もふく mourning dress ................. 1471
¹ 喪章 もしょう mourning badge/band ....... 1459
①喪中 もちゅう in mourning ................... 0035
² 喪失 そうしつ loss, forfeit ................... 0563
² 喪神する そうしんする lose consciousness .. 0316

| 1863 | Visualize as the face of a **MOURNING** woman, covered by a *cloth* (衣) veil. A pair of sad eyes |
|---|---|
| 口 30 | stares through the veil, dolefully. ☞ 衷 1862 |
| 2459 | |
| 常 12 | |

**¹ MOURNING**
**² ABHOR**

キ
い(む) い(み) い(まわしい)

①忌中 きちゅう in mourning ................... 0035
¹ 忌服 きぶく mourning ....................... 1471
②忌む いむ abhor, loathe
² 忌むべき いむべき detestable, abominable
² 忌まわしい事件 いまわしいじけん abominable
incident ................................. 0080, 0118

| 1864 | Earlier we learned to see 己 as *kneeling self*. With 心 to suggest *heart*felt emotion, picture |
|---|---|
| 心 61 | 己 as one's kneeling in prayer and **MOURNING** a deep loss. Associate M2 **ABHOR** with this |
| | person's profound displeasure over the untimely loss. |
| 1889 | |
| 常 7 | |

| 卓 | ¹ TABLE<br>² PROMINENT<br><br>タク | ¹ 卓球 たっきゅう table tennis, ping-pong......1099<br>¹ 食卓 しょくたく dining table....................0288<br>① 卓上 たくじょう tabletop, on the table........0041<br>¹ 電卓 でんたく electronic calculator..........0155<br>② 卓越 たくえつ excellence, superiority.......1112 |
|---|---|---|

| **1865**<br>十 24<br><br>1777<br>常 8 | Visualize two people playing **TABLE** tennis: S1–2 show a player at the far end of the table; 日 shows a table with a net stretched across the center; and S7–8 show a second player at the near end of the table. Associate M2 **PROMINENT** with M1 **TABLE** via the idea of being elevated in stature. |
|---|---|

| 悼 | MOURN<br><br>トウ<br>いた(む) | 悼辞 とうじ message of condolence.........1465<br>哀悼する あいとうする condole, mourn, grieve<br>...........................................................1860<br>○ 追悼 ついとう mourning.......................1181<br>○ 死を悼む しをいたむ mourn over the death of<br>...........................................................0716 |
|---|---|---|

| **1866**<br>心 61<br><br>0443<br>常 11 | When 卓 appears with 忄, think of people grieving over a deceased person who has been laid upon a *table* for a memorial service: **MOURN**. Now practice writing 卓 and 悼 and distinguishing their meanings. |
|---|---|

| 貞 | CHASTE<br><br>テイ | 貞女 ていじょ chaste woman, faithful wife...0093<br>貞操 ていそう chastity, virginity.............1809<br>○ 貞節 ていせつ chastity, virtue; constancy,<br>principle..............................................0391<br>貞潔な ていけつな chaste and pure..........1570<br>不貞な ふていな unchaste.......................0049 |
|---|---|---|

| **1867**<br>貝 154<br><br>1792<br>常 9 | Visualize S1–2 as a **CHASTITY** clasp fastened to a virgin *shell* (貝) in order to keep it tightly closed. ☞ 負 0829 |
|---|---|

| 偵 | SPY<br><br>テイ | 偵察 ていさつ scouting, reconnaissance....0639<br>内偵する ないていする make secret inquiries,<br>scout.................................................0215<br>密偵 みってい spy, emissary.....................1383<br>○ 探偵 たんてい detective work; detective, sleuth<br>...........................................................1714 |
|---|---|---|

| **1868**<br>人 9<br><br>0122<br>常 11 | Think of 亻 as a **SPY** dispatched to follow the virgin shell that wears the *chastity* clasp (貞), just in case anyone should try to remove it. Remembering this idea, practice writing 貞 and 偵 in turn. |
|---|---|

**SUPREMACY, domination**

ハ

○覇権 はけん supremacy, hegemony.........1130
覇道 はどう military government/rule......0158
制覇する せいはする conquer; win the
championship.............................0708
連覇 れんぱ consecutive championships...0582

| 1869 | |
|---|---|
| 西 146 | |
| 2379 | |
| 常 | 19 |

西 is a *box* for containing a cattle's *leather* (革) and *meat* (月). Think of it as symbolizing man's **domination/SUPREMACY** over animals. As a shortcut, the same meaning can be recognized in 西's commanding position above 革 and 月.

---

¹ **COVER, conceal**
² **OVERTURN**

フク
おお(う) くつがえ(す) くつがえ(る)

¹ 覆面 ふくめん mask, veil.....................0175
① 顔を覆う かおをおおう cover one's face......0180
² 覆没する ふくぼつする capsize and sink....0519
② 転覆する てんぷくする overturn, upset;
overthrow.................................0224
② 船を覆す ふねをくつがえす capsize a ship...0669

| 1870 | |
|---|---|
| 西 146 | |
| 2376 | |
| 常 | 18 |

*Box* (西) + *return/repeat* (復, see 0865). To associate this with M2 **OVERTURN**, let *return* suggest "turning over" the box. Now imagine **turning over** the *box* to **CONCEAL** something beneath it. Make an effort to remember that the next entry is the only one containing 复 that is not pronounced フク.

---

¹ **FULFILL**
² **PUT ON FOOTWEAR**

リ
は(く)

¹ 履行する りこうする fulfill, perform, carry out
...............................................0055
① 履歴 りれき personal history, career.........0853
¹ 履歴書 りれきしょ curriculum vitae...0853, 0853
② 履く はく put on footwear, wear (shoes)
² 草履 ぞうり Japanese sandals, zori..........0144

| 1871 | |
|---|---|
| 戸 44 | |
| 2736 | |
| 常 | 15 |

*Door* (戸) + *return/repeat* (復). Let this remind you of a *repetitive* action that takes place in a *doorway*: **PUT ON FOOTWEAR**. You might think of "repeating" the action once for each foot, or *repeating* it every time you go out the door. Associate **PUT ON FOOTWEAR** with **FULFILL** via the idea of "filling someone's shoes."

---

**BELONG TO; be subordinate to**

ゾク

○付属する ふぞくする be attached/annexed to,
belong to ...............................0064
所属する しょぞくする belong to, be attached to
...............................................0249
従属 じゅうぞく subordination, dependency 0869
○金属 きんぞく metal...........................0029
属する ぞくする belong to, be one of

| 1872 | |
|---|---|
| 戸 44 | |
| 屬 | |
| 2711 | |
| 常 | 12 |

禹 resembles 風 WIND, but for the sake of learning the kanji in which it appears, you are better off simply visualizing it as a doorman (S4 is his cap)—that is, a **subordinate** who works at the *door* (戸). Think of 禹 as **BELONGING TO** the house or firm represented by the *door*, in the sense of hiring out his services exclusively to it.

**CHARGE WITH**

ショク

○嘱託する　しょくたくする　entrust with.........1539
　委嘱する　いしょくする　charge, commission/
　　entrust with.................................0396

**1873**
口 30
嘱
0650
常 15

Now see the *mouth* (口) of a superior at the left issuing directives to the *subordinate* (door-man) at the right: **CHARGE WITH**.

---

**¹ BY CHANCE**
**² COUPLE**

グウ

① 偶然に　ぐうぜんに　by chance, accidentally...0760
¹ 偶発的な　ぐうはつてきな　accidental, contingent
　..........................................0148, 0169
② 配偶者　はいぐうしゃ　spouse, mate.....0799, 0107
² 偶数　ぐうすう　even number................0309

**1874**
人 9

0115
常 11

See 禺 as a *monkey* (not to be confused with 禹 above). Its head and body frame are obvi-ous enough, but seeing its tail in S10–11 takes a little more imagination. Now imagine the *man* (亻) and *monkey* (禺) as a kind of odd **COUPLE**, brought together by **CHANCE** despite their glaring differences.

---

**NOOK**

グウ
すみ

一隅　いちぐう　corner, nook.................0002
○隅々　すみずみ　every nook and cranny
片隅　かたすみ　corner, nook................0922
隅から隅まで　すみからすみまで　every nook and
　cranny

**1875**
阜 170

0568
常 12

Picture the *monkey* (禺) swinging and knuckling its way around every **NOOK** and cranny of the *hills* (阝).

---

**CREVICE, space, spare time**

ゲキ
すき

間隙　かんげき　crevice, gap, opening........0448
○隙間　すきま　crevice, gap, opening..........0448
隙を見付ける　すきをみつける　seize the chance
　.....................................0083, 0064
寸隙　すんげき　spare moment................0381

**1876**
阜 170
隙
0614
常 13

Visualize the narrow waist point in the middle of 阝 as a small opening (i.e., a small **CREVICE** or **space**) in the *hills*. 小 at the top and bottom emphasize the smallness of the opening, while 日 refers to the *sun*light passing through it. ☞ 除 0996

| | ¹ TREAT, receive<br>² ENCOUNTER | ①待遇する たいぐうする treat, receive, entertain ........0386<br>¹ 優遇する ゆうぐうする treat favorably, receive warmly ........0780<br>②遇う あう encounter, come across<br>² 奇遇 きぐう chance encounter ........1329<br>² 境遇 きょうぐう one's lot, circumstances, situation in life ........1548 |
|---|---|---|
| | グウ<br>あ(う)* | |

| **1877** | Here we observe the *monkey* (禺) driving out on his *truck* (辶) to **receive** a guest (the kanji refers generally to the **TREATMENT** one shows to others). If you think of the *monkey* running into his guest somewhere along the road, it should be easy to remember M2 **ENCOUNTER**. Be careful to distinguish this kanji from 迎 1139 WELCOME. |
|---|---|
| 辵 162 | |
| **2702** | |
| 常 12 | |

| | **FOOLISH** | ○愚劣な ぐれつな stupid, silly, foolish ........1743<br>愚鈍な ぐどんな stupid, silly ........1102<br>愚問 ぐもん silly question ........0452<br>○愚か おろか foolish, stupid<br>愚かしい おろかしい foolish, silly |
|---|---|---|
| | グ<br>おろ(か) | |

| **1878** | *Monkey* (禺)'s *mind* (心): **FOOLISH**. Now note that all the kanji containing 禺 are read グウ, except the present entry, which is read グ. As always, take care to remember the exception: this one is **FOOLISH** for missing the pattern set by the others. Take a moment to practice writing and distinguishing this set of four kanji based on 禺. |
|---|---|
| 心 61 | |
| **2467** | |
| 常 13 | |

| | **SERGEANT** | ○軍曹 ぐんそう sergeant ........0583<br>海曹 かいそう petty officer (navy) ........0106<br>陸曹 りくそう noncommissioned officer (army) ........1432<br>曹長 そうちょう sergeant officer, sergeant major ........0091 |
|---|---|---|
| | ソウ | |

| **1879** | Think of this as the insignia on the uniform of a **SERGEANT**. Do not confuse the upper portion with 曲 0503. The next two entries incorporate 曹 and follow its *on-yomi*. |
|---|---|
| 日 73 | |
| **2394** | |
| 常 11 | |

| | **MEET WITH, encounter** | ○遭難する そうなんする meet with disaster ...0712<br>遭難信号 そうなんしんごう distress signal, SOS ........0712, 0063, 0300<br>遭遇する そうぐうする encounter, come across ........1877<br>○遭う あう meet with, encounter<br>酷い目に遭う ひどいめにあう have a bad time ........1628, 0021 |
|---|---|---|
| | ソウ<br>あ(う) あ(わせる) | |

| **1880** | Imagine that the *sergeant* (曹), as he drives along in his *truck* (辶), comes upon someone or something unexpectedly: **MEET WITH**/encounter. In comparison with 逢う (あう, meet with, see, encounter; 1379) and 遇う (あう, encounter, come across; 1877), 遭う (あう) more often refers to encountering some kind of misfortune. ☞ 遷 0785 |
|---|---|
| 辵 162 | |
| **2725** | |
| 常 14 | |

| | TUB, tank | |
|---|---|---|
| | | ○浴槽 よくそう bathtub........................1036 |
| | | 水槽 すいそう water tank.............0027 |
| | | 貯水槽 ちょすいそう water tank........0442, 0027 |
| | ソウ | 油槽 ゆそう oil tank.....................0433 |
| | | 浄化槽 じょうかそう tank for purifying water |
| | | ...............................0979, 0120 |

| 1881 | *Sergeant*(曹) bathing in a *wooden*(木) **TUB** in the officers' club. |
|---|---|
| 木 75 | |
| 0981 | |
| 常 15 | |

| | HINDER, obstruct | |
|---|---|---|
| | | ○妨害する ぼうがいする disturb, hinder, obstruct, impede........................0413 |
| | | 妨害放送 ぼうがいほうそう radio jamming |
| | | ...............0413, 0574, 0455 |
| | ボウ | ○妨げる さまたげる hinder, disturb, obstruct |
| | さまた(げる) | 睡眠を妨げる すいみんをさまたげる disturb one's sleep........................1008, 1009 |

| 1882 | Review 防 0174. Here, 方 deliberately **HINDERS**/**obstructs** other men from approaching the *woman*(女). |
|---|---|
| 女 38 | |
| 0209 | |
| 常 7 | |

| | ¹ SONNY BOY ² COLLOQUIAL PERSON SUFFIX | |
|---|---|---|
| | | ¹坊ちゃん ぼっちゃん sonny, boy; greenhorn, baby |
| | | ¹赤ん坊 あかんぼう baby.............0774 |
| | | ²食いしん坊 くいしんぼう glutton............0288 |
| | ボウ ボッ- | ²風来坊 ふうらいぼう wanderer, vagabond, hobo |
| | | ...............0425, 0274 |
| | | 坊主 ぼうず Buddhist priest/monk, bonze; shaven head; sonny, boy.........0365 |

| 1883 | Recall the image of 方 as a person running. With 土, imagine 方 as a little boy, intimately familiar to you, running freely about your *grounds*: **SONNY BOY**. The reading ボウ sounds like **BOY**. Practice writing this kanji along with 防 0174, 訪 0454, 紡 0835, and 妨 1882, testing yourself on their meanings. |
|---|---|
| 土 32 | |
| 0205 | |
| 常 7 | |

| | BESIDE | |
|---|---|---|
| | | ○傍観者 ぼうかんしゃ bystander, onlooker....1128 |
| | | 傍系 ぼうけいの collateral, subsidiary, affiliated.........................1077 |
| | ボウ | 勉強の傍らCDを聞く べんきょうのかたわら シーディーをきく listen to a CD while studying |
| | かたわ(ら) そば* | ...............1274, 0423, 0453 |
| | | 傍に そばに by the side of |

| 1884 | Our three most important graphemes for *person*, arranged one **BESIDE** the other. Note that 旁, unlisted by itself, is the kanji for *tsukuri* (the right-hand, usually sound-bearing component of a kanji). |
|---|---|
| 人 9 | |
| 0127 | |
| 常 12 | |

| | **AT, in, on** | 東京に於いて　とうきょうにおいて　in Tokyo...0107 |
|---|---|---|
| | | ○その点に於いて　そのてんにおいて　on that point, in that regard.....................0349 |
| | オ | 日本に於けるカナダ人　にほんにおけるカナダじん　Canadians in Japan.............0001, 0031, 0015 |
| | おい(て)　お(ける) | |

| 1885 | Here 方 implies *direction* or *locality*. The element at the right shows the exact position where two items (S7–8) are located. Think of these two items as being located **AT** that position (i.e., **in** that place or **on** that spot.) Note that though 於 appears in the word 於いて (おいて), there is no such word as 於く (おく). |
|---|---|
| 方 70 | |
| 0755 | |
| 名 8 | |

| | **¹ CHAMBER** | ①暖房　だんぼう　heating.......................1127 |
|---|---|---|
| | **² TUFT, tassel** | ①冷房　れいぼう　cooling, air conditioning....0675 |
| | | ¹ 女房　にょうぼう　wife; court lady.............0093 |
| | ボウ | ¹ 文房具　ぶんぼうぐ　stationery, writing materials .........................................0101, 0837 |
| | ふさ | ②一房の髪　ひとふさのかみ　a tuft of hair..0002, 1792 |

| 1886 | *Person running* (方) through a *doorway* (戸) into a **CHAMBER**. To remember M2 **TUFT**/tassel, you might imagine that there are tassels hanging from the top of the doorway, which brush the person's head as he runs through it. |
|---|---|
| 戸 63 | |
| 1702 | |
| 常 8 | |

| | **FAN** | ○扇子　せんす　folding fan......................0094 |
|---|---|---|
| | | 扇風機　せんぷうき　electric fan........0425, 0473 |
| | | 換気扇　かんきせん　ventilation fan.....1269, 0126 |
| | セン | 扇状地　せんじょうち　alluvial delta......0616, 0187 |
| | おうぎ | 舞扇　まいおうぎ　dancer's fan...............0961 |

| 1887 | Like *doors* (戸) and birds' *wings* (羽), a **FAN** is a broad, flat object that turns or flaps. |
|---|---|
| 戸 63 | ☞ 扉 1888 |
| 1704 | |
| 常 10 | |

| | **HINGED DOOR** | ○門扉　もんぴ　leaves/doors of a gate.........0447 |
|---|---|---|
| | | 開扉する　かいひする　open the door........0450 |
| | | 鉄扉　てっぴ　iron door......................0564 |
| | ヒ | ○扉を開く　とびらをひらく　open a door..........0450 |
| | とびら | 自動扉　じどうとびら　automatic door...0081, 0540 |

| 1888 | 戸 depicts a *doorframe*, and 非 a pair of doors hinged at both sides of the doorway and joining in the middle, like the two-directional doors of a café or old-fashioned saloon: **HINGED DOORS**. ☞ 扇 1887 |
|---|---|
| 戸 63 | |
| 1705 | |
| 常 12 | |

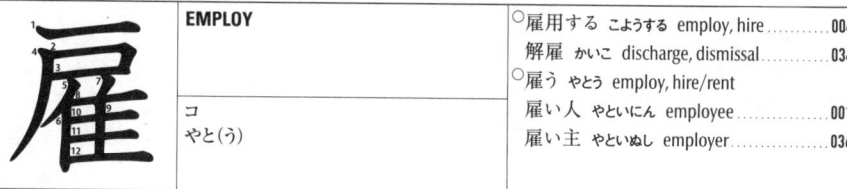

**EMPLOY**

コ
やと(う)

○雇用する こようする employ, hire .......... 0047
解雇 かいこ discharge, dismissal .......... 0345
○雇う やとう employ, hire/rent
雇い人 やといにん employee .......... 0015
雇い主 やといぬし employer .......... 0365

| 1889 | Picture a miniature hotel that **EMPLOYS** a *small bird* (隹) as a *door* (戸)man. ☞ 顧 1890 |
|---|---|
| 隹 172 | |
| 1706 | |
| 常 12 | |

**LOOK BACK (ON); take into consideration**

コ
かえり(みる)

○回顧する かいこする look back on, retrospect .......... 0050
後顧 こうこ looking back, worry .......... 0114
○顧みる かえりみる look back
顧問 こもん adviser, consultant .......... 0452
顧客 こきゃく customer, patron, client .......... 0787

| 1890 | One's *head* (頁), i.e., memory, **LOOKING BACK ON** one's days as a doorman (雇, see previous entry). ☞ 雇 1889 |
|---|---|
| 頁 181 | |
| 1677 | |
| 常 21 | |

**SCRAPS, scum**

くず

削り屑 けずりくず shavings .......... 1292
切り屑 きりくず scraps, chips .......... 0086
パン屑 パンくず breadcrumbs
屑籠 くずかご wastebasket .......... 0509
○屑入れ くずいれ wastebasket .......... 0039

| 1891 | Recall from 尾 0488 and 屈 1834 that 尸 can sometimes mean *buttocks*. The present entry thus depicts *fragments* (肖) stuck to *buttocks*: **SCRAPS/scum**. 肖 is interchangeable with the image that appears under 尸 here. ☞ 宵 1293 |
|---|---|
| 尸 44 | |
| 屑 | |
| 2680 | |
| 名 10 | |

**DROPPINGS, shit**

フン
くそ

○糞便 ふんべん excrement .......... 0890
糞詰まり ふんづまり constipation .......... 0515
馬糞 ばふん (=まぐそ) horse manure .......... 0336
糞食らえ! くそくらえ! Eat shit! .......... 0288
鼻糞 はなくそ snot .......... 1558

| 1892 | *Rice* (米) goes in the top, and something *different* (異) comes out the bottom: **DROPPINGS/shit**. A related and even more intuitive character, not introduced in this course, is 屎 (*on* reading: シ; *kun* reading: くそ). It combines with the next entry in the word 屎尿 (しにょう, human waste). ☞ 翼 0883 |
|---|---|
| 米 119 | |
| 外 17 | |

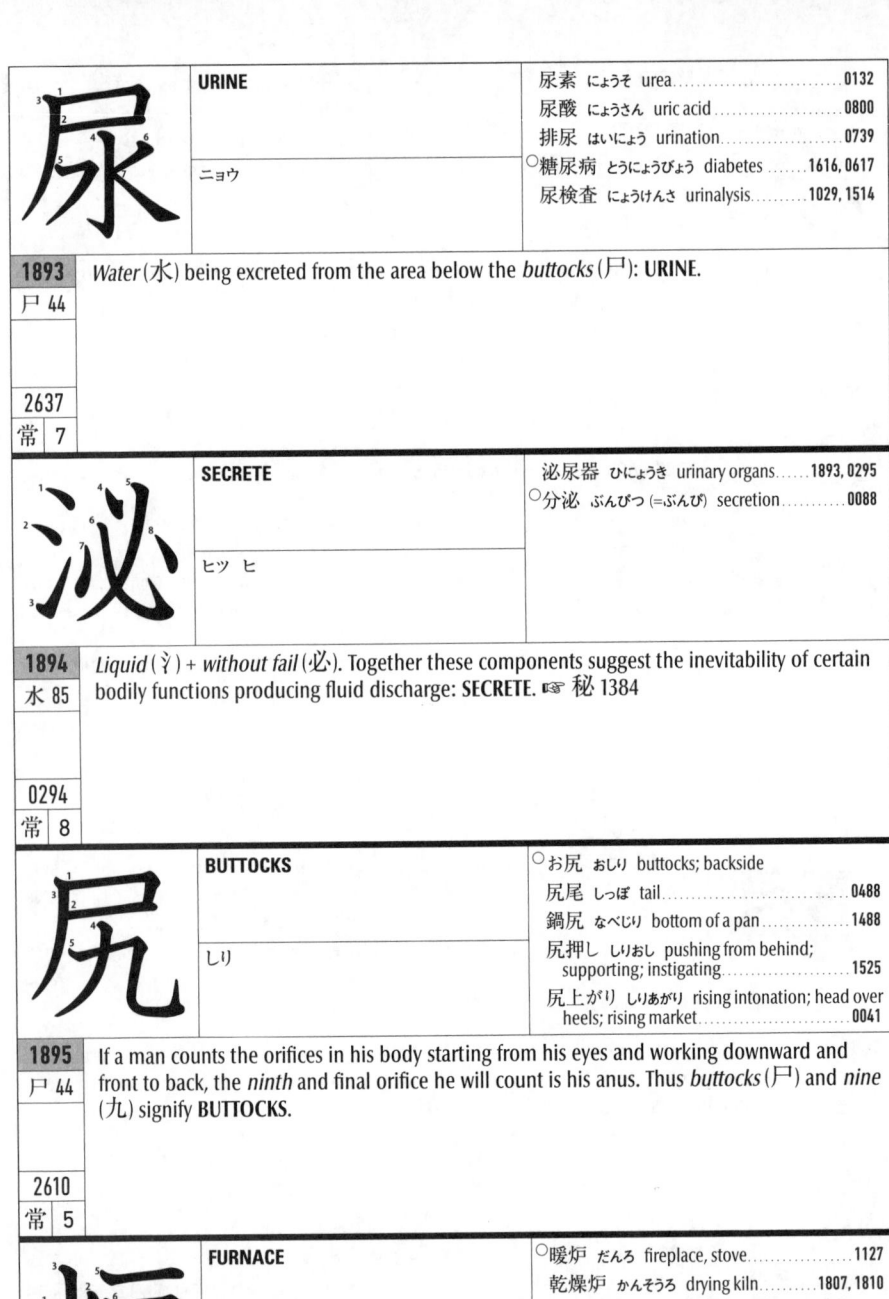

## 尿 URINE

ニョウ

尿素 にょうそ urea ........................0132
尿酸 にょうさん uric acid ....................0800
排尿 はいにょう urination ..................0739
○糖尿病 とうにょうびょう diabetes .......1616, 0617
尿検査 にょうけんさ urinalysis ..........1029, 1514

**1893**
尸 44

Water (水) being excreted from the area below the *buttocks* (尸): URINE.

2637
常 7

## 泌 SECRETE

ヒツ ヒ

泌尿器 ひにょうき urinary organs ......1893, 0295
○分泌 ぶんぴつ (=ぶんぴ) secretion ..........0088

**1894**
水 85

*Liquid* (氵) + *without fail* (必). Together these components suggest the inevitability of certain bodily functions producing fluid discharge: **SECRETE.** ☞ 秘 1384

0294
常 8

## 尻 BUTTOCKS

しり

○お尻 おしり buttocks; backside
尻尾 しっぽ tail ...............................0488
鍋尻 なべじり bottom of a pan ...............1488
尻押し しりおし pushing from behind;
　　　supporting; instigating ....................1525
尻上がり しりあがり rising intonation; head over
　　　heels; rising market ...........................0041

**1895**
尸 44

If a man counts the orifices in his body starting from his eyes and working downward and front to back, the *ninth* and final orifice he will count is his anus. Thus *buttocks* (尸) and *nine* (九) signify **BUTTOCKS**.

2610
常 5

## 炉 FURNACE

ロ

○暖炉 だんろ fireplace, stove ..................1127
乾燥炉 かんそうろ drying kiln ..........1807, 1810
原子炉 げんしろ nuclear reactor .......0208, 0094
香炉 こうろ incense burner .................1781

**1896**
火 86

*Fire* (火) behind a *door* (戸): **FURNACE.**

爐
0772
常 8

| | KILN | |
|---|---|---|
| | ヨウ かま | |

○窯業 ようぎょう ceramics, ceramic industry...0498
○窯元 かまもと pottery; source/maker of pottery .........0136
窯印 かまじるし potter's mark.............0231
穴窯 あながま "cave kiln" [sloping tunnel-like kiln] ..............0397

| 1897 | See 羊 here not as a *sheep* but as a baking rack inside a **KILN**, with two ceramic pieces stacked on top. 穴 *hole/cave* suggests an open chamber, heated by 灬 *fire*. ☞ 窪 1900 |
|---|---|
| 穴 116 | |
| 2081 | |
| 常 15 | |

| | IRON POT, cauldron | |
|---|---|---|
| | かま | |

鍋釜 なべかま pots and pans...............1488
○釜敷き かましき pot rest................1507
茶釜 ちゃがま tea kettle.............0603
お釜 おかま pot; buttocks; [slang] male homosexual
釜山 プサン Pusan [city in Korea].......0037

| 1898 | Visualize as an **IRON POT** that hangs from a pair of wires (金 suggests *metal*). ☞ 爺 1899 |
|---|---|
| 金 167 | |
| 釜 | |
| 1808 | |
| 常 10 | |

| | OLD MAN, grandpa | |
|---|---|---|
| | ヤ じじ じじい じい | |

老爺 ろうや one's old man [boss]...........0629
糞爺 くそじじい geezer, old goat...........1892
○お爺(=お祖父)さん おじいさん grandfather, grandpa, old-timer ............0641, 0100
エロ爺 エロじじい erotic old man, pervert
親爺 おやじ dad, one's old man; old man ...0276

| 1899 | See the lower portion as a variation on 耶, suggesting husband (from 旦那 [だんな]). Above the husband is 父, suggesting a still higher *father* figure: **OLD MAN/grandpa**. ☞ 釜 1898 |
|---|---|
| 父 88 | |
| 外 13 | |

| | SINK, cavity | |
|---|---|---|
| | ワ くぼ(む) くぼ(まる) くぼ | |

窪地 くぼち depressed ground, hollow .....0187
窪み くぼみ hollow, cavity, depression
笑窪 えくぼ dimple.............0579
屋根が窪んでいる やねがくぼんでいる the roof has sunk/caved in...........0252, 0284
○道の窪 みちのくぼ sink in the road.........0158

| 1900 | Water (氵) dripping into a *cave* (穴), eroding layers of *earth* (土): **SINK/cavity**. ☞ 涯 1902, 窯 1897, 窟 1843 |
|---|---|
| 穴 116 | |
| 2063 | |
| 名 14 | |

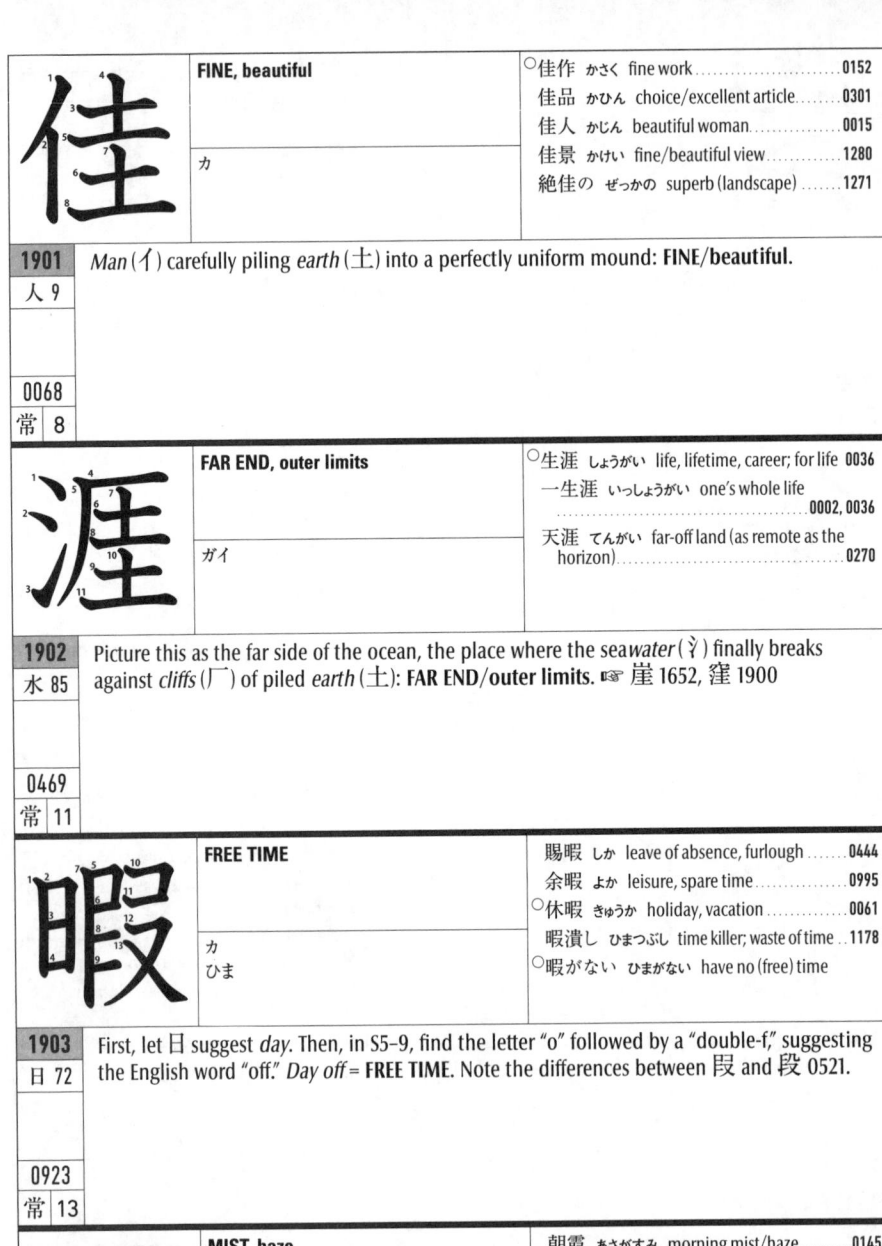

| | | FINE, beautiful | | ○佳作 かさく fine work .......................0152 |
| 佳 | カ | | | 佳品 かひん choice/excellent article........0301 |
| | | | | 佳人 かじん beautiful woman..............0015 |
| | | | | 佳景 かけい fine/beautiful view...........1280 |
| | | | | 絶佳の ぜっかの superb (landscape) .......1271 |

| **1901** | Man (亻) carefully piling *earth* (土) into a perfectly uniform mound: **FINE/beautiful**. |
| 人 9 | |
| 0068 | |
| 常 8 | |

| | | FAR END, outer limits | | ○生涯 しょうがい life, lifetime, career; for life 0036 |
| 涯 | ガイ | | | 一生涯 いっしょうがい one's whole life |
| | | | | .....................................0002, 0036 |
| | | | | 天涯 てんがい far-off land (as remote as the |
| | | | | horizon)...............................0270 |

| **1902** | Picture this as the far side of the ocean, the place where the sea *water* (氵) finally breaks |
| 水 85 | against *cliffs* (厂) of piled *earth* (土): **FAR END/outer limits.** ☞ 崖 1652, 窪 1900 |
| 0469 | |
| 常 11 | |

| | | FREE TIME | | 賜暇 しか leave of absence, furlough ........0444 |
| 暇 | カ | | | 余暇 よか leisure, spare time...............0995 |
| | ひま | | | ○休暇 きゅうか holiday, vacation ............0061 |
| | | | | 暇潰し ひまつぶし time killer; waste of time ..1178 |
| | | | | ○暇がない ひまがない have no (free) time |

| **1903** | First, let 日 suggest *day*. Then, in S5–9, find the letter "o" followed by a "double-f," suggesting |
| 日 72 | the English word "off." *Day off* = **FREE TIME**. Note the differences between 叚 and 段 0521. |
| 0923 | |
| 常 13 | |

| | | MIST, haze | | 朝霞 あさがすみ morning mist/haze.........0145 |
| 霞 | カ | | | 煙霞 えんか mist/haze and smoke; beauties of |
| | かすみ かす(む) | | | nature.................................0768 |
| | | | | 年て霞んだ目 としてかすんだめ eyes dimmed |
| | | | | with age...........................0117, 0021 |
| | | | | 春霞 はるがすみ spring haze ...............0362 |
| | | | | 霞ヶ関 かすみがせき Kasumigaseki [district in Tokyo, |
| | | | | location of numerous government ministries] 0451 |

| **1904** | In the next five entries, 雨 refers generally to *atmospheric moisture*. Because this entry |
| 雨 173 | means **MIST**, we should simply let 叚 visually represent densely concentrated water droplets. |
| | Note how the numerous short horizontal strokes on both sides of 叚 seem to replicate the |
| 2450 | water droplets in 雨 (S5–8). |
| 名 17 | |

| | ATMOSPHERE | ○霧囲気 ふんいき atmosphere, mood 0435, 0126 |
| --- | --- | --- |
| | フン | |

**1905**
雨 173

Minutely *divided* (分) *raindrops* (霝), referring to the "vapor" (Greek: *atmos*) that fills the air: **ATMOSPHERE.** ☞ 霧 1906

2414
常 12

---

| | FOG | 霧笛 むてき foghorn......................1530 |
| --- | --- | --- |
| | | ○濃霧注意報 のうむちゅういほう dense fog advisory..................0512, 0368, 0151, 1472 |
| | ム | 煙霧 えんむ smog.......................0768 |
| | きり | 霧吹き きりふき sprayer, atomizer...........1764 |
| | | ○霧雨 きりさめ (=きりあめ) drizzle...........0154 |

**1906**
雨 173

Review 務 0687. The present entry refers to a thick concentration of *atmospheric moisture* (霝)—so thick one must *strike* (夂) with *plows* (力) and *halberds* (矛) to make one's way through it: **FOG.** ☞ 露 1907, 霧 1905

2452
常 19

---

| | ¹ **DEW** | ①露の滴 つゆのしずく dewdrop...............1119 |
| --- | --- | --- |
| | ² **EXPOSE** | ² 露出 ろしゅつ exposure, disclosure; (photographic) exposure.......................0038 |
| | | ² 暴露 ばくろ exposure, disclosure............1346 |
| | ロ ロウ | ②露天 ろてん open-air, outdoor...........0270 |
| | つゆ | ○日露 にちろ Japan and Russia, Japanese-Russian...................0001 |

**1907**
雨 173

*Atmospheric moisture* (霝) condensing on the *road* (路): **DEW.** Associate this with M2 **EXPOSE** via the idea of being **EXPOSED** to the elements. Note that this character is also used phonetically for ロ, as in V5. ☞ 霧 1906

2454
常 21

---

| | FROST | ○霜害 そうがい frost damage...................0413 |
| --- | --- | --- |
| | | 降霜 こうそう (fall of) frost...................1377 |
| | | 霜柱 しもばしら frost columns...............0867 |
| | ソウ | ○霜焼け しもやけ frostbite, chilblains........0769 |
| | しも | 霜降り しもふり pepper-and-salt; marbled meat...................1377 |

**1908**
雨 173

*Atmospheric moisture* (霝) congealing on *tree* (木)tops and *eye* (目)lashes: **FROST.**

2451
常 17

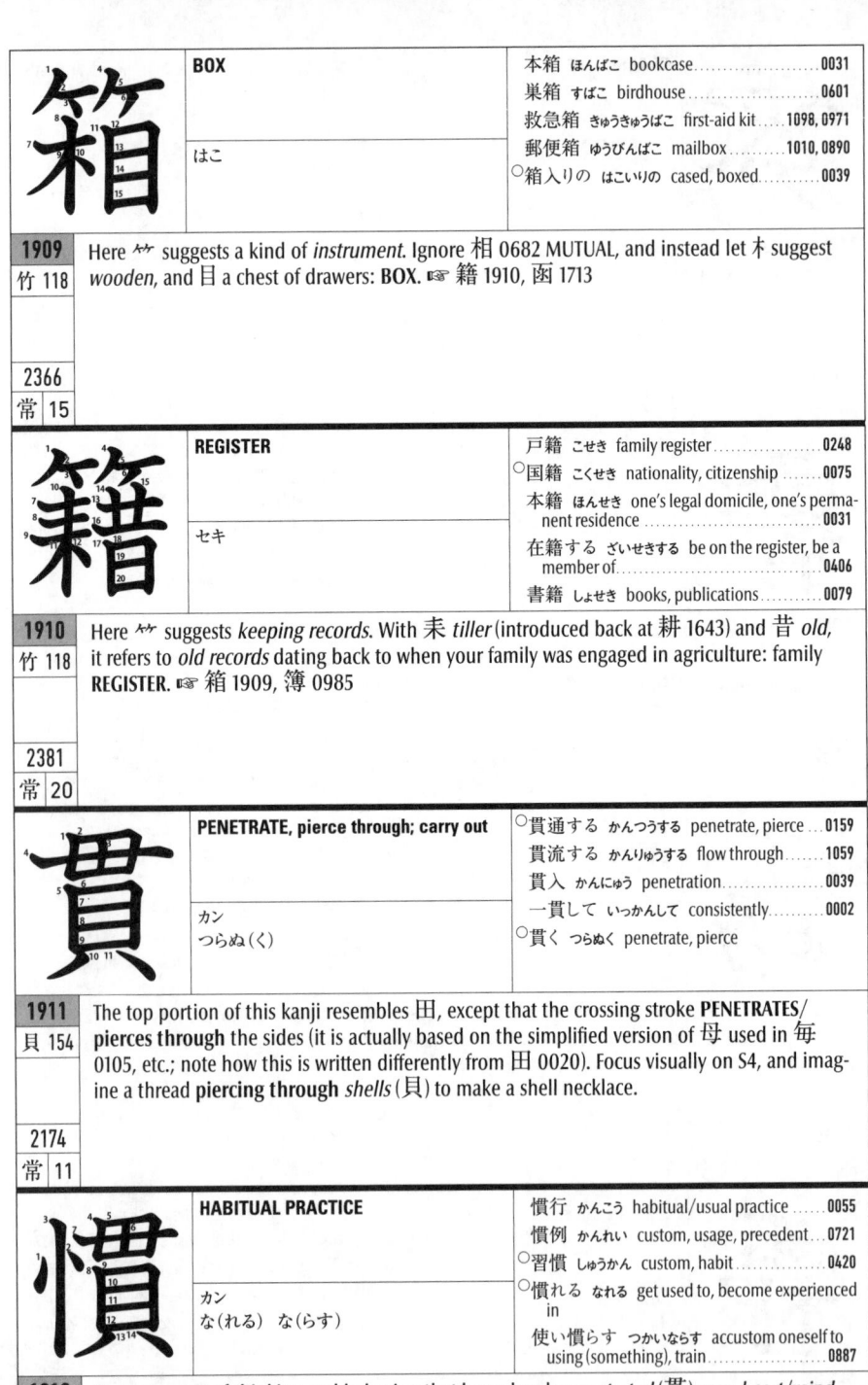

## 箱 BOX

はこ

| | | |
|---|---|---|
| 本箱 ほんばこ bookcase | | 0031 |
| 巣箱 すばこ birdhouse | | 0601 |
| 救急箱 きゅうきゅうばこ first-aid kit | | 1098, 0971 |
| 郵便箱 ゆうびんばこ mailbox | | 1010, 0890 |
| ○箱入りの はこいりの cased, boxed | | 0039 |

**1909**
竹 118

Here 竹 suggests a kind of *instrument*. Ignore 相 0682 MUTUAL, and instead let 木 suggest *wooden*, and 目 a chest of drawers: BOX. ☞ 籍 1910, 函 1713

2366
常 15

---

## 籍 REGISTER

セキ

| | | |
|---|---|---|
| 戸籍 こせき family register | | 0248 |
| ○国籍 こくせき nationality, citizenship | | 0075 |
| 本籍 ほんせき one's legal domicile, one's permanent residence | | 0031 |
| 在籍する ざいせきする be on the register, be a member of | | 0406 |
| 書籍 しょせき books, publications | | 0079 |

**1910**
竹 118

Here 竹 suggests *keeping records*. With 耒 *tiller* (introduced back at 耕 1643) and 昔 *old*, it refers to *old records* dating back to when your family was engaged in agriculture: family **REGISTER**. ☞ 箱 1909, 簿 0985

2381
常 20

---

## 貫 PENETRATE, pierce through; carry out

カン
つらぬ(く)

| | | |
|---|---|---|
| ○貫通する かんつうする penetrate, pierce | | 0159 |
| 貫流する かんりゅうする flow through | | 1059 |
| 貫入 かんにゅう penetration | | 0039 |
| 一貫して いっかんして consistently | | 0002 |
| ○貫く つらぬく penetrate, pierce | | |

**1911**
貝 154

The top portion of this kanji resembles 田, except that the crossing stroke **PENETRATES/pierces through** the sides (it is actually based on the simplified version of 母 used in 毎 0105, etc.; note how this is written differently from 田 0020). Focus visually on S4, and imagine a thread **piercing through** *shells* (貝) to make a shell necklace.

2174
常 11

---

## 慣 HABITUAL PRACTICE

カン
な(れる) な(らす)

| | | |
|---|---|---|
| 慣行 かんこう habitual/usual practice | | 0055 |
| 慣例 かんれい custom, usage, precedent | | 0721 |
| ○習慣 しゅうかん custom, habit | | 0420 |
| ○慣れる なれる get used to, become experienced in | | |
| 使い慣らす つかいならす accustom oneself to using (something), train | | 0887 |

**1912**
心 61

Suggests ways of thinking and behaving that have deeply *penetrated* (貫) your *heart/mind* (忄): **HABITUAL PRACTICES**.

0624
常 14

| | ¹ SUMMIT<br>² RECEIVE HUMBLY, eat<br><br>チョウ<br>いただ(く) いただき | ¹頂点 ちょうてん apex, peak .................. 0349<br>①頂上 ちょうじょう summit, peak, top; climax 0041<br>¹絶頂 ぜっちょう summit, peak; apex, climax 1271<br>②頂く いただく receive humbly, be given; eat, drink |

**1913**
頁 181

Review 頁 0156, then 訂 1024 and 打 1025. Here, "*nail*(丁) + *head*(頁)" suggests the head or topmost part of a nail—think of this as its **SUMMIT**. You can also write this kanji to communicate that you **RECEIVE HUMBLY**, for with it you convey that you receive something as if it were placed upon your head. ☞ 項 1915

0125
常 11

---

| | RECEIVE HUMBLY<br><br>タイ<br>いただ(く)* | ②頂戴する ちょうだいする [humble] receive, accept, take; eat, drink ...................... 1913 |

**1914**
戈 62

Like the last entry, this means **RECEIVE HUMBLY** and suggests having something placed upon one's head. Here see 異 humbly having something placed upon his head by 戈, which we saw earlier at 裁 1317–裁 1319. We might imagine that he is being crowned with the "Order of the Spear" (戈). An *on-yomi* compound for タイ appears at 冠 1969. ☞ 載 1318

2815
常 18

---

| | CLAUSE<br><br>コウ | ○項目 こうもく clause, item, provision.......... 0021<br>事項 じこう matters, facts; articles, items ... 0080<br>要項 ようこう important points; gist.......... 0547<br>条項 じょうこう articles (and clauses), terms 0119<br>第九条第二項 だいきゅうじょうだいにこう Section 9, Subsection 2............... 1191, 0011, 0119, 0003 |

**1915**
頁 181

See 工 as a scroll that has been unfurled vertically: S1 and S3 are the rods at each end, and S2 is the unfurled scroll. See 頁 *head* holding the scroll, examining the individual **CLAUSES** written on it. Recall that though 頁 appears at the right, it is a semantic element, so use the *hen* form as your phonetic clue (here, 工, コウ). ☞ 頂 1913, 頃 1916

0521
常 12

---

| | ¹ TIME<br>² ABOUT<br><br>ころ ごろ -ごろ | ¹この頃 このごろ now, these days; lately<br>①若い頃は わかいころは when (I was) young 0404<br>¹日頃 ひごろ habitually, every day.......... 0001<br>¹もう彼が帰る頃だ もうかれがかえるころだ It's about time for him to come home ... 0597, 1018<br>²昼頃 ひるごろ about noon .................. 0466 |

**1916**
頁 181

This character usually refers to a **TIME** or period in the past. Picture ヒ as a small child, and see the *head* (頁) looking back at the **TIME** when it was small. M2 **ABOUT** relates with M1 **TIME** in that it refers to an approximate time. ☞ 傾 1917, 項 1915

0124
常 11

**INCLINE, lean**

ケイ
かたむ（く）　かたむ（ける）　かし（げる）＊

傾斜する　けいしゃする　incline, slant, tilt ....0999
○傾向　けいこう　tendency, trend; disposition 0183
傾聴する　けいちょうする　listen closely.......1669
○傾く　かたむく　[vi] incline, lean; tend to; decline
傾げる　かしげる　[vt] incline, lean, tilt

| 1917 | Here focus on little ヒ, trapped between イ and 頁. It must choose which one toward which to **INCLINE** (it chooses 頁). ☞ 頃 1916 |
| 人 9 | |
| 0132 | |
| 常 13 | |

---

**STUBBORN**

ガン

○頑固な　がんこな　stubborn, obstinate, bigoted
...............................0260
頑強な　がんきょうな　stubborn, unyielding...0423
頑丈な　がんじょうな　solid, firm; strong ......0657
頑健　がんけん　robust health ................1610

| 1918 | 元 0136 suggests a firm *basis* or *origin*. Together with 頁, it indicates a *head* that is **STUB-BORNLY** rooted in its *original* idea. ☞ 願 0214 |
| 頁 181 | |
| 0953 | |
| 常 13 | |

---

**DISTRIBUTE WIDELY**

ハン

○頒布　はんぷ　distribution, circulation .......0204
頒価　はんか　distribution price..............0548

| 1919 | *Divide* (分) by *heads* (頁); in other words, distribute evenly to all individuals: **DISTRIBUTE WIDELY**. |
| 頁 181 | |
| 0955 | |
| 常 13 | |

---

**SUDDENLY, immediately**

トン
とみ（に）＊

頓に　とみに　suddenly, quickly
頓知　とんち　quick wit........................0560
○頓死　とんし　sudden death..................0716
頓挫　とんざ　setback, impasse................1699
整頓する　せいとんする　arrange neatly, tidy up
...............................0308

| 1920 | Review 屯 1100. In the present entry, the *stationed troops* (屯) **SUDDENLY** come face-to-face (i.e., *head-to-head*, 頁) with enemy forces. ☞ 頰 1935 |
| 頁 181 | |
| 0957 | |

常 13

**MANIFEST**

ケン

○顕著な けんちょな notable, conspicuous; clear, obvious.............................0707
顕示する けんじする show, reveal...........0311
顕在化する けんざいかする be actualized, come to the surface.....................0406, 0120
露顕 ろけん discovery, detection, exposure 1907
顕彰する けんしょうする give recognition, exalt, honor...............................1460

**1921**
頁 181

顯

1605
常 18

Here we observe the *sun* (日) shining its rays directly down (业) upon something, right before one's *head* (頁): **MANIFEST**. Note the similarity with 湿 0200.

---

**DOMINION**

リョウ

○領土 りょうど territory, domain...............0030
領域 りょういき territory, domain, sphere, province, field.......................1154
占領する せんりょうする capture, occupy, take possession of.......................0348
領収書 りょうしゅうしょ receipt, voucher 1155, 0079
大統領 だいとうりょう president........0033, 1058

**1922**
頁 181

1133
常 14

Here think of 頁 as a *head* of state, issuing *commands* (令) over the lands under his or her jurisdiction: **DOMINION**. The strong verticality of S5 (in typical typefaces) emphasizes the *head's* authoritative top-down control.

---

**REPEATEDLY, frequently**

ヒン しき(り)*

○頻繁に ひんぱんに frequently, very often...1575
頻発する ひんぱつする occur frequently....0148
頻出 ひんしゅつ frequent appearance.......0038
頻度 ひんど frequency......................0280
○頻りに しきりに repeatedly, frequently

**1923**
頁 181

頻

1569
常 17

*Walk* (歩) + *head* (頁): Imagine a person or animal of your choosing *walking* **REPEATEDLY** on top of your *head*. Hear the trot-trot-trot of the frequently **REPEATED** steps atop your head: ひんぴん、ひんぴん、ひんぴん … (as in the compound 頻々と [ひんぴんと, frequently; in rapid succession]).

---

**MAKE PROGRESS**

チョク
はかど(る)*

○進捗する しんちょくする make progress.....0191
○捗る はかどる make progress

**1924**
手 64

捗

0386
常 10

Refers to **MAKING PROGRESS** in one's work: let 扌 suggest working with one's *hands*, and 歩 (*walk*) suggest forward progress. Note that the *walk* portion of this kanji uses the old form of 歩 (歩, which has one fewer stroke). This kanji was not officially standardized with 歩 when it was added to the Joyo list.

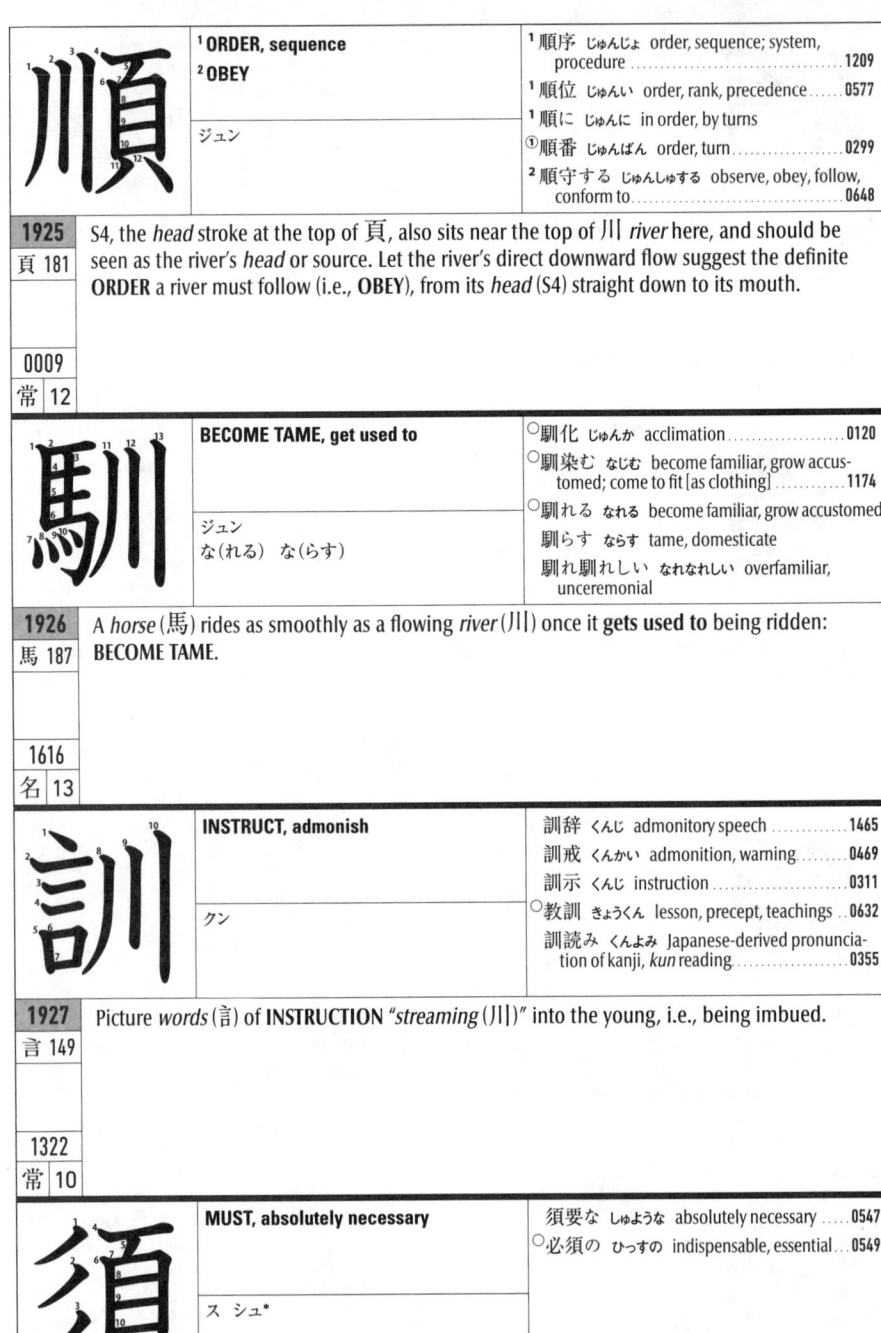

| 順 ジュン | ¹ ORDER, sequence<br>² OBEY | ¹ 順序 じゅんじょ order, sequence; system,<br>    procedure ................................... 1209<br>¹ 順位 じゅんい order, rank, precedence...... 0577<br>¹ 順に じゅんに in order, by turns<br>① 順番 じゅんばん order, turn.................. 0299<br>² 順守する じゅんしゅする observe, obey, follow,<br>    conform to.................................. 0648 |

**1925**
頁 181

S4, the *head* stroke at the top of 頁, also sits near the top of 川 *river* here, and should be seen as the river's *head* or source. Let the river's direct downward flow suggest the definite **ORDER** a river must follow (i.e., **OBEY**), from its *head* (S4) straight down to its mouth.

0009
常 12

| 馴 ジュン な(れる) な(らす) | **BECOME TAME, get used to** | ○馴化 じゅんか acclimation..................... 0120<br>○馴染む なじむ become familiar, grow accus-<br>    tomed; come to fit [as clothing] ............ 1174<br>○馴れる なれる become familiar, grow accustomed<br>馴らす ならす tame, domesticate<br>馴れ馴れしい なれなれしい overfamiliar,<br>    unceremonial |

**1926**
馬 187

A *horse* (馬) rides as smoothly as a flowing *river* (川) once it **gets used to** being ridden: **BECOME TAME**.

1616
名 13

| 訓 クン | **INSTRUCT, admonish** | 訓辞 くんじ admonitory speech ............. 1465<br>訓戒 くんかい admonition, warning........ 0469<br>訓示 くんじ instruction .................... 0311<br>○教訓 きょうくん lesson, precept, teachings .. 0632<br>訓読み くんよみ Japanese-derived pronuncia-<br>    tion of kanji, *kun* reading.................. 0355 |

**1927**
言 149

Picture *words* (言) of **INSTRUCTION** "*streaming* (川)" into the young, i.e., being imbued.

1322
常 10

| 須 ス シュ* | **MUST, absolutely necessary** | 須要な しゅような absolutely necessary ..... 0547<br>○必須の ひっすの indispensable, essential... 0549 |

**1928**
頁 181

See 彡 as the lines of vision coming down from the *head* (頁) toward an object below it: an object that it **MUST** have. The direct, intent lines of vision indicate that the head looks upon a certain object as an **absolute necessity**. ☞ 顔 0180

0526
常 12

| ¹ AMOUNT<br>² PICTURE FRAME<br>³ FOREHEAD<br><br>ガク<br>ひたい | ①金額　きんがく　amount of money, sum.......0029<br>¹ 総額　そうがく　total amount, sum total.......0557<br>¹ 巨大な額　きょだいながく　colossal amount<br>............................................................0483, 0033<br>②額縁　がくぶち　(picture) frame..............0610<br>③広い額　ひろいひたい　broad forehead, high brow<br>............................................................0238 |

| **1929**<br>頁 181<br><br>額<br><br>1604<br>常 18 | *Guest*(客) *head*(頁): let this suggest the **AMOUNT** (of money) charged per *head* to *guests* at an inn. This kanji's original meaning was **FOREHEAD**, so you might think of the front-desk clerk counting guests' **FOREHEADS** to calculate their bill. Associate M2 **PICTURE FRAME** with the rectangular shape of the **FOREHEAD**. |

| ¹ RELY ON<br>² ASK<br><br>ライ<br>たの(む)　たの(もしい)　たよ(る) | ①信頼する　しんらいする　rely on, have confidence<br>in, trust............................................0063<br>①頼る　たよる　rely on, trust<br>¹ 頼もしい　たのもしい　reliable, trustworthy<br>②頼む　たのむ　ask, request<br>² 依頼する　いらいする　request; commission; rely<br>on, depend on............................................0701 |

| **1930**<br>頁 181<br><br>頼<br><br>1458<br>常 16 | Here picture the *bundle* (束) as a kind of pillow, which the *head* (頁) lies on. Think of the *head* not just <u>lying</u> on the pillow, but <u>RELYING ON</u> it. ☞ 瀬 1931 |

| **SHALLOWS, rapids**<br><br>せ | 浅瀬　あさせ　shoal, shallows.................1587<br>早瀬　はやせ　rapids, swift current............0143<br>瀬を下る　せをくだる　descend the rapids....0040<br>○瀬戸　せと　strait, channel.....................0248<br>瀬戸内海　せとないかい　the Inland Sea<br>............................................................0248, 0215, 0106 |

| **1931**<br>水 85<br><br>瀬<br><br>0717<br>常 19 | Associate "*relying on* (頼) *water* (氵)" with stretches of a nautical journey where one's safety is particularly reliant on the water's mercy: **SHALLOWS/rapids**. ☞ 頼 1930 |

| **GORGE**<br><br>キョウ | 峡谷　きょうこく　gorge, ravine, canyon, valley 1034<br>山峡　さんきょう　(=やまかい)　gorge, ravine, glen<br>............................................................0037<br>峡湾　きょうわん　fjord............................1500<br>○海峡　かいきょう　straits, narrows, channel, sound<br>............................................................0106<br>地峡　ちきょう　isthmus.........................0187 |

| **1932**<br>山 46<br><br>峡<br><br>0318<br>常 9 | Distinguish 夹 from 来 0274 COME. See its two horizontal strokes (S4 and S7 here) as closing in on the two short strokes (ﾊ) and *pinching* them—any tighter and they'll be crushed. With 山, this suggests a narrow canyon *pinched* between two *mountains*: a **GORGE**. |

### NARROW, tight

キョウ
せま(い)　せば(める)　せば(まる)

○狭量な きょうりょうな narrow-minded........0538
偏狭な へんきょうな narrow-minded, intolerant;
　parochial...............................................1081
狭苦しい せまくるしい narrow and close,
　cramped ...............................................0405
○狭い部屋 せまいへや small room....0068, 0252
範囲を狭める はんいをせばめる narrow down
　the range.......................................0727, 0435

| 1933 | The constrained space between the two *pinching* (夹) horizontal strokes (ソ) is so **NARROW** |
| 犬 94 | that even a *dog* (犭) gets *pinched*. Note that all four kanji based on 夹 are pronounced キョウ. |

狭

0355
常 | 9

---

### HOLD BETWEEN, pinch

キョウ
はさむ

挟撃 きょうげき attack on both sides, pincer
　movement...............................................1026
○挟む はさむ hold between, pinch
箸で漬け物を挟む はしでつけものをはさむ hold
　a pickle with chopsticks .........1443, 0834, 0172
ビラを挟み込む ビラをはさみこむ insert a
　handbill...................................................0192

| 1934 | See the *hand* (扌) *pinching* (夹) the two short strokes (ソ), i.e., **HOLDING** them **BETWEEN** |
| 手 64 | its fingers. Note the traditional form for this entry and the two before it. The old form夾 still |
|  | appears in the next entry, which was not officially standardized with 峡, 狭, and 挟 when it |
|  | was added to the Joyo list. |

挟

0335
常 | 9

---

### CHEEKS

キョウ*
ほお　ほほ

頬髭 ほおひげ sideburns, whiskers...........1793
頬骨 ほおぼね (=きょうこつ) cheekbone......0465
○頬笑み (=微笑み) ほほえみ smile....0579, 2189
頬紅 ほおべに rouge............................1044
頬杖 ほおづえ resting one's head in one's hands
　.........................................................0658

| 1935 | The **CHEEKS** are the part of the *head* (頁) that people *pinch* (夹). However, 頬 is probably |
| 頁 181 | easiest to recognize simply by seeing S2–3 and S4–5 as dimpled **CHEEKS**. ☞ 煩 1937, 頓 1920 |

頬

1460
常 | 16

---

### JAW, chin

ガク
あご

顎骨 がっこつ (=あごぼね) jawbone ..........0465
顎髭 あごひげ beard............................1793
二重顎 にじゅうあご double chin.......0003, 0539
○上顎 うわあご (=じょうがく) upper jaw; palate 0041
○下顎 したあご (=かがく) lower jaw ...........0040

| 1936 | A *head* (頁) with a prominent **JAW**/chin, clearly visible in 咢: see S1–6 as two eyes, S7–8 as |
| 頁 181 | lips, and the top part of S9 as the **JAW**/chin (the bottom part of S9 shows the neck). There are |
|  | numerous kanji based on 咢 that are not listed in this book (諤 TELL IT LIKE IT IS, 鰐 ALLIGA- |
|  | TOR, 齶 JAW, 愕 SURPRISED); the last of these appears in a sample compound at 驚 0807. |

1607
常 | 18

| 煩 | **VEXING** | ○煩雑な はんざつな vexatious, troublesome, complicated ... 0379<br>煩労 はんろう trouble, bother, exertion ... 0542<br>煩う わずらう worry about, be vexed<br>○煩わしい わずらわしい vexatious, troublesome, complicated<br>心を煩わす こころをわずらわす worry oneself over ... 0056 |
| | ハン ボン<br>わずら(う) わずら(わす) | |

**1937** 火 86

Focus visually on S2, a flame leaping up from the *fire* (火) right toward the *head* stroke (at the top of 頁), irritating it. See the flame getting altogether too close, **VEXING** the *head*. ☞ 頬 1935

0937 常 13

| 串 | **SKEWER** | ○串焼き くしやき grilled on a skewer ... 0769<br>焼き串 やきぐし skewer ... 0769<br>金串 かなぐし metal skewer ... 0029<br>串に刺した野菜 くしにさしたやさい vegetables on a skewer ... 0935, 0534, 0988 |
| | くし | |

**1938** | 2

Two pieces of food, **SKEWERED**. ☞ 亜 0545

2973 常 7

| 患 | **AFFECTED BY DISEASE** | ○患者 かんじゃ patient ... 0107<br>患部 かんぶ diseased part, affected area ... 0068<br>○患う わずらう be afflicted with<br>喉を患う のどをわずらう have trouble in one's throat ... 1674<br>長患い ながわずらい lingering illness ... 0091 |
| | カン<br>わずら(う) | |

**1939** 心 61

*Skewered* (串) *heart* (organ) (心): **AFFECTED BY DISEASE**. ☞ 悪 0546

2395 常 11

| 疾 | ¹ **DISEASE**<br>² **FAST** | ①疾患 しっかん sickness, disease ... 1939<br>¹疾病 しっぺい sickness, disease ... 0617<br>②疾走 しっそう sprint, dash ... 0140<br>²疾駆する しっくする ride fast, drive a horse fast ... 1388<br>²疾風 しっぷう gale, strong wind ... 0425 |
| | シツ | |

**1940** 疒 104

Suggests an *illness* (疒) shooting through the body as swiftly as an *arrow* (矢): **DISEASE**; **FAST**. ☞ 痴 1941, 疫 1942

2793 常 10

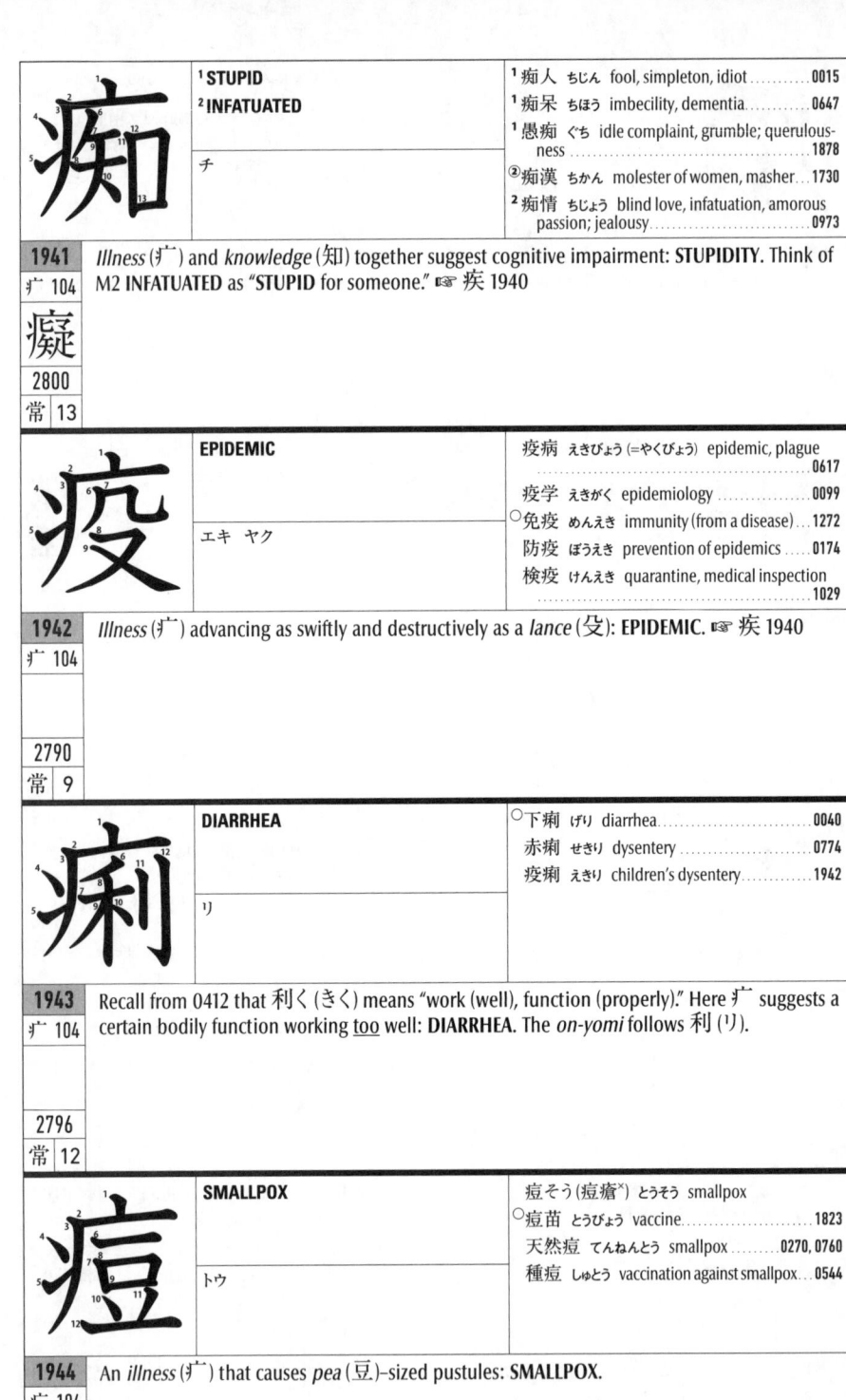

| 痴 | ¹ **STUPID**<br>² **INFATUATED**<br><br>チ | ¹ 痴人 ちじん fool, simpleton, idiot ........... 0015<br>¹ 痴呆 ちほう imbecility, dementia ........... 0647<br>¹ 愚痴 ぐち idle complaint, grumble; querulousness ........... 1878<br>② 痴漢 ちかん molester of women, masher ... 1730<br>² 痴情 ちじょう blind love, infatuation, amorous passion; jealousy ........... 0973 |

**1941** 疒 104

癡 2800 常 13

*Illness* (疒) and *knowledge* (知) together suggest cognitive impairment: **STUPIDITY**. Think of M2 **INFATUATED** as "**STUPID** for someone." ☞ 疾 1940

| 疫 | **EPIDEMIC**<br><br>エキ ヤク | 疫病 えきびょう (=やくびょう) epidemic, plague ........... 0617<br>疫学 えきがく epidemiology ........... 0099<br>○免疫 めんえき immunity (from a disease) ... 1272<br>防疫 ぼうえき prevention of epidemics ... 0174<br>検疫 けんえき quarantine, medical inspection ........... 1029 |

**1942** 疒 104

2790 常 9

*Illness* (疒) advancing as swiftly and destructively as a *lance* (殳): **EPIDEMIC**. ☞ 疾 1940

| 痢 | **DIARRHEA**<br><br>リ | ○下痢 げり diarrhea ........... 0040<br>赤痢 せきり dysentery ........... 0774<br>疫痢 えきり children's dysentery ........... 1942 |

**1943** 疒 104

2796 常 12

Recall from 0412 that 利く (きく) means "work (well), function (properly)." Here 疒 suggests a certain bodily function working <u>too</u> well: **DIARRHEA**. The *on-yomi* follows 利 (リ).

| 痘 | **SMALLPOX**<br><br>トウ | 痘そう (痘瘡ˣ) とうそう smallpox<br>○痘苗 とうびょう vaccine ........... 1823<br>天然痘 てんねんとう smallpox ........... 0270, 0760<br>種痘 しゅとう vaccination against smallpox ... 0544 |

**1944** 疒 104

2798 常 12

An *illness* (疒) that causes *pea* (豆)-sized pustules: **SMALLPOX**.

**ULCER, boil**

ヨウ

○潰瘍 かいよう ulcer.................................1178

| 1945 | An *illness* (疒) that is *difficult* (昜) to cure: **ULCER**. Additional sample compounds appear at 胃 1975 and 腫 2022. ☞ 腸 1985 |
| 疒 104 | |

2801
常 14

**CANCER**

ガン

子宮癌 しきゅうがん uterine cancer....0094, 1242
○乳癌 にゅうがん breast cancer.................0160
喉頭癌 こうとうがん laryngeal cancer..1674, 0162
発癌性 はつがんせい carcinogenic..0148, 0128
抗癌剤 こうがんざい anti-cancer drug 1639, 1261

| 1946 | In combination with *disease* (疒), 喦 suggests a growing *mountain* (山) of self-replicating **CANCER** cells (品). |
| 疒 104 | |

外 17

**BECOME THIN**

ソウ
や(せる)

○痩身 そうしん lean body; weight loss.........0060
○痩せる やせる become thin
痩せ衰える やせおとろえる become emaciated
................................................1861
夏痩せ なつやせ summer weight loss......0363
痩せ我慢する やせがまんする suffer out of pride
................................................0221, 1134

| 1947 | Note 叟 in the traditional form, which we saw earlier at 捜 1527. Both it and the simplified form, shown in the head character, can be visualized as a backbone and ribs, with a pair of crossed legs beneath them. In this entry, then, we observe an *illness* (疒) making a person's ribs visible—the illness of **BECOMING THIN**. |
| 疒 104 | |

2797
常 12

**TIRED**

ヒ
つか(れる) -づか(れ)

○疲労 ひろう fatigue...........................0542
○疲れる つかれる get tired
疲れ果てる つかれはてる be exhausted....0599
気疲れ きづかれ nervous strain, worry......0126
旅行疲れ りょこうづかれ fatigue from traveling
................................................0569, 0055

| 1948 | *Illness* (疒) + *skin* (皮): this does not refer to skin disease, but rather to **TIREDNESS**. One way to remember this is to think of **TIREDNESS** as causing certain changes in the color and texture of the skin, such as "bags under the eyes." |
| 疒 104 | |

2792
常 10

| | BE SUBJECTED TO; be covered in | ○被害者 ひがいしゃ victim..............0413, 0107<br>被告人 ひこくにん defendant..........0698, 0015<br>被保険者 ひほけんしゃ insured person<br>..................................0646, 1031, 0107 |
|---|---|---|
| | ヒ<br>こうむ(る) | ○損害を被る そんがいをこうむる suffer a loss<br>..................................1595, 0413<br>恩恵を被る おんけいをこうむる share in the<br>benefit..................................1728, 0581 |

| 1949 | *Skin*(皮) being covered in *clothing*(ネ). Associate the physical state of **being covered in** something with the abstract state of **BEING SUBJECTED TO** something. |
|---|---|
| 衣 145 | |
| 1077 | |
| 常 10 | |

---

| | OPEN OUT, reveal | 披露する ひろうする announce, introduce 1907<br>○披露宴 ひろうえん reception..........1907, 1294<br>お披露目 おひろめ début..............1907, 0021 |
|---|---|---|
| | ヒ | |

| 1950 | Picture the *hand*(扌) **OPENING OUT** so as to **reveal** its *skin*(皮, i.e., that of its palm). ☞ 抜 1951 |
|---|---|
| 手 64 | |
| 0270 | |
| 常 8 | |

---

| | ¹PULL OUT<br>²STAND OUT/above | ①抜本的な ばっぽんてきな radical, drastic<br>..................................0031, 0169<br>¹抜粋 ばっすい extract, excerpt, selection ...1622<br>①抜く ぬく pull out, extract<br>¹抜ける ぬける come/fall out/off; withdraw<br>²抜群の ばつぐんの preeminent, outstanding<br>..................................1408 |
|---|---|---|
| | バツ<br>ぬ(く) -ぬ(く) ぬ(き) ぬ(ける)<br>ぬ(かす) ぬ(かる) | |

| 1951 | Here imagine a *friend*(友)'s *hand*(扌) **PULLING** one **OUT** of a precarious or embarrassing situation. M2 **STAND OUT** is an extended meaning. ☞ 披 1950 |
|---|---|
| 手 64 | |
| 拔 | |
| 0219 | |
| 常 7 | |

---

| | HOLD BACK, deduct; note, memo | 控除 こうじょ (tax) deduction, subtraction...0996<br>馬を控える うまをひかえる hold back a horse 0336<br>○控えめな ひかえめな modest, temperate,<br>reserved<br>控え室 ひかえしつ anteroom, waiting room 0253<br>領収書の控え りょうしゅうしょのひかえ counterfoil<br>of a receipt..................1922, 1155, 0079 |
|---|---|---|
| | コウ<br>ひか(える) ひか(え) | |

| 1952 | Review 空 0398. In the present entry, imagine a suicidal person standing on an exposed I beam, threatening to jump. You reach out with your *hand*(扌) to **HOLD** him **BACK**. This kanji can also refer to taking **notes**, from the idea of "holding onto" something that has been said, rather than letting it disappear forever. |
|---|---|
| 手 64 | |
| 0453 | |
| 常 11 | |

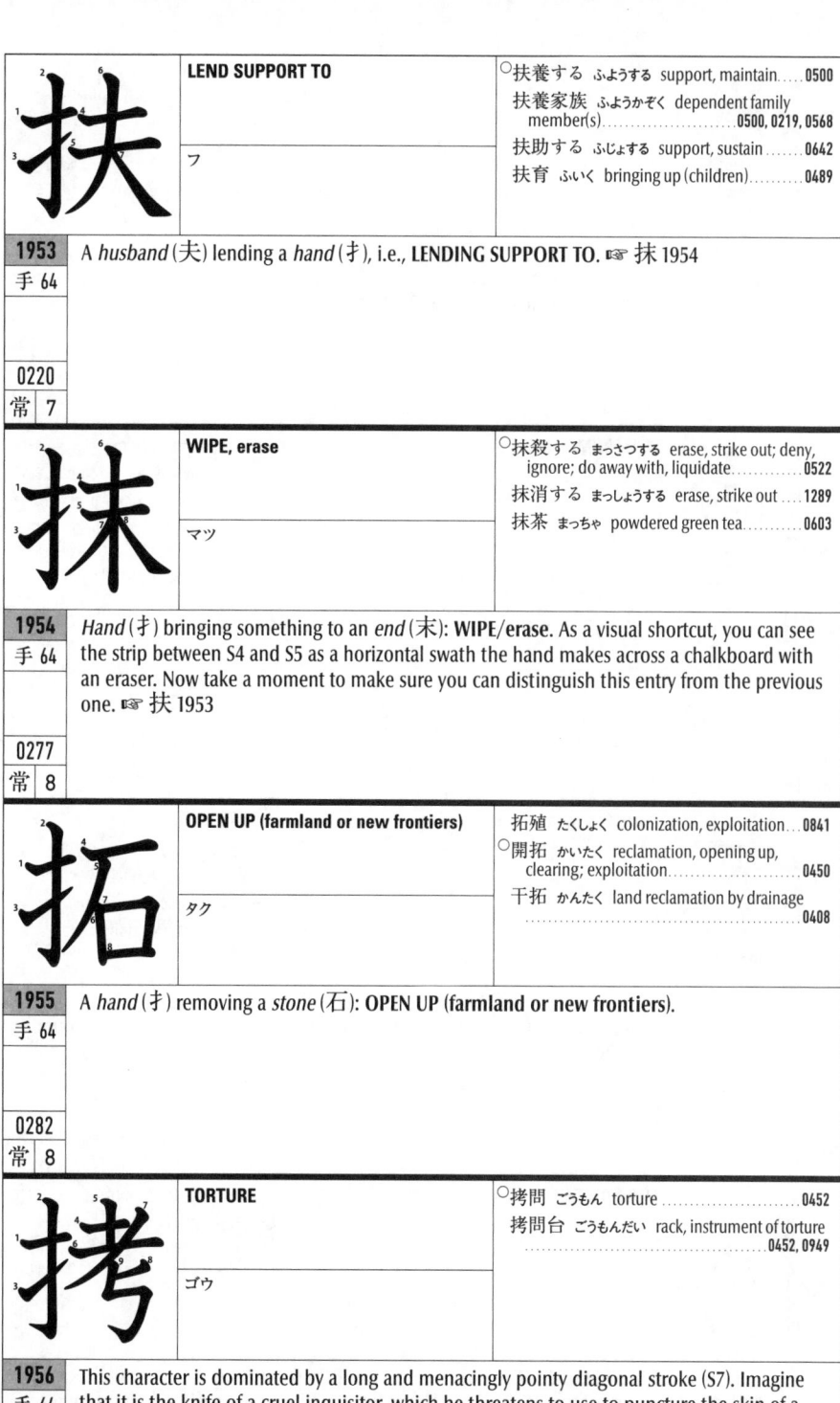

| 扶 | **LEND SUPPORT TO**<br><br>フ | ○扶養する ふようする support, maintain.....0500<br>扶養家族 ふようかぞく dependent family member(s)......................0500, 0219, 0568<br>扶助する ふじょする support, sustain.......0642<br>扶育 ふいく bringing up (children)..........0489 |
|---|---|---|
| **1953**<br>手 64<br><br>0220<br>常 7 | A *husband*(夫) lending a *hand*(扌), i.e., **LENDING SUPPORT TO**. ☞ 抹 1954 | |
| 抹 | **WIPE, erase**<br><br>マツ | ○抹殺する まっさつする erase, strike out; deny, ignore; do away with, liquidate............0522<br>抹消する まっしょうする erase, strike out ....1289<br>抹茶 まっちゃ powdered green tea..........0603 |
| **1954**<br>手 64<br><br>0277<br>常 8 | *Hand*(扌) bringing something to an *end*(末): **WIPE/erase**. As a visual shortcut, you can see the strip between S4 and S5 as a horizontal swath the hand makes across a chalkboard with an eraser. Now take a moment to make sure you can distinguish this entry from the previous one. ☞ 扶 1953 | |
| 拓 | **OPEN UP (farmland or new frontiers)**<br><br>タク | 拓殖 たくしょく colonization, exploitation...0841<br>○開拓 かいたく reclamation, opening up, clearing; exploitation......................0450<br>干拓 かんたく land reclamation by drainage ................................0408 |
| **1955**<br>手 64<br><br>0282<br>常 8 | A *hand*(扌) removing a *stone*(石): **OPEN UP (farmland or new frontiers)**. | |
| 拷 | **TORTURE**<br><br>ゴウ | ○拷問 ごうもん torture .....................0452<br>拷問台 ごうもんだい rack, instrument of torture ................................0452, 0949 |
| **1956**<br>手 64<br><br>0332<br>常 9 | This character is dominated by a long and menacingly pointy diagonal stroke (S7). Imagine that it is the knife of a cruel inquisitor, which he threatens to use to puncture the skin of a heretic's *hand*(扌), and to drive right through its bones into the wooden table of the inquisition room: **TORTURE**. | |

**TALL BUILDING**

ロウ

○楼閣 ろうかく multistoried building .........0792
望楼 ぼうろう watchtower, observation tower
.................................................1066
五層楼 ごそうろう five-story building
.........................................0007, 1224
高楼 こうろう lofty building; skyscraper .....0185

| 1957 | Once harvested, field grains must be stored high above the ground to keep them out of the |
|---|---|
| 木 75 | reach of animals. In this entry, visualize a *woman* (女) storing *rice* (米) high atop a towering |
| 樓 | *wooden* (木) structure: **TALL BUILDING**. ☞ 数 0309 |
| 0931 | |
| 常 13 | |

**PLATFORM, rostrum**

ダン タン

○演壇 えんだん platform, rostrum .............0914
教壇 きょうだん teacher's platform, rostrum...0632
詩壇 しだん poetical circles, world of poetry...0389
土壇場 どたんば place of execution; eleventh
hour .................................0030, 0445
壇に登る だんにのぼる get on the platform...1054

| 1958 | Visualize 亶 as a rostrum or **PLATFORM**, built on an *earth* (土) foundation. |
|---|---|
| 土 32 | |
| 0682 | |
| 常 16 | |

**TOWER, pagoda**

トウ

鉄塔 てっとう steel tower; pylon .............0564
管制塔 かんせいとう control tower ....1839, 0708
エッフェル塔 エッフェルとう Eiffel Tower
仏塔 ぶっとう pagoda, Buddhist pagoda....0811
○五重の塔 ごじゅうのとう five-story pagoda
.........................................0007, 0539

| 1959 | Visualize 荅 as a communications tower: 合 represents the tower structure, while ⼗⼗ repre- |
|---|---|
| 土 32 | sents the antennas on its roof. The present entry adds 土 to suggest a deep and sturdy founda- |
| | tion, and means **TOWER/pagoda**. |
| 0517 | |
| 常 12 | |

**LOAD ON BOARD**

トウ

○搭載する とうさいする load, embark .........1318
搭乗する とうじょうする board, get on a plane,
embark.................................1005
搭乗券 とうじょうけん boarding pass...1005, 0456

| 1960 | Here, visualize the *hand* (扌) **LOADING** the antennas (⼗⼗) **ON BOARD** the *tower* (荅). Remem- |
|---|---|
| 手 64 | bering this idea, practice writing 塔 and 搭 in turn, and learn to associate their meanings |
| | with the variable element. |
| 0541 | |
| 常 12 | |

| | | | |
|---|---|---|---|
| 寡 | **¹ FEW** **² WIDOW(ER)** | | |
| | カ | ¹寡少の かしょうの few, little, scanty..........0677 ①寡占 かせん oligopoly.....................0348 ¹寡黙な かもくな silent, taciturn, reticent....0762 ¹寡聞 かぶん being ill-informed............0453 ②寡婦 かふ (=やもめ) widow.................1017 | |

| **1961** | It is useful to associate this kanji with a **WIDOW**'s poverty. Picture S4–9 (like 百 0016 HUN-DRED with an extra zero) as her last thousand dollars, which she carefully stores on a special covered (宀) shelf (S10), *dividing* (分) it into tiny sums for her expenses. Thus seen, the kanji represents not only **WIDOW**, but also **FEW**. |
|---|---|
| 宀 40 | |
| 2059 | |
| 常 14 | |

| 賓 | **GUEST** | ○賓客 ひんきゃく (=ひんかく) guest, guest of honor ............................................0787 |
|---|---|---|
| | ヒン | 来賓 らいひん guest, visitor.................0274 国賓 こくひん state guest.....................0075 迎賓館 げいひんかん guesthouse.....1139, 0291 |

| **1962** | Visualize S4–8 as a uniformed doorman standing at the entrance to a well-to-do family's *house* (宀). S4 shows his doorman's cap, S6–7 his epaulets, and S8 his arm pointing toward our left, solicitously pointing the way for the family's wealthy **GUEST** (貝). This kanji is easily identified by the distinctive image of the welcoming doorman's arm. |
|---|---|
| 貝 154 | |
| 賓 | |
| 2077 | |
| 常 15 | |

| 飾 | **DECORATE** | 装飾する そうしょくする ornament, adorn, decorate.................................1591 |
|---|---|---|
| | ショク かざ(る) かざ(り) | ○修飾する しゅうしょくする decorate, ornament; [grammar] modify............................1676 粉飾 ふんしょく makeup, maquillage........1619 ○飾る かざる decorate; affect; display 首飾り くびかざり necklace..................0157 |

| **1963** | Earlier we learned to visualize 𠂉 as a person holding out an object (e.g., see 施 0571, 旗 0573, and 乞 1805). Here, see 𠂉 holding out a *cloth* (巾) and placing it over a *dining* (食) table: **DECORATE**. |
|---|---|
| 食 184 | |
| 餝 | |
| 1530 | |
| 常 13 | |

| 飽 | **SATIATED; tired of** | 飽食する ほうしょくする satiate oneself, eat one's fill.....................................0288 |
|---|---|---|
| | ホウ あ(きる) あ(かす) | ○飽満 ほうまん satiety, surfeit............0179 ○飽きる あきる be satiated, grow tired of 聞き飽きる ききあきる be fed up listening to..0453 飽きっぽい あきっぽい be fickle |

| **1964** | Here 包 *wrap* suggests a filled sack. *Eat* (食) + *filled sack*: **SATIATED**. Recall that all kanji incorporating 包 are pronounced ホウ. |
|---|---|
| 食 184 | |
| 1528 | |
| 常 13 | |

| | | STARVE | 餓死 がし death from starvation............0716 |
|---|---|---|---|
| 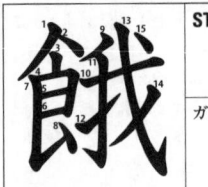 | | ガ | |
| **1965**<br>食 184 | | So hungry, one would *eat*(食) one*self*(我): **STARVING.** The *on-yomi* compound to memorize appears in the next entry. | |
| **1546**<br>常 15 | | | |

| | | STARVE | ○飢餓 きが starvation, hunger, famine.......1965 |
|---|---|---|---|
| | | | 飢民 きみん starving people ............0477 |
|  | | キ<br>う(える) | ○飢える うえる starve |
| | | | 飢え うえ hunger, starvation |
| | | | 飢え死に うえじに (death by) starvation ....0716 |
| **1966**<br>食 184 | | So hungry, one would *eat*(食) the *table*(几): **STARVING.** | |
| **1490**<br>常 10 | | | |

| | | DESK | ○机上 きじょう top of the desk; academic, theoretical...................0041 |
|---|---|---|---|
| | | | 机上の空論 きじょうのくうろん armchair theorizing.............0041, 0398, 0942 |
|  | | キ<br>つくえ | 机下 きか under the desk............0040 |
| | | | 事務机 じむづくえ office desk........0080, 0687 |
| **1967**<br>木 75 | | *Wooden*(木) *table*(几): **DESK.** | |
| **0726**<br>常 6 | | | |

| | | REDUNDANT, superfluous | 冗長な じょうちょうな verbose, redundant, prolix ...........0091 |
|---|---|---|---|
| | | | 冗員 じょういん superfluous personnel......0317 |
|  | | ジョウ | |
| **1968**<br>冖 14 | | Recall that 几 can also mean *tablecloth.* Here, we observe a *covering*(冖) placed over a *tablecloth*: **REDUNDANT.** The *on-yomi* compound to memorize appears at 談 1977. | |
| 冗 | | | |
| **1716**<br>常 4 | | | |

| CROWN | ○王冠 おうかん crown, diadem, cap..............0072 |
|---|---|
| | 戴冠式 たいかんしき coronation (ceremony) |
| | ..............................................1914, 0109 |
| カン | 冠者 かんじゃ (=かじゃ) young man (come of age) 0107 |
| かんむり | 冠婚葬祭 かんこんそうさい ceremonial occasion |
| | (coming of age, marriage, funeral, ancestral |
| | worship)..................1721, 0717, 0637 |
| | ワ冠 わかんむり wa (ワ)-shaped grapheme atop |
| | certain kanji (such as 冠) |

| 1969 | Picture the *outstretched arm* (寸) placing a **CROWN** (S3) upon someone's head (S4). 冖 rein- |
|---|---|
| 冖 14 | forces the meaning by suggesting *covering*, and **CROWNS** the whole affair for good measure. |
| | Being mindful that a **CROWN** is a *covering* and not a *roof* will help you remember that it is |
| | written with 冖, not 宀. The Japanese name for 冖 appears in V5. |
| 1790 | |
| 常 9 | |

| SEPARATE | 分離する ぶんりする separate; be separated |
|---|---|
| | ..................................................0088 |
| | 剝離 はくり exfoliation, peeling off..........0609 |
| リ | ○離婚 りこん divorce............................1721 |
| はな(れる) はな(す) | 離陸 りりく takeoff.............................1432 |
| | ○離れる はなれる separate; be separated |

| 1970 | Recall 凶 0296 EVIL MISFORTUNE. Now because the lower part of 离 resembles 内 (うち) |
|---|---|
| 隹 172 | (which can refer to one's own home or workplace), we can associate it with a home or work- |
| | place that has experienced evil misfortune. Think of the *small bird* (隹) deciding to **SEPARATE** |
| | himself from such a place. |
| 1663 | |
| 常 18 | |

| CHEST | 胸囲 きょうい chest measurement...........0435 |
|---|---|
| | ○胸部 きょうぶ breast, chest .................0068 |
| | 胸郭 きょうかく thorax, chest..................1422 |
| キョウ | 度胸 どきょう courage, pluck, heart..........0280 |
| むね むな- | 胸毛 むなげ chest hair.......................0487 |

| 1971 | In the coming series of kanji 月 will be used in the sense of *body part*. Here, 匃 suggests the |
|---|---|
| 肉 130 | *body part* wherein an *elephant* (勹) stores up memories of heart-rending *misfortune* (凶): |
| | his **CHEST**. ☞ 脳 1973 |
| 0858 | |
| 常 10 | |

| SUFFER, be troubled | 煩悩 ぼんのう worldly desires, carnal desires |
|---|---|
| | ..................................................1937 |
| | ○苦悩 くのう suffering, anguish, dread........0405 |
| ノウ | ○悩ましい なやましい distressful; seductive, alluring |
| なや(む) なや(ます) | 伸び悩む のびなやむ fail to grow ..........0873 |
| | 頭を悩ます あたまをなやます rack one's brains |
| | ..................................................0162 |

| 1972 | At 桜 1249 we visualized ⺍ as "falling blossoms." Here, visualize it as "falling into *misfortune*" |
|---|---|
| 心 61 | (凶), and imagine how this must cause the *heart/mind* (忄) to **SUFFER**. ☞ 脳 1973 |
| 悩 | |
| 0380 | |
| 常 10 | |

**BRAIN**

ノウ

| | | | |
|---|---|---|---|
| 脳死 | のうし | brain death | 0716 |
| 大脳 | だいのう | cerebrum | 0033 |
| 脳裏 | のうり | brain, mind, memory | 0704 |
| 頭脳 | ずのう | brain; brains, head | 0162 |
| ○首脳 | しゅのう | head, leader | 0157 |

| 1973 | In the strict, physiological sense, the *body part* (月) directly affected by "falling into *misfortune*" (see previous entry) is the **BRAIN**. Practice writing this and 悩, learning to associate SUFFERING (a matter of the spirit) with 忄, and **BRAIN** (a physical organ) with 月. ☞ 胸 1971, 悩 1972 |
|---|---|
| 肉 130 | |
| 脳 | |
| 0888 | |
| 常 11 | |

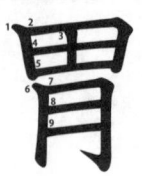

**INTERNAL ORGAN**

ゾウ

| | | | |
|---|---|---|---|
| 臓器 | ぞうき | internal organs, viscera | 0295 |
| ○内臓 | ないぞう | internal organs, viscera | 0215 |
| 心臓 | しんぞう | heart | 0704 |
| 臓物 | ぞうもつ | entrails, giblets | 0172 |

| 1974 | *Body parts* (月) stored inside the *storehouse* (蔵), i.e., **INTERNAL ORGANS**. ☞ 蔵 0695 |
|---|---|
| 肉 130 | |
| 臓 | |
| 1022 | |
| 常 19 | |

**STOMACH**

イ

| | | | |
|---|---|---|---|
| 胃弱 | いじゃく | dyspepsia, indigestion | 0424 |
| ○胃袋 | いぶくろ | stomach | 0702 |
| 胃癌 | いがん | gastric cancer | 1946 |
| 胃潰瘍 | いかいよう | stomach ulcer | 1945 |

| 1975 | To remember this kanji, imagine food going into the *head* (田) and down into a *body part* (月) located below it: the **STOMACH**. |
|---|---|
| 肉 130 | |
| 2219 | |
| 常 9 | |

| ¹ **FLAME**<br>² **INFLAMMATION, -itis** | | | |
|---|---|---|---|

エン
ほのお

| | | | |
|---|---|---|---|
| ¹火炎 | かえん | flames, blaze | 0026 |
| ¹情炎 | じょうえん | flaming desires, burning passions | 0973 |
| ①ろうそくの炎 | ろうそくのほのお | candle flame | |
| ②炎症 | えんしょう | inflammation | 0618 |
| ²脳炎 | のうえん | encephalitis | 1973 |

| 1976 | Rising *fire* (火): **FLAME; INFLAMMATION**. |
|---|---|
| 火 86 | |
| 2145 | |
| 常 8 | |

**TALK, converse**

ダン

談話 だんわ talk, conversation; comment... 0053
冗談 じょうだん joke .................................... 1968
○相談する そうだんする consult, talk over, confer
.................................................................. 0682
座談会 ざだんかい roundtable talk, symposium
............................................................ 0749, 0226
首脳会談 しゅのうかいだん summit meeting
...................................................... 0157, 1973, 0226

| 1977 | Words (言) by the *flames* (炎) of the campfire: **TALK/converse.** |
|---|---|
| 言 149 | |
| 1419 | |
| 常 15 | |

**LIGHT, faint**

タン
あわ(い)

○淡色 たんしょく light color .................... 0528
淡彩 たんさい light coloring .................. 0990
冷淡な れいたんな cool, indifferent ........ 0675
濃淡 のうたん shading, light and shade..... 0512
淡雪 あわゆき light snow ...................... 0899

| 1978 | *Water* (氵) falling on *flames* (炎), making them **LIGHT/faint.** ☞ 災 1979 |
|---|---|
| 水 85 | |
| 0484 | |
| 常 11 | |

**NATURAL CALAMITY**

サイ
わざわ(い)

○災害 さいがい calamity, disaster, accident... 0413
天災 てんさい natural disaster ............... 0270
震災 しんさい earthquake disaster .......... 0902
災禍 さいか accident, natural disaster,
    misfortune................................... 1486
○災いする わざわいする be the ruin of (someone)

| 1979 | *Fire* (火) and smoke (巛, just this time): **NATURAL CALAMITY.** ☞ 淡 1978 |
|---|---|
| 火 86 | |
| 1888 | |
| 常 7 | |

肝

**LIVER**

カン
きも

○肝臓 かんぞう liver ............................ 1974
肝油 かんゆ liver oil ......................... 0433
肝炎 かんえん hepatitis........................ 1976
肝要な かんような important, vital, essential 0547
肝に銘じる きもにめいじる take to heart..... 1546

| 1980 | *Body part* (月) for *"drying"* (干) out (i.e., detoxifying) the bloodstream: **LIVER.** |
|---|---|
| 肉 130 | |
| 0747 | |
| 常 7 | |

| 肺 | LUNG | ○肺臓 はいぞう lungs..........................1974 |
|---|---|---|
| | | 肺肝 はいかん lungs and liver, innermost heart |
| | | ..........................1980 |
| | ハイ | 肺浸潤 はいしんじゅん infiltration of the lungs |
| | | ..........................1014, 1491 |
| | | 肺炎 はいえん pneumonia, inflammation of the lungs |
| | | ..........................1976 |
| | | 肺が弱い はいがよわい have a weak chest...0424 |

| 1981 | 月 suggests *body part*. Ignore *city/market*, and instead see 市 as a picture of two pulmonary |
|---|---|
| 肉 130 | lobes, framed by a throat (S5), collarbones (S6), and a windpipe (S9): **LUNGS**. This entry is the |
| | only one breaking the rule that kanji with 市 are pronounced シ. |
| 0825 | |
| 常 9 | |

| 胆 | GALLBLADDER, gall | 胆石 たんせき gallstone ..........................0403 |
|---|---|---|
| | | 胆汁 たんじゅう bile, gall ..........................0756 |
| | | 胆力 たんりょく courage, nerve, mettle ......0084 |
| | タン | ○大胆 だいたん boldness, daring ..........0033 |
| | | 落胆 らくたん disappointment, discouragement |
| | | ..........................0793 |

| 1982 | Straying for a moment from our focus at this point in the course, interpret 月 here as *moon*, |
|---|---|
| 肉 130 | not *body part*. With 旦, it tells us a story of one morning when the *moon* had the **gall** to stay |
| 膽 | out after *dawn*: **GALLBLADDER/gall**. |
| 0828 | |
| 常 9 | |

| 腺 | GLAND | 甲状腺 こうじょうせん thyroid gland ...1521, 0616 |
|---|---|---|
| | | ○涙腺 るいせん lachrymal gland ..............1020 |
| | | 乳腺 にゅうせん mammary gland ............0160 |
| | セン | 唾液腺 だえきせん salivary gland...........1401, 0468 |
| | | 粘液腺 ねんえきせん mucus gland ....1267, 0470 |

| 1983 | 月 *body part* + 泉 *fountain/spring*: **GLAND**. The *on-yomi* follows 泉 0207 and 線 0210. |
|---|---|
| 肉 130 | |
| 0950 | |
| 常 13 | |

| 胞 | MEMBRANOUS SAC | ○細胞 さいぼう cell..........................0239 |
|---|---|---|
| | | 細胞膜 さいぼうまく cellular membrane |
| | | ..........................0239, 1337 |
| | ホウ | 胞子 ほうし spore ..........................0094 |
| | | 肺胞 はいほう alveolus..........................1981 |
| | | 芽胞 がほう spore..........................1817 |

| 1984 | *Body part*(月) + *wrap*(包): **MEMBRANOUS SAC**. |
|---|---|
| 肉 130 | |
| 0826 | |
| 常 9 | |

| 腸 | | **INTESTINES** | ○胃腸 いちょう stomach and intestines/bowels ............................1975 |
| | | | 胃腸病学 いちょうびょうがく gastroenterology ....................1975, 0617, 0099 |
| | | チョウ | 腸炎 ちょうえん enteritis ...........1976 |
| | | | 小腸 しょうちょう small intestine ............0034 |
| | | | 盲腸 もうちょう cecum, appendix ............1061 |

| **1985** | Let "*body part*(月) + *difficult*(昜)" suggest **INTESTINAL** discomfort. ☞ 賜 0444, 瘍 1945 |
| 肉 130 | |
| 0948 | |
| 常 13 | |

| 胎 | | **¹WOMB** **²FETUS** | ¹ 母胎 ぼたい mother's womb ................0104 |
| | | | ¹ 胎内 たいない interior of the womb ........0215 |
| | | | ² 胎教 たいきょう prenatal care.............0632 |
| | | タイ | ②胎児 たいじ embryo, fetus .................0772 |
| | | | 胎動 たいどう quickening, fetal movement; indication................0540 |

| **1986** | *Body part*(月) that provides a "*platform*"(台) for the development of a **FETUS**: the **WOMB**. |
| 肉 130 | |
| 0827 | |
| 常 9 | |

| 腰 | | **WAIST** | ○腰部 ようぶ waist, hips ......................0068 |
| | | | 腰骨 こしぼね hipbone ......................0465 |
| | | | 足腰 あしこし legs and loins .................0044 |
| | | ヨウ | ○腰掛ける こしかける sit down ...............1117 |
| | | こし | 腰巻き こしまき loincloth ....................0458 |

| **1987** | When we learned 要 0547, we pictured a *woman* weighed down by a heavy *box*. The present |
| 肉 130 | entry refers to the *body part*(月) that the box causes to bend: the **WAIST**. |
| 0952 | |
| 常 13 | |

| 肘 | | **ELBOW** | テニス肘 テニスひじ tennis elbow |
| | | | 肘て人を押し分ける ひじてひとをおしわける elbow one's way through a crowd ....................0015, 1525, 0088 |
| | | ひじ | ○肘掛け ひじかけ armrest ....................1117 |
| | | | 肘掛け椅子 ひじかけいす armchair ....................1117, 1332, 0094 |

| **1988** | The *body part*(月) involved in producing an *outstretched arm*(寸): **ELBOW**. |
| 肉 130 | |
| 0746 | |
| 常 7 | |

| 膝 | **KNEE; lap** | 膝蓋骨 しつがいこつ kneecap, patella 1303, 0465 |
|---|---|---|
| | | 膝関節 しつかんせつ knee joint .......0451, 0391 |
| | | 膝を崩す ひざをくずす sit at ease............1650 |
| | シツ* | ○膝掛け ひざかけ lap robe .................1117 |
| | ひざ | 膝の上に乗せる ひざのうえにのせる put on one's lap ...............................0041, 1005 |

| 1989 | Again 月 suggests *body part*. Back at 漆 1002, we visualized 桼 as splashing drops of sap. |
|---|---|
| 肉 130 | Here, let the lower portion suggest splashing drops of "*water*(氺) on the **KNEE**," being drained. To distinguish 膝 (ひざ, knee; lap) from 肘 (ひじ, elbow), it is helpful to associate the ざ of ひざ with 座 (ざ, seat), and thus with the lower part of the body. |
| 0985 | |
| 常 15 | |

| 股 | **CROTCH, thigh** | 股関節 こかんせつ hip joint, coxa.....0451, 0391 |
|---|---|---|
| | | 股座 またぐら crotch ..........................0749 |
| | | 二股 ふたまた bifurcation, splitting; double-dealing..................................................0003 |
| | コ | 内股 うちまた inner thigh; pigeon-toed.....0215 |
| | また | うちもも inner thigh |

| 1990 | 月 means *body part*, and both 几 and 又 have **CROTCH**-like shapes. Therefore, ignore 殳 |
|---|---|
| 肉 130 | *lance* and instead perceive the meaning **CROTCH** directly from these shapes. ☞ 肢 1991, 又 0058 |
| 0785 | |
| 常 8 | |

| 肢 | **LIMB** | 肢体 したい limbs, members.................0062 |
|---|---|---|
| | | 下肢 かし lower limbs, legs ..................0040 |
| | | ○四肢 しし limbs, legs and arms .............0006 |
| | シ | 前肢 ぜんし forelimb, front leg .............0113 |
| | | 選択肢 せんたくし choice, alternative 1502, 1503 |

| 1991 | Review the first part of the annotation for 支 0373. This should allow you to perceive in the |
|---|---|
| 肉 130 | present entry a *branch*-like *body part*(月), or **LIMB**. ☞ 枝 0965, 股 1990 |
| 0786 | |
| 常 8 | |

| 胴 | **TRUNK, torso** | ○胴体 どうたい trunk, torso, hull ..............0062 |
|---|---|---|
| | | 胴巻き どうまき bellyband....................0458 |
| | | 胴衣 どうい jacket, vest.......................0700 |
| | ドウ | 胴が長い どうがながい have a long trunk...0091 |

| 1992 | When 同 appears next to 月, visualize it as the rectangular shape of a human torso, housing |
|---|---|
| 肉 130 | a couple of internal organs: **TRUNK/torso**. |
| 0857 | |
| 常 10 | |

| 脇 | ¹ ARMPIT<br>² ASIDE<br><br>わき わけ | ¹ 脇毛 わきげ underarm hair .................. 0487<br>¹ 脇に抱える わきにかかえる carry under one's arm .................. 0664<br>² 薬局の脇に やっきょくのわきに next to the drugstore .................. 0303, 0256<br>² 脇見 わきみ looking aside .................. 0083<br>② 脇に置く わきにおく put aside, disregard (for the moment) .................. 0843 |
|---|---|---|

**1993** 肉 130 — At 脅 1496 we visualized three *powerful* (劦) predators threatening prey. Here, visualize a *body part* (月) emitting an over*power*ing stench: **ARMPIT**. M2 **ASIDE** is an extended meaning. ☞ 脅 1496, 協 0543

0859 常 10

| 脂 | FAT<br><br>シ<br>あぶら | 油脂 ゆし fats and oils .................. 0433<br>脂質 ししつ lipids, fats .................. 0318<br>脂性 あぶらしょう fatty constitution .......... 0128<br>脂ぎった あぶらぎった greasy, oily |
|---|---|---|

**1994** 肉 130 — If 旨 0931 refers to the essence or substance of something, here it must refer to the "*essence of meat* (月)," that is, something one always finds when one cuts into it: **FAT**. ☞ 指 0932

0861 常 10

| 詣 | VISIT A TEMPLE<br><br>ケイ<br>もう(て) もうで もう(てる) | ○参詣する さんけいする visit a temple/shrine, pay homage .................. 1239<br>詣でる もうてる visit a temple/shrine, pay homage<br>○初詣 はつもうで one's first visit to a temple/shrine in the new year .................. 0710 |
|---|---|---|

**1995** 言 149 — Let "*words* (言) + *essence* (旨)" suggest a worshipper's speaking his true feelings to God, as in a heartfelt prayer or confession: **VISIT A TEMPLE**. This kanji is the one exception to the rule that kanji containing 旨 have the *on* reading シ.

1379 常 13

| 肪 | ANIMAL FAT<br><br>ボウ | ○脂肪 しぼう fat, grease .................. 1994 |
|---|---|---|

**1996** 肉 130 — A slab of *meat* (月) with a strip of **FAT** on one *side* (方).

0781 常 8

**SKIN**

はだ

肌身 はだみ body .................................... 0060
○肌着 はだぎ underwear ........................ 0938
肌色 はだいろ flesh color ..................... 0528
美しい肌の材 うつくしいはだのざい wood of fine grain ............................................... 0497, 0654
学者肌 がくしゃはだ scholarly bent of mind ............................................... 0099, 0107

| 1997 | *Tablecloth* (几) for the *body* (月): **SKIN**. |
| 肉 130 | |
| 0731 | |
| 常 6 | |

**SKIN**

フ

○皮膚 ひふ skin ..................................... 0595
完膚無き迄 かんぶなきまで thoroughly, beyond recognition; scathingly ......... 0633, 0048, 1806

| 1998 | *Tiger* (虍, review 虎 0912 if necessary) + *stomach* (胃). To associate this with **SKIN**, we might imagine removing a *tiger's stomach* and other viscera, in order to take home only its **SKIN**. ☞ 虜 2004, 慮 1999 |
| 肉 130 | |
| 2788 | |
| 常 15 | |

**CONSIDER**

リョ

思慮 しりょ consideration, discretion ....... 0142
考慮する こうりょする consider, deliberate 0628
○遠慮する えんりょする be reserved; hesitate; refrain ............................................... 0857
配慮 はいりょ consideration, care, concern 0799
顧慮 こりょ regard, consideration ........... 1890

| 1999 | Paint a picture in your mind's eye of a *tiger* (虍) *thinking* (思), contemplating whether to initiate a chase or wait for a better opportunity: **CONSIDER**. ☞ 膚 1998, 虜 2004 |
| 心 61 | |
| 2789 | |
| 常 15 | |

**CRUEL, tyrannical**

ギャク
しいた(げる)

残虐な ざんぎゃくな cruel, atrocious, brutal 1583
○虐待 ぎゃくたい abuse, cruelty .............. 0386
虐殺 ぎゃくさつ massacre, genocide ........ 0522
○虐げる しいたげる tyrannize, oppress
虐げられた人々 しいたげられたひとびと down-trodden people, the oppressed ........... 0015

| 2000 | Picture S7-9 as the *tiger* (虍)'s claw, which he **CRUELLY** uses to maul his victims without the slightest regard for the suffering he causes them. |
| 虍 141 | |
| 2769 | |
| 常 9 | |

| | RISK, fears | ○失敗の虞 しっぱいのおそれ risk of failure .................................0563, 0830 |
|---|---|---|
| | | 転落の虞が有る てんらくのおそれがある<br>There is a risk of falling..........0224, 0793, 0400 |
| | おそれ | 感染の虞を無くす かんせんのおそれをなくす<br>preclude the possibility of infection<br>.................................0327, 1174, 0048 |

| 2001 | Typist (呉) entering *tiger* (虍)'s lair: **RISK**. Note that おそれ is usually written 恐れ (cf. 1633). |
|---|---|
| 虍 141 | |
| 2783 | |
| 常 13 | |

| | DRAMA | 悲劇 ひげき tragedy, tragic drama ..........1856 |
|---|---|---|
| | | 喜劇 きげき comedy .........................1212 |
| | | 歌劇 かげき opera ........................0827 |
| | ゲキ | ○劇場 げきじょう theater.....................0445 |
| | | 劇を演じる げきをえんじる perform a play...0914 |

| 2002 | Imagine a *sword* (刂)–fighting **DRAMA** featuring a *tiger* (虍) and a *pig* (豕). |
|---|---|
| 刀 18 | |
| 1681 | |
| 常 15 | |

| | ¹ EMPTY, void<br>² FALSE | ¹ 虚無 きょむ nothingness; nihility...........0048 |
|---|---|---|
| | | ¹ 空虚な くうきょな empty, void; inane........0398 |
| | | ①虚栄心 きょえいしん vanity .............1245, 0056 |
| | キョ コ | ②虚偽 きょぎ falsehood, lie, fallacy...........1237 |
| | | ² 虚構 きょこう fabrication, fiction...........0917 |

| 2003 | Imagine entering the *tiger* (虍)'s lair and finding nothing but a few drops of water dripping from the ceiling and splashing on the ground (业): the lair is **EMPTY**. M2 **FALSE** is a derivative meaning. ☞ 戯 2007 |
|---|---|
| 虍 141 | |
| 虚 | |
| 2778 | |
| 常 11 | |

| | CAPTIVE | ○捕虜 ほりょ prisoner of war, captive.........1596 |
|---|---|---|
| | | 虜囚 りょしゅう captive, prisoner .............1722 |
| | リョ | |

| 2004 | *Tiger* (虍) holding *man* (男) **CAPTIVE**. ☞ 膚 1998, 慮 1999 |
|---|---|
| 虍 141 | |
| 虜 | |
| 2784 | |
| 常 13 | |

**BRAVE; in high spirits**

ユウ
いさ(む)

勇敢な ゆうかんな brave, daring, heroic .... 0809
○勇気 ゆうき courage, valor, bravery, nerve... 0126
勇猛 ゆうもう bravery, daring ............... 0767
胆勇 たんゆう courage...................... 1982
○勇む いさむ be encouraged, be in high spirits

| 2005 | Recall マ *pointing forward*. Here, picture a *man* (男) running swiftly *forward*, full of enthusiasm and courage: **BRAVE; in high spirits**. |
| 力 19 | |
| 1798 | |
| 常 9 | |

**WELL UP, gush out**

ユウ
わ(く)

○湧出 ゆうしゅつ welling, gushing............ 0038
湧く わく well up, gush out
湧き出る わきでる well up, spring forth..... 0038
湧き上がる わきあがる well up, arise........ 0041
○湧き起こる わきおこる well up, arise ........ 0430

| 2006 | Picture streams of sweat (氵) **WELLING UP/gushing out** of the high-spirited running man (勇). ☞ 洩 1588 |
| 水 85 | |
| 涌 | |
| 0563 | |
| 常 12 | |

**SPORT, play**

ギ
たわむ(れる)

○戯れる たわむれる sport, play; joke
子猫がボールに戯れている こねこがボールに
たわむれている The kitten is playing with a ball
.................................................. 0094, 1825
○遊戯 ゆうぎ game, pastime, amusement ...0570
戯曲 ぎきょく drama, play...................... 0503
悪戯 いたずら (=あくぎ) mischief, prank...... 0546

| 2007 | *False* (虚) + *spear* (戈): throwing a spear for **SPORT/play**, rather than in actual battle. ☞ 虚 2003, 織 2008 |
| 戈 62 | |
| 戯 | |
| 1654 | |
| 常 15 | |

**¹FINE**
**²FIBER**

セン

①繊細な せんさいな delicate, fine, subtle..... 0239
¹繊毛 せんもう cilia, fine hair................. 0487
²繊切り せんぎり long thin strips (of a vegetable)
.................................................... 0086
²化繊 かせん chemical fiber .................. 0120
²合繊 ごうせん synthetic fiber................ 0227

| 2008 | From 裁 1317, recall the short man (十) holding a *spear* (戈): 𢦏. Here he uses the spear as the framework of a loom (recalling 幾 0470), on which he manipulates **FINE** *thread* (糸). A helpful way to remember this character is to visualize 业 as extremely **FINE FIBERS** stretched upon the spear-loom. ☞ 戯 2007, 綴 2009 |
| 糸 120 | |
| 纖 | |
| 1289 | |
| 常 17 | |

534

| | | |
|---|---|---|
| **緻** チ | **FINE** | 精緻な せいちな minute, subtle, nice........0976<br>細緻な さいちな minute, meticulous........0239<br>○緻密な ちみつな close, minute, precise.....1383<br>巧緻な こうちな exquisite, elaborate........1047 |

| 2009<br>糸 120<br><br>1283<br>常 16 | *Thread* (糸) + *bring about* (致, review 0251 if necessary): let this suggest the deliberate process of stretching thread until it becomes **FINE**. ☞ 繊 2008 |
|---|---|

| | | |
|---|---|---|
| **嘘** キョ うそ | **LIE, fib** | ○嘘をつく うそをつく tell a lie<br>嘘つき うそつき liar |

| 2010<br>口 30<br><br><br>外 14 | Here we observe a *mouth* (口) speaking a *falsity* (虚): **LIE**. |
|---|---|

| | | |
|---|---|---|
| **噂** ソン うわさ | **RUMOR, gossip** | ○噂を流す うわさをながす spread rumors ....1059<br>噂話 うわさばなし gossip ..................0053 |

| 2011<br>口 30<br><br>噂<br>0652<br>名 15 | 尊 means HONOR/esteem (see 0802), but depicts an *outstretched arm* (寸) holding aloft a *ceremonial liquor bottle* (酋, shown in non-standardized form in the next two entries). Here, the *esteemed* figures who have taken from the bottle speak **gossip** and **RUMORS** from their liquor-loosened *mouths* (口). |
|---|---|

| | | |
|---|---|---|
| **樽** ソン たる | **BARREL** | ○ ビールの樽 ビールのたる keg of beer<br>酒樽 さかだる wine barrel/cask.............0797 |

| 2012<br>木 75<br><br><br>0992<br>名 16 | This time, picture the *outstretched arm* (寸) refilling the *ceremonial liquor bottle* (酋) from a *wooden* (木) **BARREL**. |
|---|---|

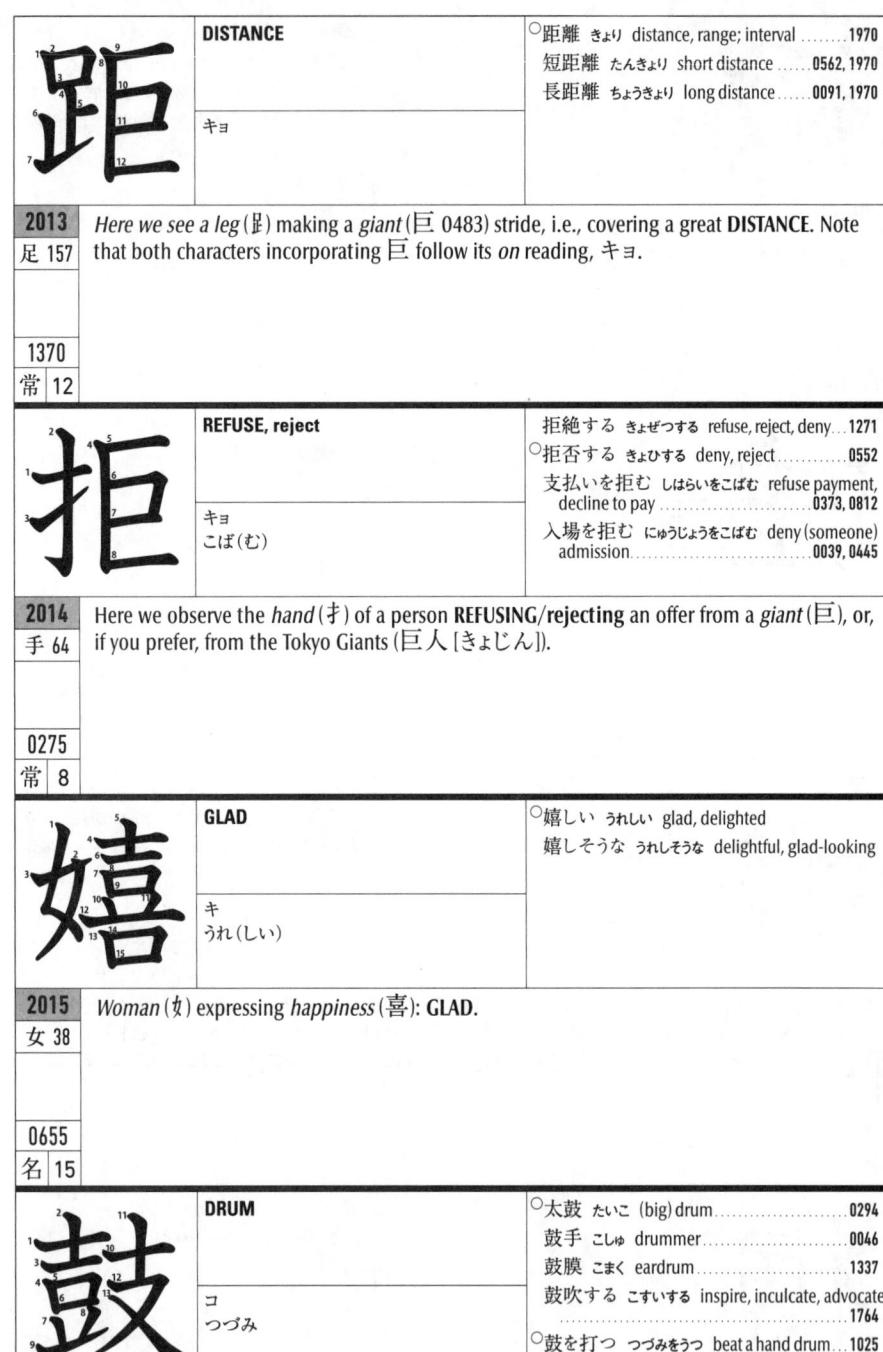

| | **DISTANCE** | ○距離 きょり distance, range; interval ..........1970 |
|---|---|---|
| | | 短距離 たんきょり short distance ......**0562, 1970** |
| | | 長距離 ちょうきょり long distance ......**0091, 1970** |
| | キョ | |

| **2013** | *Here we see a leg* (⻊) *making a giant* (巨 0483) *stride, i.e., covering a great* **DISTANCE**. Note that both characters incorporating 巨 follow its *on* reading, キョ. |
|---|---|
| 足 157 | |
| **1370** | |
| 常 12 | |

| | **REFUSE, reject** | 拒絶する きょぜつする refuse, reject, deny ...**1271** |
|---|---|---|
| | | ○拒否する きょひする deny, reject ............**0552** |
| | | 支払いを拒む しはらいをこばむ refuse payment, decline to pay ..........................**0373, 0812** |
| | キョ こば(む) | 入場を拒む にゅうじょうをこばむ deny (someone) admission ............................**0039, 0445** |

| **2014** | Here we observe the *hand* (扌) of a person **REFUSING/rejecting** an offer from a *giant* (巨), or, if you prefer, from the Tokyo Giants (巨人 [きょじん]). |
|---|---|
| 手 64 | |
| **0275** | |
| 常 8 | |

| | **GLAD** | ○嬉しい うれしい glad, delighted |
|---|---|---|
| | | 嬉しそうな うれしそうな delightful, glad-looking |
| | キ うれ(しい) | |

| **2015** | *Woman* (女) *expressing happiness* (喜): **GLAD**. |
|---|---|
| 女 38 | |
| **0655** | |
| 名 15 | |

| | **DRUM** | ○太鼓 たいこ (big) drum ......................**0294** |
|---|---|---|
| | | 鼓手 こしゅ drummer ........................**0046** |
| | | 鼓膜 こまく eardrum ........................**1337** |
| | コ つづみ | 鼓吹する こすいする inspire, inculcate, advocate ..................................................**1764** |
| | | ○鼓を打つ つづみをうつ beat a hand drum ...**1025** |

| **2016** | Recall the image of 支 0373 as a hand holding up a *branch* (支). Now imagine the hand beating the branch against the *drum* at the left (壴, introduced back at 喜 1212). |
|---|---|
| 鼓 207 | |
| 皷 | |
| **1589** | |
| 常 13 | |

**STANDING TREE**

ジュ
き*

○樹木 じゅもく tree; trees and shrubs .........0028
樹脂 じゅし resin...........................1994
樹液 じゅえき sap ...........................0468
植樹 しょくじゅ tree planting.................0840
街路樹 がいろじゅ roadside trees......0992, 0788

| 2017 木 75 | Recall from 喜 1212 that 壴 is a drum that stands on its side. Here picture the *outstretched arm* (寸) standing up the drum this way. With 木 *tree*, this provides an intuitive image for **STANDING TREE**—i.e., a tree that has not been cut down. ☞ 膨 2018 |
|---|---|
| 0987 常 16 | |

**EXPAND**

ボウ
ふく(らむ) ふく(れる)

○膨大 ぼうだい swelling, expansion ..........0033
膨満する ぼうまんする be inflated..........0179
○膨れる ふくれる expand, swell
着膨れる きぶくれる be thickly clad ........0938
膨れっ面 ふくれっつら sullen/sulky look....0175

| 2018 肉 130 | *Flesh* (月) fully stretched out like the skin of a *drum* (壴). S14-16 emphasize the outward expansion: **EXPAND.** ☞ 樹 2017 |
|---|---|
| 0999 常 16 | |

**SWELL**

チョウ

○膨脹 ぼうちょう expansion, swelling; growth, increase.................................2018

| 2019 肉 130 | *Flesh* (月) growing "*long*er" (長), i.e., **SWELLING**. Removed from the Joyo list in 2010. ☞ 腫 2022 |
|---|---|
| 0916 外 12 | |

¹ **SPREAD (out), extend (over)**
² **STRAIN, stretch**

チョウ
は(る) -は(り) -ば(り)

①膨張 ぼうちょう expansion, swelling; growth, increase.................................2018
¹ 伸張 しんちょう expansion, elongation ......0873
² 張力 ちょうりょく tension, tensile strength ...0084
○張る はる spread (out), extend (over); stretch, strain
² 頑張る がんばる be tenacious, hang in there 1918

| 2020 弓 57 | A *bow* (弓) being stretched to the fullest possible *length* (長): **SPREAD/STRETCH**. Note that kanji with the phonetic component 長 are read チョウ. |
|---|---|
| 0431 常 11 | |

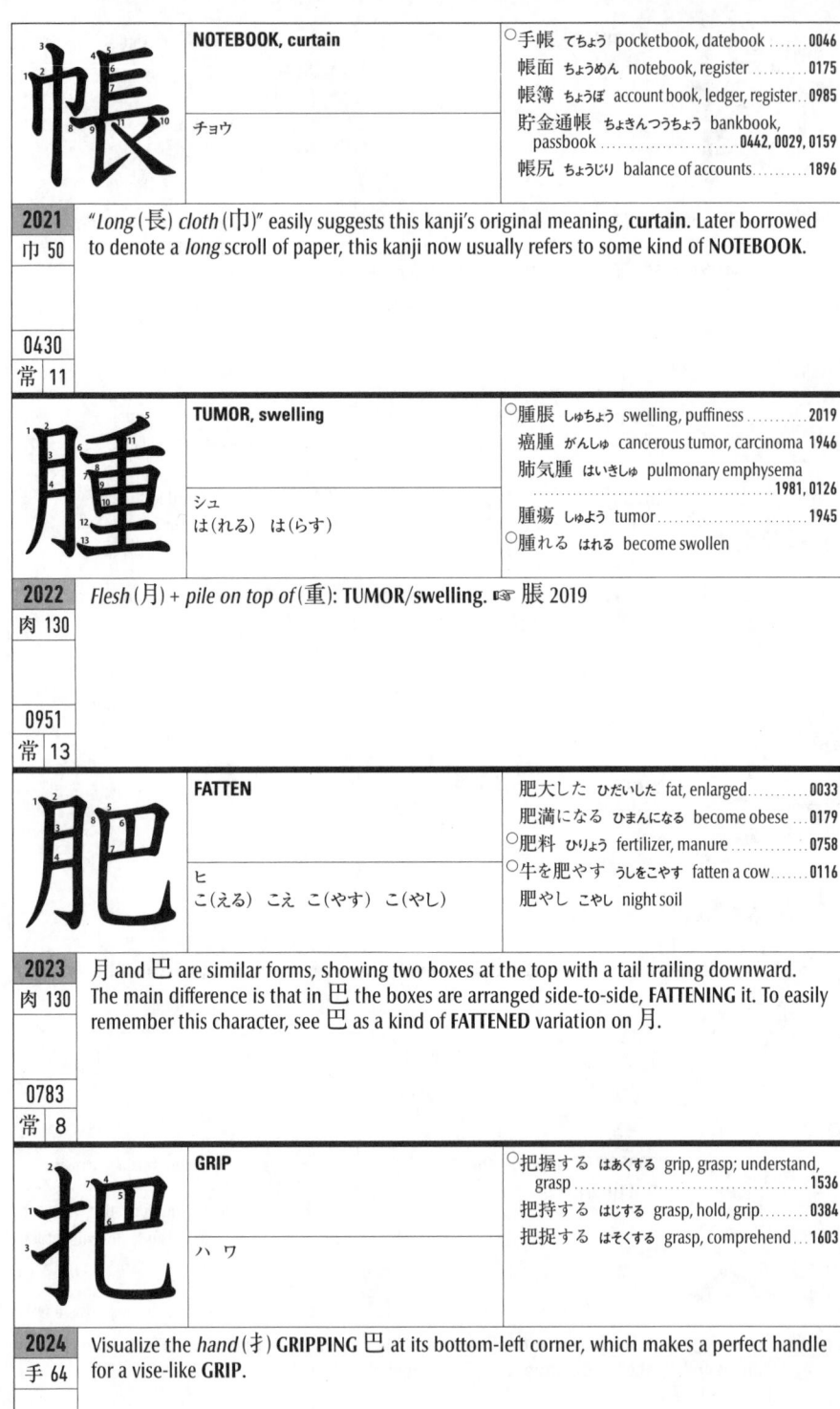

| | NOTEBOOK, curtain | |
|---|---|---|
| 帳 | チョウ | ○手帳 てちょう pocketbook, datebook .......0046<br>帳面 ちょうめん notebook, register ..........0175<br>帳簿 ちょうぼ account book, ledger, register..0985<br>貯金通帳 ちょきんつうちょう bankbook,<br>passbook ........................0442, 0029, 0159<br>帳尻 ちょうじり balance of accounts..........1896 |

| 2021<br>巾 50<br><br><br>0430<br>常 11 | "*Long* (長) *cloth* (巾)" easily suggests this kanji's original meaning, **curtain**. Later borrowed to denote a *long* scroll of paper, this kanji now usually refers to some kind of **NOTEBOOK**. |
|---|---|

| | TUMOR, swelling | |
|---|---|---|
| 腫 | シュ<br>は(れる) は(らす) | ○腫脹 しゅちょう swelling, puffiness ...........2019<br>癌腫 がんしゅ cancerous tumor, carcinoma 1946<br>肺気腫 はいきしゅ pulmonary emphysema<br>..........................................1981, 0126<br>腫瘍 しゅよう tumor.........................1945<br>○腫れる はれる become swollen |

| 2022<br>肉 130<br><br><br>0951<br>常 13 | *Flesh* (月) + *pile on top of* (重): **TUMOR**/swelling. ☞ 脹 2019 |
|---|---|

| | FATTEN | |
|---|---|---|
| 肥 | ヒ<br>こ(える) こえ こ(やす) こ(やし) | 肥大した ひだいした fat, enlarged............0033<br>肥満になる ひまんになる become obese ...0179<br>○肥料 ひりょう fertilizer, manure ..............0758<br>○牛を肥やす うしをこやす fatten a cow.......0116<br>肥やし こやし night soil |

| 2023<br>肉 130<br><br><br>0783<br>常 8 | 月 and 巴 are similar forms, showing two boxes at the top with a tail trailing downward. The main difference is that in 巴 the boxes are arranged side-to-side, **FATTENING** it. To easily remember this character, see 巴 as a kind of **FATTENED** variation on 月. |
|---|---|

| | GRIP | |
|---|---|---|
| 把 | ハ ワ | ○把握する はあくする grip, grasp; understand,<br>grasp ......................................1536<br>把持する はじする grasp, hold, grip........0384<br>把捉する はそくする grasp, comprehend...1603 |

| 2024<br>手 64<br><br><br>0222<br>常 7 | Visualize the *hand* (扌) **GRIPPING** 巴 at its bottom-left corner, which makes a perfect handle for a vise-like **GRIP**. |
|---|---|

| | **BOAST** | ○誇張する こちょうする exaggerate, overstate, magnify .................................................. **2020** |
|---|---|---|
| | | 誇示 こじ ostentation, showing off.......... **0311** |
| | | 誇大 こだい exaggeration, magnification... **0033** |
| | コ | ○誇る ほこる boast, take pride in |
| | ほこ(る) | 誇らしい ほこらしい proud |

| **2025** | We have seen S12–13 in 巧 1047, etc. Here see it, and the stroke above it, as a kind of ladder climbed by 大 *big*, representing the idea of growing too big, as in "too big for one's boots." The whole kanji, then, suggests "*talk* (言) too big," or **BOAST**. |
|---|---|
| 言 149 | |
| **1381** | |
| 常 13 | |

| | **LOOK OVER, view** | ○一覧 いちらん a glance, a reading; summary... **0002** |
|---|---|---|
| | | 御覧下さい ごらんください Please look/try ........................................................ **0862, 0040** |
| | | 観覧車 かんらんしゃ Ferris wheel ...... **1128, 0125** |
| | ラン | 展覧する てんらんする exhibit, show........ **0880** |
| | | 閲覧室 えつらんしつ reading room .... **1199, 0253** |

| **2026** | At 臨 0855 we learned to see ⼂ as a *forward gaze*, emphasized here by the stroke that follows below it. With 見 to emphasize the same idea, see the *retainer* (臣) **LOOKING OVER/ viewing.** ☞ 監 2027, 賢 2032, 腎 2033 |
|---|---|
| 見 147 | |
| 覽 | |
| **2485** | |
| 常 17 | |

| | **OVERSEE** | ○監視する かんしする watch, keep under observation ......................................... **0623** |
|---|---|---|
| | | 監査 かんさ inspection; inspector, supervisor ........................................................ **1514** |
| | | 監修 かんしゅう (editorial) supervision ...... **1676** |
| | カン | 監獄 かんごく prison........................... **0737** |
| | | 監房 かんぼう cell, ward...................... **1886** |

| **2027** | (Continuing from the previous entry) Here the *retainer* keeps watch over a *plate* (皿): **OVERSEE.** ☞ 覧 2026, 臨 0855 |
|---|---|
| 皿 108 | |
| **2483** | |
| 常 15 | |

| | **¹ APPRAISE** **² REFER TO** | ¹ 鑑賞 かんしょう appreciation, enjoyment ... **0322** |
|---|---|---|
| | | ①鑑定する かんていする appraise, estimate, identify................................................ **0045** |
| | | ² 鑑みる かんがみる take into account; heed |
| | カン | ②年鑑 ねんかん yearbook.................. **0117** |
| | かんが(みる) | ² 名鑑 めいかん list, directory................. **0269** |

| **2028** | In the next four entries, 監 will suggest *keeping watch over* or *looking to*. This entry indicates a kind of official record or standard (recorded on 金 *metal*) that the retainer *looks to* (i.e., **REFERS TO**) in order to **APPRAISE** or identify something. |
|---|---|
| 金 167 | |
| **1580** | |
| 常 23 | |

| 艦 | **WARSHIP** | 軍艦 ぐんかん warship.........................0583 |
|---|---|---|
| | | 艦隊 かんたい squadron, fleet ............0586 |
| | | 戦艦 せんかん battleship....................0461 |
| | カン | 航空母艦 こうくうぼかん aircraft carrier |
| | | .............................**1640, 0398, 0104** |
| | | ○潜水艦 せんすいかん submarine ......**1168, 0027** |

| **2029** | Boat (舟) + keep watch over (監): **WARSHIP**. |
|---|---|
| 舟 137 | |
| **1303** | |
| 常 21 | |

| 濫 | **EXCESSIVE** | 濫造 らんぞう excessive production, careless |
|---|---|---|
| | | manufacture.............................0699 |
| | | 濫伐 らんばつ overcutting of forests.........1361 |
| | ラン | 濫費 らんぴ extravagant spending ..........1189 |
| | | ○濫用する らんようする abuse, use to excess 0047 |
| | | 濫獲 らんかく excessive hunting/fishing....1659 |

| **2030** | Here picture the retainer in an observation tower, *keeping watch over* (監) rising flood *waters* (氵): **EXCESSIVE**. 濫 is interchangeable with 乱 0380 in compounds for which the latter means "excessive." ☞ 乱 0380 |
|---|---|
| 水 85 | |
| **0713** | |
| 常 18 | |

| 藍 | **INDIGO** | 青藍 せいらん indigo blue....................0130 |
|---|---|---|
| | | 藍色 あいいろ indigo blue....................0528 |
| | | 藍に染める あいにそめる dye deep blue....1174 |
| | ラン | ○藍染め あいぞめ indigo dye .................1174 |
| | あい | |

| **2031** | Here picture the retainer *keeping watch over* (監) a *plant* (艹) of a color so beautiful that he can't take his eyes off it: **INDIGO**. Now practice writing the last five entries in alternation, learning to determine their meanings from the variable component. |
|---|---|
| 艸 140 | |
| **2108** | |
| 常 18 | |

| 賢 | **WISE, intelligent** | ○賢明な けんめいな wise, intelligent; sensible |
|---|---|---|
| | | ..............................................0024 |
| | | 賢哲 けんてつ sage, wise person ............1703 |
| | ケン | 良妻賢母 りょうさいけんぼ good wife and wise |
| | かしこ(い) | mother...........................**0285, 1457, 0104** |
| | | ○賢い かしこい wise, intelligent |
| | | 悪賢い わるがしこい sly, cunning ............0546 |

| **2032** | In the next four entries, the *retainer* (臣) serves his master not with his eye, but with his *hand* (又). In this entry, he **WISELY** increases his master's fortune by stashing away *shells* (貝, i.e., *money*). ☞ 覧 2026, 腎 2033 |
|---|---|
| 貝 154 | |
| **2472** | |
| 常 16 | |

|  | **KIDNEY**<br><br>ジン | ○腎臓 じんぞう kidneys.........................1974<br>腎臓結石 じんぞうけっせき kidney stones<br>........................1974, 0516, 0403<br>腎炎 じんえん nephritis, kidney inflammation<br>........................1976<br>○肝腎な かんじんな vital, essential, main.....1980 |

| 2033<br>肉 130 | Eager to save his master's life, the *retainer*(臣) *hands*(又) him a spare *body part*(月): one of his **KIDNEYS**. ☞ 賢 2032, 覧 2026 |
| 2465<br>常 13 | |

|  | **FIRM, solid**<br><br>ケン<br>かた(い) -がた(い) | 堅牢な けんろうな solid, durable ............1737<br>○堅実な けんじつな steady, sound, reliable...0499<br>中堅 ちゅうけん mainstay, nucleus (of a company)<br>........................0035<br>○堅い かたい firm, hard<br>手堅い てがたい steady; safe; trustworthy...0046 |

| 2034<br>土 32 | Once more proving his all-around utility, the *retainer*(臣) uses his *hand*(又) to solidify the *earth*(土) foundation of his master's home: **FIRM/solid**. |
| 2457<br>常 12 | |

|  | **¹ TIGHTEN**<br>**² EXIGENT**<br><br>キン | ¹緊張 きんちょう tension, strain.................2020<br>¹緊縛する きんばくする bind tightly...........0984<br>¹緊縮 きんしゅく contraction; strict economy 0875<br>²緊迫した きんばくした tense, strained .......1182<br>②緊急な きんきゅうな urgent, pressing, emergent<br>........................0971 |

| 2035<br>糸 120 | Here the *retainer*(臣) uses his *hand*(又) to **TIGHTEN** a loose *cord*(糸). M2 **EXIGENT** is an extended meaning. Now practice writing the last four entries in alternation, and distinguishing their meanings based on the grapheme that appears at the bottom. ☞ 繁 1575 |
| 2471<br>常 15 | |

| 勃 | **SUDDENLY RISING**<br><br>ボツ | 勃然と ぼつぜんと suddenly .................0760<br>○勃発する ぼっぱつする break out, suddenly arise ........................0148<br>勃興 ぼっこう sudden rise, ascendancy .....0505<br>勃起する ぼっきする well up; stiffen, have an erection........................0430<br>勃起障害 ぼっきしょうがい erectile dysfunction<br>........................0430, 1461, 0413 |

| 2036<br>力 19 | Interpret 孛 as a *child*(子) hiding under the *ground*(土, which here is in fact 十 and 冖). Now picture the child **SUDDENLY RISING** from his underground hiding place and taking up the *plow*(力). Do not confuse 孛 with 孝 0630. |
| 1317<br>常 9 | |

| | **WORK HARD; urge on** | ○奨励 しょうれい encouragement, promotion 0615 |
| | | 激励する げきれいする encourage, urge.... 0575 |
| | | 奮励 ふんれい strenuous efforts............1656 |
| | レイ | ○勉強に励む べんきょうにはげむ study hard |
| | はげ(む) はげ(ます) | ..........1274, 0423 |
| | | 病人を励ます びょうにんをはげます cheer up an |
| | | invalid...........................0617, 0015 |

| 2037 | Here picture *ten thousand* (万) workers emerging from a tunnel inside a *cliff* (厂), pushing |
| 力 19 | the *plows* (力) with which they have been **WORKING HARD** to bore the tunnel. This charac- |
| 勵 | ter can also be used to express the idea of **urging** people **on** to such laborious efforts. |
| 1035 | ☞ 栃 2038 |
| 常 7 | |

| | **HORSE CHESTNUT (tree)** | 栃木県 とちぎけん Tochigi prefecture |
| | | ..........................0028, 0844 |
| | とち | |

| 2038 | This kanji and the next one were among those added to the Joyo list for the specific reason |
| 木 75 | that they are used in names of prefectures. Because they are used almost exclusively in these |
| 櫔 | names (VI in both entries), your time is better spent learning to read the names than learning |
| 0809 | these kanji for their own sake. ☞ 励 2037 |
| 常 9 | |

| | **BRIAR, thorn** | 茨城県 いばらきけん Ibaraki prefecture |
| | | ..........................1298, 0844 |
| | | 茨の冠 いばらのかんむり crown of thorns ...1969 |
| | いばら | |

| 2039 | (See previous entry) As with 恣 1454, the form used here differs slightly from 次, but we can |
| 艸 140 | safely ignore this difference. |
| | |
| 1952 | |
| 常 9 | |

| | **ENVIOUS** | 羨望 せんぼう envy, jealousy.............1066 |
| | | 羨む うらやむ envy, be jealous |
| | | ○羨ましい うらやましい envious, jealous; enviable |
| | セン | |
| | うらや(む) うらや(ましい) | |

| 2040 | Picture the *sheep* (羊) coveting his neighbor's (i.e., the *next* person's) possessions: **ENVIOUS.** |
| 羊 123 | For all intents and purposes, it is fine to conflate 次 with 次 *next*. ☞ 盗 1304 |
| 羨 | |
| 2055 | |
| 常 13 | |

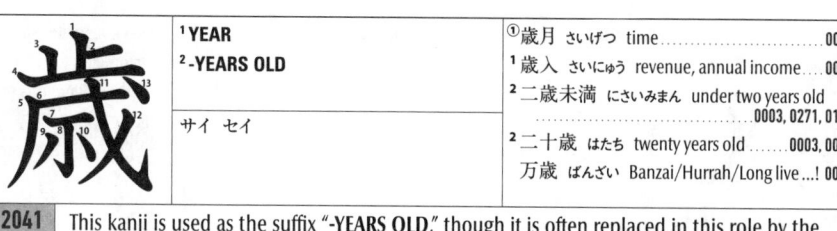

| 歳 | ¹YEAR<br>²-YEARS OLD<br><br>サイ セイ | ①歳月 さいげつ time.............................0023<br>¹ 歳入 さいにゅう revenue, annual income....0039<br>² 二歳未満 にさいみまん under two years old<br>.............................0003, 0271, 0179<br>² 二十歳 はたち twenty years old .......0003, 0005<br>万歳 ばんざい Banzai/Hurrah/Long live ...! 0018 |
|---|---|---|

| 2041<br>止 77<br><br>2190<br>常 13 | This kanji is used as the suffix "-YEARS OLD," though it is often replaced in this role by the homophonous 才 0652. It indicates the year-by-year aging process by placing 小 at the bottom (for childhood), 戌 above that (for adulthood, recalling 成人 [せいじん, adult]), and finally 止 at the very top, for the end of one's YEARS. ☞ 戚 2042 |
|---|---|

| 戚 | KIN<br><br>セキ | ○親戚 しんせき relative..........................0276 |
|---|---|---|

| 2042<br>戈 62<br><br>2997<br>常 11 | Interpret 尗 (not to be confused with 步 0679) as an image of older (上) and younger (小) *relatives* together. With 戌 *guided spear*, it suggests the passing on of duties from one generation to another within a KIN group. To distinguish from 歳 above: while one's aging process eventually *stops* (止), one's KIN group does not (no 止). ☞ 歳 2041 |
|---|---|

| 叔 | YOUNGER SIBLING OF PARENT<br><br>シュク | ○叔父 おじ (=しゅくふ) uncle (younger than one's parent) [cf. 伯 1184]..........................0100<br>○叔母 おば (=しゅくぼ) aunt (younger than one's parent) [cf. 伯 1184]..........................0104 |
|---|---|---|

| 2043<br>又 29<br><br>1168<br>常 8 | Because this kanji refers to both uncles and aunts that are younger than one's parent, we use "YOUNGER SIBLING OF PARENT" as its keyword. However, to refer to it more easily when it appears inside the three kanji that follow, we'll use *uncle* as the grapheme name. In this entry, we have "*relative* (尗) who lends you a *hand* (又)": uncle/aunt (YOUNGER SIBLING OF PARENT). ☞ 伯 1184 |
|---|---|

| 淑 | GRACEFUL, refined<br><br>シュク | 淑徳 しゅくとく feminine grace, womanly virtues 1668<br>淑女 しゅくじょ lady, gentlewoman...........0093<br>○貞淑 ていしゅく chastity, female virtue.......1867 |
|---|---|---|

| 2044<br>水 85<br><br>0483<br>常 11 | Here we add *water* (氵) to *uncle* (叔) to suggest an *uncle* of purity and refinement: GRACEFUL/refined. |
|---|---|

**LONESOME, desolate; elegant simplicity**

ジャク　セキ
さび　さび(しい)　さび(れる)

○静寂　せいじゃく　silence, quietness, stillness **0978**
閑寂　かんじゃく　quietness, tranquility ........**1365**
俳句の寂　はいくのさび　the elegant simplicity of
haiku ..................................................**0740, 0166**
○寂しい　さびしい　lonesome, desolate

| 2045 | *Uncle* (叔) by himself at *home* (宀): **LONESOME**. |
| 宀 40 | |
| 1982 | |
| 常 11 | |

¹ **SUPERVISE; urge on**
² **COMMANDER**

トク

①監督　かんとく　supervision; manager, director
.................................................................**2027**
¹ 督励する　とくれいする　urge on (one's subordi-
nates)...................................................**2037**
¹ 督促する　とくそくする　urge, press, demand. **1604**
² 提督　ていとく　admiral...........................**1679**
² 総督　そうとく　governor-general, viceroy.....**0557**

| 2046 | *Uncle* (叔) looking after the children with a watchful *eye* (目): **SUPERVISE; COMMANDER**. |
| 目 109 | |
| 2437 | |
| 常 13 | |

¹ **SLAVE**
² **GUY**

ド
やつ*

¹ 農奴　のうど　serf........................................**0511**
①守銭奴　しゅせんど　miser...............**0648, 1585**
² ずるい奴　ずるいやつ　[slang] sneaky guy,
scammer
②奴等　やつら　[slang] those guys, they........**0393**

| 2047 | Picture this *woman* (女) as an evil mistress who uses her *hand* (又) to slap a **SLAVE**. M2 **GUY** |
| 女 38 | reflects this kanji's use as an informal way to refer to a male. |
| 0164 | |
| 常 5 | |

**EXERT**

ド
つと(める)

○努力　どりょく　endeavor, effort, exertion .....**0084**
努力家　どりょくか　hard worker.........**0084, 0219**
○努める　つとめる　endeavor, try hard
努めて　つとめて　with effort, as much as possible
極力努める　きょくりょくつとめる　do one's best
.................................................................**1712, 0084**

| 2048 | (Continuing from the previous entry) Slapped by the mistress, the *slave* (奴) **EXERTS** himself |
| 力 19 | with the *plow* (力). Note that the kanji incorporating 奴 follow its *on-yomi*, ド. ☞ 怒 2049 |
| 2204 | |
| 常 7 | |

| | GET ANGRY | 憤怒 ふんど (=ふんぬ) anger, rage, resentment ................ 1815 |
|---|---|---|
| | | ○激怒 げきど wild rage, fury .................. 0575 |
| | ド | 喜怒哀楽 きどあいらく joy and anger; emotion .......... 1212, 1860, 0302 |
| | いか(る) おこ(る) | ○怒る いかる get angry |
| | | ○怒る おこる get angry; scold |

| 2049 | (Continuing from 2047–48) Slapped *slave* (奴)'s *heart* (心): **ANGRY**. Do not confuse with the name-use kanji 恕 MAGNANIMITY. ☞ 努 2048 |
|---|---|
| 心 61 | |
| 2228 | |
| 常 9 | |

| | UNDERLING | ○奴隷 どれい slave, servant ................ 2047 |
|---|---|---|
| | | 隷従 れいじゅう slavery, servitude; servile obedience ................ 0869 |
| | レイ | 隷属 れいぞく subordination .............. 1872 |
| | | 隷書 れいしょ angular style of writing Chinese characters ................ 0079 |

| 2050 | Recall 隶 *hand spraying water from hose*, introduced at 逮 1608. Now picture 士 *military man* as a man in position of authority, standing on top of an *altar* (示, which we might imagine here simply as some kind of raised platform) from which he hoses down his **UNDERLINGS**. ☞ 款 2051 |
|---|---|
| 隶 171 | |
| 隷 | |
| 1563 | |
| 常 16 | |

| | ¹ ARTICLE, subsection | ¹条款 じょうかん article, stipulation, provision 0119 |
|---|---|---|
| | ² FRIENDLY RELATIONS | ¹約款 やっかん article, stipulation, provision 0170 |
| | | ¹定款 ていかん articles of association, company contract ................ 0045 |
| | カン | ①借款 しゃっかん loan ................ 1220 |
| | | ²交款 こうかん exchange of cordialities ...... 0102 |

| 2051 | (Continuing from the previous entry) Now picture the *military man* (士) standing on the raised platform and reading out (of a *wide-open mouth*, 欠) the **ARTICLES** of a treaty of **FRIENDLY RELATIONS** between himself and his underlings. ☞ 隷 2050 |
|---|---|
| 欠 76 | |
| 1516 | |
| 常 12 | |

| | HUSK, shell | ○地殻 ちかく crust (of the earth) .............. 0187 |
|---|---|---|
| | | 甲殻類 こうかくるい Crustacea .......... 1521, 0310 |
| | | ○貝殻 かいがら shell ................ 0082 |
| | カク | 吸い殻 すいがら cigarette butt .............. 1763 |
| | から がら | 卵の殻 たまごのから eggshell ............. 1141 |

| 2052 | Simplify the next two entries by ignoring 士, 冖, and 殳, which are held constant, and focusing on the variable component at the lower left. Since 殻 refers to a grain's **HUSK** (or a shellfish's **shell**), while 穀 refers to the **GRAIN** itself, associate 禾 *rice* (next entry) with GRAIN, and 几 *tablecloth* (here) with the **HUSK** that covers it. ☞ 穀 2053 |
|---|---|
| 殳 79 | |
| 殻 | |
| 1354 | |
| 常 11 | |

**GRAIN, cereal**

コク

○穀物 こくもつ grain, cereals ................. 0172
穀類 こくるい grains ............................ 0310
五穀 ごこく the five cereals, (staple) grains .. 0007
脱穀機 だっこくき thresher ............. 1198, 0473
穀倉 こくそう granary, grain elevator ........ 0696

| 2053 | (See previous entry) ☞ 穀 2052 |
| 禾 115 | |
| 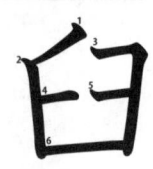 | |
| 1620 | |
| 常 14 | |

**MORTAR**

キュウ
うす

○臼歯 きゅうし molar ............................ 0674
脱臼する だっきゅうする dislocate ........... 1198
○石臼 いしうす stone mortar ................... 0403

| 2054 | You have already seen this grapheme in some old forms, including those of 児 0772 (兒) and |
| 臼 134 | 挿 1597 (插). For the few modern forms in which it still appears (such as 毀 below), it is suf- |
| | ficient to use 臼 as a visual clue. By itself, it means **MORTAR** (i.e., grinding stone). |
| 2957 | |
| 常 6 | |

**BREAK, chip**

キ
こぼ(れる)*  こわ(れる)*

○毀損する きそんする damage, harm; defame
.......................................................... 1595
毀れる こぼれる be chipped/nicked
毀れる こわれる break, get damaged [cf. 壊 1666]

| 2055 | 臼 resembles a **BROKEN** object, lying on the *ground* (土). Picture for a moment this object |
| 土 32 | before it was **BROKEN**, then imagine using this *lance* (殳) to **BREAK** it. |
| 1592 | |
| 常 13 | |

**¹ HONEST**
**² CHEAP**

レン

¹ 廉直 れんちょく integrity, uprightness ........ 0839
¹ 廉潔な れんけつな honest, incorruptible ... 1570
①破廉恥な はれんちな shameless, infamous,
　impudent ......................................... 0596, 1670
②廉価な れんかな cheap, low-priced ......... 0548
² 廉売 れんばい bargain sale .................... 0353

| 2056 | "*Shelter* (广) + *combine* (兼, see 1006)" suggests sharing a dwelling, an apt image for M2 |
| 广 53 | **CHEAP**. Associate this with M1 **HONEST** via the idea of honest, frugal living. |
| 2720 | |
| 常 13 | |

| | SICKLE | 大鎌 おおがま scythe .........................0033 |
|---|---|---|
| | かま | 鎌倉 かまくら Kamakura [city in Kanagawa prefecture; seat of national government, 1185–1333] ..............................0696 |
| | | 鎌倉時代 かまくらじだい Kamakura period [Japanese historical era, approx. 1185–1333] ..........................0696, 0383, 0071 |

| **2057** | *Combine* (兼) two pieces of *metal* (a blade and a handle) into a **SICKLE**. |
|---|---|
| 金 167 | |
| 1572 | |
| 常 18 | |

| | DISLIKE | 嫌悪 けんお hatred, dislike, repugnance .....0546 |
|---|---|---|
| | | ○機嫌 きげん mood, temper, disposition ......0473 |
| | | 交際を嫌う こうさいをきらう shun society ...........................0102, 0638 |
| | ケン ゲン | 巨人が嫌い きょじんがきらい hate the Giants (base-ball team)......................0483, 0015 |
| | きら(う) きら(い) いや | 嫌な気持ち いやなきもち unpleasant feeling ...........................0126, 0384 |

| **2058** | *Women* (女), as this character would have it, **DISLIKE** *combining* (兼) things, i.e., doing two |
|---|---|
| 女 38 | things at the same time. |
| 0583 | |
| 常 13 | |

| | HUMBLE, modest | 謙虚な けんきょな humble, modest .........2003 |
|---|---|---|
| | | ○謙譲 けんじょう modesty, humility ...........1662 |
| | ケン | 謙譲語 けんじょうご humble language/speech forms................................1662, 0222 |

| **2059** | *Combining* (兼) *words* (言) (i.e., speaking in compressed language) is a sign of **HUMILITY**. |
|---|---|
| 言 149 | |
| 1461 | |
| 常 17 | |

| | HUMBLE, modest | ○謙遜 けんそん humility, modesty ............2059 |
|---|---|---|
| | | 謙遜語 けんそんご humble language/speech forms.............................2059, 0222 |
| | ソン | 不遜な ふそんな arrogant, insolent .........0049 |
| | | 遜色 そんしょく inferiority.....................0528 |

| **2060** | Picture a *grandchild* (孫 1079) driving a modest *truck* (辶): **HUMBLE/modest**. |
|---|---|
| 辵 162 | |
| 遜 | |
| 2786 | |
| 常 14 | |

| | **TURTLE** | ○亀甲 きっこう turtle's carapace, tortoiseshell ...... 1521 |
| | | ○亀裂 きれつ crack, fissure ...... 0720 |
| | | 海亀 うみがめ (sea) turtle ...... 0106 |
| | キ | ○亀の甲羅 かめのこうら turtle's carapace, |
| | かめ | tortoiseshell ...... 1521, 0896 |

| **2061** | The stylized but still recognizable result of what began as a drawing of a **TURTLE**. |
| 龜 213 | |
| 龜 | |
| 1826 | |
| 常 11 | |

| | **TRAIN, drill** | 練習 れんしゅう practice, training ...... 0420 |
| | | 試練 しれん trial, test, probation ...... 1028 |
| | | 訓練 くんれん training, drill ...... 1927 |
| | | 熟練 じゅくれん skill, dexterity ...... 1436 |
| | レン | ○練る ねる train, drill |
| | ね(る) ね(り)- | |

| **2062** | Before being simplified, the next two entries contained 柬, not 東, which explains why they |
| 糸 120 | are read レン, not トウ. To keep things simple, we will keep using the grapheme meaning *all* |
| 練 | *the way through*, which in the present entry implies a thorough process of improving *thread* |
| | (糸) or the cloth made from it. Associate this thorough process of improvement with the |
| 1256 | figurative senses **TRAIN** or drill. |
| 常 14 | |

| | **REFINE; train** | 錬金術 れんきんじゅつ alchemy ...... 0029, 0993 |
| | | 錬鉄 れんてつ wrought iron ...... 0564 |
| | | 精錬 せいれん refining, smelting; tempering |
| | | ...... 0976 |
| | レン | 製錬 せいれん smelting ...... 0709 |
| | | ○錬成 れんせい training, drilling ...... 0070 |

| **2063** | (Continuing from the previous entry) Here, think of a similarly thoroughgoing process for |
| 金 167 | **REFINING** *metal* (金) *all the way through*. Like the previous entry, this kanji can refer to **train**- |
| 錬 | **ing** people in a skill or discipline. |
| 1553 | |
| 常 16 | |

| | **FORGE; train** | ○鍛錬する たんれんする temper, forge; train, |
| | | discipline ...... 2063 |
| | | 鍛工 たんこう metalworker, smith ...... 0108 |
| | タン | ○鍛える きたえる forge, temper; train, drill ...... 1641 |
| | きた(える) | 鍛え上げた腕 きたえあげたうで highly trained |
| | | skill ...... 0041, 0732 |
| | | 鍛冶 かじ forging, metalwork ...... 0951 |

| **2064** | *Metal* (金) + *step* (段 0521): suggests *metal*'s being **FORGED** in stages. Visualize the stages in |
| 金 167 | the four horizontal strokes at the left of 段. Like the previous two entries, this kanji can also |
| | mean **train**. |
| 1567 | |
| 常 17 | |

| | ¹ ORE<br>² MINE | ① 鉱石 こうせき ore, mineral ..................... 0403 |
|---|---|---|
| | | ¹ 鉄鉱 てっこう iron ore ......................... 0564 |
| | | ² 鉱坑 こうこう mine, shaft, pit ............... 1641 |
| | コウ | ² 鉱業 こうぎょう mining (industry) ........... 0498 |
| | | ² 炭鉱 たんこう coal mine ...................... 1647 |

**2065**
金 167

鑛

1525
常 13

"*Metal* (釒) + *wide* (広)" suggests the extensive course of a mineral vein: **ORE; MINE.**

---

| | COPPER, bronze | 銅鉱 どうこう copper ore ....................... 2065 |
|---|---|---|
| | | 銅線 どうせん copper wire ................... 0210 |
| | | 銅山 どうざん copper mine ................... 0037 |
| | ドウ | 銅像 どうぞう bronze statue/image .......... 1278 |
| | | ○銅メダル どうメダル bronze medal |

**2066**
金 167

Back at 筒 1838, we visualized 同 as a cross-sectional view of an insulated TUBE. Here, see it as a cross-section of an insulated electrical wire. 釒 refers to the *metal* used for the wire: **COPPER.**

1533
常 14

---

| | LEAD | 鉛毒 えんどく lead poisoning ............... 0133 |
|---|---|---|
| | | ○鉛筆 えんぴつ pencil ....................... 1605 |
| | | 鉛筆削り えんぴつけずり pencil sharpener |
| | エン | ........................................ 1605, 1292 |
| | なまり | 亜鉛 あえん zinc .............................. 0545 |
| | | ○鉛色 なまりいろ lead color; livid ............ 0528 |

**2067**
金 167

Review 船 0669. Here, *metal* (釒) is inserted into a *rolling hoop*: a **LEAD** pencil into a pencil sharpener.

1523
常 13

---

| | PIG IRON | ○銑鉄 せんてつ pig iron ....................... 0564 |
|---|---|---|
| | セン | |

**2068**
金 167

**PIG IRON** is iron at a stage of smelting *prior to* (先) becoming cast iron or steel. This kanji was removed from the Joyo Kanji List in 2010.

1538
外 14

| | STEEL | ○鋼鉄 こうてつ steel .......................... 0564 |
|---|---|---|
| | | 鋼板 こうはん (=こうばん) steel plate .......... 0924 |
| | | 鋼管 こうかん steel pipe/tubing ............. 1839 |
| | コウ | 製鋼 せいこう steel manufacture ............. 0709 |
| | はがね | ○鋼色 はがねいろ steel blue ................. 0528 |

| 2069 | *Metal* (釒) hard enough to bore through a *hill* (岡): **STEEL**. ☞ 鉄 0564 |
|---|---|
| 金 167 | |
| 1551 | |
| 常 16 | |

| | TOUGH, strong | 剛力 ごうりき Herculean strength; mountain carrier/guide ........................... 0084 |
|---|---|---|
| | | 金剛石 こんごうせき diamond ......... 0029, 0403 |
| | | ○剛健 ごうけん fortitude and vigor, sturdiness; manliness ........................ 1610 |
| | ゴウ | 剛直 ごうちょく moral courage, integrity ..... 0839 |
| | | 剛勇 ごうゆう bravery, prowess ............. 2005 |

| 2070 | A *sword* (刂) hacking through a *hill* (岡): **TOUGH/strong**. |
|---|---|
| 刀 18 | |
| 1495 | |
| 常 10 | |

| | ¹ ROPE ² MAIN POINTS | ¹ 綱渡り つなわたり tightrope walking/walker ........................... 0281 |
|---|---|---|
| | | ¹ 手綱 たづな bridle, reins .................... 0046 |
| | | ① 横綱 よこづな grand champion sumo wrestler ........................... 0916 |
| | コウ | ② 綱領 こうりょう main points, outline; summary ........................... 1922 |
| | つな | ² 要綱 ようこう outline, gist; general plan .... 0547 |

| 2071 | *Thread* (糸) for climbing a *hill* (岡): **ROPE**. Associate this with M2 **MAIN POINTS** via the idea of a central guiding line or principle. ☞ 網 2072 |
|---|---|
| 糸 120 | |
| 1253 | |
| 常 14 | |

| | NET | 漁網 ぎょもう fishing net .................. 0765 |
|---|---|---|
| | | 網状組織 もうじょうそしき network, reticulum ........................ 0616, 0264, 1088 |
| | | ○通信網 つうしんもう communications network ........................ 0159, 0063 |
| | モウ | 鉄道網 てつどうもう railway network ... 0564, 0158 |
| | あみ | ○金網 かなあみ wire netting, screen .......... 0029 |

| 2072 | Identical to the previous entry, except that *mountain* (山) is replaced here by *dead* (亡). Here, visualize S9-10 as two *dead* mosquitoes caught in a **NET**. Practice distinguishing 綱 and 網 based on their variable component, and associating that component with the meaning. ☞ 綱 2071 |
|---|---|
| 糸 120 | |
| 1255 | |
| 常 14 | |

**ROPE**

ジョウ
なわ

○ 縄文　じょうもん　straw-rope pattern............0101
縄文時代　じょうもんじだい　Jomon period [Japanese historical era, approx. 14,000–400 BCE]
..............................0101, 0383, 0071
○ 縄張り　なわばり　roping off; territory, turf ...2020
縄跳び　なわとび　rope jumping...............1831
沖縄　おきなわ　Okinawa (city and prefecture) 0645

| 2073 | Behold a long **ROPE** (乚) with two knots tied in it (田 and 田). Compare the right half of this character with 亀 2061. |
|---|---|
| 糸 120 | |

縄

1271
常 | 15

**BOWL**

ハチ　ハツ

火鉢　ひばち　brazier, hibachi...............0026
菓子鉢　かしばち　bowl for confectioneries
..............................0602, 0094
○ 植木鉢　うえきばち　flowerpot...........0840, 0028
鉢巻き　はちまき　headband................0458
お鉢　おはち　rice tub; one's turn

| 2074 | *Metal* (釒) *basis* (本), i.e., a metal object that supports from below: **BOWL**. |
|---|---|
| 金 167 | |

1524
常 | 13

**CHAIN**

サ
くさり

連鎖　れんさ　chain [as of reasoning], link, series
..............................0582
金鎖　きんぐさり　gold chain...............0029
○ 閉鎖する　へいさする　lock, close, shut.......0449
封鎖　ふうさ　blockade..................1837
鎖国　さこく　national isolation, exclusion of foreigners..........................0075

| 2075 | Visualize S10 and S11 as links in a *metal* **CHAIN** fastened around S9 to secure a valuable *shell* or, if you prefer, *money* (貝). ☞ 絆 2076 |
|---|---|
| 金 167 | |

1573
常 | 18

**BONDS, fetters**

ハン　バン
きずな

友愛の絆　ゆうあいのきずな　bonds of friendship
..............................0399, 0778
強い絆で結ばれている　つよいきずなでむすばれている　tied by strong bonds ..........0423, 0516

| 2076 | Visualize S7–8 as parts of a *rope* (糸) strung around the top of S11 to tie a man down: **BONDS/fetters**. ☞ 鎖 2075 |
|---|---|
| 糸 120 | |

1217
名 | 11

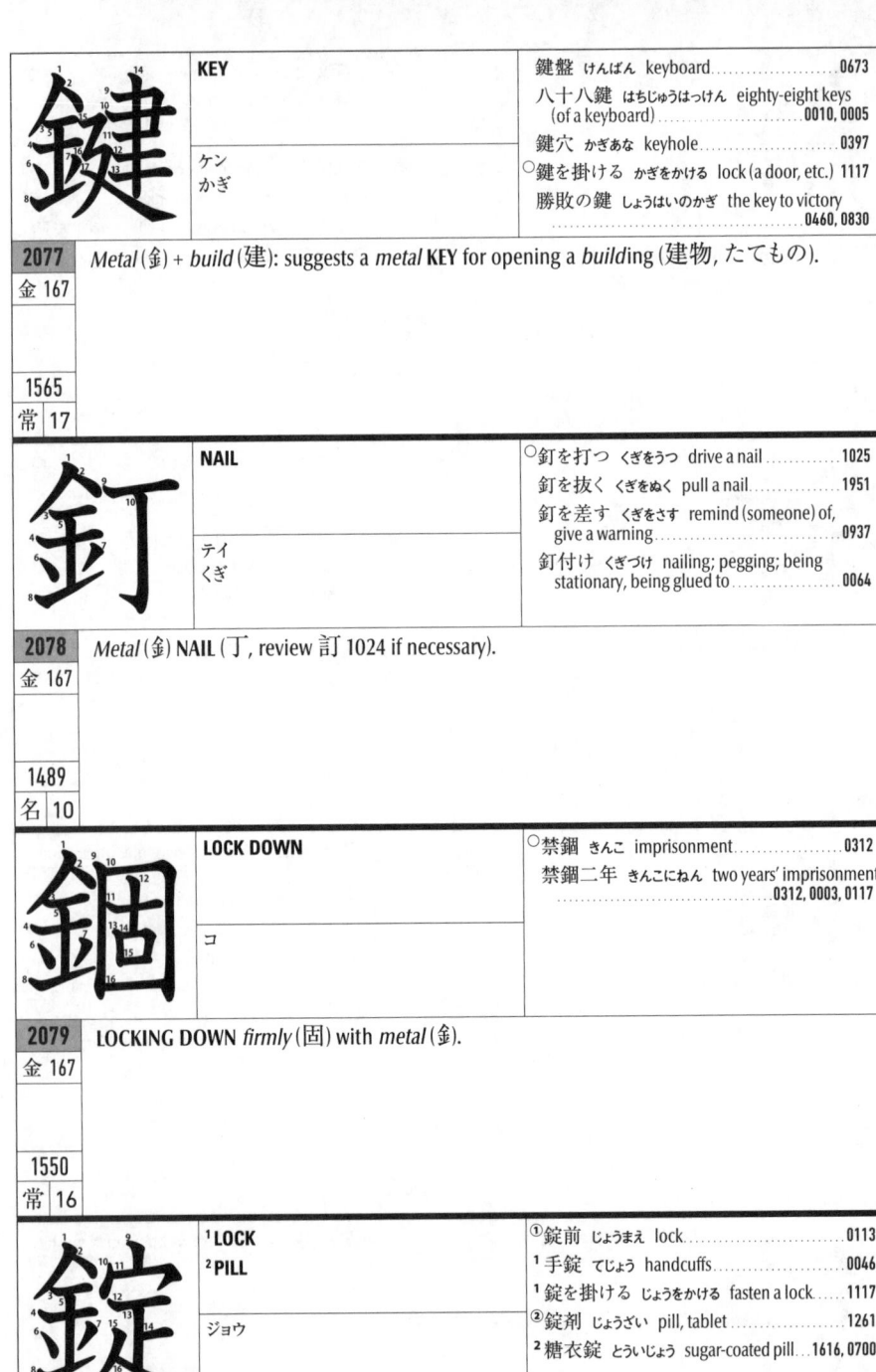

## 鍵 KEY

ケン
かぎ

鍵盤　けんばん　keyboard.....................0673
八十八鍵　はちじゅうはっけん　eighty-eight keys
　(of a keyboard)..........................0010, 0005
鍵穴　かぎあな　keyhole.......................0397
○鍵を掛ける　かぎをかける　lock (a door, etc.) 1117
勝敗の鍵　しょうはいのかぎ　the key to victory
　..............................................0460, 0830

**2077**
金 167

*Metal*(金) + *build*(建): suggests a *metal* **KEY** for opening a *build*ing (建物, たてもの).

1565
常 17

---

## 釘 NAIL

テイ
くぎ

○釘を打つ　くぎをうつ　drive a nail.............1025
釘を抜く　くぎをぬく　pull a nail................1951
釘を差す　くぎをさす　remind (someone) of,
　give a warning..................................0937
釘付け　くぎづけ　nailing; pegging; being
　stationary, being glued to.................0064

**2078**
金 167

*Metal*(金) **NAIL** (丁, review 訂 1024 if necessary).

1489
名 10

---

## 錮 LOCK DOWN

コ

○禁錮　きんこ　imprisonment.................0312
禁錮二年　きんこにねん　two years' imprisonment
　..........................................0312, 0003, 0117

**2079**
金 167

**LOCKING DOWN** *firmly*(固) with *metal*(金).

1550
常 16

---

## 錠 ¹LOCK　²PILL

ジョウ

①錠前　じょうまえ　lock.........................0113
¹手錠　てじょう　handcuffs.....................0046
¹錠を掛ける　じょうをかける　fasten a lock......1117
②錠剤　じょうざい　pill, tablet ..................1261
²糖衣錠　とういじょう　sugar-coated pill...1616, 0700

**2080**
金 167

*Metal*(金) for *fixing*(定) things in place: **LOCK**. Also means **PILL**, which is easy to remember if you think of the round, tablet-like shape of some locks.

1548
常 16

**COME APART AT THE SEAMS**

タン
ほころ（びる）

○綻びる　ほころびる　come apart at the seams; unfold, bloom; break into a smile

袖の縫い目が綻びている　そでのぬいめがほころびている　The sleeve's seam is unraveling 1531, 1380, 0021

綻び　ほころび　tear, rent seam

○破綻　はたん　bankruptcy, failure................0596

破綻国家　はたんこっか　failed state...0596, 0075, 0219

| 2081 | Picture the *thread* (糸) getting *fixed* (定) in place (i.e., getting caught on something), so that it starts unraveling: **COME APART AT THE SEAMS**. |
| 糸 120 | |
| 1263 | |
| 常 14 | |

**BELL**

レイ　リン
すず

電鈴　でんれい　electric bell..................0155

風鈴　ふうりん　wind chime..................0425

○呼び鈴　よびりん　(call) bell, doorbell...1765

鈴蘭　すずらん　lily of the valley..........1489

鈴木　すずき　Suzuki [surname]..........0028

| 2082 | *Metal* (金) **BELL** (令, see 0229). ☞ 鐘 2083 |
| 金 167 | |
| 1526 | |
| 常 13 | |

**BELL**

ショウ
かね

鐘楼　しょうろう　bell tower, belfry.........1957

○警鐘　けいしょう　alarm bell, warning........0806

鐘乳洞　しょうにゅうどう　stalactite cave 0160, 1842

○鐘の音　かねのね　a bell's toll................0150

| 2083 | Here we observe a *child* (童) standing on an adult's shoulders and tolling a large *metal* (金) **BELL**. This kanji refers to large bells that toll, not to small bells that jingle or ring (for the latter, use 鈴 2082). ☞ 鈴 2082 |
| 金 167 | |
| 1578 | |
| 常 20 | |

**PUPIL (of the eye)**

ドウ
ひとみ

○瞳孔　どうこう　pupil............................1559

瞳子　どうし　pupil............................0094

瞳の　ひとみの　pupilary

瞳を凝らす　ひとみをこらす　strain one's eyes
.................................................1351

| 2084 | Let *child* (童) suggest the smallest part of the *eye* (目): **PUPIL**. |
| 目 109 | |
| 1144 | |
| 常 17 | |

**YEARN AFTER**

ショウ ドウ*
あこが（れる）

○憧れ あこがれ yearning, longing
憧れの的 あこがれのまと object of envy; idol
........................................................0169
有名人に憧れる ゆうめいじんにあこがれる adore
a celebrity............................0400, 0269, 0015

| 2085 | |
|---|---|
| 心 61 | **YEARNING AFTER** with the *heart* (忄) of a *child* (童). A sample *on-yomi* compound appears in the next entry. |
| 0664 | |
| 常 15 | |

---

**YEARN AFTER**

ケイ

○憧憬する しょうけいする (=どうけいする) yearn after
........................................................2085
憧憬の的 しょうけいのまと (=どうけいのまと) object
of envy; idol .............................0169

| 2086 | |
|---|---|
| 心 61 | A *scene* (景 1280) that fills one's *heart* (忄) with longing: **YEARN AFTER**. |
| 0663 | |
| 常 15 | |

---

**MEAN, despicable**

ヒ
いや（しい） いや（しむ） いや（しめる）

卑屈な ひくつな mean; servile.............1834
卑劣な ひれつな mean, base, cowardly.....1743
野卑 やひ vulgarity, meanness.............0534
○卑しい いやしい mean, lowly; seedy
卑しむ いやしむ despise, look down on

| 2087 | |
|---|---|
| 十 24 | Refers to someone or something that is **MEAN** or despised. Like 単 0462, it resembles a stick figure with a box *head* (田) and simple body. See the short diagonal stroke (S7) as the figure's line of vision, pointing down from the head toward some **MEAN**, lowly thing it looks down on. ☞ 単 0462 |
| 卑 | |
| 2295 | |
| 常 9 | |

---

**MONUMENT**

ヒ

碑文 ひぶん epitaph, inscription............0101
石碑 せきひ stone monument, tombstone 0403
墓碑 ぼひ tombstone, gravestone..........1340
歌碑 かひ monument inscribed with a tanka
poem....................................0827
○記念碑 きねんひ monument..........0427, 0230

| 2088 | |
|---|---|
| 石 112 | Though we should not carry over the idea of MEAN or despicable from the previous entry, we can visualize 卑 inside this character <u>physically</u> looking down at the *stone*, for 石 represents a tombstone or other stone **MONUMENT** placed on the ground. Note that both kanji incorporating 卑 follow its *on* reading, ヒ. |
| 碑 | |
| 1122 | |
| 常 14 | |

| 痺 | PARALYSIS | ○麻痺 まひ paralysis ............................0852 |
| | | 小児麻痺 しょうにまひ infantile paralysis, poliomyelitis, polio ......0034, 0772, 0852 |
| | ヒ<br>しび(れる) | ○痺れる しびれる go numb<br>痺れ しびれ numbness |

| 2089<br>疒 104<br>痺<br>外 13 | An *illness* (疒) that, as this character would have it, causes one to be looked down on (卑): **PARALYSIS**. |

| 鬼 | DEMON, ghost | ○鬼神 きじん (=きしん, おにがみ) departed spirit, ghost; terrible god ..........................0316 |
| | | 鬼籍に入る きせきにいる pass away; join the majority ...................................1910 |
| | | 鬼婆 おにばば hag, witch ...................1452 |
| | キ<br>おに おに- | ○仕事の鬼 しごとのおに demon for work, fierce worker ............................0371, 0080 |
| | | 鬼刑事 おにけいじ crack detective ....0722, 0080 |

| 2090<br>鬼 194<br><br><br>2313<br>常 10 | An appropriately heinous image of a **DEMON**, this unlovely stick figure with its *nose* (厶) lopped off. ☞ 魔 2095 |

| 塊 | LUMP, mass | 金塊 きんかい nugget, gold ingot............0029 |
| | | 土塊 どかい (=つちくれ) dirt clod ............0030 |
| | | ○団塊 だんかい mass, lump ...................0649 |
| | カイ<br>かたまり | 団塊世代 だんかいせだい baby-boom generation............................0649, 0604, 0071 |
| | | 血の塊 ちのかたまり clot of blood ...........0198 |

| 2091<br>土 32<br><br><br>0579<br>常 13 | "*Demon* (鬼)–*soil* (土)": **LUMPY** soil. |

| 醜 | UGLY | ○醜悪な しゅうあくな ugly, repulsive............0546 |
| | | 醜聞 しゅうぶん scandal.......................0453 |
| | | 美醜 びしゅう beauty or ugliness............0497 |
| | シュウ<br>みにく(い) | ○醜い みにくい ugly |

| 2092<br>酉 164<br><br><br>1469<br>常 17 | A *demon* (鬼), *liquored* (酉): an **UGLY** spectacle. |

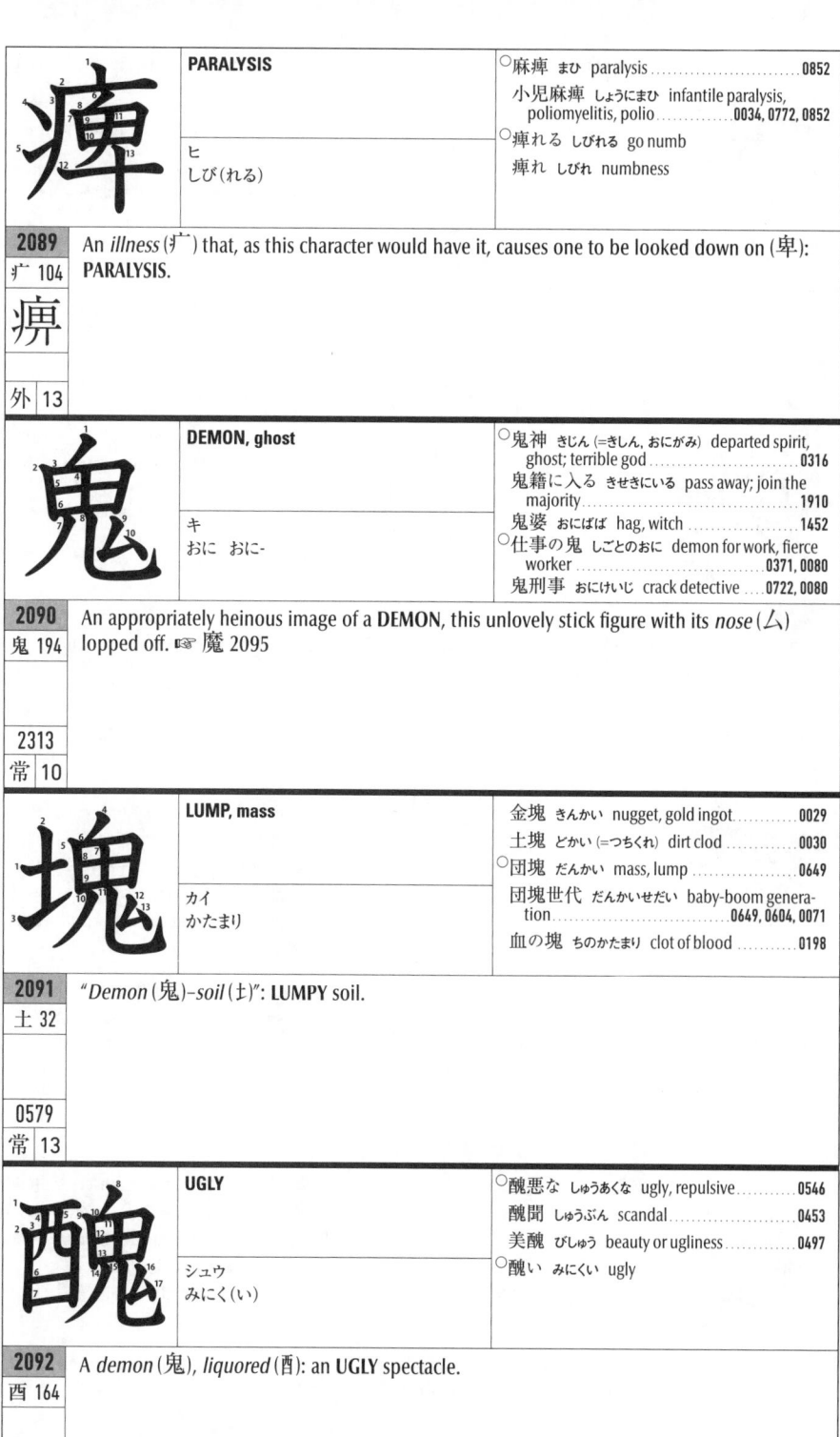

**SOUL, spirit**

コン
たましい

○闘魂 とうこん fighting spirit ................1363
商魂 しょうこん salesmanship, commercial
  enthusiasm ....................................0351
魂胆 こんたん secret intention, ulterior motive
  ...........................................................1982
鎮魂曲 ちんこんきょく requiem .........1719, 0503
○大和魂 やまとだましい soul of Japan; Japanese
  spirit .........................................0033, 0236

| 2093 | *"Demon-cloud"*: SOUL/spirit. |
| 鬼 194 | |
| 0975 | |
| 常 14 | |

**CHARM**

ミ

○魅力 みりょく charm, appeal ................0084
魅力的な みりょくてきな charming, fascinating
  ...........................................................0084, 0169
魅惑 みわく fascination, enchantment, charm
  ...........................................................1153
魅了する みりょうする charm, fascinate .....0958

| 2094 | See 未 *not yet* as a CHARM the *demon* (鬼) has *not yet* utilized. See his limb reaching way over to the right (S8), clutching this powerful CHARM, waiting for just the right moment to cast it upon you ... <u>not yet</u> ... <u>not yet</u> ... |
| 鬼 194 | |
| 2844 | |
| 常 15 | |

**DEMON, devil**

マ

悪魔 あくま devil, demon, Satan .............0546
邪魔 じゃま hindrance, obstruction .........1819
魔窟 まくつ den of iniquity [thieves] ........1843
○魔法 まほう magic, sorcery, witchcraft ....0139
魔術 まじゅつ magic, sorcery, witchcraft.....0993

| 2095 | Review 麻 0852 through 暦 0854, which contain important notes regarding 麻. Here and in two other entries that follow shortly, we return to 广. In this entry, we observe a *demon* (鬼) on *hemp*. The drug's effect goes beyond that of liquor (in 醜 2092); indeed, it turns him from a mere DEMON into a devil. ☞ 鬼 2090 |
| 鬼 194 | |
| 2747 | |
| 常 21 | |

**FEAR**

イ
おそ(れ)  おそ(れる)

畏怖する いふする fear; be in awe (of) ...1634
畏敬する いけいする revere, hold in awe...0805
○畏縮する いしゅくする cower, shrink from...0875
○畏れる おそれる fear [cf. 恐 1633]
畏れ おそれ fear [cf. 恐 1633]

| 2096 | Behold the FEARful image of a man dressed in a flowing cloak (from 衣) with a featureless four-square *head* (田), resembling a demon (鬼). ☞ 恐 1633, 界 0612 |
| 田 102 | |
| 2218 | |
| 常 9 | |

| | PRINT | ○印刷 いんさつ printing ........................0231 |
|---|---|---|
| | サツ<br>す(る) -ず(り) -ずり | 増刷 ぞうさつ additional printing, reprinting ........................1223<br>第四版三刷 だいよんはんさんさつ fourth edition, third printing..............1191, 0006, 0923, 0004<br>○刷る する print<br>校正刷り こうせいずり galley proofs...0103, 0043 |

| 2097<br>刀 18 | Here visualize *slicing* (刂) a *cloth* (巾), laying it on a *door* (戸, used as a flat surface), and then **PRINTING** a design on it. |
|---|---|
| 1169<br>常 8 | |

| | RUB, chafe | ○擦過傷 さっかしょう abrasion, scratch...0464, 1307 |
|---|---|---|
| | サツ<br>す(る) す(れる) -ず(れ) | ○擦り傷 すりきず abrasion, scratch............1307<br>靴擦れ くつずれ shoe sore..................0593<br>股擦れ またずれ saddle sore................1990<br>擦れ違う すれちがう pass by each other, brush past................................................0663 |

| 2098<br>手 64 | Ignore the meaning *inspect*, and simply see 察 as a very jagged surface. Picture the *hand* (扌) **RUBBING** itself up against the serrated, snaggy points along the left side of 察, and imagine the feeling of painful **chafing** and abrasion. |
|---|---|
| 0707<br>常 17 | |

| | RUB AGAINST | ○摩擦 まさつ friction; rubbing, chafing ......2098 |
|---|---|---|
| | マ | 摩耗する まもうする wear away, wear out...1644<br>摩滅 まめつ wear, defacement..............1149<br>摩天楼 まてんろう skyscraper..........0270, 1957 |

| 2099<br>手 64 | (Continuing from the previous entry) Now picture 手 **RUBBING AGAINST** abrasive *hemp* (麻), and imagine the same harsh scratching sensation. ☞ 磨 2100 |
|---|---|
| 2740<br>常 15 | |

| | POLISH | 磨滅 まめつ wear, defacement..............1149 |
|---|---|---|
| | マ<br>みが(く) | ○研磨する けんまする grind, polish; study hard, brush up ............................................0724<br>○磨く みがく polish, grind<br>磨き上げる みがきあげる polish up..........0041<br>歯磨き はみがき toothpaste; brushing one's teeth ............................................0674 |

| 2100<br>石 112 | Now imagine **POLISHING** a *stone* (石) with a *hemp* (麻) brush. This character is interchangeable with the previous entry in some compounds. ☞ 摩 2099 |
|---|---|
| 2744<br>常 16 | |

| | CONCAVE | ○凹面 おうめん concave surface..............0175 |
| --- | --- | --- |
| 凹 | | 凹地 おうち hollow, pit.....................0187 |
| | | 凹レンズ おうレンズ concave lens |
| | オウ | 凹版印刷 おうはんいんさつ intaglio printing |
| | ぼこ* | ...............0923, 0231, 2097 |

| 2101 | CONCAVE shape. |
| --- | --- |
| 凵 17 | |
| 2924 | |
| 常 5 | |

| | CONVEX | ○凸面 とつめん convex surface...............0175 |
| --- | --- | --- |
| 凸 | | 凸角 とっかく convex angle..................0342 |
| | | お凸 おてこ brow, forehead |
| | トツ | 凹凸 おうとつ unevenness, irregularities....2101 |
| | てこ* | ○凸凹 でこぼこ unevenness, roughness; |
| | | imbalance..................2101 |

| 2102 | CONVEX shape. |
| --- | --- |
| 凵 17 | |
| 2928 | |
| 常 5 | |

| | DEDICATE, offer | ○奉納する ほうのうする dedicate (to a deity), offer |
| --- | --- | --- |
| 奉 | | ...............1156 |
| | | 奉献する ほうけんする offer (to a shrine)....1157 |
| | | 奉公 ほうこう public service; domestic service, |
| | ホウ ブ | apprenticeship..................0089 |
| | たてまつ(る) | 奉戴する ほうたいする be presided over, live |
| | | under; accept reverentially................1914 |
| | | ○奉る たてまつる dedicate, offer respectfully |

| 2103 | 夫 evokes an image of a row of small torii gates, as one often sees lined up covering path- |
| --- | --- |
| 大 37 | ways in Shinto shrines (if you haven't seen such a pathway, do an image search for "Fushimi |
| | Inari Taisha" or "Fushimi Inari Shrine," where the most famous of these pathways is located). |
| | The association is relevant, for 奉 is always written on these small torii gates, which people |
| 2215 | or companies **DEDICATE** to a shrine. See S6–8 as a man holding a new torii gate offering in |
| 常 8 | his outstretched arms, and setting it in place: an ideal image for **DEDICATE/offer**. ☞ 捧 2108, 奏 2104 |

| | PLAY MUSIC | ○演奏する えんそうする perform, play........0914 |
| --- | --- | --- |
| 奏 | | 伴奏 ばんそう accompaniment.............0743 |
| | | 独奏 どくそう solo...........................0346 |
| | ソウ | 吹奏楽 すいそうがく wind (instrument) music, |
| | かな(てる) | brass music..................1764, 0302 |
| | | ○ピアノを奏てる ピアノをかなてる play the piano |

| 2104 | S8–9 are all that differs from the previous entry. There, the vertical S8 suggested the dedicator's |
| --- | --- |
| 大 37 | upright body, whereas here, it splits into the two curving strokes 8 and 9. This makes the |
| | lower part of the character resemble the upper part in miniature, so that 奏 can be seen |
| | as an adult-child duet on the koto: the large diagonal strokes are adult's hands, **PLAYING** |
| | **MUSIC** on a full-size koto; the short diagonal strokes represent child's hands, **PLAYING MUSIC** |
| 2233 | on a child-size koto (the horizontal strokes show the strings). Let the point of divergence |
| 常 9 | between 奏 and 奉 suggest the meaning of each character. ☞ 奉 2103 |

| | TRANQUIL | ○泰平 たいへい tranquility, perfect peace....0334 |
|---|---|---|
| | | 泰然たる たいぜんたる calm, composed; firm ................................................0760 |
| | タイ | 安泰 あんたい peace, security, tranquility...0096 |
| | | 泰国 たいこく Thailand .....................0075 |
| | | 日泰 にったい Japan and Thailand, Japanese-Thai ................................................0001 |

| 2105 | With 氺 *water* at the bottom, this entry is a bit easier to distinguish from the previous two. |
|---|---|
| 水 85 | It presents a scene of calming waters under a shelter: **TRANQUIL**. Do not confuse this entry or the previous one with the name-use kanji 秦, used in reference to the QIN DYNASTY of China and in the Japanese surname Hata. ☞ 漆 1002 |
| 2239 | |
| 常 10 | |

| | SALARY | ○俸給 ほうきゅう salary, pay ....................0526 |
|---|---|---|
| | | 年俸 ねんぽう annual salary.................0117 |
| | ホウ | 減俸 げんぽう salary cut......................1148 |

| 2106 | An *offer* (奉) made to a *man* (イ): **SALARY**. |
|---|---|
| 人 9 | |
| 0096 | |
| 常 10 | |

| | ROD, stick | ○鉄棒 てつぼう iron rod; horizontal bars......0564 |
|---|---|---|
| | | 棒状 ぼうじょう rod-shaped.................0616 |
| | | 棒立ち ぼうだち standing bolt upright......0067 |
| | ボウ | 棒で殴る ぼうでなぐる hit with a rod/club...1387 |
| | | 相棒 あいぼう pal, mate, companion, partner ................................................0682 |

| 2107 | *Offerings* (奉) from a *tree* (木): **RODS** and **sticks**! |
|---|---|
| 木 75 | |
| 0894 | |
| 常 12 | |

| | OFFER RESPECTFULLY | ○捧げる ささげる hold up; offer; dedicate |
|---|---|---|
| | | 捧げ物 ささげもの offering, sacrifice ........0172 |
| | ホウ | 捧呈する ほうていする dedicate, offer ......0587 |
| | ささ(げる) | 捧持する ほうじする hold up, bear ..........0384 |

| 2108 | Remember by association with 奉 2103. 扌 reinforces the idea of **OFFERING** by suggesting |
|---|---|
| 手 64 | the sense of "*handing to*." ☞ 奉 2103 |
| 0447 | |
| 名 11 | |

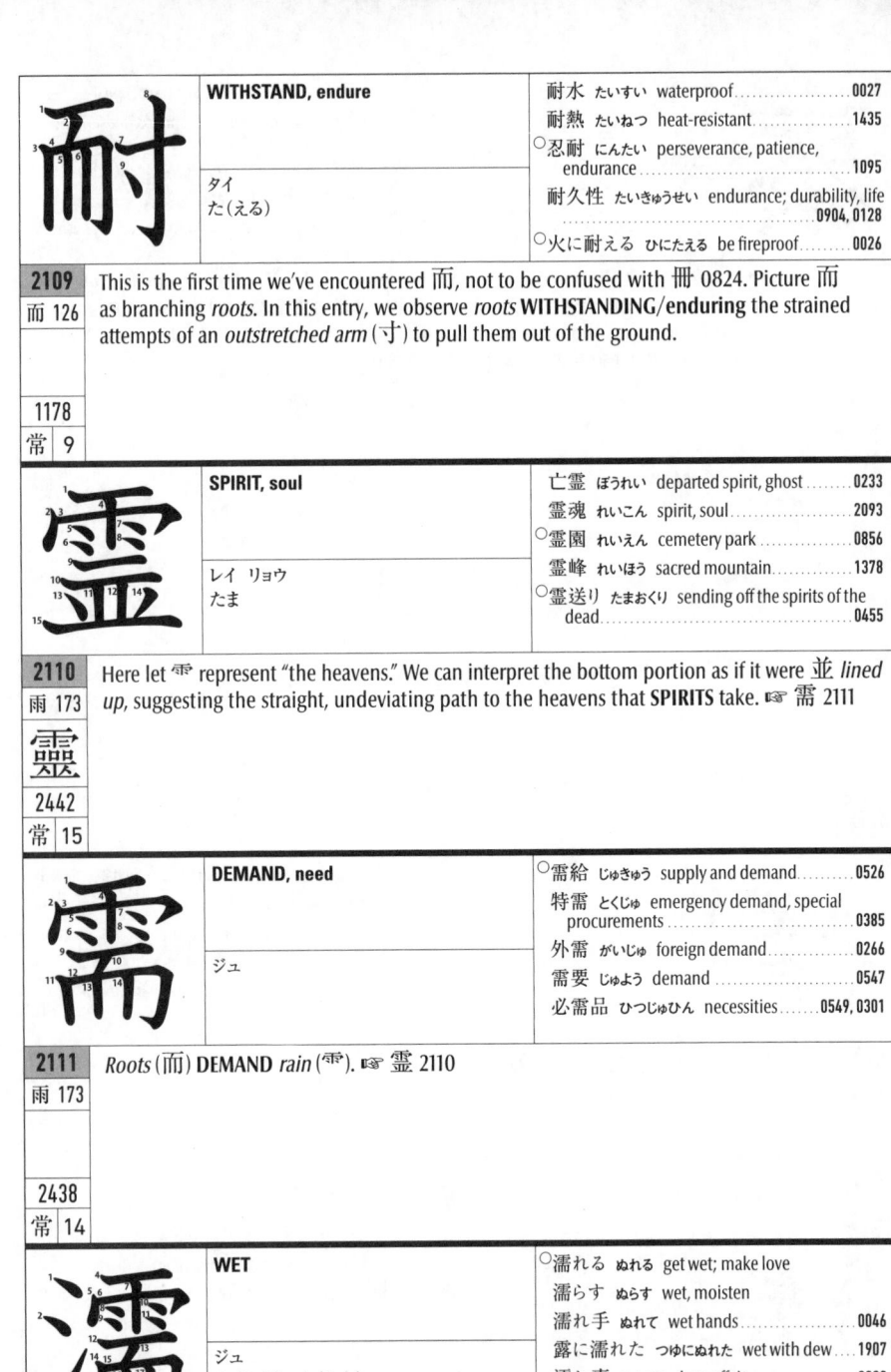

| | | |
|---|---|---|
| **WITHSTAND, endure**<br><br>タイ<br>た(える) | 耐水 たいすい waterproof.....................0027<br>耐熱 たいねつ heat-resistant................1435<br>○忍耐 にんたい perseverance, patience,<br>　　endurance...............................1095<br>耐久性 たいきゅうせい endurance; durability, life<br>........................................0904, 0128<br>○火に耐える ひにたえる be fireproof.........0026 |

| 2109 | This is the first time we've encountered 而, not to be confused with 冊 0824. Picture 而 as branching *roots*. In this entry, we observe *roots* **WITHSTANDING**/**enduring** the strained attempts of an *outstretched arm* (寸) to pull them out of the ground. |
|---|---|
| 而 126 | |
| 1178 | |
| 常 9 | |

| | | |
|---|---|---|
| **SPIRIT, soul**<br><br>レイ　リョウ<br>たま | 亡霊 ぼうれい departed spirit, ghost.........0233<br>霊魂 れいこん spirit, soul.....................2093<br>○霊園 れいえん cemetery park................0856<br>霊峰 れいほう sacred mountain..............1378<br>○霊送り たまおくり sending off the spirits of the<br>　　dead....................................0455 |

| 2110 | Here let 雨 represent "the heavens." We can interpret the bottom portion as if it were 並 *lined up*, suggesting the straight, undeviating path to the heavens that **SPIRITS** take. ☞ 需 2111 |
|---|---|
| 雨 173 | |
| 靈 | |
| 2442 | |
| 常 15 | |

| | | |
|---|---|---|
| **DEMAND, need**<br><br>ジュ | ○需給 じゅきゅう supply and demand..........0526<br>特需 とくじゅ emergency demand, special<br>　　procurements............................0385<br>外需 がいじゅ foreign demand..............0266<br>需要 じゅよう demand.....................0547<br>必需品 ひつじゅひん necessities.......0549, 0301 |

| 2111 | *Roots* (而) **DEMAND** *rain* (雨). ☞ 霊 2110 |
|---|---|
| 雨 173 | |
| 2438 | |
| 常 14 | |

| | | |
|---|---|---|
| **WET**<br><br>ジュ<br>ぬ(れる)　ぬ(らす) | ○濡れる ぬれる get wet; make love<br>濡らす ぬらす wet, moisten<br>濡れ手 ぬれて wet hands.................0046<br>露に濡れた つゆにぬれた wet with dew....1907<br>濡れ事 ぬれごと love affair.................0080 |

| 2112 | In response to the roots' *demand* (需), *water* (氵): **WET** roots. ☞ 漏 2118 |
|---|---|
| 水 85 | |
| 0709 | |
| 名 17 | |

| | |
|---|---|
| **CONFUCIANISM** | 儒教 じゅきょう Confucianism ............... 0632 |
| | ○儒学 じゅがく Confucianism ................. 0099 |
| ジュ | 儒仏 じゅぶつ Confucianism and Buddhism |
| | ............................................................. 0811 |

| 2113 | Confucian philosophy is less concerned with questions of the soul and the afterlife than it |
|---|---|
| 人 9 | is with the problems of humans in this world. This outlook is aptly expressed in the kanji |
| | for **CONFUCIANISM**, which refers to the *demands* (需) of *man* (イ). Note that the East Asian |
| | terms for Confucianism (VI–2) in fact make no reference to Confucius (孔子, see 1559). |
| 0153 | |
| 常 16 | |

| | |
|---|---|
| **EDGE, extremity** | ○極端 きょくたん extreme, extremity, pole .... 1712 |
| | 炉端 ろばた fireside ............................... 1896 |
| | 尖端 せんたん pointed end, tip; spearhead; |
| タン | vanguard ............................................ 1563 |
| はし は はた -ばた | 先端 せんたん front end, tip; vanguard ..... 0134 |
| | ○紐の端 ひものはし end of a string ........... 0591 |

| 2114 | This is the only kanji in this course in which 立 appears as a *hen*. To remember that it means |
|---|---|
| 立 117 | **EDGE**/extremity, picture the man *standing* precariously at the **EDGE** of a *mountain* (山), |
| | holding on for dear life to some exposed tree *roots* (而). |
| 1131 | |
| 常 14 | |

| | |
|---|---|
| **ONE** (in legal documents) | 壱億円 いちおくえん a hundred million yen |
| | ...................................................... 0622, 0013 |
| イチ | |

| 2115 | This kanji belongs to the special set used for writing numbers in bank notes and other legal |
|---|---|
| 士 33 | documents, as a way to prevent people from adding strokes to easily altered characters (such |
| | as 一). Here picture a *military man* (士) who owns only **ONE** *spoon* (ヒ, the one in his mess |
| 壹 | kit), which he therefore keeps well *covered* (冖). ☞ 一 0002 |
| 1879 | |
| 常 7 | |

| | |
|---|---|
| **BUDDHIST NUN** | ○尼僧 にそう nun, sister; (Buddhist) priestess |
| | ............................................................. 1226 |
| | 禅尼 ぜんに Zen nun ........................... 1076 |
| ニ | 修道尼 しゅうどうに nun ............... 1676, 0158 |
| あま | ○尼寺 あまでら nunnery, convent ............ 0382 |

| 2116 | Picture a **BUDDHIST NUN** trying to escape from a nunnery by digging a hole under the |
|---|---|
| 尸 44 | (locked) *door* (尸) with a *spoon* (ヒ). |
| 2611 | |
| 常 5 | |

| 泥 | **MUD** | ○泥土 ていど mud, mire.....................0030 |
| | | 泥水 でいすい (=どろみず) muddy water, liquid mud.....................0027 |
| | | 雲泥の差 うんでいのさ great difference [as |
| | デイ | between clouds and mud]..........0897, 0937 |
| | どろ | ○泥沼 どろぬま bog; quagmire.............1105 |
| | | 泥棒 どろぼう thief, crook...................2107 |

| **2117** | (Continuing from the previous entry) In the process of digging her way out of the nunnery, |
| 水 85 | the *nun* (尼) strikes *water* (氵), creating **MUD**. The reading デイ is unique in this course. |
| **0288** | |
| 常 8 | |

| 漏 | **LEAK** | ○漏洩 ろうえい leakage, disclosure ...........1588 |
| | | 漏電 ろうでん short circuit, leakage .........0155 |
| | | 漏出 ろうしゅつ leak.............................0038 |
| | ロウ | ○ガスが漏れている ガスがもれている gas is |
| | も(る) も(れる) も(らす) | leaking |
| | | 小便を漏らす しょうべん(=しょんべん)をもらす |
| | | wet one's pants.....................0034, 0890 |

| **2118** | *Rainwater* (雨, 氵) coming through the *door* (戸): **LEAK**. ☞ 濡 2112 |
| 水 85 | |
| **0635** | |
| 常 14 | |

| 氾 | **FLOOD** | 氾濫 はんらん flood; oversupply.............2030 |
| | | |
| | ハン | |

| **2119** | *Water* (氵) + *broken body* (巳): **FLOOD**. ☞ 汎 1632 |
| 水 85 | |
| **0172** | |
| 常 5 | |

| 彙 | **CATALOG** | ○語彙 ごい vocabulary, glossary..............0222 |
| | | 語彙力 ごいりょく (the breadth of) one's |
| | | vocabulary.............................0222, 0084 |
| | イ | 辞彙 じい dictionary.........................1465 |
| | | 彙報 いほう bulletin.........................1472 |

| **2120** | Visualize S1–5 as some kind of device being used to measure *fruit* trees (果), in an effort to |
| ヨ 58 | compile systematic information about them, i.e., to **CATALOG** them. |
| **2036** | |
| 常 13 | |

| 某 | **A CERTAIN** | 某日 ぼうじつ a certain day .................. 0001 |
| | | ○某氏 ぼうし a certain person .............. 0476 |
| | | 某所 ぼうしょ a certain place ............. 0249 |
| | ボウ | 某女 ぼうじょ Ms. So-and-so ................ 0093 |
| | | 某博士 ぼうはかせ Dr. X ................ 0983, 0350 |

| **2121** | You should usually avoid remembering a kanji's meaning with a memorized phrase. For this entry, however, the definition is itself a phrase ("**A CERTAIN**"), so you might simply learn the words, "**A CERTAIN** *tree* (木) with *sweet* (甘) nectar." By using this cryptic phrase, a bee colony avoids identifying the tree, and so keeps the nectar to itself. ☞ 果 0599 |
| 木 75 | |
| 2216 | |
| 常 9 | |

| 謀 | **SCHEME, plot** | ○謀略 ぼうりゃく stratagem, scheme, plot .... 0791 |
| | | 陰謀 いんぼう scheme, plot, conspiracy .... 1311 |
| | | 共謀 きょうぼう conspiracy, collusion ........ 0356 |
| | ボウ ム | 深謀 しんぼう deeply laid plan .............. 1715 |
| | はか(る) | ○謀る はかる scheme, plot, contrive |

| **2122** | (Continuing from the previous entry) Imagine a clandestine **SCHEME**/**plot** among the bees to acquire the tree's sweet nectar. In discussing (言) their **SCHEME**, they maintain strict secrecy regarding the tree's location by referring to it only as "*a certain* tree with sweet nectar." ☞ 課 0600 |
| 言 149 | |
| 1439 | |
| 常 16 | |

| 媒 | **MEDIATE** | 媒介 ばいかい mediation, intervention, intermediation ............................. 0611 |
| | | 媒質 ばいしつ medium ...................... 0318 |
| | | ○媒体 ばいたい medium ...................... 0062 |
| | バイ | 触媒 しょくばい catalyst ...................... 0344 |
| | | 霊媒 れいばい (spiritualistic) medium ...... 2110 |

| **2123** | (Continuing from 2121–22) Now picture the worker bees flying back and forth between the *certain* tree with sweet nectar and their queen (女): **MEDIATE**. |
| 女 38 | |
| 0518 | |
| 常 12 | |

| 尉 | **OFFICER** | ○大尉 たいい captain ........................ 0033 |
| | | 中尉 ちゅうい first lieutenant ............... 0035 |
| | イ | 少尉 しょうい second lieutenant ........... 0677 |

| **2124** | This kanji can be visualized as the entrance to an **OFFICER**s' club. Through its *doorway* 尸, we can see one of the tables inside (here shown as an *altar* 示). At the right is a doorman with an *outstretched arm* (寸), showing the **OFFICER**s in. |
| 寸 41 | |
| 1504 | |
| 常 11 | |

**CONSOLE, cheer up**

イ
なぐさ(める)　なぐさ(む)

○慰霊　いれい　comforting the spirits of the dead ............................................ 2110

慰霊祭　いれいさい　memorial service ... 2110, 0637

弔慰　ちょうい　condolence, sympathy ........ 1186

○慰める　なぐさめる　console, cheer up

慰み　なぐさみ　amusement, pastime

| 2125 | When soldiers are killed in battle, the duty of notifying their families falls to an *officer* (尉). Here we observe an *officer* trying his best to **CONSOLE** a broken *heart* (心). |
| 心 61 | |
| 2497 | |
| 常 15 | |

**DAIRY PRODUCTS**

ラク

酪農　らくのう　dairy farming ................... 0511

酪農家　らくのうか　dairy farmer ......... 0511, 0219

○酪製品　らくせいひん　dairy products ... 0709, 0301

乳酪　にゅうらく　dairy products ............... 0160

酪酸　らくさん　butyric acid .................... 0800

| 2126 | Recall that 酉 can mean either *liquor* or *ferment*. In this entry, we thus obtain "*ferment* + *cabin* (各)," suggesting the production of yogurt and cheese in a barn: **DAIRY PRODUCTS**. |
| 酉 164 | |
| 1398 | |
| 常 13 | |

**FERMENT**

コウ

酵素　こうそ　ferment; enzyme ................ 0132

○酵母　こうぼ　yeast; ferment ................... 0104

酵母菌　こうぼきん　yeast fungus ........ 0104, 1729

発酵　はっこう　fermentation, zymosis ........ 0148

| 2127 | *Ferment* (酉) + *filial piety* (孝): picture the child (子) piously **FERMENTING** liquor for his alcoholic parent to drink. |
| 酉 164 | |
| 1413 | |
| 常 14 | |

**SOY SAUCE; salted/fermented food**

ショウ

○醤油　しょうゆ　soy sauce ...................... 0433

生醤油　きじょうゆ　pure soy sauce ..... 0036, 0433

魚醤油　うおじょうゆ　sauce made from fermented fish ................................................ 0492, 0433

| 2128 | Your starting point here should be the word しょうゆ (**SOY SAUCE**), which is easy to remember from its homophony with the English word derived from it, "soy." You can then recognize this kanji by the presence of 将 0614, which indicates the *on* reading ショウ, and *ferment* (酉), which refers to the sauce's fermentation from soybeans. ☞ 奨 0615 |
| 酉 164 | |
| 醤 | |
| 外 17 | |

**VINEGAR**

サク
す

酢酸 さくさん acetic acid....................0800
○酢の物 すのもの pickled dish ............0172
酢料理 すりょうり pickled dish ........0758, 0532
ポン酢 ポンず *ponzu* (sauce made from soy sauce and citrus juice)

| 2129 | *Liquor* (酉) that cuts like a *saw* (乍): **VINEGAR**. |
| 酉 164 | |
| 醋 | |
| 1373 | |
| 常 12 | |

**SHOCHU (Japanese distilled liquor)**

チュウ

○焼酎 しょうちゅう shochu (Japanese distilled liquor)....................0769

| 2130 | *Outstretched arm* (寸), reaching for a *bottle* (酉) of **SHOCHU**. |
| 酉 164 | |
| 1329 | |
| 常 10 | |

**POUR WINE**

シャク
く(む)

○媒酌 ばいしゃく matchmaking................2123
手酌 てじゃく self-service in sake drinking...0046
晩酌 ばんしゃく evening drink................1275
○酌む くむ drink, have a drink
酒を酌み交わす さけをくみかわす drink together, help one another to sake...0797, 0102

| 2131 | Picture the *elephant* (勹) **POURING WINE** from the *liquor bottle* (酉) at the left. Visualize the half-empty bottle in S10, which he's tipping just now, decanting a glass of red for his guest. |
| 酉 164 | |
| 1331 | |
| 常 10 | |

**ANGLE**

チョウ
つ(る) つ(り) つ(り)-

沖釣り おきづり offshore fishing............0645
釣り糸 つりいと fishing line ................0112
○釣り銭 つりせん change (for money) ...1585
お釣り おつり change (for money)
釣鐘 つりがね hanging bell ................2083

| 2132 | (Continuing from the previous entry) Here the *elephant* aims downward with a wire tied to a *metal* (釒) fishhook, angling it (as shown in S11) toward the surface of a pond: **ANGLE**. |
| 金 167 | |
| 1496 | |
| 常 11 | |

| | (RAISE) LIVESTOCK | ○家畜 かちく domestic animals, livestock....0219 |
|---|---|---|
| | | 畜産業 ちくさんぎょう stock-raising industry |
| | | ............................................................0181, 0498 |
| | | 牧畜 ぼくちく livestock farming, cattle breeding |
| | チク | ............................................................0576 |
| | | 鬼畜 きちく devil ..............................2090 |
| | | 畜生 ちくしょう beast; Damn it!.........0036 |

**2133**
田 102

Review 育 0489 RAISE, from which we'll borrow the image of a rearing parent's head and broad shoulders (S1–2). Here it represents a breeder, raising a *child* (幺) of the *fields* (田): **LIVESTOCK.** ☞ 蓄 2134

1801
常 | 10

| | STORE UP | ○蓄積 ちくせき accumulation, stockpiling....0832 |
|---|---|---|
| | | 貯蓄する ちょちくする save (money), lay aside |
| | | ............................................................0442 |
| | | 備蓄 びちく saving for emergency, storing....0715 |
| | | 含蓄 がんちく implication, significance, |
| | チク | suggestiveness ................................1771 |
| | たくわ(える) | ○燃料を蓄える ねんりょうをたくわえる store up fuel |
| | | ............................................................0761, 0758 |

**2134**
艹 140

Here we observe the rearing breeder **STORING UP** *grass* (艹) for his *livestock* (畜) to eat. ☞ 畜 2133

2038
常 | 13

| | PROFOUND, occult | 玄妙な げんみょうな abstruse, occult, mysterious |
|---|---|---|
| | | ............................................................1746 |
| | | ○玄関 げんかん entrance, (front) door........0451 |
| | | 玄米 げんまい unpolished rice..............0234 |
| | ゲン | 玄人 くろうと expert, master hand ..........0015 |

**2135**
玄 95

Now we'll leave behind "breeder," and once again see 亠 as a rearing parent. Observe how he shelters his *child* (幺) from the world, hiding her in deep darkness beneath his broad shoulders: **PROFOUND/occult.** ☞ 亥 2158

1722
常 | 5

| | DAZZLING; dizzying | ○眩しい まぶしい dazzling, glaring |
|---|---|---|
| | | 眩しい日光 まぶしいにっこう glaring sunlight |
| | | ............................................................0001, 0137 |
| | | 眩い まばゆい dazzling, glaring |
| | ゲン | 眩惑される げんわくされる be dazzled; be |
| | まぶ(しい) まばゆ(い) | bewildered ....................................1153 |

**2136**
目 109

Now imagine the child emerging from *profound/occult* (玄) darkness and suddenly exposing her *eyes* (目) to bright light: **DAZZLING.**

外 | 10

| MUTTER | ○呟く つぶやく mutter, mumble; murmur<br>呟き つぶやき muttering, mumbling; murmuring |
|---|---|
| ゲン<br>つぶや(く) | |

**2137**
口 30

*Mouth* (口) speaking in an *occult* (玄) manner (i.e., unintelligibly): **MUTTERING**. Note that all four kanji incorporating 玄 in the phonetic position, including the two that appear a few entries further ahead, follow its *on* reading, ゲン. ☞ 咳 2163

外 8

| WHISPER | ○囁く ささやく whisper, murmur<br>囁き ささやき whispering, murmuring |
|---|---|
| ささや(く) | |

**2138**
口 30

Three *ears* (耳) gather closely around a **WHISPERING** *mouth* (口). This easily remembered image represents a class of high stroke-count but intuitive kanji that have become an appealing choice for writers since the invention of keyboard kanji input.

外 21

| SPEAK, chat | ○喋る しゃべる speak, talk, chatter<br>日本語で喋る にほんごでしゃべる speak in<br>Japanese ............................0001, 0031, 0222<br>ペラペラと喋る ペラペラとしゃべる blabber,<br>have a big mouth<br>お喋り おしゃべり talk, chat, chitchat |
|---|---|
| チョウ<br>しゃべ(る) | |

**2139**
口 30

Let 枼 represent 葉 0605 LEAF. Now picture thin, light, fluttering *leaves* being blown from the *mouth* (口), symbolizing light, fluent conversation: **SPEAK/chat**.

0502
名 12

| LIKEN | ○比喩 ひゆ simile, metaphor ..............0123<br>直喩 ちょくゆ simile..........................0839<br>隠喩 いんゆ metaphor ......................1312<br>引喩 いんゆ allusion..........................0422 |
|---|---|
| ユ | |

**2140**
口 30

喻

0508
常 12

俞 is the old form of 俞 (*package of sliced meat*), not standardized with 輸 0945, etc. when the present entry was added to the Joyo list. Read both forms interchangeably. Here we observe a *mouth* (口) **LIKENING** something metaphorically to *sliced meat*, perhaps by calling it "the best thing since *sliced meat*," if you will.

| | ¹ DEPRESSION, gloom<br>² CONGESTED, pent up | | ¹ 鬱々とした うつうつとした gloomy, pessimistic |
|---|---|---|---|
| | | | ① 鬱病 うつびょう depression ..................0617 |
| | | | ¹ 憂鬱 ゆううつ depression, melancholy ......0779 |
| | ウツ | | ¹ 鬱陶しい うっとうしい gloomy, depressing; dull, cloudy ................................1372 |
| | | | ² 鬱血 うっけつ blood congestion ............0198 |

| 2141<br>木 75<br>欝<br>2528<br>常 29 | Illustrates the same point about high stroke count kanji mentioned in 囁 above. Simply associate this kanji's oppressively crowded, dense, confined look with feelings of **DEPRESSION** and **CONGESTION**. Use the upper part of 凵 as a visual focus for producing these sensations. |
|---|---|

| 弦 | STRING (of a bow or musical instrument) | ○弦楽 げんがく string music ..................0302 |
|---|---|---|
| | | 調弦 ちょうげん tuning ......................0306 |
| | | 管弦楽団 かんげんがくだん orchestra ................................1839, 0302, 0649 |
| | ゲン<br>つる | 弓弦 ゆみづる (=ゆづる) bowstring ..........0421 |

| 2142<br>弓 57<br><br>0257<br>常 8 | In the next two entries, I suggest you ignore 玄 *profound/occult*, and use visual shortcuts instead. Here, visualize S5 as a **STRING** the *child* (幺) attaches to the *bow*. |
|---|---|

| 舷 | GUNWALE | 舷側 げんそく side of a ship ..................0626 |
|---|---|---|
| | | 舷窓 げんそう porthole ......................0558 |
| | | 舷門 げんもん gangway ......................0447 |
| | ゲン | ○左舷 さげん port (left side of a ship) ..........0401 |
| | | ○右舷 うげん starboard (right side of a ship) 0402 |

| 2143<br>舟 137<br><br>1227<br>常 11 | Here see S8 as the upper edge along the side of the *boat* (舟): **GUNWALE**. ☞ 舵 2144 |
|---|---|

| 舵 | RUDDER, helm | ○舵手 だしゅ helmsman, coxswain ............0046 |
|---|---|---|
| | | 舵機 だき rudder ............................0473 |
| | | 方向舵 ほうこうだ rudder ............0173, 0183 |
| | ダ<br>かじ | ○舵を取る かじをとる take the helm ..........0059 |
| | | 舵取り かじとり guidance; leader ............0059 |

| 2144<br>舟 137<br><br>1226<br>名 11 | Visualize ヒ as a **RUDDER** protruding from the stern of a *boat* (舟), and 宀 as the helmsman's arm, reaching out to adjust the **RUDDER**'s direction. ☞ 蛇 2297, 舷 2143 |
|---|---|

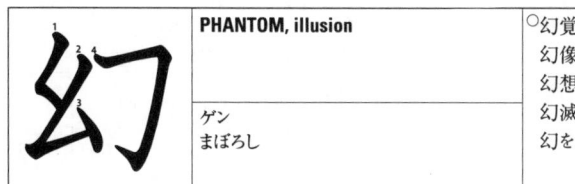

| PHANTOM, illusion | |
|---|---|
| | 幻覚 げんかく illusion, hallucination........0325 |
| | 幻像 げんぞう phantom, vision, illusion ....1278 |
| | 幻想 げんそう fantasy, illusion .............0683 |
| ゲン | 幻滅 げんめつ disillusionment ............1149 |
| まぼろし | 幻を追う まぼろしをおう pursue phantoms...1181 |

| | |
|---|---|
| **2145** | Lacking the "ear" stroke (see 局 0256), 刁 is not an *elephant*, but only the **illusion** of one. It is only a **PHANTOM** elephant, a figment of the *child* (幺)'s imagination. ☞ 幼 2147 |
| 幺 52 | |
| 0159 | |
| 常 4 | |

| QUIET AND SECLUDED; deep hidden | |
|---|---|
| | 幽谷 ゆうこく deep ravine, secluded valley...1034 |
| | 幽寂 ゆうじゃくな quiet, sequestered......2045 |
| | 幽玄な ゆうげんな profound; occult.........2135 |
| ユウ | 幽霊 ゆうれい ghost, apparition ............2110 |
| | 幽鬼 ゆうき departed soul, ghost...........2090 |

| | |
|---|---|
| **2146** | Two *children* (幺幺), each hiding deep in the quiet seclusion of a *mountain* (山) chasm: **QUIET AND SECLUDED; deep hidden.** |
| 幺 52 | |
| 2592 | |
| 常 9 | |

| VERY YOUNG | |
|---|---|
| | 幼児 ようじ young child, infant .............0772 |
| | 幼年 ようねん infancy, childhood...........0117 |
| | 老幼 ろうよう old people and children ......0629 |
| ヨウ | 幼い おさない very young, infantile |
| おさな(い) | 幼馴染み おさななじみ childhood friend |
| | .............................................1926, 1174 |

| | |
|---|---|
| **2147** | Here think of the *plow* (力) as a tool for cutting. With 幺, this suggests a *child* just now *cutting* its teeth: **VERY YOUNG** child. ☞ 劾 2160, 幻 2145 |
| 幺 52 | |
| 0168 | |
| 常 5 | |

| CHILD | |
|---|---|
| | 稚気 ちき childishness .....................0126 |
| | 稚拙な ちせつな childish, unskillful.........1833 |
| | 稚児 ちご infant, child .....................0772 |
| チ | 幼稚な ようちな childish, infantile, crude...2147 |
| | 幼稚園 ようちえん kindergarten .......2147, 0856 |

| | |
|---|---|
| **2148** | In the next several entries try to visualize the *small bird* (隹) performing various actions (or in one case, having an action done to it). In this entry, we observe a *small bird* carrying *rice* (禾) home to its **CHILD.** The reading チ is easy to associate with **CHILD.** ☞ 椎 2152 |
| 禾 115 | |
| 稚 | |
| 1114 | |
| 常 13 | |

| | FIBER; hold together | 繊維 せんい fiber, textile ............... **2008** |
|---|---|---|
| | | ○維持する いじする maintain, keep (up), preserve ............... **0384** |
| | | 維新 いしん renovation, restoration ............... **0275** |
| | イ | 明治維新 めいじいしん Meiji Restoration (1868) ............... **0024, 0950, 0275** |

| 2149 | Small bird (隹) carrying thread (糸) FIBERS for holding together its nest. |
|---|---|
| 糸 120 | |
| 1251 | |
| 常 14 | |

| | ¹ INFER<br>² PUSH FORWARD | ¹ 推定する すいていする presume, infer ...... **0045** |
|---|---|---|
| | | ① 推測 すいそく conjecture, supposition ...... **0627** |
| | | ¹ 推し量る おしはかる conjecture, surmise, guess ............... **0538** |
| | スイ | ② 推進する すいしんする propel, drive; promote ............... **0191** |
| | お(す) | ² 会長に推す かいちょうにおす recommend (someone) for the post of president ... **0226, 0091** |

| 2150 | Hand (扌) PUSHING small bird (隹) FORWARD. Noting V4, you might think of it as the same small bird as the one in 進 0191 ADVANCE, now needing a friendly PUSH in order to start advancing. Also means **INFER**, in the sense of pushing a logical argument forward from evidence to a conclusion. |
|---|---|
| 手 64 | |
| 0465 | |
| 常 11 | |

| | PILE UP | ○堆積 たいせき accumulation, pile ............ **0832** |
|---|---|---|
| | | 堆積岩 たいせきがん sedimentary rock ............... **0832, 1649** |
| | | 堆肥 たいひ compost pile ............... **2023** |
| | タイ | (氷)堆石 (ひょう)たいせき moraine ..... **1690, 0403** |
| | うずたか(い)* | 堆い うずたかい piled high |

| 2151 | Small bird (隹) PILING UP earth (土). |
|---|---|
| 土 32 | |
| 0425 | |
| 常 11 | |

| | ¹ SPINE<br>² CHINQUAPIN | ① 椎骨 ついこつ vertebra ............... **0465** |
|---|---|---|
| | | ¹ 腰椎 ようつい lumbar vertebra ............. **1987** |
| | | ¹ 椎間板 ついかんばん intervertebral disk ............... **0448, 0924** |
| | ツイ | ² 椎茸ˣ しいたけ shiitake (mushroom) |
| | しい* | ² 椎の実 しいのみ sweet acorn ............... **0499** |

| 2152 | Picture the small bird (隹) as a woodpecker, pecking a hole in a **CHINQUAPIN** tree (木) or, alternatively, in your **SPINE**. ☞ 稚 2148 |
|---|---|
| 木 75 | |
| 0905 | |
| 常 12 | |

| | SPINE | |
|---|---|---|
| | | ○脊椎 せきつい spine, backbone.............2152 |
| | | 脊椎動物 せきついどうぶつ vertebrate |
| | | .................2152, 0540, 0172 |
| | セキ | 無脊椎動物 むせきついどうぶつ invertebrate |
| | | .........0048, 2152, 0540, 0172 |
| | | 脊椎破壊 せきついはかい vertebral destruction |
| | | ...............2152, 0596, 1666 |

| 2153 | Picture S3–6 as sets of ribs, surrounding a **SPINE** (人). 月 signals the general category *body part*. ☞ 背 0124 |
|---|---|
| 肉 130 | |
| 2317 | |
| 常 10 | |

| | CHICK, doll | |
|---|---|---|
| | | ○雛鳥 ひなどり fledgling (esp. chicken)......0340 |
| | | ○雛人形 ひなにんぎょう dolls [usu. displayed in tiers]..................0015, 0147 |
| | スウ ジュ | 雛祭り ひなまつり Doll Festival (March 3) ...0637 |
| | ひな ひよこ | 雛形 ひながた sample, model, miniature...0147 |
| | | あいつはまだ雛だ あいつはまだひよこだ He is still a greenhorn |

| 2154 | A *small bird* (隹) with a pair of tiny **CHICKS**, which resemble miniature *elephants* (ク/ク). |
|---|---|
| 隹 172 | |
| 1633 | |
| 名 18 | |

| | WHO | |
|---|---|---|
| | | 彼は誰ですか かれはだれですか Who is he? |
| | | ..........................0597 |
| | | 誰の だれの whose |
| | だれ | 誰か だれか someone, somebody |
| | | 誰でも だれでも anyone, anybody |
| | | 誰彼を問わず だれかれをとわず anyone and everyone..................0597, 0452 |

| 2155 | Think of 隹 here as a talking parakeet whose cage is placed next to the entrance to a home, where he inquires the name of callers. His vocabulary is limited to a single *word* (言): **WHO?** |
|---|---|
| 言 149 | |
| 1429 | |
| 常 15 | |

| | MERELY, only | |
|---|---|---|
| | | ○唯一の ゆいいつの the only, the sole.........0002 |
| | | 唯一無二の ゆいいつむにの the one and only, unique..........0002, 0048, 0003 |
| | | 唯心論 ゆいしんろん idealism, spiritualism |
| | ユイ イ | .................0056, 0942 |
| | | 唯美主義 ゆいびしゅぎ aestheticism |
| | | .................0497, 0365, 0926 |
| | | 唯物主義 ゆいぶつしゅぎ materialism |
| | | .................0172, 0365, 0926 |

| 2156 | **MERELY** a *small bird* (隹)'s *mouth* (口) (in size). ☞ 鳴 2157 |
|---|---|
| 口 30 | |
| 0419 | |
| 常 11 | |

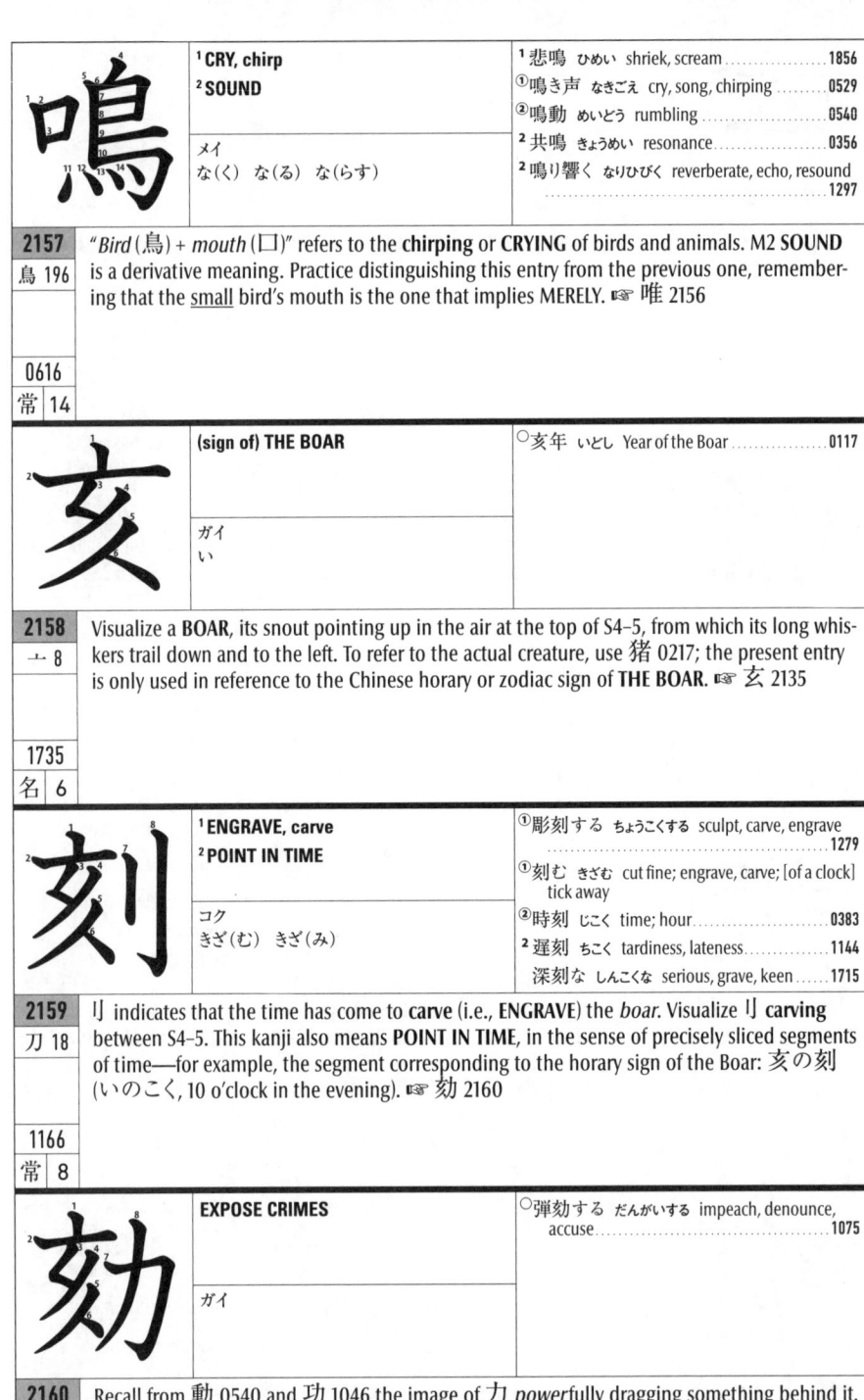

| | | |
|---|---|---|
| 鳴 | **¹ CRY, chirp**<br>**² SOUND**<br><br>メイ<br>な(く) な(る) な(らす) | ¹ 悲鳴 ひめい shriek, scream ............... 1856<br>① 鳴き声 なきごえ cry, song, chirping ......... 0529<br>② 鳴動 めいどう rumbling ............... 0540<br>² 共鳴 きょうめい resonance ............... 0356<br>² 鳴り響く なりひびく reverberate, echo, resound ............... 1297 |

| 2157<br>鳥 196<br><br>0616<br>常 14 | "*Bird* (鳥) + *mouth* (口)" refers to the **chirping** or **CRYING** of birds and animals. M2 **SOUND** is a derivative meaning. Practice distinguishing this entry from the previous one, remembering that the <u>small</u> bird's mouth is the one that implies MERELY. ☞ 唯 2156 |
|---|---|

| | | |
|---|---|---|
| 亥 | **(sign of) THE BOAR**<br><br>ガイ<br>い | ○ 亥年 いどし Year of the Boar ............... 0117 |

| 2158<br>亠 8<br><br>1735<br>名 6 | Visualize a **BOAR**, its snout pointing up in the air at the top of S4–5, from which its long whiskers trail down and to the left. To refer to the actual creature, use 猪 0217; the present entry is only used in reference to the Chinese horary or zodiac sign of **THE BOAR**. ☞ 玄 2135 |
|---|---|

| | | |
|---|---|---|
| 刻 | **¹ ENGRAVE, carve**<br>**² POINT IN TIME**<br><br>コク<br>きざ(む) きざ(み) | ① 彫刻する ちょうこくする sculpt, carve, engrave ............... 1279<br>① 刻む きざむ cut fine; engrave, carve; [of a clock] tick away<br>② 時刻 じこく time; hour ............... 0383<br>² 遅刻 ちこく tardiness, lateness ............... 1144<br>深刻な しんこくな serious, grave, keen ...... 1715 |

| 2159<br>刀 18<br><br>1166<br>常 8 | リ indicates that the time has come to **carve** (i.e., **ENGRAVE**) the *boar*. Visualize リ **carving** between S4–5. This kanji also means **POINT IN TIME**, in the sense of precisely sliced segments of time—for example, the segment corresponding to the horary sign of the Boar: 亥の刻 (いのこく, 10 o'clock in the evening). ☞ 劾 2160 |
|---|---|

| | | |
|---|---|---|
| 劾 | **EXPOSE CRIMES**<br><br>ガイ | ○ 弾劾する だんがいする impeach, denounce, accuse ............... 1075 |

| 2160<br>力 19<br><br>1165<br>常 8 | Recall from 動 0540 and 功 1046 the image of 力 *power*fully dragging something behind it. Here visualize it dragging the *boar* out from its hiding place in order to **EXPOSE** its **CRIMES**. ☞ 刻 2159, 幼 2147 |
|---|---|

| | | |
|---|---|---|
|  | **NUCLEUS, core**<br><br>カク | ○中核 ちゅうかく core, nucleus; kernel ........ 0035<br>核家族 かくかぞく nuclear family ...... 0219, 0568<br>細胞核 さいぼうかく cell nucleus ....... 0239, 1984<br>原子核 げんしかく atomic nucleus ..... 0208, 0094<br>核兵器 かくへいき nuclear weapons ... 0907, 0295 |

| **2161** | Picture the *boar* (亥) eating all the way through to the **core** of the *tree* (木), i.e., to its **NUCLEUS**. |
|---|---|
| 木 75 | |
| **0836** | |
| 常 10 | |

| | | |
|---|---|---|
|  | **BODY; skeleton**<br><br>ガイ | ○骸骨 がいこつ skeleton ...................... 0465<br>死骸 しがい corpse, carcass ................. 0716<br>遺骸 いがい corpse, (a person's) remains ... 1179<br>形骸 けいがい skeleton, shell; remains ..... 0147<br>亡骸 なきがら (a person's) remains .......... 0233 |

| **2162** | *Bones* (骨) of a *boar* (亥)'s corpse: **BODY/skeleton.** The long strokes 14 and 15 emphasize |
|---|---|
| 骨 188 | the image of exposed bones. |
| **1625** | |
| 常 10 | |

| | | |
|---|---|---|
|  | **COUGH**<br><br>ガイ<br>せき | ○咳をする せきをする [vi] cough<br>咳止め せきどめ cough suppressant ........ 0042<br>空咳 からせき dry/hacking cough ........... 0398 |

| **2163** | *Mouth* (口) + bristly *boar* (亥): raspy **COUGH.** ☞ 呟 2137 |
|---|---|
| 口 30 | |
| 外 9 | |

| | | |
|---|---|---|
|  | **CORRESPOND TO**<br><br>ガイ | ○該当する がいとうする come under, be<br>  applicable to ................................ 0141<br>当該 とうがい the said, the concerned ...... 0141<br>該案 がいあん the said proposal ............. 0097 |

| **2164** | A shortcut to perceiving the meaning **CORRESPOND TO** in this character is to see the graph- |
|---|---|
| 言 149 | emes on left and right as roughly **CORRESPONDING TO** one another (at least in the head |
| | character's handwritten form, in which S1 and S8 are both written diagonally). |
| **1377** | |
| 常 13 | |

**EXAMINE A PATIENT**

シン
み(る)

往診 おうしん house call...................0866
○診察する しんさつする examine (a patient) 0639
打診する だしんする examine by percussion;
  sound out...................1025
○患者を診る かんじゃをみる examine a patient
  ...................1939, 0107
診断 しんだん diagnosis...................0849

| 2165 | It is time for 言 to go in for a doctor's checkup. Visualize 𠆢 as the *roof* of the doctor's clinic, and 彡 as the doctor's examining successively lower parts of 言's body, as by palpating it or tapping it with a reflex hammer: **EXAMINE A PATIENT.** ☞ 計 0555, 訂 1024, 珍 2166 |
| --- | --- |
| 言 149 | |
| 1364 | |
| 常 12 | |

**RARE, curious**

チン
めずら(しい)

○珍味 ちんみ delicacy...................0273
珍品 ちんぴん rare article, curio...........0301
珍妙な ちんみょうな queer, odd, fantastic...1746
珍奇な ちんきな novel, curious; rare, strange
  ...................1329
○珍しい めずらしい rare, unusual; novel; precious

| 2166 | Here interpret 彡 as a *hair*-like pattern. This kanji thus refers to a *gem* (王) whose grain is highly unusual in showing a fine, *hair*-like pattern: **RARE** gemstone. ☞ 診 2165 |
| --- | --- |
| 玉 96 | |
| 0814 | |
| 常 9 | |

**TILE, brick**

ガ
かわら

○れん瓦 (煉×瓦) れんが brick
瓦版 かわらばん tile block print.............0923
瓦屋 かわらや tilemaker...................0252
巴瓦 ともえがわら comma-pattern tile.......0527
鬼瓦 おにがわら gargoyle tile...............2090

| 2167 | Visualize as a **TILE** at the corner of a roof. S1 marks the roof's ridge, S2 one of its hips, S3 the eaves, and the bottom of S4 a rain gutter. In the center picture a **TILE**, marked with a special design (S5) because it occupies the end of the roof's hip. To clarify this, do an image search for 鬼瓦 (おにがわら), preferably in Japanese. ☞ 互 0686 |
| --- | --- |
| 瓦 98 | |
| 2918 | |
| 常 5 | |

**PUT TOGETHER**

ヘイ
あわ(せる)

併用する へいようする use together/jointly 0047
併発 へいはつ concurrence...................0148
併記する へいきする line up together (in
  writing)...................0427
○合併する がっぺいする combine, unite, merge
  ...................0227
○併せる あわせる join together, combine, merge

| 2168 | Earlier you learned to see 开 as a torii gate. When you see 并, imagine that the two dot strokes at the top are two hands trying to push down the top crosspiece so as to merge it with the second crosspiece. 并 will thus mean *put together*. In this entry, visualize the *man* (亻) using his two hands to try to **PUT TOGETHER** the crosspieces. |
| --- | --- |
| 人 9 | |
| 0064 | |
| 常 8 | |

574

| | BOTTLE, jar | 瓶詰め　びんづめ　bottling........................0515 |
|---|---|---|
| | | 広口瓶　ひろくちびん　widemouthed bottle .............................................................0238, 0019 |
| | | ○花瓶　かびん　flower vase........................0121 |
| | ビン | 魔法瓶　まほうびん　thermos bottle......2095, 0139 |
| | | 哺乳瓶　ほにゅうびん　baby bottle.......1600, 0160 |

| **2169** |
|---|
| 瓦 98 |
| 瓶 |
| 1231 |
| 常 11 |

Many traditional roof *tiles* (瓦) are semicircular in shape. *Put together* (并) two of these and you get a round **jar** or **BOTTLE**. Note the pattern in the traditional form, shared by all the characters in this set based on 并.

| | FENCE, folding screen | ○屏風　びょうぶ　folding screen...............0425 |
|---|---|---|
| | | 枕屏風　まくらびょうぶ　bedside screen...0656, 0425 |
| | ビョウ　ヘイ | |

| **2170** |
|---|
| 尸 44 |
| 屏 |
| 外 9 |

Here, see 并 as a bunch of slats *put together* into a **FENCE** or **folding screen**. 尸 indicates the *top part of the structure*. Since 尸 also means *doorway*, it further suggests the way a **FENCE** or **folding screen** can be swung open.

| | FENCE, wall | 土塀　どべい　mud wall, plaster wall..........0030 |
|---|---|---|
| | | ○板塀　いたべい　board fence, wooden wall...0924 |
| | | れん瓦 (煉ˣ瓦) 塀　れんがべい　brick wall....2167 |
| | ヘイ | ブロック塀　ブロックべい　concrete (block) wall |
| | | 塀を巡らす　へいをめぐらす　surround with a wall, fence in ......................................1553 |

| **2171** |
|---|
| 土 32 |
| 塀 |
| 0511 |
| 常 12 |

*Earth* (土) *fence* (屏): **FENCE/wall.** ☞ 垣 1397, 壁 1466, 堀 1836

| | RICE CAKE | お餅　おもち　rice cake |
|---|---|---|
| | | ○焼き餅　やきもち　roasted rice cake; jealousy 0769 |
| | | ○煎餅　せんべい　rice cracker....................1749 |
| | ヘイ　もち | 瓦煎餅　かわらせんべい　tile-shaped rice cracker .............................................................2167, 1749 |
| | | 尻餅をつく　しりもちをつく　fall on one's rear 1895 |

| **2172** |
|---|
| 食 184 |
| 餅 |
| 1596 |
| 常 15 |

The next two entries are shown with 𩙿, the old form of 食. They were not standardized with 館 0291, etc. when they were added to the Joyo list. As usual, treat both forms as one and the same. In this entry, 𩙿/食 indicates the general category *food*, while the top two strokes of 并 depict the way **RICE CAKES** pop up over a hot fire.

| | **¹FEED** <br> **²BAIT** | ¹牛の餌 うしのえさ cow feed ................0116 |
|---|---|---|
| | | ¹雌鳥に餌をやる めんどりにえさをやる feed the hens ................1788, 0340 |
| | | ²生き餌 いきえ live bait ................0036 |
| | ジ <br> え えさ | ②餌で誘う えさでさそう lure with bait ................1783 |
| | | ²釣り針の餌を付け替える つりばりのえさをつけかえる replace the bait on one's fishhook ................2132, 0556, 0064, 1167 |

| **2173** <br> 食 184 <br> 餌 <br> 1597 <br> 常 15 | Ears (耳) may not be suitable for human *food* (飠/食), but they are perfectly acceptable as animal **FEED**, or as **BAIT**. While we show here the officially listed forms 餌 and 餌, forms using 食 are also accepted, so you needn't worry about having to write the traditional form. |
|---|---|

| | **SWALLOW, gulp** | ○呑む のむ swallow, gulp; accept; hold back |
|---|---|---|
| | | 一呑みて ひとのみて (drinking/downing) in one draft ................0002 |
| | | 条件を呑む じょうけんをのむ accept the conditions ................0119, 0118 |
| | の(む) | 涙を呑む なみだをのむ choke back one's tears ................1020 |
| | | 併呑 へいどん annexation, merger ................2168 |

| **2174** <br> 口 30 <br><br> 外 7 | The next three kanji contain not 天 but 夭, whose top stroke is written from right to left. In this entry, visualize the *mouth* (口) trying to accomplish the very difficult task of **SWALLOWING** 夭, like a snake trying to **gulp** down an ostrich egg. Like 飲 0289, 呑 is read のむ, but it refers to **SWALLOWING** and **gulping** rather than drinking. ☞ 吞 0552 |
|---|---|

| | **FERTILITY** | 沃土 よくど fertile soil, fertile land ................0030 |
|---|---|---|
| | | 沃野 よくや fertile fields ................0534 |
| | | ○肥沃な ひよくな fertile ................2023 |
| | ヨク | |

| **2175** <br> 水 85 <br><br> 0240 <br> 常 7 | Let the difference between 夭 and 天 serve as the visual clue to the meaning of this character. Focusing on the incline of S4, see 夭 as a person tilting a container to pour *liquid* (氵) nutriments into the land: **FERTILE**. |
|---|---|

| | **BEWITCHING** | ○妖術 ようじゅつ witchcraft, sorcery ................0993 |
|---|---|---|
| | | 妖婦 ようふ enchantress ................1017 |
| | | 妖雲 よううん ominous cloud ................0897 |
| | ヨウ <br> あや(しい) | 妖怪 ようかい ghost, apparition ................1255 |
| | | ○妖しい魅力 あやしいみりょく bewitching charm ................2094, 0084 |

| **2176** <br> 女 38 <br><br> 0212 <br> 常 7 | Again take your cue from the sloping line of 夭. See 夭 here as a person whose "head" (S4) turns toward the *woman* (女), caught by the spell of her **BEWITCHING** beauty. ☞ 妊 1845 |
|---|---|

| 呪 | **CHARM, curse**<br><br>ジュ<br>のろ(う) | ○呪術 じゅじゅつ sorcery, magic .............. **0993**<br>呪縛 じゅばく curse, hex ..................... **0984**<br>○呪う のろう curse |
|---|---|---|

**2177**
口 30
呪
0245
常 | 8

*Older brother* (兄)'s *mouth* (口) uttering a **curse/CHARM**.

| 艶 | **¹ CHARMING, voluptuous; glossy**<br>**² ROMANCE**<br><br>エン<br>つや なま(めかしい)* あて(やか)* | ¹妖艶な ようえんな bewitching beauty ....... **2176**<br>¹艶かしい なまめかしい charming; voluptuous<br>¹艶やかな あてやかな charming, fair<br>①艶っぽい つやっぽい coquettish, sexy<br>②艶聞 えんぶん love affair, romance .......... **0453** |
|---|---|---|

**2178**
色 139
艶
1683
常 | 19

Recall 豊 0513 ABUNDANT. With 色, we have "*abundant color*" (expressing M1 **CHARMING/ voluptuous; glossy**) or "*abundant eros*" (expressing M2 **ROMANCE**).

| | **AFFECTIONATE, compassionate**<br><br>ジ<br>いつく(しむ) | 慈愛 じあい affection, love, benevolence... **0778**<br>○慈悲 じひ mercy, compassion .............. **1856**<br>慈善 じぜん charity ....................... **1213**<br>慈雨 じう beneficial rain .................... **0154**<br>○親が子を慈しむ おやがこをいつくしむ Parents<br>care tenderly for their children ....... **0276, 0094** |
|---|---|---|

**2179**
心 61
慈
2053
常 | 13

See S1–3 as a hand facing downward (S3 shows the palm, S1–2 show two knuckles sticking up). Here then, we see a *hand* holding *two young children* (幺幺) to its *heart* (心): a vivid image of **AFFECTION**. Note that the three kanji based on 茲 are all pronounced ジ.

| 滋 | **NOURISH**<br><br>ジ | ○滋養 じよう nourishment, nutrition ......... **0500**<br>滋養分 じようぶん nutrient ............ **0500, 0088**<br>滋味に富む じみにとむ delicious, nutritious<br>............................... **0273, 1481**<br>滋賀県 しがけん Shiga prefecture ..... **1172, 0844** |
|---|---|---|

**2180**
水 85
滋
0549
常 | 12

Now see *liquid* (氵) **NOURISHING** the *two young children* (幺幺).

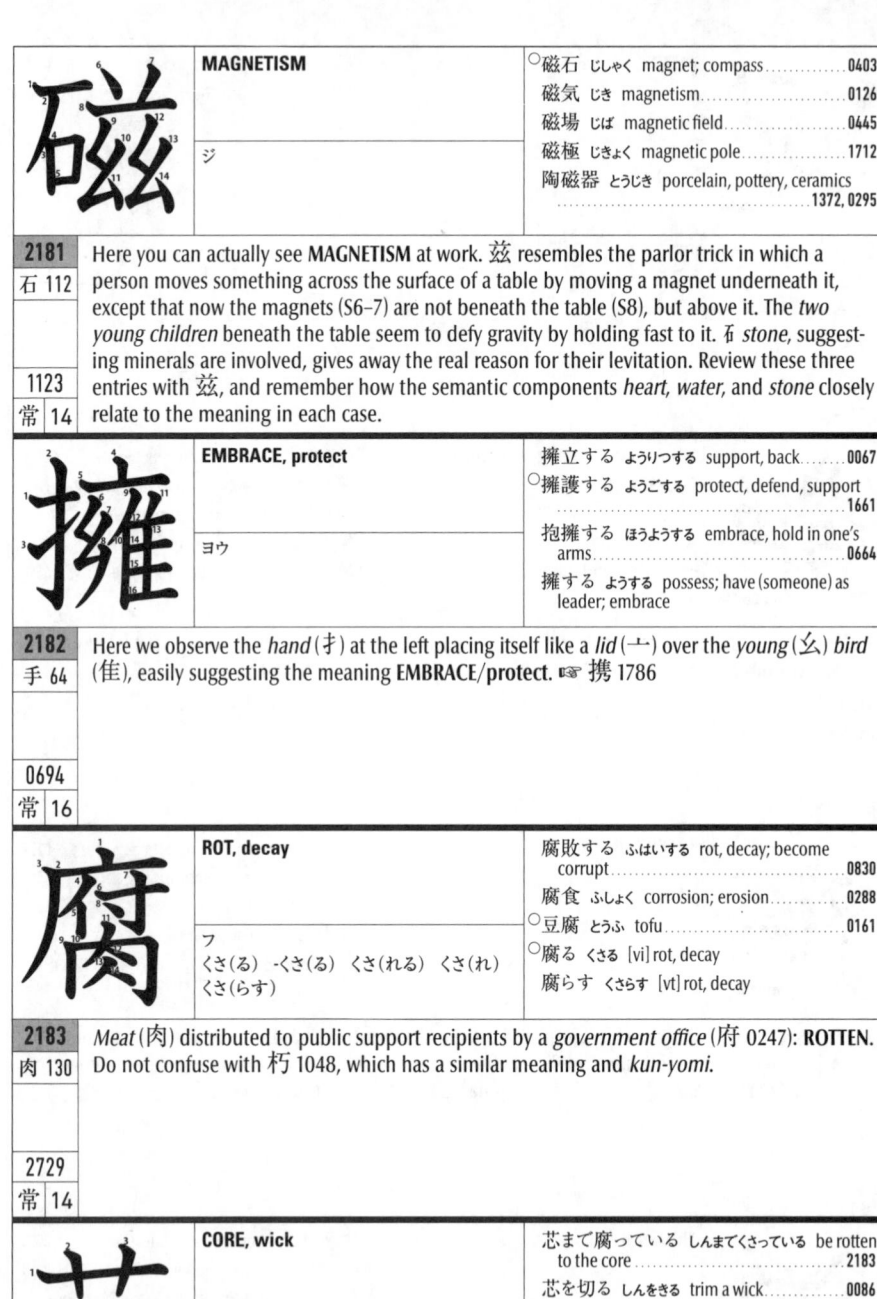

| | MAGNETISM | |
|---|---|---|
| 磁 | | ○磁石 じしゃく magnet; compass.............0403 |
| | | 磁気 じき magnetism.....................0126 |
| | | 磁場 じば magnetic field..............0445 |
| | ジ | 磁極 じきょく magnetic pole..............1712 |
| | | 陶磁器 とうじき porcelain, pottery, ceramics |
| | | .........................1372, 0295 |

**2181**
石 112

1123
常 14

Here you can actually see **MAGNETISM** at work. 兹 resembles the parlor trick in which a person moves something across the surface of a table by moving a magnet underneath it, except that now the magnets (S6–7) are not beneath the table (S8), but above it. The *two young children* beneath the table seem to defy gravity by holding fast to it. 石 *stone*, suggesting minerals are involved, gives away the real reason for their levitation. Review these three entries with 兹, and remember how the semantic components *heart*, *water*, and *stone* closely relate to the meaning in each case.

---

| | EMBRACE, protect | |
|---|---|---|
| 擁 | | 擁立する ようりつする support, back.......0067 |
| | | ○擁護する ようごする protect, defend, support |
| | | .........................1661 |
| | | 抱擁する ほうようする embrace, hold in one's |
| | ヨウ | arms..............................0664 |
| | | 擁する ようする possess; have (someone) as |
| | | leader; embrace |

**2182**
手 64

0694
常 16

Here we observe the *hand* (扌) at the left placing itself like a *lid* (宀) over the *young* (幺) *bird* (隹), easily suggesting the meaning **EMBRACE/protect**. ☞ 携 1786

---

| | ROT, decay | |
|---|---|---|
| 腐 | | 腐敗する ふはいする rot, decay; become |
| | | corrupt..............................0830 |
| | | 腐食 ふしょく corrosion; erosion...........0288 |
| | フ | ○豆腐 とうふ tofu....................0161 |
| | くさ(る) -くさ(る) くさ(れる) くさ(れ) | ○腐る くさる [vi] rot, decay |
| | くさ(らす) | 腐らす くさらす [vt] rot, decay |

**2183**
肉 130

2729
常 14

*Meat* (肉) distributed to public support recipients by a *government office* (府 0247): **ROTTEN**. Do not confuse with 朽 1048, which has a similar meaning and *kun-yomi*.

---

| | CORE, wick | |
|---|---|---|
| 芯 | | 芯まで腐っている しんまでくさっている be rotten |
| | | to the core..............................2183 |
| | | 芯を切る しんをきる trim a wick.............0086 |
| | シン | ○鉛筆の芯 えんぴつのしん pencil lead..2067, 1605 |
| | | 芯抜き器 しんぬきき corer...........1951, 0295 |
| | | 二芯ケーブル にしんケーブル duplex cable..0003 |

**2184**
艸 140

1898
常 7

*Heart* (心) of a *plant* (艹): **CORE**. As the sample vocabulary indicates, 芯 can refer to the **CORE** of things besides plants, such as the lead of a pencil, or the wick of a candle. Note that it can always be replaced by 心 0056.

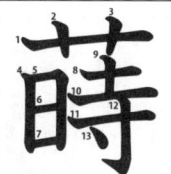

**SOW, scatter**

ジ シ
ま(く)

○蒔く　まく　sow (seed), scatter
畑に燕麦を蒔く　はたけにえんばくをまく　sow a
field with oats ....................0129, 1741, 0131
蒔絵　まきえ　(gold/silver) lacquer(ing), *makie*
..............................................0525
ばら蒔く　ばらまく　scatter; spend recklessly

| 2185 | *Plant* (艹) + *time* (時): a time to **SOW**. |
| 艹 140 | |
| 2042 | |
| 名 13 | |

**SCATTER**

サン サツ
ま(く)

○撒く　まく　scatter, sprinkle; cause to scatter, give
someone the slip
餌を撒く　えさをまく　scatter animal feed ....2173
畑に肥料を撒く　はたけにひりょうをまく　scatter
manure over a field .............0129, 2023, 0758
○撒き散らす　まきちらす　scatter about, strew;
squander........................................0808
撒水　さんすい (=さっすい)　water sprinkling...0027

| 2186 | *Hand* (扌) + *scatter* (散 0808): let this suggest **SCATTERING** with the hands, as one does with |
| 手 64 | seeds or handbills. ☞ 散 0808, 撤 2187, 徹 2188 |
| 0670 | |
| 名 15 | |

**WITHDRAW**

テツ

撤去　てっきょ　removal, dismantlement (of a
building)....................................0138
撤回　てっかい　withdrawal, retraction .......0050
撤廃　てっぱい　abolition, removal ..........0149
○撤退　てったい　withdrawal, evacuation, pullout
(of an army)..................................1091
撤兵する　てっぺいする　withdraw troops....0907

| 2187 | You should learn this one in such a way that you can distinguish it from the entries before |
| 手 64 | and after it. Unlike the one before, but like the one after, it contains 育 *raise*. When 育 |
| | appears with 扌, think of a parent's *hand* **WITHDRAWING** her child from something in which |
| | he has entered. 攵 *strike* suggests parental discipline. ☞ 徹 2188, 撒 2186 |
| 0673 | |
| 常 15 | |

**GO THROUGH (with)**

テツ

貫徹する　かんてつする　carry through, go
through with, accomplish..................1911
○徹底的　てっていてき　thorough, exhaustive
.......................................0482, 0169
一徹な　いってつな　obstinate, stubborn.....0002
徹夜　てつや　staying up all night............0467
徹する　てっする　go through (with), be thorough

| 2188 | (Continuing from the previous entry) Here 育 appears with 彳 *go*, which is our mnemonic |
| 彳 60 | clue for the meaning **GO THROUGH (with)**. Unlike in the previous entry, this time the parent |
| | does not WITHDRAW the child, but instead lets him **GO THROUGH with** something. Practice |
| | distinguishing the last three entries by their variable elements. ☞ 撤 2187, 撒 2186 |
| 0659 | |
| 常 15 | |

| | | |
|---|---|---|
| **SLIGHT, minute** | 微生物 びせいぶつ microorganism...**0036, 0172** | |
| | ○顕微鏡 けんびきょう microscope........**1921, 1547** | |
| | 微笑 びしょう smile...........................**0579** | |
| ビ | ○微妙な びみょうな subtle, delicate...........**1746** | |
| かす(か)* | 微かに見える かすかにみえる be seen dimly/ faintly.................................**0083** | |

| | |
|---|---|
| **2189** | As with the previous set of three kanji, the set of three that starts here will require us to focus |
| 彳 60 | our attention on the variable component. Ignore 彳, 山, and 攵, which are held constant. Surrounded by these three, we find in this entry a form similar to 几 *table/tablecloth*, but in fact more closely resembling π pi. We can therefore get a little irrational and use π as a |
| **0587** | mnemonic clue for **SLIGHT/minute**, since despite its infinite decimal places, π is, after all, a |
| 常 13 | **SLIGHT** number. It is easy to associate the reading ビ with "pi" (π). ☞ 徴 2190 |

| | | |
|---|---|---|
| **¹ LEVY, impose** | ¹ 徴収する ちょうしゅうする collect taxes/payment | |
| **² SIGN, symptom** | ..............................**1155** | |
| | ①徴兵 ちょうへい conscription, enlistment, draft | |
| | .................................**0907** | |
| チョウ | ² 徴候 ちょうこう symptom, sign; omen .......**1675** | |
| | ² 象徴 しょうちょう symbol...................**1277** | |
| | ②特徴 とくちょう distinctive feature, characteristic | |
| | ..............................**0385** | |

| | |
|---|---|
| **2190** | (Continuing from the previous entry) This time, associate *gem* (王) with valuables collected by |
| 彳 60 | a fiscal **LEVY** or impost. Unrelatedly, you can associate 王's other meaning of *spherical object* |
| 徴 | with M2 **SIGN**, as in a **SIGN** that one might look for in a crystal ball. ☞ 微 2189, 懲 2191 |
| **0622** | |
| 常 14 | |

| | | |
|---|---|---|
| **CHASTISE** | 懲悪 ちょうあく chastisement, punishment...**0546** | |
| | ○懲罰 ちょうばつ discipline, punishment.....**0742** | |
| | 懲役 ちょうえき penal servitude ..............**0518** | |
| チョウ | ○懲りる こりる learn a lesson; have had enough of | |
| こ(りる) こ(らす) こ(らしめる) | 懲らす(=懲らしめる) こらす (=こらしめる) chastise, punish | |

| | |
|---|---|
| **2191** | *Levying* (徴) a stiff penalty upon a *heart* (心): **CHASTISE**. As a visual shortcut, you might see |
| 心 61 | the heavy burden of four graphemes upon *heart* as a kind of **CHASTISING** punishment upon |
| 懲 | it. They do seem to be coming down on poor 心 like a ton of bricks. ☞ 徴 2190 |
| **2526** | |
| 常 18 | |

| | | |
|---|---|---|
| **ALMOST; quite, really** | 世界の殆どの国 せかいのほとんどのくに most/ almost all countries in the world 0604, 0612, 0075 | |
| | 殆ど毎週 ほとんどまいしゅう almost every week | |
| | .................................**0105, 0305** | |
| タイ ダイ* | 殆ど来ない ほとんどこない hardly ever comes | |
| ほとん(ど) | .................................**0274** | |

| | |
|---|---|
| **2192** | Picture the *platform* (台) as an operating table or sickbed, with *death* (歹) waiting nearby: |
| 歹 78 | **ALMOST** dead. The word 殆ど (ほとんど) is used like "mostly" or "hardly," in the sense of |
| | "**ALMOST** all ..." or "**ALMOST** no ..." |
| **0811** | |
| 名 9 | |

| 后 | **EMPRESS** | 皇后 こうごう empress, queen...............0077 |
|---|---|---|
| | コウ | 皇后陛下 こうごうへいか Her Majesty the Empress.................0077, 1431, 0040 |
| | | 皇太后 こうたいごう empress dowager, queen mother...............0077, 0294 |

| **2193** | Let 口 represent the emperor, in the sense of the "*mouth*piece" or public face of the imperial |
|---|---|
| 口 30 | family. See S1–3 as the **EMPRESS**, faithfully standing behind him. |
| **2574** | |
| 常 6 | |

| 垢 | **DIRT** | 垢を落とす あかをおとす wash off dirt.......0793 |
|---|---|---|
| | コウ ク | ○垢だらけ あかだらけ covered in dirt, filthy |
| | あか | 耳の垢 みみのあか earwax..................0057 |

| **2194** | Now observe how the *empress* (后) has gotten some *soil* (土) on the back of her heretofore- |
|---|---|
| 土 32 | immaculate gown, an image that emphasizes this kanji's meaning, **DIRT**. |
| 外 9 | |

| 妃 | **(married) PRINCESS** | 后妃 こうひ empress, queen..............2193 |
|---|---|---|
| | ヒ | ○妃殿下 ひでんか Her Imperial Highness ..............0881, 0040 |
| | | 王妃 おうひ queen, empress...............0072 |

| **2195** | Visualize 己 as a lady-in-waiting *kneeling* before a **married PRINCESS**. ☞ 姫 2196 |
|---|---|
| 女 38 | |
| **0182** | |
| 常 6 | |

| 姫 | **DAUGHTER OF NOBLE BIRTH** | 姫君 ひめぎみ princess, highborn young lady ......................1407 |
|---|---|---|
| | ひめ ひめ- | ○姫様 ひめさま daughter of a nobleman .....0501 |
| | | 姫宮 ひめみや princess.....................1242 |
| | | シンデレラ姫 シンデレラひめ Cinderella |
| | | 姫子松 ひめこまつ small pine .........0094, 0242 |

| **2196** | 臣 is a *retainer* assigned to keep ardent young men away from this **DAUGHTER OF NOBLE** |
|---|---|
| 女 38 | **BIRTH**. ☞ 妃 2195, 媛 1125 |
| **0368** | |
| 常 10 | |

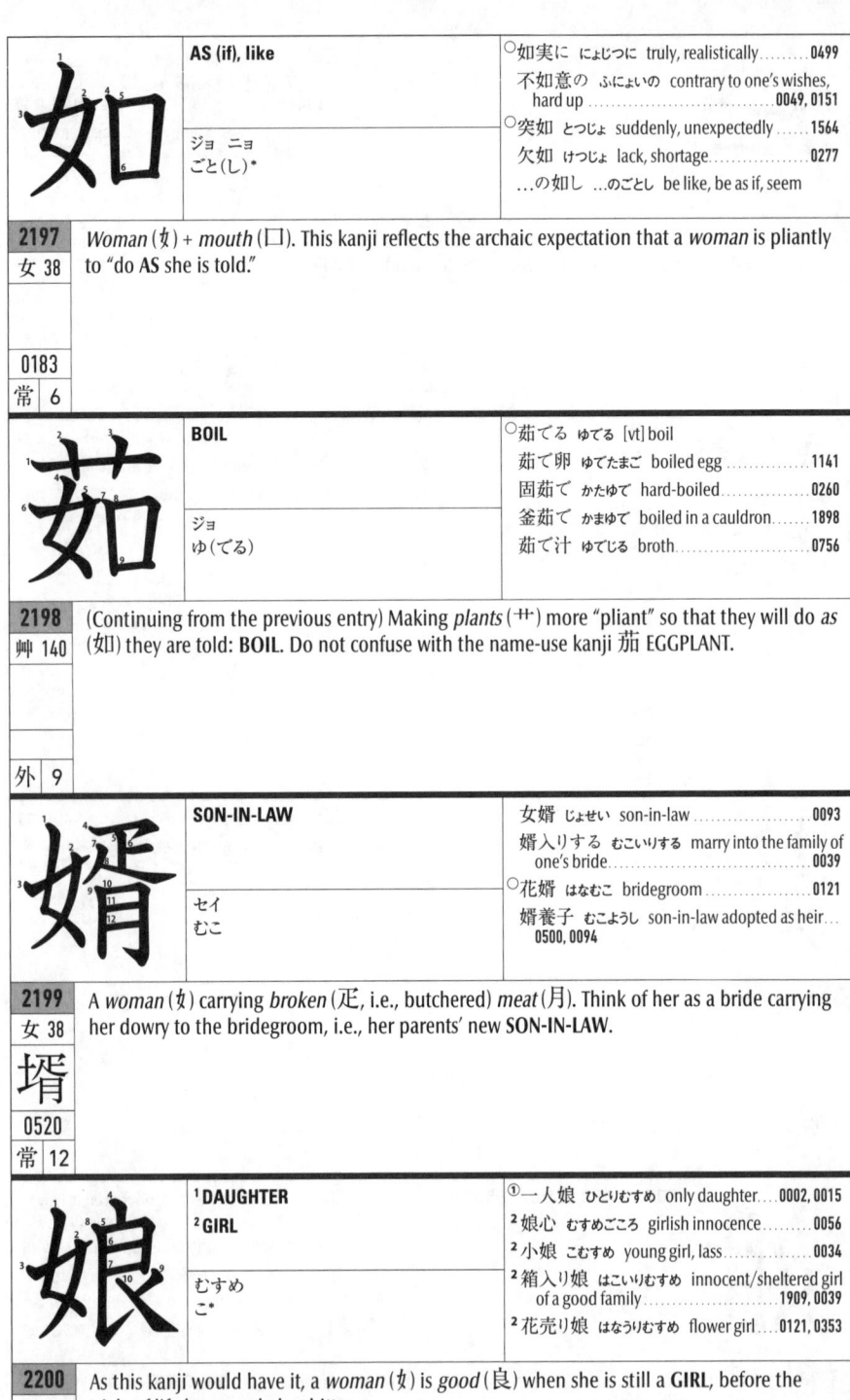

## 如

**AS (if), like**

ジョ ニョ
ごと(し)*

○如実に にょじつに truly, realistically.........0499
不如意の ふにょいの contrary to one's wishes, hard up.....................0049, 0151
○突如 とつじょ suddenly, unexpectedly......1564
欠如 けつじょ lack, shortage..................0277
…の如し …のごとし be like, be as if, seem

**2197**
女 38

*Woman* (女) + *mouth* (口). This kanji reflects the archaic expectation that a *woman* is pliantly to "do **AS** she is told."

0183
常 | 6

---

## 茹

**BOIL**

ジョ
ゆ(てる)

○茹でる ゆでる [vt] boil
茹で卵 ゆでたまご boiled egg.............1141
固茹で かたゆで hard-boiled..............0260
釜茹で かまゆで boiled in a cauldron.......1898
茹で汁 ゆでじる broth......................0756

**2198**
艸 140

(Continuing from the previous entry) Making *plants* (艹) more "pliant" so that they will do *as* (如) they are told: **BOIL**. Do not confuse with the name-use kanji 茄 EGGPLANT.

外 | 9

---

## 婿

**SON-IN-LAW**

セイ
むこ

女婿 じょせい son-in-law....................0093
婿入りする むこいりする marry into the family of one's bride...................0039
○花婿 はなむこ bridegroom.................0121
婿養子 むこようし son-in-law adopted as heir... 0500, 0094

**2199**
女 38

壻

A *woman* (女) carrying *broken* (疋, i.e., butchered) *meat* (月). Think of her as a bride carrying her dowry to the bridegroom, i.e., her parents' new **SON-IN-LAW**.

0520
常 | 12

---

## 娘

**[1] DAUGHTER**
**[2] GIRL**

むすめ
こ*

① 一人娘 ひとりむすめ only daughter....0002, 0015
[2] 娘心 むすめごころ girlish innocence.........0056
[2] 小娘 こむすめ young girl, lass...............0034
[2] 箱入り娘 はこいりむすめ innocent/sheltered girl of a good family.......................1909, 0039
[2] 花売り娘 はなうりむすめ flower girl....0121, 0353

**2200**
女 38

As this kanji would have it, a *woman* (女) is good (良) when she is still a **GIRL**, before the trials of life have made her bitter.

0367
常 | 10

| | ¹WED A MAN<br>²BRIDE | ¹再嫁 さいか second marriage................0911<br>①嫁ぎ先 とつぎさき family a woman has married<br>    into.................0134 |
|---|---|---|
| | カ<br>よめ とつ(ぐ) | ¹嫁入り よめいり wedding, marriage........0039<br>②花嫁 はなよめ bride.................0121<br>転嫁する てんかする impute, lay the blame on<br>    another.................0224 |

| 2201 | A *woman*(女) moving into her husband's *home*(家): **WED A MAN; BRIDE.** |
|---|---|
| 女 38 | |
| 0582 | |
| 常 13 | |

| | WORK, work for a living | ○稼働 かどう working, work; operation (of a<br>    machine).................0541<br>稼業 かぎょう trade, business; work; occupation<br>    .................0498 |
|---|---|---|
| | カ<br>かせ(ぐ) | ○時間を稼ぐ じかんをかせぐ gain time..0383, 0448<br>稼ぎ手 かせぎて breadwinner; good/hard<br>    worker.................0046<br>出稼ぎ でかせぎ working away from home.0038 |

| 2202 | Bringing *rice*(禾) *home*(家): **WORK (for a living).** |
|---|---|
| 禾 115 | |
| 1136 | |
| 常 15 | |

| | MOUND, hillock | 塚を築く つかをきずく pile up a mound......1635<br>○貝塚 かいづか shell mound; kitchen midden<br>    .................0082 |
|---|---|---|
| | つか -づか | 一里塚 いちりづか milepost, milestone<br>    .................0002, 0531<br>大塚 おおつか Otsuka (= Ohtsuka) [surname]<br>    .................0033 |

| 2203 | A *pig*(豕) *covering*(冖) himself in a **MOUND** of *soil*(土). |
|---|---|
| 土 32 | |
| 塚 | |
| 0509 | |
| 常 12 | |

| | ¹GREAT MAN<br>²MAGNIFICENT | ¹豪傑 ごうけつ hero, great man................1176<br>¹強豪 きょうごう veteran, champion..........0423<br>②豪華な ごうかな gorgeous, splendid, magnificent<br>    .................1012 |
|---|---|---|
| | ゴウ | ²豪壮な ごうそうな grand, magnificent, splendid<br>    .................1589<br>豪日 ごうにち Australia and Japan, Australian-<br>    Japanese.................0001 |

| 2204 | S1–5 are the roof and second-story window from 高 0185 TALL. Picture a *pig*(豕) that truly stands *tall*: **GREAT MAN; MAGNIFICENT.** Also used as the kanji abbreviation for Australia (a selected list of kanji abbreviations for countries and regions appears in Appendix 5). |
|---|---|
| 豕 152 | |
| 1838 | |
| 常 14 | |

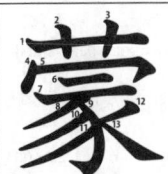

**¹ IGNORANCE, darkness**
**² PHONETIC [mō]**

モウ

①啓蒙 けいもう enlightenment, instruction...1738
②蒙古 もうこ Mongolia.........................0254
² 蒙古語 もうこご Mongolian (language)
.........................................0254, 0222
² 蒙古斑 もうこはん Mongolian spot
.........................................0254, 1854

| 2205 | See this as a *pig* (豕) lying in the **dark**, *covered* (冖) by the *grass* (艹) of the Mongolian steppe: **IGNORANCE/darkness**. Also used as the kanji abbreviation for Mongolia. Note the extra stroke between 豕 and 冖. |
| 艹 140 | |
| 2045 | |
| 名 13 | |

**CLEAR LAND FOR FARMING**

コン

○開墾 かいこん clearing, reclamation........0450
墾田 こんでん new rice field................0020
未墾の みこんの uncultivated, wild.........0271

| 2206 | At last we meet 豸, the *badger*. See S2–3 as his beady eyes and S1 as a stripe along the top of his head. The act of **CLEARING LAND FOR FARMING** is intuitively illustrated here with an image of clearing new *land* (土) at the *limit/boundary* (艮) where the farmer's land ends and the *badger*'s land begins. |
| 土 32 | |
| 2516 | |
| 常 16 | |

**¹ FAMILIAR, intimate**
**² EARNEST**

コン
ねんご(ろ)

¹ 懇願する こんがんする beg earnestly, entreat
.........................................0214
¹ 懇請する こんせいする request earnestly,
entreat.....................................0977
①懇ろな ねんごろな cordial; courteous; intimate
² 懇親 こんしん friendship, intimacy..........0276
②懇談 こんだん familiar talk/chat.............1977

| 2207 | (Continuing from the previous entry) This time, rather than crossing the *boundary* to the *badger*'s land, we cross the boundary to his *heart* (心), i.e., we become **FAMILIAR/intimate** with him. Also means **EARNEST**, from the idea of pursuing something without inhibition or pretense. |
| 心 61 | |
| 2517 | |
| 常 17 | |

**APPEARANCE, form**

ボウ

○変貌 へんぼう transformation, transfiguration
.........................................0775
容貌 ようぼう looks, personal appearance...1037
美貌 びぼう good looks, pretty features....0497
全貌 ぜんぼう full view, whole aspect.......0078

| 2208 | At the right, *white* (白) on top of *legs* (儿) suggests a *white* head. We can thus interpret this kanji as a description of a *badger* (豸)'s **APPEARANCE**. |
| 豸 153 | |
| 兒 | |
| 1408 | |
| 常 14 | |

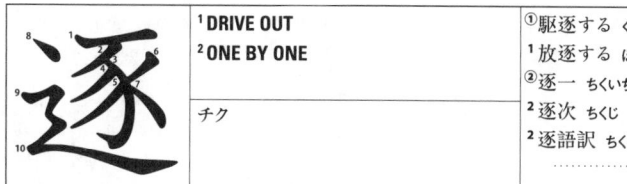

| 逐 | ¹ **DRIVE OUT** ²**ONE BY ONE** <br><br> チク | ①駆逐する　くちくする　drive away, drive out....1388 <br> ¹ 放逐する　ほうちくする　expel, banish.........0574 <br> ② 逐一　ちくいち　one by one, in detail..........0002 <br> ² 逐次　ちくじ　one by one, successively........0278 <br> ² 逐語訳　ちくごやく　word-for-word translation <br> ........................................................0222, 1505 |

| **2209** <br> 辵 162 <br><br> 2671 <br> 常 10 | Now we return to the more familiar pig (豕). Devise for yourself a memorable plot climaxing in a town's banishing all its pigs. Then picture here a pig being **DRIVEN OUT** out of town. It is important to picture the pigs being driven out **ONE BY ONE**, with special attention given to every individual. ☞ 逐 2210 |

| 遂 | **ACCOMPLISH, carry out** <br><br> スイ　と(げる) <br> つい(に)* | 遂行する　すいこうする　accomplish..........0055 <br> 完遂する　かんすいする　execute successfully, bring to completion ........................0633 <br> ○自殺未遂　じさつみすい　attempted suicide <br> ..........................................0081, 0522, 0271 <br> ○遂げる　とげる　accomplish, carry out <br> 遂に　ついに　at last, at length |

| **2210** <br> 辵 162 <br><br> 2705 <br> 常 12 | This character tells a completely different story, for here we have not simply a *pig* (豕), but a crack *pig commando* (see 隊 0586), whom we picture *advancing* (辶) forward to **carry out/ ACCOMPLISH** his special mission. ☞ 逐 2209 |

| 墜 | **DROP DOWN** <br><br> ツイ | ○墜落　ついらく　fall, crash........................0793 <br> 墜落事故　ついらくじこ　plane crash <br> ..................................................0793, 0080, 0257 <br> 墜死する　ついしする　fall to one's death.....0716 <br> 撃墜する　げきついする　shoot down.........1026 |

| **2211** <br> 土 32 <br><br> 2506 <br> 常 15 | Here we observe a *party* (隊) of pig commandos **DROPPING DOWN** from the hills toward the *earth* (土). Compared to the next entry, we should see the commandos plunging rapidly, for 墜 is mostly used in reference to plane crashes and other fatal falls. See them **DROP DOWN** like rocks with their heavy backpacks. ☞ 隊 0586, 堕 2212 |

| 堕 | **DEGENERATE, descend** <br><br> ダ | ○堕落　だらく　degeneration, corruption, decadence..................................................0793 <br> 堕胎　だたい　abortion...........................1986 |

| **2212** <br> 土 32 <br><br> 堕 <br> 2456 <br> 常 12 | Here again we see something falling toward the *earth* (土). However, compared to the last entry's "DROP DOWN," this entry's "**DEGENERATE**" suggests a more gradual sinking. For this reason, it helps here to see the outstretched hand (ナ) providing resistance, and slowing the fall to a gradual **descent**. ☞ 墜 2211, 随 2213, 惰 2217 |

**FOLLOW**

ズイ

○付随 ふずい incident to, concomitant ......0064
随行する ずいこうする attend on, accompany, follow .................................................0055
随筆 ずいひつ essay; stray notes ...........1605
随意に ずいいに voluntarily, at will .........0151
随分 ずいぶん extremely, considerably .....0088

| 2213 | The image of 有 upon (辶) is a simplification of 遀. We'll interpret the simplified form, |
| 阜 170 | which suggests *having* something on the bed of one's *truck*, as a *loaded vehicle*. In this entry, |
| 隨 | the vehicle drives up into the *hills* (阝), while the load **FOLLOWS** behind. ☞ 堕 2212, 髄 2215 |
| 0573 | |
| 常 12 | |

---

**ATTACH, be attached to, hand over**

フ

○附随 ふずい incident to, concomitant ......2213
附属する ふぞくする be attached to, belong to .................................................1872
附則 ふそく additional rules, bylaw .........0625
附着する ふちゃくする adhere/cling to, agglutinate; cohere ...........................0938
寄附する きふする contribute, donate ......1330

| 2214 | This kanji was formerly used for the intransitive verb つく, while 付 was used for the transi- |
| 阜 170 | tive つける. They have since come to be used indistinctly, and the present entry has largely |
| | fallen out of use. On the infrequent occasions when you encounter 附, interpret it the same |
| | way you would 付: **ATTACH/be attached to/hand over**. ☞ 付 0064 |
| 0307 | |
| 常 8 | |

---

**MARROW**

ズイ

○骨髄 こつずい bone marrow ................0465
脊髄 せきずい spinal cord .....................2153
髄液 ずいえき spinal fluid ......................0468
真髄 しんずい essence, quintessence, soul ...0838
精髄 せいずい essence, soul, spirit, pith ....0976

| 2215 | (Continuing from 随 2213) Picture the *loaded vehicle* (at the right) as a surgeon's loaded |
| 骨 188 | needle, advancing forward toward the center of a *bone* (骨): **MARROW**. ☞ 随 2213 |
| 髄 | |
| 1634 | |
| 常 19 | |

---

**IDLE, remiss**

タイ
おこた(る) なま(ける)

怠慢な たいまんな negligent, inattentive, remiss .................................................1134
けん怠 (倦×怠) けんたい fatigue, languor, weariness
○怠る おこたる be remiss, neglect
○怠ける なまける be lazy; neglect
怠け者 なまけもの idle/lazy fellow ..........0107

| 2216 | *Platform* (台) + *mind/heart* (心): here imagine that we are temporarily relieving the *mind* |
| 心 61 | from its duties by hiding it under a *platform* and taking it out of service: **IDLE**. |
| 1794 | |
| 常 9 | |

| 惰 | LAZY | 惰気 だき indolence, inactivity, laziness....**0126** |
|---|---|---|
| | | 惰眠 だみん indolence, idle slumber, inactivity |
| | | ....................................................**1009** |
| | ダ | °怠惰 たいだ laziness, idleness.................**2216** |
| | | 惰性 だせい inertia; force of habit.........**0128** |
| | | 惰力 だりょく inertia; force of habit.........**0084** |

| **2217** | 左 looks a little like a person holding her arm against something and leaning to one side. In |
|---|---|
| 心 61 | the head character, visualize 忄 leaning over in this way upon 月. Again letting *heart* represent |
| | a person's spirit, see the idea of **LAZINESS** in this image of a *heart* leaning over on something. |
| | ☞ 堕 2212 |
| **0531** | |
| 常 12 | |

| 佐 | ¹ ASSIST<br>² FIELD OFFICER | ①補佐する ほさする assist, help.............**1598** |
|---|---|---|
| | | ¹ 佐幕派 さばくは supporters of the shogun |
| | | ....................................................**1339, 1367** |
| | サ | ² 佐官 さかん field officer.....................**0290** |
| | | ² 大佐 たいさ (army) colonel, (navy) captain **0033** |
| | | 佐々木 ささき Sasaki [surname].............**0028** |

| **2218** | "*Left* (左)-hand *man* (イ)": **ASSISTANT**. M2 **FIELD OFFICER** is an extended meaning. |
|---|---|
| 人 9 | |
| **0051** | |
| 常 7 | |

| 玩 | PLAY WITH | °玩具 がんぐ (=おもちゃ) toy .................**0837** |
|---|---|---|
| | | 玩味する がんみする delight in, enjoy.......**0273** |
| | | 愛玩する あいがんする adore, cherish......**0778** |
| | ガン | 愛玩物 あいがんぶつ cherished object |
| | もてあそ(ぶ)* | ....................................................**0778, 0172** |
| | | °玩ぶ もてあそぶ play with [as with one's pen, |
| | | food, etc.] |

| **2219** | Visualize long S7 as an extended arm, rolling or tossing a *spherical object* (王) that is thrown |
|---|---|
| 玉 96 | underhand, such as a bowling ball or softball: **PLAY WITH**. ☞ 球 1099 |
| **0778** | |
| 常 8 | |

| 弄 | PLAY WITH | °玩弄する がんろうする toy with, make sport of |
|---|---|---|
| | | ....................................................**2219** |
| | | 愚弄する ぐろうする mock, ridicule.........**1878** |
| | | 翻弄する ほんろうする make fun of.........**1512** |
| | ロウ | 弄する ろうする play with, play a trick on |
| | もてあそ(ぶ) | °弄ぶ もてあそぶ play with [as with a person's |
| | | feelings] |

| **2220** | Normally 王 in this position would be *king*, but following the previous entry, picture it again |
|---|---|
| 玉 96 | as a *spherical object*, this time being held in *two hands* (廾): **PLAY WITH**. ☞ 奔 2222 |
| **2129** | |
| 常 7 | |

### RIDICULE

チョウ
あざけ（る）

○嘲弄する ちょうろうする ridicule, mock; disdain
..........2220
自嘲する じちょうする mock oneself..........0081
嘲笑する ちょうしょうする mock, deride..........0579
○嘲る あざける ridicule, mock; disdain

---

**2221**

口 30

嘲

0648

常 15

This kanji was not standardized with 朝 when it joined the Joyo list. To learn its meaning, start by memorizing the meaning of V4 嘲る (あざける, ridicule, mock; disdain). Then, when you see 口 (suggesting something spoken) with 朝, use the latter's *kun* reading (あさ) as a mnemonic for あざける and, by extension, **RIDICULE**.

---

### RUSH, run

ホン

○奔走する ほんそうする bustle about, exert oneself for, devote oneself to ..........0140
奔流 ほんりゅう torrent, rapids ..........1059
奔馬 ほんば galloping horse..........0336
狂奔する きょうほんする rush around; make frantic efforts ..........0736
淫奔な いんぽんな lewd, lascivious ..........1844

---

**2222**

大 37

1904

常 8

Visualize a *big man* (大) chasing a small man (十), who **RUSHES** to get under a barrier (廾) in order to save himself. ☞ 弄 2220

---

### EVIL PRACTICE

ヘイ

弊政 へいせい misgovernment, maladministration..........0246
○弊害 へいがい evil, abuse, vice ..........0413
悪弊 あくへい evil, vice, abuse ..........0546
語弊 ごへい improper expression..........0222
弊社 へいしゃ [humble] our firm..........0314

---

**2223**

廾 55

2508

常 15

Take the construction at the top to mean *dry*: see 攵 *striking* a wet *cloth* (巾) so that drops of water (S2–3 and S7–8) fly from it (note how the central line is made in two strokes, S1 and S6). When it appears above *two hands* (廾), think of compulsively *drying* the hands, a practice that leads to cracked skin: **EVIL PRACTICE.** ☞ 幣 2224, 蔽 2225

---

### ¹ CURRENCY
### ² SHINTO PAPER OFFERING

ヘイ

¹ 幣制 へいせい currency/monetary system 0708
¹ 造幣 ぞうへい coinage, mintage..........0699
¹ 貨幣 かへい money, currency, coinage..........1164
①紙幣 しへい paper currency, bank note, bill
..........0478
②御幣 ごへい hanging paper strips in a Shinto shrine, sacred staff with cut paper..........0862

---

**2224**

巾 50

2507

常 15

*Dried* (S1–12) *cloth* (巾) for using in paper **CURRENCY** and **SHINTO PAPER OFFERINGS** (see V5). ☞ 弊 2223

---

| | COVER | ○隠蔽する いんぺいする conceal, cover up ... 1312 |
|---|---|---|
| | | 遮蔽する しゃへいする shelter, shield ....... 1740 |
| | ヘイ | 遮蔽物 しゃへいぶつ shelter .......... 1740, 0172 |

| 2225 | 蔽 is the traditional form of what appears at the top of the previous two entries (the present |
|---|---|
| 艸 140 | entry was not standardized to match those when it was added to the Joyo list). Like them, |
| 蔽 | it is pronounced ヘイ. To remember the meaning **COVER**, let *dry* (敝) *grass* (艹) suggest a |
| 2084 | thatched roof. ☞ 弊 2223 |
| 常 15 | |

| | COMRADE | ○朋友 ほうゆう comrade, friend, associate ... 0399 |
|---|---|---|
| | | 朋輩 ほうばい comrade, friend, associate ... 1855 |
| | ホウ | 朋と一緒に ともといっしょに with friends/a |
| | とも | friend .............................. 0002, 1450 |

| 2226 | Two identical companions: **COMRADES**. |
|---|---|
| 月 74 | |
| 0784 | |
| 名 8 | |

| | SHELF | ○本棚 ほんだな bookshelf .................... 0031 |
|---|---|---|
| | | 食器棚 しょっきだな cupboard, sideboard |
| | | .................................. 0288, 0295 |
| | たな -だな | 神棚 かみだな household Shinto altar ...... 0316 |
| | | 網棚 あみだな luggage rack ................. 2072 |
| | | 棚卸し たなおろし inventory ................ 0861 |

| 2227 | This time 朋 are comrades holding up a *wooden* (木) **SHELF**: picture them as two vertical |
|---|---|
| 木 75 | boards separated by a few feet, with slots at S7–8 and S11–12 for inserting *wooden* boards. |
| | Now would be a good time to review the annotation for 服 1471. |
| 0895 | |
| 常 12 | |

| | FENCE, palisade | ○鉄柵 てっさく iron fence .................... 0564 |
|---|---|---|
| | | 庭に柵を巡らす にわにさくをめぐらす enclose a |
| | | garden with a fence ................ 0878, 1553 |
| | サク | 柵内立ち入るべからず さくないたちいるべからず |
| | | Do Not Cross Fence [sign] ....... 0215, 0067, 0039 |

| 2228 | Easily visualized as a *wooden* (木) **FENCE**, so ignore the meaning *book* introduced earlier for |
|---|---|
| 木 75 | 冊 (0824). |
| 柵 | |
| 0804 | |
| 常 9 | |

| | | |
|---|---|---|
| 桁 | ¹DIGIT<br>²BEAM, girder<br><br>けた | ①二桁 ふたけた two digits, double-digit......0003<br>¹四桁の番号 よんけたのばんごう four-digit number.................0006, 0299, 0300<br>¹桁違いの けたちがいの way off, incommensurable.................0663<br>²橋桁 はしげた bridge girder.................1578<br>²帆船の桁 ほぶねのけた sailboat's spar/yard.................1631, 0669 |

**2229**
木 75

Recall from 行 0055 that the spaces between the parallel lines at the top represent roads or lines of text—that is, things that follow long, straight courses. Joined with 木, this originally referred to **BEAMS** and **girders**. It later came to refer to the reeds of an abacus, from which derives its most common meaning today, **DIGIT**. ☞ 術 0993

0839
常 10

| | | |
|---|---|---|
| 栓 | STOPPER, spigot<br><br>セン | コルク栓 コルクせん cork<br>○栓抜き せんぬき bottle opener, corkscrew...1951<br>瓶の栓 びんのせん bottle stopper.................2169<br>水道の栓 すいどうのせん water spigot<br>.................0027, 0158<br>消火栓 しょうかせん fireplug, fire hydrant<br>.................1289, 0026 |

**2230**
木 75

Visualize 王 as an upward-pointing spigot or hydrant, on top of which is placed 个, a *wooden* (木) **STOPPER**.

0845
常 10

| | | |
|---|---|---|
| 詮 | INQUIRY<br><br>セン | 詮議 せんぎ discussion.................0927<br>○詮索 せんさく inquiry.................1735<br>詮索好き せんさくずき busybody......1735, 0095<br>所詮 しょせん after all.................0249 |

**2231**
言 149

詮

When this kanji was added to the Joyo list, its right-hand portion was not standardized to match 全 0078 WHOLE. To remember its meaning, let *"words (言) + whole"* suggest the thorough questioning and discussions conducted during an **INQUIRY**.

1383
常 13

| | | |
|---|---|---|
| 塞 | PLUG UP, obstruct<br><br>ソク サイ<br>ふさ(ぐ) ふさ(がる) | 塞栓 そくせん embolism.................2230<br>○閉塞 へいそく stoppage, blockage; blockade<br>.................0449<br>城塞 じょうさい fortress, stronghold.........1298<br>穴を塞ぐ あなをふさぐ fill a hole with earth..0397<br>○塞がる ふさがる be closed; be filled/occupied |

**2232**
宀 40

Review 寒 0361. Here, visualize using *earth* (土) to **PLUG UP** the space between the two people's legs. Note the differences—not limited to 宀—between this character and 基 0485. The most important compound for this character appears in the next entry. ☞ 寒 0361

2033
常 13

**BLOCK**

コウ

○梗塞 こうそく blockage; tightness; infarction ............2232
脳梗塞 のうこうそく cerebral infarction, stroke ..........1973, 2232
心筋梗塞 しんきんこうそく myocardial infarction, heart attack ....0056, 0392, 2232

| 2233 木 75 | Recall the postal delivery horse from 更 0889. In this entry, imagine using a *wooden* (木) post to corral (i.e., **BLOCK**) the horse. |

0871
常 11

**PERSIMMON**

シ*
かき

熟柿 じゅくし ripe persimmons ............1436
○渋柿 しぶがき astringent persimmons ......1234
吊るし柿 つるしがき dried persimmons....0206
樽柿 たるがき persimmons mellowed in a sake barrel.................2012

| 2234 木 75 | A *tree* (木) whose fruit are taken to *market* (市): **PERSIMMON**. |

0806
常 9

**WISTERIA**

トウ
ふじ

佐藤 さとう Sato (=Satoh) [surname] ........2218
伊藤 いとう Ito (=Itoh) [surname]..........1406
○藤棚 ふじだな wisteria trellis ...............2227
昇り藤 のぼりふじ lupine ...................1053
藤色 ふじいろ light purple, lilac............0528

| 2235 艸 140 | Recall the *shelf* image we used for 月 at 服 1471 and 棚 2227. Informed by this, picture 月 here as a trellis for **WISTERIA**, which trails in clusters down the right side of the character. ☞ 勝 0460, 騰 2236 |

2109
常 18

**RISE, jump up**

トウ

○騰貴 とうき rise (in prices)....................1177
高騰 こうとう steep rise (in prices), jump ....0185
奔騰 ほんとう price jump, boom............2222
暴騰 ぼうとう sudden (price) rise ..........1346
沸騰する ふっとうする boil, seethe, bubble 1187

| 2236 馬 187 | In the next two entries, we'll need to be more precise about how we interpret the right-hand portion: Recall that S5–10 represent *tally sticks* (see 券 0456). Now imagine striking the *horse* (馬) with the *tally sticks* so that he will jump up and over 月, a *shelf*-like horse-jumping barrier: **RISE/jump up**. ☞ 勝 0460, 藤 2235, 謄 2237 |

1024
常 20

**TRANSCRIBE, copy**

トウ

謄本 とうほん certified copy, transcript; copy of the domiciliary register ...................... 0031
○謄写 とうしゃ copy, reproduction, mimeograph ............................................ 0859
謄写版 とうしゃばん mimeograph ..... 0859, 0923

| 2237 | This time, picture **TRANSCRIBING**/**copying** someone's *words* (言) onto the *tally sticks* (关), then storing these on the *shelf* (月). ☞ 勝 0460, 謄 2236 |
| 言 149 | |

1013
常 | 17

---

**NOODLES**

メン

○麺類 めんるい noodles ...................... 0310
素麺 そうめん thin wheat noodles .......... 0132
乾燥麺 かんそうめん dried noodles ... 1807, 1810
茹で麺 ゆでめん boiled noodles ........... 2198
麺棒 めんぼう rolling pin ................. 2107

| 2238 | *Wheat* (麦) **NOODLES** on the *face* (面) of a plate. S7 looks like a long noodle being slurped off the side of the plate! |
| 麥 199 | |

麵

2828
常 | 16

---

**KIDNAP; pull**

ラ

○拉致する らちする kidnap ................... 0251
拉麺 らーめん ramen, hand-pulled noodles .................................................. 2238

| 2239 | *Hand* (扌) **pulls** *standing man* (立) away: **KIDNAP**. |
| 手 64 | |

0279
常 | 8

---

**DAZZLING**

コウ

晃々たる こうこうたる brilliant, dazzling

| 2240 | *Light* (光) shining down from the *sun* (日): **DAZZLING**. ☞ 光 0137 |
| 日 72 | |

晄

2165
名 | 10

| | AWNING, hood | 車の幌をかける くるまのほろをかける pull up the hood on the car [convertible].............0125 |
|---|---|---|
| | コウ<br>ほろ | 幌馬車 ほろばしゃ covered wagon ....0336, 0125<br>札幌 さっぽろ Sapporo [city in Hokkaido]...1694 |

| 2241 | *Cloth* (巾) to block out *dazzling* (晃) light: AWNING/hood. |
|---|---|
| 巾 50 | |
| 0586 | |
| 名 13 | |

| | *RIN* (0.001 yen) | 一厘 いちりん one *rin*......................0002 |
|---|---|---|
| | リン | |

| 2242 | When we see *cliff* (厂) and *village* (里), we should perceive a towering pile of worthless リン |
|---|---|
| 厂 27 | the villagers have disposed of over the years, now grown tall enough to overshadow the village itself. To remember the relative values of 錢 1585 (0.01 yen) and 厘—and that the latter is read リン not リ—it helps to recite the quasi-rhyme 円-錢-厘 エン-セン-リン. |
| 2589 | |
| 常 9 | |

| | RIDGE | 畝に沿って種を蒔く うねにそってたねをまく sow seeds along a furrow.............1348, 0544, 2185 |
|---|---|---|
| | うね せ* | 畝溝 うねみぞ furrow ridges.................0920<br>畝織り うねおり ribbed fabric .................1088<br>十畝 じっせ approx. 10 ares .................0005 |

| 2243 | This kanji originally referred to ridges or furrows in a farm field, and later to a unit of square |
|---|---|
| 田 102 | measure roughly equivalent to 1 are, or 100 square meters. Picture 亠 as a *long* (久) RIDGE marking the boundary of a *rice field* (田) of this dimension. |
| 畝 | |
| 1332 | |
| 常 10 | |

| | *MONME* (3.75 grams) | 一匁 いちもんめ 1 *monme*.................0002 |
|---|---|---|
| | もんめ | |

| 2244 | This "kanji" was created in Japan as a contraction of 文メ, a way of transcribing the weight |
|---|---|
| 勹 20 | unit *MONME* (3.75 grams). Recognize it by the presence of katakana メ in S3–4, associating this with the *kun* reading. It has no *on* reading, does not appear in any compounds, and was removed from the Joyo Kanji List in 2010. |
| 2913 | |
| 外 4 | |

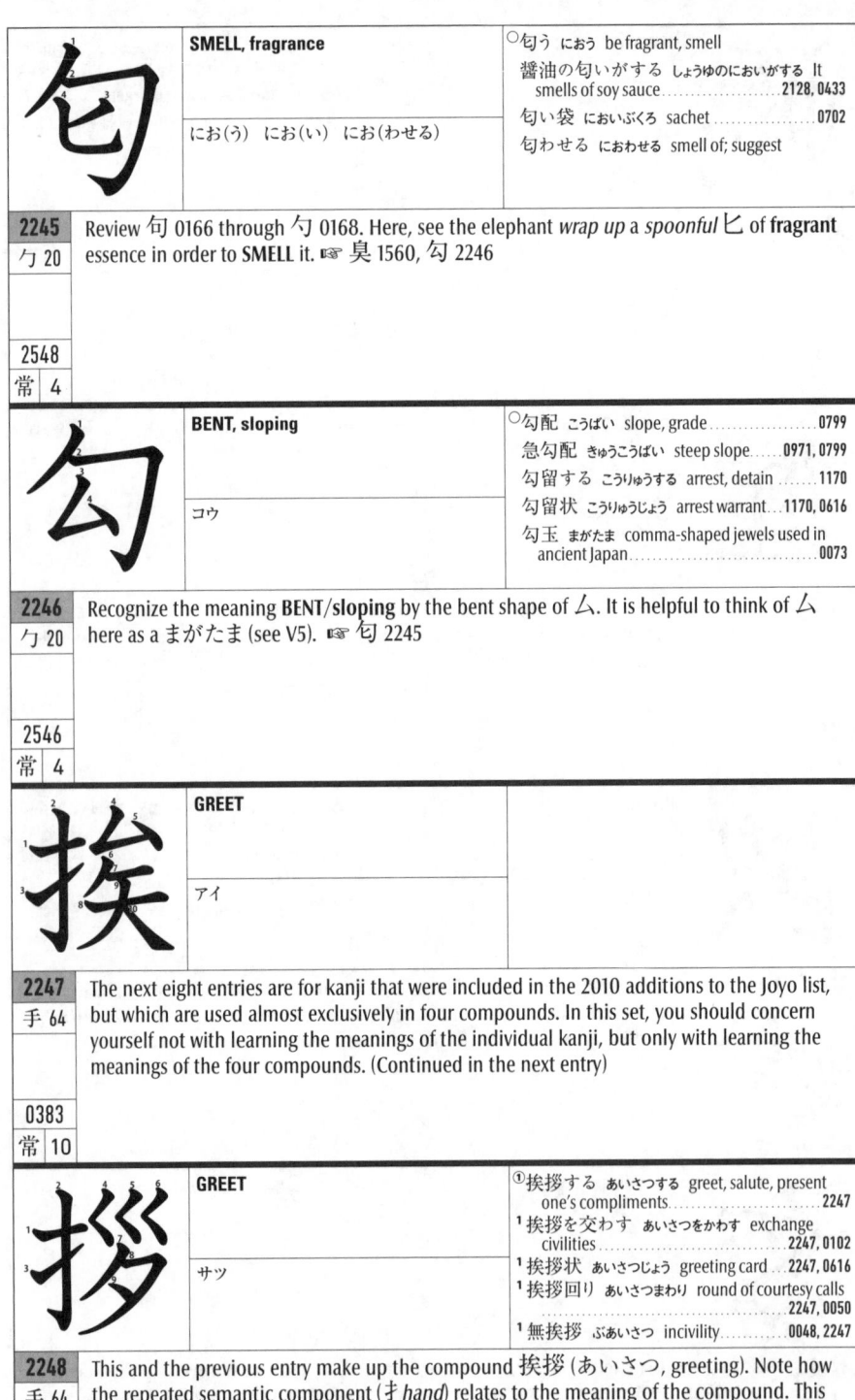

| 匂 | SMELL, fragrance | ○匂う におう be fragrant, smell |
| | | 醤油の匂いがする しょうゆのにおいがする It smells of soy sauce................2128, 0433 |
| | におう におい におわせる | 匂い袋 においぶくろ sachet.................0702 |
| | | 匂わせる におわせる smell of; suggest |

| 2245 | Review 句 0166 through 勺 0168. Here, see the elephant *wrap up* a *spoonful* ヒ of **fragrant** essence in order to **SMELL** it. ☞ 臭 1560, 勾 2246 |
| ク 20 | |
| 2548 | |
| 常 4 | |

| 勾 | BENT, sloping | ○勾配 こうばい slope, grade................0799 |
| | | 急勾配 きゅうこうばい steep slope......0971, 0799 |
| | | 勾留する こうりゅうする arrest, detain......1170 |
| | コウ | 勾留状 こうりゅうじょう arrest warrant...1170, 0616 |
| | | 勾玉 まがたま comma-shaped jewels used in ancient Japan................0073 |

| 2246 | Recognize the meaning **BENT/sloping** by the bent shape of ム. It is helpful to think of ム here as a まがたま (see V5). ☞ 匂 2245 |
| ク 20 | |
| 2546 | |
| 常 4 | |

| 挨 | GREET | |
| | アイ | |

| 2247 | The next eight entries are for kanji that were included in the 2010 additions to the Joyo list, but which are used almost exclusively in four compounds. In this set, you should concern yourself not with learning the meanings of the individual kanji, but only with learning the meanings of the four compounds. (Continued in the next entry) |
| 手 64 | |
| 0383 | |
| 常 10 | |

| 拶 | GREET | ①挨拶する あいさつする greet, salute, present one's compliments................2247 |
| | | ¹挨拶を交わす あいさつをかわす exchange civilities................2247, 0102 |
| | | ¹挨拶状 あいさつじょう greeting card ...2247, 0616 |
| | サツ | ¹挨拶回り あいさつまわり round of courtesy calls................2247, 0050 |
| | | ¹無挨拶 ぶあいさつ incivility................0048, 2247 |

| 2248 | This and the previous entry make up the compound 挨拶 (あいさつ, greeting). Note how the repeated semantic component (扌 *hand*) relates to the meaning of the compound. This pattern recurs in the next three pairs, and in numerous other compounds written with kanji that were <u>not</u> included in the Joyo Kanji List. |
| 手 64 | |
| 0336 | |
| 常 9 | |

| 暧 | **NOT CLEAR** | |
|---|---|---|
| | アイ | |

**2249** 日 72 — (See next entry)

1001 常 17

| 昧 | **DARK** | ○暧昧な あいまいな unclear, vague, equivocal .................................2249 |
|---|---|---|
| | マイ | |

**2250** 日 72 — Following the same approach as with 挨拶 above, concern yourself here only with mastering VI 暧昧な (あいまいな), using the repeated semantic component as a clue. This approach will serve you well when learning other compounds with unlisted kanji sharing the same semantic component, such as 躊躇 (ちゅうちょ, hesitation) and 軋轢 (あつれき, friction).

0794 常 9

| 瑠 | **LAPIS LAZULI** | |
|---|---|---|
| | ル | |

**2251** 玉 96 — (See next entry)

0972 常 14

| 璃 | **GLASSY SUBSTANCE** | 瑠璃 るり lapis lazuli.........................2251<br>瑠璃色 るりいろ lapis lazuli blue ............0528<br>浄瑠璃 じょうるり *joruri*, ballad drama; clear lapis lazuli .............................0979, 2251 |
|---|---|---|
| | リ | |

**2252** 玉 96 — In VI 瑠璃 the repetition of 王 *gem*—and the reading るり—are easy to associate with **LAPIS LAZULI**. If you're wondering where you saw 离 before, it was at 離 1970.

0984 常 14

# 嫉

**ENVY**

シツ

| 2253 | (See next entry) |
| --- | --- |
| 女 38 | |
| 0584 | |
| 常 13 | |

---

# 妬

**ENVY**

ト
ねた(む)

○嫉妬 しっと jealousy, envy ......................2253
　嫉妬深い しっとぶかい jealous, envious
　...............................................2253, 1715
○妬む ねたむ envy, be jealous of

| 2254 | VI 嫉妬 (しっと) seems to associate women with **ENVY** and jealousy. Disowning once more the sexist associations of some kanji, we might imagine a *woman* (女) afflicted with this particular *disease* (疾), gazing at another *woman* (女)'s *stone* (石) and **ENVIOUSLY** muttering a certain English expletive easily suggested by this compound. |
| --- | --- |
| 女 38 | |
| 0254 | |
| 常 8 | |

---

# 鹿

**DEER**

しか か

鹿革 しかがわ deerskin ......................0592
鹿の子 かのこ fawn; dapples, pattern of white
　　　spots ..........................................0094
○馬鹿 ばか fool, blockhead; nonsense ......0336
鹿児島 かごしま Kagoshima (city and prefecture)
　...............................................0772, 0341

| 2255 | This kanji depicts a **DEER** hiding inside a forest *shelter* (广). S4–7 depict the animal's head and antlers, 比 its sharply angled legs. |
| --- | --- |
| 鹿 198 | |
| 2695 | |
| 常 11 | |

---

# 塵

**DUST, trash**

ジン
ちり ごみ

粉塵 ふんじん dust ..............................1619
○塵取り ちりとり dustpan ......................0059
○塵箱 ごみばこ trash can ......................1909

| 2256 | This entry and the next two incorporate the character for *deer* (鹿) in full. Here, we observe *earth* (土) churned up by stampeding *deer*: **DUST**. |
| --- | --- |
| 鹿 198 | |
| 外 14 | |

**FOOT OF A MOUNTAIN**

ロク
ふもと

富士山を麓から登った ふじさんをふもとからのぼった (I) climbed Mt. Fuji from the base
.................................1481, 0350, 0037, 1054
山麓 さんろく foot of a mountain ...........0037

---

**2257**

鹿 198

2453

常 19

*Deer*(鹿) in its shelter at the **FOOT OF A MOUNTAIN**, just inside the tree line, i.e., the edge of the *forest*(林). You might think of ふもと as an abbreviation for "foot of a mountain," or, if you prefer, ふじさんのもと.

---

**OF GRACEFUL BEAUTY**

レイ
うるわ(しい)

麗人 れいじん beauty, belle..................0015
○奇麗な きれいな beautiful, pretty; clean; fair
.................................1329
美麗な びれいな beautiful, gorgeous.......0497
華麗な かれいな resplendent, gorgeous.....1012
○麗しい うるわしい beautiful

---

**2258**

鹿 198

1845

常 19

Someone has noticed the *deer*(鹿) and is just now admiring its **GRACEFUL BEAUTY** with wide-open eyes (S1–8, including the eyebrows).

---

**RECOMMEND**

セン
すす(める)

○推薦する すいせんする recommend, nominate
.................................2150
推薦状 すいせんじょう recommendation letter
.................................2150, 0616
自薦 じせん self-recommendation ..........0081
薦挙 せんきょ recommendation .............1247
○薦める すすめる recommend

---

**2259**

艸 140

2097

常 16

In this and the next entry, *deer*(鹿) is abbreviated to its head (and the *shelter* it sleeps in). Here, a half-eaten *bird*(鳥) sticks out of the deer's mouth. Willing to share the uneaten half, the deer **RECOMMENDS** it for our delectation—with *grass*(艹) garnish. ☞ 慶 2260

---

**FELICITATION, rejoicing**

ケイ

慶祝 けいしゅく celebration, congratulation 1200
○慶弔 けいちょう congratulations and condolences.................................1186
慶事 けいじ happy/auspicious event .......0080
同慶 どうけい (matter of) mutual congratulations.................................0182

---

**2260**

心 61

2739

常 15

This character brings to mind 憂 0779, where we removed the top portion of 愛 LOVE in the same way. Here imagine that the *deer* has sought refuge in its *shelter* in order to bear its *love* child. Picture a scene of joyful **rejoicing** and **FELICITATION**. ☞ 薦 2259

| | HELMET | 兜を脱ぐ かぶとをぬぐ take off one's helmet; acknowledge defeat ......................1198 |
|---|---|---|
| | | 兜の緒 かぶとのお helmet strap............1450 |
| | ト トウ | 兜状の かぶとじょうの helmet-shaped.......0616 |
| | かぶと | 兜虫 かぶとむし rhinoceros beetle..........0343 |

| **2261** | A long-*legged* (儿) person with a *white* (白) face, wearing a large **HELMET**. |
|---|---|
| 白 106 | |
| **2455** | |
| 名 11 | |

| | GLARE AT | ○睨む にらむ glare at, stare hard at; keep an eye on |
|---|---|---|
| | | 睨み付ける にらみつける glare at, stare at angrily/sharply...........................0064 |
| | ゲイ | 睨み倒す にらみたおす stare (someone) down |
| | にら(む) | ...........................................0941 |

| **2262** | Visualize 兒 as a two-headed person, whose two heads are turned around **GLARING AT** each other. Note, however, that without 目 at the left, 兒 is the traditional form of 児. |
|---|---|
| 目 109 | |
| 睨 | |
| 外 13 | |

| | RAT, mouse | 鼠穴 ねずみあな mouse hole.................0397 |
|---|---|---|
| | | 鼠捕り ねずみとり mousetrap; rat poison ...1596 |
| | | ○鼠色 ねずみいろ dark gray..................0528 |
| | ソ | 殺鼠剤 さっそざい rat poison..........0522, 1261 |
| | ねずみ ねず | 栗鼠 りす squirrel.............................0781 |

| **2263** | Vaguely resembles a **RAT**'s teeth, furry body, and tail. |
|---|---|
| 鼠 208 | |
| 鼡 | |
| 外 13 | |

| | DROWN, indulge in | ○溺死する できしする drown.................0716 |
|---|---|---|
| | | 溺愛する できあいする be infatuated with, love madly ...........................................0778 |
| | | 惑溺する わくできする indulge in, give way to |
| | デキ | ...........................................1153 |
| | おぼ(れる) | ○溺れる おぼれる drown; become lost in |
| | | 溺れ死ぬ おぼれじぬ drown.................0716 |

| **2264** | The right-hand portion of this kanji was not standardized with 弱 0424 WEAK when it joined the Joyo list (as usual, you should recognize both forms without distinction). We thus have "*weak* in the *water* (氵)," which means **DROWN**. It can also mean **indulge in**, from the idea of immersion. The *on* reading デキ is unique in this course. |
|---|---|
| 水 85 | |
| 溺 | |
| 0599 | |
| 常 13 | |

**LAGOON**

かた -がた

八郎潟 はちろうがた Hachiro Lagoon...**0010, 0286**
干潟 ひがた mud flat, tidal flat .............**0408**
○新潟 にいがた Niigata (city and prefecture)...**0275**

| 2265 | At the right, we have elements from both *elephant* (勹) and either *bird* (鳥) or *horse* (馬). One simple visual approach is to picture a large *bird* (an ostrich?) gyrating its head (臼) to shake off *water* (氵) as it bathes in a **LAGOON**. |
|---|---|
| 水 85 | |
| 0679 | |
| 常 15 | |

**TURBID**

ダク
にご(る) にご(す)

濁流 だくりゅう muddy stream.................**1059**
○混濁した こんだくした turbid, thick, muddy,
　　cloudy.....................................**1426**
清濁 せいだく purity and impurity; good and evil
　.............................................**0974**
○濁る にごる become turbid/impure
濁す にごす make turbid/impure

| 2266 | Picture an *elephant* (勹) pulling a *net* (罒) full of *worms* (虫) from **TURBID** *water* (氵). |
|---|---|
| 水 85 | |
| 0695 | |
| 常 16 | |

¹ **RUN DRY**
² **THIRST**

カツ
かわ(く)

①渇水 かっすい water shortage..............**0027**
¹ 枯渇する こかつする dry up, run dry; be
　exhausted, be depleted .................**1049**
² 飢渇 きかつ hunger and thirst.............**1966**
②喉が渇く のどがかわく be thirsty...........**1674**

| 2267 | Recall 匂 *smell*, from a few pages back. At the right, picture a *mischievous elephant* who loves to spend his days sniffing around here and there under the hot *sun* (日). The frequent result, as we can see in this entry, is that he ends up desperate for *water* (氵): **RUN DRY**; **THIRST**. Note the old form, which sets the pattern for this group. ☞ 湯 0446 |
|---|---|
| 水 85 | |
| 渇 | |
| 0473 | |
| 常 11 | |

**BROWN**

カツ

○褐色 かっしょく brown.........................**0528**
茶褐色 ちゃかっしょく brown, liver brown
　.............................................**0603, 0528**

| 2268 | The soiled *clothes* (衤) of the *mischievous elephant* (曷): **BROWN**. |
|---|---|
| 衣 145 | |
| 褐 | |
| 1118 | |
| 常 13 | |

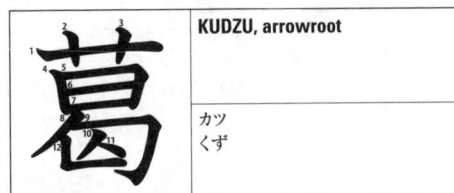

| | **KUDZU, arrowroot** | ○葛藤 かっとう entanglements, conflict, trouble ............2235 |
|---|---|---|
| | | 葛布 くずふ kudzu fiber cloth..............0204 |
| | | 葛粉 くずこ arrowroot flour..............1619 |
| | カツ<br>くず | 葛餅 くずもち cake made from arrowroot flour ............2172 |

| 2269<br>艸 140<br>葛<br>2017<br>常 12 | The *mischievous elephant* (曷) getting tangled up in a coiling *plant* (艹): **KUDZU**. This kanji was not standardized with the others in this group when it was added to the Joyo list. |
|---|---|

| | **SHOUT AT** | 喝采 かっさい applause, cheers..............0987 |
|---|---|---|
| | | 喝破する かっぱする shout someone down, declare, pronounce........................0596 |
| | | 一喝 いっかつ thundering cry, roar..........0002 |
| | カツ | ○大喝する だいかつする shout in a thunderous voice .........................0033 |

| 2270<br>口 30<br>喝<br>0417<br>常 11 | A *mouth* (口) **SHOUTING AT** the *mischievous elephant* (曷). |
|---|---|

| | **BE GRANTED AN AUDIENCE** | ○謁見 えっけん audience.........................0083 |
|---|---|---|
| | エツ | 拝謁 はいえつ audience with the emperor...1642 |

| 2271<br>言 149<br>謁<br>1420<br>常 15 | Now the *mischievous elephant* (曷) wishes to **BE GRANTED AN AUDIENCE** so that he can *say* (言) something in his own defense. |
|---|---|

| | **PUT UP, display** | 掲揚する けいようする hoist, put up, fly (a flag) ............1308 |
|---|---|---|
| | | ○掲示板 けいじばん bulletin board.....0311, 0924 |
| | | 掲載する けいさいする publish, print .......1318 |
| | ケイ<br>かか(げる) | ○掲げる かかげる put up, hoist; display in writing, publish |
| | | 国旗を掲げる こっきをかかげる hoist the national flag.........................0075, 0573 |

| 2272<br>手 64<br>掲<br>0450<br>常 11 | Picture a *hand* (扌) raising a banner high up on the back of the *mischievous elephant* (曷): **PUT UP**. As the sample vocabulary will illustrate, it is important to visualize the idea of hoisting the banner up to a high place, where it is easily visible. ☞ 揚 1308 |
|---|---|

**(sign of) THE DOG**

ジュツ
いぬ

○戌年 いぬどし Year of the Dog ..............0117

| 2273 | The conspicuous feature of this character is S3, which distinguishes it from 戊 *guided spear*. |
| 戈 62 | Simply associate that stroke with a **DOG**'s canine tooth. To refer to the actual creature, use 犬 |
| | 0293; the present entry is only used in reference to the Chinese horary or zodiac sign of **THE** |
| | **DOG**. |
| 外 6 | |

**REASONABLE, plausible**

ユウ
もっと(も)

尤度 ゆうど plausibility, likelihood..........0280
ご尤も ごもっとも You are quite right
尤もらしい もっともらしい plausible

| 2274 | You might start by focusing on this character's general balance between left and right, and |
| 尤 43 | associating that with the keyword "**REASONABLE.**" But given that this kanji appears in so few |
| | words, you should concern yourself more with learning to recognize V1–3 than learning the |
| 2604 | kanji for its own sake. Note that this form appeared earlier in 就 1283. ☞ 犬 0293 |
| 名 4 | |

¹ **GOOD FOR NOTHING**
² **CLOGS**

ダ タ*

①駄目 だめ no good, useless; No! ............0021
¹ 駄作 ださく poor piece (of writing) ........0152
¹ 駄洒落 だじゃれ poor joke [pun] ......0798, 0793
¹ 無駄な むだな no good, fruitless, wasteful 0048
②下駄 げた geta, wooden clogs..............0040

| 2275 | A *thick* (太, i.e., fat) *horse* (馬): **GOOD FOR NOTHING.** You might think of M2 **CLOGS** as |
| 馬 187 | coming from the resemblance between the sound of a person walking in clogs and the hoof- |
| | clatter of a very slow-paced horse. |
| 1617 | |
| 常 14 | |

¹ **HORSE, pony**
² **CHESS PIECE**

こま

¹ 駒座 こまざ Equuleus [constellation]........0749
¹ 当歳駒 とうさいごま one-year-old colt, yearling
..............................................0141, 2041
②将棋の駒 しょうぎのこま shogi pieces, chessmen
0614, 1796
² 駒損 こまそん (=こまぞん) loss of material [in
shogi] ..................................1595
² 持ち駒 もちごま captured piece ............0384

| 2276 | Picture the *elephant* (勹) holding in its *mouth* (口) a very small **HORSE** or **pony**, which it |
| 馬 187 | uses as a **CHESS PIECE** in a game of 将棋 (しょうぎ, Japanese chess). Now would be a good |
| | time to review 駆 1388–騒 1390. ☞ 騎 1331 |
| 1623 | |
| 常 15 | |

## 篤

1 **SERIOUS**
2 **KIND**

トク

- 1 篤学 とくがく devotion to one's studies ..... 0099
- 1 篤農家 とくのうか diligent farmer ..... 0511, 0219
- ①危篤 きとく seriously ill ..... 0726
- 2 懇篤な こんとくな cordial, kind ..... 2207
- ②篤志家 とくしか benevolent person; volunteer ..... 0369, 0219

**2277** | 竹 118 | 2370 | 常 16

A *horse* (馬) crowned with a *bamboo* (⺮) laurel for being very **SERIOUS** and **KIND**.

## 罵

**SPEAK ILL OF**

バ
ののし(る)

- ○罵る ののしる speak ill of, abuse; denounce
- 神を罵る かみをののしる blaspheme against God ..... 0316
- ○罵声 ばせい booing, jeering ..... 0529
- 罵倒する ばとうする denounce, censure ..... 0941
- 嘲罵 ちょうば insult, verbal abuse ..... 2221

**2278** | 馬 187 | 2271 | 常 15

We have long since gotten into the habit of seeing 罒 as a *net*, but in the next two entries, it would be well to see it as an *eye* (目). In this entry, picture the *eye* looking down rebukingly on the *horse* (馬) for some fault it has committed: **SPEAK ILL OF**.

## 蔑

**SCORN**

ベツ
さげす(む)　ないがし(ろ)*

- 蔑視する べっしする look down on ..... 0623
- ○軽蔑 けいべつ scorn, contempt ..... 1256
- 蔑称 べっしょう pejorative term ..... 0684
- ○蔑む さげすむ look down on
- 蔑ろにする ないがしろにする look down on, take lightly

**2279** | 艸 140 | 2068 | 常 14

This time the rebuking *eye* (罒) looks down **SCORNFULLY** upon a humble *dog* (戌 2273). 艹 suggests an eyebrow.

## 罠

**TRAP**

わな

- ○罠に落ちる わなにおちる fall into a snare/trap ..... 0793
- 鼠を罠で捕る ねずみをわなでとる catch a rat in a trap ..... 2263, 1596

**2280** | 网 122 | | 外 10

Now we revert to the usual interpretation of 罒, *net*, which we can observe here ensnaring the *public* (民) in a **TRAP**.

**RAVEN, crow**

ウ　オ
からす

○烏が鳴いている　からすがないている　the crows are cawing ................................ 2157
烏の濡れ羽色　からすのぬればいろ　glossy black (like the wet wings of a crow) ...2112, 0418, 0528
烏合の衆　うごうのしゅう　disorderly crowd, mob .............................. 0227, 1405
○烏竜茶　ウーロンちゃ　oolong tea ....... 0507, 0603

| 2281 | By now you've seen 鳥 enough to recognize that in this entry a stroke is missing from the *bird*'s head. This is the **RAVEN**, whose pitch-black coloring makes its facial features indistinguishable to us. ☞ 鳥 0340 |
|---|---|
| 火 86 | |
| 2811 | |
| 名 10 | |

**DUCK**

オウ
かも

鴨の群れ　かものむれ　a flock of ducks ....... 1408
鴨のくちばし　かものくちばし　a duck's bill
小鴨　こがも　duckling ................................ 0034
○鴨にする　かもにする　make a sucker out of

| 2282 | Visualize 甲 as the head of a **DUCK**, its long bill pointed downward. |
|---|---|
| 鳥 196 | |
| 1143 | |
| 名 16 | |

**PIGEON**

キュウ
はと

鳩舎　きゅうしゃ　pigeon house .................. 0910
○鳩便　はとびん　communication by carrier pigeon ................................................... 0890
○鳩派　はとは　doves, soft-liners ............. 1367
伝書鳩　でんしょばと　carrier/homing pigeon .......................................... 0223, 0079
九羽の鳩　きゅうわのはと　nine pigeons ... 0011, 0418

| 2283 | *Nine* (九) *birds* (鳥) gathering around to show interest in your lunch: **PIGEONS**. |
|---|---|
| 鳥 196 | |
| 0141 | |
| 名 13 | |

**CHICKEN**

ケイ
にわとり

○鶏肉　けいにく（＝とりにく）　chicken (meat) ...... 0216
養鶏　ようけい　chicken raising .................. 0500
鶏卵　けいらん　(hen's) egg .................... 1141
闘鶏　とうけい　cockfight, fighting cock ....... 1363
○鶏の餌　にわとりのえさ　chicken feed ......... 2173

| 2284 | A *husband* (夫) carrying home a **CHICKEN** by its *claws* (⼑, i.e., its feet). |
|---|---|
| 鳥 196 | |
| 1577 | |
| 常 19 | |

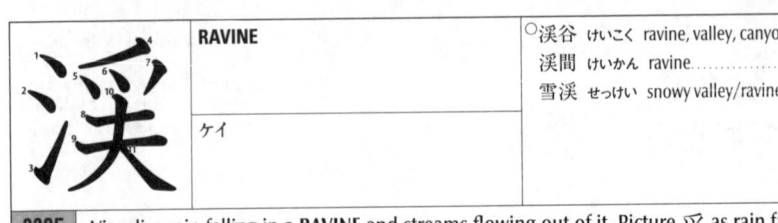

| | RAVINE | ○渓谷 けいこく ravine, valley, canyon.........1034 |
|---|---|---|
| | | 渓間 けいかん ravine.................0448 |
| | | 雪渓 せっけい snowy valley/ravine.........0899 |
| | ケイ | |

| 2285 | Visualize rain falling in a **RAVINE** and streams flowing out of it. Picture ⌒ as rain falling at the top of the ravine, and 夫 as streams flowing out into a broad valley below. As aids for recognizing the meaning, use the combination of *water* (氵) and the narrowing of 夫 toward the top. ☞ 淫 1844 |
|---|---|
| 水 85 | |
| 渓 | |
| 0474 | |
| 常 11 | |

| | HAWK | 放鷹 ほうよう hawking, falconry.............0574 |
|---|---|---|
| | | 鷹匠 たかじょう falconer.................1802 |
| | | ○鷹派 たかは hawks, hard-liners.........1367 |
| | ヨウ オウ | |
| | たか | |

| 2286 | Picture 亻 as a falconer standing under a *shelter* (广). Then see 鳥 as a **HAWK** in his service, just now bringing in a *small bird* (隹) she has captured. |
|---|---|
| 鳥 196 | |
| 2748 | |
| 名 24 | |

| | EAGLE | 白頭鷲 はくとうわし bald eagle.........0076, 0162 |
|---|---|---|
| | | 鷲の雛 わしのひな eaglet.................2154 |
| | | ○鷲掴み わしづかみ clutching.................1602 |
| | シュウ | 鷲鼻 わしばな aquiline nose [hook-nose]...1558 |
| | わし | |

| 2287 | Review 就 1283. Again let the sinking trajectory of S10 suggest *settling*, and visualize 鳥 as a large *bird settling* into its nest: **EAGLE**. |
|---|---|
| 鳥 196 | |
| 2514 | |
| 名 23 | |

| | IMPERIAL SEAL | ○御璽 ぎょじ imperial seal.................0862 |
|---|---|---|
| | ジ | |

| 2288 | 爾 looks a bit like a curly-haired sheep that has been tied up. Think of it as the golden fleece. Engraved on a *round* stone (玉), it serves as the **IMPERIAL SEAL**. |
|---|---|
| 玉 96 | |
| 2527 | |
| 常 19 | |

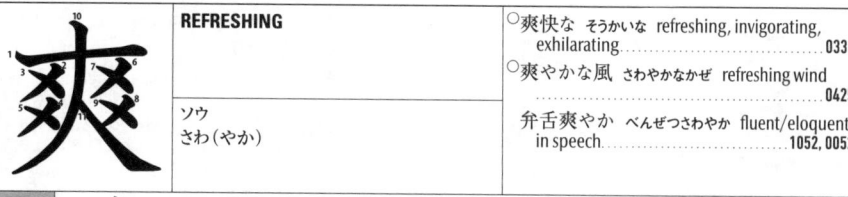

**REFRESHING**

ソウ
さわ（やか）

○爽快な　そうかいな　refreshing, invigorating, exhilarating.............................................0331
○爽やかな風　さわやかなかぜ　refreshing wind..............................................................0425
弁舌爽やか　べんぜつさわやか　fluent/eloquent in speech.............................1052, 0052

---

**2289**

爻 89

2998

常 | 11

See 爽 as person who, feeling hot, holds out her arms to let a **REFRESHING** breeze blow over her body. In reference to voice or speech, 爽 means "clear" or "fluent," like a flowing breeze.

---

¹ **STITCH TOGETHER, bind**
² **COMPOSE, spell**

テイ　テツ
と（じる）　つづ（る）

① 綴じる　とじる　bind; file
¹ 綴じ本　とじほん　bound book..............0031
¹ 手紙をファイルに綴じる　てがみをファイルにとじる　file away letters.............0046, 0478
² 詩歌を綴る　しいかをつづる　compose poetry ...........................................0389, 0827
○綴り　つづり　spelling [as of a name]; binding [as of a book]

---

**2290**

糸 120

1264

名 | 14

See all the ヌs as *threads* (糸) being **STITCH TOGETHER** to **bind** a book. M2 **COMPOSE/ spell** is easy to remember as a derivative meaning.

---

**MULBERRY**

ソウ
くわ

桑田　そうでん　mulberry plantation...........0020
　　　くわた（=くわだ）　Kuwata (= Kuwada) [surname]
○桑畑　くわばたけ　mulberry field..............0129
桑摘み　くわつみ　picking mulberry leaves...1118

---

**2291**

木 75

1814

常 | 10

See 叒 as silkworms feeding on the leaves of a **MULBERRY** *tree* (木).

---

**SILKWORM**

サン
かいこ

蚕は桑の葉しか食べない　かいこはくわのはしかたべない　Silkworms only eat mulberry leaves ...................................2291, 0605, 0288
○蚕業　さんぎょう　sericulture..............0498
蚕食する　さんしょくする　encroach; make inroads ...........................................0288
養蚕　ようさん　sericulture.....................0500

---

**2292**

虫 142

蠶
蚕

2170

常 | 10

*Heavenly* (天) *worm* (虫): **SILKWORM.** ☞ 蠶 2293

---

**EGG**

タン

○蛋白 たんぱく egg white; protein ............0076
蛋白質 たんぱくしつ protein............0076, 0318
動物性蛋白 どうぶつせいたんぱく animal protein
............0540, 0172, 0128, 0076
植物性蛋白 しょくぶつせいたんぱく vegetable
protein.................0840, 0172, 0128, 0076

| 2293 | Recall 疋 *broken/deformed*, first introduced at 旋 0572. In this entry, think of an *insect* (虫) trying to eat an **EGG** but breaking its proboscis on the shell. ☞ 蚕 2292 |
| 虫 142 | |
| 外 11 | |

**CRAB**

カイ
かに

蟹の甲羅 かにのこうら carapace of a crab
............1521, 0896
○蟹のはさみ かにのはさみ pincers of a crab
兜蟹 かぶとがに horseshoe crab............2261
蟹の横這い かにのよこばい the crab's sideward
crawl ............0916, 1554
蟹股 がにまた bowlegs .....................1990

| 2294 | Here 虫 suggests the broad category of arthropods. An *arthropod* that we must painstakingly *take apart* (解) in order to eat: **CRAB**. ☞ 蜜 1382, 触 0344 |
| 虫 142 | |
| 蠏 | |
| 2520 | |
| 名 19 | |

**MOSQUITO**

か

○蚊取り線香 かとりせんこう mosquito-repellent
incense.................0059, 0210, 1781
蚊の鳴く様な声 かのなくようなこえ very faint
voice ...................2157, 0501, 0529
蚊帳 かや (=かちょう) mosquito net..........2021
幌蚊帳 ほろがや mosquito tent.......2241, 2021

| 2295 | An *insect* (虫) coming to suck your blood while you're studying at your *writing* desk (文): **MOSQUITO**. |
| 虫 142 | |
| 1205 | |
| 常 10 | |

**(sign of) THE SERPENT**

シ
み

○巳年 みどし Year of the Serpent.............0117
初巳 はつみ first serpent day of the year....0710

| 2296 | This is the final horary sign we have to master—**THE SERPENT**. We can see half the serpent's length coiled tightly at the top, and the other half beginning to uncoil itself at the bottom. To refer to the actual creature, use the next entry. Do not confuse this kanji (or 己 0426) with the name-use kanji 已 HALT. ☞ 巴 0527 |
| 己 49 | |
| 2873 | |
| 名 3 | |

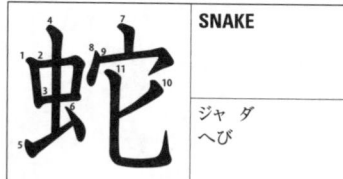

**SNAKE**

ジャ ダ
へび

蛇の目 じゃのめ umbrella with a snake's eye pattern; double circle pattern.............0021
○蛇口 じゃぐち faucet.............0019
○蛇行する だこうする meander, zigzag.......0055
○毒蛇 どくへび poisonous snake.............0133
蛇が卵を呑んだ へびがたまごをのんだ The snake swallowed an egg.............1141, 2174

| 2297 | As a shortcut, visualize S11 the same way we did the long, curling stroke in the previous entry: as the winding body of a **SNAKE**. 虫 suggests a kind of *worm*. ☞ 舵 2144 |
| --- | --- |
| 虫 142 | |
| 1230 | |
| 常 11 | |

**COCOON**

ケン
まゆ

○繭糸 けんし silk thread .............0112
○繭を掛ける まゆをかける spin a cocoon.....1117
繭玉 まゆだま festive New Year's cocoons...0073

| 2298 | A *worm* (虫, i.e., larva) eating *grass* (艹), whence it spins *thread* (糸). Using this last, it encloses itself: **COCOON**. |
| --- | --- |
| 糸 120 | |
| 2107 | |
| 常 18 | |

**BUTTERFLY**

チョウ

○蝶々 ちょうちょう butterfly
胡蝶 こちょう butterfly .............0258
高山蝶 こうざんちょう alpine butterfly...0185, 0037
紋白蝶 もんしろちょう cabbage butterfly
.............1416, 0076

| 2299 | Again let 枼 represent 葉 0605 LEAF. A *worm* (虫) feeding on a *leaf*: **BUTTERFLY**. |
| --- | --- |
| 虫 142 | |
| 1278 | |
| 名 15 | |

**RAINBOW**

コウ*
にじ

虹彩 こうさい iris .............0990
○虹色 にじいろ rainbow colors.............0528
虹の彼方に にじのかなたに over the rainbow
.............0597, 0173

| 2300 | Our journey through the kanji began at the SUN 日. It ends at a **RAINBOW**. This tiny *worm* (虫) can only see 工 from one side, so to the worm it appears as a long arch (コ). Think of it as an arch of colors, and picture the worm inching its way from one end to the other, a fitting image for our long pursuit of, and present arrival at, the end of the **RAINBOW**. |
| --- | --- |
| 虫 142 | |
| 1180 | |
| 常 9 | |

# BASIC PRINCIPLES OF STROKE DIRECTION AND STROKE ORDER

## Stroke Direction

1. Horizontal strokes go from left to right:

   ⇀

2. Vertical or slanting strokes go from top to bottom:

   ↓ ↘ ╱

   except in special combinations of a downward-slanting and an upward-slanting stroke: 冫(次)　氵(活)　氺 (暴)　氺(楽)　疒 (病)

3. A single stroke may change direction multiple times:

   亅　フ　乙　ろ　ろ　etc.

## Stroke Order

1. Top to bottom; top part to bottom part:

   三 (一　二　三),　　言 (丶　一　亠　言　言);
   客 (宀　宎　客),　　築 (ᴬᴬ　筑　築).

2. Left to right; left-hand part to right-hand part:

   州 (丶　丿　丷　州　州　州),　　脈 (月　肵　肵　脈);
   竹 (𠂊　竹),　　語 (言　語),　　例 (亻　佴　例).

3. When intersecting, horizontal strokes usually go before vertical strokes:

   十 (一　十),　　土 (一　十　土),　　大 (一　ナ　大),
   共 (一　十　廾),　花 (一　ㄜ　艹),　　用 (冂　月　用),
   耗 (亖　丰　丰),　春 (三　ヰ　夫),　　井 (二　井);

   except in 田, 王, and extensions thereof:

   田 (冂　冂　甲　田),　曲 (冂　帅　曲　曲),　角 (𠂉　角　角　角),
   王 (一　丁　干　王),　集 (广　忄　隹　隹),　青 (一　十　丰　圭).

4. Vertical stroke precedes horizontal stroke extending toward the right:
上 ( 丨 卜 上 ), 足 ( 尸 乛 尺 足 ).

5. Central strokes go first when flanked on each side by no more than two strokes:
小 ( 亅 丿 小 ),　　糸 ( 纟 纟 糸 ), →当 ( 丨 丷 丷 ),
水 ( 亅 丬 水 ),　　→衆 ( 卯 帠 衆 ), →赤 ( 亣 赤 赤 ),
→業 ( 丷 ″ ‴ 业 ), →楽 ( 白 泊 泑 ), 承 ( 孑 孟 承 );

except in 火 ( ⸜ 火 ) and 忄 ( ⸜ 忄 ).

6. Enclosing frame goes first, but "closing" line goes last:
国 ( 冂 国 国 ), 囚 ( 冂 囚 囚 ),
田 ( 冂 用 田 ), 月 ( 刀 月 月 );

but note the writing of 匚, as in 区 ( 一 フ 又 区 ).

7. Right-to-left slanting stroke goes before left-to-right:
人 ( 丿 人 ),　　→金 ( 丿 𠆢 金 ), 又 ( フ 又 ),
文 ( 亠 ナ 文 ), 故 ( 古 故 故 ), ⸜処 ( 夂 処 ).

8. Central vertical strokes that protrude at either top or bottom go last:
中 ( 口 中 ), 半 ( 丷 半 ), 事 ( 彐 事 ),
→書 ( 彐 畫 ), 平 ( 亚 平 ), 手 ( 二 手 );

but those protruding neither above nor below go after the top part:
里 ( 日 甲 里 ), 重 ( 亩 甫 重 ), 謹 ( 諽 諽 謹 ).

9. Horizontals piercing through the whole character go last:
女 ( 女 女 ), 母 ( 毋 母 ), 舟 ( 舟 舟 );

except 世 ( 一 丗 世 ).

10. 辶, 又, and 乚 go last:
進 ( 隹 進 ), 建 ( 聿 建 ), 直 ( 直 直 ).

# REGULAR *ON-YOMI* GROUPS

This appendix lists several hundred kanji whose Chinese-derived reading (音読み *on-yomi*) can be determined with a high degree of reliability based on the presence of a particular phonetic component, sometimes under specified conditions.

Because *on-yomi* are so irregular, it is generally best to learn them through the process of adding kanji compounds to your vocabulary, rather than trying to memorize them for their own sake. This rule does not apply, however, to the kanji listed in this appendix, whose readings can be learned by mastering a limited number of phonetic components. By taking advantage of these low-hanging fruit, you can make significant progress toward being able to pronounce kanji compounds and input kanji on a computer or other electronic device.

## Arrangement and Format

Groups are arranged in the order in which their phonetic components appear in the main entries, so that you may consult this appendix as you proceed through the course. Within groups, kanji are arranged in ascending order of their entry numbers. The end of each group is marked by a horizontal line.

Phonetic components appear in the left column, at the top of each group. Use these for self-testing. Superscript numerals following some phonetic components refer the user to an endnote specifying the conditions under which this component is to be associated with the reading shown. The most common condition is that the phonetic component be located at the right side of a kanji, which is the most frequent position for a kanji's pronunciation marker.

Small black circles (•) located between the phonetic component and the first kanji in the group indicate groups having one or more exceptions (see Selection Criteria, below). *On* readings appear to the right of each kanji. When the *on* reading does not match the predicted reading, it appears in parentheses, followed by a small black circle. When it matches the predicted reading but is not the only *on* reading for the kanji, it is followed by a small empty circle (○).

When studying groups having one or more exceptions or conditions, you should not only memorize the common reading, but also note the exceptions. Take care to isolate these in your memory from the rest of the group. These exceptions require special attention, because only when these are known can one be confident of knowing the pronunciation of all the others.

## Selection Criteria

This table includes groups of three or more kanji whose readings can be predicted with at least 75% accuracy based on the presence of a particular phonetic component. It also includes kanji pairs whose readings can be predicted with 100% accuracy.

Characters containing the phonetic component but not having the predicted reading counted as a full exception, even those whose reading varied from the

predicted reading only by the difference between a long and short vowel (e.g., ソ and ソウ), or that between a monophthong and a diphthong (e.g., コ and キョウ). Characters whose reading varied from the predicted reading only by the voicing or non-voicing of a consonant (e.g., ドウ vs. トウ) counted as a half-exception. Moreover, characters having the predicted reading but also having one or more other readings were counted as a half-exception *per* additional reading.

Some groups/pairs were able to meet the 75%/100% predictability standard only by specifying a condition as to the location of the phonetic component (these conditions appear in the endnotes following the table). Allowing for such conditions introduced a degree of subjectivity into the decision regarding which groups to include. In all cases, the guiding principle was to introduce only those conditions whose benefit in clearing away exceptions seemed to outweigh their cost in added complexity.

## Other Groups to Note

In the course of your study, you will note numerous groups containing a phonetic component that is more or less useful in predicting the *on-yomi*, but which are not included in this table. In particular, it is useful to note the following:

1. While the *on-yomi* of kanji that include 古 vary slightly, their vowel sounds are always short: 古, 故, 固, 湖, 枯, 鋼 (コ); 胡 (コ/ゴ); 個, 箇 (コ/カ); 居, 据, 裾 (キョ); and 苦 (ク). The 摘 (テキ) group should be considered separately.

2. 者 and 煮 are read シャ, but all others containing 者 end in a short "o": 箸, 猪, 著, 儲 (チョ); 諸, 署, 暑, 曙 (ショ); 緒 (チョ/ショ); and 都, 賭 (ト).

3. All kanji containing 青 have the *on-yomi* セイ, though not always exclusively (additional *on-yomi* shown in parentheses): 青 (ショウ), 情 (ジョウ), 清 (ショウ), 晴, 精 (ショウ), 請 (シン), and 静 (ジョウ).

4. All kanji containing 半 have the on reading ハン, though 判, 伴 and 絆 may also be read バン.

| | | | | | | | | | | | | |
|---|---|---|---|---|---|---|---|---|---|---|---|---|
| 二 · | 二 | ニ | 0003 | | 促 | ソク | 1604 | | 培 | バイ | 1264 |
| | 弐 | ニ | 0110 | 無 · | 無 | ブ° | 0048 | | 賠 | バイ | 1265 |
| | 仁 | ニ° | 1094 | | 舞 | ブ | 0961 | 代 · | 代 | タイ° | 0071 |
| 五 | 五 | ゴ | 0007 | | 撫 | ブ | 1538 | | 袋 | タイ | 0702 |
| | 吾 | ゴ | 0220 | 付 | 付 | フ | 0064 | | 貸 | タイ | 1163 |
| | 語 | ゴ | 0222 | | 府 | フ | 0247 | 白 ²· | 白 | ハク° | 0076 |
| | 悟 | ゴ | 0326 | | 符 | フ | 0982 | | 舶 | ハク | 0670 |
| 中 | 中 | チュウ | 0035 | | 腐 | フ | 2183 | | 迫 | ハク | 1182 |
| | 仲 | チュウ | 0643 | | 附 | フ | 2214 | | 泊 | ハク | 1183 |
| | 忠 | チュウ | 0644 | 受 | 受 | ジュ | 0065 | | 伯 | ハク | 1184 |
| | 沖 | チュウ | 0645 | | 授 | ジュ | 1123 | | 拍 | ハク° | 1185 |
| 足 | 足 | ソク | 0044 | 音 ¹ | 倍 | バイ | 0069 | 長 | 長 | チョウ | 0091 |
| | 捉 | ソク | 1603 | | 陪 | バイ | 1263 | | 脹 | チョウ | 2019 |

| | | | |
|---|---|---|---|
| | 張 | チョウ | 2020 |
| | 帳 | チョウ | 2021 |
| 安 | 安 | アン | 0096 |
| | 案 | アン | 0097 |
| 交 • | 交 | コウ | 0102 |
| | 校 | コウ | 0103 |
| | 較 | (カク)• | 0693 |
| | 郊 | コウ | 1412 |
| | 効 | コウ | 1413 |
| | 絞 | コウ | 1414 |
| 化 • | 化 | カ° | 0120 |
| | 花 | カ | 0121 |
| | 靴 | カ | 0593 |
| | 貨 | カ | 1164 |
| 比 | 比 | ヒ | 0123 |
| | 批 | ヒ | 0746 |
| 先 | 先 | セン | 0134 |
| | 洗 | セン | 0135 |
| | 銑 | セン | 2068 |
| 光 3 | 光 | コウ | 0137 |
| | 晃 | コウ | 2240 |
| | 幌 | コウ | 2241 |
| 朝 • | 朝 | チョウ | 0145 |
| | 潮 | チョウ | 0146 |
| | 嘲 | チョウ° | 2221 |
| 方 4 • | 防 | ボウ | 0174 |
| | 訪 | (ホウ)• | 0454 |
| | 紡 | ボウ | 0835 |
| | 妨 | ボウ | 1882 |
| | 坊 | ボウ° | 1883 |
| | 傍 | ボウ | 1884 |
| | 房 | ボウ | 1886 |
| | 肪 | ボウ | 1996 |
| 同 • | 同 | ドウ | 0182 |
| | 筒 | (トウ)• | 1838 |
| | 洞 | ドウ | 1842 |
| | 胴 | ドウ | 1992 |
| | 銅 | ドウ | 2066 |
| 高 | 高 | コウ | 0185 |

| | | | |
|---|---|---|---|
| | 稿 | コウ | 1580 |
| | 縞 | コウ | 1581 |
| 市 • | 市 | シ | 0205 |
| | 姉 | シ | 1205 |
| | 肺 | (ハイ)• | 1981 |
| | 柿 | シ | 2234 |
| 泉 | 泉 | セン | 0207 |
| | 線 | セン | 0210 |
| | 腺 | セン | 1983 |
| 家 • | 家 | カ° | 0219 |
| | 嫁 | カ | 2201 |
| | 稼 | カ | 2202 |
| 我 5 | 我 | ガ | 0221 |
| | 餓 | ガ | 1965 |
| 会 | 会 | カイ, エ | 0226 |
| | 絵 | カイ, エ | 0525 |
| 令 6 | 令 | レイ | 0229 |
| | 冷 | レイ | 0675 |
| | 齢 | レイ | 0676 |
| | 零 | レイ | 0901 |
| | 鈴 | レイ° | 2082 |
| 念 | 念 | ネン | 0230 |
| | 捻 | ネン | 1700 |
| 致 | 致 | チ | 0251 |
| | 緻 | チ | 2009 |
| 且 7 | 組 | ソ | 0264 |
| | 祖 | ソ | 0641 |
| | 租 | ソ | 1515 |
| | 粗 | ソ | 1516 |
| | 阻 | ソ | 1517 |
| 亲 | 新 | シン | 0275 |
| | 親 | シン | 0276 |
| | 薪 | シン | 1753 |
| 郎 | 郎 | ロウ | 0286 |
| | 廊 | ロウ | 0287 |
| 官 | 官 | カン | 0290 |
| | 館 | カン | 0291 |
| | 管 | カン | 1839 |
| | 棺 | カン | 1840 |

| | | | |
|---|---|---|---|
| 宿 | 宿 | シュク | 0292 |
| | 縮 | シュク | 0875 |
| 禁 | 禁 | キン | 0312 |
| | 襟 | キン | 1532 |
| 申 • | 申 | シン | 0315 |
| | 神 | シン° | 0316 |
| | 伸 | シン | 0873 |
| | 紳 | シン | 0874 |
| 感 | 感 | カン | 0327 |
| | 憾 | カン | 1216 |
| 秋 | 秋 | シュウ | 0364 |
| | 愁 | シュウ | 1316 |
| 志 | 志 | シ | 0369 |
| | 誌 | シ | 0370 |
| 委 | 委 | イ | 0396 |
| | 萎 | イ | 1456 |
| 干 • | 干 | カン | 0408 |
| | 刊 | カン | 0409 |
| | 汗 | カン | 0410 |
| | 竿 | カン | 0411 |
| | 軒 | (ケン)• | 0691 |
| | 岸 | (ガン)• | 1648 |
| | 幹 | カン | 1808 |
| | 肝 | カン | 1980 |
| 利 | 利 | リ | 0412 |
| | 梨 | リ | 1175 |
| | 痢 | リ | 1943 |
| 間 | 間 | カン | 0448 |
| | 簡 | カン | 0463 |
| 包 | 包 | ホウ | 0457 |
| | 鞄 | ホウ | 0594 |
| | 抱 | ホウ | 0664 |
| | 砲 | ホウ | 0665 |
| | 泡 | ホウ | 0666 |
| | 飽 | ホウ | 1964 |
| | 胞 | ホウ | 1984 |
| 朕 • | 勝 | (ショウ)• | 0460 |
| | 藤 | トウ | 2235 |
| | 騰 | トウ | 2236 |

| | | | | | | | | | | | |
|---|---|---|---|---|---|---|---|---|---|---|---|
| | 膽 | トウ | 2237 | | 界 | カイ | 0612 | 愛 | 愛 | アイ | 0778 |
| 咼 | 過 | カ | 0464 | 将 | 将 | ショウ | 0614 | | 曖 | アイ | 2249 |
| | 禍 | カ | 1486 | | 奨 | ショウ | 0615 | 憂 | 憂 | ユウ | 0779 |
| | 渦 | カ | 1487 | | 醤 | ショウ | 2128 | | 優 | ユウ | 0780 |
| | 鍋 | カ | 1488 | 丙 • | 病 | ヘイ° | 0617 | 票 | 票 | ヒョウ | 0782 |
| 戒 | 戒 | カイ | 0469 | | 丙 | ヘイ | 1523 | | 標 | ヒョウ | 0783 |
| | 械 | カイ | 0474 | | 柄 | ヘイ | 1524 | | 漂 | ヒョウ | 0784 |
| 幾 | 幾 | キ | 0470 | 意 10 | 憶 | オク | 0620 | 尊 | 尊 | ソン | 0802 |
| | 畿 | キ | 0471 | | 臆 | オク | 0621 | | 噂 | ソン | 2011 |
| | 磯 | キ | 0472 | | 億 | オク | 0622 | | 樽 | ソン | 2012 |
| | 機 | キ | 0473 | 則 | 則 | ソク | 0625 | 可 12• | 可 | カ | 0814 |
| 氏 8 | 氏 | シ | 0476 | | 側 | ソク | 0626 | | 何 | カ | 0815 |
| | 紙 | シ | 0478 | | 測 | ソク | 0627 | | 苛 | カ | 0816 |
| 民 | 民 | ミン | 0477 | 祭 11 | 祭 | サイ | 0637 | | 荷 | カ | 0817 |
| | 眠 | ミン | 1009 | | 際 | サイ | 0638 | | 河 | カ | 0818 |
| 氐 | 低 | テイ | 0479 | 察 | 察 | サツ | 0639 | | 阿 | (ア)• | 0819 |
| | 抵 | テイ | 0480 | | 擦 | サツ | 2098 | | 歌 | カ | 0827 |
| | 邸 | テイ | 0481 | 丈 | 丈 | ジョウ | 0657 | 司 | 司 | シ | 0820 |
| | 底 | テイ | 0482 | | 杖 | ジョウ | 0658 | | 伺 | シ | 0821 |
| 巨 | 巨 | キョ | 0483 | 般 • | 般 | ハン | 0671 | | 詞 | シ | 0822 |
| | 距 | キョ | 2013 | | 搬 | ハン | 0672 | | 飼 | シ | 0823 |
| | 拒 | キョ | 2014 | | 盤 | (バン)• | 0673 | | 嗣 | シ | 0825 |
| 農 | 農 | ノウ | 0511 | 蔵 | 蔵 | ゾウ | 0695 | | 覗 | シ | 0826 |
| | 濃 | ノウ | 0512 | | 臓 | ゾウ | 1974 | 責 • | 責 | セキ | 0831 |
| 劦 | 協 | キョウ | 0543 | 倉 | 倉 | ソウ | 0696 | | 積 | セキ | 0832 |
| | 脅 | キョウ | 1496 | | 創 | ソウ | 0697 | | 債 | (サイ)• | 0833 |
| 要 | 要 | ヨウ | 0547 | 表 | 表 | ヒョウ | 0705 | | 績 | セキ | 0836 |
| | 腰 | ヨウ | 1987 | | 俵 | ヒョウ | 1355 | 州 | 州 | シュウ | 0845 |
| 知 | 知 | チ | 0560 | 制 | 制 | セイ | 0708 | | 洲 | シュウ | 0846 |
| | 智 | チ | 1093 | | 製 | セイ | 0709 | | 酬 | シュウ | 1627 |
| | 痴 | チ | 1941 | 列 • | 列 | レツ | 0718 | 麻 | 麻 | マ | 0852 |
| 朱 | 朱 | シュ | 0566 | | 烈 | レツ | 0719 | | 魔 | マ | 2095 |
| | 珠 | シュ | 1207 | | 裂 | レツ | 0720 | | 摩 | マ | 2099 |
| | 殊 | シュ | 1208 | | 例 | (レイ)• | 0721 | | 磨 | マ | 2100 |
| 放 | 放 | ホウ | 0574 | 刑 | 刑 | ケイ | 0722 | 麻 | 歴 | レキ | 0853 |
| | 倣 | ホウ | 1353 | | 型 | ケイ | 0723 | | 暦 | レキ | 0854 |
| 呈 9 | 呈 | テイ | 0587 | 坐 | 座 | ザ | 0749 | 袁 • | 園 | エン | 0856 |
| | 程 | テイ | 0588 | | 坐 | ザ | 0750 | | 遠 | エン° | 0857 |
| 介 | 介 | カイ | 0611 | | 挫 | ザ | 1699 | | 猿 | エン | 1859 |

| | | | | |
|---|---|---|---|---|
| 复 | • | 複 | フク | 0863 |
| | | 腹 | フク | 0864 |
| | | 復 | フク | 0865 |
| | | 覆 | フク | 1870 |
| | | 履 | （リ）• | 1871 |
| 廷 | | 廷 | テイ | 0877 |
| | | 庭 | テイ | 0878 |
| | | 艇 | テイ | 0879 |
| 冓 | | 構 | コウ | 0917 |
| | | 講 | コウ | 0918 |
| | | 購 | コウ | 0919 |
| | | 溝 | コウ | 0920 |
| 義 | | 義 | ギ | 0926 |
| | | 議 | ギ | 0927 |
| | | 儀 | ギ | 0928 |
| | | 犠 | ギ | 0929 |
| 旨 | • | 旨 | シ | 0931 |
| | | 指 | シ | 0932 |
| | | 脂 | シ | 1994 |
| | | 詣 | （ケイ）• | 1995 |
| 到 | | 到 | トウ | 0940 |
| | | 倒 | トウ | 0941 |
| 俞 | | 輸 | ユ | 0945 |
| | | 諭 | ユ | 0946 |
| | | 愉 | ユ | 0947 |
| | | 癒 | ユ | 0948 |
| | | 喩 | ユ | 2140 |
| 尞 | | 療 | リョウ | 0952 |
| | | 僚 | リョウ | 0953 |
| | | 瞭 | リョウ | 0954 |
| | | 寮 | リョウ | 0955 |
| 采 | | 采 | サイ | 0987 |
| | | 菜 | サイ | 0988 |
| | | 採 | サイ | 0989 |
| | | 彩 | サイ | 0990 |
| 朮 | | 術 | ジュツ | 0993 |
| | | 述 | ジュツ | 0994 |
| 桼 | | 漆 | シツ | 1002 |
| | | 膝 | シツ | 1989 |

| | | | | |
|---|---|---|---|---|
| 乗 | | 乗 | ジョウ | 1005 |
| | | 剰 | ジョウ | 1007 |
| 𠬶 | | 侵 | シン | 1013 |
| | | 浸 | シン | 1014 |
| | | 寝 | シン | 1015 |
| 射 | | 射 | シャ | 1021 |
| | | 謝 | シャ | 1022 |
| 㑒 | • | 検 | ケン | 1029 |
| | | 験 | ケン° | 1030 |
| | | 険 | ケン | 1031 |
| | | 倹 | ケン | 1032 |
| | | 剣 | ケン | 1033 |
| 容 | | 容 | ヨウ | 1037 |
| | | 溶 | ヨウ | 1038 |
| 升 | | 升 | ショウ | 1051 |
| | | 昇 | ショウ | 1053 |
| 荒 | | 荒 | コウ | 1064 |
| | | 慌 | コウ | 1065 |
| 孫 | | 孫 | ソン | 1079 |
| | | 遜 | ソン | 2060 |
| 扁 | | 偏 | ヘン | 1081 |
| | | 遍 | ヘン | 1082 |
| | | 編 | ヘン | 1083 |
| | | 篇 | ヘン | 1084 |
| 普 | | 普 | フ | 1085 |
| | | 譜 | フ | 1086 |
| 忍 | | 忍 | ニン | 1095 |
| | | 認 | ニン | 1096 |
| 求 | | 求 | キュウ | 1097 |
| | | 救 | キュウ | 1098 |
| | | 球 | キュウ | 1099 |
| 召 [13] | | 召 | ショウ | 1103 |
| | | 招 | ショウ | 1104 |
| | | 沼 | ショウ | 1105 |
| | | 紹 | ショウ | 1106 |
| | | 詔 | ショウ | 1107 |
| | | 昭 | ショウ | 1109 |
| | | 照 | ショウ | 1110 |
| 啇 | • | 摘 | テキ | 1118 |

| | | | | |
|---|---|---|---|---|
| | | 滴 | テキ | 1119 |
| | | 嫡 | （チャク）• | 1120 |
| | | 適 | テキ | 1121 |
| | | 敵 | テキ | 1122 |
| 雚 [14] | | 観 | カン | 1128 |
| | | 勧 | カン | 1129 |
| | | 歓 | カン | 1131 |
| 隺 | | 鶴 | カク | 1132 |
| | | 確 | カク | 1133 |
| 曼 | | 慢 | マン | 1134 |
| | | 漫 | マン | 1135 |
| 加 | • | 加 | カ | 1147 |
| | | 賀 | （ガ）• | 1172 |
| | | 架 | カ | 1173 |
| 喜 | | 喜 | キ | 1212 |
| | | 嬉 | キ | 2015 |
| 善 | | 善 | ゼン | 1213 |
| | | 繕 | ゼン | 1214 |
| | | 膳 | ゼン | 1215 |
| 帯 | | 帯 | タイ | 1232 |
| | | 滞 | タイ | 1233 |
| 奐 | | 換 | カン | 1269 |
| | | 喚 | カン | 1270 |
| 肖 [15] | | 肖 | ショウ | 1288 |
| | | 消 | ショウ | 1289 |
| | | 硝 | ショウ | 1290 |
| | | 梢 | ショウ | 1291 |
| | | 宵 | ショウ | 1293 |
| 郷 | • | 郷 | キョウ° | 1295 |
| | | 饗 | キョウ | 1296 |
| | | 響 | キョウ | 1297 |
| 奇 | • | 奇 | キ | 1329 |
| | | 寄 | キ | 1330 |
| | | 騎 | キ | 1331 |
| | | 椅 | （イ）• | 1332 |
| | | 埼 | キ | 1334 |
| 業 | | 僕 | ボク | 1358 |
| | | 撲 | ボク | 1359 |
| 伐 | | 伐 | バツ | 1361 |

| | 漢字 | 読み | 番号 |
|---|---|---|---|
| | 閥 | バツ | 1362 |
| 䍃 | 揺 | ヨウ | 1369 |
| | 謡 | ヨウ | 1370 |
| | 遥 | ヨウ | 1371 |
| 夆 | 峰 | ホウ | 1378 |
| | 逢 | ホウ | 1379 |
| | 縫 | ホウ | 1380 |
| | 蜂 | ホウ | 1381 |
| 宓 | 蜜 | ミツ | 1382 |
| | 密 | ミツ | 1383 |
| 君 16 | 群 | グン | 1408 |
| | 郡 | グン | 1409 |
| 帝 | 帝 | テイ | 1418 |
| | 締 | テイ | 1419 |
| | 諦 | テイ | 1420 |
| 亭 | 亭 | テイ | 1423 |
| | 停 | テイ | 1424 |
| 昆 | 昆 | コン | 1425 |
| | 混 | コン | 1426 |
| 皆 | 皆 | カイ | 1427 |
| | 楷 | カイ | 1428 |
| | 諧 | カイ | 1429 |
| | 階 | カイ | 1430 |
| 孰 | 熟 | ジュク | 1436 |
| | 塾 | ジュク | 1437 |
| 章 | 章 | ショウ | 1459 |
| | 彰 | ショウ | 1460 |
| | 障 | ショウ | 1461 |
| 呉 | 呉 | ゴ | 1478 |
| | 娯 | ゴ | 1479 |
| | 誤 | ゴ | 1480 |
| 富 17 | 副 | フク | 1482 |
| | 幅 | フク | 1483 |
| | 福 | フク | 1484 |
| 闌 | 蘭 | ラン | 1489 |
| | 欄 | ラン | 1490 |
| 睘 | 環 | カン | 1549 |
| | 還 | カン | 1550 |
| 盾 | 盾 | ジュン | 1551 |
| | 循 | ジュン | 1552 |
| 喬 | 橋 | キョウ | 1578 |
| | 矯 | キョウ | 1579 |
| 壮 | 壮 | ソウ | 1589 |
| | 荘 | ソウ | 1590 |
| | 装 | ソウ° | 1591 |
| 甫 | 捕 | ホ | 1596 |
| | 補 | ホ | 1598 |
| | 浦 | ホ | 1599 |
| | 哺 | ホ | 1600 |
| | 舗 | ホ | 1601 |
| 建 | 建 | ケン° | 1609 |
| | 健 | ケン | 1610 |
| | 鍵 | ケン | 2077 |
| 唐 | 唐 | トウ | 1615 |
| | 糖 | トウ | 1616 |
| 凡 | 凡 | ハン° | 1629 |
| | 帆 | ハン | 1631 |
| | 汎 | ハン | 1632 |
| 亢 | 抗 | コウ | 1639 |
| | 航 | コウ | 1640 |
| | 坑 | コウ | 1641 |
| 朋 | 崩 | ホウ | 1650 |
| | 朋 | ホウ | 2226 |
| 焦 | 焦 | ショウ | 1654 |
| | 礁 | ショウ | 1655 |
| 襄 | 譲 | ジョウ | 1662 |
| | 嬢 | ジョウ | 1663 |
| | 醸 | ジョウ | 1664 |
| | 壌 | ジョウ | 1665 |
| 裏 | 壊 | カイ | 1666 |
| | 懐 | カイ | 1667 |
| 侯 | 侯 | コウ | 1673 |
| | 喉 | コウ | 1674 |
| | 候 | コウ | 1675 |
| 冒 | 冒 | ボウ | 1683 |
| | 帽 | ボウ | 1687 |
| 昌 | 昌 | ショウ | 1684 |
| | 唱 | ショウ | 1685 |
| | 晶 | ショウ | 1686 |
| 永 | 永 | エイ | 1691 |
| | 泳 | エイ | 1692 |
| | 詠 | エイ | 1693 |
| 困 | 困 | コン | 1723 |
| | 梱 | コン | 1724 |
| 因 18 | 因 | イン | 1725 |
| | 姻 | イン | 1726 |
| | 咽 | イン | 1727 |
| 堇 | 勤 | キン° | 1732 |
| | 謹 | イン | 1733 |
| | 僅 | イン | 1734 |
| 及 | 及 | キュウ | 1760 |
| | 級 | キュウ | 1762 |
| | 吸 | キュウ | 1763 |
| 朔 | 遡 | ソ | 1776 |
| | 塑 | ソ | 1777 |
| 桑 | 操 | ソウ | 1809 |
| | 燥 | ソウ | 1810 |
| | 藻 | ソウ | 1812 |
| 賁 | 噴 | フン | 1813 |
| | 墳 | フン | 1814 |
| | 憤 | フン | 1815 |
| 苗 | 苗 | ビョウ° | 1823 |
| | 描 | ビョウ | 1824 |
| | 猫 | ビョウ | 1825 |
| 屈 | 屈 | クツ | 1834 |
| | 掘 | クツ | 1835 |
| | 窟 | クツ | 1843 |
| 珏 | 班 | ハン | 1853 |
| | 斑 | ハン | 1854 |
| 忽 | 忽 | コツ | 1857 |
| | 惚 | コツ | 1858 |
| 貞 | 貞 | テイ | 1867 |
| | 偵 | テイ | 1868 |
| 禺 | 偶 | グウ | 1874 |
| | 隅 | グウ | 1875 |
| | 遇 | グウ | 1877 |
| | 愚 | （グ）° | 1878 |

| | | | | | | | | | | | |
|---|---|---|---|---|---|---|---|---|---|---|---|
| 曹 | 曹 | ソウ | 1879 | | 脳 | ノウ | 1973 | | 舷 | ゲン | 2143 |
| | 遭 | ソウ | 1880 | 奴 | 奴 | ド | 2047 | 茲 | 慈 | ジ | 2179 |
| | 槽 | ソウ | 1881 | | 努 | ド | 2048 | | 滋 | ジ | 2180 |
| 雇 | 雇 | コ | 1889 | | 怒 | ド | 2049 | | 磁 | ジ | 2181 |
| | 顧 | コ | 1890 | 卑 | 卑 | ヒ | 2087 | 散 | 撤 | テツ | 2187 |
| 段 | 暇 | カ | 1903 | | 碑 | ヒ | 2088 | | 徹 | テツ | 2188 |
| | 霞 | カ | 1904 | | 痺 | ヒ | 2089 | 微 | 徴 | チョウ | 2190 |
| 貫 | 貫 | カン | 1911 | 奉 | •奉 | ホウ° | 2103 | | 懲 | チョウ | 2191 |
| | 慣 | カン | 1912 | | 俸 | ホウ | 2106 | 狠 | 墾 | コン | 2206 |
| 夾 | 峡 | キョウ | 1932 | | 棒 | （ボウ）• | 2107 | | 懇 | コン | 2207 |
| | 狭 | キョウ | 1933 | | 捧 | ホウ | 2108 | 遀 | 随 | ズイ | 2213 |
| | 挟 | キョウ | 1934 | 需 | 需 | ジュ | 2111 | | 髄 | ズイ | 2215 |
| | 頬 | キョウ | 1935 | | 濡 | ジュ | 2112 | 敝 | 弊 | ヘイ | 2223 |
| 串 | 串 | カン | 1938 | | 儒 | ジュ | 2113 | | 幣 | ヘイ | 2224 |
| | 患 | カン | 1939 | 尉 | 尉 | イ | 2124 | | 蔽 | ヘイ | 2225 |
| 荅 | 塔 | トウ | 1959 | | 慰 | イ | 2125 | 全 21 | 栓 | セン | 2230 |
| | 搭 | トウ | 1960 | 畜 | 畜 | チク | 2133 | | 詮 | セン | 2231 |
| 几 19 | 飢 | キ | 1966 | | 蓄 | チク | 2134 | 奚 | 鶏 | ケイ | 2284 |
| | 机 | キ | 1967 | 玄 20 | 玄 | ゲン | 2135 | | 渓 | ケイ | 2285 |
| 离 | 離 | リ | 1970 | | 眩 | ゲン | 2136 | | | | |
| | 璃 | リ | 2252 | | 呟 | ゲン | 2137 | | | | |
| 凶 | 悩 | ノウ | 1972 | | 弦 | ゲン | 2142 | | | | |

## Endnotes

"PC" = phonetic component

1 PC alone at right side (excludes 部, 剖, 竸)

2 PC is character itself, or is alone at right side (excludes 原, 階, etc.)

3 PC not at left side (excludes 輝)

4 PC at right side (excludes 方, 施, etc.)

5 PC not at bottom (excludes 義, etc.)

6 PC not at left side (excludes 領)

7 PC alone at right side (excludes 宜, etc.)

8 PC is character itself, or is alone at right side (excludes 婚)

9 口 alone atop 王 (excludes 聖)

10 PC at right side (excludes 意)

11 Nothing above PC (excludes 察, 擦)

12 PC not covered by 大 (excludes 奇, etc.)

13 PC not bounded by enclosure (excludes 超)

14 PC at left side (excludes 権)

15 PC at center or right side (excludes 削)

16 PC at left side (excludes 君)

17 PC at one side (excludes 富)

18 PC not on top (excludes 恩)

19 PC alone at right side (excludes 抗, etc.)

20 PC not on top of anything (excludes 畜, 蓄)

21 PC at right side (excludes 全)

# SELECTED COMPOUNDS WITH IRREGULAR READINGS

The following list was adapted from the appendix to the proposed changes to the Joyo Kanji List (「改定常用漢字表」に関する試案, Ministry of Education, Council on Culture, Subcommittee on Japanese Language, April 2010).

| | | |
|---|---|---|
| 明日 | あす | tomorrow |
| 小豆 | あずき | adzuki bean |
| 海女 | あま | woman diver |
| 硫黄 | いおう | sulfur |
| 意気地 | いくじ | pride, self-respect; backbone |
| 田舎 | いなか | country, rural district |
| 息吹 | いぶき | breath |
| 海原 | うなばら | sea, ocean |
| 乳母 | うば | wet nurse |
| 浮気 | うわき | inconstancy; love affair; fickleness |
| 浮つく | うわつく | be fickle, be flippant, be restless |
| 笑顔 | えがお | smiling face, smile |
| 叔父／伯父 | おじ | uncle (younger than one's parent)/uncle (older than one's parent) |
| 大人 | おとな | adult |
| 乙女 | おとめ | virgin, maiden |
| 叔母／伯母 | おば | aunt (younger than one's parent)/aunt (older than one's parent) |
| お巡りさん | おまわりさん | policeman |
| お神酒 | おみき | sacred wine/sake; sake |
| 母屋／母家 | おもや | main house/wing |
| 母さん | かあさん | mother |
| 神楽 | かぐら | sacred (Shinto) music and dancing |
| 河岸 | かし | riverside; fish market |
| 鍛冶 | かじ | blacksmith |
| 風邪 | かぜ | (common) cold |
| 固唾（を飲む） | かたず（をのむ） | (to anxiously hold one's) breath |
| 仮名 | かな | kana, Japanese syllabary |
| 蚊帳 | かや | mosquito net |
| 為替 | かわせ | money order, exchange |
| 河原／川原 | かわら | dry riverbed, river beach |
| 昨日 | きのう | yesterday |
| 今日 | きょう | today |
| 果物 | くだもの | fruit |
| 玄人 | くろうと | expert, master hand |
| 今朝 | けさ | this morning |
| 景色 | けしき | scenery, landscape |
| 心地 | ここち | feeling, mood |
| 今年 | ことし | this year |
| 早乙女 | さおとめ | rice-planting girl; girl |
| 雑魚 | ざこ | small fish, small fry |
| 桟敷 | さじき | reviewing stand, box, gallery |
| 差し支える | さしつかえる | hinder, complicate; object |
| 早苗 | さなえ | rice sprouts |
| 五月雨 | さみだれ | early summer rain |
| 時雨 | しぐれ | late fall/early winter rain |
| 尻尾 | しっぽ | tail |
| 竹刀 | しない | bamboo sword |
| 老舗 | しにせ | old shop |
| 芝生 | しばふ | lawn, turf |
| 清水 | しみず | pure/clear water |

| | | |
|---|---|---|
| 三味線 | しゃみせん | samisen (three-stringed instrument) |
| 砂利 | じゃり | gravel, ballast |
| 数珠 | じゅず | Buddhist rosary |
| 上手 | じょうず | skillful, proficient |
| 白髪 | しらが | white/gray hair |
| 素人 | しろうと | amateur, novice, outsider |
| 師走 | しわす [しはす] | December |
| 数寄屋／数奇屋 | すきや | tea-ceremony arbor |
| 相撲 | すもう | sumo wrestling |
| 草履 | ぞうり | Japanese sandals, zori |
| 山車 | だし | festival car, float |
| 太刀 | たち | long sword |
| 立ち退く | たちのく | leave, depart, evacuate; take refuge; vacate, quit |
| 七夕 | たなばた | Festival of the Weaver [star Vega]; the Star Festival (July 7) |
| 足袋 | たび | Japanese [digitated] socks, tabi |
| 稚児 | ちご | infant, child |
| 一日 | ついたち | 1st day of the month |
| 築山 | つきやま | artificial hill |
| 梅雨 | つゆ | rainy season (of early summer) |
| 凸凹 | でこぼこ | unevenness, roughness; imbalance |
| 手伝う | てつだう | help, assist, lend a hand |
| 伝馬船 | てんません | lighter, jolly (boat) |
| 投網 | とあみ | casting net |
| 十重二十重 | とえはたえ | manifold, multitude |
| 父さん | とおさん | father, daddy, papa |
| 時計 | とけい | clock, watch |
| 読経 | どっきょう | sutra chanting |
| 友達 | ともだち | friends |
| 仲人 | なこうど | go-between, matchmaker |
| 名残 | なごり | parting; memory; remains |
| 雪崩 | なだれ | snowslide, avalanche |
| 兄さん | にいさん | older brother |
| 姉さん | ねえさん | older sister; waitress, girl; miss |
| 野良 | のら | the fields |
| 祝詞 | のりと | Shinto ritual prayer |
| 博士 | はかせ | doctor, PhD |
| 二十／二十歳 | はたち | twenty years old |
| 二十日 | はつか | twenty days; 20th of the month |
| 波止場 | はとば | wharf, quay |
| 一人 | ひとり | one person |
| 日和 | ひより | weather |
| 二人 | ふたり | two persons |
| 二日 | ふつか | two days; 2nd of the month |
| 吹雪 | ふぶき | snowstorm |
| 下手 | へた | unskillful, clumsy |
| 部屋 | へや | room, chamber |
| 迷子 | まいご | lost child |
| 真面目 | まじめ | serious, sober, earnest |
| 真っ赤 | まっか | deep red |
| 真っ青 | まっさお | deep blue; paleness, ghastliness |
| 土産 | みやげ | souvenir |
| 息子 | むすこ | son |
| 眼鏡 | めがね | glasses, spectacles |
| 猛者 | もさ | stalwart; veteran |
| 紅葉 | もみじ | fall colors |
| 木綿 | もめん | cotton, cotton cloth |
| 最寄り | もより | nearest, nearby |
| 八百長 | やおちょう | rigged affair, fixed game |
| 八百屋 | やおや | greengrocer; jack-of-all-trades |
| 大和 | やまと | (old name for Japan) |
| 弥生 | やよい | third month (of the lunar calendar), March |
| 浴衣 | ゆかた | informal summer kimono |
| 行方 | ゆくえ | one's whereabouts |
| 寄席 | よせ | storyteller's hall, variety hall |
| 若人 | わこうど | youth, young man |

# UNDERSTANDING KANJI COMPOUNDS

This appendix lists the principal ways that kanji are combined into compounds. Even though these word-formation patterns are generally self-evident, it is useful to take time out at a relatively early stage in your study to consider the ways kanji are put together to create meaning. I recommend you do this right after studying entry 0402 右, by which time you will be familiar with all of the kanji used in the main examples below.

Note that I have excluded *kun-yomi* compounds, whose construction tends to be even more transparent than that of *on-yomi* compounds. For more detailed explanation and for lists of illustrative examples, I refer you to Habein & Mathias's *The Complete Guide to Everyday Kanji* (Kodansha International).

## Subject–Predicate

The first kanji (A) carries out an action indicated by the second kanji (B):

| | | |
|---|---|---|
| 市立 | しりつ | "city-establish" = municipal |
| 国有 | こくゆう | "country-own" = state-owned, national |
| 人工 | じんこう | "human-manufacture" = man-made |

## Verb–Object

B is the object of an action indicated by A (these compounds mostly come from Chinese and reflect Chinese syntax):

| | | |
|---|---|---|
| 読書 | どくしょ | "read-book" = reading a book, reading |
| 防音 | ぼうおん | "defend against-sound" = soundproof |
| 決意 | けつい | "decide-mind" = resolution, determination |
| 有毒 | ゆうどく | "have-poison" = poisonous |
| 注目 | ちゅうもく | "concentrate-eye" = attention, notice |
| 駐日 | ちゅうにち | "stationed-Japan" = stationed in Japan |

## Object–Verb

A is the object of an action indicated by B (these compounds, relatively few in number, were mostly coined in Japan and reflect Japanese syntax):

| | | |
|---|---|---|
| 米作 | べいさく | "rice-cultivate" = rice crop |
| 肉食 | にくしょく | "meat-eat" = meat-eating, meat diet |

## Modifier–Modified

A functions as an adjective describing B:

| | | |
|---|---|---|
| 新人 | しんじん | "new-person" = rookie; newcomer |
| 外交 | がいこう | "outside-intercourse" = diplomacy |

| | | |
|---|---|---|
| 竹林 | ちくりん | "bamboo-forest" = bamboo forest |
| 読本 | とくほん | "read-book" = reading book, reader |
| 早朝 | そうちょう | "early-morning" = early morning |

A functions as an adverb modifying B:

| | | |
|---|---|---|
| 不快な | ふかいな | "not-pleasant" = unpleasant, disagreeable |
| 毎日 | まいにち | "every-day" = every day |
| 予防 | よぼう | "in advance-defend against" = prevention, precaution |
| 最後の | さいごの | "most-later" = last, final |
| 未定の | みていの | "not yet-decide" = undecided, pending |

## Compounding of a Single Kanji

A is repeated to create a plural:

| | | |
|---|---|---|
| 国々 | くにぐに | "country-country" = countries, nations |
| 我々 | われわれ | "self-self" = we |

A is repeated to emphasize a meaning:

| | | |
|---|---|---|
| 早々 | そうそう (＝はやばや) | "quick-quick" = quickly, without delay |
| 昔々 | むかしむかし | "former times-former times" = Once upon a time... |

## Compounding of Kanji with Similar Meanings

A and B merely confirm each other's meaning:

| | | |
|---|---|---|
| 森林 | しんりん | "thick woods-forest" = forest, woodland |
| 禁止する | きんしする | "prohibit-stop" = prohibit |
| 集合する | しゅうごうする | "gather-combine" = gather, assemble |

(The above pattern results in part from the need for multisyllabic words to avoid confusion in speech – whether in Japanese or in the original Chinese. This helps explain the existence of compounds in which one kanji seems to add little or nothing to the meaning of the other.)

A and B strengthen each other's meaning:

| | | |
|---|---|---|
| 広大な | こうだいな | "wide-big" = vast, expansive, grand |
| 万全の | ばんぜんの | "ten thousand-whole" = perfect, infallible |

A and B combine senses to denote a specific meaning:

| | | |
|---|---|---|
| 発明 | はつめい | "open up-clear" = invention, contrivance |
| 交通 | こうつう | "intercourse-pass" = traffic; transportation; communication |
| 耳目 | じもく | "ear-eye" = eyes and ears; one's attention |

## Compounding of Kanji with Opposite or Complementary Meanings

A and B together suggest opposite things, a choice, or a range between extremes:

| | | |
|---|---|---|
| 左右 | さゆう | "left-right" = right and left |
| 有無 | うむ | "there is-nothing" = existence, presence; yes or no |
| 上下 | じょうげ | "above-below" = high and low; rise and fall |
| 大小 | だいしょう | "big-small" = large and small; size |

A and B together suggest complementary things, or a general category that includes them both:

| 売買 | ばいばい | "sell-buy" = buying and selling, trade |
| 心身 | しんしん | "mind-body" = mind and body |
| 山水 | さんすい | "mountain-water" = landscape |
| 父母 | ふぼ | "father-mother" = father and mother, parents |
| 草木 | そうもく (＝くさき) | "grass-tree" = trees and plants, vegetation |

## Three-Kanji Compounds

A is a prefix to B and C:

| 私生活 | しせいかつ | "private-life" = one's private life |
| 平社員 | ひらしゃいん | "plain-employee" = mere clerk |

C is a suffix to A and B:

| 入学式 | にゅうがくしき | "school entrance-ceremony" = school entrance ceremony |
| 工事中 | こうじちゅう | "construction-middle" = under construction |

A and B are a prefix to C:

| 無人島 | むじんとう | "without humans-island" = uninhabited island |

B and C are a suffix to A:

| 竹細工 | たけざいく | "bamboo-craftsmanship" = bamboo work, bamboo crafts |

A, B, and C combine without prefix or suffix:

| 大中小 | だいちゅうしょう | "big-middle-small" = large, medium, and small |
| 年月日 | ねんがっぴ | "year-month-day" = date |

## Compounds of Greater than Three Kanji

These are combinations of smaller units:

| 生年月日 | せいねんがっぴ | "birth-date" = birth date |
| 駐車禁止 | ちゅうしゃきんし | "parking-prohibit" = No Parking |
| 公安委員会 | こうあんいいんかい | "public safety-committee" = Public Safety Commission |

## Abbreviations

東大　とうだい, short for 東京大学 (とうきょうだいがく, University of Tokyo)
日銀　にちぎん, short for 日本銀行 (にっぽんぎんこう, Bank of Japan)

## Repeating Graphical Elements

Many compounds combine two kanji with similar graphical elements (e.g., 宇宙, 清潔, 捕捉, 憧憬, 葛藤, 咽喉, 瑠璃, 紛糾, etc.) whose common element is often suggestive of the meaning of the compound. This can be used as a clue when reading, and for remembering the meanings of such compounds.

# KANJI FOR COUNTRIES AND REGIONS

Where space is at a premium, writers often abbreviate the names of countries and geographical regions using the first kanji of their old (often Chinese-based) phonetic spellings. For example, 墨 ボク may be used as an abbreviation for 墨西哥 メキシコ (Chinese pinyin: *Moxige*), such as in the phrase 日墨 (にちぼく, Japan and Mexico, Japanese-Mexican). The following table includes a selected list of these kanji, alphabetized by country/region name, with entry numbers in this book.

| | | | | | | | |
|---|---|---|---|---|---|---|---|
| 0819 | 阿 | ア | Africa | 0001 | 日 | ニチ | Japan |
| 0234 | 米 | ベイ | America, United States | 0236 | 和 | ワ | Japan |
| 0545 | 亜 | ア | Asia | 0145 | 朝 | チョウ | Korea |
| 2204 | 豪 | ゴウ | Australia | 0662 | 韓 | カン | (South) Korea |
| 1184 | 伯 | ハク | Brazil | 0336 | 馬 | マ | Malaysia |
| 0332 | 英 | エイ | Britain, England | 0179 | 満 | マン | Manchuria |
| 1147 | 加 | カ | Canada | 0536 | 墨 | ボク | Mexico |
| 0035 | 中 | チュウ | China | 2205 | 蒙 | モウ | Mongolia |
| 1012 | 華 | カ | China | 1489 | 蘭 | ラン | Netherlands, Holland |
| 1385 | 欧 | オウ | Europe | 0123 | 比 | ヒ | Philippines |
| 0811 | 仏 | フツ | France | 1907 | 露 | ロ | Russia |
| 0346 | 独 | ドク | Germany | 0795 | 西 | セイ | Spain |
| 0231 | 印 | イン | India | 0949 | 台 | タイ | Taiwan |
| 2116 | 尼 | ニ | Indonesia | 2105 | 泰 | タイ | Thailand |
| 1406 | 伊 | イ | Italy | 1112 | 越 | エツ | Vietnam |

# TABLE OF GRAPHEME MEANINGS

The meanings attached to individual graphical units are introduced and reintroduced, as you need them, throughout the main entries section. For this reason, you will not find it necessary to study the graphemes as a preliminary step to learning the kanji. However, you may on occasion find it helpful to look up the meaning(s) assigned to a grapheme, and to find the number of the entry where the grapheme is first introduced. The table that follows is provided to serve this purpose.

## Format and Arrangement

Graphemes are listed in order of increasing stroke count. Graphemes having the same stroke count are arranged by the number of the entry where each grapheme is first introduced, shown along the left side of each column. When an additional meaning for a grapheme is introduced at a later point in the main entries, a number in parentheses to the right of the meaning indicates the entry where that meaning is introduced.

## Scope and Purpose

This table is not intended to be comprehensive, but simply to be helpful to the user. It is not a complete list of character graphemes, nor is it a table of radicals according to the traditional system. It refers to "graphemes" (meaningful contrastive graphical units) rather than "radicals," because it lists these forms regardless of whether they are designated by tradition as semantic roots. For a list of the traditional radicals, I refer you to the "Quick Reference Radical Chart" in the *Kodansha Kanji Learner's Dictionary*, which shows all 214 radicals printed in each of their forms, along with their Japanese names.

   This table should also not be used for looking up the conventional meanings of the graphical elements contained herein. In keeping with this book's unconstrained approach to learning and remembering characters, some graphemes are assigned meanings that depart from tradition. For example, the form 禹 is assigned the simple, visualizable meaning "doorman," in place of its conventional meaning "mythical emperor Yu." In a few cases, a distinguishing set of strokes has been interpreted as a grapheme even though it has not traditionally been considered a distinct unit (e.g., 亠: stately crown/stately rooftop). In a few other cases, a variant form is assigned a different meaning from its parent form; for example, the 𠆢 in 倉 is interpreted as a "roof," even though it is by etymology a variant of 人 (human being). Wherever the meanings listed in this table depart from tradition, they are printed in *italics*. Conversely, traditional grapheme meanings that are not used in this course, or that apply only when the grapheme appears as a stand-alone kanji, are shown in brackets [ ]. Graphemes that are interpreted opportunistically according to the appearance of the kanji they form part of are labeled "(*various*)."

   To keep the list to a manageable length, priority was given to those graphemes

that do not appear as stand-alone kanji in this book, and therefore cannot be found in the main indexes. Next priority was given to stand-alone kanji that were deemed to require special attention for one or more of the following reasons: (a) they were assigned a special or specific interpretation when used as a component grapheme, (b) they have important variant forms, or (c) they appear as component graphemes either in a large number of kanji, or in kanji that do not appear consecutively in the main entries.

Some grapheme variants do not appear in this table. Traditional forms are only listed if they appear in one or more kanji listed in this book. Variant forms whose stroke count differs from the parent form appear both with the parent form and also separately, according to their own stroke count, with a cross-reference to the parent form. For example, four-stroke [衤] appears with its five-stroke parent 示, but also separately in the four-stroke section, with a cross-reference to 示. On the other hand, graphemes whose parent form is not listed (because it is not used in this book) are listed only under their own stroke count. For example, [艹] is only listed in the 3-stroke section, even though it derives from the six-stroke parent 艸.

## If a Certain Grapheme Cannot Be Found in This Table...

...it is likely to be one that is also a stand-alone kanji, which can therefore be found in the main indexes. Also, because of the way the kanji are arranged and cross-referenced in the main entries, users who in the course of studying come across a grapheme they have forgotten may wish to look in the preceding several entries for the necessary cross-reference, even before turning to this table.

| 1 STROKE | | |
|---|---|---|
| 0160 | L | *breast*<br>sharp hook (0313) |

| 2 STROKES | | |
|---|---|---|
| 0005 | 十 忄 | ten<br>abundant, complete<br>*cross shape, cross-shaped plant*<br>needle (0556) |
| 0010 | 八 | split<br>[eight] |
| 0015 | 人 亻 | human being, person, man |
| 0015 | 𠆢 | *roof, covering*<br>[human being, person, man] |
| 0058 | 又 | hand |
| 0065 | 冖 | cover |
| 0083 | 儿 | human legs<br>legs<br>roots (i.e., "legs" of a plant) |
| 0084 | 力 | power, strength, force<br>*plow* |
| 0085 | 刀 刂 | sword, knife<br>cut, slice |
| 0089 | 厶 | nose<br>self, private |

| | | *arm bent at elbow* (pointing down; cf. ㇇) (0238) |
|---|---|---|
| 0102 | 亠 | lid |
| 0105 | 𠂉 | *man lying flat*<br>*forward gaze* (with 臣) (0855)<br>[human being, person, man] |
| 0120 | ヒ | spoon<br>*person fallen on his rear, seated person* |
| 0149 | 厂 | cliff |
| 0159 | ㇇ | *arm bent at elbow* (pointing forward; cf. 厶)<br>*pointing forward* |
| 0166 | 勹 | wrap up, wrap around<br>*elephant* |
| 0231 | 卩 | seal<br>(cf. 㔾 ) |
| 0278 | 冫 | *second(ary)*<br>ice (0675) |
| 0296 | 凵 | open pit or container |
| 0296 | メ | *violent death*<br>*slash marks*<br>*"x" mark* |
| 0297 | 匚 匸 | *(various)*<br>hiding container (1803) |

| 0425 | 几 | wind |
| | | *wind-blown tent* |
| 0425 | 几 | table |
| | | *tablecloth* |
| 0437 | 丁 丁 | T-shaped intersection |
| | | town subsection |
| | | *nail (1024)* |
| 0528 | 宀 | *(various)* |
| 0628 | 弓 与 | *numeral 5* |
| 0726 | 巳 | *broken body* |
| | | [seal] |
| | | (cf. 卩) |
| 1114 | 卜 | *pointing downward* |
| | | [divination] |
| 1782 | 乃 | *pull away* |
| | | [possessive particle] |

**3 STROKES**

| 0019 | 口 卩 | mouth |
| | | opening |
| | | entrance |
| | | *box (0068)* |
| 0022 | 川 | river |
| 0027 | 氵 | (see 4-stroke 水) |
| 0030 | 土 圡 | soil, land, earth |
| | | place, locality, area (0320) |
| 0033 | 大 六 | big |
| 0034 | 小 | small |
| 0037 | 山 屾 屵 | mountain |
| 0045 | 宀 | roof, house, home |
| 0046 | 扌 | (see 4-stroke 手) |
| 0055 | 彳 | (see 6-stroke 行) |
| 0056 | 忄 | (see 4-stroke 心) |
| 0064 | 寸 | *outstretched arm* |
| | | [sun, a bit of] |
| 0068 | 阝 | hills |
| | | *hills around edge of town* |
| 0068 | 阝 | town |
| | | *walls around edge of town* |
| 0070 | 弋 | *spear* |
| | | [shoot] |
| 0075 | 囗 | enclosure, border |
| | | precinct |
| | | box |
| 0093 | 女 女 | woman |
| 0094 | 子 孑 | child, baby |
| 0099 | 丷 | *(various)* |
| | | [small] |
| 0108 | 工 工 | manufacture; workmanship, work |
| | | construction |
| 0112 | 幺 | child |

| 0114 | 夂 夂 夊 | (at bottom) crossed legs |
| | | *(at top) angled rooftop (0119)* |
| | | *(at top) summit (1376)* |
| 0121 | 艹 | grass, herbs |
| | | plants |
| 0137 | 屮 | *radiate from* |
| | | *converge upon* |
| | | [small] |
| 0141 | 彐 彑 | claw |
| | | *three-fingered hand* |
| | | *pitchfork, shovel* |
| 0147 | 彡 | comb, bristle |
| | | hair, fur |
| | | *(various)* |
| 0149 | 广 | slanting roof, shelter, garage |
| | | [dotted cliff] |
| 0158 | 辶 辶 | truck, dray |
| | | *move forward, conveyance* |
| 0187 | 也 | scorpion |
| 0203 | 巾 | cloth |
| 0217 | 犭 | (see 4-stroke 犬) |
| 0227 | 亼 | *snugly-fitting lid* |
| | | *fit* |
| 0233 | 亡 | deceased, die |
| 0248 | 尸 | *door* |
| | | buttocks (0488) |
| | | [corpse] |
| 0265 | 夕 | evening |
| | | moon |
| 0350 | 士 | military man, samurai |
| | | *man of learning* |
| 0408 | 干 | dry |
| 0421 | 弓 弖 | bow |
| 0426 | 己 | self |
| | | *kneeling self* |
| | | *wrap up, roll up (0457)* |
| 0469 | 廾 | two hands |
| | | twenty (1051) |
| | | *(various)* |
| 0614 | 爿 | wooden block/tablet |
| 0652 | 才 | *talented person reaching out to grab something* |
| | | [genius, talent] |
| 0700 | 衤 | (see 6-stroke 衣) |
| 0872 | 夊 | stretch one's legs |
| | | stretch |
| 1539 | 毛 | *person relaxing on floor* |
| | | [blade of grass] |
| 1629 | 凡 | *spread widely* |
| | | *carpenter's table (1633)* |
| | | [commonplace, mediocre] |

| | | |
|---|---|---|
| 0152 | 乍 | *saw* |
| | | [suddenly; while] |
| 0155 | 电 | *lightning bolt* |
| 0164 | 矛 | halberd |
| 0185 | 亠 | (see 10-stroke 高) |
| 0197 | 皿 皿 | plate |
| 0236 | 禾 | neatly bundled rice stalks, rice grain |
| 0263 | 且 | ladder, accumulate |
| 0282 | 艮 | (see 6-stroke 艮) |
| 0290 | 吕 | *government official* (cf. 6-stroke 自) |
| 0311 | 示 礻 | show |
| | | altar to the gods |
| 0315 | 申 申 | *pointing upward* |
| | | *piercing through layers* |
| | | [report to (a superior)] |
| 0319 | 宀 | *stately crown* |
| | | *stately rooftop* |
| 0352 | 罒 | net |
| | | "wide net of the law"/the authorities (0417) |
| | | eye (2278) |
| 0397 | 穴 穴 | hole, cave |
| 0403 | 石 石 | stone, rock |
| 0479 | 氏 | foundation, base |
| 0521 | 丬 | *pegged pole* |
| | | *steps, stages* |
| 0559 | 矢 矢 | arrow |
| | | *tools and measures* |
| | | *straight* |
| 0572 | 疋 | *broken, deformed* |
| | | [bolt of cloth] |
| 0617 | 疒 | illness |
| 0669 | 台 | *hoop rolling* |
| 0710 | 衤 | (see 6-stroke 衣) |
| 0814 | 可 | possible, approve |
| | | "okay" gesture |
| 0814 | 司 | officiate, administer |
| | | *desk of an official or administrator* |
| 0824 | 册 | *bookshelf* |
| | | [counter for books] |
| 0993 | 术 | *noteworthy tree* |
| 1042 | 甘 | sweet |
| 1136 | 卯 印 | rabbit |
| | | *rabbit ears* |
| 1193 | 兄 兑 | older brother |
| 1243 | 灬 | glowing, shining, brilliant (does not apply to 学, 觉, or 劳) |
| 1253 | 圣 | straight |
| 1816 | 牙 | (see 4-stroke 牙) |
| 1820 | 疋 | *fang* (cf. 4-stroke 牙) |

| | | |
|---|---|---|
| 0055 | 行 彳 亍 | go |
| | | act |
| | | *either side of a road* (as 彳亍) (0661) |
| 0057 | 耳 耳 | ear |
| 0079 | 聿 | hand writing with brush |
| 0081 | 自 | nose |
| | | self |
| 0112 | 糸 纟 | thread, string, cord, rope |
| | | line (0210) |
| | | continuity (0354) |
| 0216 | 肉 月 月 | meat, flesh |
| | | body part |
| | | (cf. 4-stroke 月) |
| 0234 | 米 米 | rice |
| 0243 | 竹 ⺮ | bamboo |
| | | bamboo instrument |
| | | counting, figuring |
| | | keeping records |
| 0250 | 至 | arrive |
| | | come to |
| 0282 | 良 | (see 7-stroke 良) |
| 0282 | 艮 艮 艮 | stop |
| | | limit, boundary |
| | | *little boy* |
| 0343 | 虫 虫 | insect, worm |
| 0418 | 羽 | feather |
| | | wing |
| 0451 | 关 | *connect with, concern* |
| | | *barricade* |
| | | *blossoms from heaven* (1251) |
| 0456 | 关 | tally stick |
| 0490 | 羊 ⺶ 羊 | sheep, goat |
| 0528 | 色 | color |
| | | eros |
| 0547 | 西 覀 | *box/basket with handle* |
| | | [west] |
| 0580 | 禺 | *mixing cauldron* |
| 0637 | 夵 | hand presenting sacrificial meat offering |
| 0668 | 舟 舟 | small boat |
| | | boat |
| 0700 | 衣 衤 衣 | |
| | | 衣 ⺻ 㐄 garment, clothing |
| 0748 | 臼 | *high-ranking official* (cf. 5-stroke 臼) |
| 0774 | 亦 | *flame-heated griddle* |
| | | [repetition] |
| 0786 | 各 | *cabin* |
| | | [each, every] |
| 0912 | 虍 虍 | tiger |
| 0935 | 束 | stab |
| 0961 | 舛 | dance |
| | | [opposite, contrary] |

| | | |
|---|---|---|
| 1582 | 戋 | *vehicle unloading cargo*<br>[spears] |
| 1643 | 耒 耒 | *three-blade rotary tiller*<br>[plow] |
| 1756 | 此 | *three men looking at something<br>   that has drawn their attention*<br>[this] |
| 1827 | 兆 | *budding stalks*<br>[showing signs of] |
| 1932 | 夹 | pinch, hold between |
| 2042 | 卡 | *relative* |
| 2054 | 臼 | *(various)*<br>[mortar] |
| 2109 | 而 | *roots*<br>[and] |
| 2168 | 并 | put together |

### 7 STROKES

| | | |
|---|---|---|
| 0044 | 足 𧾷 | foot, leg, step |
| 0051 | 言 訁 | say<br>speech, word |
| 0060 | 身 身 | body |
| 0082 | 貝 貝 | shellfish, shell<br>money, wealth |
| 0083 | 見 | see, look at |
| 0125 | 車 車 | vehicle, car<br>wheel |
| 0140 | 走 走 | run |
| 0159 | 甬 | *carry (a container) forward*<br>[wall-enclosed road] |
| 0161 | 豆 豆 | bean, pea<br>pea-sized |
| 0218 | 豕 | pig |
| 0282 | 良 𠂊 | good<br>*good little boy* |
| 0299 | 釆 釆 | *crudely tied rice bundles*<br>[divide, distinguish] |
| 0342 | 角 角 | horn, antenna |
| 0484 | 臣 | retainer |
| 0510 | 辰 | dragon |
| 0531 | 里 | village<br>*person* |
| 0647 | 呆 | swaddled baby |
| 0796 | 酉 酉 | liquor bottle, liquor<br>ferment |
| 0800 | 炎 | *sharp stimulus* |
| 0995 | 余 | remaining, excess<br>*carrying excessive load of wood* |
| 1097 | 求 | *person splashing in water*<br>[seek] |
| 1193 | 兑 | (see 5-stroke 兄) |

| | | |
|---|---|---|
| 1288 | 肖 | *sparks*<br>*fragments*<br>[likeness] |
| 1478 | 吳 | *typist*<br>[Kingdom of Wu] |
| 1596 | 甫 | *fishing net*<br>[not until] |
| 2206 | 豸 | badger |

### 8 STROKES

| | | |
|---|---|---|
| 0025 | 隹 | small bird |
| 0029 | 金 釒 | metal<br>gold<br>money |
| 0068 | 音 | *very short person standing on box* |
| 0091 | 長 | long |
| 0130 | 青 | blue<br>clear<br>pure<br>calm |
| 0154 | 雨 ⻗ | rain, raincloud, raindrops,<br>   atmospheric moisture |
| 0288 | 食 | (see 9-stroke 食) |
| 0443 | 易 | easy<br>(cf. 9-stroke 昜) |
| 0447 | 門 | gate |
| 0485 | 其 | *bind/bound*<br>*chessboard* (1796) |
| 0738 | 非 | not, non-, un-, wrong<br>*door* (0741) |
| 0808 | 昔 | *Siamese twins* |
| 0839 | 直 | straight, direct, upright<br>*put straight, correct* |
| 0942 | 侖 | careful study<br>*library* |
| 1016 | 帚 | washcloth |
| 1029 | 兔 | *stable* |
| 1272 | 免 | exemption<br>*escaping rabbit* |
| 1329 | 奇 | unusual, odd<br>*large person in odd position<br>   balancing atop object* |
| 1421 | 享 | *growing child*<br>[enjoy] |
| 1432 | 坴 | *earth's crust*<br>[land] |
| 1438 | 夌 | *emperor buried with legs crossed*<br>[surmounting a hill] |
| 1608 | 隶 | *hand spraying water hose*<br>[slave] |
| 2267 | 曷 | *mischievous elephant*<br>[interrogative adverb] |

## 9 STROKES

| | | |
|---|---|---|
| 0150 | 音 | sound |
| 0156 | 頁 | head<br>[page] |
| 0157 | 首 | head |
| 0288 | 食 𩙿 飠 | eat<br>food |
| 0301 | 品 | article<br>*(various)* |
| 0443 | 昜 | *difficult*<br>[expand; bright]<br>(cf. 8-stroke 易) |
| 0464 | 咼 | *exceed, over-*<br>[evil, dishonest] |
| 0586 | 㒸 | *pig commando*<br>[drive out] |
| 0592 | 革 革 | leather |
| 0801 | 酋 | *ceremonial liquor bottle*<br>[tribal chief] |
| 0863 | 复 | overlap, duplicate, double, fold |
| 0945 | 俞 兪 | *package of sliced meat*<br>[hollow/scoop out] |
| 1081 | 扁 | *framed bookcase*<br>[flat, level] |
| 1124 | 爰 | *give*<br>[lead to] |
| 1212 | 壴 | *drum standing on its side* |
| 1481 | 畐 | *grain silo*<br>[brimming liquor bottle] |
| 1678 | 是 | straight<br>[right, correct] |
| 1872 | 禹 | *doorman*<br>[mythical emperor Yu] |
| 1874 | 禺 | monkey |
| 1903 | 叚 | *(various)*<br>[cover with a veil] |

## 10 STROKES

| | | |
|---|---|---|
| 0185 | 高 亠口 | high, tall |
| 0336 | 馬 馬 | horse |
| 0465 | 骨 骨 | bone |
| 0507 | 竜 龍 | dragon |
| 0659 | 韋 韋 | leather |
| 0712 | 𦰩 堇 | *Han scholar-official*<br>[violet (堇)] |
| 0917 | 冓 | *scaffolding structure*<br>[put together] |
| 1132 | 隺 | *long-necked bird* |
| 1286 | 鬲 鬲 | tripod cauldron |

| | | |
|---|---|---|
| 1336 | 莫 | *no more*<br>[do/be not] |
| 1792 | 髟 | hair |

## 11 STROKES

| | | |
|---|---|---|
| 0340 | 鳥 鳥 | bird, species of bird |
| 0492 | 魚 魚 | fish |
| 0831 | 責 | responsibility, blame<br>*mounting layers* |
| 0852 | 麻 麻 | hemp |
| 1118 | 商 | *fruit merchant carrying old basket*<br>[only] |
| 1128 | 雈 | *bird pointing with arrow* |
| 1134 | 曼 | *arrogant and lazy person crossing arms and legs*<br>[handsome, broad] |
| 1222 | 曽 | *build up*<br>[before, formerly] |
| 1434 | 埶 | *the round earth*<br>[cultivation] |
| 1436 | 孰 | *well-rounded child*<br>[wall-building] |

## 12 STROKES

| | | |
|---|---|---|
| 0952 | 尞 | *big fun*<br>[burn gradually] |
| 1087 | 戠 | *spear-bearing guard standing in the sun* |
| 1358 | 菐 | *big servant*<br>[thicket] |
| 1578 | 喬 | tall |
| 1813 | 賁 | seashell swollen to bursting |
| 2223 | 敝 敝 | *dry*<br>[be worn out] |

## 13 STROKES

| | | |
|---|---|---|
| 0926 | 義 | righteousness<br>*righteous ritual of sheep sacrifice* |
| 1466 | 辟 | *criminal*<br>[law] |
| 1659 | 蒦 | grasp |
| 1662 | 㐮 | pad with fluffy lining |
| 1809 | 喿 | *fruiting tree, cotton plant*<br>[chirping] |

## 16 STROKES

| | | |
|---|---|---|
| 0507 | 龍 | (see 10-stroke 竜) |

# TABLE OF RELATED AND LOOK-ALIKE KANJI

This table arranges kanji into groups that highlight similarities and differences in their graphical forms. Use this table for review at a relatively advanced stage in your study of the kanji—for example, by testing whether you can recall each kanji's keyword(s), as well as a *kun* word or sample compound.

## Format and Arrangement

Groups are divided by horizontal lines, but have been arranged so as to allow instructive comparisons among adjacent groups in many instances. Note that many kanji appear in multiple (often adjacent) groups, while some kanji do not appear in any group.

Groups appear in ascending order of their lowest entry number. Where two or more groups begin at the same entry, they are further arranged by their highest entry number. Within each group, kanji appear in the order of their individual entry numbers, so a quick glance at these will allow you to determine how far through a group you have studied.

Groups related primarily or exclusively by a shared radical have mostly been excluded; to test yourself on these, use the Radical Index. In some cases part of a radical-based group has been included as a supplement to what appears in the Radical Index (for example, the related pair 曇 and 雲 are shown, since 曇 is not listed under Radical 173 雨).

| | | | | | | | | | | | |
|---|---|---|---|---|---|---|---|---|---|---|---|
| 五 | 0007 | 盟 | 1305 | 中 | 0035 | 定 | 0045 | 愛 | 0778 | 倍 | 0069 |
| 吾 | 0220 | 萌 | 1826 | 仲 | 0643 | 錠 | 2080 | 授 | 1123 | 位 | 0577 |
| 語 | 0222 | 曜 | 0025 | 忠 | 0644 | 綻 | 2081 | 援 | 1124 | 泣 | 0578 |
| 悟 | 0326 | 濯 | 1328 | 沖 | 0645 | 手 | 0046 | 媛 | 1125 | 拉 | 2239 |
| 六 | 0008 | 躍 | 1690 | 正 | 0043 | 毛 | 0487 | 緩 | 1126 | 成 | 0070 |
| 穴 | 0397 | 水 | 0027 | 政 | 0246 | 無 | 0048 | 暖 | 1127 | 城 | 1298 |
| 九 | 0011 | 氷 | 1690 | 整 | 0308 | 舞 | 0961 | 以 | 0066 | 誠 | 1299 |
| 丸 | 0012 | 永 | 1691 | 証 | 0550 | 焦 | 1654 | 似 | 1354 | 盛 | 1300 |
| 力 | 0084 | 東 | 0032 | 歪 | 0551 | 付 | 0064 | 部 | 0068 | 代 | 0071 |
| 刀 | 0085 | 陳 | 1373 | 症 | 0618 | 府 | 0247 | 倍 | 0069 | 袋 | 0702 |
| 刃 | 0087 | 棟 | 1688 | 征 | 0872 | 符 | 0982 | 剖 | 1262 | 貸 | 1163 |
| 千 | 0017 | 凍 | 1689 | 足 | 0044 | 腐 | 2183 | 陪 | 1263 | 伐 | 1361 |
| 干 | 0408 | 練 | 2062 | 捉 | 1603 | 附 | 2214 | 培 | 1264 | 閥 | 1362 |
| 明 | 0024 | 錬 | 2063 | 促 | 1604 | 受 | 0065 | 賠 | 1265 | 王 | 0072 |

| | | | | | | | | | | | |
|---|---|---|---|---|---|---|---|---|---|---|---|
| 玉 | 0073 | 校 | 0103 | 式 | 0109 | 索 | 1735 | 酢 | 2129 | 務 | 0687 |
| 宝 | 0074 | 較 | 0693 | 弐 | 0110 | 先 | 0134 | 電 | 0155 | 柔 | 0688 |
| 国 | 0075 | 郊 | 1412 | 武 | 0111 | 洗 | 0135 | 雷 | 0900 | 句 | 0166 |
| 白 | 0076 | 効 | 1413 | 系 | 0112 | 銑 | 2068 | 頁 | 0156 | 旬 | 0167 |
| 舶 | 0670 | 絞 | 1414 | 系 | 1077 | 洗 | 0135 | 首 | 0157 | 拘 | 1070 |
| 迫 | 1182 | 母 | 0104 | 午 | 0115 | 洪 | 0358 | 夏 | 0363 | 殉 | 1090 |
| 泊 | 1183 | 毎 | 0105 | 年 | 0117 | 元 | 0136 | 憂 | 0779 | 匂 | 2245 |
| 伯 | 1184 | 海 | 0106 | 牛 | 0116 | 示 | 0311 | 優 | 0780 | 勾 | 2246 |
| 拍 | 1185 | 毒 | 0133 | 件 | 0118 | 光 | 0137 | 頁 | 0156 | 勺 | 0168 |
| 皇 | 0077 | 侮 | 1571 | 伴 | 0743 | 当 | 0141 | 貢 | 1158 | 的 | 0169 |
| 星 | 0755 | 梅 | 1572 | 条 | 0119 | 去 | 0138 | 首 | 0157 | 約 | 0170 |
| 全 | 0078 | 悔 | 1573 | 柔 | 0688 | 法 | 0139 | 道 | 0158 | 酌 | 2131 |
| 栓 | 2230 | 敏 | 1574 | 化 | 0120 | 走 | 0140 | 導 | 0804 | 釣 | 2132 |
| 詮 | 2231 | 繁 | 1575 | 花 | 0121 | 朝 | 0145 | 通 | 0159 | 勿 | 0171 |
| 書 | 0079 | 貫 | 1911 | 靴 | 0593 | 潮 | 0146 | 痛 | 0619 | 物 | 0172 |
| 事 | 0080 | 慣 | 1912 | 貨 | 1164 | 胡 | 0258 | 踊 | 1325 | 忽 | 1857 |
| 貝 | 0082 | 者 | 0107 | 北 | 0122 | 湖 | 0259 | 勇 | 2005 | 惚 | 1858 |
| 見 | 0083 | 考 | 0628 | 背 | 0124 | 期 | 0486 | 湧 | 2006 | 方 | 0173 |
| 具 | 0837 | 老 | 0629 | 脊 | 2153 | 嘲 | 2221 | 乳 | 0160 | 防 | 0174 |
| 切 | 0086 | 孝 | 0630 | 比 | 0123 | 形 | 0147 | 浮 | 0613 | 訪 | 0454 |
| 窃 | 1566 | 者 | 0107 | 批 | 0746 | 刑 | 0722 | 孔 | 1559 | 紡 | 0835 |
| 分 | 0088 | 著 | 0707 | 皆 | 1427 | 型 | 0723 | 乳 | 0160 | 妨 | 1882 |
| 公 | 0089 | 煮 | 1192 | 此 | 1756 | 研 | 0724 | 礼 | 0313 | 坊 | 1883 |
| 長 | 0091 | 箸 | 1443 | 気 | 0126 | 発 | 0148 | 乱 | 0380 | 傍 | 1884 |
| 辰 | 0510 | 暑 | 1444 | 汽 | 0127 | 廃 | 0149 | 孔 | 1559 | 肪 | 1996 |
| 脹 | 2019 | 署 | 1445 | 青 | 0130 | 音 | 0150 | 札 | 1694 | 面 | 0175 |
| 張 | 2020 | 曙 | 1446 | 情 | 0973 | 響 | 1297 | 豆 | 0161 | 画 | 0176 |
| 帳 | 2021 | 者 | 0107 | 清 | 0974 | 闇 | 1364 | 頭 | 0162 | 両 | 0177 |
| 子 | 0094 | 猪 | 0217 | 精 | 0976 | 韻 | 1593 | 豊 | 0513 | 岡 | 0178 |
| 予 | 0163 | 都 | 0244 | 請 | 0977 | 意 | 0151 | 短 | 0562 | 満 | 0179 |
| 矛 | 0164 | 賭 | 1447 | 静 | 0978 | 憶 | 0620 | 登 | 1054 | 顔 | 0180 |
| 了 | 0958 | 諸 | 1448 | 青 | 0130 | 臆 | 0621 | 澄 | 1055 | 須 | 1928 |
| 安 | 0096 | 儲 | 1449 | 責 | 0831 | 億 | 0622 | 痘 | 1944 | 同 | 0182 |
| 案 | 0097 | 緒 | 1450 | 貴 | 1177 | 作 | 0152 | 予 | 0163 | 向 | 0183 |
| 父 | 0100 | 工 | 0108 | 麦 | 0131 | 昨 | 0153 | 預 | 0165 | 尚 | 0184 |
| 文 | 0101 | 攻 | 1045 | 表 | 0705 | 搾 | 1415 | 序 | 1209 | 司 | 0820 |
| 交 | 0102 | 功 | 1046 | 素 | 0132 | 詐 | 1794 | 矛 | 0164 | 肖 | 1288 |
| 交 | 0102 | 巧 | 1047 | | | | | | | | |

| | | | | | | | | | | | |
|---|---|---|---|---|---|---|---|---|---|---|---|
| 宵 | 1293 | 渇 | 2267 | 今 | 0228 | 至 | 0250 | 失 | 0563 | 浪 | 1477 |
| 同 | 0182 | 爪 | 0201 | 令 | 0229 | 屋 | 0252 | 夫 | 0565 | 娘 | 2200 |
| 筒 | 1838 | 瓜 | 0202 | 命 | 0232 | 室 | 0253 | 朱 | 0566 | 官 | 0290 |
| 洞 | 1842 | 孤 | 1073 | 伝 | 0223 | 到 | 0940 | 未 | 0271 | 宮 | 1242 |
| 胴 | 1992 | 弧 | 1074 | 仏 | 0811 | 倒 | 0941 | 味 | 0273 | 官 | 0290 |
| 銅 | 2066 | 巾 | 0203 | 仁 | 1094 | 窒 | 1565 | 妹 | 1206 | 館 | 0291 |
| 高 | 0185 | 布 | 0204 | 会 | 0226 | 致 | 0251 | 魅 | 2094 | 管 | 1839 |
| 稿 | 1580 | 怖 | 1634 | 絵 | 0525 | 緻 | 2009 | 昧 | 2250 | 棺 | 1840 |
| 編 | 1581 | 市 | 0205 | 合 | 0227 | 居 | 0255 | 末 | 0272 | 宿 | 0292 |
| 地 | 0187 | 姉 | 1205 | 給 | 0526 | 局 | 0256 | 抹 | 1954 | 縮 | 0875 |
| 池 | 0188 | 肺 | 1981 | 令 | 0229 | 届 | 1528 | 新 | 0275 | 犬 | 0293 |
| 他 | 0189 | 柿 | 2234 | 冷 | 0675 | 屈 | 1834 | 親 | 0276 | 状 | 0616 |
| 施 | 0571 | 泉 | 0207 | 齢 | 0676 | 固 | 0260 | 薪 | 1753 | 獣 | 0763 |
| 集 | 0190 | 線 | 0210 | 零 | 0901 | 箇 | 0261 | 欠 | 0277 | 献 | 1157 |
| 隻 | 1658 | 腺 | 1983 | 領 | 1922 | 個 | 0262 | 飲 | 0289 | 伏 | 1850 |
| 斤 | 0193 | 原 | 0208 | 鈴 | 2082 | 鋼 | 2079 | 軟 | 0689 | 吠 | 1851 |
| 近 | 0194 | 源 | 0209 | 念 | 0230 | 箇 | 0261 | 久 | 0904 | 太 | 0294 |
| 辺 | 0195 | 願 | 0214 | 捻 | 1700 | 筒 | 1838 | 炊 | 1751 | 駄 | 2275 |
| 所 | 0249 | 綿 | 0211 | 亡 | 0233 | 且 | 0263 | 吹 | 1764 | 凶 | 0296 |
| 新 | 0275 | 絹 | 0212 | 盲 | 1061 | 組 | 0264 | 次 | 0278 | 区 | 0297 |
| 質 | 0318 | 錦 | 0213 | 忘 | 1062 | 祖 | 0641 | 資 | 1165 | 図 | 0298 |
| 祈 | 0640 | 内 | 0215 | 忙 | 1063 | 助 | 0642 | 盗 | 1304 | 区 | 0297 |
| 断 | 0849 | 肉 | 0216 | 望 | 1066 | 租 | 1515 | 姿 | 1453 | 欧 | 1385 |
| 丘 | 0906 | 丙 | 1523 | 妄 | 1455 | 粗 | 1516 | 諮 | 1638 | 枢 | 1386 |
| 析 | 1697 | 猪 | 0217 | 私 | 0237 | 阻 | 1517 | 茨 | 2039 | 殴 | 1387 |
| 折 | 1698 | 豚 | 0218 | 仏 | 0811 | 狙 | 1518 | 羨 | 2040 | 駆 | 1388 |
| 斬 | 1704 | 家 | 0219 | 払 | 0812 | 且 | 0263 | 席 | 0279 | 番 | 0299 |
| 斥 | 1707 | 嫁 | 2201 | 広 | 0238 | 査 | 1514 | 度 | 0280 | 審 | 1510 |
| 匠 | 1802 | 稼 | 2202 | 拡 | 0813 | 宜 | 1519 | 渡 | 0281 | 藩 | 1511 |
| 最 | 0196 | 塚 | 2203 | 鉱 | 2065 | 畳 | 1520 | 庶 | 1739 | 翻 | 1512 |
| 撮 | 1282 | 我 | 0221 | 細 | 0239 | 名 | 0269 | 遮 | 1740 | 号 | 0300 |
| 温 | 0199 | 義 | 0926 | 紳 | 0874 | 各 | 0786 | 限 | 0282 | 考 | 0628 |
| 湿 | 0200 | 餓 | 1965 | 累 | 0884 | 銘 | 1546 | 郎 | 0286 | 与 | 0858 |
| 湯 | 0446 | 伝 | 0223 | 京 | 0245 | 天 | 0270 | 廊 | 0287 | 写 | 0859 |
| 温 | 0199 | 転 | 0224 | 景 | 1280 | 未 | 0271 | 良 | 0285 | 巧 | 1047 |
| 盟 | 1304 | 芸 | 0225 | 就 | 1283 | 末 | 0272 | 郎 | 0286 | 朽 | 1048 |
| 温 | 0199 | 会 | 0226 | 涼 | 1284 | 来 | 0274 | 食 | 0288 | 汚 | 1050 |
| 湯 | 0446 | 合 | 0227 | 鯨 | 1285 | 矢 | 0559 | 朗 | 1476 | 楽 | 0302 |

| | | | | | | | | | | | |
|---|---|---|---|---|---|---|---|---|---|---|---|
| 薬 | 0303 | 央 | 0328 | 読 | 0355 | 肢 | 1991 | 委 | 0396 | 梨 | 1175 |
| 周 | 0304 | 映 | 0329 | 共 | 0356 | 反 | 0374 | 萎 | 1456 | 痢 | 1943 |
| 週 | 0305 | 決 | 0330 | 供 | 0357 | 坂 | 0375 | 穴 | 0397 | 害 | 0413 |
| 調 | 0306 | 快 | 0331 | 洪 | 0358 | 阪 | 0376 | 空 | 0398 | 普 | 1085 |
| 数 | 0309 | 英 | 0332 | 恭 | 1345 | 飯 | 0377 | 控 | 1952 | 喜 | 1212 |
| 類 | 0310 | 並 | 0333 | 洪 | 0358 | 返 | 0378 | 友 | 0399 | 善 | 1213 |
| 楼 | 1957 | 普 | 1085 | 港 | 1501 | 仮 | 0921 | 有 | 0400 | 害 | 0413 |
| 禁 | 0312 | 平 | 0334 | 昔 | 0359 | 版 | 0923 | 左 | 0401 | 割 | 0416 |
| 襟 | 1532 | 評 | 0745 | 惜 | 1218 | 板 | 0924 | 右 | 0402 | 憲 | 0417 |
| 申 | 0315 | 半 | 0335 | 措 | 1219 | 販 | 0925 | 石 | 0403 | 寧 | 0438 |
| 神 | 0316 | 伴 | 0743 | 借 | 1220 | 雑 | 0379 | 在 | 0406 | 轄 | 1841 |
| 伸 | 0873 | 判 | 0744 | 錯 | 1221 | 粋 | 1622 | 存 | 0407 | 益 | 0414 |
| 紳 | 0874 | 畔 | 1404 | 冬 | 0360 | 砕 | 1623 | 友 | 0399 | 溢 | 0415 |
| 申 | 0315 | 絆 | 2076 | 修 | 1676 | 枠 | 1624 | 抜 | 1951 | 羽 | 0418 |
| 由 | 0432 | 尺 | 0337 | 寒 | 0361 | 酔 | 1625 | 左 | 0401 | 翌 | 0419 |
| 甲 | 1521 | 尽 | 0338 | 塞 | 2232 | 寸 | 0381 | 佐 | 2218 | 習 | 0420 |
| 員 | 0317 | 冬 | 0360 | 秋 | 0364 | 寺 | 0382 | 右 | 0402 | 翌 | 0419 |
| 買 | 0352 | 駅 | 0339 | 愁 | 1316 | 時 | 0383 | 若 | 0404 | 笠 | 0754 |
| 員 | 0317 | 択 | 1503 | 主 | 0365 | 持 | 0384 | 苦 | 0405 | 弓 | 0421 |
| 韻 | 1594 | 沢 | 1504 | 住 | 0366 | 特 | 0385 | 干 | 0408 | 弱 | 0424 |
| 損 | 1595 | 訳 | 1505 | 駐 | 0367 | 待 | 0386 | 刊 | 0409 | 溺 | 2264 |
| 党 | 0319 | 釈 | 1506 | 注 | 0368 | 侍 | 0388 | 汗 | 0410 | 己 | 0426 |
| 堂 | 0320 | 鳥 | 0340 | 往 | 0866 | 詩 | 0389 | 竿 | 0411 | 記 | 0427 |
| 常 | 0321 | 島 | 0341 | 柱 | 0867 | 等 | 0393 | 軒 | 0691 | 紀 | 0428 |
| 賞 | 0322 | 烏 | 2281 | 住 | 0366 | 時 | 0383 | 岸 | 1648 | 改 | 0429 |
| 償 | 0323 | 角 | 0342 | 仕 | 0371 | 蒔 | 2185 | 乾 | 1807 | 起 | 0430 |
| 掌 | 0324 | 触 | 0344 | 任 | 0372 | 待 | 0386 | 幹 | 1808 | 配 | 0799 |
| 覚 | 0325 | 解 | 0345 | 志 | 0369 | 得 | 0387 | 肝 | 1980 | 忌 | 1864 |
| 感 | 0327 | 蟹 | 2294 | 誌 | 0370 | 徒 | 0870 | 刊 | 0409 | 妃 | 2195 |
| 憾 | 1216 | 店 | 0347 | 記 | 0427 | 即 | 0390 | 刑 | 0722 | 由 | 0432 |
| 感 | 0327 | 占 | 0348 | 支 | 0373 | 却 | 0733 | 判 | 0744 | 届 | 1528 |
| 減 | 1148 | 点 | 0349 | 反 | 0374 | 脚 | 0734 | 汗 | 0410 | 宙 | 1529 |
| 滅 | 1149 | 貼 | 1266 | 友 | 0399 | 即 | 0390 | 汁 | 0756 | 笛 | 1530 |
| 威 | 1150 | 粘 | 1267 | 皮 | 0595 | 節 | 0391 | 斗 | 0757 | 袖 | 1531 |
| 或 | 1152 | 士 | 0350 | 支 | 0373 | 既 | 1820 | 料 | 0758 | 井 | 0434 |
| 惑 | 1153 | 仕 | 0371 | 枝 | 0965 | 節 | 0391 | 科 | 0759 | 囲 | 0435 |
| 域 | 1154 | 売 | 0353 | 技 | 0966 | 筋 | 0392 | 斜 | 0999 | 丼 | 0436 |
| 城 | 1298 | 続 | 0354 | 伎 | 0967 | 季 | 0395 | 利 | 0412 | 丁 | 0437 |

| | | | | | | | | | | | |
|---|---|---|---|---|---|---|---|---|---|---|---|
| 寧 | 0438 | 砲 | 0665 | 眠 | 1009 | 遅 | 1144 | 没 | 0519 | 憧 | 2085 |
| 町 | 0439 | 泡 | 0666 | 低 | 0479 | 群 | 1408 | 設 | 0520 | 量 | 0538 |
| 灯 | 0440 | 飽 | 1964 | 抵 | 0480 | 幸 | 1470 | 殺 | 0522 | 糧 | 1618 |
| 庁 | 0441 | 胞 | 1984 | 邸 | 0481 | 達 | 1475 | 般 | 0671 | 重 | 0539 |
| 貯 | 0442 | 巻 | 0458 | 底 | 0482 | 翔 | 1513 | 殿 | 0881 | 垂 | 1004 |
| 訂 | 1024 | 圏 | 0459 | 巨 | 0483 | 羞 | 1671 | 殴 | 1387 | 重 | 0539 |
| 打 | 1025 | 遷 | 0785 | 距 | 2013 | 魚 | 0492 | 疫 | 1942 | 種 | 0544 |
| 亭 | 1423 | 港 | 1501 | 拒 | 2014 | 鮮 | 0493 | 股 | 1990 | 腫 | 2022 |
| 停 | 1424 | 選 | 1502 | 臣 | 0484 | 蘇 | 0494 | 殻 | 2052 | 動 | 0540 |
| 釘 | 2078 | 勝 | 0460 | 姫 | 2196 | 漁 | 0765 | 穀 | 2053 | 働 | 0541 |
| 易 | 0443 | 藤 | 2235 | 基 | 0485 | 鯨 | 1285 | 毀 | 2055 | 勤 | 1732 |
| 賜 | 0444 | 騰 | 2236 | 期 | 0486 | 曲 | 0503 | 段 | 0521 | 勲 | 1778 |
| 賜 | 0444 | 謄 | 2237 | 旗 | 0573 | 典 | 0504 | 鍛 | 2064 | 労 | 0542 |
| 贈 | 1227 | 戦 | 0461 | 其 | 1757 | 農 | 0511 | 殺 | 0522 | 営 | 1243 |
| 場 | 0445 | 弾 | 1075 | 欺 | 1795 | 豊 | 0513 | 刹 | 0523 | 蛍 | 1244 |
| 湯 | 0446 | 禅 | 1076 | 棋 | 1796 | 曹 | 1879 | 刈 | 0524 | 栄 | 1245 |
| 揚 | 1308 | 単 | 0462 | 碁 | 1797 | 遭 | 1880 | 巴 | 0527 | 誉 | 1246 |
| 暢 | 1309 | 巣 | 0601 | 毛 | 0487 | 槽 | 1881 | 肥 | 2023 | 挙 | 1247 |
| 陽 | 1310 | 卑 | 2087 | 尾 | 0488 | 興 | 0505 | 把 | 2024 | 拳 | 1248 |
| 瘍 | 1945 | 過 | 0464 | 育 | 0489 | 輿 | 0506 | 巳 | 2296 | 協 | 0543 |
| 腸 | 1985 | 禍 | 1486 | 充 | 1056 | 竜 | 0507 | 色 | 0528 | 脅 | 1496 |
| 門 | 0447 | 渦 | 1487 | 羊 | 0490 | 滝 | 0508 | 危 | 0726 | 脇 | 1993 |
| 間 | 0448 | 鍋 | 1488 | 洋 | 0491 | 籠 | 0509 | 免 | 1272 | 亜 | 0545 |
| 問 | 0452 | 骨 | 0465 | 詳 | 0495 | 襲 | 1849 | 声 | 0529 | 悪 | 0546 |
| 聞 | 0453 | 滑 | 1493 | 祥 | 0496 | 辰 | 0510 | 眉 | 0530 | 串 | 1938 |
| 簡 | 0463 | 骸 | 2162 | 美 | 0497 | 農 | 0511 | 里 | 0531 | 患 | 1939 |
| 蘭 | 1489 | 髄 | 2215 | 業 | 0498 | 濃 | 0512 | 理 | 0532 | 要 | 0547 |
| 欄 | 1490 | 夜 | 0467 | 実 | 0499 | 震 | 0902 | 埋 | 0533 | 妄 | 1455 |
| 潤 | 1491 | 液 | 0468 | 養 | 0500 | 振 | 0903 | 野 | 0534 | 腰 | 1987 |
| 送 | 0455 | 戒 | 0469 | 様 | 0501 | 賑 | 0905 | 裏 | 0704 | 必 | 0549 |
| 迭 | 1211 | 械 | 0474 | 南 | 0794 | 娠 | 1846 | 厘 | 2242 | 秘 | 1384 |
| 券 | 0456 | 幾 | 0470 | 義 | 0926 | 唇 | 1847 | 黒 | 0535 | 泌 | 1894 |
| 巻 | 0458 | 畿 | 0471 | 議 | 0927 | 辱 | 1848 | 墨 | 0536 | 歪 | 0551 |
| 圏 | 0459 | 磯 | 0472 | 儀 | 0928 | 吉 | 0514 | 黙 | 0762 | 否 | 0552 |
| 勝 | 0460 | 機 | 0473 | 犠 | 0929 | 詰 | 0515 | 童 | 0537 | 呑 | 2174 |
| 包 | 0457 | 氏 | 0476 | 差 | 0937 | 結 | 0516 | 章 | 1459 | 処 | 0553 |
| 鞄 | 0594 | 紙 | 0478 | 着 | 0938 | 投 | 0517 | 鐘 | 2083 | 拠 | 0554 |
| 抱 | 0664 | 民 | 0477 | 看 | 0939 | 役 | 0518 | 瞳 | 2084 | 計 | 0555 |

| | | | | | | | | | | | |
|---|---|---|---|---|---|---|---|---|---|---|---|
| 針 | 0556 | 笑 | 0579 | 菓 | 0602 | 教 | 0632 | 衛 | 0661 | 霜 | 1908 |
| 計 | 0555 | 筈 | 1442 | 裸 | 0711 | 享 | 1421 | 韓 | 0662 | 称 | 0684 |
| 討 | 1023 | 箸 | 1443 | 果 | 0599 | 亭 | 1423 | 違 | 0663 | 弥 | 0685 |
| 訂 | 1024 | 専 | 0580 | 某 | 2121 | 勃 | 2036 | 緯 | 0660 | 互 | 0686 |
| 診 | 2165 | 恵 | 0581 | 課 | 0600 | 酵 | 2127 | 経 | 1257 | 瓦 | 2167 |
| 総 | 0557 | 博 | 0983 | 謀 | 2122 | 完 | 0633 | 抱 | 0664 | 蔵 | 0695 |
| 窓 | 0558 | 縛 | 0984 | 世 | 0604 | 院 | 0634 | 拘 | 1070 | 臓 | 1974 |
| 知 | 0560 | 簿 | 0985 | 葉 | 0605 | 奈 | 0635 | 丹 | 0667 | 倉 | 0696 |
| 智 | 1093 | 薄 | 0986 | 喋 | 2139 | 宗 | 0636 | 舟 | 0668 | 創 | 0697 |
| 痴 | 1941 | 籍 | 1910 | 蝶 | 2299 | 宗 | 0636 | 凡 | 1629 | 告 | 0698 |
| 医 | 0561 | 連 | 0582 | 葉 | 0605 | 踪 | 1322 | 船 | 0669 | 造 | 0699 |
| 匹 | 1801 | 軍 | 0583 | 棄 | 0606 | 崇 | 1645 | 沿 | 1348 | 酷 | 1628 |
| 匠 | 1802 | 運 | 0584 | 帯 | 1232 | 祭 | 0637 | 鉛 | 2067 | 衣 | 0700 |
| 匿 | 1803 | 蓮 | 0585 | 緑 | 0607 | 際 | 0638 | 般 | 0671 | 依 | 0701 |
| 諾 | 1804 | 揮 | 0933 | 録 | 0608 | 察 | 0639 | 搬 | 0672 | 袋 | 0702 |
| 失 | 0563 | 輝 | 0934 | 剝 | 0609 | 擦 | 2098 | 盤 | 0673 | 褒 | 0703 |
| 秩 | 1210 | 隊 | 0586 | 緑 | 0607 | 保 | 0646 | 盤 | 0673 | 裏 | 0704 |
| 迭 | 1211 | 墜 | 2211 | 縁 | 0610 | 呆 | 0647 | 盆 | 1302 | 装 | 1591 |
| 朱 | 0566 | 呈 | 0587 | 介 | 0611 | 守 | 0648 | 歯 | 0674 | 表 | 0705 |
| 株 | 0567 | 程 | 0588 | 界 | 0612 | 団 | 0649 | 齢 | 0676 | 俵 | 1355 |
| 珠 | 1207 | 聖 | 0589 | 畏 | 2096 | 守 | 0648 | 噛 | 1852 | 制 | 0708 |
| 殊 | 1208 | 是 | 1678 | 浮 | 0613 | 狩 | 0766 | 少 | 0677 | 製 | 0709 |
| 族 | 0568 | 丑 | 0590 | 将 | 0614 | 対 | 0650 | 砂 | 0678 | 裂 | 0720 |
| 旅 | 0569 | 紐 | 0591 | 将 | 0614 | 村 | 0651 | 省 | 0681 | 剌 | 0935 |
| 遊 | 0570 | 革 | 0592 | 奨 | 0615 | 村 | 0651 | 雀 | 1742 | 難 | 0712 |
| 施 | 0571 | 靴 | 0593 | 醤 | 2128 | 材 | 0654 | 劣 | 1743 | 漢 | 1730 |
| 旋 | 0572 | 鞄 | 0594 | 状 | 0616 | 枕 | 0656 | 抄 | 1744 | 嘆 | 1731 |
| 旗 | 0573 | 皮 | 0595 | 壮 | 1589 | 杖 | 0658 | 秒 | 1745 | 勤 | 1732 |
| 放 | 0574 | 破 | 0596 | 荘 | 1590 | 枚 | 1695 | 妙 | 1746 | 謹 | 1733 |
| 激 | 0575 | 彼 | 0597 | 装 | 1591 | 才 | 0652 | 沙 | 1747 | 僅 | 1734 |
| 傲 | 1353 | 波 | 0598 | 病 | 0617 | 財 | 0653 | 炒 | 1750 | 准 | 0713 |
| 敷 | 1507 | 疲 | 1948 | 丙 | 1523 | 材 | 0654 | 歩 | 0679 | 準 | 0714 |
| 傲 | 1508 | 被 | 1949 | 柄 | 1524 | 沈 | 0655 | 渉 | 0680 | 死 | 0716 |
| 贅 | 1509 | 披 | 1950 | 則 | 0625 | 枕 | 0656 | 頻 | 1923 | 葬 | 0717 |
| 牧 | 0576 | 抜 | 1951 | 側 | 0626 | 丈 | 0657 | 捗 | 1924 | 怨 | 0728 |
| 枚 | 1695 | 果 | 0599 | 測 | 0627 | 杖 | 0658 | 相 | 0682 | 苑 | 0729 |
| 泣 | 0578 | 課 | 0600 | 孝 | 0630 | 偉 | 0659 | 想 | 0683 | 宛 | 0730 |
| 涙 | 1020 | 巣 | 0601 | 厚 | 0631 | 緯 | 0660 | 租 | 1515 | 碗 | 0731 |

| | | | | | |
|---|---|---|---|---|---|
| 腕 0732 | 狩 0766 | 額 1929 | 崎 1333 | 摩 2099 | 殿 0881 |
| 列 0718 | 猛 0767 | 酪 2126 | 埼 1334 | 磨 2100 | 異 0882 |
| 烈 0719 | 煙 0768 | 西 0795 | 司 0820 | 歴 0853 | 翼 0883 |
| 裂 0720 | 焼 0769 | 酉 0796 | 伺 0821 | 暦 0854 | 累 0884 |
| 例 0721 | 暁 0770 | 酒 0797 | 詞 0822 | 臨 0855 | 塁 0885 |
| 倒 0941 | 噴 1813 | 洒 0798 | 飼 0823 | 覧 2026 | 糞 1892 |
| 厄 0725 | 墳 1814 | 酸 0800 | 嗣 0825 | 監 2027 | 吏 0886 |
| 危 0726 | 憤 1815 | 俊 1440 | 覗 0826 | 鑑 2028 | 使 0887 |
| 範 0727 | 焼 0769 | 竣 1441 | 負 0829 | 艦 2029 | 史 0888 |
| 犯 0735 | 燥 1810 | 猶 0801 | 敗 0830 | 濫 2030 | 更 0889 |
| 狂 0736 | 旧 0771 | 尊 0802 | 貞 1867 | 藍 2031 | 便 0890 |
| 獄 0737 | 児 0772 | 噂 2011 | 責 0831 | 賢 2032 | 硬 0891 |
| 非 0738 | 亦 0773 | 樽 2012 | 積 0832 | 腎 2033 | 梗 2233 |
| 排 0739 | 変 0775 | 遵 0803 | 債 0833 | 堅 2034 | 能 0892 |
| 排 0739 | 蛮 0776 | 導 0804 | 漬 0834 | 緊 2035 | 態 0893 |
| 俳 0740 | 恋 0777 | 敬 0805 | 績 0836 | 園 0856 | 熊 0894 |
| 罪 0741 | 跡 1321 | 警 0806 | 債 0833 | 遠 0857 | 罷 0895 |
| 罰 0742 | 赤 0774 | 驚 0807 | 借 1220 | 猿 1859 | 羅 0896 |
| 批 0746 | 赦 1320 | 散 0808 | 漬 0834 | 遠 0857 | 雲 0897 |
| 輩 1855 | 愛 0778 | 撒 2186 | 清 0974 | 還 1550 | 曇 0898 |
| 悲 1856 | 曖 2249 | 撒 2187 | 潰 1178 | 卸 0861 | 丘 0906 |
| 帥 0747 | 栗 0781 | 徹 2188 | 具 0837 | 御 0862 | 兵 0907 |
| 師 0748 | 票 0782 | 微 2189 | 真 0838 | 複 0863 | 岳 0908 |
| 座 0749 | 標 0783 | 徴 2190 | 直 0839 | 腹 0864 | 浜 0909 |
| 坐 0750 | 漂 0784 | 懲 2191 | 植 0840 | 復 0865 | 舎 0910 |
| 挫 1699 | 遷 0785 | 敢 0809 | 殖 0841 | 覆 1870 | 捨 1072 |
| 卒 0751 | 栗 0781 | 厳 0810 | 値 0842 | 履 1871 | 舗 1601 |
| 率 0752 | 慄 1716 | 可 0814 | 置 0843 | 往 0866 | 寅 0913 |
| 傘 0753 | 各 0786 | 何 0815 | 県 0844 | 征 0868 | 演 0914 |
| 笠 0754 | 客 0787 | 苛 0816 | 州 0845 | 従 0869 | 黄 0915 |
| 率 0752 | 路 0788 | 荷 0817 | 洲 0846 | 徒 0870 | 横 0916 |
| 牽 1736 | 格 0789 | 河 0818 | 酬 1627 | 縦 0871 | 構 0917 |
| 然 0760 | 絡 0790 | 阿 0819 | 継 0848 | 延 0872 | 講 0918 |
| 燃 0761 | 略 0791 | 歌 0827 | 断 0849 | 誕 0876 | 購 0919 |
| 黙 0762 | 閣 0792 | 奇 1329 | 繍 1614 | 廷 0877 | 溝 0920 |
| 獣 0763 | 落 0793 | 寄 1330 | 床 0851 | 庭 0878 | 講 0918 |
| 猟 0764 | 賂 1229 | 騎 1331 | 麻 0852 | 艇 0879 | 譲 1662 |
| 漁 0765 | 露 1907 | 椅 1332 | 魔 2095 | 展 0880 | 旨 0931 |

| | | | | | | | | | | | |
|---|---|---|---|---|---|---|---|---|---|---|---|
| 指 | 0932 | 采 | 0987 | 眼 | 1092 | 統 | 1058 | 赴 | 1114 | 架 | 1173 |
| 脂 | 1994 | 菜 | 0988 | 侵 | 1013 | 流 | 1059 | 訃 | 1115 | 染 | 1174 |
| 詣 | 1995 | 採 | 0989 | 浸 | 1014 | 硫 | 1060 | 朴 | 1116 | 梨 | 1175 |
| 刺 | 0935 | 彩 | 0990 | 寝 | 1015 | 荒 | 1064 | 掛 | 1117 | 傑 | 1176 |
| 策 | 0936 | 杉 | 0991 | 掃 | 1016 | 慌 | 1065 | 摘 | 1118 | 俊 | 1440 |
| 論 | 0942 | 街 | 0992 | 婦 | 1017 | 系 | 1077 | 滴 | 1119 | 貴 | 1177 |
| 倫 | 0943 | 掛 | 1117 | 帰 | 1018 | 係 | 1078 | 嫡 | 1120 | 潰 | 1178 |
| 輪 | 0944 | 術 | 0993 | 戻 | 1019 | 孫 | 1079 | 適 | 1121 | 遺 | 1179 |
| 輸 | 0945 | 述 | 0994 | 涙 | 1020 | 遜 | 2060 | 敵 | 1122 | 遣 | 1180 |
| 諭 | 0946 | 桁 | 2229 | 射 | 1021 | 偏 | 1081 | 観 | 1128 | 追 | 1181 |
| 愉 | 0947 | 余 | 0995 | 謝 | 1022 | 遍 | 1082 | 勧 | 1129 | 迫 | 1182 |
| 癒 | 0948 | 除 | 0996 | 撃 | 1026 | 編 | 1083 | 権 | 1130 | 弔 | 1186 |
| 喩 | 2140 | 徐 | 0997 | 繋 | 1576 | 篇 | 1084 | 歓 | 1131 | 沸 | 1187 |
| 台 | 0949 | 叙 | 0998 | 拭 | 1027 | 普 | 1085 | 鶴 | 1132 | 費 | 1189 |
| 治 | 0950 | 斜 | 0999 | 試 | 1028 | 譜 | 1086 | 確 | 1133 | 弟 | 1190 |
| 冶 | 0951 | 途 | 1000 | 誠 | 1299 | 職 | 1087 | 慢 | 1134 | 第 | 1191 |
| 始 | 0956 | 塗 | 1001 | 検 | 1029 | 織 | 1088 | 漫 | 1135 | 剃 | 1192 |
| 沿 | 1348 | 漆 | 1002 | 験 | 1030 | 識 | 1089 | 卯 | 1136 | 兄 | 1193 |
| 胎 | 1986 | 添 | 1344 | 険 | 1031 | 忍 | 1095 | 抑 | 1137 | 只 | 1194 |
| 怠 | 2216 | 膝 | 1989 | 倹 | 1032 | 認 | 1096 | 仰 | 1138 | 税 | 1195 |
| 療 | 0952 | 泰 | 2105 | 剣 | 1033 | 忽 | 1857 | 迎 | 1139 | 鋭 | 1196 |
| 僚 | 0953 | 垂 | 1004 | 谷 | 1034 | 求 | 1097 | 柳 | 1140 | 説 | 1197 |
| 瞭 | 0954 | 乗 | 1005 | 欲 | 1035 | 救 | 1098 | 卯 | 1141 | 脱 | 1198 |
| 寮 | 0955 | 兼 | 1006 | 浴 | 1036 | 球 | 1099 | 卯 | 1136 | 閲 | 1199 |
| 承 | 0959 | 華 | 1012 | 俗 | 1039 | 屯 | 1100 | 貿 | 1169 | 祝 | 1200 |
| 蒸 | 0960 | 垂 | 1004 | 裕 | 1040 | 純 | 1101 | 留 | 1170 | 況 | 1201 |
| 燕 | 1741 | 睡 | 1008 | 容 | 1037 | 鈍 | 1102 | 溜 | 1171 | 悦 | 1202 |
| 舞 | 0961 | 郵 | 1010 | 溶 | 1038 | 頓 | 1920 | 疎 | 1142 | 克 | 1203 |
| 隣 | 0962 | 錘 | 1011 | 甘 | 1042 | 召 | 1103 | 速 | 1143 | 競 | 1204 |
| 瞬 | 0963 | 唾 | 1401 | 紺 | 1043 | 招 | 1104 | 遅 | 1144 | 呪 | 2177 |
| 夢 | 0964 | 乗 | 1005 | 某 | 2121 | 沼 | 1105 | 辻 | 1145 | 喜 | 1212 |
| 岐 | 0968 | 剰 | 1007 | 謀 | 2122 | 紹 | 1106 | 迅 | 1146 | 嬉 | 2015 |
| 峠 | 0969 | 兼 | 1006 | 媒 | 2123 | 詔 | 1107 | 訊 | 1637 | 鼓 | 2016 |
| 急 | 0971 | 廉 | 2056 | 升 | 1051 | 昭 | 1109 | 加 | 1147 | 樹 | 2017 |
| 争 | 0972 | 鎌 | 2057 | 弁 | 1052 | 照 | 1110 | 賀 | 1172 | 膨 | 2018 |
| 浄 | 0979 | 嫌 | 2058 | 昇 | 1053 | 超 | 1111 | 架 | 1173 | 善 | 1213 |
| 算 | 0980 | 謙 | 2059 | 充 | 1056 | 招 | 1104 | 収 | 1155 | 繕 | 1214 |
| 鼻 | 1558 | 眠 | 1009 | 銃 | 1057 | 拐 | 1784 | 叫 | 1769 | 膳 | 1215 |

| | | | | | | | | | | |
|---|---|---|---|---|---|---|---|---|---|---|
| 曽 | 1222 | 勉 | 1274 | 栽 | 1319 | 峰 | 1378 | 郭 | 1422 | 幸 | 1470 |
| 増 | 1223 | 晩 | 1275 | 戴 | 1914 | 逢 | 1379 | 熟 | 1436 | 幸 | 1470 |
| 層 | 1224 | 許 | 1276 | 繊 | 2008 | 縫 | 1380 | 塾 | 1437 | 服 | 1471 |
| 憎 | 1225 | 詐 | 1794 | 騎 | 1331 | 蜂 | 1381 | 亭 | 1423 | 報 | 1472 |
| 僧 | 1226 | 象 | 1277 | 駒 | 2276 | 蜜 | 1382 | 停 | 1424 | 執 | 1473 |
| 贈 | 1227 | 像 | 1278 | 模 | 1336 | 密 | 1383 | 昆 | 1425 | 摯 | 1474 |
| 賦 | 1230 | 景 | 1280 | 膜 | 1337 | 蜜 | 1382 | 混 | 1426 | 呉 | 1478 |
| 賊 | 1231 | 影 | 1281 | 漠 | 1338 | 蟹 | 2294 | 皆 | 1427 | 娯 | 1479 |
| 帯 | 1232 | 憬 | 2086 | 幕 | 1339 | 旦 | 1392 | 楷 | 1428 | 誤 | 1480 |
| 滞 | 1233 | 就 | 1283 | 墓 | 1340 | 但 | 1393 | 諧 | 1429 | 虞 | 2001 |
| 帝 | 1418 | 蹴 | 1324 | 募 | 1341 | 担 | 1394 | 階 | 1430 | 富 | 1481 |
| 為 | 1236 | 驚 | 2287 | 暮 | 1342 | 壇 | 1958 | 陛 | 1431 | 副 | 1482 |
| 偽 | 1237 | 隔 | 1286 | 慕 | 1343 | 胆 | 1982 | 陸 | 1432 | 幅 | 1483 |
| 参 | 1238 | 融 | 1287 | 添 | 1344 | 亘 | 1395 | 睦 | 1433 | 福 | 1484 |
| 惨 | 1239 | 肖 | 1288 | 恭 | 1345 | 恒 | 1396 | 勢 | 1434 | 双 | 1498 |
| 呂 | 1240 | 消 | 1289 | 暴 | 1346 | 垣 | 1397 | 熱 | 1435 | 綴 | 2290 |
| 侶 | 1241 | 硝 | 1290 | 爆 | 1347 | 宣 | 1398 | 熟 | 1436 | 桑 | 2291 |
| 宮 | 1242 | 梢 | 1291 | 漠 | 1338 | 喧 | 1399 | 塾 | 1437 | 江 | 1499 |
| 桜 | 1249 | 削 | 1292 | 漢 | 1730 | 宜 | 1519 | 陵 | 1438 | 湾 | 1500 |
| 妥 | 1250 | 宵 | 1293 | 礎 | 1349 | 曄 | 1400 | 菱 | 1439 | 港 | 1501 |
| 咲 | 1251 | 屑 | 1891 | 疑 | 1350 | 唾 | 1401 | 翁 | 1451 | 乙 | 1522 |
| 朕 | 1252 | 郷 | 1295 | 凝 | 1351 | 坪 | 1403 | 婆 | 1452 | 乞 | 1805 |
| 茎 | 1253 | 饗 | 1296 | 擬 | 1352 | 畔 | 1404 | 姿 | 1453 | 迄 | 1806 |
| 径 | 1254 | 響 | 1297 | 俺 | 1356 | 伊 | 1406 | 恣 | 1454 | 乾 | 1807 |
| 怪 | 1255 | 塩 | 1306 | 庵 | 1357 | 君 | 1407 | 妻 | 1457 | 押 | 1525 |
| 軽 | 1256 | 傷 | 1307 | 僕 | 1358 | 群 | 1408 | 凄 | 1458 | 抽 | 1526 |
| 経 | 1257 | 揚 | 1308 | 撲 | 1359 | 郡 | 1409 | 章 | 1459 | 捜 | 1527 |
| 斉 | 1258 | 掲 | 2272 | 脈 | 1366 | 那 | 1410 | 彰 | 1460 | 捜 | 1527 |
| 斎 | 1259 | 陽 | 1310 | 派 | 1367 | 邦 | 1411 | 障 | 1461 | 挿 | 1597 |
| 済 | 1260 | 陰 | 1311 | 缶 | 1368 | 釜 | 1898 | 辛 | 1462 | 裾 | 1534 |
| 剤 | 1261 | 隠 | 1312 | 揺 | 1369 | 爺 | 1899 | 宰 | 1463 | 据 | 1535 |
| 剖 | 1262 | 穏 | 1313 | 謡 | 1370 | 絞 | 1414 | 辣 | 1464 | 握 | 1536 |
| 衡 | 1268 | 穂 | 1314 | 遥 | 1371 | 紋 | 1416 | 辞 | 1465 | 託 | 1539 |
| 衝 | 1567 | 稲 | 1315 | 陶 | 1372 | 蚊 | 2295 | 壁 | 1466 | 宅 | 1540 |
| 換 | 1269 | 愁 | 1316 | 陳 | 1373 | 帝 | 1418 | 璧 | 1467 | 詫 | 1541 |
| 喚 | 1270 | 悠 | 1677 | 陣 | 1374 | 締 | 1419 | 癖 | 1468 | 宇 | 1542 |
| 免 | 1272 | 裁 | 1317 | 隆 | 1376 | 諦 | 1420 | 避 | 1469 | 芋 | 1543 |
| 逸 | 1273 | 載 | 1318 | 降 | 1377 | 享 | 1421 | 辛 | 1462 | 寿 | 1544 |

| | | | | | | | | | | | |
|---|---|---|---|---|---|---|---|---|---|---|---|
| 鑄 | 1545 | 挿 | 1597 | 岸 | 1648 | 帽 | 1687 | 吸 | 1763 | 概 | 1821 |
| 錢 | 1585 | 補 | 1598 | 岩 | 1649 | 昌 | 1684 | 吹 | 1764 | 慨 | 1822 |
| 鏡 | 1547 | 浦 | 1599 | 嵐 | 1651 | 唱 | 1685 | 吐 | 1766 | 苗 | 1823 |
| 境 | 1548 | 哺 | 1600 | 崖 | 1652 | 晶 | 1686 | 叶 | 1767 | 描 | 1824 |
| 環 | 1549 | 舖 | 1601 | 催 | 1653 | 永 | 1691 | 吟 | 1770 | 猫 | 1825 |
| 還 | 1550 | 筆 | 1605 | 崩 | 1650 | 泳 | 1692 | 含 | 1771 | 兆 | 1827 |
| 盾 | 1551 | 津 | 1606 | 朋 | 2226 | 詠 | 1693 | 迷 | 1773 | 眺 | 1828 |
| 循 | 1552 | 律 | 1607 | 棚 | 2227 | 折 | 1698 | 謎 | 1774 | 逃 | 1829 |
| 息 | 1556 | 逮 | 1608 | 柵 | 2228 | 誓 | 1701 | 逆 | 1775 | 桃 | 1830 |
| 憩 | 1557 | 康 | 1611 | 崖 | 1652 | 逝 | 1702 | 遡 | 1776 | 跳 | 1831 |
| 鼻 | 1558 | 庸 | 1612 | 窪 | 1900 | 哲 | 1703 | 塑 | 1777 | 挑 | 1832 |
| 臭 | 1560 | 廉 | 2056 | 佳 | 1901 | 斬 | 1704 | 勳 | 1778 | 拙 | 1833 |
| 嗅 | 1561 | 建 | 1609 | 涯 | 1902 | 漸 | 1705 | 薰 | 1779 | 屈 | 1834 |
| 奧 | 1562 | 健 | 1610 | 焦 | 1654 | 暫 | 1706 | 香 | 1781 | 掘 | 1835 |
| 尖 | 1563 | 鍵 | 2077 | 礁 | 1655 | 斥 | 1707 | 秀 | 1782 | 堀 | 1836 |
| 突 | 1564 | 肅 | 1613 | 奮 | 1656 | 訴 | 1708 | 誘 | 1783 | 窟 | 1843 |
| 窒 | 1565 | 繡 | 1614 | 奪 | 1657 | 探 | 1714 | 透 | 1785 | 塀 | 2171 |
| 窈 | 1566 | 唐 | 1615 | 隻 | 1658 | 深 | 1715 | 携 | 1786 | 筒 | 1838 |
| 究 | 1710 | 糖 | 1616 | 獲 | 1659 | 懼 | 1717 | 擁 | 2182 | 管 | 1839 |
| 契 | 1568 | 粧 | 1617 | 穫 | 1660 | 慎 | 1718 | 雄 | 1787 | 窟 | 1843 |
| 喫 | 1569 | 粉 | 1619 | 護 | 1661 | 鎮 | 1719 | 雌 | 1788 | 窪 | 1900 |
| 潔 | 1570 | 紛 | 1620 | 讓 | 1662 | 塡 | 1720 | 些 | 1789 | 淫 | 1844 |
| 繁 | 1575 | 糾 | 1621 | 釀 | 1663 | 囚 | 1722 | 柴 | 1790 | 溪 | 2285 |
| 繫 | 1576 | 凡 | 1629 | 壤 | 1664 | 困 | 1723 | 紫 | 1791 | 妊 | 1845 |
| 緊 | 2035 | 凩 | 1630 | 壞 | 1665 | 梱 | 1724 | 髮 | 1792 | 妖 | 2176 |
| 茂 | 1577 | 帆 | 1631 | 懷 | 1666 | 因 | 1725 | 髭 | 1793 | 班 | 1853 |
| 蔑 | 2279 | 汎 | 1632 | 德 | 1667 | 姻 | 1726 | 甚 | 1798 | 斑 | 1854 |
| 橋 | 1578 | 恐 | 1633 | 聽 | 1668 | 咽 | 1727 | 勘 | 1799 | 哀 | 1860 |
| 矯 | 1579 | 築 | 1635 | 侯 | 1669 | 恩 | 1728 | 堪 | 1800 | 衰 | 1861 |
| 箋 | 1582 | 尋 | 1636 | 喉 | 1673 | 索 | 1735 | 操 | 1809 | 衷 | 1862 |
| 殘 | 1583 | 抗 | 1639 | 候 | 1674 | 牽 | 1736 | 燥 | 1810 | 喪 | 1863 |
| 棧 | 1584 | 航 | 1640 | 是 | 1675 | 牢 | 1737 | 繰 | 1811 | 卓 | 1865 |
| 錢 | 1585 | 坑 | 1641 | 提 | 1678 | 之 | 1755 | 藻 | 1812 | 悼 | 1866 |
| 踐 | 1586 | 耕 | 1643 | 堤 | 1679 | 乏 | 1758 | 牙 | 1816 | 貞 | 1867 |
| 淺 | 1587 | 耗 | 1644 | 題 | 1680 | 芝 | 1759 | 芽 | 1817 | 偵 | 1868 |
| 洩 | 1588 | 籍 | 1910 | 匙 | 1681 | 及 | 1760 | 雅 | 1818 | 屬 | 1872 |
| 湧 | 2006 | 灰 | 1646 | 冒 | 1683 | 扱 | 1761 | 邪 | 1819 | 囑 | 1873 |
| 捕 | 1596 | 炭 | 1647 | | | 級 | 1762 | 既 | 1820 | 偶 | 1874 |

| | | | | | | | | | | | |
|---|---|---|---|---|---|---|---|---|---|---|---|
| 隅 | 1875 | 肌 | 1997 | 怒 | 2049 | 端 | 2114 | 維 | 2149 | 随 | 2213 |
| 遇 | 1877 | 胸 | 1971 | 隷 | 2050 | 尼 | 2116 | 推 | 2150 | 髄 | 2215 |
| 愚 | 1878 | 悩 | 1972 | 款 | 2051 | 泥 | 2117 | 堆 | 2151 | 惰 | 2217 |
| 雇 | 1889 | 脳 | 1973 | 殻 | 2052 | 漏 | 2118 | 椎 | 2152 | 弄 | 2220 |
| 顧 | 1890 | 炎 | 1976 | 穀 | 2053 | 尉 | 2124 | 雛 | 2154 | 奔 | 2222 |
| 暇 | 1903 | 談 | 1977 | 鋼 | 2069 | 慰 | 2125 | 誰 | 2155 | 弊 | 2223 |
| 霞 | 1904 | 淡 | 1978 | 剛 | 2070 | 畜 | 2133 | 唯 | 2156 | 幣 | 2224 |
| 霜 | 1908 | 災 | 1979 | 綱 | 2071 | 蓄 | 2134 | 鳴 | 2157 | 蔽 | 2225 |
| 箱 | 1909 | 股 | 1990 | 網 | 2072 | 玄 | 2135 | 併 | 2168 | 鹿 | 2255 |
| 籍 | 1910 | 肢 | 1991 | 卑 | 2087 | 眩 | 2136 | 瓶 | 2169 | 塵 | 2256 |
| 順 | 1925 | 膚 | 1998 | 碑 | 2088 | 呟 | 2137 | 屏 | 2170 | 麓 | 2257 |
| 馴 | 1926 | 慮 | 1999 | 痺 | 2089 | 弦 | 2142 | 塀 | 2171 | 麗 | 2258 |
| 訓 | 1927 | 虞 | 2001 | 鬼 | 2090 | 舷 | 2143 | 餅 | 2172 | 薦 | 2259 |
| 頼 | 1930 | 劇 | 2002 | 塊 | 2091 | 玄 | 2135 | 沃 | 2175 | 慶 | 2260 |
| 瀬 | 1931 | 虜 | 2004 | 醜 | 2092 | 亥 | 2158 | 妖 | 2176 | 瀉 | 2265 |
| 峡 | 1932 | 虚 | 2003 | 魂 | 2093 | 刻 | 2159 | 慈 | 2179 | 濁 | 2266 |
| 狭 | 1933 | 戯 | 2007 | 魅 | 2094 | 劾 | 2160 | 滋 | 2180 | 渇 | 2267 |
| 挟 | 1934 | 繊 | 2008 | 魔 | 2095 | 核 | 2161 | 磁 | 2181 | 褐 | 2268 |
| 頬 | 1935 | 緻 | 2009 | 畏 | 2096 | 骸 | 2162 | 后 | 2193 | 葛 | 2269 |
| 煩 | 1937 | 嘘 | 2010 | 奉 | 2103 | 咳 | 2163 | 垢 | 2194 | 喝 | 2270 |
| 串 | 1938 | 励 | 2037 | 奏 | 2104 | 該 | 2164 | 如 | 2197 | 謁 | 2271 |
| 患 | 1939 | 栃 | 2038 | 泰 | 2105 | 診 | 2165 | 茹 | 2198 | 掲 | 2272 |
| 扶 | 1953 | 歳 | 2041 | 俸 | 2106 | 舷 | 2143 | 豪 | 2204 | 篤 | 2277 |
| 抹 | 1954 | 戚 | 2042 | 棒 | 2107 | 舵 | 2144 | 蒙 | 2205 | 罵 | 2278 |
| 塔 | 1959 | 叔 | 2043 | 捧 | 2108 | 蛇 | 2297 | 墾 | 2206 | 蔑 | 2279 |
| 搭 | 1960 | 淑 | 2044 | 耐 | 2109 | 幻 | 2145 | 懇 | 2207 | 罠 | 2280 |
| 飢 | 1966 | 寂 | 2045 | 霊 | 2110 | 幽 | 2146 | 逐 | 2209 | 鶏 | 2284 |
| 机 | 1967 | 督 | 2046 | 需 | 2111 | 幼 | 2147 | 遂 | 2210 | 渓 | 2285 |
| 冗 | 1968 | 奴 | 2047 | 濡 | 2112 | 劾 | 2160 | 墜 | 2211 | 蚕 | 2292 |
| 冠 | 1969 | 努 | 2048 | 儒 | 2113 | 稚 | 2148 | 堕 | 2212 | 蛋 | 2293 |

# TABLE OF NONSTANDARD FORMS

The table that begins on the facing page lists nonstandard forms of kanji introduced in this text. Most are traditional forms, which you will encounter in proper nouns, in texts written prior to 1946, and in words containing kanji belatedly added to the Joyo Kanji List. Familiarity with them will also help you read many non-Joyo kanji, which often appear in their traditional form.

At an intermediate stage of study, use this table to get a general idea of the relationship between the standard and nonstandard forms. At an advanced stage of study, use it to test your ability to identify the meanings and readings of the nonstandard forms. When practicing writing, however, always use *standard* forms.

## Arrangement and Format

Characters are grouped by the stroke count of their nonstandard forms. Within a stroke count section, they are arranged by the stroke count of their radical (as it appears in the nonstandard form), then by the entry number of the corresponding standard form.

Nonstandard forms appear to the left of the arrows, standard forms (with their entry numbers) to the right.

## Traditional Forms That Have Not Been "Standardized"

By contrast with the kanji listed on the following pages, those listed below appear in the main entries section in their *traditional* forms, which have not officially been replaced. Most are kanji that were added to the Joyo Kanji List in 2010 (unofficial standardized forms in parentheses):

籠 (篭), 剝 (剥), 箸 (箸), 賭 (賭), 嗅 (嗅), 箋 (箋), 惧 (惧), 塡 (填),
僅 (僅), 煎 (煎), 謎 (謎), 遡 (遡), 淫 (淫), 捗 (捗), 頰 (頬), 遜 (遜),
喩 (喩), 餅 (餅), 餌 (餌), 嘲 (嘲), 蔽 (蔽), 詮 (詮), 溺 (溺), 葛 (葛).

The rest are Jinmeiyo or unlisted kanji:

溢 (溢), 鞄 (鞄), 篇 (篇), 辻 (辻), 饗 (饗), 逢 (逢), 儲 (儲), 揃 (揃),
這 (這), 迄 (迄), 屑 (屑), 噂 (噂), 樽 (樽), 睨 (睨).

When writing any of the previous two sets of kanji, it is both common and accepted to use the standardized forms, even if they have not officially replaced the traditional forms.

## 3 STROKES

个 → 箇 0261
个 → 個 0262
巛 → 川 0022
互 → 工 0108
门 → 門 0447

## 4 STROKES

及 → 及 1760
仂 → 働 0541
内 → 内 0215
丹 → 丹 0667
卆 → 卒 0751
戶 → 戸 0248
主 → 主 0365

## 5 STROKES

丗 → 世 0604
册 → 冊 0824
仝 → 同 0182
包 → 包 0457
夘 → 卯 1136
囘 → 回 0050
宂 → 冗 1968
本 → 本 0031
平 → 平 0334

## 6 STROKES

㐂 → 喜 1212
亙 → 亘 1395
全 → 全 0078
住 → 住 0366
決 → 決 0330
冲 → 沖 0645
冰 → 氷 1690
込 → 込 0192
向 → 問 0452
夛 → 多 0267
収 → 収 1155
羽 → 羽 0418

## 7 STROKES

事 → 事 0080
虍 → 虎 0912
佛 → 仏 0811
免 → 免 1272
苅 → 刈 0524
注 → 注 0368
品 → 品 0301
叫 → 叫 1769
帋 → 紙 0478
赱 → 走 0140
壮 → 壮 1589
弃 → 棄 0606
邨 → 村 0651
歩 → 歩 0679
每 → 毎 0105
甼 → 町 0439
皃 → 貌 2208
糺 → 糾 1621

## 8 STROKES

兩 → 両 0177
邱 → 丘 0906
亞 → 亜 0545
舎 → 舎 0910
兒 → 児 0772
具 → 具 0837
劵 → 券 0456
卷 → 巻 0458
卑 → 卑 2087
泪 → 涙 1020
拂 → 払 0812
拐 → 拐 1784
拔 → 抜 1951
芽 → 芽 1817
咏 → 詠 1693
咒 → 呪 2177
届 → 届 1528
㫗 → 低 0479
徃 → 往 0866

## 9 STROKES

京 → 京 0245
侮 → 侮 1571
凾 → 函 1713
勉 → 勉 1274
卽 → 即 0390
卻 → 却 0733
挘 → 拍 1185
恠 → 怪 1255
恆 → 恒 1396
姙 → 妊 1845
栅 → 柵 2228
拜 → 拝 1642
迯 → 逃 1829
珎 → 珍 2166
者 → 者 0107
脉 → 脈 1366
祈 → 祈 0640
祉 → 祉 1485
竒 → 奇 1329
盃 → 杯 1696
毒 → 毒 0133
畍 → 界 0612
畊 → 耕 1643
畞 → 畝 2243
突 → 突 1564

## 10 STROKES

乘 → 乗 1005
倂 → 併 2168
凉 → 涼 1284
海 → 海 0106
涉 → 渉 0680
涌 → 湧 2006
挾 → 挟 1934
莖 → 茎 1253
莊 → 荘 1590
郞 → 郎 0286
悅 → 悦 1202
悔 → 悔 1573
狹 → 狭 1933
峯 → 峰 1378
峽 → 峡 1932
弱 → 弱 0424
徑 → 径 1254
晄 → 晃 2240
效 → 効 1413
氣 → 気 0126
烟 → 煙 0768
益 → 益 0414
眞 → 真 0838
神 → 神 0316
祖 → 祖 0641
祝 → 祝 1200
祕 → 秘 1384
竝 → 並 0333
級 → 級 1762
耻 → 恥 1670
臭 → 臭 1560
缺 → 欠 0277
舩 → 船 0669
釡 → 釜 1898

## 11 STROKES

條 → 条 0119
假 → 仮 0921
冨 → 富 1481
區 → 区 0297

參 → 参 1238
淨 → 浄 0979
凄 → 凄 1458
渕 → 淵 1492
淺 → 浅 1587
萠 → 萌 1826
陷 → 陥 1375
埜 → 野 0534
國 → 国 0075
圈 → 圏 0459
專 → 専 0580
將 → 将 0614
巢 → 巣 0601
屛 → 屏 2170
崕 → 崖 1652
帶 → 帯 1232
從 → 従 0869
敎 → 教 0632
敕 → 勅 1108
敏 → 敏 1574
晝 → 昼 0466
晚 → 晩 1275
脫 → 脱 1198
朗 → 朗 1476
脣 → 唇 1847
敍 → 叙 0998
殺 → 殺 0522
產 → 産 0181
祥 → 祥 0496
畧 → 略 0791
研 → 研 0724
翌 → 翌 0419
習 → 習 0420
處 → 処 0553
虛 → 虚 2003
賈 → 質 0318
賎 → 財 0653
閇 → 閉 0449
髙 → 高 0185
麥 → 麦 0131
麪 → 麺 2238

| | | | | |
|---|---|---|---|---|
| 獨→独 0346 | 薰→薫 1779 | 疊→塁 0885 | 類→類 0310 | 疊→畳 1520 |
| 器→器 0295 | 隱→隠 1312 | 斷→断 0849 | | 竊→窃 1566 |
| 蘭→園 0856 | 壓→圧 0186 | 曙→曙 1446 | **20 STROKES** | 聽→聴 1669 |
| 學→学 0099 | 嶽→岳 0908 | 櫪→枥 2038 | 蘭→蘭 1489 | 覽→覧 2026 |
| 憲→憲 0417 | 彌→弥 0685 | 歸→帰 1018 | 壞→壌 1665 | 讀→読 0355 |
| 戰→戦 0461 | 應→応 0850 | 禮→礼 0313 | 孃→嬢 1663 | 鑄→鋳 1545 |
| 曉→暁 0770 | 戲→戯 2007 | 蟲→虫 0343 | 寶→宝 0074 | 響→響 1297 |
| 曆→暦 0854 | 擊→撃 1026 | 謹→謹 1733 | 嚴→厳 0810 | 鶴→鶴 1132 |
| 橫→横 0916 | 舉→挙 1247 | 豐→豊 0513 | 爐→炉 1896 | |
| 概→概 1821 | 膽→胆 1982 | 轉→転 0224 | 犧→犠 0929 | **23 STROKES** |
| 遲→遅 1144 | 檢→検 1029 | 醫→医 0561 | 獻→献 1157 | 變→変 0775 |
| 歷→歴 0853 | 營→営 1243 | 醬→醤 2128 | 繼→継 0848 | 戀→恋 0777 |
| 燈→灯 0440 | 禪→禅 1076 | 鎭→鎮 1719 | 譱→善 1213 | 纖→繊 2008 |
| 燒→焼 0769 | 穗→穂 1314 | 雜→雑 0379 | 覺→覚 0325 | 罐→缶 1368 |
| 穐→秋 0364 | 穉→稚 2148 | 顏→顔 0180 | 觸→触 0344 | 鑛→鉱 2065 |
| 稽→稽 1494 | 黏→粘 1267 | 龜→亀 2061 | 譽→誉 1246 | 顯→顕 1921 |
| 縣→県 0844 | 總→総 0557 | | 譯→訳 1505 | 驛→駅 0339 |
| 螢→蛍 1244 | 縱→縦 0871 | **19 STROKES** | 釋→釈 1506 | 驗→験 1030 |
| 衞→衛 0661 | 繁→繁 1575 | 勸→勧 1129 | 鬪→闘 1363 | 體→体 0062 |
| 諭→諭 0946 | 褻→褻 0703 | 瀧→滝 0508 | 騷→騒 1390 | 髓→髄 2215 |
| 誼→喧 1399 | 聲→声 0529 | 瀨→瀬 1931 | 黨→党 0319 | |
| 諸→諸 1448 | 舊→旧 0771 | 蕷→蘇 0494 | 齡→齢 0676 | **24 STROKES** |
| 踴→踊 1325 | 謌→歌 0827 | 懷→懐 1667 | | 囑→嘱 1873 |
| 輶→輸 0945 | 謠→謡 1370 | 壞→壊 1666 | **21 STROKES** | 艷→艶 2178 |
| 豫→予 0163 | 譁→嘩 1400 | 懲→懲 2191 | 攝→摂 1235 | 觀→観 1128 |
| 豬→猪 0217 | 謁→謁 2271 | 獸→獣 0763 | 攜→携 1786 | 讓→譲 1662 |
| 錄→録 0608 | 蹈→踏 1326 | 邊→辺 0195 | 屬→属 1872 | 釀→醸 1664 |
| 錢→銭 1585 | 鍊→錬 2063 | 癡→痴 1941 | 權→権 1130 | 靈→霊 2110 |
| 靜→静 0978 | 隷→隷 2050 | 穩→穏 1313 | 櫻→桜 1249 | |
| 餘→余 0995 | 點→点 0349 | 繪→絵 0525 | 欄→欄 1490 | **25 STROKES** |
| 餝→飾 1963 | 齋→斎 1259 | 繫→繋 1576 | 歡→歓 1131 | 灣→湾 1500 |
| 頻→頻 1923 | | 繡→繍 1614 | 續→続 0354 | 廳→庁 0441 |
| 默→黙 0762 | **18 STROKES** | 繩→縄 2073 | 辯→弁 1052 | 鹽→塩 1306 |
| 龍→竜 0507 | 雙→双 1498 | 蠏→蟹 2294 | 鐵→鉄 0564 | 蠻→蛮 0776 |
| | 擴→拡 0813 | 證→証 0550 | 驅→駆 1388 | |
| **17 STROKES** | 藝→芸 0225 | 贊→賛 1166 | 飜→翻 1512 | **26 STROKES** |
| 濕→湿 0200 | 藥→薬 0303 | 贈→贈 1227 | 鷄→鶏 2284 | 欝→鬱 2141 |
| 濱→浜 0909 | 藏→蔵 0695 | 辭→辞 1465 | | 蠶→蚕 2292 |
| 潛→潜 1168 | 獵→猟 0764 | 關→関 0451 | **22 STROKES** | |
| 濟→済 1260 | 嚙→噛 1852 | 難→難 0712 | 臟→臓 1974 | |

## APPENDIX 9

# SUMMARY OF CHANGES TO THE JOYO KANJI LIST (2010)

In June 2010 the National Diet of Japan approved changes to the official Joyo (regular-use) Kanji List (常用漢字表). One hundred ninety-six kanji were added to the list, an act that recognized not only the usefulness of these kanji, but also the growing convenience of using kanji since the advent of keyboard input. The criteria used for deciding whether to add a kanji to the list included (a) its frequency of use, (b) its overall functionality, especially its capacity for generating compounds, (c) its importance to culture or daily life, (d) whether it is used in compounds that are ambiguous if written in mixed kanji-kana form, (e) whether it has an *on* reading, and (f) its importance as a component part inside other kanji. Kanji used only in proper nouns were excluded, but an exception was made for kanji used in the names of Japanese prefectures (e.g., 阪 and 岡) or in other geographic terms of similar importance to the Japanese language (e.g., 韓 and 畿).

The 196 newly listed kanji, with the numbers of their entries in this book, appear below.

挨 2247　曖 2249　宛 0730　嵐 1651　畏 2096　萎 1456　椅 1332　彙 2120　茨 2039　咽 1727　淫 1844　唄 0828　鬱 2141　怨 0728

媛 1125　艶 2178　旺 1301　岡 0178　臆 0621　俺 1356　苛 0816　牙 1816　瓦 2167　楷 1428　潰 1178　諧 1429　崖 1652　蓋 1303

骸 2162　柿 2234　顎 1936　葛 2269　釜 1898　鎌 2057　韓 0662　玩 2219　伎 0967　亀 2061　毀 2055　畿 0471　臼 2054　嗅 1561

巾 0203　僅 1734　錦 0213　惧 1717　串 1938　窟 1843　詣 0894　憬 1995　稽 2086　隙 1494　桁 1876　拳 1248　鍵 2077

舷 2143　股 1990　虎 0912　錮 2079　勾 2246　梗 2233　喉 1674　乞 1805　傲 1508　駒 2276　頃 1916　痕 1323　沙 1747　挫 1699

采 0987　塞 2232　埼 1334　柵 2228　刹 0523　拶 2248　斬 1704　恣 1454　摯 1474　餌 2173　鹿 2255　叱 1768　嫉 2253　腫 2022

呪 2177　袖 1531　羞 1671　蹴 1324　憧 2085　拭 1027　尻 1895　芯 2184　腎 2033　須 1928　裾 1534　凄 1458　醒 1626　脊 2153

戚 2042　煎 1749　羨 2040　腺 1983　詮 2231　箋 1582　膳 1215　狙 1518　遡 1776　曽 1222　爽 2289　瘦 1947　踪 1322　捉 1603

遜 2060　汰 1748　唾 1401　堆 2151　戴 1914　誰 2155　旦 1392　綻 2081　緻 2009　酎 2130　貼 1266　嘲 2221　捗 1924　椎 2152

爪 0201　鶴 1132　諦 1420　溺 2264　填 1720　妬 2254　賭 1447　藤 2235　瞳 2084　栃 2038　頓 1920　貪 1159　丼 0436　那 1410

奈 0635　梨 1175　謎 1774　鍋 1488　匂 2245　虹 2300　捻 1700　罵 2278　剝 0609　箸 1443　氾 2119　汎 1632　阪 0376　斑 1854

眉 0530　膝 1989　肘 1988　訃 1115　阜 0970　蔽 2225　餅 2172　蔑 1467　哺 2279　蜂 1600　貌 1381　頰 2208　睦 1935　睦 1433

勃 2036　昧 2249　枕 0656　蜜 1382　冥 1592　麺 2238　冶 0951　弥 0685　闇 1364　喩 2140　湧 2006　妖 2176　瘍 1945　沃 2175

拉 2239　辣 1464　藍 2031　璃 2252　慄 1716　侶 1241　瞭 0954　瑠 2251　呂 1240　賂 1229　弄 2220　籠 0509　麓 2257　脇 1993

The following five kanji were removed from the Joyo Kanji List (entry numbers in parentheses): 勺 (0168), 錘 (1011), 銑 (2068), 脹 (2019), 匁 (2244).

The new Joyo Kanji List also recognizes 28 new readings (entry numbers in parentheses):

1. 委 (0396)　ゆだ(ねる)／委ねる
2. 育 (0489)　はぐく(む)／育む
3. 応 (0850)　こた(える)／応える
4. 滑 (1493)　コツ
　　　　　　　(e.g., 滑稽な／こっけいな)
5. 関 (0451)　かか(わる)／関わる
6. 館 (0291)　やかた　館
7. 鑑 (2028)　かんが(みる)　鑑みる
8. 混 (1426)　こ(む)／混む
9. 私 (0237)　わたし／私
10. 臭 (1560)　にお(う)／臭う
11. 旬 (0167)　シュン (e.g., 旬の魚／しゅん
　　　　　　　のさかな)
12. 伸 (0873)　の(べる)／述べる
13. 振 (0903)　ふ(れる)／振れる
14. 粋 (1622)　いき／粋

15. 逝 (1702)　い(く)／逝く
16. 拙 (1833)　つたな(い)／拙い
17. 全 (0078)　すべ(て)／全て
18. 創 (0697)　つく(る)／創る
19. 速 (1143)　はや(まる)／速まる
20. 描 (1824)　か(く)／描く
21. 他 (0189)　ほか／他
22. 中 (0035)　ジュウ (e.g., 一日中／いちに
　　　　　　　ちじゅう)
23. 放 (0574)　ほう(る)／放る
24. 務 (0687)　つと(まる)／務まる
25. 癒 (0948)　い(える)／癒える
　　　　　　　いや(す)／癒す
26. 要 (0547)　かなめ／要
27. 絡 (0790)　から(める)／絡める
28. 類 (0310)　たぐ(い)／類い

The new list has also eliminated three readings:
1. 畝 (2243)　せ　　2. 疲 (1948)　つか(らす)／疲らす　　3. 浦 (1599)　ホ

and changed one reading:
1. 側 (0626)　かわ → がわ


# Nonstandardized Characters

Among the 196 characters added to the revised Joyo Kanji List, several were simplified or "standardized," if you will, to match kanji already on the list (for example, 曾 was listed as 曽, so as to match 層 and 増). A couple of dozen other newly listed kanji were not standardized in this way (for example, 剥 was not standardized to match 緑 and 録). The policy was not to impose these non-standardized forms on the public as the only acceptable forms for these kanji, but merely to list these kanji in the forms in which they are used most often (you should thus feel at liberty to use standardized forms for these kanji in your own writing). While the inclusion of these non-standardized forms creates an additional challenge for the learner, it also serves to highlight the importance of learning to recognize kanji variants. These will continue to exist for as long as people use kanji.

The following are newly listed characters that were *not* officially simplified/standardized (*unofficial* simplified/standardized forms in parentheses):
籠 (篭), 剥 (剝), 箸 (箸), 賭 (賭), 嗅 (嗅), 箋 (牋), 惧 (懼), 塡 (填), 僅 (僅), 煎 (煎), 謎 (謎), 遡 (遡), 淫 (婬), 捗 (捗), 頰 (頬), 遜 (遜), 喩 (喻), 餅 (餅), 餌 (餌), 嘲 (嘲), 蔽 (蔽), 詮 (詮), 溺 (溺), 葛 (葛).

The following are newly listed characters that *were* simplified/standardized (non-simplified/standardized forms in parentheses):
艶 (艷), 亀 (龜), 曽 (曾), 痩 (瘦), 麺 (麵), 弥 (彌).

# TABLE OF JINMEIYO KANJI

This table lists the Jinmeiyo (name-use) kanji arranged by stroke count (those introduced in this text appear with their entry numbers). I have excluded kanji recently added to the Joyo list, which, based on precedent, can be expected to disappear from the Jinmeiyo list. I have also excluded traditional forms of Joyo kanji, which are included in the Jinmeiyo list because of their use in names; these can be found in the Table of Nonstandard Forms.

The Jinmeiyo list recognizes standardized variants of some kanji within its own set, shown below in parentheses (those introduced in this text are shown with their entry numbers): 豬 (猪 0217); 曾 (曽 1222); 遙 (遥 1371); 亙 (亘 1395); 萠 (萌 1826); 晄 (晃 2240); 巖 (巌); 渚 (渚); 琢 (琢); 祐 (祐); 祿 (禄); 禎 (禎); 穣 (穣); 凛 (凜); 堯 (尭); 檜 (桧); 槇 (槙); 禰 (祢); 禱 (祷). In some cases, the Jinmeiyo list does not include a kanji's standardized variant. Of these, four appear in this text, classified as "off-list" kanji (繋 1576, 掴 1602, 繍 1614, and 醤 2128). When used in words (rather than names), such kanji are more likely to appear in standardized form.

**2 STROKES**

乃 1754
卜

**3 STROKES**

叉 1755
之 2296
巳
也
已

**4 STROKES**

允 0590
丑
云
壬
廿
巴 0527
勿 0171
尤 2274

**5 STROKES**

卯 1136
瓜 0202
禾
叶 1767
乎
弘
仔
凧 1630
只 1194
汀
疋
戊

**6 STROKES**

旭 1391
伊 1406
夷
亥
曳 2158
匡
圭
迂
此 1756
而
汐 0268
庄
丞
尖
托 1563
弛
辻
凪
汝 1145
亦
牟
肋 0773
亙 1395

**7 STROKES**

芦
杏
迁
牡
芥
汲
灸
亨
芹
玖
吾 0220
宏
劫
坐 0750
冴
孜
灼
杖 0658
宋
辰 0510
辿
佃
杜
酉
沌 0796
芭
庇
芙
吻
甫 1806
迄
佑
邑
李
伶
呑

**8 STROKES**

阿 0819
或 1152
奄
苑 0729
於 1885
茄
迦
茅
侃
杵
堯
欣
沓
祁
庚
昂
杭 1857
忽
昏 1789
些
肴
竺
昌 1684
其 1757
陀

梁淋凰峻彗徠晨梛毬眸笙絆羚脩菫萠逞菜　2076

**12 STROKES**

葵渥絢粟厥閏瑛堰甥凱萱粥雁稀卿喬欽喰　1068

---

惚砦笹皐雫悉偲淳渚捷菖埴逗萱雀舵琢猪紬梯萄寅惇捺這菱畢彪彬婉菩捧萌淀琉

1858　1291　1742　2144　0217　0913　1554　1439　2108　1826

---

隼挽桧豹圃哩祐凌狼倭晏晄晟栞莉赳俱

1891　0781　2240　1790

**11 STROKES**

逢梓庵惟桶晦笠梶椛兜掬釧裃訣倦牽絃袴梧

1379　1357　0754　2261　1736

---

峨浬莞桔砧桐矩屑栗桂倖晃浩紘朔晒柴紗峻恕哨晋秦訊栖穿閃啄耽悌挺釘砥套秤莫畠

0258　0846　0156　2192　1637　2078

**10 STROKES**

烏荻　2281

---

胡巷哉珊洲茸柘祢柏毘柊彦頁殆柾俣姪耶宥柚祐洛亮玲俐勁奎昴洸洵珈珀俠

---

苔坦帖兎宕杷函柷朋沫孟怜侑昊穹苺茉迪

1713　2226

**9 STROKES**

娃茜按郁胤姥珂俄臥廻恢恰柑竿祇笈衿

0411　1533

# 幡磐蕃樋廟撫蕪篇鋒劉諒遼魯蕨凜諄黎凜熙

1538
1084

## 16 STROKES

鮎謂窺叡燕樫鴨橘鋸諺醐錆縞錫輯鞘錐

1741
2282
1581

# 蓬鳳槙蔓箕漣漱綺綸颯槇遙摑蔣

0594
1900

## 15 STROKES

鞍噹蝦駕嬉毅誼蕎慧糊撒醇樟蕉諏撰噲蝶槻鄭撞播

2011
2015
2186
2299
1309
2290
0905

# 綾蔭榎嘉魁樺鞄窪膏閣瑳榊爾嘗裳榛翠頗摺碩槍漕綜聰豎歎暢槌蔦綴禎鳶賑箔肇緋碧輔

1926
2283
2241
1171
0585
1541
0731

# 牒椿禎鼎遁楢馴楠煤塙楓幌蓑稔蒙靖傭楊蓉溜稜煉蓮詫碗暉椰滉煌瑤祿稟詢頌

## 14 STROKES

幹

0415
1400
2185
1389

# 湊椋貫遙裡琳祿椀惺琥皓翔釉堯焰

1160
1371
1513

## 13 STROKES

葦溢碓嘩蒲禽跨瑚嵯裟獅蒐舜楯瑞嵩楚蒼楕馳

# 寓隈戟喧捲硯腔犀堺斯惹竣渚湘廚棲疏惣揣琢巽湛智筑註喋堵董敦琶萩筈斐琵葡茸淵焚

1399
1537
1093
2139
1442
1492
1752

黛醍欅蹄薙蕗　2012
憐橙澪燎蕾

**17 STROKES**

磯　0472
襖
霞
徽　1904
鞠

鍬檣鴻壕薩燦篠駿曙　1446
燭檀擢濡瓢　2112
瞥輿螺　0506
嶺

藻檜

**18 STROKES**

鵜鎧鯉穡雛　2154
蹟叢鞭麿儲櫂燿簞蟬　1449

醬

**19 STROKES**

蟹　2294
櫛
蘇　0494
鯛寵襦曝鵬蘭　1489
簾櫓麒禱繡繫

顥

**20 STROKES**

馨巖纂瀬耀

**21 STROKES**

鰯轟纏灘蠟

**22 STROKES**

饗　1296

讚穰驍鷗

**23 STROKES**

鱒鷲巖　2287

**24 STROKES**

鷺鷹鱗麟　2286

# TABLE OF *HYOGAI* KANJI

Kanji that do not belong to either the Joyo or Jinmeiyo lists are known as 表外 (ひょ うがい, off-list) kanji. This table lists all the *hyogai* kanji introduced in this text, arranged by stroke count and shown with their entry numbers.

Included in this classification are four kanji, marked with an asterisk, that are standardized versions of kanji included in the Jinmeiyo Kanji List (繋 1576, 捆 1602, 繡 1614, and 醤 2128). When used in words (as opposed to names), such kanji are more likely to appear in standardized form.

| 1 STROKE | | | | | | | |
|---|---|---|---|---|---|---|---|
| ○ | 0014 | | | | | | |

| 3 STROKES | |
|---|---|
| 勺 | 0168 |

| 4 STROKES | |
|---|---|
| 匁 | 2244 |

| 5 STROKES | |
|---|---|
| 叩 | 1360 |

| 6 STROKES | |
|---|---|
| 吊 | 0206 |
| 戌 | 2273 |

| 7 STROKES | |
|---|---|
| 呆 | 0647 |

| | |
|---|---|
| 牢 | 1737 |
| 吠 | 1851 |
| 呑 | 2174 |

| 8 STROKES | |
|---|---|
| 眩 | 2137 |

| 9 STROKES | |
|---|---|
| 歪 | 0551 |
| 洒 | 0798 |
| 剃 | 1192 |
| 洩 | 1588 |
| 咳 | 2163 |
| 屏 | 2170 |
| 垢 | 2194 |
| 茹 | 2198 |

| 10 STROKES | |
|---|---|
| 紐 | 0591 |
| 眩 | 2136 |
| 罠 | 2280 |

| 11 STROKES | |
|---|---|
| 壷 | 1402 |
| 捆* | 1602 |
| 匙 | 1682 |
| 梱 | 1724 |
| 蛋 | 2293 |

| 12 STROKES | |
|---|---|
| 覗 | 0826 |
| 脹 | 2019 |

| 13 STROKES | |
|---|---|
| 爺 | 1899 |

| | |
|---|---|
| 痺 | 2089 |
| 睨 | 2262 |
| 鼠 | 2263 |

| 14 STROKES | |
|---|---|
| 嘘 | 2010 |
| 銑 | 2068 |
| 塵 | 2256 |

| 15 STROKES | |
|---|---|
| 噛 | 1852 |

| 16 STROKES | |
|---|---|
| 錘 | 1011 |
| 髭 | 1793 |

| 17 STROKES | |
|---|---|
| 繋 * | 1576 |

| | |
|---|---|
| 繡 * | 1614 |
| 糞 | 1892 |
| 癌 | 1946 |
| 醤 * | 2128 |

| 18 STROKES | |
|---|---|
| 贅 | 1509 |

| 21 STROKES | |
|---|---|
| 囁 | 2138 |

# STROKE COUNT INDEX

This index lists each kanji by its total stroke count. Use this index if you don't know any of a kanji's readings and are not confident that you can quickly find it in the Radical Index.

## Format and Arrangement

Within each stroke count section, kanji are arranged first by their radicals (displayed along the left side of each column) and then by their entry numbers. Radicals appear in ascending order of their own stroke count. To make it easier to locate the radicals, radical variants that differ significantly in appearance from their parent forms are listed independently, according to their own stroke count. For example, 肘 is listed with the four-stroke radical 月, even though the parent form of its radical is six-stroke 肉. To determine a kanji's traditional radical, consult its main entry.

If you do not find a kanji listed here under its stroke count, you may be looking for the standardized version of a kanji that has not officially been standardized. Check for it under an alternative stroke count, or in the list of non-standardized forms appearing at the bottom of the Table of Nonstandard Forms.

## Counting Strokes

To make it easier to use this index, memorize the stroke counts of the following graphemes with easily mistaken stroke counts: 子 (3), 阝/阝 (3), 辶 (3), 廴 (3), 夂 (3), 夊 (4) and 臣 (7).

It is also useful to memorize the stroke counts of frequently encountered, high-stroke-count graphemes, such as ⺮ (6), 糸 (6), 車 (7), 貝 (7), 言 (7), 酉 (7), 金 (8), ⻗ (8), 頁 (9), and 馬 (10). For detailed information on how to count strokes, refer to the Appendix "How to Count Strokes" in the *Kodansha Kanji Learner's Dictionary*.

| **1 STROKE** | | | 乙 | 九 | 0011 | 又 | 又 | 0058 | 丶 | 丸 | 0012 | 十 | 千 | 0017 |
|---|---|---|---|---|---|---|---|---|---|---|---|---|---|---|
| 一 | 一 | 0002 | 亅 | 了 | 0958 | | | | | 之 | 1755 | 扌 | 才 | 0652 |
| 乙 | 乙 | 1522 | 二 | 二 | 0003 | **3 STROKES** | | | 丿 | 久 | 0904 | 口 | 口 | 0019 |
| ○ | ○ | 0014 | 人 | 人 | 0015 | 一 | 三 | 0004 | | 及 | 1760 | 土 | 土 | 0030 |
| | | | 入 | 入 | 0039 | | 万 | 0018 | 乙 | 乞 | 1805 | 士 | 士 | 0350 |
| **2 STROKES** | | | 八 | 八 | 0010 | | 下 | 0040 | 亠 | 亡 | 0233 | 夕 | 夕 | 0265 |
| 一 | 七 | 0009 | 刀 | 刀 | 0085 | | 上 | 0041 | 几 | 凡 | 1629 | 大 | 大 | 0033 |
| | 丁 | 0437 | 力 | 力 | 0084 | | 丈 | 0657 | 刀 | 刃 | 0087 | 女 | 女 | 0093 |
| 丿 | 乃 | 1754 | 十 | 十 | 0005 | | 与 | 0858 | 勹 | 勺 | 0168 | 子 | 子 | 0094 |

| | | |
|---|---|---|
| | 呟 | 2137 |
| | 呪 | 2177 |
| 口 | 国 | 0075 |
| | 固 | 0260 |
| 土 | 垂 | 1004 |
| | 坪 | 1403 |
| 夕 | 夜 | 0467 |
| 大 | 奈 | 0635 |
| | 奇 | 1329 |
| | 奉 | 2103 |
| | 奔 | 2222 |
| 女 | 委 | 0396 |
| | 姓 | 0431 |
| | 始 | 0956 |
| | 姉 | 1205 |
| | 妹 | 1206 |
| | 妻 | 1457 |
| | 妬 | 2254 |
| 子 | 学 | 0099 |
| | 季 | 0395 |
| 宀 | 定 | 0045 |
| | 宝 | 0074 |
| | 官 | 0290 |
| | 実 | 0499 |
| | 宗 | 0636 |
| | 宛 | 0730 |
| | 宜 | 1519 |
| | 宙 | 1529 |
| ⺌ | 尚 | 0184 |
| 尸 | 居 | 0255 |
| | 届 | 1528 |
| | 屈 | 1834 |
| 山 | 岡 | 0178 |
| | 岳 | 0908 |
| | 岬 | 1335 |
| | 岸 | 1648 |
| | 岩 | 1649 |
| 干 | 幸 | 1470 |
| 广 | 府 | 0247 |
| | 店 | 0347 |
| | 底 | 0482 |
| 廴 | 延 | 0872 |
| 弓 | 弥 | 0685 |
| | 弦 | 2142 |
| 彳 | 彼 | 0597 |
| | 往 | 0866 |
| | 征 | 0868 |
| | 径 | 1254 |
| 心 | 念 | 0230 |
| | 忠 | 0644 |
| | 忽 | 1857 |
| ネ | 祈 | 0640 |
| | 祉 | 1485 |
| 王 | 玩 | 2219 |
| 耂 | 者 | 0107 |
| 戈 | 或 | 1152 |
| 戸 | 所 | 0249 |
| | 房 | 1886 |
| 手 | 承 | 0959 |
| 攵 | 放 | 0574 |
| 方 | 於 | 1885 |
| 日 | 明 | 0024 |
| | 昔 | 0359 |
| | 易 | 0443 |
| | 昇 | 1053 |
| | 旺 | 1301 |
| | 昆 | 1425 |
| | 昌 | 1684 |
| 月 | 育 | 0489 |
| | 服 | 1471 |
| | 肩 | 1495 |
| | 肯 | 1497 |
| | 股 | 1990 |
| | 肢 | 1991 |
| | 肪 | 1996 |
| | 肥 | 2023 |
| | 朋 | 2226 |
| 木 | 東 | 0032 |
| | 林 | 0240 |
| | 松 | 0242 |
| | 果 | 0599 |
| | 枕 | 0656 |
| | 板 | 0924 |
| | 枝 | 0965 |
| | 采 | 0987 |
| | 枢 | 1386 |
| | 枠 | 1624 |
| | 枚 | 1695 |
| | 杯 | 1696 |
| | 析 | 1697 |
| 欠 | 欧 | 1385 |
| 止 | 武 | 0111 |
| | 歩 | 0679 |
| 殳 | 殴 | 1387 |
| 毋 | 毒 | 0133 |
| 火 | 炒 | 1750 |
| | 炊 | 1751 |
| | 炉 | 1896 |
| | 炎 | 1976 |
| 片 | 版 | 0923 |
| 牛 | 物 | 0172 |
| | 牧 | 0576 |
| 田 | 画 | 0176 |
| 白 | 的 | 0169 |
| 目 | 直 | 0839 |
| | 盲 | 1061 |
| 矢 | 知 | 0560 |
| 穴 | 空 | 0398 |
| | 突 | 1564 |
| 虍 | 虎 | 0912 |
| 衣 | 表 | 0705 |
| 金 | 金 | 0029 |
| 長 | 長 | 0091 |
| 門 | 門 | 0447 |
| 阜 | 阜 | 0970 |
| 雨 | 雨 | 0154 |
| 斉 | 斉 | 1258 |
| 青 | 青 | 0130 |
| 非 | 非 | 0738 |


## 9 STROKES


| | | |
|---|---|---|
| 一 | 歪 | 0551 |
| ノ | 乗 | 1005 |
| 亠 | 亭 | 1423 |
| 亻 | 信 | 0063 |
| | 保 | 0646 |
| | 便 | 0890 |
| | 侵 | 1013 |
| | 俗 | 1039 |
| | 係 | 1078 |
| | 侶 | 1241 |
| | 俊 | 1440 |
| | 促 | 1604 |
| | 侯 | 1673 |
| 冖 | 冠 | 1969 |
| 刂 | 前 | 0113 |
| | 則 | 0625 |
| | 剃 | 1192 |
| | 削 | 1292 |
| 力 | 勅 | 1108 |
| | 勇 | 2005 |
| | 勃 | 2036 |
| 十 | 南 | 0794 |
| | 卑 | 2087 |
| 卩 | 卸 | 0861 |
| 厂 | 厚 | 0631 |
| | 厘 | 2242 |
| 又 | 叙 | 0998 |
| 氵 | 活 | 0054 |
| | 海 | 0106 |
| | 洗 | 0135 |
| | 洪 | 0358 |
| | 洋 | 0491 |
| | 洒 | 0798 |
| | 洲 | 0846 |
| | 浄 | 0979 |
| | 派 | 1367 |
| | 浅 | 1587 |
| | 洩 | 1588 |
| | 津 | 1606 |
| | 洞 | 1842 |
| 扌 | 持 | 0384 |
| | 指 | 0932 |
| | 拭 | 1027 |
| | 括 | 1069 |
| | 拾 | 1071 |
| | 挑 | 1832 |
| | 挟 | 1934 |
| | 拷 | 1956 |
| | 拶 | 2248 |
| 艹 | 草 | 0144 |
| | 茶 | 0603 |
| | 荒 | 1064 |
| | 荘 | 1590 |
| | 茨 | 2039 |
| | 茹 | 2198 |
| 辶 | 送 | 0455 |
| | 退 | 1091 |
| | 追 | 1181 |
| | 迷 | 1773 |
| | 逆 | 1775 |
| | 逃 | 1829 |
| 阝 | 限 | 0282 |
| | 郎 | 0286 |
| | 郊 | 1412 |
| 忄 | 恨 | 1217 |
| | 恒 | 1396 |
| | 悔 | 1573 |
| 犭 | 独 | 0346 |
| | 狩 | 0766 |
| | 狭 | 1933 |
| 口 | 品 | 0301 |
| | 咲 | 1251 |
| | 咽 | 1727 |
| | 哀 | 1860 |

阝
院 0634
除 0996
陣 1374
陥 1375
降 1377
郡 1409
陛 1431

忄
悟 0326
悦 1202
悩 1972

口
員 0317
唄 0828
唆 1441
哺 1600
唐 1615
哲 1703
唇 1847

土
埋 0533

夂
夏 0363

女
娯 1479
娠 1846
姫 2196
娘 2200

子
孫 1079

宀
家 0219
害 0413
容 1037
宮 1242
宵 1293
宴 1294
宰 1463

寸
将 0614
射 1021

尸
展 0880
屑 1891

山
島 0341
峰 1378
差 0937

工
巾
席 0279

---

師 0748
帯 1232
庫 0694

广
座 0749
庭 0878

弓
弱 0424

彳
従 0869
徒 0870
徐 0997

心
恵 0581
恋 0777
恣 1454
息 1556
恐 1633
恥 1670
恩 1728

小
ネ
恭 1345
祥 0496

王
珠 1207
班 1853

戸
扇 1887

手
挙 1247
拳 1248

攵
敏 1574

斗
料 0758

方
旅 0569

无
既 1820

日
書 0079
時 0383
晃 2240

月
能 0892
朕 1252
脈 1366
朗 1476
脅 1971
胸 1992
胴 1993
脂 1994

---

脊 2153

木
案 0097
校 0103
根 0284
株 0567
栗 0781
格 0789
桜 1249
栽 1319
梅 1572
桟 1584
柴 1790
桃 1830
核 2161
桁 2229
栓 2230
桑 2291

歹
殉 1090
殊 1208

殳
氺
灬
殺 0522
泰 2105
烈 0719
烏 2281

牛
特 0385

田
留 1170
畔 1404
畜 2133
畝 2243

疒
病 0617
症 0618
疾 1940
疲 1948

皿
目
益 0414
真 0838
眠 1009
眩 2136

石
破 0596
砲 0665

---

禾
称 0684
秩 1210
秘 1384
租 1515

ネ
袖 1531
被 1949

罒
罠 2280

竹
笑 0579

米
粉 1619
粋 1622

糸
素 0132
紙 0478
紐 0591
紡 0835
純 1101
納 1156
紋 1416
紛 1620
索 1735

羽
耒
翁 1451
耕 1643
耗 1644

至
舟
致 0251
般 0671
航 1640

虫
蚕 2292
蚊 2295

衣
言
衰 1861
記 0427
討 1023
託 1539
訊 1637
訓 1927

貝
財 0653
貢 1158

走
車
辰
酉
起 0430
軒 0691
辱 1848
配 0799

---

酌 2130
酢 2131

金
針 0556
釜 1898
釘 2078

佳
隻 1658

食
飢 1966

馬
馬 0336

骨
骨 0465
骸 2162

高
高 0185

鬼
鬼 2090

竜
竜 0507

## 11 STROKES

乙
乾 1807

亠
ヘ
牽 1736

イ
側 0626
偏 1081
偽 1237
停 1424
健 1610
偵 1868
偶 1874

丷
曽 1222

刂
剰 1007
副 1482

力
動 0540
務 0687
勘 1799

氵
液 0468
渉 0680
清 0974
渋 1234
済 1260
涼 1284
添 1344
混 1426
深 1715

| | | |
|---|---|---|
| 扌 | 擬 | 1352 |
| | 擦 | 2098 |
| 口 | 嚇 | 1151 |
| 灬 | 嚴 | 0810 |
| 心 | 懇 | 2207 |
| 戈 | 戴 | 1914 |
| 王 | 環 | 1549 |
| 日 | 曙 | 1446 |
| | 曖 | 2249 |
| 月 | 臆 | 0621 |
| 火 | 燥 | 1810 |
| 灬 | 爵 | 1672 |
| 牛 | 犧 | 0929 |
| 疒 | 療 | 0952 |
| | 癌 | 1946 |
| 目 | 瞭 | 0954 |
| | 瞳 | 2084 |
| 矢 | 矯 | 1579 |
| 石 | 磯 | 0472 |
| | 礁 | 1655 |
| 米 | 糞 | 1892 |
| 糸 | 績 | 0836 |
| | 縮 | 0875 |
| | 繁 | 1576 |
| | 繡 | 1614 |
| | 纖 | 2008 |
| 羽 | 翼 | 0883 |
| 耳 | 聰 | 1669 |
| 臼 | 輿 | 0506 |
| 見 | 覽 | 2026 |
| 言 | 講 | 0918 |
| | 謝 | 1022 |
| | 謹 | 1733 |

| | | |
|---|---|---|
| | 謎 | 1774 |
| | 謙 | 2059 |
| | 膽 | 2237 |
| 貝 | 購 | 0919 |
| 車 | 轄 | 1841 |
| 酉 | 醜 | 2092 |
| | 醬 | 2128 |
| 金 | 鍋 | 1488 |
| | 鍛 | 2064 |
| | 鍵 | 2077 |
| 門 | 闇 | 1364 |
| 雨 | 霞 | 1904 |
| | 霜 | 1908 |
| 頁 | 頻 | 1923 |
| 魚 | 鮮 | 0493 |
| 齒 | 齡 | 0676 |

**18 STROKES**

| | | |
|---|---|---|
| 亻 | 儲 | 1449 |
| 氵 | 濫 | 2030 |
| 艹 | 藩 | 1511 |
| | 藍 | 2031 |
| | 藤 | 2235 |
| 心 | 懲 | 2191 |
| 日 | 曜 | 0025 |
| 玉 | 璧 | 1467 |
| 疒 | 癒 | 0948 |
| | 癖 | 1468 |
| 目 | 瞬 | 0963 |
| 石 | 礎 | 1349 |
| 禾 | 穫 | 1660 |
| 衤 | 襟 | 1532 |
| 竹 | 簡 | 0463 |

| | | |
|---|---|---|
| 米 | 糧 | 1618 |
| 糸 | 織 | 1088 |
| | 繕 | 1214 |
| | 繭 | 2298 |
| 羽 | 翻 | 1512 |
| 耳 | 職 | 1087 |
| 臣 | 臨 | 0855 |
| 西 | 覆 | 1870 |
| 見 | 觀 | 1128 |
| 貝 | 贈 | 1227 |
| | 贅 | 1509 |
| 金 | 鎮 | 1719 |
| | 鎌 | 2057 |
| | 鎖 | 2075 |
| 門 | 闘 | 1363 |
| 隹 | 難 | 0712 |
| | 離 | 1970 |
| | 雛 | 2154 |
| 韋 | 韓 | 0662 |
| 頁 | 顏 | 0180 |
| | 類 | 0310 |
| | 題 | 1681 |
| | 顯 | 1921 |
| | 額 | 1929 |
| | 顎 | 1936 |
| 馬 | 驗 | 1030 |
| | 騎 | 1331 |
| | 騷 | 1390 |

**19 STROKES**

| | | |
|---|---|---|
| 氵 | 瀨 | 1931 |
| 艹 | 蘇 | 0494 |
| | 蘭 | 1489 |

| | | |
|---|---|---|
| | 藻 | 1812 |
| 月 | 臓 | 1974 |
| 火 | 爆 | 1347 |
| 玉 | 璽 | 2288 |
| 灬 | 羅 | 0896 |
| 竹 | 簿 | 0985 |
| 糸 | 繰 | 1811 |
| 色 | 艷 | 2178 |
| 虫 | 蟹 | 2294 |
| 西 | 覇 | 1869 |
| 言 | 警 | 0806 |
| | 譜 | 1086 |
| | 識 | 1089 |
| 足 | 蹴 | 1324 |
| 金 | 鏡 | 1547 |
| 雨 | 霧 | 1906 |
| 音 | 韻 | 1594 |
| 頁 | 願 | 0214 |
| 骨 | 髄 | 2215 |
| 魚 | 鯨 | 1285 |
| 鳥 | 鶏 | 2284 |
| 鹿 | 麓 | 2257 |
| | 麗 | 2258 |

**20 STROKES**

| | | |
|---|---|---|
| 心 | 懸 | 1080 |
| 木 | 欄 | 1490 |
| 立 | 競 | 1204 |
| 竹 | 籍 | 1910 |
| 言 | 議 | 0927 |
| | 護 | 1661 |
| | 讓 | 1662 |
| 酉 | 釀 | 1664 |

| | | |
|---|---|---|
| 金 | 鐘 | 2083 |
| 音 | 響 | 1297 |
| 馬 | 騰 | 2236 |

**21 STROKES**

| | | |
|---|---|---|
| 口 | 囁 | 2138 |
| 舟 | 艦 | 2029 |
| 足 | 躍 | 1327 |
| 雨 | 露 | 1907 |
| 頁 | 顧 | 1890 |
| 鬼 | 魔 | 2095 |
| 鳥 | 鶴 | 1132 |

**22 STROKES**

| | | |
|---|---|---|
| 竹 | 籠 | 0509 |
| 衣 | 襲 | 1849 |
| 食 | 饗 | 1296 |
| 馬 | 驚 | 0807 |

**23 STROKES**

| | | |
|---|---|---|
| 金 | 鑑 | 2028 |
| 鳥 | 鷲 | 2287 |

**24 STROKES**

| | | |
|---|---|---|
| 鳥 | 鷹 | 2286 |

**29 STROKES**

| | | |
|---|---|---|
| 木 | 鬱 | 2141 |

# RADICAL INDEX

This index lists each kanji by its traditional "radical," or semantic root grapheme. It may be convenient to use this index when you do not know any readings for a kanji and can identify its radical. The radical most often appears at the left side of a left-right kanji, at the top of a top-bottom kanji, or as an enclosure. Important exceptions include

(a) Radicals that often/always appear at the right (radical number in parentheses):
刂 (18)　　卩 (26)　　欠 (76)　　攵 (66)　　阝 (163)　　隹 (172)　　頁 (181)

(b) Radicals that often/always appear at the bottom (radical number in parentheses):
儿 (10)　　心 (61)　　灬 (86)　　貝 (154)

For many kanji, identifying the radical is straightforward. For example, we can easily guess the radicals of 吟 (口), 宰 (宀), and 廉 (广) by following the basic rule of using the left-hand, topmost, or enclosing grapheme. For many other kanji, however, this rule does not help us correctly identify the portion of the kanji traditionally designated as its radical (for example, the traditional radical of 聞 is not the enclosure 門, but the enclosed element 耳). Because of this unpredictability, it is best to use this index only when you do not know any of a kanji's readings but are reasonably confident you can identify its radical. When you do not know the radical either, use the Stroke Count Index.

## Format and Arrangement

Each section heading displays the radical's number and parent form, followed in parentheses by an important abbreviated form, if any (abbreviated forms that do not differ significantly from their parent forms are not likely to appear). The numbers running along the left side of each column indicate each kanji's residual stroke count (the stroke count after excluding the radical). The four-digit numbers at the right side are entry numbers.

Radicals are arranged by the stroke count of their parent forms, using their conventional numbers from 1 to 214 (missing numbers belong to radicals not designated as the root grapheme of any kanji in this course). Within each radical group, kanji are arranged in order of their residual stroke counts, and then alphabetically by their readings as shown in this text—first any *on* reading(s), then any *kun* reading(s).

Because this index has been prepared in accordance with the traditional radical system, it lists radicals according to the stroke counts of their parent forms. Note the correspondence between the following abbreviated and parent forms, listed in order of their radical numbers (stroke counts in parentheses):

## Lost Radicals

In the orthographic reforms that followed World War II, some kanji were simplified so as to lose their traditional radicals. These kanji can be found here both under the traditional radical (with the traditional form of the kanji shown in parentheses), and under a replacement radical drawn from the simplified form (with a cross-reference to the old radical). In both cases, the entry number is followed by a superscript circle (°).

## RADICAL 18 刀 (刂) (continued)

| | | |
|---|---|---|
| | 刹 | 0523 |
| | 刷 | 2097 |
| | 制 | 0708 |
| | 刺 | 0935 |
| | 到 | 0940 |
| 7 | 削 | 1292 |
| | 則 | 0625 |
| | 剃 | 1192 |
| | 前 | 0113 |
| 8 | 剖 | 1262 |
| | 剛 | 2070 |
| | 剝 | 0609 |
| | 剣 | 1033 |
| | 帰 [RAD. 77] | 1018° |
| | 剤 | 1261 |
| 9 | 副 | 1482 |
| | 剰 | 1007 |
| 10 | 割 | 0416 |
| | 創 | 0697 |
| 13 | 劇 | 2002 |

## RADICAL 19 力

| | | |
|---|---|---|
| 0 | 力 | 0084 |
| 3 | 加 | 1147 |
| | 功 | 1046 |
| 4 | 劣 | 1743 |
| 5 | 努 | 2048 |
| | 助 | 0642 |
| | 励 | 2037 |
| | 労 | 0542 |
| 6 | 劾 | 2160 |
| | 効 | 1413 |
| 7 | 勃 | 2036 |
| | 勅 | 1108 |
| | 勇 | 2005 |
| 8 | 勉 | 1274 |
| 9 | 動 | 0540 |
| | 勘 | 1799 |
| | 務 | 0687 |
| 10 | 募 | 1341 |
| | 勤 | 1732 |
| | 勝 | 0460 |
| 11 | 勧 | 1129 |
| | 勢 | 1434 |
| 13 | 勲 | 1778 |

## RADICAL 20 勹

| | | |
|---|---|---|
| 1 | 勺 | 0168 |
| 2 | 勾 | 2246 |
| | 勿 | 0171 |
| | 匁 | 2244 |
| | 匂 | 2245 |
| 3 | 包 | 0457 |

## RADICAL 21 匕

| | | |
|---|---|---|
| 2 | 化 | 0120 |
| 3 | 北 | 0122 |

## RADICAL 22 匚

| | | |
|---|---|---|
| 4 | 匠 | 1802 |

## RADICAL 23 匸

| | | |
|---|---|---|
| 2 | 匹 | 1801 |
| | 区 | 0297 |
| 5 | 医 [RAD. 164] | 0561° |
| 8 | 匿 | 1803 |

## RADICAL 24 十

| | | |
|---|---|---|
| 0 | 十 | 0005 |
| 1 | 千 | 0017 |
| 2 | 午 | 0115 |
| | 升 | 1051 |
| 3 | 半 | 0335 |
| 6 | 協 | 0543 |
| | 卒 | 0751 |
| | 卓 | 1865 |
| 7 | 卑 | 2087 |
| | 南 | 0794 |
| 10 | 博 | 0983 |

## RADICAL 25 卜

| | | |
|---|---|---|
| 3 | 占 | 0348 |

## RADICAL 26 卩 (㔾)

| | | |
|---|---|---|
| 3 | 卯 | 1136 |
| 4 | 印 | 0231 |
| | 危 | 0726 |
| 5 | 却 | 0733 |
| | 卵 | 1141 |
| | 即 | 0390 |
| 6 | 巻 (卷) | 0458° |
| 7 | 卸 | 0861 |

## RADICAL 27 厂

| | | |
|---|---|---|
| 2 | 厄 | 0725 |
| 7 | 厚 | 0631 |
| | 厘 | 2242 |
| 8 | 原 | 0208 |

## RADICAL 28 厶

| | | |
|---|---|---|
| 3 | 去 | 0138 |
| 6 | 参 | 1238 |

## RADICAL 29 又

| | | |
|---|---|---|
| 0 | 又 | 0058 |
| 2 | 反 | 0374 |
| | 及 (及) | 1760° |
| | 収 [RAD. 66] | 1155° |
| | 双 [RAD. 172] | 1498° |
| | 友 | 0399 |
| 6 | 受 | 0065 |
| | 取 | 0059 |
| | 叔 | 2043 |
| 7 | 叙 [RAD. 66] | 0998° |

## 3 STROKES

## RADICAL 30 口

| | | |
|---|---|---|
| 0 | 口 | 0019 |
| 2 | 台 [RAD. 133] | 0949° |
| | 号 [RAD. 141] | 0300° |
| | 可 | 0814 |
| | 古 | 0254 |
| | 叩 | 1360 |
| | 句 | 0166 |
| | 叶 | 1767 |
| | 司 | 0820 |
| | 史 | 0888 |
| | 只 | 1194 |
| | 叱 | 1768 |
| | 召 | 1103 |
| | 右 | 0402 |
| 3 | 吊 | 0206 |
| | 同 | 0182 |
| | 各 | 0227 |
| | 吉 | 0786 |
| | 后 | 0514 |
| | 向 | 2193 |
| | 叫 | 0183 |
| | 吸 | 1769 |
| | 名 | 1763 |
| | 吏 | 0269 |
| | 吐 | 0886 |
| | 吠 | 1766 |
| 4 | 吞 | 1851 |
| | 含 | 2174 |
| | 吟 | 1771 |
| | 呉 | 1770 |
| | 吾 | 1478 |
| | 否 | 0220 |
| | 呆 | 0552 |
| | 告 | 0647 |
| | 君 | 0698 |
| | 呂 | 1407 |
| | 吹 | 1240 |
| | 呈 | 1764 |
| 5 | 呟 | 0587 |
| | 咳 | 2137 |
| | 呪 | 2177 |

### RADICAL 38 女

| | | |
|---|---|---|
| 0 | 女 | 0093 |
| 2 | 奴 | 2047 |
| 3 | 妃 | 2195 |
| | 如 | 2197 |
| | 好 | 0095 |
| | 妄 | 1455 |
| 4 | 妨 | 1882 |
| | 妥 | 1250 |
| | 妙 | 1746 |
| | 妊 | 1845 |
| | 妖 | 2176 |
| 5 | 委 | 0396 |
| | 妹 | 1206 |
| | 妻 | 1457 |
| | 姓 | 0431 |
| | 姉 | 1205 |
| | 始 | 0956 |
| | 妬 | 2254 |
| 6 | 威 | 1150 |
| | 姻 | 1726 |
| | 姿 | 1453 |
| 7 | 娯 | 1479 |
| | 姫 | 2196 |
| | 娘 | 2200 |
| | 娠 | 1846 |
| 8 | 婆 | 1452 |
| | 婦 | 1017 |
| | 婚 | 1721 |
| 9 | 媒 | 2123 |
| | 媛 | 1125 |
| | 婿 | 2199 |
| 10 | 嫁 | 2201 |
| | 嫌 | 2058 |
| | 嫉 | 2253 |
| 11 | 嫡 | 1120 |
| 12 | 嬉 | 2015 |
| 13 | 嬢 | 1663 |

### RADICAL 39 子

| | | |
|---|---|---|
| 0 | 子 | 0094 |
| 1 | 孔 | 1559 |
| 3 | 字 | 0098 |
| | 存 | 0407 |
| 4 | 孝 | 0630 |
| 5 | 学 | 0099 |
| | 季 | 0395 |
| 6 | 孤 | 1073 |
| 7 | 孫 | 1079 |

### RADICAL 40 宀

| | | |
|---|---|---|
| 3 | 安 | 0096 |
| | 守 | 0648 |
| | 宅 | 1540 |
| | 宇 | 1542 |
| 4 | 完 | 0633 |
| | 牢 | 1737 |
| 5 | 宛 | 0730 |
| | 宙 | 1529 |
| | 宜 | 1519 |
| | 宝 | 0074 |
| | 実 | 0499 |
| | 官 | 0290 |
| | 宗 | 0636 |
| | 定 | 0045 |
| 6 | 客 | 0787 |
| | 宣 | 1398 |
| | 室 | 0253 |
| 7 | 宴 | 1294 |
| | 害 | 0413 |
| | 家 | 0219 |
| | 宮 | 1242 |
| | 宰 | 1463 |
| | 宵 | 1293 |
| | 容 | 1037 |
| 8 | 寅 | 0913 |
| | 寂 | 2045 |
| | 寄 | 1330 |
| | 密 | 1383 |
| | 宿 | 0292 |
| 9 | 富 | 1481 |
| | 寓 | 0361 |
| 10 | 寒 | 1041 |
| | 寛 | 1015 |
| | 寝 | 2232 |
| 11 | 塞 | 1961 |
| | 寡 | 1382 |
| | 蜜 | 0438 |
| | 寧 | 0639 |
| 12 | 察 | 0955 |
| | 写 (寫) | 0859° |
| | 審 | 1510 |

### RADICAL 41 寸

| | | |
|---|---|---|
| 0 | 寸 | 0381 |
| 3 | 寺 | 0382 |
| 4 | 寿 [RAD. 33] | 1544° |
| | 対 | 0650 |
| 6 | 封 | 1837 |
| | 専 | 0580 |
| 7 | 射 | 1021 |
| | 将 | 0614 |
| 8 | 尉 | 2124 |
| 9 | 尋 | 1636 |
| | 尊 | 0802 |
| 12 | 導 | 0804 |

### RADICAL 42 小 (⺌)

| | | |
|---|---|---|
| 0 | 小 | 0034 |
| 1 | 少 | 0677 |
| 3 | 尖 | 1563 |
| | 当 [RAD. 102] | 0141° |
| 5 | 尚 | 0184 |
| 6 | 単 [RAD. 30] | 0462° |
| 8 | 巣 [RAD. 47] | 0601° |
| 9 | 営 [RAD. 86] | 1243° |
| 14 | 厳 [RAD. 30] | 0810° |

### RADICAL 43 尢

| | | |
|---|---|---|
| 1 | 尤 | 2274 |
| 9 | 就 | 1283 |

### RADICAL 44 尸

| | | |
|---|---|---|
| 1 | 尺 | 0337 |
| 2 | 尼 | 2116 |
| | 尻 | 1895 |
| 3 | 尽 [RAD. 108] | 0338° |
| 4 | 尾 | 0488 |
| | 局 | 0256 |
| | 尿 | 1893 |
| 5 | 屈 | 1834 |
| | 居 | 0255 |
| | 届 | 1528 |
| 6 | 屏 | 2170 |
| | 屋 | 0252 |
| 7 | 屑 | 1891 |
| | 展 | 0880 |
| 9 | 属 | 1872 |
| 11 | 層 | 1224 |
| 12 | 履 | 1871 |

### RADICAL 45 屮

| | | |
|---|---|---|
| 1 | 屯 | 1100 |

### RADICAL 46 山

| | | |
|---|---|---|
| 0 | 山 | 0037 |
| 4 | 岐 | 0968 |
| 5 | 岳 | 0908 |
| | 岩 | 1649 |
| | 岸 | 1648 |
| | 岬 | 1335 |
| | 岡 | 0178 |
| 6 | 峡 | 1932 |
| | 峠 | 0969 |
| 7 | 峰 | 1378 |
| | 島 | 0341 |
| 8 | 崖 | 1652 |

| | | | | | | | | |
|---|---|---|---|---|---|---|---|---|
| 恒 | 1396 | 慢 | 1134 | 3 扱 | 1761 | 拭 | 1027 |
| 恨 | 1217 | 慮 | 1999 | 4 拔 | 1951 | 拾 | 1071 |
| 恐 | 1633 | 憂 | 0779 | 扶 | 1953 | 7 挨 | 2247 |
| 恭 | 1345 | 憎 | 1225 | 技 | 0966 | 挫 | 1924 |
| 恩 | 1728 | 12 憤 | 1815 | 把 | 2024 | 捕 | 1596 |
| 恋 | 0777 | 憬 | 2086 | 批 | 0746 | 振 | 0903 |
| 恣 | 1454 | 憩 | 1557 | 抗 | 1639 | 搜 | 1527 |
| 息 | 1556 | 憲 | 0417 | 折 | 1698 | 揷 | 1597 |
| 7 悪 | 0546 | 憧 | 2085 | 抄 | 1744 | 捉 | 1603 |
| 悦 | 1202 | 13 懐 | 1667 | 承 | 0959 | 挫 | 1699 |
| 悟 | 0326 | 憾 | 1216 | 択 | 1503 | 8 描 | 1824 |
| 患 | 1939 | 懇 | 2207 | 投 | 0517 | 排 | 0739 |
| 悩 | 1972 | 憶 | 0620 | 抑 | 1137 | 捧 | 2108 |
| 悠 | 1677 | 14 懲 | 2191 | 5 抽 | 1526 | 授 | 1123 |
| 8 惧 | 1717 | 16 懸 | 1080 | 拝 | 1642 | 掛 | 1117 |
| 悲 | 1856 | | | 拍 | 1185 | 捆 | 1602 |
| 情 | 0973 | **RADICAL 62 戈** | | 披 | 1950 | 揭 | 2272 |
| 惚 | 1858 | 2 戌 | 2273 | 抱 | 0664 | 控 | 1952 |
| 惨 | 1239 | 成 | 0070 | 拐 | 1784 | 掘 | 1835 |
| 惜 | 1218 | 3 我 | 0221 | 拡 | 0813 | 捻 | 1700 |
| 悼 | 1866 | 戒 | 0469 | 拘 | 1070 | 採 | 0989 |
| 惑 | 1153 | 4 或 | 1152 | 拠 | 0554 | 接 | 0847 |
| 9 愛 | 0778 | 7 戚 | 2042 | 拒 | 2014 | 捨 | 1072 |
| 惰 | 2217 | 9 戦 | 0461 | 抹 | 1954 | 掌 | 0324 |
| 愚 | 1878 | 11 戯 | 2007 | 押 | 1525 | 措 | 1219 |
| 意 | 0151 | 13 戴 | 1914 | 拉 | 2239 | 掃 | 1016 |
| 慈 | 2179 | | | 拙 | 1833 | 据 | 1535 |
| 感 | 0327 | **RADICAL 63 戸** | | 招 | 1104 | 推 | 2150 |
| 慌 | 1065 | 0 戸 | 0248 | 拓 | 1955 | 探 | 1714 |
| 愁 | 1316 | 3 戻 | 1019 | 担 | 1394 | 9 握 | 1536 |
| 想 | 0683 | 4 房 | 1886 | 抵 | 0480 | 援 | 1124 |
| 愉 | 0947 | 所 | 0249 | 6 挑 | 1832 | 換 | 1269 |
| 10 慕 | 1343 | 6 扇 | 1887 | 拷 | 1956 | 揮 | 0933 |
| 慨 | 1822 | 8 扉 | 1888 | 持 | 0384 | 揃 | 1537 |
| 慄 | 1716 | | | 括 | 1069 | 提 | 1679 |
| 慎 | 1718 | **RADICAL 64 手 (扌)** | | 拳 | 1248 | 搭 | 1960 |
| 態 | 0893 | 0 才 | 0652 | 挙 | 1247 | 揚 | 1308 |
| 11 慰 | 2125 | 手 | 0046 | 挾 | 1934 | 揺 | 1369 |
| 慣 | 1912 | 2 打 | 1025 | 捗 | 2248 | 10 搬 | 0672 |
| 慶 | 2260 | 払 | 0812 | 指 | 0932 | 携 | 1786 |

| | | | | | | |
|---|---|---|---|---|---|---|
| | 采 | 0987 | | 梢 | 1291 | |
| | 析 | 1697 | 8 | 棒 | 2107 | |
| | 枝 | 0965 | | 椅 | 1332 | |
| | 松 | 0242 | | 棺 | 1840 | |
| | 枢 | 1386 | | 検 | 1029 | |
| | 東 | 0032 | | 棋 | 1796 | |
| | 桦 | 1624 | | 極 | 1712 | |
| 5 | 某 | 2121 | | 森 | 0241 | |
| | 柱 | 0867 | | 植 | 0840 | |
| | 栄 | 1245 | | 棚 | 2227 | |
| | 柄 | 1524 | | 棟 | 1688 | |
| | 柔 | 0688 | | 椎 | 2152 | |
| | 架 | 1173 | 9 | 楽 | 0302 | |
| | 枯 | 1049 | | 業 | 0498 | |
| | 柳 | 1140 | | 楷 | 1428 | |
| | 查 | 1514 | | 棄 | 0606 | |
| | 栅 | 2228 | | 楼 | 1957 | |
| | 染 | 1174 | 10 | 概 | 1821 | |
| | 柿 | 2234 | | 構 | 0917 | |
| | 栃 | 2038 | | 模 | 1336 | |
| 6 | 案 | 0097 | | 様 | 0501 | |
| | 梅 | 1572 | 11 | 標 | 0783 | |
| | 株 | 0567 | | 権 | 1130 | |
| | 核 | 2161 | | 横 | 0916 | |
| | 格 | 0789 | | 槽 | 1881 | |
| | 桁 | 2229 | 12 | 樹 | 2017 | |
| | 校 | 0103 | | 機 | 0473 | |
| | 根 | 0284 | | 橋 | 1578 | |
| | 桜 | 1249 | | 樽 | 2012 | |
| | 栗 | 0781 | 16 | 欄 | 1490 | |
| | 栽 | 1319 | 25 | 鬱 | 2141 | |
| | 柴 | 1790 | | | | |
| | 栈 | 1584 | | | | |
| | 栓 | 2230 | | | | |
| | 桑 | 2291 | | | | |
| | 桃 | 1830 | | | | |
| 7 | 械 | 0474 | | | | |
| | 梗 | 2233 | | | | |
| | 梱 | 1724 | | | | |
| | 梨 | 1175 | | | | |

---

**RADICAL 76 欠**

| | | |
|---|---|---|
| 0 | 欠 | 0277 |
| 2 | 次 | 0278 |
| 4 | 欧 | 1385 |
| 7 | 欲 | 1035 |
| 8 | 欺 | 1795 |
| | 款 | 2051 |
| 10 | 歌 | 0827 |
| 11 | 歓 | 1131 |

---

**RADICAL 77 止**

| | | |
|---|---|---|
| 0 | 止 | 0042 |
| 1 | 正 | 0043 |
| 2 | 此 | 1756 |
| 4 | 武 | 0111 |
| | 步 | 0679 |
| 9 | 歳 | 2041 |
| 10 | 歴 | 0853 |
| 14 | 帰（歸） | 1018° |

---

**RADICAL 78 歹**

| | | |
|---|---|---|
| 2 | 死 | 0716 |
| 5 | 殆 | 2192 |
| 6 | 殉 | 1090 |
| | 殊 | 1208 |
| | 残 | 1583 |
| 8 | 殖 | 0841 |

---

**RADICAL 79 殳**

| | | |
|---|---|---|
| 4 | 殴 | 1387 |
| 5 | 段 | 0521 |
| 6 | 殺 | 0522 |
| 7 | 殻 | 2052 |
| 9 | 殿 | 0881 |

---

**RADICAL 80 母**

| | | |
|---|---|---|
| 0 | 母 | 0104 |
| 2 | 毎 | 0105 |
| 4 | 毒 | 0133 |

---

**RADICAL 81 比**

| | | |
|---|---|---|
| 0 | 比 | 0123 |

---

**RADICAL 82 毛**

| | | |
|---|---|---|
| 0 | 毛 | 0487 |

---

**RADICAL 83 氏**

| | | |
|---|---|---|
| 0 | 氏 | 0476 |
| 1 | 民 | 0477 |

---

**RADICAL 84 气**

| | | |
|---|---|---|
| 2 | 気 | 0126 |

---

**RADICAL 85 水（氵）**

| | | |
|---|---|---|
| 0 | 水 | 0027 |
| 1 | 永 | 1691 |
| | 氷 | 1690 |
| 2 | 氾 | 2119 |
| | 汁 | 0756 |
| | 求 | 1097 |
| 3 | 池 | 0188 |
| | 汎 | 1632 |
| | 汗 | 0410 |
| | 江 | 1499 |
| | 污 | 1050 |
| | 汐 | 0268 |
| 4 | 没 | 0519 |
| | 沈 | 0655 |
| | 沖 | 0645 |
| | 決 | 0330 |
| | 汽 | 0127 |
| | 沙 | 1747 |
| | 汰 | 1748 |
| | 沢 | 1504 |
| | 沃 | 2175 |
| 5 | 注 | 0368 |
| | 泥 | 2117 |
| | 泳 | 1692 |
| | 沿 | 1348 |
| | 沸 | 1187 |
| | 波 | 0598 |
| | 泊 | 1183 |
| | 泌 | 1894 |
| | 泡 | 0666 |
| | 法 | 0139 |
| | 治 | 0950 |
| | 河 | 0818 |
| | 況 | 1201 |

| | | |
|---|---|---|
| 6 | 独 | 0346 |
| | 狭 | 1933 |
| | 狩 | 0766 |
| 8 | 猫 | 1825 |
| | 猪 | 0217 |
| | 猛 | 0767 |
| | 猟 | 0764 |
| 9 | 献 | 1157 |
| | 猶 | 0801 |
| 10 | 猿 | 1859 |
| 11 | 獄 | 0737 |
| 12 | 獣 | 0763 |
| 13 | 獲 | 1659 |

**5 STROKES**

### RADICAL 95 玄

| | | |
|---|---|---|
| 0 | 玄 | 2135 |
| 6 | 率 | 0752 |

### RADICAL 96 玉（王）

| | | |
|---|---|---|
| 0 | 玉 | 0073 |
| | 王 | 0072 |
| 3 | 弄 | 2220 |
| 4 | 玩 | 2219 |
| 5 | 珍 | 2166 |
| 6 | 班 | 1853 |
| | 珠 | 1207 |
| 7 | 現 | 0706 |
| | 球 | 1099 |
| | 理 | 0532 |
| 8 | 琴 | 1772 |
| 10 | 璃 | 2252 |
| | 瑠 | 2251 |
| 13 | 璧 | 1467 |
| | 環 | 1549 |
| 14 | 璽 | 2288 |

### RADICAL 97 瓜

| | | |
|---|---|---|
| 0 | 瓜 | 0202 |

### RADICAL 98 瓦

| | | |
|---|---|---|
| 0 | 瓦 | 2167 |
| 6 | 瓶 | 2169 |

### RADICAL 99 甘

| | | |
|---|---|---|
| 0 | 甘 | 1042 |
| 4 | 甚 | 1798 |

### RADICAL 100 生

| | | |
|---|---|---|
| 0 | 生 | 0036 |
| 6 | 産 | 0181 |

### RADICAL 101 用

| | | |
|---|---|---|
| 0 | 用 | 0047 |

### RADICAL 102 田

| | | |
|---|---|---|
| 0 | 田 | 0020 |
| | 甲 | 1521 |
| | 申 | 0315 |
| | 由 | 0432 |
| 2 | 町 | 0439 |
| | 男 | 0092 |
| 3 | 画 | 0176 |
| 4 | 畑 | 0129 |
| | 畏 | 2096 |
| | 界 | 0612 |
| 5 | 畜 | 2133 |
| | 畔 | 1404 |
| | 留 | 1170 |
| | 畝 | 2243 |
| 6 | 異 | 0882 |
| | 略 | 0791 |
| 7 | 番 | 0299 |
| | 畳 | 1520 |
| 8 | 当（當） | 0141° |

### RADICAL 103 疋

| | | |
|---|---|---|
| 7 | 疎 | 1142 |
| 9 | 疑 | 1350 |

### RADICAL 104 疒

| | | |
|---|---|---|
| 4 | 疫 | 1942 |
| 5 | 病 | 0617 |
| | 疲 | 1948 |
| | 疾 | 1940 |
| | 症 | 0618 |
| 6 | 痕 | 1323 |
| 7 | 痢 | 1943 |
| | 痩 | 1947 |
| | 痘 | 1944 |
| | 痛 | 0619 |
| 8 | 痴 | 1941 |
| | 痺 | 2089 |
| 9 | 瘍 | 1945 |
| 12 | 癌 | 1946 |
| | 療 | 0952 |
| 13 | 癖 | 1468 |
| | 癒 | 0948 |

### RADICAL 105 癶

| | | |
|---|---|---|
| 4 | 発 | 0148 |
| 7 | 登 | 1054 |

### RADICAL 106 白

| | | |
|---|---|---|
| 0 | 白 | 0076 |
| 1 | 百 | 0016 |
| 3 | 的 | 0169 |
| 4 | 皆 | 1427 |
| | 皇 | 0077 |
| 6 | 兜 | 2261 |

### RADICAL 107 皮

| | | |
|---|---|---|
| 0 | 皮 | 0595 |

### RADICAL 108 皿

| | | |
|---|---|---|
| 0 | 皿 | 0197 |
| 4 | 盆 | 1302 |
| 5 | 益 | 0414 |
| 6 | 盛 | 1300 |
| | 盗 | 1304 |
| 8 | 盟 | 1305 |
| 9 | 尽（盡） | 0338° |
| 10 | 盤 | 0673 |
| | 監 | 2027 |

### RADICAL 109 目

| | | |
|---|---|---|
| 0 | 目 | 0021 |
| 3 | 直 | 0839 |
| | 盲 | 1061 |
| 4 | 眉 | 0530 |
| | 冒 [RAD. 13] | 1683° |
| | 盾 | 1551 |
| | 看 | 0939 |
| | 県 [RAD. 120] | 0844° |
| | 省 | 0681 |
| | 相 | 0682 |
| 5 | 眩 | 2136 |
| | 眠 | 1009 |
| | 真 | 0838 |
| 6 | 眺 | 1828 |
| | 眼 | 1092 |
| 8 | 睦 | 1433 |
| | 睨 | 2262 |
| | 督 | 1008 |
| | 睡 | 2046 |
| 12 | 瞳 | 2084 |
| | 瞭 | 0954 |
| 13 | 瞬 | 0963 |

### RADICAL 110 矛

| | | |
|---|---|---|
| 0 | 矛 | 0164 |

### RADICAL 111 矢

| | | |
|---|---|---|
| 0 | 矢 | 0559 |
| 3 | 知 | 0560 |
| 7 | 短 | 0562 |
| 12 | 矯 | 1579 |

| | | |
|---|---|---|
| 9 | 親 | 0276 |
| 10 | 覧 | 2026 |
| 11 | 観 | 1128 |

**RADICAL 148 角**

| | | |
|---|---|---|
| 0 | 角 | 0342 |
| 6 | 解 | 0345 |
| | 触 | 0344 |

**RADICAL 149 言**

| | | |
|---|---|---|
| 0 | 言 | 0051 |
| 2 | 訃 | 1115 |
| | 計 | 0555 |
| | 訂 | 1024 |
| 3 | 訊 | 1637 |
| | 記 | 0427 |
| | 訓 | 1927 |
| | 託 | 1539 |
| | 討 | 1023 |
| 4 | 訪 | 0454 |
| | 許 | 1276 |
| | 設 | 0520 |
| | 訟 | 1709 |
| | 訳 | 1505 |
| 5 | 詠 | 1693 |
| | 評 | 0745 |
| | 詐 | 1794 |
| | 詞 | 0822 |
| | 診 | 2165 |
| | 詔 | 1107 |
| | 証 | 0550 |
| | 訴 | 1708 |
| 6 | 該 | 2164 |
| | 詣 | 1995 |
| | 詰 | 0515 |
| | 誇 | 2025 |
| | 誠 | 1299 |
| | 詮 | 2231 |
| | 詩 | 0389 |
| | 試 | 1028 |
| | 詳 | 0495 |
| | 詫 | 1541 |
| | 話 | 0053 |
| | 誉 | 1246 |
| 7 | 読 | 0355 |
| | 誤 | 1480 |
| | 語 | 0222 |
| | 認 | 1096 |
| | 誓 | 1701 |
| | 説 | 1197 |
| | 誌 | 0370 |
| | 誘 | 1783 |
| 8 | 調 | 0306 |
| | 諾 | 1804 |
| | 談 | 1977 |
| | 誰 | 2155 |
| | 謁 | 2271 |
| | 課 | 0600 |
| | 論 | 0942 |
| | 請 | 0977 |
| | 諸 | 1448 |
| | 誕 | 0876 |
| 9 | 謀 | 2122 |
| | 諧 | 1429 |
| | 諮 | 1638 |
| | 諦 | 1420 |
| | 謡 | 1370 |
| | 諭 | 0946 |
| 10 | 謙 | 2059 |
| | 謹 | 1733 |
| | 講 | 0918 |
| | 謎 | 1774 |
| | 謝 | 1022 |
| | 謄 | 2237 |
| 12 | 譜 | 1086 |
| | 警 | 0806 |
| | 識 | 1089 |
| 13 | 議 | 0927 |
| | 護 | 1661 |
| | 讓 | 1662 |

| | | |
|---|---|---|
| 16 | 変(變) | 0775° |

**RADICAL 150 谷**

| | | |
|---|---|---|
| 0 | 谷 | 1034 |

**RADICAL 151 豆**

| | | |
|---|---|---|
| 0 | 豆 | 0161 |
| 6 | 豊 | 0513 |

**RADICAL 152 豕**

| | | |
|---|---|---|
| 4 | 豚 | 0218 |
| 6 | 象 | 1277 |
| 7 | 豪 | 2204 |
| 9 | 予(豫) | 0163° |

**RADICAL 153 豸**

| | | |
|---|---|---|
| 7 | 貌 | 2208 |

**RADICAL 154 貝**

| | | |
|---|---|---|
| 0 | 貝 | 0082 |
| 2 | 負 | 0829 |
| | 貞 | 1867 |
| 3 | 貢 | 1158 |
| | 財 | 0653 |
| 4 | 貪 | 1159 |
| | 販 | 0925 |
| | 貧 | 1161 |
| | 貨 | 1164 |
| | 貫 | 1911 |
| | 責 | 0831 |
| 5 | 買 | 0352 |
| | 貿 | 1169 |
| | 貯 | 0442 |
| | 貼 | 1266 |
| | 賀 | 1172 |
| | 費 | 1189 |
| | 貴 | 1177 |
| | 貫 | 1160 |
| | 弐(貳) | 0110° |
| | 貸 | 1163 |

| | | |
|---|---|---|
| 6 | 賃 | 1162 |
| | 賂 | 1229 |
| | 資 | 1165 |
| | 賄 | 1228 |
| | 賊 | 1231 |
| 7 | 賑 | 0905 |
| 8 | 賠 | 1265 |
| | 売(賣) | 0353° |
| | 賦 | 1230 |
| | 賓 | 1962 |
| | 賛 | 1166 |
| | 賜 | 0444 |
| | 質 | 0318 |
| | 賞 | 0322 |
| 9 | 賢 | 2032 |
| | 賭 | 1447 |
| 10 | 購 | 0919 |
| 11 | 贅 | 1509 |
| | 贈 | 1227 |

**RADICAL 155 赤**

| | | |
|---|---|---|
| 0 | 赤 | 0774 |
| 4 | 赦 | 1320 |

**RADICAL 156 走**

| | | |
|---|---|---|
| 0 | 走 | 0140 |
| 2 | 赴 | 1114 |
| 3 | 起 | 0430 |
| 5 | 超 | 1111 |
| | 越 | 1112 |
| 8 | 趣 | 1113 |

**RADICAL 157 足**

| | | |
|---|---|---|
| 0 | 足 | 0044 |
| 5 | 距 | 2013 |
| 6 | 跳 | 1831 |
| | 路 | 0788 |
| | 跡 | 1321 |
| | 践 | 1586 |
| 7 | 踊 | 1325 |

# READINGS INDEX

This index lists the kanji in *a-i-u-e-o* order by their *on* (Chinese-derived) and *kun* (native) readings. This is a convenient index to use whenever you know at least one of a kanji's readings. When you do not know any readings for a kanji, use the Radical Index or the Stroke Count Index.

When a kanji has both an *on* reading and a *kun* reading, it is generally more convenient to start with the *kun* reading, which is less likely to have homophones.

## Format and Arrangement

This index contains all the readings given in the main entries, listed in the order of the *kana* syllabary (described in the appendix on kana in *The Kodansha Kanji Learner's Dictionary*). *On* readings precede *kun* readings (コ, こ), ordinary readings precede prefixes (こ, こ-), and prefixes precede suffixes (こ-, -こ). Readings are divided into sections by their initial syllable. In this division, readings that start with voiced sounds (ご, ぞ, だ, ば, etc.) have their own sections; e.g., readings that begin with コ or こ appear in one section (under the heading "こ"), while readings that begin with ゴ or ご appear in the next section (under the heading "ご").

Homophones appear in ascending order of their stroke counts, then by their radical numbers, then by their entry numbers in this course. When more than ten kanji share the same reading, the stroke counts are indicated by small numerals to the left of the kanji. The four-digit numerals to the right of the kanji are the entry numbers.

As in the main entries, *on* readings appear in katakana and *kun* readings in hiragana. Unlike the main entries, *okurigana* readings do not appear in parentheses.

| あ | | | | | | | | |
|---|---|---|---|---|---|---|---|---|
| ア | 亜 0545 | あいだ | 間 0448 | あか | 赤 0774 | あかるむ | 明 0024 |
| | 阿 0819 | あう | 会 0226 | | 垢 2194 | あがり | 上 0041 |
| あ- | 吾 0220 | | 合 0227 | あか- | 赤 0774 | -あがり | 上 0041 |
| アイ | 哀 1860 | | 逢 1379 | あかい | 赤 0774 | あがる | 上 0041 |
| | 挨 2247 | | 遇 1877 | あかし | 証 0550 | | 挙 1247 |
| | 愛 0778 | | 遭 1880 | あかす | 明 0024 | | 揚 1308 |
| | 曖 2249 | -あう | 合 0227 | | 飽 1964 | -あがる | 上 0041 |
| あい | 合 0227 | あえず | 敢 0809 | あかつき | 暁 0770 | あき | 空 0398 |
| | 藍 2031 | あえて | 敢 0809 | あからむ | 赤 0774 | | 秋 0364 |
| あい- | 合 0227 | あお | 青 0130 | | 明 0024 | あきなう | 商 0351 |
| | 相 0682 | あお- | 青 0130 | あからめる | 赤 0774 | あきらか | 明 0024 |
| -あい | 合 0227 | あおい | 青 0130 | あかり | 明 0024 | あきらめる | 諦 1420 |
| | | あおぐ | 仰 1138 | あかるい | 明 0024 | あきる | 飽 1964 |

685

| | | |
|---|---|---|
| -ぐさ | 草 | 0144 |
| -ぐみ | 組 | 0264 |
| -ぐも | 雲 | 0897 |
| ぐらい | 位 | 0577 |
| -ぐるしい | 苦 | 0405 |
| グン | 軍 | 0583 |
| | 郡 | 1409 |
| | 群 | 1408 |

**け**

| | | | |
|---|---|---|---|
| ケ | | 化 | 0120 |
| | | 仮 | 0921 |
| | | 気 | 0126 |
| | | 怪 | 1255 |
| | | 家 | 0219 |
| | | 華 | 1012 |
| | | 稀 | 1068 |
| | | 懸 | 1080 |
| け | | 毛 | 0487 |
| ケイ | 5 | 兄 | 1193 |
| | 6 | 刑 | 0722 |
| | 7 | 形 | 0147 |
| | | 系 | 1077 |
| | 8 | 京 | 0245 |
| | | 径 | 1254 |
| | | 怪 | 1255 |
| | | 茎 | 1253 |
| | 9 | 係 | 1078 |
| | | 型 | 0723 |
| | | 契 | 1568 |
| | | 計 | 0555 |
| | 10 | 恵 | 0581 |
| | 11 | 啓 | 1738 |
| | | 掲 | 2272 |
| | | 渓 | 2285 |
| | | 蛍 | 1244 |
| | 12 | 敬 | 0805 |
| | | 景 | 1280 |
| | 13 | 傾 | 1917 |
| | | 携 | 1786 |

| | | | |
|---|---|---|---|
| | | 継 | 0848 |
| | | 詣 | 1995 |
| | 14 | 境 | 1548 |
| | 15 | 憬 | 2086 |
| | | 慶 | 2260 |
| | | 稽 | 1494 |
| | 16 | 憩 | 1557 |
| | 17 | 繋 | 1576 |
| | 19 | 警 | 0806 |
| | | 鶏 | 2284 |
| | 20 | 競 | 1204 |
| けがす | | 汚 | 1050 |
| けがらわしい | | 汚 | 1050 |
| けがれる | | 汚 | 1050 |
| けす | | 消 | 1289 |
| けずる | | 削 | 1292 |
| けた | | 桁 | 2229 |
| ケツ | | 欠 | 0277 |
| | | 穴 | 0397 |
| | | 血 | 0198 |
| | | 決 | 0330 |
| | | 頁 | 0156 |
| | | 結 | 0516 |
| | | 傑 | 1176 |
| | | 潔 | 1570 |
| | | 煙 | 0768 |
| けむい | | 煙 | 0768 |
| けむり | | 煙 | 0768 |
| けむる | | 煙 | 0768 |
| けもの | | 獣 | 0763 |
| ける | | 蹴 | 1324 |
| けわしい | | 険 | 1031 |
| ケン | 4 | 犬 | 0293 |
| | 6 | 件 | 0118 |
| | 7 | 見 | 0083 |
| | 8 | 券 | 0456 |
| | | 肩 | 1495 |
| | 9 | 建 | 1609 |
| | | 県 | 0844 |
| | | 研 | 0724 |
| | 10 | 倹 | 1032 |

| | | | |
|---|---|---|---|
| | | 兼 | 1006 |
| | | 剣 | 1033 |
| | | 拳 | 1248 |
| | | 軒 | 0691 |
| | 11 | 牽 | 1736 |
| | | 健 | 1610 |
| | | 険 | 1031 |
| | 12 | 喧 | 1399 |
| | | 圏 | 0459 |
| | | 堅 | 2034 |
| | | 検 | 1029 |
| | | 間 | 0448 |
| | 13 | 嫌 | 2058 |
| | | 献 | 1157 |
| | | 絹 | 0212 |
| | | 遣 | 1180 |
| | 15 | 権 | 1130 |
| | 16 | 憲 | 0417 |
| | | 賢 | 2032 |
| | 17 | 謙 | 2059 |
| | | 鍵 | 2077 |
| | 18 | 繭 | 2298 |
| | | 顕 | 1921 |
| | | 験 | 1030 |
| | 20 | 懸 | 1080 |

**げ**

| | | | |
|---|---|---|---|
| ゲ | | 下 | 0040 |
| | | 牙 | 1816 |
| | | 外 | 0266 |
| | | 夏 | 0363 |
| | | 解 | 0345 |
| ゲイ | | 芸 | 0225 |
| | | 迎 | 1139 |
| | | 睨 | 2262 |
| | | 鯨 | 1285 |
| ゲキ | | 隙 | 1876 |
| | | 劇 | 2002 |
| | | 撃 | 1026 |
| | | 激 | 0575 |

| | | | |
|---|---|---|---|
| ゲツ | | 月 | 0023 |
| ゲン | 4 | 元 | 0136 |
| | | 幻 | 2145 |
| | 5 | 玄 | 2135 |
| | 7 | 言 | 0051 |
| | 8 | 眩 | 2137 |
| | | 弦 | 2142 |
| | 9 | 限 | 0282 |
| | 10 | 原 | 0208 |
| | | 拳 | 1248 |
| | | 眩 | 2136 |
| | 11 | 現 | 0706 |
| | | 眼 | 1092 |
| | | 舷 | 2143 |
| | 12 | 減 | 1148 |
| | 13 | 嫌 | 2058 |
| | | 源 | 0209 |
| | 17 | 厳 | 0810 |
| | 18 | 験 | 1030 |

**こ**

| | | | |
|---|---|---|---|
| コ | 3 | 己 | 0426 |
| | | 乞 | 1805 |
| | 4 | 戸 | 0248 |
| | 5 | 去 | 0138 |
| | | 古 | 0254 |
| | 8 | 呼 | 1765 |
| | | 固 | 0260 |
| | | 拠 | 0554 |
| | | 股 | 1990 |
| | | 虎 | 0912 |
| | 9 | 孤 | 1073 |
| | | 弧 | 1074 |
| | | 故 | 0257 |
| | | 胡 | 0258 |
| | | 枯 | 1049 |
| | 10 | 個 | 0262 |
| | | 庫 | 0694 |
| | | 娘 | 2200 |
| | 11 | 壺 | 1402 |

| | | | |
|---|---|---|---|
| 7 似 1354 | 11 授 1123 | 助 0642 | 10 訊 1637 |
| 児 0772 | 12 就 1283 | 序 1209 | 陣 1374 |
| 8 事 0080 | 14 需 2111 | 叙 0998 | 12 尋 1636 |
| 侍 0388 | 16 儒 2113 | 茹 2198 | 13 腎 2033 |
| 治 0950 | 樹 2017 | 徐 0997 | 14 塵 2256 |
| 9 持 0384 | 17 濡 2112 | 除 0996 | |
| 10 時 0383 | 18 雛 2154 | ジョウ 3 上 0041 | **す** |
| 除 0996 | ジュウ 2 十 0005 | 4 冗 1968 | ス 子 0094 |
| 12 滋 2180 | 4 中 0035 | 6 成 0070 | 主 0365 |
| 13 慈 2179 | 5 汁 0756 | 7 条 0119 | 守 0648 |
| 蒔 2185 | 6 充 1056 | 杖 0658 | 寿 1544 |
| 辞 1465 | 7 住 0366 | 状 0616 | 素 0132 |
| 14 磁 2181 | 9 拾 1071 | 8 定 0045 | 須 1928 |
| 15 餌 2173 | 柔 0688 | 9 乗 1005 | 数 0309 |
| 19 璽 2288 | 重 0539 | 城 1298 | 蘇 0494 |
| 路 0788 | 10 従 0869 | 浄 0979 | す 州 0845 |
| -じ 爺 1899 | 紐 0591 | 11 剰 1007 | 洲 0846 |
| じい 直 0839 | 11 渋 1234 | 常 0321 | 巣 0601 |
| ジカ 直 0839 | 14 銃 1057 | 情 0973 | 酢 2129 |
| ジキ 食 0288 | 16 獣 0763 | 盛 1300 | スイ 4 水 0027 |
| ジク 軸 0692 | 縦 0871 | 12 場 0445 | 5 出 0038 |
| じじ 爺 1899 | ジュク 塾 1437 | 畳 1520 | 7 吹 1764 |
| じじい 爺 1899 | 熟 1436 | 13 蒸 0960 | 8 垂 1004 |
| ジッ- 十 0005 | ジュツ 戌 2273 | 14 静 0978 | 炊 1751 |
| ジツ 日 0001 | 述 0994 | 15 縄 2073 | 9 帥 0747 |
| 実 0499 | 術 0993 | 16 壌 1665 | 10 粋 1622 |
| -じみる 染 1174 | ジュン 6 巡 1553 | 嬢 1663 | 衰 1861 |
| -じめ 締 1419 | 旬 0167 | 錠 2080 | 11 推 2150 |
| ジャ 邪 1819 | 9 盾 1551 | 20 譲 1662 | 酔 1625 |
| 蛇 2297 | 10 准 0713 | 醸 1664 | 12 遂 2210 |
| ジャク 若 0404 | 殉 1090 | ジョク 辱 1848 | 13 睡 1008 |
| 弱 0424 | 純 1101 | -じるし 印 0231 | 15 穂 1314 |
| 寂 2045 | 12 循 1552 | ジン 2 人 0015 | 16 錘 1011 |
| 雀 1742 | 順 1925 | 3 刃 0087 | 酸 0800 |
| 着 0938 | 13 準 0714 | 4 仁 1094 | すい 枢 1386 |
| ジャン 雀 1742 | 馴 1926 | 6 尽 0338 | スウ 崇 1645 |
| ジュ 7 寿 1544 | 15 潤 1491 | 迅 1146 | 数 0309 |
| 8 受 0065 | 遵 0803 | 9 甚 1798 | 雛 2154 |
| 呪 2177 | ジョ 女 0093 | 神 0316 | すう 吸 1763 |
| 10 従 0869 | 如 2197 | | すえ 末 0272 |

せめる 攻 1045
責 0831
せる 競 1204
セン 3 千 0017
川 0022
5 仙 1003
占 0348
6 先 0134
尖 1563
9 宣 1398
専 0580
染 1174
洗 0135
泉 0207
9 浅 1587
10 扇 1887
栓 2230
11 旋 0572
船 0669
12 揃 1537
13 戦 0461
煎 1749
羨 2040
腺 1983
詮 2231
践 1586
14 箋 1582
銭 1585
銑 2068
15 潜 1168
線 0210
遷 0785
選 1502
16 薦 2259
17 繊 2008
鮮 0493

ぜ

ゼ 是 1678
ゼイ 税 1195

説 1197
贅 1509
-ぜき 関 0451
ゼツ 舌 0052
絶 1271
ぜに 銭 1585
ぜろ ○ 0014
ゼン 全 0078
前 0113
善 1213
然 0760
禅 1076
漸 1705
膳 1215
繕 1214

そ

ソ 8 狙 1518
阻 1517
9 祖 0641
10 租 1515
素 0132
11 曽 1222
措 1219
粗 1516
組 0264
12 疎 1142
訴 1708
13 塑 1777
想 0683
鼠 2263
14 遡 1776
18 礎 1349
19 蘇 0494
ソウ 4 双 1498
6 争 0972
壮 1589
早 0143
7 走 0140
8 宗 0636

炒 1750
9 奏 2104
相 0682
草 0144
荘 1590
送 0455
10 倉 0696
捜 1527
挿 1597
桑 2291
11 曽 1222
巣 0601
掃 1016
曹 1879
爽 2289
窓 0558
12 創 0697
喪 1863
瘦 1947
葬 0717
装 1591
13 僧 1226
想 0683
14 層 1224
総 0557
遭 1880
15 槽 1881
踪 1322
16 操 1809
17 燥 1810
霜 1908
18 贈 1227
騒 1390
19 藻 1812
そう 沿 1348
添 1344
そうろう 候 1675
そえる 添 1344
ソク 7 即 0390
束 0307

足 0044
9 促 1604
則 0625
10 息 1556
捉 1603
速 1143
11 側 0626
12 測 0627
13 塞 2232
そこ 底 0482
そこなう 損 1595
-そこなう 損 1595
そこねる 損 1595
-そこねる 損 1595
そそぐ 注 0368
そそのかす 唆 1441
そだち 育 0489
そだつ 育 0489
そだてる 育 0489
ソツ 卒 0751
率 0752
そで 袖 1531
そと 外 0266
そなえる 供 0357
備 0715
そなわる 備 0715
その 其 1757
苑 0729
園 0856
そば 傍 1884
そまる 染 1174
そむく 背 0124
そむける 背 0124
そめる 染 1174
-そめる 染 1174
そら 空 0398
そらす 反 0374
そる 反 0374
剃 1192
それ 其 1757

| | | | | | | | | | | | | |
|---|---|---|---|---|---|---|---|---|---|---|---|---|
| | 呑 | 2174 | なく | 泣 | 0578 | なめらか | 滑 | 1493 | におわせる | 匂 | 2245 |
| | 貪 | 1159 | | 鳴 | 2157 | なやます | 悩 | 1972 | にがい | 苦 | 0405 |
| | 鈍 | 1102 | なぐさむ | 慰 | 2125 | なやむ | 悩 | 1972 | にがす | 逃 | 1829 |
| | 曇 | 0898 | なぐさめる | 慰 | 2125 | ならい | 習 | 0420 | にがる | 苦 | 0405 |
| どんぶり | 丼 | 0436 | なぐる | 殴 | 1387 | ならう | 倣 | 1353 | にぎやか | 賑 | 0905 |
| | | | -なげ | 投 | 0517 | | 習 | 0420 | にぎる | 握 | 1536 |
| **な** | | | なげかわしい | 嘆 | 1731 | ならす | 馴 | 1926 | にぎわう | 賑 | 0905 |
| ナ | 那 | 1410 | なげく | 嘆 | 1731 | | 慣 | 1912 | ニク | 肉 | 0216 |
| | 奈 | 0635 | なげる | 投 | 0517 | | 鳴 | 2157 | にくい | 憎 | 1225 |
| | 南 | 0794 | なごむ | 和 | 0236 | ならびに | 並 | 0333 | にくしみ | 憎 | 1225 |
| | 納 | 1156 | なごやか | 和 | 0236 | ならぶ | 並 | 0333 | にくむ | 憎 | 1225 |
| な | 名 | 0269 | なさけ | 情 | 0973 | ならべる | 並 | 0333 | にくらしい | 憎 | 1225 |
| | 菜 | 0988 | なし | 梨 | 1175 | なる | 成 | 0070 | にげる | 逃 | 1829 |
| -な | 名 | 0269 | | 成 | 0070 | | 鳴 | 2157 | にごす | 濁 | 2266 |
| ナイ | 乃 | 1754 | | 為 | 1236 | なれる | 馴 | 1926 | にごる | 濁 | 2266 |
| | 内 | 0215 | -なす | 成 | 0070 | | 慣 | 1912 | にし | 西 | 0795 |
| ない | 亡 | 0233 | なぞ | 謎 | 1774 | なわ | 縄 | 2073 | にしき | 錦 | 0213 |
| | 無 | 0048 | ナッ- | 納 | 1156 | なわ- | 苗 | 1823 | にじ | 虹 | 2300 |
| ないがしろ | 蔑 | 2279 | なつ | 夏 | 0363 | ナン | 男 | 0092 | にせ | 偽 | 1237 |
| なえ | 苗 | 1823 | なつかしい | 懐 | 1667 | | 南 | 0794 | ニチ | 日 | 0001 |
| なえる | 萎 | 1456 | なつかしむ | 懐 | 1667 | | 納 | 1156 | になう | 担 | 1394 |
| なお | 尚 | 0184 | なつく | 懐 | 1667 | | 軟 | 0689 | にぶ- | 鈍 | 1102 |
| なおす | 治 | 0950 | なつける | 懐 | 1667 | | 難 | 0712 | にぶい | 鈍 | 1102 |
| | 直 | 0839 | なでる | 撫 | 1538 | なん | 何 | 0815 | にぶる | 鈍 | 1102 |
| -なおす | 直 | 0839 | など | 等 | 0393 | なん- | 何 | 0815 | ニャク | 若 | 0404 |
| なおる | 治 | 0950 | なな | 七 | 0009 | | | | にやす | 煮 | 1188 |
| | 直 | 0839 | ななつ | 七 | 0009 | **に** | | | ニュウ | 入 | 0039 |
| なか | 中 | 0035 | ななめ | 斜 | 0999 | ニ | 二 | 0003 | | 乳 | 0160 |
| | 仲 | 0643 | なに | 何 | 0815 | | 仁 | 1094 | ニョ | 柔 | 0688 |
| | 腹 | 0864 | なに- | 何 | 0815 | | 尼 | 2116 | | 女 | 0093 |
| なかば | 半 | 0335 | なの | 七 | 0009 | | 弐 | 0110 | | 如 | 2197 |
| なかれ | 勿 | 0171 | なべ | 鍋 | 1488 | | 児 | 0772 | ニョウ | 女 | 0093 |
| ながい | 永 | 1691 | なま | 生 | 0036 | | 荷 | 0817 | | 尿 | 1893 |
| | 長 | 0091 | なま- | 生 | 0036 | に | 煮 | 1188 | にらむ | 睨 | 2262 |
| ながす | 流 | 1059 | なまける | 怠 | 2216 | -に | 荷 | 0817 | にる | 似 | 1354 |
| -ながす | 流 | 1059 | なまめかしい | 艶 | 2178 | にい- | 新 | 0275 | | 煮 | 1188 |
| ながめる | 眺 | 1828 | なまり | 鉛 | 2067 | にえる | 煮 | 1188 | にわ | 庭 | 0878 |
| ながれ | 流 | 1059 | なみ | 並 | 0333 | におい | 匂 | 2245 | にわとり | 鶏 | 2284 |
| ながれる | 流 | 1059 | | 波 | 0598 | | 臭 | 1560 | ニン | 人 | 0015 |
| なき- | 亡 | 0233 | なみだ | 涙 | 1020 | におう | 匂 | 2245 | | 任 | 0372 |
| | | | | | | | 臭 | 1560 | | | |

| Reading | Kanji | No. |
|---|---|---|
| はげる | 剝 | 0609 |
| はこ | 函 | 1713 |
|  | 箱 | 1909 |
| はこぶ | 運 | 0584 |
| はさむ | 挟 | 1934 |
| はし | 端 | 2114 |
|  | 箸 | 1443 |
|  | 橋 | 1578 |
| はしら | 柱 | 0867 |
| はしる | 走 | 0140 |
| はじ | 恥 | 1670 |
| はじまる | 始 | 0956 |
| はじめ | 初 | 0710 |
| はじめて | 初 | 0710 |
| はじめる | 始 | 0956 |
| -はじめる | 始 | 0956 |
| はじらう | 恥 | 1670 |
| はじる | 恥 | 1670 |
| はす | 蓮 | 0585 |
| はず | 筈 | 1442 |
| はずかしい | 恥 | 1670 |
| はずかしめる | 辱 | 1848 |
| はずす | 外 | 0266 |
| はずむ | 弾 | 1075 |
| はずれる | 外 | 0266 |
| はせる | 馳 | 1389 |
| はた | 畑 | 0129 |
|  | 旗 | 0573 |
|  | 端 | 2114 |
|  | 機 | 0473 |
| はたけ | 畑 | 0129 |
| はたす | 果 | 0599 |
| -はたす | 果 | 0599 |
| はたらく | 働 | 0541 |
| はだ | 肌 | 1997 |
| はだか | 裸 | 0711 |
| ハチ | 八 | 0010 |
|  | 鉢 | 2074 |
| はち | 蜂 | 1381 |
| はちす | 蓮 | 0585 |
| ハッ- | 法 | 0139 |
| ハツ | 発 | 0148 |
|  | 鉢 | 2074 |
|  | 髪 | 1792 |
| はつ | 初 | 0710 |
| はつ- | 初 | 0710 |
| はて | 果 | 0599 |
| はてる | 果 | 0599 |
| -はてる | 果 | 0599 |
| はと | 鳩 | 2283 |
| はな | 花 | 0121 |
|  | 華 | 1012 |
|  | 鼻 | 1558 |
| はなし | 話 | 0053 |
| はなす | 放 | 0574 |
|  | 話 | 0053 |
|  | 離 | 1970 |
| はなつ | 放 | 0574 |
| はなはだ | 甚 | 1798 |
| はなはだしい | 甚 | 1798 |
| はなれる | 放 | 0574 |
|  | 離 | 1970 |
| はね | 羽 | 0418 |
| はねる | 跳 | 1831 |
| はは | 母 | 0104 |
| はば | 幅 | 1483 |
| はばむ | 阻 | 1517 |
| はぶく | 省 | 0681 |
| はま | 浜 | 0909 |
| はや | 早 | 0143 |
| はや- | 早 | 0143 |
|  | 速 | 1143 |
| はやい | 早 | 0143 |
|  | 速 | 1143 |
| はやし | 林 | 0240 |
| はやす | 生 | 0036 |
| はやまる | 早 | 0143 |
|  | 速 | 1143 |
| はやめる | 早 | 0143 |
|  | 速 | 1143 |
| はら | 原 | 0208 |
|  | 腹 | 0864 |
| -はらい | 払 | 0812 |
| はらう | 払 | 0812 |
| はらす | 晴 | 0975 |
|  | 腫 | 2022 |
| はり | 針 | 0556 |
| -はり | 張 | 2020 |
| はる | 春 | 0362 |
|  | 張 | 2020 |
|  | 貼 | 1266 |
| はるか | 遥 | 1371 |
| はれ | 晴 | 0975 |
| はれ- | 晴 | 0975 |
| はれる | 晴 | 0975 |
|  | 腫 | 2022 |
| ハン | 3 凡 | 1629 |
|  | 4 反 | 0374 |
|  | 5 半 | 0335 |
|  | 氾 | 2119 |
|  | 犯 | 0735 |
|  | 6 帆 | 1631 |
|  | 汎 | 1632 |
|  | 7 伴 | 0743 |
|  | 判 | 0744 |
|  | 坂 | 0375 |
|  | 阪 | 0376 |
|  | 8 板 | 0924 |
|  | 版 | 0923 |
|  | 10 班 | 1853 |
|  | 畔 | 1404 |
|  | 般 | 0671 |
|  | 11 絆 | 2076 |
|  | 販 | 0925 |
|  | 12 斑 | 1854 |
|  | 飯 | 0377 |
|  | 13 搬 | 0672 |
|  | 煩 | 1937 |
|  | 頒 | 1919 |
|  | 15 範 | 0727 |
|  | 16 繁 | 1575 |
|  | 18 藩 | 1511 |

**ば**

| Reading | Kanji | No. |
|---|---|---|
| バ | 馬 | 0336 |
|  | 婆 | 1452 |
|  | 罵 | 2278 |
| ば | 場 | 0445 |
| ばあ | 婆 | 1452 |
| バイ | 売 | 0353 |
|  | 倍 | 0069 |
|  | 梅 | 1572 |
|  | 培 | 1264 |
|  | 陪 | 1263 |
|  | 媒 | 2123 |
|  | 買 | 0352 |
|  | 賠 | 1265 |
| ばえ | 栄 | 1245 |
| -ばえ | 映 | 0329 |
| ばかす | 化 | 0120 |
| バク | 麦 | 0131 |
|  | 博 | 0983 |
|  | 幕 | 1339 |
|  | 漠 | 1338 |
|  | 暴 | 1346 |
|  | 縛 | 0984 |
|  | 爆 | 1347 |
| ばける | 化 | 0120 |
| -ばた | 端 | 2114 |
| -ばたけ | 畑 | 0129 |
| バチ | 罰 | 0742 |
| バツ | 末 | 0272 |
|  | 伐 | 1361 |
|  | 抜 | 1951 |
|  | 罰 | 0742 |
|  | 閥 | 1362 |
| -ばらい | 払 | 0812 |
| -ばり | 張 | 2020 |
|  | 貼 | 1266 |
| -ばれ | 晴 | 0975 |